CASH to Accrual

ACCOUNTING PRINCIPLES

ROGER H. HERMANSON, Ph.D., C.P.A.
Research Professor of Accounting
Georgia State University

JAMES DON EDWARDS, Ph.D., C.P.A.
J. M. Tull Professor of Accounting
School of Accounting
The University of Georgia

R. F. SALMONSON, Ph.D., C.P.A.
Professor of Accounting
Michigan State University

ACCOUNTING PRINCIPLES

1980

BUSINESS PUBLICATIONS, INC. Dallas, Texas 75243
Irwin-Dorsey Limited Georgetown, Ontario L7G 4B3

ISBN 0-256-02258-5
Library of Congress Catalog Card No. 79–53354
Printed in the United States of America

1 2 3 4 5 6 7 8 9 0 K 7 6 5 4 3 2 1 0

Preface

Accounting Principles is designed for use in first-year accounting courses at two-year colleges, four-year colleges, and universities. The authors' goal is to present accounting information as an essential element of the decision-making process in a business environment. The material describes basic standards and principles that underlie accounting information, indicates how accounting information is accumulated, and explains how such information can be used in the decision-making process.

The text includes both introductory financial and managerial accounting topics. The authors recognize that students taking this course may seek a variety of careers. Some students may continue their studies in business administration, others may choose accounting as a major, and still others may take accounting as part of their liberal arts education. All of these students will find the ability to use and interpret accounting information valuable both in their careers and their personal lives.

The text is divided into eight parts: Introduction; Processing Accounting Information; Assets and Liabilities; Accounting Theory and Partnerships; Corporations; Analysis of Financial Statements; Accounting in Manufacturing Companies; and Planning, Control, and Decision Making. The chapters in each of these parts have been developed to assist the instructor in teaching and the student in learning a new language—accounting, the language of business. After completing the first five chapters, the instructor may alter the sequence of chapters that follow or may elect to omit some chapters so that certain topics may be emphasized. In the financial accounting chapters, pronouncements of various authoritative bodies (the Financial Accounting Standards Board, the Securities and Exchange Commission, and the American Institute of Certified Public Accountants) have been incorporated and explained as simply as possible. An appendix contains an introduction to inflation accounting. This material may be assigned or omitted, as the instructor chooses.

Each chapter has at least one demonstration problem followed by questions, exercises, two series of problems, and from one to four decision problems. There is sufficient end-of-chapter material to provide the instructor with several alternative assignments while covering the concepts included in the chapter.

An extensive array of supplementary material for student use accompanies the text.

The list of check figures gives key figures for the A and B Series problems.

Students can determine whether they are "on the right track" in working a problem by comparing their solutions with the key figure given for a particular problem.

The study guide corresponding by chapter to the text contains chapter goals, an outline, and questions and exercises. Its purpose is to strengthen the student's understanding of the chapter immediately after reading the chapter. Normally, the student should work the study guide material after studying the new terms for a chapter but before turning to the questions, exercises, and problems for that chapter. Many of the questions and exercises are in fill-in-the-blank format. The answers are contained in the back of the study guide so that answers may be checked by the student.

Two sets of working papers are available for use in working assigned problems and decision problems. One set is for use with Chapters 1–14 and the other set is for use with Chapters 15–28. The working papers in many instances are partially filled out to reduce the pencil pushing required to solve the problems.

Three practice sets are available to the student. The first practice set illustrates the use of business papers for a retailing company using periodic inventory procedure. The second practice set illustrates special journals and includes a work sheet for a retailing company using periodic inventory procedure. These two may be used any time after Chapter 6. The third illustrates the accounting system used by a manufacturing company using perpetual inventory procedure and may be used any time after Chapter 22. Each of these practice sets should take six to ten hours to complete.

Many teaching aids are also available to instructors. Instructors may obtain transparency solutions to problems, a series of tests, a comprehensive solutions manual, and a manual of questions which may be used for quizzes or as additional or alternative examination questions. All of these instructional aids have been developed to assist the instructor and are described in detail in the preface of the *instructor's solutions manual.*

We are grateful to several individuals who have contributed to the development of this test. Special appreciation goes to: G. Michael Crooch, Oklahoma State University-Stillwater; James T. Hood, Northeast Louisiana University-Monroe; Anthony T. Krzystofik, University of Massachusetts-Amherst; Arthur T. Roberts, Texas Tech University-Lubbock; and Jackson A. White, University of Arkansas-Little Rock.

December 1979

Roger H. Hermanson
James Don Edwards
R. F. Salmonson

Contents

Depreciation on the financial statements. Measurements of plant and equipment on the balance sheet. Capital and revenue expenditures: *Expenditures capitalized in asset accounts. Expenditures capitalized as charges to accumulated depreciation. Expenditures charged to expense. Distinguishing between capital and revenue expenditures.*

PART FOUR: ACCOUNTING THEORY AND PARTNERSHIPS

PART FIVE: CORPORATIONS

sheet presentation of subscriptions receivable and stock subscribed. Issuance of par value stock. Capital stock issued for property or services. Paid-in capital in excess of par (or stated) value— common or preferred account. Documents, books, and records relating to capital stock: *Stockholders' ledger. The minutes book.* Values commonly associated with capital stock: *Par value. Stated value. Market value. Liquidation value. Redemption value. Book value.*

Paid-in (or contributed) capital: *Paid-in capital—recapitalization. Paid-in capital—treasury stock transactions. Paid-in capital—donations.* Retained earnings. Paid-in capital and retained earnings in the balance sheet. Retained earnings appropriations: *Retained earnings appropriations in the balance sheet.* The statement of retained earnings. Dividends: *Cash dividends. Stock dividends. Stock splits. Recording stock dividends. Legality of dividends.* Treasury stock: *Acquisition and reissuance of treasury stock. Treasury stock in the balance sheet. Stockholders' equity in the balance sheet.* Net earnings—inclusions and exclusions: *Extraordinary items. Prior period adjustments. Accounting for tax effects. Accounting changes. Illustrative statements.*

Bonds: *Why a company might decide to issue bonds. Advantages and disadvantages of borrowing.* Bonds payable: *Accounting for the issuance of bonds. Recording bond interest. The price received for a bond issue. Bonds issued at a discount. Accounting for bond discount. Bonds issued at a premium. Accounting for bond premium. Bonds issued at face value between interest dates. Bonds issued at other than face value between interest dates.* Redeeming outstanding bonds: *Use of a sinking fund to redeem bonds.* Balance sheet illustration. Investments in bonds and stocks of other companies: *Bond investments. Accounting for bond investments. Valuation of debt securities held. Stock investments.* **Appendix:** Future worth and present value: *Future worth. Present value. Present value of an annuity. Determining the price of a bond. The effective rate of interest method for amortizing the discount.*

Parent and subsidiary corporations: *Eliminations.* Consolidated balance sheet at time of acquisition: *Acquisition at book value. Acquisition of subsidiary at a cost above or below book value. Acquisition of less than 100 percent of subsidiary. Earnings, losses, and dividends of a subsidiary.* Consolidated financial statements at a date after acquisition. Purchase versus pooling of interests: *Purchase versus pooling of interests illustrated. Abuses of pooling of interests method. Uses and limitations of consolidated statements.* **Appendix:** A set of consolidated financial statements for an actual company.

PART SIX: ANALYSIS OF FINANCIAL STATEMENTS

The statement of changes in financial position: *Basic objectives and form. Uses of the statement of changes in financial position. Content of the statement of changes in financial position. Preparing the statement of changes in financial position. Statement of changes in financial position which emphasizes cash flow.* The cash flow statement: *Preparing the cash flow statement.*

Objectives of financial statements. Comparative financial statements: *Nature and purpose. Methods of comparison—illustrated. Trend percentages.* Ratios: *Liquidity ratios. Tests of equity position and solvency. Profitability tests. Market tests.* Limitations and other considerations in evaluating financial position and earning power: *Need for comparable data. Influence of external factors. Need for comparative standards. The most serious limitation to the usefulness of financial statements.*

PART SEVEN: ACCOUNTING IN MANUFACTURING COMPANIES

PART EIGHT: PLANNING, CONTROL, AND DECISION MAKING

The operating budgets illustrated. The flexible operating budget. Preparing the financial budget for the Leed Company. The financial budgets illustrated.

The behavior of costs. Cost-volume-earnings analysis. The break-even chart. Margin of safety. The contribution margin concept. Some practical aspects of cost-volume-earnings analysis: *Cost-volume-earnings analysis for the multiproduct firm. Methods for estimating mixed costs. The meaning of units as a measure of volume. The nature of fixed costs. Assumptions made in cost-volume-earnings analysis.*

Short-term decision making. Cost and revenue concepts used in differential analysis. Special cost studies for decision making: *Product pricing. Special orders.* Elimination of products. Eliminating a department. Discontinuing sales to a certain type of customer. Further processing of joint products. Make-or-buy decisions: *Maximizing utilization of a scarce resource.* The effect of corporate income taxation on management decision making. Net earnings before taxes versus taxable income: *The investment credit. Tax rates. Decisions affected by tax considerations. Accounting methods used for tax purposes.* Interperiod income tax allocation.

Introduction to capital budgeting. Project selection: A general view: *Time value of money. Net cash benefits.* Project selection: Payback period. Project selection: Unadjusted rate of return. Project selection: Net present value method and the profitability index. Project selection: The time-adjusted rate of return. Investments in working capital. The postaudit.

The impact of inflation: *The unstable dollar. The need to adjust historical costs. Accounting responses to inflation.* Financial statements under historical cost/constant dollar accounting: *Historical cost/constant dollar accounting illustrated.* The SEC requirements. The FASB requirements: *The required disclosures. Disclosure formats. Inventory and cost of goods sold computations. Property, plant, and equipment and depreciation computations. A concluding note. Usefulness of the newly required disclosures.*

ACCOUNTING PRINCIPLES

PART ONE

INTRODUCTION

Chapter 1

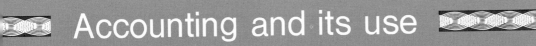

Accounting and its use

in business decisions

Accounting is a narrow discipline with very broad applications. In fact, it is useful in every organization which owns and uses economic resources. One such organization is the business firm. As it relates to such an organization, accounting has been called *the language of business.* But it also serves as a language to provide financial information about other types of organizations such as governments, churches, fraternities, and hospitals.

Accounting also is useful in making decisions involving our personal finances. For instance, you may be deciding whether your savings should be invested in a savings account in a bank, in government bonds, or in the shares of stock issued by business corporations. You may feel that your savings can be safely invested in a savings account or in a government bond. But you feel less secure about investing in shares of stock. To make an informed decision you need information about the economic activities of business firms. It is here that accounting enters the picture, since accounting is a primary source of information on economic activity of organizations.

ACCOUNTING DEFINED

Accounting[1] *is the process used to measure and report to various users relevant financial information regarding the economic activities of an organization or unit.*[2] This information is primarily financial in nature; that is, it is stated in money terms.

When persons first study accounting, they often confuse bookkeeping and accounting. Bookkeeping involves the recording of business activities and is a very mechanical process. Accounting includes bookkeeping, but goes well beyond it in scope. Among other actions, accountants prepare financial statements, conduct audits, design accounting systems, prepare special studies, prepare forecasts and budgets, do income tax work, and analyze and interpret financial information.

Specifically, accounting consists of a number of functions. Accountants *observe* events and *select* (or identify) those events that are considered evidence of economic activity. (The purchase and sale of goods and services are examples.) Then they *measure* these selected events in financial terms. As the next step, they *record* these measurements to provide a permanent history of the financial activities of the organization. In order to *report* upon what has happened, accountants *classify* their measurements of recorded events into meaningful groups. The preparation of accounting reports requires that accountants *summarize* these measurements even further. Finally, accountants may be asked to *interpret* the contents of their statements and reports. Interpretation may involve explanation of the uses, meaning, and limitations of accounting information. It may also involve drawing attention to key items through percentage and ratio analysis.

Accounting may also be defined as an *information system* designed to

---

[1] When undertaking initial study of any discipline, new terms are usually encountered. To aid in becoming familiar with the language of accounting, these terms (at their first occurrence in each chapter) are set in boldface, italic type and are also listed and defined at the end of the chapter.

[2] A complete discussion of the objectives of financial reporting is contained in FASB, "Objectives of Financial Reporting by Business Enterprises," *Statement of Financial Accounting Concepts No. 1* (Stanford, Conn., 1978). Further reference will be made to this in Chapter 13.

provide, through financial statements, relevant financial information. In designing the system, accountants keep in mind the types of users of the information (owners, creditors, etc.) and the kinds of decisions they make that require financial information. Usually, the information provided relates to the economic resources owned by an organization, the claims against these resources, the changes in both resources and claims, and the results of using these resources for a given period of time.

EMPLOYMENT OPPORTUNITIES IN ACCOUNTING

Accountants typically are employed in (1) public accounting, (2) private industry, or (3) the not-for-profit sector. Within each of these areas, specialization is possible; an accountant may, for example, be considered an expert in auditing, systems development, budgeting, cost accounting, or tax accounting.

Public accounting

If an accountant has passed an examination prepared and graded by the *American Institute of Certified Public Accountants (AICPA)* and has met certain other requirements, such as having a certain number of years of experience, he or she may be licensed by the state to practice as a *certified public accountant (CPA)*. As an independent, professional person, a CPA may offer clients auditing, management advisory, and tax services. Although the business enterprise is the primary client, individuals and not-for-profit organizations may also be clients.

Auditing. When a business seeks a loan or seeks to have its securities traded on a stock exchange, it is usually required to provide statements on its financial affairs. Users of these statements may accept and rely upon them more freely when they are accompanied by an *auditor's opinion or report.* This auditor's opinion or report contains the opinion of the CPA regarding the fairness of the statements.[3] To have the knowledge necessary for an informed opinion, the CPA conducts an examination of the client's accounting and related records and seeks supporting evidence from external sources, such as the amount on deposit in a bank.

Management advisory services. Often from knowledge gained in an audit, CPAs offer suggestions to their clients on how to improve their operations. From these and other contacts, CPAs may be engaged to provide a wide range of management advisory services. Such services are likely to be accounting related, such as the design and installation of an accounting system, the electronic processing of accounting data, inventory control, budgeting, or financial planning.

Tax services. CPAs often provide expert advice for the preparation of federal, state, and local tax returns. The objective here is to use legal means to minimize the amount of taxes paid. But of equal importance, because of high tax rates and complex tax laws, is tax planning. Proper tax planning requires that the tax effects, if any, of every business decision be known before the decision is made. There may be little chance to change its effects after the decision has been made.

---

[3] For an example of an actual auditor's report, see the Appendix to Chapter 18. Included in that Appendix is a complete set of financial statements of the type presented to external users.

Private or industrial accounting	Accountants employed by a single business are called private or industrial accountants. They may be the employer's only accountant, or one of several hundred or more. They may or may not be CPAs. If they have passed an examination prepared and graded by the National Association of Accountants—an organization for accountants employed in private industry—they will possess a Certificate in Management Accounting (CMA).

Industrial accountants may be specialists in providing certain services. They may, for example, be concerned with recording events and transactions involving outsiders and in the preparation of financial statements. Or they may be engaged in gathering and controlling the costs of goods produced by their employer. They may be specialists in budgeting—that is, in the development of plans relating to future operations. Many private accountants become specialists in the design and installation of systems for the processing of accounting data. Others are internal auditors and are employed by a firm to see that its policies and procedures are followed in its departments and divisions. These latter individuals may earn the designation, certified internal auditor (CIA), granted by the Institute of Internal Auditors.

Accounting in the not-for-profit sector	Many accountants, including CPAs, are employed by not-for-profit organizations, including governmental agencies at the federal, state, and local levels. The governmental accountant often is concerned with the accounting for and control of tax revenues and their expenditure. Accountants are also employed by governmental agencies whose task is the regulation of business activity—for example, the regulation of public utilities by a state public service commission.

Many accountants (including CPAs) are also employed in the academic arm of the profession. Here attention is directed toward the teaching of accounting and to research into the uses, limitations, and improvement of accounting information and of the theories and procedures under which it is accumulated and communicated.

THE NEED FOR ACCOUNTING INFORMATION: The decision-making process	The need for accounting information in making economic decisions has been noted, but little has been said about the decision-making process.

Basically, as shown in Illustration 1.1, any decision-making process involves (1) recognizing the existence of a problem, (2) determining the alternative courses of action considered solutions to the problem, (3) predicting the outcome of each alternative, (4) selecting the preferred consequence as determined by reference to the decision maker's personal preferences or previously set goals, and (5) taking action to see that the alternative chosen is implemented.

The problem is caused, at least in part, by events occurring in the real world of human activity and scarce resources. Its existence must be recognized or there will be no decision. The nature of the problem must be understood so that alternatives, which are possible solutions to the problem, can be determined. The list of alternatives should be complete, or the best solution may be overlooked.

Illustration 1.1: A model
of the decision-making
process

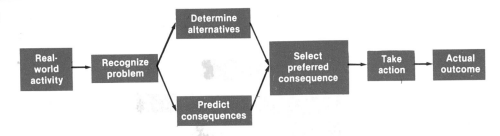

Since they represent future expected happenings, the consequences related to each alternative must be predicted. Because individuals differ, they are likely to have different personal preferences. Thus, different decision makers may make different decisions even though they predict the same consequences from the same alternatives.

Acting upon a decision causes new events in the real world. New problems will arise in the future. These problems, in turn, bring about a recycling of the whole process.

As a practical illustration, assume that a bank faces a problem. It has received requests for loans from Company A and Company B. It is in doubt as to which loan will meet its objectives as to risk, interest earnings, use of the money, date of repayment, ability to repay, and similar matters.

To solve the problem, the bank gathers information that helps it *predict the outcomes of granting each loan.* The predicted outcome of each loan is based on such factors as the rate of interest that can be charged, how the money will be used, and when it will be repaid. Projected results of the alternatives are compared with set objectives of the bank, and a decision is reached. This decision may be influenced by the personal preferences of the person making it. This person may conclude that as far as the bank is concerned, a loan to A does not differ much from a loan to B. But he or she may have a strong preference for loaning money to A because it intends to acquire pollution control equipment, while B intends to acquire new smelting equipment.

In any event, a decision is made; and the bank's position with its environment is now changed. New problems will arise requiring new information and further decisions.

In predicting the outcomes of the granting of each of the above loans, the bank relied upon accounting information. Virtually every attempt to predict the future involves a review of the past. And so, in making its predictions, the bank has relied upon the accounting records of the past financial activities of each company.

In this example, the bank is considered an external user of accounting information. But the same decision process is used, with accounting again supplying part of the information, in deciding on an internal matter. For example, a store manager may have to decide whether or not to add a new line of merchandise. Internal decisions using accounting information are now examined briefly.

Internal decisions

In most companies, persons at various levels of management make decisions that require accounting information. These decisions can be classified into four major types:

1. Financing decisions—deciding what amounts of capital are needed and whether it is to be secured from owners or creditors.
2. Resource allocation decisions—deciding how the total capital of a firm is to be invested, such as the amount invested in machinery.
3. Production decisions—deciding what products are to be produced, by what means, and when.
4. Marketing decisions—setting selling prices and advertising budgets; determining where a firm's markets are and how they are to be reached.

Managerial accounting.   Managerial accounting provides information for the above types of decisions. It ranges from the very broad (long-range planning) to the quite detailed (why costs varied from their planned levels). The information must meet two tests. It must be useful and not cost more to gather than it is worth. It generally relates to a part of a firm, such as a plant or a department, because this is where most of the decisions are made. It is used to measure the success of managers in, for example, controlling costs and to motivate them to help a firm achieve its goals. And it is forward-looking, often involving planning for the future.

External users and their decisions

The external users of accounting information and the types of questions for which answers are sought can be classified as follows:

1. Owners and prospective owners and their advisers (financial analysts and investment counselors). Should an ownership interest be acquired in this firm? Or, if one is now held, should it be increased, decreased, or retained at its present level? Has the firm earned satisfactory profits?
2. Creditors and lenders. Should a loan be granted to the firm? Will the firm be able to pay its debts as they become due?
3. Employees and their unions. Does the firm have the ability to pay increased wages? Can it do so without raising prices? Is the firm financially able to provide permanent employment?
4. Customers. Will the firm survive long enough to honor its product warranties? Can a firm install costly pollution control equipment and still remain profitable? Are profit margins reasonable?
5. Governmental units. Is this firm, a public utility, earning a fair profit on its capital investment? How much taxes does it pay? In total, is business activity at a desired level for sound growth without inflation?
6. The general public. Are profit margins too high? Are they an increasing or decreasing part of national income? Are the firms in this industry contributing to inflation?

Except for uses by governmental units, the information needs of the above users are met by providing a set of general-purpose financial statements. These statements are the end product of a process known as financial accounting.

Financial accounting. Financial accounting provides statements on a firm's financial position, changes in this position, and on the results of operations (profitability). Many companies publish these statements in an *annual report.* This report contains the auditor's opinion as to the fairness of the financial statements, as well as other information about the company's activities, products, and plans.

Financial accounting information relates to the firm as a whole, since outsiders can make decisions only on matters pertaining to the entire firm, such as whether or not to extend credit to it. Such information is historical in nature, being a report upon what has happened. Because interfirm comparisons are often made, the information supplied must conform to certain standards called generally accepted accounting principles.

But a clear-cut distinction cannot be drawn between financial and managerial accounting information. Management officials are keenly aware of the fact that their jobs may depend upon how the figures come out in the annual report. Also, much of what is called managerial accounting information is first accumulated in an accounting system designed with financial reporting in mind.

Although accounting information is essential in the management of a not-for-profit organization, primary attention in this text is devoted to business firms.

THE DEVELOPMENT OF FINANCIAL ACCOUNTING STANDARDS

As noted above, the financial statements a business firm issues to external parties must conform to certain standards. *Generally accepted accounting principles (GAAP)* are standards and principles which have developed largely in accounting practice or have been established by an authoritative body. Brief mention is made at this point of four of the prominent accounting authorities.

American Institute of Certified Public Accountants (AICPA)

The AICPA has been the dominant factor in the development of accounting standards over the past half century. In a 20-year period ending in 1959, its Committee on Accounting Procedure issued 51 *Accounting Research Bulletins* recommending certain principles or practices. From 1959 through 1973, the committee's successor, the *Accounting Principles Board (APB)*, issued 31 numbered *Opinions* which CPAs generally were *required* to follow. Through its monthly magazine, *The Journal of Accountancy*, its research division, and its other divisions and committees, the AICPA continues to influence the development of accounting standards and practices.

Financial Accounting Standards Board (FASB)

The APB was replaced in 1973 with a new, independent, seven-member, full-time *Financial Accounting Standards Board (FASB)*. The FASB has issued numerous *Statements of Financial Accounting Standards* and numerous interpretations of FASB statements of standards. The FASB is widely accepted as the major influence, in the private sector, in the development of new financial accounting standards.

U.S. Securities and Exchange Commission (SEC)

Created under the Securities and Exchange Act of 1934, the Securities and Exchange Commission (SEC) administers a number of important acts dealing with the interstate sale of securities. The SEC has the power to prescribe in detail the accounting practices followed by companies required by law to file financial statements with it. This includes virtually every major U.S. business corporation. But rather than exercise this power, the SEC has adopted a policy of working closely with the accounting profession, especially the FASB, in the development of accounting standards.

American Accounting Association (AAA)

Consisting largely of college instructors of accounting, the *American Accounting Association (AAA)* has sought to encourage research and study at a theoretical level into the concepts, standards, and principles of accounting. It publishes statements on such matters and supports the research efforts of individuals. In recent years, its quarterly magazine, *The Accounting Review,* has carried many articles reporting on research into the uses of accounting information.

The federal taxation of income must also be noted as a factor in the development of accounting standards. The accounting required for such purposes, although not usually required for financial reporting, will be discussed and illustrated from time to time in this text.

FORMS OF BUSINESS ORGANIZATION

There are three basic forms of organization for a business enterprise. They are the *single proprietorship, partnership,* and *corporation.* The early stages of this book will use the single proprietorship in its illustrations of basic accounting concepts. This is the simplest and most common form of business organization. Later chapters will use the partnership and corporation forms of organization so as to expose you to all three forms of business enterprise. Virtually the same accounting concepts apply to all three forms of organization.

Single proprietorship. A *single proprietorship is a business owned by an individual and often managed by that same individual.* Many small service type businesses (such as physicians, lawyers, barbers, and electricians) and retail establishments (such as clothing stores, antique shops, and novelty stores) are single proprietorships. There are no legal formalities in organizing such a business, and usually only a limited amount of capital (money) is required to begin operations. While there is no legal distinction between the business and the owner as entities, since the owner is responsible for personal and business debts, there is an accounting distinction. The financial activities of the business, such as selling services to the public, are kept separate from the personal financial activities, such as making a payment on an auto used exclusively for nonbusiness purposes. The business is considered an *entity* separate from the owner.

Partnership. A *partnership is a business owned by two or more persons associated as partners.* It is often managed by those same persons. The partnership is created by a partnership agreement setting forth the terms of the partnership. Preferably, the agreement should be in writing, but it may be oral. Included in the agreement will be such things as the initial investment of each partner, the duties of each partner, the means of dividing earnings or losses between the partners each year, and the settlement to be made upon the death or withdrawal of a partner. A partnership often evolves out of one or more single proprietorships. For instance, Mr. X and Ms. Y, both CPAs, may each operate as single proprietorships. Each sees the need to have another CPA to serve clients during vacations. Also, there may be a need to combine their strong points (X is a tax person and Y is an auditor) to improve service to their clients. They may decide to combine their single proprietorships into a partnership. Partnerships, like single proprietorships, are commonly found in the service and retail fields.

Corporation. A *corporation is a business that may be owned by a few persons or by thousands of persons and is incorporated under the laws of one of the 50 states.* It often is managed by persons other than the owners, although major owners sometimes serve as officers (managers) of the corporation. Ownership in a corporation is divided into units known as shares of stock. Thus, the owners are called stockholders. Ownership interest is easily transferred by selling one's shares of stock to another. Organized exchanges (such as the New York Stock Exchange) exist for this purpose. Corporations may evolve from single proprietorships or partnerships, although sometimes they are formed directly. The corporate form is more likely to appear where huge amounts of capital are needed to start the business, where a wide range of talents is needed to manage the business, and where the owners desire to limit their personal liability. Unlike the single proprietorship and partnership forms, the corporation is a separate *legal entity* from its owners. The owners are *not* personally responsible for the debts of the corporation.

FINANCIAL STATEMENTS OF BUSINESS ENTERPRISES

A modern business firm has many objectives or goals. They include providing well-paying jobs and comfortable working conditions for its employees and being a good citizen. But the two primary objectives of every business firm are *profitability* and *solvency.* Unless a firm can produce satisfactory earnings and pay its debts as they become due, any other objectives a firm may have will never be realized simply because the firm will not survive. The financial statements that reflect a firm's solvency (the balance sheet) and its profitability (the earnings statement) are illustrated and discussed below.

The balance sheet

The *balance sheet* presents measures of the assets, liabilities, and owner's equity in a business firm *as of a specific moment in time. Assets* are things of value; they constitute the *resources* of the firm. They have value to the firm because of the uses to which they can be put or the things that can be acquired by exchanging them. Illustration 1.2 shows the balance sheet of the Brent Swimming Pool Service Company on July 31, 1981. It began operations on July 1, 1981. The assets of the Brent Swimming Pool Service Company amount to $35,670. They consist of current assets of cash, accounts receivable (amounts due from customers), and property, plant, and equipment consisting of a truck, cleaning equipment, and office equipment. Current assets consist of cash and other short-lived assets that are reasonably expected to be converted into cash or to be consumed or used up in the operations of the business,

BRENT SWIMMING POOL SERVICE COMPANY
Balance Sheet
July 31, 1981

Assets			Liabilities and Owner's Equity		
Current Assets:			Current Liabilities:		
Cash	$12,470		Accounts payable	$ 600	
Accounts receivable	700		Notes payable	3,000	
		$13,170			$ 3,600
Property, Plant, and Equipment:			Owner's Equity:		
			William Brent, capital		32,070
Truck	$ 6,000				
Cleaning equipment	14,000				
Office equipment	2,500				
		22,500	Total Liabilities and Owner's		
Total Assets		$35,670	Equity		$35,670

within a short period, usually one year.[4] Property, plant, and equipment refers to relatively long-lived assets that are to be used in the production or sale of other assets or performance of services rather than being sold.

Liabilities are the debts owed by a firm. Typically, they must be paid at certain known moments in time. The liabilities of the Brent Swimming Pool Service Company are both relatively short-lived current liabilities. They consist of *accounts payable* (amounts owed to suppliers) and *notes payable* (written promises to pay) totaling $3,600.

The Brent Swimming Pool Service Company is a single proprietorship. It is customary to refer to the proprietor's interest in the business firm as the owner's equity. As will be explained later, the owner's equity consists of $30,000 of invested capital and net earnings for the month of July of $2,070. Note that the balance sheet heading includes (1) the name of the organization, (2) the title of the statement, and (3) the date of the statement. Also, note that the claims upon or interests in assets (liabilities and owner's equity) equal the assets—an equality explained later in this chapter.

The earnings statement

The purpose of the *earnings statement* (often called an income statement) is to report upon the profitability of a business organization *for a stated period of time*. The heading of an earnings statement includes (1) the name of the company, (2) the title of the statement, and (3) the time period covered by the statement. In accounting, profitability is measured by comparing the revenues generated in a period with the expenses incurred to produce those revenues. *Revenue results from the sale of goods or the providing of services to customers. It produces an inflow of assets, usually cash or receivables, to the*

---

[4] Technically speaking, the time period is one operating cycle or one year, whichever is longer. An operating cycle is the length of time that it takes cash spent for merchandise to be sold to come back to the selling company in the form of collections from its customers. Thus, in some industries (distilling, for example) the operating cycle extends for a number of years.

**Illustration 1.3:
Earnings statement**

```
BRENT SWIMMING POOL SERVICE COMPANY
              Earnings Statement
           For the Month of July 1981

Service revenues ......................          $5,700

Expenses:
Wages .........................    $2,600
Gas and oil .......................     400
Rent ..........................          300
Advertising .......................      200
Utilities .........................      100
Interest .........................        30    3,630
Net Earnings ......................             $2,070
```

firm. Expense is the sacrifice made or the cost incurred to produce revenue. It is measured by the assets surrendered or consumed in serving customers. If revenues exceed expenses, net earnings result. If the reverse is true, the business is said to be operating at a loss. Illustration 1.3 contains the earnings statement of the Brent Swimming Pool Service Company for the month of July 1981. It shows that revenues were generated by serving customers in the amount of $5,700. Expenses for the month amounted to $3,630, resulting in net earnings for the month of $2,070.

THE FINANCIAL ACCOUNTING PROCESS

Having introduced two of the three principal financial statements, attention is now directed to the process underlying such statements. (Discussion of the third statement, the statement of changes in financial position, is delayed until Chapter 19.)

The accounting equation

It has been noted that in the balance sheet presented in Illustration 1.2 the total assets of the Brent Swimming Pool Service Company are equal to the total of its liabilities and owner's equity. This equality shows that the assets of a business are equal to the equities in those assets; that is, *Assets = Equities.* Assets have already been defined simply as things of value to a business. They are further defined as those economic resources owned by a business which can be measured. All desired things, except those available in unlimited quantity without cost or effort, are economic resources.

Equities are interests in, or claims upon, assets. For example, assume that you purchased a new car for $6,000 by withdrawing $600 from your savings account and borrowing $5,400 from your credit union. Your equity in the automobile is $600, and that of your credit union is $5,400. The $5,400 can be further described as a *liability.* Your $600 equity is often described as the *owner's equity* or the residual equity or interest in the asset. Since, in the case of a single proprietorship, owner's equity is the residual equity, the basic equation is:

$$\text{Assets} - \text{Liabilities} = \text{Owner's Equity}$$

Another form of the equation, which we will be using is:

$$\text{Assets} = \text{Liabilities} + \text{Owner's Equity}$$

This equation must always be in balance. The sum of the interests in assets must always be equal to the assets themselves. It is logical to hold that all economic resources belong to someone or to some organization.

As a business engages in economic activity, the dollar amounts and the composition of its assets, liabilities, and owner's equity change. But the equality of the basic equation always holds.

Transaction analysis

Our society is characterized by *exchange*. That is, the bulk of the goods and services produced are exchanged rather than consumed by their producers. From this it follows that economic activity can be observed from the exchanges that take place. In accounting, these exchanges (as well as other changes) are called *transactions*. They provide much of the raw data entered in the accounting system. There are several reasons why this is so. First, an exchange is an observable event providing evidence of activity. Second, an exchange takes place at an agreed-upon price, and this price provides an *objective* measure of the economic activity that has occurred. Thus, the analysis of transactions is an important part of financial accounting.

To illustrate the analysis of transactions and their effects upon the basic accounting equation, the activities of the Brent Swimming Pool Service Company that led to the statements in Illustrations 1.2 and 1.3 are presented below.

Investment of owner's capital.   Assume that the Brent Swimming Pool Service Company was formed on July 1, 1981, and that in its first transaction the owner invested $30,000 cash. The transaction increased the assets (cash) of the company by $30,000 and increased its owner's equity by $30,000. Consequently, the transaction yields a basic accounting equation containing the following:

$$\text{Assets} = \text{Liabilities} + \text{Owner's Equity}$$

(Cash,	(William Brent,
$30,000)	capital, $30,000)

Borrowing of debt capital.   As its next transaction, the company borrowed $6,000 from Mrs. Brent's father, giving its written promise to repay the amount in one year. After including the effects of the second transaction, the basic equation is:

$$\text{Assets} = \text{Liabilities} + \text{Owner's Equity}$$

(Cash,	(Notes payable,	(William Brent,
$36,000)	$6,000)	capital, $30,000)

Purchase of assets for cash.   As its third transaction, the Brent Swimming Pool Service Company spent $6,000 for a truck, $14,000 for cleaning equipment, and $1,500 for some office equipment. In this transaction the Brent Swimming Pool Service Company received a truck priced at $6,000, cleaning equipment priced at $14,000, and office equipment priced at $1,500.

It gave up cash of $21,500. This transaction thus does not change the totals in the basic equation; it merely changes the composition of the assets. The equation now is as follows:

Assets		=	Liabilities		+	Owner's Equity	
Cash	$14,500						
Truck	6,000						
Cleaning						William	
equipment ...	14,000		Notes			Brent,	
Office			payable ...	$6,000		capital ...	$30,000
equipment ...	1,500			$6,000	+		$30,000
	$36,000	=					

Purchase of an asset and incurring a liability. Assume that as its fourth transaction the Brent Swimming Pool Service Company purchased $1,000 of office equipment, agreeing to pay for it within ten days after it receives a bill for it. This transaction increases liabilities in the form of accounts payable (which are amounts owed to creditors for items purchased from them) by $1,000. The items making up the totals in the accounting equation now appear as follows:

Assets		=	Liabilities		+	Owner's Equity	
Cash	$14,500						
Truck	6,000						
Cleaning			Notes				
equipment ...	14,000		payable ...	$6,000		William	
Office			Accounts			Brent,	
equipment ...	2,500		payable ...	1,000		capital ...	$30,000
	$37,000	=		$7,000	+		$30,000

Revenue and expense transactions

Thus far the transactions presented have consisted of exchanges or of the acquisition of assets either by borrowing or by owner investment. But a business is not formed merely to acquire assets. Rather, it seeks to use the assets entrusted to it to secure still greater amounts of assets. This is accomplished by providing customers with goods or services, with the expectation that the value of the assets received from customers will exceed the cost of the assets consumed in serving them. The sales of goods or services to customers have been defined as *revenues.* Thus, revenues are a source of assets. The costs of serving customers are called *expenses.* As stated earlier, expenses are measured by the cost of the assets surrendered or consumed in producing revenues. *If revenues exceed expenses, net earnings* exist. If not, a *net loss* has been suffered.

The earning of revenues for cash. Assume that cleaning services are performed for customers and $4,800 cash is received as a result (transaction 5). The cash balance increases by $4,800, and the owner's capital increases by $4,800, because revenues increase the owner's capital.

Including the effects of the revenue transaction upon the financial status of the Brent Swimming Pool Service Company yields the following basic equation:

Assets		=	Liabilities		+	Owner's Equity	
Cash	$19,300						
Truck	6,000					William	
Cleaning			Notes			Brent,	
equipment ..	14,000		payable	$6,000		capital .	$34,800 (including
Office			Accounts				$4,800 of
equipment ..	2,500		payable	1,000			service revenue)
	$41,800	=		$7,000	+		$34,800

The expectation is that revenue transactions will yield net earnings. If net earnings are not withdrawn by the owner, they become an addition to the owner's capital account. Later chapters will show that because of complexities in handling large numbers of transactions, revenues will be shown as affecting the owner's capital only at the end of an accounting period. The procedure shown above is a shortcut used to explain why the accounting equation remains in balance.

The earning of revenues on account. Assume that as its sixth transaction the company performs services for customers who agree to pay $900 at a later date. The transaction consists of an exchange of services for a promise by the customer to pay later. It is similar to the preceding transaction in that owner's equity is increased because revenues have been earned. It differs because cash has not been received. But a thing of value, an asset, has been received. This is the claim upon the customer, the right to collect at a later date. Technically, such claims are called *accounts receivable.* But the important point is that accounting does recognize them as assets and does record them. The accounting equation, including this item, is as follows:

Assets		=	Liabilities		+	Owner's Equity	
Cash	$19,300						
Accounts							
receivable ..	900						
Truck	6,000					William	
Cleaning			Notes			Brent,	
equipment ..	14,000		payable	$6,000		capital	$35,700 (including
Office			Accounts				$5,700 of
equipment ..	2,500		payable	1,000			service revenue)
	$42,700	=		$7,000	+		$35,700

Collection of an account receivable. Assume that $200 is collected from customers "on account" (transaction 7). The transaction consists of the giving up of claims upon customers in exchange for cash. The effects of the transaction are to increase cash by $200 to $19,500 and to decrease accounts receivable by $200 to $700. Note that this transaction consists solely of a change in the composition of the assets, not of an increase in assets resulting from the generation of revenue.

Payment of wages. The payment of wages of $2,600 (transaction 8) consists of an exchange of cash for employee services. Typically, the employee services have already been received by the time payment is made. Thus, the accountant treats the transaction as a decrease in an asset and a decrease in owner's equity, caused by incurring an expense.

Payment of rent and utilities. Let us further assume (as transactions 9 and 10) that the company paid cash of $300 as rent for truck storage space and office space and that it paid its utilities bill for July in the amount of $100. These transactions will be treated by the accountant as having the same effect upon the financial position of the company. They cause a decrease in the asset, cash, of $400 and a decrease in owner's equity of $400 because of the incurrence of rent expense of $300 and utilities expense of $100.

Including all of the above items into the accounting equation, it now reads:

Assets		=	Liabilities		+	Owner's Equity	
Cash	$16,500					William Brent,	
Accounts receivable	700					capital	$32,700 (including service revenue of $5,700 less wages expense of $2,600, rent expense of $300, and utilities expense of $100)
Truck	6,000		Notes				
Cleaning equipment	14,000		payable	$6,000			
Office equipment	2,500		Accounts payable	1,000			
	$39,700 =			$7,000 +			$32,700

Gas and oil expense and advertising expense. Because of their similar effects, transactions 11 and 12 of the company may be treated together. Assume that the company received a bill for gasoline, oil, and other supplies consumed during the month in the amount of $400 and a bill for $200 for advertising in July. Both transactions involve an increase in a liability, accounts payable, and a decrease in owner's equity because of the incurrence of an expense. The accounting equation of the Brent Swimming Pool Service Company now reads:

Assets		=	Liabilities		+	Owner's Equity	
Cash	$16,500					William Brent,	
Accounts receivable	700					capital	$32,100 (including service revenue of $5,700 less the following expenses— wages, $2,600; rent, $300; utilities, $100; gas and oil, $400; and advertising, $200)
Truck	6,000		Notes				
Cleaning equipment	14,000		payable	$6,000			
Office equipment	2,500		Accounts payable	1,600			
	$39,700 =			$7,600 +			$32,100

Payment of an accounts payable. Next (transaction 13), the company paid the $1,000 balance due on the purchase of the office equipment (transaction 4). This reduced the cash by $1,000 and reduced the debt owed to the equipment supplier, recorded as an account payable, by $1,000. Thus, assets and liabilities are both reduced by $1,000.

Payment of a notes payable. Finally (transaction 14), in reviewing his needs for cash at the end of the month, Mr. Brent decided that he would not need as much cash as he now holds. So he paid $3,000 on the note owed to his father-in-law, plus interest of $30 for the month. Thus, cash was decreased by $3,030, notes payable was decreased by $3,000, and owner's equity was decreased by $30 (the amount of interest expense).

The basic equation as it stands after including the effects of transactions 13 and 14 is shown in the last line of Illustration 1.4.

SUMMARY OF TRANSACTIONS

The effects of the transactions entered into by the Brent Swimming Pool Service Company in its first month upon its assets, liabilities, and owner's equity are summarized in Illustration 1.4. The itemized data in the owner's equity column (except for the owner's investment of $30,000) are the revenue and expense items reported in the earnings statement in Illustration 1.3. This summary further shows how the *basic equation* of Assets = Equities is subdivided into the three major elements of financial accounting: *assets, liabilities,* and *owner's equity.* The totals shown at the bottom of the illustration also can be found in Illustration 1.2.

Illustration 1.4:
Summary of transactions

BRENT SWIMMING POOL SERVICE COMPANY
Summary of Transactions
Month of July 1981

Trans-action	Explanation	Cash +	Accounts Receiv-able +	Truck +	Cleaning Equip-ment +	Office Equip-ment	= Notes Payable +	Accounts Payable	+ William Brent, Capital
	Beginning balances ...	$ –0–	$–0–	$ –0–	$ –0–	$ –0–	$ –0–	$ –0–	$ –0–
1	Investment of cash by owner	+30,000							+30,000
2	Borrowed money on note	+6,000					+6,000		
3	Purchased equipment for cash	–21,500		+6,000	+14,000	+1,500			
4	Purchased equipment on account					+1,000		+1,000	
5	Service revenue for cash	+4,800							+4,800(service revenue)
6	Service revenue on account		+900						+900(service revenue)
7	Collection on account..	+200	–200						
8	Paid wages	–2,600							–2,600(wages expense)
9	Paid rent	–300							–300(rent expense)
10	Paid utilities bill	–100							–100(utilities expense)
11	Bill for gas and oil used							+400	–400(gas and oil expense)
12	Bill for July advertising							+200	–200(advertising expense)
13	Paid equipment bill	–1,000						–1,000	
14	Payment on note and interest	–3,030					–3,000		–30(interest expense)
	Ending balances	$ 12,470 +	$ 700 +	$ 6,000 +	$ 14,000 +	$ 2,500 =	$ 3,000 +	$ 600 +	$ 32,070
				$35,670		=		$3,600	+ $32,070

WITHDRAWALS BY OWNER

We have seen that owner's equity is increased by capital contributed by the owner and by revenues earned through operations. We also saw that owner's equity is decreased by expenses incurred in producing revenues. Withdrawals of cash or other assets and payment of the owner's personal bills out of company funds also reduce owner's equity. Thus if the owner withdrew $1,000 cash from the business, the effect would be to reduce cash and owner's equity by that amount. This amount is not an expense but is instead a distribution of earnings.

UNDERLYING ASSUMPTIONS OR BASIC CONCEPTS

The accountant, in seeking to provide useful information on economic activity, relies upon some underlying assumptions or basic concepts. Those which have been covered, explicitly or implicitly, thus far in this chapter are summarized below.

Entity (accounting entity)

The data gathered in an accounting system relate to a specific business unit or entity. This entity is deemed to have an existence separate and apart from its owners, creditors, employees, and other interested parties.

Transactions

Those events or happenings that affect the assets, liabilities, owner's equity, revenues, and expenses of an entity are called transactions and are recorded in the accounting system. For the most part, transactions consist of exchanges.

Duality

Every transaction has a two-sided or dual effect upon each of the parties engaging in it. Consequently, if information is to be complete, both sides or both effects of every transaction must be included in the accounting system.

Money measurement

Economic activity is recorded and reported in terms of a common unit of measurement—the dollar. If not expressed in a common unit of measurement, accounting reports would be much less useful, if not unintelligible. Changes in the value of the dollar are usually ignored.

Cost

Most of the numbers entered in an accounting system are the bargained prices of exchange transactions. The result is that most assets (excluding cash and receivables) are recorded and reported at their cost of acquisition. Changes in the values of the assets are (with certain exceptions) usually ignored. This practice is usually defended on the grounds of objectivity and the absence of evidence that the acquiring firm would have been willing to pay more. The historical cost basis of asset valuation has come under severe criticism in recent years, due largely to the "double-digit" inflation experienced.

Periodicity

To be useful, information must be (among other things) timely and current. To provide such information, accountants subdivide the life of an entity into periods and report upon its activities for those periods. The requirement of periodic reporting will require the use of estimates, thus making every accounting report somewhat tentative in nature.

Continuity

Unless strong evidence exists to the contrary, the accountant assumes that the entity will continue operations into the indefinite future. Consequently, assets that will be used up or consumed in future operations need not be reported at their current liquidation values.

The underlying assumptions or basic concepts of accounting will be discussed further in Chapter 13.

NEW TERMS INTRODUCED IN CHAPTER 1

Accounting—the process used to measure and report to various users relevant financial information regarding the economic activities of an organization or unit. *Financial accounting* relates to the process of supplying financial information to parties external to the reporting entity. *Managerial accounting* relates to the process of supplying financial information for internal management use. As a field of employment, accounting is usually divided into *public accounting,* where accounting and related services are offered to the general public for a fee; *private (or industrial) accounting,* where the accountant performs services for one business employer; and *governmental accounting,* where the accountant is employed by and renders services for a governmental agency.

Accounting equation—basically, Assets = Equities; in slightly expanded form: Assets = Liabilities + Owner's Equity.

Accounting Principles Board (APB)—an organization created by the AICPA and empowered to speak for it on matters of accounting principle; replaced by the Financial Accounting Standards Board.

Accounts payable—amounts owed to creditors for items or services purchased from them.

Accounts receivable—amounts owed to a concern by its customers.

American Accounting Association (AAA)—a professional organization of accountants many of whom are college or university instructors of accounting.

American Institute of Certified Public Accountants (AICPA)—a professional organization of certified public accountants, most of whom are in public accounting practice.

Annual report—a pamphlet or document of varying length containing financial and other information about and distributed by a company to its stockholders.

Assets—things of value or economic resources; things possessing service potential or utility to their owner that can be measured and expressed in money terms.

Auditing—that branch of the accounting profession that is concerned with checking, reviewing, testing, and verifying the accounting work of others, generally with the objective of expressing a formal opinion on the fairness of the resulting information.

Auditor's opinion or report—the formal written statement by a public accountant (usually a CPA) attesting to the fairness of the information contained in a set of financial statements; for an example, see the Appendix to Chapter 18.

Balance sheet—a formal statement of the assets, liabilities, and owner's equity of an entity as of a specific date.

Certified public accountant (CPA)—an accountant who has been awarded a certificate and granted the right to be called a certified public accountant as a result of having passed a special examination and having met other requirements such as experience and education.

Continuity (going concern)—the assumption by the accountant that, unless specific evidence exists to the contrary, a business firm will continue to operate into the indefinite future.

Corporation—a legal form of organization often adopted by businesses; a business which is owned by many stockholders and frequently directed by hired managers.

Cost—the sacrifice made or the resources given up to acquire some desired thing; the basis of valuation of the bulk of the assets of a business.

Duality—the assumption by the accountant that every transaction has a dual or two-sided effect upon the party or parties engaging in it.

Earnings statement—a formal array or summary of the revenues and expenses of an organization for a specified period of time.

Entity—a unit that is deemed to have an existence separate and apart from its owners, creditors, employees, and other interested parties and for which an accounting is undertaken.

Equities—broadly speaking, all claims to or interests in assets (liabilities and owner's equity).

Expenses—the sacrifice made, usually measured in terms of the cost of the assets surrendered or consumed, to generate revenues.

Financial Accounting Standards Board (FASB)—the highest ranking nongovernmental authority on the development of accounting standards or principles.

Generally accepted accounting principles (GAAP)—accounting standards and principles which have developed largely in accounting practice or have been established by an authoritative body.

Liabilities—debts or obligations that usually possess a known or determinable amount, maturity date, and party to whom payment is to be made.

Money measurement—expression of a property of an object in terms of a number of units of a standard monetary medium, such as the dollar.

Net earnings—the amount by which the revenues of a period exceed the expenses of the same period.

Net loss—the amount by which the expenses of a period exceed the revenues of the same period.

Notes payable—written promises to pay to other parties definite sums of money at certain or determinable dates, usually with interest at specified rates.

Partnership—a business firm owned by two or more persons associated as partners.

Periodicity—the assumption that the life of an entity can be divided into periods of time and that useful information can be provided as to the activities of the entity for those periods.

Revenues—result from the sale of goods or providing of services to customers, and they produce an inflow of assets.

Single proprietorship—a business firm owned by one person.

Transactions—recordable happenings or events (usually exchanges) that affect the assets, liabilities, owner's equity, revenues, or expenses of an entity.

U.S. Securities and Exchange Commission—a governmental agency created by the Congress to administer certain acts and having the authority to prescribe the accounting and reporting practices of firms required to file financial statements with it.

DEMONSTRATION PROBLEM

On June 1, 1981, Marty Paulk formed the Le Bon Coeur Riding Stable. The following transactions occurred during June:

June 1	The owner invested $10,000 cash in the business.
4	A horse stable and riding equipment were rented (and paid for) for the month at a cost of $1,200.
8	Horse feed for the month was purchased on credit, $800.
15	Fees of $3,000 for the month were charged to those owning horses who were boarding their horses at the stable. (This amount was due on July 10.)
20	Miscellaneous expenses of $600 for June were paid.
24	The owner withdrew $500 cash.
29	Land was purchased from a savings and loan association by borrowing $40,000 from that association. The loan is due to be repaid in five years. Interest payments are due at the end of each month beginning July 31.
30	Salaries of $700 for the month were paid.
30	Riding and lesson fees were billed to customers in the amount of $2,400. (They are due on July 10.)

Required:

a. Prepare a summary of the above transactions (see Illustration 1.4). Use columns headed Cash, Accounts Receivable, Land, Accounts Payable, Loan Payable, and Marty Paulk, Capital. Determine balances after each transaction to show that the basic equation balances.

b. Prepare an earnings statement for the month of June 1981.

c. Prepare a balance sheet as of June 30, 1981.

Solution to demonstration problem

a.

		Assets			=	Liabilities		+	Owner's Equity
Date	Explanation	Cash	Accounts receivable	Land		Accounts payable	Loan payable		Marty Paulk, capital
June 1	Owner investment	$10,000			=				$10,000
4	Rent expense	−1,200							−1,200
		$ 8,800			=				$ 8,800
8	Feed expense					$+800			−800
		$ 8,800			=	$ 800		+	$ 8,000
15	Boarding fees		$+3,000						+3,000
		$ 8,800	$ 3,000		=	$ 800		+	$11,000
20	Miscellaneous expenses	−600							−600
		$ 8,200	$ 3,000		=	$ 800		+	$10,400
24	Owner withdrawal	−500							−500
		$ 7,700	$ 3,000		=	$ 800		+	$ 9,900
29	Purchased land by borrowing			$+40,000			$+40,000		
		$ 7,700	$ 3,000	$ 40,000	=	$ 800	$ 40,000	+	$ 9,900
30	Salaries paid	−700							−700
		$ 7,000	$ 3,000	$ 40,000	=	$ 800	$ 40,000	+	$ 9,200
30	Riding and lesson fees billed		+2,400						+2,400
		$ 7,000	$ 5,400	$ 40,000	=	$ 800	$ 40,000	+	$11,600

b.

the good heart

```
                    LE BON COEUR RIDING STABLE
                        Earnings Statement
                   For the Month Ended June 30, 1981

Revenues:
Horse boarding fees .........................................    $3,000
Riding and lesson fees ......................................     2,400
      Total revenues ........................................            $5,400

Expenses:
Rent expense ................................................    $1,200
Feed expense ................................................       800
Miscellaneous expenses ......................................       600
Salaries expense ............................................       700
      Total expenses ........................................             3,300
Net Earnings ................................................            $2,100
```

c.

```
                    LE BON COEUR RIDING STABLE
                          Balance Sheet
                          June 30, 1981

                            Assets

Current Assets:
Cash ........................................................    $7,000
Accounts receivable .........................................     5,400
      Total Current Assets ..................................           $12,400
Land ........................................................            40,000
            Total Assets ....................................           $52,400

                  Liabilities and Owner's Equity

Current Liabilities:
Accounts payable ............................................           $   800

Long-Term Liabilities:
Loan payable ................................................            40,000

Owner's Equity:
Marty Paulk, capital ........................................            11,600
            Total Liabilities and Owner's Equity ............           $52,400
```

QUESTIONS

1. Define accounting. What does the term "relevant" mean when speaking of accounting information? Give an example of relevant information.

2. Accounting has often been called the "language of business." In what respects would you agree with this designation? How might it be argued that it is deficient?

3. What is the relationship between accounting as an information system and economic resources?

4. Define asset, liability, and owner's equity.

5. How do liabilities and owner's equity differ? In what respects are they similar?

6. How do accounts payable and notes payable differ? How are they similar?

7. What is revenue?

8. Define expense. How is expense measured?

9. How does accounting information usually enter into the decision-making process?

10. Name four organizations that have played or are playing an important role in the development of accounting standards. Describe each briefly.

11. What is a CPA? What are some of the services usually provided by a CPA?

12. What is the role of the accountant in private industry? What are some of the services provided by the industrial accountant?

13. Identify and briefly describe the three forms of organization for a business entity.

14. What is a balance sheet? This statement generally seeks to provide information relative to what aspect of a business?

15. What is an earnings statement? This statement generally provides information on what aspect of a business?

16. What is a transaction? What use does the accountant make of transactions? Why?

17. What is the accounting equation? Why must it always balance?

18. Give an example from your personal life that you believe illustrates your use of accounting information in reaching a decision.

19. What is the accounting entity assumption? Why is it needed?

20. What is the duality assumption of accounting? Why is it needed?

21. You are a young married person who three years ago purchased a home by borrowing $20,000 on a mortgage. You recently received an inheritance of $25,000 and are considering paying off the mortgage. What types of financial information would you seek in helping you arrive at a decision?

22. You have been elected to the board of deacons of your church. At the first meeting you attend, mention is made of building a new church. What accounting information would the board need in deciding whether or not to go ahead?

EXERCISES

E–1. Give examples of transactions that would have the following effects upon the elements in a firm's accounting system:

a. Increase cash; decrease some other asset.

b. Decrease cash; increase some other asset.

c. Increase an asset; increase a liability.

d. Increase an expense; decrease an asset.

e. Increase an asset other than cash; increase revenue.

f. Decrease an asset; decrease a liability.

E–2. Assume that owner's capital increased from operations by $26,000 from June 30, 1981, to June 30, 1982. Assume expenses for the year were $60,000. Compute the revenue for the year.

E–3. On December 31, 1981, M Company had assets of $360,000, liabilities of $260,000, and owner's equity of $100,000. During 1982 it earned revenues of $120,000 and incurred expenses of $98,000. Compute the owner's equity amount on December 31, 1982.

E–4. For each of the happenings below, determine whether or not it has an effect upon the basic accounting equation. For those that do, present an analysis of the transaction showing clearly its two sides or dual nature.

a. Purchased some supplies for cash, $1,000. The supplies will be used next year.

b. Purchased a truck for $10,000, payment to be made next month.

c. Paid $200 cash for the current month's utilities.

d. Paid for the truck purchased in *(b)*.

e. Employed Don Kettler as a salesperson at $2,000 per month. He is to start work next week.

f. Signed an agreement with a bank in which the bank agreed to lend the company up to $200,000 any time within the next two years.

E–5. Which of the following transactions results in an increase in an expense? Why?

a. Cash of $20,000 is paid to employees for services received during the month.

b. Cash of $1,000 paid to a supplier in settlement of a promise to pay given when some advertising supplies were purchased.

c. Paid $10,000 of principal plus $400 of interest on a note payable.

d. Paid $50 cash as a refundable deposit when an additional telephone was installed.

E-6. At the start of a year a company had liabilities of $36,000 and owner's equity of $100,000. Net earnings for the year were $30,000, and $10,000 cash was withdrawn by the owner. Compute owner's equity at the end of the year and total assets at the beginning of the year.

E-7. Selected data for the York Company for the year 1981 are as follows (including all earnings statement data):

Revenue from services rendered on account	$ 55,000
Revenue from services rendered for cash	15,000
Cash collected from customers on account	42,000
Owner's equity, 1/1/81	80,000
Expenses incurred on account	30,000
Expenses incurred for cash	20,000
Cash withdrawn by owner......................	5,000
Additional investment by owner for cash	10,000
Owner's equity, 12/31/81	105,000

a. Compute net earnings for 1981 using an earnings statement approach.

b. Compute net earnings for 1981 by analyzing the changes in owner's equity between January 1 and December 31, 1981.

PROBLEMS, SERIES A

P1-1-A. The Jay Block Company, which provides financial advisory services, engaged in the following transactions during the month of May:

May 1 Received $50,000 cash investment from the owner.
2 The company borrowed $8,000 cash from the bank on a note.
7 The company bought $45,600 of computer equipment for cash.
11 Cash received for services performed to date was $3,800.
14 Services performed for customers who agree to pay within a month were $2,500.
15 Employee services received in operating the business to date were paid in cash, $3,300.
19 The company paid $3,500 on the note to the bank.
31 Interest paid to the bank for May was $35.
31 Customers of May 14 paid $800 of the amount they owe the company.
31 An order was received from a customer for services to be rendered next week which will be billed at $2,000.

Required:

Prepare a summary of the above transactions (see Illustration 1.4). Use money columns headed Cash, Accounts Receivable, Equipment, Notes Payable, and Jay Block, Capital. Determine balances after each transaction to show that the basic equation balances.

P1-2-A. The Jane Hewes Company engaged in the following transactions in April:

Apr. 1 The owner invested $20,000 cash in the business.
4 The company bought land for cash, $11,550.
15 Cash received for services performed to date was $400.

Apr. 16 Amounts due from customers for services performed totaled $550.
30 Of the receivables (see April 16), $320 were collected in cash.
30 Various costs of operating the business during the month of $650 were incurred and were to be paid for in 30 days.
30 An order was placed for equipment advertised at $3,000.

Required:

a. Prepare a summary of transactions (see Illustration 1.4). Use money columns headed Cash, Accounts Receivable, Land, Accounts Payable, and Jane Hewes, Capital. Determine balances after each transaction.

b. Prepare a balance sheet as of April 30.

P1-3-A. Following are the transactions for August 1981 of the Palace Theater, a theater owned by James Roberts:

Aug. 2 Paid current month's rent of building, $8,000.
7 Cash ticket revenue for the week, $4,800.
14 Cash ticket revenue for the week, $5,600.
15 Cash withdrawal by owner, $1,000.
21 Cash ticket revenue for the week, $3,200.
24 Paid month's advertising bill, $3,800.
27 Sundry expenses paid, $1,400.
31 Paid rental on films shown during month, $10,000.
31 Received $12,400 cash from operators of concessions for operating in theater during August.
31 Cash ticket revenue for August 22–31, $8,400.
31 Paid $1,500 cash to guarantee receipt of a special film to be shown in September.
31 Paid payroll for the month, $13,200.

Required:

Prepare an earnings statement for August 1981.

P1–4–A. Analysis of the transactions of the Jackson Drive-In Theater, owned by Samuel Jackson, for the month of June 1981 discloses the following:

Ticket revenue	$26,600
Rent of premises and equipment	5,000
Film rental paid	8,900
Receipts from concessionaires (percentage basis)	5,000
Advertising expense	3,100
Wages and salaries	7,800
Utilities expense	2,350

Asset and liability amounts at June 30 include the following:

Cash	$40,000
Land	8,000
Accounts payable	10,400

The balance in the Samuel Jackson capital account on June 1 was $33,150.

Required:

a. Prepare an earnings statement for the month of June 1981.

b. Prepare a balance sheet as of June 30, 1981.

Summarized, the activities for the month of May 1981 are as follows:

1. The owner invested an additional $30,000 cash in the business.
2. Collected $20,000 on accounts receivable.
3. Paid $16,000 on accounts payable.
4. Sold land costing $50,000 for $75,000 cash.
5. Decorating services were rendered to customers: for cash, $40,000; and on account, $30,000.
6. Employee services and other operating costs were incurred: for cash, $15,000; and on account, $40,000.
7. The owner withdrew $4,000 cash.
8. Paid building rent for year beginning on June 1, 1981, $24,000.
9. Placed an order for new equipment expected to cost $80,000.

Required:

a. Prepare a summary of transactions (see Illustration 1.4) using column headings for items appearing in the above balance sheet plus one for prepaid rent (an asset). Determine balances after each transaction.

b. Prepare an earnings statement for the month of May 1981.

c. Prepare a balance sheet as of May 31, 1981.

P1–5–A.

BETTY MASON COMPANY
Balance Sheet
April 30, 1981

Assets

Current Assets:

Cash	$14,000	
Accounts receivable	20,000	$ 34,000
Land		150,000
Total Assets		$184,000

Liabilities and Owner's Equity

Current Liabilities:

Accounts payable	$ 16,000

Owner's Equity:

Betty Mason, capital	168,000
Total Liabilities and Owner's Equity	$184,000

P1–6–A. Given below are comparative balance sheets and the earnings statement of the J. Ross Company.

J. ROSS COMPANY
Balance Sheet

	May 31, 1981	June 30, 1981
Assets		
Cash	$10,000	$11,000
Accounts receivable	–0–	4,000
Supplies	6,000	2,000
Total Assets	$16,000	$17,000
Liabilities and Owner's Equity		
Liabilities	$ 4,000	$ 2,000
J. Ross, capital	12,000	15,000
Total Liabilities and Owner's Equity	$16,000	$17,000

J. ROSS COMPANY
Earnings Statement
For the Month Ended June 30, 1981

Revenue from services rendered		$16,000
Expenses:		
Salaries	$8,000	
Supplies used	4,000	12,000
Net Earnings		$ 4,000

The owner withdrew $1,000 cash in June.

Required:

State the probable causes of the changes in each of the balance sheet accounts from May 31 to June 30, 1981.

PROBLEMS, SERIES B

P1–1–B. The Jack Beam Company completed the following transactions in September 1981:

Sept. 1 The company is organized and receives $20,000 cash investment from the owner.

5 The company bought equipment for cash at a cost of $5,400.

7 The company performed services for customers who agreed to pay $2,000 in one week.

14 The company received the $2,000 from the transaction of September 7.

20 Equipment which cost $800 was acquired today; payment was postponed until September 28.

28 $600 is paid on the liability incurred on September 20.

30 Employee services for the month, $700, are paid.

30 Placed an order for new equipment advertised at $5,000.

Required:

Prepare a summary of transactions (see Illustration 1.4) for the company for the above transactions. Use money columns headed Cash, Accounts Receivable, Equipment, Accounts Payable, and Jack Beam, Capital. Determine balances after each transaction.

P1–2–B. The Elaine Boggs Company completed the following transactions in June 1981:

June 1 The company was organized and received $40,000 cash investment from the owner.

4 The company paid $32,000 cash for land.

7 The company borrowed $6,000 cash from its bank on a note.

9 Cash received for services performed to date is $3,000.

12 Costs of operating the business so far this month are paid in cash, $2,100.

June 18   Services performed for customers who agree to pay within a month amounted to $3,600.
    25   The company repaid $2,710 of its loan from the bank, including $10 of interest.
    30   Expenses of operating the business from June 13 to date are $2,550 and were paid in cash.
    30   An order was received from a customer for services to be performed tomorrow, which will be billed at $2,000.

Required:

a. Prepare a summary of transactions (see Illustration 1.4). Determine balances after each transaction. Include money columns for Cash, Accounts Receivable, Land, Notes Payable, and Elaine Boggs, Capital.

b. Prepare a balance sheet as of June 30, 1981.

P1–3–B.

Required:

From the following selected transaction data for the Norman Breer Company, prepare an earnings statement for the month of May 1981:

May 1   Paid May rent on the parking structure, $10,000.
     8   Cash received for eight days' parking services, $4,840.
    15   Cash received for week's parking services, $6,040.
    16   Paid employee wages for the first half of May, $2,400.
    17   Received cash from additional investment by owner, $5,000.
    19   Paid advertising expenses for May, $800.
    22   Cash received for week's parking services, $7,920.
    31   Paid wages for last half of May, $3,000.
    31   Cash received for nine days' parking services, $7,040.
    31   Purchased motorized sweeper to clean parking structure, $6,000 cash.
    31   Paid June rent on the parking structure, $10,000.

P1–4–B. Following are summarized transaction data for the Nancy Lopez Company for the year ending June 30, 1981:

Rent revenue from building owned	$200,000
Interest revenue from bonds owned	36,000
Dividend revenue from stocks owned	28,000
Interest revenue from bank savings accounts	1,800
Building repairs	8,200
Building cleaning, labor cost	9,100
Property taxes on the building	10,300
Insurance on the building	3,500
Commissions paid to rental agent	15,000
Legal fees (for preparation of tenant leases)	3,600
Heating	8,400
Electricity	15,100
Cleaning supplies on hand	3,000
Cost of new awnings installed	5,000

Of the $200,000 of rent revenue above, $10,000 was not collected in cash until July 5, 1981.

Required:

Prepare an earnings statement for the year ended June 30, 1981.

P1–5–B. The following data are for the Ronald Wilson Company. The balance sheet for the company for September 30, 1981, was:

Assets

Cash	$68,000
Accounts receivable	6,000
	$74,000

Equities

Accounts payable	$18,000
Ronald Wilson, capital	56,000
	$74,000

Transactions:

Oct. 1   The accounts payable owed as of September 30 ($18,000) are paid.
      7   The company received cash of $1,400 for parking by daily customers during the week.
     10   The company collected $4,800 of the accounts receivable in the balance sheet at September 30.
     14   Cash receipts for the week from daily customers were $2,200.
     15   Parking revenue earned but not yet collected from fleet customers, $1,000.
     16   The company paid wages of $800 for the period October 1–15.
     19   The company paid advertising expenses of $400 for October.
     21   Cash receipts for the week from daily customers were $2,400.
     24   The company incurred sundry expenses of $280 which will be due November 10.
     31   Cash receipts for the last ten days of the month from daily customers were $2,800.
     31   The company paid wages of $1,000 for the period October 16–31.
     31   Billings to monthly customers totaled $7,200 for October.
     31   The company paid rent for the premises for October, $6,400.

Required:

a. Prepare a summary of transactions (see Illustration 1.4) using column headings for items given in the above balance sheet. Determine balances after each transaction.

b. Prepare an earnings statement for October 1981.

c. Prepare a balance sheet as of October 31, 1981.

P1–6–B. Given below are the comparative balance sheets and the earnings statement of the Kent Andrews Company:

KENT ANDREWS COMPANY
Balance Sheet

Assets	April 30, 1981	May 31, 1981
Current Assets:		
Cash	$16,000	$18,000
Accounts receivable	24,000	30,000
Prepaid rent	6,000	4,000
Total Assets	$46,000	$52,000
Liabilities and Owner's Equity		
Liabilities	$12,000	$10,000
Kent Andrews, capital	34,000	42,000
Total Liabilities and Owner's Equity	$46,000	$52,000

KENT ANDREWS COMPANY
Earnings Statement
For the Month Ended May 31, 1981

Revenues from services rendered		$30,000
Expenses:		
Salaries and wages	$20,000	
Rent	2,000	22,000
Net Earnings		$ 8,000

All revenues earned are on account. The liabilities are for unpaid salaries and wages.

Required:

State the probable causes of the changes in each of the balance sheet accounts from April 30 to May 31, 1981.

BUSINESS DECISION PROBLEM

Upon graduation from high school, Bill Loma went to work for a builder of houses and small apartment buildings. During the next six years Bill earned a reputation as an excellent employee—hard working, dedicated, and dependable—and as a very capable all-around employee in the light construction industry. He could handle almost any job requiring carpentry, electrical, or plumbing skills.

Bill then decided to go into business for himself under the name of Bill's Fix-It Shop. He invested cash, some power tools, and a used truck in his business. He completed many repair and remodeling jobs for both home-owners and apartment owners. The demand for his services was so large that he had more work than he could handle. He operated out of his garage which he had converted into a shop, adding several new pieces of power woodworking equipment.

Two years after going into business for himself Bill is faced with a decision of whether to continue in his own business or to accept a position as construction supervisor for a home builder. He has been offered an annual salary of $25,000 and a package of "fringe benefits" (medical and hospitalization insurance, pension contribution, vacation and sick pay, and life insurance) worth approximately $5,000 per year. The offer is very attractive to Bill. But he dislikes giving up his business since he has thoroughly enjoyed "being his own boss," even though it has led to an average workweek well in excess of the standard 40-hour week.

Bill now comes to you for assistance in gathering the information needed to help him make a decision. Adequate accounting records have been maintained for his business by an experienced accountant.

Required:

Indicate the nature of the information Bill needs if he is to make an informed decision. Pay particular attention to the information likely to be found in the accounting records for his business that would be useful. Does the accounting information available enter directly into the decision? Explain. Would you expect that Bill could sell his business assets for more or less than their recorded amount? Why?

PART TWO

PROCESSING ACCOUNTING

INFORMATION

Chapter 2

Recording business

transactions

This chapter introduces the basic parts in the accounting system—the ledger (book) of accounts and the journal—and illustrates their use in recording business transactions. Knowledge of the underlying recording process should yield greater understanding of the end products—the financial statements.

In Chapter 1 the effects of transactions were shown as increases or decreases in the elements in the basic accounting equation. This approach was adopted solely to obtain easy understanding of some basic relationships. It is far too cumbersome to be used in actual practice, since even a small business enters into a huge number of transactions every week, month, or year.

THE ACCOUNTING SYSTEM: The account

A business may engage in thousands of transactions. The data in these transactions must be classified and summarized before they become useful information. Making the accountant's task somewhat easier is the fact that most business transactions are repetitive in nature and can be classified into groups having common characteristics. For example, there may be thousands of receipts or payments of cash. As a result, a part of every transaction affecting cash will be recorded and summarized in an account. An *account* will be set up whenever the data to be recorded in it are believed to be useful information to some party having a valid interest in the business. Thus, every business will have a Cash account in its accounting system simply because knowledge of the amount of cash owned is useful information.

An account may take on a variety of forms, from a printed format in which entries are written by hand to an invisible encoding on a piece of magnetic tape. Every account format must provide for increases and decreases in the item for which the account was established. The account balance, the difference between the increases and decreases, may then be determined.

The number of accounts in a given accounting system will depend upon the information needs of those interested in the business. The primary requirement is that the account provide useful information. Thus, one account may be set up for cash rather than separate accounts for cash in the form of coins, cash in the form of currency, and cash in the form of deposits in banks, simply because the amount of cash is useful information while the form of cash is not.

The T-account

The way an account functions is shown by use of a T-account. It is used in this text for illustrative purposes only (it is not a replica of a form of account actually used) and derives its name because it looks like the letter T. The name of the item accounted for (such as cash) is written across the top of the T. Increases are recorded on one side and decreases on the other side of the vertical line of the T.

Recording changes in assets and equities. Increases in assets are recorded on the left side of the account, decreases on the right side. For reasons to be explained later, the process is reversed for equity accounts (debt and owner's equity), for which increases are recorded on the right side. Thus, a company would record the receipt of $10,000 invested by its owner, John Stevens, as follows (the number in parentheses is used to tie the two sides of the transaction together):

Cash		John Stevens, Capital	
(1) 10,000			(1) 10,000

The transaction involves an increase in the asset, cash, which is recorded on the left side of the Cash account, and an increase in owner's equity, which is recorded on the right side of the John Stevens, Capital account.

Because liabilities are also equities, changes in them are recorded in the same manner as for owner's equity—increases on the right side, decreases on the left. Note that the asset amounts are shown on the left side of the account and the left side of the balance sheet; equity (liabilities and owner's equity) amounts are shown on the right side of the account and the right side of the balance sheet. But for easy recollection of these rules, all that one need remember is that increases in assets are recorded on the left side of the account and increases in equities are recorded on the right side of the account.

Recording changes in expenses and revenues. To understand the logic behind the recording of changes in expense and revenue accounts recall that all expenses and revenues could be recorded directly in the owner's capital account. Thus, (2) the receipt of $1,000 of cash from customers for services rendered and (3) the payment of $600 of cash to employees as wages could be recorded as follows:

Cash		John Stevens, Capital	
(2) 1,000	(3) 600	(3) 600	(2) 1,000

But since their amounts are likely to be significant information, separate accounts are kept for revenues and expenses. The recording rules for these are as follows:

1. Since revenues increase owner's equity (and increases in owner's equity are recorded on the right side), it follows that increases in revenues should be recorded on the right side, decreases on the left.
2. Similarly, since expenses decrease owner's equity (and decreases in owner's equity are recorded on the left side), it follows that increases in expenses are recorded on the left, decreases on the right.

Following these rules, the service revenue and the wages would be recorded in the following manner:

Cash		Service Revenue	
(2) 1,000	(3) 600		(2) 1,000

Wages Expense	
(3) 600	

At the end of the accounting period the balances in the expense and revenue accounts are transferred to the owner's capital account. This is discussed and illustrated in the next chapter.

Withdrawals by the owner

If a business is successful, the owner is able to withdraw cash from the business to pay for living expenses and other items. These withdrawals are not an expense of the business but are a distribution of assets to the owner. But they have the same effect on owner's equity as an expense in that they reduce the owner's equity in the business. Just as investments increase the owner's equity, withdrawals reduce it. They are exact opposites.

Withdrawals could be shown directly as a reduction of the owner's capital account balance by entering its amount on the left side of that account. But a clearer record is available if a separate drawing account (for instance, John Stevens, Drawing) is used to record all amounts withdrawn.

A withdrawal of $100 cash by John Stevens would be shown as follows:

Cash		John Stevens, Drawing	
	(4) 100	(4) 100	

Debits and credits. The accountant uses the term *debit* in lieu of saying "place an entry on the left side of the account" and *credit* for "place an entry on the right side of an account." Debit (abbreviated Dr.) means simply left side; credit (abbreviated Cr.), right side.

Note that since assets and expenses are increased by debits or debit entries, these accounts normally have *debit* (or left side) *balances.* Conversely, liability, owner's equity, and revenue accounts are increased by credits or credit entries and normally have *credit* (or right side) *balances.* (For purposes of the rules of debit and credit, the owner's drawing account is like an expense account. It is increased by debits and decreased by credits.)

The balance of any account is obtained by summing the debits to the account, summing the credits to the account, and subtracting the smaller sum from the larger. If the sum of the debits exceeds the sum of the credits, the account has a debit balance. For example, the Cash account has a debit balance of $10,300, computed as total debits of $11,000 less total credits of $700, in the following T-account:

Cash			
(1)	10,000	(3)	600
(2)	1,000	(4)	100

For the most part, the amounts entered into the accounts are formed in the transactions entered into by the business. Business transactions are first analyzed to determine the effects (in terms of increase or decrease) that they have upon the assets, liabilities, owner's equity, revenues, or expenses of the business. Then these increases or decreases are translated into debits and credits. For example, an increase in an asset is recorded as a debit in the proper asset account. A synonym for "debit an account" is "charge an account." When an asset account is debited or charged, depending upon the transaction, there may be any of five credits:

1. Another asset account may be credited, that is, decreased.
2. A liability account may be credited, that is, increased.

3. The owner's equity account may be credited, that is, increased.
4. A revenue account may be credited, that is, increased.
5. An expense account may be credited, that is, decreased.

This double-entry procedure keeps the accounting equation in balance. Every transaction can be analyzed similarly into debits and credits.

The rules of debit and credit (*rule of double entry*) may be presented in account form as follows:

Debits	Credits
1. Increase assets.	1. Decrease assets.
2. Decrease liabilities.	2. Increase liabilities
3. Decrease owner's equity.	3. Increase owner's equity.
4. Decrease revenues.	4. Increase revenues.
5. Increase expenses.	5. Decrease expenses.

These rules may also be summarized as shown below. Note the treatment of expense accounts as if they were merely subsets of the debit side of the owner's capital account. And remember that increases in expenses do reduce what would otherwise be a larger growth in owner's capital; and if expenses are reduced, the owner's capital will increase. The exact reverse holds true for revenues.

Assets	=	*Liabilities*	+	*Owner's Equity*

An Asset Account		A Liability Account		Owner's Equity Account	
Debit	Credit	Debit	Credit	Debit	Credit
+	−	−	+	−	+
In-creases	De-creases	De-creases	In-creases	Decreases	Increases

Expense Accounts		Revenue Accounts	
Debit	Credit	Debit	Credit
+	−	−	+
In-creases	De-creases	De-creases	In-creases

The ledger

Accounts are classified into two general groups: (1) the balance sheet accounts (assets, liabilities, and owner's equity) and (2) the earnings statement accounts (revenues and expenses). *The accounts are collectively referred to as the **ledger**,* whether kept in a bound volume, handwritten in loose-leaf form, or magnetically encoded on plastic tape.

The list of the names of the accounts is known as the ***chart of accounts.*** Each account typically has an identification number as well as a name. For example, assets might be numbered from 100 to 199, liabilities from 200 to 299, owner's equity items from 300 to 399, revenues from 400 to 499, and expenses from 500 to 599. (The accounts usually appear in this order in the ledger.) The accounts would then be arranged in numerical sequence in the ledger. The use of account numbers helps to identify and locate accounts when recording data.

Having completed this introduction to accounts and the recording process, attention is now directed to the journal and to journal entries, as the means whereby data are entered into an accounting system.

The journal

Under double-entry accounting, every business transaction has a dual effect on the accounts of the business entity. And with the rare exception of transactions such as an exchange of land for land, every recorded business transaction will affect at least two ledger accounts. Since each ledger account shows only the increases and decreases in the item for which it was established, the entire effects of a single business transaction will not appear in any one account. For example, the Cash account contains only data on changes in cash and does not show the exact accounts credited for receipts of cash or the exact accounts debited for cash payments.

Therefore, if transactions are recorded directly in the accounts, it is difficult to determine the entire effects of any transaction upon an entity by looking at the accounts. Thus, the accountant uses a book or a record known as a journal. *A journal contains a chronological record of the transactions of a business.* Because each transaction is initially recorded in a journal, a journal is called a book of *original entry.* Here every business transaction is analyzed for its effects upon the entity. These effects are expressed in terms of debit and credit—the inputs of the accounting system.

The general journal. The simplest form of journal, the general journal, is illustrated and discussed in this chapter. Other forms or types of journals are discussed in Chapter 6. As shown in Illustration 2.1, a general journal contains columns for—

1. The date. The year and then the month and day appear with the first entry on each general journal page. For other entries on that page only the day of the month is shown.
2. The exact name of the account to be debited and the exact name of the account to be credited. The credit is shown on the line after the debit and is indented to the right. (Any necessary explanation of a transaction

Illustration 2.1:
General journal

GENERAL JOURNAL					*Page 1*
Date		Accounts and Explanation	L.F.	Debit	Credit
1981 Jan.	1	Cash .... John Stevens, Capital .... The owner invested cash in the business.	100 300	10,000	10,000
	5	Cash .... Service Revenue .... Services were performed for customers for cash.	100 400	1,000	1,000

appears on the line(s) below the transaction, indented halfway between the debit and credit entries.)

3. The Ledger Folio (L.F.) column; this column will be explained in the section below headed "Cross-indexing."

4. The debit column, in which the money amount of the debit is placed on the same line as the name of the account debited.

5. The credit column, in which the money amount of the credit is placed on the same line as the name of the account credited.

A blank line separates the entries for individual transactions.

Journalizing

Journalizing is the entering of a transaction in a journal. Information to be journalized comes from source materials or documents such as invoices, cash register tapes, timecards, and checks. The activity recorded on these documents must be analyzed to determine whether a recordable transaction has occurred. If so, the specific accounts affected, the dollar amounts of the changes, and their direction (whether increases or decreases) must also be determined. Then all of these changes must be translated into terms of debit and credit and entered in the journal.

Posting

In a sense, a *journal entry* is a set of instructions. It directs the entry of a certain dollar amount as a debit in a specific account. It also directs entry of a certain dollar amount as a credit in a specific account. *The carrying out of these instructions is known as posting.* In Illustration 2.2, the first entry directs that $10,000 be posted as a debit to the Cash account and as a credit to the John Stevens, Capital account. (The arrows in the illustration show how these amounts have been posted to the correct accounts.) The three-column balance type of account is shown in that illustration. In contrast to the two-sided T-account format shown so far, the three-column format has columns for debit, credit, and balance. One advantage of this form is that the balance of the account is shown after each item has been posted.

Postings to the ledger accounts may be made (1) at the time the transaction is journalized; (2) at the end of the day, week, or month; or (3) as each journal page is filled.

Cross-indexing

The number of the ledger account to which the posting was made is placed in the Ledger Folio (L.F.) column of the journal (see the arrow from account number 100 to the debit in the first entry in the general journal). The number of the journal page *from* which the entry was posted is placed in the Folio column of the ledger account (see the arrow from page 1 in the general journal to J-1 in the Folio column of the general ledger). The date of the transaction is also shown in the general ledger (see the arrows from the date in the general journal to the dates in the general ledger). Posting is always from the journal to the ledger account. *Cross-indexing is the placing of the account number in the journal and the placing of the journal page number in the account,* as shown in Illustration 2.2.

Cross-indexing aids the tracing of any recorded transaction, either from

Illustration 2.2:
General journal and
general ledger; posting
and cross indexing

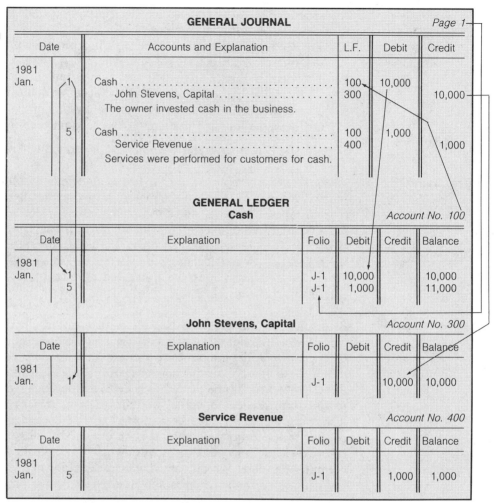

the journal to the ledger or from the ledger to the journal. Cross-reference numbers usually are not placed in the L.F. column of the journal until the entry is posted; thereafter, the cross-index numbers indicate that the entry has been posted.

An understanding of the posting and cross-indexing process can be obtained by tracing the entries from the journal to the ledger. The ledger accounts need not contain explanations of all the entries, since any needed explanations can be obtained from the journal. But if the transaction is one of a nonroutine nature, it may be helpful to write a description in the account also.

The explanation of a journal entry should be complete enough to describe fully the transaction and to prove the entry's accuracy and at the same time be concise. If a journal entry is self-explanatory, the explanation may be omitted.

Compound journal entries

The analysis of a transaction often shows that more than two accounts are directly affected. The required journal entry will involve more than one debit and/or credit. *A journal entry which involves more than one debit and/or credit is a compound journal entry.* An entry with one debit and one credit is a simple journal entry.

Assume that John Stevens purchases $8,000 of machinery from the Myers Company, paying $2,000 cash with the balance due on open account. The compound journal entry for Stevens is as follows:

Machinery	8,000	
Cash		2,000
Accounts Payable		6,000
Machinery purchased from Myers Company, Invoice No. 42.		

The functions and other advantages of using a journal are summarized below. The journal—

1. Sets forth the transactions of each day.
2. Records the transactions in chronological order.
3. Shows the analysis of each transaction in terms of debit and credit.
4. Supplies an explanation of each transaction when necessary.
5. Serves as a source for future reference to accounting transactions.
6. Removes lengthy explanations from the accounts.
7. Makes possible posting to the ledger at convenient times.
8. Assists in maintaining the ledger in balance.
9. Aids in the tracing of errors.
10. Promotes the division of labor (for example, one person may enter the journal entries and another may post them).

The accounting system in operation

Presented below is an illustration of an accounting system that might be employed by a small decorating service company, the Susan Dana Company, owned by Susan Dana. The company's balance sheet at December 31, 1980, is as follows:

SUSAN DANA COMPANY
Balance Sheet
December 31, 1980

Assets		Liabilities and Owner's Equity	
Current Assets:		Current Liabilities:	
Cash	$15,000	Accounts payable	$ 2,000
Accounts receivable	4,500		
Total Current Assets	$19,500	Owner's Equity:	
		Susan Dana, capital	33,500
Property, Plant, and Equipment:			
Furniture and equipment	$ 6,000		
Office fixtures	10,000		
Total Property, Plant, and Equipment	$16,000	Total Liabilities and	
Total Assets	$35,500	Owner's Equity	$35,500

The balance sheet reflects ledger account balances as of the close of business on December 31, 1980. These are, of course, the opening balances on January 1, 1981, and are shown as such in the illustrated ledger accounts. The furniture and equipment and office fixtures were purchased on December 31, 1980.

The Susan Dana Company's chart of accounts is as follows:

Account No.	Account title	Account No.	Account title
1	Cash	30	Advertising Expense
2	Accounts Receivable	32	Sales Salaries
3	Commissions Receivable	33	Miscellaneous Selling Expense
6	Furniture and Equipment	34	Office Rent Expense
7	Accumulated Depreciation— Furniture and Equipment	35	Administrative Salaries
		36	Office Supplies Expense
8	Office Fixtures	37	Miscellaneous Administrative Expense
9	Accumulated Depreciation— Office Fixtures		
		38	Depreciation Expense—Furniture and Equipment
11	Accounts Payable		
15	Susan Dana, Capital	39	Depreciation Expense—Office Fixtures
16	Susan Dana, Drawing		
20	Service Revenue		
21	Commissions earned		

Now assume that the following is a complete list (somewhat condensed) of the transactions entered into by the Susan Dana Company in January 1981:

Jan. 2 Paid January rent for office, $1,000.
   3 Purchased additional office furniture for cash, $1,500.
   4 Received an invoice from the Burk Agency, $200, for planning January's advertising.
   6 Paid $2,000 on account.
   8 Paid the advertising bill received on January 4.
   9 Purchased office supplies for $200 cash. The supplies are to be used in January.
   10 Collections on account, $4,500.
   15 Sales of services on account for the first half of the month, $7,600. Sales of decorating services would normally be recorded daily, but, for obvious reasons, the illustration must be shortened.
   17 Paid miscellaneous selling expenses, $600.
   23 Received an invoice from the *New York News* for advertising in the first half of January, $300.
   31 Sales of services on account for the rest of the month, $3,000.
   31 Paid sales salaries of $3,600 and administrative salaries of $4,200 for the month. (Payroll taxes and deductions are to be dealt with later.)
   31 Paid miscellaneous administrative expenses, $400.
   31 Susan Dana withdrew $1,000 cash.

The general journal of the Susan Dana Company for January 1981 is presented below. The chart of accounts presented above contains the account titles and numbers used (only those accounts which have a beginning balance or are affected by the transactions shown above for January are shown). To present the general journal as it would appear when completed, account numbers have been inserted in the L.F. (or reference) column. As already noted, these numbers typically would be inserted only after the posting of the item to the proper ledger account.

GENERAL JOURNAL						*Page 1*
Date		Accounts and Explanation		L.F.	Debit	Credit
1981 Jan.	2	Office Rent Expense . . . . Cash . . . . Rent for January 1981.		34 1	1,000	1,000
	3	Furniture and Equipment . . . . Cash . . . . Purchased additional furniture.		6 1	1,500	1,500
	4	Advertising Expense . . . . Accounts Payable . . . . Advertising expense on account.		30 11	200	200
	6	Accounts Payable . . . . Cash . . . . Payments on account.		11 1	2,000	2,000
	8	Accounts Payable . . . . Cash . . . . Paid invoice of January 4.		11 1	200	200
	9	Office Supplies Expense . . . . Cash . . . . Office supplies purchased and used.		36 1	200	200
	10	Cash . . . . Accounts Receivable . . . . Collections on account.		1 2	4,500	4,500
	15	Accounts Receivable . . . . Service Revenue . . . . Sales of services for the first half of the month.		2 20	7,600	7,600
	17	Miscellaneous Selling Expense . . . . Cash . . . . Paid other selling expenses.		33 1	600	600
	23	Advertising Expense . . . . Accounts Payable . . . . Advertising expense on account.		30 11	300	300
	31	Accounts Receivable . . . . Service Revenue . . . . Sales of services in rest of January.		2 20	3,000	3,000
	31	Sales Salaries . . . . Administrative Salaries . . . . Cash . . . . Paid salaries for January.		32 35 1	3,600 4,200	7,800
	31	Miscellaneous Administrative Expense . . . . Cash . . . . Paid other administrative expenses.		37 1	400	400

GENERAL JOURNAL *(continued)*					Page 1
Date		Accounts and Explanation	L.F.	Debit	Credit
1981 Jan.	31	Susan Dana, Drawing	16	1,000	
		Cash	1		1,000
		Owner withdrew cash.			

Presented below are the general ledger accounts of the Susan Dana Company.

GENERAL LEDGER
Cash — Account No. 1

Date		Explanation	Folio	Debit	Credit	Balance
1981 Jan.	1	Balance				15,000
	2		J-1		1,000	14,000
	3		J-1		1,500	12,500
	6		J-1		2,000	10,500
	8		J-1		200	10,300
	9		J-1		200	10,100
	10		J-1	4,500		14,600
	17		J-1		600	14,000
	31		J-1		7,800	6,200
	31		J-1		400	5,800
	31		J-1		1,000	4,800

Accounts Receivable — Account No. 2

Date		Explanation	Folio	Debit	Credit	Balance
1981 Jan.	1	Balance				4,500
	10		J-1		4,500	–0–
	15		J-1	7,600		7,600
	31		J-1	3,000		10,600

Furniture and Equipment — Account No. 6

Date		Explanation	Folio	Debit	Credit	Balance
1981 Jan.	1	Balance				6,000
	3		J-1	1,500		7,500

Office Fixtures — Account No. 8

Date		Explanation	Folio	Debit	Credit	Balance
1981 Jan.	1	Balance				10,000

GENERAL LEDGER *(continued)*

Accounts Payable *Account No. 11*

Date		Explanation	Folio	Debit	Credit	Balance
1981 Jan.	1	Balance				2,000
	4		J-1		200	2,200
	6		J-1	2,000		200
	8		J-1	200		–0–
	23		J-1		300	300

Susan Dana, Capital *Account No. 15*

Date		Explanation	Folio	Debit	Credit	Balance
1981 Jan.	1	Balance	↘			33,500

Susan Dana, Drawing *Account No. 16*

Date		Explanation	Folio	Debit	Credit	Balance
1981 Jan.	31		J-1	1,000		1,000

Service Revenue *Account No. 20*

Date		Explanation	Folio	Debit	Credit	Balance
1981 Jan.	15		J-1		7,600	7,600
	31		J-1		3,000	10,600

Advertising Expense *Account No. 30*

Date		Explanation	Folio	Debit	Credit	Balance
1981 Jan.	4		J-1	200		200
	23		J-1	300		500

Sales Salaries *Account No. 32*

Date		Explanation	Folio	Debit	Credit	Balance
1981 Jan.	31		J-1	3,600		3,600

Miscellaneous Selling Expense *Account No. 33*

Date		Explanation	Folio	Debit	Credit	Balance
1981 Jan.	17		J-1	600		600

GENERAL LEDGER *(concluded)*

Office Rent Expense — *Account No. 34*

Date		Explanation	Folio	Debit	Credit	Balance
1981 Jan.	2		J-1	1,000		1,000

Administrative Salaries — *Account No. 35*

Date		Explanation	Folio	Debit	Credit	Balance
1981 Jan.	31		J-1	4,200		4,200

Office Supplies Expense — *Account No. 36*

Date		Explanation	Folio	Debit	Credit	Balance
1981 Jan.	9		J-1	200		200

Miscellaneous Administrative Expense — *Account No. 37*

Date		Explanation	Folio	Debit	Credit	Balance
1981 Jan.	31		J-1	400		400

Control of the recording process

You may wonder why accountants record increases in assets (and expenses) as debits and increases in equities (and revenues) as credits. It would be possible to devise a scheme whereby all accounts were increased by entries on the debit side. At the end of any given period, then, all accounts would have positive debit balances. But, under such a scheme, how would accountants know whether or not the basic equation of Assets = Equities were true? Furthermore, a valuable automatic check for arithmetic errors would be missing. If they wished to check upon the arithmetic accuracy of their work, they would have to repeat virtually every step in the initial recording process. Fortunately, there is an easier way.

Increases in assets (and expenses) are recorded as debits and increases in equities (and revenues) as credits. This yields two sets of accounts—those with debit balances and those with credit balances. If the totals of these two groups are equal, the accountant has some assurance that the arithmetic part of the recording process has been properly carried out. The double-entry system of accounting requires that the debits must equal the credits in the entry to record every transaction. This equality of debits and credits for each transaction will always hold because both sides of every transaction are recorded. It is this equality of debits and credits, not of increases and decreases, that provides the important control means. If every transaction is recorded in terms of equal debits and credits, it follows that the total of the accounts with debit balances must equal the total of the accounts with credit balances.

The trial balance

The arithmetic accuracy of the recording process is generally tested by preparing a trial balance. *A trial balance is a listing of the accounts and their debit or credit balances.* The trial balance for the Susan Dana Company is shown in Illustration 2.3. Note the listing of the account titles on the left (account numbers could be included, if desired), the column for debit balances, the column for credit balances, and the equality of the two totals.

The inequality of the totals of the debits and credits columns would automatically signal the presence of an error. To find the cause of such an error the accountant should work backwards through the steps in the account-

Illustration 2.3: A trial balance

SUSAN DANA COMPANY Trial Balance January 31, 1981	Debits	Credits
Cash	$ 4,800	
Accounts receivable	10,600	
Furniture and equipment	7,500	
Office fixtures	10,000	
Accounts payable		$ 300
Susan Dana, capital		33,500
Susan Dana, drawing	1,000	
Service revenue		10,600
Advertising expense	500	
Sales salaries	3,600	
Miscellaneous selling expense	600	
Office rent expense	1,000	
Administrative salaries	4,200	
Office supplies expense	200	
Miscellaneous administrative expense	400	
	$44,400	$44,400

ing process (e.g., start by re-adding the trial balance columns, then compare the trial balance figures with the account balances, and so on). The equality of the two totals does not necessarily mean that the accounting has been error-free. Serious errors may have been made. These include the complete omission of an important transaction or the recording of an entry in the wrong account (for example, the recording of an asset as an expense, or vice versa).

A trial balance may be prepared at any time—at the end of the day, a week, a month, a quarter, or a year. Typically, one is prepared whenever financial statements are to be prepared. Thus, the trial balance provides a listing of the accounts for statement preparation. A trial balance that is out of balance will also indicate the period in which an error was made.

Adjusting entries

Continuing the Susan Dana Company illustration, assume that its owner is especially concerned with the profitability of the company for the month.

Preparing financial statements for January creates the problem for the accountant of making sure that the accounts properly reflect operations for the month and the financial status at the end of the month. Because economic activity can take place without a transaction occurring, the accounts must be analyzed to determine whether any updating adjustments are required. The entries to record these updating adjustments are called *adjusting entries* and are discussed in depth in Chapter 3.

But, to illustrate briefly here, a study of the Susan Dana Company's accounts would reveal that no expense is shown for the use of the office fixtures and the furniture and equipment (which were acquired on December 31, 1980). Assets such as these will not continue to provide benefits or services indefinitely. Wear and tear resulting from their use will eventually cause them to be disposed of as worthless. Since the assets were used in January, it seems logical to assign some part of the cost of such assets as an expense of the month of January. This expense is called *depreciation.* Assume that by spreading the recorded costs of $10,000 for the office fixtures and $7,500 for the furniture and equipment over their estimated useful lives, the monthly depreciation expenses are $100 and $125. The required journal entry to record these expenses (assume made on page 2 of the general journal) is:

Date	Accounts and Explanation	L.F.	Debit	Credit
1981				
Jan. 31	Depreciation Expense—Office Fixtures	39	100	
	Depreciation Expense—Furniture and Equipment	38	125	
	Accumulated Depreciation—Office Fixtures	9		100
	Accumulated Depreciation—Furniture and Equipment	7		125
	Depreciation for the month of January.			

Note that the amount of depreciation is not credited directly to the asset accounts but rather to separate accumulated depreciation accounts. As is explained in Chapter 3, these accounts are special subdivisions of the credit side of the asset accounts established for depreciable assets. They are used primarily because of the tentative nature of the depreciation expense recorded. Illustration 2.5 shows how these accounts are reported in the balance sheet.

Assume that another adjustment is needed to record commissions earned by the Susan Dana Company, but not yet collected, in the amount of $6,000. Susan Dana earned these commissions in January by acting as a selling agent for the Brown Wholesale Company, which delivered the merchandise sold by Susan Dana directly to the customers. The required entry is:

Date	Accounts and Explanation	L.F.	Debit	Credit
1981				
Jan. 31	Commissions Receivable	3	6,000	
	Commissions Earned	21		6,000
	Commissions earned in the month of January.			

Commissions Earned is a revenue account and will appear in the earnings statement. Commissions receivable is a current asset that will appear in the balance sheet.

These two adjusting entries are posted in the same manner that every journal entry is posted. The debits would be posted as debits to the named accounts, the credits as credits, and the proper balances brought forward. After posting these entries, the accounts to which they were posted would appear as follows:

Commissions Receivable						Account No. 3
Date		Explanation	Folio	Debit	Credit	Balance
1981 Jan.	31		J-2	6,000		6,000

Accumulated Depreciation—Furniture and Equipment						Account No. 7
Date		Explanation	Folio	Debit	Credit	Balance
1981 Jan.	31		J-2		125	125

Accumulated Depreciation—Office Fixtures						Account No. 9
Date		Explanation	Folio	Debit	Credit	Balance
1981 Jan.	31		J-2		100	100

Commissions Earned						Account No. 21
Date		Explanation	Folio	Debit	Credit	Balance
1981 Jan.	31		J-2		6,000	6,000

Depreciation Expense—Furniture and Equipment						Account No. 38
Date		Explanation	Folio	Debit	Credit	Balance
1981 Jan.	31		J-2	125		125

Depreciation Expense—Office Fixtures						Account No. 39
Date		Explanation	Folio	Debit	Credit	Balance
1981 Jan.	31		J-2	100		100

Financial statements

The financial statements desired by the owner are presented in Illustrations 2.4 and 2.5. As shown by the earnings statement in Illustration 2.4, the company showed net earnings of $5,875 for the month.

In Illustration 2.5 the net earnings are added to the beginning balance in the owner's capital account and the withdrawal was deducted to arrive

Illustration 2.4: An
earnings statement

SUSAN DANA COMPANY
Earnings Statement
For the Month Ended January 31, 1981

Revenues:		
Service revenue	$10,600	
Commissions earned	6,000	$16,600
Expenses:		
Advertising	$ 500	
Sales salaries	3,600	
Miscellaneous selling expense	600	
Office rent	1,000	
Administrative salaries	4,200	
Office supplies	200	
Miscellaneous administrative expense	400	
Depreciation expense—furniture and equipment	125	
Depreciation expense—office fixtures	100	10,725
Net earnings		$ 5,875

*would
use 3
columns*

Illustration 2.5:
A balance sheet

SUSAN DANA COMPANY
Balance Sheet
January 31, 1981

Assets

Current Assets:			
Cash		$ 4,800	
Accounts receivable		10,600	
Commissions receivable		6,000	
Total Current Assets			$21,400
Property, Plant, and Equipment:			
Office fixtures	$10,000		
Accumulated depreciation	100	$ 9,900	
Furniture and equipment	$ 7,500		
Accumulated depreciation	125	7,375	
Total Property, Plant, and Equipment			17,275
Total Assets			$38,675

Liabilities and Owner's Equity

Current Liabilities:			
Accounts payable			$ 300
Owner's Equity:			
Susan Dana, capital, January 1		$33,500	
Add net earnings for January		5,875	
		$39,375	
Deduct owner withdrawal		1,000	
Susan Dana, capital, January 31			38,375
Total Liabilities and Owner's Equity			$38,675

at the ending balance of that account. This was done to show that net earnings are added to the owner's capital account at the end of the period and withdrawals are deducted. In actual practice only the ending balance would be shown in the balance sheet.

The financial accounting process once again is back to its end products, the financial statements. Thus far, the accounting process has been shown to consist of (1) analyzing economic activity, (2) journalizing transactions, (3) posting to ledger accounts, (4) preparing a trial balance, (5) adjusting the accounts, and (6) preparing financial statements.

Use of dollar signs

Dollar signs are to be used in financial statements. A dollar sign should appear by the first amount in each column, by each subtotal listed below an underlining, and by the final total. Dollar signs are not used in journals or ledgers. They may be used in trial balances, but are not required.

When amounts are in even dollar amounts, the cents column may be left blank, or zeros or a dash may be used. When lined accounting pads are used, there is no need to use commas or a period in recording an amount. When using unlined paper, both commas and a period should be used.

NEW TERMS INTRODUCED IN CHAPTER 2

Account—a device, means, classifying tool, or storage unit used to classify and summarize money measurements of business activity in an accounting system. The three-column account is normally used. It contains columns for debit, credit, and balance.

Adjusting entries—journal entries made at the end of an accounting period that update the accounts in an accounting system for economic activity that has taken place but has not yet been recorded in the accounts.

Chart of accounts—the complete listing of the names and account numbers of all of the accounts in the ledger; somewhat comparable to a table of contents.

Charge—means the same as the word "debit."

Credit—the right side of any account; when used as a verb, to enter a dollar amount on the right side of an account.

Credit balance—the balance in an account when the sum of the credits to the account exceeds the sum of the debits to that account.

Credit entry—an entry on the right side of an account; credits increase liability, owner's equity, and revenue accounts and decrease asset and expense accounts.

Cross-indexing—the act of placing in the journal the number of the ledger account to which an entry was posted and placing in the ledger account the page number of the journal on which the entry can be found.

Debit—the left side of any account; when used as a verb, to enter a dollar amount on the left side of an account.

Debit balance—the balance in an account when the sum of the debits to the account exceeds the sum of the credits to that account.

Debit entry—an entry on the left side of an account; debits increase asset and expense accounts and decrease liability, owner's equity, and revenue accounts.

Depreciation—that portion of the cost of a long-lived tangible asset used in a business that is allocated to each period of the asset's life. (For further discussion, see Chapter 3).

Journal—a chronological record of business transactions showing the changes to be recorded as a result of each transaction; the simplest form of journal is the two-column general journal.

Journal entry—a complete analysis of the effects of a business transaction as expressed in terms of debit and credit and recorded in a journal. A compound journal entry is a journal entry with more than one debit and/or credit.

Journalizing—a step in the accounting recording process that consists of entering a transaction in a journal.

Ledger—the complete collection of all of the accounts of an entity; often referred to as the general ledger.

Posting—the transfer of entries from a journal to a ledger.

Rule of double entry—the accounting requirement that every transaction be recorded in an entry that has equal debits and credits.

T-account—an account resembling the letter T, which is used for illustrative purposes only. Debits are entered on the left side of the account and credits are entered on the right side of the account.

Trial balance—a list of all of the accounts in a ledger (excluding those with zero balances) at a given point in time, with debit balances listed in one column and credit balances listed in a second column to the right of the first column.

DEMONSTRATION PROBLEM

The Le Bon Coeur Riding Stables, owned by Marty Paulk, had the following balance sheet on June 30, 1981:

LE BON COEUR RIDING STABLE		
Balance Sheet		
June 30, 1981		
Assets		
Current Assets:		
Cash	$7,000	
Accounts receivable	5,400	
Total Current Assets		$12,400
Land		40,000
Total Assets		$52,400
Liabilities and Owner's Equity		
Current Liabilities:		
Accounts payable		$ 800
Long-Term Liabilities:		
Loan payable		40,000
Owner's Equity:		
Marty Paulk, capital		11,600
Total Liabilities and Owner's Equity		$52,400

Transactions for the month of July 1981 were as follows:

July 1 The owner invested additional cash of $25,000.
    1 Paid for a prefabricated building constructed on the land at a cost of $24,000. The building is expected to last ten years and will have no value after that time.
    8 Paid the account payable of $800.
   10 Collected the accounts receivable of $5,400.
   12 Horse feed to be used in July purchased on credit for $1,100.
   15 Boarding fees for July were charged to customers in the amount of $4,500. (This amount is due on August 10.)
   24 Miscellaneous expenses of $800 for July were paid.
   28 The owner withdrew $700 cash.
   31 Paid interest expense on the savings and loan association loan of $200.
   31 Salaries of $1,400 for the month were paid.
   31 Riding and lesson fees were billed to customers in the amount of $3,600. (They are due on August 10.)

Required:

a. Prepare the journal entries to record the transactions for July 1981. (Do not record depreciation expense until after the trial balance has been prepared.)

b. Post the journal entries to the ledger accounts after entering the beginning balances in those accounts. Insert cross-indexing references in the journal and ledger. Use the following chart of accounts:

Cash	100
Accounts Receivable	101
Land	112
Building	114
Accumulated Depreciation—Building	115
Accounts Payable	200
Loan Payable	205
Marty Paulk, Capital	300
Marty Paulk, Drawing	301
Horse Boarding Fees	400
Riding and Lesson Fees	401
Feed Expense	501
Salaries Expense	502
Depreciation Expense—Building	503
Interest Expense	504
Miscellaneous Expense	510

c. Prepare a trial balance.

d. Journalize and post the entry for depreciation for July on the building.

e. Prepare an earnings statement for July.

f. Prepare a balance sheet as of July 31.

Solution to demonstration problem

a.

GENERAL JOURNAL					Page 1
Date	Account Titles and Explanation	Folio	Debit		Credit
1981 July 1	Cash .... Marty Paulk, Capital .... Additional cash invested by owner.	100 300	25,000		25,000
1	Building .... Cash .... Paid for building.	114 100	24,000		24,000
8	Accounts Payable .... Cash .... Paid accounts payable.	200 100	800		800
10	Cash .... Accounts Receivable .... Collected accounts receivable.	100 101	5,400		5,400
12	Feed Expense .... Accounts Payable .... Purchased feed on credit.	501 200	1,100		1,100
15	Accounts Receivable .... Horse Boarding Fees .... Billed boarding fees for July.	101 400	4,500		4,500
24	Miscellaneous Expense .... Cash .... Paid miscellaneous expenses for July.	510 100	800		800
28	Marty Paulk, Drawing .... Cash .... Owner withdrew cash.	301 100	700		700
31	Interest Expense .... Cash .... Paid interest.	504 100	200		200
31	Salaries Expense .... Cash .... Paid salaries for July.	502 100	1,400		1,400
31	Accounts Receivable .... Riding and Lesson Fees .... Billed riding and lesson fees for July.	101 401	3,600		3,600

b.

GENERAL LEDGER
Cash

Account No. 100

Date			Explanation	Folio	Debit	Credit	Balance
1981							
June	30		Balance				7,000
July	1			J-1	25,000		32,000
	1			J-1		24,000	8,000
	8			J-1		800	7,200
	10			J-1	5,400		12,600
	24			J-1		800	11,800
	28			J-1		700	11,100
	31			J-1		200	10,900
	31			J-1		1,400	9,500

Accounts Receivable

Account No. 101

Date			Explanation	Folio	Debit	Credit	Balance
1981							
June	30		Balance				5,400
July	10			J-1		5,400	-0-
	15			J-1	4,500		4,500
	31			J-1	3,600		8,100

Land

Account No. 112

Date			Explanation	Folio	Debit	Credit	Balance
1981							
June	30		Balance				40,000

Building

Account No. 114

Date			Explanation	Folio	Debit	Credit	Balance
1981							
July	1			J-1	24,000		24,000

Accumulated Depreciation—Building

Account No. 115

Date			Explanation	Folio	Debit	Credit	Balance
1981							
July	31			J-2		200	200

Accounts Payable

Account No. 200

Date			Explanation	Folio	Debit	Credit	Balance
1981							
June	30		Balance				800
July	8			J-1	800		-0-
	12			J-1		1,100	1,100

GENERAL LEDGER *(continued)*

Loan Payable
Account No. 205

Date			Explanation	Folio	Debit	Credit	Balance
1981 June	30		Balance				40,000

Marty Paulk, Capital
Account No. 300

Date			Explanation	Folio	Debit	Credit	Balance
1981 June	30		Balance				11,600
July	1			J-1		25,000	36,600

Marty Paulk, Drawing
Account No. 301

Date			Explanation	Folio	Debit	Credit	Balance
1981 July	28			J-1	700		700

Horse Boarding Fees
Account No. 400

Date			Explanation	Folio	Debit	Credit	Balance
1981 July	15			J-1		4,500	4,500

Riding and Lesson Fees
Account No. 401

Date			Explanation	Folio	Debit	Credit	Balance
1981 July	31					3,600	3,600

Feed Expense
Account No. 501

Date			Explanation	Folio	Debit	Credit	Balance
1981 July	12			J-1	1,100		1,100

Salaries Expense
Account No. 502

Date			Explanation	Folio	Debit	Credit	Balance
1981 July	31			J-1	1,400		1,400

GENERAL LEDGER *(concluded)*

Depreciation Expense—Building   *Account No. 503*

Date		Explanation	Folio	Debit	Credit	Balance
1981 July	31		J-2	200		200

Interest Expense   *Account No. 504*

Date		Explanation	Folio	Debit	Credit	Balance
1981 July	31		J-1	200		200

Miscellaneous Expense   *Account No. 510*

Date		Explanation	Folio	Debit	Credit	Balance
1981 July	24		J-1	800		800

c.

LE BON COEUR RIDING STABLE
Trial Balance
July 31, 1981

	Debits	Credits
Cash	$ 9,500	
Accounts receivable	8,100	
Land	40,000	
Building	24,000	
Accounts payable		$ 1,100
Loan payable		40,000
Marty Paulk, capital		36,600
Marty Paulk, drawing	700	
Horse boarding fees		4,500
Riding and lesson fees		3,600
Feed expense	1,100	
Salaries expense	1,400	
Interest expense	200	
Miscellaneous expense	800	
	$85,800	$85,800

d.

	GENERAL JOURNAL *(continued)*			Page 2
Date	Account Titles and Explanation	Folio	Debit	Credit
1981 July 31	Depreciation Expense—Building . . . . Accumulated Depreciation—Building . . . . . . To record depreciation for July ($24,000 ÷ 120 months = $200 per month).	503 115	200	200

e.

LE BON COEUR RIDING STABLE
Earnings Statement
For the Month Ended July 31, 1981

Revenues:
Horse boarding fees $4,500
Riding and lesson fees 3,600
    Total revenues $8,100

Expenses:
Feed expense $1,100
Salaries expense 1,400
Interest expense 200
Depreciation expense 200
Miscellaneous expense 800
    Total expenses 3,700
Net Earnings $4,400

f.

```
                    LE BON COEUR RIDING STABLE
                          Balance Sheet
                          July 31, 1981
                              Assets
Current Assets:
Cash ............................................      $ 9,500
Accounts receivable ..............................       8,100
     Total Current Assets .......................                        $17,600

Property, Plant, and Equipment:
Land ............................................               $40,000
Building ........................................    $24,000
Less: Accumulated depreciation ..................        200     23,800
     Total Property, Plant, and Equipment ........                       63,800
          Total Assets ..........................                       $81,400

                   Liabilities and Owner's Equity
Current Liabilities:
Accounts payable ................................                        $ 1,100

Long-Term Liabilities:
Loan payable ....................................                        40,000
     Total Liabilities ..........................                       $41,100

Owner's Equity:
Marty Paulk, capital, July 1 ....................               $11,600
Add: Additional investment ......................    $25,000
     Net earnings for July ......................      4,400     29,400
                                                               $41,000
Deduct: Owner withdrawal ........................                 700
Marty Paulk, capital, July 31 ...................                        40,300
     Total Liabilities and Owner's Equity ........                      $81,400
```

QUESTIONS

1. Define debit and credit. Name the types of accounts which are—

a. Increased by debits.

b. Decreased by debits.

c. Increased by credits.

d. Decreased by credits.

Do you think this system makes sense? Can you conceive of other possible methods for recording changes in accounts?

2. Describe a ledger and a chart of accounts. How do these two compare with a book and its table of contents?

3. Why are expense and revenue accounts used when all revenues and expenses could be shown directly in the owner's equity account?

4. What is the purpose of the owner's drawing account and how is it increased?

5. What types of accounts appear in the trial balance? What are the purposes of the trial balance?

6. You have found that the total of the debit column of the trial balance of the Landers Company is $100,000 while the total of the credit column is $90,000. What are some of the possible causes of this difference?

7. Store equipment was purchased for $1,500. Instead of debiting the Store Equipment account, the debit was made to Delivery Equipment. Of what help will the trial balance be in locating this error? Why?

8. Differentiate between the trial balance, chart of accounts, balance sheet, and earnings statement.

9. A student remembered that the side toward the window in the classroom was the debit side of an account. The student took an examination in a room where the windows were on the other side of the room and became confused and consistently reversed debits and credits. Would the student's trial balance have equal debit and credit totals? If there were no existing balances in any of the accounts to begin with, would the error prevent the student from preparing correct financial statements? Why?

10. Are the following possibilities conceivable in an entry involving only one debit and one credit? Why?

a. Increase a liability and increase an expense.

b. Increase an asset and decrease a liability.

c. Increase a revenue and decrease an expense.

d. Decrease an asset and increase another asset.

e. Decrease an asset and increase a liability.

f. Decrease a revenue and decrease an asset.

g. Decrease a liability and increase a revenue.

11. Describe the nature and purposes of the general journal. What does "journalizing" mean? Give an example of a compound entry in the general journal.

12. Describe the act of posting. What difficulties could arise if no cross-indexing existed between the general journal and the ledger accounts?

13. Which of the following cash payments would involve the recording of an expense? Why?

a. Paid vendors for office supplies previously purchased on account.

b. Paid an automobile dealer for a new auto for a salesperson.

c. Paid the current month's rent.

d. Paid salaries for the last half of the current month.

14. Where and when should dollar signs be used in accounting records?

EXERCISES

E-1. Give the entry required for each of the following transactions:

a. Cash was received for services performed for customers, $600.

b. Services were performed for customers on open account, $900.

E-2. Give the entry required for each of the following transactions:

a. Stuart Childs invested $40,000 cash in his business.

b. A loan was arranged with a bank. The bank increased the company's checking account balance by $20,000 after the owner signed a written promise to return the $20,000, plus interest at 9 percent, six months from the date of the loan.

E-3. Explain each of the sets of debits and credits shown in the accounts below. There are ten transactions to be explained. Each set is designated by the small letters to the left of the amount. For example, the first transaction is the owner's investment of cash in the business on January 1 and is denoted by the letter *(a)*.

Cash

(a)	70,000	*(e)*	50,000
(d)	600	*(f)*	200
		(g)	1,200
		(i)	10,000

Accounts Payable

(e)	50,000	*(b)*	50,000
		(h)	400

Rent Expense

(f)	200	

Accounts Receivable

(c)	600	*(d)*	600
(j)	4,700		

Henry Lawson, Capital

	(a)	70,000

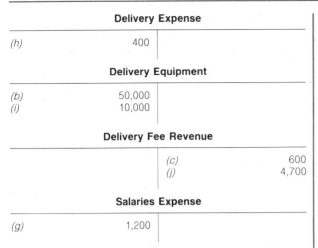

Delivery Expense

(h)	400		

Delivery Equipment

(b)	50,000		
(i)	10,000		

Delivery Fee Revenue

		(c)	600
		(j)	4,700

Salaries Expense

(g)	1,200		

E–4. Assume that the ledger accounts given in Exercise E–3 are as they appear at December 31, 1981. Prepare the trial balance as of that date.

E–5. Assume that the depreciation on the delivery equipment for the year ended December 31, 1981, is $5,000. Prepare the earnings statement for 1981 and the balance sheet as of the end of 1981, assuming that the data given in Exercise E–3 are for the Henry Lawson Company.

E–6. Give the entry (without dollar amounts) for a transaction which would involve each of the following combinations of types of accounts:

a. An asset and a liability.

b. An expense and an asset.

c. A liability and an expense.

d. Owner's equity and an asset.

e. Two asset accounts.

f. An asset and a revenue.

E–7. Kent Beyers owns and manages a bowling alley called Ten Pin Lanes. He also maintains his own accounting records and was about to prepare financial statements for the year 1981. When he prepared the trial balance from the ledger accounts, the total of the debits column was $517,900 and the total of the credits column was $515,900. What are the possible reasons why the totals of the debits and credits columns are out of balance? How would you proceed to find the source of the error?

PROBLEMS, SERIES A

P2–1–A. The transactions listed below are those of the Ben Ford Company for the month of April 1981.

Required:

a. Mentally analyze each transaction in terms of debit and credit and then enter them directly in suitable T-accounts. To identify each part of each transaction also enter the date of the transaction in the accounts.

b. Prepare a trial balance as of April 30, 1981.

Transactions:

Apr. 1 Cash of $30,000 was received as the owner's investment in the business.
  3 Rent was paid for April, $200.
  6 A delivery truck was purchased for $3,500, cash.
  7 Office equipment was purchased on account from the Rogers Company for $4,800.
  14 Wages were paid, $700.
  15 $2,900 was received for services performed.
  18 An invoice was received from Mike's Gas Station for $25 for gas and oil used.
  23 A loan was arranged with the bank for $5,000. The cash was received, and a note was signed promising to return the $5,000 plus $55 interest on May 30, 1981.

Apr. 29 Purchased a delivery truck for $4,600 on account.
  30 Wages of $900 were paid.

(Note: You may ignore depreciation expense and interest expense for the month since these are adjusting entries which would be made after the trial balance has been prepared.)

P2–2–A. Set up the following T-accounts for the Figure Trim Company: Cash; Accounts Receivable; Land; Building; Exercise Equipment; Accounts Payable; Notes Payable, Bank; Nancy Drew, Capital; Service Sales; Salaries Expense; and Office Supplies Expense.

Required:

a. Enter the transactions given below in the accounts. Date each transaction entry as indicated. Ignore depreciation expense for the period.

b. Prepare a trial balance after entering the last transaction.

Transactions:

Apr. 1 Cash of $40,000 was invested in the business by the owner.

Apr. 5   The company borrowed $25,000 from its bank and is-
          sued its note payable to the bank.
      9   Paid $15,000 cash for land.
      11 Paid $47,500 cash for a building located on the land,
          above.
      14 Purchased $6,000 of exercise equipment, on account.
      17 Paid cash of $400 for office supplies to be consumed
          in April.
      25 Sales of service, on account, were $2,500.
      30 Sales of service, for cash, for the month, were $1,000.
      30 Paid salaries for April, $700.

P2–3–A. The Klean Shirt Company, owned by Jim Jen-
kins, entered into the following transactions in August
1981:

Aug. 2   Received cash investment by owner, $40,000.
      3   Paid rent for August on a building (and laundry equip-
          ment) rented, $700.
      4   Paid rent for August on a delivery truck, $500.
      6   Laundry service revenue was $6,000 cash.
      8   Secured an order from a country club for laundry ser-
          vices, $5,000. The services are to be performed next
          month.
      13 Laundry services were performed on account for vari-
          ous customers, $8,000.
      15 Received and paid a bill for $87 for gasoline and oil
          used in operations.
      23 Cash collected from customers on account, $5,500.
      31 Paid $2,700 to employees for services performed in
          August.
      31 Received the electric and gas bill for the month of Au-
          gust, $75.

Required:

Prepare general journal entries for the above transactions.

P2–4–A. Given below is the trial balance of Compu-
Service Company, a computer service company owned
by Barry Rich:

COMPU-SERVICE COMPANY
Trial Balance
June 30, 1981

	Debits	Credits
Cash	$ 26,500	
Accounts receivable	17,000	
Office equipment	50,000	
Accumulated depreciation		$ 10,000
Accounts payable		5,400
Notes payable (dated 6/30/81, due 7/31/81)		10,000
Barry Rich, capital		47,700
Barry Rich, drawing	5,000	
Service revenue		60,000
Office rent expense	6,000	
Advertising expense	2,200	
Salaries expense	25,740	
Supplies expense	540	
Miscellaneous expense	120	
	$133,100	$133,100

The unrecorded depreciation for the year ended June
30, 1981, on the office equipment is $15,000.

Required:

a. Prepare the adjusting journal entry to record the depreciation for the year.

b. Prepare the earnings statement for the year ended
June 30, 1981.

c. Prepare the balance sheet as of June 30, 1981.

P2–5–A. The Speedy Delivery Company was formed
on January 1, 1981, by its owner, George Gibson. Its chart
of accounts is as follows:

Account No.	Account name
101	Cash
102	Accounts Receivable
106	Unexpired Insurance
107	Prepaid Taxes and Licenses
111	Delivery Trucks
112	Garage Equipment
113	Office Equipment
221	Accounts Payable
222	Notes Payable
331	George Gibson, Capital
332	George Gibson, Drawing
441	Delivery Service Sales
551	Garage Rent Expense
552	Gasoline and Oil Used
553	Repairs to Delivery Trucks
554	Salaries Expense
556	General Office Expense

Required:

a. Prepare ledger accounts for all the above accounts.

b. Journalize the transactions given below for January
1981. (Do not prepare adjusting entries for depreciation
expense or other adjustments.)

c. Post the journal entries to the ledger accounts.

d. Prepare a trial balance as of January 31, 1981.

Transactions:

Jan. 1   The company received $40,000 cash and $20,000 of
          garage equipment as an original investment of the
          owner.
      2   Paid garage rent for the month of January, $500.
      4   Purchased office equipment on account, $1,200.
      6   Purchased three delivery trucks at $7,500 each; pay-
          ment was made by giving cash of $12,500 and a 30-
          day note for the remainder.
      8   A corrected invoice for the office equipment purchased
          January 4 showed that the correct total was $1,100,
          not $1,200.
      10 Paid $150 cash for annual licenses for the delivery
          trucks and $15 for title registration fees.

Jan. 12 Purchased insurance for one year on the delivery trucks. The cost of the policy of $900 was paid in cash.

15 Received and paid January telephone and electric service bills, $80.

15 Paid salaries for first half of January, $300.

17 Cash sales of delivery service to date amounted to $150.

20 Received bill for gasoline purchased and used in January, $15. GAS & Oil Used - D C - AP

23 Purchased one delivery truck for cash, $9,000. Paid $50 cash for the annual license and $5 for title registration fees.

25 Cash sales of delivery services from the 18th through the 25th were $240.

27 Purchased an adding machine on account, $300.

31 Paid salaries for last half of January, $400.

31 Open account sales of delivery service amounted to $950.

31 Paid for repairs to a delivery truck, $10 cash.

31 George Gibson withdrew $400 cash from the business.

P2–6–A. The trial balance of the Tennis Palace at the end of the first 11 months of its fiscal year is given below.

TENNIS PALACE
Trial Balance
May 31, 1981

Account No.	Account name	Debits	Credits
100	Cash	$ 54,120	
102	Accounts receivable	54,500	
121	Equipment	40,000	
121A	Accumulated depreciation ..		$ 20,000
210	Accounts payable		12,500
220	Notes payable		10,000
310	Betty Smith, capital, June 30, 1980		71,200
320	Betty Smith, drawing	11,000	
400	Membership and lesson revenue		135,000
510	Tennis professionals' salaries expense	33,000	
520	Advertising expense	14,000	
530	Lesson supplies expense ..	1,500	
540	Equipment repairs	1,000	
550	Office salaries expense	11,000	
560	Building rent expense	22,000 +2000	
570	Telephone and utilities expense	1,400	
580	Entertainment expense	580	
590	Depreciation expense	4,400	
600	Interest expense	200	
		$248,700	$248,700

Required:

a. Open three-column ledger accounts for each of the accounts in the trial balance. Place the word "Balance" in the explanation space and enter the date June 1, 1981, on this same line.

b. Prepare general journal entries for the transactions given below for June 1981.

c. Post the journal entries to the general ledger accounts.

d. Prepare a trial balance as of June 30, 1981.

e. Prepare the adjusting journal entry to record the depreciation on the equipment for June, $400, and post this entry to the ledger accounts.

f. Prepare an earnings statement for the year ended June 30, 1981.

g. Prepare the balance sheet as of June 30, 1981.

Transactions:

June 1 Paid building rent for June, $2,000.

2 Paid vendors on account, $12,000.

5 Purchased a new cash register on account, $1,500.

7 Sold memberships on account, $18,000.

10 Paid the note payable of $10,000 plus interest of $100.

13 Cash collections from customers on account, $24,000.

19 Received a bill for equipment repairs, $150.

24 Paid the June telephone bill, $55, and the June electric bill, $65.

28 Received a bill for June advertising, $1,100.

29 Paid the equipment repair bill received on the 19th, $150.

30 Gave tennis lessons for cash, $3,000.

30 Paid office salaries, $1,000, and tennis professionals' salaries, $3,000.

30 Sales of memberships on account since June 7, $12,000.

30 Costs incurred in entertaining prospective members, $170.

30 The owner withdrew $1,000 cash.

P2–7–A. Steve Isreal lost his job as a carpenter with a contractor when a recession hit the building trades industry. He decided to form his own company and do home repairs.

The following is a summary of the transactions of the business during the first three months of operations in 1981:

Jan. 15 Steve invested $5,000 in the business.

20 Purchased an old automobile for cash at a cost of $1,600.

Feb. 10 Owner withdrew $1,000 for living expenses.

25 Received payment of $2,200 for remodeling a basement into a recreation room. (The homeowner purchased all of the building materials.)

Mar. 5 Paid cash to place an advertisement in the local newspaper, $55.

18 Owner withdrew $900 for personal living expenses.

Apr. 10 Received $3,200 for converting a room over a garage into an office for a college professor. (The professor purchased all of the materials for the job.)

Jan. 15–Apr. 15   Paid for gas and oil expenses for automobile, $350.

Jan. 15–Apr. 15   Miscellaneous business expenses were paid, $225.

Jan. 15–Apr. 15   The owner paid for various personal expenses by writing checks on the business. (You will have to determine this amount from the other data given.)

Depreciation of $100 is applicable to the business use of the automobile during the three-month period. The ending cash balance in the business was $3,500.

Required:

a. Prepare journal entries for the above transactions.

b. Post the journal entries to T-accounts.

c. Prepare an earnings statement for the three-month period ended April 15, 1981.

d. Prepare a balance sheet as of April 15, 1981.

PROBLEMS, SERIES B

P2–1–B.

Required:

a. Open T-accounts for the Janitorial Services Company, owned by Gene Thurber, and enter therein transactions given below for the month of August 1981. Place the date of each transaction in the accounts.

b. Prepare a trial balance as of August 31, 1981. (Ignore depreciation expense since this would be journalized after the trial balance had been prepared.)

Transactions:

Aug. 1   The owner invested cash, $15,000.

3   Borrowed $5,000 from the bank on a note.

4   Purchased a truck for $5,300 cash.

6   Janitorial services were performed for customers who promised to pay later, $3,600.

7   Employee services received and paid for, $700.

10   Collections were made for the services performed on August 6, $800.

14   Supplies were purchased for use in future months, $500. They will be paid for next month.

17   A bill for $100 was received for gas and oil used to date.

25   Janitorial services were performed for customers who paid immediately, $4,500.

31   Wages paid were $1,500.

31   The owner withdrew $400.

P2–2–B.

Required:

a. Open proper T-accounts for the Kwik-Fix TV Repair Service Company, owned by Walter Cline, and enter therein the transactions given below for the month of July 1981. For identification, place the date of each transaction in the accounts.

b. Prepare a trial balance as of July 31, 1981. (Ignore depreciation expense.)

Transactions:

July 2   The owner invested $5,000 cash in the business.

3   The company paid rent for July, $250.

5   A truck was purchased for $3,000 cash.

9   A bill for $500 for advertising for July was received and paid.

14   Cash of $700 was received for fees for TV repair services to customers.

15   Wages of $200 for the first half of July were paid in cash.

20   The company sold TV repair services on open account to the Wells Company, $400. The account is to be paid August 10.

22   Office furniture was acquired on account from the Maddox Company; the price was $400.

25   The owner withdrew $300 cash.

30   Cash of $2,250 was received as fees for TV repair services to customers.

31   Wages of $200 for the second half of July were paid in cash.

P2–3–B. Presented below are the transactions of the Sorg Realty Company, owned by James Sorg (partially summarized for the sake of brevity), for the month of March 1981.

1. The owner invested $10,000 cash.
2. Paid $1,800 as the rent for March on an office building.
3. Paid $300 as the rent for March on two automobiles.
4. Paid $200 for office supplies received and used in March.
5. Earned commissions of $15,000 on real estate transactions. No cash is received on this date.
6. Collected cash of $12,000 from clients on account.
7. Received a bill for $300 for advertising appearing in the local newspaper in March.
8. Paid cash for gas and oil consumed in March, $425.
9. Paid $8,000 to employees for services provided in March.
10. The owner withdrew $500 cash.

Required:

Prepare the general journal entries that would be required to record the above transactions in the records of the Sorg Realty Company. (Ignore depreciation expense.)

P2–4–B. The trial balance prepared as of the end of the Ace Delivery Service Company's calendar-year accounting period is as follows:

ACE DELIVERY SERVICE COMPANY
Trial Balance
December 31, 1981

	Debits	Credits
Cash	$ 4,000	
Accounts receivable	12,500	
Delivery equipment	28,000	
Accumulated depreciation— delivery equipment		$ 6,000
Office equipment	8,500	
Accumulated depreciation— office equipment		800
Accounts payable		9,000
Notes payable		10,000
Joe Bendo, capital		26,100
Joe Bendo, drawing	12,000	
Delivery service revenue		33,000
Rent expense	1,200	
Supplies expense	700	
Advertising expense	1,000	
Wages and salaries expense	17,000	
	$84,900	$84,900

The unrecorded depreciation expense for the year 1981 is $5,000 on the delivery equipment and $800 on the office equipment.

Required:

a. Prepare the general journal entries needed to record the depreciation expense for the year.

b. Prepare an earnings statement for the year ended December 31, 1981.

c. Prepare the balance sheet as of December 31, 1981.

P2–5–B. The Carpet Cleaning Company, owned by Kate Bowman, began business on July 1, 1981. The following account numbers and titles constitute the chart of accounts for the company:

Account No.	Account name
101	Cash
102	Accounts Receivable
111	Office Equipment
112	Cleaning Equipment
113	Service Truck
221	Accounts Payable
222	Notes Payable
331	Kate Bowman, Capital
332	Kate Bowman, Drawing
441	Cleaning Service Sales
551	Salaries Expense
552	Insurance Expense
553	Service Truck Expense
554	Rent Expense
555	Utilities Expense
556	Cleaning Supplies Expense

Required:

a. Prepare ledger accounts for all of the above accounts.

b. Journalize the transactions given below for July 1981. (Ignore depreciation expense.)

c. Post the journal entries to the ledger accounts.

d. Prepare a trial balance.

Transactions:

July 1 The owner invested $30,000 cash in the business.
      5 Office space was rented for July, and $600 cash was paid for the rental.
      8 Desks and chairs were purchased for the office on account, $3,000.
    10 Cleaning equipment was purchased for $4,200; a note was given, to be paid in 30 days.
    15 Purchased a service truck for $18,000, paying $12,000 cash and giving a 60-day note to the dealer for $6,000.
    18 Paid for cleaning supplies received and already used, $300.
    23 Cash cleaning service sales, $1,800.
    27 Insurance expense for July was paid, $450 cash.
    30 Paid for gasoline and oil used by the service truck in July, $60.
    31 Billed customers for cleaning services rendered, $4,200.
    31 Paid salaries for July, $5,400.
    31 Paid utilities bills for July, $550.
    31 The owner's house mortgage payment was paid from business funds, $425.

P2–6–B. The Green Lawn Care Company, owned by Bill Womack, was formed several years ago. The company's trial balance at the end of the first 11 months of its fiscal year is presented below:

GREEN LAWN CARE COMPANY
Trial Balance
June 30, 1981

Account No.	Account name	Debits	Credits
1	Cash	$ 49,160	
2	Accounts receivable	52,400	
11	Office equipment	5,600	
11A	Accumulated depreciation—office equipment		$ 690
12	Trucks	68,600	
12A	Accumulated depreciation—trucks		23,000
21	Accounts payable		22,400
31	Bill Womack, capital, July 31, 1980		50,000
32	Bill Womack, drawing	22,000	
40	Lawn care revenue		180,000
41	Shrubbery care revenue		67,340
51	Salaries expense	43,900	
52	Chemical supplies expense	49,600	
53	Advertising expense	12,200	
54	Automobile operating expense...............	14,600	
55	Office rent expense	10,000	
56	Office supplies expense	800	
57	Telephone and utilities	1,540	
58	Customer entertainment	1,700	
59	Depreciation expense—office equipment	330	
60	Depreciation expense—automobiles	11,000	
		$343,430	$343,430

Required:

a. Open three-column ledger accounts for each of the accounts in the trial balance under the date of July 1, 1981. Place the word "Balance" in the explanation space of each account.

b. Prepare general journal entries for the transactions given below for July 1981.

c. Post the journal entries to the general ledger accounts.

d. Prepare a trial balance as of July 31, 1981.

e. Prepare adjusting journal entries to record the depreciation for July: autos, $1,000; and office equipment, $30. Post these entries to the appropriate ledger accounts.

f. Prepare an earnings statement for the year ended July 31, 1981. Be sure to include the effects of the adjustments in **(e)**.

g. Prepare the balance sheet as of July 31, 1981.

Transactions:

July 2 Paid office rent for June and July, $2,000.
  5 Paid the accounts payable of $22,400.
  8 Paid advertising for the month of July, $800.
  10 Purchased a new office desk on account, $700.
  13 Purchased $140 of office supplies on account.
  15 Collected cash from customers on account, $47,200.
  20 Paid for customer entertainment, $50.
  22 The office supplies purchased on July 13 were incorrectly entered; the correct cost was $160.
  25 Collected an additional $4,000 from customers on account.
  26 Paid for gasoline used in the automobiles in July, $180.
  28 Billed customers for services; lawn care $31,500, shrubbery care $21,500.
  30 Paid for July chemical supplies, $13,200.
  31 Paid July salaries, $10,200.
  31 The owner withdrew $2,000 cash.

BUSINESS DECISION PROBLEM

A friend of yours, Tom Jones, is quite excited over the opportunity he has to purchase the land, building, equipment and several miscellaneous assets of the Ten Pins Bowling Lanes for $125,000. Tom tells you that the owner (who is moving because of poor health) reports that the business earned a profit of $25,000 in 1981 (last year). Tom believes that an annual profit of $25,000 on an investment of $125,000 is a really good deal. But, before completing the deal, he asks you to look it over. You agree and discover the following:

1. The owner has computed his annual profit for 1981 as the sum of his cash withdrawals plus the increase in the Cash account—withdrawals of $15,000 + increase in cash account of $10,000 = $25,000 profit.

2. As buyer of the business Tom will take over responsibility for repayment of a $100,000 loan (plus interest) on the land, building, and equipment. These three assets were acquired seven years ago at a cost of $10,000, $240,000, and $96,000 respectively. The building has a useful life of 40 years, while the equipment has an estimated useful life of 8 years.

3. An analysis of the Cash account shows the following for 1981:

Rental revenues received		$140,000
Cash paid out in 1981 for—		
Wages paid to employees in 1981	$80,000	
Utilities paid for 1981	6,000	
Advertising expenses paid	5,000	
Supplies purchased and used in 1981	8,000	
Interest paid on loan	6,000	
Loan principal paid	10,000	
Owner withdrawals	15,000	130,000
Increase in cash balance for the year		$ 10,000

4. You also find that the December utility bill of $1,000 and an advertising bill of $1,500 have not been paid.

Required:

a. Prepare a written report for Tom giving your appraisal of the offer to sell the Ten Pins Bowling Lanes. Comment on the owner's method of computing the annual "profit" of the business.

b. Include in your report a statement of the assets employed in the business and an approximate earnings statement for 1981.

Chapter 3

Adjusting the accounts

Previous chapters have discussed and shown how and why the accountant relies upon transactions as the basic source of input data. They have also shown how transactions are analyzed, journalized, and summarized in accounts.

The need to adjust the accounts prior to the preparation of financial statements was discussed only briefly. This chapter discusses more fully the need for adjusting entries and presents and illustrates closing entries. It explains why the closing of the revenue and expense accounts, called nominal accounts, is necessary at the end of the accounting period. It also discusses and illustrates the possible use of reversing entries.

THE NEED FOR ADJUSTING ENTRIES

The earnings statement of an entity for a period must report all its revenues and all of the expenses incurred to generate those revenues. If it does not, it is certainly incomplete and inaccurate and possibly misleading. Similarly, a balance sheet that does not report all of an entity's assets, liabilities, and owner's equities may be misleading.

Since interested parties need timely information, financial statements must be prepared periodically. In order to prepare such statements, the accountant must arbitrarily divide an entity's life into time periods and attempt to assign economic activity to specific periods. This requires the preparation of *adjusting entries*—that is, entries to record economic activity that has taken place but which has not yet resulted in a transaction or other recordable event. Since a transaction has not occurred, some adjusting entries are based in part upon estimates which later events may prove to be in error. This is a price that must be paid if timely information is to be secured.

Thus, adjusting entries are necessary under the accrual basis of accounting. They are even required (to a much lesser extent) under cash basis accounting as normally applied.

Cash versus accrual basis accounting

Some relatively small business firms and professional groups, such as physicians, lawyers, and accountants, may account for their revenues and expenses on a cash basis. This means that (except for depreciation expense) expenses and revenues usually are not recorded until cash is received or paid out. Thus, for example, services rendered to clients in 1981 for which cash was collected in 1982 would be treated as 1982 revenues. Similarly, expenses incurred in 1981 for which cash was disbursed in 1982 would be treated as 1982 expenses. Because of these improper assignments of revenues and expenses, the *cash basis of accounting* is generally considered unacceptable. It is acceptable only under those circumstances in which the results approximate those obtained under the accrual basis of accounting.

As already illustrated, *the accrual basis of accounting recognizes revenues when sales are made or services are rendered even though cash is not yet received. Expenses are recognized as incurred regardless of whether or not cash is paid out.* Even under the accrual basis, transactions are the source of input into the accounting system. Thus, adjusting entries are needed to bring the accounts up to date before financial statements can be prepared.

Time of preparation of adjusting entries

Adjusting entries must be prepared whenever financial statements are to be prepared. Thus, if monthly financial statements are prepared, monthly adjusting entries are required. By custom, and in some instances by law, business firms report to their owners at least annually. Consequently, adjusting entries will be required at least annually.

CLASSES OF ADJUSTING ENTRIES

The adjusting entries illustrated and explained in this chapter can be grouped first into two broad classes. *One* class consists of those entries that relate to data previously recorded in the accounts. These entries involve the transfer of data from asset and liability accounts to expense and revenue accounts or from expense and revenue accounts to asset and liability accounts. The *second* class consists of entries relating to activity on which nothing has been previously recorded in the accounts. These entries involve the first recording of assets and liabilities and the related expenses and revenues. Since each class involves both expenses and revenues, there are four major types of adjusting entries, namely, those involving (1) asset/expense adjustments, (2) asset/revenue adjustments, (3) liability/expense adjustments, and (4) liability/revenue adjustments.

Asset/expense adjustments

One of the four major classes of adjusting entries involves recognition of the complete or partial expiration of the ability of an asset to render services (thus making it less valuable to its owner) as a result of its use in generating revenues. Because of its relative importance, five examples of this type of adjusting entry are presented below, specifically, for (1) insurance, (2) prepaid rent, (3) depreciation, (4) supplies, and (5) bad debts.

Insurance. When the premium on an insurance policy is paid in advance of the period covered by the policy, an asset is created that expires and becomes an expense with the passage of time. To illustrate, the advance payment of the $7,200 premium on a one-year insurance policy that covers the period from August 1, 1981, to July 31, 1982, creates an asset called unexpired, or prepaid, insurance on August 1, 1981. An asset exists because benefits—insurance protection—will be received in the future. The journal entry to record this transaction is:

```
1981
Aug.  1   Unexpired Insurance .....................................  7,200
              Cash .............................................              7,200
          To record advance payment of annual insurance premium.
```

Assume that the company has a calendar-year accounting period and that it records adjusting entries only at the end of its accounting period. By December 31, a part of the period covered by the policy has expired. Therefore, a part of the *service potential* (or benefits embodied in the asset) has expired. The asset now provides less future benefit than when acquired. The future services that an asset can render are what make the asset "a thing of value" to a business. This reduction of the asset's ability to provide services must be recognized. The cost of the services received from the asset is treated as an expense. Since the policy provides the same services for every month of its one-year life, it seems logical to assign an equal amount of cost to each month. Thus, with 5 of the 12 months of coverage provided by payment of the premium having elapsed, 5/12 of the annual premium is charged to expense on December 31. The journal entry and the accounts after posting appear as follows:

```
1981
Dec. 31   Insurance Expense ....................................... 3,000
              Unexpired Insurance ...................................        3,000
              To record expense for five months, August 1 to December 31,
              1981.
```

Unexpired Insurance						Account No. 104
Date			Explanation	Folio	Debit	Credit	Balance

Date		Explanation	Folio	Debit	Credit	Balance
1981						
Aug.	1	Cash paid	J-7*	7,200		7,200
Dec.	31	Adjustment	J-12		3,000	4,200

* Note: In this and all future illustrations, the folio references are assumed.

Insurance Expense						Account No. 408

Date		Explanation	Folio	Debit	Credit	Balance
1981						
Dec.	31	Adjustment	J-12	3,000		3,000

The insurance expense of $3,000 is reported in the earnings statement for the year ended December 31, 1981, as one of the expenses incurred in generating that year's revenues. The remaining amount of the annual premium, $4,200, is reported as a current asset. This type of asset is often referred to as a *prepaid expense*. The $4,200 is a measure of the cost of the asset, unexpired insurance. Unexpired insurance is an asset because it provides future benefits. The $4,200 is shown as a current asset because it will be consumed in the course of normal operations in the next operating cycle of the business or one year, whichever is longer.

In initially recording the purchase of the $7,200 of insurance, the accountant could have debited Insurance Expense rather than Unexpired Insurance. If this were the case, the adjusting entry would have been a debit to Unexpired Insurance and a credit to Insurance Expense for $4,200. This would have resulted in a balance of $4,200 in the asset account and $3,000 in the expense account, as shown in the T-accounts below. Thus, the end result is the same either way. We can see that in many situations the adjusting entry depends on which account the accountant originally debited or credited.

Insurance Expense				Unexpired Insurance		
1981		1981		1981		
Aug. 1	7,200	Dec. 31	4,200	Dec. 31	4,200	
Bal.	3,000					

Prepaid rent. Prepaid rent is another example of the continuous incurrence of an expense which results from using up a previously recorded asset. When rent is paid in advance for any substantial period of time, the prepayment is debited to the Prepaid Rent account (an asset account) at the date it is paid. Because the benefits resulting from the expenditure are yet to be received, the expenditure creates an asset. Services from the facilities being rented are received *continuously* through time. Thus, the expense is incurred *continuously* as time elapses. An entry could be made frequently, even daily, to record the expense incurred. But typically the entry is not made until financial statements are to be prepared. At that time an entry is made transferring from the asset account to an expense account the cost of that portion of the asset that has expired.

The measurement of rent expense usually presents no problems. Generally, the rental contract specifies the amount of rent per unit of time. If the contract states an annual rental, 1/12 of this annual rental is charged to each month. This is true even though there are varying numbers of days in some months. The variations are not considered significant enough to be taken into consideration.

To illustrate, assume that rent of $1,200 was paid in advance on September 1, 1981, for one year beginning on that date. The entry made at that time was:

```
1981
Sept.  1  Prepaid Rent .........................................  1,200
               Cash  ...........................................           1,200
          To record advance payment of one year's rent.
```

Assuming that the company has a calendar-year accounting period ending December 31, 1981, an adjusting entry must be prepared. Since one third of the period covered by the prepaid rent (4 of 12 months) has elapsed, one third of the $1,200 of prepaid rent is charged to expense. The required adjusting entry and the accounts after posting appear as follows:

```
1981
Dec. 31  Rent Expense ..............................................  400
               Prepaid Rent .........................................           400
          To record rent expense for four months.
```

Prepaid Rent						Account No. 110
Date		Explanation	Folio	Debit	Credit	Balance
1981 Sept. Dec.	1 31	Cash paid Adjustment	J-8 J-12	1,200	400	1,200 800

Rent Expense						Account No. 410
Date		Explanation	Folio	Debit	Credit	Balance
1981 Dec.	31	Adjustment	J-12	400		400

Rent expense is one of the operating expenses incurred in generating revenues. The $400 rent expense would appear in the earnings statement for the year ended December 31, 1981. The remaining amount of the prepaid rent is reported as a current asset in the balance sheet for December 31, 1981. The $800 is a measure of the cost of the asset, prepaid rent. Prepaid rent is a current asset because it will be consumed in the course of normal operations in one year or in the next operating cycle of the business.

Depreciation. The concept of depreciation was introduced briefly in Chapter 2. Depreciation is another example of the continuous incurrence of an expense which results from the *gradual using up* of a previously recorded asset. The overall period of time involved in using up a depreciable asset, a building for example, is less definite than in the case of an insurance premium or prepaid rent. The life of a depreciable asset must be *estimated* in advance, and individuals are not able to peer 10 to 50 years into the future with any real degree of accuracy. Nevertheless, the pattern of incurring an expense because of the expiration of an asset is basically the same. The cost of the asset (less estimated salvage value) is divided by the estimated number of periods in the life of the asset to find the amount of asset cost to be charged as an expense to each time period. This process is called *depreciation accounting.* The cost allocated to each time period is called *depreciation expense.* The method of depreciation discussed and illustrated here is known as the *straight-line method.* (Other methods are presented and discussed in Chapter 10.) The three factors involved in the computation of depreciation are the following:

1. The cost of the asset.
2. The estimated useful life of the asset.
3. The estimated salvage or scrap value of the asset.

The *depreciation formula* for straight-line depreciation is as follows:

$$\text{Annual depreciation} = \frac{\text{Cost} - \text{Estimated salvage value}}{\text{Number of years of useful life}}$$

The difference between the cost of an asset and its estimated salvage value is sometimes referred to as an asset's *depreciable amount.* This difference is the net cost of using the asset during its useful life. It must be allocated to the various periods in the asset's life.

Depreciation is sometimes expressed as an annual percentage rate determined by dividing the annual amount of depreciation by the cost of the asset. For instance, $1,000 \div $10,000 = 10$ percent.

The accumulated depreciation account. The depreciation expense for a period is not credited directly to the asset account but to a contra (asset) account called the *accumulated depreciation account.* A *contra asset account* appears as a deduction from the asset to which it relates in the balance sheet. This account is merely a special subdivision of the credit side of the related plant asset account. The debit balance in the plant asset account minus the credit balance in the related accumulated depreciation contra account equals the cost of the benefits yet to be received from the asset. (This is sometimes called the *book value* or the cost not yet allocated as an expense.)

Crediting depreciation to an accumulated depreciation account rather than directly to the asset account is justified largely on the grounds that recorded amounts of depreciation are quite tentative due to the use of estimates. To provide more complete information on the balance sheet, depreciable asset accounts are shown at their original acquisition cost and the accumulated depreciation is shown also. The balance in the related accumulated depreciation account increases each year by the amount of depreciation recorded until it finally reaches an amount equal to the cost of the asset (less estimated salvage value), unless the asset is disposed of prematurely.

Depreciation accounting illustrated. To illustrate the accounting for depreciation, assume that at December 31, 1981, a company owns one delivery truck that cost $4,200. The truck was purchased on January 1, 1981. It is expected to have a useful life of five years; scrap value is estimated at $200. Therefore, the depreciation expense for one year equals ($4,200 − $200) ÷ 5, or $800. This is the amount of depreciation expense allocable to the year 1981.

Depreciation for 1981 is recorded by the following entry:

```
1981
Dec. 31   Depreciation Expense—Delivery Equipment . . . . . . . . . . . . . . . . . . .      800
               Accumulated Depreciation—Delivery Equipment  . . . . . . . . . . .              800
          To record the depreciation expense for the year.
```

The ledger accounts will appear as follows:

Delivery Equipment					Account No. 130	
Date		Explanation	Folio	Debit	Credit	Balance
1981 Jan.	1	One truck	J-8	4,200		4,200

Accumulated Depreciation—Delivery Equipment					Account No. 131	
Date		Explanation	Folio	Debit	Credit	Balance
1981 Dec.	31	Adjustment	J-14		800	800

Depreciation Expense—Delivery Equipment					Account No. 418	
Date		Explanation	Folio	Debit	Credit	Balance
1981 Dec.	31	Adjustment	J-14	800		800

At December 31, 1981, after the adjustment, $3,200 of the cost of the truck remains to be allocated to expense while the truck is used during future years.

Accumulated depreciation in the balance sheet. In the balance sheet at December 31, 1981, the asset accounts include the following:

Assets

Plant, Property, and Equipment:
Delivery equipment $4,200
    Less: Accumulated depreciation—delivery equipment   800
                                                        $3,400

The portion of the cost of the asset not yet charged to expense at the end of the first year is $3,400. Since expected scrap value is $200, only $3,200 is expected to be charged to expense in future years. Since another $800 of depreciation would be recorded at the end of 1982, the balance sheet at the end of that year would show the following:

Assets

Plant, Property, and Equipment:
Delivery equipment $4,200
    Less: Accumulated depreciation—delivery equipment   1,600
                                                        $2,600

At the end of the fifth year, $4,000 of depreciation will have been recorded. If the estimates were correct, the asset will be retired from service and sold for $200. If this occurs, the required entry would read:

Cash   200
Accumulated Depreciation—Delivery Equipment   4,000
    Delivery Equipment   4,200
    To record retirement and sale of one delivery truck.

Depreciation expense is an operating expense and is *reported in the earnings statement.* Depreciation may be classified as either selling expense or administrative expense depending on the nature of the asset being depreciated. Depreciation on salespersons' automobiles would be a selling expense, while depreciation on an administrative office building would be administrative expense.

Supplies.   Every business consumes assets referred to as supplies in its operations. Supplies may be classified as office supplies (paper, stationery, carbon paper, pencils), as selling supplies (gummed tape, string, paper bags or cartons, wrapping paper) or, possibly, as cleaning supplies (soap, disinfectants). They are frequently bought in bulk and consumed or used gradually through time.

To illustrate, assume that office supplies were bought at various times throughout the year and recorded by debiting an asset account, Office Supplies on Hand, and crediting Cash. At the end of the year, the Office Supplies on Hand account shows a debit balance of $1,400. An actual physical inventory shows that only $400 worth of supplies are on hand. Thus, an adjusting entry is required to bring the accounts up to date. The entry will recognize the reduction in the asset and the incurrence of an expense through the using up of office supplies. From the information given, the asset balance should be $400 and the expense incurred, $1,000. By making the following adjusting entry, the accounts will be adjusted to those balances:

```
1981
Dec. 31  Office Supplies Expense ...................................  1,000
             Office Supplies on Hand ..............................            1,000
         To record supplies used during the year.
```

While the entry to record the usage of supplies could be made when the supplies are issued from the storeroom, it is usually not worth the expense to account so carefully for such small items.

The Office Supplies Expense account would appear as an operating expense in the earnings statement. Office Supplies on Hand would be reported as a current asset in the balance sheet often lumped with similar items and entitled Prepaid Expenses.

Bad debts.   No matter how carefully a company screens applications for credit from its customers, if it renders services or sells goods on a credit basis it will encounter the problem of bad debts—uncollectible accounts receivable. Currently, actual bad debts range from a small fraction of accounts receivable to an amount considerably larger, depending, at least in part, upon economic conditions.

To illustrate the problems encountered in accounting for bad debts, assume that the December 31, 1981, trial balance of a company in its first year of operations shows accounts receivable of $50,000. Assume further that the manager of the company, using trade association data, estimates that 4 percent of the accounts receivable will never be collected. This information would require the following adjusting entry:

```
1981
Dec. 31  Bad Debts Expense ......................................  2,000
             Allowance for Doubtful Accounts .......................            2,000
         To record estimated bad debts for the year as 4 percent of accounts
         receivable.
```

This entry accomplishes two things: (1) it brings about a proper matching of bad debts expense with revenue, since the uncollectible accounts arising from 1981 sales are recognized as an expense in 1981; and (2) the accounts receivable as of December 31, 1981, are properly valued at their net realizable value, the amount of cash expected to be collected. The *Allowance for Doubtful Accounts account* balance is deducted from accounts receivable in the current assets section of the balance sheet as follows:

Assets

```
Current Assets:
Accounts receivable .............................................................  $50,000
    Less: Allowance for doubtful accounts ...................................    2,000
                                                                                $48,000
```

The topic of accounting for bad debts is covered in greater depth in Chapter 8. The purpose of the discussion here was merely to illustrate the adjusting entry.

Asset/revenue adjustments

In some instances, agreements are entered into which create a right to collect assets through time. Periodically, the amounts are collected. Examples of this type of adjustment include the accruals made for commissions earned (illustrated in Chapter 2), interest revenue, and rent revenue.

Interest revenue.   The interest received periodically on investments such as bonds and savings accounts is literally earned by the lender or investor moment by moment. Rarely is payment of the interest made on the last day of the accounting period. Thus, the accounting records normally will not show the amount of interest revenue earned nor the total assets owned by the investor unless an adjusting entry is made. An entry at the end of the accounting period is needed which debits a receivable account (an asset) and credits a revenue account to record the asset owned and the interest earned.

For example, assume that a company invests some funds in an interest-paying security. The interest is received twice a year on May 1 and November 1 in the amount of $1,800 on each date. If the investment was purchased on May 2, 1981, Interest Revenue is credited with the $1,800 of cash received on November 1. At December 31, 1981, an additional two months' interest of the six months' interest to be received on May 1, 1982, has been earned. An entry must be made to show the amount of interest earned and the asset, the right to receive this interest, at December 31, 1981. The entry to record the accrual of revenue is:

```
Accrued Interest Receivable . . . . . . . . . . . . . . . . . . . . . . . . . . . . . . . . . . . . . . . . .    600
      Interest Revenue . . . . . . . . . . . . . . . . . . . . . . . . . . . . . . . . . . . . . . . . . . . . . .            600
         To record two months' interest revenue.
```

The ledger accounts appear as follows:

Accrued Interest Receivable						*Account No. 107*
Date		Explanation	Folio	Debit	Credit	Balance
1981 Dec.	31	Adjustment	J-14	600		600

Interest Revenue						*Account No. 506*
Date		Explanation	Folio	Debit	Credit	Balance
1981 Nov.	1	Cash received	J-13		1,800	1,800
Dec.	31	Adjustment	J-14		600	2,400

The $600 debit balance in Accrued Interest Receivable is reported as a current asset in the December 31, 1981, balance sheet. (The term *accrued* refers to an enforceable claim which comes into existence over time. It accumulates gradually with the passage of time.) The $2,400 credit balance in Interest Revenue is the interest earned during the year. *Under accrual basis accounting, it does not matter whether cash was collected during the year or not.* The interest revenue earned still is reported in the earnings statement for the year.

Entry in next period. The collection of $1,800 of cash on May 1, 1982, is recorded as follows:

```
1982
May 1  Cash .................................................  1,800
            Accrued Interest Receivable ...........................       600
            Interest Revenue .....................................     1,200
        Collected interest for six months ending May 1.
```

Note how the preparation of the adjusting entry properly assigns the revenue earned to the proper accounting period. The $1,800 collected represents interest earned in the six months ending May 1, 1982. But two of these months fell in calendar year 1981. Therefore, one third of $1,800 should be treated as 1981 revenue and the balance as 1982 revenue. The entries prepared yield exactly these results.

Rent revenue. Rental agreements usually require rent to be paid at the beginning of the rental period. But occasionally a situation may exist that requires the accrual of rent revenue and the recognition of an asset.

To illustrate, assume that a company rents the second floor of a building it owns to another party for a monthly rental of $2,400, with the first rental payment due on January 16, 1982. Occupancy is granted on December 16, 1981. Assuming a calendar-year accounting period, the adjusting entry required on December 31, 1981, is:

```
1981
Dec. 31  Accrued Rent Receivable ................................  1,200
            Rent Revenue ........................................     1,200
        To record accrual of one half of a month's rent revenue.
```

The accrued rent receivable of $1,200 would be reported as a current asset in the balance sheet, while the rent revenue would be reported in the earnings statement.

Entry in next period. When the first monthly rental payment of $2,400 is received on January 16, 1982, the cash received would be accounted for as a $1,200 collection of the balance in the Accrued Rent Receivable account and a $1,200 collection of January rent revenue. Thus, the adjusting entry provides for assigning the first $2,400 of rent earned to the proper periods, as well as correctly stating assets on December 31, 1981. The entry required on January 16, 1982, to record the rent collected is as follows:

```
1982
Jan. 16  Cash ................................................  2,400
            Accrued Rent Receivable ...........................     1,200
            Rent Revenue .......................................     1,200
        Collected the rent for one month.
```

Liability/expense adjustments

In order to report on net earnings and financial position properly, adjustments involving liability and expense accounts are often required. Discussed below are the adjustments relating to salaries and federal income taxes, although similar adjustments may be required for other forms of taxes, interest, and pension obligations.

Salaries. The recording of employee services usually involves a debit to an expense account and a credit to cash (payroll withholdings and payroll taxes are ignored here but are discussed in Chapter 12). If the receipt of employee services is recognized only when paid, an adjusting entry may be required at the end of an accounting period to record those services received for which payment has not been made.

To illustrate, assume that the Office Salaries Expense account shows a debit balance at the end of January 1981 of $8,800. This consists of four weekly payrolls (Monday through Saturday) of $2,200 each (paid on Saturday). But, assuming the last day of January falls on a Wednesday, the expense account does not show salaries earned by employees for the last three days of the month. Nor do the accounts show the employer's obligation to pay these salaries. If financial statements are to be prepared for the month of January, the following adjusting entry is needed:

```
1981
Jan. 31   Office Salaries Expense.....................................   1,100
              Accrued Office Salaries Payable .........................            1,100
          To accrue one half of a week's office salaries.
```

The two accounts involved now appear as follows:

Office Salaries Expense   Account No. 422

Date		Explanation	Folio	Debit	Credit	Balance
1981						
Jan.	6	1st week cash	J-3	2,200		2,200
	13	2d week cash	J-4	2,200		4,400
	20	3d week cash	J-4	2,200		6,600
	27	4th week cash	J-5	2,200		8,800
	31	Adjustment	J-5	1,100		9,900

Accrued Office Salaries Payable   Account No. 309

Date		Explanation	Folio	Debit	Credit	Balance
1981						
Jan.	31	Adjustment	J-5		1,100	1,100

The adjusting journal entry brings the month's salaries expense up to its correct amount for earnings statement purposes. The credit records the liability to employees for services for balance sheet purposes. The accrued office salaries payable amounting to $1,100 is shown in the current liability section of the balance sheet.

Liability/revenue adjustments

This class of adjustments covers those situations in which the customer transfers assets (usually cash) to the selling company prior to the receipt of merchandise or services. This is called *revenue received in advance.* Such receipts are debited to Cash and usually credited to an account entitled Revenue Received in Advance, Prepaid Revenue, or Unearned Revenue. Better terminology would be Advances by Customers to show clearly the liability nature of the account. The seller is obligated either to deliver the goods, provide the services, or return the customer's money. The liability is canceled, and revenue is earned by delivering the agreed-upon goods or performing the services.

Advance payments could be received for items such as tickets, rent, and magazine or newspaper subscriptions. Because of their similarity, only the advance receipt of subscriptions will be illustrated and discussed.

Subscription revenue. Assume that during 1981 a company received a total of $48,000 at various times as payment in advance for a number of one-year subscriptions to a monthly magazine. An entry debiting Cash and crediting Subscriptions Received in Advance was made to record each amount of cash collected. The liability established when the cash was received will be gradually converted into revenue as the magazines contracted for are delivered. Thus, an adjusting entry to update the accounts is usually required before financial statements are prepared. Assuming that 40 percent of the magazines paid for in advance have been delivered by year-end, the required adjusting entry is:

```
1981
Dec. 31   Subscriptions Received in Advance  ......................  19,200
              Subscription Revenue  .............................         19,200
            To record subscription revenue earned in 1981.
```

The subscription revenue of $19,200 is, of course, reported in the earnings statement for 1981. The $28,800 ($48,000 − $19,200) balance in the Subscriptions Received in Advance account is reported as a current liability in the balance sheet. The $28,800 will be earned and transferred to a revenue account in 1982.

Since the process of preparing financial statements after adjusting entries have been journalized and posted was illustrated in Chapter 2, it need not be dealt with here. Rather, attention will be directed toward the next steps in the financial accounting process.

CLOSING ENTRIES

After adjusting entries have been journalized and posted, up-to-date information of two major types is found in the accounts: (1) information relating to the activities occurring during the period just ended and (2) information on the financial condition of the entity at the end of the period.

The first type of information is found largely in the expense and revenue accounts. These accounts have already been discussed as temporarily established subdivisions of the Owner's Equity account. The expense and revenue accounts help the accountant fulfill a most important task—the determination of periodic net earnings. After the financial statements for the period have been prepared, these temporary accounts have served their purpose. They must now be brought to a zero balance so that information for the next accounting period can be entered in them.

The balance in each expense and revenue account is transferred by journal entry to the *Expense and Revenue Summary account.* This is a *clearing* account used only at the end of the accounting period to summarize the expenses and revenues for the period. Since revenue accounts have credit balances, they are debited and Expense and Revenue Summary is credited. Conversely, since expense accounts have debit balances, they are credited and Expense and Revenue Summary is debited. The Expense and Revenue Summary account now contains either a debit (net loss) or credit (net earnings) balance. It is then debited or credited as required to bring it to a zero balance, and the owner's capital account is credited or debited in order to keep the entry in balance. Finally, the owner's drawing account is closed by debiting the owner's capital account and crediting the owner's drawing account. This *closing* process is often referred to as "closing the books."

Closing entries illustrated

To illustrate the preparation of closing entries, assume that the ledger of a business owned and operated by William Brent contains the following earnings statement accounts:

Service Revenue	$196,000
Depreciation Expense—Machinery	120,000
Salaries Expense	40,000
Miscellaneous Expense	16,000
Real Estate Taxes	5,000

The required closing entries, assuming a December 31, 1981, closing, are as follows:

1981			
Dec. 31	Service Revenue	196,000	
	Expense and Revenue Summary		196,000
	To close the revenue account.		
31	Expense and Revenue Summary	181,000	
	Depreciation Expense—Machinery		120,000
	Salaries Expense		40,000
	Miscellaneous Expense		16,000
	Real Estate Taxes		5,000
	To close the expense accounts.		
31	Expense and Revenue Summary	15,000	
	William Brent, Capital		15,000
	To close the Expense and Revenue Summary account.		

Further, assume that the owner's drawing account shows a debit balance of $5,000. It is closed directly to the owner's capital account as follows:

1981			
Dec. 31	William Brent, Capital	5,000	
	William Brent, Drawing		5,000
	To close the owner's drawing account.		

The owner's drawing account is not closed to the Expense and Revenue Summary account because the owner's drawings are not an expense of the business. Drawings represent amounts withdrawn by the owner. They are not an expense because they are not intended to produce revenues.

The above entries are posted in the normal manner and, if properly prepared and posted, will reduce all of the revenue and expense accounts to zero balances so that they can be used to accumulate data needed to determine the next period's net earnings. The drawing account is also brought to a zero balance so it will be ready to accept entries for the owner's drawings in the coming year.

The Expense and Revenue Summary and William Brent, Capital accounts as they appear after the above closing entries have been posted are presented below. The beginning balance of $65,000 in the William Brent, Capital account is assumed, as are the account numbers and the posting cross-reference (Folio J-15). Note that the Expense and Revenue Summary account shows clearly the net earnings for the period—the final amount transferred, or closed, to the William Brent, Capital account. The balance in the William Brent, Capital account of $75,000 is the amount of capital shown in the balance sheet for December 31, 1981.

Expense and Revenue Summary						*Account No. 600*
Date			Explanation	Folio	Debit	Credit	Balance
1981 Dec.	31		Revenues	J-15		196,000	196,000
	31		Expenses	J-15	181,000		15,000
	31		To close	J-15	15,000		—0—

William Brent, Capital						*Account No. 317*
Date			Explanation	Folio	Debit	Credit	Balance
1981 Jan.	1		Balance				65,000
Dec.	31		Net earnings	J-15		15,000	80,000
	31		Drawings	J-15	5,000		75,000

Post-closing trial balance

After the closing process has been completed, the only open accounts in the ledger are the balance sheet accounts. Since these accounts contain the opening balances for the coming accounting year, they must, of course, be in balance. The preparation of a *post-closing trial balance* thus serves as a means of checking upon the accuracy of the closing process (the preparation and posting of closing entries and the bringing forward of account balances). At the same time it ensures that the books are in balance at the start of the new accounting period.

As in the case of a trial balance, a post-closing trial balance is simply a listing of all of the open accounts in a system or ledger. The total of the accounts with debit balances must be equal to the total of the accounts with credit balances, or an error has been made.

THE ACCOUNTING CYCLE SUMMARIZED

The financial accounting process consists of a number of functions beginning with observation of economic activity and ending with interpretation of reports and statements upon such activity. In this process are a number of steps that relate to the formal accounting system and its use in accumulating, processing, and reporting useful financial information. These steps, which have been illustrated and discussed in this and previous chapters, are referred to collectively as the *accounting cycle.* They are as follows:

1. Journalizing transactions (and other events) in the journal.
2. Posting journal entries to the accounts.
3. Taking a trial balance of the accounts.
4. Journalizing the adjusting entries.
5. Posting the adjusting entries to the accounts.
6. Preparing financial statements.
7. Journalizing the closing entries.
8. Posting the closing entries to the accounts.
9. Taking a post-closing trial balance.

Completion of many of the steps that fall at the end of an accounting period may be made somewhat easier through use of a work sheet. The use of a work sheet is discussed and illustrated in the next chapter.

In addition to the above steps, some accountants prepare reversing entries. These entries are discussed in the next section of this chapter.

REVERSING ENTRIES

For certain types of adjusting entries, *reversing entries* (given the name because they reverse the effects of the adjusting entry to which they relate) may be prepared as of the first day of the next accounting period. The purpose of a reversing entry is to make simpler the entry relating to that same item in the next accounting period.

To illustrate, we will use the facts relating to the accrual of interest presented earlier in the section "Interest revenue." In that discussion, a company invested funds in an interest-paying security on May 2, 1981. The interest is to be received on May 1 and November 1 of each year in the amount of $1,800 on each date. The first interest check was received on November 1, 1981, and was properly recorded. An adjusting entry was made at December 31, 1981 (the end of the accounting period), to recognize the interest earned between November 1 and December 31. Below are illustrated the entries from December 31, 1981, through May 1, 1982, assuming (1) no reversing entry is used and (2) a reversing entry is used.

(1)			(2)		
No reversing entry to be used.			*Reversing entry to be used.*		
1981			1981		
Dec. 31	Accrued Interest Receivable 600		Dec. 31	Accrued Interest Receivable 600	
	Interest Revenue	600		Interest Revenue	600
	To record two months interest revenue			To record two months' interest revenue.	

(The closing entries would be the same in either case.)

1982			1982		
Jan. 1	No entry,		Jan. 1	Interest Revenue 600	
				Accrued Interest Receivable	600
				To reverse the adjusting entry made on 12/31/81.	

May 1	Cash	1,800		May 1	Cash	1,800	
	Accrued Interest				Interest Revenue		1,800
	Receivable		600		Collected interest for six		
	Interest revenue		1,200		months ending May 1.		
	Collected interest for six						
	months ending May 1.						

You will notice that whether a reversing entry is to be used or not, the adjusting and closing entries for 1981 are identical. The use of a reversing entry (which is the exact reverse of the debit and credit used in the adjusting entry) on January 1 enables the entry made on May 1 to be simpler. The accountant does not have to remember that accrued interest receivable of $600 has already been recorded on this investment. When the $1,800 check arrives, the entry is simply a debit to Cash and a credit to Interest Revenue.

When the accounts are maintained on a computer (which is a very common situation), the computer program may have been designed to debit Cash and credit Interest Revenue every time an interest check is received. The use of a reversing entry on January 1 permits the May 1 entry to be recorded in this way.

The end result in the accounts is the same whether a reversing entry is used or not. To prove this, the accounts as they would appear are shown below. The adjusting and closing entries from 1981 are ignored since they were the same under either method.

(1)				(2)			
No reversing entry to be used.				*Reversing entry to be used.*			

	Cash				**Cash**		
5/1/82	1,800			5/1/82	1,800		

	Accrued Interest Receivable				**Accrued Interest Receivable**		
Beg. bal.	600	5/1/82	600	Beg. bal.	600	1/1/82	600

	Interest Revenue				**Interest Revenue**		
		5/1/82	1,200	1/1/82	600	5/1/82	1,800

Not all adjusting entries may be reversed on the first day of the next accounting period. Ideal candidates are where cash is going to be paid or received in the following period for an item which accrues over time and resulted in an adjusting entry. Examples of such items would include accrued wages, rent, and interest. Adjustments for items which will not result in a subsequent receipt or payment of cash (such as the adjustment for depreciation) usually are not reversed. A general rule to follow is reverse all adjusting journal entries that increase assets or liabilities but do not reverse adjusting journal entries that decrease assets or liabilities. In applying this rule, assets with contra accounts should be viewed net.

Reversing entries are optional and relate to bookkeeping technique.

Whether they are used or not has no effect on the financial statements. Students may encounter the use of reversing entries in more advanced accounting courses or in actual practice. An understanding of reversing entries is not essential to understanding the remainder of this text since they will not be utilized.

<table>
<tr><td>

NEW TERMS INTRODUCED IN CHAPTER 3

</td><td>

Accounting cycle—a series of steps related to accumulating, processing, and reporting useful financial information that are performed during an accounting period. The steps include journalizing transactions, posting, taking a trial balance, adjusting the accounts, preparing financial statements, closing the accounts, and taking a postclosing trial balance.

Accrual basis of accounting—a method of earnings determination under which revenues are recorded when goods are delivered or services are rendered, and expenses are recorded in the same period as the revenues which they helped to create are recognized.

Accrued (assets and liabilities)—those assets and liabilities which exist at the end of an accounting period but which have not been recorded up to the time at which adjusting entries are to be prepared. They represent rights to receive, or obligations to make, payments which are not legally due at the balance sheet date. Examples are accrued interest receivable, accrued rent receivable, accrued salaries (or wages) payable, and accrued interest payable.

Accumulated depreciation account—a contra asset account which shows the sum of all amounts taken as depreciation on the asset up to the balance sheet date.

Adjusting entries—journal entries made to record the accrued effects of economic activity. They are made at the end of the accounting period to bring the accounts to their proper balances before financial statements are prepared.

Allowance for Doubtful Accounts account—an account showing the estimated amount of outstanding accounts receivable not expected to be collected; a contra asset account shown as a deduction from accounts receivable in the balance sheet.

Book value—the net amount of an asset. For depreciable assets, book value equals cost less the related accumulated depreciation.

Cash basis of accounting—a procedure under which revenue is recorded when cash is received and expenses are recorded when cash is paid.

Closing—the act of transferring the balances in the expense and revenue accounts to the Expense and Revenue Summary account and then to the owner's capital account. The balance in the owner's drawing account is transferred to the owner's capital account.

Contra asset account—an account shown as a deduction from the asset to which it relates in the balance sheet.

Depreciation accounting—the process of allocating and charging to expense the cost of a limited-life, long-term asset (such as a building) over its useful life.

Depreciation expense—the portion of the cost of a depreciable asset charged to expense in a given accounting period.

Depreciation formula—the procedure employed in calculating periodic depreciation, generally cost less estimated salvage value divided by the number of years of expected useful life, which is the procedure employed to determine the annual depreciation charge under the straight-line method.

</td></tr>
</table>

Expense and Revenue Summary account—a clearing account used to summarize all revenue and expense account balances at the end of an accounting period.

Interim statements—financial statements prepared at intervals shorter than one year, such as monthly and quarterly.

Post-closing trial balance—a trial balance taken after the expense and revenue (and drawing) accounts have been closed.

Prepaid expense—an asset which is awaiting assignment to expense. An example is unexpired insurance.

Revenue received in advance—a flow of assets received from customers in advance of the rendering of services or the delivery of goods; since the revenue has not been earned, it is a liability; often called *prepaid revenue or unearned revenue,* although preferred terminology would be *advances by customers.*

Reversing entries—journal entries made on the first day of the next accounting period to reverse the effects of the adjusting entries to which they relate. Their purpose is to make easier the recording of a subsequent transaction relating to those same items. They may only be used for certain types of adjusting entries—usually those accruals where cash is to be paid or received in the next accounting period.

Service potential—the benefits embodied in assets. The future services that assets can render are what make assets "things of value" to a business.

DEMONSTRATION PROBLEM

The trial balance of the Korman Company at December 31 of the current year includes, among other items, the following account balances:

	Debits	Credits
Accounts receivable	$ 42,000	
Allowance for doubtful accounts		$ 500
Office supplies inventory	3,000	
Unexpired insurance	3,900	
Prepaid rent	12,600	
Buildings	100,000	
Accumulated depreciation—buildings		16,625
Salaries expense	62,000	

Additional data:

1. It is estimated that $1,000 should be added to the Allowance for Doubtful Accounts.
2. The inventory of supplies on hand at December 31 amounts to $1,200.
3. The debit balance in the Unexpired Insurance account is the advance premium for one year from October 1 of the current year.
4. The debit balance in the Prepaid Rent account is for a one-year period that began May 1 of the current year.
5. The annual rate of depreciation for the buildings is based on the cost shown in the Buildings account less an estimated scrap value of $5,000. The estimated useful lives of the buildings are 40 years each.
6. Since the last payday, office employees have earned additional salaries of $3,000.

Required:

Prepare the adjusting journal entries at December 31.

Solution to demonstration problem

KORMAN COMPANY
General Journal

19—				
Dec. 31	Bad Debts Expense	1,000	
	Allowance for Doubtful Accounts		1,000
	To record estimated bad debts.		
31	Office Supplies Used	1,800	
	Office Supplies Inventory		1,800
	To record office supplies expense ($3,000 − $1,200).		
31	Insurance Expense	975	
	Unexpired Insurance		975
	To record expired insurance ($3,900 × 3/12).		
31	Rent Expense	8,400	
	Prepaid Rent		8,400
	To record rent expense ($12,600 × 8/12).		
31	Depreciation Expense—Buildings	2,375	
	Accumulated Depreciation—Buildings		2,375
	To record depreciation at 2.5 percent of depreciable cost [0.025 × ($100,000 − $5,000)].		
31	Salaries Expense	3,000	
	Accrued Salaries Payable		3,000
	To record accrued salaries.		

QUESTIONS

1. In what important way do the pre-closing trial balance and the post-closing trial balance differ? Why is the post-closing trial balance prepared?

2. Assuming that the closing process has been accomplished properly, which of the following statements is true? Why?

a. After closing, expense and revenue accounts never have a balance other than zero.

b. After closing, balance sheet accounts always have a balance other than zero.

3. Your uncle knows you are taking a course in accounting in college, and he asks you to come over and help him. It seems his new bookkeeper has journalized all of the business transactions for the month and has posted the journal entries to the ledger accounts. The bookkeeper now admits a difficulty in knowing how to proceed in completing the accounting process for the month.

Your uncle asks you to tell the bookkeeper what should now be done to complete the process.

4. Why are adjusting entries necessary? Why not treat every cash disbursement as an expense and every cash receipt as revenue when the cash changes hands?

5. Give an example of each of the following:

a. Equal growth of an expense and a liability.

b. Earning of revenue received in advance.

c. Equal growth of an asset and revenue.

d. Equal growth of an expense and decrease in an asset.

6. "Adjusting entries would not be necessary if the *pure* cash basis of accounting were followed (assuming no mistakes were made in recording cash transactions as they occurred). Under the pure cash basis, all receipts which are of a revenue nature are considered revenue when received and all expenditures (even for a building) which are of an expense nature are considered expenses when paid. It is the use of the accrual basis of accounting, where an effort is made to match expenses (incurred but not necessarily paid for in the same period) against the revenues (earned but not necessarily received in the same period) they create, that makes adjusting entries necessary." Do you agree with this statement? Why?

7. Why don't accountants keep all the accounts at their proper balances continuously throughout the period so that adjusting entries would not have to be made before financial statements are prepared?

8. A fellow student makes the following statement: "It is easy to tell whether a company is using the cash or accrual basis of accounting. When an amount is paid for future rent or insurance services, a firm that is using the cash basis will debit an expense account while a firm that is using the accrual basis will debit an asset account." Is the student correct?

9. You notice that the Supplies on Hand account has a debit balance of $2,700 at the end of the accounting period. How would you determine the extent to which this account needs adjustment?

10. It may be said that some assets are converted into expenses as they expire and that some liabilities become revenues as they are earned. Give examples of asset and liability accounts for which the statement is true. Give examples of asset and liability accounts to which the statement does not apply.

11. The accountant often speaks of expired costs. Do costs literally expire?

12. What does the word "accrued" mean? Is there a conceptual difference between interest payable and accrued interest payable?

13. It is more difficult to match expenses incurred with revenues earned than it would be to match expenses paid with revenues received. Do you think that the effort is worthwhile?

14. Describe the nature and purpose of a reversing entry.

EXERCISES

E–1.a. If a one-year insurance policy is purchased on and provides coverage from September 1 for $2,400 and the following entry is made at that time:

Unexpired Insurance	2,400	
Cash		2,400

What adjusting entry is necessary at December 31?

b. Give the adjusting entry which would be necessary at December 31 if the entry to record the purchase of the policy on September 1 had been:

Insurance Expense	2,400	
Cash		2,400

c. Show by the use of T-accounts that the end result is the same under either **(a)** or **(b).**

E–2. At December 31, 1981, an adjusting entry was made as follows:

Prepaid Rent	500	
Rent Expense		500

You know that the gross amount of rent paid was $1,200 and that it covers a one-year period. Determine:

a. The opening date of the year to which the $1,200 of rent applies.

b. The entry that was made on the date the rent was paid.

E–3. A building is being depreciated by an amount of $14,000 per year. You know it had an original cost of $155,000 and was expected to last ten years. How must the $14,000 have been determined? Give the entry for the sale of the building at the end of the ten-year period assuming the building was sold for its expected salvage value.

E–4. Office supplies were purchased for cash on May 2, 1981, for $800. Show two ways in which the entry for this purchase could be recorded and then show the adjusting entry that would be necessary for each, assuming that $200 of the supplies remained at the end of the year.

E–5. Prepare the adjusting entry on December 1, 1981, to record estimated bad debts of $1,000.

E–6. The cash balance at the beginning of the year was $17,000. During the year $80,000 was paid out for assets and expenses and $20,000 was invested in the business by the owner. The cash balance at the end of the year was $28,000. The balance in accounts receivable decreased by $6,000 during the year. How much service revenue was earned during the year? There were no receipts or disbursements except those specifically mentioned or implied above.

E–7. A firm borrows $10,000 on November 1 for 120 days with interest payable at the maturity of the loan at the rate of 9 percent per annum. Prepare the adjusting entry required on December 31. (It should be noted that by December 31, one half of the term of the loan has expired.)

E–8. A firm buys bonds as an investment. If the semiannual interest amounts to $600 and is paid on March 1 and September 1, what is the adjusting entry required on December 31 to record the interest revenue earned?

E–9. State the effect that each of the following would have on the amount of net earnings reported for 1981 and 1982. The company's accounting period ends on December 31.

a. No adjustment is made for accrued salaries of $800 as of December 31, 1981.

b. The collection of $600 for services yet unperformed as of December 31, 1981, is credited to a revenue account and not adjusted. The services are performed in 1982.

E–10. After adjustment, selected account balances of the Borto Company are:

	Debits	Credits
Service revenue		$40,000
Commissions expense	$21,000	
Advertising expense	4,000	
Office expense	13,000	
Borto, drawing	1,500	

In journal form, give the entries required to close the books for the period.

E–11. Using the facts presented in Exercise E–8, show how the March 1, 1982, receipt of interest would be recorded assuming (1) no reversing entry is used and (2) a reversing entry is used on January 1, 1982 (show this entry also). Now show by the use of T-accounts that the end result is the same whether a reversing entry is used or not.

PROBLEMS, SERIES A

P3–1–A.

Required:

For each of the following cases:

a. Prepare the adjusting journal entry, dating it December 31, 1981.

b. Set up three-column ledger accounts in skeleton form (without all the details), enter balances as given, if any, and post the adjusting entries made in part **(a)**.

c. Prepare and post closing entries. You will need a separate Expense and Revenue Summary account for each case.

d. State the correct figures for the balance sheet. Show related accounts in each case as they should appear on that statement.

e. State the correct figures for the earnings statement.

	Account name	Trial balance	Information for adjustments
Case 1:	Equipment	$80,000	Depreciation is computed at the rate of 15 percent per period.
	Accumulated Depreciation—Equipment	12,000	
Case 2:	Interest Expense	3,000	Unpaid interest incurred on borrowed money amounts to $400.
Case 3:	Unexpired Insurance	16,800	Of the unexpired insurance in the trial balance, only $4,400 is for additional protection after December 31.

P3–2–A. The trial balance of the John Barker Company at December 31 of the current year includes, among other items, the following account balances:

	Debits	Credits
Unexpired insurance	$ 3,648	
Buildings	79,000	
Accumulated depreciation— buildings		$15,800
Salaries expense	55,000	
Prepaid rent	12,000	

Additional data:

1. The debit balance in the Unexpired Insurance account is the advance premium for one year from September 1 of the current year.
2. The buildings are being depreciated at the rate of 4 percent a year, with no salvage value expected.
3. Salaries accrued at December 31 amount to $3,200.
4. The debit balance in Prepaid Rent is for a one-year period that started March 1 of the current year.

Required:

Prepare the adjusting journal entries at December 31.

P3–3–A. Among the account balances shown in the trial balance of the Jane Pollock Company at December 31 of the current year are the following:

	Debits	Credits
Office supplies inventory	$ 1,740	
Unexpired insurance	2,400	
Accounts receivable	74,000	
Allowance for doubtful accounts		$ 800
Buildings	42,000	
Accumulated depreciation—buildings		9,750

Additional data:

1. The inventory of supplies on hand at December 31 amounts to $300.
2. The balance in the Unexpired Insurance account is for a two-year policy effective on June 1 of the current year.
3. It is estimated that $1,400 should be added to the Allowance for Doubtful Accounts.
4. The annual rate of depreciation for the buildings is based on the cost shown in the Buildings account, less scrap value estimated at $4,500. When acquired, the lives of the buildings were estimated at 50 years each.

Required:

a. Prepare the adjusting journal entries at December 31.

b. Open three-column ledger accounts for each of the accounts involved, enter the balances as shown in the trial balance, post the adjusting entries, and bring down balances.

P3–4–A.

Required:

a. Set up the following three ledger accounts: Accounts Receivable, Bad Debts Expense, and Allowance for Doubtful Accounts.

b. Journalize the following transactions and post to the accounts (do not post to accounts not given):

Aug.	1–31	Service revenue on account amounted to $66,000.
	1–31	Cash collected on account amounted to $16,000.
	31	One percent of accounts receivable on August 31 was estimated to be uncollectible.
Sept.	1–30	Service revenue on account amounted to $72,000.
	1–30	Cash collected on account amounted to $30,000.
	30	Increased the balance in the Allowance for Doubtful Accounts account to 1 percent of the balance in the Accounts Receivable account.

P3–5–A. The Sam Higgins Company occupies rented quarters on the main street of the city. In order to get this location it was necessary for the company to rent a store larger than needed, so a portion of the area is subleased (rented) to Paul's Restaurant.

Required:

Present the period-end adjusting entries required by the statements of fact presented below. Show your calculations of the amounts as explanations of your entries.

The following partial trial balance was taken from the company's ledger as of the close of business on December 31, 1981. All of the original entries applicable to the statements of fact were posted to one or more of these accounts.

SAM HIGGINS COMPANY
Partial Trial Balance
December 31, 1981

	Debits	Credits
Cash	$20,000	
Accounts receivable	25,000	
Allowance for doubtful accounts		$ 500
Unexpired insurance	2,850	
Store equipment	22,000	
Accumulated depreciation— store equipment		2,400
Notes payable		5,000
Service revenue		150,000
Supplies expense	2,700	
Rent expense	3,600	
Store salaries expense	24,500	
Rent revenue		1,100

Data to be considered:

1. The wages of the store clerks amount to $90 per day and were last paid through Wednesday, December 27. December 31 is a Sunday. The store is closed on Sundays.
2. The Allowance for Doubtful Accounts balance needs to be increased by $3,000.
3. An analysis of the Store Equipment account disclosed:

Balance, January 1, 1981	$16,000
Addition, July 1, 1981	6,000
Balance, December 31, 1981,	
per trial balance	$22,000

The company estimates that this equipment will last 20 years from the date it was acquired and that the salvage value will be zero.

4. The store carries one combined insurance policy which is taken out once a year effective August 1. The premium on the policy now in force amounts to $1,800 per year.
5. Unused store supplies on hand at December 31, 1981, have a cost of $180.
6. December's rent of $100 from Paul's Restaurant has not yet been received.
7. The note payable is for ten months, has an interest rate of 10 percent per annum, and is dated July 1, 1981.

P3–6–A. On June 1, 1981, John Schmidt opened a swimming pool cleaning and maintenance service business. He vaguely recalled the process of making journal entries and establishing ledger accounts from a high school bookkeeping course he had taken some years ago. At the end of June, he prepared an earnings statement for the month of June, but he had the feeling that he had not proceeded correctly. He contacted his brother, Jay, a recent college graduate majoring in accounting, for assistance.

Jay immediately noted that his brother had kept his records on a cash basis. So he set about to bring the books to a full accrual basis.

Required:

a. Prepare the entries for the following transactions as John must have recorded them under the cash basis of accounting.

b. Prepare the necessary adjusting entries as Jay must have prepared them to bring the books to a full accrual basis of accounting.

c. Calculate the change in the net earnings for June brought about by changing from the cash to the accrual basis of accounting.

Transactions:

June 1 Received cash of $9,000 from various customers in exchange for service agreements to clean and maintain their pools for the months of June, July, August, and September.
  5 Paid rent for automotive and cleaning equipment to be used during the period June through September, $2,000. The payment covered the entire period.
  8 Purchased a two-year liability insurance policy effective June 1 for $2,640 cash.
  10 Received an advance of $2,500 from a Florida building contractor in exchange for an agreement to help service pools in the contractor's housing development during the months of October through May.
  16 Paid wages for the first half of June, $2,800.
  17 Paid $120 for advertising to be run in a local newspaper for two weeks in June and four weeks in July.
  19 Paid the rent of $4,000 under a four-month lease on a building rented and occupied on June 1.
  20 Borrowed $4,000 from the bank on a 90-day, 9 percent note.
  26 Purchased $1,800 of supplies for cash. (Only $300 of these supplies were used in June.)
  29 Billed various customers for services rendered, $4,200.
  30 Unpaid employee services received in the last half of June amounted to $2,600.
  30 Received a bill for $200 for gas and oil used in June.

PROBLEMS, SERIES B

P3–1–B.

Required:

For each of the following cases:

a. Prepare the adjusting journal entry, dating it December 31, 1981.

b. Set up three-column ledger accounts in skeleton form (without all the details) enter balances as given, if any, and post the adjusting entries made in part *(a)*.

c. Prepare and post closing entries. You will need a separate Expense and Revenue Summary account for each case.

d. State the correct figure for the balance sheet. Show related accounts in each case as they should appear on that statement.

e. State the correct figures for the earnings statement.

Account name	Trial balance	Information for adjustments
Case 1: Office building	$840,000	Depreciation is computed each period at the rate of 2 percent of cost less salvage value. Salvage is estimated at $40,000.
Accumulated depreciation— office building	160,000	
Case 2: Wage expense	98,000	Wages earned by employees since last payday are $1,560.
Case 3: Office supplies inventory ...	5,000	Of the office supplies purchased, only $1,800 worth remains at the end of the period.

P3–2–B. The trial balance of the Short Company at December 31 of the current year includes, among other items, the following account balances:

	Debits	Credits
Unexpired insurance	$24,000	
Prepaid rent.........................	28,800	
Accounts receivable	82,000	
Allowance for doubtful accounts		$1,400
Office supplies inventory	5,600	

Examination of the records shows that adjustments should be made for the following items:

1. Of the unexpired insurance in the trial balance, $10,000 is for coverage during the months after December 31 of the current year.
2. The balance in the Prepaid Rent account is for a 12-month period that started October 1 of the current year.
3. It is estimated that $3,000 should be added to the Allowance for Doubtful Accounts balance.
4. Office supplies used during the year amount to $3,600.

Required:

Prepare the adjusting journal entries at December 31.

P3–3–B. Tavenner Company has the following account balances, among others, in its trial balance at December 31 of the current year:

	Debits	Credits
Office supplies inventory	$ 1,240	
Prepaid rent.........................	2,400	
Accounts receivable	25,000	
Allowance for doubtful accounts		$ 600
Service revenue		87,000
Salaries expense	41,000	

Additional data:

1. The inventory of supplies on hand at December 31 amounts to $90.

2. The balance in the Prepaid Rent account is for a one-year period starting October 1 of the current year.
3. It is estimated that $870 should be added to the Allowance for Doubtful Accounts balance.
4. Since the last payday, the employees of the company have earned additional salaries in the amount of $1,810.

Required:

a. Prepare the adjusting journal entries at December 31.

b. Open three-column ledger accounts for each of the accounts involved, enter the balances as shown in the trial balance, and post the adjusting journal entries.

P3–4–B.

Required:

Given the following information for the Taylor Company, calculate the correct net earnings for 1981 and 1982. The reported net earnings for 1981 and 1982 were $60,000 and $82,000, respectively. No adjusting entries were made at year-end for any of the transactions given below:

a. A fire insurance policy to cover a three-year period from the date of payment was purchased on March 1, 1981, for $3,600. The Insurance Expense account was debited at the date of purchase.

b. Subscriptions for magazines in the amount of $72,000 to cover an 18-month period from May 1, 1981, were received on April 15, 1981. The Subscriptions Revenue account was credited when the payments were received.

c. A building costing $150,000 and having an estimated useful life of 60 years and a scrap value of $30,000 was purchased and put into service on July 1, 1981.

d. On September 1, 1981, $6,000 was borrowed from the bank to be repaid on September 1, 1983, with 10 percent annual interest.

e. A $3,000 loan was made to a customer on November 1, 1981, to be repaid in three months with 5 percent annual interest.

f. On January 12, 1982, wages of $9,600 were paid to employees. The account debited was Wages Expense. One third of the amount paid was earned by employees in December of 1981.

P3–5–B. The Elizabeth Riley Company adjusts and closes its books each December 31. It is to be assumed that the accounts for all prior years have been properly adjusted and closed. Given below are a number of the company's account balances prior to adjustment on December 31, 1981:

	Debits	Credits
Accounts receivable	$66,000	
Allowance for doubtful accounts		$ 170
Unexpired insurance	2,625	
Office supplies inventory	2,150	
Building	85,000	
Accumulated depreciation—		
building		32,000
Unearned rent revenue		900
Salaries expense	23,000	
Service revenue		92,500

Additional data (number your entries to match these items):

1. It is estimated that $925 should be added to the balance in the Allowance for Doubtful Accounts.
2. The Unexpired Insurance account balance represents the remaining cost of a four-year insurance policy dated June 30, 1979, having a total premium of $4,200.
3. The physical inventory of the office supply stockroom indicates that the supplies on hand had a cost of $675.
4. The building was originally acquired on January 1, 1964, at which time it was estimated that it would last 40 years and have a scrap value of $5,000.
5. Salaries earned since the last payday but unpaid at December 31 amount to $875.
6. Interest earned but not collected on bonds during the year amounts to $75. This interest is not due to be paid to the company until March 1, 1982.
7. The Unearned Rent Revenue account arose through the prepayment of rent by a tenant in the building for 12 months beginning October 1, 1981.

Required:

Prepare the adjusting entries indicated by the additional data. While explanations may be omitted, computations should be included.

P3–6–B. The Wiesenhutter Publishing Company began operations on December 1, 1981. The company's bookkeeper intended to use the cash basis of accounting. Consequently, the bookkeeper recorded all cash receipts and disbursements for items relating to operations in revenue and expense accounts. No adjusting entries were made prior to preparing the financial statements for December. You are called in at the end of December to show the bookkeeper how to adjust the accounts to the accrual basis.

Required:

a. Prepare journal entries for the following transactions as the bookkeeper prepared them.

b. Prepare the adjusting entries necessary at the end of the month to place the books on an accrual basis.

c. Compute the increase or decrease in net earnings which results from using the accrual basis of accounting rather than the cash basis.

Transactions:

Dec. 1 Wiesenhutter invested $10,000 cash in the firm.
   3 Received $12,000 for magazine subscriptions to run for two years from this date. The magazine is published monthly on the 23rd.
   4 Paid for advertising to be run in a national periodical for each of six months (starting this month). The cost was $4,500.
   7 Purchased an insurance policy to cover a two-year period beginning December 15, $3,600.
  11 Borrowed $6,000 from the bank on a 60-day, 6 percent per annum note dated today.
  12 Paid the annual lease on the building, $6,000, effective through November 30, 1982.
  15 Received $18,000 cash for two-year subscriptions starting with the December issue.
  15 Salaries for the period December 1–15 amounted to $4,000. Salaries are paid on the 5th and 20th of each month for the preceding half of the month.
  20 Salaries for the period December 1–15 are paid.
  23 Supplies purchased for cash, $1,800. (Only $150 of these were subsequently used in 1981.)
  27 Printing costs applicable equally to the next six issues beginning with the December issue were paid in cash, $12,000.
  31 Cash sales of the December issue, $7,000.
  31 Unpaid salaries for the period December 16–31 amounted to $4,400.
  31 Sales on account of December issue, $3,000.

BUSINESS DECISION PROBLEM 3–1

Shown below are a balance sheet and an earnings statement for the Miller Real Estate Company.

MILLER REAL ESTATE COMPANY
Balance Sheet
December 31, 1981

Assets

Cash		$20,000
Accounts receivable	$ 6,000	
Less: Allowance for		
doubtful accounts	800	5,200
Office supplies on hand		1,000
Unexpired insurance		900
Office equipment	$ 4,000	
Less: Accumulated		
depreciation	2,000	2,000
Building	$30,000	
Less: Accumulated		
depreciation	7,000	23,000
Total Assets		$52,100

Liabilities and Owner's Equity

Liabilities:	
Accounts payable	$ 3,000
Bank loan payable	5,000
Accrued interest payable	200
Unearned rental	
commissions	3,400
Owner's Equity:	
H. B. Miller, capital	40,500
Total Liabilities and	
Owner's Equity	$52,100

MILLER REAL ESTATE COMPANY
Earnings Statement
For the Year Ended December 31, 1981

Revenues:		
Sales commissions		$63,000
Rental commissions		5,000
Total revenues		$68,000
Expenses:		
Advertising	$ 720	
Salaries	25,000	
Office supplies	1,500	
Bad debts	400	
Insurance	1,800	
Utilities	1,900	
Depreciation on office		
equipment	500	
Depreciation on building	1,000	
Interest	400	
Miscellaneous	280	
Total expenses		33,500
Net Earnings		$34,500

Required:

a. Why would H. B. Miller, the owner and manager of the company, be interested in the above financial statements?

b. Why would the banker who loaned the company $5,000 be interested in the above financial statements?

c. What does the earnings statement reveal?

BUSINESS DECISION PROBLEM 3–2

On December 31, 1981, John Jones's bookkeeper quit his job without even notifying Mr. Jones of his net earnings for 1981. The bookkeeper had taken Mr. Jones's accounting records home with him the previous night and failed to bring them to work on December 31, 1981. However, Mr. Jones found the following closing entries on a pad in the bookkeeper's desk:

1981
Dec. 31	Service Revenue	86,000	
	Expense and Revenue		
	Summary		86,000

Dec. 31	Expense and Revenue		
	Summary	37,000	
	Rent Expense		3,600
	Salaries Expense		24,000
	Advertising Expense		1,800
	Utilities Expense		2,400
	Depreciation on		
	Automobiles		2,000
	Depreciation on Office		
	Equipment		500
	Insurance Expense		2,520
	Miscellaneous Expense		180

Mr. Jones knows that his capital account balance was $40,000 on January 1, 1981, and that he withdrew $20,000 for personal use during 1981.

Required:

a. Using the information given above, prepare an earnings statement and a statement of owner's equity for the year ended December 31, 1981.

b. What effect do the closing journal entries have on the earnings statement accounts?

c. What effect do the closing journal entries have on the balance sheet accounts?

d. Did the bookkeeper make all of the necessary closing entries? If not, what other entries should be made?

Chapter 4

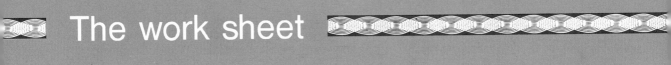

The work sheet

THE WORK SHEET AND THE ACCOUNTING CYCLE

In completing the accounting cycle many of the steps may be included on a work sheet. A *work sheet* is a large columnar sheet of paper that is a convenient means for entering the trial balance and summarizing the information needed for making adjusting and closing entries and preparing the financial statements. The work sheet is not a part of the permanent accounting records. It is constructed in pencil so that errors can be corrected easily before the information contained in it becomes a part of the permanent accounting records.

The work sheet is where the accounts in the trial balance are adjusted, balanced, and arranged for the preparation of the financial statements. Once the work sheet has been completed it serves as a convenient means from which adjusting and closing entries may be taken and entered in the journal. The work sheet may be used to assist in the preparation of the formal financial statements.

THE WORK SHEET FOR A SERVICE COMPANY

In manually operated accounting systems containing large numbers of accounts, the accounting activities to be completed at the end of a financial reporting period may be organized and handled more efficiently through use of a work sheet. A work sheet is simply a sheet of paper containing a number of columns and lines for recording account titles, item descriptions, and dollar amounts. Since it is used internally only, it can take on a variety of forms. But to be of any real value, it will, as a minimum, contain columns for a trial balance, adjusting entries, an earnings statement, and a balance sheet. An expanded version of a work sheet is presented in Illustration 4.1 and is discussed below.

Illustration 4.1: Partially completed work sheet— Trial Balance columns

JIM HUSKEY COMPANY
Work Sheet
For the Month Ended June 30, 1981

Line No.	Acct. No.	Account Titles	Trial Balance Debit	Trial Balance Credit	Adjustments Debit	Adjustments Credit
1	101	Cash	14,870			
2	102	Accounts receivable	3,500			
3	102A	Allowance for doubtful accounts		100		
4	112	Store supplies	720			
5	114	Unexpired insurance	480			
6	120	Furniture and fixtures	2,400			
7	120A	Accumulated depreciation		200		
8	201	Accounts payable		5,100		
9	301	Jim Huskey, capital		16,000		
10	310	Jim Huskey, drawing	3,000			
11						
12	401	Service revenue		7,800		
13	514	Service salaries expense	1,800			
14	515	Advertising expense	700			
15	517	Miscellaneous service expense	430			
16	521	Office salaries expense	800			
17	525	Miscellaneous administrative expense	500			
18			29,200	29,200		

The Trial Balance columns   Instead of preparing a separate trial balance, the open accounts in the ledger are entered in the first pair of columns entitled Trial Balance in the work sheet prepared for the Huskey Company for the month ended June 30, 1981. The columns are summed, and the equality of the debits and credits in the ledger is shown by entering the totals ($29,200) immediately after the last items in the trial balance. The trial balance is shown on the work sheet in Illustration 4.1.

The Adjustments columns   All of the adjustments required to bring the accounts up to date prior to the preparation of financial statements are entered on the work sheet in the Adjustments columns (see Illustration 4.2). Each adjustment is cross-referenced; the debit and credit parts of each entry are keyed by placing a key number or letter to the left of each amount. For example, the adjustment debiting Insurance Expense and crediting Unexpired Insurance is identified by the number *(1)*. A brief explanation at the bottom of the work sheet is keyed using the same numbering or lettering system as the one identifying the debits and credits in each entry. These explanations are optional. They will not be repeated in subsequent illustrations in this chapter. The assumed adjustments for the Jim Huskey Company are as follows:

    Entry *(1)* records the expiration of $40 of insurance premiums paid in advance which relate to coverage for the month of June; the debit and credit keyed with the number *(1)* comprise the entry made to recognize the asset expiration and the related expense.

Adjusted Trial Balance		Earnings Statement		Balance Sheet		Line No.
Debit	Credit	Debit	Credit	Debit	Credit	
						1
						2
						3
						4
						5
						6
						7
						8
						9
						10
						11
						12
						13
						14
						15
						16
						17
						18

JIM HUSKEY COMPANY
Work Sheet
For the Month Ended June 30, 1981

Line No.	Acct. No.	Account Titles	Trial Balance		Adjustments	
			Debit	Credit	Debit	Credit
1	101	Cash	14,870			
2	102	Accounts receivable	3,500			
3	102A	Allowance for doubtful accounts		100		(3) 160
4	112	Store supplies	720			(2) 600
5	114	Unexpired insurance	480			(1) 40
6	120	Furniture and fixtures	2,400			
7	102A	Accumulated depreciation		200		(4) 20
8	201	Accounts payable		5,100		
9	301	Jim Huskey, capital		16,000		
10	310	Jim Huskey, drawing	3,000			
11						
12	401	Service revenue		7,800		
13	514	Service salaries expense	1,800			
14	515	Advertising expense	700			
15	517	Miscellaneous service expense	430			(6) 130
16	521	Office salaries expense	800		(5) 120	
17	525	Miscellaneous administrative expense	500			
18			29,200	29,200		
19	519	Insurance expense			(1) 40	
20	516	Store supplies expense			(2) 600	
21	520	Bad debts expense			(3) 160	
22	518	Depreciation expense			(4) 20	
23	202	Accrued salaries payable				(5) 120
24	113	Travel advances			(6) 130	
25					1,070	1,070
26						
27						
28						

Adjustments:
(1) To record the expired portion of the insurance for the month of June.
(2) To record supplies used in June.
(3) To record the estimated bad debts expense for June.
(4) To record the depreciation of furniture and fixtures for June.
(5) To record the liability and expense for salaries payable.
(6) To adjust the travel expense.

Entry *(2)* records the fact that supplies costing $600 were used during the month, as determined by a physical inventory.

Entry *(3)* increases the allowance for doubtful accounts balance by $160.

Entry *(4)* records depreciation expense for the month, which is determined by dividing the cost of the furniture and fixtures ($2,400) by their estimated useful life of ten years and dividing the result by 12.

Entry *(5)* records the expense and the liability resulting from the fact that there were unpaid office salaries of $120 at the end of the month.

Adjusted Trial Balance		Earnings Statement		Balance Sheet		Line No.
Debit	Credit	Debit	Credit	Debit	Credit	
						1
						2
						3
						4
						5
						6
						7
						8
						9
						10
						11
						12
						13
						14
						15
						16
						17
						18
						19
						20
						21
						22
						23
						24
						25
						26
						27
						28

Entry *(6)* indicates that at the time it advanced money to an employee to travel on company business, Jim Huskey Company debited the amount advanced to Miscellaneous Service Expense (and credited Cash). But, since the travel will take place in July, the $130 advance is not an expense of June. It is an asset, a prepaid expense, and must be removed from the expense account and set up as an asset. The debit and credit, keyed with the number *(6)*, accomplish this.

One advantage of a work sheet is that it assembles all of the accounts in one place, where they may be studied easily to determine the need for possible adjustment. As a result, entries are not likely to be overlooked.

After all of the adjusting entries are entered in the Adjustments columns, the two columns are totaled and their equality noted as a partial check of the arithmetic accuracy of the work completed thus far.

The Adjusted Trial Balance columns

After the adjustments have been entered, the adjusted balance of each account is determined and entered in the Adjusted Trial Balance columns (see Illustration 4.3). For example, the Allowance for Doubtful Accounts has a balance of $100, unadjusted, to which was added $160 in adjusting entry *(c),* leaving a credit balance of $260. This $260 is shown in the credit column of the pair of columns headed Adjusted Trial Balance.

All accounts having balances are extended to the Adjusted Trial Balance columns. Note carefully how the rules of debit and credit apply as to whether an entry increases or decreases the balance in the account. For example, Store Supplies has a debit balance of $720 which is decreased by a credit of $600 to a total of $120—the correct balance for financial reporting purposes.

Note also that some of the account balances in the trial balance do not change, such as Cash and Furniture and Fixtures. The balances in these accounts are simply extended to the Adjusted Trial Balance column in the work sheet.

Illustration 4.3: Partially completed work sheet— Adjusted Trial Balance columns

JIM HUSKEY COMPANY
Work Sheet
For the Month Ended June 30, 1981

Line No.	Acct. No.	Account Titles	Trial Balance Debit	Trial Balance Credit	Adjustments Debit	Adjustments Credit
1	101	Cash	14,870			
2	102	Accounts receivable	3,500			
3	102A	Allowance for doubtful accounts		100		(3) 160
4	112	Store supplies	720			(2) 600
5	114	Unexpired insurance	480			(1) 40
6	120	Furniture and fixtures	2,400			
7	120A	Accumulated depreciation		200		(4) 20
8	201	Accounts payable		5,100		
9	301	Jim Huskey, capital		16,000		
10	310	Jim Huskey, drawing	3,000			
11						
12	401	Service revenue		7,800		
13	514	Service salaries expense	1,800			
14	515	Advertising expense	700			
15	517	Miscellaneous service expense	430			(6) 130
16	521	Office salaries expense	800		(5) 120	
17	525	Miscellaneous administrative expense	500			
18			29,200	29,200		
19	519	Insurance expense			(1) 40	
20	516	Store supplies expense			(2) 600	
21	520	Bad debts expense			(3) 160	
22	518	Depreciation expense			(4) 20	
23	202	Accrued salaries payable				(5) 120
24	113	Travel advances			(6) 130	
25					1,070	1,070
26						
27						
28						

The balances in the Adjusted Trial Balance columns are summed. The equality of the accounts with debit balances and those with credit balances is noted as a check upon the arithmetic accuracy of the work completed.

The Earnings Statement columns

All of the accounts in the Adjusted Trial Balance columns that will appear in the earnings statement (the expense and revenue accounts) now are extended to the Earnings Statement columns—revenues as credits and expenses as debits (see Illustration 4.4). Each column is subtotaled, revealing expenses (debits) of $5,040 and revenues (credits) of $7,800. This means that the net earnings for the period amounted to $2,760 ($7,800 − $5,040). This amount is entered in the debit column to bring the two column totals into agreement. Note the similarity of the debit here to the debit in the Expense and Revenue Summary account to close or transfer net earnings to the Jim Huskey, Capital account. A net loss would, of course, be recorded in the opposite manner—that is, as a credit in the Earnings Statement columns.

Adjusted Trial Balance		Earnings Statement		Balance Sheet		Line No.
Debit	Credit	Debit	Credit	Debit	Credit	
14,870						1
3,500						2
	260					3
120						4
440						5
2,400						6
	220					7
	5,100					8
	16,000					9
3,000						10
						11
	7,800					12
1,800						13
700						14
300						15
920						16
500						17
						18
40						19
600						20
160						21
20						22
	120					23
130						24
29,500	29,500					25
						26
						27
						28

Illustration 4.4: Partially completed work sheet—Earnings Statement columns

JIM HUSKEY COMPANY
Work Sheet
For the Month Ended June 30, 1981

Line No.	Acct. No.	Account Titles	Trial Balance Debit	Trial Balance Credit	Adjustments Debit	Adjustments Credit
1	101	Cash	14,870			
2	102	Accounts receivable	3,500			
3	102A	Allowance for doubtful accounts		100		(3) 160
4	112	Store supplies	720			(2) 600
5	114	Unexpired insurance	480			(1) 40
6	120	Furniture and fixtures	2,400			
7	120A	Accumulated depreciation		200		(4) 20
8	201	Accounts payable		5,100		
9	301	Jim Huskey, capital		16,000		
10	310	Jim Huskey, drawing	3,000			
11						
12	401	Service revenue		7,800		
13	514	Service salaries expense	1,800			
14	515	Advertising expense	700			
15	517	Miscellaneous service expense	430			(6) 130
16	521	Office salaries expense	800		(5) 120	
17	525	Miscellaneous administrative expense	500			
18			29,200	29,200		
19	519	Insurance expense			(1) 40	
20	516	Store supplies expense			(2) 600	
21	520	Bad debts expense			(3) 160	
22	518	Depreciation expense			(4) 20	
23	202	Accrued salaries payable				(5) 120
24	113	Travel advances			(6) 130	
25					1,070	1,070
26		Net earnings				
27						
28						

The Balance Sheet columns

All of the asset, liability, and owner's equity accounts are extended to the Balance Sheet columns—assets as debits and the others as credits. Note that the beginning, rather than the ending, balance in the Jim Huskey, Capital account is carried into these columns (see Illustration 4.5). The net earnings for the month of June of $2,760 is entered in both the Earnings Statement columns and the Balance Sheet columns. The net earnings of $2,760 is the balancing figure for the Earnings Statement columns and is carried over to the credit column in the Balance Sheet columns. Net earnings is shown in the credit column because it is an increase in the owner's equity. The net earnings will be added to the beginning Jim Huskey, Capital account balance, and the Jim Huskey, Drawing account balance will be deducted to get the ending amount of capital for the balance sheet.

Adjusted Trial Balance		Earnings Statement		Balance Sheet		Line No.
Debit	Credit	Debit	Credit	Debit	Credit	
14,870						1
3,500						2
	260					3
120						4
440						5
2,400						6
	220					7
	5,100					8
	16,000					9
3,000						10
						11
	7,800		7,800			12
1,800		1,800				13
700		700				14
300		300				15
920		920				16
500		500				17
						18
40		40				19
600		600				20
160		160				21
20		20				22
	120					23
130						24
29,500	29,500	5,040	7,800			25
		2,760				26
		7,800	7,800			27
						28

The completed work sheet

When the work sheet is completed, all of the information needed to prepare the financial statements is readily available. It need only be recast into a more formal format.

Note, also, that it would be a relatively routine matter to journalize the adjusting and closing entries in the journal and then post them to the accounts. The adjusting entries can be readily prepared from information in the Adjustments columns. The closing entries can be made from the items in the Earnings Statement columns and the drawing item in the Balance Sheet columns. But, since financial statements can be prepared from the Earnings Statement columns and Balance Sheet columns of the work sheet, such entries are not likely to be entered formally in the journal and posted to the accounts at any time other than at the formal annual closing of the books.

Line No.	Acct. No.	Account Titles	Trial Balance		Adjustments	
			Debit	Credit	Debit	Credit
		JIM HUSKEY COMPANY Work Sheet For the Month Ended June 30, 1981				
1	101	Cash	14,870			
2	102	Accounts receivable	3,500			
3	102A	Allowance for doubtful accounts		100		(3) 160
4	112	Store supplies	720			(2) 600
5	114	Unexpired insurance	480			(1) 40
6	120	Furniture and fixtures	2,400			
7	120A	Accumulated depreciation		200		(4) 20
8	201	Accounts payable		5,100		
9	301	Jim Huskey, capital		16,000		
10	310	Jim Huskey, drawing	3,000			
11						
12	401	Service revenue		7,800		
13	514	Service salaries expense	1,800			
14	515	Advertising expense	700			
15	517	Miscellaneous service expense	430			(6) 130
16	521	Office salaries expense	800		(5) 120	
17	525	Miscellaneous administrative expense	500			
18			29,200	29,200		
19	519	Insurance expense			(1) 40	
20	516	Store supplies expense			(2) 600	
21	520	Bad debts expense			(3) 160	
22	518	Depreciation expense			(4) 20	
23	202	Accrued salaries payable				(5) 120
24	113	Travel advances			(6) 130	
25					1,070	1,070
26		Net earnings				
27						
28						

Thus, one of the real advantages of using a work sheet is that interim (monthly and quarterly) financial statements can be prepared without going through the work of journalizing and posting adjusting and closing entries.

EARNINGS STATEMENT

The preparation of the formal financial statements from the work sheet is the next step in the accounting cycle. The information needed for the earnings statement can be taken from the Earnings Statement columns in the work sheet. The earnings statement in Illustration 4.6 is based upon the information in Illustration 4.5.

STATEMENT OF OWNER'S EQUITY AND BALANCE SHEET

The *statement of owner's equity,* Illustration 4.7, is prepared by using the beginning capital account balance, adding the net earnings or deducting the net loss, and then subtracting the withdrawals of the owner. The ending capital balance is then carried forward to the balance sheet to indicate the equity

Adjusted Trial Balance		Earnings Statement		Balance Sheet		Line No.
Debit	Credit	Debit	Credit	Debit	Credit	
14,870				14,870		1
3,500				3,500		2
	260				260	3
120				120		4
440				440		5
2,400				2,400		6
	220				220	7
	5,100				5,100	8
	16,000				16,000	9
3,000				3,000		10
						11
	7,800		7,800			12
1,800		1,800				13
700		700				14
300		300				15
920		920				16
500		500				17
						18
40		40				19
600		600				20
160		160				21
20		20				22
	120				120	23
130				130		24
29,500	29,500	5,040	7,800			25
		2,760			2,760	26
		7,800	7,800			27
				24,460	24,460	28

of Jim Huskey in the firm. In Chapter 2 this information was shown as a part of the balance sheet. Normally, only the ending balance of the owner's capital account would be shown on the balance sheet.

The balance sheet is then completed from the information in the Balance Sheet columns of the work sheet. The balance sheet for Jim Huskey Company is shown in Illustration 4.8.

ADJUSTING ENTRIES RECORDED

The financial statements now have been completed. Adjusting entries were entered on the work sheet and were used to determine the proper balances of the accounts for inclusion in the financial statements. Now it is necessary to enter the adjusting entries in the journal and post them to the ledger. Information for the adjusting entries can be found in the Adjustments columns of the work sheet.

Illustration 4.6: Earnings statement

JIM HUSKEY COMPANY
Earnings Statement
For the Month Ended June 30, 1981

Revenue:		
Service revenue		$7,800
Expenses:		
Service salaries	$1,800	
Advertising	700	
Miscellaneous service	300	
Office salaries	920	
Miscellaneous administrative	500	
Insurance	40	
Store supplies	600	
Bad debts	160	
Depreciation	20	
Total expenses		5,040
Net Earnings		$2,760

Illustration 4.7: Statement of owner's equity

JIM HUSKEY COMPANY
Statement of Owner's Equity
For the Month Ended June 30, 1981

Jim Huskey, capital, June 1, 1981	$16,000
Net earnings for June	2,760
Total	$18,760
Less: Drawings	3,000
Jim Huskey, capital, June 30, 1981	$15,760

Illustration 4.8: Balance sheet

JIM HUSKEY COMPANY
Balance Sheet
June 30, 1981

Assets

Cash		$14,870
Accounts receivable	$3,500	
Less: Allowance for doubtful accounts	260	3,240
Travel advances		130
Store supplies		120
Unexpired insurance		440
Furniture and fixtures	$2,400	
Less: Accumulated depreciation	220	2,180
Total Assets		$20,980

Liabilities and Owner's Equity

Liabilities:	
Accounts payable	$ 5,100
Accrued salaries payable	120
Total Liabilities	$ 5,220
Owner's Equity:	
Jim Huskey, capital	15,760
Total Liabilities and Owner's Equity	$20,980

The recording of the adjusting entries in the general journal would appear as follows:

Adjusting entries

1981
June 30 Insurance Expense 40
          Unexpired Insurance 40
    Insurance expense for June.

   30 Store Supplies Expense 600
          Store Supplies 600
    Store supplies used during June.

   30 Bad Debts Expense 160
          Allowance for Doubtful Accounts 160
    To record estimated bad debts for June.

   30 Depreciation Expense—Furniture and Fixtures 20
          Accumulated Depreciation—Furniture and Fixtures 20
    To record depreciation for the month of June.

   30 Office Salaries Expense 120
          Accrued Salaries Payable 120
    To record expenses for office salaries and the liability.

   30 Travel Advances 130
          Miscellaneous Service Expense 130
    To record advances as an asset because they are not yet an expense.

CLOSING ENTRIES

The expense and revenue accounts have served their purpose for the month of June and should be closed. Closing the expense and revenue accounts reduces them to zero balances so that there will be a fresh start during the next period. The closing process is an essential element in the measurement process in accounting to determine the profitability—net earnings—of a firm. The closing entries require that—

1. The Revenue account is debited and the Expense and Revenue Summary account is credited.
2. The Expense and Revenue Summary account is debited for the total of *all* of the expense accounts listed in the work sheet in the Earnings Statement debit column, and each of the expense accounts is credited.
3. The balance of the Expense and Revenue Summary account ($2,760) is debited to that account and credited to the owner's capital account. Net earnings are recorded as a credit in the capital account, thereby increasing the owner's capital. A net loss would be recorded as a debit in the capital account, thus decreasing the owner's capital.
4. The balance in the owner's drawing account is closed to the capital account by debiting the owner's capital account and crediting the drawing account. The amount in the drawing account can be found in the Balance Sheet debit column.

The closing entries for the Jim Huskey Company are as follows:

Closing entries

1981		
June 30	Service Revenue 7,800	
	Expense and Revenue Summary	7,800
	To close the revenue account.	
30	Expense and Revenue Summary............................ 5,040	
	Service Salaries Expense	1,800
	Advertising Expense	700
	Miscellaneous Service Expense	300
	Office Salaries Expense	920
	Miscellaneous Administrative Expense	500
	Insurance Expense	40
	Store Supplies Expense	600
	Bad Debts Expense..................................	160
	Depreciation Expense	20
	To close the expense accounts.	
30	Expense and Revenue Summary............................ 2,760	
	Jim Huskey, Capital	2,760
	To close net earnings to capital.	
30	Jim Huskey, Capital 3,000	
	Jim Huskey, Drawing	3,000
	To close the owner's drawing account.	

NEW TERMS INTRODUCED IN CHAPTER 4

Statement of owner's equity—a financial statement that summarizes the transactions affecting an owner's capital account balance. It starts with the beginning capital account balance, adds net earnings or deducts a net loss, and then subtracts the owner's withdrawals to arrive at the ending capital account balance.

Work sheet—an informal accounting statement used to summarize the trial balance and information needed to prepare the financial statements and the adjusting and closing entries.

DEMONSTRATION PROBLEM

The demonstration problem for Chapters 1 and 2 used information for the Le Bon Coeur Riding Stable to illustrate concepts. Financial statements were prepared without benefit of a work sheet. This problem illustrates the use of a work sheet for the month ended July 31, 1981. Also the closing process is illustrated. The trial balance for the Le Bon Coeur Riding Stable as of July 31, 1981, was as follows:

```
                        LE BON COEUR RIDING STABLE
                                Trial Balance
                                July 31, 1981

                                                        Debits      Credits
Cash .................................................   $ 9,500
Accounts receivable .................................      8,100
Land ................................................     40,000
Building ............................................     24,000
Accounts payable ....................................                $ 1,100
Loan payable ........................................                 40,000
Marty Paulk, capital ................................                 36,600
Marty Paulk, drawing ................................        700
Horse boarding fees .................................                  4,500
Riding and lesson fees ..............................                  3,600
Feed expense ........................................      1,100
Salaries expense ....................................      1,400
Interest expense ....................................        200
Miscellaneous expense ...............................        800
                                                        $85,800     $85,800
```

Additional data:

Depreciation expense for the month was $200.

Required:

a. Prepare a ten-column work sheet for the month ended July 31, 1981.

b. Journalize the closing entries.

(Note: The adjusting journal entry and the financial statements which would be prepared are shown in the solution to the Demonstration Problem for Chapter 2.)

Solution to demonstration problem

a.

LE BON COEUR RIDING STABLE
Work Sheet
For the Month Ended July 31, 1981

Account Titles	Trial Balance Debit	Trial Balance Credit	Adjustments Debit	Adjustments Credit	Adjusted Trial Balance Debit	Adjusted Trial Balance Credit	Earnings Statement Debit	Earnings Statement Credit	Balance Sheet Debit	Balance Sheet Credit
Cash	9,500				9,500				9,500	
Accounts receivable	8,100				8,100				8,100	
Land	40,000				40,000				40,000	
Building	24,000				24,000				24,000	
Accounts payable		1,100				1,100				1,100
Loan payable		40,000				40,000				40,000
Marty Paulk, capital		36,600				36,600				36,600
Marty Paulk, drawing	700				700				700	
Horse boarding fees		4,500				4,500		4,500		
Riding and lesson fees		3,600				3,600		3,600		
Feed expense	1,100				1,100		1,100			
Salaries expense	1,400				1,400		1,400			
Interest expense	200				200		200			
Miscellaneous expense	800				800		800			
	85,800	85,800								
Depreciation expense—building			*(1)* 200		200		200			
Accumulated depreciation—building				*(1)* 200		200				200
			200	200	86,000	86,000	3,700	8,100		
Net earnings							4,400			4,400
							8,100	8,100	82,300	82,300

Adjustments:
    (1) To record depreciation of building for July.

b.

Date			Accounts and Explanation	L.F.	Debit	Credit
1981						
July	31		Horse Boarding Fees	400	4,500	
			Riding and Lesson Fees	401	3,600	
			Expense and Revenue Summary	600*		8,100
			To close revenue accounts.			
	31		Expense and Revenue Summary	600	3,700	
			Feed Expense	501		1,100
			Salaries Expense	502		1,400
			Depreciation Expense—Building	503		200
			Interest Expense	504		200
			Miscellaneous Expense	510		800
			To close expense accounts.			
	31		Expense and Revenue Summary	600	4,400	
			Marty Paulk, Capital	300		4,400
			To close Expense and Revenue Summary account.			
	31		Marty Paulk, Capital	300	700	
			Marty Paulk, Drawing	301		700
			To close the owner's drawing account.			

* Assumed account number.

QUESTIONS

1. Describe the purposes for which the work sheet is prepared.

2. You have taken over a set of accounting books for a small business as a part-time job. At the end of the first accounting period you have partially completed the work sheet by entering the proper ledger accounts and balances in the Trial Balance columns. You turn to the manager and ask, "Where is the list of additional information I can use in entering the adjusting entries?" The manager indicates there is no such list. (In all the textbook problems you have done you have always been given this information.) How would you obtain the information for this real-life situation? What are the consequences of not making all of the adjustments required at the end of the accounting period?

3. At what step in the accounting cycle is a work sheet usually prepared?

4. How are the amounts in the Adjusted Trial Balance columns of a work sheet derived?

5. The work sheet for the Bridges Company contains only the following five adjustments in its Adjustments columns:

(1) Expiration of insurance, $600.
(2) Depreciation of equipment, $2,000.
(3) Depreciation of building, $5,000.
(4) Bad debts expense, $1,000.
(5) Salaries and wages accrued, $1,500.

The Trial Balance columns show totals of $800,000. What are the totals of the Adjusted Trial Balance columns?

6. After the Adjusted Trial Balance columns of a work sheet have been totaled, which account balances are extended to the Earnings Statement columns, and which account balances are extended to the Balance Sheet columns?

7. How is the statement of owner's equity prepared?

8. What is the purpose of closing entries? What accounts are not affected by closing entries?

9. A company has net earnings of $2,500 for the year. In which columns of the work sheet would net earnings appear?

10. Is it possible to prepare interim financial statements without journalizing and posting adjusting and closing entries? How?

EXERCISES

E–1. The three major column headings on a work sheet are Trial Balance, Earnings Statement, and Balance Sheet. For each of the following items, determine under which major column heading it would appear and whether it would be a debit or credit. (For instance, cash would appear under the debit side of the Trial Balance and Balance Sheet columns.)

a. Accounts receivable.

b. Accounts payable.

c. Interest revenue.

d. Advertising expense.

e. H. E. Blank, capital.

f. Fees earned.

g. Net earnings for the month.

E–2. If a set of columns were included in a work sheet for the statement of owner's equity, illustrate how it would be used. Assume a beginning balance in owner's capital of $14,000 and net earnings for the year of $6,000.

E–3. In Exercise E–2, if there were a debit balance of $9,000 in the owner's capital account as of the beginning of the year and a net loss of $8,000 for the year, show how these would be treated.

E–4. The Donovan Company reports net earnings of $25,000 for the current year. Examination of the work sheet and supporting data indicates that the following items were ignored:

1. Accrued salaries were $1,500 at December 31.
2. Depreciation on equipment acquired on July 1 amounted to $2,000.
3. Bad debts expense for the year was estimated at $500.

a. Based upon the above information, what adjusting journal entries should have been made at December 31?

b. What are the correct net earnings?

E–5. The trial balance of the C. A. Burnett Company at December 31, 1981, contains the following account balances (the accounts are listed in alphabetical order to

increase your skill in sorting amounts to the proper work sheet columns).

C. A. BURNETT COMPANY
Trial Balance Account Balances

Accounts payable	$ 10,500
Accounts receivable	44,000
Accumulated depreciation—building	12,500
Accumulated depreciation—equipment	4,500
Allowance for doubtful accounts	400
Building	50,000
C. A. Burnett, capital	32,500
C. A. Burnett, drawing	20,000
Cash	15,000
Equipment	18,000
Office supplies on hand	2,000
Salaries and wages expense	48,000
Service revenue	140,000
Unexpired insurance	1,800
Utilities expense	1,600

Using the account balances given above and the additional information presented below, prepare a work sheet for the C. A. Burnett Company.

Additional data:

1. The balance in the Allowance for Doubtful Accounts account is to be increased by $300.
2. Office supplies on hand at December 31, 1981, have a cost of $600.
3. The balance in the Unexpired Insurance account represents the cost of a two-year insurance policy covering the period from January 1, 1981, through December 31, 1982.
4. Depreciation rates: 2.5 percent for the building and 5 percent for the equipment.

E–6. Refer to the work sheet prepared in Exercise 5–6. Prepare the adjusting and closing journal entries.

E–7. The following account balances appeared in the Earnings Statement columns of the work sheet prepared for the R. T. Bradshaw Company for the year ended December 31, 1981.

	Earnings Statement	
	Debit	Credit
Service revenue		$300,000
Advertising expense	$ 1,200	
Salaries and wages expense	110,000	
Utilities expense	2,000	
Insurance expense	800	
Rent expense	6,000	
Office supplies expense	2,000	
Depreciation expense—		
equipment	4,000	
Interest expense	500	
Interest revenue		1,000
	$126,500	$301,000
Net Earnings	174,500	
	$301,000	$301,000

Prepare the closing journal entries. Assume the R. T. Bradshaw, Drawing account has a balance of $25,000 on December 31, 1981.

PROBLEMS, SERIES A

P4–1–A. Given below is the adjusted trial balance of the Rosa Cord Company:

ROSA CORD COMPANY
Adjusted Trial Balance
December 31, 1981

	Debits	Credits
Cash	$ 13,000	
Accounts receivable	34,000	
Allowance for doubtful accounts		$ 700
Office equipment	100,000	
Accumulated depreciation—		
office equipment		30,000
Accounts payable		10,800
Notes payable		20,000
Rosa Cord, capital		55,400
Rosa Cord, drawing	28,000	
Service revenue		180,000
Office rent expense	12,000	
Bad debts expense	600	
Advertising expense	5,000	
Salaries expense	90,000	
Supplies expense	1,500	
Insurance expense	1,200	
Depreciation expense—		
office equipment	10,000	
Interest expense	1,000	
Miscellaneous expense	600	
	$296,900	$296,900

Required:

Prepare the closing journal entries.

P4–2–A. The adjusted trial balance for the W. H. Park Company at December 31, 1981, is shown below:

W. H. PARK COMPANY
Adjusted Trial Balance
December 31, 1981

	Debits	Credits
Cash	$ 15,000	
Accounts receivable	10,000	
Allowance for doubtful accounts		$ 200
Accrued interest receivable	100	
Notes receivable	2,000	
Unexpired insurance	480	
Prepaid rent	1,200	
Office supplies on hand	300	
Equipment	25,000	
Accumulated depreciation—		
equipment		6,250
Building	60,000	
Accumulated depreciation—		
building		7,500
Land	18,120	
Accounts payable		30,000
Notes payable		5,000
Accrued interest payable		375
Accrued salaries and wages payable		3,500
W. H. Park, capital		50,000
W. H. Park, drawing	35,000	
Service revenue		150,000
Bad debts expense	100	
Insurance expense	960	
Rent expense...................	4,800	
Advertising expense	600	
Depreciation expense—		
equipment	1,250	
Depreciation expense—		
building	1,500	
Office supplies expense	1,140	
Salaries and wages expense	75,000	
Interest expense	375	
Interest revenue		100
	$252,925	$252,925

Required:

  a. Prepare an earnings statement.

  b. Prepare a statement of owner's equity.

  c. Prepare a balance sheet.

  d. Prepare the closing journal entries.

 P4–3–A.

Required:

  Using the following trial balance and additional information:

  a. Prepare a ten-column work sheet.

  b. Prepare adjusting journal entries.

  c. Prepare closing journal entries.

A. B. MARYLAN REALTY COMPANY
Trial Balance
December 31, 1981

	Debits	Credits
Cash	$ 5,500	
Accounts receivable	17,000	
Allowance for doubtful accounts		$ 200
Prepaid rent	4,800	
Equipment	13,300	
Accumulated depreciation—		
equipment		2,200
Accounts payable		6,500
A. B. Marylan, capital		15,000
A. B. Marylan, drawing	4,800	
Sales commissions		67,000
Salespersons' salaries expense	33,500	
Administrative expense	10,050	
Rent expense	1,950	
	$90,900	$90,900

Additional data:

1. One percent of the sales commissions is estimated to be uncollectible.
2. The prepaid rent is for the period July 1, 1981, to June 30, 1982.
3. The equipment is depreciated at the rate of 10 percent per year.
4. Salaries accrued: sales, $1,200; and administrative, $1,800.

P4–4–A.

Required:

  From the following trial balance and additional information:

  a. Prepare a ten-column work sheet for the year ended December 31, 1981.

  b. Prepare adjusting journal entries.

  c. Prepare closing journal entries.

H. T. HERBERT COMPANY
Trial Balance
December 31, 1981

	Debits	Credits
Cash	$ 12,500	
Accounts receivable	20,000	
Allowance for doubtful accounts		$ 250
Notes receivable	2,500	
Unexpired insurance	1,500	
Office supplies on hand	1,000	
Building	40,000	
Accumulated depreciation—		
building		20,000
Equipment	15,000	
Accumulated depreciation—		
equipment		10,000
Accounts payable		5,000
H. T. Herbert, capital		20,000
H. T. Herbert, drawing	9,000	
Service revenue		80,000
Salaries and wages expense	30,000	
Advertising expense	1,400	
Utilities expense	2,000	
Miscellaneous selling expense	350	
	$135,250	$135,250

Additional data:

1. The allowance for doubtful accounts should be increased to 2 percent of year-end accounts receivable.
2. Accrued interest on notes receivable is $125.
3. Insurance expense for the year is $1,200.
4. A physical inventory shows that office supplies costing $200 are on hand at December 31, 1981.
5. The building is depreciated at the rate of 10 percent per year.
6. The equipment is depreciated at the rate of 8⅓ percent per year.
7. Accrued salaries and wages are $2,000.

P4–5–A.

Required:

  From the following trial balance and supplementary information, prepare:

  a. A ten-column work sheet for the year ended December 31, 1981.

  b. The required closing entries.

Supplementary data:

1. The building is to be depreciated at the rate of 2 percent per year.
2. Depreciate the store fixtures 10 percent per year.
3. The Allowance for Doubtful Accounts account balance is to be increased by $1,365.
4. Accrued interest on notes receivable is $150.
5. Accrued interest on the mortgage note is $250.
6. Accrued sales salaries are $700.
7. Unexpired insurance is $200.
8. Prepaid advertising is $500.
9. Included in the cash on hand is a check for $25 which was cashed for an ex-employee in 1981 and which is worthless.

SAYKES COMPANY
Trial Balance
December 31, 1981

	Debits	Credits
Cash on hand and in bank	$ 36,350	
Accounts receivable	41,250	
Allowance for doubtful accounts		$ 850
Notes receivable	3,750	
Land	30,000	
Building	55,000	
Accumulated depreciation— building		16,500
Store fixtures	27,800	
Accumulated depreciation— store fixtures		5,560
Accounts payable		18,950
Mortgage note payable		25,000
Saykes, capital		95,090
Saykes, drawing	10,000	
Service revenue		119,450
Sales salaries expense	32,000	
Advertising expense	6,000	
Office salaries expense	37,000	
Insurance expense	1,450	
Interest revenue		200
Interest expense	1,000	
	$281,600	$281,600

P4–6–A.

Required:

Given the following trial balance and supplementary information, prepare:

a. A ten-column work sheet for the year ended December 31, 1981.

b. An earnings statement.

c. A statement of owner's equity.

d. A balance sheet.

e. Adjusting and closing entries.

RIVERS REALTY
Trial Balance
December 31, 1981

	Debits	Credits
Cash	$18,000	
Prepaid rent	3,600	
Unexpired insurance	960	
Office equipment	3,000	
Accumulated depreciation— office equipment		$ 720
Automobile	8,000	
Accumulated depreciation— automobile		2,000
Accounts payable		360
Unearned management fees		1,560
Lee Rivers, capital		42,580
Lee Rivers, drawing	23,500	
Revenue from commissions		30,000
Revenue from management fees		2,400
Salary expense	19,980	
Advertising expense	300	
Automobile expense	1,780	
Office supplies expense	300	
Miscellaneous expense	200	
	$79,620	$79,620

Supplementary data:

1. Insurance expense for the year, $480.
2. Rent expense for the year, $2,400.
3. Depreciation rates: office equipment, 12 percent; and automobile, 20 percent.
4. Salaries earned but unpaid at December 31, $3,330.
5. Office supplies on hand at December 31, $100.
6. The unearned management fees were received and recorded on October 1, 1981. The advance payment covered six months' management of an apartment building.

PROBLEMS, SERIES B

P4–1–B. Given below is the adjusted trial balance of the Edward Lake Company:

EDWARD LAKE COMPANY
Adjusted Trial Balance
June 30, 1981

	Debits	Credits
Cash	$ 48,000	
Accounts receivable	40,000	
Allowance for doubtful accounts		$ 1,000
Office equipment	35,000	
Accumulated depreciation— office equipment		14,000
Automobiles	40,000	
Accumulated depreciation— automobiles		20,000
Accounts payable		53,000
Edward Lake, capital		88,700
Edward Lake, drawing	5,000	
Commissions earned		130,000
Office salaries expense	25,000	
Salespersons' commission expense	90,000	
Bad debts expense	800	
Automobile operating expense	4,000	
Rent expense	4,800	
Supplies expense	600	
Utilities expense	2,000	
Depreciation expense— office equipment	3,500	
Depreciation expense— automobiles	8,000	
	$306,700	$306,700

Required:

Prepare the closing journal entries.

P4–2–B. The adjusted trial balance of the Isbel Company is shown below:

ISBEL COMPANY
Adjusted Trial Balance
December 31, 1981

	Debits	Credits
Cash	$ 58,600	
Accounts receivable	24,000	
Allowance for doubtful accounts		$ 1,400
Accrued interest receivable	200	
Notes receivable	10,000	
Unexpired insurance	1,200	
Office supplies on hand	900	
Land	16,000	
Buildings	95,000	
Accumulated depreciation— buildings		20,000
Office equipment	14,000	
Accumulated depreciation— office equipment		4,000
Accounts payable		19,000
Accrued salaries payable		4,250
Accrued interest payable		450
Notes payable		32,000
T. G. Isbel, capital		80,000
T. G. Isbel, drawing	20,000	
Commissions and fees earned		186,260
Advertising expense	7,000	
Salespersons' commissions expense	37,000	
Salespersons' travel expense	6,440	
Bad debts expense	720	
Depreciation expense— building	4,250	
Office salaries expense	44,200	
Depreciation expense— office equipment	1,400	
Office supplies expense	1,900	
Insurance expense	1,800	
Building repair expense	950	
Utilities expense	1,700	
Interest expense	900	
Interest revenue		800
	$348,160	$348,160

Required:

a. Prepare an earnings statement.

b. Prepare a statement of owner's equity.

c. Prepare a balance sheet.

d. Prepare the closing journal entries.

P4–3–B.

Required:

Using the following trial balance and additional information:

a. Prepare a ten-column work sheet.

b. Prepare the adjusting journal entries.

c. Prepare the closing journal entries.

THE WAYNE COMPANY
Trial Balance
December 31, 1981

	Debits	Credits
Cash	$ 56,000	
Accounts receivable	88,000	
Allowance for doubtful accounts		$ 4,000
Prepaid rent	7,200	
Unexpired insurance	2,400	
Equipment	80,000	
Accumulated depreciation— equipment		40,000
Accounts payable		30,000
J. D. Wayne, capital		131,600
J. D. Wayne, drawing	24,000	
Fees earned		350,000
Commissions expense	250,000	
Administrative expense	36,000	
Sundry operating expenses	12,000	
	$555,600	$555,600

Additional data:

1. The Allowance for Doubtful Accounts should be increased by 1 percent of fees earned.
2. The Prepaid Rent was for the period January 1, 1981, to December 31, 1982.
3. The depreciation on the equipment is 10 percent a year.
4. The unexpired insurance was for the period April 1, 1981, to March 31, 1982.
5. Accrued commissions payable total $3,000 at December 31.

P4–4–B.

Required:

From the following trial balance and additional information:

a. Prepare a ten-column work sheet for the year ended December 31, 1981.

b. Prepare adjusting journal entries.

c. Prepare closing journal entries.

L. B. REED CLEANING SERVICE
Trial Balance
December 31, 1981

	Debits	Credits
Cash	$ 28,000	
Accounts receivable	25,000	
Allowance for doubtful accounts		$ 200
Unexpired insurance	4,800	
Prepaid rent	9,000	
Office equipment	10,000	
Accumulated depreciation— office equipment		3,500
Cleaning equipment	30,000	
Accumulated depreciation— cleaning equipment		8,750
Service trucks	75,000	
Accumulated depreciation— service trucks		23,438
Accounts payable		12,000
Notes payable		5,000
L. B. Reed, capital		46,662
L. B. Reed, drawing	30,000	
Cleaning service revenue		240,000
Salaries expense	85,000	
Service trucks expense	3,000	
Cleaning supplies expense	8,000	
Office supplies expense	3,500	
Utilities expense	3,000	
Wages expense	25,000	
Interest expense	250	
	$339,550	$339,550

Additional data:

1. Two and one-half percent of the accounts receivable at year-end are expected to be uncollectible.
2. The balance in the Unexpired Insurance account represents the remaining cost of a five-year insurance policy purchased on January 2, 1980. The account was last adjusted on December 31, 1980.
3. The balance in the Prepaid Rent account represents the amount paid on January 2, 1981, to cover rent for the period from January 2, 1981, through June 30, 1982.
4. The plant assets are being depreciated at the following annual rates: office equipment, 10 percent; cleaning equipment, 8⅓ percent; and service trucks, 12.5 percent.
5. Accrued interest on the note payable is $100. (Debit Interest Expense and credit Accrued Interest Payable.)
6. Accrued salaries at December 31, 1981, are $2,500; accrued wages are $500.
7. A physical inventory shows that the following amounts of supplies are on hand at December 31, 1981: cleaning supplies, $1,500; and office supplies $500.

P4–5–B.

Required:

From the trial balance and additional data given below, prepare:

a. A ten-column work sheet for the year ended December 31, 1981.

b. The December 31, 1981, closing entries, in general journal form.

WRIGHT COMPANY
Trial Balance
December 31, 1981

	Debits	Credits
Cash on hand and in bank	$ 35,320	
Accounts receivable	72,520	
Allowance for doubtful accounts		$ 2,760
Notes receivable	85,000	
Store supplies inventory	1,200	
Store equipment	44,000	
Accumulated depreciation—		
store equipment		8,800
Accounts payable		39,400
Notes payable		12,000
Wright, capital		224,820
Wright, drawing	15,000	
Service revenue		238,680
Interest revenue		500
Interest expense	300	
Sales salaries expense	69,200	
Advertising expense	39,000	
Store supplies expense	1,480	
General office expense	4,940	
Fire insurance expense	2,400	
Office salaries expense	40,400	
Officers' salaries expense	80,000	
Legal and auditing expense	5,000	
Telephone and telegraph		
expense	2,400	
Rent expense	28,800	
	$526,960	$526,960

The company consistently followed the policy of initially debiting all prepaid items to expense accounts.

Additional data as of December 31, 1981:

1. Fire insurance unexpired, $700.
2. Store supplies on hand, $850.
3. Prepaid rent expense (store only), $3,500.
4. Depreciation rate on store equipment, 10 percent per year.
5. Increase Allowance for Doubtful Accounts account balance to $4,586.
6. Accrued sales salaries, $2,000.
7. Accrued office salaries, $1,500.

P4–6–B.

Required:

Given the following trial balance and supplementary information, prepare:

a. A ten-column work sheet for the year ended December 31, 1981.

b. An earnings statement.

c. A statement of owner's equity.

d. A balance sheet.

e. Adjusting and closing entries.

FOSTER COMPANY
Trial Balance
December 31, 1981

	Debits	Credits
Cash	$ 27,700	
Accounts receivable	30,800	
Allowance for doubtful accounts		$ 1,200
Office supplies inventory	2,000	
Prepaid rent	6,120	
Prepaid advertising	1,440	
Unexpired insurance	2,200	
Office equipment	3,800	
Accumulated depreciation—		
office equipment		1,380
Furniture and fixtures	14,600	
Accumulated depreciation—		
furniture and fixtures		4,140
Accounts payable		12,600
Notes payable		2,000
Kay Foster, capital		50,000
Kay Foster, drawing	21,260	
Service revenue		100,000
Salaries expense	49,400	
Utilities expense	10,000	
Miscellaneous expense	2,000	
	$171,320	$171,320

Supplementary data:

1. Office supplies on hand, at December 31, 1981, $500.
2. Rent expense for 1981, $5,304.
3. Advertising expense for 1981, $1,152.
4. Insurance expense for 1981, $1,200.
5. Bad debts expense for 1981, $100.
6. Depreciation rates: 12 percent for office equipment; and 10 percent for furniture and fixtures.
7. Accrued interest on notes payable, $75.
8. Accrued salaries, $2,100.

BUSINESS DECISION PROBLEM

Thelma and Reed Stanley met while both were employed in the interior trim and upholstery department of an auto manufacturer. After their marriage, they decided to earn some extra income by doing small jobs involving canvas, vinyl, and upholstered products. Their work was, considered excellent, and at the urging of their customers, they decided to go into business for themselves operating out of the basement of the house they owned. To do this, they invested $5,000 cash in their business. They spent $3,500 for a sewing machine (expected life is ten years) and $500 for other miscellaneous tools and equipment (expected life is five years). They undertook only custom work, with the customer purchasing the required materials so as to avoid stocking any inventory other than supplies. An advance deposit was generally required on all jobs.

The business seemed to be successful from the start, as both worked long hours. But they felt something was wrong. They worked hard and charged competitive prices. Yet there seemed to be barely enough cash available for withdrawal from the business to cover immediate personal needs. Summarized, the checkbook of the business for 1981, their second year of operation, shows:

Balance, January 1, 1981		$ 800
Cash received from customers:		
For work done in 1980	$ 1,500	
For work done in 1981	24,000	
For work to be done in 1982	2,000	27,500
		$28,300
Cash paid out:		
Two-year insurance policy		
dated January 1, 1981	$ 800	
Utilities	2,000	
Supplies	6,000	
Other expenses	3,000	
Taxes, including sales taxes	1,100	
Owner withdrawals	14,500	27,400
Balance, December 31, 1981		$ 900

The Stanleys feel, considering how much they worked, that they should have earned more than the $14,500 of cash they withdrew from their business. This is $9,000 less than their combined income when they were employed by the auto manufacturer. They are seriously considering giving up their business and going back to work for the auto manufacturer. They turn to you for advice. You discover the following:

1. Of the supplies purchased in 1981, $1,000 were used on jobs billed to customers in 1981; none was used for any other work;
2. Work completed in 1981 and billed to customers for which cash had not yet been received by year-end amounted to $4,500 (which is considered fully collectible).

Required:

Prepare a written report for the Stanleys, responding to their belief that their business is not sufficiently profitable. (Hint: Prepare an earnings statement for 1981 and include it in your report.)

Chapter 5

Merchandising transactions

and introduction to

inventories

The previous three chapters dealt with accounting for the activities of companies that earned their revenues by rendering services to customers for fees or commissions. In contrast to service-type businesses, merchandising businesses acquire goods for resale to customers. The fundamental accounting concepts applicable to service-type businesses also apply to merchandising businesses. But some additional accounts and techniques are needed to account for purchases and sales of a merchandising business.

SALES REVENUE

The amount of sales revenue of a merchandising company indicates the extent to which the company is satisfying its customers' needs. Sales revenue (or net sales) generally consists of gross (total) sales less sales returns, sales allowances, and sales discounts.

Sales

The main revenue of a merchandising company results from sales of merchandise. Basically, a sale consists of the transfer of legal ownership of goods (called passage of title) from one party to another. It is usually accompanied by physical delivery of the goods. Each time a sale is made, a revenue account called Sales is increased (credited) by the amount of the selling price of the goods sold. The accompanying debit is to Cash if the terms of sale are cash or to Accounts Receivable if the goods are sold on account. For example, a $10,000 sale on account would be recorded as follows:

Accounts Receivable	10,000	
Sales		10,000
To record the sale of merchandise on account.		

Typically, the above entry will be based on a business document called a *sales invoice,* such as the one shown in Illustration 5.1. The sales invoice is prepared after the accounting department receives notification from the shipping department of the shipment of the goods to the customer or in a retail company when the sales invoice is created at the point of sale.

Why record revenue at time of sale?   Recording revenue at the time of sale can be justified since legal title to the goods has passed and the

Illustration 5.1: Sales invoice

BRYAN WHOLESALE CO.   Invoice No.:   1258
476 Mason Street, Detroit, Michigan   Date: Dec. 19, 1981

Customer's Order No.:   218
Sold to: Baier Company
Address: 2255 Hannon Street
               Big Rapids, Michigan   Date Shipped: Dec. 19, 1981
Terms: Net 30   Shipped by: Nagel Trucking Co.

Description	Quantity	Price per unit	Amount
True-tone CB radios Model No. 5868–24393	200	$50	$10,000
Total		.	$10,000

goods are now the responsibility and property of the buyer. Also, the selling price of the goods has been verified, the seller's part of the contract has been completed, the goods have been exchanged for another asset (cash or accounts receivable), and the costs incurred can be determined.

Sales returns, sales allowances, and sales discounts are deducted from gross sales to arrive at net sales.

Sales returns

Goods delivered to a customer in the belief that a sale had been made may be returned to the seller for a variety of reasons. These include wrong color, wrong size, wrong style, wrong amounts, or inferior quality. In fact, in some firms such as retail furniture stores, goods may be returned simply because the customer did not like them. The seller's policy may be "satisfaction guaranteed." A *sales return* is a cancellation of a sale. Conceivably, it could be recorded as a debit in the Sales account. But the amount of sales returns may be useful information to owners or other interested parties. Thus, they are recorded in a separate account entitled *Sales Returns and Allowances,* which is a contra revenue account to Sales. For example, if $300 of goods sold on account (for which payment has not yet been received) and $150 of goods sold for cash are returned by the customers, the required entry would be:

Sales Returns and Allowances	450	
Accounts Receivable		300
Cash		150

To record sales returns from customers.

Sales allowances

Sales allowances are deductions from original invoiced sales prices. They may be granted to a customer for any of a number of reasons, including inferior quality or damage or deterioration in transit. As was true for sales returns, sales allowances could be recorded directly as debits in the Sales account because they do cancel a part of the recorded selling price. But, because their amounts may be useful information, they are either recorded in a separate Sales Allowances account or recorded in a combined Sales Return and Allowances account. In either case, the account is a contra account (a reduction account) to Sales. It is not an expense account even though it has a debit balance.

To illustrate the recording of a sales allowance, assume that a $400 allowance is granted to a customer for damage resulting from improperly packed merchandise. If the customer has not yet paid the account, the required entry would read:

Sales Returns and Allowances	400	
Accounts Receivable		400

To record sales allowance granted for damaged merchandise.

Sales discounts

Whenever goods are sold on account, the terms of payment are specified clearly on the sales invoice. For example, in the invoice in Illustration 5.1, the terms are stated as "net 30" (which is sometimes written simply as "n/30"). This means that the $10,000 amount of the invoice must be paid on or before 30 days after December 19, 1981, or on or before January 18, 1982. If the terms read "n/10/E.O.M.," the invoice would be due on the tenth day of the month following the month of sale—January 10 in the case of the invoice in Illustration 5.1. Credit terms vary from industry to industry according to trade practices.

In many instances, when credit periods are long, sellers will offer a cash discount in an attempt to induce early payment of an account. Theoretically, a *cash discount* is an adjustment to the gross invoice price to arrive at the actual cost—the cash price—of the merchandise. These discounts, usually ranging from 1 to 3 percent of the gross invoice price of the merchandise, may or may not be taken by the purchaser. To the purchaser, they are purchase discounts; to the seller, they are sales discounts.

Cash discount terms are often stated as follows:

2/10, n/30—which means a discount of 2 percent of the gross invoice price of the merchandise may be taken if payment is made within ten days following the invoice date. The gross invoice price is due 30 days from the invoice date.

2/E.O.M., n/60—which means a 2 percent discount may be deducted if the invoice is paid by the end of the month. The gross invoice amount is due 60 days from the date of the invoice.

Recording sales discounts.   The granting of sales discounts, then, is another factor that reduces the amount of cash actually collected from the sale of goods. But even when cash discount terms are offered, a seller may record an invoice at gross invoice price. To illustrate the conventional manner for recording sales discounts, assume that a sale on account of $2,000 was made on July 12; terms are 2/10, n/30. A check in payment of the account was received on July 21 in the amount $1,960. The required entries are:

July 12	Accounts Receivable		2,000	
	Sales			2,000
	To record sale on account.			
July 21	Cash		1,960	
	Sales Discounts		40	
	Accounts Receivable			2,000
	To record collection on account, less discount.			

The *Sales Discounts account* is a contra account to Sales and should be shown as a deduction from gross sales in the earnings statement. It is not an expense incurred in generating revenue. Rather, its purpose is to reduce recorded revenue to the amount actually realized from the sale—the net invoice price.

Illustration 5.2 contains a partial earnings statement showing how sales, sales returns and allowances, and sales discounts might be reported.

Interest rate implied in cash discounts.   A simple analysis will aid in deciding whether money should be used, even borrowed, to take advantage of discounts. For example, assume that $10,260 must be paid within

HANLON COMPANY
Partial Earnings Statement
For the Year Ended June 30, 1981

Revenues:		
Gross sales		$282,345
Less: Sales discounts	$ 5,548	
Sales returns and allowances.............................	15,436	20,984
Net sales		$261,361

30 days or $10,054.80 must be paid within 10 days to settle an invoice in the amount of $10,260; terms, 2/10, n/30. By advancing payment 20 days from the final due date, a discount of $205.20 can be secured. The interest expense incurred to borrow $10,054.80 at 8 percent per year for 20 days is $44.69. In this case, management would save $160.51 ($205.20 − $44.69) by borrowing the money and paying the invoice within the discount privilege period.

In terms of an annual rate of interest, the 2 percent rate of discount for 20 days is roughly equivalent to a 36 percent annual rate: $(360 \div 20) \times 2$ percent. The formula is:

$$\text{Equivalent annual rate of interest} = \frac{\text{The number of days in a year (assumed to be 360)}}{\text{The number of days from the end of the discount period until the final due date}} \times \text{The percentage rate of discount}$$

All cash discount terms can be converted into their approximate annual interest rate equivalents by use of this formula. Thus, a firm could afford to pay up to 18 $[(360 \div 20) \times 1]$ percent on borrowed funds to take advantage of discount terms of 1/10, n/30.

DETERMINING COST OF GOODS SOLD

Basically, there are two methods for determining the cost of the goods sold. One method, called *perpetual inventory procedure*, usually is used by manufacturing companies (to be covered in later chapters) and those selling merchandise that has a high individual unit value, such as automobiles, furniture, and appliances. For retail companies selling goods such as these latter items, it is a relatively easy task to maintain records of the cost of each unit of merchandise and in this way determine the cost of each unit sold. The inventory records are designed and maintained in such a manner as to provide close control over the actual goods on hand by showing exactly what goods should be on hand.

The main emphasis in this text (except in the manufacturing accounting chapters) will be on periodic procedure rather than perpetual procedure. It is sufficient here to note that the entries required under perpetual procedure to record the purchase of three identical refrigerators (except for serial number tags) at a cost of $320 each and the subsequent sale of one refrigerator on account for $450 are:

Merchandise Inventory	960	
Accounts Payable		960
To record purchase of three refrigerators on account.		
Accounts Receivable	450	
Sales		450
To record sale on account.		
Cost of Goods Sold	320	
Merchandise Inventory		320
To record cost of refrigerator sold.		

A perpetual record may also be kept of the number of units of inventory on hand.

At the end of the accounting period a *physical inventory* is taken. This means that a count is made of the number of units of inventory on hand. Under perpetual inventory procedure this physical count can be compared with the unit records (if they exist). Also, when the units counted are multiplied times their cost, a comparison can be made with the amount recorded in the Merchandise Inventory account.

The alternative approach to determining cost of goods sold, called *periodic inventory procedure*, is described, discussed, and illustrated in the remainder of this chapter.

Cost of goods sold, periodic procedure

Companies selling merchandise that has a low value per unit, such as nuts and bolts, nails, Christmas cards, pencils, and many similar items, often find that the extra costs of record keeping under perpetual procedure more than outweigh the benefits. Close control of such items is not necessary nor is it economically wise. For these firms, periodic inventory procedure is used. Under this procedure the Merchandise Inventory account is not debited for each purchase and credited for each sale as it is under perpetual inventory procedure. Adjustment is made only at the end of the accounting period. Records of the exact number of units on hand usually are not maintained. The record keeping is reduced considerably, but so is the control over inventory items.

At the end of the period, when the physical inventory is taken, there is no account balance against which the actual physical count can be checked. The Merchandise Inventory account does not show the cost of the goods that should be on hand since it has not been changed since the beginning of the accounting period.

Also under periodic procedure, no attempt is made to determine the cost of the goods sold for each sale at the time of the sale. Instead, the cost of all of the goods sold for all of the sales made in a period is determined at the end of the period. To do so requires knowledge of three items: (1) the cost of the goods on hand at the beginning of the period, (2) the cost of the goods purchased during the period, and (3) the cost of the unsold goods on hand at the end of the period. This information would be shown in the following manner:

Cost of goods on hand at the beginning of the period	$ 24,000
Add: Cost of goods purchased during the period	140,000
Cost of goods available for sale during the period	$164,000
Deduct: Cost of unsold goods on hand at the end of the period	20,000
Cost of goods sold during the period	$144,000

This schedule shows that the firm started the period with $24,000 of merchandise on hand and purchased an additional $140,000, making a total of $164,000 of goods that could have been sold during the period. But $20,000 remained unsold at the end of the period, which implies that $144,000 was the cost of goods sold during the period.

PURCHASES OF MERCHANDISE

Under periodic inventory procedure, purchases of merchandise which is to be offered for sale to customers are recorded by debits to the Purchases account instead of debits to the Merchandise Inventory account. The Purchases account is increased by debits and it is usually listed with the earnings statement accounts in the chart of accounts because the balance in the account is transferred to other accounts at the end of every accounting period. By recording purchases in a separate account, the owner has knowledge of the cost of the merchandise purchased during the accounting period. This is the only information provided by the account, since it tells nothing about whether or not the goods have been sold.

To illustrate, assume that Stan Hollis Retail Food Stores purchased $30,000 of merchandise from Wholesaler C on account and $20,000 for cash. The required entries are:

Purchases	30,000	
Accounts Payable		30,000
To record purchase of merchandise on account.		

Purchases	20,000	
Cash		20,000
To record purchase of merchandise for cash.		

All purchases of merchandise are debited to the *Purchases account,* which appears—with a debit balance—in both the ledger and the trial balance.

Transportation costs

Whenever goods are purchased, costs will be incurred to deliver them to the buyer. The term *f.o.b. shipping point* means free on board at the shipping point; that is, the buyer incurs all transportation costs after the merchandise is loaded on railroad cars or trucks at the point of shipment. The term *f.o.b. destination* means that the seller incurs all transportation charges to the destination of the shipment. In general, title to the goods passes from the seller to the buyer at the point at which the buyer becomes responsible for the transportation charges.

When the seller pays the freight before the goods arrive at their destination, the term *freight prepaid* is used. When the buyer pays the freight bill upon the arrival of the goods, the term *freight collect* is used.

If the goods are shipped f.o.b. shipping point, freight collect, the buyer pays the freight bill and is responsible for the freight costs. The entry on the buyer's books is (assuming a $100 delivery charge):

```
Transportation-In ...................................................  100
    Cash ............................................................       100
    To record payment of freight bill on goods purchased.
```

The $100 is actually a part of the cost of the merchandise acquired and could be debited to the Purchases account. But a more complete record of the costs incurred is obtained through use of a separate *Transportation-In account.* (Under perpetual procedure the debit would be to Merchandise Inventory.) There is no entry for freight on the seller's books.

If the goods are shipped f.o.b. destination, freight prepaid, the seller pays the freight bill and is responsible for it. No separate transportation cost is billed to the buyer. No entry is required on the buyer's books. The transportation cost undoubtedly was taken into consideration by the seller in setting selling prices. The following entry is required on the seller's books:

```
Transportation-Out ................................................  100
    Cash ............................................................       100
    To record freight cost on goods sold.
```

The *Transportation-Out account* is an expense account, showing one of the expenses incurred in making the sale to the customer.

Purchase returns and allowances

For any of a number of reasons, such as wrong size or color, a buyer may return merchandise to a seller, giving rise to what is known as a purchase return. Similarly, a seller may grant an allowance or reduction in the price of goods shipped to the buyer because of defects, damage, or blemishes. This concession is referred to by the buyer as a purchase allowance. Both returns and allowances serve to reduce the buyer's debt to the seller and to reduce the cost of the goods purchased. But more importantly, the owner may be quite interested in knowing the dollar amount of returns and allowances as the first step in controlling the costs incurred in returning unsatisfactory merchandise or negotiating purchase allowances. For this reason, purchase returns and allowances are recorded in a separate *Purchases Returns and Allowances account* as follows:

```
Accounts Payable ..................................................  350
    Purchase Returns and Allowances ...............................       350
    To record return of damaged merchandise.
```

(Under perpetual inventory procedure the credit would be to Merchandise Inventory to keep the account at its correct balance.)

Purchase discounts

Merchandise is often purchased under credit terms that permit the buyer to deduct a stated discount if the invoice is paid within a specified period of time. Usually such transactions are accounted for as follows:

```
May  4  Purchases ..................................................  2,000
            Accounts Payable ......................................       2,000
            To record purchase on account; terms, 2/10, n/30.
```

```
May 14   Accounts Payable ........................................   2,000
             Cash ...................................................          1,960
             Purchase Discounts ...................................             40
         To record payment on account within discount period.
```

A *purchase invoice* is a document prepared by the seller of merchandise and sent to the buyer that contains the details of a sale, such as units, price, terms, and manner of shipment. The purchase invoice is recorded at gross invoice price. The purchase discount is recorded only when the invoice is paid within the discount period and the discount is taken. The *Purchase Discounts account* is a contra account to Purchases. (Under perpetual inventory procedure the credit for $40 would be to Merchandise Inventory.) Its purpose is to reduce the recorded gross invoice cost of the purchase to the price actually paid. It is reported in the earnings statement as a deduction from purchases.

Net price procedure.   A theoretically preferable, although not widely used, method of accounting for purchase discounts involves recognition in the accounts only of discounts *not* taken. To illustrate, assume that goods with a gross invoice price of $2,000 are purchased under terms of 2/10, n/30. The purchase is recorded at net invoice price, as follows:

```
June 4   Purchases ............................................   1,960
             Accounts Payable ...................................          1,960
         To record $2,000 purchase; terms, 2/10, n/30.
```

This entry is preferable theoretically because it states the cost of the goods at the amount of cash for which they could be acquired. It also states the liability, accounts payable, at the amount of cash for which it could be settled.

If the discount is taken, the entry is a debit to Accounts Payable and a credit to Cash for $1,960. Note that under this procedure discounts taken do not appear in the accounts.

With discount rates around 2 percent, effective management of cash calls for procedures that ensure that all invoices are paid within their discount privilege period. The failure to take a discount should be highlighted as a deviation from company policy. Note that the following entry, which would be made if the discount were missed, does exactly this. It calls the owner's attention to discounts *not* taken by recording them in a *Discounts Lost account* if the invoice is paid after the discount period has passed:

```
June 30   Discounts Lost .........................................      40
          Accounts Payable ......................................   1,960
              Cash ................................................          2,000
          To record payment of an account and the discount lost.
```

The Discounts Lost account actually contains losses from inefficiency. It is reported among "other expenses", toward the bottom of the earnings statement.

Purchase discounts and transportation charges.   Purchase discounts are based on the invoice price of the goods. They are not affected by transportation charges, regardless of whether the buyer or the seller is responsible for freight charges.

**Merchandise
inventories**

Merchandise inventory is the quantity of goods on hand and available for sale at any given time. To determine the cost of the goods sold in any accounting period, information is needed as to the cost of the goods on hand at the start of the period (beginning inventory) as well as the cost of the goods on hand at the close of the period (ending inventory). But for any one year the task really consists only of determining the cost of the ending inventory. Because one accounting period follows another, the ending inventory of one period is the beginning inventory of the following period.

Under periodic inventory procedure, the cost of the ending inventory is determined by (1) actually counting the physical units of merchandise on hand, on display, and in the storeroom; (2) multiplying the number of units of each kind of merchandise by its unit cost; and (3) summing the costs of the various kinds of merchandise to obtain the cost of the total inventory.

Once obtained, the cost of the ending inventory is (1) reported in the earnings statement as a deduction from the cost of the goods available for sale to arrive at the cost of the goods sold, (2) entered in the Merchandise Inventory account in the ledger by way of an adjusting entry, and (3) reported as an asset in the balance sheet prepared at the end of the accounting period. The first two of these uses are illustrated below.

Cost of goods sold.   When information is available on the cost of the beginning and ending inventories and on the various elements making up the net cost of purchases, the cost of goods sold in a period can be determined and reported as shown in Illustration 5.3.

Adjusting entries for cost of goods sold.   To yield the information contained in Illustration 5.3, the underlying ledger accounts and their balances were as follows:

Merchandise Inventory, June 30, 1980	$ 24,433 Dr.
Purchases	167,688 Dr.
Purchase Returns and Allowances	8,101 Cr.
Purchase Discounts	3,351 Cr.
Transportation-In	10,453 Dr.

Illustration 5.3: Determination of cost of goods sold

Cost of goods sold:			
Merchandise inventory, June 30, 1980			$ 24,433
Purchases		$167,688	
Less: Purchase returns and allowances	$8,101		
Purchase discounts	3,351	11,452	
Net purchases		$156,236	
Add: Transportation-in		10,453	
Net cost of purchases			166,689
Cost of goods available for sale			$191,122
Merchandise inventory, June 30, 1981			31,010
Cost of goods sold			$160,112

The cost of the ending inventory, $31,010, also is known. But until further entries are made, the accounts actually contain raw, unadjusted data.

They do not clearly distinguish between that portion of the above items that should be considered an expense for the period and that portion that should be reported as an asset in the balance sheet. The required adjusting entries for inventory and cost of goods sold could be prepared in several different ways, one of which is:

June 30	Cost of Goods Sold		191,122	
	Purchase Returns and Allowances		8,101	
	Purchase Discounts		3,351	
	Merchandise Inventory			24,433
	Purchases			167,688
	Transportation-In			10,453
	To transfer the beginning inventory and the accounts comprising net purchases to the Cost of Goods Sold expense account.			
30	Merchandise Inventory		31,010	
	Cost of Goods Sold			31,010
	To set up ending inventory and reduce Cost of Goods Sold by the cost of goods not sold.			

(As an alternative, the above two entries could be combined with all items remaining the same except that the debit to Cost of Goods Sold would be $160,112 and there would be a net debit to Merchandise Inventory of $6,577.)

The accounts are shown below (with posting references and account numbers omitted) as they appear after the above adjusting entries are posted. Note that the beginning balance in the Merchandise Inventory account of $24,433 is dated June 30, 1980, which shows clearly that the ending inventory of the prior year is the beginning inventory of the current year. Observe also that this balance remains unchanged throughout the year, a distinguishing feature of periodic inventory procedure.

Merchandise Inventory

Date		Explanation	Folio	Debit	Credit	Balance
1980 June	30	Balance				24,433
1981 June	30	Transfer to Cost of Goods Sold			24,433	-0-
	30	Set up ending inventory		31,010		31,010

Purchases

Date		Explanation	Folio	Debit	Credit	Balance
1980 July	1 to					
1981 June	30			167,688		167,688
	30	Transfer to Cost of Goods Sold			167,688	-0-

Purchase Returns and Allowances

Date		Explanation	Folio	Debit	Credit	Balance
1980 July	1 to					
1981 June	30				8,101	8,101
	30	Transfer to Cost of Goods Sold		8,101		-0-

Purchase Discounts

Date		Explanation	Folio	Debit	Credit	Balance
1980 July	1 to					
1981 June	30				3,351	3,351
	30	Transfer to Cost of Goods Sold		3,351		-0-

Transportation-In

Date		Explanation	Folio	Debit	Credit	Balance
1980 July	1 to					
1981 June	30			10,453		10,453
	30	Transfer to Cost of Goods Sold			10,453	-0-

Cost of Goods Sold

Date		Explanation	Folio	Debit	Credit	Balance
1981 June	30	Goods available for sale		191,122		191,122
	30	Set up ending inventory			31,010	160,112

The balances shown in the Purchases, Purchase Returns and Allowances, Purchase Discounts, and Transportation-In accounts are the amounts of each of these items accumulated for the entire year. The balances could result from the posting of dozens of entries to each of these accounts.

Now observe how the first of the adjusting entries given above transfers into the Cost of Goods Sold account the net cost of all of the goods available for sale during the year. The second adjusting entry then removes from the Cost of Goods Sold account the cost of goods unsold at year-end and establishes this amount as the ending inventory. This entry leaves in the Cost of Goods Sold account the amount of expense incurred during the year for merchandise delivered to customers. The Cost of Goods Sold account is now closed as follows:

June 30 Expense and Revenue Summary 160,112
           Cost of Goods Sold   160,112
           To close Cost of Goods Sold to Expense and Revenue
           Summary.

THE WORK SHEET FOR A MERCHANDISING COMPANY

The example in Illustration 5.4 shows how a work sheet is prepared for a merchandising company and focuses upon the merchandise-related accounts. In other respects it is the same as for a service company.

Recall that use of a work sheet assists in the preparation of the adjusting and closing entries. Also, the work sheet contains all of the information needed for the preparation of the formal financial statements.

The trial balance of the Lyons Company in Illustration 5.4 is taken from its ledger accounts at the end of January. The inventory of $7,000 in the trial balance is its beginning inventory.

The sales and sales-related accounts and the purchases and purchases-related accounts summarize the merchandising activity for January 1981.

Adjusting the accounts

Two adjusting entries—entry (a) and (b)—are needed to arrive at the cost of goods sold for January. Entry (a) credits the Merchandise Inventory account, the Purchases account, and the Transportation-In account and debits Purchase Returns and Allowances, Purchase Discounts, and the Cost of Goods Sold account for the balance. This balance is the cost of goods available for sale in January. Entry (b) sets up the ending inventory by debiting the Merchandise Inventory account and reduces the balance in the Cost of Goods Sold account to the cost of goods actually sold in January. The $8,000 cost of the ending inventory was determined by taking a physical inventory, that is, actually counting the goods on hand.

Completing the work sheet

All revenue accounts in the work sheet are carried to the credit Earnings Statement column. All revenue deductions and all expense accounts, including the Cost of Goods Sold account, are carried to the debit Earnings Statement column. The amount needed to balance the Earnings Statement columns is the net earnings or net loss for the period. (For the Lyons Company, the net earnings are $4,843 for the month of January. It is carried to the credit Balance Sheet column.)

The drawing account balance is carried to the debit Balance Sheet column. All assets are carried to the debit Balance Sheet column. All liabilities and owners' equity items are carried to the credit Balance Sheet column.

Financial statements

Once the work sheet has been completed, the formal financial statements are prepared from the information in the work sheet. Next, the adjusting and closing entries are entered in the journal and posted to the ledger. This process clears the accounting records for the next accounting period.

Earnings statement. The earnings statement is prepared from the information in Illustration 5.4. The focus in this earnings statement is on

Illustration 5.4: Work sheet

			LYONS COMPANY Work Sheet For the Month Ended January 31, 1981		
Acct. No.	Account Titles			Trial Balance	
				Debit	Credit
1	.Cash			18,663	
3	Accounts receivable			1,880	
4	Merchandise inventory, January 1			7,000	
6	Accounts payable				700
7	Lyons, capital				25,000
8	Lyons, drawing			2,000	
9	Sales				13,600
10	Sales returns and allowances			20	
11	Sales discounts			44	
12	Purchases			6,000	
13	Purchase returns and allowances				100
14	Purchase discounts				82
15	Transportation-in			75	
15	Selling expenses			2,650	
17	Administrative expenses			1,150	
				39,482	39,482
	Cost of goods sold				
	Merchandise inventory, January 31*				
	Net earnings				

* If desired, the $8,000 in the Adjustments column and in the Balance Sheet columns may be placed on the same line as the $7,000 beginning inventory figure.

	Adjustments		Adjusted Trial Balance		Earnings Statement		Balance Sheet	
	Debit	Credit	Debit	Credit	Debit	Credit	Debit	Credit
			18,663				18,663	
			1,880				1,880	
		(1) 7,000						
				700				700
				25,000				25,000
			2,000				2,000	
				13,600		13,600		
			20		20			
			44		44			
		(a) 6,000						
	(1) 100							
	(1) 82							
		(a) 75						
			2,650		2,650			
			1,150		1,150			
	(1) 12,893	(b) 8,000	4,893		4,893			
	(2) 8,000		8,000				8,000	
	21,075	21,075	39,300	39,300	8,757	13,600		
					4,843			4,843
					13,600	13,600	30,543	30,543

the determination of the cost of goods sold; the other expenses are shown in summary.

```
                          LYONS COMPANY
                         Earnings Statement
                  For the Month Ended January 31, 1981

Revenues:
Gross sales ...........................................                    $13,600
    Less: Sales returns and allowances ..............    $   20
          Sales discounts .........................         44                 64
Net sales ...........................................                     $13,536

Cost of goods sold:
Merchandise inventory, January 1, 1981 .............             $ 7,000
Purchases ..........................................    $6,000
    Less: Purchase returns and allowances ............  $100
          Purchase discounts .....................        82        182
Net purchases .....................................             $5,818
Add: Transportation-in .............................                75
Net cost of purchases ..............................              5,893
Goods available for sale ...........................            $12,893
Merchandise inventory, January 31, 1981 ...........              8,000
          Cost of goods sold .......................                        4,893
Gross margin .......................................                       $8,643

Operating expenses:
Selling expenses ...................................            $ 2,650
Administrative expenses ............................             1,150
          Total operating expenses .................                        3,800
Net Earnings .......................................                       $ 4,843
```

Statement of owner's equity.   The statement of owner's equity shows the increase in equity resulting from net earnings and the decrease in equity resulting from the owner's withdrawals. These data are sometimes provided in the balance sheet itself or not at all.

```
                          LYONS COMPANY
                      Statement of Owner's Equity
                  For the Month Ended January 31, 1981

Lyons, capital, January 1, 1981 ........................................    $25,000
Net earnings for the month ............................................      4,843
    Total ...........................................................       $29,843
Lyons, drawing ......................................................        2,000
Lyons, capital, January 31, 1981 ......................................     $27,843
```

Balance sheet.   The balance sheet contains the assets, liabilities, and owner's equity items from the work sheet. The Lyons capital account balance comes from the statement of owner's equity.

```
                        LYONS COMPANY
                         Balance Sheet
                        January 31, 1981

                            Assets

Cash .........................................................  $18,663
Accounts receivable ..........................................    1,880
Merchandise inventory ........................................    8,000
       Total Assets ..........................................  $28,543

              Liabilities and Owner's Equity

Liabilities:
Accounts payable .............................................  $   700
Owner's Equity:
Lyons, capital, January 31 ...................................   27,843
       Total Liabilities and Owner's Equity ..................  $28,543
```

Adjusting entries.   The emphasis here has been on the determination of the cost of goods sold expense. The information needed to prepare the entries to establish cost of goods sold is taken from the information in the Adjustments columns in the work sheet.

```
Cost of Goods Sold ..........................................  12,893
Purchase Returns and Allowances .............................     100
Purchase Discounts ..........................................      82
      Merchandise Inventory .................................            7,000
      Purchases .............................................            6,000
      Transportation-In .....................................               75
   To transfer all merchandise costs to Cost of Goods Sold.

Merchandise Inventory .......................................   8,000
      Cost of Goods Sold ....................................            8,000
   To record the ending inventory and reduce Cost of Goods Sold by the
cost of goods not sold.
```

Closing entries.   The closing entries clear the expense and revenue accounts for the period and record the net earnings or loss in the owner's capital account. The entries to complete the closing process are:

```
Sales .......................................................  13,600
      Sales Returns and Allowances ..........................               20
      Sales Discounts .......................................               44
      Expense and Revenue Summary ...........................           13,536
   To close net sales.

Expense and Revenue Summary .................................   8,693
      Cost of Goods Sold ....................................            4,893
      Selling Expenses ......................................            2,650
      Administrative Expenses ...............................            1,150
   To close expenses.

Lyons, Capital ..............................    b words ......   4,843
      Expense and Revenue Summary ...........................            4,843
   To close net earnings to capital.

Lyons, Capital ..............................................   2,000
      Lyons, Drawing ........................................            2,000
   To close owner's withdrawals.
```

EARNINGS STATEMENT FOR A MERCHANDISING COMPANY (DETAILED)

The previously presented data on sales (Illustration 5.2) and cost of goods sold (Illustration 5.3), together with additional assumed data on operating expenses and other expenses and revenue, are shown in the earnings statement in Illustration 5.5 (sometimes referred to as a multiple-step earnings statement). Note that the statement has four sections: (1) operating revenues, (2) cost of goods sold, (3) operating expenses, and (4) nonoperating revenues and expenses (other revenue and other expense).

The term *operating revenues* refers to the revenues generated by the major activities of the business—usually the sale of products or services or both. All other revenues are *nonoperating revenues*. They are not related to the acquisition and sale of the products or services regularly offered for sale. They usually are of an incidental nature, such as those illustrated—gain on sale of equipment and interest revenue.

Operating expenses are those incurred in the normal buying, selling, and administrative functions of a business. In reality, cost of goods sold is an operating expense and the major one in merchandising companies. But it is customary to highlight the amount by which sales revenues exceed the cost of goods sold. The difference is called *gross margin*. Gross margin is often also expressed as a percentage rate and is computed by dividing gross margin by net sales. In Illustration 5.5, the gross margin rate is approximately 38.7 percent ($101,249/$261,361). This rate is watched closely, since a small fluctuation can cause a large change in net earnings.

Operating expenses are usually classified as either *selling or administrative* expenses. *Selling expenses* are those incurred that relate to the sale and delivery of a product or service. *Administrative expenses* are those incurred in the overall management of a business. Examples of both types are given in Illustration 5.5.

Note should also be made of the difference between transportation-in and transportation-out. The latter is an expense incurred to help sell a product, while transportation-in is a part of the cost of the merchandise acquired during the period.

The more important relationships in the earnings statement of a merchandising firm can be summarized in equation form as follows:

1. *Net sales* = Gross sales − Sales returns and allowances − Sales discounts.
2. *Cost of goods sold* = Inventory at beginning of period + (Purchases + Transportation-in − Purchase returns and allowances − Purchase discounts) − Inventory at end of period.
3. *Gross margin* = Net sales − Cost of goods sold. .
4. *Net earnings from operations* = Gross margin − Operating (selling and administrative) expenses.
5. *Net earnings* = Net earnings from operations + Other revenue − Other expenses.

The basic aspects of accounting for and reporting on merchandising activities have now been presented. Left for discussion at this time are certain related matters that merit individual attention. They are trade discounts, items

Illustration 5.5: Earnings statement for a merchandising company

HANLON COMPANY
Earnings Statement
For the Year Ended June 30, 1981

Revenues:

Gross sales			$282,345
Less: Sales discounts		$ 5,548	
Sales returns and allowances		15,436	20,984
Net sales			$261,361

Cost of goods sold:

Merchandise inventory, June 30, 1980			$ 24,433
Purchases		$167,688	
Less: Purchase returns and allowances	$8,101		
Purchase discounts	3,351	11,452	
Net purchases		$156,236	
Add: Transportation-in		10,453	
Net cost of purchases			166,689
Goods available for sale			$191,122
Merchandise inventory, June 30, 1981			31,010
Cost of goods sold			160,112
Gross margin			$101,249

Operating expenses:

Selling expenses:

Sales salaries and commissions		$ 26,245	
Salespersons' travel expense		2,821	
Transportation-out		2,729	
Advertising		3,475	
Rent		2,400	
Supplies used		1,048	
Utilities		1,641	
Depreciation—store equipment		750	
Other selling expense		412	$ 41,521

Administrative expenses:

Salaries, office		$ 29,350	
Rent		1,600	
Insurance		1,548	
Supplies used		722	
Contributions		500	
Depreciation—office equipment		600	
Other administrative expense		347	34,667
Total operating expenses			76,188
Net earnings from operations			$ 25,061

Other revenue:

Interest revenue		$ 256	
Gain on sale of equipment		1,175	1,431
			$ 26,492

Other expenses:

Interest expense			721
Net Earnings			$ 25,771

of merchandise that should and that should not be included in inventory, and inventory losses.

Nature and computation of trade discounts

A *trade discount* is a deduction from the list or catalog price of an article. It is a means used to determine the actual selling price of an item. Trade discounts probably will be shown on the seller's invoice but not recorded in the seller's accounting records. Nor are they to be recorded on the books of the purchaser. Assume an invoice with the following data:

List price, 200 swimsuits at $6	$1,200
Less: Trade discount, 30%	360
Gross invoice price	$ 840

The vendor records the sale at $840. The purchaser records a purchase of $840.

Trade discounts are used:

1. To reduce the cost of catalog publication. If separate discount lists are given the salespersons whenever prices change, catalogs may be used for a long period of time.
2. To grant quantity discounts.
3. To be able to quote different prices to different types of customers, such as to retailers and wholesalers.

A list price may be subject to several trade discounts. If so, the discount is called a *chain discount.* For example, assume that the list price of an article is $100 subject to trade discounts of 20 percent and 10 percent. The actual price is $100 − .2($100) = $80; $80 − .1($80) = $72. The same results can be obtained by multiplying the list price by the complements of the discounts allowed. For example, $100 × 0.8 × 0.9 = $72.

Inventory exclusions and inclusions

In taking a physical inventory, care must be exercised to ensure that all goods owned, regardless of where they are located, are counted and included in the inventory. Thus, goods shipped to a potential customer "on approval" should not be recorded as sold. They should be included in inventory. Similarly, goods delivered on a *consignment basis* (sent by the shipper to another party, who will make an effort to sell the goods for the shipper) should not be recorded as sold. Here the intent is that the goods remain the property of the shipper (consignor) until sold by the consignee. Such goods must be included in the shipper's inventory.

Merchandise in transit at the end of an accounting period must be recorded as a purchase by the buyer and included in inventory *if title to the goods has passed.* Generally, whether title has passed can be determined from the freight terms under which the goods were shipped. Goods in the hands of the delivering agent (airfreight line, railroad, or trucking or steamship company) are (1) the property of the seller if shipped f.o.b. destination, and (2) the property of the buyer if shipped f.o.b. shipping point. Briefly stated, the goods belong to the party who must bear the transportation charges.

On occasion, goods may remain in the possession of the seller after they have been sold. Usually, such goods have been packaged and placed in a convenient place awaiting pickup by the buyer. If title has actually passed, the goods must be excluded from the seller's inventory.

Goods which are unsalable due to damage, deterioration, or obsolescence should not be included in inventory. If goods are salable only at a reduced price, the dollar amount attached to the goods must be reduced. As a general rule this amount should not exceed the selling price of the goods less any expected costs of selling the items. This procedure charges the amount of the write-down of the goods to the accounting period in which the loss occurs.

Inventory losses

Under periodic inventory procedure, the difference between goods available for sale and the ending inventory is called the *cost of goods sold*. It is assumed that all of the goods available for sale except those on hand at the end of the accounting period were sold. But it is not necessarily true that all of the missing goods were sold. Some goods are subject to shrinkage, spoilage, or theft. Losses from shoplifting are estimated at billions of dollars annually in the United States. Under periodic inventory procedure, such losses are automatically buried in the cost of goods sold.

To illustrate, assume that the cost of certain goods available for sale was $200,000 and the actual ending inventory is $60,000. This suggests that the cost of the goods sold to customers was $140,000. But assume further that it is known that $2,000 of goods were shoplifted. If such goods had not been stolen, the ending inventory would have been $62,000 and the cost of goods sold only $138,000. Thus, the cost of goods sold of $140,000 includes the cost of the merchandise delivered to customers and the cost of merchandise stolen.

NEW TERMS INTRODUCED IN CHAPTER 5

Administrative expenses—operating expenses incurred in the overall management of a business.

Cash discount—to the seller, a sales discount; to the buyer, a purchase discount; a deduction allowed from the gross invoice price that can be taken only if the invoice is paid within a specified period of time; typically, cash discounts vary from less than 1 percent to 3 percent.

Chain discount—where a list price is subject to several trade discounts.

Consignment basis—goods sent by a shipper to another party, who will make an effort to sell the goods for the shipper.

Cost of goods sold—an expense consisting of the cost to the seller of goods sold to customers; computed as Beginning inventory + (Purchases + Transportation-in − Purchase returns and allowances − Purchase discounts) − Ending inventory.

Discounts Lost account—an account used to show discounts not taken when purchased merchandise is recorded at net invoice price.

F.o.b. destination—freight terms that mean goods are shipped to their destination without charge to the buyer; in other words, the seller bears the transportation charges.

F.o.b. shipping point—freight terms that mean goods are placed in the hands of the transport company without charge to the seller; the buyer is responsible for all transportation costs that follow.

Freight collect—terms that require the buyer to pay the freight bill when the goods are delivered.

Freight prepaid—terms that indicate the seller has paid the freight bill at the time of shipment.

Gross margin—Net sales − Cost of goods sold.

Merchandise in transit—goods in the hands of a transport company on an inventory-taking date.

Merchandise inventory—the quantity of goods on hand and available for sale at any given time.

Net earnings from operations—Gross margin − Operating expenses.

Net sales—Gross sales − Sales returns and allowances − Sales discounts.

Nonoperating expenses—expenses incurred that are not related to the acquisition and sale of the products or services regularly offered for sale; for example, interest expense.

Nonoperating revenues—revenues not related to the sale of products or services regularly offered for sale; for example, interest revenue.

Operating expenses—expenses incurred in the normal buying, selling, and administrative functions of a business.

Operating revenues—revenues resulting from the sale of products or services regularly offered for sale.

Passage of title—a legal term used to indicate transfer of legal ownership of goods.

Periodic inventory procedure—a system of accounting for merchandise acquired for sale to customers wherein the cost of such merchandise sold and the amount of such merchandise on hand are determined only through the taking of a physical inventory.

Perpetual inventory procedure—a system of accounting for merchandise acquired for sale to customers wherein the cost of such merchandise sold and the amount of such merchandise on hand can be determined at any time by reference to the Cost of Goods Sold and Merchandise Inventory accounts.

Physical inventory—a count is made of the number of units of inventory on hand.

Purchase Discounts account—an account used under periodic inventory procedure to record the amount of discounts taken when payment is made within a specified period of time; properly viewed as a reduction in the recorded cost of purchases.

Purchase invoice—a document prepared by the seller of merchandise and sent to the buyer that contains the details of a sale, such as the number of units, unit price, total price billed, terms of sale, and manner of shipment; a purchase invoice from the seller's point of view is a sales invoice.

Purchase Returns and Allowances account—an account used under periodic inventory procedure to record the cost of merchandise returned to a seller and to record reductions in selling prices granted by a seller because merchandise was not satisfactory to a buyer; viewed as a reduction in the recorded cost of purchases.

Purchases account—an account used under periodic inventory procedure to record the cost of merchandise purchased during the current accounting period.

Sales allowances—deductions from the originally agreed-upon sales price of merchandise granted by the seller to the buyer because the merchandise sold was not fully satisfactory to the buyer; to the buyer, a purchase allowance.

Sales discounts—a reduction of the amount due from a buyer granted by the seller for prompt payment; theoretically, an adjustment of recorded sales price; to the buyer, a purchase discount.

Sales Discounts account—an account used to record sales discounts taken by customers; a contra account to Sales.

Sales invoice—see purchase invoice.

Sales returns—from the seller's point of view, merchandise returned by a buyer for any of a variety of reasons; to the buyer, a purchase return.

Sales Returns and Allowances account—a contra account to Sales used to record the selling price of merchandise returned by buyers or reductions in selling prices granted.

Selling expenses—operating expenses incurred in the sale and delivery of merchandise or in the rendering of services to customers.

Trade discount—a deduction from the list or catalog price of merchandise to arrive at the gross invoice selling price; granted for quantity purchases or to particular categories of customers (e.g., retailers and wholesalers).

Transportation-In account—an account used under periodic inventory procedure to record transportation costs incurred in the acquisition of merchandise in addition to the cost of the merchandise purchased.

Transportation-Out account—an account showing the expenses incurred in shipping goods to customers when shipping terms are f.o.b. destination.

DEMONSTRATION PROBLEM

CAMP'S MUSIC STORE
Trial Balance
July 31, 1981

	Debits	Credits
Cash	$ 24,780	
Accounts receivable	5,000	
Allowance for doubtful accounts		$ 400
Merchandise inventory	31,400	
Unexpired insurance	720	
Prepaid rent	4,800	
Office equipment	12,000	
Allowance for depreciation—office equipment		4,500
Accounts payable		8,000
Clay Camp, capital		12,000
Clay Camp, drawing	20,000	
Sales		300,000
Sales returns and allowances	1,000	
Purchases	199,200	
Purchase returns and allowances		1,400
Advertising expense	1,000	
Rent expense	1,800	
Salaries expense	23,200	
Utilities expense	1,400	
	$326,300	$326,300

Clay Camp has prepared the above trial balance for Camp's Music Store. The following information was gathered which will be used to prepare adjusting entries:

1. Bad debts expense for the year ended July 31, 1981, is estimated to be $1,196.
2. A 12-month fire insurance policy was purchased for $720 on April 1, 1981, the date on which insurance coverage began.
3. On February 1, 1981, Camp paid $4,800 for the next 12 months' rent. The payment was recorded in the Prepaid Rent account.
4. Depreciation rate on office equipment is 12.5 percent.
5. Merchandise Inventory at July 31, 1981, was $26,400.

Required:

a. Prepare a ten-column work sheet for Camp's Music Store for the fiscal year ended July 31, 1981.

b. Prepare an earnings statement for the fiscal year ended July 31, 1981.

c. Prepare a balance sheet for July 31, 1981.

d. Prepare closing entries.

Solution to demonstration problem

a.

CAMP'S MUSIC STORE
Work Sheet
For the Year Ended July 31, 1981

Account Name	Trial Balance	
	Debit	Credit
Cash	24,780	
Accounts receivable	5,000	
Allowance for doubtful accounts		400
Merchandise inventory	31,400	
Unexpired insurance	720	
Prepaid rent	4,800	
Office equipment	12,000	
Allowance for depreciation—office equipment		4,500
Accounts payable		8,000
Clay Camp, capital		12,000
Clay Camp, drawing	20,000	
Sales		300,000
Sales returns and allowances	1,000	
Purchases	199,200	
Purchase returns and allowances		1,400
Advertising expense	1,000	
Rent expense	1,800	
Salaries expense	23,200	
Utilities expense	1,400	
	326,300	326,300
Bad debts expense		
Fire insurance expense		
Depreciation on office equipment		
Cost of goods sold		
Net earnings		

Adjustments		Adjusted Trial Balance		Earnings Statement		Balance Sheet	
Debit	Credit	Debit	Credit	Debit	Credit	Debit	Credit
		24,780				24,780	
		5,000				5,000	
	(1) 1,196		1,596				1,596
(5) 26,400	(5) 31,400	26,400				26,400	
	(2) 240	480				480	
	(3) 2,400	2,400				2,400	
		12,000				12,000	
	(4) 1,500		6,000				6,000
			8,000				8,000
			12,000				12,000
		20,000				20,000	
			300,000		300,000		
		1,000		1,000			
	(5) 199,200						
(5) 1,400							
		1,000		1,000			
(3) 2,400		4,200		4,200			
		23,200		23,200			
		1,400		1,400			
(1) 1,196		1,196		1,196			
(2) 240		240		240			
(4) 1,500		1,500		1,500			
(5) 229,200	(5) 26,400	202,800		202,800			
262,336	262,336	327,596	327,596	236,536	300,000		
				63,464			63,464
				300,000	300,000	91,060	91,060

b.

```
                    CAMP'S MUSIC STORE
                    Earnings Statement
              For the Year Ended July 31, 1981

Revenues:
Gross sales .......................................                    $300,000
    Less: Sales returns and allowances .................                 1,000
    Net sales .....................................                    $299,000

Cost of goods sold:
Merchandise inventory, August 1, 1980 ................     $ 31,400
Purchases ....................................  $199,200
    Less: Purchase returns and allowances ..............     1,400
Net cost of purchases ............................                197,800
Cost of goods available for sale ......................          $229,200
Merchandise inventory, July 31, 1981 .................            26,400
        Cost of goods sold .........................                            202,800
Gross margin .....................................                            $ 96,200

Operating expenses:
Advertising ....................................          $   1,000
Rent ..........................................              4,200
Salaries .......................................             23,200
Utilities .......................................             1,400
Bad debts ....................................              1,196
Fire insurance .................................              240
Depreciation on office equipment ...................          1,500
        Total operating expenses .....................                           32,736
Net Earnings ...................................                              $ 63,464
```

c.

CAMP'S MUSIC STORE
Balance Sheet
July 31, 1981

Assets

Current Assets:			
Cash		$24,780	
Accounts receivable	$5,000		
Less: Allowance for doubtful accounts	1,596	3,404	
Merchandise inventory		26,400	
Unexpired insurance		480	
Prepaid rent		2,400	
Total Current Assets			$57,464
Property, Plant, and Equipment:			
Office equipment		$12,000	
Less: Allowance for depreciation		6,000	
Total Property, Plant, and Equipment			6,000
Total Assets			$63,464

Liabilities and Owner's Equity

Liabilities:			
Accounts payable			$ 8,000
Owner's Equity:			
Clay Camp, capital, August 1, 1980		$12,000	
Add: Net earnings		63,464	
		$75,464	
Less: Drawings		20,000	
Clay Camp, capital, July 31, 1981			55,464
Total Liabilities and Owner's Equity			$63,464

d.

Closing entries

1981			
July 31	Sales	300,000	
	Sales Returns and Allowances		1,000
	Expense and Revenue Summary		299,000
	To close net sales.		
31	Expense and Revenue Summary	235,536	
	Cost of Goods Sold		202,800
	Advertising Expense		1,000
	Rent Expense		4,200
	Salaries Expense		23,200
	Utilities Expense		1,400
	Bad Debts Expense		1,196
	Fire Insurance Expense		240
	Depreciation on Office Equipment		1,500
	To close expense accounts.		
31	Expense and Revenue Summary	63,464	
	Clay Camp, Capital		63,464
	To close net earnings to capital.		
31	Clay Camp, Capital	20,000	
	Clay Camp, Drawing		20,000
	To close drawing account.		

QUESTIONS

1. What account titles are likely to appear in the accounting system of a merchandising company that do not appear in the system employed by a service enterprise?

2. Explain the difference between trade discounts and cash discounts. What are chain discounts and purchase discounts?

3. A financial manager is engaged in explaining a firm's policy to you and states, "Our firm is in a tight financial position. No one will lend us money to take advantage of our discounts. But even though we can't pay within the discount period, I do the next best thing. I pay each bill as soon as I can thereafter." Do you agree that this is the next best approach? Why?

4. Determine the effect on net earnings of each of the following:

a. Ending inventory is overstated.

b. Purchases are understated.

c. Purchase discounts are overstated.

d. Transportation-in is overstated.

e. Beginning inventory is understated.

5. You find yourself in conversation with a business executive who employs perpetual (rather than periodic) inventory procedure. The executive says, "Sure, it's cumbersome to keep perpetual inventory records, but it's much easier than having to physically count your inventory at the end of every year as you have to under periodic procedure." What would be your response?

6. Is it possible that a firm may use perpetual procedure for some of the products it sells and periodic procedure for others? Explain.

7. Perpetual inventory procedure is said to afford control over inventory. Explain exactly what this control consists of and how it is provided.

8. What kind of an account is the Purchases account? What useful purpose does it serve?

9. How can it be argued that the net price procedure of accounting for merchandise acquisitions permits application of the management by exception principle?

10. What are some of the problems encountered in taking a physical inventory? How does the accountant solve them?

11. What is a contra account? Why is it employed? What are some examples?

12. What is gross margin? Why might management be interested in the percentage of gross margin?

13. What is a multiple-step earnings statement? What are the major sections in a multiple-step earnings statement, and what is the nature of the items included in each?

EXERCISES

E–1. Prepare a table with the following columnar headings: (a) name of account, (b) increased by (debit or credit), (c) decreased by (debit or credit), and (d) normal balance (debit or credit). Complete this table for the following accounts: Sales, Sales Returns and Allowances, Sales Discounts, Accounts Receivable, Purchases, Purchase Returns and Allowances, Purchase Discounts, Discounts Lost, Cost of Goods Sold, Accounts Payable, and Transportation-In.

E–2. a. The Dorian Company purchased merchandise from the Long Company on account, and before paying its account returned damaged merchandise with an invoice price of $1,050. Assuming use of periodic inventory procedure, prepare entries on both firms' books to record the return.

b. Prepare the required entries assuming that the Long Company granted an allowance of $350 on the damaged goods instead of accepting the return.

E–3. What is the last payment date on which the cash discount can be taken on goods sold on March 5 for $32,000; terms, 3/10/E.O.M., n/60? Assume that the bill is paid on this date and prepare the correct entry on both the seller's and buyer's books to record the payment.

E–4. You have purchased merchandise with a list price of $2,000. Because you are a wholesaler you are granted trade discounts of 30, 20, and 10 percent. The cash discount terms are 2/E.O.M., n/60. How much will you pay if you pay by the end of the month of purchase? How much will you pay if you do not pay until the following month?

E–5. Merchandise with a gross invoice price of $5,000 was purchased by you under terms of 3/10, n/60, on January 2, 1981. You believe that by March 3, 1981, you could pay a loan taken out to take advantage of the discount. What is the highest annual rate of interest you could afford to pay on the loan and be as well off as if you had taken the discount? Use the formula in the text.

E–6. The Z Company uses periodic inventory procedure. Determine the cost of goods sold for the company assuming purchases during the period were $4,000, transportation-in was $30, purchase returns and allowances were $100, beginning inventory was $2,500, purchase discounts were $200, ending inventory was $1,300, and sales returns and allowances were $500.

E–7. The Cattermole Company purchased goods for $2,300 on June 14 under the following terms: 3/10, n/30; f.o.b. shipping point, freight collect. The bill for the freight amounted to $75. Assume that the invoice was paid within the discount period and prepare all entries required on Cattermole's books using gross price procedure.

E–8. Refer to the data in Question E–7 above and assume that the invoice was paid on July 11. Prepare the entry to record the payment made on that date.

E–9. Given the balances shown in the partial trial balance, indicate how the balances would be treated in the work sheet. The ending inventory is $8,000.

μ

Account Name	Trial Balance		Adjustments		Adjusted Trial Balance		Earnings Statement		Balance Sheet	
	Debit	Credit	Debit	Credit	Debit	Credit	Debit	Credit	Debit	Credit
Merchandise inventory	10,000									
Sales		70,000								
Sales returns and allowances	4,000									
Sales discounts	1,500									
Purchases	50,000									
Purchase returns and allowances		2,000								
Purchase discounts		1,000								
Transportation-in	3,000									

PROBLEMS, SERIES A

7200.⁰⁰ COST

P5–1–A. Compute the approximate annual rate of interest implicit in each of the following terms under the assumption that the discount is not taken and the invoice is paid when due:

a. 3/10, n/60.

b. 1/10, n/30.

c. 2/E.O.M., n/60, goods purchased on January 15.

In view of your computations, comment on the desirability of borrowing to take advantage of discounts.

P5–2–A. The Faherty Company purchased merchandise with a list price of $10,000, f.o.b. destination, freight prepaid, from Grove Company, on August 15, 1981. Trade discounts of 20 and 10 percent were allowed, and credit terms were 2/10, n/30. Grove Company paid the freight charges of $250 on August 16. On August 17, Faherty Company requested a purchase allowance of $470 because some of the merchandise had been damaged in transit. On August 20, it received a credit memorandum from Grove Company granting the allowance.

Required:

Record all the entries required on the books of both the buyer and the seller assuming that both firms use periodic inventory procedure. Also assume that payment is made on the last day of the discount period.

P5–3–A.

Required:

a. Journalize the following transactions for Company K and gross price procedure for invoices.

b. Journalize the following transactions for Company D. Both companies follow periodic procedure of recording inventories.

Transactions:

Mar. 12   Company K purchased merchandise from Company D, $13,500; terms, 2/10/E.O.M.
20   Company K returned $4,500 of the merchandise to Company D.
Apr. 7   Company D received proper payment in full from Company K.
16   Company K had requested and on this date received a credit memorandum granting a gross allowance of $800 from Company D, due to improper quality of merchandise purchased on March 12.

P5–4–A. The purchasing department of the Garretson Company asked for and received the following price quotations on 1,400 units of a given product that it wished to buy:

Freeman, Inc.—List price: $3.80 each, less 15 percent. Terms: 2/10, n/30, f.o.b. shipping point. (Transportation charges are determined to be $180.)
Goodman Corp.—List price: $3.40 each. Terms: n/30, f.o.b. destination. (Transportation charges are determined to be $175.)
Klein Corp.—List price: $5.50 each, less 20, 15, and 10 percent quantity discounts. Terms: 3/10, n/45, f.o.b. destination. (Transportation charges are determined to be $265.)
Heintz Co.—List price: $4.35, less 15 and 10 percent. Terms: n/30, f.o.b. shipping point. (Transportation charges are determined to be $250.)

Required:

State which bid should be accepted and support your conclusion with a schedule showing the net cost of each bid.

P5–5–A. On August 1, 1981, the Jennings Company sold merchandise to the Lesikar Company, $6,000 list price, f.o.b. destination. (The seller prepaid the freight of $80 on August 1, 1981.) Other terms were trade discounts of 30 and 10 percent and cash discount of 2/10/E.O.M., n/60. On August 8, 1981, the Lesikar Company returned

$1,000 (at list price) of the merchandise. The balance due was paid on September 9, 1981.

Required:

Journalize all entries required on the books of both the buyer and the seller, assuming that both use periodic inventory procedure and gross price procedure.

P5–6–A.

Required:

From the data given below for the Knowles Company (which uses periodic inventory procedure):

a. Prepare journal entries for the summarized transactions (omit explanation).

b. Post the journal entries to the proper ledger accounts (after entering the balances as of December 31, 1981).

c. Prepare and post entries to record cost of goods sold. Omit explanations.

d. Prepare an earnings statement for the year ended December 31, 1982.

e. Prepare a balance sheet as of December 31, 1982.

KNOWLES COMPANY
Balance Sheet
December 31, 1981

Assets

Cash	$19,000
Accounts receivable	33,000
Merchandise inventory	28,000
Total Assets	$80,000

Liabilities and Owner's Equity

Accounts payable	$21,000
Knowles, capital	59,000
Total Liabilities and Owner's Equity	$80,000

Summarized transactions for 1982

Sales for cash	$ 67,000
Sales on account (gross)	148,000
Purchases on account (gross)	160,000
Sales discounts	2,000
Sales returns (charge sales)	4,500
Purchase returns	2,200
Purchase discounts	2,400
Cash collected on accounts receivable	137,500
Cash payments on accounts payable	129,000
Land purchased (gave one half in cash and long-term note for one half)	62,000
Selling expenses incurred and paid for	19,600
Administrative expenses incurred and paid for	18,200
Interest expense on long-term note on land incurred and paid for	1,200

Additional data:

Merchandise inventory at December 31, 1982, per physical listing is $34,400.

P5-7-A.

Required:

From the following information:

a. Journalize the transactions on the records of the Lewis Company using gross price procedure.

b. Post the entries to the proper ledger accounts.

c. Prepare a trial balance as of May 31.

d. Journalize the adjusting entries, assuming the May 30 inventory is $14,000.

e. Post the adjusting entries to the proper accounts.

f. Prepare a partial earnings statement for May, through the gross margin figure.

The company was organized on May 1 and uses periodic inventory procedure.

Transactions:

May	1	Ron Lewis invested $200,000 in his new business.
	1	Purchased merchandise on account from the Linane Company, $13,000; terms, n/10/E.O.M., f.o.b. shipping point.
	3	Sold merchandise for cash, $8,000.
	6	Paid transportation charges on May 1 purchase, $200 cash.
	7	Returned $1,000 of merchandise to the Linane Company due to improper size.
	10	Requested and was granted an allowance of $500 by the Linane Company for improper quality of certain items.
	14	Sale on account to Roan Company, $5,000; terms, 2/20, n/30.
	16	Cash refund on returns of sales made on May 3, $50.
	18	Purchase on account from White Company invoiced at $8,100, including $100 of transportation charges prepaid by White; terms, 2/15, n/30, f.o.b. shipping point.
	19	Roan Company returned $100 of merchandise purchased on May 14.
	24	Returned $800 of defective merchandise to White Company and requested and was granted a transportation allowance of $10 on the original purchase.
	28	Roan Company remitted balance due on sale of May 14.
	31	Paid White Company for the purchase of May 18 after adjusting for transaction of May 24.

P5-8-A. Lubbers Company does not maintain a complete accounting system, but you believe the following account balances are accurate representations of the company's assets and liabilities at the stated dates:

	December 31	
	1981	*1982*
Cash	$ 4,125	$ 8,250
Accounts receivable	14,250	10,500
Merchandise inventory	24,000	30,250
Land	5,750	5,750
Accounts payable (for merchandise)	16,250	19,750

An analysis of the company's checkbook for 1982 shows the following:

1. Total cash received from customers (the only cash receipts), $102,500.
2. Payments to vendors for merchandise purchased, $65,250; the balance of the cash disbursements was for 1982 expenses, all of which were paid in cash in 1982.

Required:

Determine the amount of the 1982 sales, cost of goods sold, other expenses, purchases, gross margin, and net earnings, and the owner's equity (in total) as of December 31, 1981, and 1982.

P5-9-A.

Required:

From the following trial balance and supplementary data prepare—

a. A ten-column work sheet for the year ended December 31, 1981.

b. The required closing entries.

Supplementary data:

1. The building is to be depreciated at the rate of 2 percent per year.
2. Depreciate the store fixtures 10 percent per year.
3. The Allowance for Doubtful Accounts is to be increased by one half of 1 percent of net sales. (Round amount up to nearest full dollar.)
4. Accrued interest on notes receivable is $150.
5. Accrued interest on the mortgage note is $250.
6. Accrued sales salaries are $700.
7. Unexpired insurance is $200.
8. Prepaid advertising is $500.
9. Included in the cash on hand is a check for $25 which was cashed for an ex-employee in 1981 and which is worthless.
10. Cost of merchandise inventory on hand December 31, 1981, $27,750.

WHEELER COMPANY
Trial Balance
December 31, 1981

	Debits	Credits
Cash on hand and in bank	$ 8,600	
Accounts receivable	41,250	
Allowance for doubtful accounts		$ 850
Notes receivable	3,750	
Merchandise inventory,		
January 1, 1981	20,800	
Land	30,000	
Building	55,000	
Accumulated depreciation		
—building		16,500
Store fixtures	27,800	
Accumulated depreciation		
—store fixtures		5,560
Accounts payable..................		18,950
Mortgage note payable		25,000
Wheeler, capital		85,090
Sales		275,750
Sales returns and allowances	1,000	
Sales discounts	1,850	
Purchases	156,450	
Purchase returns and allowances		700
Purchase discounts		1,300
Transportation-in	3,650	
Sales salaries	32,000	
Advertising expense...............	6,000	
Transportation-out	2,300	
Officers' salaries	37,000	
Insurance expense.................	1,450	
Interest revenue		200
Interest expense	1,000	
	$429,900	$429,900

PROBLEMS, SERIES B

P5–1–B. Compute the approximate annual rate of interest implicit in each of the following terms if the discount is not taken and the invoice is paid when due.

a. 2/10, n/30.

b. 1/10, n/45.

c. 3/E.O.M., n/90, goods purchased on July 16.

P5–2–B. On July 2, 1981, the Luecke Company purchased merchandise with a list price of $9,200 from the MacEachern Company. The terms were 3/E.O.M., n/60; f.o.b. shipping point, freight collect. Trade discounts of 15, 10, and 5 percent were granted by the MacEachern Company. The Luecke Company paid the freight bill of $240 on July 5. On July 5 it was discovered that merchandise with a list price of $800 had been damaged seriously in transit; these items were returned for full credit.

Required:

Assume that the Luecke Company makes payment on the last day of the discount period and prepare all the necessary entries for the Luecke Company. Assume periodic inventory procedure and gross price procedure are used.

P5–3–B. The following are events and transactions of the Marcelle Company during April 1981:

Apr. 1 The planning department requested the purchasing department to order 1,000 units of a given material.

3 The purchasing department sent out requests for quotations to companies E, M, and W.

7 Quotations received are as follows:
E—List price: $4.20 each, less 30 and 20 percent. On all orders for more than 500 units, an additional 10 percent discount is allowed on the total order. Terms: 3/10, n/30, f.o.b. destination.

Apr. 7   M—List price: $4.80 each, less 35 and 30 percent. Terms: 2/10, n/30, f.o.b. shipping point.

      W—List price: $2.10 each. Terms: n/30, f.o.b. destination. (The shipping cost under each bid is determined to be $50, $20, and $30, respectively.)

    8   Placed order with lowest bidder.

  15   Invoice received covering above merchandise; freight was prepaid.

  16   Receiving department report stated that merchandise is as ordered. Invoice is checked and found to be correct. (Record invoice at its gross amount.)

  24   Invoice is paid.

Required:

Prepare dated journal entries for the above, where appropriate, including computations showing the actual cost in each bid, assuming that Marcelle Company uses periodic inventory procedure.

P5–4–B.

Required:

Assuming that both companies use periodic inventory procedure and gross price procedure—

a. Journalize the following transactions for Company S.

b. Journalize the following transactions for Company T.

Transactions:

May 18   Company S sold to Company T merchandise with a sales price of $24,000; terms, 2/10/E.O.M.

    29   Company T returned $3,000 of the merchandise to Company S.

June 3   Company T requested a gross allowance of $2,000 from Company S due to defective merchandise. Company S issued a credit memo granting the allowance.

    7   Company T paid the net amount due.

P5–5–B. The McDowell Company purchased merchandise on March 1, 1981, from the Miggans Company at a list price of $5,000, f.o.b. shipping point. Trade discounts of 30, 25, and 5 percent were granted. Cash discount terms were 2/E.O.M., n/60. The buyer paid the freight of $124 on March 4, 1981. The buyer notified the seller that a $600 credit should be granted against the amount due because of damaged merchandise. The seller agreed and sent the buyer a credit memorandum on March 25, 1981.

Required:

Record all entries, assuming payment on March 26, on the books of both the buyer and seller, assuming that both use periodic inventory and gross price procedures.

P5–6–B.

Required:

From the following information:

a. Prepare an earnings statement for the year ended December 31, 1981.

b. Prepare a balance sheet as of December 31, 1981.

c. Prepare the adjusting journal entries.

THE PAXTON COMPANY
Trial Balance
December 31, 1981

	Debits	Credits
Cash in bank	$ 10,550	
Accounts receivable	28,500	
Notes receivable, trade	4,000	
Merchandise inventory, January 1, 1981	22,350	
Unexpired insurance	900	
Store supplies inventory	350	
Land	30,250	
Accounts payable		$ 7,000
Notes payable		13,500
Interest payable		550
Paxton, capital		62,500
Sales		205,000
Purchases	113,000	
Sales returns	2,850	
Purchase returns		1,200
Sales discounts	3,650	
Purchase discounts		2,050
Sales salaries	32,000	
General selling expenses	1,600	
General administrative expenses	3,950	
Office salaries	20,250	
Rent, administrative	4,350	
Rent, selling	6,100	
Interest revenue		200
Interest expense	1,150	
Delivery expense	4,300	
Heat and light for sales purposes	1,200	
Telephone, office	700	
	$292,000	$292,000

The merchandise inventory on hand at December 31, 1981, had a cost of $23,100.

P5–7–B.

Required:

From the data given below for the Mountain Company (which uses periodic inventory procedure):

a. Prepare journal entries for the transactions.

b. Post the journal entries to the proper ledger accounts.

c. Journalize and post the adjusting entries.

d. Prepare an earnings statement for the month ended May 31, 1981.

e. Prepare a balance sheet as of May 31, 1981.

Transactions:

1981

May 1   The Mountain Company is organized as a single proprietorship. Wayne Mountain invests the following assets in the business: $105,000 cash, $40,000 of merchandise, and $25,000 of land.

5   The company purchases and pays cash for merchandise having a gross cost of $45,000, from which a 2 percent cash discount was granted.

8   Cash of $1,050 is paid to a trucking company for delivery of the merchandise purchased May 5. The goods were sold f.o.b. shipping point.

14   The company sells merchandise on open account, $75,000; terms, 2/10, n/30.

16   Of the merchandise sold May 14, $3,300 is returned for credit.

19   Salaries for services received are paid as follows: to office employees, $3,300; and to salespersons, $8,700.

23   The company collects the amount due on $30,000 of the accounts receivable arising from the sales of May 14.

25   The company purchases and pays cash for merchandise costing $36,000 gross, less a 2 percent discount.

27   Of the merchandise purchased May 25, $6,000 gross is returned to the vendor, who gives the Mountain Company a check for the proper amount.

28   A trucking company is paid $750 for delivery to the Mountain Company of the goods purchased May 25. The goods were sold f.o.b. shipping point.

29   The company sells merchandise on open account, $3,600; terms, 2/10, n/30.

30   Cash sales are $18,000 gross, less a 2 percent discount.

30   Cash of $24,000 is received from the sales of May 14.

31   Paid store rent for May, $4,500.

Additional data:

The inventory on hand at the close of business on May 31 is $69,700 at cost.

P5–8–B. From the following information for the Reeves Company, prepare:

a. Journal entries for the summarized transactions for 1981. Omit explanations.

b. An earnings statement for the year ended December 31, 1981.

c. A balance sheet as of December 31, 1981.

A suggestion: You may want to set up rough T-accounts and enter the December 31, 1980, balances given below and post your journal entries to arrive at ending balances.

REEVES COMPANY
Account Balances
December 31, 1980

	Debits	Credits
Cash on hand and in banks	$ 47,500	
Accounts receivable	82,500	
Merchandise inventory	70,000	
Accounts payable		$ 52,500
Reeves, capital		147,500
	$200,000	$200,000

Summarized transactions for 1981

Cash Sales	$167,500
Sales on account at gross invoice prices	370,000
Purchases on account at gross invoice prices	400,000
Accounts receivable collected (net of cash discounts of $30,000)	343,750
Sales returns (from open account sales)	11,250
Purchase returns (from open account purchases)	5,500
Accounts payable paid (net of cash discounts of $6,000)	322,500
Selling expenses incurred and paid	49,000
Administrative expenses incurred and paid	45,500
Land purchased (cash, $82,500; long-term note, $52,500)	135,000
Interest expense incurred and paid	3,000

Additional data:

The merchandise inventory at December 31, 1981, was $86,000. The company uses periodic inventory procedure.

P5–9–B. The owner of Lil's Supply House has asked you for help in preparing financial statements for the year 1981. A ledger of accounts is not maintained by the owner, but instead the owner keeps a detailed list of the amounts due from customers, the amounts owed vendors, and all cash received and paid out and the reasons therefore. With this help you are able to develop the following account balances:

	December 31	
	1980	1981
Cash	$ 4,000	$ 8,000
Accounts receivable	14,000	10,000
Merchandise on hand	22,000	30,000
Land, at cost	6,000	6,000
Accounts payable (for merchandise)	16,000	19,000

Your summary of cash receipts and disbursements for 1981 is as follows:

1. Total cash receipts, solely from customers, $110,000.
2. Payments to vendors for merchandise purchased, $60,000; all other cash payments were for 1981 expenses. There were no unpaid expenses at December 31, 1981.

Required:

Compute the following amounts for 1981: sales, purchases, cost of goods sold, other expenses, gross margin, and net earnings. Also, determine the amount of owner's equity at December 31, 1980, and 1981.

P5–10–B.

Required:

From the trial balance and additional data given below, prepare:

a. A ten-column work sheet for the year ended December 31, 1981.

b. The December 31, 1981, closing entries, in general journal form.

PETERS COMPANY
Trial Balance
December 31, 1981.

	Debits	Credits
Cash on hand and in bank	$ 35,320	
Accounts receivable	72,520	
Allowance for doubtful accounts		$ 2,760
Notes receivable	10,000	
Merchandise inventory, January 1, 1980	42,600	
Sales store supplies inventory	1,200	
Store equipment	44,000	
Accumulated depreciation—store equipment		8,800
Accounts payable		39,400
Notes payable		12,000
Peters, capital		209,820
Sales		461,180
Sales returns	2,580	
Interest revenue		500
Interest expense	300	
Purchases	250,420	
Purchase returns		2,020
Transportation-in	3,920	
Sales salaries	69,200	
Advertising	39,000	
Sales store supplies expense	1,480	
General office expense	4,940	
Fire insurance expense	2,400	
Office salaries	40,400	
Officers' salaries	80,000	
Legal and auditing expense	5,000	
Telephone and telegraph	2,400	
Rent expense	28,800	
	$736,480	$736,480

The company consistently followed the policy of initially debiting all prepaid items to expense accounts.

Additional data as of December 31, 1981:

1. Fire insurance unexpired, $700.
2. Sales store supplies on hand, $850.
3. Prepaid rent expense (store only), $3,500.
4. Depreciation rate on store equipment, 10 percent per year.
5. Increase in allowance for doubtful accounts, $1,826.
6. Accrued sales salaries, $2,000.
7. Accrued office salaries, $1,500.
8. Merchandise inventory, $75,000.

BUSINESS DECISION PROBLEM 5–1

The Walters Company received invoices for the following merchandise purchases at the specified sales terms during the current year:

Invoice No.	Amount of purchase	Terms of sale
1	$30,000	1/10, n/30
2	50,000	2/10, n/30
3	75,000	3/20, n/60
4	60,000	2/15, n/60
5	50,000	2/10, n/30

The company did not take advantage of the cash discounts. Each of the invoices was paid at the end of the allowable credit period. The company could have borrowed money at 8 percent interest from a local bank.

Required:

a. Compute the approximate equivalent annual rate of interest incurred on each of the invoices by not taking advantage of cash discounts.

b. Compute the net dollar amount that the Walters Company could have saved if it had borrowed money at 8 percent and paid the invoices on the last day of the discount period.

c. What recommendation would you make to the owner of the company concerning the company's policy on cash discounts?

BUSINESS DECISION PROBLEM 5–2

Bill Deal decided to open a men's clothing store called Deal's Men's Shop. On January 2, 1981, Bill invested the following assets in his business: $2,000 of cash, $5,000 of merchandise inventory, and $6,000 of store equipment. During 1981, Bill made the following cash disbursements:

$30,000 for merchandise purchases
20,000 for operating expenses
10,000 for withdrawals for Bill's personal use

On December 31, 1981, Bill prepared the following balance sheet:

DEAL'S MEN'S SHOP
Balance Sheet
December 31, 1981

Assets

Current Assets:		
Cash	$16,000	
Accounts receivable	8,000	
Merchandise inventory	7,500	
Total Current Assets		$31,500
Property, Plant, and Equipment:		
Store equipment	$ 6,000	
Less: Accumulated depreciation	1,000	
Total Property, Plant, and Equipment		5,000
Total Assets		$36,500

Liabilities and Owner's Equity

Liabilities:		
Accounts payable (merchandise purchases)	$ 5,000	
Accrued wages payable	1,000	
Total Liabilities		$ 6,000
Owner's Equity:		
Bill Deal, capital		30,500
Total Liabilities and Owner's Equity		$36,500

Required:

a. Using the information given above, prepare an earnings statement for the year ended December 31, 1981. Show how each of the following items is determined: net earnings, cost of goods sold, operating expenses, and sales.

b. Prepare schedules to explain the change in each of the balance sheet account balances.

BUSINESS DECISION PROBLEM 5–3

Don Clark taught physical education classes at Pine Valley High School for 20 years. In 1980, Don's uncle died and left Don $100,000. Don quit his teaching job in December of 1980 and opened a hardware store in January of 1981. On January 2, 1981, Don deposited $60,000 in a checking account opened in the store's name, Clark's Hardware Store. During the first week of January, Don rented a building and paid the first year's rent of $4,800 in advance. Also during that week, he purchased the following assets for cash:

Delivery truck costing $10,000.
Store equipment costing $5,000.
Office equipment costing $3,000.
Merchandise inventory costing $10,000.

During the remainder of the first six months of 1981, Don received cash of $70,000 from customers and disbursed cash of $42,000 for merchandise purchases and $15,000 for operating expenses.

Don had never had an accounting course, but he had heard the term *net earnings*. He decided to compute his net earnings for the first six months of 1981 and prepared the following schedule:

Cash receipts		$ 70,000
Cash disbursements:		
Delivery truck	$10,000	
Store equipment	5,000	
Office equipment	3,000	
Prepaid rent	4,800	
Merchandise purchases	52,000	
Operating expenses	15,000	(89,800)
Net Loss		$(19,800)

Required:

a. Do you agree with Don Clark's statement that his hardware store suffered a net loss of $19,800 for the six months ended June 30, 1981? If not, show how you would determine the net earnings (or net loss).

Assume that the annual depreciation rates are as follows:

Delivery truck, 20%.
Store equipment, 10%.
Office equipment, 12.5%.

Also assume that you obtain the following information:

Clark owes $8,000 to creditors for merchandise purchases.
Customers owe Clark $10,000.
Merchandise costing $6,000 is on hand.

b. Is it possible to prepare a balance sheet on June 30, 1981, or does Mr. Clark have to wait until December 31, 1981, to prepare a balance sheet? If a balance sheet can be prepared on June 30, 1981, prepare one.

Chapter 6

Internal control and the

processing of data:

Manual and electronic

This chapter covers internal control and processing of data. Internal control is discussed first. Then noncomputerized means of journalizing transactions are presented and discussed. The journals presented are referred to as special journals. Finally, computerized systems for processing data are discussed.

INTERNAL CONTROL

A system of internal control includes all the procedures and actions taken by an organization to (1) protect its assets against theft and waste, (2) ensure compliance with company policies and federal law,[1] (3) evaluate the performance of personnel in all parts of the company to promote efficiency of operations, and (4) ensure accurate and reliable operating data and accounting reports. The system provides direction to all activity within the organization and ensures that all units are functioning as intended.

Various aspects of internal control are dealt with throughout the text. For instance, Chapter 5 dealt with merchandise transactions and mentioned some of the control documents that are used. Control documents which are used include:

a. Purchase requisition—a form sent by a department manager to the purchasing department requesting that department to purchase various items which are needed.
b. Purchase order—a form used by the purchasing department to order items from another company.
c. Invoice—an itemized statement (or bill) sent by the supplier of goods or services to the purchaser of those goods or services. It is considered to be a purchase invoice to the purchaser and a sales invoice to the seller.
d. Receiving report—a form prepared by the receiving department showing the description, quantity, and condition of items received.

A copy of each of these documents is sent to the accounting department. As a group they serve as authorization to pay the invoice. In the absence of these documents the company might fail to pay a legitimate invoice, might pay fictitious invoices, or might pay certain invoices more than once. Purchase requisitions, purchase orders, invoices, and receiving reports should be serially numbered for greater control. An expanded coverage of the control aspects of the payment of invoices is contained in the voucher system discussion in Chapter 7. Various other procedures for protecting cash are discussed in that chapter. Likewise, control aspects concerning other assets are discussed in later chapters. The control aspects of budgets are discussed in Chapter 25.

---

[1] In December 1977 the Foreign Corrupt Practices Act of 1977 went into effect. Under this law all companies in the United States (as well as their officers, directors, agents, employees, and stockholders) are prohibited from bribing foreign governmental or political officials. Also, publicly held corporations are required to meet certain requirements concerning internal control and record keeping.

Some features of organization and some broad policies and procedures which lead to a strong system of internal control include:

a. Those responsible for safeguarding an asset should not maintain the accounting records for that asset. Also, responsibility for related transactions should be divided between individuals so that the work of one serves as a check on the other. In this way, collusion between at least two parties would be necessary to steal assets and cover up the theft in the accounting records.

b. Complete and accurate accounting records should be maintained on a current basis. When records are inadequate, this serves as an invitation to theft by dishonest employees.

c. Whenever possible, responsibilities should be assigned and duties subdivided in such a way that only one person is responsible for a given function or asset. Then, if a shortage occurs, responsibility cannot be denied and blamed on someone else.

d. Employees should be rotated in their job assignments when possible. Mere knowledge that this will be done may discourage certain employees from engaging in long-term schemes to steal from the company. Also, if such theft does occur, the scheme may be uncovered by the employee who is later rotated into that job. Related to job rotation is the requirement that all employees be required to take an annual vacation. Many schemes which have been used by employees to steal from their company will collapse if not attended to on a daily basis.

e. Where feasible, devices such as check protectors (which perforate the amount of a check into the check), cash registers, and time clocks should be used to record amounts in such a way that employees cannot alter them.

f. An internal auditing function should be performed, especially in large, complex companies. The internal auditing staff investigates the operating efficiency throughout the company. The staff is constantly alert for breakdowns in the system of internal control and makes recommendations for improvement of the system.

g. Honest, competent employees should be hired and then trained concerning internal control procedures. They should be made to understand the importance of following the procedures.

h. In spite of all the above features, it is impossible to construct a foolproof system. If collusion between dishonest employees exists, the system can be beaten. Therefore, it is advisable to carry adequate casualty insurance on assets and to carry fidelity bonds on those employees handling cash and other negotiable assets. With these coverages the company can recover at least a portion of any loss from the insurance or bonding company.

The masses of raw data generated by even a small business are largely unintelligible until processed—that is, recorded, analyzed, classified, summarized, and reported. Such processing facilitates the introduction of internal control over operations and must be undertaken if accurate financial statements are to be prepared. The processing of data will now be discussed.

THE PROCESSING OF DATA—MANUAL SYSTEM

The following purposes are accomplished by the orderly and efficient processing of accounting data:

1. The results of operations and the financial position of the firm can be determined and reported on a timely basis in financial statements.
2. Bills can be paid when due.
3. Shipments of merchandise can be made in the proper quantities and descriptions.
4. The conduct of other business also can be orderly and purposeful rather than disorganized.
5. Reports required by governmental units can be prepared.

BASIC ELEMENTS OF A MANUAL ACCOUNTING SYSTEM

Because of the number of transactions involved, an accounting system which includes only one book of original entry—the general journal—will not be efficient for even a relatively small business. The first step toward more efficient processing of data usually consists of the development of several special journals. These will allow for a division of labor and also for a reduction in posting time because of the grouping of similar types of transactions. Many different formats or types of journals could be used. The ones presented here are illustrative only. The special journals illustrated are the sales, purchases, cash receipts, cash disbursements, and payroll journals. A voucher system utilizing a voucher register and check register is introduced in Chapter 7. The journals actually used by a company depend upon the nature of the transactions engaged in by the company and upon the imagination of the person designing them.

Special journals are also used to aid control. For instance, one of the primary reasons for using specialized journals for sales and purchases is to assist in accounting for receivables and payables so that debit-credit information and balances are available for each creditor and each customer. The cash receipts and cash disbursements journals (and the voucher system illustrated in Chapter 7) provide handy information regarding receipts and disbursements so that control may exist over these cash flows. A *payroll journal* (illustrated in Chapter 12) provides detailed employee payment information in one place for management's use in controlling related matters.

Before discussing these further, it is necessary to understand controlling accounts and subsidiary accounts.

Controlling accounts and subsidiary accounts

A *controlling account* is an account in the general ledger that is supported by a detailed classification of accounting information in a subsidiary record. For example, an up-to-date record must be maintained for each customer to show the business done with that person and the amount owed. Therefore, outside the general ledger, an account is maintained for each individual customer, showing the debits and credits to that account and the balance due. The sum of the balances due from all customers equals the balance of the Accounts Receivable controlling account in the general ledger.

The individual account for each customer is known as a *subsidiary ac-count*; all of the individual customers' accounts make up the *subsidiary accounts receivable ledger,* or customers' ledger. A *subsidiary ledger,* then, is a group of related accounts showing the details of the balance of a controlling account in the general ledger. Subsidiary ledgers are separated from the general ledger in order *(a)* to relieve the general ledger of a mass of detail and thereby shorten the general ledger trial balance, *(b)* to promote the division of labor in the task of maintaining the ledgers, and *(c)* to strengthen the system of internal control. A subsidiary ledger may be used whether or not special journals are used.

When a transaction occurs that affects a controlling account and a subsidiary account, it is journalized in such fashion that it will be posted *(a)* to the general ledger and *(b)* to a subsidiary account. The usual way is to enter the transaction in a special column in a journal.

The key to effective operation and control of a subsidiary ledger is found in the posting procedure. The use of special columns in the journals makes it possible to post each transaction to an individual account in a subsidiary ledger during the period. Since the column totals are posted to the controlling accounts at the end of the period (usually a month), a comparison of the controlling account balance with the sum of the individual subsidiary account balances aids in determining that all amounts have been posted to the subsidiary accounts.

A few examples of frequently maintained subsidiary ledgers and the names of the related general ledger controlling accounts are as follows:

Subsidiary ledger	*General ledger controlling account*
Accounts receivable ledger (account for each customer)	Accounts Receivable
Accounts payable ledger (account for each creditor)	Accounts Payable
Equipment ledger (account for each item of equipment)	Office Equipment Delivery Equipment Store Fixtures, etc.

The number of subsidiary ledgers maintained will vary according to the information requirements of each company. Control accounts and subsidiary ledgers generally will be set up for control purposes where there are many transactions in a given account and where information on the details of these transactions is needed on a continuing basis.

Grouping of similar transactions in journals

Special journals are designed to systematize the original recording of the major recurring transactions. A *sales journal* is set up to record the journal entries for sales of merchandise on account. A *cash receipts journal* is established to record cash receipts transactions. A *purchases journal* is established to record the journal entries for purchases of merchandise on account. A *cash disbursements journal* is used to record cash disbursements. The *general journal* remains for all transactions that cannot be entered in one of the special journals. All five are records of original entry containing data which will be posted to ledger accounts. In the Folio column of the accounts, abbreviations are used to identify the source of the posting, for example, PJ for the purchases journal, and CDJ for the cash disbursements journal as shown:

	Abbreviation
Sales journal	SJ
Purchases journal	PJ
Cash receipts journal	CRJ
Cash disbursements journal	CDJ
General journal	GJ

The sales journal.   Normally, sales are for cash or on open account. The sales journal for the John Mason Company in Illustration 6.1 is used only for sales of merchandise on account. Cash sales should be recorded in the cash receipts journal. Sales of other assets should be recorded in the cash receipts journal (if cash is received at the time of sale) or in the general journal.

The simplest form of sales journal has only one money column, entitled Accounts Receivable Dr. and Sales Cr. Variations in the sales journal can be made. Special columns could be inserted for items such as state sales taxes, federal excise taxes, and sales returns and allowances. And a departmental breakdown can be obtained by providing a Sales Cr. column for each department in a company.

Posting sales.   The posting of sales from the sales journal in Illustration 6.1 involves entering the total of the money column headed Accounts Receivable Dr. and Sales Cr. as a credit to the general ledger Sales account. The folio reference of SJ-1 (sales journal, p. 1) is also entered in the Sales account, and the number (301) is written in the sales journal under the total of the money column to show that the $250 was posted as a credit to Sales. Since there generally is no subsidiary sales ledger, the individual items comprising sales are not posted.

Posting accounts receivable.   To post accounts receivable from the sales journal in Illustration 6.1, the total of the money column ($250) is posted as a debit to the Accounts Receivable control account in the general ledger with a folio reference of SJ-1. The number (111) is entered under the total of the money column in the sales journal to show that the amount has been posted and where it was posted. The individual amounts in the money column are posted to each individual customer's account in the subsidiary ledger so that the account will show the amount currently due from the customer. As each individual amount is posted, a check mark ($\sqrt{}$) is placed in the column headed $\sqrt{}$ opposite the amount to show that it has been posted. Subsidiary accounts are usually kept in alphabetical order and may not have account numbers. When the posting of the accounts receivable has been completed, the Accounts Receivable control account will show a balance of $250, which is equal to the sum of the balances in the Accounts Receivable subsidiary

Illustration 6.1: Sales journal

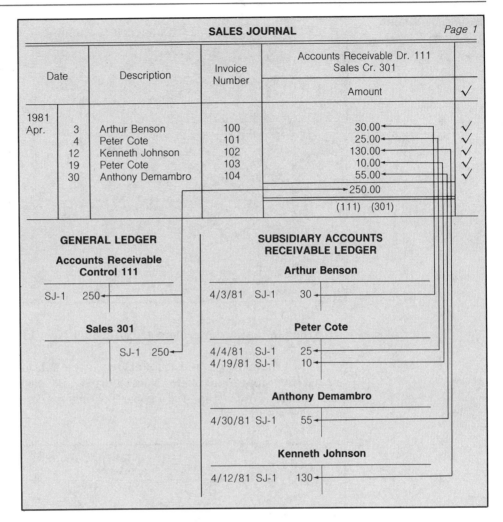

ledger accounts, assuming no previous balances in the control account or the subsidiary accounts.

Subsidiary ledger accounts usually are not numbered but are kept in alphabetical order, since their composition is constantly changing.

The cash receipts journal. The cash receipts journal, which might be used in combination with the sales journal, is shown in Illustration 6.2. Any number of different designs may be used for this journal also. For instance, if some of the items appearing in the *Sundry accounts* (miscellaneous accounts) Cr. column are frequently credited, it would be advisable to set up a separate column for each of these items.

Since the amounts appearing in the Sundry Accounts Cr. column usually pertain to different accounts, the column total is not posted and a check mark ($\checkmark$) is placed immediately below the amount. The individual items

Illustration 6.2: Cash receipts journal

101 Cash Dr.	726 Sales Discounts Dr.	Date		Description	310 Sales Cr.	111 Accounts Receivable Cr. Amount	✓	Sundry Accounts Cr. Acct. No.	Amount	✓
		1981 Apr.	1	Cash sales	10,700.00					
10,700.00										
29.40	0.60		6	Arthur Benson—Invoice No. 100		30.00	✓			
10,775.00			7	Cash sales	10,775.00					
6,000.00			10	Sold land at cost to Wells Corporation				138*	6,000.000	✓
10,600.00			14	Cash sales	10,600.00					
25.00			19	Peter Cote—Invoice No. 101		25.00	✓			
127.40	2.60		20	Kenneth Johnson—Invoice No. 102		130.00	✓			
11,045.00			25	Cash sales	11,045.00					
200.00			26	Cash received from sale of scrap				303*	200.00	✓
49,501.80	3.20				43,120.00	185.00			6,200.00	
(101)	(726)				(301)	(111)				✓

CASH RECEIPTS JOURNAL — *Page 5*

* 138 Land.
* 303 Miscellaneous Revenue.

are posted to the accounts indicated (Account Nos. 138 and 303 in Illustration 6.2).

The general ledger and accounts receivable subsidiary ledger shown below are as they appear after the sales journal and cash receipts journal have been posted. Notice that the proper posting marks have been made in the cash receipts journal.

PARTIAL GENERAL LEDGER

Cash — *Account No. 101*

Date		Explanation	Folio	Debit	Credit	Balance
1981 Apr.	1	Beginning balance (assumed)				10,000.00
	30		CRJ-5	49,501.80		59,501.80

Accounts Receivable — *Account No. 111*

Date		Explanation	Folio	Debit	Credit	Balance
1981 Apr.	30		SJ-1	250.00		250.00
	30		CRJ-5		185.00	65.00

Land — *Account No. 138*

Date		Explanation	Folio	Debit	Credit	Balance
1981 Apr.	1	Beginning balance (assumed)				18,000.00
	10		CRJ-5	.	6,000.00	12,000.00

PARTIAL GENERAL LEDGER *(continued)*
John Mason, Capital   *Account No. 250*

Date		Explanation	Folio	Debit	Credit	Balance
1981 Apr.	1	Beginning balance (assumed)				28,000.00

Sales   *Account No. 301*

Date		Explanation	Folio	Debit	Credit	Balance
1981 Apr.	30		SJ-5		250.00	250.00
	30		CRJ-5		43,120.00	43.370.00

Miscellaneous Revenue   *Account No. 303*

Date		Explanation	Folio	Debit	Credit	Balance
1981 Apr.	30		CRJ-5		200.00	200.00

Sales Discounts   *Account No. 726*

Date		Explanation	Folio	Debit	Credit	Balance
1981 Apr.	30		CRJ-5	3.20		3.20

SUBSIDIARY ACCOUNTS RECEIVABLE LEDGER
Arthur Benson

Date		Explanation	Folio	Debit	Credit	Balance
1981 Apr.	3		SJ-1	30.00		30.00
	6		CRJ-5		30.00	-0-

Peter Cote

Date		Explanation	Folio	Debit	Credit	Balance
1981 Apr.	4		SJ-1	25.00		25.00
	19		SJ-1	10.00		35.00
	19		CRJ-5		25.00	10.00

Anthony Demambro

Date		Explanation	Folio	Debit	Credit	Balance
1981 Apr.	30		SJ-1	55.00		55.00

SUBSIDIARY ACCOUNTS RECEIVABLE LEDGER *(continued)* Kenneth Johnson						
Date		Explanation	Folio	Debit	Credit	Balance
1981 Apr.	12 20		SJ-1 CRJ-5	130.00	130.00	130.00 -0-

A list of accounts receivable would contain the $10 due from Peter Cote and the $55 due from Anthony Demambro, which is, of course, in agreement with the balance of $65 in the Accounts Receivable controlling account.

It is possible to combine the sales and cash receipts journals illustrated earlier. But posting and journalizing convenience is not the only consideration. Remember that one of the reasons for creating special journals is so that several persons can work with them at the same time. Having separate sales and cash receipts journals does allow more persons to work with the data in the journals at the same time. A decision in any particular case has to be made so as to maximize the overall efficiency of working with the journals.

The purchases journal.   Most business firms are aware that in order to have an acceptable level of control over cash disbursements they must pay all bills by check. Assuming this to be the case here, all purchases are made on account and therefore are included in the purchases journal (even if the length of delay in payment is only long enough to write the check). The payment is then shown in the cash disbursements journal.

The total in the money column of the purchases journal in Illustration 6.3 (where periodic procedure is assumed) is posted to the Purchases account as a debit and to the Accounts Payable account as a credit at the end of

Illustration 6.3: Purchases journal

PURCHASES JOURNAL				Page 10	
Date	Terms	Invoice Number	Creditor	Purchases Dr. 801 Accounts payable Cr. 201	
				Amount	✓
1981 Apr. 1	2/10, n/30	862	Smith Corporation	196.00	✓
7	1/15, n/60	121	Lasky Company	99.00	✓
12	2/20, n/60	561	Booth Corporation	4,900.00	✓
15	2/10, n/30	1042	Gooch Corporation	2,940.00	✓
21	3/15, n/60	633	Wyngarden Company	9,700.00	✓
26	2/10, n/30	734	Mertz Company	98.00	✓
30	2/10, n/30	287	Nelson Company	3,920.00	✓
30	2/20, n/60	568	Booth Corporation	1,470.00	
				23,323.00	
				(801)(201)	

the month. The individual amounts in the column are posted to the accounts in the accounts payable subsidiary ledger.

There are, of course, a number of designs whicn could be used. For example, if there are separate departments, a separate purchases column could be provided for each department. A column could be inserted for purchase returns and allowances if they are encountered frequently. Since a Purchase Returns and Allowances account normally has a credit balance, an Accounts Payable debit column would have to be included also.

All amounts of purchases have been entered net of discount in the illustration. This procedure is described briefly in Chapter 5. Any discounts missed should be considered penalties due to inefficiency and recorded in a Discounts Lost account.

The cash disbursements journal. Since it is assumed that all cash disbursements are made by check, the cash disbursements journal in Illustration 6.4 contains a column in which to record the number of each check written. Payments on accounts payable and salaries payable constitute the majority of items paid in the illustration.

In companies with many employees, a separate payroll bank checking account probably would be established. Then the cash disbursements journal

Illustration 6.4: Cash disbursements journal

201 Accounts Payable Dr. Amount	√	219 Salaries Payable Dr.	821 Discounts Lost Dr.	822 Supplies Expense Dr.	Sundry Accounts Dr. Acct. No.	Amount	√	Date		Description	Check No.	101 Cash Cr.
								1981				
				42.00				Apr.	2	Brooklyn Square Paint Company	524	42.00
									3	Insurance policy to cover May		
					123*	1,200.00	√			1981—April 30, 1982	525	1,200.00
					140*	500.00	√		4	Furniture—office	526	500.00
					823*	200.00	√			Rent for April 1981	527	200.00
196.00	√								8	Smith Corporation—Invoice	528	196.00
										No. 862		
				10.00					14	Allan Park Stationery Company	529	10.00
99.00	√								18	Lasky Company—Invoice No. 121	530	99.00
4,900.00	√								21	Booth Corporation—Invoice No. 561	531	4,900.00
9,700.00	√								27	Wyngarden Company—Invoice	532	9,700.00
										No. 633		
2,940.00	√		60.00						28	Gooch Corporation—Invoice	533	3,000.00
										No. 1042		
		1,553.60							30	Clarke Frankson	534	1,553.60
		1,172.90								Mead Stacy	535	1,172.90
		803.10								Jason Evans	536	803.10
		720.20								Marshall Watson	537	720.20
		403.00								Cleveland Avoy	538	403.00
		341.02								James Jackson	539	341.02
		366.60								Stuary Bently	540	366.60
		377.14								Robert Aleo	541	377.14
17,835.00		5,737.56	60.00	52.00		1,900.00						25,584.56
(201)		(219)	(821)	(822)		(√)						(101)

CASH DISBURSEMENTS JOURNAL   Page 5

* 123—Unexpired insurance.
* 140—Furniture and Equipment.
* 823—Rent Expenses.

would show only one amount for payroll, the total amount of salaries payable. The entry would debit Payroll Cash and credit Cash (general). A separate payroll check register might then be maintained to record the payment of salaries out of the payroll checking account. The payroll journal is illustrated in Chapter 12.

The column totals for the cash, accounts payable, salaries payable, discounts lost, and supplier expenses are posted to accounts in the general ledger. Individual items in the Accounts Payable column are posted to accounts in the subsidiary accounts payable ledger. Individual items in the Sundry Accounts column are posted to the appropriate accounts in the general ledger.

Of course, it would be possible to combine the purchases and cash disbursements journals. But this limits the number of persons who can work with the data in the journals at any one time.

The general journal and other journals. Every transaction that will not fit conveniently into the special journals is entered in the general journal. For instance, the general journal (or a special payroll journal) could be used to record salaries expense as follows:

Salaries Expense xxx
    Federal Income Tax withheld   xx
    Social Security Tax withheld   xx
    Salaries Payable   xxx

Payroll is discussed in more detail in Chapter 12.

Summary of the advantages of using special journals

To summarize, the following advantages are obtained from the use of special journals.

a. *Time is saved in journalizing.* Only one line is used for each transaction; a full description is not necessary. The amount of writing is reduced because it is not necessary to repeat the account names printed at the top of the special column or columns.

b. *Time is saved in posting.* Many data are posted as totals of columns.

c. *Detail is eliminated from the general ledger.* Column totals are posted to the general ledger, and the detail is left in the journals.

d. *Division of labor is promoted.* Several persons can work simultaneously on the accounting records. This specialization and division of labor pinpoints responsibility and eases the location of errors.

e. *Use of accounting machines is facilitated.* The mass of routine transactions recorded in special journals frequently makes the use of accounting machines economical.

f. *Management analysis is aided.* The journals themselves can be useful to management in analyzing classes of transactions (such as credit sales).

The next section discusses the use of computers in accounting. It demonstrates that the accounting *functions* performed with a computer system are not unlike those found in pen-and-ink and machine accounting systems. But use of the computer changes the *form* of accounting records. Journals and ledgers appearing in the form illustrated in this chapter are no longer used as recording or accumulation devices, although computer *printout* may be in a form similar to the special journals illustrated.

THE PROCESSING OF DATA—ELECTRONIC SYSTEM

THE COMPUTER
The search for greater speed, accuracy, and storage capacity has presented a persistent challenge to both the designers of information systems and the accounting profession. This challenge has been met over the years through the increasing use of more sophisticated devices. The most recent device has been the computer. Use of the computer has permitted human participation to be limited to the preparation of input (transaction) data and the set of instructions telling the computer how these data should be processed. If properly programmed, the computer is capable of journalizing and posting many transactions in any order and with great speed and a high degree of accuracy. The distinguishing feature of a computer is its ability to accept instructions for the processing of any transaction data, to store those instructions, and to execute them any number of times precisely in the desired sequence. The computer uses elementary numerical logic to alter the sequence of instructions by observing the outcome of a numeric or alphabetic comparison. An example of the use of such a comparison is an instruction to test whether the cash balance is zero before each transaction and to continue processing cash disbursements only if the balance is greater than zero. The computer has the capability to remain exceedingly accurate even at very high calculating speeds. Since sets of operating instructions are given to the computer at the outset, human effort is conserved. The performance of repetitive tasks, routine numerical decision making, and certain types of logical decision making is taken over by the computer.

The computer consists of three basic components: *a storage unit, an arithmetic unit,* and *a processing unit. Peripheral equipment* can be attached to these units. The peripheral equipment is used mainly to feed unprocessed information into and receive processed information from the computer. Examples of peripheral equipment are tape drives, card readers, and printers. The way in which these components are connected and controlled varies from computer to computer.

The *storage unit* (sometimes called core storage) of a computer is its internal *memory* system. It is the most expensive component of acquisition cost for the computer. To determine the optimum size of internal core storage, speed and cost factors must be considered. Generally, the greater the speed and storage required, the greater the cost. Problems requiring more storage space than originally provided in the computer can utilize peripheral devices such as disks, drums, or tape units for temporary external storage.

The *arithmetic unit* of a computer contains devices which perform arithmetic operations and generally process the data. This unit does the computing.

The *processing unit* of a computer is the governing unit which interprets the *program* (the set of *instructions* submitted to the computer which specifies

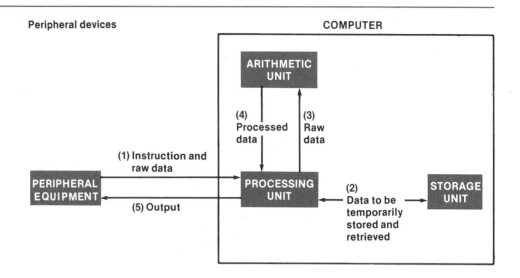

the operations to be performed and their correct sequence), makes decisions, and alters the sequence if so instructed by the program. This unit can do only what it is told to do by the program. If it reaches a situation for which it has been given no explicit instructions, it will instruct the computer to halt operations. After finding and correcting the problem situation, the computer operator can restart the processing by means of a *console* which allows the operator to exercise control over the computer when necessary.

Illustration 6.5 shows a schematic design of a simple computer system. The processing unit controls the operation of the system. The peripheral equipment is not part of the computer but is used to transmit (1) data into and out of the computer as directed by the processing unit. The processing, arithmetic, and storage units are contained within the computer. The processing unit sends the data to the storage unit until there is free time to process the data. At that time the data are recalled (2) from storage and transferred (3) to the arithmetic unit where the required arithmetic operations are performed. Upon completion, the processed data (4) are either sent back to the storage unit or if there is no more processing to be done using the data they will be sent to the peripheral equipment. The peripheral equipment will then print the processed output in a predefined format.

The computer must be given very explicit instructions for every possible event. It cannot find a solution to problems which arise during the execution process. It can execute only the steps which a programmer has devised to reach a solution.

Flowcharts

A *flowchart* is a graphic representation of the sequential order of the steps involved in the solution of a problem. It is prepared by the systems analyst or programmer prior to the actual preparation of the program or final design of a system. The symbols used are connected by lines with arrows to indicate the processing sequence.

APPLICATIONS OF ELECTRONIC DATA PROCESSING TO ACCOUNTING

The discussion so far has covered some of the data processing and computer equipment which is available and the manner in which problems are programmed and executed. Typical examples of electronic data processing applications in accounting are in the areas of payroll, accounts receivable, accounts payable, and inventory.

Nearly all applications of data processing, and particularly those which involve the accounting process, make considerable use of *files*. A *file* is any grouping of similar items of data arranged in some identifiable order. For example, the accounts receivable ledger is a file: the data are the individual invoices and other open items, and the sequence may be by customer number. The use of files is particularly relevant since the program causes the same basic processing to be performed on each of the many employee records in the payroll file, customer records in the *accounts receivable file*, vendor records in the *accounts payable file*, and parts records in the inventory file. The processing which occurs is undertaken to update these files; the end result is a new cumulative file created by the computer.

EVALUATING A COMPUTER PROPOSAL

The outlay for an electronic data processing system may be one of the largest capital expenditures that a firm may make. The proposal must be evaluated carefully. But how does one put a value on such things as improved, more timely information? Also, can the cost of the system be accurately estimated? Such questions are not easy to answer, but the huge expenditures for electronic data processing systems require that they receive more attention than they have in the past.

The cost side of the decision may be hard to estimate, yet it is the more concrete area with which to work. First, a detailed analysis of the basic costs of leasing and buying must be made. Second, an analysis of other one-time expenses should be made. These expenses include such items as special auxiliary equipment, special storage and operating equipment, and extra personnel cost due to the changeover period. This is an area in which it is very easy to overlook the full impact of a purchase decision. Finally, an estimate of normal operating expenses will be made. Questions to be answered include the following: How many programmers will be needed? Will the computer be used on one, two, or three shifts? What is the expected volume? What will be the cost of supplies? Recent studies have shown that equipment rental costs account for only about one third to one half of the normal operating expenses of a large-scale computer system. Other costs include program maintenance (including programmers); computer operations (supplies, operators, some programming); and new program development. The trend is for personnel cost to increase in proportion to equipment cost.

As difficult as it is to evaluate the cost of a proposal, the quantification of potential benefits is much more difficult. Some of the main benefits often cited for electronic data systems are the following: (1) reduces clerical costs; (2) increases quality and timeliness of management information; (3) enables scientific management techniques to be used, for example, operations research and linear programming; and (4) improves service for the firm and its customers. Of the four advantages cited, only the first can be objectively measured.

One of the main areas of reducing clerical costs has been in the accounting function, which explains why accountants were so heavily involved in the early installation of computer systems. But the areas of even greater benefit may be in the other three areas. Better information and better service may allow a firm to develop a competitive advantage. The likelihood of these possible benefits and their full implications for the organization must be evaluated carefully and critically. Such questions are difficult, but all too often they have been ignored.

OTHER INFORMATION TOOLS

The range of equipment that the accountant may be working with is very large, ranging from a hand-posted invoice register to the large, fast, present-day computers. Some of the available alternatives, in addition to the computer, are discussed briefly.

Hand-posted system

All accounting entries are recorded by hand; journals are summarized and posted to the general ledger. This is typical of many of today's smaller businesses in which the accounting function is handled by the accountant and possibly one or two clerks. This system was illustrated in the early part of this chapter.

Bookkeeping machine system

The basic nature of this system is not much different from the handposted system. The system is generally set up in such a way that those transactions recurring most often are recorded on the bookkeeping machines. Typical applications include sales postings, receivables postings, and payroll. Some bookkeeping machines include a storage capacity.

Service bureaus

Many firms have found it economical to have certain transactions (e.g., payroll, inventory, and accounts receivable) processed by a local service bureau. A *service bureau* is primarily a large computer facility that rents out time for data processing. Often, the service bureaus are independent companies, although occasionally firms with excess computer time will offer services along this line (e.g., banks). Service bureaus usually can meet the specific output requirements of a firm if some advance planning is done.

Time-sharing terminals— remote batch

Significant advances have been made in the field of computer time sharing. It is now possible to have a remote terminal in almost every business firm. The terminals are connected through telephone lines or radio waves to a host computer operated by an independent company. The company's programs are filed at the host computer and can be called by the person operating the remote terminal. Again, typical applications involve large amounts of transactions data (e.g., printing and summarizing sales invoices, updating inventory records, updating account receivable records, and so on). Note that the remote terminal must serve as both an input and output device. Because of this, the length of time before output is received is longer than processing by other means.

This has been a brief introduction to the use of computers in accounting. The Appendix which follows includes more information on computers for those who desire it.

APPENDIX: ADDITIONAL INFORMATION ON COMPUTERS

Input and storage devices

The *punched card* (Illustration 6.6) is the basic input medium for some electronic data processing (EDP) systems. A card reader senses the data according to the holes contained in the card. Each of the numbers has a single punch in the row corresponding to its value. Each letter is represented by two punches. Some special characters require three punches.

Punching is normally done with a *keypunch* (Illustration 6.7) which is similar to a typewriter. A keypunch operator reads data from *source documents* such as sales tickets, invoices, and inventory records, and, with this machine, punches the data into specified positions on the cards.

The punched cards and source documents then go to a verifier which is similar to a keypunch in appearance. The operator of this machine keys

Illustration 6.6: Punched card

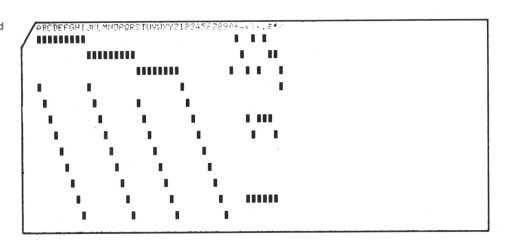

Illustration 6.7: Keypunch

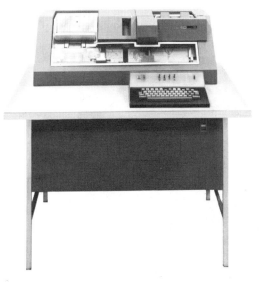

the same data into the card, but the machine, rather than punching, checks for accuracy. If the "punches" of the verifier agree with the punches in the card, a notch is placed on the right side of the card. If the two punches do not match in a given column, a notch is placed above that column. An incorrect card is then corrected or a new one punched, and in either case it is verified again before being processed further.

A collator (Illustration 6.8) is a multipurpose machine which is used to check the sequence of a file of cards, merge two files into a specified sequence, select matched or unmatched cards, and edit.

Since today's high-speed computers can process data much more rapidly than they can read data, it is desirable to speed up the input process whenever possible. The punched card has been the most convenient medium for original input, but it is also one of the slowest media. The speed with which the data contained on punched cards can be read into the computer is much slower than the processing speed of the computer. If punched cards were used as the direct input medium, then much computer time would be wasted in waiting for the data to be read in. Because of this, considerable effort has been expended in recent years to improve the speed of data transfer into the computer. Where punched cards are used as the main means of data input, most installations with large computers will use a *minicomputer* (or a series of minicomputers) to read the data and transfer them to magnetic tape or magnetic disks which can then be read into the main computer at a much faster rate. Since the *central processing unit* is an expensive piece of equipment, the increased efficiency of data processing can offset the additional costs of storing the data on tape or disks. This is especially true as most computer systems have typically been "input bound" or "output bound" with

Illustration 6.8: Collator

the rate of transfer into and out of the computer being the limiting constraint on the amount of processing that could be done.

The three major input media into computer core are *magnetic tape, magnetic disks,* and *magnetic drums.* Magnetic tape is the least expensive and the least flexible, while magnetic disks and magnetic drums are more expensive and more flexible.

Magnetic tape (Illustration 6.9) is similar to the tape used for an ordinary tape recorder but is wider, of a much higher quality, and more expensive. Data are stored very compactly on the reel of tape. When a reel of tape is used, it is mounted onto a *tape drive* which is under the control of a computer (Illustration 6.10). The tape drive can be used to read from or write on the tape. Magnetic tape is a convenient and compact storage medium as well as a useful input and output medium. The major disadvantage of magnetic tape as an input-output medium for computers is its serial access feature. This means that if the tape drive is reading from the beginning of a tape and data near the end of the tape are needed, the tape drive must physically move all of the intervening tape past the reading head before the desired data are located. This process can take as long as 4 or 5 minutes.

Magnetic tape is widely used in business data processing because in many cases it is desirable to read a whole file (contained on tape) into central processing. An example would be the updating of an accounts receivable *master file* where each individual account in the file is updated by a current transaction—either a cash payment, sale, or other adjustment.

There are many instances in the current business world where sequential processing is not adequate. For instance, the airline reservation system would never have been feasible if it were dependent on sequential processing. The need to reduce *access time* has led to the development of *random access storage* devices. The random access feature eliminates the need for the sequential

Illustration 6.9: Magnetic tape

Illustration 6.10: Tape drive

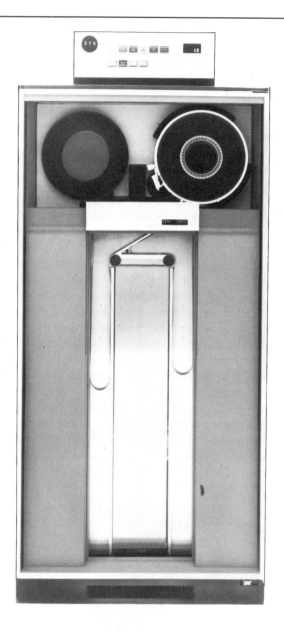

processing of data before the desired information is found. Each item of information has a specific predetermined address which can be located directly; no other data need be read or processed. The address consists of a number which designates the location of the data. Desired information can be retrieved after a time interval which is, in general, much shorter than that experienced with serial access equipment. Access *(retrieval)* time is reduced to fractions of a second. The word "random" indicates that the data can be retrieved in a random order; no consideration need be given to the sequential ordering of the data or data requests.

Magnetic disks and *magnetic drums* are random access storage devices. Both can be used as secondary storage devices; that is, they are separate from the central processor. Data are stored on magnetic disks much like songs are stored on a long-playing record album. Magnetic drums are shaped more like a barrel with the data written on the outside surface. Magnetic drums usually permit faster access than disks, but the faster access comes at a higher price. Each medium is capable of storing a large amount of data and is much cheaper than central core storage.

The fastest and most expensive type of storage device is magnetic core storage. *Magnetic core* is part of the computer and is primarily a temporary storage device used in the processing of a particular program. As such, it should not be considered as a main storage device. The amount of core storage needed in any installation can be determined only after a thorough analysis of all processing needs and future demands.

The decision as to which types and amounts of storage are required in any computer installation is one which involves trade-offs between speed and cost. In some cases, a serial access device (the least expensive but generally slowest) may be as efficient as the more expensive random access input and storage device. A firm which uses the computer in such a way as to require the use of most of the sequential data on a tape would gain little by reading

Illustration 6.11: IBM System/38

Courtesy of IBM.

the same sequence with more expensive equipment. But an inventory system which must be able to provide information on the status of any of 10,000 parts at any time may well justify the extra cost of a random access memory device. In this case the use of tapes is almost certain to involve a great deal of tape movement that is not needed. Illustration 6.11 depicts a system that uses magnetic disk.

The illustration shows the IBM System/38 with attached disk units, magnetic tape system, card reader, card punch, printer, and console typewriter.

Small computers

The IBM System/3 computer (Illustration 6.12) is a smaller third-generation computer than IBM's System/360 and System/370. The smaller computer is best suited for smaller businesses. The major advantages of the smaller computer are its low cost, compactness, and flexibility; it also provides random access storage.

There are basically two types of systems for the smaller computer—a card system and a disk system. One of the unique items appearing with the System/3 is a 96-column card. The 96-column card holds 20 percent more characters than the 80-column card, but it is only one third the size of an 80-column card.

A multifunction card unit is also available with the System/3. This piece of equipment combines the functions of a card reader, punch, sorter, collator, and interpreter in one compact device.

Illustration 6.12: IBM System/3 computer

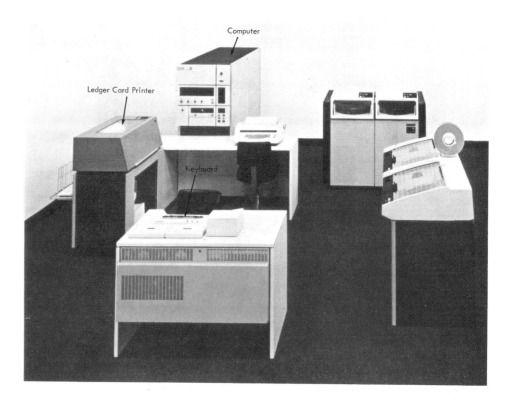

One model of the System/3 uses an operator keyboard console as the primary input device. This model is also useful for commercial data processing—especially accounts receivable, billing, inventory control, and sales analysis.

In comparison to IBM's System/360, the System/3 is much smaller in size—it occupies only slightly more space than an office desk. Thus, it seems natural that the System/3 can be rented or purchased for a much smaller amount of money than the System/360. Although the System/3 was designed primarily to meet the needs of small businesses, it can be used as a processing terminal by medium-sized and large organizations. For instance, the System/3 can be used as a processing terminal at branch offices so that data can be communicated from the System/3 (at branch offices) to an IBM System/360 located at the main office.

The primary types of input media for the System/3 are magnetic disks, the 96-column card, and direct data entry through a keyboard that looks like a typewriter. On the other hand, the System/360 uses 80-column cards, magnetic tape, magnetic disks, magnetic drums, data cell, and direct data entry as the primary input devices.

The System/3 is easier for small business to use than the System/360. It was designed to be used by people who have not had any prior experience with computers. RPG II, which stands for Report Program Generator, is a problem-oriented programming language that was developed especially for the IBM System/3. It is a very easy-to-learn and easy-to-use programming language. COBOL, FORTRAN, BASIC, and Assembler languages can also be used with certain models of the System/3. With the System/3, RPG II is typically used for accounting applications and BASIC for mathematical applications. COBOL, FORTRAN, RPG, Assembler, and PL/1 (Programming Language 1) are programming languages that can be used with the System/360. PL/1 is a relatively new language designed for both commercial and scientific applications.

One important characteristic of the System/360 is its capacity for growth which seems virtually unlimited, particularly in comparison with the System/3 whose growth possibilities are definitely limited. In addition, the System/3 can execute only 28 basic instructions whereas the System/360 can execute approximately 200 instructions. Thus, as a small business expands, the owner or manager will probably decide to rent or purchase a larger computer, such as a System/360.

Programming a problem for computer processing

So far the computer has been discussed only in terms of its ability to process data according to a set of instructions which somehow has been accepted and stored in its memory. The detailed manner in which these instructions are given to the computer in the form of a program is beyond the scope of this text. But a brief introduction to programming will be useful in order that the steps which precede data processing activities can be understood.

Nearly all modern *digital computers* perform operations internally by testing the position of electronic switches which have two alternatives (much like a light switch which can only be on or off). All of the many complex operations which a computer can perform are accomplished by nothing more than combinations of these two positions, or *binary* switches, in various patterns or circuits. The combination of all instructions in a program constitutes a master circuit, which the computer then executes one step at a time.

Since it is very difficult to communicate with the computer in terms of these binary switches, it is customary for a computer system to be able to interpret computer languages and transform instructions written in them into internal circuitry. For example, each computer has its own machine language, which is a series of special codes by which elementary processing operations are specified. These languages have the advantage of being converted very rapidly by the computer into internal instructions, but machine language programs are difficult to prepare and use. Ordinarily a machine's language cannot be transferred from one computer to another (even to other computer models produced by the same manufacturer).

Another group of languages has been written with the goal of making the transition from one machine to another less difficult. Languages such as FORTRAN and COBOL, known as *compiler* languages, can be interpreted by many computers with only minor modifications required between systems. *FORTRAN* (for FORmula TRANslator) was developed especially to be compatible with scientific work; FORTRAN instructions are similar to algebraic formulas. *COBOL* (for Common Business-Oriented Language) was developed with instructions consisting of English phrases, so that combinations of instructions form readable sentences and paragraphs (see Illustration 6.13). COBOL is especially adaptable to handling large business files. Probably about 95 percent of business data programming of the nonscientific nature now is done in COBOL. When programs which have been written in a compiler language are submitted to a computer, a specialized program known as a compiler translates the program into the appropriate machine language which the computer can interpret more efficiently. The computer languages, then, are intermediary languages which serve to bridge the gap between everyday speech and mathematics on the one hand and machine languages on the other. It should be noted, however, that it is possible to write programs in terms of machine languages, and occasionally this is done.

Illustration 6.13 gives a portion of a program written in COBOL to create a new file containing the new balances of an accounts receivable file after adding in the current transactions. The program is simplified because it assumes that each item in the master file will have a corresponding transaction entered. Also, some of the data and equipment specifications normally expected in a COBOL program are not included in the illustration. Nevertheless, the illustration should provide an understanding of what a COBOL program is like.

Paragraph-1 tells the computer to read in the transaction file, one record at a time, and store the data into memory. Paragraph-2 instructs the computer to read in the master file, one record at a time, and store in core (the whole file is not read at once, rather each item is read one at a time). Then a comparison is made to see if the transaction and master record belong to the same account. If they are not the same, control is transferred to Paragraph-

Illustration 6.13: Partial
program for updating
an accounts receivable
balance file

```
PROCEDURE DIVISION.
PARAGRAPH-1.
    READ TRANSACTIONS AT END GO TO PARAGRAPH-3.
PARAGRAPH-2.
    READ MASTER AT END GO TO PARAGRAPH-3.
    IF ID-NO IN TRANSACTION-REC IS NOT EQUAL TO ID-NO IN
        MASTER-REC GO TO PARAGRAPH-3.
ADD NEW-ENTRY TO OLD-BALANCE GIVING NEW-BALANCE.
    MOVE NEW-BALANCE TO BALANCE.
    MOVE NAME IN MASTER TO NAME IN NEW-RECORD.
    DISPLAY NEW-RECORD UPON PRINT-ER.
    GO TO PARAGRAPH-1.
PARAGRAPH-3.
    STOP RUN.
```

Illustration 6.13: Partial program for updating an accounts receivable balance file

3 and the program stops. If they are the same, the program instructs the computer to add the new entry to the old accounts receivable balance to create a new balance which will be printed out. The new entry can be either positive or negative. After the record is printed out, the computer is instructed to go to Paragraph-1 and start again. The program will continue until all of the transactions and the master file are read, at which time the program will stop.

Although this example is highly simplified, it is somewhat typical of a business data processing application. Note the similarity between COBOL sentences and regular English sentences.

Executing a program

Once a particular problem has been translated into one of the available computer languages (such as COBOL) and the data have been transmitted to and stored within the computer, it is possible to instruct the computer to execute this program. During the execution of any program, the computer may be occupied with any one of three major activities: input, processing, and output.

The *input* phase includes all of those operations which result when the program requires data which must be provided by some external source such as a tape unit, magnetic disks, or card reader. Input involves the transmission of data from this external source to the internal storage of the computer.

The processsing phase is totally internal. During this phase the computer executes the computational and analytical instructions contained in the program in the order which has been specified. If any logical tests are included in the program, it is possible for the data to cause the order or the content of these instructions to be altered.

The *output* phase results in the writing of processed information on some external medium, usually a magnetic tape. Any output created in this manner then may be processed through an auxiliary computer in order to convert the tape impulses into printed pages or punched cards. The interrelationship of these stages and the equipment involved is shown in Illustration 6.14.

With any real problem, it is unlikely that these three phases can be accomplished in their entirety in any simple sequence. In fact, there may be

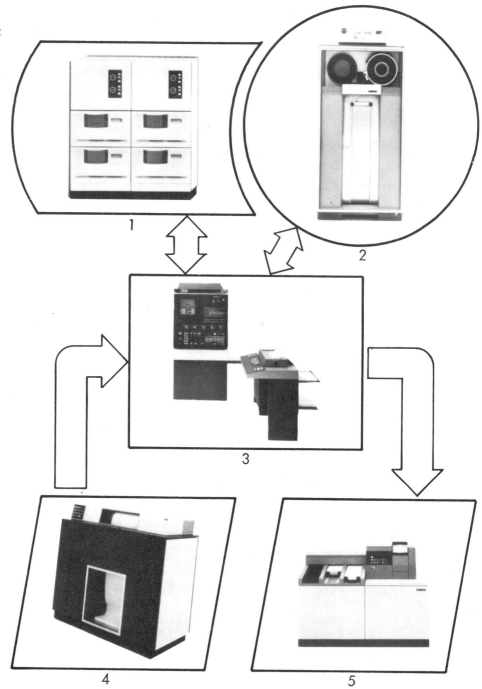

Illustration 6.14: A computer system using IBM 370 equipment (1. magnetic disks, 2. magnetic tape, 3. reader, 4. computer, 5. printer)

several input phases during the execution of a program, just as there may be any number of individual processing or output operations. Typically, a whole series of input-processing-output cycles will constitute the total program. The manner in which these are combined is a question of efficiency and speed.

NEW TERMS INTRODUCED IN CHAPTER 6

Accounts payable file—a file showing the amounts owed to vendors.

Accounts receivable file—a file showing the amounts owed by customers.

Access time—the time interval required to locate data stored within the computer system and deliver it to the designated place.

Arithmetic unit—a central component of a computer; it performs computations and comparisons.

Binary—pertaining to characteristic or property involving a selection, choice, or condition in which there are two possibilities.

Cash disbursements journal—a special journal in which all outflows of cash are recorded.

Cash receipts journal—a special journal in which all inflows of cash are recorded.

Central processing unit—the unit of a computing system that includes the circuits controlling the interpretation and execution of instructions.

COBOL—COmmon Business-Oriented Language. A compiler language used to program problems for processing in a computer and generally associated with business problems.

Compiler—a specialized computer program (an example of software) which translates programs written in compiler languages into the appropriate machine language which the computer can interpret.

Console—the component of an electronic computer system which enables an operator to communicate manually with the system and start, stop, or alter operations.

Controlling account—an account in the general ledger that is supported by a detailed classification of accounting information in a subsidiary record.

Digital computer—a device used for the step-by-step performance of arithmetic and logical operations on numbers. An electronic digital computer performs these operations with electronic circuitry.

File—a group of related data treated as a separate unit. This may be a group of cards or a reel of magnetic tape.

Flowchart—a graphic representation of the sequence of steps involved in the solution of a problem.

FORTRAN—FORmula TRANslator—a compiler language code used to program a problem for processing in a computer and generally associated with scientific problems.

General journal—a general purpose journal to be used for all transactions that cannot be entered in one of the special journals.

Input—data which are transmitted from an external source to the internal storage of the computer.

Instruction—coded information which causes the computer's control unit to perform specified operations.

Keypunch—a machine used to transfer raw data from source documents to a punched card.

Magnetic core—a ring-shaped storage device used in the computer's internal memory system. Information is stored by changing the direction of magnetization of one or more cores.

Magnetic disk—a storage device which contains magnetically recorded data on the surface of a rotating disk.

Magnetic drum—a storage device which contains magnetically recorded data on the surface of a rotating cylinder.

Magnetic tape—a storage device which contains magnetically recorded data on the surface of a plastic ribbon coated with electronically sensitive materials.

Master file—a file containing relatively permanent information which is used as a source of reference and is generally updated periodically.

Memory—see Storage unit.

Minicomputer—a smaller, lower cost computer; usually limited, because of its smaller core storage, to peripheral uses or small businesses.

Output—data which are transferred from the computer after processing. The data may be printed out on reports, punched out on cards, or recorded on an external magnetic storage device.

Payroll journal—a special journal used to record data concerning wages and salaries of employees. Payment also may be shown in the journal.

Peripheral equipment—machines used to prepare and feed information into and receive information from the main internal processing components.

Printout—output in the form of printed pages.

Processing unit—the basic component of a computer; it controls the execution of the program.

Program—a detailed set of instructions in coded form designed for the solution of a problem.

Punched card—a heavy stock paper card containing pre-positioned holes which represent data. This is a basic input-output device.

Purchases journal—a special journal in which all purchases on account of merchandise for resale are recorded.

Random access storage—memory devices such as magnetic drums, magnetic disks, and magnetic cores which can supply information in a time interval which is usually substantially smaller than that possible with serial access devices. No sequential reading of data is required.

Retrieval time—see Access time.

Sales journal—a special journal in which all sales of merchandise on account are recorded.

Service bureau—a large computer facility that rents out time for data processing.

Source documents—documents such as invoices, sales tickets, and cash register tapes which serve as the basis for recording financial transactions in the processing system.

Storage unit—a primary component of a computer; it serves to record and retain data until they are required by and transferred to other areas of the computer.

Subsidiary ledger—a group of related accounts showing the details of the balance of a controlling account in the general ledger.

Sundry accounts—miscellaneous accounts.

Tape drive—the mechanism used to move the magnetic tapes as instructed by the computer's program.

Time-sharing—a technique or system for furnishing computer services to multiple users simultaneously, usually providing rapid responses to each of the users.

DEMONSTRATION PROBLEM

The chapter mentioned (but did not illustrate) that the sales journal and cash receipts journal could be combined.

Required:

Using the data in Illustrations 6.1 and 6.2, prepare a combined sales and cash receipts journal for the John Mason Company. Show all the posting marks as they would be made.

Solution to demonstration problem

COMBINED SALES AND CASH RECEIPTS JOURNAL

101 Cash Dr.	726 Sales Discounts Dr.	111 Accounts Receivable Dr. Amount	✓	Date	Description	Invoice No.	301 Sales Cr.	111 Accounts Receivable Cr. Amount	✓	Sundry Accounts Cr. Acct. No.	Amount	✓
				1981								
10,700.00				Apr. 1	Cash sales		10,700.00					
		30.00	✓	3	Arthur Benson	100		30.00				
		25.00	✓	4	Peter Cote	101		25.00				
29.40	.60			6	Arthur Benson	100				30.00	✓	
10,775.00				7	Cash sales		10,775.00					
6,000.00				10	Sold investments at cost					138*	6,000.00	✓
		130.00	✓	12	Kenneth Johnson	102		130.00				
10,600.00				14	Cash sales		10,600.00					
		10.00	✓	19	Peter Cole	103		10.00				
25.00				19	Peter Cote	101				25.00	✓	
127.40	2.60			20	Kenneth Johnson	102				130.00	✓	
11,045.00				25	Cash sales		11,045.00					
200.00				26	Sold scrap					303*	200.00	✓
		55.00	✓	30	Anthony Demambro	104		55.00				
49,501.80	3.20	250.00					43,370.00	185.00			6,200.00	
(101)	(726)	(111)					(301)	(111)			(✓)	

* 138 Land.
* 303 Miscellaneous Revenue.

QUESTIONS

1. What purposes should a system of internal control accomplish?

2. Name some control documents that are used in merchandise transactions.

3. Identify some features which, if present, would strengthen the internal control system.

4. The processing of data is usually very costly. Why bother with this task?

5. You have applied for a position with a CPA firm in its management services division. Your role will be one of performing services for clients other than the normal auditing and tax services. The partner who is interviewing you asks, "What criteria will you use in deciding whether or not a particular client should be advised to mechanize (computerize) a major share of his data processing?" Your reply?

6. How are an organization chart and a system of internal accounting control related? Why might a firm, even if its management knew how to set up a fool-proof system of internal accounting control, not choose to do so?

7. Describe the purpose of each of the following journals by giving the types of entries that would be recorded in each: sales, purchases, cash receipts, cash disbursements, payroll, and general. Assume the same formats as were illustrated in the chapter.

8. Is the balance of a controlling account equal to the total of its subsidiary accounts at all times? Explain.

9. Why don't the subsidiary accounts receivable and accounts payable accounts usually have account numbers?

10. How can you tell whether the special journal has been completely posted? Describe the posting marks which appear.

11. In the purchases journal illustrated in the chapter, purchases were recorded net of discount. If they had been recorded at gross, what changes would have been made in the design of the cash disbursements journal?

12. A fellow student remarks, "Whoever first thought of dividing the general journal into special journals did so in an effort to reduce posting time and to make data available to more persons at any one time. The next logical step in the process is to eliminate manual journalizing and posting altogether and use a retrieval system which makes information available to any person in the company at any time. In many firms computerized systems are used to accomplish this." Do you agree?

13. How does the use of data processing equipment affect the accounting cycle and objectives of accounting?

14. Discuss the following statement: "Computers are accurate and save time. They, therefore, should be applied to the processing of all accounting data."

15. What is the difference between a management information system and an accounting system?

16. What are the three basic units of a computer and what are their functions?

17. What are the major benefits of a computer system? Can the benefits be evaluated?

18. What is the starting point in designing an information system?

EXERCISES

E-1. Concerning internal control, which of the following statements is incorrect?

a. An example of internal control is where one individual counts the day's cash receipts and a different person compares the total with the total of the cash register tapes.

b. Once an internal control system has been established, it should be effective as long as the formal organization remains unchanged.

c. Broadly speaking, internal control is the general methodology by which the management of an organization is carried on.

d. The purposes of internal control are to check the accuracy of accounting data, safeguard assets against theft, promote efficiency of operations, and ensure that management's policies are being followed.

E-2. You are employed by a company that has three selling departments. You are asked to design a sales journal which will provide a departmental breakdown of credit sales. Give the column headings that you would use and describe how postings would be made.

E-3. State whether each of the following is true or false. If a statement is false, correct the italicized words.

a. When the controlling account balance and the total of the subsidiary accounts are in agreement, it means that *no errors exist in any of these accounts.*

b. The computer may greatly reduce the use of *journals and ledgers appearing in the form illustrated in the chapter.*

E-4. Match each transaction in column A with the appropriate journal in which it would be recorded in column B. Assume each of the journals listed is used as a book of original entry and is designed as illustrated in the chapter.

Column A	*Column B*
1. Acquired merchandise on account.	*a.* Sales journal.
2. Recorded the estimated amount of bad debts.	*b.* Cash receipts journal.
	c. Purchases journal.
3. Recorded the payment of wages.	*d.* Cash disbursements journal.
4. Sold merchandise on account.	*e.* General journal.
5. Sold merchandise for cash.	*f.* Payroll journal.
6. Collected cash on account.	

7. Gave a note to a trade creditor.
8. Received a cash dividend.
9. Sold land and received a note.
10. Paid rent for the month.
11. Received a credit memorandum from a trade creditor.
12. Sent a purchase order to a trade creditor.
13. Paid a trade creditor after the discount period had expired, thereby missing the discount.
14. Recorded payroll for the month.

E-5. Which of the following figures would not be posted to a ledger account?

a. The Cash credit column total in the cash disbursements journal. *yes*

b. The Sundry debit column total in the cash disbursements journal. *No .*

c. The Purchases debit column total in the purchases journal. *yes*

d. The Accounts Receivable debit column total in the sales journal. *yes*

E-6. Describe the first four things you might do if you were to analyze a company's information needs.

PROBLEMS, SERIES A

P6-1-A. On June 30, 1981, the Accounts Receivable controlling account on the books of the Grimes Company was equal to the total of the accounts in the subsidiary accounts receivable ledger. The balances were as follows: Accounts Receivable controlling account (Account No. 131), $8,590; Ferguson, Inc., $3,300; Hanson Products, Inc., $1,540; and Oliva Company, $3,750.

The purpose of this problem is to illustrate both the controlling account principle and the use of separate sales and cash receipts journals.

Prepare a sales journal (see Illustration 6.1) and cash receipts journal (Illustration 6.2). Also set up a general journal.

Required:

Using the following information:

a. Completely journalize each of the transactions in the appropriate journals.

b. Post only the amounts pertaining to accounts receivable to the subsidiary accounts and to the controlling account. You will have to set up some additional subsidiary accounts. Keep all subsidiary accounts in alphabetical order. You will need additional accounts for the Cowden Company, Dorsey Company, and Wills Company.

c. Prepare a schedule of accounts receivable at July 31, 1981, and compare it with the balance of the controlling account at July 31, 1981.

Transactions (ignore the fact that usually the terms to all customers are the same):

July 1   Sales of merchandise on account to Oliva Company, $600; Invoice No. 306; terms, n/30.
   3   Cash sales, $1,725.
   5   Received cash for land sold at its original cost of $2,500.
   5   Received $2,250 cash as partial collection of amount due today from Ferguson, Inc. No discount was allowed.
   8   Received a 30-day, 6 percent note for $1,050 from Ferguson, Inc., in settlement of its account.
   9   Sold merchandise to the Wills Company, $450; Invoice No. 307; terms, 3/10, n/30.
   11   Received $1,509.20 from Hanson Products, Inc. A discount of 2 percent of the account balance was granted.
   16   Sold merchandise to the Cowden Company, $500; Invoice No. 308; terms, n/30.
   18   Sold merchandise to Hanson Products, Inc., $900; Invoice No. 309; terms, n/30.
   20   Issued a credit memorandum to Hanson Products, Inc., for $125 on goods returned to Grimes on Invoice No. 309.
   22   Sold $600 of merchandise to Ferguson, Inc.; Invoice No. 310; terms, n/10.
   23   Received cash of $2,000 on balance due today from Oliva Company. No discount was taken.
   25   Sold $750 of merchandise to Ferguson, Inc.; Invoice No. 311; terms, n/10.
   27   Allowed Ferguson, Inc., credit of $50 on goods sold July 25 and damaged in transit due to faulty packing by Grimes Company.
   31   Sold $650 of merchandise to the Dorsey Company; Invoice No. 312; terms, 2/10, n/30.
   31   Cash sales, $10,300.

P6–2–A. On June 30, 1981, the Accounts Payable controlling account on the books of the Grimes Company was equal to the total of the accounts in the subsidiary accounts payable ledger. The balances were as follows: Accounts Payable controlling account (Account No. 201), $7,750; Cote Company, $3,525; Larson Corporation, $1,225; and Richards Company, $3,000.

The purpose of this problem is to illustrate both the controlling account principle and the use of separate purchases and cash disbursements journals.

Prepare a purchases journal (see Illustration 6.3) and a cash disbursements journal (Illustration 6.4). Also set up a general journal.

Required:

Using the data given below:

a. Completely journalize each of the transactions in the appropriate journal.

b. Post only the amounts pertaining to accounts payable to the subsidiary accounts and to the controlling account. You should arrange all subsidiary accounts in alphabetical order. You will need additional accounts for Aleo Corporation, Ball Company, Hodge Company, and Smith Corporation.

c. Prepare a schedule of accounts payable at July 31, 1981, and compare it with the balance of the controlling account at the same date.

Transactions:

July 1   Purchased merchandise costing $2,500 from the Ball Company; Invoice No. 562; terms, 2/10, n/30. All purchases are recorded net of discount.
   2   Paid the Cote Company $2,500 on account with Check No. 101. No discount was available when the purchase was originally made.
   3   Paid rent with Check No. 102 for the month of July, $300.
   5   Gave the Larson Corporation a 60-day, 6 percent note for the amount owed. A 2 percent discount had been available but was not granted. (The original purchase was for $1,250.)
   6   Purchased merchandise costing $1,250 from the Cote Company; Invoice No. 261; terms, 2/10, n/30.
   9   Paid $1,225 to the Ball Company on the July 1 purchase with Check No. 103.
   11   Paid $1,000 for a life insurance policy on top executives to cover the period from August 1, 1981, to July 31, 1982. Used Check No. 104.
   14   Paid $1,250 to the Ball Company on the July 1 purchase, Check No. 105.
   17   Purchased merchandise costing $2,000 from the Ball Company; Invoice No. 581; terms, 2/10, n/30.
   21   Received a credit memorandum from the Richards Company for $500 on merchandise returned to it. No discount was available as of the date of purchase.
   23   Purchased merchandise costing $750 from the Aleo Corporation; Invoice No. 1031; terms, n/30.
   25   Paid $1,500 to Richards Company on account with Check No. 106. No discount was allowed as of the date of purchase.
   27   Purchased merchandise costing $1,750 from the Smith Corporation; Invoice No. 328; terms, 2/10, n/30.
   29   Paid the Ball Company $1,000 on the purchase of July 17, Check No. 107.
   31   Purchased merchandise costing $2,000 from the Hodge Company; Invoice No. 168; terms, 2/20, n/60.

P6–3–A. The Demonstration Problem of this chapter included an illustration of a combined sales and cash receipts journal and the chapter mentioned (but did not illustrate) the use of a combined purchases and cash disbursements journal.

Required:

a. Set up a *combined* sales and cash receipts journal similar to that shown in the Demonstration Problem.

b. Design a *combined* purchases (Illustration 6.3) and cash disbursements (Illustration 6.4) journal.

c. Set up a two-column general journal.

d. Journalize the transactions shown in Problems 6–1–A and 6–2–A in the journals you have created.

e. Post the amounts to the general ledger accounts shown below. You do not have to post to subsidiary accounts, but place the appropriate posting marks in the journals as if you had.

f. Prepare a trial balance as of July 31, 1981.

g. Why are combined journals not always used?

Account No.	Account title	Assumed June 30, 1981, balances
130	Cash	$ 7,500
131	Accounts Receivable	8,590
132	Notes Receivable	–0–
133	Unexpired Insurance	–0–
150	Land	2,500
		$18,590
200	Accounts Payable	$ 7,750
201	Notes Payable	–0–
250	B. Grimes, Capital	10,840
		$18,590
300	Sales	
304	Sales Returns and Allowances	
307	Sales Discounts	
400	Purchases	
405	Purchase Returns and Allowances	
406	Discounts Lost	
407	Rent Expense	

P6–4–A. The Stevens Company uses five journals as records of original entry. They are as follows: sales journal, purchases journal, cash receipts journal, cash disbursements journal, and general journal. At December 31, 1981, the column totals in the sales journal were as follows:

| Accounts Receivable | Sales | | | | | |
	Men's Clothing	Women's Clothing	Appliances	Furniture	Bargain Basement	Other
225,500	40,000	45,000	35,000	60,000	30,000	15,500

The column totals in the purchases journal at December 31, 1981, were as follows:

Purchases						Accounts Payable
Men's Clothing	Women's Clothing	Appliances	Furniture	Bargain Basement	Other	
52,500	54,000	27,500	51,000	37,500	21,750	244,250

The totals of the cash receipts journal columns were as follows:

Cash	Sales Discounts	Sales						Accounts Receivable	Sundry Accounts
		Men's Clothing	Women's Clothing	Appliances	Furniture	Bargain Basement	Other		
333,000	3,075	22,500	25,000	20,000	32,500	12,000	13,500	192,825	17,750

The entries in the Sundry Accounts column result from the collection of $13,000 of rental revenue, $4,500 on notes receivable, and $250 of interest revenue. The totals of the cash disbursements journal columns were:

Accounts Payable	Discounts Lost	Salaries Payable	Sundry Accounts	Cash
190,000	1,500	27,500	22,775	241,775

The entries in the Sundry Accounts column result from the payment of $1,275 for ordinary repairs to the buildings and $21,500 for the purchase of a warehouse.

The general journal includes the following entries at various dates during the year:

Notes Receivable	3,000	
Accounts Receivable		3,000
Office Equipment	4,000	
Notes Payable		4,000
Accounts Payable	250	
Notes Payable		250
Salaries Expense	34,000	
Federal Income Tax Withheld		5,575
Social Security Tax Withheld		925
Salaries Payable		27,500

An abbreviated trial balance of the general ledger immediately prior to posting the above journals for the year was as follows:

STEVENS COMPANY
Trial Balance
December 31, 1981

	Debits	Credits
Cash	$ 35,000	
Accounts receivable	27,500	
Notes receivable	2,500	
Inventory—men's clothing	7,500	
Inventory—women's clothing	9,000	
Inventory—appliances	6,000	
Inventory—furniture	14,000	
Inventory—bargain basement	3,500	
Inventory—other	2,500	
Office equipment (combined)	6,000	
Buildings (combined)	112,500	
Accounts payable		$ 21,750
Notes payable		125
L. Stevens, capital		204,125
	$226,000	$226,000

Required:

a. Present the general ledger of the Stevens Company, including the balances in the above trial balance and postings based on the other data given in the problem. After posting, prepare a trial balance.

b. Given the following data, compute the gross margin for each of the departments (ignore sales discounts):

Department	Ending inventory
Men's clothing	$10,000
Women's clothing	7,500
Appliances	2,500
Furniture	5,000
Bargain basement	1,500
Other	2,000

P6–5–A. The Crawford Company uses special journals for purchases, sales, cash receipts, and cash disbursements, as well as a general journal. These journals follow the same general design as those illustrated in this chapter.

Required:

a. Enter the following transactions for December 1981 in the proper journals. Purchases are recorded at net. (All journals are to be numbered page 4.)

b. Post the entries to the general ledger accounts shown below. (There would be beginning balances in the accounts, but they may be ignored.)

c. Prepare a trial balance as of the end of the period.

General ledger accounts:

1. Cash.
2. Accounts Receivable.
3. Notes Receivable.
4. Office Equipment.
5. Accounts Payable.
6. Salaries Payable.
7. Federal Income Tax Withheld.
8. Social Security Tax Withheld.
9. Notes Payable.
10. Sales.
11. Sales Discounts.
12. Purchases.
13. Discounts Lost.
14. Salaries Expense.
15. Advertising Expense.
16. Rental Revenue.

Transactions:

Dec. 1 Bought goods for resale from Mason Company, $2,800; Invoice No. C1109; terms, 2/10, n/30.

2 Purchased goods for resale from Lenz Company, $1,600; Invoice No. 1888Z; terms, ten days.

3 Bought office equipment for use from Krogman Company, $3,880; Invoice No. 854. Gave a 30-day, 4 percent note in payment.

5 Bought goods for resale from Gordon Company, $2,200; Invoice No. X9784; terms, 2/10, n/30.

6 Cash sales, $2,840.

7 Collected rent revenue for December, $3,800.

8 Sold $2,000 of merchandise on account to Davitt, Inc.; Invoice No. 3345; terms, 2/10, n/30.

9 Collected $3,000 on an overdue account receivable from T. Raia.

10 Sold $2,800 of merchandise on account to Porter Company; Invoice No. 3346; terms, 2/10, n/30.

11 Sold $3,200 of merchandise on account to Zinn Company; Invoice No. 3347; terms, 2/10, n/30.

12 Paid Mason Company for purchase of December 1 with Check No. 201.

Dec. 12 Paid Lenz Company for purchase of December 2 with Check No. 202.

14 Paid Gordon Company for purchase of December 5 with Check No. 203.

15 Received a 5 percent, 60-day note in settlement of an old account receivable from M. Conrad, $4,400.

16 Cash sales, $7,880.

17 Incurred salaries expense for first half of month of $8,200. Out of this gross amount $800 was withheld for federal income tax and $200 was withheld for social security taxes. (Record this entry in the general journal.) This amount payable was paid with Check Nos. 204–214.

18 Collected amount due on sale of December 8 to Davitt, Inc.

20 Collected amount due on sale of December 10 to Porter Company.

21 Collected amount due on sale of December 11 to Zinn Company.

22 Received a 5 percent, 60-day note in settlement of an old account receivable from T. Elliot, $2,820.

23 Cash sales, $5,000.

24 Paid *Jamestown Post Journal* for advertising expense, $3,020 (Check No. 215).

26 Sold $2,400 of merchandise on account to Zinn Company; Invoice No. 3348; terms, 2/10, n/30.

26 Sold $5,600 on account to Baker Company; Invoice No. 3349; terms, 2/10, n/30.

27 Sold $11,880 on account to Cole Company; Invoice No. 3350; terms, 2/10, n/30.

31 Incurred salaries expense of $12,000. Out of this amount $900 was withheld for federal tax and $300 for social security tax. The amounts due were paid with Check Nos. 216–226. (Journalize the expense incurred in the general journal and the payment in the cash disbursements journal.)

P6–6–A. Jim Brunswick, the owner and operator of the Strike-Spare Bowling Lanes, has been using a general journal to record all business transactions. The posting task has taken an increasing amount of his time. He asks your assistance in designing special journals which would make the task less time consuming.

His wife is to handle all of the credit purchases, cash disbursements, and adjusting entries in her office at home. Jim or his assistant will record all sales and cash receipts at the bowling lanes.

Sales are classified as follows: Bowling Fees, Equipment, Supplies, Shoe Rental, and Miscellaneous Services. (The adjoining restaurant and bar are owned and operated by another party.) Sales are made for both cash and credit. No sales discounts are offered.

Purchases are made from various suppliers. They are recorded at gross invoice price. Perpetual inventory procedure is used for bowling equipment. The entries debiting Cost of Goods Sold and crediting Merchandise Inventory—Equipment are to be made in the general journal. Periodic inventory procedure is used for supplies.

The assistant is paid once a week. The entry establishing the amount payable is to be made in the general journal.

Required:

a. Determine which special journals should be used.

b. Show the column headings which could be used in each of the special journals. Illustrate the use of the special journals by journalizing a sufficient number of assumed transactions for 1981 so that at least one number appears in each of the columns you have designed.

c. Describe the posting of each of the special journals you have designed.

P6–7–A.

Required:

Cite some of the factors that you feel would be important in deciding whether a company should utilize an accounting (bookkeeping) machine; a time-sharing facility; a service bureau; or a computer system installed at the firm.

PROBLEMS, SERIES B

P6–1–B. On August 31, 1981, the Accounts Receivable controlling account on the books of the Colt Company was equal to the total of the accounts in the subsidiary accounts receivable ledger.

The balance on August 31, 1981, in the Accounts Receivable controlling account (Account No. 120) is $45,000. The balances in the Accounts Receivable subsidiary ledger accounts are Ball Corporation, $18,000; Sanders Company, $15,000; and West Corporation, $12,000.

The purpose of this problem is to illustrate both the controlling account principle and the use of separate sales and cash receipts journals.

Prepare a sales journal (see Illustration 6.1) and cash receipts journal (Illustration 6.2). Then set up a general journal.

Required:

Using the following information:

a. Journalize completely the transactions in the appropriate journals.

b. Post only the amounts pertaining to accounts receivable to the subsidiary accounts and to the controlling account. You will have to prepare additional subsidiary accounts and should keep them all in alphabetical order. You will need additional accounts for Allen Company, Niles Corporation, and York Company.

c. Prepare a schedule of accounts receivable at September 30, 1981, and compare it with the balance of the controlling account at that same date.

Transactions (ignore the fact that normally the terms to all customers are the same):

Sept. 1 Received $6,860 from the Sanders Company. A discount of $140 had been taken.

Sept. 2 On this date, merchandise was sold for $11,000 to the Allen Company; Invoice No. 501; terms, 2/20, n/30.
4 Cash sales, $25,000.
7 Received $9,000 on account from the Ball Corporation. No discount was taken.
8 Received $20,000 cash for land sold at a gain of $5,000.
10 Received a 60-day, 5 percent note from Ball Corporation for the remainder of the amount due.
12 Sold merchandise to the Sanders Company, $9,000; Invoice No. 502; terms, n/30.
15 Received payment for $5,000 worth of the merchandise purchased on September 2 by the Allen Company. The discount was taken on this payment.
18 Sold merchandise to the Niles Corporation, $34,000; Invoice No. 503; terms, n/30.
21 Cash sales, $57,000.
23 Issued a credit memorandum to Niles Corporation for $1,000 for goods returned.
26 Sold merchandise to the York Company, $10,000; Invoice No. 504; terms, 2/20, n/30.
29 Received $10,000 cash from the Niles Corporation to apply against the amount due on Invoice No. 503.
30 Cash sales, $39,000.

P6–2–B. On August 31, 1981, the Accounts Payable controlling account on the books of the Colt Company was equal to the total of the accounts in the subsidiary accounts payable ledger. The balances were as follows: Accounts Payable controlling account (Account No. 220), $36,000; Frewsburg Company, $16,000; Maplehurst Corporation, $12,160; and Warren Corporation, $7,840.

The purpose of this problem is to illustrate both the controlling account principle and the use of separate purchases and cash disbursements journals.

Prepare a purchases journal (see Illustration 6.3) and

cash disbursements journal (Illustration 6.4). Also set up a two-column general journal.

Required:

Using the data given below:

a. Completely journalize each of the transactions in the appropriate journals.

b. Post only the amounts pertaining to accounts payable to the subsidiary accounts and to the controlling account. You will have to create some additional subsidiary accounts. You should arrange all subsidiary accounts in alphabetical order. You will need additional accounts for Bemus Point Corporation, Celeron Company, Jamestown Corporation, Kane Company, and Moonbrook Company.

c. Prepare a schedule of accounts payable at September 30, 1981, and compare it with the balance of the controlling account at the same date.

Transactions:

Sept. 1 Purchased merchandise costing $15,000 from the Celeron Company; Invoice No. 542; terms, 2/10, n/30. All purchases are recorded net of discount.

3 Paid the Warren Corporation $8,000 with Check No. 451. The original discount of 2 percent was not taken, as the discount period had expired.

4 Paid rent for the month of September, $500, with Check No. 452.

5 Paid the Frewsburg Company $9,000 on account with Check No. 453. No discount was available as of the date of purchase.

6 Gave the Frewsburg Company a $7,000, 30-day, 5 percent note for the balance due.

7 Purchased merchandise costing $8,000 from the Jamestown Corporation; Invoice No. 982; terms, 2/10, n/30.

8 Purchased merchandise costing $9,000 from the Warren Corporation; Invoice No. 1522; terms, 2/10, n/30.

9 Received a credit memorandum from the Jamestown Corporation for $1,000 of the $8,000 of merchandise purchased.

12 Paid the Celeron Company the amount due on the purchase of September 1 with Check No. 454.

15 Purchased merchandise costing $12,000 from the Bemus Point Corporation; Invoice No. 841; terms, n/30.

17 Paid Warren Corporation the amount due on the purchase of September 8 with Check No. 455.

20 Purchased merchandise costing $13,000 from the Warren Corporation; Invoice No. 1566; terms, 2/10, n/30.

22 Purchased merchandise costing $7,000 from the Moonbrook Company; Invoice No. 1910; terms, n/30.

25 Paid $8,000 on account to the Bemus Point Corporation on the purchase of September 15 with Check No. 456.

29 Received a credit memorandum for $3,000 from the Warren Corporation relating to the purchase of September 20.

30 Purchased merchandise having a cost of $5,000 from the Kane Company; Invoice No. 2125; terms, n/60.

P6–3–B. The Demonstration Problem of this chapter included an illustration of a combined sales and cash receipts journal and the chapter mentioned (but did not illustrate) the use of a combined purchases and cash disbursements journal.

Required:

a. Set up a *combined* sales and cash receipts journal similar to that shown in the demonstration problem.

b. Design a *combined* purchases (see Illustration 6.3) and cash disbursements (Illustration 6.4) journal.

c. Set up a two-column general journal.

d. Journalize the transactions shown in Problems 6–1–B and 6–2–B in the journals you have created.

e. Post the amounts to the general ledger accounts shown below. You do not have to post to subsidiary accounts, but place the appropriate posting marks in the journals as if you had.

f. Prepare a trial balance as of September 30, 1981.

g. Why are combined journals not always used?

Account No.	Account name	Assumed balances on August 31, 1981
110	Cash	$ 40,000
120	Accounts Receivable	45,000
132	Notes Receivable	–0–
150	Land	15,000
		$100,000
220	Accounts Payable	$ 36,000
221	Notes Payable	–0–
250	A. Colt, Capital	64,000
		$100,000
300	Sales	
303	Sales Returns and Allowances	
307	Sales Discounts	
400	Purchases	
404	Purchase Returns and Allowances	
406	Discounts Lost	
407	Rent Expense	
408	Gain on Sale of Land	

P6–4–B. The Jeffries Company uses five journals as records of original entry. They are as follows: sales journal, purchases journal, cash receipts journal, cash disbursements journal, and general journal. At December 31, 1981, the column totals in the sales journal were as follows:

Accounts Receivable	Sales					
	Men's Clothing	Women's Clothing	Shoes	Cosmetics and Jewelry	Sporting Goods	Miscellaneous
40,500	10,000	12,500	4,200	4,000	7,800	2,000

The column totals in the purchases journal at December 31, 1981, were as follows:

Purchases						Accounts Payable
Men's Clothing	Women's Clothing	Shoes	Cosmetics and Jewelry	Sporting Goods	Miscellaneous	
14,000	19,000	6,000	7,500	13,900	4,000	64,400

The totals of the cash receipts journal columns were as follows:

Cash	Sales Discounts	Sales						Accounts Receivable	Sundry Accounts
		Men's Clothing	Women's Clothing	Shoes	Cosmetics and Jewelry	Sporting Goods	Miscellaneous		
70,100	560	6,000	8,000	3,300	6,000	3,200	4,000	36,000	4,160

The entries in the Sundry Accounts column result from the collection of $3,000 on notes receivable, $160 of interest revenue, and $1,000 of revenue from the operation of a delivery service for other companies. The totals of the cash disbursements journal columns were as follows:

Accounts Payable	Discounts Lost	Salaries Payable	Sundry Accounts	Cash
55,700	1,400	9,700	7,900	74,700

The entries in the Sundry Accounts column result from the payment of $960 for a delivery truck and $6,940 for the purchase of a garage.

The two-column general journal includes the following summarized entries during the fiscal year:

Notes Receivable	4,040	
Accounts Receivable		4,040
Buildings	8,700	
Notes Payable		8,700

Salaries Expense	12,060	
Federal Income Tax Withheld		2,050
Social security Tax Withheld		310
Salaries Payable		9,700

An abbreviated trial balance of the general ledger immediately prior to posting the above journals for the year was as follows:

JEFFRIES COMPANY
Trial Balance
December 31, 1981

	Debits	Credits
Cash	$17,500	
Accounts receivable	12,000	
Notes receivable	4,400	
Inventory—men's clothing	6,000	
Inventory—women's clothing	10,000	
Inventory—shoes	1,000	
Inventory—cosmetics and jewelry	4,000	
Inventory—sporting goods	5,500	
Inventory—miscellaneous	1,300	
Office equipment (combined)	3,300	
Buildings (combined)	30,300	
Accounts payable		$10,100
Notes payable		1,000
A. Jeffries, capital		84,200
	$95,300	$95,300

Required:

a. Present the general ledger of the Jeffries Company, including the balances in the above trial balance and postings based on the other data given in the problem.

After posting, prepare a trial balance.

b. Assuming the following ending inventory amounts, prepare a statement showing the gross margin of each department (ignore sales discounts):

Department	Ending inventory
Men's clothing	$ 7,500
Women's clothing	5,000
Shoes	2,000
Cosmetics and jewelry	7,000
Sporting goods	10,000
Miscellaneous	1,000

P6–5–B. Roxa, Inc., uses special journals for purchases, sales, cash receipts, and cash disbursements as well as a general journal. These journals follow the same general design as those illustrated in this chapter.

Required:

a. Enter the following transactions for August 1981 in the proper journals. Purchases are recorded at net.

b. Post the entries to the general ledger accounts shown below. (All journal pages are to be numbered page 5. There would be beginning balances in the accounts but they may be ignored.)

c. Prepare a trial balance as of the end of the period.

General ledger accounts:

1. Cash.
2. Accounts Receivable.
3. Notes Receivable.
4. Office Equipment.
5. Accounts Payable.
6. Salaries Payable.
7. Federal Income Tax Withheld.
8. Social Security Tax Withheld.
9. Notes Payable.
10. Sales.
11. Sales Discounts.
12. Purchases.
13. Discounts Lost.
14. Salaries Expense.
15. Delivery Expense.
16. Advertising Expense.
17. Rental Revenue.

Transactions:

Aug. 1 Sold Allen, Inc., $3,000 of merchandise; terms, 2/10, n/30; Invoice No. WI-A1.
3 Bought merchandise from the Dunn Company; Invoice No. 33-NP; terms, ten days, $2,100.
5 Cash sales, $9,500.
9 Rent revenue received, $400.
10 Salaries expense incurred was $2,750. Amounts withheld were $150 for federal income tax and $100 for social security tax. (Record this in the general journal.) The net amount payable was also paid on this date with Check Nos. 121–131.
11 Collected from Allen, Inc., for sale of August 1. Discount allowed.
11 Paid for office equipment received today, $1,200 (Check No. 132).
12 Paid Dunn Company for purchase of August 3 (Check No. 133).
14 Sold $2,000 of merchandise to Landry, Inc.; Invoice No. WI-A2; terms, 2/10, n/30.
15 Sold $700 of merchandise to Franks Company; Invoice No. WI-A3; terms, 2/10, n/30.
15 Bought merchandise from Dunn Company, $990; Invoice No. 34-VX; terms, 2/10, n/30.
17 Bought merchandise from Green Company, $1,500; Invoice No. 98-VX; terms, 2/10, n/30.
18 Bought office equipment today for $950 and gave a 30-day, 4 percent note in payment.
19 Received a note receivable (6 percent, 90 days) for an old account receivable (Fred Williams) in the amount of $350.
19 Cash sales, $1,800.
20 Collected $770 on an overdue account receivable from James Lynn.
21 Cash sales, $1,120.
22 Cash sales, $300.

Aug. 23 Collected net amount due from Landry, Inc., on sale of August 14.

24 Collected net amount due from Franks Company on sale of August 15.

26 Paid Dunn Company on invoice of August 15 (Check No. 134).

26 Paid Green Company on invoice of August 17 (Check No. 135).

26 Incurred salaries expense of $3,000. Amounts withheld were $200 for federal income tax and $100 for social security tax (Record this in the general journal.) The net amount payable was paid on·this date with Check Nos. 136–146.

28 Paid delivery expense in cash, $400 (Check No. 147).

28 Paid advertising expense in cash, $800 (Check No. 148).

29 Sold $3,700 worth of merchandise to the Franks Company; Invoice No. WI-A4; terms, 2/10, n/30.

30 Sold $4,900 worth of merchandise to Landry, Inc.; Invoice No. WI-A5; terms, 2/10, n/30.

31 Bought merchandise from the Dunn Company, $890; Invoice No. 137-NP; terms, ten days.

P6–6–B. Bill Strausbaugh, the golf professional at the Plushmore Country Club, has been using a general journal to record all business transactions. But the volume of business has been increasing, and he seeks your assistance in devising some special journals. He wants his wife to keep track of all receipts, disbursements, and adjusting entries in her office at home. He and his assistant are to record all credit sales and purchases at the golf shop.

Sales are classified as follows: Golf Equipment, Golf Supplies, Apparel, Lessons, Cart Rental, and Miscellaneous Services. Sales are made for both cash and on account. No sales discounts are offered.

Purchases are made from many different suppliers. They are recorded at gross invoice price. Periodic inventory procedure is used for apparel and golf supplies; perpetual inventory procedure is used for golf equipment. The ·entries debiting Cost of Goods Sold and crediting Merchandise Inventory—Equipment are to be made in the general journal.

The golf pro's assistant is paid each week. The general journal is. to be used to record the amount payable.

Required:

a. Determine which special journals should be used.

b. Show the column headings which could be used in each of the special journals. Illustrate the use of each special journal by journalizing enough assumed transactions for 1981 so that at least one number appears in each of the columns you have designed.

c. Describe the posting of each of the special journals you have designed.

P6–7–B.

Required:

Discuss the importance of the "user" in an information system. Identify those people you feel are the main users of accounting information. Explain how the computer may be helpful in meeting some of their needs.

BUSINESS DECISION PROBLEM 6–1

During World War II a managerial accountant in the United States was called back to active duty with the Army. An acquaintance of the accountant forged papers and assumed the identity of the accountant. He obtained a position in a small firm as the only accountant. Eventually he took over (from the manager) the functions of approving bills for payment, preparing and signing checks, and almost all other financial duties. On one weekend he traveled to some neighboring cities and prepared and mailed invoices made out to the company he worked for. On Monday morning he returned to work and began receiving, approving, and paying the invoices he had prepared. The following weekend he returned to the neighboring cities and cashed and deposited the checks in bank accounts under his own signature card. After continuing this practice for several months, he withdrew all of the funds and never was heard from again. Discuss some of the steps which could have been taken to prevent this theft. Remember that it is a small firm with limited financial resources.

BUSINESS DECISION PROBLEM 6–2

You are the manager of a restaurant which serves liquor. Your accountant comes in once a year and prepares financial statements and the tax return. In the current year you have a feeling that even though business seems good, net earnings are going to be lower. You ask the accountant to prepare condensed statements on a monthly basis. All sales are priced to yield an estimated gross margin of 40 percent. You and your accountant and several of the accountant's assistants take physical inventories at the end of each of the four months indicated below. The resulting sales, cost of goods sold, and gross margins are as follows:

What would you suspect after analyzing these reports? What sales control procedures would you recommend to correct the bad situation? How could the monthly reports have been summarized so that the relationships would have been more obvious?

	March		April		May		June	
	Restaurant	Bar	Restaurant	Bar	Restaurant	Bar	Restaurant	Bar
Sales	$29,040	$42,400	$31,240	$34,200	$30,480	$31,200	$33,000	$28,400
Cost of goods sold	18,620	25,200	19,040	24,800	18,380	24,600	20,400	24,900
Gross margin	$10,420	$17,200	$12,200	$ 9,400	$12,100	$ 6,600	$12,600	$ 3,500

PART THREE

ASSETS AND LIABILITIES

Chapter 7

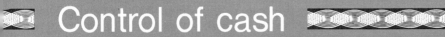

Control of cash

Cash includes currency, coin, negotiable instruments (such as checks, bank drafts, and money orders), amounts in checking or savings accounts at a bank, and demand certificates of deposit at a bank. Cash does *not* include such items as postage stamps, IOUs, and notes receivable. Cash is usually divided into cash on hand and cash in banks. But in financial reporting these are combined into one amount and reported as "cash."

Many business transactions involve cash. Also, cash is the most useful item for someone to steal since it can be used to obtain anything else. Therefore management must keep close control over cash and account for it carefully.

The objectives of management in regard to cash are the following:

1. Account for all cash transactions accurately so that management will have correct information regarding cash.
2. Make sure there is enough cash to pay bills as they come due.
3. Avoid holding excessive amounts of idle cash which could be invested in productive assets to increase earnings.
4. Prevent the loss of cash due to theft or fraud.

Most of a firm's cash transactions involve a bank checking account. It deposits its daily receipts into a checking account and writes checks on that account to pay its bills. Periodically, the firm's account and the bank's account are reconciled to make sure that no errors have been made. Therefore, in this chapter significant attention is given to the checking account portion of cash. But first, we examine the procedures used to control cash receipts and cash disbursements to prevent error, theft, and fraud. Petty cash and the voucher system are the other topics covered in this chapter.

CONTROLLING CASH RECEIPTS

From the moment cash is received until it is deposited in the bank, it should be safeguarded completely. While cash is of no more importance than inventory, it is stolen more easily because it can be concealed and is not readily identifiable.

The methods used to control cash receipts vary with each business. Therefore, the following description of the internal control of cash receipts may be varied in practice to suit the individual needs of each business. A few basic principles for controlling cash receipts follow.

1. A record of all cash receipts should be prepared as soon as the cash is received. Most thefts of cash receipts occur before a record is made of the receipt. Once a record is made, improper uses are more readily traceable.
2. All cash receipts should be deposited intact in the bank, preferably on the next business day or in the bank's night depository on the same day. Cash disbursements should not be made from cash receipts but only by check or from petty cash funds. In many retail stores, refunds for returned merchandise are made from the cash register. If this practice is followed, refund tickets should be prepared and approved by another employee.
3. The person who handles the cash receipts should not record them in

the accounting records, and the company accountant should not have access to the cash receipts.

4. If possible—and it is possible in all but small concerns—the internal function of receiving cash should be separated from the internal function of disbursing cash.

CONTROLLING CASH DISBURSEMENTS

The functions of handling cash receipts and cash disbursements should be completely separated. The procedures to control cash disbursements are the following:

1. With the exception of petty cash disbursements, all disbursements should be by check. No cash receipts should be disbursed.
2. All checks should be prenumbered—consecutively—and all should be controlled and accounted for by a responsible individual.
3. Preferably, two signatures should appear on each check.
4. If possible, the person who approves payment should not be one of those who signs the checks.
5. Each check should be supported by approved invoices or approved vouchers (authorizations to draw the checks).
6. The person authorizing the disbursement of cash should be certain that payment is in order and that it is made to the proper payee.
7. Invoices and vouchers should be indelibly stamped "paid," together with the date and check number. This minimizes the risk of paying the same debt more than once.
8. The person signing the checks should not have access to returned checks paid by the bank.
9. The bookkeeper should obtain the bank statement and the paid checks and prepare the bank reconciliation statement.
10. All voided and spoiled checks should be retained and mutilated to prevent their unauthorized use.

The operation of a voucher system which may be used to provide close control over cash disbursements is discussed later in this chapter. The special journals used in such a system are a voucher register and a check register.

THE BANK CHECKING ACCOUNT: The signature card

A bank must account to its depositors for all funds received from and spent for them. Certain business papers are involved.

A bank requires a new depositor to complete a signature card giving signatures of persons authorized to sign checks on the account. The signature card is retained at the bank to identify the signatures as they appear on returned checks drawn on the bank.

Bank deposit tickets

When a deposit is made in the bank, the depositor prepares a *deposit ticket.* Deposit tickets come in many forms but generally include the name of the account, the account number, the amount of cash deposited, and a listing of the checks deposited. In modern machine-based bank accounting systems, each depositor is given a number of deposit tickets imprinted with the depositor's name and account number. When making a deposit, the depositor receives a machine-imprinted receipt showing the date and the amount of the deposit.

The bank check

There are three parties to every bank check transaction: (1) the depositor issuing the check, (2) the bank on which the check is drawn, and (3) the party to whose order the check is made payable.

A check is a written order on a bank to pay a specific sum of money to the party designated (called the payee) or to his or her order. It is signed by the person issuing the check.

The type of check often used by modern business firms is prenumbered when printed. It is prepared in sets of an original and as many copies as are needed. The lower section of the check is known as a *remittance advice* and is detached prior to the depositing of the check. The remittance advice contains information explaining the check.

The checking account statement

The bank furnishes each checking account depositor with a *bank statement,* one form of which is shown in Illustration 7.1. Usually it is issued once each month.

The bank statement shows *(a)* each deposit made during the period, *(b)* each check which cleared during the period, and *(c)* a daily balance of the account whenever it changes. Any debit memoranda (amounts deducted from the account, such as for *service charges*) and credit memoranda (amounts added to the account, such as for the proceeds of notes collected for the depositor by the bank) also will be shown.

Copies of the deposit tickets and the checks paid by the bank during the month will also be returned to the depositor with the bank statement.

Reconciling the bank statement and Cash account balances

The balance shown by the bank statement usually will differ from the balance for the same date in the depositor's ledger account for cash in bank. The reasons for this difference include the following:

1. Items that cause a larger balance to be shown on the bank's statement than in the depositor's ledger account:
    a. Checks issued by the depositor which are still outstanding; the payees have not presented the checks to the bank for payment.
    b. Deposits made in the depositor's account by the bank for which entries have not been made on the depositor's books. For example, the bank may collect a note for the depositor, add it to the depositor's balance, and advise the depositor of the collection immediately; the depositor may not yet have recorded the amount in its accounting records.
2. Items that cause a smaller balance to be shown on the bank's statement than in the depositor's ledger account:
    a. Deposits recorded on the depositor's books which are in transit (have not yet been recorded by the bank). They are picked up as deposits on the next period's bank statement.
    b. Bank charges for services rendered by the bank to the depositor which

Illustration 7.1: Bank statement

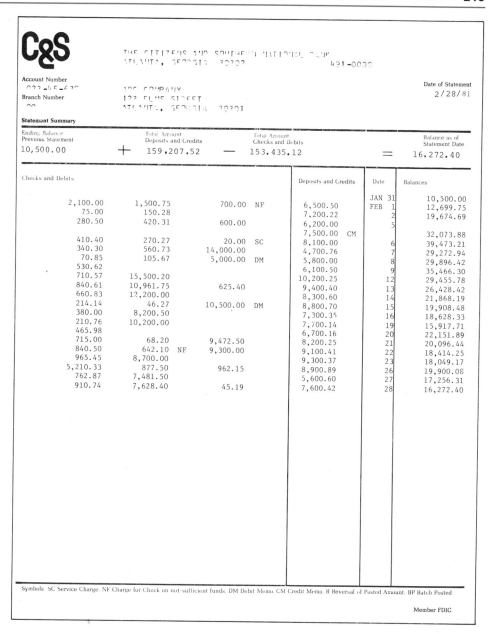

have been deducted from the bank balance but which have not been credited to cash on the books of the depositor. Notice of these deductions is included with the bank statement in the form of debit memoranda. Examples of these deductions are service charges for checks and deposits (when the daily balance in an account is below the minimum required by the bank) and charges for collecting notes.

c. Deductions for *N.S.F.* (not sufficient funds) *checks.* These are checks which were received from customers and were deposited. When the check arrived at the bank which was ordered to pay the funds there were insufficient funds to cover the check. Since the customer has not satisfied the debt, the company needs to reestablish the account receivable.

Incorrect entries on the bank's books or on the depositor's books may cause errors in either balance. As a result of these various items, neither the bank statement nor the depositor's ledger account shows the exact expendable balance of cash that should appear on the balance sheet. Correcting entries should be made to reflect items 1 *(b),* 2 *(b),* and 2 *(c)* on the depositor's records, along with the correction of errors made on the depositor's records.

The bank reconciliation statement

A *bank reconciliation statement* is prepared to explain the difference between the cash balance on the books and on the bank statement. Both the bank statement balance and the balance in the Cash ledger account are adjusted to the true balance of expendable cash that should appear on the balance sheet as shown in Illustration 7.2.

Illustration 7.2: Bank reconciliation statement

| ATLANTA COMPANY |
| Bank Reconciliation Statement |
| August 31, 1981 |

Balance per bank statement			Balance per ledger		
August 31, 1981	$23,195.85		August 31, 1981		$22,009.85
Add: Deposit in transit	1,057.05		Add: Note collected		
	$24,252.90		by bank		800.00
					$22,809.85
Less: Outstanding checks	1,645.55		Less: Bank charges	$ 2.50	
			N.S.F. check . .	200.00	202.50
Adjusted balance,			Adjusted balance,		
August 31, 1981	$22,607.35		August 31, 1981		$22,607.35

The first step in preparing the reconciliation statement is to examine the bank statement and the debit and credit memoranda, if any, returned with the statement. The depositor's accounting records should be examined to see if the items referred to in these memoranda have been recorded. If they have not, they must be added to or deducted from the balance in the Cash account, as shown by the adjustments for $800 for the note collected, $2.50 for bank service charges, and $200 for the N.S.F. check in Illustration 7.2.

The second step is to sort the canceled checks returned by the bank into numerical order. The outstanding checks are identified by a process of elimination. The numbers of the checks which have cleared and been returned by the bank are compared with the numbers of the checks issued. Tick marks (√) are used in the books to indicate those returned. The checks issued for which no canceled checks have been returned from the bank are the *outstanding checks.* Checks outstanding at the start of the month which have cleared the bank during the month may be traced to the reconciliation statement prepared at the end of the preceding month. Any checks outstanding at the end of the preceding month which have not yet been returned during the current month are, of course, still outstanding at the end of the current month.

The next step in preparing the reconciliation statement is to see if there are any *deposits in transit* to the bank. The receipts for the last day of the month might have been deposited in the night depository box at the bank. Thus, they would be reported as a deposit by the bank as of the next day. The debits to the Cash account can be traced to the individual deposits per the bank statement.

Deposits in transit and outstanding checks, together with the bank service charges indicated on the bank statement, will often account entirely for the difference between the balance in the bank statement and the balance in the Cash account. Any omissions and errors in the depositor's books are corrected by proper entries. These entries should be made prior to the preparation of the financial statements. If any errors made by the bank are discovered in preparing the reconciliation statement (such as charging a check against the wrong account), they should be called to the attention of the bank.

To illustrate the preparation of a bank reconciliation statement, assume that the bank statement of the Atlanta Company at August 31, 1981, showed a balance of $23,195.85; the Cash account balance of the depositor at the same date was $22,009.85. By comparing the canceled checks returned by the bank with the accounting records, the following checks were found to be outstanding at the end of the month:

Check No.	Amount
556	$ 840.00
570	354.25
571	451.30
	$1,645.55

An examination of the debit and credit memoranda returned with the bank statement reveals a credit memorandum showing that the bank had collected a customer's note for the Atlanta Company and had credited the amount collected, $800, to the company's account. (A credit memorandum is evidence of an addition to a depositor's account which arises from a transaction other than a normal deposit.) For this service, the bank charged the Atlanta Company $2.50 and so advised the company by including a debit memorandum for that amount with the canceled checks returned on August 31, 1981. There was another debit memorandum in the amount of $200 for an N.S.F. check received from Rook Company on August 10 and deposited on that date.

A tracing of the deposits shown in the accounting records to the bank statement revealed that cash receipts for August 31, $1,057.05, did not appear as a deposit on that date. Examination of the deposit ticket showed that the bank recorded the deposit on September 1.

The statement reconciling the balance per the bank statement with the balance per Cash account as of August 31, 1981 (Illustration 7.2), shows that the cash available for immediate disbursement is not $22,009.85 or $23,195.85, but $22,607.35. Consequently, the following journal entries must be prepared and posted:

Cash	800.00	
Notes Receivable		800.00
To record note collected by bank.		
Bank Service Charges	2.50	
Cash		2.50
To record bank collection charges.		
Accounts Receivable (Rook Company)	200.00	
Cash		200.00
To record N.S.F. check which was deducted from our account.		

The earnings statement for the period ended August 31, 1981, should include the expense of $2.50. The balance sheet as of August 31, 1981, should show a cash balance of $22,607.35.

When more than one checking account is maintained by a company, each account must be reconciled separately with the statement received from the bank covering the account.

Certified checks

Because a check might not be paid when presented to the bank upon which drawn, a payee may demand that the check be certified. A *certified check* is a regular check drawn by a depositor and taken by the depositor to his or her bank for certification. The bank will stamp "certified" across the face of the check and insert the name of the bank and the date; the certification will be signed by a bank official. The bank will do this only after determining that the depositor's balance is large enough to cover the check, and the check will be deducted from the depositor's balance immediately. The check then becomes a liability of the bank. For this reason it will be accepted without question.

Transfer bank accounts

A company operating in many widely scattered locations and having accounts with many local banks should use special procedures to avoid accumulating too much idle cash. One such procedure involves the use of special-instruction bank accounts. For example, transfer accounts may be set up in the local banks. These banks automatically transfer to a central bank (by wire or bank draft) all amounts on deposit in excess of a stated amount (which may be zero). In this way funds not needed for local operations are sent quickly to the company's headquarters where they can be invested.

PAYROLL CHECKING ACCOUNTS

Many firms maintain a separate payroll account, especially when many employees are paid by check. In general, a payroll checking account is used in the following fashion. Before each payday, the net payroll is computed, a check is drawn on the general commercial bank account for that amount, and the check is deposited in the payroll bank account. Individual payroll checks are issued to the employees. When these are cashed they are cleared against the payroll bank account.

The use of a payroll account has several advantages, as follows:

1. A distinctive payroll check form may be used, with spaces provided on an attached apron for the amounts of gross earnings, the various payroll deductions, and the net cash paid.
2. Payroll checks, identifiable as such, are easily cashed by employees.
3. The work of reconciling the bank balances may be divided among employees. One check is drawn against the general commercial bank account. The hundreds or thousands of payroll checks issued each payday are drawn on the payroll bank account. Occasionally, payroll checks are lost or negotiated many times before clearing the bank. Including these items in the payroll reconciliation simplifies the reconciliation of the general Cash account.
4. Only one authorization is prepared, calling for one check drawn against the general commercial bank account; therefore, payroll checks are issued without separately prepared and signed authorizations.
5. The individual payroll checks need not be entered in the regular cash disbursements record; the payroll check numbers are inserted in the payroll journal or record, and a repetition of the entering of the checks is avoided.

The payroll account is frequently operated on an imprest basis with a round dollar amount of, say, $1,000 deposited over and above immediate payroll needs. During the period between regular payroll dates there will be a balance available for such payroll checks as may be issued for advances to employees or for final pay upon termination of employment.

CASH SHORT AND OVER

Occasionally, errors are made in returning change to customers. In these cases the amount of cash will be short of, or in excess of, the amount shown by the total of a cash register tape or an adding machine tape total of sales slips for a day.

Assume that a store clerk accidentally shortchanges a cash customer to the extent of $1. Total cash sales for the day were $704.50. At the end of the day, the total actual cash will be $1 over the sum of the sales tickets or the total of the cash register tape. The journal entry to record the day's cash sales is as follows:

Cash	705.50	
Sales		704.50
Cash Short and Over		1.00
To record cash sales for the day.		

The Cash Short and Over account is an expense (debit balance) or revenue (credit balance) account. It is credited if the cash received is greater than the correct amount and debited if the cash received is less than the correct amount. The balance of the account at the end of the period will be treated as an "other expense" or "other revenue" in the earnings statement.

PETTY CASH FUNDS

While it is desirable that all disbursements be made by check, most concerns find it convenient to make certain small payments in cash. Disbursements for delivery charges, postage stamps, taxi fares, employees' supper money when working overtime, and other small items usually require a small amount of cash on hand.

To permit such small disbursements to be made in cash and at the same time to maintain adequate control over cash disbursements, firms often establish a *petty cash fund* of some round dollar amount such as $50 or $100. One individual in the company is placed in charge of the fund and is responsible for the entire sum.

Imprest petty cash funds

A petty cash fund could be established on a basis whereby an entry would be made to record every change in the fund. Thus, when the fund is established, an entry could be made debiting Petty Cash and crediting Cash. If cash is expended for delivery charges, an entry could be made debiting Transportation-In (or Transportation-Out, as the case may be) and crediting Petty Cash. If maintained on this basis, the records of the company would soon be cluttered with numerous entries for small amounts. For this reason, petty cash funds are almost always maintained on an *imprest* basis. This means that only periodically is the petty cash fund reimbursed out of general cash. At the same time, the expenses are recorded. All future discussion will assume the establishment and maintenance of petty cash funds on this basis.

When the petty cash fund is established, a check is prepared, payable to the order of the person who is to be the petty cash cashier, and an entry is made as follows:

Petty Cash Fund 100
    Cash 100
      To record drawing a check to establish a petty cash fund of $100.

The fund should be sufficiently large to take care of petty cash disbursements for a reasonable period of time, for example, one month. The check is cashed, and the fund now is ready for disbursements to be made from it.

A *petty cash voucher,* Illustration 7.3, should be prepared for each disbursement from the petty cash fund. If the person receiving the cash can furnish an invoice, it should be stapled to the petty cash voucher. The petty

Illustration 7.3: Petty cash voucher

PETTY CASH VOUCHER NO. 359			
To Local Cartage, Inc.		Date June 29, 1981	
EXPLANATION	ACCT. NO.	AMOUNT	
Freight on parts	27	2	27
APPROVED BY *a. E. S.*		RECEIVED PAYMENT *Ken Black*	

cash cashier at all times is accountable for cash and petty cash vouchers totaling to the amount of the fund.

Replenishing the fund

Whenever the balance in the petty cash fund is at a relatively low level, it is replenished. A check is drawn, payable to the cashier of the fund, for the amount of the vouchers. It is debited to the various expense accounts (and occasionally other accounts) indicated by a summarization and credited to cash.

To illustrate, assume that when summarized, the vouchers in a given fund show petty cash fund expenditures of $22.75 chargeable to Transportation-In, $50.80 for postage stamps, and $19.05 chargeable to Delivery Expense, for a total of $92.60. A check in that amount would be drawn, payable to the cashier of the fund, and would be debited to the accounts indicated above. The entry would read:

Transportation-In	22.75	
Stamps and Stationery	50.80	
Delivery Expense	19.05	
Cash		92.60
To record check drawn to replenish petty cash fund.		

After the check for $92.60 has been endorsed and cashed, the amount of cash in the fund is at the established amount, $100. After the petty cash vouchers have been audited (by someone other than the custodian of the fund) and approved and the fund replenished, the vouchers should be stamped or mutilated so that they cannot be reused.

Generally, the Petty Cash account is debited only when the fund is created or increased in size and credited only when the fund is discontinued or decreased in size. But at the end of the accounting period (assume it is December 31) it is necessary to bring all expenses for the period into the accounts for earnings determination purposes and for proper balance sheet reporting. This must be done even if the fund is not replenished at that time. Therefore, at the end of the year, if the fund contains $80 of cash and a voucher for office supplies for $20, the following entry should be made:

Dec. 31	Office Supplies Expense	20	
	Petty Cash		20
	To adjust the office supplies expense account and petty cash.		

The amount of the entry is for the total of the expense vouchers in the petty cash fund. The $80 petty cash balance would be reported as part of the total representing all of the company's cash balances.

Assuming that $10 additional expenditures have been paid out of the petty cash fund for office supplies prior to January 10, the journal entry to record its replenishment on that date would read as follows:

Jan. 10	Office Supplies Expense	10	
	Petty Cash	20	
	Cash		30
	To replenish the petty cash fund.		

The above entry restores the petty cash fund to its original $100 balance.

THE VOUCHER SYSTEM

In very small companies where the owner has an intimate knowledge of all transactions and where he or she personally signs all checks, there need be no great concern over the proper handling of cash disbursements. In larger companies where the owners or top-management people have no direct part in the payment process, close control over this function should be provided via a formalized system of internal control. While the owner who has an intimate knowledge of all transactions might use special journals to reduce journalizing and posting time, he or she would not have need for the formalized system of internal control over disbursements (called a voucher system) presented here. The voucher system utilizes two special journals which have not yet been described.

With a *voucher system,* internal control over cash disbursements is achieved in the following way: each transaction that will involve the payment of cash is entered on a voucher and recorded in a voucher register some time before payment is made. A *voucher* is a form with spaces provided for data concerning the liability being set up (such as invoice number, invoice date, creditor's name and address, description of the goods or services, terms of payment, and amount due). It also has spaces for signatures of those approving the obligation for payment. The voucher usually forms a "jacket" for the invoice and other supporting documents. Each voucher goes through a rigorous process of examination and eventual approval or disapproval. By the time a voucher is approved for payment, one can be quite certain that the liability for payment is legitimate, since various persons have attested to the propriety and accuracy of the claim.

The voucher system eliminates entirely the formal subsidiary accounts payable ledger. The file of unpaid vouchers serves as the subsidiary accounts payable ledger.

When the voucher system is used, the term "vouchers payable" is usually substituted for the term "accounts payable" in the accounts. When financial statements are prepared, the more conventional term "accounts payable" is preferable.

The system of internal control is strengthened by a separation of duties. For instance, the person or persons who authorize the incurrence of liabilities should not also prepare and distribute checks. The receipt of assets or services resulting from the incurrence of a liability must be acknowledged and approved by (a) the receiving department, or (b) others who do not have authority to prepare and distribute checks. The persons who have authority to sign checks should do so only when approved vouchers authorizing each check are presented. The possibilities of errors and of recording unauthorized liabilities or cash disbursements thereby are minimized.

Types of vouchers

The voucher system for recording liabilities that will result in cash disbursements is so named because every such transaction will result in the preparation of a voucher. In a broad sense a voucher is any written document that serves as a receipt or as evidence of authority to act. In a narrow sense—as applied to the voucher system—a voucher is a form that confirms a liability and thus serves as the basis for an accounting entry. Vouchers are numbered consecutively for control purposes.

In some lines of business the terms of discount and of payment run from the date of the invoice. When this is the case a voucher should be prepared for each invoice, as in Illustration 7.4, and should be filed according

Illustration 7.4: A voucher

ATWELL SUPPLY COMPANY
Atwell Plaza
Atwell, Texas 78712

VOUCHER

VOUCHER NO. ___141___
OUR P.O. NO. ___2514___
VENDOR'S INVOICE ___416___
PAID BY CHECK NO. ___587___
DATE PAID ___7/18/81___

Payable To: Gregory Corporation
48 Cadillac Square
Detroit, Michigan 48226

DATE		ACCT. NO.	DESCRIPTION	QUANTITY	UNIT PRICE	TOTAL
July	14	126	X-16 Transistors	100	$2.00	$200.00
			TOTAL			$200.00
			DISCOUNT	2%		4.00
			NET PAYABLE			$196.00

TERMS 2/10, n/30
EXPLANATIONS:

AUDITED AS TO CORRECTNESS a.T.	APPROVED FOR PAYMENT L. J. W.	ENTERED IN VOUCHER REGISTER R.E.J	DATE ENTERED 7/14/81

to the date on which the discount period terminates or payment is due. Such a file may be called a tickler file.

When discount and payment terms are computed from the end of the month, it is possible to modify the voucher and reduce the number of vouchers prepared and, therefore, the number of entries made in the voucher register. All invoices received from each creditor may be accumulated and listed on one voucher at the month-end, since all will probably be paid by one check. The details of the various invoices may be summarized on one voucher.

Special journals used

Voucher register. A *voucher register* is a multicolumn journal containing special debit columns for the accounts most frequently debited when a liability is incurred. Stated in a different manner, a voucher register contains a chronological and serial record of all vouchers prepared. It includes a brief description of the transactions and indicates the accounts involved. One line is allotted to each voucher.

A special Vouchers Payable Cr. column in the voucher register summarizes all vouchers approved. The total of the Vouchers Payable column in the voucher register is posted to the liability controlling account, *Vouchers Payable,* at the end of each month. The two items appearing in the General Ledger Accounts Cr. column would be posted to the accounts indicated as credits. The column totals of the next seven columns would be posted to

Illustration 7.5: A voucher register

Line No.	Voucher Date 1981		Voucher No.	Payee	Explanation	Terms	Date Paid		Check No.	Vouchers Payable Cr. 101	General Ledger Account Name
1	May	2	223	Hanley Company	Ring binders	2/10,n/30	May	12	1350	980.00	
2		4	224	Moore Transport	Transportation, binders			5	1347	13.00	
3		6	225	White Stationery Company	Office supplies	2/10,n/30		12	1351	102.00	
4		8	226	Specialty Advertisers	Advertising			8	1348	1,200.00	
5		10	227	Blanch Company	Note and interest			10	1349	1,010.00	
6		12	228	Internal Revenue Service	Income tax withheld, April 1981			12	1352	2,200.00	
7		14	229	Swanson Company	Filler paper	2/10,n/30		26	1356	3,920.00	
8		16	230	Rizzo Company	Office desk	n/30		25	1355	640.00	
9		18	231	Warren Company	Spiral binders	2/10,n/30		28	1357	4,900.00	
10		20	232	First National Bank	Interest on mortgage note			20	1353	154.00	
11		22	233	Falcone Company	Books	n/30				10,000.00	
12		24	234	Petty cash	Reimbursement			24	1354	132.00	
13		26	235	Swanson Company	Discount lost (No. 229).			26	1356	80.00	
14		28	236	Celoron Company	Drawing sets	2/20,n/30				9,800.00	
15		31	237	Payroll account	Salaries and wages			31	1358	21,600.00	F.I.C.A. Tax Liability
16											Federal Income Tax Withheld
										56,731.00	

the indicated accounts as debits. The three items in the General Ledger Accounts Dr. column would be posted to the indicated accounts as debits.

Illustration 7.5 is presented to show the entry of vouchers in the special journal for vouchers payable in cases where one voucher is prepared for each invoice. As each voucher is prepared and entered in the voucher register (Illustration 7.5), the voucher is placed in the *unpaid voucher file*. As each is paid, the voucher (or a duplicate copy of it) is transferred to the *paid voucher file*. A notation of the payment is made in the Date Paid and Check Number columns of the voucher register as illustrated.

Check register. A *check register* (or check record) is a special journal containing a chronological and serial record of all checks issued. One line is allotted to each check. No check may be issued unless it is authorized by

Page No. *15*
Month *May 1981*

Accounts Cr. Acct. No.	Amount Cr.	✓	Discounts Lost Dr. 122	Merchandise Purchases Dr. 131	Transportation In Dr. 144	Salaries and Wages Dr. 158	Office Expense Dr. 175	Advertising Expense Dr. 262	Interest Expense Dr. 306	General Ledger Accounts Dr. Account Name	Acct. No.	Amount Dr.	✓
				980.00									
					13.00								
							102.00						
								1,200.00					
									10.00	Notes Payable	103	1,000.00	
										Federal Income Tax Withheld	108	2,200.00	
				3,920.00									
										Office Equipment	42	640.00	
				4,860.00	40.00								
									154.00				
				10,000.00									
					31.88		60.12	40.00	*				
			80.00										
				9,800.00									
107	400.00					24,000.00							
108	2,000.00												
	2,400.00		80.00	29,560.00	84.88	24,000.00	162.12	1,240.00	164.00			3,840.00	

an approved voucher. Thus, the interrelationship of the voucher register and the check register is evident.

The check register, Illustration 7.6, sets forth the entry and procedure when a check is issued in payment of each voucher. When invoices are entered net (after discount deductions) in the voucher register, a check register usually has only one money column. The total of this column is posted as a debit to Vouchers Payable and a credit to Cash. If an invoice is paid after the discount privilege period has expired, another voucher should be prepared for the amount of the discount (see line 13 in Illustration 7.5).

If invoices are entered gross (before discount deductions) in the voucher register, a Purchase Discounts Cr. column also should be provided in the check register. In this latter instance, separate columns would be necessary for the debit to Vouchers Payable and credit to Cash, since the dollar amounts posted to these two accounts would be different by the amount of the discount taken.

The voucher register and the check register are the two primary journals in a voucher system from which postings are made to the Vouchers Payable controlling account. And when a voucher system is employed, these two registers replace the more traditional purchases and cash disbursements journals.

Illustration 7.6: Check register

| | | | CHECK REGISTER | | | Page No. 24 |
						Month May, 1981
Line No.	Date 1981		Payee	Voucher No.	Check No.	Vouchers Payable Dr., Cash Cr.
1	May	5	Moore Transport	224	1347	13.00
2		8	Specialty Advertisers	226	1348	1,200.00
3		10	Blanch Company	227	1349	1,010.00
4		12	Hanley Company	223	1350	980.00
5		12	White Stationery Company	225	1351	102.00
6		12	Internal Revenue Service	228	1352	2,200.00
7		20	First National Bank	232	1353	154.00
8		24	Petty Cash	234	1354	132.00
9		25	Rizzo Company	230	1355	640.00
10		26	Swanson Company	235 } 229 }	1356	4,000.00
11		28	Warren Company	231	1357	4,900.00
12		31	Payroll account	237	1358	21,600.00
						36,931.00

Files maintained in a voucher system

Unpaid and paid voucher files.   As stated earlier, two files are always maintained when a voucher system is used: the *unpaid voucher file,* referred to earlier as the tickler file, and the *paid voucher file.*

The unpaid voucher file contains all vouchers that have been prepared and approved as proper liabilities but which have not yet been paid. When credit terms run from the invoice date, they are filed according to their due dates. When credit terms run from the end of the month, the invoices of each creditor are included in one voucher and then filed by due date.

The paid voucher file contains all vouchers which have been paid. They are filed by their voucher numbers in numerical order. Filed in this manner, they constitute a permanent and convenient reference for anyone desiring to check the details of previous cash disbursements. The unpaid voucher file serves as (or takes the place of) the subsidiary accounts payable ledger. The total of the vouchers in the unpaid vouchers file should equal the total of the "open" items (those not paid) in the voucher register and also equal the balance in the Vouchers Payable account.

Procedure for preparing a voucher

The preparation of a voucher begins with the receipt of an invoice from a creditor, or with approved evidence that a liability has been incurred and cash will be disbursed. The procedure followed from that point is typically as follows. Basic data such as the invoice number, invoice date, creditor's name and address, description of the goods or services, terms of payment, and amount due are entered on the voucher from the invoice. The invoice, voucher, and receiving report are sent to the persons responsible for verifying the correctness of the description of the goods as to quantity and quality, the dollar amounts, and other details. Each of these persons initials the voucher when he or she is satisfied as to its correctness. When the voucher and accompanying documents are received by the accounting department, a notation is made on the voucher as to the proper accounts to be debited and credited. After a final review by an authorized person, the proper entry is made in the voucher register and the voucher is filed in the unpaid voucher file.

Under the voucher system an invoice or other business document is *not* the basis for making a journal entry; rather, it is the basis for preparing a voucher. The voucher is the basis for making the journal entry in the voucher register. All vouchers are entered serially in the voucher register.

Procedure for paying a voucher

When the voucher comes due for payment, it is removed from the unpaid voucher file. A check is prepared for the amount payable. The check, voucher, and supporting documents then typically are sent to the treasurer. The treasurer (or a representative) examines all of the documents. If they are found to be in order, the treasurer initials the voucher (to show that final approval has been given) and signs the check. The treasurer then mails the check, and usually a remittance advice showing the details of payment, to the creditor. The voucher is returned to the accounting department.

On receipt of the voucher the accounting department makes an entry in the check register showing the date paid, check number, voucher number, and amount paid. The date paid and check number also are inserted in the voucher register and on the voucher itself. The voucher then is filed in the paid voucher file.

NEW TERMS INTRODUCED IN CHAPTER 7

Bank reconciliation statement—a statement which shows the items and amounts which cause a bank's record of a depositor's account balance to differ from the depositor's record.

Bank service charges—amounts deducted by a bank from a depositor's account as payment for services rendered.

Bank statement—a statement issued (usually monthly) by a bank describing the activities in a depositor's checking account.

Cash—currency, coins, undeposited negotiable instruments (such as checks, bank drafts, and money orders), amounts in checking or savings accounts at a bank, demand certificates of deposit at a bank, and anything else a bank will accept for immediate deposit.

Cash short and over—a miscellaneous expense (debit balance) or revenue (credit balance) account used for recording the difference between actual cash receipts and the amount of cash that should be on hand.

Certified check—a regular check drawn by a depositor and taken to his or her bank for certification. The check is deducted from the depositor's balance immediately and becomes a liability of the bank. Thus, it will be accepted without question.

Checking account—a balance maintained with a bank subject to withdrawal on demand.

Check register—a special journal containing a chronological and serial record of all checks issued.

Deposit in transit—cash receipts of a depositor recorded as receipts in one period but recorded as a deposit by the bank in a succeeding period.

Deposit ticket—a document showing the name and number of the account into which the deposit is made, the date, and the items comprising the deposit.

N.S.F. check—a check which the bank has refused to pay because the writer of the check does not have sufficient funds in his or her checking account to cover the check.

Outstanding checks—checks issued by a depositor which have not yet been paid by the bank upon which drawn.

Paid voucher file—a permanent file where vouchers which have been paid are filed in numerical sequence.

Petty cash fund—a usually nominal sum of money established as a separate fund from which minor cash disbursements for valid business purposes are to be made. When established on an *imprest* basis, the cash in the fund plus the vouchers covering disbursements must always equal the balance at which the fund was established and at which it is carried in the ledger accounts.

Petty cash voucher—a form with spaces provided for recording data about disbursements from the petty cash fund. The data recorded often includes the amount and purpose of the disbursement, to whom it was made, and a signature authorizing the disbursement.

Remittance advice—a form attached to a check informing the payee why the drawer of the check is making this payment.

Transfer bank account—a bank account controlled by special instructions which require the bank to forward immediately any funds in excess of a stated amount to a central bank.

Unpaid voucher file—serves as a subsidiary accounts payable ledger under a voucher system; unpaid vouchers are filed according to their due dates.

Voucher—a form with spaces provided for data concerning the liability being recorded (such as invoice number, invoice date, creditor's name and address, terms, description of the goods or services, and amount due); also has spaces for approval signatures, the date of the check used for payment, and the check number.

Voucher register—a special journal in which prenumbered vouchers are recorded in numerical sequence. In addition to a credit column for Vouchers Payable, it normally has various columns for debits such as Merchandise Purchases, Salaries, and Transportation-In. See Illustration 7.5.

Vouchers Payable—an account title often substituted for Accounts Payable in the ledger when a voucher system is in use.

Voucher system—a procedure used to ensure tight internal control over all cash disbursements.

DEMONSTRATION PROBLEM

The following data pertain to the Nunn Company:

1. Balance per the bank statement, dated March 31, 1981, is $8,900.
2. Balance of the Cash in Bank account on the company's books as of March 31, 1981, is $8,938.
3. Bank deposit of March 31 for $2,600 was not included in the deposits per the bank statement.
4. Outstanding checks as of March 31 totaled $2,100.
5. Service and collection charges for the month amount to $20.
6. The bank erroneously charged the Nunn Company account for a $400 check of the Munn Company. The check was included in the canceled checks returned with the bank statement.
7. During March, the bank credited Nunn Company with the proceeds, $2,020, of a note which it had collected for the company. Face of the note was $2,000.
8. A $150 check received from a customer was returned with the bank statement marked N.S.F.
9. During March the bank paid a $1,000, 9 percent, 60-day note of the Nunn Company and charged it to the company's account per instructions received. Nunn Company had not recorded the payment of this note.
10. An examination of the cash receipts and the deposit tickets revealed that the bookkeeper erroneously recorded a customer's check of $263 as $236.

Required:

a. Prepare a bank reconciliation statement as of March 31, 1981.

b. Prepare the journal entries necessary to adjust the accounts as of March 31, 1981.

Solution to demonstration problem

a.

NUNN COMPANY			
Bank Reconciliation Statement			
March 31, 1981			
Balance per bank statement, March 31, 1981		$8,900	
Add: Deposit in transit	$2,600		
Munn Company check charged in error	400	3,000	$11,900
Less: Outstanding checks			2,100
Adjusted balance, March 31, 1981			$ 9,800
Balance per ledger, March 31, 1981		$8,938	
Add: Note and interest collected	$2,020		
Error in recording check received	27	2,047	$10,985
Less: Service and collection charges		$ 20	
N.S.F. check		150	
Nunn Company note and interest			
charged against account		1,015	1,185
Adjusted balance, March 31, 1981			$ 9,800

b.

Cash	862	
Accounts Receivable ($150 − $27)	123	
Notes Payable	1,000	
Interest Expense	15	
Bank Charges	20	
Notes Receivable		2,000
Interest Revenue		20
To record adjustments to Cash account.		

QUESTIONS

1. What are the four objectives sought in effective cash management?

2. Cite four essential features in a system of internal control over cash receipts.

3. The bookkeeper of a given company was stealing remittances received from customers in payment of their accounts. To cover the theft, the bookkeeper made out false credit memoranda indicating returns and allowances made by or granted to the customers. What feature of a system of internal control, if operative, possibly would have prevented this defalcation?

4. Cite six essential features in a system of internal control over cash disbursements.

5. The difference between a company's Cash ledger account balance and the balance in the bank statement is usually a matter of timing. Do you agree or disagree? Why?

6. Why might a company's management wish to determine the cash position daily?

7. Explain how the use of transfer bank accounts can bring about effective cash management.

8. Indicate the manner in which a payroll bank account is operated.

9. Describe the operation of an imprest petty cash fund and the advantages obtained from its use. Be sure to indicate exactly how control is effected through the use of the imprest system.

10. What can be accomplished with a voucher system that is not accomplished through the use of a purchases journal and a cash disbursements journal?

11. What should the relationship be between the balance in the Vouchers Payable account, the "open" items in the voucher register, and the total of all vouchers in the unpaid voucher file?

EXERCISES

E–1. The bank statement for the Baker Company at the end of August showed a balance of $68,600. Checks outstanding totaled $21,000, and deposits in transit totaled $30,500. If these are the only pertinent data available to you, what was the correct amount of cash against which the Baker Company could have written checks as of the end of August?

E–2. From the following data prepare a bank reconciliation statement and determine the correct available cash balance for the Sikes Company as of October 31, 1981:

Balance per bank statement,	
October 31, 1981	$4,658
Ledger account balance	3,676
Note collected by bank not	
yet entered in ledger	1,000
Bank charges not yet entered	
by Sikes Company	6
Deposit in transit	560
Outstanding checks:	
No. 327	128
No. 328	96
No. 329	240
No. 331	84

E–3. From the following information for the Clerk Company:

a. Prepare a bank reconciliation statement as of September 30, 1981.

b. Give the necessary journal entries to correct the Cash account.

Balance per bank statement,	
September 30, 1981	$16,300
Ledger account balance as of	
September 30, 1981	14,650
Note collected by bank	1,000
Bank charges	10
Deposits in transit	924
N.S.F. check deposited and	
returned	84
Check of Clark Company	
deducted in error	50
Outstanding checks	1,718

E–4. As of March 1 of the current year the Pate Company had outstanding checks of $15,000. During March the company issued an additional $57,000 of checks. As of March 31 the bank statement showed that $51,000 of checks had cleared the bank during the month. What is the amount of outstanding checks as of March 31?

E–5. The Dexter Company's bank statement as of August 31, 1981, shows total deposits into the company's account of $25,670 and a total of 14 deposits. On July 31 deposits of $1,350 and $1,050 were in transit. The total cash receipts for August amounted to $26,375, and the company's records show 13 deposits made in August. What is the amount of deposits in transit at August 31?

E–6. On August 31, 1981, the Mark Company's petty cash fund contained:

Coin and currency	$42.50
IOU from office boy	5.00
Vouchers covering expenditures for—	
Postage	20.00
Taxi fares	8.50
Entertainment of a customer	23.00

The Petty Cash account shows a balance of $100. If financial statements are prepared for each calendar month, what journal entry is required on August 31?

E–7. Use the data in Exercise 6 above. If the fund were replenished on August 31, 1981, what journal entry would be required? Which of the accounts debited would not appear in the earnings statement?

E–8. You are the chief accountant of the Magnuson Company. An invoice has just been received from the Arnott Company in the amount of $2,000, with terms of 2/10, n/30. List the procedures you would follow in processing this invoice up through the point of filing it in the unpaid vouchers file.

E–9. Refer to the situation described in Exercise E–8. Assume that the time for payment of the voucher has arrived and the payment is to be made within the discount period. List the actions that would be taken if the company uses a Discounts Lost account.

E–10. What would be a reasonable procedure had the discount period elapsed before payment was made in Exercise E–9 above?

E–11. List the posting steps that would be used to post the data shown in Illustration 7.5. How many numbers would actually be posted?

PROBLEMS, SERIES A

7–1–A. The bank statement for the Wesson Company's general checking account with the First National Bank for the month ended August 12, 1981, showed an ending balance of $5,309, service charges of $10, an N.S.F. check returned of $210, and the collection of a $1,000 note plus interest of $10. Further investigation revealed that a wire transfer of $1,800 from the bank account maintained by a branch office of the company had not been recorded by the company as having been deposited in the First National Bank account. In addition, a comparison of deposits with receipts showed a deposit in transit of $2,100. Checks outstanding amounted to $1,506, while the cash ledger balance was $3,313.

Required:

a. Prepare a bank reconciliation statement for the Wesson Company account for the month ended August 12, 1981.

b. Prepare all necessary journal entries.

7–2–A. The following data pertain to the Mellis Company:

1. Balance per the bank statement dated June 30, 1981, is $40,760.
2. Balance of the Cash in Bank account on the company books as of June 30, 1981, is $11,980.
3. Outstanding checks as of June 30, 1981, are $20,000.
4. Bank deposit of June 30 for $3,140 was not included in the deposits per the bank statement.
5. The bank had collected a $30,000, 6 percent, 30-day note and the interest which it credited to the Mellis Company account. The bank charged the company a collection fee of $20 on the above note.
6. The bank erroneously charged the Mellis Company account for a $14,000 check of the Meliss Company. The check was found among the canceled checks returned with the bank statement.
7. Bank service charges for June, exclusive of the collection fee, amounted to $100.
8. Among the canceled checks was one for $690 given in payment of an account. The bookkeeper had recorded the check at $960 in the company records.
9. A check of Crosley, a customer, for $4,200, deposited on June 20, was returned by the bank marked N.S.F. No entry has been made to reflect the returned check on the company records.
10. A check for $1,680 of Moran, a customer, which had been deposited in the bank, was erroneously recorded by the bookkeeper as $1,860.

Required:

Prepare a bank reconciliation statement as of June 30, 1981. Also prepare any necessary adjusting journal entries.

P7–3–A. The following data pertain to the Tennis Company. The reconciliation statement as of June 30, 1981, showed a deposit in transit of $1,350 and three checks outstanding:

No. 553	$ 600
No. 570	1,100
No. 571	800

During July the following checks were written and entered in the Cash account:

No. 572	$ 750
No. 573	825
No. 574	1,410
No. 575	635
No. 576	1,263
No. 577	845
No. 578	1,150
No. 579	1,410
No. 580	180
No. 581	2,427
No. 582	2,400
No. 583	924

As of July 31, all the checks which were written, except No. 578, were mailed to the payees. Check No. 578 was kept in the vault pending receipt of a statement from the payee. Four deposits were made at the bank as follows:

July 7	$7,500
14	9,600
14	5,700
28	6,900

The bank statement, which was received on August 2, correctly included all deposits and showed a balance as of July 31 of $25,260. The following checks were returned: Nos. 570, 571, 572, 573, 574, 575, 576, 577, 580, and 581. With the paid checks there were three debit memoranda for—

1. Fee of $4 for the collection on July 30 of a $1,100 noninterest-bearing note payable to the Tennis Company for which a credit memorandum was enclosed.
2. Monthly service charge of $5.
3. Payment of $750 noninterest-bearing note of the Tennis Company.

The bank included a credit for $3,000 dated July 29. The bank telephoned the company on the morning of August 3 to explain that this credit was in error because it represented a transaction between the bank and the Tenist Company.

The balance in the Cash account on the books of the Tennis Company as of July 31 is $15,435.

Required:

Prepare a bank reconciliation statement for the Tennis Company as of July 31, 1981. Also prepare any necessary adjusting entries.

P7–4–A. Burch Company's bank reconciliation statement of July 13, 1981, included the following information:

Bank balance, July 13, 1981		$20,850
Balance per books, July 13, 1981		19,245
Outstanding checks:		
No. 423	$ 350	
No. 425	1,225	
No. 430	1,400	
No. 442	1,505	4,480
Deposit in transit		2,875

Burch Company's records show the following receipts and disbursements for the month ended August 13, 1981:

Cash receipts

July	10	$2,350
	26	3,500
Aug.	10	7,000
	13	5,250

Cash disbursements

Check No. 443	$1,750
No. 444	2,100
No. 445	1,575
No. 446	1,500
No. 447	1,750

The bank statement covering the month ended August 13 showed:

Balance, July 13, 1981		$20,850
Deposits (4)		15,725
		$36,575
Checks deducted (6)	$8,505	
Service charges	7	8,512
Balance, August 13, 1981		$28,063

The checks returned by the bank were Nos. 423, 425, 442, 443, 444, and 445.

Required

a. Compute the unadjusted cash balance per books as of August 13, 1981.

b. Prepare a bank reconciliation statement as of August 13, 1981.

c. Prepare any necessary adjusting journal entries as of the same date.

P7–5–A. The bank statement of the Lumkin Company's checking account with the First National Bank shows:

Balance, June 30, 1981		$24,610
Deposits		36,400
		$61,010
Less: Checks deducted	$36,000	
Service charges	10	36,010
Balance, July 31, 1981		$25,000

The following additional data are available:

1. A credit memorandum included with the canceled checks returned indicates the collection of a note by the bank for the Lumkin Company, $2,000.
2. An N.S.F. check in the amount of $920 is returned by the bank and included in the total of checks deducted on the bank statement.
3. Deposits in transit as of July 31, $5,000, and as of June 30, $2,400.
4. Checks outstanding as of June 30, all of which cleared the bank in July, $3,400; checks outstanding as of July 31, $8,200.
5. Balance per ledger account as of July 31, $19,094.
6. Deposits of Lumpkan Company credited to Lumkin Company account by bank, $2,000.
7. Check of Lumpkan Company charged against Lumkin Company account by bank, $400.
8. Deposit of July 21 recorded by the company as $637, and by the bank at actual amount of $673. The receipts for the day were from collections on account.

Required:

a. Prepare a bank reconciliation statement as of July 31, 1981, for the Lumkin Company.

b. Determine the amount of cash receipts for the month of July shown by the Lumkin Company's accounts prior to adjustment.

c. Determine the amount of checks drawn by Lumkin in the month of July.

d. Prepare any adjusting journal entries needed at July 31, 1981.

P7–6–A. The treasurer of the Dexter Company prepared the following correct bank reconciliation statement as of April 30, 1981:

Balance per bank statement,
    April 30 .... $58,795
    Add: Deposit in transit 3,670
                         $62,465
    Deduct: Outstanding checks 18,100
Adjusted balance $44,365

Balance per books,
    April 30 .... $45,380
    Less: N.S.F. check $1,000
          Service charges 15   1,015
Adjusted balance $44,365

The bank statement for the month of May shows:

Balance, May 1, 1981 .... $ 58,795
Deposits 110,400
                         $169,195
Checks cleared.................... $165,040
Service charges 35   165,075
Balance, May 31, 1981 .... $ 4,120

The May deposits shown on the bank statement include the proceeds of a $30,000 note payable drawn by the treasurer of the Dexter Company payable to the bank in 60 days. No entry was made for the note in the company's books. The total cash receipts as shown by the Dexter Company records amount to $81,800, and the total checks recorded amount to $76,640. This latter total does not include one check drawn and signed by the treasurer payable to himself. The treasurer has disappeared. No record of this check appears anywhere in the company's records. Checks outstanding on May 31, 1981, total $16,700.

Required:

a. What is the corrected cash balance as of April 30?

b. Compute the unadjusted cash balance as of May 31 shown by the company's records.

c. Compute the amount of the undeposited receipts, if any, as of May 31.

d. Compute the amount of the check drawn payable to the treasurer.

e. Prepare a bank reconciliation statement as of May 31.

f. Prepare any necessary adjusting entries.

g. State the particular feature of a good system of internal control which is designed to prevent abstractions of funds such as illustrated here.

P7–7–A. First Company uses an imprest payroll checking account, with a $1,000 balance. This balance is used for payroll advances and to pay employees whose services

are terminated between payroll payment dates. Following are selected transactions of the First Company during 1981:

June 15 Payroll department determines that the payroll and payroll deductions for the first half of the month of June are:

Office salaries	25,000
Sales salaries and commissions	41,000
Sales office salaries.........	20,000
	$86,000

Payroll deductions:		
Federal incomes taxes withheld	$11,000	
Social security taxes withheld	2,000	
Community Fund contributions withheld	3,000	16,000
Net payroll		$70,000

   17 A check in the amount of the net payroll is drawn on the general checking account and deposited in the payroll checking account.
   20 Payroll checks are issued.
   24 One employee's services are terminated. The salary of this office employee for the partial period is $300, and the only deduction is for $45 of income taxes to be withheld. A payroll check is issued.

The bank statement for the payroll account shows a balance of $1,350.63. Checks outstanding are for $278.25 and $327.38.

Required:

a. Prepare general journal entries to record those transactions which would be formally recorded in the records of the First Company.

b. Determine the actual (not the book) balance in the payroll checking account at June 30. Why is it not the imprest balance of $1,000?

c. Prepare a bank reconciliation statement for the payroll checking account as of June 30, 1981.

P7–8–A. Following are selected transactions of the Richter Company during 1981:

Mar. 1 Established a petty cash fund of $500 which will be under the control of the assistant office manager and is to be operated on an imprest basis.

Apr. 3 Fund is replenished on this date. Prior to replenishment, the fund consisted of the following:

Coin and currency	$284.58
Payroll check issued by Richter Company to part-time office boy, Joe Johnson, properly endorsed by Johnson	27.98

Petty cash vouchers indicating
disbursements for—
Postage stamps 70.00
Supper money for office employees
working overtime 24.00
Office supplies 21.80
Window washing service 40.00
Flowers for wedding of employee 10.00
Flowers for hospitalized employee 10.00
Employee IOU 10.00

The employee's IOU is to be deducted from the employee's next paycheck.

Required:

Present journal entries for the above transactions. Use the Cash Short and Over account for any shortage or overage in the fund.

P7–9–A. The Netter Company was organized January 1 of the current year. It uses a voucher register and a check register with the same column headings as in Illustrations 7.5 and 7.6, except that there are only four debit columns headed Merchandise Purchases, Transportation-In, Discounts Lost, and General Ledger Accounts.

Required:

Enter the following approved transactions for the month of January in these registers. Total and rule the registers. Start with Voucher No. 1 and Check No. 1. Vouchers are prepared for the net amount of the invoice. For discounts lost, a new voucher is prepared for the amount of the discount.

Transactions:

Jan. 1 Received an invoice from the Modern Company in the amount of $2,400 for office equipment. Terms were 2/10, n/30, f.o.b. shipping point.
3 Received an invoice from the Bailey Company for merchandise in the amount of $4,200. Terms were 2/10, n/30.
5 Received an invoice from the Simpson Company for merchandise in the amount of $2,700. Terms were 2/10, n/30.
7 Paid $360 to the Lund Advertising Service for services received in January.
10 Paid $270 of freight charges to the James Company. Of this, $60 was applicable to the office equipment received on January 1 and the rest to merchandise received from the Bailey Company.
14 Paid the Simpson Company the amount due.
20 Paid the Bailey Company the correct amount due.

Jan. 31 Paid the Thomas Company the net amount of $24,210 for merchandise received today.
31 The January 1 Modern Company voucher was misfiled and had not been paid as of the end of the month.

P7–10–A. The Hultman Company has been organized for several years and uses a voucher register and a check register with the same column headings as in Illustrations 7.5 and 7.6, except that there are only four debit columns headed Merchandise Purchases, Transportation-In, Discounts Lost, and General Ledger Accounts. The last voucher number used was 9743, and the last check issued was No. 2096. As of August 31, 1981, there were three vouchers in the unpaid voucher file:

Voucher No. 9696	$ 660
Voucher No. 9741	1,330
Voucher No. 9742	570
	$2,560

The total of the unpaid voucher file agreed with the credit balance in the Vouchers Payable control account.

The following transactions occurred during September, 1981. Vouchers are prepared for the net amount of the invoice. For any discounts lost a new voucher is prepared for the amount of the discount.

Transactions:

Sept. 3 Paid a $600 note that matured this date plus $10 interest to the Citizens Bank.
5 Received an invoice for $700 from the Reese Company for merchandise. Terms were 2/10, n/30.
6 Paid Voucher No. 9696 to the Tims Company, $660.
10 Received an invoice for $294 from the Zink Company for merchandise. Terms were 2/10, n/30.
15 Paid the Reese Company the amount owed it on its invoice of September 5.
17 Paid $130 to the Jacklin Company for advertising placed in September.
30 Paid $8,900 to the Arlin Company. This included $178 chargeable to the Transportation-In account. The balance paid was the net cost of merchandise received today. Terms were 2/10, n/30.
30 Paid the Zink Company the amount due on the purchase of September 10.

Required:

Enter these transactions in the voucher register and the check register. Total and rule the registers as of September 30. List the unpaid vouchers at September 30 and compare the total with the balance in the Vouchers Payable control account (Account No. 250) at that date after posting the proper amounts thereto.

PROBLEMS, SERIES B

P7–1–B. The bank statement for Turner Company's account with the First National Bank for the month ended April 14, 1981, showed a balance of $10,886. On this date the company's Cash account balance was $9,527. Returned with the bank statement were (1) a debit memo for service charges of $10; (2) a debit memo for a customer's N.S.F. check of $100; and (3) a credit memo for a $2,200 wire transfer of funds on April 14 from the State Bank, the local bank used by the company's branch office. Further investigation revealed that outstanding checks amounted to $1,300, the cash receipts of April 14 of $1,621 did not appear as a deposit on the bank statement, and the canceled checks included a check for $410 (drawn by the president of the company to cover travel expenses on a recent trip) which the company has yet to record.

Required:

a. Prepare a bank reconciliation statement for the month ended April 14, 1981.

b. Prepare any necessary journal entries.

P7–2–B. The following information pertains to the Harris Company. The June 30 bank reconciliation statement was as follows:

	Cash account	Bank statement
Balances on June 30	$25,524.48	$25,744.48
Add: Deposit not credited by bank		371.40
Total		$26,115.88
Deduct: Outstanding checks:		
No. 724 . . . . $ 24.60		
No. 886 . . . . 20.00		
No. 896 . . . . 191.40		
No. 897 . . . . 250.20		
No. 898 . . . . 105.20		591.40
Adjusted cash balance, June 30	$25,524.48	$25,524.48

The July bank statement was as follows:

Balance on July 1 . . .		$25,744.48	
Deposits during July .		6,370.52	$32,115.00
Canceled checks returned:			
No. 724	$ 24.60		
No. 896	191.40		
No. 897	250.20		
No. 898	105.20		
No. 899	25.14		
No. 900	1,914.00		
No. 902	1,262.56		
No. 904	58.68	$ 3,831.78	
N.S.F. check of Manley Company		72.04	3,903.82
Bank statement balance, July 31 .			$28,211.18

The cash receipts deposited in July, including receipts of July 31, amounted to $7,904.40. Checks written in July:

No. 899	$ 25.14
No. 900	1,914.00
No. 901	37.00
No. 902	1,262.56
No. 903	79.60
No. 904	58.68
No. 905	1,458.00
No. 906	20.00

The cash balance per the ledger on July 31 was $28,-573.90.

Required:

Prepare a bank reconciliation statement and any necessary adjusting entries.

P7–3–B. The following information is taken from the books and records of the Shenton Company.

Balance per ledger, July 31, 1981	$23,242
Collections received on the last day of July and debited to "Cash in Bank" on books but not entered by bank until August	5,312
Debit memo for customer's check returned unpaid (uncollectible check is on hand but no entry for the return has been made on the books)	500
Debit memo for bank service charge for July	15
Checks issued but not paid by bank	5,034
Credit memo for proceeds of a note receivable which was left at the bank for collection but which has not been recorded on the books as collected ($8 of this is interest revenue)	800
Check for an account payable entered on books as $480 but issued and paid by the bank in the correct amount of $840.	
Balance per bank statement, July 31, 1981	22,889

Required:

Prepare a bank reconciliation statement and the necessary journal entries to adjust the accounts.

P7–4–B. The following data for March 1981 are summarized from the accounts of Norwood Company. The accountant also acts as cashier.

Cash receipts

Mar. 2	$1,100
4	3,200
5	1,300
11	2,800
13	3,500
14	4,200
19	1,000
20	800
27	60
29	320

Cash disbursements

Check No. 911	$ 884
No. 912	1,226
No. 913	1,458
No. 914	888
No. 915	1,614
No. 916	2,400
No. 917	3,800
No. 918	2,700
No. 919	750
No. 920	700

At March 1 the checks outstanding were:

No. 209	$ 90
No. 792	1,600
No. 796	558
No. 910	1,262

There were no deposits in transit. The balance of the Cash in Bank account per books was $15,350 at March 31. The bank statement for the month of March is as follows:

BANK STATEMENT

Date	Checks	Deposits	Balance
Mar. 1			17,000
3		1,100	18,100
4	884		
4	1,226		15,990
6		4,500	20,490
9	1,614		
9	888		17,988
16		10,500	28,488
19	2,400		
19	2,700		23,388
24		1,800	25,188
25	558		
25	1,262		23,368
26	3,800		
26	1,000 N.S.F.		18,568

Mar. 27	1,000 D.M.		17,568
29		380	17,948
31	4 D.M.		17,944

The debit memoranda (D.M.) are for the payment of a company note and for the monthly service charge.

Required:

a. Prepare a bank reconciliation statement as of March 31, 1981.

b. Journalize the entry or entries necessary to correct the books.

c. Comment on the company's control of cash receipts.

P7–5–B. The following information pertains to the bank reconciliation statement to be prepared for the Barker Company as of May 31, 1981:

1. Balance per bank statement as of May 31, 1981, was $10,980.
2. Balance per the Barker Company's Cash account at May 31, 1981, was $11,914.
3. A late deposit on May 31 did not appear on the bank statement, $950.
4. Outstanding checks as of May 31 totaled $1,100.
5. During May the bank credited Barker Company with the proceeds, $1,510, of a note which it had collected for the company. Face of the note was $1,500.
6. Service and collection charges for the month amount to $4.
7. Comparison of the canceled checks with copies of these checks reveals that one check in the amount of $234 had been recorded in the books at $342. The check had been issued in payment of an account payable.
8. A review of the deposit slips with the bank statement showed that a deposit of $500 of Borker and Company has been credited to the Barker Company account.
9. A $60 check received from a customer, R. Perry, was returned with the bank statement marked N.S.F.
10. During May the bank paid a $3,000, 6 percent, 60-day note of the Barker Company and charged it to the company's account per instructions received. Barker Company had not recorded the payment of this note.
11. An examination of the cash receipts and the deposit tickets revealed that the bookkeeper erroneously recorded a customer's check of $324 as $432.

Required:

a. Prepare a bank reconciliation statement as of May 31, 1981.

b. Prepare the journal entries necessary to adjust the accounts as of May 31, 1981.

P7–6–B. The bank reconciliation statement for the Minoza Company for April 30, 1981, was as follows:

	Cash account	Bank statement
Balance as of April 30, 1981..	$ 65,252	$107,424
Deposit in transit		2,900
		$110,324
Outstanding checks		52,400
Service charges . . . . $ 48		
Note paid on demand 7,280	7,328	
Adjusted balance on April 30, 1981.	$ 57,924	$ 57,924

The bank statement for May shows:

Balance, May 1, 1981		$107,424
Deposits		141,448
		$248,872
Checks cleared	$243,800	
Service charges	60	243,860
Balance, May 31, 1981		$ 5,012

The total cash receipts for May amount to $140,836. The total checks drawn amount to $155,000. This total does not include one check drawn and signed by and payable to the treasurer of the company, who has disappeared. No record of this check appears anywhere in the company's records. Checks outstanding on May 31 total $36,600.

Required:

a. Compute the balance in the Cash account as shown by the company's records, excluding the check drawn payable to the treasurer.

b. Compute the amount of receipts for May not deposited, if any.

c. Compute the amount of the check drawn payable to the treasurer.

d. Prepare a bank reconciliation statement as of May 31, 1981.

e. Prepare any required adjusting entries.

f. What one procedure, if followed, might have prevented the theft of funds by the treasurer?

P7–7–B. West Company employs a special checking account upon which its payroll checks are drawn. Employees are paid on the 5th and the 20th of each month the salaries earned in the preceding half-month. The following transactions occur in December:

1. A check for $1,000 is drawn and deposited in the payroll checking account to cover advances to employees and checks issued to employees whose services are terminated. The payroll checking account is to be operated on an imprest basis.

2. The payroll for the last half of November consists of the following:

Gross wages of employees		$26,200
Less: Income taxes withheld	$3,500	
Social security taxes withheld	400	3,900
Net payroll		$22,300

3. On December 4 a check is drawn in the amount of the net payroll and deposited in the payroll checking account.

4. Payroll checks aggregating the amount of the net payroll are issued to employees.

5. A payroll check in the amount of $40 is issued to John Jackson as an advance on the wages he will be receiving on December 20.

6. The payroll for the first half of the month of December is the same as given above. The advance to John Jackson is deducted from his payroll check.

7. A general account check is drawn and deposited in the payroll account.

8. The payroll checks are issued.

Required:

Present in general journal form all entries which must be journalized in the records of the West Company as a result of the above transactions.

P7–8–B. The following data pertain to the petty cash fund of the Hardman Company:

Nov. 2 A $400 check is drawn, cashed, and the cash placed in the care of the assistant office manager to be used as a petty cash fund maintained on an imprest basis.

Dec. 17 The fund is replenished. An analysis of the fund shows:

Coins and currency	$ 98.27
Petty cash vouchers for—	
Delivery expenses	115.65
Freight-in	174.08
Postage stamps purchased	10.00

31 The end of the accounting period falls on this date. The fund was not replenished. Its contents on this date consist of—

Coins and currency	$334.70
Petty cash vouchers for—	
Delivery expenses	21.10
Postage stamps	24.20
Employee's IOU	20.00

Required:

Present journal entries to record the above transactions. Use the Cash Short and Over account for any shortage or overage in the fund.

P7–9–B. The Gustav Company was organized January 1 of the current year, 1981. It uses a voucher register and a check register with the same column headings as in Illustrations 7.5 and 7.6, except that there are only four debit columns headed Merchandise Purchases, Transportation-In, Discounts Lost, and General Ledger Accounts.

Required:

Enter the following approved transactions for the month of January in these registers and total and rule the registers. Start with Voucher No. 1 and Check No. 1. Vouchers are prepared for the net amount of the invoice. For discounts lost, a new voucher is prepared for the amount of the discount.

Transactions:

Jan. 2 Received merchandise from the Lind Company on terms of 2/10, n/30. The invoice received was in the amount of $10,400.
3 Paid transportation charges to Moyer Trucking Company on purchase of January 2, $174.
6 Paid Wilson Display Company $6,600 for billboard advertising for a three-month period beginning February 1, 1981.
15 Paid the Lind Company for the purchase of January 2.
17 Received merchandise from Bradly Company on terms of 2/10, n/30. The invoice received was for $8,400.
18 Received merchandise from Burns Company on terms of 2/10, n/30. The invoice received was for $36,400. Paid net amount today to establish a good credit rating.
23 Received invoice for $3,600 from Office Equipment, Inc., for office equipment recently received. Terms are 2/10, n/30.

P7–10–B. The Byrnes Company has been organized for several years and uses a voucher register and a check register with the same column headings as in Illustrations 7.5 and 7.6, except that there are only four debit columns headed Merchandise Purchases, Transportation-In, Discounts Lost, and General Ledger Accounts. The last voucher used was No. 432, and the last check issued was No. A727. As of December 31, 1981, there were three vouchers in the unpaid voucher file:

Voucher No. 388	$ 5,760
Voucher No. 401	11,200
Voucher No. 431	3,280
	$20,240

The total of the unpaid voucher file agreed with the credit balance in the Vouchers Payable control account. The following transactions occurred during January 1982. Vouchers are prepared for the net amount of the invoice. For discounts lost, a new voucher is prepared for the amount of the discount.

Transactions:

Jan. 2 An invoice in the amount of $5,600 was received from the Drake Company for office equipment already received. Terms were 2/10, n/30, f.o.b. shipping point.
3 Paid a $3,200 note that matured this date plus $64 interest. Payee: Citizens' Bank.
4 Received an invoice for $4,000 from the Dundee Company for merchandise recently received. Terms were 2/10, n/30.
5 Paid Voucher No. 388 to the Engle Company, $5,760.
7 Paid $560 to the Rapid Service for transportation. Of this amount $160 applied to the purchase from the Dundee Company and the balance applied to the purchase of office equipment from the Drake Company.
11 Paid the Drake Company for the purchase of January 2.
14 Paid Voucher No. 431 to the Baker Company, $3,280.
15 Paid $880 to the Ericson Company for advertising services received in January.
20 Paid the Dundee Company for the purchase of January 4.
22 Received an invoice for $12,000 from the Dundee Company for merchandise; terms, 2/10, n/30.
31 Paid the Hanley Company $70,400. This included $1,408 chargeable to Transportation-In. The balance paid was the net cost of merchandise received today. Terms were 2/10, n/30.

Required:

Set up a voucher register and a check register as described and enter the above transactions. Total and rule the registers at January 31. List the unpaid vouchers at January 31 and compare the total with the balance in the Vouchers Payable control account (Account No. 250) at that date, after posting has been completed.

BUSINESS DECISION PROBLEM 7–1

Walter Green was set up in business by his father, who purchased the business of an elderly acquaintance wishing to retire. One of the few changes in personnel made by Walter was to install a college classmate as the office manager–bookkeeper–cashier–sales manager.

During the course of the year, Walter found it necessary

to borrow money from the bank (with his father as co-signer) because, although the business seemed profitable, there was a continuous shortage of adequate cash. The investment in inventories and receivables grew substantially during the year. Finally, after a year had elapsed, Walter's father employed a certified public accountant to audit the records of Walter's business. The CPA reported that the office manager–bookkeeper–cashier–sales manager had been stealing funds and had been using a variety of schemes to cover his actions. More specifically he had—

1. Pocketed cash receipts from sales and understated the cash register readings at the end of the day or altered the copies of the sales tickets retained.
2. Abstracted checks mailed to the company in payment of accounts receivable, credited the proper accounts, and then created fictitious receivables to keep the records in balance.

3. Issued checks to fictitious suppliers and deposited them in accounts bearing these names with himself as signer of checks drawn on these accounts; the books were kept in balance by charging the purchases to the inventory account.
4. Abstracted petty cash funds by drawing false vouchers purporting to cover a variety of expenses incurred.
5. Prepared false sales returns vouchers indicating the return of cash sales to cover further thefts of cash receipts.

Required:

For each of the above items, indicate at least one feature of a good system of internal control which would have prevented the losses due to dishonesty.

BUSINESS DECISION PROBLEM 7–2

The outstanding checks of the Barnes Company at November 30, 1981, are:

No. 229	$250.00
No. 263	272.25
No. 3678	169.75
No. 3679	201.00
No. 3680	350.50

During the month checks numbered 3681–3720 are issued and all of these checks clear the bank except Nos. 3719 and 3720 for $240.75 and $181.50, respectively. Checks No. 3678, 3679, and 3680 also clear the bank.

The bank statement on December 31 shows a balance of $5,986. Service charges amount to $5 and two checks are returned by the bank, one marked N.S.F. in the amount of $28.50 and the other marked "No account" in the amount of $500.

Salinas recently retired as the office manager–cashier–bookkeeper for the company and was replaced by Clark. Clark noted the absence of a system of internal control but was momentarily deterred from embezzling for lack of a scheme of concealment. Finally, Clark hit upon several schemes. The $500 check marked "No account" by the bank is the product of one scheme. Clark took cash receipts and replaced them with a check drawn upon a nonexistent account to make it appear that a customer had given the company a worthless check.

The other scheme was more subtle. Clark pocketed cash receipts to bring them down to an amount sufficient to prepare the following reconciliation statement:

Balance, Cash account		
Dec. 31, 1981		$6,806.70
Deduct:		
Worthless check	$500.00	
N.S.F. check	28.50	
Service charges	5.00	533.50
Adjusted balance		$6,273.20
Balance per bank		
statement, Dec.		
31, 1981		$5,986.00
Add: Deposit in		
transit		709.45
		$6,695.45
Deduct: Out-		
standing checks:		
No. 3719	$240.75	
No. 3720	181.50	422.25
Adjusted balance		$6,273.20

Required:

a. State the nature of the second scheme hit upon by Clark. How much in total does it appear Clark has stolen by use of the two schemes together?

b. Prepare a correct bank reconciliation statement as of December 31, 1981.

c. Suggest procedures which would have defeated the attempts of Clark to steal funds and conceal these actions.

BUSINESS DECISION PROBLEM 7–3

Carol Bell recently acquired an importing business from a friend. The business employs ten salesclerks and four office employees. A petty cash fund of $500 has been established on an imprest basis. All of the 14 employees are allowed to make disbursements from the fund. Vouchers are not used, and no one keeps a record of the disbursements. The petty cash is kept in a large shoe box in the office.

Required:

Discuss the operation of the petty cash fund from an internal control point of view. Indicate the weaknesses that currently exist, and suggest how the internal control system can be improved.

Chapter 8

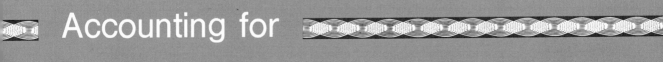

Accounting for

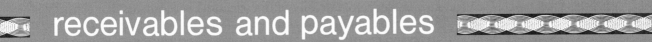

receivables and payables

The term *receivables* is often used in a broad sense in accounting to include any sum of money due to be received from any party for any reason resulting from a past transaction.

The term *payables* similarly is used to describe any amount of money due to be paid to any party for any reason resulting from a past transaction.

The purpose of this chapter is to discuss those receivables and payables which are not discussed in other parts of this text. Special attention is given to allowance for doubtful accounts, which is related to accounts receivable. Also, notes receivable and notes payable (and the interest receivable and interest payable which result from them) are discussed.

ACCOUNTS RECEIVABLE

The selling and buying of goods and services on credit has become common practice in the United States economy. A company which does not extend credit to its customers can expect to lose customers to companies that do offer credit terms. The receivables arising from the sale of goods and services (called "trade receivables") should be shown separately in the balance sheet from those arising from other transactions, such as loans to officers of the company.

Before granting credit to customers, whether they be individuals or other business firms, an evaluation of their credit rating generally is made. There are companies (called credit agencies) which provide these credit ratings upon request. Use of such information can reduce the proportion of sales to customers who cannot or will not pay their account when due.

Revenue from sales usually is recorded at the time of the completion of the sale. This point of sale generally is assumed to be the time of delivery of the goods to the customer. There are two main reasons for this: (1) the revenue is earned, that is, the seller usually has completed or substantially completed his or her part of the agreement; and (2) the revenue is realized, that is, an exchange has taken place with an outsider and the amount of revenue is known because of the receipt of cash or the customer's promise to pay cash. The asset usually received is an account receivable, although cash or, occasionally, a note may be received.

The recording of revenue at the time of the receipt of a promise to pay is the source of a number of special accounting aspects not found in companies selling for cash only. These include sales discounts and uncollectible accounts, as well as the expenses of operating a credit and collection department. Also, any company selling merchandise is likely to have sales returns and sales allowances. Many of these items may not arise until the period following the period of sale. A question arises as to how to properly match these items against the recognized sales revenue which causes them to come into existence.

Uncollectible accounts or bad debts

For companies doing business on a credit basis, certain accounts will not be collected. The desired matching of uncollectible accounts or bad debts against sales revenue is accomplished through making an adjusting entry at the end of the period. The entry debits Bad Debts Expense and credits Allowance for Doubtful Accounts.

The purpose of the debit to *Bad Debts Expense* is to bring about a proper matching of the bad debts against revenue. For example, this proper matching consists of matching against the revenues of 1981 all accounts arising from 1981 sales which will ultimately prove uncollectible in 1981, 1982, or some other year. The purpose of the credit to *Allowance for Doubtful Accounts* (a contra account to Accounts Receivable) is to reduce accounts receivable to their proper amount for balance sheet purposes, that is, the amount that ultimately will be collected—their net realizable value.

There are two basic methods of directly or indirectly estimating the amount of bad debts to be charged to a given accounting period.

Percentage of sales method.   This method involves calculating the amount which has proven uncollectible from each year's credit sales. This ratio of uncollectible accounts to credit sales is then used in estimating the amount for the bad debts adjusting entry. If cash sales are small or are a fairly constant percentage of total sales, the entry may be based on total net sales.

To illustrate, assume that the Rankin Company has found that 1 percent of its net sales is uncollectible. On the basis of this experience, each period the company may charge an amount equal to 1 percent of the net sales for the period to expense and add a like amount to the Allowance for Doubtful Accounts. If net sales for 1981 are $400,000, the entry will read:

Bad Debts Expense 4,000
    Allowance for Doubtful Accounts 4,000
    To record bad debts expense.

Assuming that the gross amount of accounts receivable is $100,000 and there was no previous balance in the allowance account, net accounts receivable would appear as follows on the balance sheet:

Accounts receivable $100,000
    Less: Allowance for doubtful accounts   4,000
Net accounts receivable . . . . $ 96,000

The gross and net amounts of accounts receivable should be shown in the current asset section of the balance sheet. The gross amount is equal to all customers' accounts with debit balances. (The total of all accounts with credit balances, if any, should be shown under current liabilities under the caption "Credit balances in customers' accounts.")

At the date of setting up the allowance, the specific accounts that will become uncollectible are not known. As stated above, the use of the allowance permits charging expense at the end of the period for open accounts that may become uncollectible in the future.

Sometimes the Allowance for Doubtful Accounts account has a balance before adjustment. Under this first method any existing balance in the allowance account will *not* influence the size of the bad debts adjusting entry.

This method is theoretically preferable because it bases the estimate of expense solely on the sales revenue of the same period and gives the most precise matching of expense and revenue.

Percentage of accounts receivable method.   This method is designed to adjust the Allowance for Doubtful Accounts balance to a certain percentage of accounts receivable. It may use one overall percentage or may use a different percentage for each age category of receivable. To illustrate the use of one overall percentage, assume that on the basis of past experience the Jax Company estimates that 5 percent of its outstanding receivables of $100,000 as of December 31, 1981, will utlimately prove to be uncollectible. The Allowance for Doubtful Accounts has a *debit* balance of $1,000. The journal entry to adjust the balance in the allowance account to its required $5,000 *credit* balance is as follows:

Bad Debts Expense 6,000
    Allowance for Doubtful Accounts   6,000
To adjust allowance for possible uncollectible accounts.

Alternatively, an *aging* schedule may be used so as to apply a different percentage for each age category of receivable. An aging schedule is presented in Illustration 8.1, showing how the age of each customer's account is determined. As can be seen from Illustration 8.1, under this method the age of the accounts is the basis for estimating uncollectibility. For example, only 1 percent of the accounts not yet due (sales made less than 30 days prior to the end of the accounting period) is expected to be uncollectible. At the other extreme, 50 percent of all accounts 91–180 days past due is expected to become worthless. The journal entry amount is still affected by the amount already in the allowance account prior to adjustment. For instance, Illustration 8.1 shows that $24,400 is needed in the allowance. If the account already has a credit balance of $5,000, for instance, the adjusting entry would be made for only $19,400.

**Illustration 8.1:
Accounts Receivable
aging schedule**

Customer	Debit Balance	Not Due	Number of Days Past Due				Amount Needed in Allowance
			1–30	31–60	61–90	91–180	
		Estimated Uncollectible Percentage					
		1%	5%	10%	25%	50%	
X	$ 8,000					$ 8,000	$ 4,000
Y	16,000		$ 12,000	$4,000			1,000
Z	4,000				$800	3,200	1,800
All others	800,000	$560,000	240,000				17,600
	$828,000	$560,000	$252,000	$4,000	$800	$11,200	$24,400

DARCY COMPANY
Analysis of Accounts Receivable
December 31, 1981

**Write-off of
uncollectible
accounts**

Once a company has established an Allowance for Doubtful Accounts, accounts which are identified as being uncollectible are charged against the allowance. Using the assumed account receivable of Smith (which arose in

1981) as an example and assuming that $4,000 of the account is identified as being uncollectible, the entry to record this fact in January 1982 is:

Allowance for Doubtful Accounts 4,000
    Accounts Receivable 4,000
    To write off an uncollectible account.

Posting this entry does not change the estimated net collectible amount of the asset, accounts receivable. To illustrate: If accounts receivable amount to $20,000 and the allowance is $2,000, the net receivables are $18,000. If a $1,000 account is written off, the receivables and allowance balances are $19,000 and $1,000, respectively, or $18,000 net.

It should also be noted that it is quite possible for the Allowance for Doubtful Accounts account to have a debit balance if it is adjusted only once a year. Companies do not often carry accounts receivable which are one year or more old in their accounts. Consequently, by the end of 1981, all accounts which arose from 1980 sales will have been collected or written off. If estimates were exact (which is not likely), the allowance balance would be zero. But it may develop a debit balance if previous estimates were too small. Also, some accounts arising from 1981 sales have probably been charged off. The result is very likely to be a debit balance in the Allowance account before adjusting.

Bad debts recovered

The first indication that an account has been charged off in error usually occurs when a check applying to that account is received in the mail. The cash receipt will be recorded by debiting Cash and crediting Accounts Receivable. To illustrate, assume that on October 8, 1982 Smith's check for $4,000 is received in the mail. The entry is:

Cash 4,000
    Accounts Receivable, Smith 4,000
    To record the collection of an account receivable.

When it is discovered that Smith's account had been written off to the allowance, the following entry to correct the error is required:

Accounts Receivable, Smith 4,000
    Allowance for Doubtful Accounts 4,000
    To reverse the original write-off of Smith's account.

If only a part of a previously written off account is collected, the preferable procedure is to reinstate only that portion of the account actually collected, unless there is evidence that the entire account will be collected.

Use of credit cards

The losses from bad debts and the cost and bother of checking on customers' credit, maintaining a subsidiary accounts receivable ledger, and collecting from customers have become very significant for some retailers. To avoid these negative factors some of these retailers have agreed to accept national *credit cards* such as VISA, American Express, and Master Charge.

Credit cards such as these are issued by banks or some other credit-granting agency. Under this system the retailer allows the customer to use a credit card for purchases. The retailer checks the number against a list of canceled credit cards, and for purchases over a certain amount must call the credit granting agency for permission to grant the credit. The charge slips are then sent to the credit agency and the retailer receives payment, usually within a few days. A substantial discount (of between 3 to 7 percent) is deducted by the credit agency in making the payment. Thus, if the retailer sends a charge slip for a $100 sale (assuming a 5 percent discount is in effect), only $95 will be paid to the retailer. The retailer records the sale as follows:

```
Accounts Receivable, VISA ...........................................     95
Credit Card Discount Expense ........................................      5
    Sales ...........................................................          100
        To record a sale of goods to a customer using a VISA credit card.
```

When payment is received from the credit card company, the following entry is made:

```
Cash.................................................................     95
    Accounts Receivable, VISA .......................................           95
        To record receipt of $95 from VISA.
```

Another advantage to the retailer of using such a system is that accounts receivable are outstanding for a much shorter period. Payment from the agency issuing the credit card is received within a few days while payment from customers who do not use credit cards generally is received anywhere from 10 to 60 days after purchase (or never).

The credit card company bills the customer for all of the charge sales he or she has charged to the credit card during the month. If the customer fails to pay, the agency issuing the credit card (and not the retailer who sold the goods) suffers the loss.

Accounts receivable arising from installment sales

Many retail stores sell merchandise to customers on an *installment* basis. This means that they allow the customer to pay for the merchandise by making payments of a certain amount each month over a period of time extending as long as 24 to 36 months. Sometimes an initial down payment is required. Substantial interest payments are generally added to the cash selling price in determining the payments to be made. The seller has the right to repossess the merchandise if payments are not made when due. Repossessed merchandise would be recorded at its current market value when repossessed. The effect of the installment method on accounting earnings and taxable income are covered in Chapter 13.

NOTES RECEIVABLE AND NOTES PAYABLE

A *promissory note* is an unconditional promise in writing, made and signed by the borrower (the *maker*), obligating the borrower to pay the lender (the *payee*) or someone else who legally acquires the note a certain sum of money on demand or at a definite time. An example of a promissory note is shown in Illustration 8.2.

A company may have notes receivable or notes payable arising from transactions with suppliers or customers. Notes may also arise from loans

Illustration 8.2: Promissory note

```
$ 2,000.00                                    June 1              , 19  81

Sixty days- - - - - - - - - - - - - - - - - - AFTER DATE  We        PROMISE TO PAY TO

THE ORDER OF      MOTOR WHEEL CORPORATION

Two Thousand and no/100- - - - - - - - - - - - - - - - - - - - - - - DOLLARS

AT Motor Wheel Corporation, Lansing, Michigan

FOR VALUE RECEIVED WITH INTEREST AT THE RATE OF   10%    PER ANNUM FROM June 1, 1981

        This note is one of a series of    1      notes of even date herewith, numbered    487     to    --      inclusive, and
all of said notes shall become immediately due and payable at the option of the holder hereof on default being made in the payment of any one at maturity.

NO. 487        DUE  July 31, 1981          THE PETERSON COMPANY
                                             John J. Lucia, Treasurer
```

involving a bank or an individual. The accounting for these transactions is covered in this section.

Calculation of interest

Most notes have an explicit charge for interest. Interest is the fee charged for use of money through time. It is an expense to the maker of the note and revenue to the payee of the note. For the sake of convenience (and possibly profit), in commercial transactions interest is commonly calculated on the basis of 360 days per year. The elapsed time in a fraction of a year between two stated days is computed by counting the exact number of days, omitting the day the money is borrowed but counting the day it is paid back. A note falling due on a Sunday or a holiday is due on the following business day.

Assume that we desire to calculate the interest on a $1,000 note; the interest rate is 6 percent, and the life of the note is 60 days. The calculation is as follows:

$$\text{Principal} \times \text{Rate of interest} \times \text{Time} = \text{Interest}$$
$$\$1,000 \times 6/100 \times 60/360 = \$10$$

Notice that when the interest rate is 6 percent and the life of the note is 60 days, you can find the amount of interest by moving the decimal point in the principal two places to the left. This is often referred to as the 6 percent, 60-day rule. For instance, assuming that the following notes are all 6 percent, 60-day notes, the interest on each is:

Principal	Interest
$ 1,000	$ 10.00
1,250	12.50
168,000	1,680.00

Determination of maturity date

The maturity date may be found by one of several methods depending on the wording used in the note:

1. *On demand.* "On demand, I promise to pay. . . ." In this case, the maturity date is at the option of the holder and cannot be computed.

2. *On a stated date.* "On July 18, 1980, I promise to pay. . . ." The date is designated, and a computation is not necessary to determine it.

3. *At the end of a stated period.*
    a. "One year after date, I promise to pay. . . ." If the maturity is expressed in years, the note matures on the same day of the same month as the date of the note in the year of maturity.
    b. "Four months after date, I promise to pay. . . ." If the maturity is expressed in months, the note will mature on the same date in the month of maturity. For example, one month from July 18, 1980, is August 18, 1980, and two months from July 18, 1980, is September 18, 1980. If a note is issued on the last day of a month and the month of maturity has fewer days than the month of issuance, the note matures on the last day of the month of maturity. A one-month note dated January 30, 1980, matures on February 29, 1980.
    c. "Ninety days after date, I promise to pay. . . ." If the maturity is expressed in days, the exact number of days must be counted. The first day (date of origin) is omitted and the last day (maturity date) is included in the count. For example, a 90-day note dated October 19, 1980, matures on January 17, 1981.

Life of note (days)		90 days
Days remaining in October not counting		
date of origin of note:		
Days to count in October (31–19)	12	
Total days in November	30	
Total days in December	31	73
Maturity date in January		17

Notes arising from business transactions

Sometimes a note results from the conversion of an open account. To illustrate, assume that on October 6, 1980, Cooper (the payee) receives from Price (the maker) a 60-day, $18,000 note; the interest rate is 9 percent, and the note results from the earlier sale (on October 4) of merchandise by Cooper to Price. The interest will be earned over the life of the note and will not be paid until maturity, December 5, 1980. The entries for both the payee and the maker are as follows:

Cooper, payee

Oct. 4	Accounts Receivable, Price	18,000	
	Sales		18,000
	To record sale.		
Oct. 6	Notes Receivable	18,000	
	Accounts Receivable, Price		18,000
	To record receipt of note.		
Dec. 5	Cash	18,270	
	Notes Receivable		18,000
	Interest Revenue		270
	To record receipt of principal and interest.		

Price, maker

Oct. 4	Purchases	18,000	
	Accounts Payable, Cooper		18,000
	To record purchase.		
Oct. 6	Accounts Payable, Cooper	18,000	
	Notes Payable		18,000
	To record giving of note.		
Dec. 5	Notes Payable	18,000	
	Interest Expense	270	
	Cash		18,270
	To record payment of principal and interest.		

Dishonored note. A note is dishonored if the maker fails to pay it at maturity. The payee of the note may debit either Accounts Receivable or *Dishonored Notes Receivable* and credit Notes Receivable for the face of the note. If interest is due, the uncollected interest should be debited to the same account to which the dishonored note is debited and credited to Interest Revenue. The maker should merely debit the amount of interest incurred to Interest Expense and credit Interest Payable.

To illustrate, assume that Price did not pay the note at the maturity date. The entries on the books of the payee and the maker are as follows:

Cooper, payee

Dec. 5	Dishonored Notes Receivable	18,270	
	Notes Receivable		18,000
	Interest Revenue		270
	To record dishonoring of note receivable.		

Price, maker

Dec. 5	Interest Expense	270	
	Interest Payable		270
	To record interest on note payable.		

Sometimes when a note cannot be paid at maturity, the maker either pays the interest on the original note or includes it in the face of a new note given to take the place of the old note. When it becomes obvious that the maker will never pay the note, the amount in the Dishonored Notes Receivable account pertaining to that note should be written off to Bad Debts Expense, Loss on Dishonored Notes, or some similar account. If notes were taken into account when making the annual provision for doubtful accounts, the debit should be to the Allowance for Doubtful Accounts account.

Notes payable arising from need for short-term financing

There are various reasons why a business may need short-term financing. Included among these are (1) delay in the receipt of cash caused by granting customers credit terms on amounts due (although this is at least partially offset by the use of credit on its purchases to delay the payment of cash); (2) seasonal buildup of inventory, such as that occurring in department stores just before the Christmas holidays; and (3) expansion in operations caused by the expectation of a future increase in sales. We shall discuss some of the ways in which a business can acquire short-term financing.

Noninterest-bearing notes. In instances when a company presents its noninterest-bearing note to a bank with a request for a loan, the bank computes the amount of interest it charges for the use of its money on the face value of the note, deducts the amount computed from the face value, and gives the balance, the proceeds, to the company. The amount deducted is often called a bank discount. The process of computing the amount is referred to as discounting. To illustrate this process, assume that a bank discounts a company's $20,000, 90-day, noninterest-bearing note at 9 percent. The 9 percent interest is the bank's charge for the use of its money. The discount is $450, and this sum is deducted from the $20,000 and the remainder of $19,550 given to the company.

If the above transaction occurred on December 1, 1980, it would be recorded by the company as follows:

```
Dec.  1  Cash ................................................  19,550
             Notes Payable—Discount ...............................     450
             Notes Payable ......................................           20,000
             To record borrowing on note payable.
```

Note that the company does not receive $20,000 but $19,550. Since the company will pay $450 for the use of this sum for a period of 90 days, a rate of interest higher than 9 percent is actually being paid. (If $450 is the interest on $20,000 at 9 percent for 90 days, then $450 is more than 9 percent on $19,550 for 90 days.) Note also that the bank must discount this note in order to introduce interest into the transaction. At maturity the bank will receive $20,000. The *Notes Payable—Discount* account is used as a valuation contra account to reduce notes (traditionally carried at face value) to their net present value.

Assuming that December 31, 1980, is the end of the company's accounting period, interest expense for the month of December is recorded as follows:

```
Dec. 31  Interest Expense ........................................  150
             Notes Payable—Discount ...............................          150
             To record interest on note payable.
```

In the current liability section on the December 31, 1980, balance sheet, the note and the discount appear as follows:

```
Notes payable ..................................  $20,000
Less: Discount ................................       300
                                                 $19,700
```

When the note is paid at maturity, the entry is as follows (maturity date is March 1, 1981):

```
Mar.  1  Notes Payable .........................................  20,000
             Interest Expense ......................................     300
             Cash ...............................................           20,000
             Notes Payable—Discount ............................              300
             To record payment of note at maturity.
```

This entry reduces the Notes Payable—Discount and Notes Payable accounts to zero balances. Notice that the difference between the cash paid out ($20,000) and that originally received ($19,550) is equal to the total interest expense ($450). The interest is related to a 90-day period, 30 days of which fall in the year ending December 31, 1980, and 60 days in the following year. Thus, the amount charged to interest expense should be $150 in 1980 and $300 in 1981.

Interest-bearing notes. Alternatively, the company could have given a $20,000, 90-day, 9 percent interest-bearing note. At the date of borrowing, the required entry is as follows:

```
Cash ...................................................... 20,000
    Notes Payable .........................................        20,000
    To record borrowing on note payable.
```

At maturity the company pays both the face amount of the note and interest at the rate stated in the note on the face amount (a total of $20,450). When this method is used, the company is paying the actual stated percentage rate of interest.

Discounting notes receivable. When a company issues its own note payable to a bank, it is directly liable to the bank at the maturity date of the loan. Such notes payable are shown in the balance sheet as liabilities.

Instead of borrowing directly, a company may use another method of obtaining short-term financing from a bank. It may select a note receivable held by it, endorse it, and receive cash by discounting it at a bank. Thus, a note receivable discounted arises. A company which discounts a note receivable is contingently, instead of directly, liable to the lending bank. It must pay the bank the amount due at maturity only if the maker of the note fails to pay the obligation.

The cash proceeds of notes receivable discounted are computed as follows:

1. Determine the *maturity value* of the note (face value plus interest).
2. Determine the discount period; that is, count the exact number of days from the date of discounting to the date of maturity. Exclude the date of discounting but include the date of maturity in the count.
3. Using the rate of discount charged by the bank, compute the bank discount on the maturity value for the discount period.
4. Deduct the bank discount from full value at maturity. The result is the cash proceeds.

The contingent liability is usually shown in the accounts by recording the note discounted in a Notes Receivable Discounted account at the face value of the note, even though the contingent liability extends to the interest also. If the original maker does not pay the bank at the maturity date, the borrower who discounts the note will have to pay the principal and interest.

Example. Assume that on May 4, 1980, Clark Company received a $10,000 note from Kent Company bearing interest at 9 percent and maturing in 60 days from May 4. On May 14, 1980, Clark Company discounted the note at the Michigan National Bank at 10 percent. The discount and the cash proceeds are determined as follows:

Face value of note	$10,000.00
Add: Interest at 9% for 60 days	150.00
Maturity value	$10,150.00
Less: Bank discount on $10,150 at 10% for 50 days	140.97
Cash proceeds	$10,009.03

The entry is as follows:

```
May 14   Cash . . . . . . . . . . . . . . . . . . . . . . . . . . . . . . . . . . . . . . . . . . . . . . . .   10,009.03
              Notes Receivable Discounted . . . . . . . . . . . . . . . . . . . .            10,000.00
              Interest Revenue  . . . . . . . . . . . . . . . . . . . . . . . . . . . . .                    9.03
                 To record discounting of note receivable.
```

If the proceeds had been less than the book value of the note, the difference would have been debited to an Interest Expense account.

Balance sheet presentation of notes receivable discounted. In the Clark Company example, a balance sheet prepared for Clark Company as of June 30, 1980, should show a contingent liability in the amount of $10,000 for notes receivable discounted. Assume that the total of all notes receivable is $70,000. An acceptable method of presenting this information in the balance sheet is:

Assets

```
Current Assets:
  Cash  . . . . . . . . . . . . . . . . . . . . . . . .   $xx,xxx
  Accounts receivable . . . . . . . . . . . . .    xx,xxx
  Notes receivable (Note 1) . . . . . . . .    60,000
```

Notes to Financial Statements:
    Note 1: At June 30, 1980, the company is contingently liable for $10,000 of customers' notes receivable (in addition to the $60,000 shown) which it has endorsed and discounted at the local bank.

Discounted notes receivable paid by maker. When a note receivable has been discounted, it is usually the duty of the endorsee (the holder) to present the note to the maker for payment at maturity. If the maker pays the endorsee (the bank in the above illustration) at maturity, the endorser (the company which discounted the note) is thereby relieved of its contingent liability. If the note is not paid at maturity, the endorsee can collect from the endorser which, in turn, can try to collect from the maker.

Assume that Kent Company, in the above example, pays the $10,000 note plus interest of $150 to the Michigan National Bank on July 3, 1980, the note's maturity date. Clark Company, which discounted the note at the bank, can no longer be held liable on the note and, therefore, will make the following entry:

```
July 3   Notes Receivable Discounted . . . . . . . . . . . . . . . . . . . . . . . . . . . . .   10,000
              Notes Receivable  . . . . . . . . . . . . . . . . . . . . . . . . . . . . . . . . .                10,000
                 To remove the note and the contingent liability from the accounts.
```

This entry reduces the balance of each of these accounts to zero.

Discounted notes receivable not paid by maker. If Kent Company dishonors its note, the Michigan National Bank will collect the principal ($10,000), interest ($150), and any protest fee (assume it to be $5) from Clark Company. Clark Company will have to make two entries as follows:

```
July 3   Notes Receivable Discounted ...........................   10,000
              Notes Receivable ......................................            10,000
         To remove the note and the contingent liability from the accounts.

     3   Dishonored Notes Receivable ...........................   10,155
              Cash ................................................            10,155
         To record the cash deducted from our account by the bank on
         the note dishonored by Kent.
```

Clark Company will then try to collect $10,155 from Kent Company. If this cannot be done, the $10,155 will be removed from the Dishonored Notes Receivable account and treated as a loss from bad debts.

Long-term notes   Notes may be either short term or long term. They are usually short term. But when they are long term (have maturities exceeding approximately one year) they are to be recorded at their present cash value.[1] To illustrate, assume the existence of a $1,000 face value note, bearing no explicit rate of interest, which is due one year from its date. Even though this does not "exceed approximately one year" and technically would not have to be recorded at its present value, it is assumed the company chooses to do so. Assume that the rate of interest to be used in reducing this note to its present value is 6 percent. To solve for the present value one should ask the following question: What amount if invested at 6 percent would grow to $1,000 one year from now? If x equals that amount, the calculation is:

$$x + .06x = \$1,000$$
$$1.06x = \$1,000$$
$$x = \frac{\$1,000}{1.06} = \$943.40$$

Assuming the note payable results from the purchase of a machine on December 31, 1980, it is recorded as follows:

```
Machinery ................................................   943.40
Notes Payable—Discount .................................    56.60
     Notes Payable .......................................            1,000.00
Gave note to purchase machinery.
```

At the due date, $1,000 is paid to the payee and $56.60 is recorded as interest expense. The required entry at the due date, December 31, 1981, is:

```
Notes Payable ...........................................   1,000.00
Interest Expense ........................................      56.60
     Notes Payable—Discount ..............................              56.60
     Cash ................................................           1,000.00
Paid note payable.
```

The accounting for the interest in this type of transaction is quite similar to that used when a company discounts its own note at the bank.

Most long-term notes do bear an explicit rate of interest. When such a note arises from an arm's-length transaction, it is assumed that the rate of interest stipulated by the parties represents fair and adequate compensation

---

[1] Accounting Principles Board, "Interest on Receivables and Payables," *APB Opinion No. 21* (New York: AICPA, August 1971).

to the supplier of funds. In these instances, the note payable is recorded at the purchase price of the asset acquired. An example of such a transaction is the mortgage note payable.

Mortgage note payable.   Sometimes companies give their own notes to finance the acquisition of a plant asset. Such a note is usually a long-term liability and is secured by a mortgage on the property acquired. A mortgage is an obligation to give up the property that has been pledged to the payee in case the maker defaults on the payments. Most of us become familiar with this form of financing when we purchase a house. Business firms also sometimes use this method of financing when they acquire assets such as buildings.

This form of financing can be illustrated by looking at a situation where a business is acquiring a building. The borrower makes a constant lump-sum payment each month (exclusive of real estate taxes), which at first pays mostly interest and very little principal. Assume that the mortgage is $35,000, the interest rate is 8 percent, and the life of the note is 25 years. There are mortgage payment schedule books which indicate that the monthly payment for principal and interest is $271. Here is how the first two months' and the last month's payments are applied:

	Monthly payment	Interest	Principal	Principal balance
Date of purchase	—	—	—	$35,000.00
First month	$271	$233.33	$ 37.67	34,962.33
Second month	271	233.08	37.92	34,924.41
300th month	271	2.00	269.00	-0-

Notice that interest is calculated on the latest principal balance. For instance, when the first $271 payment is made, interest is calculated as follows:

$$\frac{\$35,000 \times 0.08}{12} = \$233.33$$

It is necessary to divide by 12 because the interest rate is 8 percent per year and the calculation of the amount is for one month. The excess of the payment over the interest is applied against the principal ($37.67 in the first payment above). Thus, the principal balance decreases slowly (but more rapidly each month), so that the last $271 payment at the end of 25 years pays interest of approximately $2 on the remaining principal balance of approximately $269 and reduces the principal balance to zero.

NEW TERMS INTRODUCED IN CHAPTER 8

Aging (of accounts receivable)—a process of classifying accounts receivable according to their age in appraising the accounts for purposes of establishing or adding to the balance in an Allowance for Doubtful Accounts account.

Allowance for doubtful accounts—a contra account to accounts receivable designed to reduce gross accounts receivable to their net realizable value.

Bad debts expense—an operating expense a business incurs when it sells on credit. It results from nonpayment of accounts receivable.

Credit cards—charge cards such as VISA, American Express, and Master Charge which are used by customers to charge their purchases of goods and services.

Discounting notes receivable—the act of transferring a note receivable with recourse to a bank. With recourse means that the bank can collect from the company which transferred the note to the bank if the maker does not pay at maturity. The proceeds are equal to the maturity value less the discount (amount charged by the bank). The discount is computed as the maturity value times the annual discount rate times the number of days the bank must hold the note to maturity divided by 360. In computing the number of days, the maturity date is included while the date of discount is excluded.

Dishonored notes receivable account—an account showing notes which the makers failed to pay at maturity and which have not yet been written off.

Installment sales—sales of merchandise to customers under terms which allow the customer to pay equal monthly payments over an extended period of time, up to 36 months.

Maker—the person preparing and signing a promissory note.

Maturity value—the amount the holder of a negotiable instrument is entitled to receive at the due date. Included in the amount are the principal and accrued interest, if any.

Note, promissory—an unconditional promise made in writing by one person to another, signed by the maker, engaging to pay on demand or at a definite time a sum certain (a certain sum) in money to order or to bearer.

Notes payable—discount—a contra account used to reduce Notes Payable to their net present value. The amount in the discount account is converted into interest expense as time passes.

Payable—any amount of money due to be paid to any party for any reason resulting from a past transaction.

Payee—the person to whose order payment is promised or ordered on a note or other negotiable instrument.

Percentage of accounts receivable method—a method of determining the desired size of the allowance for doubtful accounts and, indirectly, the bad debts expense for the period. This method has two variations. One is to use an overall percentage, and the other is to use the aging technique.

Percentage of sales method—a method of estimating the expected amount of uncollectible accounts from a given period's credit sales and, indirectly, of determining the balance in the Allowance for Doubtful Accounts account.

Receivables—sums of money due to be received for any reason resulting from past transactions.

DEMONSTRATION PROBLEM

Part a. A $15,000, 90-day, 12 percent note dated June 15, 1981, was received by the Long Company from the Short Company in payment of its account.

Required:

Prepare the journal entries in the records of the Long Company for each of the following:

1. Receipt of the note, June 15, 1981.
2. The Long Company discounted the note on July 15, 1981, at 10 percent at the Citizens' National Bank.
3. The Short Company paid the note at maturity.
4. Assume that the Short Company did not pay the note at maturity. The Citizens' National Bank charged the note, plus a protest fee of $8, to the Long Company. The Long Company decided that the note was uncollectible.

Part b. The Best Company estimates its bad debts expense to be 1 percent of sales. Sales in 1981 are $750,000.

Required:

Prepare the journal entries for the following transactions:

1. The company prepares the adjusting entry for bad debts for the year 1981.
2. On January 15, 1982, the company decided that the account for James Ryan in the amount of $500 is uncollectible.
3. On February 12, 1982, James Ryan's check for $500 arrives.

Solution to demonstration problem

Part a.

1. 1981
    June 15 Notes Receivable 15,000.00
                  Accounts Receivable 15,000.00
                  To record receipt of a note from Short Company.

2. July 15 Cash 15,192.50
                  Notes Receivable Discounted 15,000.00
                  Interest Revenue 192.50
                  To record the discounting.

                  Computation of cash proceeds:
                    Maturity value $15,450.00
                    (Days until maturity = 60)
                    Discount $15,450 × 10% × 60 days 257.50
                                            $15,192.50

3. Sept. 13 Notes Receivable Discounted 15,000.00
                  Notes Receivable 15,000.00
                  To remove the note and contingent liability.

4. Sept. 13 Dishonored Notes Receivable 15,458.00
                  Cash 15,458.00
                  To record the charge made against our account for the Short Company note of $15,000, interest of $450, and protest fee of $8.

        13 Notes Receivable Discounted 15,000.00
                  Notes Receivable 15,000.00
                  To remove the note and contingent liability.

13	Allowance for Doubtful Accounts*	15,458.00	
	Dishonored Notes Receivable		15,458.00

To write off the Short Company note as uncollectible.

* This debit assumes that notes receivable were taken into consideration when an allowance was established. If it has not, a debit to Bad Debts Expense or Loss from Dishonored Notes Receivable should be made.

Part b.

1. 1981

Dec. 31	Bad Debts Expense	7,500	
	Allowance for Doubtful Accounts		7,500

To record estimated bad debts for the year.

2. 1982

Jan. 15	Allowance for Doubtful Accounts	500	
	Accounts Receivable, James Ryan		500

To write off the account of James Ryan as uncollectible.

3. 1982

Feb. 12	Cash	500	
	Accounts Receivable, James Ryan		500

To record the collection of James Ryan's account receivable.

Feb. 12	Accounts Receivable, James Ryan	500	
	Allowance for Doubtful Accounts		500

To correct the write-off of James Ryan's account on January 15.

QUESTIONS

1. What are the two major purposes to be accomplished in establishing an allowance for possible uncollectible accounts?

2. In view of the fact that it is impossible to estimate the exact amount of uncollectible accounts receivable for any one year in advance, what exactly does the Allowance for Doubtful Accounts account contain after a number of years?

3. How might information in an aging schedule prove useful to management for purposes other than estimating the size of the required allowance for doubtful accounts?

4. In view of the difficulty in estimating future events, would you recommend that accountants wait until collections are made from customers before recording sales revenue? Or wait until known accounts prove to be uncollectible before charging an expense account?

5. The credit manager of a company has established a policy of seeking to eliminate completely all losses from uncollectible accounts. Is this a desirable objective for a company? Explain.

6. For a company using the allowance method of accounting for uncollectible accounts, which of the following affects its reported net earnings: (1) the establishment of the allowance, (2) the writing off of a specific account, (3) the recovery of an account previously written off as uncollectible?

7. Explain why an account receivable might have a credit balance. What is the proper treatment of such an item in the financial statement?

8. Why might a retailer agree to sell by credit card when such a substantial discount is taken by the credit card agency in paying the retailer?

9. At what value should merchandise which had been sold on an installment basis be recorded when repossessed?

10. Differentiate between dishonored notes receivable and notes receivable discounted. How is each shown in the statement of financial position?

11. Describe two ways involving a note payable in which amounts can be borrowed from a bank.

12. Why might a situation arise in which the bank rate of discount is less than the rate in a customer's note which the holding company discounts at the bank?

13. At what amount should long-term notes payable be recorded?

14. How is interest calculated on a mortgage note payable each month?

EXERCISES

E–1. How should the following situation be shown in the balance sheet? The subsidiary accounts receivable ledger of the Matson Company shows a total of $124,000. An examination of the accounts shows one account of $15,000 due from the president of the company. The composition of this account is as follows:

a. Due from sale of merchandise, $4,000.

b. A loan of $11,000.

E–2. How should the following appear in the balance sheet of the Bee Company on December 31, 1980? Why?

Accounts receivable (including credit balances of
$700) $123,000
Accounts payable (including advance payments to
vendors of $500) 87,000

E–3. On December 28, 1980, Jordan Company received a check for $2,500 as a 10 percent down payment on an order for merchandise from the Argonne Company. Argonne is not indebted to Jordan at this time. The receipt was recorded by debiting Cash and crediting Argonne's Accounts Receivable account. The merchandise was not delivered until January 5, 1981. On December 31, 1980, the trial balance amount of accounts receivable was $172,000. Indicate the proper balance sheet presentation of the above data.

E–4. The accounts of the Baldon Company as of December 31, 1980, show Accounts Receivable, $90,000; Allowance for Doubtful Accounts, $500; Sales, $540,000; and Sales Returns and Allowances, $10,000. Prepare journal entries to adjust for possible uncollectible accounts under each of the following assumptions:

a. Uncollectible accounts are estimated at one half of 1 percent of net sales.

b. The allowance is to be increased to 3 percent of accounts receivable.

E–5. On April 1, 1980, Brackton Company, which employs the allowance method of accounting for uncollectible accounts, wrote off Bill Combs' account receivable of $352. On December 14, 1980, the company received a check for that amount from Combs marked "in full of account." Prepare the necessary entries for all of the above.

E–6. Compute the required size of the Allowance for Doubtful Accounts account for the following receivables:

Accounts receivable	Age (months)	Probability of collection
$100,000	Less than 1	0.95
40,000	1 to 3	0.80
20,000	3 to 6	0.70
5,000	6 to 12	0.40
1,000	12 and over	0.10

E–7. You have read the rule that when the terms of an obligation are 6 percent for 60 days you can look at the face amount of the obligation and move the decimal point two places to the left to find the dollar amount of interest. Prove that this rule is true.

E–8. Bauer gives a 90-day, $15,000, 8 percent note to Beebe in exchange for merchandise. Give the entry that each will make on the maturity date, assuming payment is made.

E–9. Give the entries that Bauer and Beebe (see Exercise E–8) would make at the maturity date assuming that Bauer defaults.

E–10. Determine the maturity dates for notes with each of the following lives:

Issue date	Life
January 13, 1980	1 year
January 31, 1980	1 month
June 4, 1980	30 days
December 1, 1979	90 days

E-11. Austin Company gives a 120-day, $5,000, 6 percent note to Chase Company on July 6, 1980. Chase Company discounts the note at the bank on August 20, 1980. The rate of discount is 6 percent. Determine the entries each company would make on the date of discounting.

E-12. In Exercise E-11, if Austin Company fails to make payment on the maturity date, what entries are required on the books of each company?

E-13. Day Kreuzburg goes to the bank and asks to borrow $1,000 at 6 percent for a 60-day period. Give the

entry which should be made to record the proceeds received for each of the following alternatives:

a. He signs a note for $1,000. Interest is deducted from the face amount in determining the proceeds.

b. He receives $1,000 and signs a note for that amount. The interest is to be paid at the maturity date.

E-14. Give the entry or entries which would be made at the maturity date for each of the alternatives given in Exercise E-13 assuming the loan is repaid before the end of the accounting period.

PROBLEMS, SERIES A

P8-1-A. Presented below are selected accounts of the Robinson Company as of December 31, 1980. Prior to closing the accounts, the $2,000 account of Lake Company is to be written off (this was a credit sale of February 12, 1980).

Accounts receivable	$ 160,000
Allowance for doubtful accounts	2,000 Dr.
Sales	1,120,000
Sales returns and allowances	20,000

Required:

a. Present journal entries to record the above and to record the bad debts expense for the period, assuming the estimated expense is 2 percent of net sales.

b. Give the entry to record the estimated expense for the period if the allowance is to be adjusted to 5 percent of outstanding receivables instead of as in **(a)** above.

P8-2-A. The accounts receivable (all arising under sales terms of n/30) of the Bently Company at December 31, 1980, total $200,000. The age composition of $180,000 of these accounts is:

Age	Amount
Not yet due	$142,000
1–30 days past due	18,000
31–60 days past due	8,000
61–90 days past due	6,000
91–120 days past due	4,000
Over 120 days past due	2,000
	$180,000

Given below are the four other accounts which account for the remaining $20,000 of accounts receivable:

Company A

Date		Explanation	Folio	Debit	Credit	Balance
1980						
Jan.	1	Balance forwarded (12/27/79 sale)				2,000
Feb.	7		SJ-14	8,000		10,000
	10		CRJ-3		2,000	8,000
Mar.	1		CRJ-6		2,000	6,000
July	5		SJ-17	1,200		7,200
	8		CRJ-20		2,000	5,200
Nov.	3		CRJ-31		400	4,800

Company B

Date		Explanation	Folio	Debit	Credit	Balance
1980						
Jan.	10		SJ-5	5,000		5,000
Feb.	1		CRJ-3		-2,500	2,500
Mar.	4	Allowance granted 1/10 sale	GJ-5		-1,000	1,500
June	2		CRJ-16		-500	1,000
	6		SJ-16	300		1,300
July	3		CRJ-19		- 500	800
Sept.	12		SJ-30	900		1,700
	15		CRJ-22		200	1,500
Nov.	30		CRJ-32		400	1,100

Company C

Date		Explanation	Folio	Debit	Credit	Balance
1980						
July	5		SJ-17	1,500		1,500
Aug.	2		CRJ-20		500	1,000
	28		SJ-28	1,000		2,000
Sept.	5		CRJ-21		500	1,500
Oct.	5		CRJ-28		500	1,000
	6		SJ-32	12,700		13,700
Nov.	3		CRJ-31		2,000	11,700

Company D

Date		Explanation	Folio	Debit	Credit	Balance
1980						
Aug.	22		SJ-26	1,000		1,000
Sept.	5		CRJ-21		1,000	-0-
	12		SJ-30	1,200		1,200
	30		SJ-31	500		1,700
Oct.	5		CRJ-28		1,700	-0-
	28		SJ-34	1,300		1,300
Nov.	2	Adjustment granted	GJ-17		100	1,200
	7		CRJ-31		1,000	200
	10		SJ-36	1,800		2,000
Dec.	5		CRJ-34		1,800	200
	11		SJ-38	2,200		2,400

Note: The abbreviations in the Folio column stand for the following: CRJ = Cash Receipts Journal; SJ = Sales Journal; and GJ = General Journal. These journals are illustrated in Chapter 6.

Required:

a. Prepare an aging schedule for the accounts receivable of the Bently Company. Compute the required Allowance for Doubtful Accounts balance assuming estimated percentages of uncollectable accounts of ½, 1, 2, 5, 10, and 25 percent, respectively, for the six classifications given above.

b. Prepare the necessary adjusting journal entry assuming the allowance has a debit balance of $600.

P8–3–A. The W. Smothers Company is a retail store which sells men's clothing. On its merchandise sales to customers it allows them to pay cash or charge the purchase with a VISA credit card. When the charge slips are forwarded to the credit agency, a discount of 5 percent is deducted in making payment.

Summarized transactions for the first week of September 1980 were as follows:

1. Sold men's clothing:
   For cash, $4,200.
   On VISA credit cards, $8,600.
2. Received payment from the credit card agency for $8,200 of the purchases on VISA credit cards in (1) above.
3. The agency notified the retailer that $400 was charged on credit cards which appeared on its list of canceled cards, for which it could not make payment. The Smothers Company was unable to locate the persons making those purchases. ~~No allowance for doubtful accounts exists, since no bad debts were expected~~.

Required:

a. Prepare journal entries to record the transactions given.

b. Comment on the advantages of accepting credit cards for purchases and on how the retailer can avoid the loss it suffered during September.

P8-4-A. The Rymer Company received on July 24, 1980, a note from the Watt Company with the following description:

Face amount	$30,000
Life of note	90 days
Date of note	7/24/80
Interest rate on note	10%
Date of discounting note at the bank	8/23/80
Rate of discount charged by the bank	12%

Required:

Determine:

a. The maturity date of the note.

b. The maturity value of the note.

c. The number of days from the discount date to the maturity date.

d. The dollar amount of the discount.

e. The cash proceeds received by the company.

f. The entry to record the receipt of the proceeds at the date of discount.

P8-5-A. Using the simplified method illustrated in the text, compute the interest when the terms are as follows:

	Interest rate	Life	Face amount
a.	6%	60 days	$ 7,245
b.	2	90 days	10,000
c.	1	50 days	3,000
d.	9	40 days	8,000
e.	12	20 days	4,500

P8-6-A. The Reetz Company has an accounting period of one year, ending on July 31. On July 1, 1980, the balances of certain ledger accounts are Notes Receivable, $24,800, Notes Receivable Discounted, $12,000, and Notes Payable, $40,000. The balance in Notes Receivable consists of the following:

Face amount	Maker	Date of note	Life	Interest rate	Date discounted	Discount rate
$12,000	May Co.	5/15/80	60 days	12%	6/1/80	12%
4,000	Brad Co.	6/1/80	60 days	12	—	—
8,800	Ross Co.	6/15/80	30 days	10	—	—
$24,800						

The note payable is a 60-day bank loan dated May 20, 1980. Interest Expense was debited for the discount, which is at a rate of 6 percent.

Required:

Prepare dated journal entries for the following transactions and necessary July 31 adjustments.

Transactions:

July 1 The Reetz Company discounted its own $12,000, 60-day, noninterest-bearing note at the State Bank. The discount rate is 10 percent and the note is dated today.

3 Received a 20-day, 12 percent note, dated today, from the Jones Company in settlement of an account receivable of $2,400.

6 Purchased merchandise from the May Company, $19,200, and issued a 60-day, 12 percent note, dated today, for the purchase.

8 Sold merchandise to the Wood Company, $16,000. A 30-day, 12 percent note, dated today, is received to cover the sale.

14 The $12,000 note discounted on June 1, 1980, is paid by the May Company directly to the holder in due course.

15 The Ross Company sent a $4,000, 30-day, 12 percent note, dated today, and a check to cover its notes of June 15, 1980, and interest in full to this date.

18 The Wood Company note of July 8 is discounted at the State Bank for the remaining life of the note. The discount rate is 12 percent.

19 The note payable dated May 20, 1980, is paid in full.

23 The Jones Company dishonored its note of July 3, due today.

26 The Jones Company sent a check for the interest on the dishonored note and a new 30-day, 12 percent note dated July 23, 1980.

30 The Brad Company note dated June 1, 1980, is paid with interest in full.

PROBLEMS, SERIES B

P8–1–B. As of December 31, 1980, the Bridges Company's accounts prior to adjustment show:

Accounts receivable	$ 84,000
Allowance for doubtful accounts	3,000
Sales	900,000

Bridges Company follows a practice of estimating uncollectible accounts at 1 percent of sales.

On February 23, 1981, the account of Don Cole in the amount of $3,200 is considered uncollectible and is written off. On August 12, 1981, Cole remits $500 and indicates that he intends to pay the balance due as soon as possible. By December 31, 1981, no further remittance has been received from Cole.

Required:

a. Prepare journal entries to record all of the above transactions and adjusting entries.

b. Give the entry necessary as of December 31, 1980, if the Bridges Company estimated its uncollectible accounts at 8 percent of outstanding receivables rather than at 1 percent of sales.

P8–2–B. The accounts receivable (all arising under sales terms of n/30) of the Potts Company as of December 31, 1980, total $280,000. The age composition of $250,000 of these accounts is:

Age	Amount
Not yet due	$205,000
Past due:	
1–30 days	30,000
31–60 days	8,000
61–90 days	2,000
91–120 days	1,000
Over 120 days	4,000
	$250,000

Given below are the three other accounts which account for the remaining $30,000 of accounts receivable:

James, Inc.

Date		Explanation	Folio	Debit	Credit	Balance
1980						
Jan.	1	Balance forward				3,000
		(12/28/79 sale)				
	8		CRJ-2		3,000	–0–
	11		SJ-1	4,000		4,000
Feb.	5		CRJ-2		4,000	–0–
Sept.	18		SJ-9	5,000		5,000
	26	Adjustment granted	GJ-9		700	4,300
Oct.	5		CRJ-10		4,000	300
	8		SJ-10	2,500		2,800
Nov.	3		CRJ-11		2,500	300
	15		SJ-11	3,200		3,500
Dec.	4		CRJ-12		3,200	300
	18		SJ-12	4,300		4,600
	21		SJ-12	2,000		6,600

Knobloch Company

Date		Explanation	Folio	Debit	Credit	Balance
1980						
Apr.	5		SJ-4	2,200		2,200
May	5		CRJ-5		2,200	–0–
Aug.	3		SJ-8	2,100		2,100
Sept.	5	Return	GJ-9		500	1,600
	11		CRJ-9		1,600	–0–
Oct.	15		SJ-10	6,300		6,300
Nov.	7		CRJ-11		1,500	4,800
	10		SJ-11	500		5,300
Dec.	15		CRJ-12		1,000	4,300

Kyle Company

Date		Explanation	Folio	Debit	Credit	Balance
1980						6,200
Jan.	1	Balance forward				
	8		CRJ-1		6,200	–0–
Feb.	18		SJ-2	11,000		11,000
Mar.	6		CRJ-3		11,000	–0–
May	19		SJ-5	2,200		2,200
June	1		SJ-6	1,100		3,300
	7		CRJ-6		2,200	1,100
	23		SJ-6	20,500		21,600
July	5		CRJ-7		21,600	–0–
Oct.	15		SJ-10	23,000		23,000
Nov.	3		CRJ-11		4,000	19,000
	9		SJ-11	5,400		24,400
	18	Return 10/15 sale	GJ-11		300	24,100
Dec.	5		CRJ-12		8,000	16,100
	17		SJ-12	3,000		19,100

Note: The abbreviations in the Folio column stand for the following: CRJ = Cash Receipts Journal; SJ = Sales Journal; and GJ = General Journal. These journals are illustrated in Chapter 6.

Required:

a. Prepare an aging schedule classifying the accounts as per the age groups given above.

b. Assuming the Allowance for Doubtful Accounts has a debit balance of $2,100, prepare the necessary adjusting journal entry for estimated uncollectible accounts as of December 31, 1980, if the amount of uncollectible accounts is estimated at ½, 1, 2, 5, 10, and 25 percent, respectively, of the age groups given above.

c. What has apparently happened with regard to $300 of the balance of the James, Inc., account? What is the probability of collecting this balance?

P8–3–B. The Andrews Company discounted its own $5,000, noninterest-bearing, 180-day note on November 16, 1980, at the Chautauqua County Bank at a discount rate of 12 percent.

Required:

Prepare dated journal entries for—

a. The original discounting on November 16.

b. The adjustment required at the end of the company's calendar-year accounting period.

c. Payment at maturity.

P8–4–B. On June 1, 1980, the Stevens Company received a $6,000, 120-day, 8 percent note from the Thomas Company dated June 1, 1980. On August 15, 1980, the note was discounted at the bank. The rate of discount was 12 percent.

Required:

Determine:

a. The maturity value of the note.

b. The number of days from the discount date to the maturity date.

c. The dollar amount of the discount.

d. The cash proceeds received by the company.

e. The proper entry to record the receipt of proceeds at the date of discount.

P8–5–B. Following are selected transactions of the Brown Company:

Oct. 31 Discounted its own 30-day, $10,000, noninterest-bearing note at the First State Bank at 12 percent.

Nov. 8 Received a $5,000, 30-day, 9 percent note from the Best Company in settlement of an account receivable. The note is dated November 8.

15 Purchased merchandise by issuing its own 90-day note for $4,800. The note is dated November 15 and bears interest at 12 percent.

20 Discounted the Best Company note at 12 percent at the First State Bank.

30 The First State Bank notified the Brown Company that it had charged the note of October 31 against the company's checking account.

Required:

Assume that all notes falling due after November 30 were paid in full on their due dates by the respective makers. Prepare dated journal entries for the Brown Company for all of the above transactions (including the payment of the notes after November 30) and all necessary adjusting entries assuming a fiscal year accounting period ending on November 30.

P8–6–B. The Giersch Company is in the power boat manufacturing business. As of September 1, the balance in its Notes Receivable account is $46,000. The balance in the Notes Receivable Discounted account is $14,000, and the balance in Dishonored Notes Receivable is $10,110. A schedule of the notes (including the dishonored note) is as follows:

Face amount	Maker	Date	Life	Interest rate	Comments
$20,000	C. Davis Co.	6/1/80	120 days	12%	
12,000	A. Box Co.	6/15/80	90 days	8	
14,000	C. Bean Co.	7/1/80	90 days	10	Discounted 8/16/80 at 6%
10,000	Y. Sole Co.	7/1/80	60 days	6	Dishonored, interest, $100; protest fee, $10
$56,000					

Required:

Prepare dated journal entries for the following 1980 transactions.

Transactions:

Sept. 5 The C. Davis Company note is discounted at the Fulton County Bank. The discount rate is 10 percent.

10 Received $6,110 from the Y. Sole Company as full settlement of the amount due from it. The company does not charge losses on notes to the Allowance for Doubtful Accounts account.

? The A. Box Company note is collected when due.

? The C. Davis Company note is not paid at maturity. The bank deducts the balance from the Giersch Company's bank balance. A protest fee of $8 is also deducted.

? C. Bean Company pays its note at maturity.

30 Received a new 60-day, 12 percent note from the C. Davis Company for the total balance due on the dishonored note. The note is dated as of the maturity date of the dishonored note. The Giersch Company accepts the note in good faith.

BUSINESS DECISION PROBLEM 8–1

Tom Larson runs a hardware store, selling items for both cash and on account. During 1980, which seemed to be a typical year, some of his operating and other data were as follows:

Sales:

For cash	$200,000
On credit	400,000
Cost of obtaining credit reports on customers	$ 600
Cost incurred in paying a part-time bookkeeper to keep the accounts receivable subsidiary ledger up to date	$ 2,000
Costs associated with preparing and mailing invoices to customers and other collection activities	$ 3,000
Bad debts arising from uncollectible accounts	$ 7,500
The average outstanding accounts receivable balance (on which Tom estimates he could have earned 10% if it had been invested in other assets)	$ 30.000

A national credit card agency has approached Tom and tried to convince him that instead of carrying his own accounts receivable he should only accept its credit card for sales on credit. The agency would pay Tom within two days of his submitting sales charges. It would deduct 6 percent from the amount and pay him 94 percent.

Required:

a. Using the data given, prepare an analysis showing whether or not it would pay Tom to switch to the credit card method of selling on credit.

b. What other factors should be taken into consideration?

BUSINESS DECISION PROBLEM 8–2

Mike Bondo operates a large fruit and vegetable stand on the outskirts of a city. In a typical year he sells $1,000,000 of goods to regular customers. His sales are 40 percent for cash and 60 percent on credit. He carries all of the credit himself. Only after a customer has a total of $200 unpaid balance on which no payments have been made for two months does he refuse that customer credit for future purchases. His income before taxes is approximately $350,000. The total of uncollectible accounts for a given year are about 10 percent of credit sales, or $60,000.

You are one of Mike's regular customers. He knows that you are taking a course in accounting in college and has asked you to tell him your opinion of several alternatives which have been recommended to him to reduce or eliminate $60,000 per year bad debt loss. The recommended alternatives are as follows:

1. Do not sell on credit.
2. Sell on credit by national credit card only.
3. Allow customers to charge only until their account balance reaches $50.
4. Allow a bill collector to "go after" bad debts. He would keep half of what he collects.
5. Require all credit customers to sign a note so that Mike can discount these at the local bank.

Required:

Give Mike your opinion as to the advisability of following any of these alternatives.

Chapter 9

Measuring and reporting
inventories

In Chapter 5 the amount of merchandise on hand at any point in time was called the merchandise inventory of a specific business. Cost was used as a basis for measuring and reporting its amount. Illustrations showed (1) how the inventory amount was used in computing cost of goods sold and (2) how inventory was presented as an asset on the balance sheet. But a number of important questions about inventory have not yet been answered. They include (1) What cost elements should be included in inventory? (2) What methods may be used to determine the cost of ending inventory?

THE NATURE AND SIGNIFICANCE OF INVENTORY: Definition of inventory

Inventory is one of the largest and most important assets owned by a merchandising or manufacturing business. In certain companies it may be several times the size of other assets.

What is included in inventory varies with the nature of the business. Retail and wholesale merchandising businesses buy merchandise from others and sell it in the condition in which it is acquired. Thus, they have only one important item of *inventory—merchandise held for resale.*

Manufacturing companies generally have three inventory items—*raw materials, work in process,* and *finished goods.* The finished goods inventory of a manufacturer is similar to a merchandiser's inventory. Both finished goods and merchandise inventory are ready for sale to customers. On the other hand, raw materials and work in process inventories require more processing before they can be sold.

Since current assets are listed in the balance sheet in order of liquidity (with the most liquid first), inventories usually are listed after accounts receivable. In addition, factory, store, and office supplies sometimes are listed as supplies inventory, even though such items actually are *not* offered for sale to customers.

Broadly speaking, inventory can be defined as the sum of those items of tangible property which (1) are held for sale in the ordinary course of business, (2) are in process of production for such sale, or (3) are to be currently consumed in the production of goods or services which will be available for sale.[1]

Importance of proper inventory measurement

An accurate measurement of the ending inventory is necessary to reflect the proper net earnings for the period. When the periodic inventory system is used, ending inventory is subtracted from cost of goods available for sale to determine the cost of goods sold. Cost of goods sold is then deducted from revenues to compute gross margin and net earnings. Thus, if ending inventory is misstated, cost of goods sold, gross margin, and net earnings will also be misstated. Also, since the inventory amount is shown as a current asset in the balance sheet, any misstatement in its measurement means that statement is in error.

If the ending inventory is overstated, then current assets are overstated, and total assets are similarly overstated. At the same time, cost of goods

---

[1] Committee on Accounting Procedure, American Institute of Certified Public Accountants, "Accounting Research Bulletin No. 43," *Accounting Research and Terminology Bulletins, Final Edition* (New York, 1961), p. 27.

sold is understated with a resulting overstatement of gross margin, net earnings, and owner's equity. To illustrate (assuming periodic inventory procedure):

	For the year ended December 31, 1981			
	Ending inventory correctly stated		Ending inventory overstated	
Sales		$800,000		$800,000
Cost of goods available for sale	$600,000		$600,000	
Ending inventory	70,000	530,000	80,000	520,000
Gross margin		$270,000		$280,000

As shown, when ending inventory is overstated by $10,000, gross margin is overstated by $10,000. Current assets and total assets will also be overstated by $10,000.

Net earnings, whether misstated or not, are closed to the capital account (owner's equity). If net earnings are misstated, capital is misstated in an amount and direction which brings the balance sheet into balance even though the inventory is misstated. In other words, capital and inventory are both stated incorrectly by the same amount and in the same direction. In the example above, inventory and capital are both overstated by $10,000. Thus, the balance sheet totals balance but at the incorrect amount.

Assuming a correct ending inventory for the next year (ending December 31, 1982), the preceding illustration is continued below (last year's ending inventory is this year's beginning inventory):

	For the year ended December 31, 1982			
	Beginning inventory correctly stated		Beginning inventory overstated	
Sales		$850,000		$850,000
Beginning inventory, January 1	$ 70,000		$ 80,000	
Purchases	530,000		530,000	
Cost of goods available for sale	$600,000		$610,000	
Less: Ending inventory, December 31	50,000		50,000	
Cost of goods sold		550,000		560,000
Gross margin		$300,000		$290,000

An overstated beginning inventory understates gross margin by an equal amount. Likewise, an understated beginning inventory overstates gross margin. The overall results of the two periods (1981 and 1982) are summarized as follows:

	1981 and 1982 inventories correct	1981 ending inventory overstated
Gross margin, 1981	$270,000	$280,000
Gross margin, 1982	300,000	290,000
Gross margin, 1981 and 1982	$570,000	$570,000

The above table shows clearly that inventory errors affect gross margin and net earnings and that an error in one period's ending inventory automatically causes an error in the opposite direction in the next period. Thus, it is important to understand the significance of the measurement of the inventory in the determination of a major expense (cost of goods sold) and then net earnings.

THE COST OF INVENTORY: Possible inclusions

The cost of inventory includes all outlays that are necessary to obtain the goods and place them in their existing condition and location. Thus, cost includes:

1. The price on the invoice received from the seller.
2. Insurance in transit (when ultimately paid by the buyer).
3. Transportation charges from the seller to the buyer (when ultimately paid by the buyer).
4. Handling costs.

When the periodic inventory system is used, the Purchases account is normally debited for the invoice price of the goods acquired. Preferably, the cost of insurance in transit and transportation-in should be debited to separate accounts.

Inventory and purchase discounts. The method used to account for purchase discounts affects the measurement of inventory and cost of goods sold. As described in Chapter 5, the company may record the purchase at the *gross* invoice price at the time of acquisition, with a purchase discount recorded if payment is made within the discount period. Alternatively, the *net* invoice price may be debited to the appropriate account at the time of acquisition and a Discounts Lost account debited for the discount lost if payment is made after expiration of the discount period. Under the net price method, although discounts lost are technically losses, they usually are treated as an element of financial expense. They are classified among the "other expenses" in the earnings statement.

Inventory measurement under varying prices

The general rule. *Accounting Research Bulletin No. 43* states that the "primary basis of accounting for inventories is cost . . ." and that "a departure from the cost basis . . . is required when the utility of the goods is no longer as great as . . ." their cost. Thus, inventories are usually reported in the balance sheet at a dollar amount described as *cost or market, whichever is lower.*

But this general rule does not indicate how the cost of goods available for sale should be assigned to ending inventory and cost of goods sold when goods have been acquired at different unit costs. For instance, suppose a retailer has three units of a given product on hand. One unit was acquired at $20, another at $22, and the third at $24. Now the retailer sells two of the units for $30 each. What is the cost of the two units sold? Is it $42, the cost of the first and second units; $44, the cost of the first and third units; or $46, the cost of the second and third units? Or is it $44, determined as two units at an average cost of $22? Four inventory costing methods have

Illustration 9.1: Beginning
inventory, purchases,
and sales

Beginning inventory and purchases				Sales			
Date	Units	Unit cost	Total cost	Date	Units	Price	Total
Jan. 1	10	$8.00	$ 80	Mar. 10	10	$12.00	$120
Mar. 2	10	8.50	85	July 14	20	12.00	240
May 28	20	8.40	168	Sept. 7	10	14.00	140
Aug. 12	10	9.00	90	Nov. 22	20	14.00	280
Oct. 12	20	8.80	176				
Dec. 21	10	9.10	91				
	80		$690		60		$780

been developed to solve this type of problem. They are (1) specific identification; (2) first-in, first-out (Fifo); (3) last-in, first-out (Lifo); and (4) average.

The data in Illustration 9.1 are assumed with regard to the beginning inventory, purchases, and sales of a given product in order to illustrate the determination of inventory cost. Total goods available for sale consist of 80 units with a total cost of $690. Sixty of the available units were sold, producing sales revenue of $780. Twenty units were left on hand in inventory.

Methods of determining cost of inventory

Specific identification. This method can be used when it is known that a particular cost attaches to an identifiable unit of product. It can be easily applied when large items such as automobiles are purchased and sold. When the *specific identification* method is used, each item is identified by means of a serial number plate or identification tag.

To illustrate, assume that the 20 units of product on hand at the end of the year in the above illustration can be identified as 10 from the August 12 purchase and 10 from the December 21 purchase. The ending inventory is shown in Illustration 9.2. *The $181 cost of the ending inventory is subtracted from the total cost of goods available for sale of $690 to get the cost of goods sold of $509.*

The earnings statement would report the *cost of goods sold* under the *specific identification* method in the following manner:

Cost of goods available for sale	$690
Less: Ending inventory	181
Cost of goods sold	$509

The cost of goods sold of $509 would be an expense in the earnings statement and the $181 of ending inventory would be a current asset in the

Illustration 9.2: Ending
inventory under
specific identification

Purchased	Units	Unit cost	Total cost
August 12	10	$9.00	$ 90
December 21	10	9.10	91
Total	20		$181

balance sheet. This accounts for the total cost of goods available for sale of $690.

When the specific identification method is used, cost of goods sold and inventory are stated in terms of the actual cost of the actual units sold and on hand. The method is criticized because it may result in identical units being included in inventory at different prices. For example, television sets may vary only in serial number, but they may be stated at different costs if purchased at different times. Likewise, cost of goods sold may show identical units of product sold entered at different costs. But many people would argue that this is entirely logical under the cost basis of accounting and that this method is the most theoretically sound of all the methods.

It is often stated that earnings can be manipulated when specific identification is used. For example, assume a company has three units of a given product which are identical except for different serial numbers. The three units were acquired at different times at different prices. The first unit cost $2,000; the second, $2,100; and the third, $2,200. Now one unit is sold for $2,800. The units are all alike; therefore, the customer does not care which unit is selected. But the earnings reported on the sale will differ; they will be either $800, $700, or $600, depending upon which unit is shipped. It should be obvious that earnings can be controlled by shipping different units. If higher earnings are desired, ship the unit which cost $2,000. If lower earnings are desired, ship the unit which cost $2,200.

The main disadvantage of the specific identification method is that it cannot be used in many cases. Either the units cannot be identified or trying to identify them would be too costly. For example, it would be too difficult and too costly to apply the method to the nails sold by a hardware store if the nails are purchased in hundred-pound kegs and sold by the pound. It would also be difficult to use the specific identification method in an ice cream parlor that purchases ice cream in five-gallon cans and sells it in cones, pints, and quarts. These difficulties cause the accountant to make assumptions about the flow of costs through a business.

First-in, first-out (Fifo).   When this method is used, the accountant assumes that the first units purchased are the first ones sold. In other words, the oldest goods are sold first. In many businesses, the first units in must be the first ones out to avoid large losses from spoilage. Fresh dairy products and fresh vegetables and fruits are excellent examples. In such cases, the assumed first-in, first-out flow of costs corresponds with the actual physical flow of goods. The first-in, first-out method may be used under either periodic or perpetual inventory procedure. Perpetual Fifo is discussed later in this chapter.

Fifo applied under periodic inventory procedure.   When Fifo is used with periodic procedure, inventory is measured by the latest (most recent) purchase prices. The goods on hand are assumed to be from the latest purchases. The older goods are the first ones out. That is, they have been sold, while the newer goods are still on hand. But it should be noted that Fifo can be used to measure inventory even when the physical flow of goods is not first-in, first-out.

The first-in, first-out method can be applied to the data in Illustration 9.1 to measure the cost of ending inventory. Begin by listing the latest purchase and move back through the year listing purchases until enough units have been listed to agree with the total number of twenty units in inventory. The inventory cost is computed in Illustration 9.3. The ending inventory consists of the latest purchases. The Fifo cost of the ending inventory, $179, is subtracted from the total cost of goods available for sale, $690, to get the cost of goods sold of $511.

Illustration 9.3: Fifo cost of ending inventory under periodic procedure

Purchased	Units	Unit cost	Total cost
December 21	10	$9.10	$ 91
October 12	10	8.80	88
Total	20		$179

The earnings statement under the Fifo inventory costing method would report the *cost of goods sold* in the following manner:

Cost of goods available for sale	$690
Less: Ending inventory	179
Cost of goods sold	$511

The cost of goods sold of $511 would be an expense in the earnings statement, and the $179 of ending inventory would be a current asset in the balance sheet. This accounts for the total cost of goods available for sale of $690.

Last-in, first-out (Lifo).   Under Lifo the costs of the last units purchased are the first costs charged against revenues. As a result, the cost of goods sold consists of the cost of the most recent purchases while the ending inventory consists of the cost of the oldest purchases. Lifo can be used for federal income tax purposes. But Lifo may be used for tax purposes only if it is used in the general financial statements. Lifo may be used to measure inventory whether or not goods actually flow in a last-in, first-out manner.

Lifo applied under the periodic inventory procedure.   When Lifo is used with periodic procedure, ending inventory is measured by the earliest purchase prices. In fact, ending inventory may consist of costs incurred many years ago. The cost of goods sold, on the other hand, consists of the most recent purchase prices.

The last-in, first-out method can be applied to the data in Illustration 9.1 to measure the cost of the ending inventory. Begin by listing the units in the beginning inventory; continue listing subsequent purchases until enough units have been listed to agree with the total number of twenty units in the ending inventory. Illustration 9.4 shows how the Lifo method is used to measure inventory cost. The Lifo cost of the ending inventory, $165, is subtracted from the cost of goods available for sale, $690, to show a cost of goods sold of $525. Thus the costs charged against revenue are the most recent costs.

Illustration 9.4: Lifo cost of ending inventory under periodic procedure

Purchased	Units	Unit cost	Total cost
Beginning inventory	10	$8.00	$ 80
March 2....................................	10	8.50	85
Total	20		$165

The ending inventory consists of the oldest costs. It includes the cost of the March 2 purchase and the cost of the beginning inventory which may have been incurred several years ago.

The earnings statement under the Lifo inventory costing method would report the cost of goods sold in the following manner:

Cost of goods available for sale	$690
Less: Ending inventory	165
Cost of goods sold	$525

The cost of goods sold of $525 would be an expense in the earnings statement, and the $165 of ending inventory would be a current asset in the balance sheet. This accounts for the total cost of goods available for sale of $690.

Fifo and Lifo compared.   Much has been written about the relative merits of Fifo and Lifo. Lifo appeals to many companies because prices have risen almost constantly in this country since the early 1930s. An example will make this point clear.

Suppose Company B has one unit of Product Y on hand which cost $20. The unit is sold for $30; other selling expenses total $7. The tax rate is 50 percent. The unit is replaced for $22 before the end of the accounting period. Using Fifo, net earnings are computed as follows:

Net sales...	$30.00
Cost of goods sold	20.00
Gross margin	$10.00
Expenses	7.00
Net operating margin..............................	$ 3.00
Federal income taxes (50% rate)	1.50
Net Earnings....................................	$ 1.50

According to the above schedule, the company is selling Product Y at a price which is high enough to produce net earnings. But consider the following:

Cash secured from sale	$30.00
Expenses and taxes paid ($7.00 + $1.50)	8.50
Cash available for replacement	$21.50
Cost to replace..................................	22.00
Additional cash required to replace inventory	$ 0.50

Thus, Company B is reporting net earnings of $1.50, but it cannot replace its inventory unless it obtains more cash. Note the different results when Lifo is used to measure inventory:

Net sales	$30.00
Cost of goods sold	22.00
Gross margin	$ 8.00
Expenses	7.00
Net operating margin	$ 1.00
Federal income taxes (50% rate)	0.50
Net Earnings	$ 0.50

Cash secured from sale	$30.00
Expenses and taxes paid ($7.00 + $0.50)	7.50
Cash available for replacement	$22.50
Cost to replace..................................	22.00
Cash available after replacement	$ 0.50

Tax effect of Lifo. We have seen from the above example that the use of Lifo increased cost of goods sold by $2 and decreased taxes by $1. This example shows why many companies have changed to Lifo because of the rather constant price increases experienced in this country in the last few years.

Those who favor Lifo argue that Lifo tends to match costs and revenues better than does Fifo. When Lifo is used, the earnings statement reports sales and the most current cost of making those sales.

Manipulation possible under Lifo. On the other hand, those who favor Fifo argue that Lifo matches the cost of certain unsold goods against sales revenue. Also, in a period of rising prices, the use of Lifo tends to understate inventory. In addition, the use of Lifo allows management to manipulate net earnings. To obtain smaller net earnings, management purchases an abnormal amount of goods at the end of the current period (at current high prices) for sale in the next period. Under Lifo, these higher costs will be charged to cost of goods sold in the current period. To obtain larger net earnings, management delays making the normal amount of purchases until the next period and charges the older and lower costs to cost of goods sold.

Average methods. An average inventory cost can be determined under either perpetual or periodic procedure. But the computations differ with the procedure used. Under periodic inventory procedure a weighted-average method is used. Under perpetual procedure a moving-average method is used. (This latter method is not illustrated in this text.)

Using periodic inventory procedure, the number of units purchased is added to the number of units in beginning inventory to obtain the total number of units available for sale during the year. The total cost of the purchases is added to the cost of the beginning inventory to arrive at the total cost of goods available for sale during the year. Then the total cost of goods available for sale is divided by the total number of units available for sale to obtain a *weighted-average* unit cost. This weighted-average unit cost is then multiplied by the total number of twenty units in the ending inventory to determine the cost of the inventory. Illustration 9.5, using the data from Illustration 9.1, shows how this procedure is applied.

Purchased	Units	Unit cost	Total cost
Jan. 1	10	$8.00	$ 80.00
Mar. 2	10	8.50	85.00
May 28	20	8.40	168.00
Aug. 12	10	9.00	90.00
Oct. 12	20	*8.80	176.00
Dec. 21	10	9.10	91.00
	80		$690.00

Weighted-average unit cost is $690 ÷ 80, or $8.625.
Ending inventory then is $8.625 × 20 .... 172.50
    Cost of goods sold $517.50

At the end of the period, the cost of goods sold in the earnings statement would be reported in the following manner:

Cost of goods available for sale	$690.00
Less: Ending inventory	172.50
Cost of goods sold	$517.50

The cost of goods sold of $517.50 would be reported as an expense in the earnings statement. The $172.50 of ending inventory would be reported as a current asset in the balance sheet.

Using the weighted-average method, each unit of a product is assigned the same amount of cost regardless of whether the cost is to be charged to cost of goods sold or carried forward in inventory. Also, when this method is used, the cost of goods sold and the cost of inventory cannot be determined until the end of the period.

Differences in cost methods summarized.   Using the data in Illustration 9.1, Illustration 9.6 shows the cost of goods sold, ending inventories, and gross margins of the four basic cost methods of measuring ending inventory.

Note that each of the above methods produces a different inventory measurement and gross margin. Since prices generally increased during the period, Lifo shows the highest cost of goods sold and the lowest gross margin.

Which is the "correct" method?   *All four methods are acceptable; there is no single correct one.* Different methods look attractive under different

Illustration 9.6:
Summary of effects of
employing different
inventory methods with
same basic data

	Specific identifi- cation	Fifo	Lifo	Weighted average
Sales	$780.00	$780.00	$780.00	$780.00
Cost of goods sold:				
Beginning inventory	$ 80.00	$ 80.00	$ 80.00	$ 80.00
Purchases	610.00	610.00	610.00	610.00
Cost of goods available for sale	$690.00	$690.00	$690.00	$690.00
Ending inventory	181.00	179.00	165.00	172.50
Cost of goods sold	$509.00	$511.00	$525.00	$517.50
Gross margin	$271.00	$269.00	$255.00	$262.50

conditions. For instance, Lifo results in matching current costs with current revenue. Also, Lifo reduces the amount of taxes payable currently in a period of rising prices.

On the other hand, Lifo often charges against revenues the cost of goods not actually sold. It also allows net earnings to be manipulated by changing the time at which additional purchases are made. Fifo and specific identification result in a more precise matching of historical cost with revenue. Earnings may be manipulated under both the specific identification method and the simple weighted-average method. Under the latter method, the purchase of a large amount of goods at a relatively high price after the last sale of the period will change the average unit cost of the goods charged to the Cost of Goods Sold account. Only under Fifo is the manipulation of earnings not possible.

Inventories at less than cost

As already noted, *Accounting Research Bulletin No. 43* requires a departure from the cost basis for inventories when the utility of the goods is less than their cost. Such loss of utility may be evidenced by damage or obsolescence or by a decline in the selling price of the goods.

Net realizable value.   Damaged, obsolete, or shopworn goods should not be carried in inventory nor reported in the financial statements at more than their net realizable value. *Net realizable value* is defined as estimated selling price less costs to complete and dispose of the goods. For example, assume that an auto dealer has on hand one auto that has been used as a demonstrator. The auto was acquired at a cost of $4,000 and had an original sales price of $4,800. But, because it has been used and it is now late in the model year, the net realizable value of the auto is estimated at:

Estimated selling price	$3,800
Estimated maintenance and selling costs	300
Net realizable value	$3,500

The auto would be written down for inventory purposes from $4,000 to $3,500. In this way, the $500 would be treated as an expense in the period in which the decline in utility occurred. If net realizable value exceeds cost, the item would of course be carried at cost. Accountants generally frown upon recognizing profits before goods are sold.

The lower-of-cost-or-market method.   Measuring inventories at the lower of cost or market has long been accepted in accounting. The method assumes that if the purchase price in the market in which the firm buys has fallen, the selling price has also fallen or will fall. But this is not always a valid assumption.

The term "market" as used here means replacement cost in terms of the quantity usually purchased. To apply the method, it is still necessary to determine cost (by specific identification. Fifo, Lifo, or an average method).

Under this method market values are used only when they are less than cost. For instance, if the ending inventory has a cost of $40,000 and a market value of $45,000, this increase in market value is not recognized. To do so would be to recognize revenues before the time of sale.

On the other hand, if market value is $39,600, the inventory can be written down to market value. A $400 loss is recognized on the grounds that the inventory has lost part of its revenue-generating ability. Thus, the write-down recorded anticipates a reduced selling price when the goods are actually sold.

Application of the lower-of-cost-or-market method. In the accounting records, the lower-of-cost-or-market method may be applied to each item in inventory, to each class in inventory, or to total inventory. Illustration 9.7 shows the application of the method to individual items and to total inventory.

If the lower-of-cost-or-market method is used on an item-by-item basis, the ending inventory would be $5,000. The lower of cost or market is determined item by item but is applied on the total of all items in the inventory—thus the $5,000 for inventory in Illustration 9.7. The $5,000 ending inventory would be deducted from the cost of goods available for sale on the earnings statement and would be reported in the current assets section of the balance sheet.

Illustration 9.7: Application of lower-of-cost-or-market method

Item	Quantity	Unit cost	Unit market	Total cost	Total market	Lower of cost or market
1	100 units	$10	$9.00	$1,000	$ 900	$ 900
2	200 units	8	8.75	1,600	1,750	1,600
3	500 units	5	5.00	2,500	2,500	2,500
				$5,100	$5,150	$5,000

Gross margin method of estimating inventory

The *gross margin method* can be used to estimate the amount of inventory for the following purposes:

1. To obtain an inventory cost to be used in the monthly or quarterly financial statements.
2. To verify a previously determined ending inventory amount.
3. To determine the amount recoverable from an insurance company when inventory is destroyed by fire or stolen.

The gross margin method is based on the assumption that the rate of gross margin is about the same each period. The method is satisfactory only if this assumption is true.

The gross margin method provides only an estimate of the cost of goods sold and the ending inventory. It is not usable by itself for year-end statements because it assumes that the gross margin rate in the current period is the same as in prior periods. At year-end, it is necessary to use a physical inventory in conjunction with one of the previously described methods for determining the actual inventory, cost of goods sold, gross margin, and net earnings for the current year. Without so doing, the gross margin method is not valid for future years because there would be no way to determine the "normal" rate of gross margin to be used in future computations. But an actual physical count is usually performed only at the end of the year, not during the year.

To illustrate the gross margin method of computing inventory, assume that the Field Company has for several years maintained a rate of gross margin on sales of 30 percent. The following data for 1981 are available: the January 1 inventory was $40,000; purchases of merchandise were $480,000; and sales of merchandise were $700,000. The inventory for December 31, 1981, can be estimated as follows:

Inventory, January 1, 1981		$ 40,000
Purchases		480,000
Cost of goods available for sale		$520,000
Less estimated cost of goods sold:		
Sales	$700,000	
Gross margin (30% of $700,000)	210,000	
Estimated cost of goods sold		490,000
Estimated inventory, December 31, 1981		$ 30,000

The estimated ending inventory is determined by deducting the estimated cost of goods sold from the cost of goods available for sale. The gross margin method is an effective method of determining the ending inventory for the preparation of monthly financial statements.

Retail method of estimating inventory

Another method of estimating inventory, the *retail inventory method*, is used by a wide variety of companies that sell goods directly to the ultimate consumer. In such companies, each item of merchandise usually is marked or tagged with its retail or selling price with the result that the goods are referred to and inventoried at their retail prices.

In skeletal form, the retail method consists first of determining the ending inventory at retail prices:

> Beginning inventory at retail prices
> + Purchases at retail prices
> = Goods available for sale at retail prices
> − Sales (which are, of course, at retail prices)
> = Ending inventory at retail prices

To convert the ending inventory at retail prices to cost, the relationship between cost and retail prices must be known. This requires that information on the beginning inventory and purchases be accumulated so that goods available for sale can be expressed in terms of *cost* and *retail prices.* This *cost/retail* price ratio is then applied to sales to determine cost of goods sold and to the ending inventory at retail to reduce it to cost as is shown in Illustration 9.8.

The $280,000 sales amount is derived from the accounting records. The $168,000 is the cost of the goods sold during the month computed by applying the cost/retail price ratio of 60 percent to the sales of $280,000. Deducting $168,000 and $280,000 from the $204,000 and $340,000 amounts on the "goods available for sale" line yields the January 31, 1981, inventory at cost and at retail.

Illustration 9.8: Inventory calculation using the retail method

	Cost	Retail price
Inventory, January 1, 1981	$ 24,000	$ 40,000
Purchases, net	180,000	300,000
Goods available for sale	$204,000	$340,000
Cost/retail price ratio: $204,000/$340,000 = 60%		
Sales		280,000
Cost of goods sold: 60% of $280,000	168,000	
Inventory, January 31, 1981	$ 36,000	$ 60,000

PERPETUAL INVENTORY PROCEDURE

The emphasis thus far in this chapter has been on periodic inventory procedure. Under periodic inventory procedure, when merchandise is acquired the Purchases account is debited and no entry is made in the Cost of Goods Sold account when merchandise is sold. The cost of goods sold is determined at the end of the accounting period, and the Inventory account is brought up to date by recording the ending inventory.

When a company has an inventory that has a high unit cost such as automobiles, trucks, tractors, or television sets, *perpetual inventory* procedure is used. Merchandise inventory is the largest asset in some business firms such as automobile dealerships. Here the use of an effective internal control system is important to provide adequate protection for the company's inventory, and a perpetual inventory system can provide that effective control.

Perpetual inventory procedure can be operated manually or by using computers. In either system, there will be a card identifying each item in the inventory. An automobile dealer will have a perpetual inventory card for each of the cars in the inventory even if there are dozens or even hundreds of cars in stock. The card in Illustration 9.9 contains some of the basic information that can be on file.

The inventory costing procedure used in this illustration is first-in, first-out. By looking at the inventory card, one can determine the beginning inventory, $2,400, the units purchased, the per unit cost, the number of units sold, and the cost of these units. At any time, the owner of the firm can

Illustration 9.9: Perpetual inventory card

	Item TV-96874				Maximum 26				
	Location				Minimum 6				

	Purchased			Sold			Balance		
1981 Date	Units	Unit cost	Total	Units	Unit cost	Total	Units	Unit cost	Total
July 1							8	$300	$2,400
5	10	$300	$3,000				18	300	5,400
7				5	$300	$1,500	13	300	3,900
12	10	300	3,000				23	300	6,900
19				8	300	2,400	15	300	4,500
26				3	300	900	12	300	3,600

determine the number of units on hand and the cost of those units. This information assists management in controlling the investment in inventory and in maintaining the quantities within the upper and lower limits that have been pre-established.

Journal entries for perpetual inventory procedure

The Merchandise Inventory account is updated at the time of each sale or purchase under the perpetual inventory method. The Cost of Goods Sold account is debited and Merchandise Inventory is credited each time a sale is made.

The entry to record the purchase on July 5 (see Illustration 9.9) would be as follows:

```
Merchandise Inventory ...........................................   3,000
     Accounts Payable—ABC Manufacturing .........................            3,000
     To record the purchase of ten units of merchandise.
```

This purchase transaction is reflected in the inventory control card as shown in Illustration 9.9.

To record the sales transaction of July 7, the journal entries would be as follows:

```
Accounts Receivable ...........................................   2,250
     Sales ........................................................            2,250
     To record the sale of five units at $450 each.

Cost of Goods Sold ............................................   1,500
     Merchandise Inventory ......................................            1,500
     To record the cost of the five units sold.
```

Similar journal entries would be made for each series of purchases and sales for all of the items in the inventory. The ending inventory per the perpetual inventory cards is verified by a physical count of the units on hand at the end of each year.

NEW TERMS INTRODUCED IN CHAPTER 9

Fifo (first-in, first-out)—a method of pricing inventory under which the costs of the first goods acquired are the first costs charged to cost of goods sold when goods are actually sold.

Gross margin method—a method for estimating inventory. Gross margin percentages from previous periods are applied to sales of the current period to arrive at an estimated amount of gross margin and cost of goods sold. Cost of goods sold is deducted from cost of goods available for sale to arrive at estimated ending inventory.

Lifo (last-in, first-out)—a method of pricing inventory under which the costs of the last goods acquired are the first costs charged to cost of goods sold when goods are actually sold.

Lower-of-cost-or-market method—a method of pricing inventory under which cost or market, whichever is lower, is selected for each item, each group, or for the whole inventory.

Net realizable value—estimated selling price of merchandise less estimated cost of completion and disposition.

Retail inventory method—a procedure for estimating the cost of the ending inventory by applying the ratio of cost to retail price to the ending inventory at retail.

Specific identification—an inventory pricing method which involves the assignment of a known actual cost to a particular identifiable unit of product.

Weighted-average method—a method of pricing inventory under which the total number of units purchased plus those in the beginning inventory is divided into the total cost of goods available for sale to arrive at a weighted unit cost. The ending inventory is carried at this cost per unit.

DEMONSTRATION PROBLEM

Following are data related to the beginning inventory and purchases of a given item of product of the Van Company for the year 1981:

January 1 inventory	5,000 @ $2.00
March 15	4,000 @ $2.10
May 10	7,000 @ $2.25
August 12	5,000 @ $2.40
November 20	3,000 @ $2.60

During the year, 20,000 units were sold. The periodic inventory procedure is used.

Required:

Compute the ending inventory under each of the following methods:

a. Fifo.

b. Lifo.

c. Weighted average.

Solution to demonstration problem

a. Ending inventory under Fifo:

Purchased	Units	Unit cost	Total cost
November 20	3,000	$2.60	$ 7,800
August 12	1,000	2.40	2,400
	4,000		$10,200

b. Ending inventory under Lifo:

Purchased	Units	Unit cost	Total cost
January 1 inventory	4,000	$2.00	$ 8,000

c. Ending inventory under weighted average:

Purchased	Units	Unit cost	Total cost
January 1 inventory	5,000	$2.00	$10,000
March 15	4,000	2.10	8,400
May 10	7,000	2.25	15,750
August 12	5,000	2.40	12,000
November 20	3,000	2.60	7,800
	24,000		$53,950

Weighted average unit cost is $53,950 ÷ 24,000, or $2.25.
Ending inventory cost is $2.25 × 4,000 = $9,000.

QUESTIONS

1. Why does an understated ending inventory understate net earnings for the period by the same amount?

2. Why does an error in ending inventory affect two accounting periods?

3. What cost elements are included in inventory?

4. How should purchase discounts lost be shown in the earnings statement?

5. What does it mean to "take a physical inventory"?

6. Indicate how a company can manipulate the amount of net earnings it reports if it uses the Lifo method of inventory measurement. Why is the same manipulation not possible under Fifo?

7. What is net realizable value, and how is it used?

8. Why is it considered acceptable accounting practice to recognize a loss by writing down an item of merchandise in inventory to market, but unacceptable to recognize a gain by writing up an item of merchandise in inventory?

9. Under what operating conditions will the gross margin method of computing an inventory produce approximately correct amounts?

10. What are three uses of the gross margin method?

11. How can the retail method be used to estimate inventory?

EXERCISES

(Exercises E–1 and E–2 review concepts covered in Chapter 5.)

E–1. The Grantham Company uses periodic inventory procedure, maintains an account to show discounts lost, and records purchases at their net prices. Prepare entries for the following transactions:

May 1 Received merchandise from the Adam Corporation, $2,000; terms, 2/10, n/30.
  3 Received merchandise from the Eve Corporation, $1,200; terms, 2/10, n/30.
  8 Paid the Adam Corporation invoice.
  15 Paid the Eve Corporation invoice.

E–2. The Vinson Company uses the net invoice price in its statements and records. Using periodic inventory procedure, journalize the following transactions:

a. Purchased on account and received eight units of merchandise at $100 each; terms, 2/10, n/30.

b. Received and paid cash for a large supply of sales tickets, letterheads, and so forth; invoice price, $600 less 2 percent cash discount.

c. Ordered six units of merchandise at $150 each; terms, 2/10, n/30.

d. Paid cash for one unit of office equipment; terms, 2/10, n/30. The invoice read:

One checkwriter	$400	
Less 2% discount	8	$392
Express charges		6
Cash paid		$398

e. Paid transportation charges of $20 on the eight units of merchandise received in **(a)**.

f. Paid the invoice for transaction **(a)** after the discount period had expired.

g. Sold one unit of merchandise acquired in transaction **(a)** for $210 cash.

E–3. The Charm Company inventory records show a January 1 inventory of 1,000 units at $8 (total $8,000) and the following purchases:

	Units	Amount
Feb. 14	300	@ $7.40 = $2,220
Mar. 18	800	@ $7.25 = $5,800
July 21	600	@ $7.70 = $4,620
Sept. 27	600	@ $7.40 = $4,440
Nov. 27	200	@ $7.85 = $1,570

The December 31 inventory was 1,400 units.

a. Present a short schedule showing the measurement of the ending inventory using the Fifo method.

b. Do the same using the Lifo method.

E–4. The Vine Company's inventory of a certain product was 8,000 units with a cost of $11 each on January 1, 1981. During 1981 numerous units of this product were purchased and sold. Also during 1981 the purchase price of this product fell steadily until at year-end it was $9. The inventory at year-end was 12,000 units. State which of the two methods of inventory measurement, Lifo or Fifo, would have resulted in the higher reported net earnings and explain briefly.

E–5. The Camel Company had the following inventory transactions during 1981:

a. January 1 inventory on hand, 200 units at $4 = $800.

b. January sales were 40 units.

c. February sales totaled 60 units.

d. March 1, purchased 100 units at $4.20.

e. Sales for March through August were 80 units.

f. September 1, purchased 20 units at $4.80.

g. September through December sales were 90 units.

Record the journal entries affecting the *inventory* account assuming periodic inventory procedure is used and a physical inventory on December 31, 1981, showed 50 units on hand. Price the ending inventory at its weighted-average cost.

E–6. Your assistant has compiled the following schedule to assist you in determining the decline in inventory from cost to the lower of cost or market, item by item:

	Item			
	A	B	C	D
Units	200	200	600	1,000
Unit cost	$18	$8	$6	$10.20
Unit market	$17	$9	$6	$10.40
Total cost	$3,600	$1,600	$3,600	$10,200
Total market	$3,400	$1,800	$3,600	$10,400

Compute the cost of the ending inventory using the lower-of-cost-or-market method applied to individual items.

E–7. Royce Company follows the practice of taking a physical inventory at the end of each calendar-year accounting period to establish the ending inventory amount for financial statement purposes. Its financial statements for the past few years indicate a normal gross margin of 30 percent. On July 18, a fire destroyed the entire store building and contents. The records were in a fireproof vault and are intact. These records, through July 17, show:

Merchandise inventory, January 1	$ 100,000
Merchandise purchases	2,100,000
Purchase returns	40,000
Transportation-in	125,000
Sales	3,200,000
Sales returns	100,000

The company was fully covered by insurance and asks you to determine the amount of its claim for loss of merchandise.

PROBLEMS, SERIES A

P9–1–A. Farmington Company reported net earnings in 1981 of $130,000, in 1982 of $135,000, and in 1983 of $145,000. Analysis of its inventories shows that certain clerical errors were made so that inventory figures were as follows:

	Incorrect	Correct
December 31, 1981	$40,000	$45,000
December 31, 1982	38,000	35,000

Required:

a. Compute the amount of net earnings for each of the three years assuming that the clerical errors in computing the inventory had not been made.

b. Determine the total net earnings for the three years with the use of the incorrect inventories and compare this with the total net earnings determined when correct inventories were used.

P9–2–A. An examination of the records of the Hyslop Company on December 31, 1981, disclosed the following with regard to merchandise inventory for 1981 and prior years:

1. December 31, 1978: Inventory understated $40,000.
2. December 31, 1979: Inventory of $28,000 was included twice.
3. December 31, 1980: Inventory of $25,000 was omitted.
4. December 31, 1981: Inventory is correct.

The reported net earnings for each year were as follows:

1978	$235,000
1979	284,000
1980	307,000
1981	281,000

Required:

a. What are the correct net earnings for 1978, 1979, 1980, and 1981?

b. What is (are) the error(s) in each December 31 balance sheet?

P9–3–A. Following are selected transactions and data of the Lahiri Company:

1981
Mar. 1   Bought merchandise from A Company: invoice amount, $4,000; terms, 2/10, n/30.
    5   Bought merchandise from B Company: invoice amount, $5,000; terms, 2/10, n/30.
   11   Paid A Company for purchase of March 1.
   21   Paid B Company for purchase of March 5.
   31   The goods bought from both A Company and B Company make up the complete physical inventory.

Required (you may assume there were no opening inventory and no sales for March):

a. Present journal entries to record the above transactions and to set up the ending inventory at March 31, following a procedure which shows discounts taken. Assume periodic inventory procedure is used.

b. Repeat **(a)** above under a procedure which shows discounts lost.

c. Which procedure would you recommend, and why?

(Note: This problem reviews concepts covered in Chapter 4. You may wish to refer back to that chapter.)

P9–4–A. Following are data relating to the beginning inventory and purchases of a given item of product of the Snow Company for the year 1981:

January 1 inventory	1,400 @ $2.10
February 2	1,000 @ $2.00
April 5	2,000 @ $1.50
June 15	1,200 @ $1.25
September 30	1,400 @ $1.20
November 28	1,800 @ $1.75

During the year 6,600 units were sold. Periodic inventory procedure is used.

Required:

Compute the ending inventory and cost of goods sold under each of the following methods:

a. Fifo.

b. Lifo.

c. Weighted average.

P9–5–A. The Staubach Company was organized on January 1, 1981. Selected data for 1981–83 are as follows:

Year ended December 31	Inventory Fifo	Inventory Lifo	Annual data Purchases	Annual data Sales
1981	$1,600	$1,200	$7,200	$8,100
1982	2,000	1,400	6,000	9,500
1983	3,300	2,000	7,400	8,200

Required:

Compute the gross margin for each of the three years under Fifo and under Lifo.

P9–6–A. The Batter Company determines its net earnings using the Fifo method of inventory measurement. It reported net earnings for 1981 of $68,000; 1982, $65,400; and 1983, $67,300. Inventories on the Fifo and Lifo bases were as follows:

December 31	Fifo	Lifo
1980	$15,000	$14,000
1981	17,200	15,800
1982	16,800	15,600
1983	18,300	16,700

Required:

Compute the net earnings that would have been reported in 1981, 1982, and 1983 by the Batter Company had it used the Lifo method of inventory measurement. Assume that purchases, selling expenses, administrative expenses, and sales are $29,200; $3,000; $2,000; and $100,000, respectively, for each of the years 1981, 1982, and 1983.

P9–7–A. Given below are data relating to the ending inventory of the Tucker Company at December 31, 1981:

Item	Quantity	Unit cost	Unit market
1	6,000	$1.00	$0.95
2	12,000	0.80	0.90
3	4,000	0.75	0.80
4	10,000	1.40	1.25
5	8,000	1.25	1.30
6	2,000	0.90	0.80

Required:

a. Compute the ending inventory applying the lower-of-cost-or-market method to the total inventory.

b. Repeat **(a)** above applying the method to individual items.

P9–8–A. Baily Company employs a fiscal year ending September 30. At this time inventories are usually at a very low level because of reduced activity. The management of the company wishes to maintain full insurance coverage on its inventory at all times. The company has earned around 40 percent gross margin on net sales over the last few years. Given below are data for the seven months ending April 30, 1981:

Sales	$400,000
Sales returns	40,000
Sales discounts	10,000
Inventory, October 1, 1980	30,000
Purchases	305,000
Purchase returns	23,000
Purchase discounts	7,000
Transportation-in	15,000
Selling expenses	35,000
Administrative expenses	30,000

Required:

a. Indicate, in general, how the company can estimate its inventory at any given date.

b. State the amount of insurance coverage the company should obtain on its inventory to be fully covered at all times if the inventory is at its highest level on April 30 of each year.

P9–9–A. The sales and cost of goods sold for the Blanca Company for the past five years were as follows:

Year	Sales (net)	Cost of goods sold
1976	$693,400	$464,578
1977	749,600	502,232
1978	857,400	565,884
1979	820,600	558,008
1980	885,600	593,352

For the seven months ended July 31, 1981, the following information is available from the accounting records of the company:

Sales	$645,680
Purchases	382,400
Purchase returns	2,400
Sales returns	14,480
Inventory, January 1, 1981	79,000

In requesting the extension of credit by a new supplier, the Blanca Company has been asked to present current financial statements. It does not want to take a complete physical inventory at July 31, 1981.

Required:

a. Indicate how financial statements can be prepared without taking a complete physical inventory.

b. From the data given, estimate the inventory at July 31, 1981.

P9–10–A. The following data pertain to a certain department of the Walton Department Store for the year ended December 31, 1981:

	Cost	Retail
Merchandise inventory, January 1, 1981	$ 40,000	$ 60,000
Purchases, net	440,000	740,000
Sales		720,000

Required:

Use the retail method to compute the cost of the inventory on December 31, 1981.

PROBLEMS, SERIES B

P9–1–B. Gotham Company reported net earnings in 1981 of $119,200, in 1982 of $128,800, and in 1983 of $108,600. Analysis of its inventories shows that certain clerical errors were made so that inventory figures were the following:

	Incorrect	Correct
December 31, 1981	$24,200	$28,400
December 31, 1982	28,000	23,400

Required:

a. Compute the amount of net earnings for each of the three years assuming that the clerical errors in computing the inventory had not been made.

b. Determine the total net earnings for the three years with the use of the incorrect inventories and compare this with the total net earnings determined when correct inventories were used.

P9–2–B. As of December 31, 1981, the financial records of the Mott Company were examined for the years ended December 31, 1978, 1979, 1980, and 1981. With regard to merchandise inventory, the examination disclosed the following:

1. December 31, 1978: Inventory of $20,000 was included twice.
2. December 31, 1979: Inventory overstated $10,000.
3. December 31, 1980: Inventory of $22,000 was omitted.
4. December 31, 1981: Inventory is correct.

The reported net earnings for each year were as follows:

1978	. . . .	$38,400
1979	. . . .	54,400
1980	. . . .	67,000
1981	. . . .	84,600

Required:

a. What are the correct net earnings for 1978, 1979, 1980, and 1981?

b. What is (are) the errors in each December 31 balance sheet?

c. Comment on the implications of your corrected net earnings as contrasted with reported net earnings.

P9–3–B. Following are selected transactions and data of the Woods Company for 1981:

June 1 Bought merchandise from the Birch Company: invoice amount, $10,500; terms 2/10, n/30.
6 Bought merchandise from the Pine Company: invoice amount, $10,000; terms, 2/10, n/30.
12 Paid the Birch Company for the purchase of June 1.
15 Paid the Pine Company for the purchase of June 6.
30 The entire physical inventory consists of the goods bought from the Birch Company and the Pine Company.

Required:

a. Assuming use of periodic inventory procedure, present journal entries to record the above transactions and to set up the ending inventory at June 30 following a procedure which shows discounts taken.

b. Repeat *(a)* above under a procedure which shows discounts lost.

c. Which method would be of more value to the management of the Woods Company? Why?

(Note: This problem reviews concepts covered in Chapter 4. You may wish to refer back to that chapter.)

P9–4–B. Beatle Company, a newly organized business, embarked upon an extensive purchasing program in November 1981. It opened its doors for business on December 15, 1981. The company decided to use a calendar-year accounting period, and as of December 31, 1981, its accounts show the following:

Sales	. . . .	$ 84,000
Purchases	. . . .	900,000
Transportation-in	. . . .	102,000
Purchase discounts	. . . .	18,000

All purchases were subject to discount terms of 2/10, n/30. The cost of the inventory on December 31, 1981, at vendors' gross invoice prices was $840,000.

Required:

Present a schedule showing the computation of cost of goods sold and the gross margin for the period ending December 31, 1981, assuming that all of the purchase discounts were taken. (Note: This problem reviews concepts covered in Chapter 4. You may wish to refer back to that chapter.)

P9–5–B. The purchases and sales of a certain product for the Lawton Company for April 1981 are shown below. There was no inventory on April 1.

Purchases

Apr. 3	. . . .	1,000 units @ $2.50
10	. . . .	800 units @ $2.60
22	. . . .	1,600 units @ $2.30
28	. . . .	900 units @ $2.40

36,090

Sales

Apr. 4	. . . .	600 units
11	. . . .	500
16	. . . .	500
26	. . . .	400
30	. . . .	600

Required:

a. Compute the ending inventory of the above product as of April 30 under each of the following methods: (1) Fifo, (2) Lifo, and (3) weighted average.

b. Give the journal entries to record the purchases and the cost of goods sold for the month under both Fifo and Lifo methods applied under periodic procedure.

P9–6–B. Listed below are the purchases and sales of a certain product made by the Cooper Company during 1981 and 1982. The company had 10,000 units of this product on hand at January 1, 1981, with a cost of $2 per unit.

Purchases

1981		
Feb. 20	. . . .	2,000 @ $2.00
Apr. 18	. . . .	5,000 @ $1.95
Aug. 28	. . . .	5,000 @ $1.90
Dec. 22	. . . .	4,000 @ $1.92
1982		
Jan. 26	. . . .	3,000 @ $1.95
Mar. 6	. . . .	5,000 @ $2.00
Aug. 12	. . . .	3,000 @ $2.10
Nov. 15	. . . .	4,000 @ $2.20

66

Sales

1981		
Feb. 2	. . . .	3,000 @ $3.00
Apr. 23	. . . .	4,000 @ $2.50
Sept. 3	. . . .	4,000 @ $2.40
Dec. 24	. . . .	3,500 @ $2.45

1982
Jan. 7 . . . . 2,500 @ $2.50
Mar. 21 . . . . 4,000 @ $2.60
Sept. 8 . . . . 2,500 @ $2.60
Dec. 2 . . . . 4,500 @ $2.75

The company uses periodic inventory procedure.

Required:

a. Compute the cost of the ending inventory and the cost of goods sold for both years assuming the use of the Fifo method of inventory measurement.

b. Repeat **(a)** above assuming the use of Lifo.

P9–7–B. Given below are the net earnings and inventories of the Ashworth Company as reported for the years indicated:

December 31	Fifo	Lifo	Net earnings
1981.	$360,000	$294,000	$ 950,000
1982.	372,000	348,000	980,000
1983.	414,000	408,000	1,020,000

The Ashworth Company has used the Fifo method of inventory measurement.

Required (ignore the possible effects of federal income taxation):

a. State the amount of net earnings that the company would have reported in 1982 and 1983 if it had used the Lifo method rather than Fifo.

b. State the amount of net earnings that the company would have reported in 1983 had it changed from Fifo to Lifo in 1983.

P9–8–B. The accountant for the Box Company prepared the following schedule of the company's inventory at December 31, 1981, and used the lower of the total cost or total market value in determining cost of goods sold.

Item	Quantity	Cost per unit	Market value per unit	Total value Cost	Market
Q	2,500	$2.00	$2.00		
R	1,000	1.50	1.40		
S	3,500	1.00	0.90		
T	3,000	0.75	0.80		

Required:

a. State whether this is an acceptable method of inventory measurement and determine the amounts computed.

b. Compute the amount of the ending inventory using the lower-of-cost-or-market method on an individual item basis.

c. State the effect upon net earnings in 1981 if the method in **(b)** was used rather than the method in **(a)**.

P9–9–B. As part of a loan agreement with a local bank, the Kirk Company must present quarterly and cumulative earnings statements for the year 1981. The company uses periodic inventory procedure and marks its merchandise to sell at a price which will yield a gross margin of 40 percent. Selected data for the first six months of 1981 are as follows:

	First quarter	Second quarter
Sales	$310,000	$315,000
Purchases	200,000	225,000
Purchase returns and allowances	12,000	13,000
Purchase discounts	3,800	3,900
Sales returns and allowances	10,000	5,000
Transportation-in	8,800	8,900
Selling expenses	31,000	30,000
Administrative expenses	21,000	19,000

The cost of the physical inventory taken December 31, 1980, was $38,000.

Required:

a. Indicate how the earnings statements may be prepared without taking a physical inventory at the end of each of the first two quarters of 1981.

b. Prepare earnings statements for the first quarter, the second quarter, and the first six months of 1981.

P9–10–B. The following data pertain to the Little Department Store for the fiscal year ended June 30, 1981:

	Cost	Retail
Merchandise inventory, July 1, 1980	$ 25,000	$ 37,000
Purchases, net	315,000	463,000
Sales		480,000

Required:

Use the retail method to compute the cost of the inventory on June 30, 1981.

BUSINESS DECISION PROBLEM 9–1

The Griffin Company, which began operations on January 2, sells a single product, Product X. The following data relate to the purchases of Product X for the year:

January	2	500 @ $2.00
February	15	800 @ $2.00
April	8	1,000 @ $2.15
June	6	400 @ $2.25
August	19	800 @ $2.30
October	5	600 @ $2.50
November 22		400 @ $2.80

Periodic inventory procedure is used. On December 31, a physical inventory of Product X shows that 800 units are on hand.

Mr. Griffin is trying to decide which of the following inventory costing methods he should adopt: weighted average, Fifo, or Lifo. Since Mr. Griffin is short of cash, he wants to minimize the amount of income taxes payable.

Required:

In this case, which of the three inventory costing methods will minimize the amount of income taxes payable? What will be the cost of goods sold and the cost of ending inventory under this method?

BUSINESS DECISION PROBLEM 9–2

Harry Rawlins owns and operates a sporting goods store. On February 2, 1981, the store suffered extensive fire damage and all of the inventory was destroyed. Mr. Rawlins uses periodic inventory procedure and has the following information in his accounting records which luckily were not damaged by the fire:

January 1 inventory	$10,000
Purchases:	
January 8	4,000
January 20	6,000
January 30	8,000
Sales:	
January	30,000
February 1	2,000

Mr. Rawlins also knows that his gross margin rate has been 40 percent the last three years.

The insurance company has offered to pay $7,000 to settle Mr. Rawlins' inventory loss unless he can adequately prove that he suffered a greater loss.

Required:

Should Mr. Rawlins settle for $7,000? If not, how can he prove to the insurance company that he suffered a greater loss? What is the estimated amount of this loss?

Chapter 10

Plant and equipment:

Depreciation

PLANT AND EQUIPMENT IN GENERAL

The term *plant and equipment* refers to tangible long-lived assets (assets whose useful lives are expected to last for several periods) obtained for use in business operations instead of for resale. Land, buildings, machinery, delivery equipment, and office equipment are typical examples of plant and equipment (also referred to as *plant assets* or *property, plant, and equipment*). This chapter deals with (1) the initial costs of acquiring long-lived assets, (2) depreciation expense, and (3) later expenditures on these assets. Certain other matters dealing with these assets are covered in the next chapter.

To be properly classified as plant and equipment, an asset must be used in the production or sale of another asset or service. For example, a delivery truck or equipment held for sale by a dealer is classified as inventory whereas the same truck or equipment used in producing or selling a product is classified as plant and equipment. Similarly, land held for speculation is classified as a long-term investment, whereas land used in business operations is classified as plant and equipment. In addition, once an asset is retired from service and held for sale or left idle, the asset is no longer classifiable as plant and equipment.

Plant and equipment can be viewed as consisting of bundles of service potential, many of which are consumed or used up over a period of time. For instance, a new delivery truck may represent 100,000 miles of transportation service. Likewise, a new building may represent 40 years of shelter and sales space. To match periodic revenues and related expenses as accurately and logically as possible, it is necessary to measure the part of the service potential of plant and equipment which expired during the period. While it is often difficult to determine the exact length of these assets' useful lives, some estimate must be made so that the amount of expense (the amount of expired service potential) may be determined.

Types of plant and equipment

Plant and equipment can be broadly classified as land and depreciable property. Since land does not deteriorate with age or use, it is not depreciable. Farmland is an exception to this rule because it may lose its fertility or suffer from erosion.

All other items of plant and equipment are depreciable property. Their usefulness is reduced through wear, tear and/or obsolescence.

Cost of plant and equipment

Plant and equipment usually are recorded at cost. Cost includes all normal, reasonable, and necessary outlays to obtain and get the asset ready for use, such as invoice price, installation costs, and transportation. Traffic tickets or fines that must be paid as a result of hauling machinery to a new plant are not part of the cost of the machinery. Likewise, if the machinery is dropped and damaged while being unpacked, the cost of repairing the damage is not included in the cost of the machinery.

Land and land improvements.   The cost of land includes the purchase price; option cost; real estate commissions; cost of title search; fees for recording the title transfer; unpaid taxes assumed by the purchaser; cost of surveying, clearing, grading, and landscaping; and local assessments for sidewalks, streets, sewers, and water mains. Sometimes land purchased as a building site contains an old building that must be removed. In such cases, the entire purchase price should be debited to the Land account. The Land account should also be debited for the cost of removing the old building less any proceeds received from the sale of salvaged materials.

As stated above, land purchased as a building site is considered to have an unlimited life and is therefore not depreciable. But *land improvements* such as driveways, fences, parking lots, lighting systems, and sprinkler systems have limited lives and are therefore depreciable. Hence, the costs of land and land improvements should be recorded in two separate accounts.

Building. If a building is purchased, its cost includes the purchase price, the costs of repairing and remodeling the building for the purposes of the new owner, unpaid taxes assumed by the purchaser, legal costs, and real estate brokerage commissions paid. When land and buildings are purchased together, the total cost should be divided so that separate ledger accounts may be established for land and for buildings. This may be done by a competent appraiser. One of the reasons for dividing the cost is to establish the proper balances in the appropriate accounts. This is especially important since reported earnings will be affected by the later depreciation recorded on the buildings.

If a building is constructed, the cost may be more difficult to determine. But it usually includes payments to contractors, architects' fees, building permits, taxes during construction, salaries of officers supervising construction, and insurance during construction.

To illustrate, assume that Bonner Company purchased an old farm on the outskirts of Bridgeport, Connecticut, as a factory site. The company paid $150,000 for this property. In addition, the company agreed to pay unpaid taxes from previous periods (called back taxes) of $8,000 on this property. Attorneys' fees and other legal costs related to the purchase of the farm amounted to $1,200. The farm buildings were demolished at a net cost of $10,000 (cost of removal less salvage value), and a factory was constructed at a cost of $200,000. Building permits and architects' fees totaled $15,000. Finally, the company paid an assessment of $6,000 to the city for water mains, sewers, and street paving. The costs of the land and factory building are computed as follows:

	Land	Building
Cost of factory site	$150,000	
Back taxes	8,000	
Attorneys' fees and other legal costs	1,200	
Demolition	10,000	
Factory construction		$200,000
Building permits and architects' fees		15,000
City assessment	6,000	
	$175,200	$215,000

All of the costs relating to the purchase of the farm and the razing of the old buildings are assignable to the Land account because none of the old buildings purchased with the land is to be used. The real goal was to purchase the land, but the land was not available without taking the buildings also.

Instead of the situation described above, suppose one or more of the existing buildings were going to be adapted through a remodeling program for use by Bonner Company. Then it would have been necessary to determine what part of the cash purchase price of the farm, the back taxes, and the legal fees was allocable to such buildings and what portion was allocable to the land. These costs would have been allocated on the basis of appraised values. For instance, assume that the land was appraised at three fourths of the total value and the buildings at one fourth. Then three fourths of the acquisition cost would be assigned to the land and one fourth to the buildings.

Machinery.   If machinery is purchased, its cost includes the net invoice price, transportation charges, insurance in transit, cost of installation, the costs of any attachments or accessories, testing costs, if any, and other costs needed to put it into condition and location for use. If a company builds a machine for its own use, the cost includes material, labor, and an amount equal to the increase in factory costs caused by the construction of the machine. This cost of the machine should be recorded in the Machinery account (even if it is less than what the company would have paid if it had purchased the machine) since it represents resources sacrificed to acquire the machine.

To illustrate, assume that after pricing machinery of the type needed, the Henkel Company decided to build its own machine. The cost of construction was $20,000. The f.o.b. (free on board) shipping point price of a similar machine purchased from the usual source is $23,000, and transportation charges to the Henkel Company's plant amount to another $1,000. The machine should be recorded in the accounts at $20,000—the amount of resources actually sacrificed to acquire the machine.

Delivery equipment.   The cost of delivery equipment includes all costs necessary to place the equipment in a condition and location for its intended use. Included in the cost are the f.o.b. shipping point price, transportation charges, costs of accessories, and special paint and decoration costs.

Office equipment.   The cost of office equipment includes the net invoice purchase price and all costs necessary to place the equipment in a condition and location for use.

Noncash acquisitions and gifts of plant and equipment

Plant and equipment usually are acquired by purchase for cash or on account. They may also be acquired through an exchange for securities or other assets or as gifts. When plant and equipment are acquired under these conditions, it is necessary to determine the amount at which they initially should be recorded. Several possible bases may be used, such as fair market value, appraised value, and book value.

Fair market value.   If noncash assets are received in an exchange for securities or other noncash assets having a known market value, the cost of the assets received is considered equal to the fair market value of the securities or assets given up. If the securities or assets given up do not have a known market value, the cash purchase price at which the asset received could have been acquired should be used as the cost of the acquired asset. It would also be considered the amount received for the securities or assets given up.

Appraised value.   Noncash assets sometimes are acquired as gifts. Although these assets do not cost the recipient anything, they are usually recorded in the accounts. If similar assets are not regularly traded and a market value cannot be determined for them, they may be recorded at an appraised value determined by a professional appraiser or by management.

Book value.   The *book value* of an asset is its original cost less accumulated depreciation. The book value of an asset given up is an acceptable basis for measuring a newly acquired asset only if a better basis is not available. The book value of an old asset is usually a poor and misleading indication of the economic value of a new asset. When assets are received in a noncash exchange, it is the accountant's job to find the best measure of their value. The general rule followed is to use the fair market value of the assets received or of the assets given up, whichever is more clearly evident.

DEPRECIATION OF PLANT AND EQUIPMENT

Depreciation in accounting is an estimate, usually expressed in terms of cost, of the amount of service potential of a depreciable asset which expired in a given period. Major causes of depreciation are physical deterioration, inadequacy for future needs, and obsolescence.

Physical deterioration results from use, wear and tear, and the action of the elements. Even if a good maintenance and repair policy is in effect, a plant asset will eventually have to be discarded. If a company grows more rapidly than anticipated, existing plant assets may become *inadequate*. In such a case, the company will not be able to meet all of the demands for its product or service. *Obsolescence* refers to the process of becoming out of date or obsolete. A machine may be in excellent physical condition but also be obsolete because more efficient, economical, and higher quality machines have become available. Both inadequacy and obsolescence are difficult to predict, but they must be taken into consideration in determining depreciation.

Depreciation accounting distributes in a systematic and rational manner the cost of a depreciable plant asset, less its salvage value, over the asset's estimated useful life. Thus, *depreciation is a process of allocation and not of valuation*. Depreciation is recorded by debiting the depreciation expense account and crediting the accumulated depreciation account. The accounting treatment of the amounts of depreciation recorded depends upon the type of services which the asset provides. If the services received are classified as selling or administrative, the depreciation is usually expensed in the period recognized. If manufacturing services are received, the depreciation may be treated as a part of the manufacturing cost. In such an instance, it becomes an expense (as part of cost of goods sold) when the manufactured goods are sold to customers. The depreciation recorded on one asset may be considered part of the cost of another asset—for example, when a truck is used in the construction of a building.

Depreciation is one of the costs of operating a business. The use of plant assets in the operation of a business represents the change from a plant asset cost to an operating cost. Depreciation is a noncash cost because it does not require the actual outlay of cash. The cost of plant and equipment is recovered from customers by charging them enough for the product to cover all expenses, including depreciation. Costs are recovered only when total revenue is at least equal to total expenses, which of course is the normal situation for firms which remain in business.

Factors affecting depreciation estimates

To estimate periodic depreciation, the following three factors must generally be considered:

1. Cost.
2. Estimated *salvage value.* Salvage or scrap value is the amount estimated to be recoverable (less disposal cost) on the date the asset will be disposed of or retired.
3. Estimated useful life. This may be expressed in years, months, working hours, or units of production.

It is not possible to measure the exact amount of depreciation to be allocated to each period of an asset's life. Thus, there are several methods for computing depreciation. When evaluating the various depreciation methods it is important to remember the main causes of depreciation—physical deterioration, inadequacy, and obsolescence. These three factors should be taken into consideration in estimating salvage value and useful life as well as in selecting the appropriate depreciation method. For example, a machine may be capable of producing units for 20 years, but it is expected to be obsolete in 6 years. Thus, its estimated useful life is 6—not 20—years.

Depreciation methods

Straight-line depreciation.   There are many ways to compute depreciation. One of the methods most commonly used is the straight-line method which we introduced earlier. The straight-line method distributes the same dollar amount of depreciation to expense each period. Under this method the passage of time is considered to be the main factor in allocating cost. It assumes that wear, obsolescence, and deterioration of the plant assets are directly proportional to elapsed time. This assumption may not be true.

The formula for computing depreciation under the straight-line method is:

$$\text{Depreciation per period} = \frac{\text{Cost} - \text{Estimated salvage value}}{\text{Number of accounting periods in estimated life}}$$

To illustrate, for a machine costing $27,000 with an estimated life of ten years and an estimated salvage value of $2,000, the depreciation per year is ($27,000 − $2,000) ÷ 10, or $2,500. The schedule in Illustration 10.1 presents the annual depreciation entries, the balance in the accumulated depreciation accounts, and the book (or carrying) value of this machine. Book value is the difference between original cost and the balance of the accumulated depreciation account.

Illustration 10.1:
Depreciation schedule—
straight-line method

End of year	Depreciation expense Dr.; Accumulated depreciation Cr.	Total accumulated	Book value
			$27,000
1	$ 2,500	$ 2,500	24,500
2	2,500	5,000	22,000
3	2,500	7,500	19,500
4	2,500	10,000	17,000
5	2,500	12,500	14,500
6	2,500	15,000	12,000
7	2,500	17,500	9,500
8	2,500	20,000	7,000
9	2,500	22,500	4,500
10	2,500	25,000	2,000*
	$25,000		

* Estimated salvage value.

Units-of-production depreciation.   If usage is the main factor causing the expiration of the asset, depreciation may be based on physical output. The depreciation charge per unit of output may be found by dividing the original cost of the asset, less any salvage value, by the estimated number of units to be produced during the asset's life. The periodic depreciation is then obtained by multiplying the rate per unit by the actual number of units produced during the period.

To illustrate, assume that on January 1, 1981, Lee Company purchased a machine at a total cost of $27,000. The machine is expected to have a ten-year useful life and a salvage value of $2,000. It is estimated that the machine will produce five million units of product throughout its useful life. The depreciation charge per unit of product produced is $0.005 computed as follows:

$$\frac{\text{Depreciation per unit}}{\text{of product}} = \frac{\text{Cost} - \text{Estimated salvage value}}{\text{Estimated units of production}}$$

$$= \frac{\$27,000 - \$2,000}{5,000,000} = \$0.005$$

If the machine produces 100,000 units in 1981, the depreciation charge under the units-of-production method will be $500 ($0.005 × 100,000). Similarly, if 250,000 units are produced in 1982, the depreciation charge will be $1,250 ($0.005 × 250,000).

Accelerated depreciation methods

The 1954 Revenue Act permitted taxpayers to use a fixed percentage declining-balance method or a sum-of-the-years'-digits method of computing depreciation. These methods are often called *accelerated depreciation* and are still used. Under these methods, larger amounts of depreciation are recorded in the earlier years of an asset's life than in the later years. Business managers often prefer these methods because the increased depreciation in the early years reduces taxable earnings. This, in turn, reduces the amount of federal income taxes which must be paid in those years.

There is also theoretical support for these methods. Their use seems especially appropriate when the service-rendering or revenue-producing ability of the asset declines over time, when the value of the asset declines more in early years and less in later years of its life, and when repairs and other maintenance costs increase over time.

Double-declining-balance method of depreciation. Under this method the straight-line rate of depreciation is doubled and the doubled rate is applied to the declining balance of the asset—its net book value. Salvage value is ignored. Illustration 10.2 gives an example of an asset costing $27,000 with an estimated life of ten years and a salvage value of $2,000. In this example, the 10 percent straight-line rate of depreciation (100 percent ÷ 10 years = 10 percent per year) is doubled, giving a depreciation rate of 20 percent.

Illustration 10.2:
Double-declining-
balance method
depreciation schedule

End of year	Depreciation expense Dr.; Accumulated depreciation Cr.	Total accumulated	Book value
			$27,000.00
1. (20% of $27,000)	$5,400.00	$ 5,400.00	21,600.00
2. (20% of $21,600)	4,320.00	9,720.00	17,280.00
3. (20% of $17,280)	3,456.00	13,176.00	13,824.00
4. (20% of $13,824)	2,764.80	15,940.80	11,059.20
5. (20% of $11,059.20)	2,211.84	18,152.64	8,847.36
6. (20% of $8,847.36)	1,769.47	19,922.11	7,077.89
7. (20% of $7,077.89)	1,415.58	21,337.69	5,662.31
8. (20% of $5,662.31)	1,132.46	22,470.15	4,529.85
9. (20% of $4,529.85)	905.97	23,376.12	3,623.88
10. (20% of $3,623.88)	724.78*	24,100.90	2,899.10

* This amount could be $1,623.88 so as to reduce the book value down to the estimated salvage value of $2,000.

When the double-declining-balance method is used to compute the annual depreciation amount, the annual amount is allocated to the months within the year on a straight-line basis. For example, the depreciation per month in the first year for the asset in Illustration 10.2 is $450 ($5,400 ÷ 12). In the second year, it is $360 ($4,320 ÷ 12) per month.

Sum-of-the-years'-digits depreciation. This method also produces larger depreciation charges in the early years of an asset's life. The years of estimated life of an asset are added together and used as the denominator in a fraction. The number of years of life remaining at the beginning of the accounting period is the numerator. Cost, less estimated salvage value, is then multiplied by this fraction to compute the periodic depreciation. This is illustrated below for a plant asset which costs $27,000, has an estimated useful life of ten years, and salvage value of $2,000.

Sum-of-the-years' digits: 1 + 2 + 3 + 4 + 5 + 6 + 7 + 8 + 9 + 10 = 55.

Depreciation:
Year 1: $^{10}\!/_{55}$ of $25,000 .... $ 4,545.45
Year 2: $^{9}\!/_{55}$ of $25,000 .... 4,090.91
Year 3: $^{8}\!/_{55}$ of $25,000 .... 3,636.36
Year 4: $^{7}\!/_{55}$ of $25,000 .... 3,181.82
Year 5: $^{6}\!/_{55}$ of $25,000 .... 2,727.27
Year 6: $^{5}\!/_{55}$ of $25,000 .... 2,272.73
Year 7: $^{4}\!/_{55}$ of $25,000 .... 1,818.18
Year 8: $^{3}\!/_{55}$ of $25,000 .... 1,363.64
Year 9: $^{2}\!/_{55}$ of $25,000 .... 909.09
Year 10: $^{1}\!/_{55}$ of $25,000 .... 454.55
Total depreciation $25,000.00

At the beginning of Year 1 there are ten years of life remaining. Thus, the ratio used to compute the depreciation charge for Year 1 is $^{10}\!/_{55}$.

The mathematical formula for finding the sum-of-the-years' digits for any given number of periods is:

$$S = \frac{n(n+1)}{2}$$

where S is the sum-of-the-years' digits and n is the number of periods in the asset's life. Thus, the sum-of-the-years' digits for ten years is 55, computed as follows:

$$\frac{10(10+1)}{2} = \frac{110}{2} = 55$$

Depreciation on assets acquired or retired during an accounting period

When plant assets are acquired or retired during an accounting period, depreciation is usually computed to the nearest month. Thus, an asset purchased on or before the 15th day of the month is treated as if it were purchased on the first of the month. An asset purchased after the 15th day of the month is treated as if it were purchased on the first day of the following month. For instance, assume that a company which operates on a calendar-year accounting period acquires a machine on March 14, 1981. The machine has a $26,000 cost, a $2,000 salvage value, and a ten-year estimated useful life. Under the straight-line method, the depreciation expense for 1981 would be $2,000 ($24,000 × 0.10 × $^{10}\!/_{12}$). However, if the machine had been purchased on March 16, the straight-line depreciation expense for 1981 would be $1,800 ($24,000 × 0.10 × $^{9}\!/_{12}$).

When accelerated depreciation methods are used, more computations are necessary when assets are acquired or retired during an accounting period. For example, assume that a machine is acquired on July 1, 1981. The machine has a $40,000 cost, a $1,000 salvage value, and a ten-year estimated useful life. Double-declining-balance depreciation is used. For the year ending December 31, 1981, the depreciation expense is $4,000 ($40,000 × 0.20 × ½). The 1982 depreciation expense would be $7,200 computed as follows:

$$\frac{1}{2} \times (\$40,000 \times 0.20) = \$4,000$$
$$+ \frac{1}{2} \times [(\$40,000 - \$8,000) \times 0.20] = \underline{3,200}$$
$$1 \text{ Year} \qquad\qquad \underline{\$7,200}$$

Revisions of life estimates

When it is found that the estimate of the life of an asset is incorrect, the annual depreciation charge under the straight-line method may be changed as follows: the net book value (less salvage) of the asset at the beginning of the current period is divided by the estimated number of life periods remaining. The result is the revised annual depreciation charge applicable to the current and succeeding years.

For example, assume that a machine cost $30,000, has an estimated salvage value of $3,000, and has an estimated useful life of eight years. At the end of the fourth year of the machine's life, the balance in its accumulated depreciation account is $13,500. At the beginning of the fifth year, it is estimated that the asset will last six more years (salvage value remains at $3,000). The revised annual depreciation charge is $2,250 [($30,000 − $13,500 − $3,000) ÷ 6].

Depreciation on the financial statements

When depreciation is recorded, a depreciation expense account is debited. The depreciation expense appears in the earnings statement as one of the expenses of generating revenue. The periodic depreciation is credited to an accumulated depreciation account. The accumulated depreciation account is used so that the original cost of the asset will continue to be shown in the asset account. The total cost and accumulated depreciation are shown separately on the balance sheet as follows:

Plant and Equipment:

Store equipment	$ 12,000	
Less: Accumulated depreciation	2,000	$ 10,000
Building	$100,000	
Less: Accumulated depreciation	20,000	80,000
Land		40,000
Total Plant and Equipment		$130,000

The presentation of cost less accumulated depreciation provides a financial statement reader with a better understanding of a company's financial position than does the presentation of just book value (remaining undepreciated cost). For instance, reporting $100,000 of assets with $60,000 of accumulated depreciation says something quite different from $40,000 of new assets.

Some financial statement readers mistakenly assume that the amount of accumulated depreciation represents funds available for replacing old assets with new assets. But accumulated depreciation is simply the part of an asset's cost that has been charged to depreciation expense. Accumulated depreciation has a credit balance and is a contra asset account. An informed reader should realize that cash is required to replace assets, and that the amount of cash a company owns is shown as a current asset on its balance sheet. There is no cash represented in the accumulated depreciation account.

MEASUREMENTS OF PLANT AND EQUIPMENT ON THE BALANCE SHEET

As stated above, plant and equipment are reported on the balance sheet at their original cost less accumulated depreciation. The going-concern concept is the justification for reporting remaining undepreciated cost instead of market values. Under the *going-concern concept,* it is assumed that the company will continue in business and use the plant and equipment in business operations instead of selling them. Thus, market values are not considered relevant for use in the primary financial statement.[1] Furthermore, the accounting requirement of *realization* does not allow recording market prices greater than cost until the asset is sold. It also is not proper to recognize a loss by writing down the asset to a market value lower than cost if the cost of the asset is expected to be fully recovered from the future revenues the asset will produce.

CAPITAL AND REVENUE EXPENDITURES

It is often necessary to make expenditures for plant assets other than when they are acquired. The accounting treatment of such expenditures may consist of charging the amount to (1) an asset account, (2) an accumulated depreciation account, or (3) an expense account.

Expenditures which are added to the asset account or charged to the accumulated depreciation account are often called *capital expenditures*. These expenditures increase the book value of the plant assets. On the other hand, expenditures immediately expensed are called *revenue expenditures*. The differences between these two are discussed below.

Expenditures capitalized in asset accounts

Betterments or *improvements* to existing assets are called capital expenditures. They are properly chargeable to asset accounts because they add to the service-rendering ability of the assets. Betterments or improvements increase the *quality* of services which can be obtained from an asset. For instance, installing an air conditioner in an auto which did not previously have one is a betterment. Air conditioned transportation instead of merely transportation is the result.

Expenditures capitalized as charges to accumulated depreciation

Occasionally expenditures are made on plant assets which will extend the *quantity* of services *beyond the original estimate* but not the quality of services they produce. Because they will benefit an increased number of future periods, these expenditures are properly capitalized. But because there is no visible, tangible addition to or improvement in the quality of services, they are often charged to the accumulated depreciation account. Such expenditures are viewed as canceling a part of the existing accumulated depreciation.

To illustrate, assume that after operating the press for four years, the company in the preceding illustration spent $3,750 to recondition it. The effect of the reconditioning is to increase the life of the machine to a total of 14 years from an original estimate of 10 years. The journal entry to record the major repair is:

```
Accumulated Depreciation—Machinery ..............................  3,750
    Cash (or Accounts Payable) ...................................          3,750
    Cost of reconditioning press.
```

When it was acquired, the press had an estimated life of ten years with no expected salvage value. At the end of the fourth year the balance in its accumulated depreciation account under the straight-line method is $12,100 [($30,250 ÷ 10) × 4]. After the $3,750 debit to the accumulated depreciation

---

[1] Reporting market values in supplementary financial statements is permissible.

account, the balances in the asset account and its related accumulated depreciation account are as follows:

Cost of press	$30,250
Accumulated depreciation	8,350
Book value (end of four years)	$21,900

The remaining book value of $21,900 is divided equally among the ten remaining years in amounts of $2,190 per year under the straight-line method. The effect of the expenditure, then, is to increase the carrying amount of the asset by reducing its contra account, accumulated depreciation.

Expenditures for major repairs which do not extend the life of the asset are also sometimes charged to accumulated depreciation (which increases future depreciation charges). The purpose is to avoid distortion of net earnings which might result if such expenditures were expensed in the year incurred. In this way the cost of major repairs is spread over a number of years.

To illustrate, assume the same facts as in the above example except that the expenditure did not extend the life of the asset. Because of the size of the $3,750 expenditure it was charged to accumulated depreciation. The $21,900 remaining book value would be spread over the remaining six years of life. Annual charges would be $3,650 ($21,900 ÷ 6) under the straight-line method.

Expenditures charged to expense

Recurring and/or minor expenditures that neither add to the quality of service-rendering abilities of the asset nor extend the quantity of services beyond the original estimate are treated as expenses. Thus, regular maintenance (lubricating a machine) and ordinary repairs (replacing a broken fan belt) are expensed immediately as revenue expenditures. For example, if the company above spends $190 to repair the press after using it for some time, that amount should be debited to Maintenance Expense.

In many companies, any expenditure below an arbitrary minimum, such as $25, is charged to expense regardless of its service-rendering abilities. The purpose for doing this is to avoid having to recalculate the depreciation schedule for the asset for such a small expenditure.

Distinguishing between capital and revenue expenditures

It is often very difficult in an actual situation to distinguish between capital and revenue expenditures by applying the above criteria. For instance, some expenditures seem to affect both the quality and quantity of services. If a revenue expenditure is improperly capitalized during a period, asset costs are overstated, expenses are understated, and net earnings and owner's equity are overstated. During the rest of the asset's life, net earnings will be understated because of incorrect depreciation charges. If a capital expenditure is improperly charged to an expense account, the book value of the asset is understated. In addition, expenses are overstated for that period, and net earnings and owner's equity are understated. In the periods that follow, expenses will be understated and net earnings overstated because depreciation expense will be understated in those periods.

To illustrate, assume that on January 2, 1981, the Ross Company purchased a machine for cash at an invoice price of $30,000. In addition, the company paid $500 of freight charges and $800 of installation charges. The invoice price of the machine was correctly debited to the Machinery account, but the freight and installation costs were debited to Maintenance Expense. The machine has an estimated useful life of ten years. If this error is not discovered and corrected, net earnings for 1981 will be understated by $1,170. The $1,300 overstatement of maintenance expense will cause net earnings to be understated by $1,300. But the asset account has been understated, and hence depreciation has been based on too small a figure. If the asset costs were properly capitalized, the depreciation charge for 1981 would be $130 ($1,300/10) larger. Net earnings for 1981 are, therefore, understated by the net amount of $1,170 ($1,300 − $130). If the error is not corrected, depreciation for 1982 will be understated by $130, and net earnings for 1982–90 will be overstated by $130 each year.

NEW TERMS INTRODUCED IN CHAPTER 10

Accelerated depreciation—an accounting procedure under which the amounts of depreciation recorded in the early years of an asset's life are greater than those recorded in later years.

Betterment—replacement of an existing asset or part of an asset with a superior or improved asset or part.

Book value—cost less accumulated depreciation of a plant asset.

Capital expenditure—an expenditure made, usually with regard to plant assets, which is to be capitalized because of the benefits it will render in subsequent periods.

Depreciation—an estimate, usually expressed in terms of cost, of the amount of service potential of a plant asset that expired in a period. The double-declining-balance method of computing annual depreciation consists of finding the straight-line rate, doubling it, and applying it to the net book value which the asset had at the beginning of the year. The straight-line method assigns equal amounts of depreciation to equal periods of time. The sum-of-the-years'-digits method assigns depreciation in decreasing amounts to successive periods of time; the formula used consists of multiplying cost (less estimated salvage) by a fraction, the denominator of which is the sum of the numbers from one to the number of years of useful life expected from an asset and the numerator of which is the number of periods of life remaining from the beginning of the year. The units-of-production method assigns equal amounts of depreciation to each unit of product produced by an asset.

Depreciation accounting—distributes in a systematic and rational way the cost of a depreciable plant asset, less its salvage value, over the asset's estimated useful life.

Improvement—an alteration or structural change in a depreciable asset which results in a better asset, that is, one which has greater durability, productivity, or efficiency. Costs of improvements are properly capitalizable.

Inadequacy—inability of a plant asset to produce enough product to meet current demands.

Land improvements—improvements to real estate which have a limited life and are subject to depreciation such as driveways, fences, and parking lots.

Obsolescence—the decline in usefulness of an asset brought about by invention and technological progress.

Plant and equipment—tangible long-lived assets obtained for use in business operations instead of for resale.

Physical deterioration—results from use, wear and tear, and the action of the elements.

Revenue expenditure—a normal recurring expenditure made on plant assets to keep them in operating condition which is expected to benefit only the current period.

Salvage value—the amount estimated to be recoverable (less disposal cost) on the date the plant asset will be disposed of or retired.

DEMONSTRATION PROBLEM

The McBride Company acquired a machine on January 2, 1981, at a total cost of $82,000. The machine was estimated to have a useful life of ten years and a scrap value of $2,000. It was also estimated that the machine would produce one million units of product during its life. The machine produced 90,000 units in 1981 and 125,000 units in 1982.

Required:

Compute the amounts of depreciation to be recorded in 1981 and 1982 under each of the following:

- **a.** Straight-line method.
- **b.** Double-declining-balance method.
- **c.** Sum-of-the-years'-digits method.
- **d.** Units-of-production method.

Solution to demonstration problem

- **a.** Straight-line method:
  1981: ($82,000 − $2,000) ÷ 10 = $8,000
  1982: ($82,000 − $2,000) ÷ 10 = $8,000

- **b.** Double-declining-balance method:
  1981: $82,000 × 20% = $16,400
  1982: ($82,000 − $16,400) × 20% = $13,120

- **c.** Sum-of-the-years'-digits method:

  1981: ($82,000 − $2,000) × $\dfrac{10}{55}$ = $14,545

  1982: ($82,000 − $2,000) × $\dfrac{9}{55}$ = $13,091

- **d.** Units-of-production-method:
  1981: [($82,000 − $2,000)/1,000,000] × 90,000 = $7,200
  1982: [($82,000 − $2,000)/1,000,000] × 125,000 = $10,000

QUESTIONS

1. What is the main distinction between inventory and plant and equipment?

2. Which of the following items are properly classifiable as plant and equipment on the balance sheet?

a. Advertising to inform the public about new energy-saving programs at a manufacturing plant.

b. A truck acquired by a manufacturing company to be used to deliver the company's products to wholesalers.

c. An automobile acquired by an insurance company to be used by one of its salespersons.

d. Adding machines acquired by an office supply company to be resold to customers.

e. The cost of constructing and paving a driveway which has a useful life of ten years.

3. Barnes Company recently bought, for $200,000, a plot of land on which to construct a new warehouse. Legal fees connected with the transaction were $2,200. Back taxes on the property amounted to $8,000, for which Barnes Company assumed the liability. Estimates from various demolition crews indicate that the cost of razing the old warehouse currently on the property will be $9,000. What is the cost of the land to date? To what account will the cost of razing the old warehouse be charged when incurred?

4. Why should periodic depreciation be recorded on all plant assets except land?

5. In any exchange of noncash assets, the accountant's task is that of finding the most appropriate valuation to assign to the assets received. What is the general rule for determining the most appropriate valuation in such a situation?

6. Define the terms *inadequacy* and *obsolescence* as used in accounting for plant and equipment.

7. What four factors must be known in order to compute depreciation on a plant asset?

8. If a machine has an estimated useful life of nine years, what will be the total digits to use in calculating depreciation under the sum-of-the-years'-digits method?

9. What does the balance in the accumulated depreciation account represent? Can this balance be used to replace the related plant asset?

10. What is the justification for reporting plant assets on the balance sheet at undepreciated cost rather than market value?

11. Distinguish between *capital expenditures* and *revenue expenditures.*

12. For each of the following, state whether the expenditure made should be charged to an expense, an asset, or an accumulated depreciation account:

a. Cost of installing air-conditioning equipment in a leased building.

b. Biennial painting of an owned factory building.

c. Cost of replacing the roof on a 10-year-old building which was purchased new and has an estimated total life of 40 years. Replacement of the roof was anticipated in setting the annual depreciation charge on the building.

d. Cost of rewinding the armature of an electric motor.

EXERCISES

E–1. Hrizik Company acquired, for $320,000 cash, real property consisting of a tract of land and two buildings. The company intended to raze the old factory building and remodel and use the old office building. To allocate the cost of the property acquired, the company had the property appraised. The appraised values were land, $120,000; factory building, $120,000; and office building, $160,000. The factory building was demolished at a net cost of $16,000. The office building was remodeled at a cost of $32,000. The cost of a new identical office building was estimated to be $180,000. Present a schedule or schedules showing the determination of the amounts at which the assets acquired should be carried in the Hrizik Company accounts. Show calculations.

E–2. Moran Company purchased a heavy factory machine for $10,000 less a 2 percent cash discount. One of the company's employees drove a truck containing the machine to the company's factory. The company was fined $200 because the employee failed to obtain a permit to transport the machine on city streets. Installation and testing costs totaled $1,000. What is the cost of the factory machine?

E–3. The Hayes Company purchased some office furniture on March 1, 1981, for $6,200 cash. Cash of $100 was paid for freight and cartage costs. The furniture is being depreciated over a four-year life under the straight-line method, assuming a $300 salvage value. The company employs a calendar-year accounting period and records depreciation for the full month in which an asset is installed. On July 1, 1982, $40 was spent to refinish the furniture. Prepare journal entries for the Hayes Company to record all of the above data, including the annual depreciation adjustments, through 1982.

E–4. Martin Company purchased a new machine on January 2, 1981, at a cash cost of $60,000. The machine is estimated to have a life of five years, with no salvage value at the end of that time. If federal income taxes are levied at a rate of 50 percent of net earnings, how much would the income taxes payable for the years 1981 and 1982 be reduced if the company chose the double-declining-balance method of computing depreciation rather than the straight-line method?

E–5. On January 2, 1981, a new machine was acquired for $50,000. The machine has an estimated salvage value of $2,000 and an estimated useful life of ten years. The machine is expected to produce a total of 500,000 units of product throughout its useful life. Compute depreciation for 1981 and 1982 using each of the following methods:

a. Straight line.

b. Units of production. (Assume 30,000 and 50,000 units were produced in 1981 and 1982, respectively.)

c. Double-declining balance.

d. Sum-of-the-years' digits.

E–6. Cagle Company acquired equipment costing $15,000 on April 1, 1981. The equipment has an estimated salvage value of $1,000 and an estimated useful life of seven years. The machine is being depreciated using the sum-of-the-years'-digits method. Compute the depreciation for the years ended December 31, 1981, and 1982.

E–7. The Danfield Company acquired a delivery truck on January 2, 1981, for $28,000. The truck has an estimated salvage value of $1,500 and an estimated useful life of eight years. The truck is being depreciated on a straight-line basis. At the beginning of 1984, it is estimated that the truck has a remaining useful life of seven years? What is the depreciation charge for 1981 and for 1984?

E–8. Classify each of the following as either a capital expenditure or a revenue expenditure:

a. Painting of office building at a cost of $400. The building is painted every year.

b. Addition of a new plant wing at a cost of $100,000.

c. Expansion of a paved parking lot at a cost of $60,000.

d. Replacement of a stairway with an escalator at a cost of $16,000.

e. Lubricating a machine at a cost of $200.

f. Replacing a broken fan belt at a cost of $150.

PROBLEMS, SERIES A

P10–1–A. The Land Building Company purchased a two-square-mile farm from the owner under the following terms: cash paid, $405,000; mortgage note assumed, $200,000; and interest accrued on mortgage note assumed, $5,000.

The company paid $46,000 for brokerage and legal services to acquire the property and secure clear title. It planned to subdivide the property into residential lots and construct houses on these lots. Clearing and leveling costs of $18,000 were paid. Crops on the land were sold for $12,000. A house on the land, to be moved by the buyer, was sold for $4,200. The other buildings were razed at a cost of $8,000, and salvaged material was sold for $8,400.

Approximately six acres of the land were deeded to the township for roads, and another ten acres were deeded to the local school district as a site for a future school. After the subdivision was completed, this land would have an approximate value of $1,600 per acre. The company secured a total of 1,200 salable lots from the remaining land.

Required:

Present a schedule showing in detail the composition of the cost of the 1,200 salable lots.

P10–2–A. When you were hired as manager of the Easy Street Company on January 1, 1982, the company bookkeeper gave you the following information regarding one of its equipment accounts:

Equipment—Machine C

1981				1981			
Jan. 1	Disposition cost of Machine B	500		Jan. 1	Cash from sale of Machine B	400	
1	Material used in building Machine C	15,000		Dec. 31	Depreciation on Machine C for year ended,		
1	Labor used in building Machine C	10,000			12/31/81 (10% of $28,500)	2,850	
1	Cost of installing Machine C	1,900					
1	Net earnings from building Machine C rather than purchasing it	1,500					

Required:

Construct the theoretically correct equipment account for Machine C.

P10–3–A. Grape Company purchased land and a building having appraised values of $120,000 and $200,000, respectively. The terms of the sale were that Grape would pay $163,000 in cash and assume responsibility for a $100,000 mortgage note, $5,000 of accrued interest, and $12,000 of unpaid property taxes. Grape intends to use the building as an office building.

Required:

Prepare a journal entry to record the purchase.

P10–4–A. Bunsen Company acquired a machine on July 1, 1981, at a cash cost of $48,000 and immediately spent $2,000 to install it. The machine was estimated to have a useful life of eight years and a scrap value of $3,000 at the end of this time. It was further estimated that the machine would produce 500,000 units of product during its life. In the first year the machine produced 100,000 units.

Required:

Prepare journal entries to record depreciation for the fiscal year ended June 30, 1982, if the company used:

a. The straight-line method.

b. The sum-of-the-years'-digits method.

c. The double-declining-balance method.

d. The units-of-production method.

P10–5–A. Fulton Company purchased a machine on January 2, 1980, at an invoice price of $62,600. Transpor-

tation charges amounted to $700, and $1,500 was spent to install the machine. Costs of removing an old machine to make room for the new amounted to $600; and $200 was received for the scrapped material from the old machine.

Required:

a. State the amount of depreciation that would be recorded on the machine for the first year on the straight-line basis, on the double-declining-balance basis, and on the sum-of-the-years'-digits basis, assuming an estimated life of eight years and no salvage value expected.

b. Give the journal entry needed at December 31, 1982, to record depreciation assuming a revised total life expectancy for the machine of 12 years; assume that depreciation has been recorded through December 31, 1981, on a straight-line basis.

P10–6–A. Trap Company purchased a machine at a cash cost of $35,000. An electric motor was purchased for cash and attached to the machine at a total cost of $26,000. The machine was installed in a production center on the first floor at a cost of $8,000 on July 1, 1981. Its estimated life was 15 years, with no salvage value expected. On July 1, 1986, the machine and motor unit was moved from its first-floor location to the second floor and the entire unit installed at a cost of $16,000. The estimated life of the unit in its second-floor location is ten years, with no salvage value expected.

Required:

Compute the depreciation charge for the year ending June 30, 1987, using the straight-line method.

PROBLEMS, SERIES B

P10–1–B. White Company planned to erect a new factory building and a new office building in Atlanta, Georgia. Preliminary studies showed two possible sites as available and desirable. Further studies showed the second site to be preferable. A report on this property showed an appraised value of $300,000 for land and orchard and $200,000 for a building.

After considerable negotiation, the company and the owner reached the following agreement. White Company was to pay $260,000 in cash, assume a $150,000 mortgage note on the property, assume the interest accrued on the mortgage note of $3,200, and assume unpaid property taxes of $12,000. White company paid $33,000 cash for brokerage and legal services in acquiring the property.

Shortly after acquisition of the property, White Company sold the fruit on the trees for $4,400, remodeled the building into an office building at a cost of $64,000, and removed the trees from the land at a cost of $15,000. Construction of the factory building is to begin in a week.

Required:

Prepare schedules showing the proper valuation of the assets acquired by the White Company.

P10–2–B. The Broad Company has the following entries in its Building account:

31, 1981) the company installed new machinery costing $400,000 on the first floor of the building. Regular operations began on January 2, 1982.

Required:

a. Compute the correct balance for the Building account as of December 31, 1982. The building is expected to last 40 years. The company employs a calendar-year accounting period.

b. Prepare the necessary journal entries to correct the records of the Broad Company at December 31, 1982. No depreciation entries are required.

P10–3–B. The Snow Company acquired a heavy factory machine on July 1, 1981. The machine had an invoice price of $36,000, but the company received a 3 percent cash discount by paying the bill on the date of acquisition. An employee of the Snow Company hauled the machine down a city street without a permit. As a result, the company had to pay a $300 fine. Installation and testing costs totaled $3,580. The machine is estimated to have a $1,500 salvage value and a seven-year useful life.

				Debits
1981				
May	5	Cost of land and building purchased	$400,000
	5	Broker fees incident to purchase	18,000
1982				
Jan.	3	Contract price of new wing added to south end of building	110,000
	15	Cost of new machinery, estimated life ten years	400,000
June	10	Real estate taxes for six months ended 6/30/82	9,000
Aug.	10	Cost of landscaping and building parking lot for employees in back of building	12,400
Sept.	6	Replacement of broken windows	400
Oct.	10	Repairs due to regular usage	4,600
				Credits
1981				
Dec.	31	Transfer to Land account, as per allocation of purchase cost authorized in minutes of board of directors	60,000
1982				
Jan.	5	Proceeds from lease of second floor for six months ended 12/31/81	10,000

The original property was acquired on May 5, 1981. The Broad Company immediately engaged a contractor to construct a new wing on the south end of the building. While the new wing was being constructed, the company leased the second floor as temporary warehouse space to the Goody Company. During this period (July 1 to December

Required:

a. Prepare the journal entry to record the acquisition of the machine.

b. Prepare the journal entry to record depreciation for 1981 under the double-declining-balance method.

c. Assume that at the beginning of 1984, it is estimated that the machine will last another six years. Prepare the journal entry to record depreciation for 1984.

P10–4–B. Boston Company acquired equipment on January 2, 1981, at a cash cost of $125,000. Transportation charges amounted to $1,000, and installation and testing costs totaled $4,000. The equipment was damaged while being installed, and the cost of repairing the damage was $500.

The equipment was estimated to have a useful life of nine years and a salvage value of $2,000 at the end of its life. It was further estimated that the equipment would be used in the production of 640,000 units of product during its life. During 1981, 142,000 units of product were produced.

Required:

Prepare journal entries to record depreciation for the year ended December 31, 1981, if the company used—

a. The straight-line method.

b. The sum-of-the-years'-digits method.

c. The double-declining-balance method.

d. The units-of-production method.

P10–5–B. The Kash Company's fiscal year ends May 31. The company has its own fleet of delivery vehicles. Included are the following:

Description	Date acquired	Cost	Expected life	Expected salvage value
Sedan No. 3	June 1, 1980	$ 8,000	4 years	$1,200
Truck No. 2	June 1, 1976	12,000	100,000 miles	1,000
Truck No. 5	Jan. 1, 1982	28,000	150,000 miles	2,800
Trailer No. 8	Apr. 1, 1979	16,000	400,000 miles	–0–

Mileage readings at May 31 show the following:

	1981	1982
Sedan No. 3	15,000 miles	28,000 miles
Truck No. 2	120,000	150,000
Truck No. 5	–0–	20,000
Trailer No. 8	50,000	75,000

Required:

Set up schedules showing in full detail the amount of depreciation to be recorded for the year ended May 31, 1982, on each of the above assets. (Use the straight-line method for Sedan No. 3 and the units-of-production [number of miles driven] method for the other vehicles.)

P10–6–B. A machine belonging to the McGraw Company that cost $30,000 has an estimated life of 20 years. After ten years, an extremely important machine part, representing about 40 percent of the original cost, is worn out and replaced. The replacement cost is $9,000, and the useful life of the new part is the same as the remaining useful life of the machine.

Required:

a. Prepare journal entries to record the replacement of the old part with the new part. (Assume depreciation has already been brought up to date.)

b. Compute the annual depreciation charge after replacement, using the straight-line method.

BUSINESS DECISION PROBLEM 10–1

The Sloan Company has the following entries in its Building account:

			Debits
1981			
Jan.	2	Cost of land and old buildings purchased	$200,000
	2	Legal fees incident to purchase	4,000
	2	Fee for title search	500
	12	Cost of demolishing old buildings on land	8,000
June	16	Cost of insurance during construction of new building	2,000

July	30	Payment to contractor upon completion of new building	450,000
Aug.	5	Architect's fees for design of new building	20,000
Sept.	15	City assessment for sewers and sidewalks	7,000
Oct.	6	Cost of landscaping	4,000
Nov.	1	Cost of driveways and parking lots	25,000

Credits

Jan.	15	Proceeds received upon sale of salvaged materials from old buildings	$ 2,000.00
Dec.	31	Depreciation for 1981 at 2½%	17,962.50

You are in charge of auditing the Sloan Company's Building account. In addition to the entries in the account, you are given the following information:

1. The company began using the new building on September 1, 1981. The building is estimated to have a 40-year useful life and no salvage value.
2. The company began using the driveways and parking lots on November 1, 1981. The driveways and parking lots are estimated to have a ten-year useful life and no salvage value.
3. The straight-line depreciation method is used to depreciate all the company's plant assets.

Required:

a. Prepare a schedule which shows separately the cost of land, buildings, and land improvements.

b. Compute the amount of depreciation expense for 1981.

c. What journal entries are required to correct the accounts at December 31, 1981? (Assume that Depreciation Expense, Buildings was debited for the entire amount of depreciation credited to the Buildings account. Also assume that closing entries have not been made.)

BUSINESS DECISION PROBLEM 10–2

On January 2, 1981, Wagner Company acquired new equipment costing $160,000. The equipment has an estimated salvage value of $4,000 and an estimated useful life of 15 years. It is estimated that the machine will produce 4,000,000 units of product during its lifetime. During 1981, 260,000 units of product were produced. After deducting all expenses except depreciation on the new equipment and income taxes, the company has earnings of $100,000.

Required for the year 1981:

a. Compute depreciation on the equipment for 1981 using each of the following methods:

1. Straight line.
2. Double-declining balance.
3. Sum-of-the-years' digits.
4. Units of production.

b. Assuming the company's income tax rate is 40 percent, prepare a schedule showing net earnings after taxes under each of the four depreciation methods.

c. Which method results in the smallest amount of income taxes? Which method results in the largest amount of income taxes?

BUSINESS DECISION PROBLEM 10–3

Coaster Company and Stone Company are alike in all respects except the following: Coaster Company uses double-declining-balance depreciation whereas Stone Company uses straight-line depreciation. On January 2, 1981, both companies acquired the following plant assets with the related costs, salvage values, and useful lives:

Plant asset	Cost	Salvage value	Useful life
Building	$200,000	Negligible	40 years
Land	80,000	—	—
Machinery	160,000	Negligible	16 years

The companies reported the following net earnings for the years 1981, 1982, and 1983:

	Net Earnings	
Year	Coaster Company	Stone Company
1981	$38,000	$39,500
1982	40,000	41,000
1983	44,000	44,500

Robert Reynolds is interested in buying one of the companies. He notices that Stone Company's earnings exceed Coaster Company's earnings each year. But Coaster Company has more working capital than Stone Company. Reynolds has engaged you to advise him on buying one of the companies.

Required:

a. Compute the amount of depreciation recorded by each of the companies in 1981, 1982, and 1983.

b. Compute the amount of tax savings Coaster Company obtains by using double-declining-balance depreciation instead of straight-line depreciation. (Assume a 50 percent tax rate.)

c. Which company would you advise Mr. Reynolds to buy? Why?

Chapter 11

Plant and equipment, natural
resources, and intangible assets

In the preceding chapter, the discussion focused on certain problems encountered in accounting for plant and equipment such as determining the cost of plant and equipment, estimating depreciation of plant and equipment, and distinguishing between capital and revenue expenditures. This chapter will examine accounting for (1) plant and equipment at their time of disposition, (2) natural resources, and (3) intangible assets.

DISPOSITION OF PLANT ASSETS

Plant and equipment eventually wear out, become inadequate, or become obsolete and must be sold, retired, or traded in on new assets. Upon disposition of a plant asset, the asset's cost and accumulated depreciation must be removed from the accounts.

Sale of plant assets

When a plant asset is sold, there may be a gain or loss on the sale. The gain or loss is determined by comparing the asset's book value (cost less accumulated depreciation) and its sales price. If the sales price is greater than the asset's book value, there is a gain. If the sales price is less than the asset's book value, there is a loss. Of course, if the sales price is equal to the asset's book value, there is no gain or loss.

To illustrate accounting for the sale of a plant asset, assume that equipment costing $30,000 and having accumulated depreciation of $12,000 is to be sold. If the equipment is sold for $20,000, a gain of $2,000 is realized as computed below:

Equipment cost	$30,000
Accumulated depreciation	12,000
Book value	$18,000
Sales price	20,000
Gain realized	$ 2,000

The journal entry to record the sale is:

Cash	20,000	
Accumulated Depreciation—Equipment	12,000	
Equipment		30,000
Gain on Sale of Plant Assets		2,000
To record sale of equipment at a price greater than book value.		

If the equipment is sold for $16,500, a loss of $1,500 ($18,000 book value − $16,500 sales price) is realized, and the journal entry to record the sale is:

Cash	16,500	
Accumulated Depreciation—Equipment	12,000	
Loss on Sale of Plant Assets	1,500	
Equipment		30,000
To record sale of equipment at a price less than book value.		

If the equipment is sold for $18,000, there is no gain or loss, and the journal entry to record the sale is:

Cash	18,000	
Accumulated Depreciation—Equipment	12,000	
Equipment		30,000
To record sale of equipment at a price equal to book value.		

Accounting for depreciation to date of disposition. When a plant asset is sold or otherwise disposed of, it is important to record the depreciation to the date of sale or disposition. For example, if an asset were sold on July 1 and depreciation was last recorded on December 31, depreciation for six months (January 1–June 30) should be recorded. If depreciation is not recorded for that period, operating expenses will be understated and the gain on the sale of the asset understated or the loss overstated.

To illustrate, assume that on August 1, 1982, Ray Company sold a machine for $1,500. The machine cost $12,000 and was being depreciated at the rate of 10 percent per year. As of December 31, 1981, after closing, the machine's accumulated depreciation account had a balance of $9,600. Before a gain or loss can be determined and before an entry can be made to record the sale, the following entry must be made to record depreciation for the seven months ended July 31, 1982:

Depreciation Expense—Machinery	700	
Accumulated Depreciation—Machinery		700
To record depreciation for seven months ($12,000 × 0.10 × 7⁄12).		

Now the $200 loss on the sale can be computed as shown below:

Machine cost	$12,000
Accumulated depreciation ($9,600 + $700)	10,300
Book value	$ 1,700
Sales price	1,500
Loss realized	$ 200

The journal entry to record the sale is:

Cash	1,500	
Accumulated Depreciation—Machinery	10,300	
Loss on Sale of Plant Assets	200	
Machinery		12,000
To record sale of machinery at a price less than book value.		

Retirement of plant assets without sale

When a plant asset is retired from productive service, it is necessary to remove the asset's cost and accumulated depreciation from the plant asset accounts. For example, Hayes Company should make the following journal entry when it retires a fully depreciated machine that cost $15,000 and had no salvage value:

Accumulated Depreciation—Machinery	15,000	
Machinery		15,000
To record the retirement of a fully depreciated machine.		

Occasionally a plant asset is continued in use after it has been fully depreciated. In such a case, the asset's cost and accumulated depreciation should *not* be removed from the accounts until the asset is sold, traded, or retired from service. But no more depreciation should be recorded on a fully depreciated asset. The purpose of depreciation accounting is to charge a plant asset's cost to expense. Thus, the total depreciation expense may never exceed the plant asset's cost.

Sometimes a plant asset is retired from service or discarded before it is fully depreciated. If the asset is scrapped for salvaged material—even though the material will not be sold immediately—the value of the material should be debited to a Salvaged Materials account. To illustrate, assume that a machine with an original cost of $7,000 and accumulated depreciation of $6,200 is retired and the scrap value of the machine is estimated at $375. The journal entry to record the retirement is:

Salvaged Materials	375	
Accumulated Depreciation—Machinery	6,200	
Loss on Retirement of Plant Assets	425	
Machinery		7,000
To record retirement of machinery.		

Destruction of plant assets

Plant assets are sometimes wrecked in accidents or destroyed by fire, flood, storm, or other causes. Losses are normally incurred in such situations. For example, assume that an uninsured building costing $40,000 with accumulated depreciation of $12,000 is completely destroyed by a fire. The journal entry is:

Fire Loss	28,000	
Accumulated Depreciation—Building	12,000	
Building		40,000
To record fire loss.		

If the building were insured, only the amount of the fire loss in excess of the amount to be recovered from the insurance company would be debited to the Fire Loss account. To illustrate, assume that in the example above the building was partially insured and that $22,000 was recoverable from the insurance company. The journal entry is:

Receivable from Insurance Company	22,000	
Fire Loss	6,000	
Accumulated Depreciation—Building	12,000	
Building		40,000
To record fire loss and amount expected to be recovered from insurance company.		

Exchanges of plant assets

Certain plant assets, such as automobiles, trucks, and office equipment, are often acquired by trading in an old asset. In such cases, a trade-in allowance is usually granted on the old asset and the balance of the price is paid in cash. The accountant must determine the amount at which the new asset is to be recorded and the amount of gain or loss, if any, to be recognized on the exchange. Such transactions should be accounted for at the fair market value of the assets involved, and a gain or loss should be recognized.[1] Thus, the asset received normally would be recognized at the fair value of the old asset given up plus the amount of cash paid. A loss occurs if the fair value of the old asset is less than the book value of the old asset. A gain occurs if fair value of the old asset is greater than the book value of the old asset. But when similar assets are involved, an exception sometimes is made, as described below.

---

[1] APB, "Accounting for Nonmonetary Transactions," *APB Opinion No. 29* (New York: AICPA, May 1973), par. 16.

Exchanges of dissimilar assets.

When dissimilar assets (such as a factory machine and a delivery truck) are exchanged, both gains and losses are recognized. The new asset is recorded at an amount equal to the fair market value of the old asset at the time of the exchange plus the amount of cash paid. This would, of course, be equal to the cash price of the new asset. To illustrate, assume that an old factory machine is exchanged for a new delivery truck. The machine cost $40,000 and has a related accumulated depreciation balance of $33,000. The truck has a cash price of $50,000. The truck is acquired by trading the machine and paying $47,000 cash. A $4,000 loss is realized on the exchange, as computed below:

Machine cost	$40,000
Accumulated depreciation	33,000
Book value	$ 7,000
Trade-in allowance (fair value) ($50,000 − $47,000)	3,000
Loss realized	$ 4,000

Notice that in this exchange the trade-in allowance is the difference between the cash price of the new asset and the amount of cash paid. The journal entry to record the exchange is:

Delivery Truck	50,000	
Accumulated Depreciation—Factory Machinery	33,000	
Loss on Exchange of Plant Assets	4,000	
Factory Machinery		40,000
Cash		47,000
To record loss on exchange of dissimilar plant assets.		

To illustrate the recognition of a gain on the exchange of dissimilar plant assets, assume that the fair market value of the old asset (the trade-in allowance) in the above illustration was $8,000 instead of $3,000 and that $42,000 was paid in cash. The gain would be $1,000 ($8,000 fair market value less $7,000 book value). The journal entry to record the exchange would be:

Delivery Truck	50,000	
Accumulated Depreciation—Factory Machinery	33,000	
Factory Machinery		40,000
Cash		42,000
Gain on Exchange of Plant Assets		1,000
To record gain on exchange of dissimilar plant assets.		

Exchanges of similar assets.

When similar assets (such as an old delivery truck and a new delivery truck) are exchanged, *losses are recognized but gains are not recognized.* If a loss is indicated on an exchange of similar assets, the new asset is recorded at its cash price (which would equal the fair value of the old asset plus the cash paid), and the loss *is* recognized. However, if a gain is indicated on an exchange of similar assets, the new asset is recorded at the sum of the cash paid and the book value of the old asset, and the gain *is not* recognized.

To illustrate accounting for exchanges of similar assets, assume that $47,000 cash and Delivery Truck No. 1 which cost $40,000 and has a related accumulated depreciation balance of $33,000 are exchanged for Delivery Truck

No. 2 which has a cash price (fair market value) of $50,000. A loss of $4,000 is realized on the exchange, as computed below:

Cost of Delivery Truck No. 1	$40,000
Accumulated depreciation	33,000
Book value	$ 7,000
Trade-in allowance ($50,000 − $47,000)	3,000
Loss on exchange of plant assets	$ 4,000

The journal entry to record the exchange is:

Delivery Trucks (Cost of No. 2)	50,000	
Accumulated Depreciation—Delivery Trucks	33,000	
Loss on Exchange of Plant Assets	4,000	
Delivery Trucks (Cost of No. 1)		40,000
Cash		47,000
To record loss on exchange of similar plant assets.		

Notice that exchanges of similar plant assets are recorded just like exchanges of dissimilar plant assets provided a loss occurs on the exchange.

In the preceding example, assume that Delivery Truck No. 1 and $42,000 cash had been given in exchange for Delivery Truck No. 2. A gain of $1,000 is indicated on the exchange, as computed below:

Cost of Delivery Truck No. 1	$40,000
Accumulated depreciation	33,000
Book value	$ 7,000
Trade-in allowance ($50,000 − $42,000)	8,000
Gain indicated	$ 1,000

The journal entry to record the exchange is:

Delivery Trucks (Cost of No. 2)	49,000	
Accumulated Depreciation—Delivery Trucks	33,000	
Delivery Trucks (Cost of No. 1)		40,000
Cash		42,000
To record exchange of similar plant assets.		

Notice that a gain is not recognized on the exchange of similar assets. The new asset is recorded at the book value of the old asset ($7,000) plus the amount of cash paid ($42,000). The gain is deducted from the cost of the new asset. Thus, the cost basis of the new delivery truck is equal to its cash price of $50,000 less the $1,000 gain. The $49,000 cost basis of the delivery truck is used in recording depreciation on the truck and in determining any gain or loss on its disposition.

The justification for not recognizing gains on exchanges of similar plant assets is that ". . . revenue should not be recognized merely because one productive asset is substituted for a similar productive asset but rather should be considered to flow from the production and sale of the goods or services to which the substituted productive asset is committed."[2] In effect, the gain on exchanges of similar plant assets is realized in the form of increased net earnings because of smaller depreciation charges on the newly acquired asset. In the preceding example, depreciation is less if it is based on the $49,000

---

[2] Ibid., par. 16.

cost basis of the truck than if it is based on the $50,000 cash price of the truck. Thus, future net earnings per year are larger.

Tax rules and plant asset exchanges.   The Internal Revenue Code does not allow recognition of *gains or losses* for tax purposes when similar productive assets are exchanged. For tax purposes, the cost basis of the new asset is the book value of the old asset plus any additional cash paid. The additional cash outlay is called *boot.*

In comparing accounting and tax methods, accounting principles and income tax laws agree on the treatment of gains, but they disagree on the treatment of losses. Thus, the previous example involving a $4,000 loss on the exchange of delivery trucks, must be recorded as follows for tax purposes:

Delivery Trucks (No. 2)	54,000	
Accumulated Depreciation—Delivery Trucks	33,000	
Delivery Trucks (No. 1)		40,000
Cash		47,000
To record exchange of similar plant assets for tax purposes.		

Because of the differences between accounting principles and income tax laws, two sets of depreciation records must be kept if a *material loss* (relatively significant) occurs on an exchange of similar plant assets. One set of records will be based on the accounting valuation of the new asset (fair market value of the old asset plus cash paid) and will be used for determining net earnings for financial reporting purposes. The second set of records will record the tax basis of the new asset (book value of the old asset plus cash paid), which will be used for determining the depreciation deduction for tax purposes.

Under the accounting principle of materiality, two sets of records do not have to be kept if the loss on the exchange is immaterial, or insignificant. In the case of an immaterial loss, the new asset can be recorded at the book value of the old asset plus the amount of cash paid for both tax purposes and financial reporting purposes. For example, assume a company that earns $1,000,000 suffers a $25 loss on an exchange of plant assets. In relation to $1,000,000, $25 is considered immaterial. Thus, the company can record the newly acquired asset at the sum of the book value of the old asset and the amount of cash paid. Only one set of records is required.

Exchange of a note for a plant asset

Sometimes a plant asset is acquired in exchange for a note. In such a case, the asset is recorded at the face value of the note if the note's face value is approximately equal to the asset's cash price *and* the stated interest rate is at or near the prevailing rate. For example, assume that a machine having a cash price (fair value) of $5,000 is acquired in exchange for a one-year note having a face value of $5,000 and bearing a 10 percent rate of interest. This is the prevailing rate at the time of the exchange. The exchange would be recorded as follows:

Machinery	5,000	
Notes Payable		5,000
Acquired a machine in exchange for a one-year, $5,000, 10 percent note payable.		

On the other hand, if any one of the following conditions exists, the asset should be recorded at its cash price or the present value (explained below) of the note, whichever is more clearly determinable:

(1) an interest rate is not stated;
(2) the stated interest rate is not reasonable; or
(3) the face value of the note is materially different from the cash price of the asset.[3]

If any one of the three conditions exists and the note is recorded at its face value, assets, liabilities, and interest expense will be misstated.

To illustrate, assume that on December 31, 1980, Haley Company acquired factory equipment in exchange for a five-year $20,000 noninterest-bearing note. The cash price of the equipment cannot be readily determined. The prevailing rate of interest at the time of the exchange is 10 percent. Thus, the *present value* of the note is $12,420. The present value of $20,000 to be received five years from now when the prevailing interest rate is 10 percent is computed as follows:

Present value of $1 to be received at the end of five years when the interest rate is 10% (locate the amount in the fifth row of the 10% column in Table 2, Appendix B, at the end of this text)	0.621
X Face value of the note	$20,000
Present value of the note	$12,420

(If you desire a detailed coverage of present value concepts at this time, refer to the Appendix at the end of Chapter 17.)

The journal entry to record the exchange is:

Factory Equipment	12,420	
Discount on Notes Payable	7,580	
Long-Term Notes Payable		20,000
To record exchange of noninterest-bearing note for factory equipment.		

The cost of the factory equipment is $12,420—the present value of the note at the time of the exchange. Both the calculation of depreciation and the calculation of a gain or loss on the sale or other disposition of the asset are based on the $12,420 cost. The discount of $7,580 represents the interest element of the transaction. If a balance sheet is prepared immediately after the exchange, the liability would be shown at its present value as follows:

Long-Term Liabilities:	
Long-term notes payable	$20,000
Less: Unamortized discount	7,580
Book value (which is the present value at the date of the exchange)	$12,420

At the end of each year during the five-year life of the note, part of the discount is amortized to interest expense. The amount of each year's

---

[3] APB, "Interest on Receivables and Payables," *APB Opinion No. 21* (New York: AICPA, August 1971), par. 12.

discount amortization is determined by multiplying the note's carrying value (face value less unamortized discount) at the beginning of each year by the rate of interest prevailing at the time of the exchange. The schedule in Illustration 11.1 shows the amount of discount amortization for each year, the unamortized discount at the end of each year, and the note's carrying value at the beginning and end of each year. Of course, the carrying value at the beginning of one year is the same as the carrying value at the end of the preceding year.

Illustration 11.1

Year	(1) Carrying value at beginning of year	(2) Discount amortization	(3) Unamortized discount at end of year	(4) Carrying value at end of year
1980			$7,580	$12,420
1981	$12,420	$1,242	6,338	13,662
1982	13,662	1,366	4,972	15,028
1983	15,028	1,503	3,469	16,531
1984	16,531	1,653	1,816	18,184
1985	18,184	1,816*	–0–	20,000

* Adjusted for rounding.
(2) = (1) × 10%.
(3) = Previous balance in (3) − current amount in (2).
(4) = $20,000 − current amount in (3) or previous balance in (4) + current amount in (2).

In Illustration 11.1, the discount amortization is determined by multiplying the carrying value at the beginning of the year by 10 percent—the interest rate prevailing at the time of the exchange. The unamortized discount at the end of each year is determined by subtracting the discount amortization for each year from the unamortized discount at the end of the preceding year. The carrying value at the end of each year is determined by subtracting the unamortized discount at the end of each year from the $20,000 face value of the note. The carrying value at the end of the year is also the sum of the carrying value at the beginning of the year plus the discount amortization for the year. For example, the discount amortization for 1981 is $1,242 ($12,420 × 0.10). The unamortized discount at the end of 1981 is $6,338 ($7,580 − $1,242). The carrying value at the end of 1981 is $13,662 ($20,000 − $6,338, or $12,420 + $1,242).

The journal entry to record the discount amortization for 1981 is:

Interest Expense	1,242	
Discount on Notes Payable		1,242
To record discount amortization for 1981.		

On the December 31, 1981, balance sheet, the liability under the note would be reported as follows:

Long-Term Liabilities:	
Long-term notes payable	$20,000
Less: Unamortized discount	6,338
Book value	$13,662

Each year, the carrying value of the note increases by the amount of discount amortization for the year. At the end of the fifth year, 1985, the carrying value of the note is $20,000—that is, the face or maturity value of the note. Upon payment of the note, the following journal entry is recorded:

Long-Term Notes Payable 20,000
   Cash 20,000
     To record payment of noninterest-bearing note.

SUBSIDIARY PLANT ASSET RECORDS

Most business firms maintain an asset account and related accumulated depreciation account in the general ledger for each major class of depreciable plant and equipment—buildings, factory machinery, office equipment, delivery equipment, and store equipment. The general ledger account for office equipment contains entries for such items as typewriters, desks, adding machines, dictating equipment, chairs, and filing cabinets. A single general ledger account cannot maintain detailed information about each individual item of office equipment. Thus, many firms use subsidiary plant asset ledgers or record cards to maintain better control over plant and equipment.

A subsidiary ledger consisting of plant asset record cards is maintained for each major class of plant and equipment. Thus, there will be a subsidiary ledger for factory machinery, office equipment, and other such assets. Each subsidiary record card will contain detailed information about a single item of property, such as a desk or a typewriter. The information on the card should include the following: description of asset, identification or serial number, location of asset, date of acquisition, cost, estimated useful life, depreciation, accumulated depreciation, insurance coverage, repairs, and gain or loss on the final disposition of the asset. The identification or serial number shown on the asset's record card should also be stenciled on or otherwise attached to the asset to enhance control over plant and equipment. Then a physical inventory can be taken periodically to determine whether or not all items shown in the accounting records actually exist, are still where they should be, and are being used. A company that does not use subsidiary records and identification numbers and conduct physical inventories may find it difficult to determine whether assets have been discarded or stolen.

The balance in the general ledger control account for each major class of plant and equipment should equal the total of the amounts shown on all the subsidiary record cards for that class of plant and equipment. Each time a plant asset is acquired, exchanged, or disposed of, an entry should be posted to both a general ledger control account and an appropriate subsidiary record card.

Subsidiary plant asset record cards show the total cost and accumulated depreciation to be written off upon the disposition of plant assets. They provide supporting evidence for depreciation deductions and gains and losses reported on income tax returns and the earnings statement. They can also be used as a basis for obtaining the proper amount of insurance coverage and for substantiating claims for losses sustained on insured plant assets.

Since subsidiary plant asset records are costly to maintain, most companies do not keep such records for assets that cost less than an established minimum of say $50 or $100. The principle of materiality provides the justification for immediately expensing plant assets which cost less than the minimum.

NATURAL RESOURCES

Ore deposits, mineral deposits, oil reserves, gas deposits, and timber stands supplied by nature are known as *natural resources* or *wasting assets*. In their natural state, they represent inventories of raw materials which will be consumed or exhausted through extraction or removal of their physical properties. But, on the balance sheet, natural resources are classified as a separate group of noncurrent assets under such headings as "Timber stands" or "Oil reserves."

Natural resources should be recorded in the accounts at the cost of acquisition plus the cost of development. They should be reported on the balance sheet at total cost less accumulated depletion.

Depletion is the exhaustion of a natural resource. It results from the physical removal of part of the resource. The amount of depletion which is recognized in a period is an estimate of the cost of the amount of the resource which is removed during the period. It is recorded by debiting the Depletion account and either crediting the resource account directly or an accumulated depletion account. This depletion cost is combined with other mining or removal costs to determine the total cost of the resource mined. This total cost is then divided between cost of goods sold and the inventory of ore on hand according to the amount of ore sold. Thus, it is possible that all, some, or none of the depletion recognized in a period will be expensed in that period. The part not considered an expense will be part of the cost of a current asset—inventory.

Depletion charges may be computed by dividing the total cost by the estimated number of units—tons, barrels, or board feet—in the property. For example, assume that in 1981, $900,000 was paid for a mine estimated to contain 900,000 tons of ore. The unit (per ton) depletion charge would be $1 per ton ($900,000 ÷ 900,000 tons). If 100,000 tons of ore were mined in 1981, the depletion charge would be 100,000 × $1, or $100,000. The journal entry to record the depletion charge would be:

Depletion of Mineral Deposits	100,000	
Accumulated Depletion—Mineral Deposits		100,000
To record depletion for 1981.		

The Mineral Deposits account could also be credited directly. The Depletion account contains the material component of the cost of the ore mined. It is combined with labor and other mining costs to arrive at the total cost of the ore mined. This total cost is then allocated to cost of goods sold and inventory.

To illustrate, assume that in addition to the $100,000 depletion cost, mining labor costs totaled $300,000 and other mining costs (such as depreciation, property taxes, supplies, and power) totaled $80,000. The total cost of mining 100,000 tons of ore in 1981 is $480,000. Therefore, the cost per ton is $4.80 ($480,000 ÷ 100,000). If 80,000 tons were sold in 1981, the earnings statement would show cost of ore sold at $384,000 ($4.80 × 80,000), and the balance sheet would show inventory of ore on hand (a current asset) at

$96,000 ($4.80 × 20,000). The balance sheet would also report the cost less accumulated depletion of the natural resource as follows:

Mineral deposits	$900,000
Less: Accumulated depletion	100,000
	$800,000

Depreciation of plant assets on extractive industry property.
Depreciable plant assets erected on extractive industry property are depreciated in the same manner as other depreciable assets. If such assets will be abandoned when the natural resource is exhausted, they should be depreciated over the shorter of *(a)* the life of the physical asset or *(b)* the life of the natural resource. In some cases the periodic depreciation charge is computed on the basis of the units of mineral or other resource extracted.

To illustrate, assume that a building costing $310,000 and having an estimated physical life of 20 years and an estimated salvage value of $10,000 is constructed at the site of a mine. The mine is estimated to contain 1,000,000 tons of ore and is expected to be completely exhausted within ten years. During the first year of the building's life, 150,000 tons of ore are mined. Since the life of the mine (10 years) is shorter than the life of the building (20 years), the building should be depreciated over the life of the mine—that is, 10 years. If the depreciation charge is based on the units of ore mined, the depreciation charge for the first year is $45,000, as computed below:

$$\text{Depreciation} = (\text{Cost} - \text{Salvage value}) \times \frac{\text{Units mined}}{\substack{\text{Total units in mine at} \\ \text{time of acquisition}}}$$

$$= (\$310,000 - \$10,000) \times \frac{150,000}{1,000,000}$$

$$= \$45,000$$

INTANGIBLE ASSETS

Intangible assets arise from (1) superior entrepreneurial capacity or management know-how and customer loyalty—*goodwill;* and (2) exclusive privileges granted by governmental authority—*trademarks, patents, copyrights,* and *franchises.* These intangible assets have no physical characteristics. They have value because they give business advantages or exclusive privileges and rights to their owners.

All intangible assets are nonphysical, but not all nonphysical assets are classified as intangible assets. For example, accounts receivable and prepaid expenses are nonphysical, but they are classified as current assets. Thus, intangible assets are both nonphysical and noncurrent.

Intangible assets are initially recorded at their cost of acquisition. Some companies may have extremely valuable intangibles, such as *trademarks* (symbols, designs, or brand names used with a product), which were acquired at little or no cost. Nonetheless, intangible assets should be reported on the balance sheet only if they were acquired at a cost.

Intangible assets are usually classified as follows:

1. Those that are specifically identifiable and can be acquired individually as well as in groups of assets such as patents, trademarks, and franchises.

2. Those that are not individually identifiable and may be acquired only as part of a group of assets. Because they cannot be identified individually, they are often lumped together and called goodwill.

Amortization of intangible assets. All intangible assets are subject to *amortization.* Amortization is similar to depreciation of plant assets and depletion of natural resources. Amortization is an estimate of the services or benefits received from an intangible asset in a given period. It is recorded by debiting an amortization account and crediting the intangible asset account or an accumulated amortization account.

In general, intangible assets should be amortized over the shorter of their expected economic life or their legal life. *Opinion No. 17* of the Accounting Principles Board requires that an intangible asset acquired after October 31, 1970, be amortized over a period of not more than 40 years. Straight-line amortization must be used unless another method can be shown to be superior.

Patents

A *patent* is a right granted by a government which gives the owner of the patent the exclusive right to manufacture, sell, lease, or otherwise benefit from the patent. The real value of a patent lies in its ability to produce earnings. The legal life of a patent is 17 years. Protection under the patent starts at the time of application for the patent and lasts for 17 years from the date it is granted.

A patent which is purchased should be recorded in the Patents account at cost. The cost of successfully defended patent infringement suits should also be charged to the Patents account.

The cost of a patent which is purchased should be amortized over the shorter of 17 years or its estimated useful life. If a patent cost $40,000 and is to be amortized over a useful life of ten years, the journal entry to record the amortization at the end of each year is:

```
Patent Amortization Expense .......................................  4,000
    Patents ........................................................          4,000
    To record patent amortization.
```

If, after a few years, the patent becomes worthless, the unamortized balance should be charged to expense and, if material in amount, should be set forth separately in the earnings statement.

Copyrights

A *copyright* gives its owner an exclusive right protecting writings, designs, and literary productions from being reproduced illegally. A copyright has a legal life equal to the life of the creator plus 50 years. Since most publications have a limited life, it is advisable to charge the cost of the copyright against the first edition published through charges to expense over the period of its publication.

Franchises

A *franchise* may be a contract between a government agency and a private company, such as a public utility. It may also be between two private companies, such as McDonald's Corporation and a single proprietor operating one or more McDonald's restaurants. It gives the company certain rights, ranging from those of a nominal nature to that of complete monopoly. It also places certain restrictions on the company, especially regarding rates or prices charged. If periodic payments to the grantor of the franchise are required, they should be debited to a Franchise Expense or Rent Expense account. If a lump-sum payment is made to obtain the franchise, the cost should be amortized over the shorter of the useful life of the franchise or 40 years.

Goodwill

Goodwill is best seen as an intangible value of an entity which results chiefly from its management's skill, or know-how, and favorable reputation with customers. The value of an entity may be greater than the total sum of the fair market values of its tangible assets. This means that the company is expected to be able to generate an above-average rate of earnings on each dollar of investment. Thus, the proof of the existence of goodwill can be found only in the ability of a company to produce superior or above-average earnings.

A Goodwill account will appear in the records only if goodwill has been bought and paid for in cash or other property of the purchaser. Goodwill cannot be purchased by itself. An entire business or a part of it must be purchased to obtain the accompanying intangible asset, goodwill.

To illustrate, assume that A Company purchases all of the assets of B Company. These consist of accounts receivable, inventories, land, buildings, equipment, and patents. A Company pays B Company $600,000 cash and assumes responsibility for $300,000 of debts owed by B Company. With assumed market values (not costs from B's books) as follows, the intangible value attached to B and purchased by A is $75,000:

Cash paid		$600,000
Liabilities assumed		300,000
Total price paid		$900,000
Less fair market values of individually identifiable assets:		
Accounts receivable	$100,000	
Inventories	90,000	
Land	150,000	
Buildings	250,000	
Equipment	200,000	
Patents	35,000	825,000
Goodwill		$ 75,000

The $75,000 is called goodwill and is recorded in a Goodwill account. It is treated in this way because it is difficult to identify the specific reasons for the existence of goodwill. The reasons might include good reputation, customer loyalty, product leadership, valuable human resources, and a good information system.

Amortization of goodwill.   Goodwill cannot be amortized in determining taxable earnings for tax purposes. But current accounting practice requires the amortization of goodwill over a period not to exceed 40 years. The reasoning behind this requirement is that the value of the purchased goodwill will eventually disappear. Other goodwill may be generated in its place, but the organization is not equipped to value the regenerated goodwill.

If A Company in the above example decided that the goodwill attached to B Company would last ten years, it would make annual adjusting entries debiting Goodwill Amortization Expense and crediting Goodwill for $7,500.

Leaseholds and leasehold improvements

A *lease* is a contract by which the person acquiring the lease (the lessee) makes payments to the person granting the lease (the lessor) in exchange for the right to use property for the amount of time stated in the lease.

Under certain circumstances, a lease transaction may be regarded as a purchase and should be recorded as one. This type of lease is called a *capital lease.*

If the lease does not meet the criteria for a capital lease, it is called an *operating lease.* Operating leases are not shown on the lessee's balance sheet unless an initial lump-sum payment is made when the lease is signed. Such an initial lump-sum payment, other than the first year's rent, is called a *leasehold.* An advance payment is recorded in a Leasehold account and is amortized over the life of the lease by a debit to Rent Expense and a credit to Leasehold. Straight-line amortization is commonly used.

If the lessee improves the leased property, these *leasehold improvements* will usually become the property of the lessor after the lease has expired. Leasehold improvements are assets and should be debited to a Leasehold Improvements account. The useful life of the leasehold improvements to the lessee is the shorter of the life of the improvements or the life of the lease; hence, this is the period over which the cost of the leasehold improvements should be spread. To illustrate, assume that on January 2, 1981, Y leases a building for 25 years under a nonrenewable lease at an annual rental of $20,000 payable on each December 31. Y immediately incurs a cost of $80,000 for improvements to the building, which are estimated to have a life of 40 years. The $80,000 should be amortized over 25 years, since the period of the lease is shorter than the life of the improvements and Y will not be able to use the improvements beyond the life of the lease. If only annual statements are prepared, the following journal entries will properly record the expense for the year ended December 31, 1981:

Rent Expense (or Leasehold Improvement Expense)	3,200	
Leasehold Improvements		3,200
To charge off ⅕th of $80,000.		
Rent Expense	20,000	
Cash		20,000
To record annual rent of $20,000.		

The total rental expense is thus $23,200 per year.

Although leaseholds are intangible assets, leaseholds and leasehold improvements are sometimes shown in the plant assets section of the balance sheet.

RESEARCH AND DEVELOPMENT COSTS

Prior to 1975, research and development costs were often capitalized as intangible assets when future benefits were expected from their incurrence. Since it was often difficult to determine the costs applicable to future benefits, many firms expensed all such costs as they were incurred. Other firms capitalized those costs which related to proven products and expensed the rest as incurred. As a result of these varied accounting practices, the Financial Accounting Standards Board ruled that all research and development costs, other than those directly reimbursable by government agencies and others, must be expensed at the time they are incurred. Immediate expensing is justified on the grounds that (1) the amount of costs applicable to the future cannot be measured with any high degree of precision, (2) doubt exists as to whether any future benefits will be received, and (3) even if benefits are expected they cannot be measured. As a result of the ruling, research and development costs will no longer appear as intangible assets on the balance sheet.

NEW TERMS INTRODUCED IN CHAPTER 11

Amortization—an estimate, usually expressed in terms of cost, of the service potential of an intangible asset that expired in a period, which is accounted for by periodically charging a portion of the cost of an intangible asset to expense.

Boot—the amount of cash or other assets paid in addition to the asset surrendered to acquire another asset.

Copyright—an exclusive privilege conferred upon the owner protecting writings, designs, and literary productions from unauthorized reproduction.

Depletion—the amount deducted from the cost (or other basis) of an asset of the natural resource type because of a removal of a part of the resource.

Franchise—a contract between a government subdivision and a private company or between two private companies granting the franchisee certain privileges (ranging from those of a minor nature to that of complete monopoly to service a given territory) while placing on it certain restrictions, especially in the matter of rates or prices charged.

Goodwill—the intangible value of an entity resulting primarily from the expectation that its management has the ability to produce an above-average rate of earnings per dollar of investment due to superior management know-how and customer loyalty.

Intangible asset—a noncurrent asset having no physical existence but having value because it provides business advantages or exclusive rights and privileges to its owner.

Lease—a contract under which the owner of property (the *lessor*) grants to another (the *lessee*) the right to operate and use the property for a stated period of time in exchange for stipulated payments.

Leasehold—the down payment, other than first year's rent, made at the time the lease agreement is signed.

Leasehold improvement—any physical alteration to leased property from which benefits are expected to be secured beyond the current accounting period.

Natural resources—ores, minerals, oil reserves, gas deposits, and timber stands.

Patent—an exclusive privilege granted by a government conferring on the owner of the patent the exclusive right to manufacture, sell, lease, or otherwise benefit from the patented invention.

Present value—the value today of a specified future cash flow discounted at a stipulated rate of interest.

Trademark—a symbol, design, brand name, or any other indication of easy and ready recognition attributed to a product.

Wasting assets—depletible natural resources such as mineral and petroleum deposits and timber stands.

DEMONSTRATION PROBLEM

On January 2, 1978, the Hopper Company purchased a machine for $60,000 cash. The machine has an estimated useful life of six years and an estimated salvage value of $2,000. The double-declining-balance method of depreciation is being used.

Required:

a. Compute the book value of the machine as of July 1, 1981.

b. Assume the machine is disposed of on July 1, 1981. Prepare the journal entries to record the disposition of the machine under each of the following unrelated assumptions:

1. The machine is sold for $10,000 cash.
2. The machine is sold for $15,000 cash.
3. The machine and $60,000 cash are exchanged for a new machine that has a cash price of $65,000.
4. The machine is completely destroyed by fire. Cash of $8,000 is expected to be recovered from the insurance company.

Solution to demonstration problem

a.

	HOPPER COMPANY Schedule to Compute Book Value July 1, 1981		
Cost			$60,000
Less accumulated depreciation:			
Depreciation for 1978 ($60,000 × 33⅓%)	$20,000		
Depreciation for 1979 ($60,000 − $20,000) × 33⅓%	13,333		
Depreciation for 1980 ($60,000 − $33,333) × 33⅓%	8,889		
Depreciation for first half of 1981 ($60,000 − $42,222) × 33⅓% × ½	2,963	45,185	
Book value			$14,815

b.

1.
Cash	10,000	
Accumulated Depreciation—Machinery	45,185	
Loss on Sale of Plant Assets	4,815	
Machinery		60,000
To record sale of machinery at a loss.		

2.
Cash	15,000	
Accumulated Depreciation—Machinery	45,185	
Machinery		60,000
Gain on Sale of Plant Assets		185
To record sale of machinery at a gain.		

```
3.  Machinery (New) .............................................  65,000
      Accumulated Depreciation—Machinery ..........................  45,185
      Loss on Sale of Plant Assets ................................   9,815
        Machinery (Old) ..........................................                  60,000
        Cash .....................................................                  60,000
    To record exchange of machines.

4.  Receivable from Insurance Company ............................   8,000
      Accumulated Depreciation—Machinery ..........................  45,185
      Fire Loss ...................................................   6,815
        Machinery ................................................                  60,000
    To record loss of machinery.
```

QUESTIONS

1. When depreciable plant assets are sold for cash, how is the gain or loss measured?

2. A plant asset that cost $15,000 and has a related accumulated depreciation account balance of $15,000 is still being used in business operations. Would it be appropriate to continue recording depreciation on this asset? Explain. When should the asset's cost and accumulated depreciation be removed from the accounting records?

3. A piece of factory equipment and $10,000 cash are exchanged for a delivery truck. How should the cost basis of the delivery truck be measured?

4. A plant asset is disposed of by exchanging it for a new asset of a similar type. How should the cost basis of the new asset be measured under generally accepted accounting principles?

5. A plant asset is exchanged for an asset of a similar type. What is the cost basis of the new asset for tax purposes?

6. Assume that a plant asset is acquired in exchange for a long-term note. Under what conditions would it be appropriate to record the plant asset at the face value of the note? Under what conditions would it *not* be appropriate to record the plant asset at the face value of the note? How should the plant asset be recorded under these conditions?

7. What advantages can accrue to a company that maintains subsidiary plant asset records?

8. a. Distinguish between depreciation, depletion, and amortization. Name two assets which are subject to depreciation; to depletion; and to amortization.

b. Distinguish between tangible and intangible assets and classify the above-named assets accordingly.

9. A building with an estimated physical life of 40 years was constructed at the site of a coal mine. The coal mine is expected to be completely exhausted within 20 years. Over what length of time should the building be depreciated, assuming the building will be abandoned after all the coal has been extracted?

10. What are the characteristics of intangible assets? Give an example of an asset which has no physical existence but is not classified as an intangible asset.

11. Over what length of time should intangible assets be amortized?

12. You note that a certain store seems to have a steady stream of regular customers, a favorable location, courteous employees, high-quality merchandise, and a reputation for fairness in dealing with customers, employees, and suppliers. Does it follow automatically that this business has goodwill? Explain.

13. What is the difference between a leasehold (under an operating lease contract) and a leasehold improvement? Is there any difference in accounting procedures applicable to each?

14. Brush Company leased a tract of land for 40 years at an agreed annual rental of $10,000. The effective date of the lease was July 1, 1981. During the last six months of 1981 Brush constructed a building on the land at a cost of $250,000. The building was placed in operation on January 2, 1982, at which time it was estimated to have a physical life of 50 years. Over what period of time should the building be depreciated? Why?

15. What reasons justify the immediate expensing of most research and development costs?

EXERCISES

E-1. Plant equipment originally costing $36,000 on which $24,000 of depreciation has been accumulated is sold for $9,000. Prepare the journal entry to record the sale.

E-2. A machine costing $8,000 on which $6,000 of depreciation has been accumulated is completely destroyed by fire. What journal entry should be made to record the machine's destruction and the resulting fire loss under each of the following unrelated assumptions:

a. The machine is *not* insured.

b. The machine *is* insured, and it is estimated that $1,500 will be recovered from the insurance company.

E-3. King Company owns an automobile acquired on July 1, 1980, at a cash cost of $5,200; at that time, it was estimated to have a life of four years and a $400 salvage value. Depreciation has been recorded through June 30, 1983, on a straight-line basis. On July 1, 1983, the auto is traded for a new auto. The old auto has a fair value of $1,000. Cash of $4,600 is paid. Prepare the journal entry to record the trade-in under generally accepted accounting principles.

E-4. Equipment costing $22,000, on which $15,000 of accumulated depreciation had been recorded, was disposed of on January 2, 1981. What journal entries are required to record the equipment's disposition under each of the following unrelated assumptions?

a. The equipment was sold for $9,000 cash.

b. The equipment was sold for $5,800 cash.

c. The equipment was retired from service and hauled to the junkyard. No material was salvaged.

d. The equipment was exchanged for similar equipment having a cash price of $30,000. A trade-in allowance of $10,000 was received, and the balance was paid in cash.

e. The equipment was exchanged for similar equipment having a cash price of $30,000. A trade-in allowance of $5,000 was received, and the balance was paid in cash.

(Record this transaction twice: first, for tax purposes; and, second, for financial reporting purposes.)

E-5. On January 2, 1981, the Bristol Company acquired a factory machine in exchange for a two-year, $50,000 noninterest-bearing note. The cash price of the machine was not readily determinable. The prevailing rate of interest at the time of the exchange was 8 percent. Prepare journal entries to record the following:

a. The exchange of the note for the machine.

b. The amortization of the discount on December 31, 1981. Record a full year's amortization.

c. The amortization of the discount on December 31, 1982.

d. The payment of the note on January 2, 1983.

E-6. Ace Company paid $1 million for the right to extract all of the mineral-bearing ore, estimated at 5 million tons, from a certain tract of land. During the first year, Ace Company extracted 500,000 tons of the ore and sold 400,000 tons. What part of the $1,000,000 should be charged to expense during the first year?

E-7. The Hannah Company purchased a patent on January 1, 1965, at a total cost of $68,000. In January 1976 the company successfully prosecuted an infringement of its patent rights. The legal fees amounted to $15,000. What will be the amount of patent cost amortized in 1981? (The useful life of the patent is the same as its legal life—17 years.)

E-8. Pebble Company leased a building under an operating lease contract for a 20-year period beginning January 1, 1981. The company paid $80,000 in cash and agreed to make annual payments equal to 1 percent of the first $500,000 of sales and one half of 1 percent of all sales over $500,000. Sales for 1981 amounted to $1,500,000. Payment of the annual amount will be made on January 12, 1982. Prepare journal entries to record the cash payment of January 1, 1981, and the proper expense to be recognized for the use of the leased building for 1981.

PROBLEMS, SERIES A

P11-1-A. The Allen Company began operations in January of 1979. The following transactions related to plant and equipment accounts occurred between 1979 and 1982.

1979
Jan. 2 Purchased the following:
    1. A machine for $32,000 cash;
    2. Office equipment for $18,000 cash; and

Jan.   3. A delivery truck for $3,000 cash and a two-year $10,000 note bearing a 10 percent rate of interest payable annually. The cash price of the delivery truck was $13,000.

Dec. 31   Recorded one year's depreciation on the plant assets purchased on January 2. The following information was used to determine depreciation for the year:

Asset	Estimated useful life	Estimated salvage value	Depreciation method
Machine	10 years	$1,000	Double-declining balance
Office equipment	8	–0–	Straight line
Delivery truck	5	500	Sum-of-the-years' digits

Dec. 31   Paid a year's interest on the note. (Ignore two days' interest that is chargeable to 1980.)

1980
Oct.   1   The delivery truck was completely destroyed in an accident.
Dec. 31   Recorded depreciation for 1980 on the machine and the office equipment.
       31   Accrued the interest on the note.

1981
Jan.   2   Paid the note and interest.
Sept. 1   The office equipment was sold for $10,000 cash.
Dec. 31   Recorded depreciation for 1981 on the machine.

1982
Oct.   1   Exchanged the machine and $30,000 cash for a similar new machine which had a cash price of $40,000. (Tax method was not used.)
Dec. 31   Recorded depreciation on the new machine which has an estimated useful life of ten years and no salvage value. Double-declining-balance depreciation was used.

Required:

Prepare journal entries to record the above transactions.

P11–2–A. Keith Company purchased a new 1981 model automobile on September 1, 1981. The cash price of the new car was $5,200, and the company received a trade-in allowance of $1,000 for a 1979 model. The 1979 model had been acquired on September 1, 1979, at a cost of $4,800. Depreciation had been recorded through December 31, 1980, on a double-declining-balance basis, with four years of useful life expected. At the time of the trade, the 1979 automobile had a cash value (fair value) of $1,000.

Required:

Prepare journal entries to record the exchange of the automobiles under **(a)** the tax method and **(b)** the theoretically correct accounting method.

P11–3–A. On July 1, 1981, the English Company had the following balances in its plant asset and accumulated depreciation accounts:

	Asset	Accumulated depreciation
Land	$100,000	
Leasehold	75,000	
Buildings	938,000	$129,250
Equipment	408,000	130,000
Trucks	71,000	21,325

Additional data:

1. The leasehold covers a plot of ground leased on July 1, 1976, for a period of 25 years under an operating lease.

2. The office building is on the leased land and was completed on July 1, 1977, at a cost of $288,000. Its physical life is set at 40 years. The factory building is on the owned land and was completed on July 1, 1976, at a cost of $650,000. Its life is also set at 40 years.

3. Equipment is depreciated at 6⅔ percent per year.

4. The company owns three trucks—A, B, and C. Truck A, purchased on July 1, 1979, at a cost of $16,000, had an expected life of three years and a scrap value of $1,000. Truck B, purchased on January 2, 1980, at a cost of $25,000, had an expected life of four years and a scrap value of $2,000. Truck C, purchased on January 2, 1981, at a cost of $30,000, had an expected life of five years and a scrap value of $3,000.

The following events occurred in the fiscal year ended June 30, 1982:

1981
July 1   Rent for July 1, 1981–June 30, 1982, on leased land is paid, $9,500.
Oct. 1   Truck A is traded in on Truck D. Cash price of the new truck is $32,000. Cash of $27,000 is paid. Truck D has an expected life of four years and a scrap value of $1,750.

1982
Feb. 2   Truck B is sold for $14,000 cash.
June 1   Truck C is completely demolished in an accident. The truck was not insured.

Required:

Prepare journal entries to record the above transactions and the necessary June 30, 1982, adjusting entries. Use the straight-line depreciation method.

P11–4–A. On December 31, 1980, the Upton Company acquired factory equipment in exchange for a five-year, $150,000, noninterest-bearing note. The cash price of the equipment was not readily determinable. The prevailing rate of interest at the time of the exchange was 12 percent.

Required:

a. Prepare a schedule for years 1981–85 which contains the following information: (1) carrying value of note at beginning of year, (2) discount amortization for year, (3) unamortized discount at end of year, and (4) carrying value of note at end of year.

b. Prepare journal entries to record the following (omit explanations):

1. The exchange of the note for the equipment.
2. The amortization of the discount at the end of each year from 1981–85.
3. The payment of the note on December 31, 1985.

P11–5–A. Barnes Company acquired a mine for $4,500,000. The mine contained an estimated 4.5 million tons of ore. It was also estimated that the land would have a value of $400,000 when the mine was exhausted and

that only four million tons of ore could be economically extracted. A building was erected on the property at a cost of $600,000. The building had an estimated useful life of 35 years and no scrap value. Specialized mining equipment was installed at a cost of $825,000. This equipment had an estimated useful life of seven years and an estimated $21,000 salvage value. The company began operating on July 1, 1981. During the fiscal year ended June 30, 1982, 400,000 tons of ore were extracted. The company decided to use the units-of-production basis to record depreciation on the building and the sum-of-the-years'-digits method to record depreciation on the equipment.

Required:

Prepare journal entries to record the depletion and depreciation charges for the fiscal year ended June 30, 1982. Show calculations.

P11–6–A. The Hackett Company purchased a patent for $60,000 on January 2, 1981. The patent was estimated to have a useful life of ten years. The $60,000 cost was properly charged to an asset account and amortized in 1981. On July 1, 1982, the company incurred legal and court costs of $18,000 in a successful defense of the patent in an infringement suit.

Required:

Compute the patent amortization cost for 1982.

PROBLEMS, SERIES B

P11–1–B. On January 2, 1979, the Colson Company purchased a delivery truck for $21,000 cash. The truck has an estimated useful life of six years and an estimated salvage value of $1,000. The double-declining-balance method of depreciation is being used.

Required:

a. Prepare a schedule which shows how the truck's book value on January 1, 1982, would be computed.

b. Assume the truck is to be disposed of on July 1, 1982. What journal entry is required to record depreciation for the six months ended June 30, 1982?

c. Prepare the journal entries to record the disposition of the truck under each of the following unrelated assumptions:

1. The truck is sold for $3,000 cash.
2. The truck is sold for $7,000 cash.

3. The truck is retired from service, and it is expected that $1,500 will be received from the sale of salvaged materials.
4. The truck and $20,000 cash are exchanged for office equipment having a cash price of $28,000.
5. The truck and $22,000 cash are exchanged for a new delivery truck which has a cash price of $30,000.
6. The truck is completely destroyed in an accident. Cash of $2,800 is expected to be recovered from the insurance company.

P11–2–B. Young Moving Company purchased a new moving van on October 1, 1981. The cash price of the new van was $22,000, and the company received a trade-in allowance of $4,000 for a 1979 model. The balance was paid in cash. The 1979 model had been acquired on October 1, 1979, at a cost of $18,000. Depreciation had been recorded through December 31, 1980, on a double-declining-balance basis, with three years of useful life expected. At the time of trade, the 1979 van had a cash value of $4,000.

Required:

Present journal entries to record the exchange of the moving vans.

P11–3–B. On January 1, 1981, the Weber Company had the following balances in its plant asset and accumulated depreciation accounts:

	Asset	Accumulated depreciation
Land	$ 40,000	
Leasehold	50,000	
Buildings	219,600	$18,375
Equipment	192,000	89,100
Trucks	28,800	14,025

Additional data:

1. The leasehold covers a plot of ground leased on January 1, 1977, for a period of 20 years.
2. Building No. 1 is on the owned land and was completed on July 1, 1980, at a cost of $126,000. Its life is set at 40 years. Building No. 2 is on leased land and was completed on July 1, 1977, at a cost of $93,600. Its life is also set at 40 years.
3. Equipment is depreciated at 12.5 percent per year.
4. Truck A, purchased on January 1, 1979, at a cost of $9,600, had an expected life of 2½ years and a scrap value of $600. Truck B, purchased on July 1, 1979, at a cost of $8,400, had an expected life of two years and a scrap value of $1,400. Truck C, purchased on July 1, 1980, at a cost of $10,800, had an expected life of three years and a scrap value of $1,350.

The following events occurred in 1981:

Jan. 2   Rent for 1981 on leased land is paid, $5,600.
Apr. 1   Truck B is traded in on Truck D. Cash price of the new truck is $9,600. A trade-in allowance of $1,800 is granted ($1,800 is also the cash value of Truck B). The balance is paid in cash. Truck D has an expected life of 2½ years and a scrap value of $600. (Do not use tax method.)
      1   Truck A is sold for $1,800 cash.

Required:

Prepare journal entries to record the 1981 transactions and the necessary December 31, 1981, adjusting entries, assuming a calendar-year accounting period. Use the straight-line depreciation method.

P11–4–B. On December 31, 1980, the Schley Company acquired a delivery truck in exchange for a three-year, $30,000, noninterest-bearing note. The cash price of the truck was not readily determinable. The prevailing rate of interest at the time of the exchange was 10 percent.

Required:

a. Prepare a schedule for years 1981–83 which contains the following information: (1) carrying value of note at beginning of year, (2) discount amortization for year, (3) unamortized discount at end of year, and (4) carrying value of note at end of year.

b. Prepare journal entries to record the following (omit explanations):

1. The exchange of the note for the truck.
2. The amortization of the discount at the end of each of the years 1981, 1982, and 1983.
3. The payment of the note on December 31, 1983. (Ignore the two days of interest that could be charged.)

P11–5–B. The Klay Mining Company, on January 2, 1981, acquired ore deposits at a cash cost of $1,785,000. The ore deposits contain an estimated three million tons. Present technology will allow the economical extraction of only 85 percent of the total deposit. Machinery, equipment, and temporary sheds are installed at a cost of $306,000. These assets will have no further value to the company when the ore body is exhausted; they have a physical life of 12 years. In 1981, 350,000 tons of ore are extracted. The company expects the mine to be exhausted in ten years, with sharp variations in annual production.

Required:

a. Compute the depletion charge for 1981.

b. Compute the depreciation charge for 1981 under each of the following methods: (1) straight line, (2) sum-of-the-years' digits, (3) double-declining balance, and (4) units of production.

c. Which depreciation method do you believe to be most appropriate in the circumstances cited?

P11–6–B. The Monticello Company spent $41,650 to purchase a patent on January 2, 1981. It is assumed that the patent will be useful during its full legal life. In January 1982 the company successfully prosecuted an infringement of its patent rights at a cost of $8,000. Also in January 1982, the company paid $12,000 to obtain patents that could, if used by competitors, make the earlier Monticello patents useless. The purchased patents will never be used.

Required:

Give the entries to record the information relative to the patents in 1981 and 1982.

BUSINESS DECISION PROBLEM 11–1

Laborteaux Company acquired Machine A for $50,000 on January 2, 1979. Machine A had an estimated useful life of four years and no salvage value. The machine was depreciated on the double-declining-balance basis. On January 2, 1981, Machine A was exchanged for Machine B. Machine B had a cash price of $60,000. In addition to Machine A, cash of $50,000 was given up in the exchange. The company recorded the exchange in accordance with income tax regulations but failed to record the exchange in accordance with generally accepted accounting principles. Machine B has an estimated useful life of five years and no salvage value. The machine is being depreciated under the straight-line method.

Required:

a. What journal entry did the Laborteaux Company make when it recorded the exchange of machines? (Show computations.)

b. What journal entry should the Laborteaux Company have made to record the exchange of machines in accordance with generally accepted accounting principles?

c. Assume the error is discovered on December 31, 1982, before adjusting journal entries are made. What journal entries should be made to correct the accounting records? What adjusting journal entry should be made to record depreciation for 1982? (Ignore income taxes.)

d. What effect did the error have on reported net earnings for 1981? (Ignore income taxes.)

e. How should Machine B be reported on the December 31, 1982, balance sheet?

BUSINESS DECISION PROBLEM 11–2

Hazelwood is trying to decide whether to buy Company A or Company B. Both Company A and Company B have assets and liabilities with the following book values and fair market values:

	Book value	Fair market value
Accounts receivable	$100,000	$100,000
Inventories	400,000	600,000
Land	150,000	350,000
Buildings	300,000	700,000
Equipment	120,000	200,000
Patents	80,000	100,000
Accounts payable	200,000	200,000
Notes payable	50,000	50,000

The only difference between Company A and Company B is that Company A has net earnings which are about average for the industry while Company B has net earnings which are greatly above average for the industry.

Required:

a. Assume Hazelwood can buy Company A for $1,800,000 or can buy Company B for $2,300,000. Prepare the journal entry to record the acquisition assuming Hazelwood buys (1) Company A and (2) Company B. What accounts for the difference between the purchase price of the two companies?

b. Assume Hazelwood can buy either company for $1,800,000. Which company would you advise Hazelwood to buy? Why?

Chapter 12

Payroll accounting (and personal federal income tax)

For many businesses the cost associated with payroll is the largest expense they incur. Thus, payroll accounting is a very important function for these businesses. Another reason for the close attention directed to payroll accounting is that the federal and state governments require employers to maintain payroll records showing the amount each employee has earned and the amounts which have been withheld from the employees' paychecks. There are also regular reports regarding payroll which must be filed with the federal and state government. Periodic payment of the amounts withheld is required.

The payroll accounting system is a part of the general accounting system. Its purposes are to—

1. Process data such as names, social security numbers, hours worked, rates of pay, and deductions for items such as taxes, union dues, and health insurance.
2. Provide accurate paychecks when due.
3. Provide an explanation to each employee showing gross pay, deductions, and net pay.
4. Produce necessary employee earnings records, withholding statements, and reports to government agencies.
5. Protect against fraud in payroll transactions.

This chapter describes the important features of payroll accounting including internal control over payroll transactions, the nature and amount of items withheld from employees' wages, the forms used in payroll accounting, and the means for recording payroll information. An Appendix to this chapter describes the individual federal income tax.

INTERNAL CONTROL OVER PAYROLL TRANSACTIONS

In a small business the owner-manager can often handle the entire payroll procedure. Where companies become too large for the owner to handle the payroll, a separation of duties regarding payroll is one way to strengthen internal control. Ideally, in these situations the functions of timekeeping, preparing the payroll, keeping payroll records, and distributing the pay to employees should be performed by different individuals or in separate units of the organization.

An accurate method should be used for recording the time that each employee works if compensation is based on time worked. One such method used for hourly employees is the use of a time clock. When employees report for work, they take their *timecard* from a rack located near the time clock and insert it in the time clock. The date and time are punched onto the card. When the employee leaves, the same procedure is used. Safeguards must be used to ensure that no employee punches in or out for another employee. The timecards serve as a source document to be used in calculating gross pay.

The timecards are sent to the individual or unit (such as the payroll department) responsible for preparing the payroll. The names of authorized employees, their pay rates, and authorized deductions are also available. The individual payroll records are updated, and the payroll checks are prepared. Periodically, any necessary governmental reports regarding payroll are prepared.

The payroll checks are sent to the treasurer for his or her signature. Documents to support the correctness of the checks may accompany the payroll checks. When the treasurer is satisfied that the payments are proper, the checks are signed. The payroll checks are then distributed to the employees by the personnel department or a paymaster. Ideally, each employee should sign for and receive his or her check in person from the one designated to distribute the checks.

Payroll fraud

Some of the schemes involving payroll which have occurred in the past to defraud the employer include the following:

1. Paying employees more than they have earned and then receiving a kickback of at least part of the overpayment from them after they have cashed their checks.
2. Making payroll checks out to fictitious or former employees and then cashing these checks to obtain the cash.
3. Preparing duplicate payroll checks and then cashing the duplicate checks to obtain the funds.
4. Overstating payroll deductions and confiscating the difference. For instance, assume that the health insurance deduction is actually $18.20, but it is recorded as $20.20 and the $2.00 difference for each employee is retained by the perpetrator of the fraud.

Because of these schemes, great care must be taken to ensure that only the actual employees of the company are being paid, and in the proper amount. The separation of duties described above aids in accomplishing this. When this separation exists, it is difficult to arrange and cover up fraudulent transactions. The work of one person serves as a check on the others. For instance, if a person in the payroll department falsifies the hours worked for an employee in an attempt to overpay that employee, the changed hours will be in disagreement with the stamped time clock record. If the timekeeping function existed within the payroll department, a phony timecard could be created to support the fraudulent transaction.

The maintenance of accurate employment and payroll records also is crucial. For instance, the payroll department must be informed of hirings and terminations as soon as possible. Current copies of documents authorizing payroll deductions should be on hand so that the legitimacy of deductions can be checked whenever necessary.

The fact that each employee's social security number must be on hand, an employee earnings record must be maintained, and periodic payroll reports must be submitted to the federal government has reduced the probability of payroll frauds. But the company must be alert to the possibility and protect against that possibility.

MISCELLANEOUS MATTERS REGARDING GROSS EARNINGS OF EMPLOYEES

Employees are those (such as internal auditors, production workers, and salespersons) whose activities are under the direction and supervision of the employer in an employer-employee relationship. They are distinguished from independent contractors (such as a lawyer, independent auditor, or consultant) who are not controlled or supervised directly by the one paying them. Amounts paid to employees are subject to federal income tax withholding, social security, and unemployment taxes, while fees paid to independent contractors are not.

The *Wages and Hours Law* requires that employees engaged in interstate commerce be paid at least 1½ times their normal rate for hours worked in excess of 40 hours per week. This law also requires that at least the minimum wage be paid to these employees. (As of this writing, the minimum wage was scheduled to be $3.10 per hour in 1980 and $3.35 per hour in 1981.) Some union contracts also call for premium rates of pay (such as double time for work on Sundays) for a certain portion of the hours worked. Details on hours worked must be maintained with extreme accuracy to ensure that these requirements are being met. In the absence of such records, later assessments for overtime pay may be made against the employer, based largely on the word of former or present employees (a penalty also may be imposed).

The term *wages* generally is used to refer to the gross earnings of an employee who is paid by the hour. Such employees are paid only for the actual number of hours worked. The term *salaries* generally is used to refer to the gross earnings of an employee who is paid by the week or month. Such an employee is paid that flat amount whether he or she works more or less hours than normal during the period.

DEDUCTIONS FROM GROSS EARNINGS

The *deductions from gross earnings* commonly made include amounts withheld for federal income tax, social security tax, state income tax, and other items which will be discussed.

Federal income tax

Under the federal pay-as-you-go income tax collection system, most individuals must pay (partially or in full) their federal income taxes on wages as they are received throughout the year rather than waiting until they file an income tax return. The tax is withheld by the employer from the wages of employees at the time wage payments are made. The *federal income taxes withheld* are remitted periodically by the employer to a depository bank or to the Internal Revenue Service.

The amount of the income tax to be withheld from the pay of each employee depends upon (1) the amount of the employee's earnings, (2) the frequency of the payroll period, and (3) the income exempt from taxation as determined by the number of exemptions claimed by the employee on his or her *Employee's Withholding Allowance Certificate (Form W-4)*, Illustration 12.1. The amount of each personal exemption is built into the withholding tax rates and tables.

After the end of each calendar year, an employer must furnish each employee certain information necessary to aid in preparing his or her personal federal income tax return. The information is contained in the *Wage and*

Illustration 12.1: Employee's Withholding Allowance Certificate (Form W-4)

Form **W-4**
(Rev. May 1977)
Department of the Treasury
Internal Revenue Service

Employee's Withholding Allowance Certificate

(Use for Wages Paid After May 31, 1977)

This certificate is for income tax withholding purposes only. It will remain in effect until you change it. If you claim exemption from withholding, you will have to file a new certificate on or before April 30 of next year.

Type or print your full name
Ronald Mark Kyle

Your Social security number
107 24 4260

Home address (number and street or rural route)
52 Allendale Road

City or town, State, and ZIP code
Dunwoody, Georgia 30338

Marital Status

☐ Single   ☒ Married
☐ Married, but withhold at higher Single rate

Note: If married, but legally separated, or spouse is a nonresident alien, check the single block.

1 Total number of allowances you are claiming   4
2 Additional amount, if any, you want deducted from each pay (if your employer agrees) .... $
3 I claim exemption from withholding (see instructions). Enter "Exempt"

Under the penalties of perjury, I certify that the number of withholding exemptions and allowances claimed on this certificate does not exceed the number to which I am entitled. If claiming exemption from withholding, I certify that I incurred no liability for Federal income tax for last year and that I anticipate that I will incur no liability for Federal income tax for this year.

Signature ▶ *Ronald Mark Kyle*   Date ▶ July 18   , 19 78

Illustration 12.2: Wage and Tax Statement (Form W-2)

1 Control number		2 Employer's State number			For Official Use Only
	222				

3 Employer's name, address, and ZIP code

Beacham-Moorhead Ace Hardware
7360 Roswell Road
Sandy Springs, Georgia 30328

4 Sub-total ☐	Cor-rection ☐	Void ☐

Make No Entry Here
See Note on the Back of Copy D

7 Employer's identification number
14 162184

10 Employee's social security number	11 Federal income tax withheld	12 Wages, tips, other compensation	13 FICA tax withheld	14 Total FICA wages
107 24 4260	1,211.60	13,000	780	13,000

15 Employee's name (first, middle, last)	16 Pension plan coverage? Yes Ⓝⓞ	17 *	18 FICA tips
Ronald Mark Kyle			

52 Allendale Road
Dunwoody, Georgia 30338

19 Employee's address and ZIP code

Wage and Tax Statement   **1978**

Copy A For Social Security Administration
*See Instructions for Forms W-2 and W-2P and back of Copy D

Form **W-2**

Department of the Treasury—Internal Revenue Service

Tax Statement (Form W-2) shown in Illustration 12.2. The completed form must be distributed by the end of January following each year. One copy is sent to the Internal Revenue Service by the employer. The other three copies are given to the employee. The employee retains one copy, includes one with his or her federal income tax return, and includes one with his or her state income tax return (if applicable). The Internal Revenue Service uses its copy in determining whether or not taxpayers have filed proper income tax returns.

Accounting for federal income tax withheld.   To illustrate the accounting entries for federal income tax withheld from employees, assume that there is one employee whose gross wage is $250 per week, and that the tax to be withheld is $23.30, determined from a withholding table supplied by the Internal Revenue Service. An example of such a table is the *wage bracket withholding table* shown in Illustration 12.3. The weekly accounting entries will be as follows:

Salary Expense	250.00	
Federal Income Tax Withheld		23.30
Accrued Salaries Payable		226.70
To record the accrual of salaries.		

Accrued Salaries Payable	226.70	
Cash		226.70
To record the payment of salaries.		

For those who wish to pursue the topic, the Appendix to this chapter contains a discussion of the individual federal income tax. This tax is the reason for the above entries.

Illustration 12.3: Wage bracket withholding table

MARRIED Persons — WEEKLY Payroll Period

And the wages are—		And the number of withholding allowances claimed is—										
At least	But less than	0	1	2	3	4	5	6	7	8	9	10 or more
		The amount of income tax to be withheld shall be—										
145	150	14.30	11.70	9.10	6.50	4.40	2.20	.10	0	0	0	0
150	160	15.70	13.10	10.50	7.90	5.50	3.30	1.20	0	0	0	0
160	170	17.50	14.90	12.30	9.70	7.10	4.80	2.70	.50	0	0	0
170	180	19.30	16.70	14.10	11.50	8.90	6.30	4.20	2.00	0	0	0
180	190	21.10	18.50	15.90	13.30	10.70	8.10	5.70	3.50	1.40	0	0
190	200	22.90	20.30	17.70	15.10	12.50	9.90	7.30	5.00	2.90	.70	0
200	210	24.70	22.10	19.50	16.90	14.30	11.70	9.10	6.50	4.40	2.20	0
210	220	26.50	23.90	21.30	18.70	16.10	13.50	10.90	8.30	5.90	3.70	1.50
220	230	28.40	25.70	23.10	20.50	17.90	15.30	12.70	10.10	7.50	5.20	3.00
230	240	30.60	27.50	24.90	22.30	19.70	17.10	14.50	11.90	9.30	6.70	4.50
240	250	32.80	29.60	26.70	24.10	21.50	18.90	16.30	13.70	11.10	8.50	6.00
250	260	35.00	31.80	28.60	25.90	23.30	20.70	18.10	15.50	12.90	10.30	7.70
260	270	37.20	34.00	30.80	27.70	25.10	22.50	19.90	17.30	14.70	12.10	9.50
270	280	39.40	36.20	33.00	29.80	26.90	24.30	21.70	19.10	16.50	13.90	11.30
280	290	41.80	38.40	35.20	32.00	28.90	26.10	23.50	20.90	18.30	15.70	13.10
290	300	44.30	40.70	37.40	34.20	31.10	27.90	25.30	22.70	20.10	17.50	14.90
300	310	46.80	43.20	39.60	36.40	33.30	30.10	27.10	24.50	21.90	19.30	16.70
310	320	49.30	45.70	42.10	38.60	35.50	32.30	29.10	26.30	23.70	21.10	18.50
320	330	51.80	48.20	44.60	41.00	37.70	34.50	31.30	28.20	25.50	22.90	20.30
330	340	54.30	50.70	47.10	43.50	39.90	36.70	33.50	30.40	27.30	24.70	22.10
340	350	56.80	53.20	49.60	46.00	42.40	38.90	35.70	32.60	29.40	26.50	23.90
350	360	59.30	55.70	52.10	48.50	44.90	41.30	37.90	34.80	31.60	28.40	25.70
360	370	62.10	58.20	54.60	51.00	47.40	43.80	40.10	37.00	33.80	30.60	27.50
370	380	64.90	60.80	57.10	53.50	49.90	46.30	42.60	39.20	36.00	32.80	29.60
380	390	67.70	63.60	59.60	56.00	52.40	48.80	45.10	41.50	38.20	35.00	31.80
390	400	70.50	66.40	62.40	58.50	54.90	51.30	47.60	44.00	40.40	37.20	34.00
400	410	73.30	69.20	65.20	61.20	57.40	53.80	50.10	46.50	42.90	39.40	36.20
410	420	76.10	72.00	68.00	64.00	59.90	56.30	52.60	49.00	45.40	41.80	38.40
420	430	78.90	74.80	70.80	66.80	62.70	58.80	55.10	51.50	47.90	44.30	40.70
430	440	81.80	77.60	73.60	69.60	65.50	61.50	57.60	54.00	50.40	46.80	43.20

Social security (F.I.C.A.) tax

The *social security tax* was created by passage of the Federal Insurance Contributions Act (F.I.C.A.). The basic plan for management of the social security fund is simple. During their years of employment covered by the act, employed persons, their employers, and self-employed persons pay a certain percentage of their earnings (up to the limit specified in the act) into a special fund. This fund is used to pay retirement benefits to the covered persons who reach age 62 and retire. When earnings stop because the covered worker has retired or died, or in certain cases has been disabled, benefit payments are made to the worker or the family from the fund to take the place of the earnings the worker has lost. Certain hospital and post-hospital care costs for almost everyone over 65 also are payable out of social security funds. Additional voluntary medical insurance is also available for those individuals 65 and over who enroll for it.

Social security (F.I.C.A.) taxes are levied against both the employer and the employee. The amount of tax that must be withheld from the salary of each covered employee for 1979 was 6.13 percent of the first $22,900 of wages paid in that year. This rate and base are subject to frequent change, so to make things easier we will use a rate of 6 percent and a base of $25,000 in our examples and in the exercises and problems at the end of the chapter. The rates and bases scheduled to go into effect as of this writing for 1980–87 are shown in Illustration 12.4. Using the rates and bases shown one can see that the maximum tax would increase from $1,404 in 1979 to $3,046 in 1987.

The employer must bear a tax equal to that withheld from each employee. Thus, the total social security tax in 1979 amounted to 12.26 percent of the first $22,900 of the wages of each covered employee—half borne by the employee and half by the employer. If eligible for coverage under the act, a self-employed person pays the entire social security tax at a rate somewhat higher than that paid by an employee (8.10 percent in 1979). But the program, rates, coverage, and benefits may—at any time—be changed by Congress.

Illustration 12.4: Social security rates and bases

Year	Rate	Base
1980	6.13	$25,900
1981	6.65	29,700
1982	6.70	31,800*
1983	6.70	33,900*
1984	6.70	36,000*
1985	7.05	38,100*
1986	7.15	40,200*
1987	7.15	42,600*

* These amounts are estimates since the actual increases will depend on cost-of-living benefit increases in the preceding calendar year. Congress may, of course, revise these at any time it chooses.

Accounting entries required for social security taxes.   To illustrate the accounting entries for social security taxes, assume that an employee receives a salary of $250 per week. The amount to be deducted from the salary of the employee each week is 6 percent of $250 ($15). Also assume that the income tax withheld is $23.30. The entries to record the accrual and payment of the employee's salary on the records of the employer are as follows:

Salary Expense	250.00	
Social Security Tax Liability		15.00
Federal Income Tax Withheld		23.30
Accrued Salaries Payable		211.70
To record the accrual of salaries.		
Accrued Salaries Payable	211.70	
Cash		211.70
To record the payment of salaries.		

Both the Social Security Tax Liability account and the Federal Income Tax Withheld account represent amounts owed to the federal government which are payable to the Internal Revenue Service.

In addition to the amounts withheld for each employee, the employer is liable for its portion of the social security tax. In this case, the employer's expense also is 6 percent of $250 or $15. To record the employer's portion of the social security tax, the following entry is made:

```
Payroll Taxes Expense . . . . . . . . . . . . . . . . . . . . . . . . . . . . . . . . . . . . . . . . . . .   15
    Social Security Tax Liability . . . . . . . . . . . . . . . . . . . . . . . . . . . . . . . . . . . . . .        15
        To record the employer's portion of social security taxes.
```

This entry normally is part of the month-end adjustment procedure rather than being made weekly as shown above.

Both the employer's and the employee's portions of the tax are recorded

Illustration 12.5:
Employer's Quarterly
Federal Tax Return
(Form 941)

Form **941** (Rev. April 1978) Department of the Treasury Internal Revenue Service	**Employer's Quarterly Federal Tax Return**		
1 First Quarter Only.—Number of employees (except household) employed in the pay period that includes March 12th ▶		6	
2 Total wages and tips subject to withholding, plus other compensation ⟶		23,010	00
3 Total income tax withheld from wages, tips, annuities, gambling, etc. (see instructions)		2,826	20
4 Adjustment of withheld income tax for preceding quarters of calendar year			
5 Adjusted total of income tax withheld ▶		2,826	20
6 Taxable FICA wages paid . . . . . $ 23,010.00 multiplied by 12.1% = TAX		2,784	21
7 Taxable tips reported . . . . . $ multiplied by 6.05% = TAX			
8 Total FICA taxes (add lines 6 and 7) ⟶		2,784	21
9 Adjustment of FICA taxes (see instructions)			
10 Adjusted total of FICA taxes ⟶		2,784	21
11 Total taxes (add lines 5 and 10)		5,610	41
Deposit period ending:	I. Tax liability for period / II. Date of deposit / III. Amount deposited		
from previous quarter.			

Total for quarter (add items A, B, and C)		
E Final deposit made for quarter. (Enter zero if the final deposit made for the quarter is included in item D)		

12 Total deposits for quarter (including final deposit made for quarter) and overpayment from previous quarter. (See instructions on page 4)	5,610	41

Note: If undeposited taxes at the end of the quarter are $200 or more, deposit the full amount with an authorized financial institution or a Federal Reserve bank according to the instructions on the back of the Federal Tax Deposit Form 501. Enter this deposit in the Record of Federal Tax Deposits and include it in line 12.

13 Undeposited taxes due (subtract line 12 from line 11—this should be less than $200). Pay to Internal Revenue Service and enter here ▶		
14 If line 12 is more than line 11, enter overpayment here ▶ $ and check if to be: ☐ Applied to next return, or ☐ Refunded.		
15 If you are not liable for returns in the future, write "FINAL" (See instructions) ▶ Date final wages paid ▶		

Under penalties of perjury, I declare that I have examined this return, including accompanying schedules and statements, and to the best of my knowledge and belief it is true, correct, and complete.

Date ▶ April 24, 1979   Signature ▶ *George C. Beacham*   Title ▶ owner

	T
	FF
	FD
	FP
	I
	T

Your name, address, employer identification number, and calendar quarter of return. (If not correct, please change)

Name (as distinguished from trade name)
George C. Beacham

Date quarter ended
March 31, 1979

Trade name, if any
Beacham-Moorhead Ace Hardware

Employer identification number
14 162184

Address and ZIP code
7360 Roswell Road
Atlanta, Georgia 30328

If address is different from prior return, check here ▶

Please file this form with your Internal Revenue Service Center.
(See instructions on "Where to file")

Form **941** (Rev. 4–78)

in the Social Security Tax Liability account. The balance in the account is carried on the records as a current liability until paid to the Internal Revenue Service.

The journal entry made when the taxes are paid is (assume that only the above amounts are involved):

Social Security Tax Liability	30.00	
Federal Income Tax Withheld	23.30	
Cash		53.30
To record the payment of taxes to the IRS.		

Illustration 12.5 shows the *Employer's Quarterly Federal Tax Return (Form 941)* which is used to report the amount of social security and withholding taxes for a quarter. It is due within one month of the end of each calendar quarter. The employer reports *(a)* total wages subject to withholding, *(b)* federal income taxes withheld, *(c)* total wages subject to social security taxes, *(d)* the amount of social security taxes due (from the employer and employees), and *(e)* the combined amount of income tax withheld and social security taxes due.

Unemployment taxes

The Federal Unemployment Tax Act (F.U.T.A.) provides for a cooperative federal-state system of unemployment compensation. The *federal unemployment tax* is a tax imposed on salaries and wages to help finance the joint federal-state unemployment program.

Unemployment benefits to qualified unemployed persons are paid by each of the states and territorial governments. The unemployment laws of the several states and territories vary only in minor respects; their general similarity is due to the fact that the Federal Unemployment Tax Act sets forth certain minimum standards that must be met by each state.

Federal unemployment tax rate. The federal unemployment tax rate generally has varied between 3 and 3.5 percent. As of January 1, 1979, it was 3.4 percent, levied on the first $6,000 of wages paid to an employee. This rate will be used as an example in all further discussion. The Federal Unemployment Tax Act provides that each employer may have a credit of up to 2.7 percentage points against its federal unemployment tax for amounts paid to the state. This, in effect, leaves the federal unemployment tax at 0.7 of 1 percent (3.4% − 2.7%) on the first $6,000 of wages paid to each employee. The entire federal unemployment tax is borne by the employer; no tax is levied on the employee.

State unemployment taxes. Most states set the *state unemployment tax* rate at 2.7 percent of the first $6,000 of earnings per employee. This basic rate and base will be used in this text. Gaining a merit rate by not laying off employees can reduce this state rate for an employer to as little as 0.5 percent in some states and even to zero in other states. (An employer earning a lower merit rate still can deduct a credit of 2.7 percent against its federal unemployment tax rate.) Almost all state laws levy a state unemployment tax only against the employer.

Each pay period, or once each month, the employer should prepare accounting entries for the federal and state unemployment taxes in the following form:

```
Payroll Taxes Expense ............................................................   xxx
    Federal Unemployment Tax Payable ...................................          xxx
    State Unemployment Tax Payable ....................................          xxx
    To record payroll tax expense.
```

Taxes based on employee earnings are summarized as follows:

Tax	Paid by	Rate
Social security (F.I.C.A.)	Both employer and employee pay at current rate	6.13% of first $22,900 each employee earns annually*
Income tax†	Employee	Varies with earnings and exemptions
State unemployment	Employer	2.7% of first $6,000 each employee earns annually‡
Federal unemployment	Employer	0.7% of first $6,000 each employee earns annually§

* This rate and base are for 1979. We will assume a rate of 6 percent and a base of $25,000 in the exercises and problems in this chapter.

† If combined F.I.C.A. and withholding taxes exceed $100 per month, they must be deposited monthly with a federal depository bank.

‡ Some states have a higher rate and/or base than this. Also, most states allow a reduction from the basic rate to firms with low labor turnover.

§ The federal rate varies, but in this text it is assumed to be 3.4 percent. An allowance of 2.7 percent is granted for amounts paid to the state, thus reducing the effective rate to 0.7 percent.

Other deductions from gross pay

Some union contracts require that the company deduct union dues from gross pay as a convenience to the employees and the union. Amounts are then paid by the company to the union.

Hospital insurance and life insurance premiums may also be deducted from gross pay. This is especially true where group insurance plans are in effect. The amounts deducted are paid directly to the insurance companies.

Deductions are sometimes authorized to pay back amounts borrowed from the employees' credit union. Also amounts to be saved may be deducted and deposited in an employee account with the credit union.

Pledges to charities such as the United Way Fund are often handled through payroll deduction. Amounts deducted are paid directly to the designated charity.

Other deductions are conceivable. For instance, deductions may be made for pension or retirement plans, where the employee is obligated to pay at least a portion of the cost of the plan. Other possible deductions include those to pay for merchandise purchased by the employee from the company and to accumulate funds to purchase U.S. savings bonds.

INDIVIDUAL EARNINGS RECORD

This chapter has mentioned various federal laws which result in amounts being withheld from employees' paychecks, minimum rates of pay for overtime hours, and payroll taxes levied on the employer. These laws require that adequate payroll records be maintained on each employee by the employer so that a determination can be made that these laws are being applied correctly.

Illustration 12.6:
Employee's
individual
earnings record

Position	Sales		SEX M X F	EXEMPTION CLASS	NAME — LAST Kyle		FIRST Ronald		MIDDLE Mark
Date Employed February 20, 1974			MARITAL M X S	NUMBER OF Exemptions 4	ADDRESS 52 Allendale Road Dunwoody, Georgia 30338				
HOURS FULL TIME WEEK 40	WORK WEEK BEGINS DAY Monday		REGULAR EARNINGS $ 250/wk	HOUR RATE $ 6.25	PHONE NO. 394-1776	SOCIAL SECURITY NO. 107 24 4260		Spouse Barbara	

Date of Birth
July 14, 1936

EMPLOYEES EARNINGS RECORD

LINE NO	19 79 PERIOD ENDING	TIME WORKED DAYS	HOURS	RATE PER Hr.	EARNINGS REGULAR	EXTRA FOR OVERTIME	TOTAL	DEDUCTIONS Fed.Inc. Tax	S.S. TAX	State Inc.Tax	Hosp. Ins.	NET PAID AMOUNT	CHECK NO.	Cumulative EARNINGS
FORWARDED														
1	Jan. 5	5	40	6.25	250 00		250 00	23 30	15 00	3 31	20 00	188 39	642	250 00
2	12	5	40	"	250 00		250 00	23 30	15 00	3 31	20 00	188 39	648	500 00
3	19	5	40	"	250 00		250 00	23 30	15 00	3 31	20 00	188 39	654	750 00
4	26	5	40	"	250 00		250 00	23 30	15 00	3 31	20 00	188 39	660	1000 00
5														
6	MONTH TOTAL	20	160		1000 00		1000 00	93 20	60 00	13 24	80 00	753 56		
7	Feb. 2	5	40	"	250 00		250 00	23 30	15 00	3 31	20 00	188 39	666	1250 00
8	9	5	40	"	250 00		250 00	23 30	15 00	3 31	20 00	188 39	672	1500 00
9	16	5	40	"	250 00		250 00	23 30	15 00	3 31	20 00	188 39	678	1750 00
10	23	5	40	"	250 00		250 00	23 30	15 00	3 31	20 00	188 39	684	2000 00
11														
12	MONTH TOTAL	20	160		1000 00		1000 00	93 20	60 00	13 24	80 00	753 56		
13	Mar. 2	5	40	"	250 00		250 00	23 30	15 00	3 31	20 00	188 39	690	2250 00
14	9	6	44	"	250 00	37 50	287 50	28 90	17 25	3 45	20 00	217 90	696	2537 50
15	16	6	44	"	250 00	37 50	287 50	28 90	17 25	3 45	20 00	217 90	702	2825 00
16	23	5	40	"	250 00		250 00	23 30	15 00	3 31	20 00	188 39	708	3075 00
17	30	5	40	"	250 00		250 00	23 30	15 00	3 31	20 00	188 39	714	3325 00
18	MONTH TOTAL	27	208		1250 00	75 00	1325 00	127 70	79 50	16 83	100 00	1000 97		
19	QUAR TOTAL				3250 00	75 00	3325 00	314 10	199 50	43 31	260 00	2508 09		

For this reason, employers maintain an *employee's individual earnings record* for each present employee showing such information as name, social security number, address, phone number, date employed, date of birth, sex, marital status, number of exemptions claimed, pay rate, and present job within the company. For each pay period it also shows the hours worked, gross pay, deductions, and net pay. A cumulative total of gross pay during the year also may be included to aid in determining when to stop deducting social security taxes and when to stop accruing the employer's payroll taxes for both social security and unemployment. Illustration 12.6 shows an example of an employee's individual earnings record which might be used. For former employees much of the above information is retained plus the termination date and reason.

THE PAYROLL JOURNAL

Sometimes a formal *payroll journal* is maintained to record data for payroll accounting. A payroll journal may contain a debit column for each category of salary (e.g., sales, delivery, and office). Credit columns may be included for such accounts as Federal Income Tax Withheld, Social Security Tax Withheld, State Income Tax Withheld, Hospital Insurance, Union Dues Withheld, Retirement Plan, and Salaries Payable, which are all liabilities, representing amounts that must be paid out either to employees or to others on the employees' behalf. Illustration 12.7 shows such a journal.

Illustration 12.7: Payroll journal

PAYROLL JOURNAL

Date Week Ended	Employee	Exemptions Claimed	Salaries Expense (or gross pay)	Deductions				Salaries Payable (or net pay)	Check No.	Distribution		
				Federal Income Tax Withheld	Social Security Tax Withheld	State Income Tax Withheld	Hospital Insurance			Sales Salaries	Delivery Salaries	Office Salaries
1979 Jan. 5	Ronald Kyle	4	250.00	23.30	15.00	3.31	20.00	188.39	642	250.00		
	Rick Larson	2	210.00	21.30	12.60	2.11	10.00	163.99	643		210.00	
	Louis Marshall	4	400.00	57.40	24.00	9.80	20.00	288.80	644	400.00		
	Arthur Niles	3	340.00	46.00	20.40	6.87	15.00	251.73	645	340.00		
	Sally Wallen	3	300.00	36.40	18.00	5.14	15.00	225.46	646			300.00
	Betty Yates	2	270.00	33.00	16.20	4.57	10.00	206.23	647	270.00		
			1,770.00	217.40	106.20	31.80	90.00	1,324.60		1,260.00	210.00	300.00

Notice that a Check No. column was included to show which check subsequently was used to pay the liability. The format of such a journal could be changed to include the number of hours worked per day or per week, the number of overtime hours, and pay rates and the computation of gross earnings.

Some companies maintain a payroll journal only as a memorandum record, which means no postings are made from it. In these firms the entry for payroll would have to be made in some other journal, such as the general journal. The entry would be made for the totals of the columns shown in Illustration 12.7 and would be as follows:

```
1979
Jan. 5  Sales Salaries Expense ...........................  1,260.00
        Delivery Salaries Expense .......................    210.00
        Office Salaries Expense .........................    300.00
            Federal Income Tax Withheld .....................           217.40
            Social Security Taxes Payable ...................           106.20
            State Income Taxes Withheld .....................            31.80
            Hospital Insurance ..............................            90.00
            Salaries Payable................................          1,324.60
        To record the payroll for the week ending January 6.
```

USE OF A SPECIAL PAYROLL CHECKING ACCOUNT

Chapter 6 described the use and advantages of a separate *payroll checking account.* Use of such an account is very common in companies having a large number of employees.

If a separate payroll checking account were being used in the above example, a check for $1,324.60 would be written on the Cash account and would be deposited in the special payroll checking account. The following entry would be made either in the check register or cash disbursements journal (if one of these is in use) or in the general journal:

```
1979
Jan. 5  Salaries Payable ...................................  1,324.60
            Cash ..........................................          1,324.60
        To transfer funds into the payroll checking account to cover
        the January 6 payroll.
```

The payroll checks would be issued and would be charged against the special payroll checking account balance when they cleared at the bank where the account is maintained. A special payroll check register could be used to record the payroll checks. But many firms prefer to merely list the check numbers in the payroll journal (as shown in Illustration 12.7), using it to keep track of the check numbers.

If a special payroll checking account is not in use, the payroll checks will be written on the general Cash account, and each one would appear in the check register or cash disbursements journal (if one of these is in use) or in the general journal.

The payroll checks usually have a detachable portion which shows information such as gross pay, deductions, and net pay. It may also show hours worked and rate of pay. Illustration 12.8 shows an example of such a payroll check.

Illustration 12.8: Payroll check

Employee	Hours Worked	Rate per Hour	Regular Earnings	Extra for Overtime	Gross Earnings	Fed. Inc. Tax W/H	Soc. Sec. Tax	State Inc. Tax W/H	Hosp. Ins.	Net Pay
Ronald Mark Kyle	40	6.25	250.00		250.00	23.30	15.00	3.31	20.00	188.39

Retain this stub for your records – Detach before cashing check

```
                    ACE        BEACHAM-MOORHEAD ACE HARDWARE                        335
                  HARDWARE             7360 ROSWELL RD.
                                    ATLANTA, GEORGIA  30328
                                                                                   64-1240
                                                       January 5,      19 79         611

PAY TO THE
ORDER OF     Ronald Mark Kyle                                            $ 188.39

   One hundred eighty-eight and 39/100s --------------------------------------------- DOLLARS

   The CITIZENS and SOUTHERN BANK
            NORTH SPRINGS OFFICE
          ATLANTA, GEORGIA
                                                     George C. Beacham
FOR _____

      "000335"    ":0611""1240:  038 82  131"
```

END OF PERIOD ACCRUALS FOR PAYROLL

There is common agreement that it is necessary to accrue wages which have been earned between the last payday and the end of the accounting period. But a question arises as to whether it is necessary to also accrue payroll taxes.

Since payroll taxes are levied on wages actually paid during a period, there is no legal liability for payroll taxes on wages which have accrued (but not been paid) during the period. Thus, one could argue that there is no need to accrue payroll taxes on these unpaid wages. But the matching concept used in accounting states that expenses should be recognized (recorded) in the period in which they are incurred. Since the wages were incurred in this period, it seems logical that the payroll taxes on those wages should also be recognized in the adjusting entry made at the end of the period. Some companies follow the legal, practical view and do not accrue payroll taxes at the end of the period. Others follow the theoretical view and do accrue these taxes. Since the amounts involved are often rather small, either treatment may be used without affecting the decisions of a statement user.

Assume that the Beacham-Moorhead Ace Hardware Company does accrue payroll taxes at the end of the accounting period and that accrued wages for December are $885 ($630 sales salaries, $105 delivery salaries, and $150 office salaries). The entry to record the accrual of wages and payroll taxes would be as follows:

Dec. 31	Sales Salaries Expense	630.00	
	Delivery Salaries Expense	105.00	
	Office Salaries Expense	150.00	
	Payroll Taxes Expense	53.10	
	Social Security Taxes Payable		53.10
	Accrued Wages Payable		885.00
	To accrue wages and employer's payroll taxes.		

Only the payroll taxes levied against the employer would be accrued. The only one to include in this example would be the employer's portion of social security taxes (6 percent times $885). The state and federal unemployment taxes are levied only on the first $6,000 paid to each employee. All of the employees of the Beacham-Moorhead Ace Hardware Company would have exceeded the $6,000 level of earnings earlier in the year. If there had been $100 of accrued wages at the end of the period on which state and federal unemployment taxes accrued, the entry would have been:

Payroll Taxes Expense	3.40	
State Unemployment Taxes Payable		2.70
Federal Unemployment Taxes Payable		0.70
To accrue employer's unemployment taxes.		

The employees' share of social security taxes and their federal income tax become liabilities of the employer only when they have been withheld. Since no amounts for these items have been withheld from accrued wages, these liabilities would not be part of the adjusting entry.

MORE EFFICIENT METHODS FOR PAYROLL ACCOUNTING

The payroll procedures described in this chapter are used very effectively in many small businesses. The illustration used was a hardware store with six employees.

When there are many employees, the method described would be rather inefficient. A more efficient method would be desirable.

One possibility for medium-sized businesses is to use what is called a *pegboard system of payroll accounting.* Such a system aligns the payroll check, the individual earnings record, and the payroll journal in such a way that all three are completed with one writing. Instead of having to record gross pay, deductions, and net pay three different times for each employee it is only done once. Of course, the forms must be designed so as to be completely compatible. Use of such a system can reduce clerical time dramatically.

Other methods for increasing efficiency are by utilizing a payroll machine to serve the same function as the pegboard system or to utilize a computer. The business executive must consider the benefits and costs in selecting between any of these systems.

APPENDIX: PERSONAL FEDERAL INCOME TAXES

One of the deductions from gross wages mentioned in the chapter was for federal income taxes. The purpose of this Appendix is to give an introductory understanding of personal federal income taxes. The coverage here incorporates changes introduced up through the Revenue Act of 1978.

The requirements as to who must file a federal income tax return are somewhat complicated. In 1979 the income level at which a tax return must be filed was $3,300 for a single person and $5,400 for married persons under 65 filing a joint return.

Illustration 12.9 shows how taxable income is determined for an individual taxpayer.

The taxpayer's income from sources such as wages, dividends, interest,

**Illustration 12.9:
Determination of taxable
income for an individual
taxpayer**

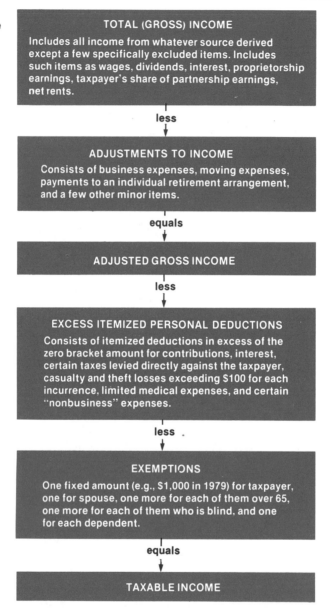

TOTAL (GROSS) INCOME

Includes all income from whatever source derived
except a few specifically excluded items. Includes
such items as wages, dividends, interest, proprietorship
earnings, taxpayer's share of partnership earnings,
net rents.

less

ADJUSTMENTS TO INCOME

Consists of business expenses, moving expenses,
payments to an individual retirement arrangement,
and a few other minor items.

equals

ADJUSTED GROSS INCOME

less

EXCESS ITEMIZED PERSONAL DEDUCTIONS

Consists of itemized deductions in excess of the
zero bracket amount for contributions, interest,
certain taxes levied directly against the taxpayer,
casualty and theft losses exceeding $100 for each
incurrence, limited medical expenses, and certain
"nonbusiness" expenses.

less

EXEMPTIONS

One fixed amount (e.g., $1,000 in 1979) for taxpayer,
one for spouse, one more for each of them over 65,
one more for each of them who is blind, and one
for each dependent.

equals

TAXABLE INCOME

proprietorship earnings, partnership earnings, and net rents is totaled and is
called *total income* or *gross income.*

Unless an item of income is specifically exempted by law, it must be included
in total (gross) income. One of the items which is included in total income,
but which receives favored tax treatment, is long-term capital gains. (Capital
gains and losses are explained later.) Only a few types of income are exempted,
including interest on state and municipal bonds, social security benefits, and

workmen's compensation insurance benefits. Also, gifts, inheritances, and proceeds of life insurance policies are not taxable to the recipient.

Total (gross) income less certain adjustments to income is equal to *adjusted gross income.* These adjustments are for business expenses relating to the production of gross income, moving expenses, payment to an individual retirement arrangement, alimony paid, and forfeited interest penalty (when the interest was included in gross income) for premature withdrawal of funds from certain investments.

Allowable personal deductions may be taken for charitable contributions, interest, certain taxes levied directly against the taxpayer, casualty and theft losses exceeding $100 for each incurrence, *limited* medical expenses, and certain "nonbusiness" expenses. Only *itemized deductions* in excess of what is called a *zero bracket amount* can be deducted from adjusted gross income. These are called *excess itemized deductions.* The zero bracket amount (which replaced the old standard deduction) is $3,400 for joint returns, $2,300 for single and head of household returns, and $1,700 for married persons filing separately. *Exemptions* at $1,000 each are deducted to arrive at taxable income. Briefly, the exemptions an employee can claim are as follows:

One for the taxpayer and one for the spouse (if married and assuming the filing of a joint return, which will be explained later) plus:

1. One more for each of them who is 65 or over.
2. One more for each of them who is blind.
3. One more for each closely related person (son or daughter, or descendant of either; father or mother, or ancestor of either; stepson or stepdaughter; brother, sister, stepbrother, or stepsister; stepfather or stepmother; son or daughter of a sister or brother; brother or sister of father or mother; brother- or sister-in-law, father- or mother-in-law, son- or daughter-in-law) or person (excluding certain unrelated persons) living in taxpayer's home as a member of the household and who is dependent on the taxpayer. The person claimed as a dependent must have less than $1,000 gross income during the year unless he or she is under 19 or is a full-time student. The person must also, in most cases, receive more than one half of his or her support from the taxpayer to qualify as a dependent.

Capital gains and losses

Since long-term gains on the sale of capital assets receive favored tax treatment, taxpayers are continually searching for ways to report income as *long-term capital gains.* To qualify gains as long term, the capital assets giving rise to these gains must have been held for more than one year. Prior to the Revenue Act of 1978, taxpayers excluded 50 percent of their net capital gain from gross income. The Revenue Act of 1978 increased the deduction to 60 percent so that only 40 percent of long-term capital gains is taxed. Gains that do not qualify as long-term are classified as short-term gains and are taxed as ordinary income.

Capital assets commonly held by taxpayers include stocks, bonds, houses, and land. The tax code defines capital assets as all items of property *other than* inventories in a trade or business, trade accounts and notes receivable, copyrights, government obligations due within one year and issued at a discount, and real or depreciable property used in a trade or business.

Even though real or depreciable items of property used in a trade or business and certain other properties are *not* capital assets, the gains may be considered net long-term capital gains for tax purposes. The recognized gains on the sale or exchange of these assets would have to exceed the recognized losses from such sales for them to be recognized as net long-term capital gains. These assets are often described as section "1231" assets, referring to the number of the section of the Internal Revenue Code which grants this treatment.

The gain or loss is equal to the difference between the selling price of the capital asset and its "basis." Generally, the basis is equal to cost less depreciation taken, but the rules governing the proper determination of the basis are extremely complex and are beyond the scope of this book.

An individual age 55 or over may exclude from total (gross) income up to $100,000 (or $50,000 in the case of married persons who file separate returns) of any gain on the sale of a principal residence.

Long-term capital gains are taxed as follows: Assume that a taxpayer has net long-term capital gains of $4,000 and that the taxpayer's marginal tax bracket is 46 percent. The tax paid on the gain would be:

$$4,000 \times 40 \text{ percent} \times 46 \text{ percent} = \$736$$

Calculation of taxable income

The following illustration for arriving at taxable income for the year 1979 is for an individual filing a joint return who is in business and who also has other income. He is married, and he and his wife, both under age 65, have two children under 19 years of age. The parents provide more than one half of the children's support.

Interest received on bank deposits	$ 500
Business income	38,000
Long-term capital gain ($10,000 of which only 40% is included)	4,000
Total (gross) income	$42,500
Less adjustment for payments to an individual retirement arrangement	4,000
Adjusted gross income	$38,500
Itemized personal deductions:	
Medical and dental .... $ 150	
Taxes (property taxes on residence, state income tax, and state sales tax) 1,690	
Interest paid 2,200	
Contributions to church 1,550	
Casualty or theft loss (uninsured fire loss—excess over $100) 850	
Total $6,440	
Less zero bracket amount	3,400
Excess itemized deductions	$ 3,040
Total (also called tax table income)	35,460
Exemptions: Taxpayer, wife, two children at $1,000 each	4,000
Taxable income	$31,460

Calculation of tax due

Once taxable income has been calculated, tax rate tables are used to calculate the tax due. The tax rate tables for 1979 are shown in Illustration 12.10.[1] Notice that there are four tables which are to be used depending on the taxpayer's marital status. The only one which is not self-explanatory is the one for *heads of household*. Generally, persons in this category are certain unmarried or legally separated persons (and those married to nonresident aliens) who maintain a residence for a relative or a dependent.

Illustration 12.10: Tax rates for 1979

1979 tax rates: Married individuals filing joint return or surviving spouses				1979 tax rates: Married individuals filing separate returns		
Taxable income		Tax	% on excess	Taxable income	Tax	% on excess
$0– $ 3,400		—	—	$0– $ 1,700	—	—
Over	3,400	—	14	Over 1,700	—	14
	5,500	294	16	2,750	$ 147	16
	7,600	630	18	3,800	315	18
	11,900	1,404	21	5,950	702	21
	16,000	2,265	24	8,000	1,133	24
	20,200	3,273	28	10,100	1,637	28
	24,600	4,505	32	12,300	2,253	32
	29,900	6,201	37	14,950	3,101	37
	35,200	8,162	43	17,600	4,081	43
	45,800	12,720	49	22,900	6,360	49
	60,000	19,678	54	30,000	9,839	54
	85,600	33,502	59	42,800	16,751	59
	109,400	47,544	64	54,700	23,772	64
	162,400	81,464	68	81,200	40,732	68
	215,400	117,504	70	107,700	58,752	70

1979 tax rates: Unmarried individuals				1979 tax rates: Heads of households		
Taxable income		Tax	% on excess	Taxable income	Tax	% on excess
$0– $ 2,300		—	—	$0– $ 2,300	—	—
Over	2,300	—	14	Over 2,300	—	14
	3,400	$ 154	16	4,400	$ 294	16
	4,400	314	18	6,500	630	18
	6,500	692	19	8,700	1,026	22
	8,500	1,072	21	11,800	1,708	24
	10,800	1,555	24	15,000	2,476	26
	12,900	2,059	26	18,200	3,308	31
	15,000	2,605	30	23,500	4,951	36
	18,200	3,565	34	28,800	6,859	42
	23,500	5,367	39	34,100	9,085	46
	28,800	7,434	44	44,700	13,961	54
	34,100	9,766	49	60,600	22,547	59
	41,500	13,392	55	81,800	35,055	63
	55,300	20,982	63	108,300	51,750	68
	81,800	37,677	68	161,300	87,790	70
	108,300	55,697	70			

---

[1]Actually, taxpayers with income below a certain level must use tax tables different from the ones illustrated here. For our purposes we will assume that all taxpayers may use the tables shown.

In the above example taxable income was \$31,460. To calculate the tax, the table for married individuals filing joint return or surviving spouses would be used. The amount of *income tax* would be computed as follows:

$$\text{Tax} = \$6,201 + 37 \text{ percent of amount over } \$29,900$$
$$= \$6,201 + 0.37(\$1,560)$$
$$= \$6,201 + 577.20$$
$$= \$6,778.20$$

There is a maximum marginal tax rate of 50 percent on all personal services income. Personal services income includes wages, salaries, professional fees, pensions and annuities (arising from performing personal services), and deferred compensation and other compensation for personal services actually rendered.

Certain direct credits may be taken (deducted directly from tax due) in arriving at the amount of tax which must be paid. Some of the more significant credits which may be taken are for contributions to candidates for public office, child and dependent care expenses, investment credit (10 percent credit on purchases of new capital equipment), home energy conservation, and alternative energy equipment.

The investment tax credit works this way. If equipment for a trade or business is purchased at a cost of \$10,000 and qualifies under this provision, a \$1,000 (10 percent) credit may be taken as a direct reduction of tax due.

The last two credits became available under the Energy Act of 1978. The tax credit for home energy conservation allows a credit for certain energy conservation expenditures such as insulation, storm windows and doors, caulking and weatherstripping, and clock thermostats. The credit is 15 percent of qualified expenditures up to \$2,000, or a maximum credit of \$300 for all years (not for each year). The tax credit for alternative energy equipment is for installing solar, wind, or geothermal energy equipment in principal residences. The credit is 30 percent of the first \$2,000 in costs and 20 percent of the next \$8,000, for a maximum credit of \$2,200 for all years.

This has been a brief introduction to some of the provisions of personal federal income tax. The law is changed frequently and is so complex that one must specialize in taxes to become an expert.

NEW TERMS INTRODUCED IN CHAPTER 12

Adjusted gross income—gross income minus business expenses and a few other minor items.

Capital assets—all items of property *other than* inventories in a trade or business, trade accounts and notes receivable, copyrights, government obligations due within one year and issued at a discount, and real or depreciable property used in a trade of business.

Deductions from gross income—all business expenses other than those incurred by an employee, plus five categories of expenses incurred by an employee, such as moving expenses.

Deductions (itemized)—deductions from adjusted gross income for items such as contributions, interest, taxes, casualty losses, limited medical expenses, child and dependents' care expenses, and "nonbusiness" expenses.

Employee's individual earnings record—a record maintained by an employer for each employee showing details such as hours worked, pay rate, gross pay, deductions, net pay, and personal biographical data (see Illustration 12.6).

Employee's Withholding Allowance Certificate (Form W-4)—the form on which an employee indicates the number of exemptions to be used in calculating federal and state income tax withheld (see Illustration 12.1).

Employer's Quarterly Federal Tax Return (Form 941)—a form used to report the amount of social security and withholding taxes for a quarter (see Illustration 12.5).

Excess itemized deductions—the amount by which itemized deductions exceed the zero base amount.

Exemptions—a fixed amount ($1,000 in 1979) the taxpayer may deduct from adjusted gross income for the taxpayer, the spouse, one more for each of them over 65, one more for each of them who is blind, and one for each dependent.

Federal income tax withheld—the amount withheld for federal income tax by the employer from the employees' gross wages. Periodic remittances are made by the employer to the federal government.

Federal unemployment tax—a tax of 3.4 percent levied on the first $6,000 of wages paid per employee. A credit of up to 2.7 percent may be taken for amounts paid to a state unemployment fund, thus reducing the rate to 0.7 percent.

Heads of household—certain unmarried or legally separated persons (and those married to nonresident aliens) who maintain a residence for a relative or a dependent.

Income taxes—taxes based upon taxable income and levied by governmental bodies on individuals (and others).

Long-term capital gains—gains resulting from the sale of capital assets (and certain other assets) which have been held more than one year. Favored federal income tax treatment is accorded these gains.

Payroll checking account—a separate checking account used only for payroll checks. Each payday an amount is transferred from the general cash account to cover the amount of the payroll checks. One of the purposes is to keep the "clutter" of outstanding payroll checks from making more complex the reconciliation of the general Cash account.

Payroll journal—a formal record showing the details of each payroll including for each employee the gross pay, deductions, net pay, and check number. It may be used as a book of original entry (in which case postings to accounts would be made from it) or it may be only a memorandum record.

Pegboard system of payroll accounting—a system which aligns the payroll check, the individual earnings record, and the payroll journal in such a way that all three are completed simultaneously (with one writing).

Social security (F.I.C.A.) tax liability—the amount deducted from an employee's wages to pay into a special fund used to pay retirement and other benefits. In 1979 the rate was 6.13 percent on the first $22,900 of wages paid. The employer also pays a similar amount. In the text we use a rate of 6 percent on the first $25,000 of wages paid to simplify calculations.

State unemployment tax—a tax of 2.7 percent (typically) of the first $6,000 of earnings per employee. A merit rate for not laying off employees may reduce the percent below 2.7 percent.

Time card—used to maintain a record of when an employee reports to and leaves work. It is used as a source document for calculating gross pay.

Total (gross) income—includes all income from whatever source derived except a few specifically excluded items.

Wage and Tax Statement (Form W-2)—a form which the employer must furnish to each employee after the end of the year showing gross wages, amounts withheld, and net pay. It is used by the employee in preparing his or her personal federal income tax return (see Illustration 12.2).

Wage bracket withholding table—a table supplied by the IRS which shows the amount of income tax to be withheld given the wage and number of withholding allowances claimed (see Illustration 12.3).

Wages and Hours Law—requires that employees engaged in interstate commerce be paid at least 1½ times their normal rate for hours worked in excess of 40 hours per week. It also requires that at least the minimum wage be paid.

Zero bracket amount—an amount which is built into the tax tables as a deduction which all can take. Itemized deductions can be deducted from adjusted gross income only to the extent they exceed the zero bracket amount.

DEMONSTRATION PROBLEM

The Fargo Company employs four persons as salespersons (all are married) and pays them weekly salaries as shown below. The number of exemptions and weekly deductions for hospital insurance for each employee are also given.

	Weekly salary	Exemptions	Hospital insurance
Robbin Lucia	$375	3	15
Jo Ann Morgan	400	2	15
Robert Pearson	390	4	20
John Travis	265	2	15

Each employee has 5 percent withheld for state income tax and 8 percent withheld for the retirement plan. Use the wage bracket withholding table in Illustration 12.3 to determine the federal income taxes to be withheld.

Required:

a. Prepare the payroll journal for the week ending January 11, 1980, using headings which will accomplish the purpose. (The check numbers used are 604–7.) Use 6 percent rate for social security.

b. Assuming that the payroll journal is a memorandum record only, prepare the general journal entry to record the payroll.

c. Prepare the entry to transfer funds from general cash to the special payroll checking account.

d. Prepare the entry to record the employer's payroll taxes using the rates given in this chapter. (In actual practice this often is done only at the end of the month.)

e. Prepare the entry to record payment January 14 of the federal income taxes and social security taxes due to be paid to the federal government. (In actual practice this often is done only at the end of the month or quarter, depending on the amounts involved.)

Solution to demonstration problem

a.

				Deductions						
Date Week Ended	Employee	Exemptions Claimed	Salaries Expense	Federal Income Tax Withheld	Social Security Tax Payable	State Income Tax Withheld	Hospital Insurance	Retirement Plan	Salaries Payable	Check No.
1980 Jan. 11	Robbin Lucia	3	375.00	53.50	22.50	18.75	15.00	30.00	235.25	604
	Jo Ann Morgan	2	400.00	65.20	24.00	20.00	15.00	32.00	243.80	605
	Robert Pearson	4	390.00	54.90	23.40	19.50	20.00	31.20	241.00	606
	John Travis	2	265.00	30.80	15.90	13.25	15.00	21.20	168.85	607
			1,430.00	204.40	85.80	71.50	65.00	114.40	888.90	

Table heading: **PAYROLL JOURNAL**

b.

1980			
Jan. 11	Salaries Expense	1,430.00	
	Federal Income Tax Withheld........................		204.40
	Social Security Tax Payable		85.80
	State Income Tax Withheld...........................		71.50
	Hospital Insurance Payable		65.00
	Retirement Plan Premiums Payable		114.40
	Salaries Payable		888.90
	To record the payroll for the week ending January 11.		

c.

1980			
Jan. 11	Salaries Payable	888.90	
	Cash		888.90
	To record the transfer of funds to cover the January 11 payroll.		

d.

1980			
Jan. 11	Payroll Taxes Expense	134.42	
	Social Security Tax Payable		85.80
	State Unemployment Tax Payable		38.61
	Federal Unemployment Tax Payable		10.01
	To record payroll taxes on the January 11 payroll.		

e.

1980			
Jan. 14	Federal Income Tax Withheld	204.40	
	Social Security Tax Payable	171.60	
	Cash		376.00
	To record payment of federal income tax withheld and social security tax payable from the January 11 payroll.		

QUESTIONS

1. Describe some of the purposes of a payroll accounting system.

2. List the various functions regarding payroll and give a method for establishing internal control over these functions.

3. Describe how the system of internal control works. (Begin with the time and end with the issuance of the paycheck.)

4. Identify some schemes involving payroll which have been used to defraud a company.

5. Why is it important to distinguish between employees and independent contractors? Give an example of each.

6. What requirements does the Wages and Hours Law place on employers? Why should accurate records be maintained as to hours worked by employees?

7. List the possible deductions from gross pay which are common.

8. What is the purpose of the Employee's Withholding Allowance Certificate (Form W-4)?

9. What purposes does the Wage and Tax Statement (Form W-2) serve?

10. Against which parties are social security taxes levied and in what amounts?

11. What is the purpose of the Employer's Quarterly Federal Tax Return (Form 941)?

12. What are the federal and state rates for unemployment tax? What is a merit rate and what effect does it have on the credit granted by the federal government for amounts paid to the state?

13. Why should an employer maintain an individual earnings record for each employee?

14. Describe two ways in which the payroll journal might be utilized in the payroll accounting system.

15. Under what conditions would the use of a special payroll checking account be desirable? How does such an account operate?

16. What are the arguments for and against accruing employer's payroll taxes at the end of the accounting period?

17. What payroll procedures might be employed which would be more efficient than the system described in the chapter? Why are these other methods not always used in a given system?

(Questions 18–21 are based on the Appendix.)

18. Define the term, adjusted gross income, as it is used for personal income tax purposes.

19. For what kinds of expenditures may personal deductions be taken on one's personal federal income tax? What effect does the zero bracket amount have on the total personal deductions which may be deducted from adjusted gross income?

20. What are exemptions and by how much does each one reduce taxable income?

21. Why does a taxpayer wish a gain to qualify as a long-term capital gain and how will it so qualify?

EXERCISES

E–1. The Gomez Company employs four persons whose weekly wages and exemptions are as follows:

	Wage	Exemptions
John Sampson	$350	5
Thomas McPherson	220	3
John Lauber	300	4
Robert Conrad	410	2

Using Illustration 12.3, determine the correct amount to withhold for federal income tax per week.

E–2. Using the data in Exercise E–1, calculate how many weeks it would take before the employer would no longer incur federal or state unemployment taxes on each individual.

E–3. Using the data in Exercise E–1 and assuming a rate of 6 percent and a maximum base of $25,000, how much would the employer withhold from each of the employees for the entire year? How much would the employer's social security tax expense be for the year?

E–4. The January 19, 1979, gross payroll for salaries of the Mateer Corporation is $1,600. The total federal income tax withheld is $325. The employees' share of F.I.C.A. taxes withheld is $96. What is the correct entry at the time of payment, assuming no prior recording of salaries? (Ignore federal and state unemployment taxes.)

E–5. Rubin Bixby is trying to decide whether to hire four workers at $30,000 each per year, or 12 workers on a part-time basis at $10,000 each per year, to perform a particular job. Using the rates given in the chapter, calculate the difference in the employer's payroll tax expense under the two alternatives.

E–6. The H. Williams Company is in a state which has a state unemployment rate of 2.7 percent. Due to a record of stable employment, the company has earned a merit rate of 2.1 percent. Total wages on which it incurred federal and state unemployment taxes for the month of March were $12,000. Prepare an entry to record federal and state unemployment taxes for the month.

E–7. At the end of December the M. Harris Company had accrued wages of $1,000 ($500 for sales salaries, $300 for office salaries, and $200 for maintenance wages). The company makes the accrual for payroll taxes on accrued wages. Assume that no employee has earned over $25,000 (including the above wages) and that unemploy-

ment taxes still accrue only on the maintenance wages. Prepare the necessary adjusting entry to accrue the wages and payroll taxes.

E–8. Using the data in Exercise E–8, what entry would the company make if it did not follow the practice of accruing payroll taxes on accrued wages?

(Exercises E–9 and E–10 are based on the Appendix.)

E–9. Paul Daly is 68 years old, and his wife is 65 years old and blind. They have three sons, ages 22, 24, and 29. The son who is 22 is a full-time student in college and earns $3,000 per year. His parents contribute $4,000 per year toward his living expenses. The other two sons are self-supporting. How many exemptions are Paul and his wife entitled to on their joint return?

E–10. John Franks has gross income of $70,000, adjustments to gross income of $4,000, excess itemized deductions of $6,500, and six personal exemptions. He is filing a joint return with his wife who has no income. How much is their tax liability? (Use the tax schedule in Illustration 12.10.)

PROBLEMS, SERIES A

P12–1–A.

Required:

a. The Daly Company has 36 employees and an annual payroll of $371,600: 8 employees earn $30,000 each per year, and 28 employees earn an equal amount each per year. What is the annual social security tax (1) for the employees and (2) for the employer? (Use the 6 percent rate and $25,000 maximum base mentioned in the chapter.)

b. What is the amount of the federal and state unemployment tax per year, assuming a federal rate of 3.4 percent and a state rate of 2.7 percent for this employer?

c. Which of the preceding items would constitute expenses on the records of the Daly Company?

P12–2–A. The Olson Company pays its employees once each month. The payroll data for October are as follows:

Gross payroll . . . . $41,200 (One employee is above the $6,000 limit. Prior to October, the employee's gross salary was $27,000; and the employee's gross October salary was $3,000.)

Income tax withheld . . .   4,400
F.I.C.A. tax . . . .   ?
State income tax . . . . . .   3% of gross salary

Required:

Prepare entries to record:

a. The October payroll.

b. The employer's social security tax for October (use 6 percent rate and $25,000 base).

c. The employer's federal and state unemployment taxes assuming that the federal rate is 3.4 percent and that the state rate is 2.7 percent.

d. Payment of the various taxes.

P12–3–A. The Bently Company employs six persons in its fast-food franchise operation. The names of the employees, weekly wages, and number of exemptions claimed are as follows:

Employee	Weekly wage	Number of exemptions
Bikram Garcha	$410	4
Norman Harbaugh	275	2
Fred Massey	250	3
Becky Rogers	375	1

Marc Schaefer   225   2
Paula Stephan   146   5

State income tax is withheld from employees at the rate of 4 percent on all wages paid.

Required:

a. Prepare a payroll journal with the following headings: Date Week Ended, Employee, Exemptions Claimed, Salaries Expense, Federal Income Tax Withheld, Social Security Tax Payable, State Income Tax Withheld, Salaries Payable, and Check No.

b. Using the withholding table and rates given in the chapter (including the 6 percent rate for social security taxes), enter the payroll data in the payroll journal for the week ending January 9, 1981. Check numbers used were 405–10.

c. Assuming the payroll journal is used only as a memorandum record, prepare an entry as it would appear in the general journal to record the payroll.

d. Prepare the entry to record the employer's payroll taxes for social security and unemployment.

e. Prepare the entry to record the transfer of funds to the special payroll checking account on January 9.

P12–4–A. At the end of the year (1981) the Thornton Company has $30,000 of accrued wages ($15,000 sales salaries, $9,000 delivery wages, and $6,000 office salaries). Of this total, $25,000 are subject to social security tax and $8,000 are subject to unemployment taxes.

Required:

a. Describe the two alternatives the company may follow in making the adjusting entry and explain why these alternatives exist.

b. Prepare the adjusting entry under the two alternatives. (Use the 6 percent rate mentioned in the text for social security.)

P12–5–A (based on the Appendix). William Brantly was about to calculate his taxable income for 1979. He gathered together the following information:

Gross wages	$40,000
Interest received	800
Long-term capital gain	9,000
Contribution to individual retirement system	5,000
Medical and dental expenses	150
Property taxes on residence	1,900
State sales tax	350
State income tax	2,400
Interest paid	4,200
Contributions to church	1,800
Casualty loss (excess over $100)	400

Mr. Brantly is married and files a joint return. He has two young children who live with him.

Required:

Calculate the amount of taxable income for 1979 for Mr. Brantly.

P12–6–A (based on the Appendix). The following data pertain to four individuals for 1979:

			Expenditures on—		
Individual	*Tax status*	*Taxable income*	*Assets qualifying for the investment credit*	*Energy conservation*	*Qualified alternative energy equipment*
A	Married filing jointly	$66,000	5,000		3,000
B	Head of household	52,000		2,500	
C	Married filing separately	36,000			
D	Unmarried	40,000	4,500	1,400	

Required:

Using the data given and the tables in Illustration 12.10, calculate the amount of federal income tax due. None of the individuals had ever before taken a credit for energy conservation or alternative energy equipment. Assume that the maximum marginal tax on personal service income does not apply.

PROBLEMS, SERIES B

P12–1–B. The Smith Company has an annual payroll of $580,000. There are 10 employees who earn $28,000 each and 40 part-time employees, each of whom earns an equal amount.

Required:

a. What are the total employee and employer portions of the F.I.C.A. tax for the year? (Use the 6 percent rate and $25,000 maximum base.)

b. What are the amounts of federal and state unemployment tax per year, assuming that the federal rate is 3.4 percent and the state rate is 2.7 percent for this company?

c. What is the total expense incurred by the employer for these items?

P12–2–B. Throughout the first quarter of the year the Thuss Company employed seven machinists at $1,200 each per month and an assistant manager at $1,500 per month. The monthly payroll was paid on the last of each month. On January 31 the company withheld $1,230 of federal income taxes from employees, along with the proper social security tax.

Required:

Journalize:

a. The payroll for January.

b. The employer's social security tax for January, assuming a 6 percent rate and $25,000 maximum base.

c. The employer's federal and state unemployment taxes, assuming a federal rate of 3.4 percent and a state rate of 2.7 percent for this company.

d. The entry to record payment of the various taxes.

P12–3–B. The Tasty Bakery employs five persons. Their names, weekly wages, number of exemptions claimed, and hospital insurance premiums are as follows:

Employee	Weekly wage	No. of exemptions	Hospital insurance premiums
Marge Authier	$180	3	$15
Alice Cummins	145	1	10
Becky Hooten	200	1	15
Betty McDowell	230	2	15
Louetta Nowlin	155	1	10

State income tax is withheld from employees at the rate of 5 percent on all wages paid.

Required:

a. Prepare a payroll journal with the following headings: Date Week Ended, Employee, Exemptions Claimed, Salaries Expense, Federal Income Tax Withheld, Social Security Tax Payable, State Income Tax Withheld, Hospital Insurance, Salaries Payable, and Check No.

b. Using the withholding table and rates given in the chapter (including the 6 percent rate for social security taxes), enter the payroll data in the payroll journal for the week ending May 30, 1980. Check numbers used were 210–14.

c. Prepare the general journal entry to record the transfer of funds to the special payroll checking account on May 30.

d. Prepare the general journal entry to record the employer's payroll taxes for social security and unemployment.

e. Using T-accounts post the totals of the payroll journal and the entries made in **(c)** and **(d).** Do not bother to enter the dates since they are all May 30, 1980.

P12–4–B. The Sundell Company operates an indoor tennis complex. At the end of 1981 the company has accrued wages of $18,000 ($9,000 for professional tennis staff, $5,000 for administrative staff, and $4,000 for maintenance personnel). Of these wages, $12,000 are subject to social security taxes and $5,000 are subject to unemployment taxes.

Required:

a. Describe two alternative ways in which the company can prepare the adjusting entry. Explain why these alternatives exist.

b. Prepare the adjusting entry under the two alternatives. (Use a 6 percent rate for social security tax.)

P12–5–B (based on the Appendix). Elizabeth Powers is gathering together her income tax information for 1979. She is single and has no other dependents. She accumulated the following data:

Business income	$60,000
Royalties received	3,000
Interest received	1,200
Long-term capital gain	15,000
Contribution to individual retirement system	7,000
Medical and dental expense	150
Property taxes on residence	2,600
State sales tax	420

State income tax	3,200
Interest paid	6,500
Contributions to church and other charitable organizations	2,800
Theft loss (excess over $100)	2,100

Required:

Calculate Elizabeth Power's taxable income for 1979.

P12–6–B (based on the Appendix). The following data pertain to four individuals for 1979:

Required:

Using the data given and the tables in Illustration 12.10, calculate the amount of federal income tax due. None of the individuals had ever before taken a credit for energy conservation or alternative energy equipment. Assume that the maximum marginal tax on personal service income does not apply.

			Expenditures on—		
Individual	Tax status	Taxable income	Assets qualifying for the investment credit	Energy conservation	Qualified alternative energy equipment
1	Unmarried	$37,000	$5,000		$3,000
2	Surviving spouse	54,000		4,000	
3	Head of household	58,000		1,200	
4	Married filing separately	25,000	4,000		2,500

BUSINESS DECISION PROBLEM 12–1

Peter Cote operates a fine restaurant and employs 15 employees. He is interested in food preparation, supervision of waiters, and customer relations. He has little aptitude for record keeping. As a result he hired Michael Robbins to do all of the paper work for the business. This includes preparing the payroll, keeping payroll records, signing the payroll checks, distributing the payroll checks, and reconciling the bank account. The payroll checks are written on the general Cash account rather than a special payroll checking account.

Business seems to be good, but the cash position keeps getting tighter. Wages expense seems to be somewhat higher than Mr. Cote believes it should be. Mr. Robbins assures Mr. Cote that all is well regarding payroll. Mr. Cote suspects that something is wrong regarding the payroll function.

Required:

a. What could be wrong?

b. What would you recommend to Mr. Cote to correct the situation?

BUSINESS DECISION PROBLEM 12–2

Joe Mason owns and runs a motel and has 10 employees. He has one opportunity to acquire a chain of five other motels (with an additional 50 employees). A second opportunity exists to acquire a second chain of 20 other motels (with an additional 200 employees). He will only consider acquiring the second chain if he acquires the first chain.

Mr. Mason is wondering about which type of payroll system to use given the fact that he may have 10, 60, or 260 employees. Estimated costs of three alternative payroll systems are as follows:

	Clerical cost per employee/week	Cost of forms per employee/week	Service charge per week
Manual system	$1.50	$0.20	0
Pegboard system	0.50	0.30	$ 10*
Computer Service Bureau	0.25	0.10	100

*An initial charge for pegboard equipment expressed as a weekly charge.

Required:

Calculate the cost per week of using each of the three systems for 10, 60, and 260 employees, respectively. Which is the least costly alternative payroll system for each alternative number of employees?

PART FOUR

ACCOUNTING THEORY AND

PARTNERSHIPS

Chapter 13

Accounting theory

underlying financial statements

Accounting theory consists of "a set of basic concepts and assumptions and related principles that explain and guide the accountant's actions in identifying, measuring, and communicating economic information."[1] But the exact nature of the basic concepts and related principles has been debated for years. And the debate continues today even though numerous references can be found to "generally accepted accounting principles" (GAAP). To date, all attempts to present a concise statement of GAAP have produced only disagreement and frustration.

This has led to many attempts to start at the beginning by stating the objectives of financial accounting and reporting. Here the belief is that if one carefully studies the environment and knows what objectives are sought, one can discover which principles lead to the attainment of the stated objectives. Or, stated in another way, a principle can be determined as follows: Given the environment, if you seek this objective, proceed in this manner. The directive "proceed in this manner" is the principle. The FASB has taken the first steps in this approach in "Objectives of Financial Reporting by Business Enterprises."[2]

THE OBJECTIVES OF FINANCIAL REPORTING

According to the FASB, the first objective of financial reporting is:

> Financial reporting should provide information that is useful to present and potential investors and creditors and other users in making rational investment, credit, and similar decisions. The information should be comprehensible to those who have a reasonable understanding of business and economic activities and are willing to study the information with reasonable diligence.[3]

The terms *investors* and *creditors* are used broadly and include many others (such as employees, labor unions, security analysts, brokers, and lawyers) who are interested in how investors and creditors are faring. Financial reporting should provide information to all who are willing to learn to use it properly. And, even though the Board's objectives are couched in terms of the corporate form of business organization, they apply equally well to single proprietorships and partnerships.

The second objective states:

> Financial reporting should provide information to help present and potential investors and creditors and other users in assessing the amounts, timing, and uncertainty of prospective cash receipts from dividends [owner withdrawals] or interest and the proceeds from the sale, redemption, or maturity of securities or loans. Since investors' and creditors' cash flows are related to enterprise cash flows, financial reporting should provide information to help investors, creditors, and others assess the amounts, timing, and uncertainty of prospective net cash inflows to the related enterprise.[4]

This objective ties the cash flows to investors (owners) and creditors

---

[1] American Accounting Association, *A Statement of Basic Accounting Theory* (Sarasota, Fla., 1966), pp. 1–2.

[2] FASB, "Objectives of Financial Reporting by Business Enterprises," *Statement of Financial Accounting Concepts No. 1* (Stamford, Conn., 1978).

[3] Ibid., par. 34.

[4] Ibid., p. viii.

to the cash flows of the enterprise, a tie-in that appears entirely logical. Enterprise cash inflows are the source of cash for dividends (owner withdrawals), interest, and for redemption of maturing debt.

The third objective states:

> Financial reporting should provide information about the economic resources of an enterprise, the claims to those resources (obligations of the enterprise to transfer resources to other entities and owners' equity), and the effects of transactions, events, and circumstances that change its resources and claims to those resources.[5]

A number of conclusions can be drawn from the above objectives, and a study of the environment in which financial reporting is carried out. Financial reporting should provide information about an enterprise's past performance because such information is used as a basis for prediction of future enterprise performance. Financial reporting should focus upon earnings and its components, despite the emphasis upon cash flows. Earnings computed under the accrual basis provide a better indicator of ability to generate favorable cash flows than do statements of cash receipts and payments. Financial reporting does not seek to measure the value of a business but to provide information that may be useful to those who do. Financial reporting does not seek to evaluate management's performance, predict earnings, assess risk, or estimate earning power, but it may provide information to those who wish to do so. These are some of the conclusions reached in *Statement of Financial Accounting Concepts No. 1*. And, as the Board states, these statements "are intended to establish the objectives and concepts that the Financial Accounting Standards Board will use in developing standards of financial accounting and reporting."[6]

How successful the Board will be in the approach adopted remains to be seen. But it appears likely that an obstacle barring success in previous efforts to specify accounting principles has been removed, namely, conflicting objectives. Disagreement over accounting principles is bound to exist if the same principles are to achieve conflicting objectives. For example, management may wish to minimize reported earnings for tax purposes while maximizing them to support a loan application. It should be obvious that alternative accounting principles must be available to attain such conflicting objectives. Some examples are given in a later section of this chapter dealing with the major principles of accounting.

QUALITATIVE OBJECTIVES

There is general agreement that in order to be useful, financial information must meet certain *qualitative objectives*.[7] These objectives are discussed below.

Relevance

For information to be relevant it must be pertinent or bear upon a decision. *Relevance* is the *primary* qualitative objective. If information is not relevant,

---

[5] Ibid.

[6] Ibid., p. i.

[7] For discussion and summarization of a number of lists of qualitative objectives, see FASB, *Conceptual Framework for Financial Accounting and Reporting: Elements of Financial Statements and Their Measurement* (Stamford, Conn., 1976), chap. 7. For the ordering of these objectives into a different hierarchy, see FASB, *Exposure Draft Proposed Statement of Financial Accounting Concepts, Qualitative Characteristics: Criteria for Selecting and Evaluating Financial Accounting and Reporting Policies* (Stamford, Conn., 1979).

it is useless even though it meets the other objectives fully. Relevant information aids investors and creditors in assessing the possible returns (cash flows) and risks related to investment or lending opportunities. It is for its lack of relevance that accounting information is under attack today. For example, it is argued that the fact that a tract of land cost its owner $1 million over 40 years ago is irrelevant (except for possible tax implications) to any user for any decision that must be made today. These attacks have encouraged research into the types of information that are relevant to users.

Relevance and materiality.   Although often cited as a principle, *materiality* is a part of the relevance objective. A statement, fact, or item is material if it is significant enough to influence the decisions of informed investors or creditors. Thus, material information is relevant information; immaterial information is irrelevant information.

One way of determining whether an item is material is to look at its relative size. A $10,000 expense in a firm with net earnings of $30,000 would seem to be material. But the same amount in a much more profitable firm may not be material. If an item is considered immaterial, it may be handled without regard to accounting principles. Thus, the cost of a wastebasket may be charged to expense in the period in which it is acquired rather than set up as an asset and depreciated over its useful life. Material items must be handled in accordance with generally accepted accounting principles.

But there is more to materiality than dollar amounts. The very nature of an item may make it material. For example, it may be quite significant to know that a firm is securing its overseas business by bribing officials of a foreign government. Or that U.S. firms are making illegal political contributions. How to assess the significance of such actions is proving to be a serious problem for accountants.

Relevance and substance over form.   In some instances the economic substance of a transaction may conflict with its legal form. For example, a contract which is legally a lease may, in fact, be a purchase. This is true for a three-year contract to rent an auto at a stated monthly rental, with the lessee to receive title to the auto at the end of the lease upon payment of a nominal sum (say, $1). Because it is likely to be relevant to economic decision making, the accountant records economic substance rather than legal form.

Understandability

This objective is important on the simple grounds that information must be understood if it is to be useful. Information should be presented in a form and expressed in terminology that investors and creditors understand. But the complexity of economic activity makes it impossible to reduce reports on it to simple terms. Investors and creditors must aid their own cause by acquiring knowledge of business and economic activity and of financial accounting and reporting. They must also be willing to devote time and effort to the study of financial statements.

Quantifiability

Financial accounting primarily is concerned with economic resources and obligations and changes in both. Those activities, resources, and obligations that can be quantified (expressed in numbers) are of primary concern to financial accounting. Quantified data generally are more useful than verbal data. It usually is more useful to know exactly how much cash one possesses than to know that one has some cash. This concern for quantified data means that accounting pays little attention to unmeasurable economic concepts of satisfaction, utility, and welfare. Nor is accounting directly concerned with the sociological and psychological aspects of economic activity.

Verifiability

Financial information is considered verifiable when it could be substantially duplicated by other independent measures using the same measurement methods. The requirement that financial information be based upon objective evidence is based upon the demonstrated needs of users for reliable, unbiased financial information. This is needed especially when parties with opposing interests (credit seekers and credit grantors) rely upon the same information. The reliability of information is enhanced if it is verifiable.

But financial information will never be free of subjective opinion and judgment. It will always possess varying degrees of verifiability. Some measurements can be supported by canceled checks and invoices. Others, such as periodic depreciation charges, never can be verified because of their very nature. Thus, financial information in many instances is verifiable only in that it represents a consensus as to what would be reported if the same procedures had been followed by other accountants.

Neutrality

Financial accounting information should be neutral—it should not favor one group over another. It should meet the common needs of many users rather than the particular needs of specific users. It is not sufficient that the information be verifiable, since biased information can be verified. For example, inventories under the lower-of-cost-or-market method can be verified. But, since only declines in, and not increases in, market value have been recognized, one may question whether they meet the objective of neutrality.

Timeliness

The utility of information decreases with age. It is likely to be much more useful to know what the net earnings for 1980 were in early 1981 than to receive this information a year later. And if information is to be of any value in decision making, it must be available before the decision is made. If not, it is useless. In determining what constitutes timely information, consideration must be given to the other qualitative objectives and to the cost of gathering information. For example, a timely estimated amount for uncollectible accounts may be more valuable than a later, verified actual amount.

Comparability

When comparable financial information is presented, the differences and similarities noted will arise from the matters being reported upon and not from their accounting treatment. Comparable information will reveal relative strengths and weaknesses in a single company through time and between two or more companies at the same point in time.

The accounting requirement of consistency leads to comparability of financial information for a single company through time. Consistency generally requires adherence to the same accounting principles and reporting practices through time. It bars indiscriminate switching of principles or methods (such as changing depreciation methods every year). It does not bar changes in principles if the information needs of users are better served by the change. But disclosure of the change and, if material, its effects are required.[8]

Comparability between companies is more difficult to achieve because the same activities may be accounted for in different ways. For example, B may use the Lifo and accelerated depreciation methods, while C accounts for identical activities using Fifo and straight-line depreciation methods. A high degree of intercompany comparability will not exist until it is required that the same activities be accounted for in the same manner.

Completeness

Completeness requires that all financial accounting information meeting the other qualitative objectives be reported. Full disclosure is to be made of all significant information in a manner that is understandable to and does not mislead informed investors, creditors, and other users. Such full disclosure generally requires presentation of a balance sheet, an earnings statement, a statement of changes in financial position, and necessary supporting schedules. Such statements are to be complete with items properly classified and segregated, such as reporting sales revenue separately from other revenues. The required disclosures may be made in (1) the body of the financial statements, (2) in the notes to such statements, (3) in special communications, and (4) in the president's letter in the annual report.

In addition to changes in accounting principles, disclosure usually must be made of a number of other items. These include unusual activities (loans to officers); changes in expectations (losses on inventory); depreciation expense for the period; long-term obligations entered into that are not recorded by the accountant (a 20-year lease on a building); new arrangements with certain groups (pension and profit-sharing plans for employees); significant events that occur after the date of the statements (loss of a major customer); and the accounting policies (major principles and their manner of application) followed in preparing the financial statements.[9] Because of its emphasis upon disclosure, this objective is often called the full-disclosure principle. Much of what constitutes full disclosure already has been illustrated in preceding chapters. For an actual example, see the Appendix to Chapter 18.

UNDERLYING ASSUMPTIONS OR CONCEPTS

Some of the *underlying assumptions* or concepts of accounting were presented and discussed briefly in Chapter 1. A more complete discussion is presented below.

Entity

All accounting information pertains to a specific unit or area of interest called the *entity*. This entity is viewed as having an existence apart from its owners, creditors, employees, and other interested parties. For the corporation, this

---

[8] APB, "Accounting Changes," *APB Opinion No. 20* (New York: AICPA, July 1971).

[9] APB, "Disclosure of Accounting Policies," *APB Opinion No. 22* (New York: AICPA, April 1972).

separate existence is confirmed by law. But the boundaries of the accounting entity may differ from those of the legal entity, since financial information may relate to a corporation and its subsidiary corporations as a single business. An accounting entity may exist where it is not supported by a legal entity, as in a single proprietorship. Here the business, not the individual, is the accounting entity. Financial statements must identify the entity for which they are prepared; and their content must be limited to reporting the activities, resources, and obligations of that entity.

Continuity (going concern)

In financial accounting, the entity is viewed as continuing indefinitely in operation unless evidence to the contrary exists. This assumption is justified because experience shows that continuity at least until the end of another reporting period is highly probable for most entities. Yet if liquidation appears likely, financial information should not be reported based on the assumption of continuity.

The expectation of continuity often is used to justify the use of cost rather than market value as a basis for measuring assets. While significant for an entity in liquidation, market values are alleged to be of no significance to an entity that intends to use rather than sell its assets. On the other hand, the expectation of continuity permits the accountant to record certain items as assets. For example, printed advertising matter may be on hand to be used to promote a special sale next month. It may have little, if any, value to anyone but its owner. But it is recorded as an asset because its owner is expected to continue operating long enough to benefit from it.

Money measurement

Accounting measurements normally will be expressed in money terms. The unit of measure (the dollar in the United States) is identified in the financial statements.

This does not mean that all measurements of economic activity must be stated in monetary terms to be useful. It may, for example, be useful to know that a plant is operating at 50 percent of its capacity. But the full economic significance of this bit of information cannot be known until it is translated into money terms.

The monetary unit, the dollar, also provides accountants with a common unit of measure in reporting upon economic activity. Think, for a moment, about preparing a balance sheet without using the dollar as a unit of measure. Without using the monetary unit, how does one add buildings, equipment, and inventory? Even if prepared, such a statement would probably be of little value.

Stable unit. In making money measurements, accountants typically have ignored fluctuations in the value of the unit of measure—the dollar. Thus, they have used the *stable dollar* assumption. This means that a portion of the cost of a building acquired in 1940 is deducted, without adjustment for change in the value of the dollar, from revenues earned in, and expressed in, 1980 dollars in arriving at the net earnings for 1980. The 1940 and 1980 dollars are treated as equal units of measure, even though substantial price inflation has occurred between the two years. The inflation experienced in the 1970s once again caused renewed interest to be expressed in the problem of adjusting financial statements for changes in the general level of prices. The question at issue is whether accountants should continue to report in historical, unadjusted dollars or adopt another unit of measure—a constant dollar of equal general purchasing power. For further discussion and illustration of accounting and reporting under changing price levels, see the Appendix to this book.

Periodicity (time periods)

To provide useful financial information to investors and creditors at various points in the life of an entity, accountants must subdivide the life of an entity into periods and prepare reports on the activities of those periods. In order to aid comparisons, the time periods usually are of equal length. The length of the period must be stated in the financial statements. Such financial statements are prepared under the accrual basis, which requires approximation and the exercise of judgement.

Accrual basis.   Financial statements better reflect the financial status and operations of a firm when prepared under the accrual rather than the cash basis of accounting. Under the cash basis, which is used primarily in small service-rendering firms, revenues and most expenses are recorded at the time of cash receipt or cash payment. Under the *accrual basis,* changes in resources (assets) and obligations (equities), including revenues and expenses, are recorded much more closely to the time that they actually occur. For example, revenues are recorded when services are rendered or products are sold and delivered, even if not paid for immediately in cash. Similarly, expenses are recorded as incurred in the period benefited—for example, employee services are recorded in the period received, which may not be the same period in which payment is made. The accrual basis reflects the fact that considerable economic activity can occur that is not matched by a concurrent cash flow.

Approximation and judgment.   Accounting measurements are often estimates. To provide periodic financial information, estimates must often be made of such things as expected uncollectible accounts and the useful lives of depreciable assets. Periodic depreciation charges can never be anything but estimates. Because they depend on future events, estimates of the net realizable value of accounts receivable must be uncertain and tentative. This uncertainty precludes precise measurement and makes estimates necessary.

Yet, because they represent the exercise of judgment by an informed accountant, these estimates are often quite accurate. And it is this need to exercise judgment that prevents one from stating the financial accounting process as a set of inflexible rules, an example of which might be: Depreciate all trucks over three years regardless of their useful lives.

Exchange prices

Because most goods and services are exchanged rather than consumed by their producers, accountants have long relied upon exchanges as indicators of, and exchange prices as measures of, economic activity. Typically, past exchange prices are used and called historical costs when applied to many assets. But, at times, a current exchange price or a future exchange price may be used. For example, both replacement cost and expected selling price are used in determining "market" under the lower-of-cost-or-market inventory method. But, on the whole, financial accounting is concerned largely with past exchange prices, that is, with historical costs.

But this appears to be changing. Due largely to the more than 10 percent annual rate of inflation in the mid-70s, accountants are becoming more interested in "current value accounting." They are asking whether some other attribute of assets and liabilities such as current market value, rather than historical cost, should be measured and reported in providing relevant financial information. Among those in use or advocated are the following.[10]

1. *Historical cost/historical proceeds.* Initially, this is the amount of cash paid to acquire an asset *(historical cost);* for some assets, historical cost is subject to depreciation or amortization. For liabilities, this is the amount of cash received when a debt was incurred (historical proceeds).

2. *Current cost/current proceeds.* **Current cost** is the amount of cash that would have to be paid currently to acquire an asset already owned. It is *current reproduction cost* for an identical asset; it is *current replacement cost* for an asset with equivalent productive capacity. *Current proceeds* refers to the amount of proceeds that would be obtained if the same obligation were incurred currently.

3. *Current exit value in orderly liquidation.* **Current exit value** is the amount of cash that would be obtained from an orderly, not rushed, sale of an asset. It is also the amount of cash that would have to be paid out currently to eliminate a liability. It is current market value for both assets and liabilities.

4. *Expected exit value in due course of business.* **Expected exit value** is the amount of cash expected from conversion of an asset in the due course of business, less the direct costs of effecting the conversion. As applied to accounts receivable and inventories, this is the familiar net realizable value. It is also the amount of cash expected to be paid to eliminate a liability in the due course of business including the direct costs necessary to make those payments. Or, it is the nondiscounted amount of expected cash outlays.

5. *Present value of expected cash flows.* This is the *present value* of the future cash inflows expected from an asset in the due course of business less the present value of the cash outflows necessary to obtain those inflows. It is also the present value of the future cash outflows to eliminate a liability in the due course of business including the cash outflows necessary to make those payments. The present value concept was mentioned briefly in Chapter 8 and is covered in the Appendix to Chapter 17.

It is well beyond the scope of this text to attempt a full discussion of these attributes. But several points can be noted. Attribute No. 1 is the familiar historical cost upon which accounting has long been based. The FASB has decided to retain this for the basic financial statements. (Statements prepared using constant dollars of equal general purchasing are to appear as supplemental statements only.) Attribute No. 2 has received considerable support in

---

[10] Adapted from FASB, *Conceptual Framework,* p. 193.

the literature and has been recommended for implementation in the United Kingdom. Also, as stated in its *Accounting Series Release No. 190,* the Securities and Exchange Commission requires that certain companies required to file financial statements with the Commission disclose in their annual reports (in footnotes or in a separate section) the current replacement cost of inventories, cost of goods sold, productive capacity (plant assets, except land), and depreciation, depletion, and amortization. Attribute No. 3 is currently used to value the marketable securities of investment companies and brokers and dealers in securities. As mentioned above, attribute No. 4 is actually net realizable value and is currently used for accounts receivable and inventories. Because it is based upon estimates of future cash flows, attribute No. 5 is highly subjective when applied to certain of these flows. As indicated in Chapter 8, its use is required for certain long-term notes. Also, its use will very likely be restricted to assets and liabilities having fairly certain cash flows.

MEASUREMENT IN ACCOUNTING

Accounting is often defined as a measurement process. We have already noted that accounting measurements are in terms of a monetary unit. Relying upon the basic assumptions already discussed and guided by the principles presented in the next section, the accountant seeks to—

1. Measure the assets, liabilities, and owners' equity of an accounting entity.
2. Measure the changes in assets, liabilities, and owners' equity that occur and assign these changes to particular time periods in order to compute the net earnings of the accounting entity.

Because owners' equity is a residual amount (computed as assets minus liabilities), we can focus our attention upon assets and liabilities.

Measuring assets

Assets are service potentials or future economic benefits owned by an entity. They are, for measurement purposes, classified as *monetary* or *nonmonetary.* Monetary assets include cash, accounts receivable, notes receivable, and other claims to a fixed number of dollars. Cash is measured at its denominated amount, while claims to cash are measured at their expected cash inflow, taking possible uncollectible accounts into consideration. Nonmonetary assets are expected to be converted into cash through operations. They consist of inventories, prepaid expenses, plant and equipment, and intangibles. They are measured at their cost at time of acquisition.

Measuring liabilities

Liabilities are obligations arising from past transactions and which require the entity to convey assets or perform services in the future. Generally, liabilities are measured in terms of the cash that will be paid or the value of the services that will be performed for their satisfaction.

Measuring changes in assets and liabilities

While all changes in assets and liabilities must be measured, certain changes are handled routinely by the accountant. These include an exchange of one asset for another of equal value, the acquisition of an asset on credit, and the payment of a liability. Certain changes in net assets (assets less liabilities) are also dealt with easily because they involve an additional cash investment or a cash withdrawal by the owners. But the other changes in net assets are of great concern because they involve the recognition of net earnings or net loss. Here the accountant is concerned with determining when a change has taken place as well as determining its amount. These involve the recognition of revenues and expenses and are guided by the principles discussed below.

THE MAJOR PRINCIPLES

Although there exists no complete authoritative statement of generally accepted accounting principles, accountants agree that certain principles dominate their practice. These principles are presented and discussed below.

The initial recording (or cost) principle

Stated briefly, this principle is: Transfers of resources are recorded initially in the accounting system at the time of exchange and at the prices agreed upon by the parties to the exchange. Thus, for any firm, this principle determines to a large extent (1) what goes into the accounting system—transaction data; (2) when it is recorded—at the time of exchange; and (3) the amounts—exchange prices—at which assets, liabilities, owners' equity, revenues, and expenses are recorded. As applied to certain assets, this principle is often called the *cost principle*, meaning that these assets initially are recorded at cost. But use of a term such as *exchange price principle* is to be preferred because it seems inappropriate to refer to liabilities, owners' equity, and certain assets such as cash and accounts receivable as being measured in terms of their cost. Note also that even if other attributes are reported in the financial statements, the data initially recorded in the accounting system will be exchange prices.

The matching principle

A most fundamental principle of accounting is that net earnings can be determined by matching the expenses incurred with the periodic revenues they generate. The logic of the principle stems from the fact that wherever economic resources are employed someone will want to know what was accomplished and at what cost. Every appraisal of economic activity will involve matching sacrifice with benefit. And knowledge of sacrifice and benefit usually is considered far more valuable than knowledge of the stock of resources. So it is in accounting. The earnings statement generally is considered more important than the balance sheet.

The way the matching principle is applied is discussed and illustrated below.

Revenue recognition

Revenue results in the inflow of assets from the sale of goods and services to customers. It is best measured by the amount of cash expected from the customer. A question arises as to when this revenue should be recorded, that is, credited to a revenue account. The general answer is that the revenue should be earned and realized before it is recognized.

The earning of revenue. In a broad sense, all of the activities of a firm to create additional utility constitute the earning process. The actual receipt of cash from a customer may have been preceded by many events including (1) placing advertisements, (2) calling on the customer several times, (3) submission of samples, (4) acquisition of raw materials, (5) manufacture of the goods, and (6) delivery of the goods. Costs were undoubtedly incurred for these activities. And revenue actually was being generated by these activities, even though in most instances accountants refuse to recognize it until time of sale. This is called the *earning principle.* This refusal is based upon their requirement that revenue be realized before it is recognized.

The realization of revenue.   Under the *realization principle,* revenue is considered realized at the time of sale for merchandise transactions and when services have been performed in service transactions. Legally, a sale occurs when title to the goods passes to the buyer. As a practical matter, accountants generally record revenue when goods are delivered.

The advantages of recognizing revenue at time of sale include (1) the delivery of the goods is a noticeable event; (2) the revenue is measurable; (3) the risk of loss due to price decline or destruction of the goods has passed to the buyer; (4) the revenue has been earned, or substantially so; and (5) because the revenue has been earned, expenses can be determined thus allowing net earnings to be determined. As discussed below, the disadvantage of recognizing revenue at time of sale is that the revenue may not be recorded in the period in which most of the activity creating it occurred.

Cash collection as point of revenue recognition.   Some small firms record revenues and expenses at the time of cash collection and payment. This procedure is known as the *cash basis of accounting.* It is acceptable primarily in service enterprises which do not have substantial credit transactions or inventories, and in accounting for installment sales.

Installment basis of revenue recognition.   When the selling price of goods is to be collected in installments and considerable doubt exists as to collectibility, the *installment basis or method* of accounting may be employed. Under this basis, the gross margin on a sale is treated as being realized proportionately with the cash collected from customers. If this gross margin rate is 40 percent, then 40 cents of every dollar collected on the installment accounts receivable represents realized gross margin. For example, assume a stereo system costing $300 is sold for $500, with payment to be made in ten equal installments of $50 each. If four installments are collected in the year of sale, the realized gross margin taken into net earnings is $80 ($4 \times \$50 \times 0.40$). In the next year it will be $120 ($6 \times \$50 \times 0.40$) if the final six installments are collected.

This method is accepted for tax purposes. But, because it delays the recognition of revenue beyond the time of sale, it is accepted for accounting purposes only when extreme doubt exists as to the collectibility of the installments due.

Revenue recognition on long-term construction projects.   The revenue created by completing a long-term construction project can be recognized under two methods: (1) the completed contract method or (2) the percentage-of-completion method. Under the *completed contract method,* no revenue is recognized until the period in which the contract is completed, and then all of the revenue is recognized even though the contract may have required three years to complete. The costs incurred on the project are carried forward in inventory accounts and are charged to expense in the period in which the revenue is recognized. This approach is similar to recognizing revenue at the time of sale. It suffers from the disadvantage of recognizing no revenue or net earnings from a project in periods in which a major part of the revenue-producing activity may have occurred.

Under the *percentage-of-completion method*, revenue and net earnings are recognized periodically on the basis of the estimated stage of completion of the project. To illustrate, assume that a firm has a contract to erect a dam at a price of $44 million. By the end of the first fiscal year, it had incurred costs of $30 million and expected to incur $10 million more. The contract would be considered 75 percent complete since $30 million of an expected $40 million of costs have been incurred. Consequently, $33 million of revenue and $3 million of earnings would be recognized on the contract in the fiscal year.

Revenue recognition at completion of production. Recognizing revenue at the time of completion of productive activities, called the *production basis*, is considered acceptable procedure for certain precious metals (gold) and for many farm products such as wheat, corn, and soybeans. The homogeneous nature of the products, the fact that they can usually be sold at their market prices, and the difficulties sometimes encountered in determining production costs are the reasons advanced to justify recognizing revenue prior to sale. Recognizing revenue upon completion of production is accomplished by debiting inventory and crediting a revenue account for the expected selling price of the goods produced. All of the costs incurred in the period can then be treated as expenses.

Collections of revenue before it is earned. Sometimes cash is collected before goods are delivered or services rendered; in effect, future revenues are collected. Such receipts should not be credited to a revenue account, since no revenue has been earned. Such receipts give rise to a liability, and they should be credited to an account that reveals their nature, such as Unearned Subscription Revenue or Advances by Customers. In the period in which the goods are delivered or the services performed, this account can be debited and the regular revenue account (Sales or Service Revenue) credited.

Expense recognition

Expenses are defined as the resources or service potentials consumed in generating revenue. Since resources and service potentials are assets, expenses may also be defined as asset expirations voluntarily incurred to produce revenue. The television set delivered by a dealer to a customer for cash can readily be thought of as an asset expiration to produce revenue. Similarly, the services of a television station employed to advertise a product can be thought of as expiring to produce revenue. *Losses*, on the other hand, may be distinguished as involuntary asset expirations not related to the production of revenue. Fire losses are an example.

The measurement of expense. Many assets used in operating a business are measured in terms of historical cost. It follows that many expenses, resulting from expired assets, are measured in terms of the historical cost of the assets expired. Other expenses are paid for currently and are measured in terms of their current costs. Note that in a transaction recorded as a debit to Advertising Expense and a credit to Cash, it is not the asset, cash, that expires. The actual transaction consists of an exchange of cash for advertising services—an asset. The accountant, anticipating that the services will have expired by the end of the accounting period, records the expenditure as an expense. By this short-cut, an adjusting entry will be avoided. But this is merely an expedient accounting technique. No one knowingly buys expenses, that is, expired assets.

The timing of expense recognition.[11] The matching principle implies that a cause-and-effect relationship exists between expense and revenue, that is, expense is the cause of revenue. For certain expenses, the relationship is readily seen, as in the case of goods delivered to customers. When a direct cause-and-effect relationship cannot be seen, the costs of assets with limited lives may be charged to expense in the periods benefited on a systematic and rational allocation basis. Depreciation of plant assets is an example. In other instances, the relationship between expense and revenue can only be assumed to exist, as in the case of a contribution to the local community fund. Consequently, the recognition of expense, as a practical matter, is often guided by the concepts of product costs and period costs.

Product costs are those costs incurred directly and indirectly in the acquisition and manufacture of goods. Included are the invoice costs of goods, as well as freight and insurance-in-transit costs. For manufacturing firms, product costs include all costs of raw materials as well as the direct labor and indirect costs of operating a factory to produce goods (see Chapters 22 and 23). Such costs are deemed to attach to the goods produced, are carried in inventory accounts as long as the goods are on hand, and are charged to expense when the goods are sold. Thus, a precise matching of the expense, cost of goods sold, and its related revenue results.

Period costs are the remaining costs incurred and consist primarily of selling and administrative expenses. Under this concept, expenses are matched with revenues by periods because matching by transactions is simply not possible. Thus, period costs are expensed in the period incurred because (1) they relate to the current period's revenue—the local supermarket's weekly newspaper advertisement is an example; (2) the cost must be incurred every period, and there is no measurable buildup of benefits—officers' salaries are an example here; (3) there is no measurable relationship with any portion of revenue, yet the cost must be incurred to remain in business—the cost of the annual audit is an example; and (4) the amount of cost to be carried forward cannot be measured in a nonarbitrary manner—as might be true for the costs of an employee training and apprenticeship program.

Earnings models. Since the 1930s the primary focus of financial accounting has been upon the determination of net earnings. This has led to increased attention to matching, including the recording of accruals and deferrals. The accounting model for net earnings is:

Revenues (including gains) − Expenses (including losses and taxes) = Net earnings

---

[11] For further discussion, see APB, "Basic Concepts and Principles Underlying Financial Statements of Business Enterprises," *APB Statement No. 4.* (New York: AICPA, October 1970), pars. 157–60.

This focus upon earnings determination has been illustrated repeatedly in this text. But let us illustrate briefly how the earnings determination principles dominate what is reported in the financial statements. The initial recording (cost) principle directs that assets be initially recorded at cost. The realization principle requires that increases in the value of assets not be recorded until realized through an exchange. Thus, assets are reported at cost, or cost less accumulated depreciation if they are being systematically and rationally depreciated in adherence to the matching principle. Also, in adhering to the matching principle, a firm may defer the cost of a major promotional campaign to introduce a new product. These costs are reported as assets and expensed over future periods even though they possess no value to anyone but the firm incurring them.

These effects upon the balance sheet of the matching principle have caused concern among a growing number of accountants. And this, in turn, has led some of them to call for a different earnings model—one based upon the balance sheet. It is similar to the economist's income model in that it is based upon the change in the value of the net assets (assets − liabilities) or owners' equity between two points of time, adjusted for capital investments and withdrawals. Sometimes referred to as the asset and liability view of earnings (to contrast it with the revenue and expense view), the model in equation form is:

$$OE_1 + W - CI - OE_0 = NE$$

where OE_1 is the ending owners' equity, W is owner withdrawals, CI is additional capital invested, OE_0 is beginning owners equity, and NE is net earnings. To illustrate, a firm having a beginning owners equity of $100,000, an ending equity of $200,000, owner withdrawals of $20,000, and $50,000 of additional capital invested, would have net earnings for the period of $70,000.

The two earnings models will yield the same amount of net earnings if assets, liabilities, owners' equity, revenues, and expenses are defined the same and are based upon measurements of the same attributes. As of this writing, the FASB has indicated (in an exposure draft) its preference for the balance sheet approach rather than the earnings statement approach.[12]

Modifying conventions

For several reasons, called *modifying conventions,* accounting principles may not be strictly applied. These reasons reside in the environment in which accounting is practiced. We have already noted that immaterial items may be given a practical rather than a theoretical treatment. Materiality thus can be considered a modifying convention as well as a qualitative objective. We have also noted that construction revenues may be accounted for on a percentage-of-completion rather than the completed contract (sales) basis. This yields a clearer reflection of actual activities. It is also an example of the modifying convention calling for exercise of judgment by the accounting profession as a whole. It is also in accord with the emphasis placed by accountants upon earnings determination. But the primary modifying convention is conservatism.

---

[12] For further discussion, see FASB, *Conceptual Framework,* chap. 5.

Conservatism. *Conservatism* is the accountants' response to the uncertainty faced in the environment in which accounting is practiced. It embraces the idea of being cautious or prudent. Many accounting measurements are estimates and involve the exercise of judgment. In such cases, conservatism tells the accountant "to play it safe." Playing it safe usually involves making sure that if in error, all estimates are in error in such a way as to yield lower reported net assets and net earnings than might otherwise be reported.

Conservatism may be applied with varying degrees of severity in different firms, causing decreased comparability in their financial information. This may cause investors to act in a manner not in their best interest. They may, for example, dispose of their interest in a firm because its earnings did not meet their expectations. Yet this failure may have been due solely to a conservative measurement of inventories. Thus, a fine line exists, in many instances, between conservative and incorrect accounting.

Implementing principles

Underlying the major principles discussed above is a set of *implementing (broad operating) principles*. They guide the actual operation of the accounting system. They indicate which events are to be recorded and which are not, and how the selected events are to be measured. They show how the principle of initial recording of exchange prices is to be applied to exchanges that affect assets, liabilities, owners' equity, revenues, and expenses. These principles also indicate the accounting to be applied to (1) transfers such as gifts, donations, lawsuit losses, fines, and thefts; (2) events favorable and unfavorable to the firm such as changes in the market values of assets owned; and (3) internal events such as the manufacture of goods. These implementing principles are not dealt with here because most of them are discussed in other chapters. For the same reason, the procedures or detailed accounting principles underlying the implementing or operating principles will not be discussed here. Examples of these include the Fifo method of inventory costing and the straight-line depreciation method. One of the purposes of this chapter has been to put these detailed accounting principles or procedures in place in a loose framework of the theory of financial accounting.

NEW TERMS INTRODUCED IN CHAPTER 13

Accrual basis—a system or basis of accounting that assigns measures of economic activity to the periods it occurs rather than the period of cash inflow or outflow.

Cash basis (of accounting)—a basis of accounting for expenses and revenues in which they are recorded in the period of cash payment or receipt.

Comparability—a qualitative objective of accounting information; when information is comparable, it reveals similarities and differences that are real and not the result of differing accounting treatments.

Completed contract method—a method of recognizing revenue on long-term projects in which no revenue is recognized until the project is completed; similar to recognizing revenue upon the completion of a sale.

Completeness—a qualitative objective of accounting information; requires disclosure of all significant information in a manner that aids understanding and does not mislead; sometimes called the full-disclosure principle.

Conservatism—the mental quality of being cautious or prudent; making sure that estimates, if in error, tend to understate rather than overstate net assets and net earnings.

Continuity (going concern)—the assumption that an entity will continue in operation indefinitely, thus allowing the accountant to avoid using liquidation values for assets.

Current cost—the amount of cash that would have to be paid currently to acquire an asset already owned; called *current reproduction cost* when applied to an identical asset and *current replacement cost* when applied to an asset of equivalent capacity. The amount of cash that would be received currently from the incurrence of a liability is called *current proceeds.*

Current exit value—current market value; the amount of cash that would be received from an orderly sale of an asset.

Earning principle—the requirement that revenue not be recognized prior to the time that all of the activities to create it have been completed.

Entity (accounting entity)—the specific unit or area of interest to which accounting information pertains; entities have a separate existence from owners, creditors, managers, employees, and other interested parties.

Expected exit value—the net realizable value of an asset; the amount of cash expected from an asset less any direct costs to be incurred in converting it.

Expense—service potential or economic resources consumed in the generation of revenue; matched with revenue under the principles of associating cause and effect, systematic and rational allocation, or immediate recognition.

Financial reporting objectives—the broad overriding goals sought by engaging in financial reporting; providing informed investors and creditors with information useful in making rational investment and credit decisions is an example.

Historical cost—the amount of cash paid or fair value of liability incurred or other resource surrendered to acquire an asset.

Implementing (broad operating) principles—the guides relied upon in making the major principles (such as realization) operational.

Initial recording (cost) principle—the requirement that transfers of resources be initially recorded at the time of exchange and at the prices (cost) agreed upon in the exchange.

Installment basis or method—a revenue recognition procedure in which the gross margin on an installment sale is considered realized only in proportion to the cash collected on the installment receivable.

Loss—expired service potential or economic resources that produced no revenue or other benefit; usually involuntary in nature.

Matching principle—the principle that net earnings can be determined by associating or relating the revenues generated in a period with the expenses incurred to create them.

Materiality—a qualitative objective specifying that financial accounting report only information significant enough to influence decisions or evaluations; also a modifying convention that allows the accountant to deal with immaterial items in a nontheoretical, expedient manner.

Modifying conventions—customs emerging from accounting practice that alter the results that would be obtained from a strict application of accounting principles; conservatism is an example.

Money measurement—quantification in terms of a monetary unit of measurement—

the dollar—as contrasted to quantification in terms of physical or other units of measurement—feet, inches, grams, and so on.

Neutrality—a qualitative objective that requires accounting information to be free from bias.

Percentage-of-completion method—a method of recognizing revenue on long-term projects according to the degree of completion attained; the degree of completion is often measured by comparing costs incurred with total costs expected to be incurred.

Period costs—costs incurred that cannot be traced to specific revenue and that are, as a result, expensed in the period incurred.

Periodicity (time periods)—an assumption of the accountant that the life of an entity can be subdivided into time periods for purposes of reporting upon its economic activities.

Present value—the amount obtained by discounting net future cash flows.

Product costs—costs incurred in the manufacture of goods which are accounted for as if they were attached to the goods, with the result that they are charged to expense when the goods are sold.

Production basis—a method of revenue recognition used in limited circumstances which permits the recording of revenue upon completion of production prior to sale.

Qualitative objectives—characteristics accounting information should possess to be useful.

Quantifiability (quantification)—description in terms of a scale of natural numbers.

Realization principle—a principle that directs the goods be sold or that services be rendered before revenue is recognized.

Relevance—a qualitative objective requiring that information be pertinent to or have a bearing upon a decision or an evaluation.

Stable dollar—an assumption that fluctuations in the value of the dollar are insignificant and may, therefore, be ignored.

Timeliness—a qualitative objective requiring that accounting information be provided at a time when it may be considered in reaching a decision.

Underlying assumptions—the basic concepts or premises regarding the environment which serve as a foundation for accounting principles.

Understandability—a qualitative objective requiring that the accounting information provided be comprehended, as to format and terminology, by the intended user.

Verifiability—a qualitative objective requiring that other accountants using the same measurement methods reach the same conclusion as to the magnitude of the measurements presented.

DEMONSTRATION PROBLEM

For each of the transactions or circumstances described below and the entries made, state which, if any, of the objectives, assumptions or concepts, principles, or modifying conventions of accounting were violated. If any, give the entry to correct the improper accounting, assuming the books have not been closed.

During the year, the Bessone Company—

1. Had its buildings appraised. They were found to have a market value of $410,000, although their book value was only $380,000. The accountant debited the Buildings and Accumulated Depreciation—Buildings accounts for $15,000 each and credited J. Bessone, Capital. No separate mention was made of this action in the financial statements.

2. Received from the owner, Mr. Bessone, a calculating machine worth $115 for which he no longer had a personal use. The company paid $10 to have the machine picked up and delivered to its offices. The $10 was charged to the Equipment account, and no other entry made.

3. Purchased a number of new electric pencil sharpeners for its offices at a total cost of $60. These were recorded as assets and are being depreciated over five years.

4. Changed its depreciation rates on machinery from 10 percent to 15 percent per year, increasing the amount of depreciation recorded from $6,000 to $9,000. No other action was taken and no disclosure made. Net earnings for the year amounted to $350,000.

5. Produced a number of agricultural products at a cost of $26,000. These costs were charged to expense when the products were set up in inventory at their net market value of $35,000. The difference of $9,000 was credited to a Farm Revenues Earned account.

Solution to demonstration problem

1. The realization principle, the objectives of completeness (disclosure) and verifiability, and the modifying convention of conservatism may have been violated. Consistency may also have been violated, but this cannot be determined from the information given. Such write-ups simply are not looked upon with favor in accounting.

J. Bessone, Capital	30,000	
Buildings		15,000
Accumulated Depreciation—Buildings		15,000

2. The initial recording principle was violated. The owner's additional investment should be recorded as follows:

Equipment	115	
J. Bessone, Capital		115

3. Theoretically, there were no violations unless there is one relating to the cost of compiling insignificant information. As a practical matter, the $60 could have been expensed on materiality grounds.

4. If it can be further assumed that the new rate is the proper rate, then there are no violations. Disclosure of the change in life estimates is required, but disclosure of the amount of the change would not be, since it is not material. If the change can be justified only by resorting to conservatism, it is an improper application of this doctrine.

5. There were no violations. The procedures followed are considered acceptable for farm products that are interchangeable and readily marketable. No correcting entry is needed, provided due allowance has been made for the costs to be incurred in delivering the products to the market.

QUESTIONS

1. For whom is financial reporting primarily intended? Why?

2. Investment and credit decisions generally involve a comparison of what two amounts? What is the primary role played by financial information in such decisions?

3. What are generally accepted accounting principles? What are the sources of such principles? Where might one find a list of them?

4. Why might it be desirable to have an authoritative set of generally accepted accounting principles?

5. In general, what are the qualitative objectives? Which is the primary such objective? Why?

6. What is meant by the term accrual basis of accounting? What is its alternative?

7. What two requirements generally must be met before revenue will be recognized in a period? What would you consider the ideal time to recognize revenue? Why?

8. Under what circumstances, if any, is the receipt of cash an acceptable time to recognize revenue?

9. A firm reports its marketable securities at a cost of $100,000. You note from the stock price reports in your newspaper that they have a market value of $250,000. Why are the securities reported at $100,000 and the

$150,000 not included in net earnings? Is not the firm better off by $150,000?

10. Define expense. What principles guide the recognition of expense?

11. Contrast the accountant's approach to determining net earnings with that of the economist. Are the two reconcilable? Explain.

12. What is meant by the accounting term "conservatism"? How does it affect the amounts reported in the financial statements?

13. What is the principle of initial recording or cost principle? What is the significance of adhering to this principle?

14. Name the assumptions underlying generally accepted accounting principles. Comment on the validity in recent years of the stable unit of measurement assumption.

15. Many assets are reported in the balance sheet at their historical cost. But the reporting of other attributes for some assets is now in use or has been recommended. What are these other attributes?

16. How are consistency and full disclosure related?

17. What does it mean to say that accountants record substance rather than form?

EXERCISES

E–1. A company purchased a building on January 2, 1976, for $80,000. By December 31, 1980, it has a net book value of $64,000 and a market value of $100,000. The building was completely destroyed by fire on January 1, 1981. Cash of $72,000 was received as full settlement from an insurance company.

a. Compute the gain or loss from the fire that the accountant would record.

b. Comment on whether the accountant's record is in accord with the facts and explain why it is or is not.

E–2. Cloyce Company sells its products on an installment sales basis. Data for 1980 and 1981 are as follows:

	1980	1981
Installment sales	$100,000	$120,000
Cost of installment sales	70,000	90,000
Other expenses	15,000	20,000
Cash collected from 1980 sales	60,000	30,000
Cash collected from 1981 sales		80,000

a. Compute the net earnings for 1981 assuming use of the accrual (sales) basis of revenue recognition.

b. Compute the net earnings for 1981 assuming use of the installment method of recognizing revenue and gross margin.

E–3. A company follows a practice of expensing the premium on its fire insurance policy when it is paid. In 1980 it charged to expense the $720 premium paid on a three-year policy covering the period July 1, 1980, to June 30, 1983. In 1977 a premium of $660 was charged to expense on the same policy for the period July 1, 1977, to June 30, 1980.

a. State the principle of accounting that was violated by this practice.

b. Compute the effects of this violation on the financial statements for the calendar year 1980.

c. State the grounds upon which the company's practice might be justified.

E–4. A company employs the lower-of-cost-or-market method of inventory measurement. Its beginning and ending inventories for 1980 on this basis were $20,000 and $24,000. On a strict cost basis they would have been $21,000 and $24,400.

a. State the grounds upon which the company's practice may be justified.

b. Compute the effect on net earnings for 1980 from use of the lower-of-cost-or-market method rather than the strict cost method.

E–5. The following relate to the X Company for 1980.

1. Sales on account, $100,000, of which $80,000 were collected.
2. Services rendered on account, $60,000, of which $50,000 were collected. In addition, services were rendered for which cash was received in 1979 in the amount of $1,800.
3. Sold a truck with a book value of $1,000 on December 31, 1980, and received a $1,500, 8 percent, six-month note in exchange.

State the amount of revenue earned by the company in 1980.

E–6. Match the items in Column A with the proper description in Column B.

Column A	*Column B*
1. Continuity (going concern).	*a.* An assumption relied on in the preparation of financial statements that would be unreasonable if applied to the environment of many South American countries in recent years.
2. Comparability.	*b.* Concerned with relative dollar amounts.
3. Disclosure or completeness.	*c.* The usual basis for the recording of assets.
4. Verifiability.	*d.* Required if the accounting treatment differs from that previously accorded a particular item.
5. Conservatism.	*e.* An assumption that would be unreasonable to use in reporting on a firm that had become insolvent.
6. Stable dollar.	*f.* None of these.
7. Matching.	*g.* An objective achieved for a single entity's financial information by adhering to the requirement of consistency.
8. Materiality.	*h.* A measurement that can be corroborated by qualified accountants using the same measurement methods.
9. Exchange prices.	*i.* Discourages undue optimism in measuring and reporting net assets and net earnings.
10. Entity.	*j.* Requires separation of personal from business activity in the recording and reporting processes.

PROBLEMS, SERIES A

P13–1–A. Given below are the contract prices and costs relating to all of the Boyd Company's long-term construction contracts (in millions of dollars):

		Costs incurred		
	Contract price	*Prior to 1980*	*In 1980*	*Costs yet to be incurred*
On contracts completed in 1980	$16.0		$14.0	–0–
On incomplete contracts	48.0	$8.0	16.0	$16.0

General and administrative expenses for 1980 amounted to $600,000.

Required:

a. Compute the earnings before taxes for 1980 using the completed contract method.

b. Repeat part **(a)** assuming use of the percentage-of-completion method.

P13–2–A. You are an auditor. Your audit client, Rappel Company, has prepared tentative financial statements for 1980 which are summarized as follows:

Balance Sheet

Total assets	$500,000
Total liabilities	200,000
Owner's equity	300,000

Earnings Statement

Total sales revenue	$1,200,000
Total expenses and taxes	1,150,000
Net earnings	50,000

In the course of your audit, you discover the following items:

1. Accrued salaries at the end of 1980 were not recorded.
2. Accrued rent receivable at the end of 1980 was not recorded.
3. The cost of a machine was charged to expense in 1980. The machine has a useful life of six years.
4. Your client has been bribing an official of a foreign country to secure an annual license to do business in that country.

Required:

State at what dollar amount you would consider each of the above four items to be material ($100, $500, $1,000, $2,000, $5,000, $10,000, $20,000, or some other amount). Also state the references or relationships used to arrive at your answer.

P13–3–A. Floodplain Company sells real estate lots under terms calling for a small cash down payment and monthly installment payments spread over a few years. Following are data on the company's operations for its first three years:

	1978	1979	1980
Gross margin rate	45%	48%	50%
Cash collected in 1980 from sales made in	$80,000	$100,000	$120,000

Sales in 1980 amounted to $400,000, while general and administrative expenses amounted to $100,000.

Required:

a. Compute the net earnings for 1980 assuming revenue is recognized at the time of sale.

b. Repeat part **(a)** assuming use of the installment method of accounting for sales and gross margin.

P13–4–A. In each of the circumstances described below, the accounting practices followed may be questioned. You are to indicate whether you agree or disagree with the accounting employed and to state the principles or concepts on which you would rely to justify your position.

1. The cost of certain improvements to leased property having a life of five years was charged to expense because they would revert to the lessor when the lease expires in three years.
2. The salaries paid to the top officers of the company were charged to expense in the period in which they were incurred, even though the officers spent over half of their time planning next year's activities.
3. A company spent over $4 million in developing a new product and then spent an additional $4.5 million promoting it. All of these costs were incurred and charged to expense prior to the sale of a single unit of this new product. The expensing of these costs was justified on the grounds that they had to be incurred every year—that new product development and promotion were regularly recurring.
4. No entry was made to record the belief that the market value of the land owned (carried in the accounts at $58,000) increased in value from $100,000 to $105,000, in keeping with the advance in the general level of prices.
5. No entry was made to record the fact that costs of $50,000 were expected to be incurred in fulfilling warranty provisions on products sold this year, the revenue from which was recognized this year.
6. The acquisition of a tract of land was recorded at the price paid for it of $108,000, even though the company would have been willing to pay $125,000.
7. A truck acquired at the beginning of the year was reported at year-end at 80 percent of its acquisition price, even though its market value then was only 65 percent of its original acquisition price.

P13–5–A. By following the most conservative accounting practices permitted, its accountant determined that the Blake Company would report a loss of $60,000 for 1980, its first year of operation. But the top management of the company is concerned about reporting such a loss because it is planning on seeking outside financing for some additional equipment. It calls upon you as an expert accountant to review the accounting practices followed. You discover the following information relating to the loss:

1. Construction revenue has been recorded on a completed contract basis. Six contracts with a total price of $800,000 were partially completed during the year, with costs of $120,000 incurred out of total expected costs of $480,000.
2. Only $20,000 of gross margin realized through installment collections was included in arriving at the net loss of $60,000. Installment sales for the year were $400,000; cost of goods sold was $300,000. There is little doubt about the collection of the installment receivables.
3. The ending inventory was $62,000, using Lifo. Under Fifo it would have amounted to $70,000.
4. Accelerated depreciation for the year amounted to $24,000. Under the straight-line method it would have been $16,000.

Required:

Prepare a schedule showing how the above items would change the reported net loss to net earnings if they were accounted for in an acceptable, yet less conservative way.

P13–6–A. The Brighton Company, as of December 31, 1980, had assets of $560,000, liabilities of $95,000, and owner's equity of $465,000. Net earnings for 1980 included in owner's equity were $102,000.

The adjustments presented below were ignored in computing the above figures. Unless otherwise stated, expense and revenue items were entered initially in the expense and revenue accounts.

Required:

a. Journalize the necessary adjusting entries assuming the books have not yet been closed for 1980.

b. Restate the totals for assets, liabilities, owner's equity, and net earnings.

The ignored adjustments were (or were related to) the items listed below.

1. Accrued salespersons' commissions at year-end were $12,900.
2. Accrued interest receivable on investments was $1,830 as of December 31.
3. A five-year insurance policy was purchased on July 1, 1980. The premium was $6,000.
4. The company purchased five automobiles on July 1, 1980, for $20,000. The asset account was debited. The salvage was estimated at $1,520, and the expected economic life was four years. Depreciation (on a straight-line basis) has not been recorded for the current year.
5. $40,000 was received as service revenue. Only $18,000 was earned during 1980.
6. Goods purchased by the Brighton Company for $8,000 were shipped by the seller on December 31, 1980, f.o.b. destination. No entry was made to record the purchase, and the goods were not included in inventory. (Periodic inventory procedure was used.)
7. Other goods purchased by the Brighton Company for $5,000 were shipped by the seller on December 29, 1980, f.o.b. shipping point. The entry was made to record the purchase, but the goods were not included in the physical inventory.
8. Goods having a cost of $7,000 were sold by the Brighton Company for $12,000. They were shipped to the customer on December 31, 1980, f.o.b. destination. The Brighton Company did not record the sale but did deduct the goods from the ending inventory.

PROBLEMS, SERIES B

P13–1–B. The following data relate to the John Construction Company's long-term construction projects for the year 1980:

	Completed project	Incomplete projects
Contract price	$4,500,000	$24,000,000
Costs incurred prior to 1980	–0–	4,000,000
Costs incurred in 1980	3,700,000	8,000,000
Estimated costs to complete (at 12/31/80)	–0–	8,000,000

General and administrative expenses incurred in 1980 amounted to $500,000.

Required:

Assume that the same accounting methods are used for financial accounting and for income tax purposes and—

a. Compute net earnings for 1980 under the completed contract method.

b. Repeat part **(a)** using the percentage-of-completion method.

P13–2–B. For each of the numbered items listed below, state the letter or letters of the principles used to justify the accounting procedure followed:

A—Entity.
B—Conservatism.
C—Earning principle of revenue recognition.
D—Going concern (continuity).
E—Initial recording at exchange prices principle.
F—Matching principle.
G—Period cost (or principle of immediate recognition of expense).
H—Realization principle.
 I—Systematic and rational allocation principle of expense recognition.
J—Stable dollar assumption.

1. The ending inventory was recorded at $60,000 using the lower-of-cost-or-market method. The cost of the inventory was $64,000.
2. A truck purchased in January was reported at 80 percent of its cost even though its market value at year-end was only 70 percent of its cost.
3. One half of the premium paid on January 2 for a two-year term of insurance coverage was charged to expense.
4. The collection of $10,000 of cash for services to be performed next year was reported as a current liability.
5. The president's salary was treated as an expense of the year even though most of the president's time was spent planning the next two years' activities.
6. No entry was made to record the fact that the company received an offer of $100,000 for land carried in its accounts at $60,000.
7. A supply of printed stationery, checks, and invoices with a cost of $2,000 was treated as a current asset at year-end even though it had no value to others.
8. A tract of land acquired for $35,000 was recorded at that price even though it was appraised at $40,000 and the company would have been willing to pay that amount if pushed.
9. Paid and charged to expense the $1,500 paid to Bill Bunker for rent of a truck owned by him. Bill Bunker is sole proprietor of the company.
10. Recorded the $5,000 of interest collected on $100,000 of 5 percent bonds as interest revenue even though the general level of prices increased 8 percent during the year.

P13–3–B. The following data are for the Ace Company for 1980:

Services rendered in 1980: credit sales, $220,000; cash sales, $50,000; and for cash received in 1979, $6,000. Cash collections in 1980 in addition to the above cash sales: from 1979 credit sales, $20,000; from 1980 credit sales, $180,000; and prepaid on 1981 sales, $4,000.
Expenses: 1980 cash expenses, $40,000; 1980 credit expenses, $130,000; and from 1979 prepayments, $3,000.
Cash payments in 1980 in addition to the above cash expenses: for 1979 credit expenses, $35,000; for 1980 credit expenses, $100,000; and prepayment on 1981 expenses, $2,000.

Required:

Prepare separate schedules showing total revenues, total expenses, and net earnings for 1980 under—

a. The cash basis of accounting.

b. The accrual basis of accounting.

P13–4–B. Slick Company sells a teaching machine under terms calling for a small cash down payment and monthly payments spread over three years. Following are data for the first three years of the company's operations:

	1978	1979	1980
Sales	$200,000	$300,000	$400,000
Cost of goods sold	140,000	180,000	200,000
Cash collected in 1980 from installment sales made in 1978, 1979, and 1980, respectively	60,000	80,000	130,000

General and selling expenses amounted to $120,000 in 1980.

Required:

a. Compute the net earnings for 1980 assuming revenues are recognized at the time of sale.

b. Repeat part **(a)** using the installment method of accounting for sales and gross margin.

P13–5–B. The Krull Company reported the following financial position as of December 31, 1980:

Assets	$750,000
Liabilities	150,000
Owner's equity	600,000

Net earnings were $100,000 for 1980. You discover in your audit of the company's records that—

1. The company wrote off $25,000 of its merchandise inventory to expense on the grounds that future selling prices might decline.
2. Sales orders of $20,000 were recorded as Sales Revenue and debited to Accounts Receivable.
3. No entry was made to accrue employee wages in the amount of $8,000 at the end of the year because these wages were not paid until 1981.

4. The net book value of a machine of $8,000 was charged to expense because the machine was used to make a special product which is now obsolete. The machine could be used for another ten years in the manufacture of this product. There is no other use for the machine at this time, and no future use can be seen at this time.
5. The company had its buildings appraised on December 31, 1980, and as a result recorded a $50,000 increase in its buildings account and in the owner's equity account.

Required:

a. Prepare a schedule starting with reported net earnings which shows the corrections to be made to arrive at the correct net earnings.

b. Prepare another schedule with three columns in which are entered first the amounts for assets, liabilities, and stockholders' equity for December 31, 1980. Show by means of plus and minus the needed corrections for these items to arrive at corrected amounts.

c. Justify the position you took on each of the above items by reference to generally accepted accounting principles.

P13–6–B. As of December 31, 1980, the Harden Company had assets of $362,000, liabilities of $72,000, and owner's equity of $290,000. Net earnings for 1980 included in owner's equity were $47,000.

The auditor of the company discovered that the adjustments presented below were left out of consideration when the above totals were computed. You, as auditor, are required **(a)** to journalize the necessary adjusting entries and **(b)** to state the correct totals for assets, liabilities, owner's equity, and net earnings. Closing entries have not been made for 1980. Unless otherwise stated, expense and revenue items were entered initially in the expense and revenue accounts.

The adjustments that the company omitted from consideration were as follows:

1. Depreciation on a building, which had a cost of $90,000, at the rate of 4 percent per year was not recorded.
2. The balance of the accounts receivable as of December 31, 1980, was $30,000. The normal uncollectible account loss is 2 percent of the accounts receivable at the end of the year. There is no balance in the allowance for doubtful accounts.
3. Taxes accrued on payroll were $1,200. Property taxes prepaid were $450. (Taxes Expense was debited.)
4. Salespersons' commissions due but not paid amounted to $750.
5. Discount on notes payable amounted to $300. (Interest Expense was debited for this amount.)
6. Unexpired insurance amounted to $1,200. This had been recorded as insurance expense.
7. Revenue received in advance and credited to a revenue account was $1,500.
8. Interest accrued on notes payable was $120.
9. Store supplies consumed in 1980 amounted to $720. When store supplies were purchased, they were charged to Prepaid Supplies.

BUSINESS DECISION PROBLEM

Dotman Company began business in 1977 and sells a patented product under a franchising arrangement with the company that holds the franchise for the entire state in which Dotman operates. This arrangement calls for the payment of a fee of 5 percent of the selling price on all products sold. The products are sold through salespersons, who receive a commission of 15 percent of the selling price. Sales revenue, fees, and salespersons' commissions have been recorded only after receipt of cash from customers in payment of their accounts. All other expenses are properly computed under accrual basis accounting. Computed in this manner, the net earnings for 1977, 1978, 1979, and 1980 were $18,000, $26,000, $40,000, and $42,000, respectively.

As an accountant you are called in to examine the records of the company, and you immediately suggest that the records be converted to an accrual basis of accounting to better reflect the results of operations. You determine that the outstanding accounts receivable at the end of 1977, 1978, 1979, and 1980 were $22,000, $32,000, $24,000, and $12,000, respectively.

Required:

a. Prepare a schedule showing the conversion of the cash basis amounts of net earnings to the amounts that would have been reported if sales, fees, and salespersons' commissions had been accounted for under accrual basis accounting.

b. Compare the annual net earnings amounts under the two methods and comment on the differences noted in the trend of net earnings.

Chapter 14

Partnership accounting

There are three common types of business organizations in the United States: single proprietorships, partnerships, and corporations. Up to this point in the text we have illustrated the single proprietorship form of business organization. Single proprietorships and partnerships are larger in number than corporations, but corporations possess a much larger amount of capital and produce more goods and services than unincorporated businesses.

Single proprietorships and partnerships are similar in that (1) they do not issue capital stock (as does a corporation) and (2) their existence is not legally separate from the owners (as is the case in a corporation). The two types of organizations differ in that a single proprietorship is owned by one person, whereas a partnership is owned by two or more persons. The *Uniform Partnership Act* defines a partnership as "an association of two or more persons to carry on as co-owners a business for profit." Unique features of and accounting for partnerships will be discussed in this chapter. Subsequent chapters will illustrate the corporate form.

THE PARTNERSHIP AGREEMENT

A *partnership* is a voluntary association of individuals which is based on a *partnership agreement* or contract, known as the *articles of copartnership.* This contract, which serves as the basis for the formation and operation of a partnership, should be in writing in order to avoid any misunderstanding and disagreements. Among other points, the partnership contract should specify the nature of the business, the types of partners, the capital contribution and duties of each partner, and the rights of the partners in the event of dissolution. It should also specify the location of the partnership's records; the manner in which earnings and losses are to be divided among the partners; and the salaries, interest on capital account balances, and drawings allowed each partner.

When a partnership agreement is prepared, it is difficult to anticipate all future events. If a point arises that is not covered by the contract, the provisions of the Uniform Partnership Act govern in those states which have adopted this act. Otherwise the common law as determined by decisions in past court cases governs.

CHARACTERISTICS OF A PARTNERSHIP: Voluntary association

Any natural person who possesses the right to enter into a contract may become a partner. But since a partnership is a voluntary association, persons cannot be forced into a partnership against their will. Unless otherwise specified in the articles of copartnership, each partner has one vote in the management of a partnership's affairs.

Mutual agency

Each partner is an *agent* (one who has the authority to act for another) of the partnership; as such, a partner has the power to bind the remaining partners to any contract within the apparent scope of the partnership's business. Therefore, it is the responsibility of partners to act in the best interest of the partnership and *not* in their own personal interest in all matters pertaining to the partnership.

Limited life	A partnership always has a limited life. It can be terminated at any time by the voluntary withdrawal or retirement of a partner, the death or *bankruptcy* (the condition of being unable to pay one's debts) of a partner, or the incapacity or adjudged insanity of a partner. If the partnership contract is for a specified period of time, the partnership ends at the expiration of the period. A partnership can also be terminated if the business for which it was formed is completed.
Unlimited liability	*Each* partner may be held liable for *all* the debts of the partnership. If the partnership cannot pay its debts, creditors may satisfy their claims by turning to the partners' personal assets. If a partner's personal assets are not sufficient to meet that partner's individual share of creditors' claims, the creditors can satisfy their claims from the remaining partners who are able to pay. The only personal assets of a partner exempt from the claims of creditors of the partnership are those specified in the bankruptcy laws. If one partner personally pays all of the legal debts of the partnership, that partner has a right of action against the remaining partners. This unlimited liability feature often discourages wealthy individuals from investing in partnerships.
REASONS FOR FORMATION OF PARTNERSHIPS	Partnerships are formed when (1) business capital requirements exceed the amount that may be raised by a single proprietor; (2) a single proprietor desires to obtain the talents and services of other persons who will also share in the risks or rewards of the business; or (3) a single proprietor wants to induce an employee to stay with the business by making that employee a partner. A business organization of the partnership type is usually relatively small (compared with most corporations) as measured by sales, capital, or earnings. It is used where the capital contributions of a few persons are sufficient for the needs of the business. Partnerships also exist in the professional fields—accounting, law, and medicine—where there is a personal responsibility between the firm and the client and where, because of this personal responsibility, the laws of the state may prohibit or limit incorporation by those engaged in such professions.
ADVANTAGES OF A PARTNERSHIP	The status of the partnership form of business organization is sufficiently flexible to permit reasonable accumulation of capital and talent. Also, a partnership is easier and less expensive to organize than a corporation. A partnership is not required to observe as many formalities as a corporation, nor is it subject to the corporation's extra tax burden. The partnership itself is not a taxable entity, while a corporation is. In general, the legal restrictions imposed on a partnership are not greater than those imposed on individuals.
DISADVANTAGES OF A PARTNERSHIP	Perhaps the greatest disadvantage of the partnership form of organization lies in the fact that *each* partner may be held liable for *all* the debts of the partnership. In general, stockholders of a corporation are not liable for the payment of the debts of a corporation; usually their loss cannot exceed the price paid for their capital stock. Also, any one partner may bind the partnership by making contracts in the ordinary course of business. Therefore, a

partner who fails to exercise good judgment can cause the loss of the partnership assets and also the loss of the personal wealth of the remaining partners.

As a functioning organization, the partnership becomes unwieldy when the number of partners becomes large. A partnership is subject, at any time, to momentary discontinuance through the death, adjudged incapacity, bankruptcy, withdrawal, or retirement of one of the partners.

Because partners are co-owners of the net assets of a partnership, the transfer of the capital investment of one partner, by sale or otherwise, to another person (either another partner or an outside person) may be difficult to accomplish. If partners desire to sell their individual investments in a partnership, either (1) a new partner must be obtained, with the consent of the remaining partners; or (2) the remaining partners may purchase the investment of the partner who wishes to withdraw, assuming that the latter is willing to sell that portion to the remaining partners.

To summarize, the disadvantages of a partnership are unlimited liability, mutual agency, limited life, and difficulty in transferring a partnership interest.

UNIQUE FEATURES IN PARTNERSHIP ACCOUNTING

The need for adequate accounting records is greater in a partnership than in a single proprietorship because of the division of interests that exists and because of the complications that arise in the treatment of such matters as partners' drawings and the division of earnings.

The partners' capital accounts

A capital account is maintained for each partner. The total in the partner's capital account after closing represents the partner's equity. Each partner's capital account is:

1. Credited with the original investment.
2. Credited with subsequent investments.
3. Credited (debited) with that partner's share of net earnings (loss).
4. Debited with permanent capital reductions.
5. Debited with the balance of that partner's drawing account at the end of each fiscal period.

To illustrate the use of the capital accounts for original and subsequent investments, assume that James Law and Todd Hart, who have been in business as single proprietors, form a partnership. The formation of the partnership creates a new entity. As a matter of equity, the assets contributed by each partner are recorded at their current market values at the time they are contributed. The contributions, so valued, of each partner to the partnership are listed below:

Law		*Hart*	
Cash	$ 5,600	Cash	$ 6,600
Accounts receivable	6,800	Merchandise	3,400
Merchandise	12,000	Land	8,000
Delivery equipment	3,000	Building	20,000
Accounts payable	(3,200)	Accounts payable	(2,200)

The journal entries on January 1, 1981, to record the investment of each partner are as follows:

Cash	5,600	
Accounts Receivable	6,800	
Merchandise Inventory	12,000	
Delivery Equipment	3,000	
Accounts Payable		3,200
James Law, Capital		24,200
To record the investment of Law in the partnership of Law and Hart.		
Cash	6,600	
Merchandise Inventory	3,400	
Land	8,000	
Building	20,000	
Accounts Payable		2,200
Todd Hart, Capital		35,800
To record the investment of Hart in the partnership of Law and Hart.		

If additional investments are made at a later date, they also are credited to the capital accounts. Assume that on August 1, 1981, additional investments are made as indicated by the following journal entry:

Cash	5,800	
James Law, Capital		2,400
Todd Hart, Capital		3,400
To record additional cash investments.		

On December 31, 1981, before closing the books, the capital accounts of the partners will appear as follows:

James Law, Capital

Date		Explanation	Folio	Debit	Credit	Balance
1981						
Jan.	1	Original investment			24,200	24,200
Aug.	1	Additional cash investment			2,400	26,600

Todd Hart, Capital

Date		Explanation	Folio	Debit	Credit	Balance
1981						
Jan.	1	Original investment			35,800	35,800
Aug.	1	Additional cash investment			3,400	39,200

The partners' drawing accounts

During an accounting period, partners may withdraw cash or merchandise for their personal use. The partnership agreement should specify whether withdrawals of merchandise should be priced at cost or at selling price. These withdrawals are charged to the drawing account of each partner and credited either to Purchases (if priced at cost) or Sales (if priced at selling price). The drawings are made against earnings that presumably have been earned during the fiscal period.

As a rule, partners cannot withdraw any part of their original investment without the consent of all the other partners. Whether or not partners can draw against subsequent additions to their capital depends upon the partnership agreement. Drawings definitely identified as withdrawals of investments should be debited directly to the capital account.

To illustrate drawing accounts, assume that Law and Hart have made withdrawals as indicated below:

James Law, Drawing

Date		Explanation	Folio	Debit	Credit	Balance
1981						
Feb.	7	Cash		1,600		1,600
Apr.	8	Cash		1,700		3,300
July	31	Cash		1,750		5,050
Dec.	1	Cash		1,650		6,700

Todd Hart, Drawing

Date		Explanation	Folio	Debit	Credit	Balance
1981						
Mar.	1	Cash		1,900		1,900
June	7	Cash		1,700		3,600
Sept.	18	Cash		2,000		5,600
Dec.	4	Cash		1,600		7,200

End of period entries

At the end of the fiscal period, all adjusting journal entries are made and the expense and revenue accounts are closed to the Expense and Revenue Summary account in the customary manner. This account in turn is closed to the capital accounts of the partners as are the drawing accounts.

To illustrate, assume that the net earnings of the partnership of Law and Hart for the year ended December 31, 1981, are $30,000 and that the partners divide the earnings equally. The journal entry to close the net earnings to the capital accounts is:

```
Expense and Revenue Summary ................................  30,000
     James Law, Capital  .........................................        15,000
     Todd Hart, Capital  .........................................        15,000
     To close the net earnings to the capital accounts.
```

Another step is to close the balance of the drawing accounts to the capital accounts by the following journal entries:

```
James Law, Capital ...........................................  6,700
     James Law, Drawing ........................................        6,700
     To close the December 31, 1981, drawing account balance.
```

```
Todd Hart, Capital ...........................................  7,200
     Todd Hart, Drawing .........................................        7,200
     To close the December 31, 1981, drawing account balance.
```

After the entries are posted, the drawing accounts and the capital accounts of Law and Hart appear as follows:

James Law, Drawing

Date		Explanation	Folio	Debit	Credit	Balance
1981						
Feb.	7	Cash		1,600		1,600
Apr.	8	Cash		1,700		3,300
July	31	Cash		1,750		5,050
Dec.	1	Cash		1,650		6,700
	31	To capital			6,700	–0–

James Law, Capital

Date		Explanation	Folio	Debit	Credit	Balance
1981						
Jan.	1	Original investment			24,200	24,200
Aug.	1	Additional cash investment			2,400	26,600
Dec.	31	Net earnings			15,000	41,600
	31	From drawing		6,700		34,900

Todd Hart, Drawing

Date		Explanation	Folio	Debit	Credit	Balance
1981						
Mar.	1	Cash		1,900		1,900
June	7	Cash		1,700		3,600
Sept.	18	Cash		2,000		5,600
Dec.	4	Cash		1,600		7,200
	31	To capital			7,200	–0–

Todd Hart, Capital

Date		Explanation	Folio	Debit	Credit	Balance
1981						
Jan.	1	Original investment			35,800	35,800
Aug.	1	Additional cash investment			3,400	39,200
Dec.	31	Net earnings			15,000	54,200
	31	From drawing		7,200		47,000

DIVISION OF PARTNERSHIP EARNINGS

The ratio in which partnership earnings and losses are divided is known as the *earnings and loss ratio* or the profit and loss ratio. The earnings and losses are divided in accordance with the provisions of the partnership contract. If the contract is silent with respect to the division of earnings and losses, the law assumes an equal division for all partners. This is true even if there is inequality in investments, ability, time devoted to the business, and/or risks assumed.

If each of the partners invests an equal amount of assets, has approximately equal ability, devotes the same amount of time to the business, and incurs the same risks, the earnings and losses probably should be divided equally. If variations in the foregoing factors exist between partners, the partner devoting the most time to the business, for example, might be compensated by a salary (out of net earnings) before the division of the remaining net earnings. *The salary is part of the earnings sharing agreement. It is not considered an expense of the partnership.* For example, assume net earnings are $50,000 and A is to be given credit for a salary of $10,000 before the remaining earnings are divided equally with B. A is credited with $30,000 and B with $20,000 when the Expense and Revenue Summary account is closed.

As another illustration, one partner may invest greater capital than another partner. In this case, the partner with the greater investment may insist that the partnership agreement specify that interest be allowed on capital account balances in the division of net earnings before the remainder is divided in accordance with the earnings and loss ratio.

Common methods of dividing earnings are as follows:

1. In a set ratio such as:
   a. Equally.
   b. In an agreed ratio other than equal.
   c. In the ratio of the partners' capital account balances at the beginning of the fiscal period.
   d. In the ratio of the average capital investment.
2. By allowing interest on the capital investments or salaries or both and dividing the remaining net earnings in an agreed ratio.

Assume that Rogers and Morgan have decided to form a partnership. Rogers' initial capital investment is $75,000; Morgan's is $25,000. The partners are equally capable of running the business, and they expect to share equally in the management of the business. But most of Rogers' time and attention is occupied by other business interests. Consequently, the partners have agreed that Rogers will devote only half time to partnership business, whereas Morgan will devote full time.

Under these circumstances, the most equitable method of dividing earnings and losses between the partners is to allow salaries for time devoted to the business, interest on the capital investments, and then divide the remaining net earnings equally. This method adjusts for differences in capital and time contributed by the partners. The equal division of the remaining earnings also seems equitable, since the partners share equally in the management decisions and are equally competent in operating a business of this kind. If one of the partners brings special talents to the firm, the division of partnership earnings should take this into account.

Illustrations of distributions of partnership earnings

The illustrations which follow are based on these data about the partnership of Anders and Budd: net earnings for the year ended December 31, 1981, were $60,000. During 1981 Anders' drawings were $14,000 and Budd's drawings were $22,000. The capital account balances of the partners on December 31, 1981, before the accounts were closed, were Anders, $85,000, and Budd, $134,000.

Case 1. Earnings divided only in a set ratio. If the net earnings of $60,000 were divided equally between Anders and Budd, they would each be credited with $30,000 of earnings. If the partnership agreement instead called for a division of earnings of 60 percent to Anders and 40 percent to Budd, the entry to divide the $60,000 net earnings for 1981 would credit Anders with $36,000 and Budd with $24,000.

Suppose the partnership agreement called for a division of earnings in the beginning of period capital account ratio and Anders' beginning balance was $40,000 and Budd's was $80,000. In this case, the amount of earnings credited to the capital accounts when the Expense and Revenue Summary account is closed would be $20,000 ($40,000/$120,000 × $60,000) for Anders and $40,000 ($80,000/$120,000 × $60,000) for Budd. The distribution of net earnings is computed by using fractions: each partner's beginning capital balance is a numerator and total beginning capital is the denominator.

Sometimes the earnings are divided in the average capital account ratio. Illustration 14.1 contains the assumed details in the partners' capital accounts.

The ratio of average capital amounts is computed by using the total average capital ($50,000 + $90,000 = $140,000) as the denominator of fractions having each partner's average capital as numerators. Thus, Anders is credited with $50,000/$140,000 or 35.71 percent of net earnings, and Budd with $90,000/$140,000 or 64.29 percent.

If the partners invest or withdraw capital on dates other than the first of the month, a unit of time other than a month (days or weeks) may be used to determine the average capital. If days are used, the month-dollars column becomes day-dollars and the total of the day-dollars column is divided by the number of days in the year to arrive at the average capital.

**Illustration 14.1:
Computation of
average capital**

Anders, capital

Date	Debits	Credits	Balance	Months unchanged	Month-dollars (weighted equivalent)
Jan. 1			$40,000	6	$240,000
July 1		$15,000	55,000	5	275,000
Dec. 1		30,000	85,000	1	85,000
				12	$600,000

Average capital of Anders: $600,000 ÷ 12 = $50,000.

Budd, capital

Date	Debits	Credits	Balance	Months unchanged	Month-dollars (weighted equivalent)
Jan. 1			$ 80,000	7	$ 560,000
Aug. 1		$ 4,000	84,000	3	252,000
Nov. 1		50,000	134,000	2	268,000
				12	$1,080,000

Average capital of Budd: $1,080,000 ÷ 12 = $90,000.

Case 2. Interest allowed on investments before dividing the remainder. Interest may be allowed at some agreed rate on the partners' capital investments (the balance in the capital accounts) at the beginning of the year or on their average capital amounts for the year. The *interest on capital invested* is considered a distribution of net earnings for the period and is *not* an expense to be deducted in arriving at net earnings. If there is a net loss for the year, the distribution or allocation of the interest will further increase the negative amount to be distributed to the partners.

To illustrate this method of earnings distribution, it is necessary to recall that the partners' capital account balances on January 1, 1981, were Anders, $40,000, and Budd, $80,000. Their average capital investments for 1981 were $50,000 and $90,000, respectively.

If interest at 6 percent per year is allowed on each partner's capital investment at the beginning of the year, the interest allowed is:

Anders, $40,000 at 6%	$2,400
Budd, $80,000 at 6%	4,800
Total	$7,200

If interest at 6 percent per year is allowed on each partner's average capital investment for the year 1981, the interest allowed is:

Anders, $50,000 at 6%	$3,000
Budd, $90,000 at 6%	5,400
Total	$8,400

Case 3. Salaries allowed before dividing the remainder. Partners also may agree to allow themselves salaries to compensate for differences in time devoted to the business or differences in ability. If the salary agreement is not specified in the articles of copartnership, no partner may receive a salary as a differential even if there are differences in time spent or differences in ability or risks assumed.

Salaries granted to partners are divisions of net earnings and are *not* operating expenses as are salaries paid to employees. If a salary agreement is in effect, the salaries are allocated according to the schedule below as distributions of net earnings. The net earnings amount on a partnership's earnings statement is computed without deducting amounts for interest on partners' capital and salaries to partners. These are always considered to be part of the earnings-sharing mechanism instead of expenses to be deducted in arriving at net earnings. Salaries (as well as interest on partners' capital) are allowed even if their total exceeds the amount of net earnings.

In the case of Anders and Budd, suppose that partnership net earnings are only $20,800. The earnings-sharing conditions are that Anders is allowed a salary of $16,000 per year and Budd a salary of $10,000 per year and that the remaining net earnings or net loss is divided equally. Anders receives $13,400 and Budd receives $7,400, determined as follows:

	Anders	Budd	Both	Earnings to be distributed
Net earnings				$20,800
Salaries	$16,000	$10,000	$26,000	(5,200)
Remainder (negative balance)	(2,600)	(2,600)	(5,200)	–0–
	$13,400	$ 7,400	$20,800	

Notice in the above schedule that the salaries are granted even though earnings are insufficient to cover them. The resulting negative balance is then distributed to the partners in the agreed ratio. The journal entry to record the above earnings distribution is:

```
Expense and Revenue Summary ...............................  20,800
      Anders, Capital .........................................        13,400
      Budd, Capital ..........................................         7,400
   To divide the earnings between the partners.
```

Case 4. Interest and salaries allowed before dividing the remainder.
If it is desired to compensate the partners for capital contributed, they may be allowed interest. If it is desired to compensate them for differences in time devoted to the business or in ability, they may be allowed salaries.

Assume that Anders and Budd are allowed interest at 6 percent per year on their capital account balances at January 1, 1981, and that Anders is allowed a salary of $16,000 and Budd a salary of $10,000. Any remaining net earnings or net loss is divided equally. Net earnings are $60,000. The division in this case is:

	Anders	Budd	Both	Earnings to be distributed
Net earnings				$60,000
Interest...................	$ 2,400	$ 4,800	$ 7,200	52,800
Salary	16,000	10,000	26,000	26,800
Remainder	13,400	13,400	26,800	–0–
Distribution	$31,800	$28,200	$60,000	

The entry to divide net earnings is:

```
Expense and Revenue Summary ...............................  60,000
      Anders, Capital .........................................        31,800
      Budd, Capital ..........................................        28,200
   To divide the earnings between the partners.
```

Even if the allowances for salaries or interest exceed net earnings, or if there is a net loss for the period, the partners still are given credit for their full amounts of interest and salary. For example, in the situation above if there was a net loss of $20,000 instead of net earnings of $60,000 for the year, the division would be as follows:

	Anders	Budd	Both	Earnings to be distributed
Net loss				$(20,000)
Interest	$ 2,400	$ 4,800	$ 7,200	(27,200)
Salary	16,000	10,000	26,000	(53,200)
Remainder	(26,600)	(26,600)	(53,200)	–0–
Distribution	$ (8,200)	$(11,800)	$(20,000)	

The entry to divide the net loss would be:

```
Anders, Capital...............................................    8,200
Budd, Capital ................................................   11,800
    Expense and Revenue Summary .............................              20,000
        To divide the net loss between the partners.
```

FINANCIAL STATEMENTS OF A PARTNERSHIP: Partnership earnings statement

The earnings statement of a partnership is the same in form as that for any other type of organization engaged in a similar business. It is advisable to append a section to the earnings statement showing the division of the net earnings between the partners as illustrated in the earnings statement for the partnership of Anders and Budd for the year ended December 31, 1981 (see Illustration 14.2).

Illustration 14.2: Earnings statement

ANDERS AND BUDD
Earnings Statement
For the Year Ended December 31, 1981

Sales			$600,000
Cost of goods sold:			
Inventory, January 1, 1981..........................		$ 62,000	
Purchases	$364,000		
Less: Purchase discounts	1,600	362,400	
Total		$424,400	
Inventory, December 31, 1981......................		64,000	
Cost of goods sold			360,400
Gross margin on sales			$239,600
Deduct: Operating expenses:			
Selling expenses		$ 80,000	
Administrative expenses		100,000	
Total operating expenses			180,000
Net operating earnings			$ 59,600
Other revenue:			
Interest revenue			400
Net Earnings			$ 60,000

Distribution of Net Earnings

	Anders	Budd	Total
Interest	$ 2,400	$ 4,800	$ 7,200
Salary..........................	16,000	10,000	26,000
Remainder equally.....................	13,400	13,400	26,800
Net earnings	$ 31,800	$ 28,200	$ 60,000

Partnership balance sheet

The only distinctive feature of a partnership balance sheet is the presentation of the capital accounts in the owners' equity section. Instead of a single capital account, the owners' equity section contains a separate capital account for each partner unless there are many partners.

Statement of partners' capital

At the close of each fiscal period, a *statement of partners' capital* is prepared. This statement is a summary of the transactions affecting the capital of each partner and in total for all partners. It is prepared from information in the capital accounts in the general ledger. It starts with the capital account balance at the beginning of the year and ends with the capital account balance at the end of the same year. The net earnings and net earnings distribution amounts from the earnings statement are used to arrive at the new capital account balances shown in the balance sheet. In this way, this statement acts as a link between the earnings statement and the balance sheet.

The statement of partners' capital for Anders and Budd, showing the distribution of the earnings and the capital changes, is presented in Illustration 14.3. The statement could, of course, show net earnings added to the beginning capital account balances before drawings are deducted, instead of after; either format is correct.

The purpose of the statement of partners' capital is to present details that could not readily be shown on the balance sheet. The balance sheet need indicate only the final balance of each partner's capital account when it is accompanied by this detailed analysis.

The balance sheet of a partnership composed of many partners may show only a single item and amount called "Partners' capital." Each partner's name and capital balance would be reported in a supporting schedule.

Illustration 14.3: Statement of partners' capital

ANDERS AND BUDD Statement of Partners' Capital For the Year Ended December 31, 1981			
	Anders	*Budd*	*Total*
Balance January 1, 1981	$ 40,000	$ 80,000	$120,000
Add: Additional investments	45,000	54,000	99,000
Capital account balances, December 31, 1981, before drawing charges	$ 85,000	$134,000	$219,000
Deduct: Drawings	14,000	22,000	36,000
Capital account balances before 1981 earnings distribution	$ 71,000	$112,000	$183,000
Net earnings 1981, per earnings statement:			
Interest	2,400	4,800	7,200
Salaries	16,000	10,000	26,000
Remainder equally	13,400	13,400	26,800
Capital account balances, December 31, 1981	$102,800	$140,200	$243,000

CHANGES IN PARTNERSHIP PERSONNEL

Legally, a partnership is terminated when an existing partner withdraws or retires or a new partner is admitted. In most cases the old partnership is succeeded immediately by a new partnership. The new partnership differs from the old one only to the extent of the change in the personnel of the partners. In these cases the "termination" is technical only, and the continuity of operations is undisturbed. Such a technical termination must be clearly distinguished from a permanent liquidation and winding up of a partnership.

Admission of a new partner

A new partner can gain admission to a partnership in either of two ways. The new partner can purchase an interest from one or more existing partners or can invest assets in the business.

Purchase of an interest.   When a new partner purchases an interest directly from an existing partner, the partnership's assets and liabilities remain unchanged. The accounting entry on the partnership's books simply transfers a portion of the partnership capital from an existing partner to a new partner.

To illustrate, assume that Smith and Jones are partners with capital account balances of $15,000 and $13,000, respectively. Farr purchases an $8,000 interest in the partnership capital from Jones. The journal entry on the partnership's books is:

Jones, Capital	8,000	
Farr, Capital		8,000
To transfer $8,000 of Jones's interest in the partnership assets to Farr.		

The price that Farr paid Jones personally might be more or less than $8,000, but this difference should not be reflected on the books of the partnership. The journal entry merely shows the book value of the interest that is purchased and sold.

Smith cannot prevent Jones from selling an interest to Farr. On the other hand, Farr cannot become a partner unless Smith agrees to the transfer of partnership interests. Under the Uniform Partnership Act, if Smith refuses to accept Farr as a partner, Farr is entitled to the designated share of partnership earnings and losses (and the designated share of partnership assets if the firm is liquidated) but cannot be involved in the management of the business. Under the common law, if Smith refuses to accept Farr as a partner, the partnership must be liquidated, and Farr receives only the designated share of the partnership assets.

Investment in the partnership.   When a new partner acquires an interest in a partnership by investing assets in the business, both partnership assets and total owners' equity increase. In this case, the assets given up by the new partner become the property of the partnership instead of the property of one of the partners.

To illustrate, assume that the partnership of Crowe and Lang has the following assets and equities:

Assets		Equities	
Cash	$15,000	Crowe, capital	$35,000
Other assets	55,000	Lang, capital	35,000
Total Assets	$70,000	Total Equities	$70,000

Crowe and Lang agree to admit Potter as a partner with a one-half interest in the partnership upon Potter's investment of $70,000 cash. The entry to record Potter's investment is:

```
Cash ..................................................... 70,000
    Potter, Capital ......................................              70,000
```
To record Potter's investment of $70,000 cash.

After the above entry is posted, the partnership has the following assets and equities:

Assets		Equities	
Cash	$ 85,000	Crowe, capital	$ 35,000
Other assets	55,000	Lang, capital	35,000
		Potter, capital	70,000
Total Assets	$140,000	Total Equities	$140,000

The fact that Potter has a one-half interest in the new partnership does not necessarily mean that Potter will receive one half of the earnings and losses. The sharing of earnings and losses is a separate matter upon which the partners must agree. If the new partnership contract does not specify how earnings and losses are to be divided, the assumption is that the partners intend to share earnings and losses equally.

Bonus to the old partners. If an existing partnership consistently has exceptionally high net earnings, the existing partners may require a new partner to pay a bonus for admission to the partnership. For example, Marsh and Will operate a partnership which has had above-average net earnings for the last ten years. The partners share earnings and losses in a ratio of two to one—that is, Marsh receives two thirds and Will receives one third. The partners' capital account balances show $55,000 for Marsh and $75,000 for Will. Gray wishes to join the partnership by investing $50,000. Marsh and Will agree to admit Gray as a partner with a one-fourth interest in both capital and earnings in exchange for his $50,000. Gray's equity in the partnership is $45,000, computed as follows:

```
Equities of old partners ($55,000 + $75,000) ...................     $130,000
Investment of new partner .....................................         50,000
    Total equities of new partnership .........................     $180,000
Gray's one-fourth equity ($180,000 × ¼) ......................     $ 45,000
```

The entry to record Gray's investment in the partnership is:

```
Cash ..................................................... 50,000
    Gray, Capital ......................................              45,000
    Marsh, Capital .....................................               3,333
    Will, Capital ......................................               1,667
```
To record Gray's investment in partnership.

Notice that Gray paid $50,000 for an equity of only $45,000. The $5,000 difference is a bonus to the old partners which they share in their earnings and loss ratio.

Bonus to the new partner. Sometimes an incoming partner may be able to provide cash which is desperately needed, or may have extraordinary abilities or business contacts which can help increase the partnership's earnings. In such cases, the existing partners may be willing to give the new partner a bonus—that is, an equity in the partnership greater than the new partner's investment. For example, assume Bentz and Hahn are partners with equities of $100,000 and $60,000, respectively. They share earnings and losses in a ratio of 3:2 (Bentz, ⅗, and Hahn, ⅖). Their firm desperately needs cash. Therefore, they are willing to give Kirby a one-fourth equity in the firm if Kirby will invest $40,000 cash. Kirby agrees to invest $40,000 and receives an equity of $50,000, computed as follows:

Equities of old partners ($100,000 + $60,000)...................	$160,000
Investment of new partner..	40,000
Total equities of new partnership........................	$200,000
Kirby's one-fourth equity ($200,000 × ¼).......................	$ 50,000

The entry to record Kirby's investment in the partnership is:

Cash	40,000	
Bentz, Capital...	6,000	
Hahn, Capital	4,000	
Kirby, Capital		50,000
To record Kirby's investment in partnership.		

Notice that the $10,000 bonus is contributed by the old partners in their earnings and loss ratio of 3:2. After Kirby is admitted to the partnership, the partners must agree on a new earnings and loss ratio. Remember that Kirby's one-fourth equity in the partnership capital does not necessarily entitle Kirby to receive one fourth of the earnings and losses. Interest in capital and interest in earnings and losses are two separate matters.

Withdrawal of a partner

Many articles of copartnership include clauses that prescribe the manner in which settlement is to be made when a partner withdraws from the partnership. Such clauses set forth the method to be followed in computing the fair price to be paid by the continuing partnership for the withdrawing partner's interest. The method prescribed usually involves an audit of the partnership's accounting records and a revaluation of the partnership's assets to their current market values. The revaluation of assets is reflected by increases or decreases in the partners' capital accounts. The withdrawing partner usually is allowed to withdraw assets equal to the amount in that partner's capital account after revaluation. But in some cases, a withdrawing partner may receive assets worth more or less than the book value of that partner's equity. Each of these three cases is illustrated below.

Case 1: Withdrawing partner receives book value of equity. Assume that Snow, South, and Stone are partners, sharing earnings and losses in a ratio of 3:1:1. Stone decides to withdraw from the partnership at a time when the partnership books show the following assets and equities:

Assets			Equities		
Cash		$ 30,000	Snow, capital		$ 50,000
Accounts receivable		10,000	South, capital		30,000
Merchandise inventory ..		40,000	Stone, capital		20,000
Plant and equipment	$50,000				
Less: Accumulated					
depreciation	30,000	20,000			
Total Assets		$100,000	Total Equities		$100,000

The partnership's books are audited. The merchandise inventory is revalued at $45,000, and plant and equipment is revalued at $54,000 with accumulated depreciation of $32,000. The journal entries required to record the revaluations are:

Merchandise Inventory	5,000	
Snow, Capital		3,000
South, Capital		1,000
Stone, Capital		1,000
To revalue inventory.		
Plant and Equipment	4,000	
Accumulated Depreciation		2,000
Snow, Capital		1,200
South, Capital		400
Stone, Capital		400
To revalue plant and equipment.		

Notice that the gains (and losses) from asset revaluations are shared in the partners' earnings and loss ratio. If the partnership were not terminated, the gains and losses would eventually be realized and reflected in net earnings which would then be shared by the partners in their earnings and loss ratio.

After the above entries have been posted, the partnership's assets and equities appear as follows:

Assets			Equities	
Cash		$ 30,000	Snow, capital	$ 54,200
Accounts receivable		10,000	South, capital	31,400
Merchandise inventory		45,000	Stone, capital	21,400
Plant and equipment	$54,000			
Less: Accumulated				
depreciation	32,000	22,000		
Total Assets		$107,000	Total Equities	$107,000

After the revaluations, the entry required to record Stone's withdrawal from the partnership and his receipt of cash equal to the book value of his equity is:

Stone, Capital	21,400	
Cash		21,400
To record Stone's withdrawal.		

Stone could take any combination of assets to which the partners agree. He does not have to take cash. After Stone's withdrawal, a new partnership is created, and a new earnings and loss sharing agreement must be agreed upon by Snow and South.

Case 2. Withdrawing partner receives more than the book value of equity.   Sometimes the partners may decide not to revalue the assets and adjust the accounts when a partner withdraws. In such cases, the partners may agree that the assets are undervalued and that the withdrawing partner should receive assets worth more than the book value of that partner's equity. At other times, the remaining partners may be so anxious for the partner to withdraw that they are willing to give up assets worth more than the book value of that partner's equity. In both cases, the withdrawing partner, in effect, withdraws assets equal to the book value of that partner's own equity plus part of the book value of the remaining partners' equities.

To illustrate, assume that North, East, and West are partners who share earnings and losses in a 3:2:1 ratio. East wishes to withdraw from the partnership at a time when the partnership has the following assets and equities:

Assets		Equities	
Cash	$30,000	North, capital	$50,000
Merchandise inventory	40,000	East, capital	25,000
Equipment, net	20,000	West, capital	15,000
Total Assets	$90,000	Total Equities	$90,000

The partners agree that assets are undervalued by a total of $3,000, but they do not wish to adjust the accounts to current market values. They also agree that East's capital account would increase by $1,000 if the accounts were adjusted. As a result, East is allowed to withdraw $26,000 cash. The entry to record East's withdrawal is:

East, Capital	25,000	
North, Capital	750	
West, Capital	250	
Cash		26,000
To record East's withdrawal.		

East withdrew $1,000 more than the book value of his equity. This excess amount is charged to North's and West's capital accounts on the basis of their earnings and loss ratio of 3:1.

Case 3: Withdrawing partner receives less than the book value of equity. Sometimes the partners may agree that the assets are overvalued but that they do not want to adjust the accounts. In such cases, the partners may also agree that the withdrawing partner should receive assets worth less than the book value of his or her equity. At other times, a partner who is very anxious to withdraw may be willing to accept assets worth less than the book value of that partner's own equity in order to get out of the partnership. The unwithdrawn equity is divided between the remaining partners in their earnings and loss ratio.

To illustrate, assume that Alda, Fonda, and Moore are partners who share earnings and losses in an 8:7:5 (40 percent, 35 percent, 25 percent) ratio. The partnership's assets and equities are as follows:

Assets		Equities	
Cash	$21,000	Alda, capital	$25,000
Merchandise inventory	24,000	Fonda, capital	22,000
Plant and equipment, net	20,000	Moore, capital	18,000
Total Assets	$65,000	Total Equities	$65,000

Moore is very anxious to withdraw from the partnership and is willing to accept $16,000 in settlement of her equity. Alda and Fonda agree to the settlement. The entry to record Moore's withdrawal is:

Moore, Capital	18,000	
Cash		16,000
Alda, Capital		1,067
Fonda, Capital		933
To record Moore's withdrawal.		

Moore withdrew $2,000 less than the book value of her equity. The unwithdrawn amount is credited to the capital accounts of Alda and Fonda in accordance with their earnings and loss ratio of 8:7.

LIQUIDATION OF A PARTNERSHIP

The *liquidation* and winding up of a partnership may be the result of an agreement between the partners or of the operation of the law. The following acts result in liquidation:

1. The accomplishment of the purpose for which the partnership was formed.
2. The expiration of the time for which the partnership was formed.
3. Bankruptcy of the partnership.

True liquidation occurs when a firm dissolves and ceases to exist and its assets are sold. The funds thus acquired are used to pay partnership debts. After the debts are paid, any remaining funds are distributed to the partners.

When a partnership is liquidated by selling its assets and paying its liabilities, certain questions arise regarding the distribution of the partnership assets. The partnership agreement may contain provisions relative to this matter. It may be provided, for example, that one of the partners shall be made liquidator, with power to wind up the partnership affairs, pay the debts of the firm, and make the proper distribution to the partners.

Liquidation may take place rapidly, or it may take place over a long period. If liquidation is rapid, it is likely that only a single cash distribution will be made to the partners after all assets are sold and all liabilities are paid. If liquidation is prolonged, more than one cash distribution may be made to the partners. In this case, care must be exercised to avoid overpaying any one of the partners because it might be impossible to recover the overpaid amount.

Illustration of the liquidation of a partnership

In the following illustration of the liquidation of a partnership, it is assumed that all assets were sold, all liabilities paid, and only one—the final—liquidating distribution was paid to the partners in liquidation of their capital accounts.

The partnership of Ring, Scott, and Terry decides to liquidate as of August 1, 1981. The earnings and loss ratio is as follows: Ring, 40 percent; Scott, 35 percent; and Terry, 25 percent.

The business is discontinued, and the accounts are closed on August 1, 1981. Immediately preceding liquidation, the trial balance of the firm, in condensed form, is as shown in Illustration 14.4.

**Illustration 14.4:
Condensed trial
balance**

RING, SCOTT, AND TERRY
Trial Balance
August 1, 1981

	Debits	Credits
Assets	$100,000	
Liabilities		$ 10,000
Ring, capital		30,000
Scott, capital		30,000
Terry, capital		30,000
	$100,000	$100,000

Case 1: Assets sold at a gain. The assets are sold for $105,000, and the $5,000 gain on the sale is distributed to the partners in their earnings and loss ratio. The liabilities are paid in full. The remaining cash is distributed to the partners in accordance with the balances of their capital accounts, not in the earnings and loss ratio.

The journal entries to record the foregoing facts and the liquidation of the partnership on August 1, 1981, are as follows:

Cash	105,000	
Assets		100,000
Gain on Sale of Assets		5,000
To record the sale of the assets.		
Gain on Sale of Assets	5,000	
Ring, Capital		2,000
Scott, Capital		1,750
Terry, Capital		1,250
To distribute the gain on the sale of the assets.		
Liabilities	10,000	
Cash		10,000
To record the settlement of partnership liabilities.		
Ring, Capital	32,000	
Scott, Capital	31,750	
Terry, Capital	31,250	
Cash		95,000
To distribute the remaining cash to the partners in accordance with the balances of their capital accounts.		

Case 2. Assets sold at a loss when no partner's share of the loss is greater than the balance of that partner's capital account. The assets of Ring, Scott, and Terry are sold for $80,000, and the $20,000 loss on the sale is distributed to the partners in the earnings and loss ratio. The liabilities are paid in full. The remaining cash is distributed to the partners in accordance with the balances of their capital accounts.

The journal entries to record the foregoing facts and the liquidation are as follows:

Cash	80,000	
Loss on Sale of Assets	20,000	
Assets		100,000
To record the sale of the assets.		
Ring, Capital	8,000	
Scott, Capital	7,000	
Terry, Capital	5,000	
Loss on Sale of Assets		20,000
To distribute the loss on the sale of the assets.		
Liabilities	10,000	
Cash		10,000
To record the settlement of the liabilities of the firm.		
Ring, Capital	22,000	
Scott, Capital	23,000	
Terry, Capital	25,000	
Cash		70,000
To record the distribution of the cash to the partners.		

Case 3: Assets sold at a loss when one partner's share of the loss is greater than the balance of that partner's capital account. In Case 2, the loss charged to the capital account of each partner is smaller than that partner's capital account balance. But it is possible that a partner's portion of the loss may be greater than that partner's capital account balance. When the loss is charged to the partner and a debit balance is created in that partner's capital account, the debit balance represents an amount owed to the other partners. The cash available for distribution will be insufficient to pay the other partners in full until the partner with the debit balance pays in the amount of the debit balance. If the partner with the debit balance is unable to pay in the amount owed, the remaining partners must bear this loss in the earnings and loss ratio existing between them.

To illustrate, assume that the assets of Ring, Scott, and Terry were sold for only $20,200. Entries to record the foregoing facts and the liquidation follow:

Cash	20,200	
Loss on Sale of Assets	79,800	
Assets		100,000
To record the sale of the assets.		
Ring, Capital	31,920	
Scott, Capital	27,930	
Terry, Capital	19,950	
Loss on Sale of Assets		79,800
To distribute the loss on the sale of the assets.		
Liabilities	10,000	
Cash		10,000
To record the settlement of the liabilities of the partnership.		

At this stage of the liquidation, the capital accounts of the partners have the following balances:

Ring, Capital	$ 1,920 Dr.
Scott, Capital	2,070 Cr.
Terry, Capital	10,050 Cr.

Only $10,200 cash is available for distribution to Scott and Terry, while the combined balance of their capital accounts is $12,120; $1,920 is due from Ring. Ring's debit balance must be viewed as a possible loss; consequently, Scott and Terry must divide the possible loss of $1,920 between them in their earnings and loss ratio, or 35/60 of $1,920 to Scott and 25/60 of $1,920 to Terry. Scott's possible loss, therefore, is $1,120; and Terry's possible loss is $800.

Scott will receive $950 ($2,070 − $1,120), and Terry will receive $9,250 ($10,050 − $800). The journal entry to record the distribution is as follows:

Scott, Capital	950	
Terry, Capital	9,250	
Cash		10,200
To record the distribution of the remaining cash.		

At this stage of the distribution, the capital accounts have the following balances:

Ring, Capital	$1,920 Dr.
Scott, Capital	1,120 Cr.
Terry, Capital	800 Cr.

The sum of the credit balances of Scott and Terry is equal to the debit balance in Ring's capital account. Ring's debit balance should not be closed to the capital accounts of Scott and Terry until collection from Ring has been proven impossible.

If Ring remits $1,920 on September 1, 1981, the entries are as follows:

Cash	1,920	
Ring, Capital		1,920
To record the liquidation of the debit balance in Ring, Capital account.		

Scott, Capital	1,120	
Terry, Capital	800	
Cash		1,920
To distribute the cash received from Ring.		

The work paper in Illustration 14.5 may be prepared to summarize the situation set forth in Case 3.

Illustration 14.5

	Ring	Scott	Terry	Total
Earnings and loss ratio	40 percent	35 percent	25 percent	100 percent
Capital account balance	$30,000	$30,000	$30,000	$90,000
Apportionment of loss on sale of assets	31,920	27,930	19,950	79,800
Capital balances after loss apportionment	Dr. $ 1,920	Cr. $ 2,070	Cr. $10,050	Cr. $10,200
Liquidating distribution	0	950	9,250	10,200
Capital account balances	Dr. $ 1,920	Cr. $ 1,120	Cr. $ 800	0
Ring's contribution	1,920			Cr. 1,920
Distribution to other partners		1,120	800	1,920
Balance	0	0	0	0

NEW TERMS INTRODUCED IN CHAPTER 14

Agent—one who has the authority to act for another (the partnership) or in the place of another.

Articles of copartnership—see partnership agreement.

Bankruptcy—the condition of being unable to pay one's debts.

Earnings and loss ratio—often called the profit and loss ratio. The agreed-upon way in which a partnership's earnings or losses are shared.

Interest on capital invested—a means often used in the sharing of earnings to give weight to the relative amounts of capital invested by the partners. The interest is sometimes based on the beginning of year balances in the capital accounts and sometimes on the average balances in the capital accounts. The interest is *not* an expense to be deducted in arriving at net earnings.

Liquidation—the final conclusion of a partnership and the winding up of its business affairs.

Partnership—an association of two or more persons to carry on a business as co-owners for profit.

Partnership agreement—also known as articles of copartnership (when in written form); the conditions or provisions accepted by all of the partners to serve as the basis for the formation and operation and liquidation of the partnership.

Salary granted to partners—a means often used in the sharing of earnings to reward certain partners for spending more time than other partners in running the affairs of the business. The salary is *not* an expense of the partnership in determining net earnings.

Statement of partners' capital—a financial statement which summarizes the transactions affecting the capital balance of each partner and in total for all partners.

Uniform Partnership Act—a written law adopted in many states which is applicable in resolving contested matters between partners which are not covered in the partnership agreement.

Unlimited liability—a characteristic of partnerships under which owners are liable for more than merely the amounts invested in the business, as their personal assets may also be taken to satisfy the claims of business creditors.

DEMONSTRATION PROBLEM

The Cox and Long partnership had the following earnings and loss sharing agreement:

1. Cox receives a salary of $1,000 per month.
2. Cox and Long each receive interest at 10 percent on their capital balances at the beginning of the year.
3. The remainder is divided by Cox and Long in a 2:1 ratio.

On January 1, 1981, the partners' capital account balances were Cox, $30,000, and Long, $40,000. On December 31, 1981, the partners' drawing account balances were Cox, $10,000, and Long, $8,000. Net earnings for the year ended December 31, 1981, were $20,000.

Required:

a. Prepare a schedule showing the distribution of net earnings to the partners.

b. Prepare journal entries to close the Expense and Revenue Summary account and the drawing accounts.

Solution to demonstration problem

a.

	Cox	Long	Together	Amount to be distributed
Net earnings				$20,000
Salaries	$12,000	$ –0–	$12,000	8,000
Interest:				
Cox (10% of $30,000)	3,000			
Long (10% of $40,000)		4,000	7,000	1,000
Remainder (2:1)	667	333	1,000	–0–
Distribution	$15,667	$4,333	$20,000	

b.

```
1981
Dec. 31  Expense and Revenue Summary .........................  20,000
              Cox, Capital .........................................        15,667
              Long, Capital .......................................         4,333
         To distribute balance in Expense and Revenue Summary.

      31  Cox, Capital .........................................  10,000
          Long, Capital ........................................   8,000
              Cox, Drawing .......................................        10,000
              Long, Drawing ......................................         8,000
         To close drawing accounts.
```

QUESTIONS

1. Tom Roberts currently is operating a small machine shop. He is considering forming a partnership with an employee, John Green, whom he considers an excellent worker and supervisor and with whom it is easy to associate. Prepare a brief list of the advantages and disadvantages to Roberts of the potential partnership.

2. Many matters usually are covered in the typical partnership agreement. Some of them are of little significance to the accountant, while others are quite crucial. What are some of the crucial provisions as far as the accountant is concerned?

3. Moser and Burgan are partners in a local grocery store. Both take home sufficient merchandise to feed their families. Would you suggest that the merchandise taken home be recorded at selling price or cost? Why?

4. Can you think of a set of circumstances in which you might be willing to enter into a partnership with another person, do all of the work needed to run the business, provide all of the capital, and yet be willing to allow the other person a substantial share of the net earnings?

5. Why should a partnership agreement be quite specific regarding the treatment of withdrawals by partners insofar as the sharing of earnings and losses is concerned?

6. What are three reasons for the formation of partnerships?

7. What is a statement of partners' capital?

8. Describe two different ways in which a new partner can be admitted to a partnership.

9. Why might a withdrawing partner receive assets worth more or less than the book value of his or her equity?

10. What procedures are followed in liquidating a partnership?

EXERCISES

E–1. Borman, Lovell, and Anders are partners. In 1981 net earnings are $90,000. With how much will each be credited in the earnings distribution if—

a. Nothing is said in the partnership agreement concerning the division of earnings?

b. The earnings and loss ratio is 50:30:20, respectively?

E–2. Give the entries to record the division of earnings in **(b)** of Exercise E–1. Also give the entries to record the closing of the drawing accounts assuming drawings were $15,000, $20,000, and $10,000, respectively.

E–3. Given the earnings and loss ratio in **(b)**, Exercise E–1, how would the three share a loss of $60,000?

E–4. Partner A was credited with a salary of $12,000 and interest of $6,000 on her capital account and charged with $1,000 as her share of the balance in the Expense and Revenue Summary account. She drew $14,000 during the year. What amount will she report on her tax return as her share of the partnership's earnings?

E–5. The capital account balances of X and Y stood at $10,000 and $50,000 throughout the entire year. X drew $3,000, and Y drew $3,600, and these drawings are not to be considered capital withdrawals. (Sometimes a limit is placed on drawings in any one time period, and the excess drawings are debited to the capital accounts rather than the drawing accounts.) The net earnings for the year are $10,000. If salaries are to be allowed X and Y in the amounts of $4,000 and $3,000 and the balance of the earnings distributed equally, how much will each partner receive as his or her share of the earnings for the year?

E–6. From the following data in Cavett's capital account, compute the average capital investment for the current year:

Jan. 1	Balance	$32,000
Mar. 1	Withdrew	6,000
May 1	Invested	12,000
June 1	Invested	2,000
Aug. 1	Withdrew	1,000
Dec. 1	Withdrew	3,000

E–7. R and T are partners. They agree that salaries of $500 per month are to be allowed each partner, withdrawable on the last day of each month. Interest is to be credited to each partner at the rate of 6 percent on her actual capital balance less any withdrawals in excess of the allowed salaries. The remainder of the earnings or losses is to be shared equally.

R's capital account balance at January 1 was $50,000, and she drew her monthly salary at the end of each month. In addition, she withdrew $2,000 on July 1.

T's capital account balance at January 1 was $100,000. She drew her monthly salary at the end of each month. She also drew $5,000 on April 1 and $3,000 on October 1.

Prepare a short schedule showing the distribution of earnings of $30,000 for the current year.

E–8. Calvin, Kline, and Hite are partners with capital account balances of $60,000, $70,000, and $50,000, respectively. Heath acquires one third of Calvin's interest in the partnership for $22,000 and one half of Hite's interest in the partnership for $27,500. Prepare the journal entry to record Heath's acquisition of an interest in the partnership.

E–9. Ford, Dodge, and Aspen are partners with capital account balances of $10,000, $15,000, and $25,000, respectively. The partners agree to admit King as a new partner with a one-fourth interest in both partnership capital and earnings in exchange for $10,000 cash. Determine King's equity in the resulting partnership, and prepare the journal entry to record King's investment in the partnership. (Assume the original partners had an earnings and loss ratio of 1:2:2.)

E–10. Carney, Korman, and Hardy are partners with capital account balances of $100,000, $80,000, and $50,000, respectively. They share earnings and losses in the ratio of 5:4:3. Korman decides to withdraw. The partnership revalues its assets from $230,000 to $250,000. Korman then receives cash equal to the book value of his equity after the accounts have been adjusted to current market values. Prepare the journal entry to record the increase in asset values assuming inventory was increased by $10,000 and plant and equipment (net) was increased by $10,000. Also, prepare the journal entry to record Korman's withdrawal from the partnership.

E–11. Anton, Bahr, and Conlon are partners with capital balances of $60,000, $40,000, and $20,000. The partners share earnings and losses in the ratio of 4:1:1. Conlon withdraws and is paid $25,000 by the partnership. Give the journal entry to record Conlon's withdrawal.

E–12. Arch, Butler, and Carroll are partners with capital balances of $136,000, $92,500, and $71,500. They share earnings and losses: Arch, 30 percent; Butler, 50 percent; and Carroll, 20 percent. Total assets are $300,000. The partnership is dissolved; the total assets are sold for $230,000 cash. Give the journal entries to record the sale of the assets, the division of gain or loss, and the disbursement of all cash.

E–13. The liability and capital account credit balances of the firm of Holt and Graf are as follows:

Accounts Payable	$10,000
Holt, Capital	15,000
Graf, Capital	30,000
	$55,000

All assets are sold for $49,000, and that amount of cash is on hand; the loss on the sale of the assets has not yet been charged to the partners in their earnings and loss ratio of 60 percent to Holt and 40 percent to Graf. Prepare journal entries to record the sale of the assets, the distribution of the loss and the distribution of the $49,000 to the creditors and to the partners.

E–14. The trial balance of the F–Y partnership is as follows:

	Debits	Credits
Sundry assets	$100,000	
Current liabilities		$ 10,000
Fern, capital		60,000
Yates, capital		30,000
	$100,000	$100,000

The partners agree to dissolve the partnership. Sundry assets are sold for $45,000 cash. Prepare journal entries to record all steps in the dissolution of the partnership.

E–15. A, B, and C were partners. Certain data of the firm are shown below:

	A	B	C	Total
Capital accounts prior to 1981 operations	$98,000	$27,000	$65,000	$190,000
Loss for year ended December 31, 1981				20,000
Earnings and loss ratio	40%	40%	20%	100%

The partners decided to liquidate. All liabilities were liquidated, after which the assets were sold. The cash realized from the sale of the assets was $100,000.

a. Prepare the journal entry to close the 1981 loss.

b. Prepare the journal entries for the liquidation and the distribution of the cash. Each partner had invested all his available assets in the firm prior to liquidation.

PROBLEMS, SERIES A

P14–1–A. An analysis of Sanders' capital account for the year 1981 shows a beginning balance of $30,000, a capital withdrawal of $10,000 on June 1, and an additional investment of $5,000 on November 1. A similar analysis of Sanders' partner Cannon's capital account shows a beginning balance of $5,000 and an additional investment of $20,000 on July 1. The balance in the Expense and Revenue Summary account shows net earnings for the year of $22,000.

Required:

Prepare a schedule and the required journal entry to record the distribution of the net earnings to the partners under each of the following independent assumptions:

a. Sanders and Cannon are allowed annual salaries of $8,000 and $10,000; 6 percent interest on average

capital balance is to be credited to each partner; and balance of earnings and losses to be shared equally.

b. Equal annual salaries of $10,000 to each partner; 6 percent interest on capital balances at beginning of year; and balance in a 3:2 ratio to Sanders and Cannon.

P14–2–A. Blake's capital account shows a beginning balance of $72,000 and a July 1 withdrawal of $9,000. Rice's capital account shows a beginning balance of $90,000 and a November 1 withdrawal of $18,000. The Expense and Revenue Summary account shows a debit balance of $12,000 for the year 1981.

The partnership agreement calls for salaries of $12,000 and $18,000 to Blake and Rice; interest at 6 percent on average capital balances; and balance to Blake and Rice in a 3:7 ratio.

Required:

Prepare a schedule showing the distribution of the loss for the year to the partners. No excess drawings were charged against the capital accounts. Also prepare the necessary journal entry.

P14–3–A. The balances in the capital accounts of C and D at June 30, 1981, are $120,000 and $60,000. These balances were unchanged during the year. C drew $16,000 during the year, and D drew $18,000. Net earnings for the year amount to $80,000.

Required:

Compute the earnings to be distributed to each partner at the end of the year under each of the following independent conditions:

a. Salaries allowed are $12,000 and $20,000 to C and D; remaining earnings to be divided in capital account ratio as of the beginning of the year.

b. Salaries allowed are $38,000 and $32,000 to C and D; interest on capital account balances as of the beginning of the year at 6 percent; and no other provisions are contained in the agreement with regard to sharing earnings and losses.

P14–4–A. Slim and Fat formed a partnership on March 1, 1981, by investing $20,000 and $32,000. On July 1, 1981, Slim and Fat invested additional capital of $8,000 and $12,000. At this time the partners agreed that in dividing net earnings, interest on capital account balances would be allowed at 6 percent on the investment for the period of time actually invested.

On September 1 both partners invested an additional $20,000. No drawings were made except for the monthly withdrawal of salaries at the annual rate of $14,400 and $19,200 for Slim and Fat. The net earnings for the partial year ending December 31, 1981, amounted to $48,000.

Required:

Prepare a short schedule showing the distribution of the net earnings to each of the partners.

P14–5–A. Boy and Girl, as partners, have agreed to the following distribution of net earnings:

1. Salaries of $18,000 and $24,000 to Boy and Girl.
2. A bonus to Girl of 25 percent of net earnings in excess of salaries.
3. The remainder equally.

Net earnings for the years 1980, 1981, and 1982 were $90,000, $30,000, and a loss of $15,000.

Required:

Prepare short schedules showing the distribution of earnings and losses to the partners.

P14–6–A.

BLUE AND GRAY
Trial Balance
December 31, 1981

	Debits	Credits
Cash	$ 20,500	
Accounts receivable	30,000	
Allowance for doubtful accounts		$ 500
Inventory	18,500	
Equipment	35,000	
Accumulated depreciation—equipment		8,500
Unexpired insurance	455	
Accounts payable		25,500
Blue, capital		18,500
Gray, capital		36,500
Blue, drawing	500	
Gray, drawing	6,000	
Sales		275,000
Purchases	220,000	
Selling expenses	20,000	
Administrative expenses	16,500	
Other revenue		2,955
	$367,455	$367,455

The articles of copartnership for Blue and Gray provide for the distribution of earnings and losses in the following manner:

1. Each partner is allowed 6 percent interest per year on his capital investment as of the beginning of the year.
2. Blue is allowed a salary of $15,000 and Gray a salary of $18,000 per year as a distribution of earnings.
3. The remaining earnings and losses are divided equally.

Your analysis of the books and records discloses the following data that require your consideration: the ending inventory is $15,500; 1 percent of sales is to be added to the allowance for doubtful accounts; and depreciation on the equipment should be recorded at 10 percent of cost. Blue's capital account includes a credit for $2,000 invested on July 15 of the current year. Unexpired insurance at December 31, 1981, is $40.

Required:

You are to prepare the following for the partnership:

a. Adjusting and closing journal entries.

b. An earnings statement for the year.

c. A statement of partners' capital for the year.

P14–7–A. Minerva and Cheevy are partners who share earnings and losses in a 7:3 ratio. They decide to admit Guthrie as a new partner at a time when their capital account credit balances are as follows:

Minerva, Capital	$160,000
Cheevy, Capital	80,000

Required:

Prepare journal entries to record Guthrie's admission to the partnership under each of the following unrelated conditions:

a. Guthrie acquires one half of Minerva's interest for $85,000 cash.

b. Guthrie acquires one fifth of Minerva's interest for $35,000 cash and one fourth of Cheevy's interest for $22,000 cash.

c. Guthrie invests $60,000 for a 20 percent interest.

d. Guthrie invests $40,000 for a 15 percent interest.

e. Guthrie invests $50,000 for a one-sixth interest.

P14–8–A. Martin, Nelson, and Olsen are partners who share earnings and losses in a 4:3:3 ratio. On December 31, 1981, Nelson decides to retire. At this time, the partners have capital account credit balances as follows:

Martin, Capital	$22,000
Nelson, Capital	18,000
Olsen, Capital	30,000

Required:

Prepare entries to record the retirement of Nelson under each of the following unrelated conditions. (Also prepare entries to adjust the books for changes in market values, if specified.)

a. The partners agree that assets are undervalued by $10,000 and that the books should be adjusted to reflect market values. After the books have been adjusted, Nelson receives cash equal to the balance in his capital account.

b. The partners agree that assets are undervalued by $10,000 but that the books should *not* be adjusted to reflect market values. But Nelson receives cash equal to the balance that would be in his capital account if the increases in market values had been recorded.

c. The partners agree that assets are overvalued by $6,000 and that the books should be adjusted to reflect current market values. After the books have been adjusted, Nelson receives cash equal to the balance in his capital account.

d. The partners agree that assets are overvalued by $6,000 but that the books should *not* be adjusted to reflect market values. But Nelson receives cash equal to the balance that would be in his capital account if the decreases in market values had been recorded.

P14–9–A. The XYZ Partnership was liquidated on January 1, 1981. Before selling the assets, the liability and partnership capital account credit balances were as follows:

Accounts Payable	$50,000
X, Capital	5,000
Y, Capital	20,000
Z, Capital	22,500
	$97,500

The assets were sold for $67,500 cash.

Required:

Prepare the journal entries for the liquidation of the partnership and the distribution of the cash to creditors and partners. Assume that all available assets of the partners had been invested in the firm prior to liquidation.

P14–10–A. A, B, C, and D decide to liquidate their partnership. The balance sheet of the firm at the date of liquidation was as follows:

ABCD PARTNERSHIP
Balance Sheet
June 30, 1981

Assets

Cash	$ 2,000
Other assets	15,500
Total Assets	$17,500

*Liabilities and
Owners' Equity*

Accounts payable	$ 3,500
A, Capital	4,800
B, Capital	3,200
C, Capital	4,000
D, Capital	2,000
Total Equities	$17,500

Other assets were sold for $2,700 cash.

Required:

Prepare the journal entries for the liquidation of the partnership and the distribution of cash. It cannot be determined as yet whether payment can be expected from deficient partners. Show your calculations.

P14–11–A. The partnership of Absynth, Bivalve, and Cicero is forced to liquidate due to pressure exerted by creditors. At the time of liquidation the balance sheet of the partnership was as follows:

ABSYNTH, BIVALVE, AND CICERO PARTNERSHIP
Balance Sheet
March 31, 1981

Assets

Cash	$ 20,000
Accounts receivable	80,000
Merchandise inventory	60,000
Plant and equipment	140,000
Total Assets	$300,000

*Liabilities and
Owners' Equity*

Accounts payable	$110,000
Absynth, capital	50,000
Cicero, capital	80,000
Bivalve, capital	60,000
Total Equities	$300,000

The assets were sold on April 1, 1981, for the following amounts:

Accounts receivable	$ 40,000
Merchandise inventory	30,000
Plant and equipment	50,000
Total Assets	$120,000

The partners, Absynth, Bivalve, and Cicero, share earnings and losses 40 percent, 30 percent, and 30 percent, respectively.

Required:

Prepare any necessary entries to record the complete liquidation of the partnership including the final distribution of any remaining cash to the partners. (In other words, close the partnership records.) Should a partner acquire a debit balance after loss distributions, you are to assume that he will be unable to contribute to the firm.

PROBLEMS, SERIES B

P14-1-B. An analysis of the capital accounts for 1981 of Mann and Sellers, partners, shows:

Mann

Jan. 1	Balance		$60,000
June 1	Capital withdrawal		10,000
Nov. 1	Additional investment		15,000

Sellers

Jan. 1	Balance		10,000
July 1	Additional investment		20,000

The balance in the Expense and Revenue Summary account shows net earnings of $30,000 for the year 1981.

Required:

Prepare a schedule showing the distribution of the net earnings under each of the following assumptions with regard to earnings distribution. Also prepare the entries to distribute the earnings and to close the drawing accounts. (Note: In each instance assume drawings equal to salaries allowed for each partner.)

a. Mann and Sellers are allowed annual salaries of $9,000 and $12,000; 6 percent interest on actual capital balances for actual periods the capital is invested; and balance of earnings shared equally.

b. Equal annual salaries of $12,500 to each partner; interest at 8 percent on capital balances at beginning of year; and balance in a 2:3 ratio to Mann and Sellers.

P14-2-B. The E and H partnership had the following agreement concerning earnings sharing. E receives 8 percent on her capital account balance as of the beginning of each year. H receives a salary of $1,200 per month as a distribution of earnings. The remainder is divided equally. The net earnings for 1981 were $36,000.

Required:

a. Assuming that E's and H's capital account balances at January 1, 1981, were $120,000 and $30,000, respectively, prepare a schedule and the entry necessary to distribute the net earnings.

b. Prepare the entry necessary to close the drawing accounts of the partners which had the following balances (before closing) at December 31, 1981; E, zero; and H, $14,400.

c. Present a schedule showing the changes occurring in 1981 in the capital accounts of each partner.

P14-3-B. The capital account balances (unchanged during the year) at December 31, 1981, for He and She, partners, are $120,000 and $60,000. He drew $12,000, and She drew $30,000 during the year, with all withdrawals charged to the respective drawing accounts. Net loss for the year amounts to $12,000.

Required:

Prepare short schedules showing the distribution of earnings to each of the partners for the year 1981 under each of the following assumed provisions in the partnership agreement relating to earnings distribution:

a. Salaries allowed of $12,000 and $30,000 to He and She; remaining earnings divided according to capital account balances at the beginning of the year.

b. Salaries allowed of $18,000 and $30,000; interest on capital account balances at beginning of the year at 6 percent; and no further provisions relating to earnings distribution included in the partnership agreement.

P14–4–B. Fred and Harry formed a partnership on April 1, 1981, by investing $40,000 each. Later, on July 1, each partner invested another $12,000.

The partnership agreement calls for monthly salaries of $1,200 to Fred and $1,400 to Harry, withdrawable monthly. Drawings in excess of allowed salaries are to be charged interest at the rate of 6 percent per year until paid back or covered by undrawn salary allowances. Fred drew his regular monthly salary and also withdrew $6,000 on September 1, so that his drawing account has a debit balance at December 31, 1981, of $16,800. Harry drew his regular salary and an additional $4,000 on November 1, 1981.

The partnership agreement provides for sharing the balance in the Expense and Revenue Summary account equally after allowing for salaries and the recording of interest credits for excessive withdrawals, if any.

Required:

Prepare a schedule and the necessary journal entry to record the distribution of the net earnings of the partnership at December 31, 1981, assuming earnings for the year of $35,000.

P14–5–B. Duffey and Nally are partners in a retail hardware store. Their partnership agreement calls for salaries to Duffey and Nally of $9,000 and $18,000; interest on capital accounts at 6 percent on actual balances during the year, provided drawings are not in excess of monthly salaries allowed; a bonus to Nally of 20 percent of the earnings in excess of salaries and interest allowed; the balance of the net earnings or losses to be shared equally.

During 1981 each partner drew his allowed salary, and there were no withdrawals in excess of allowed salaries. The capital accounts of the two partners remained unchanged during the year at $40,000 for Duffey and $60,000 for Nally.

Required:

Present short schedules showing the distribution of net earnings to the partners assuming that the earnings statement for 1981 shows:

a. $36,000 of net earnings.

b. $20,000 of net earnings.

c. A loss of $8,000.

P14–6–B. Poole and Rankin are partners operating a retail store. Their partnership agreement calls for annual salaries of $12,000 to Poole and $16,000 to Rankin, interest at 8 percent on capital accounts at actual balances throughout the year if drawings for the year do not exceed salaries allowed, and the balance of the earnings to be shared equally. Their June 30, 1981, trial balance follows:

	Debits	Credits
Cash	$ 40,400	
Accounts receivable	64,000	
Inventory, July 1, 1980	28,800	
Accounts payable		$ 40,800
Notes payable		20,000
Poole, capital		28,000
Rankin, capital		20,000
Poole, drawing	8,000	
Rankin, drawing	10,000	
Sales		428,000
Purchases	272,000	
Purchase returns		4,000
Employee salaries and wages	12,000	
Rent expense	52,000	
Delivery expense	16,800	
Store expense	36,800	
	$540,800	$540,800

The $20,000 note payable is a 120-day note dated April 1, 1981, and calls for interest at 10 percent per year. The inventory at June 30, 1981, is $33,200. The only change in the capital accounts during the year was an additional investment by Poole of $8,000 on January 1.

Required:

You are to prepare the following for the partnership:

a. The necessary adjusting and closing entries.

b. An earnings statement for the year ended June 30, 1981.

c. A statement of partners' capital for the year ended June 30, 1981.

d. A balance sheet for June 30, 1981.

P14–7–B. Potts, Roast, and Watts are partners who share earnings and losses in a 3:2:1 ratio. They decide to admit Post to the partnership at a time when their capital account credit balances are as follows:

Potts, Capital	$60,000
Roast, Capital	40,000
Watts, Capital	20,000

Required:

Prepare journal entries to record Post's admission to the partnership under each of the following unrelated conditions:

a. Post acquires 40 percent of Roast's interest for $18,000 cash.

b. Post acquires all of Watts' interest for $18,000 cash.

c. Post invests $80,000 for a one-half interest.

d. Post invests $30,000 for a one-fifth interest.

e. Post invests $60,000 for a 30 percent interest.

P14–8–B. On December 31, 1981, John Daniels, a member of the firm of Daniels and Ehinger, decides to retire. The partners have shared earnings and losses equally. On this date their capital account credit balances are as follows:

John Daniels	$60,000
Peter Daniels	40,000
Paul Ehinger	40,000

Required:

Prepare entries to record the withdrawal of John Daniels under each of the following assumptions. All payments are to be in cash.

a. Daniels is paid $60,000.

b. Daniels is paid $63,000.

c. Daniels is paid $55,000.

P14–9–B. Donald, John, and Charles are partners in the Dennison Company. Due to disagreements among the partners they decide to liquidate. Their ledger account balances on January 1, 1981, follow:

Cash	$ 2,000	
Accounts receivable	12,000	
Allowance for doubtful accounts		$ 1,000
Merchandise inventory	25,000	
Equipment	6,000	
Accumulated depreciation		2,000
Accounts payable		3,000
Donald, capital		20,000
John, capital		15,000
Charles, capital		4,000
	$45,000	$45,000

In the course of liquidation, the assets are sold for the following amounts:

Collection of accounts receivable (balance uncollectible)	$ 8,000
Merchandise inventory	15,000
Equipment	2,000

The liabilities are paid, the balance of cash is distributed to the partners, and the books are closed. The partners share earnings and losses as follows: Donald, 50 percent; John, 30 percent; and Charles, 20 percent.

Required:

Prepare journal entries to record the liquidation of the partnership. (If a partner has a debit balance in his capital account, assume that he is unable to contribute to the partnership.)

P14–10–B. X, Y, and Z, partners, sharing earnings and losses equally, decided to liquidate their business. The balance sheet of the firm at the date of liquidation was as follows:

X, Y, AND Z
Balance Sheet
May 31, 1981

Assets

Cash	$ 5,000
Inventory	30,000
Store equipment	5,000
Delivery equipment	3,000
Land and building	17,000
Total Assets	$60,000

Liabilities and Owners' Equity

Accounts payable	$15,000
X, capital	14,000
Y, capital	16,000
Z, capital	15,000
Total Equities	$60,000

The assets were sold June 1, 1981, for the following amounts:

Inventory	$35,000
Store equipment	3,000
Delivery equipment	5,000
Land and building	24,000

Required:

Prepare the journal entries for the liquidation of the partnership and the distribution of the cash to the partners.

P14–11–B. The following is the balance sheet of the RST partnership at the time it is forced to liquidate:

RST PARTNERSHIP
Balance Sheet
April 30, 1981

Assets

Cash	$ 10,000
Accounts receivable	20,000
Merchandise inventory	50,000
Plant and equipment	100,000
Total Assets	$180,000

*Liabilities and
Owners' Equity*

Accounts payable	$ 95,000
R, capital	35,000
S, capital	25,000
T, capital	25,000
Total Equities	$180,000

On May 1 the assets were sold for the following amounts:

Accounts receivable	$10,000
Merchandise inventory	20,000
Plant and equipment	59,000
	$89,000

R, S, and T share earnings and losses in a 3:2:1 ratio.

Required:

Prepare all necessary journal entries to liquidate the firm and close the accounts. Assume that any partners who have debit balances in their capital accounts after loss distributions are immediately able to pay in cash equal to the debit balances.

BUSINESS DECISION PROBLEM 14–1

Franklin and Cummings operate a mens' clothing store as a partnership. The partners have capital account balances of Franklin, $60,000, and Cummings, $20,000. They share earnings and losses as follows:

1. Franklin and Cummings receive annual salaries of $8,000 and $7,000, respectively.
2. The remainder is shared equally.

Net earnings for 1981 and 1982 were $20,000 and $30,000, respectively. Franklin is not satisfied with his share of the earnings. Since Franklin spends all of his time running the business and Cummings only spends about 20 hours per week of his time running the business, Franklin suggests that he should receive a salary of $10,000 and Cummings a salary of $5,000. Franklin also suggests that interest at 8 percent be allowed on beginning of year capital account balances. Any remaining earnings should be shared equally.

The partners' capital account balances on January 1, 1981, were Franklin, $50,000; and Cummings, $15,000. On January 1, 1982, the partners' capital account balances were Franklin, $70,000; and Cummings, $25,000.

Required:

a. Prepare a schedule showing the distribution of net earnings for 1981 and 1982 in accordance with the original earnings and loss sharing agreement.

b. Prepare a schedule showing how earnings and losses for 1981 and 1982 would have been distributed if Franklin's suggestions had been in effect at that time.

c. What is the difference between the earnings distributions in **(a)** and **(b)** above? Is Franklin's suggestion beneficial for him?

BUSINESS DECISION PROBLEM 14–2

Hefner and Hughes operate a dry cleaning business as a partnership. The partners' earnings and loss sharing agreement is as follows:

1. Hefner and Hughes receive annual salaries of $15,000 and $12,000, respectively.
2. Interest at 10 percent is allowed on both partners'

capital account balances at the beginning of the year.
3. The remainder is shared by Hefner and Hughes in a 3:2 ratio.

The partners' capital account balances at the beginning of 1980, 1981, and 1982 were as follows:

	1980	*1981*	*1982*
Hefner	$50,000	$65,000	$82,000
Hughes	32,000	40,000	45,000

Jackson, an employee of the partnership, has been very faithful and devoted to the business for the last ten years. For the last three years, his annual salary has been $10,000. One of the partnership's competitors is trying to lure Jackson into his business by offering him an $11,500 salary.

Hefner and Hughes decide to admit Jackson as a partner in order to entice him to stay with their business. They tell Jackson that if he will invest $10,000 in the partnership they will give him a 25 percent interest in partnership capital which currently consists of Hefner, $100,000, and Hughes, $50,000. They propose the following earnings and loss sharing agreement:

1. Salaries of $16,000, $13,000, and $12,000 to Hefner, Hughes, and Jackson, respectively.
2. The remainder in a 3:2:1 ratio (Hefner, Hughes, Jackson).

Earnings for 1980, 1981, and 1982 were $40,000, $55,000, and $80,000, respectively.

Required:

a. Prepare a schedule showing the distribution of earnings for 1980, 1981, and 1982 to Hefner and Hughes.

b. Prepare a schedule showing how earnings for 1980, 1981, and 1982 would have been distributed if Jackson had become a partner at the beginning of 1980.

c. In 1983, the partnership expects to earn $100,000. Prepare a schedule showing how earnings for 1983 will be distributed if Jackson joins the partnership on January 1, 1983.

d. Based on the information given, would you advise Jackson to join the partnership or to go to work for the partnership's competitor? Why? (Assume Jackson always has a balance of $15,000 or more in his checking account.)

e. Prepare the journal entry to record Jackson's investment in the partnership should he decide to join.

BUSINESS DECISION PROBLEM 14–3

The Bottoms Brothers Sporting Goods Store has been operated as a partnership by Jim, Todd, and Lance Bottoms for 25 years. The business has been very successful, but the Bottoms brothers all wish to retire. Thus, the brothers decide to liquidate on January 2, 1981. On that date, the partnership's asset, liability, and owners' equity accounts have the following balances:

Cash	$30,000
Merchandise inventory	80,000
Land	20,000
Building, net	30,000
Equipment, net	10,000
Accounts payable	40,000
Jim Bottoms, capital	50,000
Todd Bottoms, capital	45,000
Lance Bottoms, capital	35,000

The noncash assets are sold for the following amounts of cash:

Merchandise inventory	$70,000
Land	40,000
Buildings, net	60,000
Equipment, net	8,000

The creditors are paid, and the brothers distribute the remaining cash among themselves.

Required:

a. Assume you are the accountant for the partnership. What journal entries would you make in order to close the partnership books in January 1981? (Assume Jim, Todd, and Lance shared earnings and losses in a 5:3:2 ratio prior to liquidation.)

b. Did you distribute the remaining cash to the partners in accordance with their earnings and loss ratio of 5:3:2? If not, indicate how you actually did determine the distribution of the remaining cash.

PART FIVE

CORPORATIONS

Chapter 15

Corporations: Formation, administration, and classes of capital stock

Although fewer in number than single proprietorships and partnerships, corporations possess the bulk of our business capital and currently supply us with most of our goods and services. This chapter discusses the corporate form of business organization, its administration, and some of the unique problems encountered in accounting for and reporting on the classes of stock.

THE CORPORATION

A *corporation* is an association of individuals recognized by law as possessing an existence separate and distinct from any of these individuals. That is, it is a separate legal entity. It is an artificial, invisible, intangible being or person created by law. It is endowed with many of the rights and obligations possessed by natural persons. It can, for example, enter into contracts in its own name; buy, sell, or hold real or personal property; borrow money; hire and fire employees; sue and be sued. But it cannot vote.

Advantages of the corporation

Corporations have proved to be remarkably well-suited vehicles for obtaining the huge amounts of capital necessary to secure the economies resulting from large-scale mass production. This is accomplished by issuing shares of stock which are the units into which the ownership of the corporation is divided. The advantages individuals find in investing their savings in corporations include (1) ease of transferability of ownership simply by selling the shares owned; (2) limited liability, that is, stockholders are not personally responsible for the corporation's debts; (3) continuous existence; (4) professional management; (5) centralized authority and responsibility; and (6) limited legal exposure since stockholders are not agents of a corporation.

Disadvantages of the corporation

The corporate form of organization is not without its disadvantages. These include:

1. *Taxation.* Being a separate legal entity, the net earnings of a corporation are subject to taxation.
2. *Government regulation.* Because corporations are created by law, they are subject to greater regulation and control than the sole proprietorship or partnership.
3. *Entrenched management.* The management of a corporation may become thoroughly entrenched because it can use corporate funds to solicit proxies (votes) from stockholders.
4. *Limited ability to raise creditor capital.* The limited liability of stockholders makes a corporation an attractive device for accumulating stockholder capital. At the same time, this limited liability feature limits the amount of creditor capital a corporation may amass because creditors cannot look to the personal assets of stockholders for satisfaction of their debts if the corporation cannot pay.

Incorporating

Each state has a corporation act which permits the formation of corporations by qualified persons. The requirements of the corporation act must be met by the persons—*incorporators*—who desire to form a corporation. Most state corporation laws require a minimum of three incorporators, each of whom must be a natural person of legal age, and a majority of whom must be citizens of the United States.

If a company intends to conduct business solely within one state, it normally seeks incorporation in that state because most state laws are less severe for domestic corporations. The laws of each state view a corporation organized in that state as a domestic corporation and a corporation organized in any other state as a foreign corporation. Concerns conducting an interstate business usually incorporate in the state which has laws most advantageous to the corporation being formed, especially as regards the powers granted the corporation, the taxes levied upon it, and the reports required of it.

Articles of incorporation

The contract between the state and the incorporators and their successors is known as the *charter.* The application for the charter is known as the *articles of incorporation.* When the information requested in the application form is supplied, the articles are filed with the proper office of the state of incorporation. Upon approval by that office (frequently that of the secretary of state), the charter is granted and the corporation exists. Different states require different information in the articles of incorporation; the following list is representative of the information that must be supplied: (1) name of corporation; (2) location of principal office; (3) purposes of business; (4) number of shares of stock authorized, class or classes of shares, and voting and dividend rights of each class of shares; (5) value of assets paid in by the original *subscribers* (persons who contract to acquire shares) to shares; and (6) limitations on authority of the management and owners of the corporation.

As soon as the charter is obtained, the corporation is authorized to operate its business. The incorporators call the first meeting of the stockholders. Two of the purposes of the first meeting of the stockholders are to elect a board of directors and to adopt a code of regulations (bylaws) for the corporation.

Organization costs

Costs of organizing a corporation, such as state incorporation fees and legal fees applicable to incorporation, should be debited to an account called Organization Costs. Since these costs were incurred to benefit the corporation indefinitely, it is reasonable that they be carried as an asset. According to Accounting Principles Board *Opinion No. 17,* organization costs must be amortized over a period not to exceed 40 years. As long as the Organization Costs account is kept on the records, it should appear in the balance sheet as an intangible asset.

Directing the corporation

The corporation is managed through the delegation of authority in a line from the stockholders to the directors to the officers as shown in the organization chart in Illustration 15.1. For any given organization the lower level of the chart could differ from that shown. The stockholders elect the board of directors. The board of directors formulates the broad policies of the company and selects the principal officers, who execute the policies.

Illustration 15.1: Typical corporation's organization chart

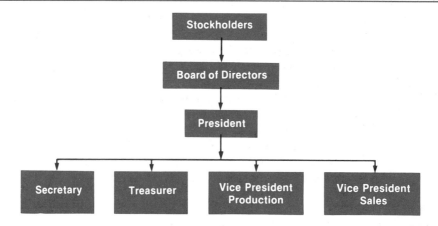

Stockholders. Stockholders, as such, do not have the right to participate actively in the management of the business, unless they serve as directors and/or officers. But stockholders do have certain basic rights; these include the right to (1) dispose of their shares (2) buy additional shares as they are issued on a proportional basis (the *preemptive right*), (3) share in dividends when declared, (4) share in assets in liquidation, and (5) participate in management indirectly by voting their shares of stock.

Normally, stockholders' meetings are held annually. At these meetings each stockholder is entitled to one vote for each share of voting stock held. If stockholders do not personally attend meetings, they may vote by proxy. A *proxy* is a document of authority, signed by the stockholder, giving another person—usually the secretary of the corporation—the authority to vote the shares. At the annual meeting, the stockholders indirectly share in the management by voting on such questions as changing the charter, increasing capital stock issues, approving pension plans, selecting auditors, and others.

Board of directors. Stockholders elect a board of directors which is primarily responsible for the formulation of broad business policies and for the protection of both stockholder and creditor interests. The board, in turn, appoints administrative officers and delegates to them the execution of the broad policies established by the board. The board also has more specific duties including (1) authorizing contracts, (2) declaring dividends, (3) establishing executive salaries, and (4) granting authorization to borrow money. The decisions of the board are recorded in the minutes of its meetings. These minutes are an important source of information to the accountant, as they serve as a basis for certain entries.

Corporate officers. Officers of a corporation usually are specified in the code of regulations and commonly are as follows:

The president is the chief executive officer of the corporation. The president is empowered by the code of regulations to appoint all necessary employees except those appointed by the board of directors.

Vice presidents are charged with the responsibility for specified functional operations, such as sales, engineering, production, and finance.

The secretary has charge of the official records of the company and records the proceedings of meetings of stockholders and directors.

The treasurer is the custodian of company funds and may be charged with general supervision of accounting.

Code of regulations (bylaws). At its first meeting, the board of directors, authorized by the stockholders, drafts and adopts a *code of regulations,* also known as the corporation's *bylaws.* The code contains, along with other information, provisions for the following: *(a)* the place, date, and manner of calling the annual stockholders' meeting; *(b)* the method for electing directors and the number of directors; *(c)* the duties and powers of the directors; and *(d)* the method for selecting officers of the corporation.

CAPITAL STOCK AUTHORIZED

The corporate charter will state the number of shares and the par value, if any, per share of each class of stock that the corporation is permitted to issue. The corporation may not intend to issue all of its authorized stock immediately. It may hold some for issuance in the future when additional capital is needed. If all authorized stock has been issued and more capital is needed, the consent of the state will be required to increase the number of authorized shares.

CAPITAL STOCK OUTSTANDING

The total ownership of a corporation rests with the holders of the outstanding shares of stock—that is, the shares authorized and issued and currently held by stockholders. If, for example, a corporation is authorized to issue 10,000 shares of common stock but has issued only 8,000 shares, the holders of the 8,000 shares own 100 percent of the corporation.

Each outstanding share of stock of a given class is identical with any other outstanding share of that class with respect to the rights and privileges possessed. Shares authorized but not yet issued are referred to as unissued shares (there are 2,000 unissued shares in the above example). No rights or privileges attach to these shares until they are issued; they are not, for example, entitled to dividends, nor can they be voted at stockholders' meetings.

CLASSES OF CAPITAL STOCK

The two ordinary classes of capital stock that may be issued by a corporation are *(a)* preferred stock and *(b)* common stock. If only one class of stock is issued, it is known as *common stock,* and the rights of the stockholder are enjoyed equally by the holders of all shares. The common stock is usually referred to as the residual equity in the corporation. This means simply that all other claims rank ahead of the claims of the common stockholder.

A corporation may also issue preferred stock with different rights and privileges than those possessed by the common stock. And different classes of preferred stock may exist with slightly different characteristics.

Preferred stock

Corporations generally issue *preferred stock* for one or more of three main reasons: (1) With several classes of stock available for issuance, more capital may be attracted from investors who have differing investment objectives. In fact some institutional investors (banks) are prohibited by law from owning common stocks but may own preferred stocks. (2) Since preferred stocks may have no voting rights, their issuance does not dilute the control of the common stockholders over the corporation. (3) The return (dividend) on preferred stocks is usually fixed. Thus, considerable financial leverage is made possible by their use. *Favorable financial leverage* means that the common stockholders obtain leverage, or a greater return, because the corporation can earn more through use of the preferred stockholders' money than the corporation has to pay out as dividends on the preferred stock.

As an example of favorable financial leverage, assume that the organizers of a corporation have two feasible ways of securing capital: (1) issue 20,000 shares of $10 par value common for $200,000, or (2) issue 10,000 shares of $10 par value common for $100,000 and 1,000 shares of $100 par value, 6 percent preferred stock for $100,000. This means that $6 per share of preferred stock will be paid annually as a *dividend* (or return to preferred shareholders). Net earnings of $30,000 per year are expected. The earnings to the common stockholders on a per share basis (net earnings less preferred dividends divided by number of common shares outstanding) are as follows:

	With preferred	Without preferred
Net earnings	$30,000	$30,000
Preferred dividends	6,000	–0–
Net earnings to common stock	$24,000	$30,000
Number of common shares outstanding	10,000	20,000
Earnings per share of common stock	$2.40	$1.50

The test of whether or not the use of financial leverage is favorable is whether it results in higher earnings per share for common shareholders. The use of the preferred stock in the above example increases the expected earnings per share on the common stock from $1.50 to $2.40. Thus, favorable financial leverage results.

When a corporation issues both preferred and common stock, the preferred stock may be:

1. Preferred as to dividends. If it is, it may be:
   a. Cumulative or noncumulative.
   b. Participating or nonparticipating.
2. Preferred as to assets in the event of liquidation.
3. Convertible or nonconvertible.
4. Callable.

Stock preferred as to dividends.   If stock is preferred as to dividends, the holders thereof are entitled to a specified dividend per share before the payment of any dividend on the common stock. The required dividend may be stated as a specific dollar amount per share per year, such as $4.40, or it may be stated as a percentage of the par value of the preferred stock. Regardless of the manner in which they are stated, dividends on preferred stock usually are paid quarterly. A dividend—in full or in part—can be paid on the preferred stock only if it is declared by the board of directors and, in some states, only if the corporation has retained earnings at least equal in dollar amount to the dividend declared.

A stock preferred as to dividends is *cumulative* if all dividends in arrears (required dividends not paid in prior years) and the current dividend on this stock must be paid before dividends can be paid on the common stock. For example, assume cumulative 4 percent preferred stock outstanding of $100,000, common stock outstanding of $100,000, and retained earnings of $10,000. No dividends have been paid for two years, including the current year. The preferred stockholders are entitled to dividends of $8,000 before any dividend can be paid to the common stockholders.

Dividends in arrears are never shown as a liability of the corporation since they are not a legal liability until declared by the board of directors. But since the amount of dividends in arrears may influence the decisions of users of a corporation's financial statements, such dividends should be, and usually are, disclosed in a footnote. An appropriate footnote might read: "Dividends in the amount of $8,000, representing two years' dividends on the company's 4 percent, cumulative preferred stock, were in arrears as of December 31, 1981."

If a preferred stock is *noncumulative,* a dividend omitted or not paid in any one year need not be paid in any future year. Because omitted dividends are usually lost forever, noncumulative preferred stocks hold little attraction for investors and rarely are issued.

Participating preferred stock.   Although it is a relatively uncommon offering, a *participating preferred stock* possesses the right to participate in dividends at a rate greater than its stated basic dividend according to carefully spelled-out provisions in the preferred stock contract. For example, a preferred stock may have a preference over common to a cumulative dividend of $5 per share per year. After the common stock has received a dividend of $2 per share in any fiscal year, the preferred may be entitled to participate in additional dividends on a share-for-share basis with the common. Thus, for every $1 per share of dividends paid to the common over the specified $2 per share, $1 per share must be paid to the preferred. If a dividend of $4 per share is to be paid to the common, $7 per share must be paid to the preferred.

If preferred stock is *nonparticipating,* as are most preferreds, it is entitled to its indicated dividend only, regardless of the size of the dividend paid on the common stock.

Stock preferred as to assets.   Most preferred stocks are preferred as to assets in the event of dissolution and liquidation of the corporation. Typically, this means that the preferred stockholders are entitled to receive the par value (or a larger stipulated liquidation value) per share before the common stockholders receive any distribution of corporate assets. If there are cumulative preferred dividends in arrears at liquidation, they usually are payable regardless of whether there are retained earnings sufficient to meet them. Stock may be preferred as to assets or dividends, or both.

Convertible preferred stock. In recent years substantial amounts of new preferred stock have been issued by corporations merging with or acquiring other corporations. The preferred stock issued is often convertible; that is, the holders of the stock may exchange it, at their option, for shares of common stock of the same corporation at a conversion ratio stated in the preferred stock contract.

Preferred stock often is issued in these mergers for two main reasons: (1) to avoid the use of bonds with their fixed interest charges which must be paid regardless of the amount of net earnings, and (2) to avoid issuing so many additional shares of common stock that earnings per share will be less in the current year than in prior years.

Investors find convertible preferred stock attractive because of the greater probability that the dividends on the preferred will be paid (as compared to dividends on common shares) and because the conversion privilege may be the source of substantial price appreciation. The latter is especially attractive to those institutional investors prohibited by law from owning common stocks.

To illustrate this latter attraction, assume that the Olsen Company issued 1,000 shares of 6 percent $100 par value convertible preferred stock at $100 per share. The stock is convertible at any time into four shares of Olsen common stock, which has a current market value of $20 per share. In the next several years the company reports sharply increased net earnings and increases the dividend on the common stock from $1 to $2 per share. Assume that the common stock now sells at $40 per share. The holders of shares of preferred stock can convert each share of preferred stock into four shares of common stock and increase the annual dividend from $6 to $8. Or they can sell their preferred shares at a substantial gain, since the preferred stock will sell in the market at approximately $160 per share, the market value of the four shares of common into which it is convertible. Or the holders may continue to hold their preferred shares in the expectation of realizing an even larger gain at a later date.

On the other hand, the issuing corporation may force conversion by calling the preferred stock for redemption. Virtually all preferred stocks, convertible or nonconvertible, are callable at the option of the issuing corporation. This means simply that the holders of nonconvertible preferred stock must surrender it to the company when requested to do so. Holders of convertible preferred may either surrender it or convert it into common shares. The preferred shares are usually callable at par value plus a small premium (the *call premium*) of 3 or 4 percent of the par value of the stock. If the stock is surrendered, the former holder receives par value, plus the call premium, plus any dividends in arrears and a prorated portion of the current period's dividend. If the market value of the common shares which can be obtained by converting the shares into common is higher than the amount that would be received in redemption, the holder would be foolish not to convert.

The many reasons why a corporation might call its preferred stock include (1) the outstanding preferred stock may require a 7 percent annual dividend at a time when capital to retire the stock can be secured by issuing a new 4 percent preferred; (2) the issuing company may have been sufficiently profitable to enable it to retire the preferred stock out of earnings; and (3) the company may wish to force conversion of a convertible preferred because the cash dividend on the equivalent common shares will be less than the dividend on the preferred.

BALANCE SHEET PRESENTATION OF STOCK

We will now illustrate the proper financial reporting of preferred and common stock, reporting of authorized and unissued shares, and a manner of describing the shares. Assume that a corporation is authorized to issue 10,000 shares of $100 par value, 6 percent, cumulative, convertible preferred stock, all of which have been issued and are outstanding; and 200,000 shares of $10 par value common stock of which 80,000 shares have been issued and are outstanding. The stockholders' equity section of the balance sheet (assuming $450,000 of retained earnings) is:

Paid-In Capital:

Preferred stock—$100 par value, 6 percent, cumulative, convertible; authorized, issued, and outstanding, 10,000 shares	$1,000,000	
Common stock—$10 par value; authorized, 200,000 shares; issued and outstanding, 80,000 shares	800,000	$1,800,000
Retained earnings		450,000
Total Stockholders' Equity		$2,250,000

A footnote to the balance sheet states the rate at which the preferred stock is convertible into common stock. If the preferred stock is participating, a footnote is included stating the terms of participation and the word "participating" is included in the description of the stock in the balance sheet.

STOCK ISSUANCES FOR CASH: Capital stock with par value

Each share of capital stock (common or preferred) is, according to the terms of the charter of the issuing corporation, of par value or without par value. The par value, if any, is stated in the charter and printed on the stock certificates issued. Par value may be of any amount—1¢, 10¢, 16⅔¢, $1, $5, or $100. Low par values, $10 or less, are commonplace in our economy.

Par value per share is no indication of the amount of stockholders' equity per share (book value per share, as it is called) that is recorded in the accounting records of the corporation. The stockholders' equity consists of paid-in capital and retained earnings, and the latter may be either positive or negative. Nor does par value give any clue as to the market value of the stock. Shares with a par value of $5 have sold in the market for well over $600, and many $100 par value preferred stocks have sold for considerably less than par. Par value is not even a reliable indicator of the price at which shares can be issued. Even in new corporations, shares are often issued at prices well in excess of par value and may even be issued for less than par value if state laws permit.

But par value does serve two purposes: (1) it is the amount per share that is credited to the capital stock account for each share outstanding, and (2) the par value of the outstanding shares is often the legal or *stated capital* of the corporation. A corporation is prohibited by law from declaring dividends or acquiring its own stock if such actions will reduce stockholders' equity below the legal capital of the corporation. For this reason, the par value of the outstanding shares does tend to serve as a buffer or cushion of capital to protect creditors from losses.

Assume that 200 shares of an authorized 1,000 shares of $100 par value common stock are issued for $23,000 cash. The following entry would be made:

```
Cash ........................................................ 23,000
    Common Stock ..............................................          20,000
    Paid-in Capital in Excess of Par Value .........................          3,000
    To record the issuance of 200 shares of stock for cash.
```

Notice that the credit to the Common Stock account is at the par value ($100) times the number of shares issued. The excess ($3,000) is credited to Paid-in Capital In Excess of Par Value, and is part of the paid-in capital contributed by the stockholders.

The stockholders' equity section of the balance sheet would appear as follows:

```
Common stock, par value, $100; $1,000 shares
    authorized; 200 shares issued and outstanding ......................   $20,000
Paid-in capital in excess of par value ...............................     3,000
    Total paid-in capital ........................................   $23,000
```

Capital stock without par value

Laws permitting the issuance of shares of *stock without par value* (sometimes referred to as no par value stock) were first enacted in New York in 1912. Similar, but not uniform, legislation has since been passed in many states. Shares of stock without par value may or may not have a stated value.

Stated value stock. The board of directors of a corporation issuing stock without par value may assign a stated value to each share of capital stock. This stated value, like par value, may be set at any amount by the board, although some state statutes specify a minimum amount such as $5 per share. Stated value may be established either before or after the shares are issued, if not specified by applicable state law.

When shares without par value but with stated value are issued, the shares are carried in the capital stock account at a uniform amount per share—the stated value. Any amounts received in excess of the stated value per share, as well as the stated value itself, represent a part of the capital of the corporation and should be credited to a paid-in capital account. The stated or legal capital of a corporation issuing stated value shares is generally equal to the aggregate of the stated value of the shares issued.

As an illustration, assume that the DeWitt Corporation, which is authorized to issue 10,000 shares of capital stock without par value, assigns a stated value of $20 per share to its stock. The 10,000 authorized shares are issued for cash at $22 per share. The entry would be as follows:

```
Cash ........................................................ 220,000
    Common Stock ..............................................          200,000
    Paid-in Capital in Excess of Stated Value ....................          20,000
    To record issuance of 10,000 shares for cash.
```

The paid-in capital section of the balance sheet would appear as follows:

Common stock without par value, stated value, $20; 10,000 shares	
authorized, issued, and outstanding	$200,000
Paid-in capital in excess of stated value	20,000
Total paid-in capital	$220,000

The $20,000 received over and above the stated value of $200,000 is carried permanently as paid-in capital because it is a part of the capital originally contributed by the stockholders. But the stated or legal capital of the DeWitt Corporation is generally held to be $200,000—the stated value of the shares issued.

Shares without par value or stated value.   If a corporation issues shares without par value which have not been assigned a stated value, the entire amount received is credited to the capital stock account. For instance, consider the above illustration of the DeWitt Corporation involving the issuance of stock without par value. If no stated value had been set, the entry would have been as follows:

Cash	220,000	
Common Stock		220,000
To record issuance of 10,000 shares for cash.		

Because shares may be issued at different times and at differing amounts, the credit to the capital stock account is not at a uniform amount per share, contrary to the case of par value or no par, stated value shares. The entire amount received for shares without par value, to which no stated value is assigned or required by state law, is the amount of *stated capital* (or legal capital).

The stockholders' equity section of the company's balance sheet would be as follows:

Common stock without par or stated value; 10,000 shares authorized,	
issued, and outstanding	$220,000
Total Stockholders' Equity	$220,000

The actual capital contributed by stockholders is $220,000. In some states, the stated capital is also $220,000.

Some general guides to the legal concept of stated capital have been presented. In any actual situation the stated capital of a corporation is governed by the laws of the state of incorporation, and these laws vary considerably.

Dividends declared on shares without par value, whether with or without a stated value, are expressed in dollars per share; dividends on par value shares may be expressed either in terms of a percentage of the par value per share or in dollars per share.

There are several reasons for issuing capital stock without par value. (1) The use of a par value may cause confusion among some investors who are unable to reconcile the constant par figure with the changes in book value and the fluctuating prices at which the stock may be quoted in the stock market. When there is no par or stated value, this source of confusion is avoided. (2) If par value stock is issued at a *discount* (at an amount below its par value), it often carries with it a contingent liability upon the shareholders to creditors of the corporation for the amount of the discount. Although this liability has not been enforced in many cases, the issuance of shares without par or stated value avoids the possibility of such a liability. (3) Most states prohibit the original issuance of stock at a discount. Use of shares without a par or stated value permits an issuance at whatever price the existing market conditions warrant. (4) In states that prohibit the original issuance of stock at a discount, schemes may be employed when par value stock is issued in exchange for property other than cash. For example, the board of directors may accept property in exchange for capital stock. The value of the property may be inflated to avoid disclosure of the discount on common stock. The issuance of shares without par or stated value removes one of the reasons for inflation of asset values.

RECORDING CAPITAL STOCK ISSUES BY SUBSCRIPTION

Stock is often sold through subscriptions. A *subscription* is a contract or agreement to acquire so many shares of stock at a certain price and to pay for the shares at a specified date or specified dates. A *subscriber* is a person contracting to acquire the shares. The steps in recording the issuance of capital stock by subscription are as follows:

1. Receipt of subscriptions for the issuance of the capital stock.
2. Collection of the subscriptions.
3. Issuance of the stock certificates.

In most states, authorized stock becomes legally (but not actually) issued at the time a subscription is accepted. A bona fide subscription contract may be regarded as an asset of the corporation. Thus, the subscriber is a shareholder. The subscriber's legal status as a shareholder is not dependent on the issuance of the stock certificate. Nevertheless, for accounting purposes capital stock is not recorded as issued until the time the stock certificate is delivered to the shareholder.

The authorization of a stock issue does not create an asset or a capital item; it merely establishes the possibility of obtaining assets through the issuance of the stock. Therefore, the authorization to issue stock is not a transaction to be recorded by journal entry. The authorization to issue stock is noted as a memorandum in the ledger (and often in the general journal) in order to avoid issuing shares in excess of the number authorized.

The stock subscribed account

A *stock certificate* is a printed or engraved document serving as evidence of the ownership of a certain number of shares of stock. When stock certificates are not issued until a subscriber has paid in full, a separate account must be maintained to show the amount of stock subscribed but not yet outstanding. This is accomplished by setting up a Common (or Preferred) Stock Subscribed account. *Subscribed stock* is stock for which subscriptions have been received, but for which stock certificates have not been issued.

To illustrate, assume that the Grayson Corporation was authorized to issue 100,000 shares of common capital stock without par value. On January 2, 1981, the corporation received subscriptions for 20,000 shares at $20 per share. The subscriptions were collected on January 10, 1981. The journal entries would be as follows:

January 2, 1981

On this day the corporation was authorized to issue 100,000 shares of common stock without par value.

```
1981
Jan.  2  Subscriptions Receivable—Common ....................  400,000
              Common Stock Subscribed  ......................              400,000
         To record subscriptions to 20,000 shares of common stock
         without par or stated value at $20 per share.

Jan. 10  Cash ...........................................  400,000
              Subscriptions Receivable—Common .................              400,000
         To record the collection of subscriptions in full.

Jan. 10  Common Stock Subscribed ..........................  400,000
              Common Stock....................................              400,000
         To record issuance of stock certificates for 20,000 shares.
```

To continue the Grayson Corporation illustration, assume that on January 15, 1981, subscriptions were received for 30,000 shares at $22 per share, and 80 percent of each of the subscriptions was collected on January 25, 1981. Certificates for these shares are to be issued when the subscriptions are collected in full.

Note that the subscriptions received January 2 were at $20 per share and those received January 15 were at $22 per share. On January 15 the board of directors of the corporation decided to assign a stated value of $20 to each share. This merely means that the board wishes the proper capital stock account to be credited at the uniform amount of $20 per share. Any amount received in the future or in the past in excess of $20 per share ($2 in this case) would be credited to a capital account called Paid-In Capital in Excess of Stated Value. This account represents a portion of the capital contributed by the stockholders, and it is capital just as is the amount credited to the capital stock accounts.

The journal entries would be as follows:

```
1981
Jan. 15  Subscriptions Receivable—Common ....................  660,000
              Common Stock Subscribed  ......................              600,000
              Paid-In Capital in Excess of Stated Value .............               60,000
         Subscriptions received for 30,000 shares of stock without par
         value at $22 per share. The stated value is $20 per share.

Jan. 25  Cash ...........................................  528,000
              Subscriptions Receivable—Common .................              528,000
         Received 80 percent on each of the subscriptions of January
         15, 1981.
```

The $600,000 balance in the Common Stock Subscribed account at January 25, 1981, represents the stated value of stock subscribed for but not yet physically issued to subscribers.

Balance sheet presentation of subscriptions receivable and stock subscribed

Illustration 15.2 shows the balance sheet prepared from the accounts shown above.

Two accounts, Subscriptions Receivable—Common (or Preferred) and Common (or Preferred) Stock Subscribed, must be displayed on any balance sheet prepared prior to collection in full of amounts owed by subscribers and issuance of the stock certificates.

The Common Stock Subscribed account should be regarded as a temporary capital stock account, with its balance representing the stated (or par) value or, for shares without par or stated value, the subscription price of shares subscribed for but not yet issued. It should be presented immediately below the Common Stock account. The two accounts should be combined to present the total of shares issued and to be issued. To this should be

Illustration 15.2

THE GRAYSON CORPORATION Balance Sheet January 25, 1981		
Assets		
Current Assets:		
Cash		$ 928,000
Subscriptions receivable—common		132,000
Total Assets		$1,060,000
Stockholders' Equity		
Paid-In Capital:		
Common stock without par value, stated value, $20 per share; 100,000 shares authorized:		
Issued and outstanding, 20,000 shares	$400,000	
Subscribed but not issued, 30,000 shares (see subscriptions receivable)	600,000	$1,000,000
Paid-in capital in excess of stated value		60,000
Total Stockholders' Equity		$1,060,000

added the balance, if any, of the Paid-In Capital in Excess of Stated (or Par) Value—Common account.

The reference to subscriptions receivable following the caption, "Subscribed but not issued, 30,000 shares" in Illustration 15.2 informs the reader that $132,000 remains to be paid in before the 30,000 subscribed shares will be issued.

Subscriptions receivable normally will be collected within a matter of days or weeks. They are, therefore, properly classified as a current asset in the balance sheet, although the account should be displayed separately and not included in the total of trade accounts receivable. In rare instances, collection of the subscriptions will not be effected within the coming operating cycle. The account is then properly classifiable as a noncurrent asset and preferably shown under the caption "Other assets" near the bottom of the assets section of the balance sheet.

Issuance of par value stock

The following examples illustrate the conventional method for recording the issuance of par value stock. The method follows the practice indicated in accounting for shares with stated value, where it was assumed that the shares were issued when subscriptions were fully paid. The examples differ from each other in the degree of completion of the various steps of subscription of stock, collection of cash, and issuance of certificates. The data used concern the Lake Company, organized as a corporation with an authorized capital stock (all common) of $500,000, divided into 5,000 shares with a par value of $100 each. The authorization is noted in memorandum form in the general journal and in the Common Stock account.

If all the capital stock is subscribed at par the entry is:

```
Subscriptions Receivable—Common ...........................  500,000
    Common Stock Subscribed ................................           500,000
    To record the subscriptions to 5,000 shares at par.
```

At the time of a 20 percent cash collection of the subscriptions, the entry is:

```
Cash .....................................................  100,000
    Subscriptions Receivable—Common .......................           100,000
    To record the partial collection of the subscriptions.
```

When subscriptions are collected in full, the certificates are issued and the following entries are prepared:

```
Cash .....................................................  400,000
    Subscriptions Receivable—Common .......................           400,000
    To record collection of the remaining subscriptions.

Common Stock Subscribed ..................................  500,000
    Common Stock .........................................           500,000
    Certificates issued for 5,000 shares paid in full.
```

If the stock had been subscribed for at a $100,000 premium (the amount in excess of par value), the entry would have been:

```
Subscriptions Receivable—Common ...........................  600,000
    Common Stock Subscribed ...............................           500,000
    Paid-In Capital in Excess of Par Value—Common ..............           100,000
    To record the subscriptions to 5,000 shares of common stock at $120
    per share.
```

If preferred stock were involved the entries would be the same except that the corresponding preferred stock account titles would be used.

Defaulted subscriptions.   The possibility exists that subscribers may be unable or unwilling to fulfill their subscription contracts. Since these contracts often call for an immediate cash payment, with the balance payable in periodic installments, the further possibility exists that the subscriber may have paid a part of the total subscription price. The laws of the state of incorporation generally govern the disposition of the amount paid in and the balance of the contract. There are three possible courses of action: (1)

the subscriber may receive as many shares as have been paid for in full, and the balance of the contract is canceled; (2) the amount paid in may be refunded (often after deducting any expenses and losses incurred in selling the shares to another party); and (3) the amount paid in may be declared forfeited to the corporation. In the latter case, the amount retained should be credited to a Paid-In Capital from Defaulted Subscriptions account to indicate the source of the capital.

CAPITAL STOCK ISSUED FOR PROPERTY OR SERVICES

When capital stock is issued for property or services a question arises: At what dollar amount should the exchange be recorded? In general, accountants seek to measure the economic significance of such exchanges by recording them at the fair value of the property or services received or of the stock issued, whichever is more clearly evident.

As an example, assume that the owners of a tract of land deed it to a corporation in exchange for 1,000 shares of $12 par value common stock which, at the time of the exchange, has a value of $14,000. The required entry is:

Land	14,000	
Common Stock		12,000
Paid-In Capital in Excess of Par Value—Common		2,000
To record the receipt of land for capital stock.		

Now, asume 100 shares of common stock with a par value of $40 per share are issued in exchange for legal services received in organizing a corporation. The attorney providing the services previously agreed to a price of $5,000 for these services. In this example, the correct entry is:

Organization Costs	5,000	
Common Stock		4,000
Paid-In Capital in Excess of Par Value—Common		1,000
To record the receipt of legal services for capital stock.		

The services should be valued at the price previously agreed on, and should be charged to an asset account because these services will benefit the corporation indefinitely. The amount by which the value of the services received exceeds the par value of the shares issued is properly credited to a Paid-In Capital in Excess of Par Value—Common account.

PAID-IN CAPITAL IN EXCESS OF PAR (OR STATED) VALUE— COMMON OR PREFERRED ACCOUNT

Amounts received in excess of the par or stated value of shares issued should be credited to an account called Paid-In Capital in Excess of Par (or Stated) Value—Common or Preferred. The board of directors can dispose of this account in a number of ways, as discussed in the next chapter. But until such action is taken, the amounts received in excess of par or stated value should be carried in separate accounts for each class of stock issued and reported in the balance sheet as follows:

Paid-In Capital:
Preferred stock—$100 par value, 6 percent
   cumulative; 1,000 shares authorized, issued,
   and outstanding $100,000
Common stock—without par value, stated
   value $5; 100,000 shares authorized, 80,000
   shares issued and outstanding 400,000 $500,000
Paid-in capital in excess of par or stated value:
   From preferred stock issuances .... $ 5,000
   From common stock issuances 20,000   25,000 $525,000
Retained earnings 200,000
       Total Shareholders' Equity $725,000

DOCUMENTS, BOOKS, AND RECORDS RELATING TO CAPITAL STOCK

Currently, as reported in the financial pages of most daily newspapers, millions of shares of corporate capital stock are traded every business day on organized stock exchanges such as the New York Stock Exchange, the American Stock Exchange, and in the over-the-counter market. These sales (or "trades") seldom involve the corporation issuing the stock as a party to the exchange, but rather are made by existing stockholders to other individual or institutional investors. These trades are followed by the physical transfer of documents known as stock certificates.

When a stockholder sells shares of stock, the new owner receives the stock certificate, duly signed over to the new owner and presents it to the issuing corporation. The certificate is canceled and attached to its corresponding stub in the stock certificate book, and a new certificate is prepared for the new owner. The number of shares of stock outstanding at any time can be determined by summing the shares shown on the open stubs (stubs without certificates attached).

Stockholders' ledger

Among the more important records maintained by a corporation is the *stockholders' ledger.* This ledger is subsidiary to, and contains the supporting detail for, the common (or preferred) stock account contained in the general ledger. It contains an account for each stockholder and as a result may, in a large corporation, consist of more than a million individual accounts. Each stockholder's account shows the number of shares owned, their certificate numbers, and the dates on which shares were acquired or sold. Entries are made in terms of the number of shares rather than dollars.

The stockholders' ledger contains the same information as the stock certificate book but summarizes it alphabetically by stockholder, since a stockholder may own a dozen or more certificates. When so summarized, a corporation can readily determine the number of shares a stockholder is entitled to vote at a stockholders' meeting, and dividend checks can be limited to one per stockholder rather than one per stock certificate.

Many large corporations with actively traded shares turn the task of maintaining reliable stock records over to an outside stock transfer agent and a stock registrar. The *stock transfer agent,* usually a bank or trust company, transfers shares between stockholders by canceling the certificates covering shares sold, issuing new stock certificates, and making appropriate entries in the stockholders' ledger. The new certificates are sent to the *stock registrar,* typically another bank, which maintains separate records of the shares outstanding. The control afforded by this type of system makes it highly unlikely that stock certificates can be issued fraudulently by an employee of a corporation and the proceeds stolen.

The minutes book

The *minutes book,* kept by the secretary of the corporation, is a written record of the actions taken at official meetings of the board of directors and at stockholders' meetings. It is the written authorization for many actions taken by corporate officers. All actions taken by the board of directors and the stockholders must be in accord with the provisions contained in the charter and in the code of regulations. The minutes book contains a variety of data, including the following:

1. A copy of the corporate charter.
2. A copy of the code of regulations (bylaws).
3. Dividends declared by the board of directors.
4. Authorization for the acquisition of major assets.
5. Authorization for borrowing.
6. Authorization for increases or decreases in capital stock.
7. Authorization for pension plans.

VALUES COMMONLY ASSOCIATED WITH CAPITAL STOCK: Par value

Par value is simply the nominal amount printed on a stock certificate. It is the amount per share at which par value stock customarily is recorded in the accounts. Under some state statutes the par value of the issued shares is the legal capital of the corporation—that is, the amount of capital which must be maintained unless formal procedures are employed to reduce this amount (reduction of par value, for example).

Stated value

Stated value is the amount per share at which the board of directors of a corporation may decide to record its capital stock if it does not have a par value. Any excess of issuance price over stated value is credited to Paid-In Capital in Excess of Stated Value—Common. Stated value is similar to par value in that it is established arbitrarily and bears no necessary relationship to the market or book value of the capital stock.

Market value

Market value is the price at which shares of capital stock are bought and sold by investors in the open market. Market price is affected directly by all the factors that influence general economic conditions, investors' expectations concerning the corporation, the money market, and the earnings of the corporation. It is the value of greatest interest to most investors, assuming there is no expectation of dissolution of the corporation or of redemption of the stock involved.

Liquidation value

Liquidation value is the amount a stockholder will receive if a corporation discontinues operations and liquidates by selling its assets, paying its liabilities, and distributing the remaining cash among the stockholders. Since the assets may be sold for more or less than the amounts at which they are recorded in the corporation's accounts, liquidation value may be more or less than book value, which is discussed below. If only one class of common stock is outstanding, each stockholder will receive, per share, the amount obtained by dividing the remaining cash by the number of shares of stock outstanding. If both common and preferred stock are outstanding, liquidation values depend on the preference features of the preferred stock.

Redemption value

Preferred stock may be issued with the stipulation that the corporation has the right to redeem it. The *redemption value* may be par, par plus dividends in arrears, or par plus dividends to redemption date plus a premium of a few dollars (such as $1 to $5) per share. The excess of the call premium over the premium received on issuance is charged to retained earnings as a distribution to the retiring preferred stockholders.

Book value

The *book value* of all of a corporation's outstanding shares is the total of the recorded net asset values of the corporation—that is, total assets minus liabilities. Or, it is simply total stockholders' equity. When only common stock is outstanding, book value per share is computed by dividing stockholders' equity by the number of shares outstanding plus shares subscribed but not yet issued, if any.

Assume that the stockholders' equity of a corporation is as follows:

Common stock without par value, stated value $10; authorized, 20,000 shares; issued and outstanding, 15,000 shares	$150,000	
Paid-in capital in excess of stated value	10,000	$160,000
Retained earnings		50,000
Total Stockholders' Equity		$210,000

The book value per share of the stock is determined as follows:

Total stockholders' equity	$210,000
Total shares outstanding	÷ 15,000
Book value per share	$ 14

When two or more classes of capital stock are outstanding, the computation of book value per share is more complex. The usual approach is to assume that the assets and liabilities would be liquidated at book value, which means that the corporation would have cash equal to its stockholders' equity to distribute among its stockholders. How much cash would be distributed for each share of stock then depends upon the rights of the preferred shareholders. Preferred shareholders typically are entitled to a specified liquidation value per share, plus cumulative dividends, if any, since most preferred stocks are preferred as to assets and are cumulative. In each case, the specific provisions in the preferred stock contract will govern.

As an illustration, the Celoron Company's stockholders' equity is as follows:

Preferred stock, $100 par value, 5,000 shares	$ 500,000
Common stock, $10 par value, 200,000 shares	2,000,000
Paid-in capital in excess of par value—common	200,000
Retained earnings	400,000
Total Stockholders' Equity	$3,100,000

The preferred stock is 6 percent, cumulative, and nonparticipating, preferred as to dividends and as to assets in liquidation to the extent of liquidation value of $100 per share, plus cumulative dividends. Dividends for the current year and the preceding three years are unpaid on the preferred stock. The book values for each class of stock are as follows:

		Total	Per share
Total stockholders' equity		$3,100,000	
Book value of preferred stock (5,000 shares):			
Liquidation value (5,000 × $100)	$500,000		
Dividends (four years at $30,000)	120,000	620,000	$124.00
Book value of common stock (200,000 shares)		$2,480,000	12.40

Suppose that all of the features attached to the preferred stock in the above example are the same except that the preferred stockholder has the right to receive $103 per share in liquidation. The book values for each class of stock would be:

		Total	Per share
Total stockholders' equity		$3,100,000	
Book value of preferred stock (5,000 shares):			
Liquidation value (5,000 × $103)	$515,000		
Dividends (four years at $30,000)	120,000	635,000	$127.00
Book value of common stock (200,000 shares)		$2,465,000	12.33

Caution must be exercised not to attach too much significance to book value. The shares of many corporations are traded regularly at market prices different than their book values.

NEW TERMS INTRODUCED IN CHAPTER 15

Articles of incorporation—the form containing information about the proposed corporation that is filed with the state by incorporators seeking to organize the corporation.

Book value (per share)—stockholders' equity per share; computed as the amount per share each shareholder would receive if the corporation were liquidated without incurring any further expense and if assets were sold and liabilities liquidated at their recorded amounts.

Call premium (on preferred stock)—the difference between the amount at which a corporation may call its preferred stock for redemption and the par value of the stock.

Capital stock authorized—the stock that a corporation is entitled to issue as designated in its charter.

Capital stock outstanding—the shares of stock which have been authorized and issued and are currently held by shareholders.

Capital stock unissued—capital stock authorized for which stock certificates have not been issued.

Charter, corporate—the contract between the state and the incorporators of a corporation or their successors granting the corporation its legal existence.

Code of regulations (bylaws)—a set of rules or regulations adopted by the board of directors of a corporation to govern the conduct of corporate affairs within the general laws of the state and the policies and purposes stated or implied in the corporate charter.

Common stock—shares of stock representing the residual equity in the corporation. All other claims rank ahead of the common shareholder.

Convertible preferred stock—preferred stock which is convertible into common stock of the issuing corporation.

Corporation—an association of individuals which, at law, is viewed as an artificial person. It is granted many of the rights and placed under many of the obligations of a natural person. As viewed through the eyes of the law of a given state, all corporations organized under the laws of that state are domestic corporations, all others are foreign.

Cumulative preferred stock—the right to receive a basic dividend each year accumulates if not paid; dividends in arrears must be paid before dividends can be paid on the common stock.

Defaulted subscription—a contract to acquire stock on which a required installment payment has not been made.

Discount on capital stock—the amount by which the par value of shares subscribed for exceeds their subscription price. The issuance of shares at a discount is illegal in most states.

Dividends in arrears—cumulative unpaid dividends.

Dividend on preferred stock—the amount paid to preferred stockholders as an annual return.

Financial leverage (favorable)—when the common stockholders earn a greater return because they obtain preferred stockholders' money at a fixed rate and use it to produce earnings at a higher rate.

Incorporators—natural persons seeking to bring a corporation into existence.

Liquidation value—the amount to be paid per share of preferred stock upon liquidation of the corporation, often equal to par value and a fixed premium.

Market value—the price at which shares of stock are exchanged in the open market.

Minutes book—the record book in which actions taken at stockholders' and board of directors' meetings are recorded.

Noncumulative preferred stock—a preferred stock on which the right to receive a dividend expires if not declared.

Nonparticipating preferred stock—a preferred stock which is entitled to its indicated dividend only, regardless of the size of the dividend paid on common stock.

Organization costs—an intangible asset consisting of the various costs incurred in bringing a corporation into existence, including legal and other service fees or costs and fees paid to the state.

Paid-in capital in excess of par (or stated) value—common or preferred—capital contributed to a corporation in addition to that assigned to the shares issued and recorded in capital stock accounts.

Participating preferred stock—a preferred stock which is entitled to receive dividends above the stated preference rate under certain conditions which are stated carefully in the preferred stock contract.

Par value—an arbitrary amount assigned to each share of a given class of stock and printed on the stock certificate.

Preemptive right—the right of a stockholder to subscribe to additional shares of the same class of stock he holds in any subsequent issuance of new shares. This right may be waived.

Preferred stock—corporate capital stock which carries certain privileges or rights not carried by all outstanding shares of stock. Preferred stock may be cumulative or noncumulative and participating or nonparticipating.

Proxy—a legal document which, when properly executed, grants to another the right to vote a given stockholder's shares at a stockholders' meeting.

Redemption value—the price per share at which a corporation may call its preferred stock for retirement.

Stated capital—an amount prescribed by law (often par value or stated value of shares outstanding) below which the stockholders' equity of a corporation will not be reduced through the declaration of dividends or other distributions of corporate assets to stockholders in exchange for their shares of stock.

Stated value—an arbitrary amount assigned by the board of directors to each share of a given class of no par value stock.

Stock certificate—a printed or engraved document serving as evidence of ownership of a certain number of shares of capital stock.

Stock preferred as to assets—a stock which is entitled to receive assets in liquidation up to a stated amount before any assets may be distributed to the common stockholders.

Stock preferred as to dividends—a stock which is entitled to receive certain dividends prior to the payment of any dividends to common stockholders.

Stock registrar—an outside agency, typically a bank, which authenticates stock issues and maintains separate records of stock outstanding.

Stock transfer agent—an outside agency, typically a bank or trust company, employed by a corporation to transfer stock between buyers and sellers.

Stock without par value (no par value stock)—capital stock without par value, to which a stated value may or may not be assigned.

Stockholders' ledger—a group of subsidiary accounts showing the number of shares of stock held by each stockholder at any one moment.

Subscribed stock—stock for which subscriptions have been received, but for which stock certificates have not been issued.

Subscriber—a person contracting to acquire shares, usually in an original issuance of stock by a corporation.

Subscription—a contract to acquire a certain number of shares of stock, at a specified price, with payment to be made at a specified date or specified dates.

Subscription price—the price at which a subscriber agrees to acquire shares of stock in a subscription agreement.

DEMONSTRATION PROBLEM

The Dey Company has paid all required preferred dividends through December 31, 1976. Its outstanding stock consists of 10,000 shares of $100 par value common and 4,000 shares of 6 percent, $100 par value preferred. During five successive years, the company's dividend declarations were as follows:

1977	$140,000
1978	84,000
1979	12,000
1980	24,000
1981	108,000

Required:

Compute the amount of dividends which would have been paid to each class of stock in each of the last five years assuming the preferred stock is:

a. Cumulative and nonparticipating.

b. Noncumulative and nonparticipating.

c. Cumulative and participating on a share for share basis after dividends of $2 per share have been paid on the common stock each year.

d. Noncumulative and participating as in **(c)** above.

Solution to demonstration problem

DEY COMPANY

		Assumptions			
Year	Dividends to	(a)	(b)	(c)	(d)
1977	Preferred	$ 24,000	$ 24,000	$51,429*	$51,429
	Common	116,000	116,000	88,571*	88,571
1978	Preferred	24,000	24,000	35,429	35,429
	Common	60,000	60,000	48,571	48,571
1979	Preferred	12,000	12,000	12,000	12,000
	Common	–0–	–0–	–0–	–0–
1980	Preferred	24,000	24,000	24,000	24,000
	Common	–0–	–0–	–0–	–0–
1981	Preferred	36,000	24,000	50,857	42,286
	Common	72,000	84,000	57,143	65,714

	Common	Preferred
* Preferred dividend (4,000 × $6)		$24,000
Common dividend (10,000 × $2)	$20,000	
Remainder (⅝ and ⅖ of $96,000)	68,571	27,429
	$88,571	$51,429

With respect to any amount of dividends in which the two classes participate (parts [c] and [d]), the allocation ratios are:

$$\text{Preferred:} \quad \frac{4,000}{14,000} \left(\frac{2}{7}\right)$$

$$\text{Common:} \quad \frac{10,000}{14,000} \left(\frac{5}{7}\right)$$

QUESTIONS

1. Cite the major advantages of the corporate form of business organization and indicate why each is considered an advantage.

2. What is meant by the allegation that corporate earnings are subject to double taxation? Cite several other disadvantages of the corporate form of organization.

3. Why is the title Organization Expense not a good one for the account which records the costs of organizing a corporation? Could you justify leaving the balance of an Organization Costs account intact throughout the life of a corporation?

4. What are the basic rights associated with a share of capital stock if there is only one class of stock outstanding?

5. With reference to preferred stock, what is the meaning of the terms *(a)* cumulative and noncumulative and *(b)* participating and nonparticipating?

6. A corporation has outstanding 1,000 shares of 4 percent $100 par value cumulative preferred stock. Dividends on this stock have not been declared for three years. Is the corporation liable to its preferred stockholders for these dividends? How should they be shown in the balance sheet, if at all?

7. Explain why a corporation might issue a preferred stock that is both convertible into common stock and callable.

8. What are the differences between par value stock and stock with no par value?

9. Corporate capital stock is seldom, if ever, issued for less than par value. Give two reasons why this is true.

10. Explain the nature of the Subscriptions Receivable account. How should it be classified in the balance sheet? On what occasions is it debited? Credited?

11. What is the general approach of the accountant in seeking the dollar amount at which to record the issuance of corporate stock for services or property other than cash?

12. Explain the nature of the account entitled Paid-In Capital in Excess of Par Value. Under what circumstances is an entry recorded in the account?

13. Explain the purpose of *(a)* the stockholders' ledger, *(b)* the minutes book, *(c)* the stock transfer agent, and *(d)* the stock registrar.

14. Explain the terms liquidation value and redemption value. To what class of stock do they usually apply?

15. Assuming there is no preferred stock outstanding, how can the book value per share of common stock be determined? Of what significance is it? What is its relationship to market value per share?

EXERCISES

E–1. Baker Company has 1,000 shares of cumulative preferred stock with a $6 annual dividend per share and 5,000 shares of common stock without par value outstanding. No dividends were paid in 1979 or 1980. At the beginning of 1981 the company had a deficit of $12,000. During 1981 it had net earnings of $60,000. If a dividend of $3 per share is declared on the common stock, what is the ending balance in retained earnings?

E–2. Blaine Corporation has 1,000 shares of $100 par value convertible preferred stock outstanding which was issued at par value. Each share is convertible into 3.5 shares of $10 stated value common stock. Give the entry to record the conversion of all 1,000 shares of preferred.

E–3. Parker Company called all of its 2,000 shares of outstanding $100 par value preferred stock. The stock

was cumulative, nonparticipating, entitled to $100 per share plus cumulative dividends in liquidation, and callable at $105. Give the entry to record the calling of the preferred stock, assuming it was issued at par value. Give the entry required if the stock had been issued at $102. In each case assume there are no unpaid cumulative dividends.

E–4. One hundred shares of $100 par value common stock are issued to the promoters of a corporation in exchange for land (which cost the promoters $7,000 one year ago) needed by the corporation for use as a plant site. Experienced appraisers recently estimated the value of the land to be $8,500. What journal entry would be appropriate to record the acquisition of the land?

E–5. James Corporation owes a trade creditor $12,000 on open account which it does not have sufficient cash to pay. The trade creditor suggests that James Corporation issue to him 1,000 shares of the company's $10 par value common stock, which is currently selling on the market at $12. What might prevent the James Corporation from engaging in this apparently quite desirable and advantageous transaction? If this bar did not exist, and the James Corporation did issue the shares as suggested by the creditor, present the entry or entries that should be made on James Corporation's books.

E–6. Why would a corporation ever consider issuing stock having a par value of $10,000 as payment in full of a bill for legal services rendered of $7,500? If such a transaction occurred, give the journal entry to record it.

E–7. The stockholders' equity section of the Aspen Company's balance sheet is as follows:

Paid-In Capital:

Common stock without par value, $5 stated value; authorized, 100,000 shares, issued and outstanding, 20,000 shares	$100,000
Subscribed but not issued, 20,000 shares	100,000
Paid-in capital in excess of stated value	40,000
Paid-In Capital	$240,000
Retained earnings	60,000
	$300,000

Compute the average price at which the common stock was subscribed. Compute the book value per share of common stock.

PROBLEMS, SERIES A

P15–1–A. On July 1, 1981, the Walters Company was authorized to issue 10,000 shares of $25 par value common stock. On July 7, subscriptions for 1,000 shares at $30 per share were received. The subscription contract required a 10 percent immediate payment, with the remainder due on July 31. No stock certificates were to be issued until the subscriptions were paid in full.

Required:

a. Present the entries to record all transactions during July 1981. Subscriptions were collected when due.

b. Present the July 1981 entries assuming the stock is without par value.

c. Present the entries for July 7, 1981, if the subscriptions for the stock without par value were accompanied with cash payment in full and the stock was issued.

P15–2–A. On July 3, 1981, the Dobbs Company was authorized to issue 10,000 shares of common stock, and 2,000 shares were issued immediately to the promoters of the company for cash at $20 per share. Another 200 shares were issued to the promoters for services rendered in organizing the company.

On July 5, 1981, $500 worth of legal and printing costs were paid. These costs related to securing the corporate charter and the stock certificates.

On July 10 subscriptions were received from the general public for 3,000 shares at $18 per share, with one half of the subscription price paid in cash immediately. The balance is due August 10, 1981.

Required:

a. Prepare the balance sheet of the Dobbs Company as of the close of July 10, 1981, assuming the authorized stock has a $10 par value.

b. Repeat *(a)* assuming the stock is without par value but is to have a $15 stated value.

c. Repeat *(a)* assuming the stock is without par or stated value.

P15–3–A. The Cowles Company issued all of its 2,000 shares of authorized preferred stock on July 1, 1979, at $103 per share. The preferred stock is without par value, has a stated value of $2.50 per share, is entitled to a cumulative basic preference dividend of $6 per share, is callable at $105 beginning in 1985, and is entitled to $100 per share in liquidation plus cumulative dividends. Cowles also issued its 4,000 authorized shares of common stock without par value but with a $10 stated value on this date at $50 per share.

On June 30, 1981, the end of its second fiscal year of operations, the company's retained earnings amounted to $70,000. No dividends have been declared or paid on either class of stock since the date of issue.

Required:

a. Prepare the stockholders' equity section of the Cowles Company's June 30, 1981, balance sheet.

b. Compute the book value in total and per share of each class of stock as of June 30, 1981, assuming the preferred stock is nonparticipating.

c. If $55,000 of dividends are to be declared as of June 30, 1981, compute the amount payable to each class of stock assuming the preferred stock is nonparticipating.

d. Repeat *(c)* assuming the preferred stock is entitled to participate equally on a share-for-share basis with the common stock in any dividends declared in any fiscal year in excess of $4 per share of common stock.

P15–4–A. On July 1, 1981, the Suffock Corporation received authorization to issue 20,000 shares of common stock without par value. On that date subscriptions were received from the general public for 7,000 shares at $30 per share. Also, on the same date, 1,000 shares were issued to Mr. Suffock and his sons for services rendered and costs incurred in organizing the corporation. The following transactions occurred during the remainder of the month of July.

July 10 Received subscriptions for another 3,000 shares at $32 per share and collected one third of each of the July 1 subscriptions for 7,000 shares.

11 Issued 2,000 shares in exchange for a tract of land.

20 Collected the balance of each of the July 1 subscriptions and issued the shares. Also, collected one half of each of the July 10 subscriptions.

30 Collected the balance of each of the July 10 subscriptions and issued the shares.

Required:

a. Assume that on September 1, 1981, the board of directors placed a stated value of $10 per share on the common stock. Present journal entries to record all of the July transactions and the entry needed on September 1.

b. Prepare journal entries to record all of the July transactions assuming that the stock issued was $25 par value stock.

P15–5–A. The Wilde Company was authorized to issue 2,000 shares of preferred stock, par value $50, and 10,000 shares of common stock, par value $20.

WILDE COMPANY
Post-Closing Account Balances
December 31, 1981

Organization costs	$ 65,000
Inventory	48,000
Common stock subscribed, 4,000 shares	80,000
Buildings and equipment	100,000
Accumulated depreciation	20,000
Cash	98,000
Accounts payable	12,000
Preferred stock, $50 par; 2,000 shares authorized, issued, and outstanding	100,000

Accounts receivable	122,000
Common stock, $20 par; 10,000 shares authorized, 6,000 shares issued and outstanding	120,000
Paid-in capital in excess of par—common	8,000
Notes payable (due June 30, 1982)	50,000
Unexpired insurance	11,500
Subscriptions receivable—common	38,400
Paid-in capital in excess of par—preferred	3,000
Retained earnings	?

Required:

From the above list of accounts and balances, present in good form the December 31, 1981, balance sheet.

P15–6–A. *Part 1.* On January 1, 1977, the retained earnings of the Finlay Company were $70,000. Net earnings for the succeeding five years were as follows:

1977	$49,000
1978	30,000
1979	2,000
1980	11,000
1981	46,000

The outstanding capital stock of the corporation consisted of 2,000 shares of $4 preferred stock with a par value of $100 per share and 8,000 shares of common stock without par value having a stated value of $50 per share. No dividends were in arrears as of January 1, 1977.

Required:

Prepare schedules showing how the net earnings for the above five years were distributed to the two classes of stock if, in each of the years, the entire current earnings (and only these earnings) were distributed as dividends and the preferred stock was:

a. Cumulative and nonparticipating.

b. Cumulative and participating on the basis of $0.02 per share of dividends to the preferred stock for every $0.01 per share of dividends paid to the common stock over $4 per share per calendar year.

c. Noncumulative and participating as in *(b)*.

d. Noncumulative and nonparticipating.

Part 2. In 1982 the board of directors and stockholders decided to dissolve the Finlay Company. All of its assets were sold, its liabilities were liquidated, and $480,000 remained for distribution to stockholders. No dividends were in arrears, and current dividends had been paid.

Required:

Prepare short schedules showing how the cash was distributed to the stockholders if—

a. The preferred stock was preferred as to assets and entitled to $105 in liquidation.

b. The preferred stock was not preferred as to assets.

P15–7–A. The McCord Company received its charter on April 1, 1981, authorizing it to issue 5,000 shares of $100 par value, $4 cumulative, convertible preferred stock; 10,000 shares of $1.50 cumulative preferred stock without par value having a stated value of $5 per share and a liquidation value of $25 per share; and 100,000 shares of common stock without par or stated value.

On April 2 promoters of the corporation acquired 50,000 shares of the common stock for cash of $10 per share, and 200 shares were issued to an attorney for services rendered in organizing the corporation. On April 3 the company issued all of its authorized shares of $4 convertible preferred stock for land valued at $200,000 and a building valued at $600,000. The property was subject to a mortgage of $300,000.

On April 4 subscriptions for 5,000 shares of the $1.50 preferred stock were received at $26 per share, with one half of the subscription price paid in cash. On April 8 the remaining 5,000 shares of $1.50 preferred stock were issued to an inventor for a patent. A subscription for 1,000 shares of common stock at $10 per share was also received, with a cash payment of $1,000 accompanying the subscription.

On April 25 the balance due on the April 4 subscriptions was collected and the shares issued. By April 30 the subscriber to 1,000 shares of common stock had failed to pay the balance of her subscription, which she had agreed to pay in ten days. Shares were issued for her down payment, and the balance of the contract was canceled.

Required:

a. Prepare general journal entries for the above transactions.

b. Prepare the stockholders' equity section of the April 30, 1981, balance sheet. Assume a deficit of $10,000.

c. Assume that each share of the $4 convertible preferred stock was convertible into six shares of common stock and that all of the preferred was converted on September 1, 1984. Give the required journal entry.

P15–8–A. Littleton, Inc., is a corporation in which all of the outstanding preferred and common stock is held by four Littleton brothers. The brothers have an agreement stating that the remaining brothers will, upon the death of a brother, purchase from his estate his holdings of stock in the company at book value. The agreement also stipulates that the land owned by the company be valued at fair market value, that inventory be valued at its current replacement cost, and that whatever other adjustments are needed to place the accounts on a sound accounting basis be made prior to computing book value.

The stockholders' equity accounts of the company on June 30, 1981, the date of the death of William Littleton, show:

Preferred stock, 6%, $100 par value, liquidation value $100; 2,000 shares authorized, issued, and outstanding	$200,000
Paid-in capital in excess of par—preferred	10,000
Common stock without par value, stated value, $5; 30,000 shares authorized, issued, and outstanding	150,000
Paid-in capital from recapitalization	150,000
Retained earnings	20,000
	$530,000

The fair market value of the land held by the company and carried in its accounts at $20,000 is $50,000, and the current replacement cost of the inventory is $16,000 more than the amount at which it is carried in the accounts, although no improper accounting is involved. It is also agreed by the three remaining brothers and the accountant representing Mrs. William Littleton that the accounts fail to include a proper accrued liability of $10,000 for pensions payable to employees. No dividends have been paid on the preferred stock, which is cumulative and nonparticipating, in the last six months. William Littleton held, at the time of his death, 1,000 shares of preferred stock and 5,000 shares of common stock of the company.

Required:

Compute the amount which the remaining brothers must pay to the estate of William Littleton for the preferred and common stock which he held at the time of his death.

PROBLEMS, SERIES B

P15–1–B. In the charter granted January 2, 1981, the Sullivan Corporation was authorized to issue 1,000 shares of common stock without par value. Subscription agreements called for immediate payment of one half of each subscription, with the remainder due on the first day of the following month. All subscriptions were collected in accordance with the agreements.

On January 5 subscriptions for 600 shares at $48 per

share were received, and on May 1 an additional 200 shares were subscribed at $60 per share.

Required:

a. Present the entries to record all the transactions of January through May 1981, assuming no stock was issued until the subscriptions were paid in full.

b. Present the May 31, 1981, balance sheet assuming there were no transactions other than those described above.

P15–2–B. In the corporate charter which it received on May 1, 1981, the Mansfield Company was authorized to issue 10,000 shares of common stock. The company issued 1,000 shares immediately to two of the promoters for $25 per share, cash.

On May 2 the company issued 200 shares of stock and paid $1,000 cash to a lawyer for legal services rendered in organizing the corporation and billed at $5,000. On May 3 subscriptions, accompanied by a 10 percent down payment, were received from the general public for 6,000 shares at $20 per share. On May 4 the company issued 2,000 shares to the principal promoter of the corporation in exchange for a patent. Another 100 shares were issued to this same person for costs incurred and services rendered in bringing the corporation into existence.

Required:

a. Prepare a balance sheet for the Mansfield Company as of May 4, 1981, assuming the authorized stock had a par value of $20 per share.

b. Prepare the stockholders' equity section of the May 4 balance sheet assuming the stock authorized had no par value but had a $10 per share stated value.

c. Repeat **(b)** assuming the stock authorized had neither par nor stated value.

P15–3–B. On January 2, 1980, the date the Jason Company received its charter, it issued all of its authorized 2,000 shares of preferred stock without par value at $104 and all of its 8,000 authorized shares of common stock without par value but with a stated value of $1 at $40 per share. The preferred stock had a stated value of $5 per share, was entitled to a basic cumulative preference dividend of $6 per share, was callable at $106 beginning in 1982, and was entitled to $100 per share plus cumulative dividends in the event of liquidation.

On December 31, 1981, the end of the second year of operations, retained earnings were $60,000. No dividends had been declared or paid on either class of stock.

Required:

a. Prepare the stockholders' equity section of the Jason Company's December 31, 1981, balance sheet.

b. Compute the book value of each class of stock, assuming the preferred stock is nonparticipating.

c. If $50,000 of dividends were declared as of December 31, 1981, compute the amount payable to each class of stock assuming the preferred stock is nonparticipating.

d. Repeat **(c)** assuming the preferred stock is entitled to participate equally on a share-for-share basis with the common stock in any dividends declared in any calendar year in excess of $2 per share of common stock.

P15–4–B. The Moore Company was authorized on September 1, 1981, to issue 100,000 shares of common stock without par value. On this date subscriptions for 60,000 shares were received from the public at $4 per share, with cash payment in full accompanying the subscriptions. Subsequent transactions were as follows:

Sept. 2 5,000 shares were issued to the three promoters for legal fees, accounting services, printing costs, state incorporation fees, and other costs incurred in promoting the corporation.

5 Certificates covering the shares subscribed for on September 1 were issued, as per stock transfer agent's report.

8 Subscriptions for an additional 20,000 shares were received at $4.50 per share.

9 10,000 shares were issued to one of the promoters for certain patents which the promoter held and believed were worth $50,000.

Oct. 1 The subscriptions of September 8 were collected in full.

5 Certificates covering the subscriptions of September 8 were issued.

9 The board of directors established a stated value of $2 per share on the common stock.

Required:

a. Present journal entries for the above transactions.

b. Present the October 9, 1981, balance sheet assuming no transactions other than those given above.

P15–5–B. Hinson, Inc., was authorized to issue 2,000 shares of $2.50 cumulative preferred stock, par value $50, and 20,000 shares of common stock, par value $25.

HINSON, INC.
Post-Closing Account Balances
December 31, 1981

Paid-in capital in excess of par—	
preferred	$ 5,000
Accounts payable...........................	30,000
Inventory	100,000
Unexpired insurance	3,000
Organization costs	50,000

Common stock subscribed, 2,000 shares	50,000
Subscriptions receivable—common	40,000
Buildings and equipment	120,000
Notes payable, due June 30, 1982	15,000
Cash	60,000
Accumulated depreciation	20,000
Preferred stock, $50 par value; 2,000 shares authorized	100,000
Paid-in capital in excess of par— common	12,000
Common stock, $25 par value; 20,000 shares authorized	200,000
Accounts receivable	152,000
Retained earnings	?

Required:

From the above list of account balances, prepare the December 31, 1981, balance sheet in good form.

P15–6–B. *Part 1.* The outstanding capital stock of the Longley Corporation consisted of 4,000 shares of $6 preferred stock, $100 par value, and 40,000 shares of $50 stated value common stock. The preferred was issued at $103, the common at $60. On January 1, 1977, the retained earnings of the company were $100,000. During the succeeding five years net earnings were as follows:

1977	$192,000
1978	128,000
1979	12,000
1980	40,000
1981	160,000

No dividends were in arrears as of January 1, 1977, and during the five years 1977–81, the board of directors declared dividends in each year equal to the net earnings of the year.

Required:

Prepare a schedule showing the dividends declared each year on each class of stock assuming the preferred stock is:

a. Cumulative and nonparticipating.

b. Cumulative and participating on the basis of $0.02 per share of dividends to the preferred stock for every $0.01 per share of dividends declared on the common stock over $3 per share per calendar year.

c. Noncumulative and participating as in *(b)*.

d. Noncumulative and nonparticipating.

Part 2. In 1982 the board of directors, with stockholder approval, decided to dissolve the Longley Corporation. All of its assets were sold, its liabilities were liquidated, and $1,780,000 of cash remained for distribution to the

stockholders. No dividends were in arrears at liquidation, and current dividends had been paid.

Required:

Prepare short schedules showing the amount of cash to be distributed to each class of stock if—

a. The preferred stock has a preference as to assets in the event of liquidation over the common stock in the amount of $105 per share plus cumulative dividends.

b. The preferred stock has no preference to assets in liquidation.

P15–7–B. Jay Company, on May 1, 1981, received a charter which authorized it to issue:

1. 2,000 shares of preferred stock without par value to which a stated value of $3 per share was assigned. The stock was entitled to a cumulative dividend of $2.40, convertible into two shares of common stock, callable at $52, and entitled to $50 per share in liquidation.
2. 1,000 shares of $100 par value, $5 cumulative preferred stock which is callable at $105 and entitled to $103 in liquidation.
3. 100,000 shares of common stock without par value to which a stated value of $10 was assigned.

Transactions:

May	1	All of the $2.40 convertible preferred was subscribed for and issued at $51 per share, cash.
	2	All of the $5 cumulative preferred was exchanged for inventory, land, and buildings valued at $22,000, $25,000, and $55,000, respectively.
	2	Subscriptions were received for 50,000 shares of common at $20 per share, with 10 percent of the subscription price paid immediately in cash.
	3	Cash of $3,000 was paid to reimburse promoters for costs incurred for accounting, legal, and printing services. In addition, 1,000 shares of common stock were issued to the promoters for their services.
	31	All of the subscriptions to the common stock were collected and the shares issued.

Required:

a. Prepare journal entries for the above transactions.

b. Assume that retained earnings were $50,000. Prepare the stockholders' equity section of the May 31, 1981 balance sheet.

c. On June 30, 1985, the company called and retired all of the $5 cumulative preferred stock, and all of the $2.40 convertible preferred stock was converted into common stock. Give the required journal entries, assuming no cumulative dividends were in arrears.

P15–8–B. Bernice Corporation has an agreement with each of its 5 preferred and 10 common stockholders that in the event of the death of a stockholder, it will purchase at book value from the stockholder's estate or heirs the shares of Bernice Corporation stock held by the deceased at the time of death. The book value is to be computed in accordance with generally accepted accounting principles.

Following is the stockholders' equity section of the Bernice Corporation's December 31, 1981, balance sheet:

$5 preferred stock without par value, $10 stated value; 1,000 shares authorized, issued, and outstanding	$ 10,000
Common stock, $20 par value; 20,000 shares authorized, issued, and outstanding	400,000
Paid-in capital in excess of stated value— preferred	100,000
Paid-in capital in excess of par value— common	20,000
Retained earnings	200,000
	$730,000

The preferred stock is cumulative and entitled to $100 per share plus cumulative dividends in liquidation. No dividends have been paid for 1½ years.

A stockholder, owner of 100 shares of preferred stock and 1,000 shares of common stock, died on December 31, 1981. You have been employed by the stockholder's widow to compute the book value of each class of stock and to determine the price to be paid for the stock held by her late husband. In reviewing the corporation's records you discover that machinery costing $10,000 on December 27, 1981, had been charged to expense and that the December 31, 1981, inventory was understated by $2,500.

Required:

Prepare a schedule showing the computation of the amount to be paid for the deceased stockholder's holdings of Bernice preferred and common stock.

BUSINESS DECISION PROBLEM 15–1

Robert Douglas recently inherited $40,000 cash which he wishes to invest in one of the following securities: common stock of the Duffy Corporation or common stock of the Gaylord Corporation. Both corporations manufacture the same types of products and have been in existence for five years. The stockholders' equity sections of the two corporations' latest balance sheets are shown below:

DUFFY CORPORATION

Common stock, $10 par value, authorized issued, and outstanding 30,000 shares	$300,000
Retained earnings	300,000
Total Stockholders' Equity	$600,000

GAYLORD CORPORATION

Preferred stock, $100 par value, 8% cumulative and nonparticipating 2,000 shares	$200,000
Common stock, $10 par value, 40,000 shares authorized, issued, and outstanding	400,000
Retained earnings	30,000
Total Stockholders' Equity	$630,000

The Duffy Corporation has paid a cash dividend of $0.50 per share each year since its creation; its common stock is currently selling for $50 per share. The Gaylord Corporation's common stock is currently selling for $40 per share. The current year's dividend and three prior years' dividends on the preferred stock are in arrears. The preferred stock has a liquidation value of $100 per share.

Required:

a. What is the book value per share of the Duffy Corporation common stock and the Gaylord Corporation common stock? Is book value the major determinant of the stock prices?

b. Based solely upon the above information, which investment would you recommend? Why?

BUSINESS DECISION PROBLEM 15–2

Southern Company and Northern Company are two companies which have extremely stable net earnings of $6,000,000 and $4,000,000, respectively. Both companies distribute all their net earnings as dividends each year. Southern Company has 100,000 shares of $100 par value, 6 percent preferred stock and 500,000 shares of $10 par value common stock outstanding. Northern Company has 50,000 shares of $50 par value, 8 percent preferred stock and 400,000 shares of $5 par value common stock out-

standing. Both preferred stocks are cumulative and non-participating.

Required:

a. Compute the annual dividend per share of preferred stock and per share of common stock for each company.

b. Based solely upon the above information, which common stock would you predict to have the higher market price per share? Why?

BUSINESS DECISION PROBLEM 15–3

Rogers and Hart are partners. At December 31, 1981, they decide to incorporate as of January 2, 1982, under the name of R and H, Inc. In the partnership, Rogers and Hart shared earnings equally. At December 31, 1981, their balance sheet was as follows:

ROGERS AND HART
Balance Sheet
December 31, 1981

Assets

Cash	$ 15,000
Receivables	31,000
Inventory	25,000
Plant and equipment	49,000
Total Assets	$120,000

Liabilities and Owners' Equity

Accounts payable	$ 10,000
Rogers, capital	55,000
Hart, capital	55,000
Total Liabilities and Owners' Equity	$120,000

The partners agreed to the following valuations of non-cash assets for transfer to the corporation: receivables, $30,000; inventory, $15,000; and plant and equipment, $55,000. After the partnership assets have been revalued, the assets and liabilities are transferred to the corporation in exchange for its stock. Each partner is to receive capital stock with a par value equal to the balance in the partner's capital account after adjustment. The corporation's charter authorizes it to issue 15,000 shares of $10 par value common stock.

Required:

a. How many shares of stock should Rogers and Hart each receive?

b. What journal entry is required to record the issuance of stock in exchange for the partnership's assets and liabilities?

Chapter 16

Corporations: Paid-in capital,

retained earnings, dividends,

and treasury stock

The preceding chapter dealt with paid-in capital resulting from the issuance of shares of stock for cash or other property or services. Attention is now directed to other sources of paid-in capital and other matters affecting stockholders' equity.

PAID-IN (OR CONTRIBUTED) CAPITAL

The term *paid-in capital,* or *contributed capital,* is a term embracing capital acquired from several different sources. No single account entitled Paid-In Capital is maintained in the ledger; instead, a separate account is established for each source of capital. Each of these accounts could carry the words paid-in capital in its title. For example, the Common Stock and the Preferred Stock accounts could quite properly be titled Paid-In Capital—Common Stock and Paid-In Capital—Preferred Stock, since both accounts record capital contributions made by stockholders. The shorter titles are used in this text because of their widespread acceptance in practice. Illustration 16.1 presents in sum-

Illustration 16.1: Sources of stockholders' equity

Source of stockholders' equity	Illustrative general ledger account titles
I. Capital contributed	
A. For, or assigned to, shares:	
1. To the extent of par or stated value or the amount received for shares without par or stated value.	Common Stock 5 Percent Preferred Stock
2. In addition to par or stated value:	
a. In excess of par.	Paid-In Capital in Excess of Par Value—Common (Preferred)
b. In excess of stated value.	Paid-In Capital in Excess of Stated Value—Common (Preferred)
c. Resulting from reduction in par or stated value of shares.	Paid-In Capital—Recapitalization
d. Resulting from reissue of treasury stock at a price above its acquisition price.	Paid-In Capital—Common (Preferred) Treasury Stock Transactions
B. Other than for shares, whether from shareholders or from others.	Paid-In Capital—Donations
II. Capital accumulated by retention of earnings.	Retained Earnings or Retained Income

mary form several sources of stockholders' equity and illustrative titles for general ledger accounts to be used to record increases and decreases in capital from each of these sources.

To illustrate the need for separate accounts to show the sources of the various types of paid-in capital, assume that a corporation issued both its preferred stock and common stock at various times and at differing premiums, aggregating $25,000 on the preferred stock and $15,000 on the common stock. If only one premium account (Paid-In Capital in Excess of Par) were established, it would not be obvious that the capital contributed by the preferred stockholders was the par value of the preferred stock plus the premium of $25,000. Nor could the capital contributed by the common stockholders be readily identified as being the par value of the common stock plus the premium of $15,000. If separate accounts for the premiums have not been maintained, a proper accounting for the retirement of all or a part of the outstanding preferred stock may not be possible without extensive review of prior years' records.

The accounts shown opposite the sources listed under IA in Illustration 16.1 represent amounts paid in by either past or present stockholders of the corporation. The contributions of capital represented by the Paid-In Capital—Donations account may have come from either stockholders or other donors, such as a chamber of commerce which has donated a plant site as a means of attracting industry to the community. Regardless of the specific source, paid-in capital is regarded as the relatively permanent portion of the stockholders' equity. On the other hand, retained earnings—typically the source of dividend distributions—is regarded as the relatively temporary portion of corporate capital. (To the extent that accumulated earnings remain undistributed over a long period of time, however, there is a degree of permanence also in the retained earnings element of the stockholders' equity.)

Paid-in capital— recapitalization

A corporation may find it necessary to make a change in its capitalization. For example, a company having 5,000 shares of common stock with a par value of $100 may find that it cannot issue additional shares at $100 because the shares will not sell at that price. To avoid issuing shares at a discount, the company decides to reduce the par value of its stock to $80. The entry to record the exchange of all the $100 shares for the new $80 shares is:

```
Common Stock—$100 Par .....................................  500,000
    Common Stock—$80 Par ...................................           400,000
    Paid-In Capital from Recapitalization .....................           100,000
  To record the exchange of 5,000 new $80 par common
  shares for 5,000 old $100 par common shares.
```

Paid-in capital— treasury stock transactions

If a corporation reacquires shares of its own outstanding capital stock at one price and later reissues them at a higher price, the corporate capital is increased by the difference between the two prices. If the reissue price is less than acquisition cost, corporate capital is decreased. Treasury stock transactions are treated at length later in this chapter.

Paid-in capital— donations

Occasionally a corporation receives gifts of assets—a gift of land from a chamber of commerce is an example. Such gifts represent *donated capital*. They increase corporate capital but not through earnings or transactions involving capital stock. The entry to record the gift of a $5,000 land site is a debit to Land and a credit to Paid-In Capital—Donations, regardless of whether the donor is a stockholder or not. The entry should be in the amount of the fair market value of the gift when received.

Dividends—withdrawals of capital by stockholders through formal action of the board of directors—are normally reductions of retained earnings. Dividends from paid-in capital are unusual. If paid-in capital is being distributed, such dividends are *liquidating dividends* and serve to reduce the "permanent" portion of the stockholders' equity. The corporation should disclose to its stockholders the source of those dividends which are not distributions of earnings. The legality of such dividends depends upon the precise source of the capital and upon the laws of the state of incorporation.

RETAINED EARNINGS

In general, the stockholders' equity or interest in a corporation is made up of two elements: (1) paid-in (or contributed) capital and (2) retained earnings. *Retained earnings* is the term used to describe the increase in stockholders' equity resulting from profitable operation of the corporation. As such, it indicates the source of certain assets received but not distributed to stockholders as dividends. Thus, both categories indicate the source of assets received by the corporation—actual investment by the stockholders and investment by the stockholders in the sense of earnings not yet withdrawn. For present purposes, the balance in the Retained Earnings account will be viewed as the net earnings of the corporation from the date of incorporation to the present less the sum of dividends declared during the same period.

When the Retained Earnings account has a debit balance, a *deficit* exists. It is shown under that title as a negative amount in the stockholders' equity section of the balance sheet. The net effect of having a deficit is that net assets have been decreased rather than increased as a result of operations and dividend declarations. The title of the general ledger account need not be changed merely because it contains a debit balance.

At the end of the accounting period the net earnings or loss of a corporation as shown in the earnings statement is transferred to retained earnings. This is done in the entry which closes the Expense and Revenue Summary account. Retained Earnings is credited for the amount of net earnings or debited for the amount of net loss. Since dividends reduce the capital accumulated through retention of earnings, they are also debited to Retained Earnings.

PAID-IN CAPITAL AND RETAINED EARNINGS IN THE BALANCE SHEET

The following stockholders' equity section of a balance sheet illustrates the presentation of the various sources of capital:

Paid-In Capital:

Preferred stock, 6% $100 par value;			
authorized, issued, and outstanding, 4,000 shares		$ 400,000	
Common stock without par value,			
stated value $5 per share; authorized, issued, and			
outstanding, 200,000 shares		1,000,000	$1,400,000
Paid-in capital in excess of par or stated value:			
From preferred stock issuances		$ 40,000	
From recapitalization of common stock		1,000,000	
From donations		10,000	1,050,000
Total Paid-In Capital			$2,450,000
Retained earnings			500,000
Total Stockholders' Equity			$2,950,000

In highly condensed published balance sheets, the details regarding the sources of the paid-in capital in excess of par or stated value are often omitted and replaced by a single item, such as:

Paid-in capital in excess of par or stated value $1,050,000

RETAINED EARNINGS APPROPRIATIONS

A *retained earnings appropriation* is a segregation or subdivision of retained earnings and is recorded by a debit to Retained Earnings and a credit to a properly named retained earnings appropriation account. The reason for the establishment of the appropriation often is indicated by the title of the appropriation account. Transferring a part of retained earnings to appropriated retained earnings has the purpose and effect of limiting dividend declarations to the remaining balance—the free or unappropriated retained earnings. It does *not* segregate a sum of cash for the purpose indicated, but does reduce the amount available for dividends. The result is that more cash is likely to be on hand for the intended purpose. In other words, the creation of a retained earnings appropriation informs stockholders that a certain amount of the assets brought into the corporation through the earning process is not to be distributed to stockholders as dividends. But no cash is being set aside by the entry. Retained earnings appropriations are established by action of the board of directors, voluntarily or in accordance with the provisions of certain contracts such as bond indentures (the contract between the issuer of bonds and the bondholders or their trustee) or loan agreements.

The following entry might be made if a bond indenture requires the restriction of $25,000 of retained earnings:

Retained Earnings	25,000	
Appropriation for Bond Indebtedness		25,000

When the retained earnings appropriation has served its purpose of restricting dividends and the bonds have been paid, it may be returned intact to Retained Earnings at the direction of the board of directors. The entry is simply a debit to the Appropriation for Bond Indebtedness account and a credit to Retained Earnings.

Retained earnings appropriations in the balance sheet

In the balance sheet, retained earnings appropriations should be shown in the stockholders' equity section as follows:

Paid-In Capital:		
Preferred stock, $50 par; 500 shares authorized,		
issued, and outstanding	$25,000	
Common stock, $5 par; 10,000 shares authorized,		
issued, and outstanding	50,000	
Total Paid-In Capital		$ 75,000
Retained Earnings:		
Appropriated:		
For bond indebtedness	$25,000	
Free and unappropriated	20,000	
Total Retained Earnings		45,000
Total Stockholders' Equity		$120,000

Note that the creation of a retained earnings appropriation does not reduce the equity of the stockholders; it merely earmarks (restricts) a portion of that equity for a specific reason.

In previous years, the term "retained earnings reserve" was used instead of "retained earnings appropriation." The latter term makes it more clear that no cash has actually been set aside.

The formal recording and reporting of retained earnings appropriations is decreasing and is being replaced by footnote explanations such as the following:

Note 7.   Retained earnings restrictions. According to provisions in the bond indenture, retained earnings available for dividends are limited to $20,000.

A formal entry normally is made only when required by contract or law.

THE STATEMENT OF RETAINED EARNINGS

Most corporations include four financial statements in their annual reports to stockholders. These statements are a balance sheet, an earnings statement, a statement of retained earnings, and a statement of changes in financial position (to be discussed in Chapter 19). The purpose of the *statement of retained earnings* is to explain the changes in retained earnings that occurred between two balance sheet dates. Usually, these changes consist of the addition of net earnings (or deduction of net loss) and the deduction of dividends and appropriations. A typical statement of retained earnings is shown in Illustration 16.2: Statement of retained earnings

Illustration 16.2:
Statement of retained earnings

WARD CORPORATION Statement of Retained Earnings For Year Ended December 31, 1981		
Unappropriated retained earnings:		
January 1, 1981 balance		$180,000
Add: Net earnings		80,000
		$260,000
Less: Dividends	$25,000	
Appropriation for plant expansion	25,000	50,000
Unappropriated retained earnings,		
December 31, 1981		$210,000
Appropriated retained earnings:		
Appropriation for plant expansion,		
balance, January 1, 1981	$50,000	
Appropriated in 1981	25,000	
Appropriated retained earnings,		
December 31, 1981		75,000
Total Retained Earnings, December 31, 1981		$285,000

DIVIDENDS

Dividends are distributions of earnings by a corporation to its stockholders. The normal dividend is a cash dividend, but additional shares of the corporation's own capital stock may also be distributed as dividends.

Since they are the means whereby the owners of a corporation share in the earnings of the corporation, dividends usually are charged against retained earnings. They must be declared by the board of directors and recorded in the minutes book. The significant dates concerning dividends are the date of *declaration,* the date of *record,* and the date of *payment.* For example, the board of directors of the Allan Corporation may declare on June 5, 1981, a cash dividend of $1.25 per share to stockholders of record on July 1, 1981, payable on July 10. The *date of declaration* is the date the board takes action in the form of a motion that dividends be paid, creating the liability for dividends payable. The *date of record* is the date established by the board to determine to whom the dividends will be paid. The stockholders on the date of record are determined from the corporation's records (a subsidiary stockholders' ledger). The *date of payment* is the date of actual payment of the dividend.

Cash dividends   If a quarterly cash dividend (of 2 percent) on $100,000 (1,000 shares of $100 par value) of 8 percent preferred stock is declared on January 21, 1981, to stockholders of record on February 5, 1981, to be paid on March 1, 1981, the entries at the declaration and payment dates are as follows:

Jan. 21	Retained Earnings 2,000	
	Dividends Payable	2,000
	Dividends declared: 2 percent on $100,000 of outstanding preferred stock, payable March 1, 1981, to stockholders of record on February 5, 1981.	
Mar. 1	Dividends Payable 2,000	
	Cash	2,000
	Paid the dividend declared on January 21, 1981.	

No entry is made on the date of record.

When a cash dividend is declared, some companies debit a Dividends account instead of Retained Earnings; at the end of the fiscal year, the Dividends account is closed to Retained Earnings. Both methods are acceptable.

Once a cash dividend is declared and notice of the dividend is given to the stockholders, it cannot be rescinded unless all stockholders agree to such action. A legally declared cash dividend is a current liability of the corporation.

Stock dividends   A corporation may declare a dividend calling for the distribution of additional shares of its capital stock. Stock dividend declarations usually call for the distribution of additional shares of the same class of stock as that held by the stockholders—in other words, additional common stock to common stockholders. The effect of the distribution of a stock dividend usually is to transfer a sum from retained earnings to permanent paid-in capital. The amount transferred for stock dividends is usually the fair market value of the distributed shares. Most states permit the use of retained earnings or paid-in capital from any other source (other than amounts already credited to capital stock) for stock dividends. But if the purpose of a stock dividend is to capitalize retained earnings, the source of the dividend should be retained earnings.

Stock dividends have no effect on the total amount of stockholders' equity. They merely decrease retained earnings and increase paid-in capital by an equal amount or transfer amounts between paid-in capital accounts. Immediately after the declaration and distribution of a stock dividend, each share of similar stock has a lower book value per share. This is because more shares are outstanding with no increase in total stockholders' equity.

Stock dividends do not affect the individual stockholder's percentage ownership in the corporation. For example, if a stockholder owns 1,000 shares in a corporation having 100,000 shares of stock outstanding, that stockholder owns 1 percent of the outstanding shares. After a 10 percent stock dividend, the stockholder will still own 1 percent of the outstanding shares—1,100 of 110,000 outstanding.

Reasons for declaring a stock dividend include:

1. Retained earnings may have become large relative to total stockholders' equity, or the corporation may simply desire a larger permanent capitalization.
2. The market price of the stock may have risen above a desirable trading range, or the corporation may wish to have a larger number of stockholders and expects to increase their number by increasing the number of shares outstanding.
3. Stock dividends may be used as a means for quieting stockholders' demands for dividends from a corporation which does not have sufficient cash to pay cash dividends.

Stock splits

The Committee on Accounting Procedure of the American Institute of Certified Public Accountants has distinguished between stock dividends and stock splits. A distribution of shares greater than 20 to 25 percent of the previously outstanding shares is assumed to have the goal of reducing the market price of the shares by increasing the number of shares outstanding and is treated as a *stock split*.

There are a number of ways of accounting for a stock split, depending on the particular circumstances. If the board of directors reduces the par or stated value of shares, only the number of shares outstanding and the par or stated value need to be changed on the records. Thus, a two for one stock split in which the par value of the shares is decreased from $20 to $10 could be recorded as follows:

Common Stock—$20 par value 100,000
    Common Stock—$10 par value   100,000
   To record a two for one stock split. 5,000 shares of $20 par value common stock were replaced by 10,000 shares of $10 par value common stock.

But a corporation may wish to double the number of its outstanding shares without changing the par or stated value of the shares. To do this, it declares a 100 percent stock dividend. It does not change the par value per share. Whenever a distribution of shares occurs and the par or stated value of the shares is not changed, the distribution is generally described as a stock dividend. But such "stock dividends" of over 20–25 percent of the previously outstanding shares are *accounted for* as stock splits. They are looked upon as capital transactions, to be kept in the capital accounts, rather than as dividends that are properly charged against Retained Earnings. The shares issued are credited to the capital stock account in an amount equal to the total par or stated value. The debit is entered in other paid-in capital accounts, to the extent possible, and in Retained Earnings only as a last resort. Thus, the net effect of a 100 percent stock dividend declared and paid by Walt

Disney Productions in 1973 on its 14,276,173 shares of $1.25 par value common stock was to transfer approximately $17,845,216 from Paid-In Capital in Excess of Par Value to Capital Stock—Common. The entries actually made could have read:

At Declaration Date

Paid-In Capital in Excess of Par Value—Common	17,845,216	
Stock Dividend Distributable		17,845,216

At Payment Date

Stock Dividend Distributable	17,845,216	
Capital Stock—Common		17,845,216

If no other paid-in capital related to the class of shares issued exists, or exists only in an amount less than the par or stated value of the shares issued, the dividend, if larger than 20–25 percent, is charged in its entirety, or in part, to Retained Earnings. The amount so charged need not exceed the par or stated value of the additional shares issued.

Recording stock dividends

A distribution of shares of less than 20 to 25 percent of the previously outstanding shares is assumed to have little effect on the market value of the shares. Thus, it is to be accounted for at the present market value of the outstanding shares. Assume a corporation is authorized to issue 20,000 shares of $100 par value common stock, of which 8,000 shares are outstanding. Its board of directors now declares a 10 percent stock dividend (800 shares). The market price of the stock is $125 per share immediately before the stock dividend is announced. Since distributions of less than 20–25 percent of the previously outstanding shares are to be accounted for at market value, the entry for the declaration of the dividend is as follows (assuming the dividend was declared on August 10, 1981):

Aug. 10	Retained Earnings	100,000	
	Stock Dividend Distributable—Common		80,000
	Paid-In Capital—Stock Dividend		20,000
	To record the declaration of a 10 percent stock dividend; shares to be distributed on September 20, 1981, to stockholders of record on August 31, 1981.		

The entry to record the issuance of the shares is as follows:

Sept. 20	Stock Dividend Distributable—Common	80,000	
	Common Stock		80,000
	To record distribution of 800 shares of common stock as authorized in stock dividend declared on August 10, 1981.		

Assume Mr. Adams, a stockholder in the company illustrated above, owns 200 shares of the stock before the stock dividend is declared. He will receive 20 shares as a stock dividend. Before the stock dividend he owns 200/8,000 of the outstanding stock; after the dividend, he owns 220/8,800. His percentage ownership of the outstanding stock does not change as a result of the dividend.

Current liabilities usually are paid out of current assets. A *stock dividend distributable (payable)* is not payable with assets; hence, it is not a liability.

If a balance sheet is prepared between the date of declaration of the 10 percent dividend and the date of issuance of the shares, the proper statement presentation of the effects of the stock dividend is as follows:

Paid-In Capital:

Common stock, $100 par value; authorized, 20,000 shares; issued and outstanding, 8,000 shares	$800,000	
Stock dividend distributable on September 20, 1981, 800 shares at par value	80,000	
Total par value of shares issued and to be issued	$880,000	
From capitalization of retained earnings through declaration of stock dividend	20,000	
Total Paid-In Capital		$ 900,000
Retained earnings		150,000
Total Stockholders' Equity		$1,050,000

Suppose that the market price is still $125 per share on the date of declaration, but the common stock is without par value and has a stated value of $50 per share. In this case, the entry to record the declaration of the stock dividend would be:

Retained Earnings	100,000	
Stock Dividend Distributable—Common		40,000
Paid-In Capital—Stock Dividend		60,000

The entry to record the issuance of the stock dividend is:

Stock Dividend Distributable—Common	40,000	
Common Stock		40,000

Legality of dividends

The corporation laws of the states differ in their provisions as to the legality of a dividend. The stated or legal capital of a corporation is established by state law as that portion of the stockholders' equity which must be maintained intact, unimpaired by dividend declarations or other distributions to stockholders. The stated capital often is established at an amount equal to the par value of the shares issued or at an amount equal to a minimum price per share issued. The objective of the statutes in prohibiting the impairment of stated capital by the declaration of dividends is to protect the creditors of the corporation, whose claims are superior to those of stockholders.

The board of directors of a corporation possesses sole power to declare dividends. The *legality* of a dividend generally depends upon the amount of the retained earnings available for dividends—not upon the net earnings of any one period or the condition of the cash balance. The *financial advisability* of declaring a dividend depends on the working capital position of the corporation. Dividends may be paid in periods in which losses are incurred, provided retained earnings and working capital position justify the dividend. In some states, dividends may be declared from current earnings even though there is an accumulated deficit.

TREASURY STOCK

Treasury stock is the corporation's own capital stock, either preferred or common, which has been issued and reacquired by the issuing corporation. It has not been canceled, and it is legally available for reissuance. Treasury stock and unissued capital stock differ in that treasury stock has been issued at some time in the past, whereas unissued capital stock has never been issued.

Treasury stock may be acquired by purchase or in settlement of a debt. The corporation laws of most states consider treasury stock as issued but not outstanding, since the shares are no longer in the possession of stockholders. Treasury shares cannot be voted, and dividends are not paid on them.

Treasury stock may be reissued without violating the preemptive right provisions of the state laws. As previously explained, if additional authorized but unissued shares are to be issued after a lapse of time from the date of original issue, the additional shares (in most states) first must be offered to existing stockholders.

Certain states require that the cost of treasury stock may not exceed the amount of retained earnings at the date of acquisition. Thus, if a corporation is subject to such a law, the retained earnings available for dividends are limited to the amount in excess of the cost of the treasury shares on hand.

Acquisition and reissuance of treasury stock

When treasury stock is acquired, the stock is recorded at cost. Reissues are credited to the Treasury Stock account at the cost of acquisition. The excess of the reissue price over cost is credited to Paid-In Capital—Treasury Stock Transactions because it represents additional paid-in capital.

For example, the Hillside Corporation, whose stockholders' equity consists solely of capital stock and retained earnings, acquires ten shares of its outstanding common stock for $55 each and two months later reissues three shares for $58 each. The entries are:

Treasury Stock—Common (10 × $55)	550	
Cash		550
Acquired ten shares of treasury stock at $55.		
Cash (3 × $58)	174	
Treasury Stock—Common (3 × $55)		165
Paid-In Capital—Treasury Stock Transactions		9
Reissued three shares of treasury stock at $58; cost $55 per share.		

If the reissue price of subsequent shares is less than the acquisition price, the difference is debited to Paid-In Capital—Treasury Stock Transactions. But that account is not permitted to develop a debit balance. By definition, no paid-in capital account can have a debit balance. If the Hillside Corporation reissues an additional two shares at $52 per share, the entry is:

Cash (2 × $52)	104	
Paid-In Capital—Treasury Stock Transactions	6	
Treasury Stock—Common (2 × $55)		110
Reissued two shares of treasury stock at $52; cost $55 per share.		

At this point, the credit balance in the Paid-In Capital—Treasury Stock Transactions account is $3. If the remaining five shares are reissued for $53 per share, the entry is:

Cash (5 × $53)	265	
Paid-In Capital—Treasury Stock Transactions	3	
Retained Earnings	7	
Treasury Stock—Common (5 × $55)		275
Reissued five shares of treasury stock at $53; cost $55 per share.		

Note that the Paid-In Capital—Treasury Stock Transactions account has been exhausted. The remaining $7 of the excess of cost over reissue price is regarded as a special distribution to the stockholders involved and is chargeable to the Retained Earnings account.

Treasury stock in the balance sheet

Treasury stock should not be shown as an asset, since its acquisition reduces the stockholders' equity. The acquisition of treasury stock consists of a return of capital to the stockholder from whom the stock is acquired.

When a corporation acquires its own capital stock as treasury stock, the purpose of the acquisition may be (1) to cancel and retire the stock, (2) to reissue it at a later time at a higher price, (3) to reduce the number of shares outstanding and thereby increase earnings per share, or (4) to use the stock to issue to employees. If the intention of the acquisition is cancellation and retirement, the treasury shares exist as such simply because they have not been retired and canceled by formal reduction of the authorized capital.

When treasury stock is held on a balance sheet date, it customarily is shown in that statement at cost and as a deduction from the sum of the paid-in capital and retained earnings, as follows:

Common stock, authorized and issued, 20,000 shares, par value $10 per share, of which 2,000 shares are in the treasury	$200,000
Retained earnings (including $22,000 restricted by acquisition of treasury stock)	80,000
Total	$280,000
Less: Treasury stock at cost, 2,000 shares	22,000
Total Stockholders' Equity	$258,000

Stockholders' equity in the balance sheet

Much of what has been discussed so far in this chapter can be summarized through presentation of the stockholders' equity section of the balance sheet of a hypothetical corporation (see Illustration 16.3).

The balance sheet shown in Illustration 16.3 shows (1) the amount of capital assigned to shares outstanding; (2) the capital contributed for outstanding shares in addition to that assigned to the shares; (3) other forms of paid-in capital; and (4) retained earnings, appropriated and unappropriated.

NET EARNINGS— INCLUSIONS AND EXCLUSIONS

Accounting has long been plagued by the problem of what should be included in the net earnings reported for a period. Should net earnings include only the revenues and expenses related to normal operations? Or should it include unusual, nonrecurring gains and losses? And further, should the net earnings for 1981, for example, include an item that can be clearly associated with a prior year, such as additional federal income taxes for 1977? Or should such items, including corrections of errors, be carried directly to retained earnings?

APB Opinion No. 9 (December 1966) sought to provide answers to the above questions. It directed that unusual or nonrecurring items that have an earnings or loss effect be classified as extraordinary items (reported in the earnings statement) or as prior period adjustment (reported in the statement of retained earnings). To provide useful information, extraordinary items were to be reported separately after net earnings from regular continuing activities.

Illustration 16.3: Stock-holders' equity section of the balance sheet

HYPOTHETICAL CORPORATION
Partial Balance Sheet
December 31, 1981

Stockholders' Equity

Paid-In Capital:

Preferred stock, $100 per value; 2,000 shares authorized, issued, and outstanding		$ 200,000
Common stock, $10 par value; authorized, 100,000 shares, issued, 80,000 shares of which 1,000 are held in treasury	$800,000	
Stock dividend distributable on common stock on January 15, 1982, 7,900 shares	79,000	879,000
Paid-in capital in excess of par value:		
From common stock issuances	40,000	
From capitalization of retained earnings through stock dividends	60,000	
From treasury stock transactions	30,000	
From donations	50,000	180,000
Total Paid-In Capital		$1,259,000
Retained Earnings:		
Appropriated:		
For bond indebtedness	$250,000	
Unappropriated (restricted to the extent of $20,000, the cost of treasury shares held; see Note A)	150,000	400,000
		$1,659,000
Less: Treasury stock, common, 1,000 shares at cost		20,000
Total Stockholders' Equity		$1,639,000

Note A: The company has been named defendant in a suit seeking damages for injuries allegedly sustained from use of a company product which was allegedly rendered unfit for its intended purpose through negligence in its manufacture. In the opinion of legal counsel, the company's liability in this matter will be nominal at most.

Extraordinary items

Abuses in the financial reporting of gains and losses as *extraordinary items* led to the issuance of *APB Opinion No. 30* (September 1973). In the Opinion, extraordinary items are redefined as those which are unusual in nature *and* which occur infrequently. Note that both conditions must be met—unusual nature and infrequent occurrence. Whether an item is unusual and infrequent is to be determined in the light of the environment in which the firm operates. Examples include gains or losses which are the direct result of a major casualty (a flood), a confiscation of property by a foreign government, or a prohibition under a newly enacted law. Such items are to be included in the determination of periodic net earnings, but disclosed separately (net of their tax effects, if any) in the earnings statement. *FASB Statement No. 4* further directs that gains and losses from the early extinguishment of debt are extraordinary items. Earnings before extraordinary items must be reported and then earnings after extraordinary items as shown in Illustration 16.4. *Earnings before extraordinary items* are earnings from operations less applicable income taxes.

Gains or losses related to ordinary business activities are not extraordinary items regardless of their size. For example, material write-downs of uncollectible receivables, obsolete inventories, and intangible assets are not extraordinary items. But such items may be separately disclosed as part of net earnings from continuing activities.

Illustration 16.4: Earnings statement

ANSON COMPANY
Earnings Statement
For the Year Ended December 31, 1981

Net sales		$41,000,000
Other revenues		2,250,000
Total revenue		$43,250,000
Cost of goods sold	$22,000,000	
Administrative, selling, and general expenses	12,000,000	34,000,000
Net earnings before income taxes		$ 9,250,000
Federal income taxes		4,625,000
Net earnings before extraordinary item and the cumulative effect of an accounting change		$ 4,625,000
Extraordinary item:		
Gain on retirement of debt	40,000	
Less tax effect	20,000	20,000
		$ 4,645,000
Cumulative effect on prior years' earnings of changing to a different depreciation method (net of tax)		20,000
Net Earnings		$ 4,665,000
Earnings per share of common stock:		
Net earnings before extraordinary item and the cumulative effect of an accounting change		$ 4.625
Extraordinary item		.020
Cumulative effect on prior years' earnings of changing to a different depreciation method		.020
Net Earnings		$ 4.665

Prior period adjustments

According to *APB Opinion No. 9, prior period adjustments* were to be reported in the statement of retained earnings. They consisted of those material adjustments which (1) are directly and specifically related to business activities of a prior period, (2) are not the result of economic events occurring after the prior period, (3) result primarily from determinations made by persons outside the business, and (4) could not be estimated with reasonable accuracy prior to this determination.

Examples of prior period adjustments included material assessments or settlements of income taxes, settlements of contracts through renegotiation, amounts paid to settle litigation or other similar claims, and corrections of accounting errors. But *FASB Statement No. 16* (June 1977) changed virtually all of this. Here the Board held that assessments of income taxes and settlements of contracts and litigations were economic events of the year of settlement and involved management determination as well as the actions of outsiders. These settlements then did not qualify as prior period adjustments. They are to be reported in the earnings statement, classified as extraordinary items only if they are unusual and nonrecurring. As a result of the Board's action, prior period adjustments will consist almost solely of corrections of accounting errors.

In the statement of retained earnings (see Illustration 16.5), prior period adjustments are treated as adjustments of the opening balance of retained

**Illustration 16.5:
Statement of retained
earnings**

ANSON COMPANY Statement of Retained Earnings For the Year Ended December 31, 1981	
Retained earnings, January 1, 1981	$5,000,000
Prior period adjustment:	
Correction of error of expensing land (net of tax effect of $100,000)	100,000
Adjusted retained earnings, January 1, 1981	$5,100,000
Add: Net earnings	4,665,000
	$9,765,000
Less: Dividends	500,000
Retained Earnings, December 31, 1981	$9,265,000

earnings. But normal recurring corrections or adjustments, which follow inevitably from the use of estimates in accounting practice, are not to be treated as prior period adjustments.

**Accounting for
tax effects**

Most extraordinary items and prior period adjustments will affect the amount of income taxes payable with the result that questions arise as to proper reporting procedure. To prevent distortions, *Opinion No. 9* recommends that extraordinary items and prior period adjustments be reported *net of their tax effects*, as shown in Illustrations 16.4 and 16.5.

**Accounting
changes**

A company's reported net earnings and financial position can be altered materially by changes in accounting methods. A change in inventory valuation method (for example, from Fifo to Lifo) or a change in depreciation method (for example, from straight-line to accelerated) would be examples of *accounting changes*. According to *APB Opinion No. 20* a company should consistently apply the same accounting methods from one period to another. But a change may be made if the newly adopted method is preferable and if the change is adequately disclosed in the financial statements. In the period in which an accounting change is made, the nature of the change, its justification, and its effect on net earnings must be disclosed in the financial statements. Also, the cumulative effect of the change on prior years' earnings (net of tax) must be shown on the earnings statement for the year of change.

Corrections of accounting errors are considered another type of accounting change. But in this case the financial reporting would be as shown in Illustration 16.5. The journal entry to record the correction (assuming income taxes, at a 50 percent rate, were underpaid to the extent of $100,000 because of the error) is:

Land	200,000	
Federal Income Taxes Payable		100,000
Prior Period Adjustment—Correction of Error in		
Expensing Cost of Land		100,000
To correct an accounting error involving land.		

**Illustrative
statements**

Financial statements reporting on the types of items discussed above are shown in Illustrations 16.4 and 16.5. They assume that the Anson Company had a taxable gain in 1981 of $40,000 from retirement of debt and that it expensed the $200,000 cost of land acquired in 1980 for both financial accounting and tax purposes. Also, the company changed depreciation methods in 1981, and the cumulative effect of the change amounted to $20,000. There are 1,000,000 shares of common stock outstanding. The current tax rate is 50 percent.

Note especially the following in Illustrations 16.4 and 16.5: (1) earnings of $4,625,000 before extraordinary item and cumulative effect of an accounting change are more representative of the continuing earning power of the firm because normal amounts of income taxes have been deducted in arriving at this amount; (2) the gain on debt retirement is reported at its actual impact upon the company—that is, net of its tax effect; (3) the correction of the $200,000 error adds only $100,000 to retained earnings because income taxes were underpaid in prior years because the mistake carried over to the tax return; and (4) earnings per share are reported both before and after the extraordinary item and the cumulative effect of an accounting change.

NEW TERMS INTRODUCED IN CHAPTER 16

Accounting changes—changes in accounting data caused by accounting errors (expensing of an asset), mistaken estimates (depreciation), and changes in principles (change from Fifo to Lifo).

Accumulated earnings—a term used synonymously with retained earnings.

Appropriation (retained earnings)—an account created as a voluntary or contractual restriction upon retained earnings and designed to inform readers of the existence of the restriction.

Contributed capital—all capital paid into a corporation, including that carried in capital stock accounts.

Date of declaration (of dividends)—the date on which the board of directors formally states its intention that the corporation will pay a dividend.

Date of payment (of dividends)—the date on which dividend checks are to be mailed or additional shares issued in the case of a stock dividend.

Date of record (of dividends)—the date at which the corporation ascertains to whom dividends are to be paid.

Deficit—a debit balance in the Retained Earnings account.

Dividend—a pro rata distribution, usually of cash, by a corporation to its stockholders, excluding distributions made in exchange for shares of stock; usually chargeable to retained earnings; legality of a dividend is satisfied if stockholders' equity exceeds stated capital after the act of declaration.

Donated capital—an increase in stockholders' equity resulting from donation of assets to the corporation.

Earnings before extraordinary items—earnings from operations less applicable income taxes (federal and state, if any).

Extraordinary items—items having an earnings or loss effect and which are unusual and nonrecurring; reported in the earnings statement net of tax effects, if any.

Liquidating dividends—dividends which are a return of contributed capital, not a distribution chargeable to retained earnings.

Net-of-tax effect—used for extraordinary items, prior period adjustments, and accounting changes whereby items are shown at the dollar amounts remaining after deducting the effects of such items on the income taxes (federal and state, if any) payable currently.

Paid-in capital—all of the contributed capital of a corporation, including that carried in capital stock accounts. When the words "paid-in capital" are included in the account title, the account contains capital contributed in addition to that assigned to the shares issued and recorded in the capital stock accounts.

Paid-In Capital—Treasury Stock Transactions—the title of the account credited when treasury stock is reissued for more than its cost; this account is also debited, to the extent of the balance therein, for deficiencies when such shares are reissued at less than cost.

Prior period adjustments—material adjustments that have an earnings or loss effect and result from accounting errors made in prior accounting periods; they are reported in the statement of retained earnings net of their tax effects, if any.

Proprietary capital—stockholders' equity.

Recapitalization (paid-in capital from)—the amount of capital removed from the capital stock account when the par or stated value of the outstanding shares is reduced.

Retained earnings—that part of stockholders' equity resulting from earnings; the account to which the results of corporate activity, including prior period adjustments, are carried and to which dividends and certain items resulting from capital transactions are charged.

Retained income—a synonym for retained earnings.

Statement of retained earnings—a formal statement showing the items causing changes in retained earnings during a stated period of time.

Stock dividend—a dividend payable in additional shares of the declaring corporation's stock.

Stock Dividend Distributable (Payable)—the stockholders' equity account credited for the par or stated value, or the value assigned by the board of directors in the case of shares without par or stated value, upon the recording of the declaration of a stock dividend.

Stock split—as used in *Accounting Research Bulletin No. 43,* a distribution of additional shares of the issuing corporation's stock without consideration and for the purpose of effecting a material reduction in the market price per share of the outstanding stock.

Treasury stock—shares of capital stock issued and returned to the issuing corporation which have not been formally canceled or retired and are available for reissue.

DEMONSTRATION PROBLEM

Following are selected transactions of the Morgan Company:

1. The company acquired 200 shares of its own $100 par value common stock, previously issued at a premium of 5 percent, for $20,600 cash.
2. Fifty of the treasury shares are reissued at $110 per share, cash.
3. Seventy of the treasury shares are reissued at $95 per share, cash.

4. Stockholders of the corporation donated 100 shares of their common stock to the company.
5. The 100 shares of treasury stock received by donation are reissued for $9,000.

Required:

Prepare the necessary journal entries to record the above transactions.

Solution to demonstration problem

1. Treasury Stock 20,600
     Cash 20,600
    Acquired 200 shares at $20,600 ($103 per share).

2. Cash 5,500
     Treasury Stock 5,150
     Paid-In Capital—Treasury Stock Transactions 350
    Reissued 50 shares at $110.

3. Cash 6,650
    Paid-In Capital—Treasury Stock Transactions 350
    Retained Earnings 210
     Treasury Stock 7,210
    Reissued 70 shares at $95.

4. Stockholders donated 100 shares of common stock to the company.

5. Cash 9,000
     Paid-In Capital—Donations 9,000
    Reissued donated shares at $90.

QUESTIONS

1. What are the two most common component parts of the stockholders' equity in a corporation? Explain the difference between them.

2. Name several sources of paid-in capital. Would it suffice to maintain one account called Paid-In Capital for all sources of paid-in capital? Why or why not?

3. Why is a dividend consisting of the distribution of additional shares of the common stock of the declaring corporation not considered earnings to the recipient stockholders?

4. What is the effect of each of the following on the total stockholders' equity of a corporation: *(a)* declaration of a cash dividend, *(b)* payment of a cash dividend already declared, *(c)* declaration of a stock dividend, and *(d)* issuance of a stock dividend already declared?

5. The following dates are associated with a cash dividend of $50,000: July 15, July 31, and August 15. Identify each of the three dates and give the journal entry required on each, if any.

6. How should a declared but unpaid cash dividend be shown on the balance sheet? A declared but unissued stock dividend?

7. What is the purpose underlying the statutes which provide for restriction of retained earnings in the amount of the cost of treasury stock? Are such statutes for the benefit of stockholders, management, or creditors?

8. Does the cost method of accounting for treasury stock resemble accounting for an asset? Is treasury stock an asset? If not, where is it properly shown in a balance sheet according to the cost method?

9. What is meant by the term stated capital? Is it primarily an accounting term or a legal term? Explain.

10. On May 10 Power sold his capital stock in the Tanner Corporation directly to Bright for $10,000, endorsing his stock certificate and giving it to Bright. Bright placed the stock certificate in her safe. On May 8 the board of directors of the Tanner Corporation declared a dividend, payable on June 5 to stockholders of record on May 17.

On May 30 Bright sent the certificate to the transfer agent of the Tanner Corporation for transfer. Who received the dividend? Why?

11. What are extraordinary items? Where and how are they reported?

12. What are prior period adjustments? Where and how are they reported?

13. Name two types of accounting changes. How is each reported?

EXERCISES

E-1. Baler Company received 100 shares of its $10 stated value common stock on December 1, 1981, as a donation from a stockholder. On December 15, 1981, it issued the stock for $2,000 cash. Give the journal entry or entries necessary for these transactions.

E-2. Alston Corporation's stockholders' equity consists of 25,000 authorized shares of $10 par value common stock, of which 10,000 shares have been issued at par, and retained earnings of $200,000. The company now splits its stock, two for one, by calling in the old shares and issuing new $5 par shares.

a. Give the required journal entry.

b. Suppose instead that the company declared and later issued a 10 percent stock dividend. Give the required journal entries, assuming that the market value on the date of declaration is $12.50 per share.

E-3. The balance sheet of B Company contains the following:

Appropriation for contingencies $200,000

a. Give the journal entry made to create this account.

b. Explain the reason for its existence and its manner of presentation in the balance sheet.

E-4. The stockholders' equity section of M Company's balance sheet on December 31, 1981, shows 100,000 shares of authorized and issued $10 stated value common stock, of which 8,000 shares are held in the treasury. On this date, the board of directors declares a cash dividend of $1 per share payable on January 21, 1981, to stockholders of record on January 10. Give dated journal entries for the above.

E-5. Arden Company's balance sheet shows total assets of $500,000, liabilities of $200,000, and stockholder's equity of $300,000. B owns 300 of Arden's 30,000 shares of outstanding common stock. Arden now declares and issues a 10 percent stock dividend. Compute the book value per share and in total of B's investment in Arden:

a. Before the stock dividend.

b. After the stock dividend.

E-6. Masters Company has outstanding 100,000 shares of common stock without par or stated value which were issued at an average price of $8 per share, and retained earnings of $400,000. The current market price of the common stock is $15 per share. Total authorized stock consists of 500,000 shares.

a. Give the required journal entry to record the declaration of a 10 percent stock dividend.

b. If, alternatively, the company declared a 30 percent stock dividend, what additional information would you need before making a journal entry to record the dividend?

E-7. Nader Company has outstanding 100,000 shares of $5 stated value common stock, all issued at $6 per share, and retained earnings of $200,000. The company now acquires 1,000 shares of its stock from the widow of a deceased stockholder for cash at book value.

a. Give the entry to record the acquisition of the stock.

b. Give the entry to record the subsequent reissuance of this stock at $10 per share.

c. Give the entry required if the stock is reissued at $7 per share and there have been no prior treasury stock transactions.

E-8. B Company has revenues of $42 million, expenses of $36 million, a tax-deductible earthquake loss (its first such loss) of $1 million, a tax-deductible downward adjustment of $3 million resulting from renegotiation of a contract completed two years ago, and an income tax rate of 50 percent. The beginning retained earnings were $10 million, and a dividend of $500,000 was declared.

a. Prepare an earnings statement for the year.

b. Prepare a statement of retained earnings for the year.

E–9. The Barton Company had owners' equity of $500,000 on May 31, 1981, and $700,000 on May 31, 1982. Additional shares of common stock were issued during the year for $100,000 cash; treasury stock was acquired at a cost of $10,000; and a cash dividend was declared and paid in the amount of $50,000. Compute the net earnings for the year ended May 31, 1982.

PROBLEMS, SERIES A

P16–1–A. The stockholders' equity of the Wells Company on June 30, 1981, consists solely of capital stock of $500,000 and retained earnings of $430,000. The stock is $100 par value common stock, with 10,000 shares authorized and 5,000 issued and outstanding.

The board of directors on June 30, 1981, declares a 10 percent cash dividend and a 10 percent stock dividend, both payable on July 31 to stockholders of record on July 15. The cash dividend applies only to the shares outstanding prior to the stock dividend. The market price of the stock on June 30 is $200 per share.

Required:

a. Present journal entries to record the declaration of both dividends, the payment of the cash dividend, and the issuance of the stock dividend.

b. Assuming no change in the amount of retained earnings except that caused by the dividends and no change in the number of shares outstanding between June 30 and July 31, compute the book value per share of common stock: (1) just prior to the declaration of dividends, (2) just after the declaration of dividends, (3) just after the payment of the cash dividend but before issuance of the stock dividend, and (4) immediately after the issuance of the stock dividend.

c. Describe, in general terms, how the presence of preferred stock in the balance sheet affects the computation of book value per share of common stock.

P16–2–A. Following are selected transactions of the Davies Corporation:

1976
Dec. 31 By action of the board of directors, $20,000 of retained earnings were appropriated to provide for future expansion of the company's main building. (On the last day of each of the four succeeding years the same action was taken. You need not make entries for these four years.)
1981
Jan. 3 Obtained, at a cost of $200, a building permit to construct a new wing on the main plant building.
July 30 Paid $106,000 to the Able Construction Company for completion of the new wing.

Aug. 4 The board of directors authorized the release of the sum appropriated for expansion of the plant building.
    4 The board of directors declared a 10 percent common stock dividend on the 25,000 shares of $40 par value common stock outstanding. The market price on this date was $44 per share.

Required:

Present journal entries to record all of the above transactions.

P16–3–A. The following information relates to the Beason Corporation for the year 1981.

Net earnings for the year	$ 480,000
Dividends declared on common stock	60,000
Dividends paid on common stock during 1981	80,000
Dividends declared on preferred stock	30,000
Dividends received on investments	10,000
Retained earnings, January 1, unappropriated	1,420,000
Appropriation for retirement of bonds	140,000
Premium received on shares of preferred stock issued during the year	8,000
Balance in "Appropriation for possible loss of a lawsuit" no longer needed on December 31 because of favorable court decision is at directors' orders returned to unappropriated retained earnings	214,000

Required:

Prepare a statement of retained earnings for the year ended December 31, 1981.

P16–4–A. The stockholders' equity section of the Valor Company's December 31, 1980, balance sheet is:

Paid-In Capital:	
Capital stock—common, $20 par; authorized, 2,000 shares, issued and outstanding, 1,000 shares	$20,000
Paid-in capital in excess of par value	1,000
Total Paid-In Capital	$21,000
Retained earnings	8,000
Total Stockholders' Equity	$29,000

On July 15, 1981, the board of directors declared a cash dividend of $2 per share, which was paid on August 1, 1981. On December 1, 1981, the board declared a stock dividend of 10 percent and the shares were issued on December 15, 1981. Market value of the stock was $24 on December 1 and $28 on December 15. Net earnings for the year 1981 were $4,700.

Required:

a. Present journal entries for the above dividend transactions.

b. Compute the book value per share on December 31, 1980, and on December 31, 1981.

P16–5–A. The trial balance of the Welby Corporation at December 31, 1981, contains the following account balances:

Bonds payable, 7%, due May 1, 1983	$1,000,000
Allowance for doubtful accounts	12,000
Common stock without par value, stated value $10; 200,000 shares authorized, issued, and outstanding	2,000,000
Retained earnings, unappropriated	228,000
Dividends payable in cash declared December 15 on preferred stock	6,000

P16–6–A. The stockholders' equity of the Ingham Company as of December 31, 1980, consisted of 10,000 shares of authorized and outstanding $10 par value common stock, paid-in capital in excess of par of $50,000, and retained earnings of $100,000. Following are selected transactions for 1981:

May	1	Acquired 2,000 shares of its own common stock at $25 per share.
June	1	Reissued 500 shares at $28.
	30	Reissued 700 shares at $23.
Oct.	1	Declared a cash dividend of $1 per share.
	31	Paid the cash dividend declared on October 1.

Net earnings for the year were $15,200. No other transactions affecting retained earnings occurred during the year.

Required:

a. Present general journal entries for the above transactions.

b. Prepare the stockholders' equity section of the December 31, 1981, balance sheet.

c. Compute the book value per share as of December 31, 1981.

P16–7–A. The stockholders' equity section of Ralph Company's December 31, 1980, balance sheet is:

Paid-In Capital:		
Preferred stock: 5%, $100 par value; authorized, 5,000 shares, issued and outstanding 2,500 shares		$250,000
Common stock without par or stated value; authorized, 50,000 shares, issued, 25,000 shares of which 500 are held in treasury		375,000
Paid-in capital in excess of par—preferred		5,000
Total Paid-In Capital		$630,000
Retained Earnings:		
Appropriated:		
For plant expansion	$ 25,000	
Unappropriated (restricted as to dividends to the extent of $10,000, the cost of the treasury stock held)	210,000	
Total Retained Earnings		235,000
		$865,000
Less: Treasury stock, common at cost (500 shares)		10,000
Total Stockholders' Equity		$855,000

Appropriation for pending litigation	280,000
Preferred stock, 6%, par value $100; 2,000 shares authorized, issued, and outstanding	200,000
Paid-in capital from donation of plant site	150,000
Paid-in capital in excess of par value— preferred	4,000

Required:

Present in good form the stockholders' equity section of the balance sheet.

Following are selected transactions occurring in 1981.

Jan.	13	Subscriptions are received for 550 shares of previously unissued common stock at $22.
Feb.	4	A plot of land is accepted as payment in full for 500 shares of common, and the stock is issued. Closing market price on this date of the common is $21 per share.
Mar.	24	All of the treasury stock is reissued at $24.50.
June	22	All stock subscriptions are collected in full, and the shares issued.

June 23   The regular semiannual dividend on the preferred stock is declared.
30   The preferred dividend is paid.
July   3   A 10 percent stock dividend is declared on the common stock. Market price on this date is $25.
18   The stock dividend shares are issued.
Oct.   4   The company acquires 105 shares of its common stock at $24.
Dec. 18   The regular semiannual dividend on the preferred and a $0.40 per share dividend on the common are declared.
31   Both dividends are paid.
31   An additional appropriation of retained earnings of $5,000 for plant expansion is authorized.

Required:

   a. Prepare journal entries to record the 1981 transactions.

   b. Prepare a statement of unappropriated retained earnings for the year 1981. The net earnings for the year were $43,125.

   c. Prepare the stockholders' equity section of the December 31, 1981, balance sheet.

   P16–8–A. Selected data and accounts of the Hammond Company for the year ended December 31, 1981, are:

Sales, net $960,000
Interest expense   80,000

Cash dividends on common stock	160,000
Selling and administrative expense	240,000
Cash dividends on preferred stock	80,000
Rent revenue	440,000
Cost of goods sold	640,000
Flood loss (has never occurred before)	240,000
Interest revenue	80,000
Other revenue	120,000
Depreciation and maintenance on rental equipment	160,000
Stock dividend on common stock	400,000
Litigation loss	480,000
Cumulative effect on prior years' earnings of changing to a different depreciation method	40,000

The applicable federal income tax rate is 50 percent. All above items of expense, revenue, and loss are includable in the computation of taxable income. The litigation loss resulted from a court award of damages for patent infringement on a product the company produced and sold in 1977 and 1978 and which was discontinued in 1978. The cumulative effect of the accounting change amounts to an increase of $40,000. Retained earnings as of January 1, 1981, were $5,600,000.

Required:

   Prepare an earnings statement and a statement of retained earnings for 1981.

PROBLEMS, SERIES B

   P16–1–B. The only two balance sheet accounts in the stockholders' equity section of the James Company's June 30, 1981, balance sheet were $750,000, representing 7,500 shares of $100 par common stock outstanding and retained earnings of $100,000. On this date, the board of directors declared a 6 percent cash dividend and a 4 percent stock dividend, both payable on August 1 to stockholders of record on July 15. The cash dividend applies only to shares outstanding prior to the stock dividend. The market price of the stock on June 30 was $110 per share.

Required:

   a. Present journal entries to record the declaration and payment of the dividends.

   b. Assuming no change in the amount of retained earnings except that occasioned by the dividends, compute the book value per share of common stock immediately before the declaration of the dividends, immediately after declaration of the dividends (the stock dividend shares

are not considered outstanding until they are issued), and immediately after payment of the dividends.

   c. Describe, in general terms, how the presence of preferred stock in the balance sheet affects the computation of book value per share of common stock.

   P16–2–B. Following are selected transactions of the Bard Corporation.

1976
Dec. 31   The board of directors authorized appropriation of $200,000 of retained earnings to provide for the future acquisition of a new plant site and the construction of a new building. (On the last day of the four succeeding years the same action was taken. You need not make entries for these four years.)

1979
Jan.   2   Purchased a new plant site for cash, $150,000.
Mar. 29   Entered into a contract for construction of a new building, payment to be made within 30 days following completion.

1981

Feb. 10 Following final inspection and approval of the new building, the Dome Construction Company was paid in full, $920,000.

Mar. 10 The board of directors authorized release of the retained earnings appropriated for the plant site and building.

Apr. 2 A 10 percent stock dividend on the 100,000 shares of $100 par value common stock outstanding was declared. The market price on this date was $110 per share.

Required:

Present journal entries for all of the above transactions.

P16–3–B. Following are selected data and accounts of the Addison Corporation at December 31, 1981:

Net earnings for the year	$270,000
Dividends declared on preferred stock	40,000
Retained earnings appropriated for future plant expansion during the year	100,000
Dividends received on stock investments	14,000
Dividends paid on common stock	40,000
Excess over stated value received for shares of common stock issued during the year	64,000
Dividends declared on common stock	36,000
Retained earnings, January 1, unappropriated	410,000
Directors ordered balance in "Appropriation for bond sinking fund," related to bond issue retired on March 31, 1981, returned to unappropriated retained earnings	200,000

Required:

Prepare a statement of unappropriated retained earnings for the year 1981.

P16–4–B. The only stockholders' equity items of the Cushion Company at June 30, 1981, are:

Common stock, $25 par; 4,000 shares authorized, 2,000 shares issued and outstanding	$ 50,000
Paid-in capital in excess of par value	25,000
Retained earnings	40,000
Total Stockholders' Equity	$115,000

On August 4, a 4 percent cash dividend was declared, payable September 3. On November 16, a 10 percent stock dividend was declared. The shares were issued on December 1. The market value of the common stock on November 16 was $40 per share and on December 1,

$42. Net earnings for the six months ended December 31, 1981, were $5,000.

Required:

a. Present journal entries for the above transactions.

b. Compute the book value per share on July 1 and December 31, 1981.

P16–5–B. Following are selected data and accounts of Jefferson, Inc., at May 31, 1981:

Estimated liability for product warranties	$ 10,000
Paid-in capital in excess of par value— preferred	6,000
Retained earnings, unappropriated	114,000
Allowance for doubtful accounts	30,000
Common stock without par value, stated value $50; 20,000 shares authorized, issued, and outstanding	1,000,000
Appropriation for retirement of bonds	100,000
Dividends payable (cash)	7,000
Paid-in capital in excess of stated value—common	50,000
7% bonds payable, due April 1, 1987	600,000
Preferred stock: 7%, par value $100; 2,000 shares authorized, issued, and outstanding	200,000
Paid-in capital donations	24,000

Required:

Present the stockholders' equity section of the company's balance sheet.

P16–6–B. The stockholders' equity of the A. Sandretto Company on December 31, 1980, consisted of 1,000 authorized and outstanding shares of $7 cumulative preferred stock, stated value $10 per share, which were originally issued at $105 per share; 100,000 shares authorized and outstanding of $5 stated value common stock which were originally issued at $5; and retained earnings of $100,000. Following are selected transactions and other data relating to 1981:

1. The company acquired 2,000 shares of its common stock at $15.
2. One thousand of the treasury shares were reissued at $13.
3. Stockholders donated 1,000 shares of common stock to the company. These shares were immediately reissued at $12 to provide working capital.
4. The first quarter's dividend of $1.75 per share was declared and paid on the preferred stock. No other dividends were declared or paid during 1981.

The company suffered a net loss of $20,000 for the year 1981.

Required:

a. Prepare journal entries for the numbered transactions above.

b. Prepare the stockholders' equity section of the December 31, 1981, balance sheet.

P16-7-B. The stockholders' equity section of the Bunde Company's October 31, 1980, balance sheet was:

Paid-In Capital:

Preferred stock: 6%, $100 par value; 1,000 shares authorized, 350 shares issued and outstanding		$ 35,000
Common stock: $10 par value; 100,000 shares authorized, 40,000 shares issued and outstanding		400,000
Paid-in capital from donation of plant site		25,000
Total Paid-In Capital		$460,000
Retained Earnings:		
Appropriated:		
Appropriation for contingencies	$20,000	
Unappropriated	55,500	
Total Retained Earnings		75,500
Total Stockholders' Equity		$535,500

During the ensuing fiscal year, the following transactions were entered into by the Bunde Company:

1. Appropriation of $20,000 of retained earnings was authorized in October 1980 because of the likelihood of an unfavorable court decision in a pending lawsuit. The suit was brought by a customer seeking damages for the company's alleged breach of a contract to supply the customer with certain products at stated prices in 1979. The suit was concluded with a court order directing the company to pay $17,500 in damages. These damages were deductible in determining income tax liability (the tax rate was 50 percent). The board ordered the damages paid and the appropriation closed.
2. The company acquired 1,000 shares of its own common stock at $15 in May 1981. On June 30 it reissued 500 of these shares at $12.
3. Dividends declared and paid during the year were 6 percent on preferred stock, and $0.30 per share on common stock. The common dividend was declared and paid in October 1981.

The company had net earnings after income taxes for the year of $19,000, excluding the loss on the lawsuit and the related tax effects.

Required:

a. Prepare general journal entries for the above transactions.

b. Prepare a statement of retained earnings for the year ended October 31, 1981.

c. Prepare the stockholder's equity section of the October 31, 1981, balance sheet.

P16-8-B. Selected accounts and other data for the Williams Company for 1981 are:

Common stock—$10 par value	$1,000,000
Sales, net	4,000,000
Selling and administrative expenses	800,000
Cash dividends declared and paid	300,000
Cost of goods sold	2,000,000
Gain on sale of securities	350,000
Depreciation expense	300,000
Interest revenue	50,000
Loss on write-down of obsolete inventory	100,000
Retained earnings (as of 12/31/80)	5,000,000
Earthquake loss	240,000
Cumulative effect on prior years of changing from straight-line to an accelerated method of computing depreciation	80,000

The applicable federal income tax rate is 50 percent. All of the items of expense, revenue, and loss are includable in the computation of the amount of income taxes payable. The tax effects of the cumulative effect of the change in depreciation methods can be ignored. The gain on sale of securities is a common item for the company, while the earthquake loss resulted from the first earthquake experienced at the company's location. In addition, the company discovered that in 1980 it had erroneously charged to expense the $400,000 cost of a tract of land purchased that year and had made the same error on its tax return for 1980.

Required:

a. Prepare an earnings statement for 1981.

b. Prepare a statement of retained earnings for 1981.

BUSINESS DECISION PROBLEM 16–1

The stockholders' equity section of the Clinton Corporation's balance sheet for June 30, 1981, is shown below:

Paid-in Capital:
Common stock—$10 par; authorized
200,000 shares, issued and outstanding
80,000 shares .... $ 800,000
Paid-in capital in excess of par value 400,000
      Total Paid-In Capital $1,200,000
Retained earnings 500,000
         Total Stockholders' Equity $1,700,000

On July 1, 1981, the corporation's directors declared a 10 percent stock dividend distributable on August 2 to stockholders of record on July 16. On November 1, 1981, the directors voted a $1.00 per share annual cash dividend payable on December 2 to stockholders of record on November 16. For four years prior to 1981, the corporation had paid an annual cash dividend of $1.05.

Joe Turk owns 8,000 shares of Clinton Corporation's common stock, which he purchased five years ago. The market value of his stock was $20 per share on July 1, 1981, and $18.18 per share on July 16, 1981.

Required:

a. What is the book value (total and per share) of Turk's shares on June 30, 1981, and on August 2, 1981 (after he receives his dividend shares)?

b. What amount of cash dividends will Turk receive in 1981? How does this amount differ from the amount of cash dividends Turk received in the previous four years?

c. For what logical reason did the price of the stock drop from $20.00 to $18.18 on July 16, 1981?

d. Is Turk better off as a result of the stock dividend and the $1.00 cash dividend than he would have been if he had just received the $1.05 dividend? Why?

BUSINESS DECISION PROBLEM 16–2

Shown below are some journal entries made by the bookkeeper for the Corly Corporation:

1. Retained Earnings 1,500
    Reserve for Doubtful Accounts ... 1,500
  To record bad debts expense.

2. Retained Earnings 6,000
    Reserve for Depreciation 6,000
  To record depreciation expense.

3. Retained Earnings 15,000
    Reserve for Plant Expansion 15,000
  To record retained earnings appropriation.

4. Retained Earnings 1,000
    Stock Dividend Distributable 1,000
  To record 10 percent stock dividend declaration (100 shares—$10 par value, $15 market value).

5. Stock Dividend Distributable 1,000
    Common Stock 1,000
  To record distribution of stock dividend.

6. Treasury Stock 4,000
    Cash 4,000
  To record acquisition of 200 $10 par value common shares at $20.

7. Cash 2,200
    Treasury Stock 2,200
  To record sale of 100 treasury shares at $22.

8. Cash 850
    Treasury Stock 850
  To record sale of 50 treasury shares at $17.

9. Common Stock 2,000
    Dividends Payable 2,000
  To record declaration of cash dividend.

10. Dividends Payable 2,000
    Cash 2,000
  To record payment of cash dividend.

Required:

Analyze the above journal entries in connection with their explanations and decide whether each is correct or incorrect. If a journal entry is incorrect, prepare the journal entry that should have been made.

BUSINESS DECISION PROBLEM 16–3

An earnings statement and statement of retained earnings for the year ended December 31, 1981, for the Wallace Company are presented below:

WALLACE COMPANY
Earnings Statement
For the Year Ended December 31, 1981

Sales		$260,000
Costs and expenses:		
Costs of goods sold	$70,000	
Selling expenses	40,000	
Depreciation expense	3,000	
Loss on early retirement of debt	10,000	123,000
Net earnings before income taxes		$137,000
Federal income taxes		68,500
Net earnings before extraordinary items		$68,500
Extraordinary items:		
Gain on sale of equipment (net of tax effect of $30,000)	$30,000	
Write-down of obsolete inventory (net of tax effect of $40,000)	(40,000)	10,000
Net Earnings		$ 58,500

WALLACE COMPANY
Statement of Retained Earnings
For the Year Ended December 31, 1981

Retained earnings, January 1, 1981		$290,000
Add: Net earnings		58,500
		$348,500
Less:		
Dividends	$32,000	
General and administrative expenses incurred during a strike (net of tax effect of $10,000)	10,000	
Earthquake loss (net of tax effect of $40,000)	40,000	82,000
Retained Earnings, December 31, 1981		$266,500

Several stockholders of the Wallace Company have complained that the above statements are not prepared in accordance with generally accepted accounting principles. As a result, the stockholders cannot compare the financial statements of the Wallace Company with those of other companies.

Required:

a. Are the above statements prepared in accordance with generally accepted accounting principles? If not, why not?

b. If your response to part ***(a)*** was negative, then prepare the earnings statement and the statement of retained earnings in accordance with generally accepted accounting principles.

Chapter 17

Corporations: Bonds

payable and investments

Bonds may be issued by a corporation as one means of financing its activities. Also a corporation may purchase bonds or stocks issued by another company to invest its own funds. This chapter discusses the accounting involved in these situations.

BONDS

A bond is one of the most common forms of long-term debt financing. When bonds are issued by a corporation, often other corporations purchase them as long-term investments. A bond is a written unconditional promise wherein the borrower promises to pay to the holder of the bond (1) the face value of the bond at the maturity date and (2) interest at a specified rate on the face value at specified dates (usually semiannually).

Bonds may be secured or unsecured. *Secured bonds* are those which have a claim against certain property of the issuer if the bonds are not paid at the maturity date. The property pledged (or mortgaged) may be real estate, machinery, merchandise, investments, or personal property. A *mortgage* is a conditional transfer of certain property given by the borrower (the mortgagor) to the lender of funds (the mortgagee) to secure the payment of a loan. Bonds which have first claim on a certain asset are called *first-mortgage bonds,* while those which have a second claim on that same asset are called *second-mortgage bonds,* and so on.

Most *unsecured bonds* are called *debenture bonds.* They are backed by the general credit of the corporation.

For interest-paying purposes, bonds may be either *registered bonds* or *coupon bonds.* Interest is paid to the owner of registered bonds by check. The owner's name is registered on the records of the issuing corporation. Interest is paid on coupon bonds when the appropriate coupon is detached and cashed on the interest date or thereafter. The registered type of bond is most frequently used by corporations today. An unregistered bond is transferred to another party by mere delivery, whereas transfer of a registered bond requires the owner's endorsement, assignment, and registration.

Any type of bond may be *convertible* if such a provision is stated in the *bond indenture* (the contract between the issuer of bonds and the bondholders or the trustee representing the bondholders). Such bonds are convertible, at the bondholder's option and under stated conditions, into stock of the issuing corporation. For example, a $1,000 convertible debenture bond might be convertible (for a stated period of its life) into 20 shares of the issuing company's common stock.

Bonds may also be *callable* if such a provision is included in the bond indenture. This provision entitles a company to buy back its bonds before the maturity date. This usually involves payment of an amount in excess of the face value. The amount above the face value is the *call premium.*

Why a company might decide to issue bonds

When a corporation needs additional long-term funds, it must decide between the issuance of additional capital stock or borrowing by issuing notes or bonds. The issuance of notes and bonds may be advantageous if the present stockholders prefer not to share ownership and corporate earnings with additional shareholders.

A bondholder is a creditor and a stockholder is an owner, but both can be viewed as investors. Many bonds are secured by the plant assets of the borrower and always rank ahead of the stock as claims on assets in liquidation. Therefore, owners of bonds are provided with greater protection for their investment than are stockholders.

Interest expense on a note or bond is a fixed cost to the borrower. It must be met when it is due if default on the loan is to be avoided. Interest on bonds must be paid on dates specified by the bond contract. Dividends on stock are declared at the discretion of the board of directors.

Advantages and disadvantages of borrowing

The advantages of operating a business with borrowed funds may be illustrated with the use of the data contained in Illustration 17.1. Both companies began operations on January 1, 1981. They were equally efficient in employing assets, since both were able to earn a 20 percent rate of return from operations (before interest and taxes) on assets acquired as of the beginning of 1981 ($4,000,000 ÷ $20,000,000). Company B, because of the bonds in its capital structure, earned $1.65 per share while Company A earned only $1.00 per share.

The differences between Company A and Company B can be explained as follows: Company B borrowed $10 million at a rate of 7 percent, which cost the company $350,000 after income taxes. Interest of $700,000 was incurred, but the $700,000 of interest reduced the amount of federal income taxes levied by $350,000. Thus, the net cost after tax is $350,000. Both companies operated equally efficiently, earning $4 million (before interest and taxes) on $20 million worth of total assets. But Company B was able to finance one half of its assets at a cost before taxes of 7 percent, while the assets secured through borrowing were earning a return of 20 percent before taxes. This additional return of $1,300,000 ($2,000,000 − $700,000) yielded an addi-

Illustration 17.1: Favorable financial leverage

COMPANIES A AND B, CONDENSED STATEMENTS Balance Sheet January 1, 1981	Company A	Company B
Total assets	$20,000,000	$20,000,000
Bonds payable, 7%		$10,000,000
Stockholders' equity (capital stock)	$20,000,000	10,000,000
	$20,000,000	$20,000,000
Earnings Statement Year Ended December 31, 1981		
Net earnings from operations for 1979	$ 4,000,000	$ 4,000,000
Interest expense		700,000
Net earnings before income taxes	$ 4,000,000	$ 3,300,000
Income taxes at 50%	2,000,000	1,650,000
Net Earnings for 1981	$ 2,000,000	$ 1,650,000
Number of shares	2,000,000	1,000,000
Earnings per share	$1.00	$1.65

tional $650,000 of net earnings after taxes (at a 50 percent rate) to the stockholders of Company B. The additional earnings were sufficient to increase earnings per share in Company B to $1.65 as contrasted to $1 for Company A.

Company B is employing what is known as *financial leverage*, or is said to be *"trading on the equity."* That is, it is using the existence of stockholders' equity as a basis for securing funds on which a fixed rate of return is paid, the use of which is intended to increase the amount of earnings per share of the common stockholders. The funds may be obtained by either issuing preferred stock or bonds. The use of preferred stock to obtain financial leverage was covered in Chapter 15. The use of bonds to secure financial leverage is illustrated here. The situation given above, where the use of leverage increased earnings per share, is called *favorable financial leverage.*

Unfavorable financial leverage can exist also, and would for Company B if earnings from operations of each company amounted to only $1 million instead of $4 million. In this case the earnings per share for Companies A and B, respectively, would be $0.25 and $0.15 (you may want to prove this to yourself).

A disadvantage of borrowing is that it reduces the ability of a company to absorb losses. Suppose that both A and B sustain losses amounting to $11 million. Company A will still have $9 million of stockholders' equity at the end of the year and can continue operations with a chance to recover. Company B will be insolvent at the end of the year (its liabilities will exceed its assets), and the stockholders of B may lose their entire investment through liquidation proceedings.

BONDS PAYABLE: Accounting for the issuance of bonds

The *bond indenture* (the overall contract between the issuer and the bondholders) sets forth the total amount of bonds that may be issued. The bonds may all be issued at one time or a portion at one date and the remainder later.

Assume that the Southern Company issued on July 1, 1981, $1,000,000 of its $1,500,000 authorized first-mortgage, 9 percent, ten-year bonds (dated July 1, 1981) at face value of $1,000,000. This transaction would be recorded in the accounts as follows:

```
July 1  Cash ...............................................   1,000,000
            Bonds Payable ................................                1,000,000
        To record the issuance of bonds.
```

Recording bond interest

Interest on most bonds is paid semiannually, as required by the provisions of the bond indenture. We will assume that the interest is paid directly by the borrower to the bondholders and that the accounting year ends on December 31. The required entries are:

```
1981
Dec. 31  Bond Interest Expense ..................................   45,000
             Accrued Bond Interest Payable ......................                45,000
         To accrue bond interest expense for the period July 1–December
         31, 1981.
```

```
1982
Jan.  1  Accrued Bond Interest Payable ..........................  45,000
            Cash ...............................................              45,000
         To record the payment of interest for the period July 1–January
         1, 1982.
```

The price received for a bond issue

The price a bond issue will bring when offered to investors, or the price at which a bond sells in the market, often may differ from its face or maturity value. Basically, a bond issue will sell at a price higher (lower) than its face or maturity value if the contract rate of interest offered in the bonds is higher (lower) than the market rate of interest. The *contract rate of interest* is the rate of interest printed on the face of the bonds. The *market rate of interest* is the minimum rate of interest which investors are willing to accept on bonds of a particular risk category. The effect of a premium or discount on a bond is to change the rate of interest offered by the bond to the effective rate desired by the investor (which is generally at, or close to, the market rate of interest). The *effective rate of interest* is the rate that an investor can earn on a particular bond issue by paying a certain price for it.

In purchasing a bond, an investor actually acquires two promises from the issuer of the bond: (1) the promise to pay the stated principal amount on a given date—the maturity date—and (2) a promise to pay periodic interest at stated intervals throughout the life of the bond. Thus, a $1,000, 20-year, 8 percent bond, dated October 1, 1981, which calls for semiannual interest payments on each April 1 and October 1, contains two promises. The issuer promises to pay $1,000 to the holder on October 1, 2001, and to pay $40 each April 1 and October 1 through October 1, 2001, beginning on April 1, 1982.

If an investing company desired an 8 percent rate of interest from such a bond, it would offer to purchase it at face value. It would invest $1,000 and receive $80 of interest per year—exactly an 8 percent rate. But suppose the company would invest in such a bond only if it could earn a 10 percent rate. Since the rate on the face of the bond (the contract or coupon rate) cannot be changed, the investing company can change the rate at which interest is actually earned only by changing the price paid for the bond. In this instance it would pay less than the face value to increase the rate received above the 8 percent. The method for determining the price which an investor would be willing to pay for a bond is discussed in the Appendix to this chapter.

Bonds issued at a discount

To illustrate the accounting for bonds issued at a discount, assume that on July 1, 1981, the Southern Company issued $1,000,000 of first-mortgage, 9 percent, ten-year bonds for $980,000, or at 98 percent of face value. The bonds call for semiannual interest payments and mature on July 1, 1991. At issuance the entry would be:

```
July 1  Cash .................................................  980,000
        Discount on Bonds Payable ..........................   20,000
            Bonds Payable ....................................             1,000,000
        To record the issuance of $1,000,000 face value bonds at
        98.
```

Note that in recording bonds payable on the issuer's books, the bonds are carried at their face value in one account and the discount (or premium) in another. It is customary in accounting to record liabilities at the amount expected to be paid at maturity, excluding interest unless it actually has accrued.

Accounting for bond discount

To the issuing corporation, bond discount represents a cost of using funds just as it is a form of additional interest earnings to the investor. Thus the total cost of borrowing includes the total interest paid in cash (ten years times $90,000) plus the total discount ($20,000) which is paid as a lump sum at maturity as part of the face value of $1,000,000. Thus, the total cost of borrowing is:

Interest paid	$90,000 × 10 = $900,000
Discount	20,000
Total cost of borrowing	$920,000

Both items must be spread equitably over the life of the bonds, although no disbursement is made for the amount of discount until the debt is paid at or before maturity.

Thus, the original amount in the Discount on Bonds Payable account should be charged to expense ($2,000 per year) over the period of time between the date on which the bonds were issued and their maturity date. The amount charged to expense is often computed on a straight-line basis; that is, equal amounts are charged to expense for equal periods of time elapsed. How often this adjusting entry will be made will depend upon how often the company prepares financial statements.

To illustrate, assume that the Southern Company, which issued $1,000,000 of ten-year, 9 percent bonds at 98, uses a calendar-year accounting period and prepares semiannual financial statements. The total discount of $20,000 must be written off over the ten years of life in the bonds. The annual charge is $2,000, and the charge per interest period (six months) is $1,000. The entry required on December 31, 1981, would be (recall that the bonds were issued on July 1, 1981):

Dec. 31 Bond Interest Expense	46,000	
Discount on Bonds Payable		1,000
Accrued Bond Interest Payable		45,000
To record the accrual of interest and amortization of the discount on bonds payable.		

Under the straight-line method illustrated, the total interest cost for each six months is the $45,000 which must be paid currently plus $1,000 of the $20,000 of discount which will be paid at maturity, or a total of $46,000.

The *straight-line discount amortization method* shown is widely used because of its simplicity and ease of application.[1] An alternative, and the

---

[1] *APB Opinion No. 21* states that the straight-line basis shown here may only be used if the results obtained are not materially different from those which would result from the effective rate of interest method. This latter method is illustrated in the Appendix to this chapter.

theoretically correct method which yields slightly different results, embraces the use of the effective rate of interest. This method is covered in the Appendix to this chapter.

Each time a balance sheet is prepared, the remaining balance in the Discount on Bonds Payable account will be shown as a deduction from Bonds Payable. The bonds payable, except for amounts maturing currently, are shown in the long-term liability section of the balance sheet. At the end of the tenth year of the bonds' life—after 20 interest payments have been made—the balance in the Discount on Bonds Payable account will be zero; the entire amount will have been charged to expense.

Bonds issued at a premium

Bonds are issued at a premium (at more than face value) when the interest rate specified on the face of the bonds is higher than the market rate of interest for similar bonds. Investors are willing to pay a premium because the periodic interest payments are larger than the minimum they would be willing to accept if they purchased bonds of this quality at face value. Thus, investors literally purchase some of the interest to be paid periodically by the issuing company. The total interest cost to the company, then, will not be the total of all of the cash interest payments made but will be this sum less the amount of premium received.

To illustrate, assume that the bonds mentioned above had been issued at 102 percent of face value. The total of the periodic interest payments to be made on the bonds is $90,000 per year for ten years, or a total of $900,000. But this will not be the total expense to the company. The investors have actually purchased in advance a part of each periodic interest payment; and in this way, they have invested more capital in the business issuing the bonds than simply the face value of the bonds. Thus, the total cost of borrowing is:

Interest paid	$90,000 × 10 = $900,000
Less premium	20,000
Total cost of borrowing	$880,000

A part of each periodic payment to the investors must be viewed as a partial return of the investors' capital.

At the date of issuance the required entry is:

July 1	Cash	1,020,000	
	Bonds Payable		1,000,000
	Premium on Bonds Payable		20,000
	To record the issuance of $1,000,000 of bonds at 102.		

Accounting for bond premium

The typical accounting treatment for bond premium is to amortize the original amount by crediting interest expense with an equal amount each accounting period between the issue date of the bonds and their maturity date. This is called straight-line amortization. To continue the above illustration, the amount of premium amortized each year would be $2,000 ($20,000 ÷ 10 years). The following entry would be recorded at the end of 1981:

```
Dec. 31  Bond Interest Expense ................................. 44,000
         Premium on Bonds Payable ...........................  1,000
              Accrued Bond Interest Payable ......................       45,000
         To record the accrual of interest and amortization of the premium
         on bonds payable.
```

The debit to Premium on Bonds Payable is $1,000. The interest cost recorded is $44,000, which would equal an annual cost of $88,000. This $88,000 can be verified in another manner. The total interest payments over the life of the bonds amount to $900,000; the premium is $20,000; and the net total interest cost, as shown above, is $880,000. Dividing this by ten years, an annual cost of $88,000 is obtained.

When a balance sheet is prepared, the remaining balance in the Premium on Bonds Payable account will be added to the amount of Bonds Payable. This amount, except for currently maturing amounts in some instances, is shown in the long-term liabilities section.

Bonds issued at face value between interest dates

Frequently, bonds are issued between interest dates. In this case, the bond investor usually pays for both the bond and the interest accrued from the last interest payment date to the date of purchase. On the interest date following the interim date of purchase, the accrued interest will be collected by the bondholder when a check is received for the interest for the entire period. The company is obligated, by contract, to pay the bondholders interest for the full six months on the interest payment date *regardless* of how long these holders have owned the bonds. Since the bond purchaser has paid for the interest which had accrued to the purchase date, it would be improper not to recognize this fact in determining the bond interest expense for the first interest period after issuance.

To illustrate, assume that the Carlson Company issues $100,000 of 9 percent bonds on May 1, 1981 (four months after the last interest date), at face value plus accrued interest. The accrued interest is equal to $100,000 \times 0.09 \times 1/3 = $3,000$. The entry to record the issuance is:

```
May 1  Cash ............................................... 103,000
            Accrued Bond Interest Payable .......................        3,000
            Bonds Payable ....................................      100,000
       To record the issuance of bonds at face and the accrued interest
       thereon.
```

Assuming no action has been taken to record the interest accrued for the two months prior to the payment of the semiannual interest, the Carlson Company will make the following entry in its accounts at the time of semiannual payment:

```
July 1  Accrued Bond Interest Payable .............................. 3,000
        Bond Interest Expense ....................................  1,500
             Cash ...............................................         4,500
        To record the payment of bond interest.
```

The net interest expense to the Carlson Company is $1,500 ($100,000 \times 0.09 \times 1/6$) which represents interest for the two months from the date of issuance to the next interest date.

Bonds issued at other than face value between interest dates

The most complex situation involving bonds occurs when bonds are issued between interest dates at either a premium or a discount. Accrued interest must be accounted for at the issuance date and a discount or a premium must be amortized at year-end.

Assume that Issuer Corporation issues ten-year, 12 percent bonds with a face value of $1,000,000 to the Purchaser Insurance Company at 92.2 on March 1, 1981. The bonds are dated January 1, 1981. The necessary entries on the issuer's books during 1981 are:

Mar.	1	Cash		942,000	
		Discount on Bonds Payable		78,000	
		Bonds Payable			1,000,000
		Accrued Interest Payable			20,000
		To record the issue of bonds at 92.2 plus two months' accrued interest.			
July	1	Accrued Interest Payable		20,000	
		Interest Expense		40,000	
		Cash			60,000
		To record the payment of six months' interest.			
Dec. 31		Interest Expense		60,000	
		Accrued Interest Payable			60,000
		To record the accrual of six months' interest.			
		Interest Expense		6,610	
		Discount on Bonds Payable			6,610
		To record the amortization of ten months' discount at $661 per month.			

With the bonds issued at a discount, entries are required to amortize the discount over the periods of *remaining life of the bonds*. The time over which the discount is spread is 118 months. Thus the amount to amortize per month is:

$$\frac{\text{Discount}}{\text{Months between issuance and maturity dates}} = \frac{\$78,000}{118 \text{ months}} = \$661 \text{ per month}$$

REDEEMING OUTSTANDING BONDS

At the maturity date the bonds are to be redeemed at their face value. Assuming interest for the last period has already been paid, the redemption of bonds with a face value of $100,000 would be recorded as follows:

Bonds Payable	100,000	
Cash		100,000
To record the redemption of bonds.		

If bonds are redeemed before their maturity date, any difference between the amount paid and the book value is treated as a gain or loss on retirement. Book value is equal to the face value plus the pro rata share of any remaining premium or minus the pro rata share of any remaining discount. For instance, if bonds with a face value of $100,000 and a remaining premium of $2,000 are redeemed before maturity at a cost of $99,000, the following entry would be made:

Bonds Payable	100,000	
Premium on Bonds Payable	2,000	
Cash		99,000
Gain on Redemption of Bonds Payable		3,000
To record the redemption of bonds.		

The gains and losses from such transactions are totaled and, if material in amount, are classified as an extraordinary item in the earnings statement, net of the related income tax effect. (This is required under *FASB Statement No. 4.*)

Bonds known as *serial bonds* are redeemed in a series in accordance with the provisions of the indenture. For instance, for ten-year bonds, $\frac{1}{10}$ may mature at the end of the first year, $\frac{1}{10}$ at the end of the second year, and so on. This allows investors to select a bond with the desired time period to meet their needs. Quite often serial bonds are issued by governmental units, such as cities. No interest accrues on a bond beyond its scheduled redemption date.

Use of a sinking fund to redeem bonds

The manner in which a *sinking fund* has been employed to redeem bonds has changed through the years. Traditionally, a sinking fund consisted of an accumulation of cash and securities (and earnings thereon) which were readily marketable. The use of these funds was restricted to the redemption of the entire bond issue at the maturity date.

Provisions in modern indentures require that payments be made on or before a given date to a *bond redemption fund,* often called a sinking fund, which will be used to immediately redeem a stipulated amount of bonds and to pay the accrued interest on them. If a *trustee* is used in such sinking fund arrangements, the trustee will determine by specific identification which bonds will be called for redemption. The expenses of the sinking fund trustee are not to be reimbursed from the sinking fund. Thus, the modern sinking fund brings about the serial redemption of outstanding bonds without actually issuing serial bonds.

To illustrate current practices regarding the use of a sinking fund, assume that on October 1, 1976, the Bradley Company issued $1 million of 25-year, 12 percent, semiannual coupon bonds at face value. Under the terms of the indenture, the company is to deliver to the trustee on September 30, 1981, and each September 30 thereafter as long as any bonds are outstanding, an amount sufficient to redeem $50,000 of the principal amount at 100 and to pay any accrued interest on the bonds called for redemption through the sinking fund. The entry to record the required payment on September 30, 1981, is:

Sinking Fund	53,000	
Cash		53,000
Payment to trustee of funds to call $50,000 of bonds at face value plus accrued interest of $3,000 ($50,000 $\times$ 0.12 $\times$ 1/2).		

The trustee calls $50,000 of bonds, pays for the bonds and the accrued interest, and notifies the company. Assuming that the accrued interest has been recorded, the entry is:

Accrued Bond Interest Payable	3,000	
Bonds Payable	50,000	
Sinking Fund		53,000

To record payment by trustee of accrued interest on, and redemption of, bonds through sinking fund.

BALANCE SHEET ILLUSTRATION

The liabilities portion (current and long term) of the balance sheet of the Sperry Corporation (Illustration 17.2) presents certain accounts discussed in this chapter.

Illustration 17.2: Liabilities portion of the balance sheet

THE SPERRY CORPORATION
Partial Balance Sheet
December 31, 1981

Current Liabilities:			
Accounts payable		$160,000	
Accrued bond interest payable		4,000	
Current maturity of long-term debt		10,000	$174,000
Long-Term Liabilities:			
Debenture bonds, 10%, due 1985	$190,000		
Less: Discount	4,000	$186,000	
First-mortgage bonds, 12%, due 1986	$200,000		
Add: Premium	2,000	202,000	388,000
Total Liabilities			$562,000

INVESTMENTS IN BONDS AND STOCKS OF OTHER COMPANIES: Bond investments

Companies may invest in the bonds and stocks of other companies. The remainder of the chapter deals with these investments.

A company can only issue bonds when some other party is willing to buy them. There are both short-term and long-term reasons for buying bonds.

The main short-term reason is to earn at least a nominal rate of return on cash that would otherwise be temporarily idle. There may be forms of investment which involve less risk, but regardless of this some companies do acquire bonds as a temporary investment. The primary risk is that the investor will have to sell the bonds at a time when the market price is relatively low (because of an increase in the market rate of interest).

Long-term reasons for investing in bonds include the desire to secure a continuing stream of revenue from the investment over a period of years and the desire to establish a financial affiliation with another company. Insurance companies often acquire bonds for the former reason. They receive insurance premiums from customers and must earn a return on these until the time comes to pay claims. Investing in capital stock is too risky, so they invest in bonds. The insurance companies usually can wait until the maturity date if need be and collect the face value of the bonds. They usually can refrain from having to sell the bonds before maturity at a temporarily depressed market price. Also, interest on bonds must be paid by the issuer, while dividends on capital stock need not be declared.

The purpose for which a corporation acquires bonds, which generally must be determined on the basis of management intent, determines how they are shown in the balance sheet. If bonds are held as a temporary investment they should be classified as current assets. Otherwise, they should be considered to be long-term and reported as noncurrent assets, under the caption "Investments."

This chapter deals primarily with the accounting treatment for the long-term type of investment in bonds by corporations.

Accounting for bond investments

If bonds are purchased at face value, the entry to record the purchase includes a debit to Bond Investments and a credit to Cash for the face value of the bonds. But bonds are often purchased at a premium or discount for reasons already covered. Recording the acquisition of bonds and the earning of interest revenue are discussed below. Rounded dollar amounts are used merely for the sake of keeping the illustrations simple.

Bonds purchased at a discount or premium.   Earlier in the chapter when bonds were *issued* at a discount or premium, the discount or premium was recorded in a separate account. But when bonds are *purchased* at a discount or premium, no separate account is used for the discount or premium.

To illustrate, assume that Northern Company on July 1, 1981, purchased $1,000,000 of 9 percent, ten-year, first-mortgage bonds of the Southern Company for $980,000 (this example is the opposite side of the transaction where bonds were issued by Southern Company at this amount on page 497). The interest dates are July 1 and January 1. The bond investment would be recorded as follows:

```
July 1   Bond Investments . . . . . . . . . . . . . . . . . . . . . . . . . . . . . . . . . . . . .   980,000
            Cash  . . . . . . . . . . . . . . . . . . . . . . . . . . . . . . . . . . . . . . . . . . .              980,000
         To record the purchase of bonds at 98.
```

The total amount carried to the Bond Investments account is the total cost of acquiring the bonds. This usually consists of the price paid for the bonds, broker's commission, and perhaps postage and other miscellaneous delivery charges. (These latter charges are ignored in the example.) No useful purpose is served by recording the face value of the bonds in one account and the difference between face value and total cost in another.

If the bonds are not going to be held to maturity, there is no need to amortize the premium or discount.[2] But *if the bonds are to be held to maturity,* the premium or discount is amortized over the remaining life of the bonds. Usually this is done on a straight-line basis. In this example the $20,000 discount is to be amortized over the ten years that the company will hold the bonds. The annual amount is $2,000, and the amount per interest period (six months) is $1,000. The entry required on December 31, 1981, would be (recall that the bonds were purchased on July 1, 1981):

```
Bond Investments  . . . . . . . . . . . . . . . . . . . . . . . . . . . . . . . . . . . . . . . .   1,000
Accrued Interest Receivable . . . . . . . . . . . . . . . . . . . . . . . . . . . . . . . . .  45,000
    Interest Revenue . . . . . . . . . . . . . . . . . . . . . . . . . . . . . . . . . . . . . . . .            46,000
    To record the accrual of interest and the amortization of the discount on
    bond investments.
```

---

[2] Some authors use the term "accumulate" when referring to the discount. We shall use the term "amortize" for both the premium and discount.

Interest receivable is calculated as follows:

$$\$1,000,000 \times 0.09 \times \tfrac{1}{2} = \$45,000 \text{ per 6 months}$$

The Northern Company's balance sheet as of December 31, 1981, would show accrued interest receivable of $45,000 as a current asset. The bonds will be shown in the investments section of that statement at $981,000.

If the bonds had been purchased at a premium of $20,000 instead of at a discount, the entry to record the purchase would have been:

```
Bond Investments ........................................  1,020,000
    Cash .................................................             1,020,000
    To record the purchase of bonds at 102.
```

The entry required at December 31 would have been:

```
Accrued Interest Receivable ....................................  45,000
    Bond Investments ..........................................             1,000
    Interest Revenue ..........................................            44,000
    To record the accrual of interest and the amortization of the premium
    on bond investments.
```

The Northern Company's balance sheet as of December 31, 1981, would have shown accrued interest receivable of $45,000 and bond investments of $1,019,000.

Bonds purchased at face value between interest dates. Assume that the $100,000 of 9 percent bonds of the Carlson Company (described on page 500) are purchased by Braxton Company on May 1, 1981, at face value plus four months of accrued interest. (They were purchased four months after the most recent interest date.) The accrued interest is equal to $100,000 \times 0.09 \times \tfrac{1}{3} = \$3,000$. The entry to record the purchase is:

```
May 1  Bond Investments ....................................  100,000
           Accrued Interest Receivable .......................    3,000
               Cash ..........................................            103,000
       To record the purchase of bonds at face plus four months of interest.
```

If no action has been taken to record the interest accrued for the two months prior to the receipt of the semiannual interest, the Braxton Company will make the following entry in its accounts at the time it receives the first interest check:

```
July 1  Cash.................................................  4,500
            Accrued Interest Receivable ......................            3,000
            Interest Revenue .................................            1,500
        To record the receipt of interest on bond investments.
```

The net interest revenue is $1,500 ($100,000 \times 0.09 \times \tfrac{1}{6}$) which is interest for the two months from the date of purchase to the first interest date.

Bonds purchased at a discount or premium between interest dates. When bonds are purchased at a discount or premium between interest dates, it is necessary to amortize the premium or discount over the period running from the acquisition date to the maturity date. It is important to note that you do not write off the discount or premium over the *entire* life of the bonds unless the bonds are to be held for their entire life.

To illustrate, assume that the Purchaser Insurance Company on March 1, 1981, bought bonds of the Issuer Corporation at 92.2. They are 12 percent bonds with a face value of $1,000,000. The bonds are dated January 1, 1981. (The other side of this transaction was given on page 501. You may want to refer back to it as you examine the entries required for the purchaser.)

The entries required for 1981 on the Purchaser Insurance Company's books are as follows:

Mar.	1	Bond Investments	922,000	
		Accrued Interest Receivable..........................	20,000	
		Cash		942,000
		To record the purchase of bonds at 92.2 plus two months' accrued interest.		
July	1	Cash	60,000	
		Accrued Interest Receivable		20,000
		Interest Revenue		40,000
		To record receipt of six months' interest.		
Dec. 31		Accrued Interest Receivable..........................	60,000	
		Interest Revenue		60,000
		To record the accrual of six months' interest.		
		Bond Investments	6,610	
		Interest Revenue		6,610
		To record the amortization of ten months' discount at $661 per month.		

$$\frac{\$78,000}{118 \text{ months}} = \$661$$

Valuation of debt securities held

The most common basis of valuation for investments in bonds is cost, whether they are current assets or long-term investments. Cost usually consists of price paid plus broker's commission. An exception to this practice is made when a *substantial* and *apparently permanent* decline in the value of the bonds occurs. Then these bond investments are written down to market by debiting Loss on Market Decline of Bond Investments and crediting Bond Investments.

Once bond investments are written down, it is *not* permissible to write them back up to even their original cost if market prices advance in the future. Gain or loss simply is recorded for the difference between the sales proceeds and the amount at which the bonds are carried in the accounts when they are sold.

Stock investments

Sometimes companies invest in the common and preferred stocks of other companies. Such investments may actually consist of marketable securities in that the stocks may be readily marketable. But these rarely are purchased as temporary investments of idle cash. When acquired, they are more likely to be either long-term investments or an attempt to speculate in the stock market.

The reasons for investing on a long-term basis in the securities of others include the desire (1) to establish an affiliation with another business, (2) to acquire control over another business, or (3) to secure a continuing stream of revenue from the investment over a period of years.

Reporting stock investments in the balance sheet.   The generally stated guides as to where these securities should be classified in the balance sheet tend to emphasize intent and may be summarized as follows.

1.   If the securities held are readily marketable, they should be shown as current assets if they *will* be converted into cash in the normal operating cycle of the business. Such securities are called *short-term marketable securities*. If they will not be converted, they should be considered noncurrent assets and reported in the investments section of the statement.
2.   If the securities are not readily marketable, they may not be classified as current assets, unless they mature in the coming operating cycle and there is no doubt as to their redemption.

The primary classification criterion is the intent of management.

Valuation of equity securities (stock investments).   The FASB in its *Statement No. 12,* "Accounting for Certain Marketable Securities," describes the method of accounting for marketable equity securities.[3] It requires the use of the lower-of-the-cost-or-market method for marketable *equity* securities (with certain limited exceptions). *Marketable equity securities* include common and preferred stocks of other corporations. Marketable equity securities are to be carried at the lower of total cost or total market for all securities classified as current *taken as a group* and for securities classified as noncurrent *taken as a group.*

Current marketable equity securities.   For the securities classified as current any excess of total cost over total market is debited to an account such as Net Unrealized Loss on Current Marketable Equity Securities, which is shown in the earnings statement. The credit is to a current asset valuation allowance account such as Allowance for Market Decline of Current Marketable Equity Securities. The entry would appear as follows (assuming cost is $16,000 and market is $15,500):

```
Net Unrealized Loss on Current Marketable Equity Securities ................. 500
     Allowance for Market Decline of Current Marketable
          Equity Securities ..........................................        500
     To record the unrealized loss from a market decline of current marketable equity
     securities.
```

The balance sheet presentation would be as follows:

```
               Current Assets:
               Current marketable equity securities (cost $16,000 less
                    allowance for market decline of $500) ................. $15,500
```

Any later recovery in total market price (up to the amount of the original cost) would be debited to the asset valuation allowance and would be credited to an account such as Net Unrealized Gain on Current Marketable Equity

---
    [3] FASB, "Accounting for Certain Marketable Securities," *FASB Statement No. 12* (Stamford, Conn., December 1975), pp. 31.

Securities, which would be shown in the earnings statement. The entry would appear as follows (assuming the market price recovered by $400):

```
Allowance for Market Decline of Current Marketable Equity Securities . . . . . . . . .   400
     Net Unrealized Gain on Current Marketable Equity Securities . . . . . . . . . . . .          400
     To record the recovery in market price on current marketable equity securities.
```

The balance sheet presentation of the asset would now be:

```
Current Assets:
Current marketable equity securities (cost $16,000 less
     allowance for market decline of $100) . . . . . . . . . . . . . . . . . .   $15,900
```

Noncurrent marketable equity securities. Any "temporary" losses on noncurrent equity securities (long-term investments) are charged against a stockholders' equity account (but not deducted from net earnings) and credited to an asset valuation allowance account. The account debited might be entitled, Net Unrealized Loss on Noncurrent Marketable Equity Securities. Thus, the entry might be as follows (assuming cost is $32,000 and market is $31,000):

```
Net Unrealized Loss on Noncurrent Marketable Equity Securities . . . . . . . . .   1,000
     Allowance for Market Decline of Noncurrent Marketable Equity
          Securities . . . . . . . . . . . . . . . . . . . . . . . . . . . . . . . . . . . . . . . . . . . . . . . . .          1,000
     To record the unrealized loss from a market decline of noncurrent marketable
     equity securities.
```

The balance sheet presentation of the asset would be:

```
Investments:
Noncurrent marketable equity securities (cost $32,000 less
     allowance for market decline of $1,000) . . . . . . . . . . . . . . . . .   $31,000
```

Later recoveries up to cost would be debited to the allowance account and credited to the unrealized loss account as follows (assume market increases by $1,700):

```
Allowance for Market Decline of Noncurrent Marketable Equity Securities . . .   1,000
     Net Unrealized Loss on Noncurrent Marketable Equity Securities . . . . . . .          1,000
     To record the recovery in market price on noncurrent marketable equity
     securities.
```

Thus, the entry would increase owners' equity by $1,000 (not $1,700) but would not increase reported earnings. If a loss on an individual noncurrent security is determined to be "permanent," it is recorded as a realized loss and deducted in measuring earnings. The entry would be (assuming a permanent loss of $1,400):

```
Realized Loss on Noncurrent Marketable Equities Securities . . . . . . . . . . . . . .   1,400
     Investment in Noncurrent Marketable Equity Securities . . . . . . . . . . . . . .          1,400
     To record the realized loss from a permanent market decline of noncurrent
     marketable equity securities.
```

Any subsequent recovery in market value would be ignored until the security is sold.

The equity method. This method should be used for an investment in common stock by an investor whose investment in voting stock gives it the ability to exercise significant influence over operating and financial policies of that company (even though the investor holds 50 percent or less of the voting stock). In the absence of evidence to the contrary, an investment of 20 percent or more indicates the ability to exercise significant influence, and an investment of less than 20 percent does not. In situations where there is the ability to significantly influence, the investor is required to use the equity method of accounting for its investment.[4] Under the equity method, the investor initially records the investment at cost and then adjusts the carrying amount to recognize its share of the other company's earnings or losses after the date of acquisition. Dividends received are deducted from the investment. In this chapter we shall assume that investments in the common stock of others represent less than 20 percent of the outstanding shares. In the next chapter the equity method is discussed and illustrated.

Entry to record acquisition.   When the common or preferred stocks of other corporations are acquired, they should be recorded at cost, which is the cash outlay or the fair value of the asset given in exchange. Since the stock acquired usually will be purchased from another investor through a broker, cost normally will consist of the price paid for the stock plus a commission to the broker. For example, assume that Brewer Corporation purchased 1,000 shares of Cowen Corporation common stock at $15 per share through a broker who charged $100 for services rendered in acquiring the stock. Brewer would record the transaction as follows:

Stock Investment	15,100	
Cash		15,100
To record purchase of 1,000 shares of Cowen common at $15 plus $100 broker's commission.		

Cash dividends on investments.   The usual accounting for the receipt of dividends on stock investments is to debit Cash and credit Dividend Revenue when the cash dividend check is actually received. This accounting for dividends is acceptable for tax purposes and is followed widely by investors.

An alternative will be required when a dividend is declared in one accounting period which will not be paid until the following period. Assume that the Cowen Corporation declared a cash dividend of 20 cents per share on December 1, 1981, to stockholders of record as of December 20, 1981, payable on January 15, 1982. Under these circumstances an entry should be made either on December 20 or as an adjusting entry on December 31 as follows:

Dividends Receivable	200	
Dividend Revenue		200
To record dividend of 20 cents per share on Cowen common stock due January 15, 1982.		

When the dividend is collected on January 15, the entry would be a debit to Cash and a credit to the Dividends Receivable account. In this manner the dividend is recorded as revenue in the period in which it is earned.

Stock dividends and stock splits.   A stock dividend consists of the distri-

---

[4] APB, "The Equity Method of Accounting for Investments in Common Stock," *APB Opinion No. 18* (New York: AICPA, March 1971).

bution by a corporation of additional shares of its stock to its stockholders. Usually the distribution consists of additional common stock to common stockholders. Such a distribution is not considered to be a revenue-producing transaction to the holders of the stock. A stock dividend is viewed simply as having the effect of dividing the stockholders' equity into a large number of smaller pieces. It simply increases the number of shares a stockholder holds, but it does not change his or her percentage of ownership of the outstanding shares.

Thus, the accounting for stock dividends consists only of a notation in the accounts of the number of shares received and a change in the average per share cost of the shares held. For example, if 100 shares of A Company common stock are held, which cost $22 per share, and the A Company distributes a 10 percent stock dividend, the number of shares held is increased to 110 and the cost per share is now $20 ($2,200 ÷ 110 shares = $20 per share).

Similarly, when a corporation *splits* its stock, called a *stock split,* the only accounting entry required is a notation indicating the receipt of the additional shares. If Smith Company owned 1,000 shares of Jones Company common stock and Jones Company split its stock on a two for one basis, Smith would own 2,000 shares after the split and the cost per share would be halved.

Sale of stock investments.   When stock holdings are sold, the gain or loss on the sale is the difference between the net proceeds received and the carrying value of the shares sold.[5] Assume, for example, that 100 shares of Thacker Company common stock are sold for $75 per share. The broker deducted a commission and other taxes and charges of $62 prior to making remittance to the seller. If the seller's cost were $5,000, the required entry is:

Cash	7,438	
Stock Investments		5,000
Gain on Sale of Investments		2,438
To record the sale of stock investments.		

The realized gain on sale of investments is shown in the earnings statement regardless of whether the securities were classified as current or noncurrent equity securities.

APPENDIX: FUTURE WORTH AND PRESENT VALUE

This Appendix discusses the concepts of future worth (or value), present value, and present value of an annuity, their use in determining the price of a bond issue, and the effective rate of interest method for amortizing the discount on bonds payable.

Future worth

Interest is compounded, called *compound interest,* when periodically its amount is computed and added to the base to form a new amount upon which the

---

[5] FASB, *Statement No. 12,* p. 5.

interest for a later period is to be computed. For example, an investment of $1,000 at 3 percent compound interest will grow to $1,060.90 in two periods at compound interest, but only to $1,060 at simple interest. At simple interest, the interest for each period will be $30 for a total of $60. At compound interest, the interest for the first period will be $30 and the amount of the investment at the end of the first period will be $1,030 ($1,000 × 1.03). Interest for the second period will be $30.90 ($1,030 × 0.03), and the amount of the investment will be $1,060.90 ($1,030 × 1.03) at the end of the second period as shown below:

Value now	Interest $1,000 × 0.03 = $30	Value in 1 year	Interest $1,030 × 0.03 = $30.90	Value in 2 years
$1,000		$1,030		1,060.90

Note that the $1,060.90 amount was derived by multiplying $1,000 × 1.03 × 1.03. Since 1.03 × 1.03 is equal to $(1.03)^2$, a shortcut can be employed in the calculation. The amount of the investment at the end of the second period is simply $1,000 × $(1.03)^2$, which equals $1,000 × 1.0609, or $1,060.90. From this the formula for the compound amount of 1 can be derived as being $(1 + i)^n$ where i is the interest rate per period and n is the number of periods involved.

The task of computing the sum (the future worth) to which any invested amount will grow at a given rate for a stated number of periods is facilitated through the use of interest tables. From Table 1, Appendix B (at the end of this text), the amount to which an investment of $1 at 3 percent for three periods will grow can be determined as being $1.092727. The amount to which an investment of $1,000 will grow is simply 1,000 times this amount.

Present value

In the illustrations above, the future worth of a given investment was found by multiplying the investment by $(1 + i)^n$, where i was the interest rate involved and n the number of periods of life. Since *present value* is exactly the reverse of a future sum, it is found by dividing the future sum by $(1 + i)^n$. Thus, the present value of $1,000 due in one period at 3 percent is equal to $1,000 ÷ (1.03). Or the computation can be expressed as $1,000 × 1/(1.03) which is equal to $1,000 × 0.970874, or $970.87. Thus, $970.87 invested at 3 percent per period will grow to exactly $1,000 in one period as follows:

Value now	Interest $970.87 × 0.03 = $29.13	Value after 1 year
$970.87		$1,000

The present value of $1,000 due in two periods then is simply $1,000 ÷ $(1.03)^2$. Here again the computation can be expressed as $1,000 × 1/$(1.03)^2$, which simplifies to $1,000 × 0.942596, or $942.60. This can be shown as follows:

Present value .... Lump sum to be received in 2 years

$942.60 ← $1,000

$1,000 × 0.942596 (found in Appendix B, Table 2, 3% column and 2 period row)

Table 2, Appendix B, at the end of this text contains the present values of $1 at different interest rates for different periods of time. The use of the table can be illustrated by determining the present value of $10,000 due in 40 periods at 3 percent. The present value of 1 due in 40 periods at 3 percent per period is given as 0.306557. The present value of $10,000 due in 40 periods at 3 percent then is $3,065.57 ($10,000 × 0.306557).

Present value of an annuity

An *annuity* may be defined as a series of equal payments (called rents) equally spaced in time. The present value or worth of such a series may be desired information for certain types of decisions. The approach to the problem of valuing annuities can be illustrated by finding the present value, at 3 percent per period, of an annuity calling for the payment of $100 at the end of each of the next three periods. It would be possible, through the use of Table 2, Appendix B, to find the present value of each of the $100 payments as follows:

Present value of $100 due in—
1 period is 0.970874 × $100 = $ 97.09
2 periods is 0.942596 × $100 =   94.26
3 periods is 0.915142 × $100 =   91.51
Total present value of
   three $100 payments . . $282.86

Such a procedure could become quite tedious if the annuity consisted of 50 to 100 or more payments. Fortunately, tables are also available showing the present values of an annuity of $1 per period for varying interest rates and periods. See Table 3, Appendix B, at the end of the text. Thus, a single figure can be obtained from the table which represents the present value of an annuity of $1 per period for three periods at an interest rate of 3 percent per period. This figure is 2.828611, and when multiplied by $100, the number of dollars in each payment, yields the present value of the annuity as $282.86. The present value of an annuity can be illustrated as follows:

Present value	Amount to be received at end of year 1	Amount to be received at end of year 2	Amount to be received at end of year 3
$282.86	$100	$100	$100

$100 × 2.828611 (found in Table 3, Appendix B, 3% column and 3 period row)

Determining the price of a bond

The concepts discussed above now will be employed to illustrate the computation of the price of a bond issue.

In determining the price of a bond, the life of the bond always is stated in terms of interest payment periods, and the effective rate used in seeking amounts from the interest tables is the annual effective rate divided by the number of interest periods in one year.

Assume that bonds with a face value of $100,000 and an interest rate of 10 percent (semiannual interest payments) are issued at a price which will yield the investor an annual return of 12 percent (or 6 percent for each interest period). The issue date is July 1, 1981, and the maturity date is July 1, 1984 (this unrealistically short life is used for the sake of keeping the illustration simple). The price the investor would pay is calculated as shown:

Present value of the promise to pay principal is $100,000 times the present value of $1 due in 6 periods at 6%, or $100,000 × 0.704961 (from Table 2, Appendix B)	$70,496.10
Present value of the promise to pay periodic interest is $5,000 times the present value of an annuity of $1 for 6 periods at 6%, or $5,000 × 4.917324 (from Table 3, Appendix B)	24,586.62
Total price	$95,082.72

Thus, the amount of the discount is $100,000 − $95,082.72 = $4,917.28.

The effective rate of interest method for amortizing the discount

The following table shows how this discount would be amortized over the life of the bonds under the *effective rate of interest method*. The yield rate must be known to make the calculations required under this method. Notice that the amount amortized increases each period rather than remaining constant as it would under the straight-line method ($819.55 per six-month period under the straight-line method).

Discount amortized by the effective rate of interest method

Date	Cash credit	Interest expense debit	Discount on bonds payable credit	Carrying value of bonds payable
7/1/81				$ 95,082.72
1/1/82	$ 5,000[1]	$ 5,704.96[2]	$ 704.96[3]	95,787.68[4]
7/1/82	5,000	5,747.26	747.26	96,534.94
1/1/83	5,000	5,792.10	792.10	97,327.04
7/1/83	5,000	5,839.62	839.62	98,166.66
1/1/84	5,000	5,890.00	890.00	99,056.66
7/1/84	5,000	5,943.34[5]	943.34	100,000.00
	$30,000	$34,917.28	$4,917.28	

[1] $100,000 × 10% × ½ = $5,000.
[2] $95,082.72 × 12% × ½ = $5,704.96.
[3] $5,704.96 − $5,000 = $704.96.
[4] $95,082.72 + $704.96 = $95,787.68.
[5] Actually this came to $5,943.40, but was reduced to make the carrying value come to $100,000.

The numbered items (1–4) at the bottom of the table show how each of the numbers for January 1, 1982, is calculated.

To illustrate use of the table, assume that an entry is to be prepared on July 1, 1982. It would appear as follows:

7/1/82	Interest Expense	5,747.26	
	Cash		5,000
	Discount on Bonds Payable		747.26

To record the payment of interest and amortize the discount for the first six months of 1982.

NEW TERMS INTRODUCED IN CHAPTER 17

Annuity—a series of equal payments spaced equally in time.

Bond indenture—the overall contract between the issuer of bonds and the bondholders or the trustee representing the bondholders.

Bond redemption fund—a fund established to bring about the gradual redemption of outstanding bonds; usually called a sinking fund.

Call premium—the price in excess of face value which a bond issuer may be required to pay to redeem bonds prior to maturity date.

Compound interest—interest calculated on the principal plus the interest earned in previous periods, as compared to simple interest in which interest is computed only on the principal.

Contract rate of interest—the rate of interest printed on the face of the bonds.

Coupon bonds—bonds with interest coupons which are to be detached and presented for payment on the interest date or thereafter.

Debenture bonds—unsecured bonds whose value depends upon the general credit of the issuer and which are a general lien against all unpledged property.

Effective interest rate method—a method in which interest expense (revenue) for a period is calculated by multiplying the book value of the bonds payable (investment in bonds) by the effective interest rate at the bond issue (purchase) date. The difference between the actual expense (revenue) and the amount paid (received), based on the nominal bond interest rate, represents the accumulation of discount or amortization of premium for the period.

Effective rate of interest—the rate of interest that an investor can earn on a particular bond issue by paying a certain price for it and that the issuer will incur by issuing it at that price.

Favorable financial leverage—an increase in earnings per share resulting from the use of borrowed funds.

Financial leverage—the effect upon earnings of the introduction, or existence, of long-term debt (or other instrument with a fixed payout) as a means of financing a business; results from the fact that interest on debt is fixed in amount regardless of the level of earnings and is deductible in arriving at taxable earnings.

Market rate of interest—the minimum rate of interest which investors are willing to accept on bonds of a particular risk category.

Marketable equity securities—include common and preferred stocks of other companies.

Marketable securities (short term)—securities which can and will be converted into cash within one year or one current operating cycle, whichever is longer. Included among these securities are certificates of deposit, 91-day Treasury bills. Treasury tax anticipation notes, commercial paper of other companies, and other governmental securities.

Mortgage—a conditional transfer of title to property to secure a debt.

Present value—the value today of a specified future cash flow (an annuity or a lump-sum amount); determined by discounting such flows at a stipulated rate of interest.

Registered bonds—bonds for which the names of the owners are recorded by the issuer or trustee.

Sinking fund—a fund into which periodic cash deposits are made for the purpose of redeeming outstanding bonds.

Straight-line (discount or premium) amortization method—a method of amortizing a discount or premium which results in the same amount being assigned to each period of the life of a bond.

Stock investments—purchases of shares of stock issued by other companies.

Stock split—a procedure by which a corporation replaces each of its outstanding shares with two or more new shares. Thus, the owner of stock of a corporation receives some multiple of the number of shares held in place of the original shares. For instance, Mr. X might receive 2,000 shares of Corporation B's shares in place of the 1,000 shares he formerly held.

Trading on the equity—the securing of a portion of the needed capital of a business through the use of securities which limit the amount of interest (or dividends) paid periodically on them (see financial leverage).

Trustee—usually a bank or trust company selected to represent the bondholders in a bond issue and enforce the provisions of the bond indenture made by the issuing company.

Unfavorable financial leverage—the reverse of favorable financial leverage.

Unsecured bonds—bonds for which no specific property is pledged as security and whose value, as a result, depends on the general credit of the issuer.

DEMONSTRATION PROBLEM

On September 1, 1981, Sullivan Corporation issued $600,000 of ten-year, 8 percent bonds dated July 1, 1981, at 100. Interest on the bonds is payable semiannually upon presentation of the appropriate coupon. All of the bonds are of $1,000 denomination. The company's accounting period ends on September 30, with semiannual statements prepared on March 31 and September 30.

All of the first coupons on each of the bonds are presented to the company's bank and paid by January 2, 1981. All but two of the second coupons on the bonds are similarly received and paid on July 1, 1981.

Required:

a. Present all necessary journal entries for the above transactions, including all adjusting entries needed at September 30, 1981.

b. Swift Company purchased $300,000 of Sullivan Corporation's bonds on September 1, 1981, as a long-term investment. The company prepares financial statements on December 31. Present all journal entries for Swift Company relating to the bonds through December 31, 1981.

Solutions to demonstration problem

a.

```
                         SULLIVAN CORPORATION
                           General Journal

1981
Sept.  1  Cash ...................................................  608,000
             Bonds Payable ......................................            600,000
             Accrued Bond Interest Payable.......................              8,000
          To record the issuance of bonds at face value plus two month's
          interest, $8,000 = ($600,000 × 0.08 × ⅙).

      30  Bond Interest Expense .................................    4,000
             Accrued Bond Interest Payable.......................              4,000
          To accrue interest for one month at 8 percent on $600,000 of
          bonds.

1982
Jan.   2  Bond Interest Expense .................................   12,000
          Accrued Bond Interest Payable .........................   12,000
             Cash ...............................................             24,000
          To record receipt and payment of interest coupon No. 1 on
          bonds outstanding.

Mar.  31  Bond Interest Expense .................................   12,000
             Accrued Bond Interest Payable.......................             12,000
          To accrue interest for three months at 8 percent on $600,000
          of bonds.

July   1  Bond Interest Expense .................................   12,000
             Accrued Bond Interest Payable.......................             12,000
          To accrue interest for three months.

       1  Accrued Bond Interest Payable .........................   23,920
             Cash ...............................................             23,920
          To record payment of all except two of interest coupon No. 2.
```

$$\left[\$24{,}000 - 2\left(\frac{\$1{,}000 \times 0.08}{2} \right) \right]$$

b.

```
                           SWIFT COMPANY
                           General Journal

1981
Sept.  1  Investment in Bonds ...................................  300,000
          Accrued Bond Interest Receivable ......................    4,000
             Cash ...............................................            304,000
          Purchased Sullivan Corporation bonds plus accrued interest as
          a long-term investment.

Dec.  31  Accrued Interest Receivable ...........................    8,000
             Interest Revenue....................................              8,000
          Accrued interest (0.08 × $300,000 × 4/12).
```

QUESTIONS

1. What is meant by the term "trading on the equity"?

2. What are the advantages of obtaining long-term funds by the issuance of bonds rather than additional shares of capital stock? What are the disadvantages?

3. Ace Corporation was authorized to issue $1.5 million, of 7 percent, ten-year bonds. On a certain balance sheet date, only $1 million of the bonds had been issued. How should these facts be displayed in the balance sheet? Why should they be disclosed?

4. When bonds are issued between interest dates, why is it appropriate that the issuing corporation should receive cash equal to the amount of accrued interest in addition to the issue price of the bonds?

5. Why might it be more accurate to describe a sinking fund as a bond redemption fund?

6. Indicate how each of the following items should be classified in a balance sheet on December 31, 1981.

a. Cash balance in a sinking fund.

b. Accrued interest on bonds payable.

c. Debenture bonds payable due in 1991.

d. Premium on bonds payable.

e. First-mortgage bonds payable, due July 1, 1982.

f. Discount on bonds payable.

g. First National Bank—Interest account.

h. Convertible bonds payable due in 1984.

7. Why would an investor whose intent is to hold bonds to maturity pay more for the bonds than their face value?

8. Explain the main problem encountered in classifying marketable securities in the balance sheet.

9. Describe the valuation bases used for marketable equity securities.

10. Explain briefly the accounting for stock dividends and stock splits from the investor's point of view.

11 (based on the Appendix). If a corporation can obtain funds at a net cost of 3 percent to buy an asset which will produce a series of annual net cash flows of $1,000 at the end of each of the next ten years, should it make the investment in this asset if its cost is $8,750? (The present value of an annuity of $1 due for ten periods at 3 percent is 8.53020284.)

EXERCISES

E–1. Interest on Martin Corporation's coupon bonds is paid by a trustee, the Third National Bank. Assuming the semiannual interest amounts to $25,000 and all of the coupons are cashed, prepare the entries to record the deposit of the cash for interest with the trustee, the accrual of the interest, and the cashing of the coupons.

E–2. The Bailey Company issued $100,000 of ten-year, 9 percent bonds dated June 1, 1981, on August 1, 1981, at 99 plus accrued interest. Prepare the entry necessary to record the issuance. Wonder Company bought one tenth of these bonds. Prepare the journal entry to record this long-term investment.

E–3. Thayer Company issued $200,000 of ten-year, 10 percent bonds at 102 on January 1, 1981, the date of the bonds.

a. Was the market rate of interest for these bonds higher or lower than 10 percent?

b. What is the amount of bond interest expense for 1981, assuming straight-line amortization of the bond premium?

E–4. If Baxter Corporation bought $40,000 of the bonds issued by Thayer Company (see Exercise E–3) as a long-term investment, what amount of interest revenue was earned in 1981 assuming straight-line amortization was used? Give the journal entry required at December 31, 1981, to amortize the premium.

E–5. If, in Exercise E–3, the bonds were issued at 95, what would the interest expense be for 1981 assuming use of the straight-line method?

E–6. The Wixon Company, pursuant to provisions of its bond indenture, acquired $20,000 of its outstanding bonds on the open market at 97 plus accrued interest. These bonds were originally issued at face and carry a 6 percent interest rate payable semiannually. The acquisition was made on September 1, and the bonds are dated December 1, 1970. Prepare the entries required to record the acquisition and the accrual of the interest to the acquisition date on the bonds acquired.

E–7. The K Company is required to make a deposit of $40,000 plus accrued interest of $1,200 on April 30,

1980, to the trustee of its sinking fund so that the trustee can redeem $40,000 of the bonds on May 1, 1980. Prepare the entries required on April 30 to record the interest accrual and sinking fund deposit and the entries on May 1 to record the bond retirement, payment of interest, and payment of trustee expenses, assuming the latter amount to be $125. (The bonds were issued at 100.)

E-8. Wells Company purchased 100 shares of Tinker Company stock at a total cost of $1,050 on July 1, 1981. At the end of the accounting year (December 31, 1981) the market value for these shares was $950. As of December 31, 1982, the market value had risen to $1,100. This is the only marketable equity security that Wells Company owns. The company classifies the securities as noncurrent assets. Give the entries which would be necessary at the date of purchase and at December 31, 1981, and 1982.

E-9. Bentley Company purchased on July 1, 1981, 100 shares of Pool Company capital stock at $47 per share plus a commission of $50. On July 15 a 10 percent stock dividend was received. Bentley received a cash dividend of 50 cents per share on August 12, 1981. On November 1 Bentley sold all of the above shares for $58 per share, less commissions and taxes of $55. Prepare entries to record all of the above in Bentley Company's accounts.

E-10. The Delex Company has marketable equity securities which have a market value at year-end that is $800 below their cost. Give the required entry if—

a. The securities are current assets.

b. The securities are noncurrent assets and the loss is considered to be temporary.

c. The securities are noncurrent assets and the loss is considered to be permanent.

d. State where each of the accounts debited in **a, b,** and **c** would be reported.

E-11 (based on the Appendix). Conceptually, what is the present worth of a lump-sum payment of $10,000 due in five years? If the going market rate of interest on investments of this type is 5 percent per year and the present value of $1 due in five years at 5 percent is 0.78352617, what is its specific worth?

E-12 (based on the Appendix). Conceptually, what is the present worth of a series of annual payments of $1,000 due at the end of each of the next five years? If the going market rate of interest on investments of this type is 5 percent per year and the present value of an annuity of $1 for five periods at 5 percent is 4.32947667, what is its specific worth?

PROBLEMS, SERIES A

P17-1-A. On December 1, 1981, Brooks Company issued $500,000 of ten-year, 9 percent bonds dated July 1, 1981, at 100. Interest on the bonds is payable semiannually on July 1 and January 1. All of the bonds are registered. The company's accounting period ends on March 31. Quarterly financial statements are prepared.

The company deposits a sum of money sufficient to pay the semiannual interest on the bonds in a special checking account in the First National Bank and draws interest payment checks upon this account. The deposit is made the day before the checks are drawn.

Required:

a. Present journal entries to record the issuance of the bonds; the December 31 adjusting entry; the January 1, 1982, interest payment; and the adjusting entry needed on March 31, 1982.

b. The Brown Corporation bought $100,000 of the Brooks Company bonds on December 1, 1981, as a long-term investment. The company's year-end is December 31. Present all journal entries for Brown Corporation for these bonds through December 31, 1981.

P17-2-A. Laundon Corporation issued $100,000 of 9 percent, ten-year bonds at 95. Interest is payable semiannually. Mann Company also issued $100,000 of 9 percent, ten-year bonds, but received a price of 105 for its bonds. These bonds also call for semiannual interest payments. Both bond issues are dated and issued on July 1, 1981.

Required:

Prepare journal entries to record the issuance of both bond issues, the interest expense, and the payment of interest for the first semiannual period. Both companies have a fiscal-year accounting period ending on June 30, and straight-line amortization is applicable. (Amortize any premium and accumulate any discount on the interest date.) Which company actually is paying the lower interest rate? Why?

P17–3–A. On October 1, 1981, Marsalis Corporation issued $200,000 of ten-year, 9 percent debenture bonds at face value. The bonds are registered, and interest is payable semiannually on October 1 and April 1. The company is required by the bond indenture to deposit with the trustee each September 30 an amount sufficient to retire at face value $20,000 of the outstanding debenture bonds plus accrued interest. Such bonds are to be called for redemption on October 1 of each year, beginning in 1982. The company has the right to deliver bonds acquired in the market in lieu of making a cash deposit, with the required deposit reduced by $1,000 plus interest of $45 for each bond so delivered.

The first three interest payments were made according to provisions of the bond indenture, and the first sinking fund deposit was made as scheduled. The trustee reported on October 1, 1982, that the required number of bonds had been called. Trustee expenses of $100 were paid on December 1, 1982.

On August 1, 1983, the company purchased $20,000 of its outstanding bonds in the market at 99¾ plus accrued interest and delivered these to the trustee in lieu of making a cash deposit on September 30, 1983.

Required:

Prepare journal entries to record all transactions on the above bonds from October 1, 1981, through August 1, 1983, including the necessary adjusting entries. The company has a calendar-year accounting period and prepares quarterly statements.

P17–4–A. Dahlberg Company issued $200,000 of 9 percent, ten-year, first-mortgage bonds at 102.36 on September 1, 1981. The bonds are dated July 1, 1981, and call for semiannual interest payments on July 1 and January 1.

Lauer Company issued $200,000 of 8 percent, ten-year, first-mortgage bonds at 96.55 on December 1, 1981. The bonds are dated July 1, 1981, and call for semiannual interest payments on July 1 and January 1.

Required:

Assuming that the accounting period ends on March 31 for both companies, present journal entries to record the issuance of the bonds, the payment of the first semiannual interest payment, and the adjusting entries needed on March 31. Use the straight-line method for amortizing the premium and discount and do so only at year-end.

P17–5–A. Temple Corporation bought $100,000 face value of the bonds of each company in Problem 17–4–A as a long-term investment. Temple's accounting year ends on March 31.

Required:

Present all journal entries necessary to record the purchases, interest payments, and any adjusting entries needed through March 31, 1982. Amortize the premium or discount only at the accounting year-end. Use the straight-line method.

P17–6–A. Following are selected transactions relating to the bonds of the McPherson Company.

1981
July 1 Authorized issue of $200,000 of 9 percent, ten-year bonds dated July 1, 1981, interest payable semiannually on January 1 and July 1.
Sept. 1 Issued $100,000 face value of the bonds at 92.92.
1982
Jan. 1 Paid the semiannual interest.
Feb. 1 Issued the remaining bonds at 102.26.
July 1 Paid semiannual interest.

Required:

Present journal entries to record all of the above transactions, including the adjusting entry needed at June 30, 1982, the end of the company's accounting period. Also, present the long-term liability section of the company's June 30, 1982, balance sheet. Use the straight-line method in amortizing the discount and premium, and amortize any premium or discount only at the end of the accounting year.

P17–7–A. Lauber, Inc., issued $1 million of bonds on January 1, 1981, at 105 percent of their face value. The bonds bear interest at the rate of 9 percent, payable semiannually, and mature on January 1, 2001. The bond indenture provides that the issuing corporation may, on any interest date subsequent to December 31, 1985, redeem all or any part of its outstanding bonds by call by paying a redemption price equal to 105 percent of face value. On January 1, 1986, after due notification as to which bonds are being called, the corporation calls and cancels $400,000 of its outstanding bonds. The company employs a calendar-year accounting period.

Required:

Prepare journal entries to record the issuance of the bonds, the accrual of the first six months' interest expense and the payment thereof (also amortize the premium on this date using the straight-line method), and the entries necessary on January 1, 1986.

P17–8–A. Knobloch Company issued $200,000 of 9 percent bonds on July 1, 1981, at face value. The bonds are dated July 1, 1981; call for semiannual interest payments on July 1 and January 1; and mature at the rate of $20,000 per year on July 1, beginning in 1986. The company's accounting period ends on September 30.

Required:

a. Present journal entries to record the interest expense and payment for the six months ending July 1, 1986; the maturing of the bonds on July 1, 1986; and the adjusting entries needed on September 30, 1986.

b. Show how the bonds will be presented in the company's balance sheet for September 30, 1986.

P17–9–A. The Bruns Company acquired on July 15, 1981, 200 shares of Reetz Company $100 par value capital stock at $97 per share plus a broker's commission of $120. On August 1, 1981, Bruns Company received a cash dividend of 60 cents per share. On November 3, 1981, it sold 100 of these shares at $105 per share less a broker's commission of $80. On December 1, 1981, the Reetz Company issued shares comprising a 100 percent stock dividend declared on its capital stock November 18.

On December 31, 1981, the end of the calendar-year accounting period, the market quotation for Reetz's common stock was $46 per share. The decline was considered to be permanent.

Required:

a. Present journal entries to record all of the above data, assuming the securities are considered temporary investments and are to be valued at the lower of cost or market.

b. If the remaining shares are to be held for affiliation purposes—Reetz Company has become a major customer—indicate how they should be shown in the balance sheet.

P17–10–A (based on the Appendix). Johnston Company issued $100,000 of 8 percent, 20-year bonds on July 1, 1981. Kenimer Company issued $100,000 of 5 percent, 20-year bonds on July 1, 1981. Both bond issues are dated July 1, 1981, call for semiannual interest payments on July 1 and January 1, and are issued to yield 6 percent (3 percent per period).

Required:

a. Compute the amount received by each company for the bonds issued. (Use the tables in Appendix B.)

b. Present entries to record the issuance of the bonds.

c. Using the effective interest rate method, present entries to recognize the interest expense and payment of

the interest for the first six months. Assume a fiscal-year ending December 31.

P17–11–A (based on the Appendix). Joyce Corporation purchased one tenth of the Johnston Company bonds (see Problem 17–10–A) as a long-term investment.

Required:

Present the journal entries for the purchase and the interest payment of January 1, and the adjusting entry required on June 30, 1982, the company's year-end. Use the effective interest rate method to amortize any premium or accumulate any discount, and do so at each interest date and at the end of the accounting period.

P17–12–A. The Bryan Company purchased the following common stocks at per share prices that included commissions on October 27, 1980:

300 shares of Aye Company common stock @ $60	$18,000
500 shares of Bee Company common stock @ $40	20,000
800 shares of Cey Company common stock @ $20	16,000
	$54,000

On December 31, 1980, the market prices per share of the above common stocks were Aye, $62; Bee, $38; and Cey, $15.

Summarized, the cash dividends received in 1981 were Aye, 300 shares @ $2; Bee, 500 shares @ $1; and Cey, 800 shares @ $0.75. Also, a 100 percent stock dividend (300 shares) was received on the Aye Company common stock.

On December 31, 1981, the per share market prices were Aye, $34; Bee, $32; and Cey, $20.

All of the changes in market prices given above are considered temporary.

Required:

a. Prepare journal entries for all of the above, including calendar year-end adjusting entries, assuming the shares of common stock acquired are considered short-term investments.

b. Assuming the securities acquired are considered long-term investments, how would the entries made in *(a)* differ?

c. For both parts *(a)* and *(b),* give the descriptions (titles) and the dollar amounts of the items that would appear in the earnings statements for 1980 and 1981.

PROBLEMS, SERIES B

P17–1–B. On June 1, 1981, Ackerman Corporation issued $900,000 of ten-year, 8 percent bonds dated April 1, 1981, at 100. Interest on the bonds is payable semiannually upon presentation of the appropriate coupon. All of the bonds are of $1,000 denomination. The company's accounting period ends on June 30, with semiannual statements prepared on December 31 and June 30.

All of the first coupons on each of the bonds are presented to the company's bank and paid by October 2, 1981. All but two of the second coupons on the bonds are similarly received and paid on April 1, 1982.

Required:

a. Present all necessary journal entries for the above transactions, including all adjusting entries needed at June 30, 1981.

b. Allen Company purchased $300,000 of Ackerman Corporation's bonds on June 1, 1981, as a long-term investment. The company prepares financial statements on September 30. Present all journal entries for Allen Company relating to the bonds through September 30, 1981.

P17–2–B. Yates, Inc., issued $200,000 of 8 percent, ten-year bonds at 98. Interest is payable semiannually. Wyatt Corporation also issued $200,000 of 8 percent, ten-year bonds, but received a price of 102 for its bonds. These bonds also call for semiannual interest payments. Both bond issues are dated and issued on July 1, 1981.

Required:

Prepare journal entries to record the issuance of both bond issues, the interest expense, and the payment of interest for the first semiannual period. Assume both companies have a calendar-year accounting period and that straight-line amortization is acceptable. Which company is actually paying the lower interest rate? Why?

P17–3–B. The Allison Company, on July 1, 1981, issued $100,000 of ten-year, 12 percent bonds dated July 1, 1981, at face value. Bond interest coupons are to be submitted semiannually on July 1 and January 1 for payment. The company is required to deposit with the trustee on each June 30, beginning in 1982, a sum sufficient to enable the trustee to call $10,000 face value of bonds for redemption on July 1 at face value plus accrued interest. The company also has the right to deliver bonds acquired in the open market to the trustee in lieu of making a cash payment. The company's accounting period ends on December 31, and semiannual statements are prepared.

The following transactions were entered into by the Allison Company:

1982
Jan. 2 Bank reports that it paid all of the semiannual interest coupons.
June 30 Paid the required deposit to trustee.
July 1 Trustee reports $10,000 of bonds acquired at face value as well as payment of accrued interest on these bonds.
      3 Bank reports that it paid semiannual interest coupons in the amount of $5,400.
Dec. 31 Paid $75 of trustee's expenses.
1983
Jan. 2 Report from bank shows that it paid all of the outstanding coupons due for payment on January 1, 1983.
June 1 Purchased $10,000 of outstanding bonds in the market at 99½ and delivered them to the trustee in lieu of the cash deposit required on June 30.

Required:

Prepare journal entries to record the issuance of the bonds and to record the data in the above transactions, including whatever adjusting entries are needed at December 31, 1981; June 30, 1982; and December 31, 1983.

P17–4–B. On December 1, 1981, Wright Company issued $200,000 of 9 percent, ten-year, first-mortgage bonds for $193,040 cash plus accrued interest. The bonds are dated August 1, 1981, and call for semiannual interest payments on August 1 and February 1.

Armstrong Corporation issued $200,000 of 9 percent, ten-year, first-mortgage bonds on August 1, 1981, for $209,520 cash plus accrued interest. The bonds are dated July 1, 1981, and call for semiannual interest payments on January 1 and July 1.

Required:

Assume the accounting period ends for both companies on March 31 and present entries to record the issuance of both bond issues, the first interest payment, and the necessary adjusting entries at March 31, 1982. Straight-line amortization is appropriate.

P17–5–B. The Wofford Corporation purchased one tenth of the bonds of each company in Problem 17–4–B as a long-term investment. Its year-end is also March 31. Present the journal entries to record the acquisition of the bonds, the first interest payment, and any necessary adjusting entries at March 31, 1982. Use the straight-line method.

P17–6–B. Following are selected transactions of the Bailey Company, which employs a fiscal year ending on June 30:

1981
July 1   Received authorization to issue $200,000 of 9 percent, ten-year bonds dated July 1, 1981. Interest is payable semiannually on January 1 and July 1.
Aug. 1   Issued, for cash, $100,000 of the bonds at 103.57.
1982
Jan. 1   Paid semiannual interest.
Mar. 1   Issued the remaining bonds for $97,760 plus accrued interest since the last interest date.
July 1   Paid semiannual interest on all bonds.

Required:

Prepare journal entries to record all of the above transactions including the adjusting entries needed at June 30, 1982. Also present the long-term liability section of the company's June 30, 1982, balance sheet. Straight-line amortization is acceptable.

P17–7–B. On January 1, 1981, Barnes, Inc., issued $100,000 of 7 percent, 20-year bonds dated January 1, 1981, at 106. Interest is payable on January 1 and July 1. The bond indenture provides that the company may retire any or all of the bonds on any interest payment date subsequent to July 1, 1985, at a price equal to 105 percent of face value. On January 1, 1986. Barnes, Inc., redeemed $40,000 of its outstanding bonds. The company's accounting period ends on December 31.

Required:

Prepare journal entries to record the issuance of the bonds, the first semiannual interest payment (the company decided on semiannual, straight-line amortization of the premium), and the entries necessary on January 1, 1986.

P17–8–B. Wilkerson Company issued $200,000 of 8 percent serial bonds on July 1, 1981, at face value. The bonds are dated July 1, 1981; call for semiannual interest payments on July 1 and January 1; and mature at the rate of $40,000 per year, with the first maturity falling on July 1, 1986. The company's accounting period ends on September 30, with quarterly statements prepared.

Required:

Present journal entries to record the interest payment of July 1, 1986; the maturing of $40,000 of bonds on July 1, 1986; and the adjusting entry needed on September 30, 1986. Also, show how the bonds will be presented in the company's balance sheet for September 30, 1986.

P17–9–B. On September 1, 1981, Landry Company purchased the following securities as long-term investments:

1. One thousand shares of Hi-Flyer Company capital stock at $61 plus broker's commission of $400.

2. Five hundred shares of Turkey Company capital stock at $98 plus broker's commission of $350.

Cash dividends of $1.25 per share on the Hi-Flyer capital stock and $1 per share on the Turkey capital stock were received on December 7 and December 10, respectively.

Market prices at December 31, 1981, are Hi-Flyer stock, $65; and Turkey stock, $91.

Required:

a. Prepare journal entries to record the above transactions.

b. Prepare the necessary adjusting entry(ies) at December 31, 1981, to adjust the carrying values assuming that market price changes are assumed to be permanent.

c. Explain what factor(s) may have caused the price of the capital stock to go up in one case and down in the other.

P17–10–B (based on the Appendix). Whitley Company issued $100,000 of 7 percent, 20-year bonds on October 1, 1981. The bonds are dated October 1, 1981, call for semiannual interest payments on October 1 and April 1, and are issued to yield 8 percent (4 percent per period).

Boucher Company issued $100,000 of 9 percent, 20-year bonds on October 1, 1981. The bonds are dated October 1, 1981, call for semiannual interest payments on October 1 and April 1, and are issued to yield 8 percent (4 percent per period).

Required

a. Compute the amount received by each company for the bonds issued. (Use the tables in Appendix B.)

b. Present entries to record the issuance of the bonds.

c. Present entries to recognize the interest expense and payment for the first six months using the effective interest rate method of amortizing the premium or discount to the periods of life in the bonds. Assume a fiscal year accounting period ending May 31.

P17–11–B (based on the Appendix). Bray Company bought one tenth of the Whitley Company's bonds (see Problem 17–10–B) as a long-term investment. Record the journal entries for the acquisition of the bonds; receipt of interest on April 1, 1982; and the adjusting entry required on September 30, 1982, the company's year-end. Use the effective interest rate method for the entries required on April 1 and September 30 for amortizing any premium or discount.

P17–12–B. Brezina Corporation purchased on July 2, 1980, 100 shares of East Company $50 par value capital stock at $80 per share, plus broker's commission of $60. A 20 percent stock dividend was received on December 15, 1981.

On July 15, 1982, a dividend of $1 per share was received. On September 15, 1982, the East Company split each of its $50 par value shares of capital stock into two $25 par value shares of capital stock.

On November 2, 1982, the Brezina Corporation sold 100 shares of East capital stock at $50, less commissions and taxes of $40.

Required:

a. Present journal entries to record all of the 1982 transactions.

b. In light of the above information, how would you recommend that the remaining shares of stock be classified in the December 31, 1983, balance sheet if still held at that date?

BUSINESS DECISION PROBLEM 17–1

A company is trying to decide whether to spend an additional $2,000,000 on plant expansion and to divide another $1,000,000 equally between financing expansion of inventories and receivables. This $3,000,000 expansion will approximately double the business volume. The new volume can all be sold at the same price per unit as present sales. Profit forecasts indicate that net earnings from operations will rise from $800,000 to $1,320,000. The tax rate will be about 40 percent. Earnings after taxes last year were $438,000. Interest expense on current obligations is $70,000 per year. There are presently 200,000 shares of common stock outstanding.

The necessary funds can be obtained in two alternative ways:

1. Finance entirely by issuance of additional common stock. The issuance price would be $75 per share.
2. Finance two thirds with bonds, one third with additional common stock. The bonds would be 20-year, 7 percent; and the issue price of the stock would be $80. Assume the bonds are issued at face value.

Required:

Should the investment be made? If so, what financing alternative would you recommend? (Hint: Calculate earnings per share for last year and under each of the alternatives for this year.)

BUSINESS DECISION PROBLEM 17–2

Part 1. The board of directors of the Jones Company has decided to issue $500,000 of mortgage bonds to raise capital for a planned expansion of operations. The directors believe that the bonds will sell at face value if they carry an 8 percent interest rate. Interest rates are expected to rise slightly over the coming few years.

Harold, one of the directors, firmly believes the bonds should carry a rate of 9 percent. This will cause the bonds to sell at a premium, and they will continue to sell at a premium even if interest rates do rise slightly. He believes this would be an indication of real financial strength. He is of the opinion that having one's bonds sell at a discount is a sign of weakness that is to be avoided if at all possible.

Joan, another director, disagrees. She thinks the bonds should carry an interest rate of about 7 percent. This will cause the bonds to sell at a discount, and investors will be attracted to this special buying opportunity. Furthermore, selling the bonds at a discount is a means of paying some of your interest in advance, she argues, indicating that she considers this quite valuable.

Required:

Prepare a brief evaluation of the positions taken by each of these two directors.

Part 2. You are the CPA engaged to audit the records of the Brown Company. You find that your client has a portfolio of marketable equity securities that have a market value (in total) that is $50,000 less than the total cost of the portfolio. You ask the vice president for finance if the client expects to sell these securities in the coming year. He answers that he doesn't know. The securities will be sold if additional cash is needed to finance operations. When you ask for a cash forecast you are told that one has been prepared that covers the next year. It shows no need to sell the marketable securities.

Required:

How would you recommend that the client's portfolio of marketable securities be classified in the balance sheet? Why? Does it really make any difference whether the securities are classified as current or noncurrent? Explain.

Chapter 18

Corporations:

Consolidated financial statements

PARENT AND SUBSIDIARY CORPORATIONS

In many cases, one corporation owns a majority (more than 50 percent) of the outstanding voting common stock of a second corporation. In such cases, both corporations exist as separate legal entities; neither of the corporations is dissolved. The corporation which owns a majority of the outstanding voting common stock of another corporation is referred to as the *parent* company; the corporation controlled by the parent company is known as the *subsidiary* company.

When a large enterprise is operated as a parent company and its controlled subsidiaries, each corporation maintains its own accounting records. But, since the parent and its subsidiaries are *controlled* by a central management and are related to each other, the parent company usually is *required* to prepare one set of financial statements as if the parent and its subsidiaries taken together constitute a single enterprise. The term *consolidated statements* refers to the financial statements that result from combining the parent's financial statement amounts with those of its subsidiaries. Preparation of consolidated statements is discussed in this chapter. Consolidated statements *must be prepared* when one company owns more than 50 percent of the outstanding voting common stock of another company (and, thus, exerts control over the other company) and the two companies are not engaged in markedly dissimilar businesses such as banking and manufacturing.

Eliminations

For the purposes of preparing consolidated financial statements, it is necessary to eliminate the amounts of intercompany transactions in order to show the assets, liabilities, and stockholders' equity accounts as if the parent and its subsidiaries were a single economic enterprise. Elimination entries are made only on a consolidated statement work sheet, not in the accounts of the parent or subsidiaries. The items remaining for the subsidiaries are combined with the corresponding items remaining for the parent in preparing the consolidated balance sheet.

One elimination will offset the parent company's investment in the subsidiary against the stockholders' equity accounts of the subsidiary. Assume that P Company organized the S Company, receiving all of S Company's $100,000 par value common stock for $100,000 cash. If a consolidated balance sheet is to be prepared, the required elimination on the worksheet is:

Common Stock—S Company	100,000	
Investment in S Company		100,000

This elimination is required because the parent company's investment in the stock of the subsidiary actually represents an equity in the net assets of the subsidiary. Thus, unless the investment is eliminated, the same resources will appear twice on the consolidated balance sheet (as the investment and as the assets of the subsidiary). The elimination also is necessary to avoid double counting the owners' equity.

Intercompany receivables and payables (due from and owed to companies in the consolidated group) are also items which must be eliminated during the preparation of consolidated statements. For example, assume the parent company owes the subsidiary $5,000 as evidenced by a $5,000 note receivable on the subsidiary's books and a $5,000 note payable on the parent's books. These balances would be eliminated by offsetting the note receivable against the note payable. No debt is owed to or due from any entity outside the consolidated enterprise. Similarly, other intercompany balances would be eliminated when consolidated statements are prepared.

CONSOLIDATED BALANCE SHEET AT TIME OF ACQUISITION: Acquisition at book value

To combine the assets and liabilities of a parent company and its subsidiaries, a *consolidated statement work sheet* similar to the one shown in Illustration 18.1 is prepared. The first two columns show the assets, liabilities, and stockholders' equity of the parent and subsidiary as they would appear on each corporation's individual balance sheet. The pair of columns labeled Eliminations allows intercompany items to be offset and consequently eliminated from the consolidated statement. The final column shows the amounts that will appear on the consolidated statement.

This particular work sheet (Illustration 18.1) was prepared to consolidate the accounts of P Company and its subsidiary, S Company, on January 1, 1981. P Company acquired S Company on January 1, 1981, by purchasing all of its outstanding voting common stock for $106,000 cash, which was the *book value* of the stock.

When P Company acquired the stock of S Company from S Company's stockholders, P Company made the following entry:

Investment in S Company	106,000	
Cash		106,000
To record investment in S Company.		

Illustration 18.1: Work sheet for consolidated balance sheet

P COMPANY AND SUBSIDIARY S COMPANY
Work Sheet for Consolidated Balance Sheet
January 1, 1981 (date of acquisition)

	P Company	S Company	Eliminations		Consolidated Amounts
			Debit	Credit	
Assets					
Cash	26,000	12,000			38,000
Notes receivable	5,000			*(b)* 5,000	
Accounts receivable, net	24,000	15,000			39,000
Inventory	35,000	30,000			65,000
Investment in S Company	106,000			*(a)* 106,000	
Equipment, net	41,000	15,000			56,000
Buildings, net	65,000	35,000			100,000
Land	20,000	10,000			30,000
	322,000	117,000			328,000
Liabilities and Stockholders' Equity					
Accounts payable	18,000	6,000			24,000
Notes payable		5,000	*(b)* 5,000		
Common stock	250,000	100,000	*(a)* 100,000		250,000
Retained earnings	54,000	6,000	*(a)* 6,000		54,000
	322,000	117,000	111,000	111,000	328,000

Two elimination entries are required in this example. The investment appears as an asset on P Company's balance sheet. By buying the subsidiary's stock, the parent in effect acquired a 100 percent equity or ownership interest in the subsidiary's net assets. Thus, if both the investment and the subsidiary's assets appear on the consolidated balance sheet, the same resources will be counted twice. The Common Stock and Retained Earnings accounts of the subsidiary also represent an equity in the subsidiary's assets. Therefore, it is necessary to offset P's investment in S Company against S Company's stockholders' equity accounts so that the subsidiary's assets and the ownership interest in these assets appear only once on the consolidated statement. This elimination is accomplished by entry *(a)* on the work sheet.

Entry *(b)* is required to eliminate the effect of an intercompany transaction (intercompany debt in this case). On the date it acquired S Company, P Company loaned S Company $5,000—which is recorded as a $5,000 note receivable on P's books and a $5,000 note payable on S's books. If the elimination entry is not made on the work sheet, the consolidated balance sheet will show $5,000 owed to the consolidated enterprise *by itself.* Actually from the viewpoint of the consolidated entity, neither an asset nor a liability exists. Therefore, entry *(b)* is made on the work sheet to eliminate both the asset and the liability.

In making *elimination entries,* it is important to understand that *the entries are made only on the consolidated statement work sheet; no elimination entries are made in the accounts of either P Company or S Company.*

Acquisition of subsidiary at a cost above or below book value

In the previous illustration, P Company acquired 100 percent of S Company at a cost equal to book value. But, in some cases, subsidiaries may be acquired at a cost greater than or less than book value. For example, assume P Company purchases 100 percent of S Company's outstanding voting common stock for $125,000. The book value of the stock is $106,000. Cost exceeds book value by $19,000. P Company may have paid more than book value for either or both of two reasons: (1) P Company may think that the subsidiary's earnings prospects justify paying a price greater than book value, or (2) P Company may believe that the fair value of the subsidiary's assets exceeds their book values.

According to the Accounting Principles Board *(APB Opinion No. 16),* in cases where cost exceeds book value because of expected above-average earnings, the excess should be labeled as *goodwill* on the consolidated balance sheet. On the other hand, if the excess is attributable to the belief that assets of the subsidiary are undervalued, then the value of the assets should be increased to the extent of the excess.[1] In Illustration 18.2, it is assumed that the $19,000 excess of cost over book value is attributable to expected above-average earnings. As a result, the excess is identified as goodwill on the balance sheet (Illustration 18.3). Elimination entry *(b)* in Illustration 18.2 is the same as for the first illustration. Entry *(a)* involves debits to the subsidiary's common stock and retained earnings accounts and to an account labeled excess of

---

[1] *APB Accounting Principles* (Chicago: Commerce Clearing House, Inc., 1973), vol. II, p. 6655.

Illustration 18.2:
Work sheet for
consolidated
balance sheet

P COMPANY AND SUBSIDIARY S COMPANY
Work Sheet for Consolidated Balance Sheet
January 1, 1981 (date of acquisition)

	P Company	S Company	Eliminations Debit	Eliminations Credit	Consolidated Amounts
Assets					
Cash	7,000	12,000			19,000
Notes receivable	5,000			(b) 5,000	
Accounts receivable, net	24,000	15,000			39,000
Inventory	35,000	30,000			65,000
Investment in S Company	125,000			(a) 125,000	
Equipment, net	41,000	15,000			56,000
Buildings, net	65,000	35,000			100,000
Land	20,000	10,000			30,000
Excess of cost over book value			(a) 19,000		19,000
	322,000	117,000			328,000
Liabilities and Stockholders' Equity					
Accounts payable	18,000	6,000			24,000
Notes payable		5,000	(b) 5,000		
Common stock	250,000	100,000	(a) 100,000		250,000
Retained earnings	54,000	6,000	(a) 6,000		54,000
	322,000	117,000	130,000	130,000	328,000

cost over book value and a credit to the parent's investment account. After these elimination entries are made, the remaining amounts are combined and extended to the column labeled consolidated amounts. The amounts in this column are then used to prepare the consolidated balance sheet shown in Illustration 18.3.

Under some circumstances, a parent company may pay less than the book value of the subsidiary's net assets. In such cases, it is highly unlikely that a "bargain" purchase has been made. The most logical explanation for the price paid is that some of the subsidiary's assets are overvalued. The Accounting Principles Board requires that the excess of book value over cost be used to reduce proportionately the value of the noncurrent assets acquired.[2] If the noncurrent assets are reduced to zero before the excess of book value over cost is fully eliminated, the remaining amount of excess should be reported as a deferred credit on the consolidated balance sheet. The *deferred credit*, which will be allocated to future operations, often is reported between liabilities and stockholders' equity on the balance sheet.

Acquisition of less
than 100 percent
of subsidiary

Sometimes a parent company acquires less than 100 percent of the outstanding voting common stock of a subsidiary. For example, assume P company acquires 80 percent of S Company's outstanding voting common stock. P Company

[2] Ibid., p. 6655.

Illustration 18.3: Consolidated balance sheet

P COMPANY AND SUBSIDIARY S COMPANY
Consolidated Balance Sheet
January 1, 1981

Assets

Current Assets:

Cash	$ 19,000	
Accounts receivable, net	39,000	
Inventory	65,000	
Total Current Assets		$123,000

Plant and Equipment:

Equipment, net	$ 56,000	
Buildings, net	100,000	
Land	30,000	
Total Plant and Equipment		186,000
Goodwill		19,000
Total Assets		$328,000

Liabilities and Stockholders' Equity

Current Liabilities:

Accounts payable		$ 24,000

Stockholders' Equity:

Common stock	$250,000	
Retained earnings	54,000	
Total Stockholders' Equity		304,000
Total Liabilities and Stockholders' Equity		$328,000

is the majority stockholder, but minority stockholders exist who own 20 percent of the stock. These minority stockholders, usually referred to as the *minority interest,* have an interest in the subsidiary's net assets and share the subsidiary's earnings with the parent company.

When preparing a consolidated balance sheet for a partially owned subsidiary, only part of the subsidiary's stockholders' equity is eliminated. That part of the common stock and retained earnings which relates to the minority stockholders is established on the consolidated work sheet as the minority interest.

Illustration 18.4 shows the elimination entries that are required when P Company purchases 80 percent of S Company's stock for $100,000. The book value of the stock acquired by P Company is $84,800 (80 percent of $106,000). The excess of cost over book values amounts to $15,200 and can be attributed to S Company's above-average earnings prospects. On the consolidated balance sheet, the $15,200 excess will be identified as goodwill (Illustration 18.5).

The minority stockholders have an equity of $21,200 (20 percent of $106,000) in the net assets of the consolidated enterprise (Illustration 18.5). The amount of the minority interest appears between the liabilities and stockholders' equity sections of the consolidated balance sheet. (Actually, there is some disagreement as to whether the minority interest is a liability or a part of stockholders' equity.)

Illustration 18.4:
Work sheet for
consolidated
balance sheet

	P Company	S Company	Eliminations Debit	Eliminations Credit	Consolidated Amounts
P COMPANY AND SUBSIDIARY S COMPANY Work Sheet for Consolidated Balance Sheet January 1, 1981 (date of acquisition)					
Assets					
Cash	32,000	12,000			44,000
Notes receivable	5,000			(b) 5,000	
Accounts receivable, net	24,000	15,000			39,000
Inventory	35,000	30,000			65,000
Investment in S Company	100,000			(a) 100,000	
Equipment, net	41,000	15,000			56,000
Buildings, net	65,000	35,000			100,000
Land	20,000	10,000			30,000
Excess of cost over book value			(a) 15,200		15,200
	322,000	117,000			349,200
Liabilities and Stockholders' Equity					
Accounts payable	18,000	6,000			24,000
Notes payable		5,000	(b) 5,000		
Common stock	250,000	100,000	(a) 100,000		250,000
Retained earnings	54,000	6,000	(a) 6,000		54,000
Minority interest				(a) 21,200	21,200
	322,000	117,000	126,200	126,200	349,200

Earnings, losses, and dividends of a subsidiary

If a subsidiary is operated profitably, there will be an increase in its net assets and retained earnings. When the subsidiary pays dividends, both the parent company and the minority stockholders will share in the distribution. Earnings and dividends will be recorded in the accounting records of the subsidiary just as they are recorded for other corporations.

Two different methods can be used by an investor to account for investments in common stock. They are the cost method and the equity method. The Accounting Principles Board has identified the circumstances under which each method can be used. The *general rules* for determining the appropriate method of accounting are summarized below:

Percent of outstanding voting common stock of investee owned by investor	Method of accounting required by Accounting Principles Board in most cases
Less than 20%	Cost
20%–50%	Equity
More than 50%:	
Consolidated subsidiary	Cost or equity
Nonconsolidated subsidiary	Equity

P COMPANY AND SUBSIDIARY S COMPANY
Consolidated Balance Sheet
January 1, 1981

Assets

Current Assets:

Cash	$ 44,000	
Accounts receivable, net	39,000	
Inventory	65,000	
Total Current Assets		$148,000

Plant and Equipment:

Equipment, net	$ 56,000	
Buildings, net	100,000	
Land	30,000	
Total Plant and Equipment		186,000
Goodwill		15,200
Total Assets		$349,200

Liabilities and Stockholders' Equity

Liabilities:

Accounts payable		$ 24,000
Minority interest		21,200

Stockholders' Equity:

Common stock	$250,000	
Retained earnings	54,000	
Total Stockholders' Equity		304,000
Total Liabilities and Stockholders' Equity		$349,200

According to the above table, the parent company can use either the cost or the equity method of accounting for its investment in a consolidated subsidiary. After consolidation, the results are identical.

Under the cost method, the investor company records its investment at cost (price paid at acquisition). Only subsidiary (investee) earnings that are distributed as dividends are recorded by the investor company (under the cost method). The investor company records dividends received from the subsidiary by debiting Cash and crediting Dividend Revenue. Thus, the investment account rarely changes under the cost method.

Under the equity method, the parent (investor) company initially records its investment at cost. Subsequently, the investment account is adjusted periodically for the parent (investor) company's share of the subsidiary's (investee's) earnings or losses as they are reported by the subsidiary. The parent company's share of the subsidiary's earnings is debited to the Investment in S Company account and credited to an account labeled Earnings of S Company. For example, assume the subsidiary S Company mentioned in the preceding illustrations earned $20,000 during 1981. P Company owns 80 percent of S Company. P Company would record its share of the earnings in the following manner:

```
Investment in S Company .......................................  16,000
    Earnings of S Company ....................................         16,000
  To record 80 percent of subsidiary's earnings.
```

The $16,000 debit to the investment account increases the parent's equity in the subsidiary. The $16,000 credit to the revenue account will be closed to the Expense and Revenue Summary account which then is closed to P Company's Retained Earnings account.

If the subsidiary incurs a loss, the parent company debits a loss account and credits the investment account for its share of the loss. For example, assume S Company incurs a loss of $10,000 in 1982. Since P Company still owns 80 percent of S Company, P Company would record its share of the loss as follows:

```
Loss of S Company .............................................  8,000
    Investment in S Company ....................................         8,000
  To record 80 percent of subsidiary's loss.
```

The $8,000 debit is closed first to the Expense and Revenue Summary which then is closed to Retained Earnings; the $8,000 *credit* reduces P Company's equity in the subsidiary.

Amortization of goodwill over a period not to exceed 40 years is required by the APB. Thus, the following entries would also be required on P Company's books in 1981 and 1982 to amortize goodwill ($15,200) over 40 years:

```
1981  Earnings of S Company .......................................  380
         Investment in S Company ...................................         380
        To amortize goodwill by deducting it.
1982  Loss of S Company ............................................  380
         Investment in S Company ...................................         380
```

P Company actually records its share of the net earnings (loss) of S Company less (plus) the amortization of goodwill from consolidation. The amortization of goodwill reduces the earnings or increases the loss. Changes in values of limited life assets are likely to require similar adjusting entries with calculations based on additional depreciation on revalued depreciable assets.

When a subsidiary declares and pays a dividend, the assets and retained earnings of the subsidiary are reduced by the amount of the dividend payment. When the parent company receives its share of the dividends, it debits the asset received (cash, in this case) and credits the investment account. For instance, assume S Company declares a cash dividend of $8,000 in 1981. P Company's share of the dividend amounts to $6,400 and is recorded as follows:

```
Cash ..........................................................  6,400
    Investment in S Company ....................................         6,400
  To record dividend received from subsidiary.
```

The receipt of the dividend reduces the parent's equity in the subsidiary as shown by the credit to the investment account.

CONSOLIDATED FINANCIAL STATEMENTS AT A DATE AFTER ACQUISITION

Under the equity method, the investment account on the parent company's books increases and decreases as the parent company records its share of the earnings, losses, and dividends reported by the subsidiary. Consequently, the balance in the investment account differs after acquisition from its balance on the date of acquisition. Therefore, the amounts eliminated on the consolidated statement work sheet will differ from year to year. As an illustration, assume the following facts:

1. P Company acquired 100 percent of the outstanding voting common stock of S Company on January 1, 1981. P Company paid $121,000 for an equity of $106,000. The excess of cost over book value (sometimes referred to as a *differential*) is attributable to S Company's above-average earnings prospects and is to be amortized over 20 years.
2. During 1981, S Company earned $20,000 from profitable operations.
3. On December 31, 1981, S Company paid a cash dividend of $8,000.
4. S Company has not paid the $5,000 it borrowed from P Company at the beginning of 1981.
5. Including S Company's earnings, P Company earned $30,250 during 1981.
6. P Company paid a cash dividend of $10,000 during December 1981.
7. P Company uses the equity method of accounting for its investment in S Company.
8. P sold goods that cost it $6,000 to S for $10,000. S sold all of these goods to outsiders for $15,000.

The financial statements for the two companies are given in the first two columns of the work sheet for consolidated financial statements for December 31, 1981, Illustration 18.6

In Illustration 18.6, notice that P Company has a balance of $19,250 in its Earnings of S Company account and a balance of $132,250 in its Investment in S Company account. The balances are the result of the following journal entries made by P Company in 1981:

Investment in S Company	121,000	
Cash		121,000
To record 100 percent investment in subsidiary.		
Investment in S Company	20,000	
Earnings of S Company		20,000
To record earnings of subsidiary.		
Earnings of S Company	750	
Investment in S Company		750
To amortize excess of cost over book value over 20 years ($15,000 ÷ 20).		
Cash	8,000	
Investment in S Company		8,000
To record dividends received from subsidiary.		

The elimination entries are explained below:

Entry *(a):*   During the year, S Company earned $20,000. P Company increased its investment account balance by $20,000. P Company also reduced its investment account balance by amortizing $750 of the excess

Illustration 18.6: Work sheet for consolidated financial statements

P COMPANY AND SUBSIDIARY S COMPANY
Work Sheet for Consolidated Financial Statements
December 31, 1981

	P Company	S Company	Eliminations Debit	Eliminations Credit	Consolidated Amounts
Earnings Statement					
Revenue from sales	397,000	303,000	(f) 10,000		690,000
Earnings of S Company	19,250		(a) 19,250		
Cost of goods sold	(250,000)	(180,000)		(f) 10,000	(420,000)
Expenses (excluding deprecia-					
tion, amortization, and taxes)	(100,000)	(80,000)			(180,000)
Depreciation expense	(7,400)	(5,000)			(12,400)
Amortization of goodwill			(d) 750		(750)
Income tax expense	(28,600)	(18,000)			(46,600)
Net earnings—carried forward	30,250	20,000			30,250
Statement of Retained Earnings					
Retained earnings—January 1:					
P Company	54,000				54,000
S Company		6,000	(c) 6,000		
Net earnings—brought forward	30,250	20,000			30,250
	84,250	26,000			84,250
Dividends					
P Company	(10,000)				(10,000)
S Company		(8,000)		(b) 8,000	
Retained earnings—December					
31—carried forward	74,250	18,000			74,250
Balance Sheet					
Assets					
Cash	38,000	16,000			54,000
Notes receivable	5,000			(e) 5,000	
Accounts receivable, net	25,000	18,000			43,000
Inventory	40,000	36,000			76,000
Investment in S Company	132,250		(b) 8,000	(c) 121,000	
				(a) 19,250	
Equipment, net	36,900	12,000			48,900
Buildings, net	61,700	33,000			94,700
Land	20,000	10,000			30,000
Excess of cost over book value			(c) 15,000	(d) 750	14,250
	358,850	125,000			360,850
Liabilities and Stockholders' Equity					
Accounts payable	19,600	2,000			21,600
Notes payable	15,000	5,000	(e) 5,000		15,000
Common stock	250,000	100,000	(c) 100,000		250,000
Retained earnings—brought					
forward	74,250	18,000			74,250
	358,850	125,000	164,000	164,000	360,850

of cost over book value. The first entry *(a)* on the work sheet eliminates the subsidiary's earnings less amortization from the investment account and P Company's revenue. It reverses the entries made on the books of P Company to recognize the parent's share of the subsidiary's earnings less amortization.

Entry *(b):*   When S Company paid its cash dividend, P Company debited Cash and credited the investment account for $8,000. The second entry *(b)* offsets parts of the entries originally made by P Company and S Company. That is, P's investment account is debited and S's dividends account is credited.

Entry *(c):*   This entry is familiar. It eliminates the original investment account balance and the subsidiary's stockholders' equity accounts as of the date of acquisition. It also establishes an amount which represents the excess of cost over book value.

After the first three entries are made, the investment account contains a zero balance from the viewpoint of the consolidated entity.

Entry *(d):*   According to *APB Opinion No. 17,* goodwill must be amortized over a period of time not to exceed 40 years. In this case, goodwill is being amortized over 20 years which results in $750 being written off as expense each year.

Entry *(e):*   This entry is also familiar. It eliminates the intercompany debt of $5,000.

Entry *(f):*   This entry eliminates the $10,000 of intercompany sales made by P to S. The records of the individual companies include the amounts shown in the first two columns with regard to these sales:

	P	*S*	*Total*	*Consoli-dated total*	*Over-state-ment*
Sales	$10,000	$15,000	$25,000	$15,000	$10,000
Cost of goods sold	6,000	10,000	16,000	6,000	10,000
Gross margin	$ 4,000	$ 5,000	9,000	$ 9,000	$ –0–

But from a consolidated entity viewpoint, sales can include only sales to outsiders. Sales to outsiders involving these goods were only $15,000, not $25,000, and cost of goods sold was only $6,000, not $10,000. Gross margin is still $9,000, so this elimination entry only removes the overstatement of sales and cost of goods sold by the $10,000 of intercompany sales.

After the eliminations have been made and goodwill has been amortized, the corresponding amounts are added together and placed in the Consolidated Amounts column. The entire net earnings row in the earnings statement section is carried forward to the net earnings row in the statement of retained earnings section. Likewise, the entire ending retained earnings row in the statement of retained earnings section is carried forward to the retained earnings row in the balance sheet section. The final column of the work sheet is then used in the preparation of the consolidated earnings statement (Illustration 18.7), the consolidated statement of retained earnings (Illustration 18.7), and the consolidated balance sheet (Illustration 18.8).

Illustration 18.7:
Consolidated
earnings
statement

P COMPANY AND SUBSIDIARY S COMPANY
Consolidated Earnings Statement
For the Year Ended December 31, 1981

Revenue from sales		$690,000
Cost of goods sold		420,000
Gross margin		$270,000
Expenses (excluding depreciation, amortization, and taxes)	$180,000	
Depreciation expense	12,400	
Amortization of goodwill	750	
Income tax expense	46,600	239,750
Net Earnings		$ 30,250

P COMPANY AND SUBSIDIARY S COMPANY
Consolidated Statement of Retained Earnings
For the Year Ended December 31, 1981

Retained earnings, January 1, 1981	$54,000
Net earnings	30,250
	$84,250
Dividends	10,000
Retained Earnings, December 31, 1981	$74,250

Illustration 18.8:
Consolidated
balance sheet

P COMPANY AND SUBSIDIARY S COMPANY
Consolidated Balance Sheet
December 31, 1981

Assets

Current Assets:		
Cash	$ 54,000	
Accounts receivable, net	43,000	
Inventory	76,000	
Total Current Assets		$173,000
Plant and Equipment:		
Equipment, net	$ 48,900	
Buildings, net	94,700	
Land	30,000	
Total Plant and Equipment		173,600
Goodwill		14,250
Total Assets		$360,850

Liabilities and Stockholders' Equity

Current Liabilities:		
Accounts payable	$ 21,600	
Notes payable	15,000	
Total Liabilities		$ 36,600
Stockholders' Equity:		
Common stock	$250,000	
Retained earnings	74,250	
Total Stockholders' Equity		324,250
Total Liabilities and Stockholders' Equity		$360,850

**PURCHASE
VERSUS
POOLING OF
INTERESTS**

In the illustrations in this chapter, it has been assumed that the parent company acquired the subsidiary's common stock in exchange for cash. Such a *business combination* is classified as a *purchase*. A purchase would also result if the acquiring company issued debt securities or assets other than cash. But, in some cases, one company issues common stock in exchange for the common stock of another company. Here it appears that the stockholders of both companies maintain an ownership interest in the combined company. Such a business combination is classified as a *pooling of interests* (if it meets all the pooling criteria cited in *APB Opinion No. 16*).

Given the circumstances surrounding a particular business combination, only one of the two methods—purchase or pooling of interests—is appropriate. It should be emphasized that the purchase and pooling of interest methods are *not* alternatives which can be applied to the same situation. *APB Opinion No. 16* specifies 12 conditions (only two of which will be described here) that must be met before a business combination can be classified as a pooling of interests. Two of the conditions are (1) that the combination be affected in one transaction or be completed within one year in accordance with a specific plan and (2) that one corporation issue only its common stock for 90 percent or more of the voting common stock of another company. If all 12 of the conditions are met, then the resulting business combination *must* be accounted for as a pooling of interests. Otherwise, the purchase method must be used to account for the combination.

When the pooling of interests method is used, the parent company's investment is recorded at the book value of the subsidiary's net assets and not at the market value of the parent's common stock given in exchange. This differs from the purchase method in which an investment is recorded at the amount of cash given up or at the fair market value of the assets or stock given up, whichever can be determined most clearly and objectively.

Since the investment is recorded at the book value of the subsidiary's net assets under the pooling of interests method, there can be no goodwill or deferred credit from consolidation. The subsidiary's retained earnings at the date of acquisition become a part of the consolidated retained earnings, whereas under the purchase method they do not become part of consolidated retained earnings. Also, under the pooling of interests method all the earnings of a subsidiary for the year during which it is acquired are included in the consolidated earnings for the year of acquisition. On the other hand, only that portion of the subsidiary's earnings which arises after the date of acquisition is included in consolidated net earnings under the purchase method.

From the above discussion, it should be apparent that significant differences exist between earnings statement and balance sheet amounts when the different methods are used. (Remember only one method is appropriate for a given set of circumstances.) For instance, under the purchase method, any excess of cost over book value must be used to increase the value of any assets that are undervalued or be recognized as goodwill from consolidation. Thus, more depreciation and amortization will be recorded under the purchase method when cost exceeds book value with the result that consoldiated net earnings are less under the purchase method than under the pooling of interests method. (Remember that under the pooling of interests method asset values are not increased and goodwill is not recognized upon consolidation.) Similarly, since the subsidiary's earnings for the entire year during which it was acquired are included in consolidated net earnings under the pooling of interests method, consolidated net earnings for the year of acquisition also would be larger under the pooling of interests method than under the purchase method (unless the combination occurred at the beginning of the accounting period). It is important that the appropriate method of accounting be used for a particular business combination.

Purchase versus pooling of interests illustrated

In this section, we will present a work sheet for consolidated statements using both the purchase and pooling of interests methods (under different sets of assumptions). We will then contrast the two sets of statements.

Assumptions (purchase method). Par Company acquired 100 percent of Sub Company's voting common stock on January 2, 1981. Par Company paid $200,000 cash for the stock, which had a book value of $190,000 ($150,000 common stock and $40,000 retained earnings). The $10,000 excess of cost over book value is attributed to the subsidiary's above-average earnings prospects. During 1981, Sub Company borrowed $8,000 from Par Company. The debt is evidenced by a note and has not been paid on December 31, 1981.

The work sheet for consolidated financial statements on December 31, 1981, is shown in Illustration 18.9.

Assumptions (pooling of interests method). Par Company acquired 100 percent of Sub Company's voting common stock on January 2, 1981. Par Company issued 15,000 shares of its own $10 par value common stock in exchange for the stock of Sub Company which had a book value of $190,000 ($150,000 common stock and $40,000 retained earnings). Par Company made the following entry to record its investment:

Investment in Sub Company	190,000	
Common Stock (15,000 shares)		150,000
Paid-In Capital—Pooling of Interests		40,000
To record investment in Sub Company.		

Notice that the investment is recorded at the book value of the subsidiary's stock, $190,000. The Common Stock account is credited for the par value of the shares issued (15,000 × $10). The remainder ($190,000 − $150,000 = $40,000) is credited to a paid-in capital account.

During 1981, Sub Company borrowed $8,000 from Par Company. The debt is evidenced by a note that has not been paid on December 31, 1981. The work sheet for consolidated financial statements on December 31, 1981, is shown in Illustration 18.10.

Notice that under the pooling of interests method the investment account balance is offset against the common stock of the subsidiary and paid-in capital—pooling of interests. The retained earnings of the subsidiary are included

Illustration 18.9: Work sheet for consolidated financial statements—purchase method

PAR COMPANY AND SUBSIDIARY SUB COMPANY
Work Sheet for Consolidated Financial Statements
(purchase method)
December 31, 1981

	Par Company	Sub Company	Eliminations Debit	Eliminations Credit	Consolidated Amounts
Earnings Statement					
Revenue from sales	400,000	150,000			550,000
Earnings of Sub Company	49,000		(a) 49,000		
Cost of goods sold	(250,000)	(75,000)			(325,000)
Expenses (excluding amortization)	(80,000)	(25,000)			(105,000)
Amortization of goodwill			(d) 1,000		(1,000)
Net earnings—carried forward	119,000	50,000			119,000
Statement of Retained Earnings					
Retained earnings—January 1:					
Par Company	200,000				200,000
Sub Company		40,000	(c) 40,000		
Net earnings—brought forward	119,000	50,000			119,000
	319,000	90,000			319,000
Dividends:					
Par Company	100,000				100,000
Sub Company		30,000		(b) 30,000	
Retained earnings—December 31— carried forward	219,000	60,000			219,000
Balance Sheet					
Assets					
Cash	100,000	80,000			180,000
Notes receivable	8,000			(e) 8,000	
Accounts receivable, net	17,000	28,000			45,000
Inventory	30,000	40,000			70,000
Investment in Sub Company	219,000		(b) 30,000	(c) 200,000	
				(a) 49,000	
Equipment, net	70,000	80,000			150,000
Excess of cost over book value			(c) 10,000	(d) 1,000	9,000
	444,000	228,000			454,000
Liabilities and Stockholders' Equity					
Accounts payable	25,000	10,000			35,000
Notes payable		8,000	(e) 8,000		
Common stock—$10 par	200,000	150,000	(c) 150,000		200,000
Retained earnings—brought forward	219,000	60,000			219,000
	444,000	228,000	288,000	288,000	454,000

Explanation of elimination entries:
(a) To eliminate earnings of subsidiary less amortization.
(b) To eliminate dividends received from subsidiary.
(c) To eliminate investment in subsidiary and subsidiary's capital accounts.
(d) To adjust excess of cost over book value by recording one year's amortization. (Goodwill is being amortized over ten years.)
(e) To eliminate intercompany debt.

Illustration 18.10: Work sheet for consolidated financial statements—pooling of interests method

PAR COMPANY AND SUBSIDIARY SUB COMPANY
Work Sheet for Consolidated Financial Statements
(pooling of interests method)
December 31, 1981

	Par Company	Sub Company	Eliminations Debit	Eliminations Credit	Consolidated Amounts
Earnings Statement					
Revenue from sales	400,000	150,000			550,000
Earnings of Sub Company	50,000		(a) 50,000		
Cost of goods sold	(250,000)	(75,000)			(325,000)
Expenses	(80,000)	(25,000)			(105,000)
Net earnings—carried forward	120,000	50,000			120,000
Statement of Retained Earnings					
Retained earnings—January 1:					
Par Company	200,000				200,000
Sub Company		40,000			40,000
Net earnings—brought forward	120,000	50,000			120,000
	320,000	90,000			360,000
Dividends:					
Par Company	100,000				100,000
Sub Company		30,000		(b) 30,000	
Retained earnings—December 31—					
carried forward	220,000	60,000			260,000
Balance Sheet					
Assets					
Cash	300,000	80,000			380,000
Notes receivable	8,000			(d) 8,000	
Accounts receivable, net	17,000	28,000			45,000
Inventory	30,000	40,000			70,000
Investment in Sub Company	210,000		(b) 30,000	(c) 190,000	
				(a) 50,000	
Equipment, net	70,000	80,000			150,000
	635,000	228,000			645,000
Liabilities and Stockholders' Equity					
Accounts payable	25,000	10,000			35,000
Notes payable		8,000	(d) 8,000		
Common stock—$10 par	350,000	150,000	(c) 150,000		350,000
Paid-in capital—pooling of interest	40,000		(c) 40,000		
Retained earnings—brought forward	220,000	60,000			260,000
	635,000	228,000	278,000	278,000	645,000

Explanation of elimination entries:
  (a) To eliminate earnings of subsidiary.
  (b) To eliminate dividends received from subsidiary.
  (c) To eliminate investment in subsidiary and common stock of subsidiary and paid-in capital from pooling of interests.
  (d) To eliminate intercompany debt.

in consolidated retained earnings. The following differences are found when the two sets of statements are contrasted:

	Purchase	Pooling of interests	Difference
Amortization of goodwill	$ 1,000	$ –0–	$ (1,000)
Net earnings	119,000	120,000	1,000
Cash	180,000	380,000	$200,000
Excess of cost over book value	9,000	–0–	(9,000)
Total			$191,000
Common stock—$10 par	200,000	350,000	$150,000
Retained earnings	219,000	260,000	41,000
Total			$191,000

Net earnings are $1,000 more under the pooling of interests method because there is no goodwill to be amortized. Cash is $200,000 more under the pooling of interest method because common stock was issued, whereas under the purchase method, $200,000 cash was paid. Under the pooling of interests method, common stock is $150,000 more because 15,000 shares of common stock were issued by Par Company to achieve the combination. Retained earnings are $41,000 larger under pooling of interests accounting because of the $1,000 difference in net earnings and because the subsidiary's retained earnings at acquisition ($40,000) are included in consolidated retained earnings.

Abuses of pooling of interests method

Prior to the issuance of *APB Opinion No. 16,* the pooling of interests method was used in cases where it really was not applicable. In other words, its use was subject to abuse. Four common abuses of pooling are indicated below:

1. Acquisition of smaller companies at year-end so that the earnings of the smaller companies can be combined with the parent's earnings (or used to offset the parent's loss) in order to increase net earnings and earnings per share.
2. Acquisition of a company having several plants whose fair market values are much greater than their book values. In this case the plants would be recorded as assets at their rather low book value, say, $200,000. The next year, one of the plants would be sold for its fair market value of, say, $800,000. The result of the sale would be a $600,000 gain which would instantly increase net earnings and earnings per share.
3. Issuance of unusual convertible securities which could be traded in one year later for either common stock or cash. Such securities were issued so that (1) the combination could be accounted for as a pooling of interests and (2) stockholders of the subsidiary could receive cash shortly if they did not want common stock.
4. Accounting for an acquisition as "part-purchase, part-pooling." In some cases, a certain number of stockholders would refuse to accept common stock or unusual convertible securities. They wanted cash immediately.

Thus, some companies accounted for part of the acquisition as a purchase and the other part as a pooling of interests.

APB Opinion No. 16 has helped to reduce these abuses of pooling.

Uses and limitations of consolidated statements

Consolidated statements are of primary importance to the stockholders, managers, and directors of the parent company. The parent company benefits from the earnings, asset increases, and other financial strengths of the subsidiary. Likewise, the parent company suffers from a subsidiary's losses or other financial weaknesses. The Appendix to this chapter includes significant portions of the consolidated financial statements of an actual company. They illustrate many of the concepts discussed in this text.

On the other hand, consolidated statements are of very limited use to the creditors and minority stockholders of the subsidiary. The subsidiary's creditors have a claim against the subsidiary alone; they cannot look to the parent company for payment. And the minority stockholders do not benefit or suffer from the parent company's operations. They benefit only from the subsidiary's earnings, asset increases, and financial strengths; they suffer only from the subsidiary's losses and financial weaknesses. Therefore, the subsidiary's creditors and minority stockholders are more interested in the subsidiary's individual financial statements than in the consolidated statements.

APPENDIX: A SET OF CONSOLIDATED FINANCIAL STATEMENTS FOR AN ACTUAL COMPANY

Presented in this Appendix are 20 pages of the 36-page Annual Report for 1978 of Interlake, Inc., and its consolidated subsidiaries. Included are (1) 1978 Highlights, (2) Financial Review, (3) Management's Responsibility for Financial Reporting, (4) a further Financial Review consisting of Management's Discussion of Summary of Operations, (5) Statement of Consolidated Income and Retained Earnings, (6) Consolidated Balance Sheet, (7) Statement of Changes in Consolidated Financial Position, (8) Notes to Consolidated Financial Statements, (9) Report of Independent Accountants, (10) Five-Year Financial Summary of Operations, and (11) Financial Information by Line of Business. These items are presented as illustrative of the financial reporting practices of a modern business corporation to its stockholders and other external parties. Several explanatory comments on some of the above items are presented below.

The item "Future Income Taxes" in the Consolidated Balance Sheet and discussed in Note 1 and Note 9 is explained and discussed in Chapter 27.

Particular attention should be paid to the rather substantial amounts of additional information and explanation presented in the Notes to the Consolidated Financial Statements. For example, Note 1 discloses the accounting policies followed in developing the amounts reported in the various statements, such as the methods of depreciation and inventory costing followed as well as the principles of consolidation employed.

A strong trend has emerged in recent years toward making more informative disclosures in corporate annual reports. Many of these added disclosures result from FASB or SEC requirements. Examples include (1) the financial review and management's discussion of the summary of operations, (2) the disclosure of the details with respect to income taxes, (3) the reporting of quarterly data, and (4) the disclosure of business segment information.

The premise underlying many of these added disclosures is simply that management knows better than anyone else what happened and why. Therefore, it should be called upon to explain. These added disclosures reflect the fact that stockholders and other users of financial statements need information that is more timely—quarterly rather than annually—and further that users need information on the various segments making up the consolidated entity.

The inclusion of a statement entitled "Management's Responsibility for Financial Reporting" is relatively new. This statement is presented to make sure that the reader understands that it is management, not the independent accountants, which is primarily responsible for the financial statements and their contents.

Note 12 shows that the company chose not to reveal detailed replacement cost information in its annual report. Such information is included in the reports filed with the SEC and is available to the public through that governmental agency.

Interlake, Inc
1978
Highlights

Interlake, Inc. is a Chicago-based international company engaged in two major businesses: metals and material handling. In metals, we manufacture and sell iron, steel, ferrous metal powders, investment and die castings, silicon metal and ferroalloys. Material handling includes packaging, shipping, storage and handling products and systems.

For The Year (In thousands)	% Change 78-77	1978	1977
Net sales	+ 20.2	$921,127	$766,614
Net income	− 44.0	10,488	18,732
Cash flow	− 12.3	36,978	42,151
Capital expenditures	+118.2	65,974	30,233
Cash dividends paid	+ .4	13,077	13,019
At Year End (In thousands)			
Working capital	+ 16.1	$163,348	$140,682
Current ratio	− 5.0	1.9 to 1	2.0 to 1
Property, plant and equipment—net	+ 12.0	237,620	212,121
Long-term debt, less current maturities	+ 59.8	136,169	85,233
Shareholders' equity	− .7	306,311	308,400
Shares outstanding	+ .6	5,959	5,925
Per Share Statistics			
Net income	− 44.2	$ 1.77	$ 3.17
Cash dividends paid	—	2.20	2.20
Shareholders' equity at year-end	− 1.2	51.41	52.05

1

Sales and Earnings by Business (In millions)

	Sales		Earnings	
	1978	1977	1978	1977
Metals				
Iron/Steel	$401.0	$353.8	$(31.6)	$ 3.9
Metal Powders	74.6	58.4	20.9	14.8
Investment/Die Castings	67.4	50.3	9.8	7.9
Silicon Metal/Ferroalloys	53.9	44.2	3.8	2.2
Material Handling				
Material Handling/Storage	227.3	174.0	11.0	3.7
Packaging	160.4	136.1	11.1	8.7
Corporate Items/Eliminations	(63.5)	(50.2)	(9.1)	(6.9)
	$921.1	$766.6	$ 15.9	$ 34.3

Interlake, Inc.

Financial Review
Chief Financial Officer's Letter

16

Robert Jacobs
Executive Vice President
Finance and Planning

Net Income
(in millions)

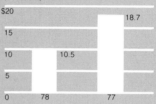

To Our Shareholders:

Significant sales increases in each of our six businesses generated record consolidated sales of $921.1 million for 1978. Operating income was higher in five businesses; however, net income declined 44% from $18.7 million in 1977 to $10.5 million in 1978. The key factors in the decline in earnings were a series of adverse conditions which affected our largest business, Iron and Steel, throughout the year, including a non-recurring provision of $15.7 million for the shutdown of the Toledo blast furnace plant and the sintering facility at the Chicago plant.

ferroalloys business reversing declining trends in these products in recent years.

A review of results by geographic area indicates record sales in domestic and foreign operations with domestic operating income impacted by the decline experienced by Iron and Steel. Foreign operations, aided by record results from Dexion's storage products operations, realized record operating income; improved economic conditions in major markets, aggressive marketing programs and effective cost controls were the keys to this record performance.

Net Sales
(in millions)

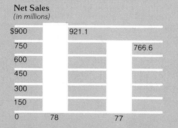

Combined operating income from the five businesses showing increases rose over 50% from 1977. Record operating income was reported by metal powders, packaging, investment/die castings and material handling/storage products. In addition, improved market conditions contributed to marked income improvement for the silicon metal/

Foreign Operations
(in millions)
- Sales
- Pre Tax Income

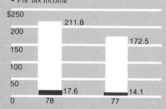

The impact of the shutdown/disposal provision on net income was partially offset by two factors: a favorable swing in the translation of the results of foreign operations and a lower effective tax rate.

Through 1976, the impact of foreign exchange activity and translation was minimal. Although Interlake has a policy of hedging major foreign currency exposures when practical, dramatic movements in foreign currency values relative to the U.S. dollar since 1976 and the prescribed accounting standard on translation have magnified the impact of foreign exchange between years. In 1977, translation of foreign subsidiary financial statements and foreign currency transactions, including hedging, penalized net income by 39¢ per common share. In 1978, the effect was a benefit to net income of 8¢ per common share.

The lower effective tax rate was primarily the result of a significant increase in investment tax credits related to the record level of capital expenditures. Investment tax credits were more than double the 1977 total, adding 62¢ to earnings per common share in 1978 compared with 29¢ in 1977. The investment tax credit is a direct reduction of federal income taxes for qualifying property placed in service during the year.

Financial Condition

Interlake remains strong financially as indicated by these key financial statistics:

	At 12/31/78	At 12/25/77
Working Capital	$163.3 million	$140.7 million
Working Capital Ratio	1.9 to 1	2.0 to 1
Quick Asset Ratio	.9 to 1	.9 to 1
Debt/Total Capitalization	31%	22%

The ratio of long term debt to total capitalization is about average for the six largest companies in the capital intensive steel industry, where Interlake has almost half of its investment, and is in line with other Moody's "A" rated companies. Record capital expenditures necessitated the increase in long-term debt during 1978 to $136.2 million at year-end, up $50.9 million. The increase largely represents the take down of the remaining $38.0 million under the 8½% loan agreement entered into in 1977 with a group of insurance companies. Industrial development and pollution control loan agreements, net of the redemption of $4.3 million of 8.8% Debentures, account for the remainder of the increase.

Capitalization

(in millions)

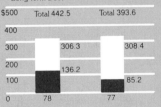

Interlake maintains short-term bank credit lines in the U.S. and abroad. At year-end, informal credit lines totaling $64.0 million, with rates at or equivalent to the prime rate, were available, against which $15.2 million was borrowed.

Cash flow from operations totaled $37.0 million in 1978, representing a decline of $5.2 million from 1977. However, the non-current portion of the shutdown/disposal provision provided an additional $13.7 million of funds. With other resources, primarily the additional long-term borrowings, total funds provided of $113.9 million exceeded uses of funds by $22.7 million.

Capital Expenditures

(in millions)

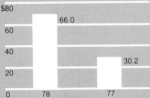

The major use of funds for 1978 was record capital expenditures of $66.0 million. This compares to an average annual rate of $25 million for the previous five years. The majority of the 1978 total was invested in the iron and steel business. A major blast furnace reline and repair of the coke ovens, with new emission control equipment, both at the Chicago plant, and the completion of the hot strip mill project at Newport to increase coil size, productivity and steel quality, accounted for $27.3 million of the $37.1 million expended in the iron and steel business. Major projects in other business segments in 1978 included:

- $9.8 million for the atomized powder metal plant at Gallatin, Tennessee
- $1.7 million for the completion of the new automatic shelf line in the U.K.
- $1.8 million for the completion of the relocation and expansion of die casting facilities at Hazleton, Pa., and initial expansion of investment casting facilities at Tilton, New Hampshire.

17

18   The second major use of funds was cash dividends of $13.1 million on common shares. The Board of Directors continued the cash dividend rate of $2.20 per common share which was initiated in the second quarter of 1976. Management believes that, consistent with the availability of adequate sources of internal and external funds, the dividend policy should reflect the broader outlook of Interlake rather than short-term fluctuations.

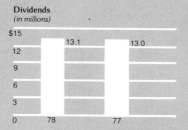

Dividends
(in millions)

Working capital increased $22.7 million to a record $163.3 million at year-end. Additions to inventories and accounts receivable, net of higher current liabilities, made up a significant part of this increase. A portion of the inventory growth was due to the operating plan to shut down the Toledo blast furnace and

allow for planned 1979 equipment outages at the Chicago blast furnace plant. As a result, pig iron inventories were increased to about three times the normal quantity and coke and semi-finished steel inventories were higher; lower Toledo ore and coal inventories at year-end partially offset these increases.

Accounts receivable additions reflect the higher sales levels achieved. However, the number of day's sales in year-end receivables increased only 3% to 44 days in 1978 although the prime interest rate increased to the highest level in four years.

Your investment in Interlake is represented by shareholders' equity which totaled $306.3 million at year-end. The $2.1 million decline from 1977 represented net income less dividends paid. The return on shareholders' equity declined to 3.4% from the average of 12% in the previous five years.

Robert Jacobs

Robert Jacobs
Executive Vice President
Finance and Planning

February 21, 1979

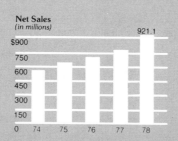

Net Sales
(in millions)

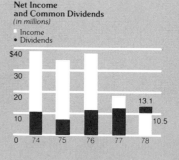

**Net Income
and Common Dividends**
(in millions)
□ Income
● Dividends

Management's Responsibility for Financial Reporting

Corporate accounting and reporting has been dramatically influenced in recent years by prescribed policies and practices from both private and governmental agencies. These pronouncements have resolved many debated issues, but also have created new problems, as with the accounting standard for translation of foreign currency financial statements and transactions. Overall, the benefits of such activities have outweighed any shortcomings and have produced an increased awareness and demand for quality and integrity in financial reporting from businessmen, investors, and the general public. In full consideration of this prevailing environment, we have prepared this Financial Review, including the financial statements of Interlake, Inc. and its consolidated subsidiaries at December 31, 1978 and related notes and management's discussion of summary of operations.

The financial statements were prepared by management in conformity with generally accepted accounting principles applied on a basis consistent with that of the prior year. The manner of presentation and integrity of the financial information are the responsibility of management. Some of the amounts included in the financial statements are estimates based on currently available information and management's best judgment of current conditions and circumstances. All of the financial information presented in the Annual Report is consistent with that in the financial statements.

Interlake's policy is to have a comprehensive system of internal accounting controls and organizational arrangements which provide for delegation of authority and appropriate divisions of responsibility to ensure the integrity of its financial reporting. The resultant system of internal accounting controls is intended to provide reasonable assurance as to the reliability of the financial records and the protection of assets against loss from unauthorized use or disposition. However, there are inherent limitations that should be acknowledged in evaluating the potential effectiveness of any system of internal accounting control. The concept of reasonable assurance is based on the recognition that the cost of a system of internal control should not exceed the benefits derived; the evaluation of those factors requires estimates and judgments by management. Management believes that Interlake's system of internal control provides such reasonable assurance.

Management is continually modifying and improving its system of accounting and controls in response to changes in business conditions and operations and comprehends in those revisions the comments and recommendations made by the independent accountants and the internal audit staff.

The financial statements have been examined by Interlake's independent accountants, Price Waterhouse & Co., who have given their unqualified opinion on the financial statements as found on page 32 of the Annual Report. Their examination was conducted in accordance with generally accepted auditing standards and was supplemented by the work of the internal auditors who have participated in these examinations. The internal auditors and the independent accountants meet at least twice each year with the Audit Review Committee of the Board of Directors to review the scope and timing of their audits and their findings. The Audit Review Committee consists of three outside directors who are charged with the responsibility to review, appraise, and report to the Board on accounting and reporting practices, the internal control system, and the audit effort by both the independent accountants and the internal auditors. The independent accountants have private and confidential access to the Audit Review Committee through its Chairman at any time they desire or request it.

In addition, Interlake has prepared and distributed to its employees statements of its policies for conducting business affairs in a lawful and ethical manner. We have developed and instituted specific internal controls and internal audit procedures to provide assurance that these policies are not violated.

19

**Capital Expenditures
and Depreciation**
(in millions)

Capital Expenditures
● Depreciation

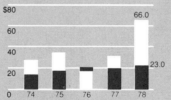

Capitalization
(in millions)
Shareholders' Equity
● Long Term Debt

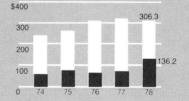

Interlake, Inc.

Financial Review
Management's Discussion of Summary of Operations

20 Net Sales

Sales reached a record $921 million in 1978 and increased $495 million or 116% in the five-year period ended December 31, 1978. The Dexion and Arwood companies acquired during this period accounted for $204 million of this sales increase. In 1974, operations and shipments generally reached capacity levels. Demand dropped in 1975 and returned to near 1974 levels in 1978. Price increases and acquisitions allowed the sales growth to continue unabated during the period of slackened demand. Sections on each of Interlake's six lines of business detailing the significant factors effecting sales are included on the following pages.

Other Revenues

Other revenues primarily include rent, royalty and interest income and gains on sales of property and equipment. Net gains on sales of vacant land and idle equipment averaged $2.5 million in the 1974-1976 period. In 1978, such gains were $2.1 million. Interest income reached a peak in 1974 and declined in subsequent years because of lower yields and lower available cash balances which resulted from major capital investments and acquisitions. In 1978, higher interest yields and short-term increases in available cash resulting from take-downs on long-term debt caused interest income to return to the 1974 level.

Costs and Expenses

Costs and expenses have increased steadily as a per cent of sales since 1974. Pricing actions since 1974 failed to recoup increasing labor, material and energy costs, particularly in the iron, steel, silicon metal and ferroalloy product lines. This condition was aggravated by low priced imports which limited demand for domestic production. In 1975, product costs benefited from a $10 million favorable settlement from a raw material supplier. In 1977 and 1978, severe winter weather, labor strikes directly reducing income from our coal and ore mining investments and related operations, and the effects of accelerated deterioration of the Chicago coke oven batteries and their repair, impacted costs severely, primarily in the iron and steel businesses.

Depreciation expense increased with the extensive program of capital expenditures which rose to a record level in 1978. Interest expense followed the increase in long-term debt required to support the higher capital expenditures. Selling and administrative expenses since the acquisition of Dexion Comino International in late 1974 have declined steadily as a per cent of sales despite inflationary pressures. Taxes other than income taxes remained at a relatively constant level as a percent of sales.

The sections by line of business include discussions of the general trends in costs and expenses and their relationship to price changes.

Shutdown/Disposal Provision

Interlake pig iron shipments steadily declined in recent years —for 1978, shipments of 253,200 tons represented a 17% decline from 1977 and only 54% of 1974 shipments. Shipments in 1978 accounted for a fraction of the capacity of the Toledo blast furnace plant, Interlake's primary producer of pig iron. Domestic demand for pig iron has suffered because of the disparity in pig iron and scrap prices. The prices of scrap, which can be used as a substitute raw material by foundries, have decreased dramatically as a percentage of pig iron prices. In 1974, the average price of scrap was 76% of the average price of pig iron; in the 1975—1978 period, this relationship has dropped to 37% as higher ore, coal, labor and energy costs spurred pig iron price increases. Demand for domestic pig iron was further lessened by foreign imports of low-priced pig iron; imports accounted for 20% of apparent domestic consumption in 1974 and rose to an estimated 46% in 1978. Confronted with these market conditions, a decision was reached in the third quarter of 1978 to consolidate Interlake's iron production at the Chicago blast furnace plant. This consolidation allows Interlake to meet expected iron demand and realize the benefits of full capacity production at one location. In December, 1978 the Toledo blast furnace operation was shut down and the ancillary coke oven facilities were sold. In addition, the sintering facility in Chicago was shut down due to the availability of additional iron units resulting from the closing of the Toledo blast furnace operation. The shutdown/disposal provision reflecting these actions covers estimated losses on the disposition of property, plant and equipment and inventories, employee severance costs and other costs.

Income Taxes

The effective rates of income taxes were:

Year	1978	1977	1976	1975	1974
Effective Tax Rate	19.4%	40.9%	38.8%	42.4%	45.1%

The effective tax rates are below the statutory rate principally because of investment tax credits, available depletion allowances, and equity in earnings of affiliated companies which varies in impact during the period. In 1978, significantly lower pre-tax income as a result of the shutdown/disposal provision magnified the impact of these items.

IRON AND STEEL

Record sales and increased shipments could not overcome the operating problems faced in 1978; as a result, the first loss for the iron and steel operations was recorded. Almost one-half of the loss is related to the shutdown/disposal provision.

Sales increased 13% in 1978 on the basis of increased selling prices and an overall 3% increase in total tons shipped. Selling price increases have not been sufficient to cover cost increases since 1974-5, especially prices received for iron, which have increased less than 10% since late 1974. Reduced demand for domestic pig iron because of low-priced imports and scrap and resulting price competition among domestic producers has limited the effectiveness of price increases. Total iron shipments to customers declined less than 1% in 1978 after larger declines in recent years. However, pig iron tonnage dropped 17% in 1978 to extend the significant declines noted since 1974. Iron usage for Interlake's steel operations represented 59%, a constant level in the last three years. The resurgence of the steel industry caused a 25% increase in molten iron shipped to our largest customer, a producer of ingot molds and stools.

Sales
(in millions)

$500	401.0
400	
300	
200	
100	
0	74 75 76 77 78

Steel shipments in 1978 increased 6% after a 2% increase in 1977. Part of this gain relates to the continuing increase in internal uses for packaging and storage products which totaled 20% in 1978 compared with 19% in 1977. Customer shipments increased 5%, led by the second year of major increases in tubular products shipments.

The reported operating loss was a direct result of
- the United Mine Workers' strike which lasted through the first quarter and curtailed operations primarily at Toledo, Ohio,
- extended labor strikes affecting our ore and coal mining interests which reduced income from these investments for the second consecutive year,
- equipment outages for major repair and capital programs.

These outages included:
- the repair of one battery of coke ovens in Chicago from June to December which reduced earnings because of

Operating Income
(in millions)

$60	
45	
30	
15	
0	74 75 76 77 78
15	
30	(31.6)

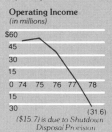

($15.7) is due to Shutdown Disposal Provision

unabsorbed production costs and premiums paid for purchased coke needed to maintain iron production,
- the installation and difficult start-up of the improved hot strip mill facilities at Newport, Kentucky,
- the first of two blast furnace relines at the Chicago Plant which resulted in lost production.

The deterioration in earnings since 1975 reflects the inadequacy of price increases to cover escalated labor, material, energy and pollution control costs. Further, in 1977 and 1978, severe winter weather, excess costs related to equipment start up and labor strikes affecting coal and ore mining income had a severe impact on operating results.

The year concluded with high customer demand, progressive improvement in the Newport hot strip mill and expected improved output from the repaired coke oven battery. However, a second furnace reline and the second coke battery repair remain to be completed.

METAL POWDERS

Sales of metal powders reached a new record level for the third consecutive year as increased demand, evidenced by an 18% growth in shipments, boosted sales 28% over 1977. Sales growth since 1975 has averaged 36% and represents the fastest growing segment of the Company. This growth resulted from expanded application of powder metal parts, primarily in the automotive industry. Price increases in 1978 accounted for about one-fourth of the sales increase.

The record shipment level in 1978 strained productive capacity at the Riverton, New Jersey plant, but generated record operating income for the fifth consecutive year. In addition to the benefits of increased sales volume, record production yielded efficiency and productivity gains. Higher costs for materials, labor and energy were offset by price increases; conditions which typified the experience of recent years. Earnings increased 41% in 1978 after a 53% gain in 1977.

Sales
(in millions)

$80	74.6
60	
40	
20	
0	74 75 76 77 78

Operating Income
(in millions)

$25	20.9
20	
15	
10	
5	
0	74 75 76 77 78

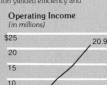

21

22 INVESTMENT CASTINGS/DIE CASTINGS

Arwood produced record results in 1978. Total sales increased 34% with acquisitions accounting for about one-third of that gain. The results of Arwood have been consolidated since the April, 1976 acquisition.

A boom in the aircraft and aerospace industries and the acquisition of the remaining interest of the former Jetshapes joint venture contributed to a sales increase in investment castings from 1977 of almost 60% after a 29% gain from the full year 1976. Significant 1978 sales gains were realized at each producing location, led by the reversal of recent sales declines at the Cleveland, Ohio plant.

Die casting sales experienced some weakness related to slackening demand in consumer product markets in each geographic area served. The sales increase of 9% can be attributed primarily to the full year's sales of the Garland, Texas die casting plant acquired in October, 1977. Despite the disruptive effect on production of the plant relocation from Syracuse, New York to expanded facilities in Hazleton, Pennsylvania, 1978 combined sales for these two locations increased 11%. Other locations reported no growth or a slight decline in sales in 1978.

Record operating income rose 24% in 1978 after a 44% gain in 1977 from the results of the full year 1976. Record sales volume contributed to the significant earnings increase experienced in investment castings; production levels were at or near capacity by year-end. Die casting earnings declined primarily because of the costs of relocating to Hazleton, where operations reached planned targets in the fourth quarter. Reduced production levels and price increases, limited by competitive conditions, also contributed to the decline in die casting earnings. In the fourth quarter, die casting results returned to 1977 levels.

Sales
(in millions)

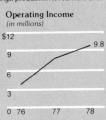

Operating Income
(in millions)

SILICON METAL/FERROALLOYS

Sales and operating income in 1978 reversed the declining trend of recent years because of increased volume and improved mix of products sold. Unfavorable market conditions in recent years, created by indiscriminate sales activities of foreign producers, have limited price increases despite accelerated costs and have reduced market opportunities for domestic producers. Selective marketing of products with profit potential, the withdrawal of one foreign country from silicon metal production, and International Trade Commission support against dumping by foreign producers led to the income resurgence in this business segment.

Price increases effected during 1978 had a negligible impact on revenues. Although unsatisfactory, this represented an improvement from the overall decline in selling prices experienced in recent years.

Increasing costs, therefore, continued to be absorbed. In addition to inflation stimulated increases in raw material and labor costs, electrical energy rates increased significantly in 1978.

Overall sales tonnage increased 31% in 1978; this compared with an average decline of 11% over the last three years. Silicon metal equalled the overall rate of increase in sales tonnage on the strength of reduced imports and increased demand from the secondary aluminum industry, a primary user of silicon metal.

The selective marketing approach generated the change in the mix of sales realized in 1978.

Ferrochromes, which represented 60% of total sales in 1974, accounted for 34% in 1977 and 17% in 1978. Renewed emphasis on ferrosilicons in 1978 was initiated by the related magnesium ferrosilicon products used in the growing INMOLD casting process. Ferrosilicon shipments increased to 22% of total sales in 1978, compared with less than 2% in the three previous years.

Sales
(in millions)

Operating Income
(in millions)

MATERIAL HANDLING/STORAGE

Increased worldwide demand produced record sales and income in 1978. Sales increased 31% in 1978 on the strength of increased shipments; prices accounted for one-fourth of this gain. Highly price-competitive markets, primarily for larger jobs, have limited the benefits of price increases in recent years.

Domestic sales gained 39% following a gain of only 9% in 1977. The growth was based on a dramatic recovery in sales of storage systems after the decline experienced in the previous two years. Pallet rack and angle products also realized significant sales increases in all major domestic markets. In total, shipments reached record levels.

Foreign sales exceeded 1977's record level by 27% with gains recorded in all geographic areas. Strengthening foreign currencies in relation to the U.S. dollar and benefits of price increases accounted for half of the improvement. Sales gains in Australia and France outperformed the overall average in 1978. Foreign sales, which represented only 26% of total sales in 1974, have dominated this line of business since the acquisition of Dexion-Comino International Limited in late 1974.

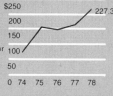

Sales
(in millions)

Income almost tripled in 1978 to establish record earnings and reversing the trend since 1975. The benefits of record shipping and production volumes compounded the increase in income. Domestic and foreign income from operations reversed year-to-year declines noted in 1977.

Income from domestic pallet rack, angle and storage systems increased significantly. However, overall domestic income continued to be impacted by losses in the conveyor business. Domestic income had declined in the previous two years as a result of lower sales volume and extremely competitive pricing.

The earnings performance in Australia, England and Germany reflected the benefits of increased sales volume.

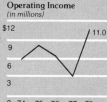

Operating Income
(in millions)

Operations in countries where Dexion is primarily a distributor, rather than a manufacturer of the Dexion product line, experienced reduced earnings levels; part of the cause was the relative strengthening of English and German currencies in which the purchases were made. Canadian results improved in 1978 despite continuing stagnant economic conditions.

The year ended with overall record backlogs.

PACKAGING

Record sales and operating income in 1978 resulted from increased steel and non-metallic strapping shipments and significantly higher earnings from foreign operations. Overall, sales increased 18% in 1978 after a modest 5% gain in 1977; the dramatically lower value of Canadian currency in 1977 and the absence of sales of discontinued products in 1976 halved the growth in 1977. However, overall steel strapping and stitching wire tonnage shipped increased 14% after averaging gains of 2% from 1975 to 1977. An aggressive marketing strategy was particularly in evidence in the U.S. where steel strapping shipments increased 21% to the highest level since 1974. Price increases generally followed material cost increases, and, in 1978, accounted for one-third of the sales growth. The benefits of price increases were limited by geographic price competition in the U.S. and Canada.

Non-metallic strapping represented this segment's fastest growing product group with a sales increase of 30% in 1978 following the 34% gain in 1977. Since 1974, non-metallic strapping sales have tripled. Customer acceptance of non-metallic strapping applications has provided sustained, strong growth in sales in the U.S., Canada and England.

Sales
(in millions)

Operating income increased 28% in 1978 to a record $11.1 million after an erratic earnings pattern in recent years. The increased strapping volume was the key factor in the earnings improvement. In addition, earnings benefited from foreign currency translation gains of $1.0 million in 1978 primarily related to the Canadian dollar inventories; in 1977, earnings were penalized by translation losses of $.7 million. 1976 income was aided by $.9 million from the net result of discontinuing certain metal forming and bronze plaque operations and the gain on the sale of related plant and equipment.

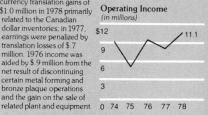

Operating Income
(in millions)

23

Interlake, Inc

Statement of Consolidated Income and Retained Earnings
For the Years Ended December 31, 1978 and December 25, 1977

24	1978 (53 Weeks)	1977 (52 Weeks)
	(In thousands except per share statistics)	
Sales and Revenues:		
Net sales	$921,127	$766,614
Other revenues	8,718	6,444
	929,845	773,058
Costs and Expenses:		
Cost of products sold (excludes items shown below)	744,306	604,064
Depreciation, depletion and amortization (Note 1)	23,012	21,058
Selling and administrative expenses	92,601	82,466
Taxes other than income taxes	26,700	22,594
Interest expense	11,600	8,592
	898,219	738,774
Income Before Non-Recurring Item, Taxes on Income and Minority Interest	31,626	34,284
Shutdown/Disposal Provision (Note 6)	15,682	—
Income Before Taxes on Income and Minority Interest	15,944	34,284
Provision for Income Taxes (Note 9)	3,100	14,010
	12,844	20,274
Minority Interest in Net Income of Subsidiary	2,356	1,542
Net Income for the Year	$ 10,488	$ 18,732
Net Income Per Share of Common Stock		
(based on average shares of 5,941,966 in 1978 and 5,915,214 in 1977)	$ 1.77	$ 3.17
Retained Earnings at Beginning of Year	$215,056	$209,343
Net Income for the Year	10,488	18,732
	225,544	228,075
Deduct Cash Dividends Paid ($2.20 per share)	(13,077)	(13,019)
Retained Earnings at End of Year	$212,467	$215,056

(See notes to consolidated financial statements)

Interlake, Inc.

Consolidated Balance Sheet
December 31, 1978 and December 25, 1977

Assets	1978	1977	25
Current Assets:	(In thousands)		
Cash	$ 7,910	$ 4,635	
Certificates of deposit	11,783	8,959	
Marketable securities, at cost which approximates market	1,044	634	
Receivables, less allowance for doubtful accounts of			
$3,480,000 in 1978 and $2,647,000 in 1977	147,103	106,701	
Inventories (Note 1):			
Raw materials and supplies	66,099	69,193	
Semi-finished and finished products	93,572	78,111	
Other current assets	13,271	9,139	
Total current assets	340,782	277,372	
Investments and Other Assets:			
Investments in and advances to associated companies (Notes 1 and 10)	44,226	46,656	
Other assets (Note 1)	35,787	23,419	
	80,013	70,075	
Property, Plant and Equipment, at cost (Notes 1 and 10):			
Land and mineral properties, less depletion	12,537	13,465	
Plant and equipment	514,435	492,291	
	526,972	505,756	
Less—Depreciation and amortization	289,352	293,635	
	237,620	212,121	
Total Assets	**$658,415**	**$559,568**	

Liabilities and Shareholders' Equity			
Current Liabilities:			
Accounts payable	$ 75,941	$ 58,367	
Accrued liabilities	69,293	50,353	
Income taxes payable (Note 9)	15,851	15,723	
Debt due within one year (Note 2)	16,349	12,247	
Total current liabilities	177,434	136,690	
Long-Term Debt (Note 2)	136,169	85,233	
Other Long-Term Liabilities	15,109	10,153	
Future Income Taxes (Note 1)	16,899	13,421	
Minority Interest in Subsidiary	6,493	5,671	
Shareholders' Equity (Note 4):			
Common stock, par value $1 a share;			
authorized 20,000,000 shares, issued 6,819,510 shares	109,992	109,870	
Retained earnings (Note 3)	212,467	215,056	
	322,459	324,926	
Less—Cost of common stock held in treasury			
(860,794 shares in 1978 and 894,515 in 1977)	16,148	16,526	
	306,311	308,400	
Total Liabilities and Shareholders' Equity	**$658,415**	**$559,568**	

(See notes to consolidated financial statements)

Interlake, Inc.

Statement of Changes in Consolidated Financial Position
For the Years Ended December 31, 1978 and December 25, 1977

	1978 (53 weeks)	1977 (52 weeks)
	(In thousands)	
Financial Resources Were Provided By:		
Net income	$ 10,488	$ 18,732
Depreciation, depletion and amortization	23,012	21,058
Equity in earnings of affiliates and joint ventures, less dividends received	1,490	(2,939)
Shutdown/disposal provision	13,739	—
Future income taxes	3,478	2,361
Other long-term liabilities	355	(666)
Working capital provided from operations	52,562	38,546
Long-term borrowings	54,350	8,832
Disposals of property, plant and equipment	5,503	815
Capital contribution to subsidiary by minority shareholder	—	3,000
Minority interest in net income of subsidiary	2,356	1,542
Other	(851)	1,471
	113,920	54,206
Financial Resources Were Used For:		
Capital expenditures	65,974	30,233
Reduction of long-term debt	3,414	2,908
Cash dividends	13,077	13,019
Investments in affiliated companies and joint ventures	(375)	2,421
Increase (decrease) in construction funds held by trustees	9,164	(1,907)
	91,254	46,674
Increase in working capital	$ 22,666	$ 7,532
Increase (Decrease) in Working Capital Comprises:		
Cash and short-term investments	$ 6,509	$ 3,316
Receivables	40,402	5,412
Inventories	12,367	16,265
Other current assets	4,132	(2,284)
Accounts payable and accrued liabilities	(36,514)	(12,762)
Income taxes payable	(128)	(4,653)
Debt due within one year	(4,102)	2,238
	22,666	7,532
Working capital at beginning of year	140,682	133,150
Working capital at end of year	$163,348	$140,682

(See notes to consolidated financial statements)

Interlake, Inc

Notes to Consolidated Financial Statements
For the Years Ended December 31, 1978 and December 25, 1977

NOTE 1—Summary of Significant Accounting Policies

Principles of Consolidation—The consolidated financial statements include the accounts of all majority-owned domestic and foreign subsidiaries. Investments in corporate joint ventures and companies owned 20% to 50% are accounted for by the equity method. Such investments are carried at cost plus equity in undistributed earnings.

Inventories—Inventories are stated at the lower of cost or market value. Cost of domestic inventories is determined principally by the last-in first-out method, which is less than current costs by $91,402,000 and $85,376,000 at December 31, 1978 and December 25, 1977, respectively. Cost of inventories of foreign subsidiaries is determined principally by the first-in first-out method.

Property, Plant and Equipment and Depreciation—For financial reporting purposes, plant and equipment are depreciated principally on a straight-line method over the estimated useful lives of the assets. Costs of significant renewals and betterments, including furnace relines, are capitalized. Depreciation claimed for income tax purposes is computed by use of accelerated methods. Income taxes applicable to differences between depreciation claimed for tax purposes and that reported in the financial statements are charged or credited to future income taxes, as appropriate. Provisions for depletion of mineral properties are based on tonnage rates which are expected to amortize the cost of such properties over the estimated amount of mineral deposits to be removed.

Goodwill—Other assets includes goodwill of $10,525,000 and $10,804,000 at December 31, 1978 and December 25, 1977, respectively. Goodwill represents the excess of the purchase price over the fair value of the net assets of acquired companies and is amortized on a straight-line method over a period of approximately thirty years.

Investment Tax Credits—The full amount of investment tax credits claimed for tax purposes is reflected in income in the year the related property is placed in service.

Pension Plans—The company has various pension plans which cover substantially all employees. The majority of employees are covered by plans which follow the basic pension pattern of the steel industry. The provision for pension costs includes current costs plus interest on and amortization of unfunded prior service costs over periods not exceeding twenty-five years. The Company's policy is to fund pension costs accrued.

NOTE 2—Long-Term Debt and Credit Arrangements

Long-term debt of the Company consists of the following:

27

	December 31, 1978	December 25, 1977
	(In thousands)	
8.8% Debentures, due annually $2,500,000 1979 to 1995, and $5,000,000 in 1996	$ 45,736	$ 50,000
8½% Senior Notes, due annually $3,000,000 1984 through 1998	45,000	7,000
Obligations under long-term lease agreements	16,650	17,300
11¼% Notes payable, due annually in varying installments from 1980 to 1998	10,000	10,000
Pollution control and industrial development loan agreements	16,350	—
Other	3,542	4,024
	137,278	88,324
Less—Current maturities	1,109	3,091
	$136,169	$ 85,233

At December 31, 1978, 8.8% debentures with a face value of $1,764,000 were held in the treasury by the Company. These may be used in meeting the 1979 sinking fund requirement and have been applied as a reduction of debt due within one year.

In 1977, the Company negotiated a note agreement with a group of insurance companies to sell $45,000,000 principal amount of its 8½% Senior Notes. Of the total, $7,000,000 was received in December, 1977 and the remainder was received in June, 1978.

The long-term lease obligations relate principally to capitalized pollution control facilities. The interest rates on these obligations vary from 6.00% to 7.88%. Principal payments begin in 1981 ($500,000) and continue in varying annual amounts through 2002.

In 1978, the Company entered into several loan agreements with state and county pollution control and industrial development authorities and borrowed $12,350,000 to finance environmental control projects and $4,000,000 to finance facility expansion and improvement projects. Interest rates on these obligations vary from 6% to 7⅛%. Principal payments of $1,700,000 and $3,500,000 are to be made in 1988 and 1993, respectively, then continue in varying amounts from 1998 to 2008.

The Company maintains informal domestic and foreign short-term bank credit lines of $64,000,000 against which $15,240,000 was borrowed at December 31, 1978. Domestic borrowings bear interest at the prime rate. Foreign borrowings bear interest at varying rates which are, generally, the overseas equivalent of the prime rate. In connection with the domestic lines of credit, the Company has entered into informal arrangements to maintain average compensating balances of 10% for the total lines and an additional 10% for any borrowings. The Company's average float exceeded the bank deposits required under these arrangements.

28 **NOTE 3—Retained Earnings**

Under the most restrictive terms of the Company's various loan agreements, the Company could not as of December 31, 1978 pay cash dividends or repurchase the Company's capital stock in amounts aggregating more than $28,600,000.

NOTE 4—Capital Stock

The Company's authorized capital stock includes 2,000,000 shares of serial preferred stock at $1 par value per share, none of which has been issued.

NOTE 5—Stock Options

The Company has two stock option plans through which options have been granted to officers and other key employees at prices equal to the fair market value at date of grant. Remaining outstanding options under the 1965 plan will expire in 1979; no further options will be granted under this plan. Under the 1975 plan, options (up to a maximum of 375,000 shares) may be granted until December 31, 1984 to purchase common stock for periods not longer than ten years from date of grant. Options become exercisable 33⅓% annually, on a cumulative basis, starting one year from date of grant.

In April, 1977 the shareholders approved the Interlake, Inc. 1977 Stock Incentive Program, consisting of a Stock Appreciation Rights Plan (activated in 1977) under which a maximum of 300,000 shares of common stock may be issued, a Stock Awards Plan and a Restricted Stock Purchase Plan. Total shares issued for the latter two plans may not exceed 100,000. Stock appreciation rights are issued in relation to specific stock options and entitle the holder to receive the value of the stock appreciation rights (the difference between market price and option price at time of exercise of the rights) in cash, shares of common stock, or a combination of the two at the Company's discretion. Exercise of a stock appreciation right results in cancellation of an equivalent number of option shares. The Stock Awards Plan was activated in 1978 and 16,600 shares were awarded with a total market value as of the dates awarded of $428,000. Shares are issued at date of award and delivered to recipients 20% immediately and 20% on each of the four succeeding anniversary dates, subject to certain restrictions. The Board of Directors has not adopted a Restricted Stock Purchase Plan. Changes in common shares under option and related stock appreciation rights for the two years are summarized as follows:

	1978		1977	
	Option Shares	Average Option Price	Option Shares	Average Option Price
Outstanding— beginning of year	211,900	$28.45	219,675	$25.41
Granted	57,900	25.63	47,150	31.38
Exercised	(7,375)	17.61	(16,100)	18.43
Surrendered for exercised rights	(55,275)	18.15	(32,075)	16.91
Cancelled or expired	(6,901)	31.67	(6,750)	28.56
Outstanding— end of year	200,249	30.77	211,900	28.45
Options exercisable at end of year	91,524	31.64	105,385	23.21
Options available for grant	161,176		212,775	

Stock appreciation rights were granted in relation to 140,050 stock option shares with an average option price of $26.94 in 1978 and in relation to 59,325 stock option shares with an average option price of $22.66 in 1977. Stock appreciation rights were outstanding in relation to 109,250 and 26,275 stock option shares at December 31, 1978 and December 25, 1977, respectively.

NOTE 6—Shutdown/Disposal Provision

A decision was made in the third quarter of 1978 to consolidate the Company's iron production in Chicago. In December, 1978 the Toledo blast furnace operation was shut down and the ancillary coke oven batteries were sold. Surplus equipment and real property related to the blast furnace operation are also to be sold. The consolidation also resulted in the shutdown of the sintering facility at the Chicago plant. No future use of this facility is contemplated.

The shutdown/disposal provision of $15,682,000 is equivalent to $1.32 per common share after applicable income taxes and covers estimated losses on the disposition of property, plant and equipment and inventories, and employee severance and other costs.

NOTE 7—Business Segment Information
(Detailed on Pages 30 and 31)

The Company operates in six lines of business: four in metals and two in material handling products. Metals include iron and steel products, metal powders, investment castings and die castings, and silicon metal and ferroalloys. Material handling consists of material handling and storage products and packaging products. The accompanying tables present financial information by line of business for the years 1978 and 1977.

Sales between lines of business are primarily priced at market value for metal products and at distributor prices for material handling products. Operating profit consists of total sales and other revenues of a product line less all related operating expenses. Income and expenses which are not related to nor appropriately allocable to lines of business, primarily interest expense, are included in general Corporate expense.

Total assets by line of business consist of those assets used directly in the operations of the product line plus an allocation of assets of central administrative offices which function primarily in servicing the lines of business. Corporate assets consist principally of cash, securities and investments in real property.

The Company's interests in iron ore mining joint ventures in Minnesota and Labrador, Canada and coal mining joint ventures in West Virginia and Kentucky, are accounted for by the equity method and are vertically integrated with the iron and steel business. Investments in material handling and storage products in Greece, India and Japan are also on an equity basis.

Sales to the largest individual customers are not material in relation to consolidated sales, nor are sales to domestic or foreign government agencies. Iron and Steel sales to unaffiliated customers, in millions, were: Iron—$96.1 and 92.4, and Steel —$245.0 and $213.8, for 1978 and 1977, respectively.

Transfers between geographic areas, which are virtually all in the material handling line of business, are made at prices which approximate the prices of similar items sold to distributors. Operating profit by geographic area is the difference between total sales and other revenues attributable to the areas and related operating expenses. Income and expenses which are not related to nor appropriately allocable to geographic areas, primarily interest expense, are included in general Corporate expense. Export sales to unaffiliated customers included in the United States sales are not material.

"Other" foreign includes operations in Canada, Mexico, Australia, Japan, Greece and India.

Total assets consist of those assets used directly in the operations in the geographic areas shown plus a nominal amount of allocated assets of central administrative offices which service these geographic areas.

NOTE 8—Pensions

Pension costs were $25,555,000 in 1978 and $21,199,000 in 1977. The increase in 1978 was attributable primarily to a change in the actuarial assumption as to the rate of future compensation increases and to increased compensation levels in the current year. In addition to the 1978 provision for pension costs, a portion of the estimated costs of the shutdown of the Toledo plant (see Note 6) is attributable to pensions and other employment costs related to terminated employees. The actuarially computed value of vested benefits exceeded the market value of the pension fund assets and balance sheet pension accruals by approximately $82,000,000 and $85,000,000 as of December 31, 1978 and December 25, 1977, respectively.

NOTE 9—Income Taxes

The provisions for taxes on income consist of:

	1978	1977
	(53 weeks)	(52 weeks)
	(In thousands)	
Currently payable:		
U.S. Federal (less investment credits of $3,699,000 in 1978 and $1,727,000 in 1977)	$ 1,418	$ 2,388
Foreign and state	8,660	7,696
Deferred	(6,978)	3,926
	$ 3,100	$14,010

The effective tax rates are lower than the statutory rate due principally to investment tax credits, equity in earnings of affiliated companies and percentage depletion allowances. Timing differences between amounts deductible for financial reporting and income tax purposes principally relate to depreciation and, in 1978, the disposal/shutdown provision and certain pension costs.

As of December 31, 1978 U.S. Federal income tax returns for the years 1965 through 1973 have been examined. A number of adjustments have been proposed, one of which involves the determination of the cost of ore from one of the Company's iron ore interests and could result in certain of these costs being disallowed as a tax deduction. The Company believes that its position on this issue has merit and that final resolution should not result in any significant adjustment.

No provision for U.S. income taxes on unremitted earnings of foreign subsidiaries has been made as it is anticipated that any U.S. taxes on dividend distributions will be substantially offset by foreign tax credits.

NOTE 10—Commitments and Contingencies

With respect to the Company's interests in two mining joint ventures, the Company is required to take its ownership proportion of production for which it is committed to pay its proportionate share of the operating costs of these projects, either directly or as a part of the product price. Such costs include, as a minimum and regardless of the quantity of ore received, annual interest and sinking fund requirements of the funded debt of these projects of approximately $3,000,000 through 1983, and lesser amounts thereafter through 1991.

The Company is involved, on a continuing basis, as a party to enforcement and other proceedings with governmental agencies relating to the application of environmental laws and regulations to certain of the Company's plants. Several of such proceedings have recently been settled on the basis of Company commitments to meet certain emission standards and to install control facilities at substantial cost. The Company anticipates that capital expenditures for installation of environmentally-related facilities (including those agreed to in settlement of proceedings) will aggregate approximately $13,000,000 over the next three years.

Note 7 (continued)

30 Information About The Company's Lines Of Business (In Millions)

	Iron/Steel		Metal Powders	
	1978	1977	1978	1977
Net sales to unaffiliated customers	$341.1	$306.2	$ 74.6	$ 58.4
Net sales to other lines of business	59.9	47.6	—	—
Total sales	$401.0	$353.8	$ 74.6	$ 58.4
Operating profit (loss)	$ (34.6)	$ (1.5)	$ 20.9	$ 14.8
Equity in net income (loss) of unconsolidated affiliates	3.0	5.4	—	—
Income (loss) before taxes	$ (31.6)	$ 3.9	$ 20.9	$ 14.8
Assets at end of year	$220.7	$199.3	$ 58.2	$ 48.0
Investment in unconsolidated affiliates	43.4	44.6	—	—
Total assets	$264.1	$243.9	$ 58.2	$ 48.0
Capital expenditures	$ 37.1	$ 17.7	$ 10.8	$ 1.9
Depreciation, depletion and amortization	11.4	10.5	1.3	1.2

Information About The Company's Operations
By Geographic Areas (In Millions)

Net sales to unaffiliated customers
Net sales to other geographic areas
    Total sales

Operating profit (loss)
Equity in net income of unconsolidated affiliates
    Income (loss) before taxes

Assets at end of year
Investment in unconsolidated affiliates
    Total assets

31

	Investment/Die Castings		Silicon Metal/ Ferroalloys		Matl. Handling/ Storage Products		Packaging		Corporate Items/ Eliminations		Consolidated	
	1978	1977	1978	1977	1978	1977	1978	1977	1978	1977	1978*	1977**
	$ 67.4	$ 50.3	$ 52.7	$ 43.4	$227.0	$173.9	$158.3	$134.4	$ —	$ —	$921.1	$766.6
	—	—	1.2	.8	.3	.1	2.1	1.7	(63.5)	(50.2)	—	—
	$ 67.4	$ 50.3	$ 53.9	$ 44.2	$227.3	$174.0	$160.4	$136.1	$ (63.5)	$ (50.2)	$921.1	$766.6
	$ 9.8	$ 7.8	$ 3.8	$ 2.2	$ 11.0	$ 4.5	$ 11.1	$ 8.7	$ (9.1)	$ (6.9)	$ 12.9	$ 29.6
	—	.1	—	—	—	(.8)	—	—	—	—	3.0	4.7
	$ 9.8	$ 7.9	$ 3.8	$ 2.2	$ 11.0	$ 3.7	$ 11.1	$ 8.7	$ (9.1)	$ (6.9)	$ 15.9	$ 34.3
	$ 34.1	$ 20.1	$ 46.9	$ 46.0	$151.0	$119.3	$ 67.0	$ 61.8	$ 36.3	$ 18.4	$614.2	$512.9
	—	1.4	—	—	.6	.7	.2	—	—	—	44.2	46.7
	$ 34.1	$ 21.5	$ 46.9	$ 46.0	$151.6	$120.0	$ 67.2	$ 61.8	$ 36.3	$ 18.4	$658.4	$559.6
	$ 3.9	$ 2.3	$ .4	$ 1.0	$ 11.3	$ 4.7	$ 2.5	$ 2.6	$ —	$ —	$ 66.0	$ 30.2
	.8	.6	2.1	2.1	4.2	3.5	2.8	2.8	.4	.4	23.0	21.1

	United States		FOREIGN						Corporate Items/ Eliminations		Consolidated	
			Western Europe		Other		Total					
	1978	1977	1978	1977	1978	1977	1978	1977	1978	1977	1978*	1977**
	$710.3	$595.3	$158.4	$125.1	$ 52.4	$ 46.2	$210.8	$171.3	$ —	$ —	$921.1	$766.6
	4.0	3.8	1.0	1.2	—	—	1.0	1.2	(5.0)	(5.0)	—	—
	$714.3	$599.1	$159.4	$126.3	$ 52.4	$ 46.2	$211.8	$172.5	$ (5.0)	$ (5.0)	$921.1	$766.6
	$ 6.0	$ 24.9	$ 9.9	$ 7.1	$ 6.3	$ 4.6	$ 16.2	$ 11.7	$ (9.3)	$ (7.0)	$ 12.9	$ 29.6
	1.6	2.3	—	—	1.4	2.4	1.4	2.4	—	—	3.0	4.7
	$ 7.6	$ 27.2	$ 9.9	$ 7.1	$ 7.7	$ 7.0	$ 17.6	$ 14.1	$ (9.3)	$ (7.0)	$ 15.9	$ 34.3
	$433.5	$373.0	$113.9	$ 89.6	$ 30.5	$ 31.9	$144.4	$121.5	$ 36.3	$ 18.4	$614.2	$512.9
	30.8	31.0	.6	.7	12.8	15.0	13.4	15.7	—	—	44.2	46.7
	$464.3	$404.0	$114.5	$ 90.3	$ 43.3	$ 46.9	$157.8	$137.2	$ 36.3	$ 18.4	$658.4	$559.6

*53 weeks
**52 weeks

32 **NOTE 11—Quarterly Results (Unaudited)**

Quarterly results of operations for 1978 and 1977 were
as follows:

Quarter	Net sales 1978	Net sales 1977	Net sales less cost of products sold 1978	Net sales less cost of products sold 1977	Net income (loss) Amount 1978	Net income (loss) Amount 1977	Net income (loss) Per share 1978	Net income (loss) Per share 1977
			(In millions, except per share amounts)					
1st	$204.2	$181.5	$ 34.9	$ 36.3	$ (1.1)	$ 2.6	$ (.19)	$ .44
2nd	231.0	201.8	47.7	45.1	8.1	6.8	1.36	1.15
3rd*	233.3	182.2	40.3	37.2	(4.9)	4.3	(.83)	.72
4th	252.6	201.1	53.9	44.0	8.4	5.0	1.43	.86
Year	$921.1	$766.6	$176.8	$162.6	$ 10.5	$ 18.7	$ 1.77	$ 3.17

*Third quarter of 1978 included fourteen weeks, all other quarters thirteen weeks.

The loss in the first quarter of 1978 was a direct result of the prolonged coal miners' strike and severe winter weather. Second quarter earnings exceeded the preceding year as a result of higher sales and production volume in all business segments except iron and steel. Results for iron and steel in the second quarter and the balance of the year were reduced by the impact of equipment outages for major capital improvements and repairs. In addition, the third quarter was charged with the shutdown/disposal provision (See Note 6) which reduced net income by $7.8 million or the equivalent of $1.32 per common share. The third quarter benefited from a $1.8 million pre-tax gain on the sale of undeveloped coal properties.

Translation of foreign currency exposures and hedging costs resulted in net income of $.5 in 1978 compared with a loss of $2.3 million in 1977. Quarterly results for the first and fourth quarters of 1978 were better than the corresponding 1977 quarters by $1.8 million and $1.4 million, respectively, due to foreign exchange fluctuations.

NOTE 12—Replacement Cost Information (Unaudited)

The Company's Annual Report (Form 10-K) filed with the Securities and Exchange Commission contains specific replacement cost information. In general, replacement cost of sales is not materially different from actual cost of sales and replacement cost depreciation expense is significantly higher than actual depreciation expense.

Report of Independent Accountants

Price Waterhouse

To the Board of Directors and Shareholders of Interlake, Inc.

In our opinion, the accompanying consolidated balance sheet and the related statement of consolidated income and retained earnings and the statement of changes in consolidated financial position present fairly the financial position of Interlake, Inc. and its subsidiaries at December 31, 1978 and December 25, 1977, and the results of their operations and the changes in their financial position for the years then ended, in conformity with generally accepted accounting principles consistently applied. Our examinations of these statements were made in accordance with generally accepted auditing standards and accordingly included such tests of the accounting records and such other auditing procedures as we considered necessary in the circumstances.

Chicago, Illinois
January 31, 1979

Price Waterhouse & Co.

For The Year	1978	1977	1976	1975	1974	33
	(Dollar amounts in thousands except per share statistics)					
Net sales of continuing operations	$921,127	$766,614	$708,876	$640,831	$593,764	
Other revenues	8,718	6,444	9,767	9,493	9,278	
	929,845	773,058	718,643	650,324	603,042	
Cost of products sold (excludes items shown below)	744,306	604,064	526,358	457,128	446,920	
Depreciation, depletion and amortization	23,012	21,058	20,960	19,287	15,337	
Selling and administrative expenses	92,601	82,466	77,907	74,985	45,996	
Taxes other than income taxes	26,700	22,594	20,928	19,284	14,428	
Interest expense	11,600	8,592	8,932	9,861	5,934	
	898,219	738,774	655,085	580,545	528,615	
Income before non-recurring item	31,626	34,284	63,558	69,779	74,427	
Shutdown/disposal provision	15,682	—	—	—	—	
Income before taxes on income	15,944	34,284	63,558	69,779	74,427	
Provision for income taxes	3,100	14,010	24,682	29,558	33,580	
	12,844	20,274	38,876	40,221	40,847	
Minority interest in consolidated subsidiary companies	2,356	1,542	971	515	584	
Income from continuing operations	10,488	18,732	37,905	39,706	40,263	
Loss from discontinued operations	—	—	—	(5,331)	(1,264)	
Net Income — Amount	$ 10,488	$ 18,732	$ 37,905	$ 34,375	$ 38,999	
Net Income — % of net sales	1.1%	2.4%	5.3%	5.4%	6.6%	
Net Income — % of average shareholders' equity	3.4%	6.2%	13.3%	13.7%	17.2%	
Average shares of common stock outstanding	5,942	5,915	5,736	5,413	5,598	
Earnings per common share —						
Income from continuing operations	$1.77	$3.17	$6.61	$7.34	$7.19	
Net income	1.77	3.17	6.61	6.35	6.97	
Capital expenditures (excluding assets of acquired businesses)	65,974	30,233	19,538	35,884	25,486	
Cash dividends per common share	2.20	2.20	2.15	1.50	1.97	
At Year End						
Working capital — Amount	$163,348	$140,682	$133,150	$109,421	$ 95,143	
Working capital — Current ratio	1.9 to 1	2.0 to 1	2.1 to 1	2.0 to 1	1.6 to 1	
Property, plant and equipment (net)	237,620	212,121	202,195	201,345	188,746	
Long-term debt (less current maturities)	136,169	85,233	78,828	85,599	74,216	
Future income taxes	16,899	13,421	11,060	12,042	13,316	
Common shareholders' equity — Amount	306,311	308,400	301,818	264,046	242,134	
Common shareholders' equity — Per common share	51.41	52.05	51.15	48.85	43.22	
Common stock price range	29⅞-21¼	39¼-26	42½-25½	26½-18	19⅝-13⅞	
Number of employees	12,659	12,126	11,329	10,502	13,391	

NOTE: 1978 was a 53-week year while prior periods were 52-week years. 1974 has been restated to exclude operating results of the Howell Division (home furnishings and gas products), which was sold in 1975. Per share statistics have been restated to reflect the 3-for-2 share split in October, 1975.

34		Net Sales			Income (Loss)			
		Unaffiliated Customers	Other Lines of Business	Total	Operating Profit	Equity* Income	Income Before Taxes	Total Assets
Iron/Steel**	1978	$341.1	$ 59.9	$401.0	$(34.6)	$ 3.0	$(31.6)	$264.1
	1977	306.2	47.6	353.8	(1.5)	5.4	3.9	243.9
	1976	305.5	35.2	340.7	25.3	7.6	32.9	230.4
	1975	281.5	33.7	315.2	46.5	4.2	50.7	213.6
	1974	305.6	45.2	350.8	41.1	4.4	45.5	204.7
Metal Powders	1978	74.6	—	74.6	20.9	—	20.9	58.2
	1977	58.4	—	58.4	14.8	—	14.8	48.0
	1976	49.0	—	49.0	9.7	—	9.7	43.7
	1975	30.4	—	30.4	4.0	—	4.0	40.6
	1974	34.0	—	34.0	3.5	—	3.5	41.4
Investment/Die Castings	1978	67.4	—	67.4	9.8	—	9.8	34.1
	1977	50.3	—	50.3	7.8	.1	7.9	21.5
	1976	27.8	—	27.8	3.7	.2	3.9	15.0
Silicon Metal/Ferroalloys	1978	52.7	1.2	53.9	3.8	—	3.8	46.9
	1977	43.4	.8	44.2	2.2	—	2.2	46.0
	1976	46.9	.7	47.6	6.3	—	6.3	48.4
	1975	48.6	.9	49.5	8.1	—	8.1	46.7
	1974	55.1	1.1	56.2	13.3	—	13.3	33.1
Material Handling/Storage	1978	227.0	.3	227.3	11.0	—	11.0	151.6
	1977	173.9	.1	174.0	4.5	(.8)	3.7	120.0
	1976	151.7	.4	152.1	8.0	(.9)	7.1	104.8
	1975	171.2	—	171.2	9.2	(.4)	8.8	96.0
	1974	79.9	—	79.9	6.6	—	6.6	110.2
Packaging	1978	158.3	2.1	160.4	11.1	—	11.1	67.2
	1977	134.4	1.7	136.1	8.7	—	8.7	61.8
	1976	128.0	1.5	129.5	10.3	—	10.3	58.0
	1975	109.1	1.1	110.2	5.7	—	5.7	62.0
	1974	119.2	1.1	120.3	9.8	—	9.8	63.3
Corporate Items/Eliminations	1978	—	(63.5)	(63.5)	(9.1)	—	(9.1)	36.3
	1977	—	(50.2)	(50.2)	(6.9)	—	(6.9)	18.4
	1976	—	(37.8)	(37.8)	(6.6)	—	(6.6)	25.9
	1975	—	(35.7)	(35.7)	(7.5)	—	(7.5)	21.2
	1974	—	(47.4)	(47.4)	(4.3)	—	(4.3)	43.7
Consolidated	1978	921.1	—	921.1	12.9	3.0	15.9	658.4
	1977	766.6	—	766.6	29.6	4.7	34.3	559.6
	1976	708.9	—	708.9	56.7	6.9	63.6	526.2
	1975	640.8	—	640.8	66.0	3.8	69.8	480.1
	1974	593.8	—	593.8	70.0	4.4	74.4	496.4

* from unconsolidated affiliates

**Net Sales to Unaffiliated Customers	1978	1977	1976	1975	1974
Iron	$ 96.1	$ 92.4	$107.3	$110.1	$103.0
Steel	245.0	213.8	198.2	171.4	202.6

Business combination—the joining together of all or nearly all of the operations of two or more firms under a single controlling management.

Consolidated statements—the financial statements that result from combining the parent's financial statement amounts with those of its subsidiaries (after certain eliminations have been made). The consolidated statements reflect the financial position and results of operations of a single economic enterprise.

Consolidated statement work sheet—an informal statement on which elimination entries are made for the purpose of showing the assets, liabilities, stockholders' equity, revenues, expenses, and dividends as if the parent and its subsidiaries were a single economic enterprise.

Deferred credit—an account, such as the excess of book value over cost, which has a credit balance but which cannot be properly classified as a contra asset, liability, or stockholders' equity account. The credit balance will be allocated to future operations.

Elimination entries—entries made on a consolidated statement work sheet, which are necessary to remove certain intercompany items and transactions in order to show the assets, liabilities, stockholders' equity, revenues, expenses, and dividends as if the parent and its subsidiaries were a single economic enterprise.

Goodwill—an intangible value attaching to a business firm due primarily to its above-average earnings prospects.

Minority interest—the claim of the stockholders who own less than 50 percent of a subsidiary's outstanding voting common stock. The minority stockholders have an interest in the subsidiary's net assets and share the subsidiary's earnings with the parent company.

Parent company—a corporation which owns more than 50 percent of the outstanding voting common stock of another corporation.

Pooling of interests—a business combination which meets certain criteria specified in *APB Opinion No. 16* including the issue of common stock in exchange for common stock; also, a method of accounting for business combinations classified as poolings of interests. Using this method, the parent company records its investment at the book value of the subsidiary's net assets.

Purchase—a business combination in which the acquiring company issues cash or other assets, debt securities, and sometimes common or preferred stock for the subsidiary's common stock. Also, a method of accounting for business combinations in which the parent company records its investment in the subsidiary at the fair market value of the assets or securities given up or at the fair market value of the common stock received, whichever can be more clearly and objectively determined.

Subsidiary—a corporation acquired and controlled by a parent corporation, with control established by ownership of more than 50 percent of the subsidiary's outstanding voting common stock.

DEMONSTRATION PROBLEM

The Stiller Company acquired all of the outstanding voting common stock of Meara Company on January 2, 1981, for $200,000 cash. On the date of acquisition, the balance sheets for the two companies were as follows:

	Stiller Company	Meara Company
Assets		
Cash	$ 50,000	$ 20,000
Accounts receivable	60,000	25,000
Notes receivable	10,000	5,000
Inventory	75,000	50,000
Investment in Meara Company	200,000	—
Plant and equipment, net	202,000	130,000
Total Assets	$597,000	$230,000
Liabilities and Stockholders' Equity		
Accounts payable	$ 50,000	$ 30,000
Notes payable	15,000	10,000
Common stock—$5 par	350,000	100,000
Retained earnings	182,000	90,000
Total Liabilities and Stockholders' Equity	$597,000	$230,000

Also on January 2, 1981, Meara Company borrowed $10,000 from Stiller Company; the debt is evidenced by a note. The excess of cost over book value is attributable to Meara Company's above-average earnings prospects.

Required:

Prepare a work sheet for a consolidated balance sheet on the date of acquisition.

Solution to demonstration problem

STILLER COMPANY AND SUBSIDIARY MEARA COMPANY
Work Sheet for Consolidated Balance Sheet
January 2, 1981 (date of acquisition)

	Stiller Company	Meara Company	Eliminations Debit	Eliminations Credit	Consolidated Amounts
Assets					
Cash	50,000	20,000			70,000
Accounts receivable	60,000	25,000			85,000
Notes receivable	10,000	5,000		(b) 10,000	5,000
Inventory	75,000	50,000			125,000
Investment in Meara Co.	200,000			(a) 200,000	
Equipment, net	202,000	130,000			332,000
Excess of cost over book value			(a) 10,000		10,000
	597,000	230,000			627,000
Liabilities and Stockholders' Equity					
Accounts payable	50,000	30,000			80,000
Notes payable	15,000	10,000	(b) 10,000		15,000
Common stock	350,000	100,000	(a) 100,000		350,000
Retained earnings	182,000	90,000	(a) 90,000		182,000
	597,000	230,000	210,000	210,000	627,000

QUESTIONS

1. What is the purpose of preparing consolidated financial statements?

2. Under what circumstances must consolidated financial statements be prepared?

3. Why is it necessary to make elimination entries on the consolidated statement work sheet? Are these elimination entries also posted to the accounts of the parent and subsidiary? Why or why not?

4. Why might a corporation pay an amount in excess of the book value of a subsidiary's stock? Why might it pay an amount less than the book value of the subsidiary's stock?

5. The item "Minority interest" often appears as one amount in the consolidated balance sheet. What does this item represent?

6. How do a subsidiary's earnings, losses, and dividends affect the investment account of the parent?

7. When must each of the following methods be used to account for a business combination?

a. Purchase.

b. Pooling of interests.

8. List three differences that exist between the purchase and pooling of interests methods of accounting for business combinations.

9. Why are consolidated financial statements of limited usefulness to the creditors and minority stockholders of a subsidiary?

EXERCISES

E-1. On February 1, 1981, the Howard Company acquired 100 percent of the oustanding voting common stock of the Bowden Company for $250,000 cash. The stockholders' equity of the Bowden Company consisted of common stock, $200,000, and retained earnings, $50,000. Prepare **(a)** the entry to record the investment in Bowden Company and **(b)** the elimination entry that would be made on the consolidated statement work sheet on the date of acquisition.

E-2. The Ramsey Corporation acquired, for cash, 80 percent of the outstanding voting common stock of Peacock Company. On the date of its acquisition, the Peacock Company's stockholders' equity consists of common stock, $175,000, and retained earnings, $65,000. The cost of the investment exceeds book value by $9,000. Prepare **(a)** the entry to record the investment in Peacock Company and **(b)** the entry to eliminate the investment for purposes of preparing consolidated financial statements on the date of acquisition.

E-3. On January 1, 1981, Company A acquired 85 percent of the outstanding voting common stock of Company B. On that date, Company B's stockholders' equity section appeared as follows:

Common stock, $20 par; 10,000 shares authorized, issued, and outstanding	$200,000
Retained earnings	50,000
Total Stockholders' Equity	$250,000

Compute the difference between cost and book value in each of the following cases:

a. Company A pays $212,500 cash for its interest in B.

b. Company A pays $250,000 cash for its interest in B.

c. Company A pays $195,000 cash for its interest in B.

d. Company A issues some of its own common stock; the resulting business combination must be accounted for as a pooling of interests.

E-4. Company Y purchased 90 percent of Company Z's outstanding voting common stock on January 2, 1981. Company Y paid $150,000 for an equity of $135,000— $90,000, common stock, and $45,000, retained earnings. The difference was due to undervalued land owned by

Z. Company Z earned $18,000 during 1981 and paid cash dividends of $6,000.

a. Compute the balance in the investment account on December 31, 1981.

b. Compute the amount of the minority interest on (1) January 2, 1981, and (2) December 31, 1981.

E–5. The Meadow Company owns 75 percent of the Foy Company. The Foy Company reported net earnings of $52,000 for 1981. On December 31, 1981, the Foy Company paid a cash dividend of $14,000. In 1982 the Foy Company incurred a net loss of $10,000. Prepare entries to reflect these events on Meadow Company's books.

E–6. On January 1, 1981, the stockholders' equity section of the Floyd Company's balance sheet is as follows:

Paid-In Capital:

Common stock—$10 par value: authorized, 100,000 shares; issued and outstanding, 75,000 shares ..	$750,000
Paid-in capital in excess of par value	125,000
Total Paid-In Capital	$875,000
Retained earnings	75,000
	$950,000

Ninety percent of Floyd Company's outstanding voting common stock was acquired by Duncan Company on January 1, 1981, for $835,000. Compute **(a)** the book value of the investment, **(b)** the difference between cost and book value, and **(c)** the minority interest.

E–7. On June 1, 1981, the Weeks Corporation issued 5,000 shares of its own $20 par value common stock for 70 percent of the outstanding voting common stock of the Wages Company. The business combination does not qualify as a pooling of interests. The book value of Wages Company's net assets is $320,000. The market value per share of Weeks Corporation stock is $50. Give the journal entry to record the investment on Weeks Company's books.

E–8. P Company acquired a 100 percent interest in the common stock of S Company on January 1, 1981. During 1981, P sold goods to S for $25,000 that cost P $15,000. S sold all of these goods to other companies for $30,000. Give the elimination entry required for the above in the consolidated working papers for the year ended December 31, 1981. Also prepare a schedule showing how you arrived at the amount of the entry.

PROBLEMS, SERIES A

P18–1–A. Farr Company acquired 75 percent of the outstanding voting common stock of Daley Company for $172,000 cash on January 1, 1980. During 1980, 1981, and 1982, Daley Company reported the following:

	Net earnings (loss)	Dividends paid
1980	$42,600	$34,600
1981	(5,400)	–0–
1982	12,900	$ 8,600

Required:

a. Prepare general journal entries to record the investment and the effect of the subsidiary's earnings, losses, and dividends on Farr Company's accounts.

b. Compute the balance in the investment account on December 31, 1982.

P18–2–A. The Robins Company acquired 100 percent of the outstanding voting common stock of the Warner Company on January 1, 1981, for $76,000 cash. On the date of acquisition, the balance sheets for the two companies were as follows:

	Robins Company	Warner Company
Assets		
Cash	$ 6,000	$14,000
Accounts receivable	14,000	18,000
Notes receivable	10,000	6,000
Inventory	25,000	15,000
Investment in Warner Company	76,000	
Equipment, net	22,000	28,000
Total Assets	$153,000	$81,000
Liabilities and Stockholders' Equity		
Accounts payable.................	$ 16,000	$ 5,000
Notes payable	12,000	
Common stock—$20 par	100,000	60,000
Retained earnings	25,000	16,000
Total Liabilities and Stockholders' Equity	$153,000	$81,000

Also on January 1, 1981, Robins Company borrowed $6,000 from Warner Company; the debt is evidenced by a note.

Required:

Prepare a work sheet for a consolidated balance sheet on the date of acquisition.

P18–3–A. On January 1, 1981, Medlin Company acquired 80 percent of the outstanding voting common stock of the Hamby Corporation for $90,000 cash. The January 1, 1981, balance sheets for the two companies are shown below:

	Medlin Company	Hamby Corporation
Assets		
Cash	$ 12,000	$ 9,000
Accounts receivable	10,000	12,000
Inventory	30,000	26,000
Investment in Hamby Corporation ...	90,000	
Equipment, net	15,000	9,000
Buildings, net	45,000	32,000
Land..........................	8,000	10,000
Total Assets	$210,000	$98,000
Liabilities and Stockholders' Equity		
Accounts payable	$ 10,000	$ 5,000
Common stock—$10 par	160,000	80,000
Retained earnings	40,000	13,000
Total Liabilities and Stockholders' Equity	$210,000	$98,000

Medlin Company was willing to pay an amount greater than the book value of Hamby Corporation's stockholders' equity for two reasons:

1. It believed that the equipment owned by Hamby Corporation was undervalued by $3,000, of which $2,400 was Medlin's 80 percent share.
2. The company believed that the remaining excess of cost over book value could be justified on the basis of the subsidiary's excellent earnings expectations.

Required:

a. Prepare a work sheet for a consolidated balance sheet on the date of acquisition.

b. Prepare a consolidated balance sheet for January 1, 1981.

P18–4–A. The Adams Company acquired 100 percent of the outstanding voting common stock of the Belcher Company on January 2, 1981, for $300,000 cash. On the date of acquisition, the balance sheets for the two companies were as follows:

	Adams Company	Belcher Company
Assets		
Cash	$ 35,000	$ 20,000
Accounts receivable	26,000	16,000
Notes receivable	40,000	10,000
Inventory	55,000	26,000
Investment in Belcher Company	300,000	
Equipment, net	72,000	50,000
Buildings, net	210,000	110,000
Land...........................	85,000	45,000
Total Assets	$823,000	$277,000
Liabilities and Stockholders' Equity		
Accounts payable	$ 13,000	$ 15,000
Notes payable	10,000	12,000
Common stock—$10 par............	600,000	200,000
Retained earnings	200,000	50,000
Total Liabilities and Stockholders' Equity	$823,000	$277,000

The excess of cost over book value is attributable to the above-average earnings prospects of Belcher Company and to the belief that Belcher Company's equipment and buildings are undervalued. The fair values are believed to be $70,000 for the equipment and $120,000 for the buildings. On the date of acquisition, Belcher Company borrowed $8,000 from Adams Company; the debt is evidenced by a note.

Required:

a. Prepare a work sheet for a consolidated balance sheet on the date of acquisition.

b. Prepare a consolidated balance sheet as of January 2, 1981.

P18–5–A. Refer back to Problem 18–4–A. Assume the following are the adjusted trial balances for the Adams Company and the Belcher Company on December 31, 1981:

	Adams Company	Belcher Company
Cash	$ 39,000	$ 35,000
Accounts receivable	42,000	20,000
Notes receivable	35,000	5,000
Inventory, December 31	55,000	31,900
Investment in Belcher Company	307,600	
Equipment, net	68,400	47,500
Buildings, net	201,600	105,600
Land	85,000	45,000
Cost of goods sold	200,000	70,000
Expenses (excluding depreciation, taxes, and amortization	80,000	30,100
Depreciation expense	12,000	6,900
Income tax expense	65,000	21,000
Dividends declared	60,000	12,000
Total debits	$1,250,600	$430,000

					Hasty Company	Boland Company
Accounts payable	$ 15,000	$ 20,000				
Notes payable	16,000	10,000				
Common stock—$10 par	600,000	200,000		**Assets**		
Retained earnings—January 1	200,000	50,000				
Revenue from sales	400,000	150,000	Cash	$ 50,000	$ 30,000
Earnings of Belcher Company	19,600		Accounts receivable	32,000	15,000
			Notes receivable	23,000	
Total credits	$1,250,600	$430,000	Inventory	90,000	50,000

There is no intercompany debt at the end of the year.

	Hasty Company	Boland Company
Investment in Boland Company	220,000	
Equipment, net	82,000	30,000
Buildings, net	190,000	120,000
Land	60,000	20,000
Total Assets	$747,000	$265,000

Required:

Prepare a work sheet for *consolidated financial statements* on December 31, 1981. (On January 2, 1981 the equipment and buildings had remaining lives of 20 and 25 years, respectively; goodwill is to be amortized over 20 years.)

Liabilities and Stockholders' Equity

	Hasty Company	Boland Company
Accounts payable	$ 37,000	$ 25,000
Notes payable		20,000
Common stock—$10 par	500,000	200,000
Paid-in capital—pooling of interests . . .	20,000	
Retained earnings	190,000	20,000
Total Liabilities and Stockholders' Equity	$747,000	$265,000

P18–6–A.

Required:

Using the work sheet prepared for Problem 18–5–A, prepare the following items:

a. Consolidated earnings statement for the year ended December 31, 1981.

b. Consolidated statement of retained earnings for the year ended December 31, 1981.

c. Consolidated balance sheet for December 31, 1981.

P18–7–A. Hasty Company acquired 100 percent of the Boland Company's voting common stock on January 2, 1981. Hasty Company issued 20,000 shares of its own $10 par value stock in exchange for all the stock of Boland Company which had a book value of $220,000 ($200,000 common stock and $20,000 retained earnings). On the date of acquisition, the balance sheets for the two companies were as follows:

On the date of acquisition, Boland Company borrowed $10,000 from Hasty Company. The debt is evidenced by a note.

Required:

a. Give the journal entry Hasty Company made on January 2, 1981, to record its investment in Boland Company.

b. Prepare a work sheet for a consolidated balance sheet on the date of acquisition.

c. Prepare a consolidated balance sheet as of January 2, 1981.

PROBLEMS, SERIES B

P18–1–B. Mincey Company acquired 68 percent of the outstanding voting common stock of Shelley Company for $510,000 on January 1, 1980. During the years 1980–82, Shelley Company reported the following:

	Net earnings (loss)	Dividends paid
1980	$86,600	$51,900
1981	22,200	13,300
1982	(1,400)	3,325

Required:

a. Prepare general journal entries to record the investment and the effect of the subsidiary's earnings, losses, and dividends on Mincey Company's accounts.

b. Compute the investment account balance on December 31, 1982.

P18–2–B. The Smith Company acquired all of the outstanding voting common stock of the Boyer Company on

January 3, 1981, for $84,000. On the date of acquisition, the balance sheets for the two companies were as follows:

	Smith Company	Boyer Company
Assets		
Cash	$ 14,000	$12,000
Accounts receivable	27,000	25,000
Notes receivable	15,000	4,000
Inventory	39,000	18,000
Investment in Boyer Company	84,000	
Equipment, net	72,000	33,000
Total Assets	$251,000	$92,000
Liabilities and Stockholders' Equity		
Accounts payable	$ 26,000	$ 8,000
Common stock—$10 par	120,000	58,000
Retained earnings	105,000	26,000
Total Liabilities and Stockholders' Equity	$251,000	$92,000

Required:

Prepare a work sheet for a consolidated balance sheet on the date of acquisition.

P18–3–B. On February 1, 1981, Landon Company acquired 75 percent of the outstanding voting common stock of the Greene Corporation for $70,000. The February 1, 1981, balance sheets for the two companies show:

	Landon Company	Greene Corporation
Assets		
Cash	$ 22,000	$17,000
Accounts receivable	18,000	14,000
Notes receivable	9,000	
Inventory	32,000	18,000
Investment in Greene Corporation	70,000	
Equipment, net	28,000	12,000
Buildings, net	42,000	28,000
Land	6,000	5,000
Total Assets	$227,000	$94,000
Liabilities and Stockholders' Equity		
Accounts payable	$ 17,000	$ 8,000
Common stock—$10 par	115,000	50,000
Retained earnings	95,000	36,000
Total Liabilities and Stockholders' Equity	$227,000	$94,000

The price paid by Landon reflects its belief that its 75 percent interest in the undervaluation of Greene's equipment and buildings was $2,000 and $3,500, respectively.

Required:

a. Prepare a work sheet for a consolidated balance sheet on the date of acquisition.

b. Prepare a consolidated balance sheet for February 1, 1981.

P18–4–B. The Noel Company acquired all of the outstanding voting common stock of the Holly Company on January 1, 1981, for $240,000. On the date of acquisition, the balance sheets for the two companies were as follows:

	Noel Company	Holly Company
Assets		
Cash	$ 50,000	$ 15,000
Accounts receivable	24,000	20,000
Notes receivable	10,000	6,000
Inventory	76,000	48,000
Investment in Holly Company	240,000	
Equipment, net	68,000	41,000
Buildings, net	185,000	92,000
Land	78,000	25,000
Total Assets	$731,000	$247,000
Liabilities and Stockholders' Equity		
Accounts payable	$ 44,000	$ 20,000
Notes payable	12,000	14,000
Common stock—$20 par	530,000	198,000
Retained earnings	145,000	15,000
Total Liabilities and Stockholders' Equity	$731,000	$247,000

The cost of the investment differs from its book value because the Noel Company thinks that the Holly Company's assets are undervalued. The Noel Company thinks the equipment, buildings, and land are undervalued by $6,000, $12,000, and $9,000, respectively.

On the date of acquisition, Holly Company borrowed $10,000 from Noel Company; the intercompany debt is evidenced by a note.

Required:

a. Prepare a work sheet for a consolidated balance sheet on the date of acquisition.

b. Prepare a consolidated balance sheet for January 1, 1981.

P18–5–B. Refer back to Problem 18–4–B. Assume the following are the adjusted trial balances for the Noel Company and the Holly Company on December 31, 1981:

	Noel Company	Holly Company
Cash	$ 48,000	$ 20,238
Accounts receivable	30,752	23,000
Notes receivable	19,000	5,000
Inventory, December 31	85,000	56,000
Investment in Holly Company	250,100	
Equipment, net	63,750	38,437
Buildings, net	175,750	87,400
Land	78,000	25,000
Cost of goods sold	448,000	120,000
Expenses (excluding depreciation and taxes)	120,000	45,000
Depreciation expense	13,500	7,163
Income tax expense	31,648	6,862
Dividends declared	26,500	9,900
Total debits	$1,390,000	$444,000
Accounts payable	$ 40,000	$ 21,000
Notes payable	15,000	10,000
Common stock—$20 par	530,000	198,000
Retained earnings	145,000	15,000
Revenue from sales	640,000	200,000
Earnings of Holly company	20,000	
Total credits	$1,390,000	$444,000

There is no intercompany debt at the end of the year.

Required:

Prepare a work sheet for consolidated financial statements on December 31, 1981. (At the beginning of 1981, the equipment and buildings had remaining lives of 16 and 20 years, respectively.)

P18–6–B. Using the work sheet prepared for Problem 18–5–B, prepare the following items:

a. Consolidated earnings statement for the year ended December 31, 1981.

b. Consolidated statement of retained earnings for the year ended December 31, 1981.

c. Consolidated balance sheet for December 31, 1981.

P18–7–B. Lavin Corporation acquired 100 percent of Allen Corporation's voting common stock on January 3, 1981. Lavin Corporation issued 50,000 shares of its own $5 par value stock in exchange for all the stock of Allen Corporation which had a book value of $300,000 ($250,000 common stock and $50,000 retained earnings). The following are the adjusted trial balances for the Lavin Corporation and the Allen Corporation on December 31, 1981:

	Lavin Corporation	Allen Corporation
Cash	$ 50,000	$ 20,000
Accounts receivable	80,000	40,000
Notes receivable	25,000	15,000
Inventory, December 31	130,000	80,000
Investment in Allen Corporation	330,000	
Equipment, net	180,000	75,000
Buildings, net	300,000	120,000
Land	205,000	100,000
Cost of goods sold	540,000	180,000
Expenses	200,000	65,000
Dividends declared	75,000	25,000
Total debits	$2,115,000	$720,000
Accounts payable	$ 100,000	$ 80,000
Notes payable	60,000	40,000
Common stock	750,000	250,000
Paid-in capital—pooling of interests	50,000	
Retained earnings, January 1	200,000	50,000
Revenue from sales	900,000	300,000
Earnings of Allen Corporation	55,000	
Total credits	$2,115,000	$720,000

Required:

Prepare a work sheet for consolidated financial statements on December 31, 1981.

BUSINESS DECISION PROBLEM 18-1

On January 2, 1981, Inman Company acquired 60 percent of the voting common stock of Houseman Corporation for $200,000 cash. Inman and Houseman are engaged in similar lines of business. Inman has hired you to help it prepare consolidated financial statements. Inman has already collected the following information for both companies as of January 2, 1981:

	Inman Company	Houseman Corporation
Assets		
Cash	$ 20,000	$ 15,000
Accounts receivable	30,000	35,000
Inventories	80,000	60,000
Investment in Houseman Corporation	200,000	
Plant and equipment	260,000	205,000
Total Assets	$590,000	$315,000

Liabilities and Stockholders' Equity		
Accounts payable	40,000	15,000
Common stock—$20 par	400,000	200,000
Retained earnings	150,000	100,000
Total Liabilities and Stockholders' Equity	$590,000	$315,000

Required:

a. Inman believes that consolidated financial statements can be prepared simply by adding together the amounts in the two individual columns. Is Inman correct? If not, why not?

b. Prepare a consolidated balance sheet for the date of acquisition.

BUSINESS DECISION PROBLEM 18-2

On July 1, 1981, Vernon Corporation acquired all the outstanding voting common stock of Warner Corporation in exchange for its own $10 par value common stock. The book value of Warner Corporation's net assets on the date of acquisition was $250,000 ($150,000 common stock and $100,000 retained earnings). Warner Corporation's net earnings for 1981 were $45,000. The business combination meets all of the twelve conditions specified in *APB Opinion No. 16.*

Required:

a. Decide whether the business combination should be accounted for as a purchase or a pooling of interests. Give reasons to support your answer.

b. What amount of the subsidiary's retained earnings at the date of acquisition should be included in consolidated retained earnings?

c. What amount of the subsidiary's net earnings for 1981 should be included in consolidated net earnings for 1981?

PART SIX

ANALYSIS OF

FINANCIAL STATEMENTS

Chapter 19

Statement of

changes in financial position;

cash flow statement

The conventional financial statements of a company—the earnings statement, the statement of retained earnings, and the balance sheet—often have not provided answers to questions that users have been asking. These questions include: How much working capital was generated by operations? Why is such a profitable firm only able to pay such meager dividends? How much was spent for new plant and equipment, and where did the funds come from to purchase it?

The statement which provides this desired information is called the statement of changes in financial position and is one of the topics of this chapter. The Accounting Principles Board decided that such a statement is to be provided as a basic financial statement for each period for which an earnings statement is presented.[1] Its companion statement, the schedule of changes in working capital, is also discussed and illustrated. The other topic covered is the cash flow statement.

The statement of changes in financial position shows flows of funds into and out of the business. The term, funds, can be viewed as being cash. But a broader view often is taken. Funds can mean working capital (current assets minus current liabilities), or it can mean all financial resources. This latter view would include (as fund flows) financing and investing transactions which do not require the use of working capital. An example would be where a building is acquired by issuing long-term debt or stock.

THE STATEMENT OF CHANGES IN FINANCIAL POSITION: Basic objectives and form

The broad objectives of the statement of changes in financial position are (1) to summarize the financing and investing activities of the enterprise including an indication of the amount of working capital provided by operations and (2) to help explain and disclose the changes in financial position that occurred during the period. The statement provides information on the financing and investing activities of the enterprise which are a vital part of the successful administration of the enterprise.[2]

Currently, the concepts, terminology, and even the form of the statement of changes in financial position are in a transitional stage. *APB Opinion No. 19* permits considerable flexibility in form. The statement of changes in financial position presented will be similar in format and terminology to those used in practice.

Typically, these statements contain two major sections. One is headed "Financial resources provided" and shows the sources of the flow of financial resources (funds) into the enterprise. The other is headed "Financial resources applied" and shows how the financial resources flowing into the enterprise were used. Illustration 19.1 shows the types of items which represent financial

---

[1] APB, "Reporting Changes in Financial Position," *APB Opinion No. 19* (New York: AICPA, March 1971), par. 7.

[2] The statement of changes in financial position may highlight the amount of cash provided by operations and still be in accord with *APB Opinion No. 19.* But current practice tends heavily to emphasize working capital from operations, and we will do the same.

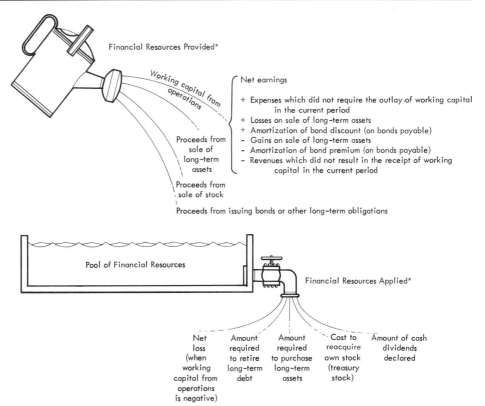

Illustration 19.1: Graphic illustration of flows represented in the statement of changes in financial position

Financial Resources Provided*

Working capital from operations

{ Net earnings
+ Expenses which did not require the outlay of working capital in the current period
+ Losses on sale of long-term assets
+ Amortization of bond discount (on bonds payable)
– Gains on sale of long-term assets
– Amortization of bond premium (on bonds payable)
– Revenues which did not result in the receipt of working capital in the current period

Proceeds from sale of long-term assets

Proceeds from sale of stock

Proceeds from issuing bonds or other long-term obligations

Pool of Financial Resources

Financial Resources Applied*

Net loss (when working capital from operations is negative)

Amount required to retire long-term debt

Amount required to purchase long-term assets

Cost to reacquire own stock (treasury stock)

Amount of cash dividends declared

* If financial resources provided exceed financial resources applied, there is an increase in working capital, and vice versa. While financial resources provided and applied which did not affect working capital are included, the amounts offset each other.

resources provided and financial resources applied. (Refer to Illustration 19.6 to examine the format of the statement.)[3]

In the past, such statements often were broadly referred to as funds flow statements and carried the formal titles of "statement of sources and applications of funds" or "statement of sources and uses of funds." Or, because such statements usually showed the flows of working capital into and out of the firm, the statement was called "statement of sources and uses of working capital." In these instances the format was to show only *working capital provided* (the sources of working capital flowing into an enterprise in a given period) and *working capital applied* (the uses of working capital during that period). Following the preference expressed in *APB Opinion No. 19,* this text will use the broader title "statement of changes in financial position."

---

[3] A schedule of working capital (to be illustrated later) may either appear as a third part of the statement of changes in financial position or may appear as a separate schedule. We have used the latter approach.

Uses of the statement of changes in financial position

The information contained in the statement of changes in financial position is useful to many parties for a variety of reasons.

Management uses.   Management may, for example, after studying such information, decide to change its dividend policy in order to conserve working capital. Or it may decide that in the light of the large amount of working capital generated by operations that a certain amount of working capital can be safely invested in plant and equipment. Or the information may show clearly the need for additional financing to take advantage of capital expenditure opportunities that promise to be highly profitable. And the statement highlights the all-important relationship between working capital generated by operations, all other sources and uses of working capital, and financial resources provided and applied which did not affect working capital.

Creditor and investor uses.   Information contained in the statement of changes in financial position also may be used by creditors and investors. These groups make decisions on whether to invest (or disinvest) in the debt or equity securities issued by a given company. *Projections* of such information can provide valuable insights into such matters as (1) whether or not dividends are likely to be increased, (2) how future capital expenditures are likely to be financed, and (3) whether or not a firm appears capable of meeting its debts as they come due. Typically, projections of the future are based upon study of the past.

Content of the statement of changes in financial position

As stated earlier, Illustration 19.1 shows the financial resources provided (inflows) and the financial resources applied (outflows) which are reported in the statement of changes in financial position. A careful study of this illustration should be helpful in understanding the concepts presented in the remainder of this chapter. Compare this illustration with Illustration 19.6 and refer to Illustration 19.6 as you read the remainder of the chapter.

Working capital from operations.   The amount of working capital generated by operations is one of the most important single figures that can be determined for most business enterprises. Over the long run, a successful business will acquire plant and other assets, retire long-term debt, and pay dividends largely from working capital generated by operations.

Nature of working capital from operations.   At this point it might be helpful to describe the nature of working capital from operations and why it is reported as it is. Typically, the measurement of working capital from operations begins with net earnings. This is because sales of goods and services bring new current assets into the business (usually cash or receivables), while expenses for the most part decrease working capital (either through decreases in current assets or increases in current liabilities). But because of the inclusion of expenses such as depreciation, which do not require the use of working capital, net earnings do not measure the amount of working capital generated by operations. Adjustments for revenues not producing working capital and expenses not consuming working capital must be made. These are called *nonworking capital charges or credits.*

The following illustration is presented to explain the adjustment needed when net earnings contain an expense not requiring working capital:

Sales (represented by receipts of cash and receivables)		$230,000
Less: Operating expenses consuming working capital (represented by credits to current asset or current liability accounts)	$180,000	
Depreciation (recorded by credits to accumulated depreciation accounts, which are related to plant assets and are *not* current assets or current liabilities)	12,000	192,000
Net Earnings		$ 38,000

The parenthetical expressions above indicate that one item presented—depreciation—does not result in either an increase or decrease in working capital. Unlike most expenses, depreciation does not decrease current assets or increase current liabilities. Since this is true, it follows that the amount of working capital generated by operations is not $38,000 (the net earnings amount) but $50,000. This amount is found as follows:

Working capital from sales	$230,000
Less: Working capital consumed by expenses	180,000
Working capital from operations	$ 50,000

A more common way of showing the working capital generated by operations in the statement of changes in financial position is as follows:

Working capital provided:	
By operations:	
Net earnings	$38,000
Add: Expenses not requiring the outlay of working capital in the current period—depreciation	12,000
	$50,000

Because the purpose of the statement of changes in financial position is to show gross flows rather than simply net changes, the first method of reporting has considerable merit. But the second method is almost always used because it is brief and can be tied in with reported net earnings.

Use of this second method has led some to refer to depreciation as a source of funds. But as explained above, depreciation is added back to net earnings only to arrive at working capital from operations. Depreciation is not a source of funds.

Depreciation is one example of an expense that does not require an outflow of working capital. Others are the amortization of patents, bond discounts or premiums, leases and leaseholds, and the recording of depletion. In fact, an adjustment is required for any expense that is recorded by a debit to an expense account and a credit to a long-term balance sheet account. The asset may be credited directly or by means of a credit to an allowance account (e.g., accumulated depreciation).

Whether or not operations produce or consume working capital in a firm operating at a net loss depends upon the size of the items included in the net loss that did not require or produce working capital. For example, if a company reports a net loss of $50,000 occurring after deducting $80,000 of depreciation, then $30,000 of working capital was provided by operations. But if a loss of $50,000 is shown with only $15,000 of depreciation deducted, then operations have consumed (rather than provided) $35,000 of working capital. Typically, the $35,000 is reported as an application of working capital.

Other significant financing and investing activities.   In addition to reporting the working capital provided by operations, the statement of changes in financial position should disclose clearly:

1.   The use of working capital to acquire long-term assets—investments; property, plant, and equipment; and intangibles.
2.   The other sources of working capital such as the sale of noncurrent assets and the issuance of long-term debt or shares of stock.
3.   The use of working capital to pay dividends to stockholders.
4.   All changes of a significant financial or investment nature which do not involve the use of working capital. These would include changes such as the conversion of long-term debt or preferred stock into common stock and the issuance of long-term debt or preferred or common stock for noncurrent assets.

Changes reported in the balance sheet which are not significant investment or financial activities do not have to be reported in the statement of changes in financial position. Examples are stock dividends and stock splits.

The schedule of changes in working capital.   *APB Opinion No. 19,* states that a statement or schedule showing the details of the net change in working capital should be presented when a statement of changes in financial position is presented. It is often presented at the bottom of the statement of changes in financial position. But we will treat it as a separate schedule, as shown in Illustration 19.4.

Preparing the statement of changes in financial position

First let us examine a very simple illustration. In fact it is so simple that we can prepare the statement of changes in financial position directly from the facts with almost no analysis.

Assume the following facts for the year 1981 for the Welby Company:

Change in working capital	+$10,000
Changes in noncurrent accounts	
Machinery	+$40,000
Land (sold at book value)	−$30,000
Retained earnings	+$20,000
Net earnings (all items included affected working capital)	$20,000

The statement of changes in financial position prepared from the data would contain the following information:

WELBY COMPANY
Statement of Changes in Financial Position
For the Year Ended December 31, 1981

Financial resources provided:	
Working capital provided:	
By operations:	
Net earnings	$20,000
Working capital provided by operations	$20,000
Other sources of working capital:	
Sale of land	30,000
Total financial resources provided	$50,000
Financial resources applied:	
Working capital applied:	
Purchase of machinery	$40,000
Total financial resources applied	$40,000
Increase in working capital	10,000
Total	$50,000

This simple illustration shows how changes in working capital and in the noncurrent accounts are reported in the statement of changes in financial position.

We will now consider a more realistic, and therefore more complex, example. The basic principles of reporting the data are the same, but the analysis is more involved.

It is assumed in the following illustration that the accountant has prepared two of the financial statements for The United States Corporation (see Illustrations 19.2 and 19.3) and is now turning to the statement of changes in financial position. Additional information will be provided as required in order to illustrate the type of analyses undertaken in the preparation of the statement of changes in financial position.

The remaining steps to be taken to prepare a statement of changes in financial position are:

1. Determine the change in working capital.
2. Prepare the working paper showing the analysis of the changes in the noncurrent accounts.
3. Use the data in the working paper to prepare the formal statement of changes in financial position.

Determining the change in working capital.   The comparative balance sheet in Illustration 19.3 has already been expanded to include a column showing the net increase or decrease in each item between December 31, 1980, and December 31, 1981. From the increase-decrease column it is a simple matter to prepare the *comparative schedule of working capital* shown in Illustration 19.4. Each of the current assets and current liabilities is listed along with its balance and its effect on working capital.

Each increase in a current asset results in an increase in working capital,

Illustration 19.2:
Statement of
earnings and
retained earnings

THE UNITED STATES CORPORATION
Statement of Earnings and Retained Earnings
For the Year Ended December 31, 1981

Gross sales		$1,475,000
Less: Sales returns and allowances		10,800
Net sales		$1,464,200
Cost of goods sold:		
Inventories, January 1	$115,300	
Net purchases	883,450	
Cost of goods available for sale	$998,750	
Inventories, December 31	127,600	
Cost of goods sold		871,150
Gross margin		$ 593,050
Less: Operating expenses:		
Bad debts expense	$ 7,320	
Depreciation expense ($3,250, buildings; $31,050, equipment)	34,300	
Salaries	215,000	
Sundry selling expenses	90,000	
Taxes, payroll and other	26,000	
General administrative expenses	123,780	
Total operating expenses		496,400
Net earnings from operations		$ 96,650
Other revenue:		
Interest earned	$ 1,950	
Gain on sale of long-term investments	1,700	3,650
		$ 100,300
Other expenses:		
Interest expense	$ 3,800	
Loss on sale of equipment	900	4,700
Net earnings before federal income taxes		$ 95,600
Deduct: Federal income taxes		45,250
Net earnings to retained earnings		$ 50,350
Retained earnings, January 1		84,100
		$ 134,450
Deduct: Dividends declared		18,000
Retained Earnings, December 31		$ 116,450

as, for example, the $5,400 increase in cash. Similarly, a net decrease in any current asset results in a decrease in working capital. Conversely, increases in current liabilities are decreases in working capital (accounts payable, for example), while decreases in current liabilities are increases in working capital.

The schedule of changes in working capital (Illustration 19.4) details the changes in the working capital of The United States Corporation. But it does not explain what caused the $30,150 net increase in working capital. One of the purposes of the statement of changes in financial position is to show these causes. As the analysis below explains, the reasons for the changes are found in the noncurrent accounts shown in the comparative balance sheet. Bear in mind that the effect of net earnings and dividends is reported in retained earnings.

Illustration 19.3:
Comparative
balance sheet

THE UNITED STATES CORPORATION
Comparative Balance Sheet
December 31, 1980, and 1981

	1981	1980	*Increase decrease**
Assets			
Current Assets:			
Cash	$ 46,300	$ 40,900	$ 5,400
Accounts receivable	119,980	107,000	12,980
Allowance for doubtful accounts	(7,820)	(6,000)	(1,820)
Marketable securities	3,000	–0–	3,000
Inventories	127,600	115,300	12,300
Prepaid expenses	3,100	4,700	1,600*
Total Current Assets	$292,160	$261,900	$30,260
Investments	$ 17,000	$ 25,000	$ 8,000*
Property, Plant, and Equipment:			
Land	$100,000	$ 80,000	$20,000
Buildings	175,000	130,000	45,000
Accumulated depreciation—buildings	(29,750)	(26,500)	(3,250)
Equipment	198,000	175,000	23,000
Accumulated depreciation—equipment	(57,650)	(43,100)	(14,550)
Total Property, Plant, and Equipment	$385,600	$315,400	$70,200
Total Assets	$694,760	$602,300	$92,460
Liabilities and Stockholders' Equity			
Current Liabilities:			
Accounts payable	$ 74,620	$ 64,900	$ 9,720
Notes payable	15,000	20,000	5,000*
Advances from customers	1,000	900	100
Accrued interest payable	800	1,070	270*
Other accrued liabilities	9,890	12,230	2,340*
Estimated federal income tax liability	12,000	14,100	2,100*
Total Current Liabilities	$113,310	$113,200	$ 110
Long-Term Liabilities:			
Mortgage note payable, 8% (on land and buildings)	$ 35,000	$ –0–	$35,000
Bonds payable, 9%, due 1983	40,000	40,000	–0–
Total Long-Term Liabilities	$ 75,000	$ 40,000	$35,000
Total Liabilities	$188,310	$153,200	$35,110
Stockholders' Equity:			
Common stock, stated value, $50 per share	$390,000	$365,000	$25,000
Retained earnings	116,450	84,100	32,350
Total Stockholders' Equity	$506,450	$449,100	$57,350
Total Liabilities and Stockholders' Equity	$694,760	$602,300	$92,460

Preparing the working paper showing the analysis of changes in the noncurrent accounts. A working paper may be used to analyze the changes in the noncurrent accounts and to prepare the statement of changes in financial position. Illustration 19.5 is the working paper for The United States Corporation. It will be used to analyze the transactions and prepare

THE UNITED STATES CORPORATION
Comparative Schedule of Working Capital
December 31, 1980, and 1981

| | December 31 | | Working capital | |
	1981	1980	Increase	Decrease
Current assets:				
Cash	$ 46,300	$ 40,900	$ 5,400	
Accounts receivable	119,980	107,000	12,980	
Allowance for doubtful accounts	(7,820)	(6,000)	(1,820)	
Marketable securities	3,000	–0–	3,000	
Inventories	127,600	115,300	12,300	
Prepaid expenses	3,100	4,700		$ 1,600
Total Current Assets	$292,160	$261,900		
Current Liabilities:				
Accounts payable	$ 74,620	$ 64,900		9,720
Notes payable	15,000	20,000	5,000	
Advances from customers	1,000	900		100
Accrued interest payable	800	1,070	270	
Other accrued liabilities	9,890	12,230	2,340	
Estimated federal income tax				
liability	12,000	14,100	2,100	
Total Current Liabilities	$113,310	$113,200		
Working capital	$178,850	$148,700		
Net increase in working capital				30,150
			$41,570	$41,570

the statement of changes in financial position. The discussion which follows will describe the items and trace them to the entries made in Illustration 19.5. Use of a working paper is optional; some accountants may choose to use it and others may not.

The steps to follow in preparing the working paper are as follows:

1. Enter the amount of working capital as of the beginning of the period in the first column and the working capital as of the end of the period in the last column.

2. Enter the account balances of all noncurrent balance sheet accounts as of the beginning of the period in the first column and as of the end of the period in the last column. Notice that the debit items are listed first, followed by the credit items.

3. Total the debits and credits in the first and last columns to determine that debits equal credits in each of the columns.

4. Write in the term "Financial resources provided" immediately below the total of the credit items. Leave sufficient space for listing all of the sources of funds. Then write in "Financial resources applied."

5. The analyzing entries are entered in columns two and three. They may be made in any order. They perform two functions: *(a)* they explain the change in each noncurrent account and *(b)* they record the sources and uses of funds. (The analyzing entries are discussed later in this chapter.)

Illustration 19.5: Working paper for statement of changes in financial position

UNITED STATES CORPORATION
Working Paper for Statement of Changes in Financial Position
For the Year Ended December 31, 1981

	Account Balances 12/31/80	Analysis of Transactions for 1981		Account Balances 12/31/81
		Debit	Credit	
Debits				
Working capital	148,700	(1) 30,150		178,850
Investments	25,000		(2) 8,000	17,000
Land	80,000	(3) 20,000		100,000
Buildings	130,000	(3) 45,000		175,000
Equipment	175,000	(5) 43,000	(4) 20,000	198,000
Totals	558,700			668,850
Credits				
Accumulated depreciation—buildings	26,500		(6) 3,250	29,750
Accumulated depreciation—equipment	43,100	(4) 16,500	(6) 31,050	57,650
Mortgage note payable, 8%	–0–		(3) 35,000	35,000
Bonds payable, 9%	40,000			40,000
Common stock	365,000		(7) 25,000	390,000
Retained earnings	84,100	(9) 18,000	(8) 50,350	116,450
Totals	558,700	172,650	172,650	668,850
Financial resources provided:				
Working capital provided by operations:				
Net earnings		(8) 50,350		
Depreciation—buildings		(6) 3,250		
Depreciation—equipment		(6) 31,050		
Loss on sale of equipment		(4) 900		
Less: Gain on sale of investments			(2) 1,700	
Other sources:				
Sale of investments		(2) 9,700		
Sale of equipment		(4) 2,600		
Issuance of common stock		(7) 25,000		
Financial resources provided which did not affect working capital:				
Assumed liability on mortgage note to acquire land and buildings		(3) 35,000		
Financial resources applied:				
Working capital applied:				
Acquisition of land and buildings			(3) 30,000	
Acquisition of equipment			(5) 43,000	
Declaration of cash dividends			(9) 18,000	
Financial resources applied which did not affect working capital:				
Land and buildings acquired by assuming the liability on a mortgage note			(3) 35,000	
Increase in working capital during 1981			(1) 30,150	
Totals		157,850	157,850	

6. Total the debit and credit columns in the middle two columns. There will be one set of totals for the balance sheet items and another set for the sources and uses of funds. The bottom portion of the working paper is used to prepare the formal statement of changes in financial position.

As described above, one of the items to be reported in the statement of changes in financial position is the net change in working capital. Consequently, once the change in working capital has been determined (see Illustration 19.4), no further attention need be paid to the individual items making up working capital—cash, accounts receivable, accounts payable, and so forth. The changes in all of these accounts are summarized and reported as one amount. (See entry [1] in Illustration 19.5). Thus, in our analysis of changes in financial position, we need not concern ourselves with whether cash increased or decreased when we analyze the changes in the noncurrent accounts. All that we need to know is whether the change affected working capital or was part of a significant financing or investing transaction. If so, it must be reported in the statement of changes in financial position.

The changes which we must analyze to see whether they should be so reported are summarized below. They consist of all of the changes shown in the noncurrent accounts in the comparative balance sheet for December 31, 1980, and December 31, 1981.

	Increase	Decrease
Investments		$8,000
Land...	$20,000	
Buildings	45,000	
Accumulated depreciation—buildings	3,250	
Equipment	23,000	
Accumulated depreciation—equipment	14,550	
Mortgage note payable	35,000	
Common stock, stated value, $50 per share	25,000	
Retained earnings	32,350	

Let us assume that the following information also is available:

1. There were no purchases of investments during the year. Investments with a cost of $8,000 were sold for $9,700.
2. One transaction took place in which land and buildings valued at $65,000 ($45,000 for the building and $20,000 for the land) were acquired, subject to a 9 percent mortgage note of $35,000.
3. During the year the corporation disposed of equipment which had an original cost of $20,000 and which had been depreciated to the extent of $16,500 at date of sale.
4. All of the common stock was issued for cash.

We are now prepared to analyze each of the above changes in the noncurrent accounts to see if it affected working capital or was part of a significant investing or financing transaction. Changes of either type must be reported in the statement of changes in financial position.

Investments.   The gain on the sale of investments must be deducted from net earnings to show the entire amount received from the sale as a source of working capital. We know that the $8,000 change in investments actually produced $9,700 of working capital. The statement of changes in financial position would show:

> Other sources of working capital:
> Sale of investments $9,700

This is accomplished by making entry (2) in the working paper (Illustration 19.5).

Land and buildings.   The increases in the land and buildings accounts were the result of a single transaction. In this transaction the acquisition of the land and buildings was financed by an increase in a long-term debt (the assumption of liability on the mortgage note of $35,000) and by the use of working capital ($30,000). The acquisition of these assets would be reported in the statement of changes in financial position as follows:

Working capital applied:
Acquisition of land and buildings $30,000

Financial resources applied which did not affect working capital:
Land and buildings acquired by assuming the liability on a mortgage note $35,000

The assumption of the liability on the mortgage note would be reported:

Financial resources provided which did not affect working capital:
Assumption of liability on mortgage note to acquire land and buildings $35,000

Entry (3) in Illustration 19.5 shows how to accomplish this reporting.

Before the issuance of *APB Opinion No. 19,* it was not uncommon to report only the $30,000 effect on working capital of transactions such as the above as an element of working capital applied. Such a procedure is now considered deficient. The merger wave of the 1960s showed very clearly that a company could engage in highly significant transactions which do not affect working capital. It could for example, double the amount of assets owned by issuing common stock for plant and equipment. Consequently, under *APB Opinion No. 19,* a transaction involving a change in a noncurrent asset and a noncurrent equity must be reported separately as both a provision of financial resources and an application of financial resources. Similarly, exchanges of one type of noncurrent asset for another and one type of noncurrent equity for another must also be reported separately as both financial resources provided and financial resources applied. Stock dividends and stock splits are exceptions.

Equipment.   The equipment account shows a net increase of $23,000 in spite of the fact that some equipment was sold during the year. Thus the net change in this account must be analyzed further to allow the reporting of the working capital provided and applied. The amount shown under "Other sources of working capital" from the sale of the equipment is the amount received at time of sale, computed as follows:

Cost of equipment sold	$20,000
Less: Accumulated depreciation	16,500
Book value of equipment sold	$ 3,500
Less: Loss on sale of equipment (from earnings statement)	900
Working capital received (sales price of the equipment)	$ 2,600

Entry (4) shows how the sale of equipment would be treated in the working paper.

The equipment account must have been debited for purchases of equipment amounting to $43,000 if the account increased $23,000 in spite of a $20,000 credit to the account. Thus, the statement of changes in financial position would show working capital applied to purchase of equipment of $43,000, as shown in entry (5).

Accumulated depreciation. The $17,800 net increase in the two accumulated depreciation accounts ($3,250 for buildings plus $14,550 for equipment) is the result of the credits from recording the depreciation charges for the year, $3,250 on buildings and $31,050 on equipment, and the debit entered to remove the $16,500 applicable to the equipment sold. Entry (6) shows that the depreciation expense amounts must be added back to net earnings since they did not consume working capital.

Mortgage note payable. The manner in which the change in the Mortgage Note Payable account will appear in the statement of changes in financial position has already been presented (see entry [3]).

Common stock. Since $25,000 of stated value common stock was issued for $25,000 cash, the statement of changes in financial position would show working capital provided by the issuance of common stock of $25,000. Had the stock been issued at an amount greater than stated value, the excess would appear as an increase in a separate stockholders' equity account. But the statement of changes in financial position would simply show the total amount received under "Other sources of working capital." This is shown in entry (7).

Retained earnings. The statement of retained earnings and the earnings statement reveal that net earnings for 1981 amounted to $50,350 (shown in entry [8]) and that dividends declared during the year amounted to $18,000 (shown in entry [9]). The difference between these two figures fully explains the $32,350 net increase in retained earnings. The net earnings amount is included as a source of working capital from operations. The dividends of $18,000 represent an application of working capital. They reduced working capital by $18,000 at the time of declaration (the creation of the current liability account, Dividends Payable, reduced working capital).

Had the Retained Earnings account changed for any other reason, the cause of the change must be determined in order to decide whether it should be reported in the statement of changes in financial position. The transfer of an amount from one stockholders' equity account to another does not affect working capital and usually is not a significant investment or financing transaction. Such transactions would not be reflected in the statement of changes in financial position.

Using the working paper to prepare the statement of changes in financial position. All information relating to working capital, the changes in working capital, and other significant financing and investing activities during 1981 has now been analyzed and shown in Illustration 19.5 (in the section below the double underlining). The resulting statement of changes in financial position is shown in Illustration 19.6. This statement shows that of the total financial resources provided, over one half consisted of working capital provided by operations. The working capital provided by operations was adequate not only to cover the dividends for the year but also to finance approximately one half of the expansion in assets, including the increase in working capital. This latter increase may be a permanent increase necessary to support the corporation's expanded activity.

Illustration 19.6:
Statement of
changes in
financial
position

THE UNITED STATES CORPORATION*
Statement of Changes in Financial Position
For the Year Ended December 31, 1981

Financial resources provided:

Working capital provided:

By operations:

Net earnings			$50,350
Add: Expenses not requiring outlay of working capital in current period:			
Depreciation—buildings	$ 3,250		
Depreciation—equipment	31,050		
Loss on sale of equipment	900	35,200	
		$85,550	
Deduct: Gain on sale of investments		1,700	
Working capital provided by operations			$ 83,850
Other sources of working capital:			
Sale of investments			9,700
Sale of equipment			2,600
Issuance of common stock			25,000
Total working capital provided			$121,150
Financial resources provided which did not affect working capital:			
Assumption of liability on mortgage note to acquire land and buildings			35,000
Total financial resources provided			$156,150
Financial resources applied:			
Working capital applied:			
Acquistion of land and buildings			$ 30,000
Acquisition of equipment			43,000
Declaration of cash dividends.			18,000
Total working capital applied			$ 91,000
Financial resources applied which did not affect working capital:			
Land and buildings acquired by assuming the liability on a mortgage note			35,000
Total financial resources applied			$126,000
Increase in working capital			30,150
Total			$156,150

* Note: In published annual reports the information similar to that presented in Illustration 19.4 could be included at the bottom of this statement or could appear as a separate statement.

Assume the statement in Illustration 19.6 and a request for a $250,000, five-year loan were presented to the United States Corporation's banker. The banker would be quick to note that the company has the ability to pay off the loan in about three years by using the working capital provided by operations. The banker would also note that the company pays dividends in an amount well under the amount of working capital generated by operations.

Statement of changes in financial position which emphasizes cash flow

The statement of changes in financial position may emphasize cash rather than working capital.[4] If so, the changes in other elements of working capital (all other current assets and the current liabilities) should be shown as sources or uses of cash in the statement.

As when the working capital concept was emphasized, the effects of other financing and investing activities should also be shown separately in such a statement of changes in financial position.

This form of the statement of changes in financial position ideally is suited to an entity which does not distinguish between current and noncurrent assets and liabilities (such firms are relatively rare). But it may be used by any entity which believes this format will be the most informative in its circumstances. Since it seldom is used in practice, illustration of this form will be left to textbooks designed for more advanced courses. Thus, when we are discussing the statement of changes in financial position we will be using the working capital format.

THE CASH FLOW STATEMENT

The analysis of working capital as described in the first part of the chapter is particularly useful for long-range planning by management and for long-run analysis by external users. A cash flow statement provides information for planning the short-range cash needs of the firm. An analysis of cash flow shows whether the firm's pattern of cash inflow from operations will enable it to pay its debts promptly. If it cannot, it may seek short-term credit to meet current debts and planned purchases of plant, property, and equipment. Thus, cash flow analysis is another important management tool and generally is prepared for internal use only.

A cash flow statement shows the cash receipts and disbursements leading to the net change in cash in a given period. In preparing a cash flow statement each item in the earnings statement is examined together with related changes in current asset, current liability, or other balance sheet accounts to determine the cash flow from the item. This converts net earnings to cash flow from operations. Additional procedures used to determine cash flow resemble those used in preparing the statement of changes in financial position under the working capital concept.

Preparing the cash flow statement

Given below are the financial statements (Illustrations 19.7 and 19.8) of the Delta Corporation and some related data. These will serve as a basis to illustrate the preparation of a cash flow statement.

---

[4] It may alternatively emphasize cash and temporary investments combined or all quick assets (see paragraph 11 of *APB Opinion No. 19*). But statements with this format are so rare that we will ignore them in our discussion.

Illustration 19.7:
Comparative
balance sheet

THE DELTA CORPORATION
Comparative Balance Sheet
June 30, 1980, and 1981

	1981	1980	Increase decrease*
Assets			
Current Assets:			
Cash	$ 30,000	$ 80,000	$ 50,000*
Accounts receivable	160,000	100,000	60,000
Inventory	100,000	70,000	30,000
Prepaid rent	20,000	10,000	10,000
Total Current Assets	$310,000	$260,000	$ 50,000
Property, Plant, and Equipment:			
Equipment	$400,000	$200,000	$200,000
Accumulated depreciation	(60,000)	(50,000)	(10,000)
Total Property, Plant, and Equipment	$340,000	$150,000	$190,000
Total Assets	$650,000	$410,000	$240,000
Liabilities and Stockholders' Equity			
Current Liabilities:			
Accounts payable	$ 50,000	$ 40,000	$ 10,000
Notes payable—bank	–0–	50,000	50,000*
Accrued salaries and wages	10,000	20,000	10,000*
Federal income tax payable	30,000	20,000	10,000
Total Current Liabilities	$ 90,000	$130,000	$ 40,000*
Stockholders' Equity:			
Common stock, $10 par	$300,000	$100,000	$200,000
Capital in excess of par	50,000	–0–	50,000
Retained earnings	210,000	180,000	30,000
Total Stockholders' Equity	$560,000	$280,000	$280,000
Total Liabilities and Stockholders' Equity	$650,000	$410,000	$240,000

Cash flow from operations. The conversion of net earnings to cash from operations is the first step in the preparation of a cash flow statement. To do this, each item in the earnings statement is analyzed for its effect on cash. Illustration 19.9 is a working paper which shows the additions and deductions necessary to do this.

Sales. Since sales are usually recorded as debits to accounts receivable prior to the receipt of cash, the change in accounts receivable must be included in determining the amount of cash received from customers. This is done in the following manner:

$$\text{Net sales} \left\{ \begin{array}{c} + \text{ Decrease in accounts receivable} \\ \text{or} \\ - \text{ Increase in accounts receivable} \end{array} \right\}$$

$$\text{and/or} \left\{ \begin{array}{c} + \text{ Increase in advances from customers} \\ \text{or} \\ - \text{ Decrease in advances from customers} \end{array} \right\} = \begin{array}{c} \text{Cash received} \\ \text{from customers} \end{array}$$

THE DELTA CORPORATION
Statement of Earnings and Retained Earnings
For the Year Ended June 30, 1981

Sales		$1,000,000
Cost of goods sold	$600,000	
Salaries and wages	200,000	
Rent	40,000	
Depreciation	20,000	
Interest	3,000	
Loss on sale of equipment	7,000	870,000
Net earnings before federal income taxes		$ 130,000
Federal income taxes		60,000
Net earnings		$ 70,000
Retained earnings, July 1, 1980		$ 180,000
		$ 250,000
Dividends		40,000
Retained Earnings, June 30, 1981		$ 210,000

Additional data:
1. Equipment with a cost of $20,000, on which $10,000 of depreciation had been recorded, was sold for cash.
2. Additional borrowings from the bank during the year amounted to $30,000.
3. Stock was issued for cash.

Thus, for the Delta Corporation cash received from customers would be $1,000,000 − $60,000 = $940,000.

The first line of Illustration 19.9 shows how this would appear in the working paper.

Cost of goods sold. Converting cost of goods sold to cash paid to vendors involves two steps as shown below:

$$\text{Cost of goods sold} \begin{Bmatrix} +\text{ Increase in inventory} \\ \text{or} \\ -\text{ Decrease in inventory} \end{Bmatrix} = \text{Purchases};$$

$$\text{Purchases} \begin{Bmatrix} +\text{ Decrease in accounts and notes payable} \\ \text{or} \\ -\text{ Increase in accounts and notes payable} \end{Bmatrix} = \begin{matrix} \text{Cash paid} \\ \text{for purchases} \end{matrix}$$

For the Delta Corporation the cash basis cost of goods sold (also shown in Illustration 19.9) is $600,000 + $30,000 − $10,000 = $620,000.

Other revenues. Converting other revenues such as interest revenue, rent revenue, subscriptions revenue, and so on to a cash basis is done as follows:

$$\text{Revenue} \begin{Bmatrix} +\text{ Decrease in the related} \\ \quad \text{accrued receivable account} \\ \text{or} \\ -\text{ Increase in the related} \\ \quad \text{accrued receivable account} \end{Bmatrix} \text{and/or}$$

$$\left.\begin{array}{c} + \text{ Increase in the related revenue} \\ \text{received in advance account} \\ \text{or} \\ - \text{ Decrease in the related revenue} \\ \text{received in advance account} \end{array}\right\} = \begin{array}{l} \text{Cash received} \\ \text{from that} \\ \text{revenue} \end{array}$$

The Delta Corporation had no revenue other than sales, but the above framework may be useful in other situations.

Other expenses. To convert an expense from the accrual basis to the cash basis the following method is used:

$$\text{Expense}\left\{\begin{array}{c} + \text{ Decrease in related} \\ \text{accrued payable account} \\ \text{or} \\ - \text{ Increase in related} \\ \text{accrued payable account} \end{array}\right\} \text{and/or}$$

$$\left.\begin{array}{c} + \text{ Increase in related} \\ \text{prepaid expense account} \\ \text{or} \\ - \text{ Decrease in related} \\ \text{prepaid expense account} \end{array}\right\} = \begin{array}{l} \text{Cash paid} \\ \text{for that} \\ \text{expense} \end{array}$$

Thus the following expenses of the Delta Corporation are converted to a cash basis as follows:

Salaries and wages: $200,000 + $10,000 (decrease in accrued salaries and wages payable) = $210,000

Rent expense: $40,000 + $10,000 (increase in prepaid rent) = $50,000

Federal income tax expense: $60,000 − $10,000 (increase in federal income taxes payable) = $50,000

There was no accrued interest payable at the beginning or end of the year. Thus, the amount of interest expense shown must have been paid in cash, and no adjustment is needed to convert interest expense to a cash basis. The $20,000 of depreciation expense and the loss on sale of equipment of $7,000 are both excluded in the determination of cash flow from operations since neither required an expenditure of cash.

All of the earnings statement items have now been analyzed, and their effect upon cash determined. Summarized, these items yield a net cash flow from operations of $7,000, as shown in Illustration 19.9.

Other sources and uses of cash. To complete the accumulation of data for the cash flow statement, each of the remaining balance sheet accounts must be analyzed for its effect on cash. This is done in a manner exactly like that used in the preparation of a statement of changes in financial position emphasizing working capital from operations. The changes in the accounts not yet analyzed are:

Notes payable—bank	$ 50,000*
Equipment	200,000
Allowance for depreciation	10,000
Common stock	200,000
Capital in excess of par	50,000
Retained earnings	30,000

* Decrease.

According to the data presented earlier, $30,000 was borrowed from the bank during the year. If $50,000 were owed to banks at the beginning of the year, $30,000 were borrowed during the year, and nothing is owed at

Illustration 19.9: Working paper to convert accrual earnings to a cash flow basis

	Accrual Basis Amounts	Add (or Deduct)	Cash Basis Amounts
THE DELTA CORPORATION Working Paper to Convert Accrual Earnings to a Cash Flow Basis For the Year Ended December 31, 1981			
Sales	$1,000,000		
Deduct decrease in accounts receivable		$(60,000)	$940,000
Cost of goods sold	600,000		
Add increase in inventory		30,000	
Deduct increase in accounts payable		(10,000)	$620,000
Salaries and wages	200,000		
Add decrease in accrued salaries and wages payable		10,000	210,000
Rent expense	40,000		
Add increase in prepaid rent		10,000	50,000
Depreciation	20,000	(20,000)	–0–
Interest	3,000		3,000
Loss on sale of equipment	7,000	(7,000)	–0–
Federal income tax expense	60,000		
Deduct increase in federal income taxes payable		(10,000)	50,000
Total expenses	$ 930,000		$933,000
Net earnings	$ 70,000		
Net cash flow from operations			$ 7,000

year-end, $80,000 must have been paid on bank loans during the year. The cash flow statement must, therefore, show $30,000 of cash received from bank loans and $80,000 of payments on bank loans.

The additional data revealed that equipment was sold for cash. Since equipment costing $20,000 was sold during the year, $220,000 of equipment must have been purchased to cause the account to increase by $200,000. The $220,000 must appear in the cash flow statement as should the $3,000 of cash received from the sale of equipment. The $10,000 increase in the accumulated depreciation account is the result of a $20,000 credit for depreciation recorded and the charge to the allowance for accumulated depreciation on equipment sold. It has no effect on cash.

Common stock was issued for cash of $250,000—the total of the increases in the Common Stock and Capital in Excess of Par accounts—and this amount will appear in the cash flow statement. The $30,000 increase in retained earnings was caused by $70,000 of net earnings less $40,000 of dividends. Since the effect on cash of the net earnings has already been determined, only the cash paid out as dividends remains to be determined. This must be $40,000 since there were no dividends payable at either the beginning or end of the year.

The analysis is now complete. Every balance sheet account has been analyzed for its effect on cash, and these effects have been classified into a number of major categories as is shown in The Delta Corporation's cash flow statement in Illustration 19.10.

Illustration 19.10: Cash flow statement

THE DELTA CORPORATION
Cash Flow Statement
For the Year Ended June 30, 1981

Cash balance, July 1		$ 80,000
Add cash received from:		
Operations	$ 7,000	
Bank loans	30,000	
Sale of equipment	3,000	
Common stock issued	250,000	290,000
		$370,000
Deduct cash paid out for:		
Payment of bank loans	$ 80,000	
Purchase of new equipment	220,000	
Dividends	40,000	340,000
Cash balance, June 30		$ 30,000

Note also that the cash flow statement explains the major reasons for the decrease of $50,000 in the company's cash balance during the year.

While the above is overly simplified and kept brief deliberately, it serves to introduce knowledge of the nature and significance of cash flow and to indicate the general approach to cash flow statement preparation.

NEW TERMS INTRODUCED IN CHAPTER 19

Cash flow from operations—the net of cash receipts and disbursements for a given period as related to items which normally appear in the earnings statement; computed by adjusting each item in the earnings statement to a cash basis.

Cash flow statement—a statement or schedule showing beginning cash balance, sources of additions to cash, reasons for cash disbursements, and ending cash balance.

Comparative schedule of working capital—a statement showing the change in working capital as well as the change in each element of working capital between two dates.

Nonworking capital charges or credits (items)—any change in any noncurrent account which does not involve a change in a current account; examples are depreciation and amortization of patents which ultimately offset retained earnings and long-term asset accounts.

Statement of changes in financial position—a statement which usually emphasizes the flows of working capital into and out of an enterprise in a given period of time; it also shows the effects of significant financial or investment transactions even though they involve only long-term accounts.

Working capital applied—the various uses of working capital in an enterprise during a given period.

Working capital provided—the various sources of working capital flowing into an enterprise in a given period.

Working capital from operations—working capital arising from the regular operations of a business; computed as net earnings plus nonworking capital charges deducted in arriving at net earnings, less nonworking capital items added, and less certain gains which are included in the total proceeds received from the sale of noncurrent assets.

DEMONSTRATION PROBLEM

The last part of the chapter showed how a cash flow statement would be prepared for the Delta Corporation.

Required:

Using the data given for the Delta Corporation prepare a statement of changes in financial position (after preparing a working paper similar to Illustration 19.5).

Solution to demonstration problem

	Account Balances 6/30/80	Analysis of Transactions for 1981		Account Balances 6/30/81
		Debit	Credit	
Debits				
Working capital	130,000	(1) 90,000		220,000
Equipment	200,000	(5) 220,000	(4) 20,000	400,000
Totals	330,000			620,000
Credits				
Accumulated depreciation	50,000	(4) 10,000	(3) 20,000	60,000
Common stock	100,000		(6) 200,000	300,000
Capital in excess of par	–0–		(6) 50,000	50,000
Retained earnings	180,000	(7) 40,000	(2) 70,000	210,000
Totals	330,000	360,000	360,000	620,000
Financial resources provided:				
Working capital provided by operations:				
Net earnings		(2) 70,000		
Add: Depreciation		(3) 20,000		
Loss on sale of equipment		(4) 7,000		
Other sources:				
Sale of equipment		(4) 3,000		
Sale of common stock		(6) 250,000		
Financial resources applied:				
Working capital applied:				
Purchase of equipment			(5) 220,000	
Declaration of cash dividends			(7) 40,000	
Increase in working capital during year			(1) 90,000	
Totals		350,000	350,000	

DELTA CORPORATION
Working Paper for Statement of Changes in Financial Position
For the Year Ended June 30, 1981

THE DELTA CORPORATION
Statement of Changes in Financial Position
For the Year Ended June 30, 1981

Financial resources provided:

Working capital provided:

By operations:

Net earnings		$70,000	
Add: Expenses not requiring outlay of working capital in current period:			
Depreciation	$20,000		
Loss on sale of equipment	7,000	27,000	
Working capital provided by operations			$ 97,000
Other sources of working capital:			
Sale of equipment			3,000
Sale of common stock			250,000
Total working capital provided			$350,000

Financial resources applied:

Working capital applied:

Purchase of equipment	$220,000
Declaration of cash dividends	40,000
Total working capital applied	$260,000
Increase in working capital	90,000
Total	$350,000

QUESTIONS

1. The term "funds" is used in many different ways in accounting. Indicate several of these usages other than that given in this chapter. What is the concept of funds as the term is used in a statement of changes in financial position?

2. If the net earnings for a given period amount to $25,000, does this mean that there is an increase in working capital of the same amount? Why or why not?

3. Give an example of how the analysis of working capital flow can aid management in its decision-making process.

4. What are the major sources of working capital in a business? What are the major uses of working capital in a business? What use of working capital might be called involuntary?

5. Does the declaration or the payment of dividends affect working capital? Why?

6. Why might a company have a positive inflow of working capital from operations in spite of operating at a net loss?

7. What effect, if any, does the amortization of premium on bonds payable have upon the statement of changes in financial position?

8. Why is an analysis of working capital flow apt to be unsuitable for short-run planning?

9. Why is it unlikely that the cash flow from operations will be equal to the net earnings for the same period?

10. What factors might cause cash to increase even though operations are conducted at a loss? What factors might cause cash to decrease even though operations are profitable?

11. In what respects does cash flow analysis differ from working capital flow analysis?

EXERCISES

E–1. Indicate how the following data should be reported in a statement of changes in financial position. A company purchased land valued at $20,000 and a building valued at $40,000 by payment of $10,000 by check, signing an interest-bearing note due in six months for $15,000, and by assuming a mortgage on the property of $35,000.

E–2. A company sold for $5,000 equipment having an original cost of $7,000 and on which $4,000 of depreciation had been recorded. The gain was included in net earnings. How should these data be shown in the statement of changes in financial position and why?

E–3. The following data are from the Automobile and the Accumulated Depreciation—Automobile accounts of a certain company:

Automobile

1981		Debit	Credit	Balance
Jan.	1 Balance brought forward			$4,000
July	1 Traded for new auto . .		$4,000	–0–
	New auto	$4,400		4,400

Accumulated Depreciation—Automobile

Jan.	1 Balance brought forward			$3,000
July	1 One-half year's depreciation		500	3,500
	Auto traded	$3,500		–0–
Dec. 31	One-half year's depreciation		550	550

The old auto was traded for a new one with the difference in values paid in cash. The earnings statement for the year shows a loss on the exchange of autos of $300.

Indicate the dollar amounts, the descriptions of these amounts, and their exact locations in a statement of changes in financial position.

E–4. Assume that the cost of goods sold for a given company for a given year is $350,000. Inventory at the beginning of the year was $51,000 and at the end of the year, $63,000; accounts payable for merchandise purchases were $38,000 and $42,000 at the beginning of the year and end of the year, respectively. What was the amount of cash paid to vendors during the year?

E–5. The earnings statement for the X Company shows rent revenue of $5,000. The Rent Received in Advance account had a beginning balance of $400 and an ending balance of $300. How much cash was received from this revenue item during the year?

E–6. Dividends payable increased from $12,000 to $15,000 during the year. Dividends of $60,000 were declared during the year. What amount should be shown in the statement of changes in financial position for dividends? In the cash flow statement? If the amounts are not the same, why do they differ?

E–7. During the course of the year a company purchased $50,000 of marketable securities as a temporary investment. The securities were sold later at a loss of $1,500, and the loss was deducted in arriving at net earnings. How would these data appear on the cash flow statement?

PROBLEMS, SERIES A

P19–1–A. Following are comparative financial position data and a statement of retained earnings for the year ended May 31, 1981, for Beasley Company (000 omitted).

May 31

	1981	1980
Debits		
Cash	$ 70	$ 56
Marketable securities	20	24
Accounts receivable, net	116	144
Inventories	140	100
Investment in subsidiary	90	80
Land	60	50
Buildings and equipment	450	380
Patents	14	16
Total	$960	$850
Credits		
Accounts payable	$ 90	$ 64
Taxes payable	16	12
Accumulated depreciation	80	60
Bonds payable	200	200
Common stock, $100 par	400	400
Retained earnings	174	114
Total	$960	$850

Statement of Retained Earnings

Balance, May 31, 1980	$114
Net earnings	100
	$214
Dividends declared	40
Balance, May 31, 1981	$174

Additional data:

a. Additional shares of stock of the subsidiary company were acquired for cash.

b. A tract of land adjacent to land owned was purchased during the year.

c. Depreciation of $32,000 and patent amortization of $2,000 were charged to expense during the year.

d. New equipment with a cost of $82,000 was purchased during the year, while fully depreciated equipment with a cost of $12,000 was scrapped and discarded.

Required:

a. Prepare a comparative schedule of working capital.

b. Prepare a statement of changes in financial position (emphasizing working capital). Try to do so without preparing a working paper so that your conceptual understanding of the statement may be strengthened.

P19–2–A.

FISHER, INC.
Comparative Balance Sheet

April 30

	1981	1980
Assets		
Cash	$ 47,000	$ 26,000
Accounts receivable	141,000	134,000
Inventory	83,000	102,000
Prepaid expenses	9,000	11,000
Plant assets	300,000	280,000
Accumulated depreciation	(65,000)	(50,000)
Total Assets	$515,000	$503,000
Liabilities and Stockholders' Equity		
Accounts payable	$ 62,000	$ 48,000
Accrued expenses payable	17,000	19,000
Federal income taxes payable	23,000	21,000
Bank loan payable	60,000	80,000
Capital stock	300,000	300,000
Retained earnings	53,000	35,000
Total Liabilities and Stockholders' Equity	$515,000	$503,000

FISHER, INC.
Earnings Statement
For Year Ended, April 30, 1981

Net sales		$740,000
Cost of goods sold	$500,000	
Salaries and wages	130,000	
Depreciation	15,000	
Rent expense	15,000	
Other	33,000	693,000
Net earnings before taxes		$ 47,000
Federal income taxes		23,000
Net Earnings		$ 24,000

Additional data:

a. Dividends of $6,000 were declared during the year.

b. Prepaid expenses consist solely of rent.

c. Accrued expenses payable at April 30, 1981, and April 30, 1980, consist entirely of accrued salaries and wages.

d. During a high level of seasonal activity an additional $30,000 was borrowed from a local bank.

e. The accounts payable arose solely from the purchase of merchandise.

Required:

a. Prepare a schedule similar to Illustration 19.9 showing the determination of the cash flow from operations.

b. Prepare a cash flow statement.

P19–3–A.

CARDER COMPANY
Comparative Balance Sheet

	April 30	
	1981	1980
Assets		
Cash	$ 61,000	$ 61,000
Marketable securities	12,000	20,000
Accounts receivable, net	98,000	60,000
Inventories	250,000	100,000
Prepaid expenses	10,000	15,000
Total Current Assets	$431,000	$256,000
Land	60,000	65,000
Buildings and equipment	330,000	250,000
Accumulated depreciation	(80,000)	(65,000)
Total Assets	$741,000	$506,000
Liabilities and		
Stockholders' Equity		
Accounts payable	$100,000	$ 60,000
Bank loans	60,000	–0–
Accrued expenses payable	32,000	15,000
Federal income taxes payable	70,000	75,000
Total Current Liabilities	$262,000	$150,000
Bonds payable (5%)	200,000	200,000
Premium on bonds payable	1,800	2,000
Capital stock—common, $100 par ...	200,000	140,000
Capital in excess of par	10,000	–0–
Retained earnings	67,200	14,000
Total Liabilities and		
Stockholders' Equity ...	$741,000	$506,000

CARDER COMPANY
Earnings Statement
For Year Ended April 30, 1981

Net sales		$800,000
Less: Cost of goods sold	$500,000	
Selling and administrative		
expenses	148,000	648,000
Net earnings from operations		$152,000
Gain on sale of land		8,000
		$160,000
Loss on sale of marketable securities .	$ 1,000	
Interest expense	10,800	
Loss on sale of equipment	4,200	16,000
Net earnings before income taxes		$144,000
Federal income taxes		70,000
Net Earnings		$ 74,000

Additional data:

a. Dividends of $20,800 were declared during the year.

b. Equipment sold during the year had an original cost of $20,000, and depreciation of $12,000 had been recorded to time of sale.

c. The capital stock was issued for a building valued at $70,000 erected on company property.

d. Premium on bonds payable of $200 was amortized during the year.

Required:

a. Compute the change in working capital.

b. Prepare a working paper similar to Illustration 19.5.

c. Prepare a statement of changes in financial position (emphasizing working capital).

P19–4–A. Use the data given in Problem 19–3–A and the following additional information:

1. Depreciation expense of $27,000 is included in selling and administrative expenses.
2. Accounts payable arose solely from the purchase of merchandise.
3. Prepaid expenses consist of prepaid store rent.
4. All of the accrued expenses payable relate to selling and administrative expenses except that the balance on April 30, 1981, includes $1,000 of accrued interest payable on bank loans.

Required:

a. Prepare a schedule showing the cash flow from operations. (A schedule similar to Illustration 19.9 is sufficient.)

b. Prepare a cash flow statement.

P19–5–A. The earnings statement for the Mitchell Company for the year ended December 31, 1981, shows:

Net sales		$660,000
Cost of goods sold	$375,000	
Operating expenses	100,000	
Major repairs.....................	60,000	
Interest expense	5,000	
Loss on sale of equipment	10,000	550,000
Net earnings before taxes		$110,000
Federal income taxes		48,000
Net Earnings		$ 62,000

A comparative balance sheet for the company shows:

	December 31	
	1981	1980
Assets		
Cash	$ 48,000	$ 40,000
Accounts receivable, net	105,000	76,000
Inventories	210,000	180,000
Prepaid expenses	16,000	6,000
Total Current Assets	$379,000	$302,000
Buildings	100,000	100,000
Accumulated depreciation— buildings	(55,000)	(50,000)
Equipment	185,000	130,000
Accumulated depreciation— equipment	(63,000)	(60,000)
Total Assets	$546,000	$422,000
Liabilities and Stockholders' Equity		
Accounts payable	$ 47,000	$ 75,000
Accrued expenses payable	16,500	14,500
Federal income taxes payable	48,000	45,000
Dividends payable	9,500	7,500
Total Current Liabilities	$121,000	$142,000
Bonds payable (5%)	100,000	100,000
Total Liabilities	$221,000	$242,000
Capital stock—par $100	$250,000	$150,000
Capital in excess of par	15,000	–0–
Retained earnings	60,000	30,000
Total Stockholders' Equity	$325,000	$180,000
Total Liabilities and Stockholder's Equity ...	$546,000	$422,000

Additional data:

1. Capital stock was issued for cash.
2. Accrued expenses payable relate solely to operating expenses.
3. The depreciation on equipment for the year amounted to $15,000. The equipment sold had an original cost of $30,000.
4. Dividends declared during the year total $32,000.
5. Accounts payable arose solely from purchases of merchandise.

Required:

a. Prepare a comparative schedule of working capital for the year 1981.

b. Prepare a working paper similar to Illustration 19.5.

c. Prepare a statement of changes in financial position (emphasizing working capital) for the year ended December 31, 1981.

P19–6–A. Use the data in Problem 19–5–A.

Required:

a. Prepare a schedule of cash flow from operations (see Illustration 19.9).

b. Present a cash flow statement.

PROBLEMS, SERIES B

P19–1–B.

ZABO CORPORATION
Comparative Balance Sheet

	June 30	
	1981	1980
Assets		
Current assets	$ 340,000	$235,000
Investment in stock of affiliated company	175,000	150,000
Buildings	380,000	280,000
Allowance for depreciation— buildings	(60,000)	(50,000)
Equipment	470,000	400,000
Allowance for depreciation— equipment	(160,000)	(120,000)
Total Assets	$1,145,000	$895,000

Liabilities and Stockholders' Equity		
Current liabilities	$ 180,000	$120,000
Five-year note payable	100,000	–0–
Capital stock, par $100	800,000	700,000
Retained earnings	65,000	75,000
Total Liabilities and Stockholders' Equity	$1,145,000	$895,000

Additional data:

1. Net earnings for year ended June 30, 1981, were $30,000.
2. Dividends declared, $40,000.
3. Stock was issued at par for cash.
4. No equipment or building retirements occurred during the year.

5. The five-year note was issued to pay for a building erected on land leased by the company.
6. Additional shares of stock of the affiliated company were acquired for cash.
7. Equipment was also purchased for cash.

Required:

a. State the change in working capital.

b. Prepare a statement of changes in financial position (emphasizing working capital). Try to do so without preparing a working paper so that your conceptual understanding of the statement might be strengthened.

P19–2–B.   GEMS, INC.
Comparative Balance Sheet

	September 30	
	1981	*1980*
Assets		
Cash	$ 78,000	$ 23,000
Accounts receivable	122,000	121,000
Inventory	100,000	78,000
Prepaid expenses	4,000	5,000
Equipment and fixtures	75,000	60,000
Accumulated depreciation	(21,000)	(15,000)
Total Assets	$358,000	$272,000

Liabilities and Stockholders' Equity		
Accounts payable	$ 48,000	$ 40,000
Accrued expenses payable	13,000	17,000
Federal income taxes payable	60,000	35,000
Dividends payable	6,000	5,000
Capital stock	100,000	100,000
Retained earnings	131,000	75,000
Total Liabilities and Stockholders' Equity	$358,000	$272,000

GEMS, INC.
Earnings Statement
For Year Ended September 30, 1981

Net sales		$750,000
Cost of goods sold	$400,000	
Selling and administrative expenses......................	220,000	620,000
Net earnings before taxes		$130,000
Federal income taxes		60,000
Net Earnings		$ 70,000

Additional data:

1. Depreciation of $6,000 is included in selling and administrative expenses.

2. Dividends declared during the year amounted to $14,000.
3. Accounts payable arose solely from the purchase of merchandise.

Required:

a. Prepare a schedule showing the cash flow from operations (see Illustration 19.9).

b. Prepare a cash flow statement.

P19–3–B.   POLASKY CORPORATION
Comparative Balance Sheet

	December 31	
	1981	*1980*
Assets		
Cash	$ 15,000	$ 20,000
Accounts receivable	122,000	98,000
Inventories	122,000	112,000
Unexpired insurance	3,000	4,000
Total Current Assets	$262,000	$234,000
Land	50,000	30,000
Buildings	200,000	100,000
Accumulated depreciation— buildings	(25,000)	(20,000)
Equipment.......................	225,000	215,000
Accumulated depreciation— equipment	(115,000)	(100,000)
Total Assets	$597,000	$459,000

Liabilities and Stockholders' Equity		
Accounts payable	$ 82,000	$ 80,000
Dividends payable	12,000	10,000
Federal income taxes payable	38,000	30,000
Accrued salaries and wages payable	4,000	3,000
Accrued expenses payable	6,000	4,000
Total Current Liabilities	$142,000	$127,000
Bonds payable—7%	100,000	100,000
Total Liabilities	$242,000	$227,000
Capital stock—common	300,000	200,000
Capital in excess of par	15,000	–0–
Retained earnings	40,000	32,000
Total Liabilities and Stockholder's Equity ...	$597,000	$459,000

POLASKY CORPORATION
Earnings Statement and Statement of Retained Earnings
For Year Ended December 31, 1981

Sales (net)		$900,000
Cost of goods sold		600,000
Gross margin		$300,000
Salaries and wages	$150,000	
Depreciation	27,000	
Insurance	2,000	
Other expenses (including interest)	50,000	
Loss on sale of equipment	1,000	230,000
Net earnings before federal income taxes		$ 70,000
Federal income taxes		38,000
Net earnings		$ 32,000
Retained earnings, December 31, 1980		32,000
		$ 64,000
Less Dividends		24,000
Retained Earnings, December 31, 1981		$ 40,000

Additional data:

1. Equipment having an original cost of $10,000 and on which $7,000 of depreciation was recorded was sold at a loss of $1,000. Equipment additions were for cash.
2. All of the additional capital stock issued during the year, plus $5,000 of cash, was exchanged for land and a building.

Required:

a. Compute the change in working capital.

b. Prepare a working paper similar to Illustration 19.5.

c. Prepare a statement of changes in financial position (emphasizing working capital).

P19–4–B. Use the data given in Problem 19–3–B. Assume that the accounts payable at the end of 1980 and 1981 arose solely from the purchase of merchandise and that the accrued expenses payable arose from the accrual of expenses included in the other expenses shown in the earnings statement.

Required:

a. Prepare a schedule showing cash flow from operations (see Illustration 19.9).

b. Prepare a cash flow statement.

P19–5–B. Given below are comparative balance sheet account balances and other data of the Brooks Corporation:

	June 30	
	1981	1980
Debit balances		
Cash	$ 64,000	$ 68,000
Accounts receivable, net	340,000	168,000
Notes receivable	42,000	54,000
Inventories	420,000	436,000
Unexpired insurance	2,400	2,800
Land	160,000	180,000
Buildings	1,120,000	620,000
Machinery and tools	440,000	240,000
Goodwill	–0–	200,000
Discount on bonds payable	4,200	5,000
Total	$2,592,600	$1,973,800
Credit balances		
Accrued liabilities	$ 14,000	$ 4,000
Accounts payable	65,000	90,000
Bank loans	29,000	33,600
Taxes payable	30,000	2,000
Accumulated depreciation of buildings, machinery, and tools	442,000	262,000
Mortgage bonds payable	200,000	100,000
Common stock, $100 par	900,000	300,000
Retained earnings	912,600	1,182,200
Total	$2,592,600	$1,973,800

Additional data:

1. Net earnings for the year ended June 30, 1981, were $35,400.
2. A 5 percent cash dividend was declared and paid in June.
3. Additional common stock was issued in April at $90, and the discount was charged to Retained Earnings.
4. The mortgage bonds were issued in conjunction with the acquisition of a new building. The bonds were accepted by the seller of the building at their face value.
5. The gain on the sale of land of $4,000 was credited to a miscellaneous revenue account.
6. Fully depreciated machinery with an original cost of $30,000 was written off during the year and scrapped.

Required:

a. Prepare a comparative schedule of working capital.

b. Prepare a working paper similar to Illustration 19.9.

c. Prepare a statement of changes in financial position (emphasizing working capital).

P19–6–B. Given below is a condensed earnings statement for the Brooks Corporation for the year ended June 30, 1981:

Net sales	$2,700,000
Cost of goods sold	2,000,000
Gross margin	$ 700,000
Selling and administrative expenses	628,800
Net operating earnings	71,200
Gain on sale of land	4,000
	$ 75,200
Interest expense	9,800
	$ 65,400
Federal income tax	30,000
Net Earnings	$ 35,400

Additional data:

1. Of the depreciation recorded for the year, $150,000 was charged to cost of goods sold and the balance to selling and administrative expenses.
2. The accrued liabilities relate solely to costs included in cost of goods sold. The accounts payable at year-end are all for material purchases except one account due of $10,000 for machinery purchased.
3. The total proceeds received from bank loans made during the year amount to $60,000.
4. The taxes payable shown consist only of federal income taxes.
5. The expired insurance premiums were charged to selling and administrative expense.
6. The notes receivable are from customers for merchandise sold to them.

Required:

From the above data and those in Problem 19–5–B, prepare:

a. A schedule showing cash flow from operations (see Illustration 19.9).

b. A cash flow statement.

BUSINESS DECISION PROBLEM 19–1

Following are comparative ledger balances for the Clayton Company:

	December 31	
	1981	*1980*
Debit balances		
Cash	$ 20,000	$ 25,000
Accounts receivable	42,000	31,000
Inventory	40,000	35,000
Land.........................	45,000	40,000
Building	60,000	60,000
Equipment	190,000	150,000
Goodwill	80,000	100,000
Total	$477,000	$441,000

	December 31	
	1981	*1980*
Credit balances		
Allowance for doubtful accounts	$ 2,000	$ 1,000
Accumulated depreciation— building	20,000	18,000
Accumulated depreciation— equipment	35,000	32,000
Accounts payable	50,000	30,000
Accrued liabilities	20,000	15,000
Capital stock	210,000	200,000
Paid-in capital—stock dividends	50,000	45,000
Paid-in capital—land donation	10,000	–0–
Retained earnings	80,000	100,000
Total	$477,000	$441,000

An analysis of the Retained Earnings account for the year reveals the following:

Balance, December 31, 1980		$100,000
Add:		
Net earnings for the year		65,000
		$165,000
Less:		
Cash dividends	$30,000	
Stock dividends	15,000	
Additional income taxes for 1978 ...	40,000	85,000
Balance, December 31, 1981		$ 80,000

Additional data:

Equipment with a cost of $20,000 on which $18,000 of depreciation had been accumulated was sold during the year at a loss of $1,000. Included in net earnings is a gain on the sale of land of $6,000.

Required:

a. The company desires to increase working capital each year by about $40,000 and to increase the dividend to $60,000. Is the company able to generate enough working capital from operations to do this?

b. Determine how much cash was generated by operations. (Even though you are not given an earnings statement this can be done by working with the net earnings amount and the current assets and liabilities.)

BUSINESS DECISION PROBLEM 19–2

Following are comparative account balances for the Sims Company:

	December 31	
	1981	*1980*
Debit balances		
Cash	$ 70,000	$ 20,000
Accounts receivable	54,000	52,000
Inventory	80,000	100,000
Land...........................	50,000	50,000
Buildings	230,000	100,000
Equipment	250,000	200,000
Patents.........................	75,000	100,000
Total	$809,000	$622,000
Credit balances		
Allowance for doubtful accounts	$ 4,000	$ 2,000
Accumulated depreciation— buildings	13,000	10,000
Accumulated depreciation— equipment	60,000	50,000
Accounts payable	80,000	50,000
Accrued liabilities	30,000	20,000
Bonds payable	200,000	200,000
Bond premium	4,000	5,000
Common stock	300,000	200,000
Capital in excess of par	20,000	10,000
Retained earnings	98,000	75,000
Total	$809,000	$622,000

Additional data:

1. Equipment with a cost of $30,000 on which $28,000 of depreciation had been accumulated was sold during the year at a gain of $5,000.
2. Net earnings for the year were $68,000 including the gain on sale of equipment, a special write-off of obsolete inventory of $17,000, and the write-off (in addition to the regular amortization) of a worthless patent of $20,000.
3. Cash dividends declared, $25,000.
4. An additional income tax assessment for 1976 of $20,000 was paid in cash and charged to retained earnings.

Required:

   a. Prepare a comparative schedule of working capital.

   b. Prepare a statement of changes in financial position (emphasizing working capital). Try to do so without preparing a working paper.

   c. Is the company able to generate enough working capital from operations to increase working capital by $50,000 per year?

   (Note: This is a rigorous problem which should be a challenge even to the very best students.)

BUSINESS DECISION PROBLEM 19–3

The first part of this chapter showed how a statement of changes in financial position would be prepared for The United States Corporation. Assume that management has made a tentative decision to issue a 100 percent stock dividend if the cash flows indicate that the company could pay twice the amount of dividends it paid in 1981.

Required:

   a. Using the data given for The United States Corporation, prepare a working paper to convert accrual earnings to a cash flow basis and then prepare a cash flow statement. (Assume that prepaid expenses pertain to general and administrative expenses and that other assumed liabilities pertain 90 percent to salaries expense and 10 percent to taxes, payroll, and others.)

   b. Will the company be able to double the level of dividend payments in the future? Discuss.

   (Note: This problem contains one aspect that was not dealt with in the chapter. A total of $5,500 was written off during the period for accounts receivable determined to be uncollectible. This amount should be deducted from net sales in the working paper. Bad debts expense should be treated similarly to depreciation expense in the working paper.)

Chapter 20

Analysis and interpretation of financial statements

OBJECTIVES OF FINANCIAL STATEMENTS

Financial statements are issued to communicate useful financial information to interested parties. If this objective is not met, the statements serve no purpose. But careful analyses and interpretations made by the user of financial statements will often clarify and add to their usefulness and thus aid communication. Thus, it is essential that the users of statements become skilled in the use of available techniques for analyzing financial statements. Several of these analytical techniques are presented in this chapter. Also, brief mention is made of price level accounting. Interested readers are referred to Appendix A at the end of the book which covers that topic in detail.

Managers, employees, current and prospective investors, current and prospective creditors, business counselors, and executives of trade associations are among those who at one time or another will be interested in the financial statements of a specific firm. For example, a commercial bank loan officer will decide whether or not to grant a loan to a firm after the firm's financial statements have been analyzed. The loan officer will pay close attention to the firm's ability to pay its debts. A current stockholder may decide to sell his or her stock in the company after analyzing the company's financial statements and comparing its earnings history with that of another firm.

The purpose of financial statement analysis is to establish and present the relationships and trends found in the data contained in financial statements. Based upon this analysis, the users will draw their own conclusions and act accordingly.

COMPARATIVE FINANCIAL STATEMENTS: Nature and purpose

Comparative financial statements present the statements of the same firm for two or more accounting periods so that changes and trends can be analyzed. The usefulness of financial statements is improved greatly when they are so presented. The nature of, and trends in, changes which affect a firm can be seen far more clearly in comparative statements than in the statements for a single period.

To illustrate, a balance sheet dated December 31, 1982, shows an accounts receivable balance of $500,000. That information by itself tells the statement user only that there is a receivables balance and that it equals $500,000. Suppose the user is also told that on December 31, 1981, the receivables balance was $250,000 and that the balance increased by $250,000 during 1982—an increase of 100 percent. Then, the balance of $500,000 on December 31, 1982, becomes more meaningful. But neither statement indicates what the balance ought to be.

Methods of comparison— illustrated

Comparisons of financial statement data can be expressed as—

1. Absolute increases and decreases for an item from one period to the next or from a base period which is more than one period removed.
2. Percentage increases and decreases for an item from one period to the next or from a base period which is more than one period removed.
3. Percentages of an aggregate total.
4. Trend percentages.
5. Ratios.

The first three of these methods have been used in preparing the following comparative financial statements which will serve as a basis for the first analyses presented in this chapter. Trend percentages are then discussed. Finally, various ratios are presented and illustrated.

The statements presented are:

Exhibit A: Comparative balance sheet, Illustration 20.1.
Exhibit B: Comparative statements of earnings and retained earnings, Illustration 20.2.
Schedule B–1:   Comparative schedules of selling and administrative expenses, Illustration 20.3.
Schedule B–2:   Comparative schedules of other expenses and revenues, Illustration 20.4.

These statements are presented here where they will be easy to find for reference while studying this chapter. The "Other expenses" and "Other revenues" categories include earnings statement items which are not directly related to the regular operations of the business.

The comparative balance sheets of the Knight Corporation, Illustration 20.1, set forth certain relationships. Management can establish these relationships by means of analysis and use them as guidelines when it makes business decisions. For example, the comparative balance sheets in Illustration 20.1 show (among other items):

1. The dollar amount of each asset, liability, and stockholders' equity item and the total of each class of assets, liabilities, and stockholders' equity on December 31, 1981, and on December 31, 1982.
2. The increase or decrease in dollar amounts of each of the items listed in (1) above, by comparison of December 31, 1982, balances with those of December 31, 1981. For example, it is shown that on December 31, 1982, as compared with December 31, 1981:
   a. Current assets have increased $37,121, while current liabilities have increased $17,280. This increase in the Knight Corporation's working capital (current assets less current liabilities) could have resulted from (1) retention of earnings, (2) conversion of plant assets to current assets through sale, (3) long-term borrowing, and/or (4) the issuance of more capital stock. Further examination of the comparative balance sheets and the earnings statement will reveal that the first and last of these possibilities have caused the improvement in the current position.
   b. Total assets have increased $84,126, while total liabilities have increased only $130. Total stockholders' equity has increased $83,996, of which $40,000 represents an increase in outstanding capital stock. Thus, retention of earnings and investments by stockholders have increased greatly the stockholders' equity in the corporation while the equity of the creditors has increased only slightly.
3. The percentage increase or decrease in each of the items listed in (1) above—December 31, 1982, balances are compared with December 31,

Illustration 20.1: Comparative balance sheets

THE KNIGHT CORPORATION Comparative Balance Sheets December 31, 1981, and 1982							*Exhibit A*
		December 31		*Increase or decrease* 1982 over 1981*		*Percentage of total assets December 31*	
		1982	*1981*	*Dollars*	*Per-centage*	*1982*	*1981*
Assets							
Current Assets:							
Cash		$ 80,215	$ 54,980	$25,235	45.9	12.6	10.0
Accounts receivable, net		124,171	132,550	8,379*	6.3*	19.5	24.0
Notes receivable		55,000	50,000	5,000	10.0	8.7	9.1
Inventories		110,825	94,500	16,325	17.3	17.4	17.1
Prepaid expenses		3,640	4,700	1,060*	22.6*	0.6	0.9
Total Current Assets		$373,851	$336,730	$37,121	11.0	58.9ᴿ	61.1
Plant and Equipment:							
Land		$ 21,000	$ 21,000	–0–	–0–	3.3	3.8
Building		205,000	160,000	$45,000	28.1	32.3	29.0
Less: Accumulated depreciation		(27,040)	(22,355)	(4,685)	21.0	(4.3)	(4.1)
Furniture and fixtures		83,200	69,810	13,390	19.2	13.1	12.7
Less: Accumulated depreciation		(20,800)	(14,100)	(6,700)	47.5	(3.3)	(2.5)
Total Plant and Equipment		$261,360	$214,355	$47,005	21.9	41.1	38.9
Total Assets		$635,211	$551,085	$84,126	15.3	100.0	100.0
Liabilities and Stockholders' Equity							
Current Liabilities:							
Accounts payable		$ 70,310	$ 64,560	$ 5,750	8.9	11.1	11.7
Notes payable		20,000	15,100	4,900	32.5	3.1	2.7
Taxes accrued		36,830	30,200	6,630	22.0	5.8	5.5
Total Current Liabilities		$127,140	$109,860	$17,280	15.7	20.0	19.9
Long-Term Liabilities:							
Mortgage notes payable, land and building, 9%, 1984		43,600	60,750	17,150*	28.2*	6.9	11.0
Total Liabilities		$170,740	$170,610	$ 130	†	26.9	30.9
Stockholders' Equity:							
Common stock, par value $10 per share		$240,000	$200,000	$40,000	20.0	37.8	36.3
Retained earnings		224,471	180,475	43,996	24.4	35.3	32.8
Total Stockholders' Equity		$464,471	$380,475	$83,996	22.1	73.1	69.1
Total Liabilities and Stockholders' Equity		$635,211	$551,085	$84,126	15.3	100.0	100.0

† Less than one half of 1 percent.
ᴿ Rounding error.

1981, balances. For example, inspection of the comparative balance sheets shows that—

Current assets have increased by 11 percent, while current liabilities have increased by 15.7 percent. Total assets have increased by 15.3 percent, while total liabilities have increased by less than one half of

Illustration 20.2: Comparative statements of earnings and retained earnings

	Year ended December 31		Increase or decrease* 1982 over 1981		Percentage of net sales	
THE KNIGHT CORPORATION Comparative Statements of Earnings and Retained Earnings For the Years Ended December 31, 1981, and 1982 *Exhibit B*						
	1982	*1981*	*Dollar*	*Per-centage*	*1982*	*1981*
Gross sales	$995,038	$775,836	$219,202	28.3	100.9	101.3
Less: Sales returns and allowances	8,650	10,321	1,671*	16.2*	0.9	1.3
Net sales	$986,388	$765,515	$220,873	28.9	100.0	100.0
Cost of goods sold:						
Inventories, January 1	$ 94,500	$ 85,150	$ 9,350	11.0	9.6	11.1
Net purchases	639,562	510,290	129,272	25.3	64.8	66.7
	$734,062	$595,440	$138,622	23.3	74.4	77.8
Inventories, December 31	110,825	94,500	16,325	17.3	11.2	12.4
Cost of goods sold	$623,237	$500,940	$122,297	24.4	63.2	65.4
Gross margin	$363,151	264,575	98,576	37.3	36.8	34.6
Less: Selling expenses, Schedule B–1	$132,510	$ 84,898	$ 47,612	56.1	13.4	11.1
Administrative expenses, Schedule B–1	120,345	98,642	21,703	22.0	12.2	12.9
	$252,855	$183,540	$ 69,315	37.8	25.6	24.0
Net operating earnings	$110,296	$ 81,035	$ 29,261	36.1	11.2	10.6
Less: Net other expenses, Schedule B–2	3,000	2,800	200	7.1	0.3	0.4
Net earnings before federal income taxes	$107,296	$ 78,235	29,061	37.1	10.9	10.2
Deduct: Federal income taxes	48,300	31,700	16,600	52.4	4.9	4.1
Net earnings, to retained earnings	$ 58,996	$ 46,535	$ 12,461	26.8	6.0	6.1
Retained earnings, January 1	180,475	146,440	34,035	23.2		
	$239,471	$192,975	$ 46,496	24.1		
Deduct: Dividends declared and paid	15,000	12,500	2,500	20.0		
Retained Earnings, December 31	$224,471	$180,475	$ 43,996	24.4		

1 percent, and total stockholders' equity has increased by 22.1 percent. These percentages express the increases and decreases in terms which may have more meaning than the increases and decreases expressed in dollar amounts.

Trend percentages

Trend percentages (also referred to as index numbers) are a useful means for comparing financial statements for several years. They emphasize changes or trends that have occurred over a period of time. They are calculated by:

1. Selecting a base year.
2. Assigning a weight of 100 percent to the amounts appearing on the base year financial statements.
3. Expressing the amounts shown on the other years' financial statements as a percentage of the base year amounts. (In other words, divide the other years' amounts by the base year amounts.)

As an example, assume the following information is given:

	1981	1982	1983	1984
Sales	$350,000	$367,500	$441,000	$485,000
Cost of goods sold	200,000	196,000	230,000	285,000
Gross margin	$150,000	$171,500	$211,000	$200,000
Operating expenses	145,000	169,000	200,000	192,000
Net Earnings before taxes	$ 5,000	$ 2,500	$ 11,000	$ 8,000

Letting 1981 be the base year, the trend percentages would be calculated as follows:

1. Divide the amounts shown for "Sales" by $350,000.
2. Divide the amounts shown for "Cost of goods sold" by $200,000.
3. Divide the amounts shown for "Gross margin" by $150,000.
4. Divide the amounts shown for "Operating expenses" by $145,000.
5. Divide the amounts shown for "Net Earnings before Taxes" by $5,000.

After all the divisions have been made, each result would be multiplied by 100 and the resulting trends would appear as follows:

	1981	1982	1983	1984
Sales	100	105	126	139
Cost of goods sold	100	98	115	143
Gross margin	100	114	141	133
Operating expenses	100	117	138	132
Net earnings before taxes	100	50	220	160

Illustration 20.3: Comparative schedules of selling and administrative expenses

THE KNIGHT CORPORATION
Comparative Schedules of Selling and Administrative Expenses
For the Years Ended December 31, 1981, and 1982   Schedule B–1

	Year ended December 31		Increase or decrease* 1982 over 1981		Percentage of net sales	
	1982	1981	Dollars	Per-centage	1982	1981
Selling expenses:						
Advertising	$ 28,632	$18,105	$10,527	58.1	2.9	2.4
Salespersons' salaries	69,225	45,900	23,325	50.8	7.0	6.0
Rent of sales office	10,150	7,200	2,950	41.0	1.0	0.9
Payroll taxes	9,366	4,050	5,316	131.3	1.0	0.5
General sales office expense and depreciation	15,137	9,643	5,494	57.0	1.5	1.3
Total selling expenses (Exhibit B)	$132,510	$84,898	$47,612	56.1	13.4	11.1
Administrative expenses:						
Officers' and office salaries	$ 90,132	$74,957	$15,175	20.2	9.1	9.8
Bad debts expense	1,100	2,500	1,400*	56.0*	0.1	0.3
Telephone and light	10,300	7,200	3,100	43.1	1.0	0.9
Taxes, payroll, and other	9,853	7,450	2,403	32.3	1.0	1.0
General administrative office expense and depreciation	8,960	6,535	2,425	37.1	1.0	0.9
Total administrative expenses (Exhibit B)	$120,345	$98,642	$21,703	22.0	12.2	12.9

Illustration 20.4: Comparative schedules of other expenses and revenues

THE KNIGHT CORPORATION Comparative Schedules of Other Expenses and Revenues For the Years Ended December 31, 1981, and 1982					Schedule B–2	
	Year ended December 31		Increase or decrease* 1982 over 1981		Percentage of net sales	
	1982	1981	Dollars	Per- centage	1982	1981
Other expenses:						
Interest expense	$9,325	$10,850	$1,525*	14.1*	0.9	1.4
Total other expenses	$9,325	$10,850	$1,525*	14.1*	0.9	1.4
Other revenues:						
Gain on sales of plant assets	6,325	8,050	1,725*	21.4*	0.6	1.0
Net other expenses (Exhibit B)	$3,000	$ 2,800	$ 200	7.1	0.3	0.4

In reviewing the trends, one should pay close attention to the trends for interrelated items. Trend percentages indicate changes and the direction of changes. They do not explain the basic reasons for the changes. But by looking at the trend percentages, management can determine which areas of the business need to be investigated.

RATIOS

It is generally recognized that logical relationships exist between certain items in the balance sheet. Logical relationships also exist between certain items in the earnings statement, and between pairs of items of which one appears in one statement and one in the other. Thus, many ratios can be computed from the same set of financial statements. These ratios can be broadly classified as (1) liquidity ratios, (2) tests of equity position and solvency, (3) profitability tests, and (4) market tests.

Liquidity ratios

Current or working capital ratio. Working capital is equal to the excess of current assets over current liabilities. The ratio which relates these two categories to each other is known as the *current ratio* or *working capital ratio*. It measures the ability of a company to meet its current liabilities. It also indicates the strength of a company's working capital position. The dollar amount of working capital does not provide an adequate index of the ability to pay current debts. The current ratio has been designed to provide a better index.

The current ratio is computed by dividing total current assets by total current liabilities:

$$\text{Current ratio} = \frac{\text{Current assets}}{\text{Current liabilities}}$$

The ratio usually is stated in terms of the number of dollars of current assets to one dollar of current liabilities (although the dollar signs usually are omitted). Thus, if current assets total $75,000 and current liabilities total $50,000, the ratio is expressed as 1.5:1 or 1.5 to 1.

To illustrate the superiority of the current ratio over working capital as a measure of debt-paying ability, consider the following example. Assume that Company A and Company B have current assets and current liabilities on December 31, 1981, as follows:

	Company A	Company B
Current assets	$11,000,000	$200,000
Current liabilities	10,000,000	100,000
Working capital	$ 1,000,000	$100,000
Current ratio	1.1:1	2:1

Company A has ten times as much working capital as Company B. But Company B has a superior debt-paying ability since it has two dollars of current assets for each dollar of current liabilities. Company A has only $1.10 of current assets for each $1 of current liabilities.

Short-term creditors are interested particularly in the working capital ratio. They expect to receive payment from the conversion of inventories and accounts receivable into cash. They are not as concerned with long-range earnings as are investors. Therefore, they concentrate on the current short-term financial position. The current ratios for the Knight Corporation are shown in Illustration 20.5.

Illustration 20.5: Current ratio

	December 31		Amount of increase
	1982	1981	
Current assets (a)	$373,851	$336,730	$37,121
Current liabilities (b)	127,140	109,860	17,280
Working capital (a − b)	$246,711	$226,870	$19,841
Current ratio (a ÷ b)	2.94:1	3.07:1	

Current assets and the operating cycle defined. Current assets consist of cash and any other assets which will be realized in cash, or sold or consumed in the course of normal operations during the normal operating cycle of the business or one year, whichever is longer. Real comprehension of the operations of a business enterprise requires a thorough understanding of this circulation process. Inventories are acquired by the disbursement of cash or the incurrence of current liabilities or both; inventories, upon sale, are converted into cash or trade receivables or both (at a gain, normally); receivables are in turn converted into cash, which is used to pay current liabilities. At the same time, other current liabilities are being created to replenish inventories, and so on. The average time intervening between the time cash is expended to acquire inventories and the time that it is received from the collection of receivables is an *operating cycle*.

Quick or acid-test ratio. The *acid-test ratio* (or *quick ratio*) is the ratio of cash, net receivables, and marketable securities (known as quick assets) to current liabilities:

$$\text{Acid-test ratio} = \frac{\text{Quick assets}}{\text{Current liabilities}}$$

Inventories and prepaid expenses are excluded from this computation because they might not be readily convertible into cash. Short-term creditors are interested particularly in this ratio since it relates the "pool" of cash and immediate cash inflows to immediate cash outflows.

For the Knight Corporation, acid-test ratios are presented in Illustration 20.6.

Illustration 20.6:
Acid-test ratio

	December 31		Amount of increase
	1982	*1981*	
Quick assets *(a)*	$259,386	$237,530	$21,856
Current liabilities *(b)*	127,140	109,860	17,280
Net quick assets *(a − b)*	$132,246	$127,670	$ 4,576
Acid-test ratio *(a ÷ b)*	2.04:1	2.16:1	

In deciding whether or not the acid-test ratio is satisfactory, a good starting point is to consider the quality of the receivables and the marketable securities. An accumulation of poor quality receivables or temporary investments on which losses are likely at the time of their disposition could cause an acid-test ratio to appear deceptively favorable. As for the Knight Corporation, there appears to be little immediate danger of insolvency since it has over $2 of quick assets for every dollar of short-term debt.

Accounts receivable turnover. *Turnover* is the relationship between the amount of an asset and some measure of its use. *Accounts receivable turnover* is computed by dividing net sales by average net accounts receivable, that is, accounts receivable after deducting the balance of the allowance for doubtful accounts.

$$\text{Accounts receivable turnover} = \frac{\text{Net sales}}{\text{Average net accounts receivable}}$$

Ideally, the divisor should be computed by averaging the end-of-month balances or end-of-week balances of net accounts receivable outstanding during the period. Often though, only the beginning-of-year and end-of-year balances are averaged, which is the method we will use. Sometimes a formula calls for the use of an average balance, but only the year-end amount is available. Then the analyst must use the year-end amount in the calculation. (These same comments apply to the other ratios described in this chapter.) The net sales figure should include only sales on account. But if cash sales are relatively small or if their proportion to total sales remains fairly constant from year to year, reliable results can be obtained by using total net sales. We will use this latter method. Illustration 20.7 shows the computations of the accounts

Illustration 20.7:
Turnover of
accounts
receivable

	1982	1981	Amount of increase or decrease*
Net sales *(a)*	$986,388	$765,515	$220,873
Accounts receivable:			
January 1	132,550	121,240	11,310
December 31	124,171	132,550	8,379*
Total	256,721	253,790	2,931
Average accounts receivable *(b)*	128,361	126,895	
Turnover of accounts receivable *(a ÷ b)*	7.68	6.03	

receivable turnover for the Knight Corporation for 1982 and 1981. (Assume that the amount of net accounts receivable on January 1, 1981, was $121,240.)

The turnover of accounts receivable indicates, on the average, how often the accounts receivable were collected. In other words, a turnover of 12 would mean that it takes about one month for accounts to be collected; a turnover of 8 would mean the collection period is longer—about 46 days (365 ÷ 8). The number of days in the year (365) divided by the turnover of accounts receivable is the average life of accounts receivable or the average collection period. The ratio measures the average liquidity of the accounts receivable and gives an indication of their quality. Comparing the collection period to the credit period granted will provide further indication of the quality of the accounts receivable.

Inventory turnover.   *Inventory turnover* is obtained by dividing the cost of goods sold for a given period by the average inventory for the same period:

$$\text{Inventory turnover} = \frac{\text{Cost of goods sold}}{\text{Average inventory}}$$

Inventory turnover for the Knight Corporation is shown in Illustration 20.8.

In attempting to secure satisfactory earnings, the costs of storage, obsolescence, and implicit interest incurred in owning inventory must be balanced against the possible loss of sales from not owning it. Other things being equal, the management which is able to maintain the higher inventory turnover rate is considered more efficient.

Illustration 20.8:
Turnover of
inventory

	1982	1981	Amount of increase
Cost of goods sold *(a)*	$623,237	$500,940	$122,297
Inventories:			
January 1	$ 94,500	$ 85,150	$ 9,350
December 31	110,825	94,500	16,325
Total	$205,325	$179,650	$ 25,675
Average inventory *(b)*	102,663	89,825	
Turnover of inventory *(a ÷ b)*	6.07	5.58	

Turnover of total assets.   *Total assets turnover* shows the relationship between dollar volume of sales and average total assets used in the business and is calculated as follows:

$$\text{Total assets turnover} = \frac{\text{Net sales}}{\text{Average total assets}}$$

It measures the efficiency of the use of the capital invested in the assets (assuming a constant margin of earnings on each dollar of sales). The larger the dollar volume of sales made per dollar of invested capital, the larger will be the earnings on each dollar invested in the assets of the business. For the Knight Corporation the total assets turnover ratios for 1982 and 1981 are shown in Illustration 20.9. (Assume total assets as of January 1, 1981, were $510,200.)

Illustration 20.9:
Turnover of
total assets

	1982	1981	Amount of increase
Net sales *(a)*	$ 986,388	$ 765,515	$220,873
Total assets:			
January 1	551,085	510,200	40,885
December 31	635,211	551,085	84,126
Total	1,186,296	1,061,285	125,011
Average total assets *(b)*	593,148	530,643	
Turnover of total assets *(a ÷ b)*	1.66	1.44	

In 1981, each dollar of total assets produced $1.44 of sales; and in 1982, each dollar of total assets produced $1.66 of sales, or an increase of $0.22 of sales per dollar of investment in the assets.

Tests of equity position and solvency

Equity ratio.   The data shown in Illustration 20.10, taken from the comparative balance sheets in Illustration 20.1, show the sources of the assets of the Knight Corporation on December 31 of 1982 and 1981. The two sources of assets are owners (stockholders) and creditors. The stockholders of the Knight Corporation have increased their proportionate equity in the assets of the company through additional investment in the company's common stock and through retention of the company's earnings.

Illustration 20.10:
Sources of
assets

	December 31, 1982		December 31, 1981	
	Amount	Percent	Amount	Percent
Current liabilities	$127,140	20.0	$109,860	19.9
Long-term liabilities	43,600	6.9	60,750	11.0
Total Liabilities	$170,740	26.9	$170,610	30.9
Common stock	$240,000	37.8	$200,000	36.3
Retained earnings	224,471	35.3	180,475	32.8
Total Stockholders' Equity	$464,471	73.1	$380,475	69.1
Total Equity (equal to total assets)	$635,211	100.0	$551,085	100.0

The *equity ratio* is equal to the proportion of owners' (stockholders') equity to total equity (or to total assets) at the end of the period:

$$\text{Equity ratio} = \frac{\text{Owners' equity}}{\text{Total equity}}$$

The Knight Corporation's equity ratio increased from 69.1 percent in 1981 to 73.1 percent in 1982. The equity ratio must be interpreted carefully. From a creditor's point of view, a high proportion of owners' equity is desirable. A high percentage indicates the existence of a large protective buffer for creditors in the event the company suffers a loss. But from an owner's point of view a high proportion of owners' equity may or may not be desirable. If borrowed funds can be used by the business to generate earnings in excess of the net after tax cost of the interest on such borrowed funds, a lower percentage of owners' equity may be desirable. For example, assume that Dorton Company has $10,000,000 of 8 percent bonds payable in its capital structure, which after taxes have a net cost of $400,000 ($10,000,000 × 0.08 × 0.5), assuming a 50 percent tax rate. If the Dorton Company can use the $10,000,000 to produce earnings in excess of the $400,000 net aftertax cost of the borrowed funds, earnings per share will increase, and it may decide that borrowing is advantageous. As discussed in earlier chapters, use of borrowed funds or preferred stock to such an advantage is termed successful "trading on the quity" or "favorable *financial leverage*."

The following is a brief illustration of the effect on the Knight Corporation if it were more highly leveraged (i.e., had a larger proportion of debt). Assume that Knight Corporation could have financed its present operations with $50,000 of 8 percent bonds instead of 5,000 shares of common stock. The effect on earnings for 1982 would be as follows, assuming a marginal federal income tax rate of 50 percent:

Earnings as presently stated (Illustration 20.2)	$58,996
Additional interest on bonds, net of tax (0.50 × 8% × $50,000)	2,000
Adjusted earnings	$56,996

As shown, net earnings would be less. But there would be 5,000 fewer shares outstanding. Therefore, earnings per share would be increased to $3 ($56,996 ÷ 19,000) from $2.46 ($58,996 ÷ 24,000). In recent years many companies have introduced larger portions of debt into their capital structures to increase earnings per share. But these companies will also show a larger drop in earnings per share when earnings go down than will those which are financed largely by common stock.

It should also be pointed out that too low a percentage of owners' equity (too much debt) may be hazardous from the owners' standpoint. A period of business recession may result in operating losses and shrinkages in the values of assets (such as receivables and inventories) leading to an inability to meet fixed payments for interest and principal on the debt. This in turn may cause stockholders to lose control of the company. The company may be forced into liquidation.

Owners' equity/debt ratio.   The relative equities of owners and creditors may be expressed in several ways. To say, for example, that creditors hold a 26.9 percent equity in the assets of the Knight Corporation on December 31, 1982, is equivalent to saying that the stockholders hold a 73.1 percent interest. In many cases, the relationship is expressed as a ratio of owners' equity to debt. Such a ratio for the Knight Corporation would be 2.23:1 ($380,475 ÷ $170,610) on December 31, 1981, and 2.72:1 ($464,471 ÷ $170,740) on December 31, 1982. (Some analysts relate only long-term debt to owners' equity in these calculations.)

Profitability tests

Determination of earning power on operating assets.   The best measure of earnings performance without regard to the sources of assets is the relationship of net operating earnings to operating assets.

Net operating earnings exclude nonoperating revenues (such as extraordinary gains on the early retirement of debt and interest earned on investments), nonoperating expenses (such as interest paid on obligations), and federal income taxes.

Operating assets are all assets actively used in producing operating revenue. Examples of excluded (that is, nonoperating) assets are land held for future use, a factory building being rented to someone else, and long-term bond investments.

Elements in earning power.   There are two elements in the determination of the percentage of earning power. They are the operating margin and the turnover of operating assets. The operating margin can be expressed in formula form as follows:

$$\text{Net operating margin} = \frac{\text{Net operating earnings}}{\text{Net sales}}$$

The total assets turnover is inadequate as an independent measure of earnings performance. But when slightly changed and used in combination with the net operating margin, it becomes an excellent measure of earnings performance as shown below. If nonoperating assets are excluded (as they should be), this ratio becomes the "turnover of operating assets" represented by the formula:

$$\text{Turnover of operating assets} = \frac{\text{Net sales}}{\text{Operating assets}}$$

The turnover of operating assets shows the dollars of sales made for each dollar invested in operating assets. The operating assets amount used is generally the year-end amount. One could argue that the average balance should be used, but it seldom is (and we will not use it).

The *earning power percentage* of a firm is equal to the net operating margin multiplied by the turnover of operating assets. The more a company earns per dollar of sales and the more sales it makes per dollar invested in operating assets, the higher will be the return per dollar invested. Earning power may be expressed by the following formula: Earning power = Net operating margin × Turnover of operating assets, or

$$\text{Earning power percentage} = \frac{\text{Net operating earnings}}{\text{Net sales}} \times \frac{\text{Net sales}}{\text{Operating assets}}$$

Since the net sales amount appears as both a numerator and a denominator, it can be canceled out, and the formula for the earning power percentage becomes:

$$\text{Earning power percentage} = \frac{\text{Net operating earnings}}{\text{Operating assets}}$$

But it is more useful for analytical purposes to leave the formula in the form which shows margin and turnover separately.

Securing desired earning power. Companies that are to survive in the economy must attain some minimum level of earning power. But this minimum can be obtained in many different ways. To illustrate, consider a grocery store and a jewelry store, each with an earning power of 8 percent on operating assets. The grocery store normally would have a low margin and a high turnover while the jewelry store would have a higher margin and a lower turnover:

	Margin	×	Turnover	=	Earning power percentage
Grocery store	1%	×	8.0 times		8%
Jewelry store	20	×	0.4		8

The earning power percentage figures for the Knight Corporation for 1982 and 1981 are calculated in Illustration 20.11.

Illustration 20.11: Earning power

	1982	1981	Amount of increase
Net operating earnings (a)	$110,296	$ 81,035	$ 29,261
Net sales (b)	986,388	765,515	220,873
Net operating margin (a ÷ b = c)	11.18%	10.59%	
Net sales (d)	$986,388	$765,515	$220,873
Total assets (all operating assets) (e)	635,211	551,085	84,126
Turnover of operating assets (d ÷ e = f)	1.55	1.39	
Earning power percentage (c × f)	17.33%	14.72%	

Earning power percentage is the best measure of the profitability of the firm without regard to the sources of the assets. It is concerned with the earning power of the company as a bundle of assets, not with the determination of which sources of the assets are favored in the division of earnings.

Net earnings as a percentage of net sales. Net earnings as a percentage of net sales is obtained by dividing the net earnings for the period by the net sales for the same period:

$$\text{Net earnings to net sales} = \frac{\text{Net earnings}}{\text{Net sales}}$$

This ratio measures the proportion of the sales dollar which remains after the deduction of all expenses. For the Knight Corporation the computations are shown in Illustration 20.12.

Illustration 20.12: Ratio of net earnings to net sales

	1982	1981	Amount of increase
Net earnings *(a)*	$ 58,996	$ 46,535	$ 12,461
Net sales *(b)*	986,388	765,515	220,873
Ratio of net earnings to net sales *(a ÷ b)*	5.98%	6.08%	

Although the ratio of net earnings to net sales indicates the net margin of earnings on each dollar of sales, a great deal of care must be exercised in its use and interpretation. The amount of net earnings is equal to net operating earnings plus nonoperating revenues and less nonoperating expenses and taxes. Thus, unlike the earning power on operating assets, the ratio of net earnings to net sales is affected by the methods used to finance the assets of the firm.

Net earnings as a percentage of average stockholders' equity. From the stockholders' point of view, an important measure of the earnings-producing ability of a company is the relationship of net earnings to stockholders' equity or the rate of return on stockholders' equity. Stockholders are interested in the ratio of operating earnings to operating assets as a measure of the efficient use of assets. But they are even more interested in knowing what part of the earnings remains for them after other capital suppliers have been paid.

Net earnings as a percentage of stockholders' equity is obtained by dividing the net earnings for the period by the average total stockholders' equity for the same period. The ratios for the Knight Corporation are shown in Illustration 20.13. (Assume that total stockholders' equity on January 1, 1981, was $321,460.)

Illustration 20.13: Ratio of net earnings to stockholders' equity

	1982	1981	Amount of increase
Net earnings *(a)*	$ 58,996	$ 46,535	$ 12,461
Total stockholders' equity:			
January 1	380,475	321,460	59,015
December 31	464,471	380,475	83,996
Total	$844,946	$701,935	$143,011
Average total stockholders' equity *(b)*	$422,473	$350,968	
Ratio of net earnings to stockholders' equity *(a ÷ b)*	13.96%	13.26%	

The increase in the ratio of net earnings to stockholders' equity from 13.26 percent to 13.96 percent would be looked upon favorably.

Earnings per share.   When preferred stock is outstanding, a portion of the net earnings must be assigned to the preferred stock with the remainder left for the common stock. To determine the rate of earnings (or dollars earned per share) on the common stock, the portion of net earnings belonging to the various classes of stock outstanding must be computed.

Most preferred stock issues provide for preference over common stock for a specific limited dividend per share with no dividend rights beyond this amount. In this case it is necessary to deduct from the net earnings for the period only the annual dividends to which preferred stockholders are entitled. The remainder is then divided by the average number of shares of common stock outstanding to compute the *earnings per share* of common stock:

$$\text{Earnings per share of common stock} = \frac{\text{Earnings available to common stockholders}}{\text{Average number of shares of common stock outstanding}}$$

When extraordinary gains or losses are included in net earnings, *Accounting Principles Board Opinion No. 9* requires that separate per share amounts be shown for net earnings before extraordinary items; for the net amount of the extraordinary items, if any (net of their tax effects); and for net earnings. Thus a company which has suffered a loss on the early retirement of debt might include the following in its earnings statement for the year:

Per share of common stock—	
Net earnings before extraordinary loss	$1.75
Loss on early retirement of debt, net of tax	(0.25)
Net Earnings	$1.50

Annual preferred dividend requirements, if any, must be deducted in computing the $1.75 as well as the $1.50.

For the Knight Corporation, which had no preferred stock outstanding in either 1982 or 1981, earnings per share of common stock are computed in Illustration 20.14.

Illustration 20.14:
Earnings
per share

	1982	1981	Amount of increase
Net earnings *(a)*	$58,996	$46,535	$12,461
Average number of shares of common stock outstanding *(b)*	22,000	20,000	2,000
Earnings per share of common stock *(a ÷ b)*	$2.68	$2.33	

Effect of shares issued for assets.   In interpreting the above illustration it is important to note that although the Knight Corporation increased its outstanding common stock by 4,000 shares in 1982, the increase in the average number of shares outstanding was only 2,000. The above computation assumes that the 4,000 shares were issued on June 30. Having 4,000 shares outstanding for one-half year is equivalent to having 2,000 shares outstanding during all of the year. Hence, the average number of shares outstanding increased by 2,000.

When new shares are issued for assets, or outstanding shares are reacquired by the company, it is best to compute the average number of shares outstanding during the period. Earnings per share of common stock are then reported on an average basis for the entire year.

To illustrate, assume that as of January 1, 1981, Barnes Corporation had 110,000 shares of common stock outstanding. On October 1, 1981, it issued 40,000 shares for cash. Earnings available to common stockholders for 1981 amount to $480,000. The average number of shares outstanding is computed as follows:

$$(110,000 \times \%_{12}) + (150,000 \times \frac{3}{12}) = 120,000$$

The computation shows 110,000 shares outstanding for nine months and 150,000 shares outstanding for the last three months.

The earnings per share are:

$$\$480,000 \div 120,000 = \$4$$

Effect of shares issued for stock dividends or stock splits.   When additional shares are issued during the period as a result of a stock dividend or stock split, no attempt is made to average the number of shares outstanding at different times during the year as is done when additional shares are issued for cash or other property. The reason is that the stock split or the stock dividend is not viewed as being a change in substance. It is simply a division of the stockholders' interest into more pieces.

When comparing earnings per share before and after a stock split or stock dividend, the earnings per share should be adjusted to the same basis. Assume a company reports earnings per share as follows: 1980, $1; 1981, $1.25; and 1982, $0.75. But a two for one stock split occurred in 1982. The first two years' figures should be adjusted for the stock split in order to be comparable to the 1982 figure. Thus, earnings per share would be $0.50 for 1980, and $0.625 for 1981. Then the proper trend can be seen:

Year	Earnings per share
1980	$0.50
1981	0.625
1982	0.75

Number of times interest is earned.   Another relationship which focuses attention upon the position of a particular class of investor—in this case, the bondholder—is the ratio of earnings available for bond interest charges to the amount of such charges. For example, if the amount of earnings before interest and income taxes is $100,000 and the bond interest expense for the period is $10,000, the ratio is 10:1. In such a case the bond interest is said to have been earned ten times.

Bondholders are interested in knowing whether the company is earning enough so that even if a drop in earnings should occur, it could continue to earn enough to meet its interest payments. It is true that interest must usually be paid regardless of whether earnings are sufficient to cover it. But it is also true that a company probably could not continue to pay interest in excess of net earnings before interest for a long period of time. Thus, the bondholders are interested in knowing the likelihood that they will continue to receive their interest.

The number of times that the present interest is earned is one measure of a company's ability to meet interest payments. And, of course, since bond interest is deductible for income tax purposes, net earnings before bond interest and income taxes is used since there would be no tax if bond interest were equal to or greater than net earnings before interest and taxes. In formula form, the ratio is:

$$\text{Number of times interest is earned} = \frac{\text{Net earnings before interest and taxes}}{\text{Interest expense}}$$

Number of times preferred dividends are earned. Preferred stockholders, like bondholders, must usually be satisfied with a fixed dollar return on their investments. They are interested in the company's ability to make preferred dividend payments each year. This can be measured by computing the number of times preferred dividends are earned. It can be computed as follows:

$$\text{Times preferred dividends earned} = \frac{\text{Net earnings after income taxes}}{\text{Preferred dividends}}$$

Suppose a company has earnings after income taxes of $48,000 and has $100,000 (par value) of 8 percent preferred stock outstanding. The number of times the preferred dividends are earned would be:

$$\frac{\$48,000}{\$8,000} = 6 \text{ times}$$

The higher this rate, the higher is the probability that the preferred stockholders will receive their dividends each year. While the analogy is far from perfect, a finance company would be much more likely to expect to continue to receive payments on a loan from an individual who is earning eight times the required periodic payment than one who is earning only twice the payment.

Market tests

Yield on common stock and price-earnings ratio. The *yield* on a stock investment is the annual earnings or dividends per share as a percentage of the current market price per share. Thus, a firm's earnings yield per share of common stock is calculated as follows:

$$\text{Earnings yield on common stock} = \frac{\text{Earnings per share}}{\text{Current market price per share}}$$

Suppose, for example, that a company had earnings per share of common stock of $2 and that the quoted market price of the stock on the New York Stock Exchange was $30. The *earnings yield* on common stock would be:

$$\frac{\$2}{\$30} = 6\frac{2}{3} \text{ percent}$$

This ratio when inverted is called the *price-earnings ratio.* In the case just cited the price-earnings ratio is:

$$\text{Price-earnings ratio} = \frac{\text{Current market price per share}}{\text{Earnings per share}} = \frac{\$30}{\$2} = 15 : 1$$

Investors would say that this stock is selling at 15 times earnings or at a multiple of 15. They might have a multiple in mind as being the proper one that should be used to judge whether the stock were underpriced or overpriced. Different investors will have different estimates of the proper price-earnings ratio for a given stock and also different estimates of the future earnings prospects of the firm. These are two of the factors which cause one investor to sell stock at a particular price and another investor to buy at that price.

    Dividend yield and payout ratios. The dividend paid per share of common stock is also of much interest to common stockholders. When the dividend is divided by the current market price per share, the result is called the *dividend yield.*

    If the company referred to immediately above paid a $1.50 per share dividend, the dividend yield would be:

$$\frac{\text{Dividend yield on}}{\text{common stock}} = \frac{\text{Dividend per share}}{\text{Current market price per share}} = \frac{\$1.50}{\$30.00} = 5 \text{ percent}$$

One additional step is to divide the dividend per share by the earnings available per share to determine the *payout ratio on common stock* as follows:

$$\text{Payout ratio} = \frac{\text{Dividend per share}}{\text{Earnings per share}} = \frac{\$1.50}{\$2.00} = 75 \text{ percent}$$

A payout ratio of 75 percent means that the company paid out 75 percent of the earnings per share in the form of dividends. Some investors are attracted by the stock of companies that pay out a large percentage of their earnings. Other investors are attracted by the stock of companies which retain and reinvest a large percentage of their earnings. The tax status of the investor has a great deal to do with this. Investors in very high tax brackets often prefer to have the company reinvest the earnings with the expectation that this will result in share price appreciation which would be taxed at capital gains rates when the shares are sold. Dividends are taxed at ordinary income rates, which may be much higher than capital gains rates.

    Yield on preferred stock. Preferred stockholders compute dividend yield in a manner similar to the computation of dividend yield for common

Illustration 20.15:
Summary of ratios

Ratio	Formula	Significance
Current ratio	Current assets ÷ Current liabilities	Test of debt-paying ability
Acid-test (quick) ratio	(Cash + Net receivables + Marketable securities) ÷ Current liabilities	Test of immediate debt-paying ability
Accounts receivable turnover	Net Sales ÷ Average Net Accounts Receivable	Test of quality of accounts receivable
Average collection period	Number of days in year ÷ Accounts receivable turnover ratio	Test of quality of accounts receivable
Inventory turnover	Cost of goods sold ÷ Average inventory	Test of whether or not a sufficient volume of business is being generated relative to inventory
Total assets turnover	Net sales ÷ Average total assets	Test of whether or not volume of business generated is adequate relative to amount of capital invested in business
Equity ratio	Owners' (Stockholders') equity ÷ Total equities	Index of long-run solvency and safety
Earning power percentage	Net operating earnings ÷ Operating assets	Measure of managerial effectiveness
Net earnings to stockholders' equity	Net earnings ÷ Average stockholders' equity	Measure of what a given company earned for its stockholders from all sources as a percentage of the stockholders' investment
Earnings per share (of common stock)	Net earnings available to common stockholders ÷ Average number of shares of common stock outstanding	Tends to have an effect on the market price per share
Number of times interest is earned	Net earnings before interest and taxes ÷ Interest expense	Indicates likelihood that bondholders will continue to receive their interest payments
Number of times preferred dividends are earned	Net earnings after income taxes ÷ Preferred dividends	Indicates the probability that preferred stockholders will receive their dividend each year
Earnings yield on common stock	Earnings per share ÷ Current market price per share	Useful for comparison with other stocks
Price-earnings ratio	Current market price per share ÷ Earnings per share	Index of whether a stock is relatively cheap or expensive
Dividend yield	Dividend per share ÷ Current market price per share	Useful for comparison with other stocks
Payout ratio on common stock	Dividend per share ÷ Earnings per share	Index of whether company pays out large percentage of earnings as dividends or reinvests most of its earnings

stockholders. Suppose a company has 2,000 shares of $100 par value, 8 percent preferred stock outstanding which has a current market price of $110 per share. The dividend yield would be computed as follows:

$$\text{Dividend yield on preferred stock} = \frac{\text{Dividend per share}}{\text{Current market price per share}} = \frac{\$8}{\$110} = 7.27 \text{ percent}$$

Through the use of dividend yield rates, different preferred stocks having different annual dividends and different market prices can be compared.

Many of the ratios presented in this chapter are summarized conveniently in Illustration 20.15.

LIMITATIONS AND OTHER CONSIDERATIONS IN EVALUATING FINANCIAL POSITION AND EARNING POWER

Comparative financial statements facilitate analysis of changes and possible trends. Generally, three to five years are necessary for evaluation. There is no substitute for informed judgment in financial analysis. Percentages and ratios are useful *guides* to aid comparisons. The financial analyst uses these tools to uncover potential strengths and weaknesses. The analyst should try to discover the *basic causes* behind changes and trends. For example, declining earnings may be due to poor management, declining product demand, poor cost control, an inefficient sales force, and so on. By examining key items on financial statements, the analyst can make informed judgments as to continued profitability.

Companies do not operate in an economic vacuum. It is important to place financial statement analysis within an industry and economic environment context. Acceptable current ratios, gross margin percentages, debt to equity ratios, and so on, vary widely depending upon environmental conditions and the industry in which the company operates. Even within an industry, legitimate variations may exist. For example, a retail discount store may operate at a relatively low gross margin percentage. This does not necessarily mean that its operating philosophy is inferior to that of its higher margin competitors. Also, within the same company over time, small percentage declines may indicate potential trouble. For example, a small percentage decline in gross margin percentage may be a danger signal because large dollar amounts may be involved.

The potential investor should realize that acquiring the ability to make informed judgments in a long process and is not acquired overnight. Using ratios and percentages mechanically is a sure road to wrong conclusions.

Need for comparable data

Analysts must be sure that their comparisons are valid—whether the comparisons be of items for different periods or dates or for items of different companies. Consistent accounting practices must be followed from period to period if interperiod comparisons are to be made. It is the accountant's responsibility, of course, to disclose any changes in method or departures from consistent practice, if they are material.

Influence of external factors

Facts and conditions not disclosed by the financial statements may affect their interpretation. A single important event may have been largely responsible for a given relationship. For example, a new product may have been unexpectedly put on the market by competitors, making it necessary for the company under study to sacrifice its stock of a product suddenly rendered obsolete. Such an event would affect the percentage of gross margin to net sales severely. Yet, there may be little or no chance that such a thing would happen again.

General business conditions within the business or industry of the company under study must be considered. A downward trend in earnings, for example, is less alarming if the trend in the industry or in business in general is also downward rather than limited to a single corporation.

Consideration should be given to the possible seasonal nature of the businesses under study. If the balance sheet date represents the seasonal peak in the volume of business, for example, the ratio of current assets to current liabilities may acceptably be much lower than if the balance sheet date is one in a season of low activity.

Need for comparative standards

Relationships between financial statement items become more meaningful when standards are available for comparison. Comparison with standards provides a starting point for the analyst's thinking and leads to further investigation and, ultimately, to conclusions and business decisions. Such standards consist of (1) those which the analyst has in his or her own mind, as a result of experience and observation; (2) those provided by the records of past performance and position of the business under study; and (3) those provided by accounting data of other enterprises—for example, data available through trade associations, universities, research organizations, and governmental units.

The most serious limitation to the usefulness of financial statements

The utility of conventional financial statements has been questioned in recent years more than ever before. There is one primary reason for this—the statements fail to reveal the impact of inflation upon the reporting entity. One of the primary rules to be followed in making comparisons is to be sure that the items being compared are comparable. The old adage is that one should not add apples and oranges and call the total either apples or oranges. Yet, the accountant does exactly this when dollars of different real worth are added or subtracted as if they were the same. And the worth of a dollar has been steadily declining as inflation surges strongly through our economy.

Considerable debate has existed over the proper response by accounting to inflation. Some argue that we should change our unit of measure from the nominal, unadjusted dollar to a dollar of constant purchasing power. Others maintain that only by adopting current values or current costs as the attribute measured will the real effects of inflation upon an entity be revealed. How each of these alternative approaches could be implemented and what they are likely to reveal is discussed in some depth in Appendix A at the end of this text.

NEW TERMS INTRODUCED IN CHAPTER 20

Acid-test ratio—the ratio of cash and near cash assets (net receivables and marketable securities) to total current liabilities.

Accounts receivable turnover—net sales divided by average net accounts receivable.

Current ratio—the ratio of current assets to current liabilities.

Dividend yield—on common or preferred stocks, current annual dividend per share divided by current market price per share.

Earning power percentage—(net operating earnings divided by net sales) × (net sales divided by operating assets). The result is equal to net operating earnings divided by net operating assets.

Earnings per share—usually computed for common stock; net earnings less annual preferred dividend requirements, if any, divided by the average number of shares of common stock outstanding.

Earnings yield—on common stock—ratio of current earnings per share to current market price per share.

Equity ratio—the ratio of owners' equity to total equities (or total assets).

Inventory turnover—cost of good sold divided by average inventory.

Net earnings as a percentage of net sales—a ratio formed by dividing net sales into net earnings.

Net earnings as a percentage of average stockholders' equity—net earnings divided by average stockholders' equity; often called *rate of return on stockholders' equity.*

Net operating earnings—the principal revenues of a company less the expenses incurred in producing them; excluded are nonoperating expenses and revenues, extraordinary gains and losses, and federal income taxes.

Number of times interest is earned—a ratio computed by dividing net earnings before interest expense and federal income taxes by interest expense.

Number of times preferred dividends are earned—a ratio computed by dividing net earnings after taxes by the annual preferred dividend requirements, whether declared and paid or not.

Operating assets—all assets used to produce the major revenues of a company.

Payout ratio on common stock—the ratio of dividends per share to earnings per share.

Price-earnings ratio—the ratio of the current market price of a share of stock to the earnings per share of the stock.

Quick ratio—same as acid-test ratio above.

Total assets turnover—net sales divided by average total assets.

Turnover—the relationship between the amount of an asset and some measure of its use; thus, Accounts receivable turnover = Net sales divided by average net accounts receivable; Inventory turnover = Cost of goods sold divided by average inventory; and Total assets turnover = Net sales divided by average total assets.

Working capital ratio—same as current ratio above.

Yield (on stock)—the annual earnings or dividends per share, expressed as a percentage of the current market price per share; Earnings yield on common stock = Ratio of earnings per share to current market price; Dividend yield on common or preferred stocks = Ratio of current annual dividend to current market price.

DEMONSTRATION PROBLEM

The balance sheet and supplementary data for the Turner Corporation are shown below:

TURNER CORPORATION
Balance Sheet
December 31, 1981

Assets

Cash		$ 50,000
Marketable securities		30,000
Accounts receivable		70,000
Inventory		150,000
Building	$400,000	
Less: Accumulated depreciation	100,000	300,000
Total Assets		$600,000

Liabilities and Stockholders' Equity

Accounts payable	$ 30,000
Bank loans payable	10,000
Mortgage notes payable, due in 1985	40,000
Bonds payable, 9%, due 12/31/84	100,000
Common stock, $100 par value	300,000
Retained earnings	120,000
Total Liabilities and Stockholders' Equity	$600,000

Supplementary data:

1. 1981 net earnings: $60,000.
2. 1981 cost of goods sold: $540,000.
3. 1982 sales: $900,000.
4. Inventory, December 31, 1980: $100,000.
5. Bond interest expense: $9,000.
6. 1981 net earnings before interest and taxes: $130,000.

Required:

Compute the following ratios:

a. Current ratio.

b. Acid-test ratio.

c. Accounts receivable turnover.

d. Inventory turnover.

e. Total assets turnover.

f. Equity ratio.

g. Earnings per share of common stock.

h. Number of times bond interest was earned.

Solution to demonstration problem

a. Current ratio:

$$\frac{\text{Current assets}}{\text{Current liabilities}} = \frac{\$300,000}{\$40,000} = 7.5:1$$

b.   Acid-test ratio:

$$\frac{\text{Quick assets}}{\text{Current liabilities}} = \frac{\$150,000}{\$40,000} = 3.75:1$$

c.   Accounts receivable turnover:

$$\frac{\text{Net sales}}{\text{Accounts receivable}} = \frac{\$900,000}{\$70,000} = 12.86 \text{ times}$$

d.   Inventory turnover:

$$\frac{\text{Cost of goods sold}}{\text{Average inventory}} = \frac{\$540,000}{\$125,000} = 4.32 \text{ times}$$

e.   Total assets turnover:

$$\frac{\text{Net sales}}{\text{Total assets}} = \frac{\$900,000}{\$600,000} = 1.5 \text{ times}$$

f.   Equity ratio:

$$\frac{\text{Stockholders' equity}}{\text{Total assets}} = \frac{\$420,000}{\$600,000} = 70 \text{ percent}$$

g.   Earnings per share of common stock:

$$\frac{\text{Net Earnings}}{\text{Number of shares of common stock outstanding}} = \frac{\$60,000}{3,000} = \$20$$

h.   Number of times bond interest was earned:

$$\frac{\text{Net earnings before interest and taxes}}{\text{Bond interest expense}} = \frac{\$130,000}{\$9,000} = 14.44 \text{ times}$$

QUESTIONS

1. The higher the accounts receivable turnover rate the better off is the company. Do you agree? Why?

2. See if you can think of a situation where the current ratio is very misleading as an indicator of short-term debt-paying ability. Does the quick ratio offer a remedy to the situation you have described? Describe a situation where the quick ratio will not suffice either.

3. Before the John Company issued $10,000 of long-term notes (due more than a year from the date of issue) in exchange for a like amount of accounts payable, its acid-test ratio was 2:1. Will this transaction increase, decrease, or have no effect on the current ratio? The equity ratio?

4. Through the use of turnover ratios explain why a firm might seek to increase the volume of its sales even though such an increase can be secured only at reduced prices.

5. Indicate which of the relationships illustrated in Chapter 20 would be best to judge:

   a. The short-term debt-paying ability of the firm.

   b. The overall efficiency of the firm without regard to the sources of assets.

   c. The return to owners of a corporation.

   d. The safety of bondholders' interest.

   e. The safety of preferred stockholders' dividends.

6. Indicate how each of the following ratios or measures is calculated:

   a. Payout ratio.

b. Earnings per share of common stock.

c. Price-earnings ratio.

d. Yield on common stock.

e. Yield on preferred stock.

f. Times interest earned.

g. Times preferred dividends earned.

h. Return on stockholders' equity.

7. How is earning power on operating assets determined? Is it possible for two companies with "operating margins" of 5 percent and 1 percent, respectively, to both have an earning power of 20 percent on operating assets? How?

8. Cite some of the possible deficiencies in accounting information especially as regards its use in analyzing a particular company over a ten-year period.

EXERCISES

E–1. Under each of the three conditions listed below, compute the current ratio after each of the transactions described. Current assets are now $100,000. (Consider each transaction independently of the others.) Current ratio before the transactions is:

a. 1:1.

b. 2:1.

c. 1:2.

Transactions:

1. $100,000 of merchandise is purchased on account.
2. Purchased $50,000 of machinery for cash.
3. Issued stock for $50,000 cash.

E–2. A company has sales of $912,500 per year. Its average accounts receivable balance is $182,500.

a. What is the average number of days an account receivable is outstanding?

b. Assuming released funds can be invested at 10 percent, how much could the company earn by reducing the collection period of the accounts receivable to 40 days?

c. What assumption must you make in order for this earnings calculation to be correct?

E–3. From the following partial earnings statement calculate the inventory turnover for the period.

Net sales		$521,450
Cost of goods sold:		
Beginning inventory	$ 50,000	
Purchases	370,000	
Goods available		
for sale	$420,000	
Less: Ending		
inventory	58,000	
Cost of goods		
sold		$362,000
Gross margin		$159,450
Operating expenses		75,000
Net Operating Earnings		$ 84,450

E–4. The Korner Company had 40,000 shares of common stock outstanding on January 1, 1981. On April 1, 1981, it issued 10,000 additional shares for cash. The earnings available for common stockholders for 1981 were $200,000. What amount of earnings per share of common stock should the company report?

E–5. A company paid bond interest of $4,000, incurred federal income taxes of $11,000, and had net earnings (after taxes) of $21,000. How many times was the bond interest earned?

E–6. The Field Company had 4,000 shares of $100 par value, 5 percent, preferred stock outstanding. Net earnings after taxes were $120,000. The market price per share was $80.

a. How many times were the preferred dividends earned?

b. What was the yield on the preferred stock assuming the regular preferred dividends were declared and paid?

PROBLEMS, SERIES A

P20–1–A. From the following data for the Edwards Company compute **(a)** the working capital; **(b)** the current ratio; and **(c)** the acid-test ratio, all as of both dates; and **(d)** comment briefly on the company's short-term financial position.

	December 31, 1982	December 31, 1981
Notes payable (due in 90 days)	$ 47,000	$ 38,500
Merchandise inventory	200,000	176,200
Cash	63,310	78,350
Marketable securities	31,000	18,750
Accrued liabilities	12,000	13,800
Accounts receivable	117,500	115,000
Accounts payable	69,400	45,300
Allowance for doubtful accounts	14,800	9,600
Bonds payable, due 1987	92,500	98,000
Prepaid expenses	4,050	4,650

P20–2–A. Dobson Products, Inc., has a current ratio on December 31, 1981, of 2:1. If the following transactions were completed on that date, indicate **(a)** whether the amount of working capital would have been increased, decreased, or unaffected by each of the transactions; and **(b)** whether the current ratio would have been increased, decreased, or unaffected by each of the transactions (consider each independently of all of the others).

1. Sold building for cash.
2. Exchanged old equipment for new equipment. (No cash was involved.)
3. Declared a cash dividend on preferred stock.
4. Sold merchandise on account (at a profit).
5. Retired mortgage notes which would have matured in 1989.
6. Issued stock dividend to common stockholders.
7. Paid cash for a patent.
8. Temporarily invested cash in government bonds.
9. Purchased inventory for cash.
10. Wrote off an account receivable as uncollectible.
11. Paid the cash dividend on preferred stock.
12. Purchased a computer and gave a two-year promissory note.
13. Collected accounts receivable.
14. Borrowed from bank on a 120-day promissory note.
15. Discounted a customer's note. A financial expense was involved.

P20–3–A. The following are comparative balance sheets of the Happer Corporation on December 31, 1981, and 1982:

HAPPER CORPORATION
Comparative Balance Sheets

	December 31, 1982	December 31, 1981
Assets		
Cash	$ 75,000	$ 85,000
Accounts receivable, net	65,000	75,000
Merchandise inventory	45,000	55,000
Plant assets, net	100,000	45,000
Total Assets	$285,000	$260,000
Liabilities and Stockholders' Equity		
Accounts payable	$ 40,000	$ 25,000
Notes payable	35,000	43,000
Common stock	110,000	110,000
Retained earnings	100,000	82,000
Total Liabilities and Stockholders' Equity	$285,000	$260,000
Other data:		
Sales	$460,000	$400,000
Gross margin	190,000	170,000
Selling and administrative expense	120,000	110,000
Interest expense	4,000	2,000
Cash dividends	38,000	15,000

During 1982, a note in the amount of $25,000 was given for equipment purchased at that price. Unlike the company's other notes, which are short term, the $25,000 note matures in 1986.

Required:

a. Prepare comparative earnings statements which show for each item its percentage of net sales.

b. Prepare comparative balance sheets which show for each item its percentage of total assets.

c. Prepare a schedule which shows the percentage of each current asset to the total of current assets as of both year-end dates.

d. Compute the current ratios as of both dates.

e. Compute the acid-test ratios as of both dates.

f. Compute the percentage of stockholders' equity to total equity (or total assets) as of both dates.

P20–4–A. The following condensed balance sheet and supplementary data are for the Carradine Company for 1982:

CARRADINE COMPANY
Balance Sheet
December 31, 1982

Assets

Current Assets:

Cash	$ 400,000	
Marketable securities	250,000	
Accounts receivable	650,000	
Inventory	420,000	$1,720,000

Plant and Equipment:

Plant assets, cost	3,000,000	
Less: Accumulated depreciation................	550,000	2,450,000
Total Assets		$4,170,000

*Liabilities and
Stockholders' Equity*

Current Liabilities:

Accounts payable	$ 300,000	
Bank loans payable (due in six months)	80,000	$ 380,000

Long-Term Liabilities:

Mortgage notes payable, due in 1988..................	$ 175,000	
Bond payable, 8%, due December 31, 1990	800,000	975,000

Stockholders' Equity:

Common stock, par value $50 per share	$2,300,000	
Reserve for bond sinking fund	115,000	
Retained earnings	400,000	2,815,000
Total Liabilities and Stockholders' Equity		$4,170,000

Supplementary data:

1. 1982 interest expense, $80,000.
2. 1982 net sales, $3,000,000.
3. 1982 cost of goods sold, $2,100,000.
4. 1982 net earnings after taxes, $200,000.
5. 1982 earnings before interest and taxes, $400,000.
6. Inventory, December 31, 1981, $625,000.

Required:

Calculate the following ratios. Where you would normally use the average amount for an item in a ratio, but the information is not available to do so, use the year-end balance. (Analysts sometimes have to do this.) Show computations.

a. Current ratio.

b. Percentage of net earnings to stockholders' equity.

c. Turnover of inventory.

d. Average collection period of accounts receivable (365 days in 1982).

e. Earnings per share of common stock.

f. Number of times bond interest was earned.

g. Stockholders' equity ratio.

h. Percentage of net earnings to total assets.

i. Turnover of total assets.

j. Acid-test ratio.

P20–5–A.

	Operating assets	Net operating earnings	Net sales
Company 1....	$ 150,000	$ 20,000	$ 220,000
Company 2....	900,000	65,000	2,000,000
Company 3....	4,000,000	525,000	3,750,000

Required:

a. Determine the operating margin, turnover of operating assets, and earning power on operating assets for each company.

b. In the subsequent year the following changes took place (no other changes occurred):

Company 1 bought some new machinery at a cost of $25,000. Net operating earnings increased by $2,000 as a result of an increase in sales of $40,000.

Company 2 sold some equipment it was using which was relatively unproductive. The book value of the equipment sold was $100,000. As a result of the sale of the equipment, sales declined by $50,000 and operating earnings declined by $1,000.

Company 3 purchased some new retail outlets at a cost of $1,000,000. As a result, sales increased by $1,-500,000 and operating earnings increased by $80,000.

1. Which company has the largest absolute change in—
   a. Operating the margin ratio?
   b. Turnover of operating assets?
   c. Earning power on operating assets?
2. Which one realized the largest dollar change in operating earnings? Explain this in the light of the earning power changes.

P20–6–A. You have managed to determine the following data:

	1982	1981
Net sales	$550,000	$425,000
Net earnings before interest and taxes	90,000	30,000
Net earnings after taxes	45,000	15,000
Bond interest expense	12,000	5,000
Stockholders' equity, January 1	375,000	250,000
Stockholders' equity, December 31	400,000	375,000

Common stock, par value $50,
   December 31   300,000   180,000

Additional shares of common stock were issued on January 1, 1982.

Required:

Compute the following for both 1981 and 1982:

a. Earnings per share of common stock.

b. Percentage of net earnings to net sales.

c. Rate of return on stockholders' equity.

d. Number of times bond interest was earned.

Compare and comment.

PROBLEMS, SERIES B

P20–1–B. The following account balances are taken from the ledger of the Toynbee Company:

	December 31, 1982	December 31, 1981
Allowance for doubtful accounts	$ 32,000	$ 25,000
Prepaid expenses	15,000	20,000
Accrued liabilities	70,000	62,000
Cash in Bank A	365,000	325,000
Bank overdraft in Bank B (credit balance)	–0–	42,500
Accounts payable	238,000	195,000
Merchandise inventory	595,000	658,000
Bonds payable, due in 1987 ..	205,000	198,000
Marketable securities	72,500	49,000
Notes payable (due in six months)	151,000	91,000
Accounts receivable	469,500	433,000

Required:

a. Compute the amount of working capital as of both year-end dates.

b. Compute the current ratio as of both year-end dates.

c. Compute the acid-test ratio as of both year-end dates.

d. Comment briefly on the company's short-term financial position.

P20–2–B. On December 31, 1981, the Brandy Company's current ratio was 3:1. Assume that the following transactions were completed on that date and indicate *(a)* whether the amount of working capital would have been increased, decreased, or unaffected by each of the transactions; and *(b)* whether the current ratio would have been increased, decreased, or unaffected by each of the transactions. (Consider each transaction independently of all the others.)

1. Purchased merchandise on account.
2. Paid a cash dividend declared on November 15, 1981.
3. Sold equipment for cash.
4. Temporarily invested cash in marketable securities.
5. Sold obsolete merchandise for cash (at a loss).
6. Issued ten-year bonds for cash.
7. Wrote off Goodwill to Retained Earnings.
8. Paid cash for inventory.
9. Purchased land for cash.
10. Returned merchandise which had not been paid for.
11. Wrote off an account receivable as uncollectible.
12. Accept d a 90-day note from a customer in settlement of customer's account receivable.
13. Declared a stock dividend on common stock.

P20–3–B. From the following data of the Prader Company:

a. Prepare comparative earnings statements which show for each item its percentage of net sales.

b. Prepare comparative balance sheets which show for each item its percentage of total assets.

c. Prepare a schedule which shows the percentage of each current asset to the total of current assets as of both year-end dates.

d. Compute the current ratios as of both dates.

e. Compute the acid-test ratios as of both dates.

f. Compute the percentage of stockholders' equity to total assets as of both dates.

THE PRADER COMPANY
Comparative Balance Sheet

	December 31, 1982	December 31, 1981
Assets		
Cash	$ 25,000	$ 16,000
Accounts receivable, net	45,000	23,000
Merchandise inventory	35,000	28,000
Plant assets, net	36,000	27,000
Total Assets	$141,000	$ 94,000
Liabilities and Stockholders' Equity		
Accounts payable	$ 19,000	$ 13,000
Notes payable	25,000	14,000
Common stock	65,000	46,000
Retained earnings	32,000	21,000
Total Liabilities and Stockholders' Equity	$141,000	$ 94,000
Other data:		
Sales	$190,000	$145,000
Gross margin	115,000	95,000
Selling and administrative expense	60,000	53,000
Interest expense	2,000	700

Cash dividends of $42,000 were paid in 1982. In 1982, plant assets were increased by giving a note of $4,500 for machinery of the same cost. The note matures October 1, 1985. All other notes are short term.

P20–4–B. The following balance sheet and supplementary data are for the Yeomen Corporation for 1982:

YEOMEN CORPORATION
Balance Sheet
December 31, 1982

Assets		
Current Assets:		
Cash	$ 150,000	
Marketable securities	80,000	
Accounts receivable	130,000	
Inventory	110,000	$ 470,000
Plant and Equipment:		
Plant assets, cost	$1,700,000	
Less: Accumulated depreciation	125,000	$1,575,000
Total Assets		$2,045,000

Liabilities and Stockholders' Equity		
Current Liabilities:		
Accounts payable	$ 85,000	
Bank loans payable	35,000	$ 120,000
Long-Term Liabilities:		
Mortgage notes payable, due in 1985	$ 45,000	
Bonds payable, 6%, due December 31, 1984	215,000	260,000
Total Liabilities		$ 380,000
Stockholders' Equity:		
Common stock, par value $50 per share	$1,100,000	
Reserve for bond sinking fund	40,000	
Retained earnings	525,000	1,665,000
Total Liabilities and Stockholders' Equity		$2,045,000

Supplementary data:

1. 1982 net earnings after taxes amounted to $150,000.
2. 1982 earnings before interest and taxes, $300,000.
3. 1982 cost of goods sold was $400,000.
4. 1982 net sales amounted to $750,000.
5. Inventory on December 31, 1981, was $75,000.
6. Interest expense for the year was $15,000.

Required:

Calculate the following ratios. Where you would normally use the average amount for an item in a ratio, but the information is not available to do so, use the year-end balance. (Analysts sometimes have to do this.) Show computations.

a. Current ratio.

b. Percentage of net earnings to stockholders' equity.

c. Turnover of inventory.

d. Average collection period of accounts receivable (365 days in 1982).

e. Earnings per share of common stock.

f. Number of times bond interest was earned.

g. Stockholders' equity ratio.

h. Percentage of net earnings to total assets.

i. Turnover of total assets.

j. Acid-test ratio.

P20–5–B. The Lake Company has net operating earnings of $80,000 and operating assets of $400,000. Its net sales are $800,000.

The accountant for the company computes the rate of

earning power on operating assets after first computing the operating margin and the turnover of operating assets.

Required:

a. Show the computations the accountant made.

b. Indicate whether the operating margin and turnover will increase or decrease and then determine what the actual rate of earning power on operating assets would be after each of the following changes. The events are not interrelated; consider each separately starting from the original earning power position. No other changes occurred.

1. Sales are increased by $20,000. There is no change in the amount of operating earnings and no change in operating assets.
2. Management found some cost savings in the manufacturing process. The amount of reduction in operating expenses was $5,000. The savings resulted from the use of less materials to manufacture the same quantity of goods. As a result average inventory was $2,000 lower than it otherwise would have been.
3. The company invested $10,000 of cash (received on accounts receivable) in a plot of land it plans to use in the future (a nonoperating asset); earnings are not affected.
4. The federal income tax rate on amounts of taxable income over $50,000 was increased from 48 percent to 60 percent. The taxes have not yet been paid.
5. The company issued bonds and used the proceeds to buy $50,000 of machinery to be used in the busi-

ness. Interest payments are $2,500 per year. Operating earnings increased by $10,000 (net sales did not change).

P20–6–B.

	1982	1981
Net sales	$420,000	$260,000
Net earnings before interest and taxes	110,000	85,000
Net earnings after taxes	55,500	63,000
Bond interest expense	9,000	8,000
Stockholders' equity, December 31 (on December 31, 1980, $200,000) .	305,000	235,000
Common stock, par value $50, December 31	260,000	230,000

Additional shares of common stock were issued on January 1, 1982.

Required:

Compute the following for both 1981 and 1982:

a. Earnings per share of common stock.

b. Percentage of net earnings to net sales.

c. Rate of return on average stockholders' equity.

d. Number of times bond interest was earned.

Compare and comment.

BUSINESS DECISION PROBLEM 20–1

Shown below are the comparative balance sheets of the Bradley Corporation for December 31, 1982, and 1981:

BRADLEY CORPORATION
Comparative Balance Sheets
December 31, 1982, and 1981

	December 31, 1982	December 31, 1981
Assets		
Cash	$ 50,000	$10,000
Accounts receivable	9,000	12,000
Inventory	40,000	42,000
Plant and equipment	28,000	30,000
Total Assets	$127,000	$94,000

Liabilities and Stockholders' Equity		
Accounts payable	$ 10,000	$10,000
Common stock	70,000	70,000
Retained earnings	47,000	14,000
Total Liabilities and Stockholders' Equity . .	$127,000	$94,000

Required:

a. What were the net earnings for 1982, assuming no dividend payments?

b. What was the primary source of the large increase in the cash balance from 1981 to 1982?

c. What are the two main sources of assets for the Bradley Corporation?

d. What other comparisons and procedures would you use to complete the analysis of the balance sheet begun above?

BUSINESS DECISION PROBLEM 20–2

The information below was obtained from the annual reports of the Morley Manufacturing Company:

	1979	1980	1981	1982
Net accounts receivable ...	$ 45,000	$ 90,000	$120,000	$165,000
Net sales	400,000	550,000	625,000	800,000

Required:

a. Assume a 360-day year. If cash sales account for 30 percent of all sales and credit terms are always 1/ 10, n/60, determine all turnover ratios possible and the number of days' sales in accounts receivable at all possible dates. (The number of days' sales in accounts receivable should be based on year-end accounts receivable and net credit sales.)

b. How effective is the company's credit policy?

BUSINESS DECISION PROBLEM 20–3

Barbra Salter is interested in investing in one of three companies (X, Y, or Z) by buying its common stock. The companies' shares are selling at about the same price. The long-term capital structures of the companies are as follows:

	Company X	Company Y	Company Z
Bonds with a 10% interest rate			$ 500,000
Preferred stock with an 8% dividend rate		$ 500,000	
Common stock, $10 par	$1,000,000	500,000	500,000
Retained earnings	80,000	80,000	80,000
Total long-term equity	$1,080,000	$1,080,000	$1,080,000
Number of common shares outstanding	100,000	50,000	50,000

Ms. Salter has consulted two investment advisors. One advisor believes that each of the companies will earn $80,000 per year before interest and taxes. The other advisor believes that each company will earn about $250,000 per year before interest and taxes.

Required:

a. Compute each of the following, assuming first the estimate made by the first advisor is used and then the one made by the second advisor is used:

1. Earnings available for common stockholders, assuming a 40 percent tax rate.
2. Earnings per share of common stock.
3. Rate of return on total stockholders' equity.

b. Which stock should Ms. Salter select if she believes the first advisor?

c. Are the stockholders as a group (common and preferred) better off with or without the use of long-term debt in the above companies?

PART SEVEN

ACCOUNTING IN

MANUFACTURING COMPANIES

Chapter 21

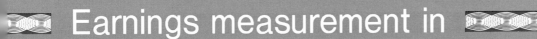
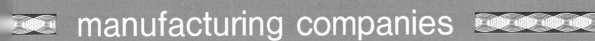

Earnings measurement in manufacturing companies

Up to this point in the text the accounting for inventory and earnings determination has been limited to retailers and wholesalers. Such firms have only one type of inventory—merchandise available for sale. Now attention is turned toward a company that makes rather than buys the goods that it sells.

COST CLASSIFICATIONS IN MANUFACTURING FIRMS

Because they involve the manufacture as well as the sale of a product, a manufacturing firm's activities are usually more extensive and complex than a merchandiser's. A manufacturer's activities can be classified broadly as (1) manufacturing or production, (2) marketing or selling, and (3) general or administrative. Since the accumulation of marketing and administrative costs under the accrual basis of accounting was dealt with in earlier chapters, only brief attention will be paid to these costs in the discussion below. Rather, attention will be focused on manufacturing costs.

The objective of a manufacturer is to use resources to produce a product that can be sold at a profit. To achieve this objective, raw materials are acquired and processed by employees and machines to convert them into finished products that are delivered to customers. For example, a furniture manufacturer converts lumber, cloth, foam rubber, and other raw materials into chairs, tables, sofas, and so on. All of these actions are taken with profit in mind.

Thus, a cost objective in measuring the costs of a manufacturer is to provide information on the cost per unit of goods manufactured. Such information is needed to determine the cost of the goods sold in earnings determination and the cost of inventories for reporting on financial position. But costs also are measured for other purposes, such as product pricing, planning, and performance evaluation.

Manufacturing costs

Cost is a money measurement of the resources used or the sacrifice made for a stated purpose. The total cost of manufacturing a product includes the costs of (1) direct materials, (2) direct labor, and (3) manufacturing overhead. These three elements of total cost are referred to as *manufacturing cost, factory cost,* or *product cost.*

Direct materials.   *The basic materials that are included in the finished product, that are clearly traceable to the product, and whose manufacture caused their usage are called direct materials.* Thus, iron ore is a direct material to a steel company, while steel is a direct material to the auto manufacturer. But some minor direct materials are often not accounted for as direct materials. For example, glue and thread used in manufacturing furniture may not be accounted for as direct materials, although they could be, simply because it is not practical to trace these items to the finished product. They would be described as *supplies* or *indirect materials* and accounted for as manufacturing overhead.

Direct materials costs include the cost of the actual quantity of materials used, priced at net invoice price, plus delivery costs. Some firms also include storage and handling costs. The method of costing inventories, such as Fifo, Lifo, and average cost, also affects the measurement of direct materials costs.

Direct labor.   *The services of employees who actually work on the materials to turn them into finished products are called direct labor.* The direct labor costs of a product include those labor costs that are clearly traceable to or readily identifiable with the product or are caused by its manufacture. Evidence that a labor cost is directly related to a product can be established by showing that the amount of labor cost incurred varies with the number of units produced. Thus, the services of the machinist, the assembler, the cutter, and the painter are classified as direct labor. But some labor services may not be accounted for as direct labor, even though they vary directly with the number of units produced. These services are broadly described as *indirect labor* and are accounted for as manufacturing overhead. Materials handling costs may be an example.

Direct labor cost is usually measured by multiplying the number of hours of direct labor services received by the hourly wage rate. The actual cost of direct labor is considerably higher than this amount because of other costs such as employer's payroll taxes, pension costs, paid vacations, paid sick leaves, and other "fringe benefits." These may amount to as much as 25 to 50 percent of the hourly wage paid. Although sometimes accounted for as part of direct labor cost, these are commonly included in manufacturing overhead.

Manufacturing overhead.   There are many alternative names for this cost category including factory indirect costs, factory burden, and manufacturing expense. However named, *the cost category includes all costs incurred in making a product, except those costs accounted for as direct materials and direct labor costs.* These manufacturing overhead costs are manufacturing costs that must be incurred but which cannot be traced directly to the units produced. As already noted, manufacturing overhead may include certain direct materials and direct labor costs because it is not practical to trace them to the units produced.

Some of the more common types of manufacturing overhead costs incurred include indirect materials, indirect labor, repairs and maintenance, depreciation of factory buildings and machinery, pensions, payroll taxes and other fringe benefits, utilities, insurance and taxes on factory property, and overtime wage premiums paid direct laborers. Indirect labor includes the salaries and wages earned by factory employees who do not work directly on the products produced but serve indirectly in their manufacture. This includes the services of timekeepers, inspectors, janitors, engineers, supervisors, materials handlers, and toolroom personnel. Overtime wage premiums are usually included in manufacturing overhead rather than being included as direct labor cost traced directly to the products worked on. The reason for this is that the need to work overtime can usually be traced to all production, not the manufacture of a given product that, by chance, happened to be the one worked on during the overtime period.

Manufacturing cost terminology.   The sum of the direct materials costs and direct labor costs incurred to manufacture a product is called *prime cost.* The sum of the direct labor costs and the manufacturing overhead costs related to a product is often referred to as *conversion cost.* As stated earlier, the sum of the three elements of cost (direct materials, direct labor, and

Illustration 21.1: Cost relationships

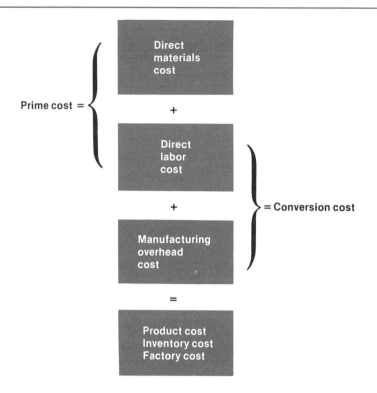

manufacturing overhead) is called *manufacturing cost, factory cost,* or *product cost.* The costs incurred to manufacture the product are "attached" to units of the product and determine the amount at which each unit of completed goods is carried in inventory until sold. The total of these costs assigned to units of product determine the amount used to measure the expense, cost of goods sold, when the products are actually sold. These cost relationships are shown in Illustration 21.1.

The product cost concept will be discussed further below. It is sufficient at this stage to recognize its general significance: classifying a cost as a product cost means that it will be recognized as an expense when the product is sold, not when the cost is recorded. Thus, the purchase of direct materials is an acquisition of an asset; the use of the direct materials creates another asset—the product; the direct materials used are recognized as an expense when the finished product is sold.

Selling and administrative costs

Selling and administrative costs differ from manufacturing costs. Selling and administrative costs are incurred in the general administration of the organization and to *dispose* of the product, not to produce it.

Selling (marketing) costs. *Selling or marketing costs* generally are classified as order-getting and order-filling costs. These terms are virtually self-explaining. Order-getting costs are costs incurred in seeking orders for products or services. They include the cost of advertising, market research, selection and training of personnel, and maintaining sales offices as well as sales salaries and commissions. Order-filling costs are the costs incurred after completion of a product until it is delivered to a customer and the resulting account receivable collected. Thus, they include costs of warehousing, delivery, installation, and servicing of a product as well as the costs of billing a customer, processing payments received, and bad debts.

Administrative (general) costs. All costs not classified as manufacturing or selling are classified as *administrative or general costs.* This category includes the costs of the top administrative functions plus those of various staff departments—accounting, finance, personnel, legal, and so on. Also included are executives' salaries and executive office expenses, donations, litigation costs, and research and development costs. How these costs are classified will differ among firms.

A cost classified as a selling and administrative cost is often called a *period cost,* as contrasted to a product cost. This means that selling and administrative costs are not attached to products and are not carried in inventory accounts. Rather, they are recorded as expenses of the period in which incurred. Thus, a sales manager's salary will be recorded as an expense in the period it is incurred. And this will hold even though the manager may be working on projects that will benefit future periods. The salary will be treated as a period cost and charged to expense because the amount to be carried forward is not material in amount, or is difficult to measure, or both.

Variable and fixed costs

Another of the most useful ways to classify the above costs is by their behavior—that is, according to how a cost changes as activity (output) changes. A cost may increase or decrease in total amount as activity increases or decreases or it may remain constant despite changes in the level of activity.

Variable costs. *Variable costs are those costs that vary in total amount directly with changes in the level of activity or output.* The best examples are found in the direct materials used in making a product. Every electric washing machine produced has one electric motor. If the motors cost $5 each, then the motor cost of one machine is $5, of two machines $10, of 100 machines $500, and so on. If the profit plans call for the production of 10,000 washing machines, then the planned cost of the motors is $50,000. Similarly, the labor cost to install the motors is a variable cost. In merchandising firms, the best examples of variable costs are cost of goods sold and sales commissions. Both will vary with the dollar volume of sales.

Fixed costs. *Fixed costs are costs that remain constant in total amount over wide variations in the level of activity.* For example, the annual license for an automobile may cost $50 whether the auto is driven 1,000 or 100,000 or some other number of miles during the year. The same may hold for the annual premium on an insurance policy on the auto. Property taxes, depreciation, rent, executives' salaries, and advertising are further examples of fixed costs. Fixed costs are often called time-related costs to distinguish them from volume-related costs.

Fixed costs present a special type of problem in determining the unit cost of producing a certain product. Since the total cost is fixed, cost *per unit* may vary widely if output varies. If the site on which a factory building is located is rented at an annual rent of $100,000, then the rental cost per ton of output is $1 if 100,000 tons are produced, $0.50 if 200,000 tons are produced, and only $0.10 if 1,000,000 tons are produced. Thus, unit cost decreases with increases in output and increases with decreases in output. This situation will be dealt with in some detail in a later chapter.

THE GENERAL COST ACCUMULATION MODEL

In manufacturing companies a primary cost objective is to measure the cost per unit to manufacture a product. Unit product costs are measured under the principle that such costs consist of (1) direct materials and direct labor plus (2) a fair share of the other factory indirect costs incurred. This cost information is needed for financial reporting and pricing and is required for income tax purposes.

Product and cost flows

The accounting systems of manufacturing firms tend to have a similar general framework because the products manufactured flow through each firm in a similar order. Raw or basic materials are acquired; direct labor services and other factory services are used to process the materials into completed products ready for sale. The accounting records are set up in such a way as to show a flow of costs through the records that matches the physical flow of product through the firm. These relationships are shown graphically in Illustration 21.2.

Physically, the products move from the raw materials warehouse to the production department. During production they are partially completed manufactured products and are called *work in process.* Eventually they become completed manufactured products and are called *finished goods.* They are then moved to the finished goods warehouse and then delivered to customers. The accounting records show the flow of costs from the Materials Inventory into Work in Process Inventory where the costs of direct labor and other factory services are added. When the products are completed, their costs are moved to the Finished Goods Inventory account and, upon sale, transferred to the Cost of Goods Sold account.

Because it has products in various stages of completion, the accounts

Illustration 21.2: Product and cost flows

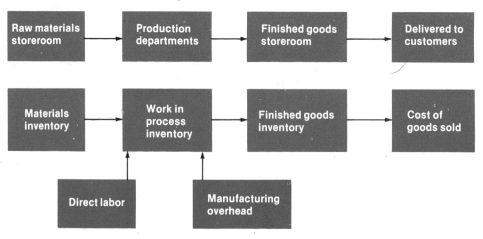

and financial statements of a manufacturer typically will show three types of inventories: Materials, Work in Process, and Finished Goods. At any given time the amount or balance in each of these accounts will depend upon many factors, including the availability of materials and the level of customer demand.

Accounting for cost and revenue flows

Knowledge of the general flow of costs and revenues through a manufacturing firm is of value in understanding a cost system. For this reason, an example using dollar amounts is presented below and summarized graphically in Illustration 21.3. The lines running between accounts show the transfer or flow of costs from one account to the next.

Illustration 21.3: Cost and revenue flowchart

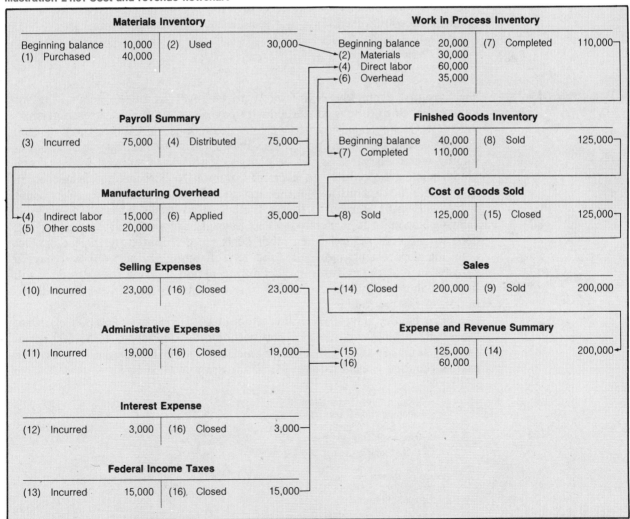

To begin the illustration, it is assumed that the inventories of the Brice Company as of July 1, 1981, were:

Materials inventory	$10,000
Work in process inventory	20,000
Finished goods inventory	40,000

The company's activities for July are summarized below, together with further explanation.

The flow of direct materials costs

During July, $40,000 of materials were purchased on account and $30,000 were issued to production from the storeroom. The entries required (numbered to key to the entries in the T-accounts in Illustration 21.3) are:

1.	Materials Inventory	40,000	
	Accounts Payable		40,000
	To record purchases of raw materials on account.		

(Note: In order to focus attention upon cost and revenue flows, the credit to Accounts Payable is not included in Illustration 21.3.)

2.	Work in Process Inventory	30,000	
	Materials Inventory		30,000
	To record direct materials issued to production.		

The flow of labor costs

Two groups of employees are likely to be involved in the accounting for labor costs. One group is concerned with *payroll accounting*—that is, determining the total wages earned, the various deductions, and the net pay of each employee. The second group engages in *labor cost accounting*—that is, determining which accounts are to be charged with what amount of labor costs. Under such a procedure, an account common to both groups is needed to tie together the separate accounting activities. In Illustration 21.3, this account is called Payroll Summary. It is a temporarily established account called a clearing account. It is debited when payrolls are prepared by the payroll department and credited when labor costs are distributed by the factory accounting department. Normally, the Payroll Summary account will have a zero balance at the end of any accounting period. During the period, it will have a balance only because of the time lag between preparation and distribution of the payroll.

The factory payrolls for July amounted to $75,000—$60,000 of direct labor, and $15,000 indirect. Payroll withholdings amounted to $3,500 social security taxes, $8,000 of federal income taxes, and $500 of union dues. The entries required (keyed [3] and [4] in Illustration 21.3) are:

3.	Payroll Summary	75,000	
	Social security Taxes Withheld		3,500
	Federal Income Taxes Withheld		8,000
	Union Dues Withheld		500
	Accrued Payroll		63,000
	To record factory payroll and various withholdings.		

4.	Work in Process Inventory	60,000	
	Manufacturing Overhead	15,000	
	Payroll Summary		75,000
	To distribute labor costs for the month.		

The accrued payroll will be paid in cash to the employees, while the amounts withheld will be paid on their behalf to the federal government and the union at a later date. Entries showing such payments are omitted here as not being relevant to our purposes, as are the various credits in entry 3. Entry 3 records the various liabilities incurred upon receipt of factory employee services. Entry 4 adds to Work in Process Inventory the cost of the labor traceable to the products being manufactured and transfers those labor costs not traceable to products to Manufacturing Overhead.

The flow of overhead costs

The indirect costs of operating the factory during the period included repairs of $1,000, property taxes of $1,500, equipment rent of $2,500, payroll taxes of $3,500, utilities of $4,000, insurance of $2,000, and factory building depreciation of $5,500. Entry 5 shows the recording of these costs:

5.	Manufacturing Overhead	20,000	
	Cash		1,000
	Accounts Payable		4,000
	Accrued Property Taxes Payable		1,500
	Unexpired Insurance		2,000
	Prepaid Rent		2,500
	Accumulated Depreciation—Factory Building		5,500
	Accrued Payroll Taxes Payable		3,500
	To record factory indirect costs for the period.		

Entries would also be made in supporting accounts or records maintained for each type of manufacturing overhead cost incurred. The credits assumed to accompany the $20,000 debit to manufacturing overhead are omitted from Illustration 21.3 as not being relevant to the showing of cost flows.

The manufacturing overhead costs are as much a part of the cost of the period's production as are the costs of direct materials and direct labor. These costs must, therefore, be added to the costs already in the Work in Process Inventory account, and this is done in entry 6:

6.	Work in Process Inventory	35,000	
	Manufacturing Overhead		35,000
	To assign overhead to work in process.		

The assignment of overhead to work in process is a problem that is dealt with later. For purposes of Illustration 21.3, it is assumed that the overhead incurred during a period is to be assigned to the production of the period.

The flow of finished goods

As shown in Illustration 21.3, for product costing purposes, Work in Process Inventory is charged with the materials, labor, and overhead costs of producing goods. When the goods are completed and transferred out of production, an entry is made to transfer their cost from Work in Process Inventory to Finished Goods Inventory. Assuming goods costing $110,000 were completed and transferred, the entry needed is:

7.	Finished Goods Inventory	110,000	
	Work in Process Inventory		110,000
	To record transfer of completed goods.		

Now let it be assumed that goods costing $125,000 were sold on account for $200,000. Entries are now required to record the sale of the goods and to record the transfer out of the Finished Goods Inventory account of the cost of the goods sold. The required entries are:

```
 8. Costs of Goods Sold ....................................    125,000
       Finished Goods Inventory ................................           125,000
       To record cost of goods sold.

 9. Accounts Receivable ....................................    200,000
       Sales ...............................................           200,000
       To record sales on account.
```

Once again, since we are concerned with costs and revenues, the debit to Accounts Receivable in entry 9 is omitted from Illustration 21.3.

To complete the explanation of the entries in the accounts in Illustration 21.3, assume that selling expenses of $23,000, administrative expenses of $19,000, interest expense of $3,000, and federal income taxes of $15,000 were incurred in July. The required entries are:

```
10. Selling Expenses ......................................    23,000
       Various asset and liability accounts ......................           23,000
       To record selling expenses incurred in July.

11. Administrative Expenses ..................................    19,000
       Various asset and liability accounts ......................           19,000
       To record administrative expenses incurred in July.

12. Interest Expense .......................................    3,000
       Accrued Interest Payable ........ ......................           3,000
       To record interest expense incurred in July.

13. Federal Income Taxes ..................................    15,000
       Federal Income Taxes Payable ........................           15,000
       To record estimated income taxes for July.
```

Subsidiary records or accounts would be kept for the various types of selling and administrative expenses incurred, but, for brevity, are omitted here. The credits in entries 10 and 11 would be to accounts such as Cash, Accounts Payable, Salaries Payable, Accumulated Depreciation, and so on. They are omitted from Illustration 21.3, as are the credits in entries 12 and 13, to keep attention directed toward costs, expenses and revenues.

Although the accounts are usually formally closed only at the end of the accounting year, entry 14 records the closing of the Sales revenue account for the month of July as an illustration of the annual entry:

```
14. Sales ................................................    200,000
       Expense and Revenue Summary ......................           200,000
       To close Sales revenue account.
```

Entries 15 and 16 are required to close the expense accounts:

```
15. Expense and Revenue Summary ..........................    125,000
       Cost of Goods Sold .....................................           125,000
       To close Cost of Goods Sold account.
```

16.	Expense and Revenue Summary	60,000	
	Selling Expenses		23,000
	Administrative Expenses		19,000
	Interest Expense		3,000
	Federal Income Taxes		15,000

To close other expense accounts.

The closing process would, of course, be completed by debiting the Expense and Revenue Summary account and crediting the Retained Earnings account for $15,000. Here again, this entry is omitted for brevity.

As a technical matter, the accounting for the costs of manufacturing operations ends with entry 7. The other entries are included to provide a complete set of illustrative entries for a manufacturing company.

FINANCIAL REPORTING BY MANUFACTURING COMPANIES

Typically, it would be difficult to determine from a statement of retained earnings and a statement of changes in financial position whether the issuing company was a merchandiser or a manufacturer. But this would not hold for a balance sheet or an earnings statement.

The balance sheet

The balance sheet (or the notes thereto) typically will disclose separately the manufacturer's inventories of materials, work in process, and finished goods as well as factory supplies. By way of contrast, a merchandiser will report a single merchandise inventory amount and, perhaps in prepaid expenses, the cost of supplies on hand. The manufacturer's statement may also show, as intangible assets, patents and trademarks relating to the products manufactured and sold. And it may contain greater detail in the property, plant, and equipment section because of the ownership of assets used in manufacturing. But these present little in the line of additional problems.

The earnings statement

The preparation of a manufacturer's earnings statement is considerably more complex than for a merchandiser. The manufacturer incurs so many additional costs in producing goods rather than buying them, ready for sale, as a merchandiser does. Because of this greater detail, a question arises as to how detailed an earnings statement should be. To a large extent, the answer depends upon to whom the statement is to be shown.

If the earnings statement is to be published in an annual report, it is usually in very condensed form, differing little from a merchandiser's earnings statement. Such a statement is shown in Illustration 21.4 which reports on

Illustration 21.4: Earnings statement of a manufacturer

BRICE COMPANY Earnings Statement For the Month Ended July 31, 1981		
Sales		$200,000
Cost of goods sold	$125,000	
Selling expenses	23,000	
Administrative expenses	19,000	
Interest expense	3,000	
Federal income taxes	15,000	185,000
Net Earnings		$ 15,000

the just discussed activities of the Brice Company which are summarized in Illustration 21.3. Although it is common practice to include comparative data (the earnings statement for July 1980) when financial statements are released to the public, such data are omitted here.

The same type of earnings statement could be used in reporting to top management and to the board of directors. When so used, it is likely to be in comparative form, containing data for the same period last year, and to contain budgeted data. It is also likely to be supported by a statement of cost of goods manufactured and sold and with the schedules showing the details of the selling and administrative expenses, complete with comparative and budgeted data.

The statement of cost of goods manufactured and sold

Illustration 21.5 contains the statement of cost of goods manufactured and sold for the Brice Company for the month of July 1981. Note how it shows the costs incurred during the month for materials, labor, and overhead and describes this total as *"Cost to manufacture."* By adding to this amount the July 1 inventory and subtracting the July 31 inventory of work in process, the *"Cost of goods manufactured"* (completed) during the period is shown. When the July 1 finished goods inventory is added to this amount, the *"Cost of goods available for sale"* is obtained. This amount less the July 31 finished goods inventory yields the *"Cost of goods sold."* At this stage, note the following similarity:

Merchandiser: Beginning merchandise inventory + Purchases − Ending merchandise inventory = Cost of goods sold

Illustration 21.5: Statement of cost of goods manufactured and sold

BRICE COMPANY Statement of Cost of Goods Manufactured and Sold For the Month Ended July 31, 1981		
Direct materials		$ 30,000
Direct labor		60,000
Manufacturing overhead:		
Indirect labor	$15,000	
Building depreciation	5,500	
Utilities	4,000	
Payroll taxes	3,500	
Equipment rent	2,500	
Insurance	2,000	
Property taxes	1,500	
Repairs	1,000	35,000
Cost to manufacture		$125,000
Work in process, July 1, 1981		20,000
		$145,000
Work in process, July 31, 1981		35,000
Cost of goods manufactured		$110,000
Finished goods, July 1, 1981		40,000
Cost of goods available for sale		$150,000
Finished goods, July 31, 1981		25,000
Cost of goods sold		$125,000

Manufacturer: Beginning finished goods inventory + Cost of goods manufactured—Ending finished goods inventory = Cost of goods sold

Careful attention should be paid to the terminology used in the statement of cost of goods manufactured and sold. Note the similarity between "Cost to manufacture" and "Cost of goods manufactured." *"Cost to manufacture"* consists of the costs of all of the resources put into production in the period. *"Cost of goods manufactured"* consists of the cost of the goods completed and includes "Cost to manufacture" and the change in the Work in Process inventory from the beginning to the end of the period.

Use of a work sheet

The work sheet illustrated in Chapter 5 for a merchandising company can also be used for a manufacturing company. The amounts shown in the trial balance for raw materials inventory, work in process inventory, and finished goods inventory will be the end of period balances (when the perpetual method is used in manufacturing companies). The amounts would be carried to the Balance Sheet debit column as shown below. The cost of goods sold amount will be included with the other expenses in the trial balance. If any balance remains in the Manufacturing Overhead account at the end of the period, it would be transferred to the Cost of Goods Sold account as an adjusting entry. The adjusted amount of cost of goods sold would be carried to the Earnings Statement debit column as shown below. All other steps in preparing the work sheet are as described in Chapter 5.

	Trial Balance		Adjustments		Adjusted Trial Balance		Earnings Statement		Balance Sheet	
	Debit	Credit	Debit	Credit	Debit	Credit	Debit	Credit	Debit	Credit
Materials inventory	xxx				xxx				xxx	
Work in process inventory	xxx				xxx				xxx	
Finished goods inventory	xxx				xxx				xxx	
Manufacturing overhead	xxx			(a) xx						
Cost of goods sold	xxx		(a) xx		xxx		xxx			

A graphic summary

The discussion of a manufacturer's activities that lead to the recognition of net earnings is summarized graphically in Illustration 21.6. Several implications of the accounting for such activities are worth stressing again.

First, the accounting for the costs of manufacturing operations is an integral part of the overall accounting system of the manufacturer. No separate system is used to accumulate manufacturing cost information.

Second, as Illustration 21.6 shows, manufacturing costs are considered product costs, are attached to the products manufactured, and are run through

Illustration 21.6: A manufacturing company's total operations

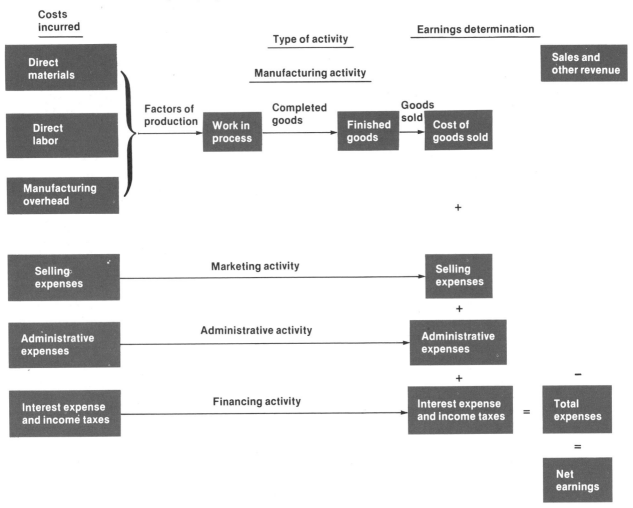

work in process and finished goods inventories. They are recognized as expenses when the products to which they attach are sold. Selling and administrative costs are treated as period costs and expensed in the period in which incurred. They are not "inventoriable" costs.

MANUFACTURING OVERHEAD RATES

To focus on the general pattern of cost flows shown in Illustration 21.3, certain problems in accounting for manufacturing overhead were not discussed. These problems arise primarily because the costs of a wide variety of factory services having no common physical basis of measurement must be allocated to many different products. By their nature and for practical reasons, such costs are not traceable to or identifiable with any given unit of product.

Before directing attention to these problems, the terms *cost center, production center,* and *service center* need to be introduced and defined. A *cost center* is an accounting unit of activity for accumulating costs having a common objective. That is, the items of cost recorded as having been incurred by a given cost center all seek to accomplish the same objective or purpose. Thus, the costs incurred in the assembly department of a furniture manufacturer seek to bring about the assembly of furniture and can, therefore, be allocated to the products assembled. A cost center in which work is performed on units of product is called a *production center.* A *service center* is a cost center in which work indirectly related to the goods produced is performed. A tool room, maintenance department, power plant, and even the company cafeteria are examples of service centers.

General procedures

Illustration 21.7 depicts graphically the general procedures followed in loading indirect factory costs on the units of product manufactured by a company producing a line of unfinished redwood patio furniture. Manufacturing operations are conducted in two production centers, cutting and assembly, and two service centers, building occupancy and general.

The general procedures followed in allocating overhead to products consist of three tasks:

Task 1. All manufacturing overhead costs incurred in a period are charged initially to one and only one service center or production center. In this way, the sum of the overhead charged to the four centers equals the total overhead incurred in a period. Thus, the cost of supplies used is charged to the center where they are consumed, indirect labor cost is charged to the center where the employee works, and so on. All overhead costs incurred to house factory operations, such as building depreciation, taxes, and insurance, are charged to the occupancy center. All overhead costs not traceable to or identifiable with one of the other three centers are charged to the general service center. Section I of Illustration 21.8 shows this initial assignment of overhead costs to the four cost centers of our patio furniture manufacturer.

Illustration 21.7: Manufacturing overhead allocated to products

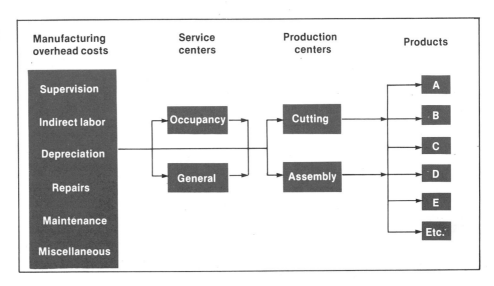

Task 2. The total overhead costs accumulated in the service centers are now reassigned to the production centers. The objective is to ultimately accumulate all overhead costs in production centers only. Some service center costs, such as those incurred to generate electricity or steam, may be charged to other cost centers on the basis of the metered amounts actually consumed. Repair costs may be charged on a "time and materials" basis. Still other costs will have to be allocated on some reasonable basis such as square feet of floor space occupied, number of employees, dollars of payroll cost, or some other measure of activity. The guiding principle is to allocate service center costs to the production centers that benefited from or caused the incurrence of these costs.

Illustration 21.8:
Allocating overhead to
products

	Production centers		Service centers		
	Cutting	Assembly	Occupancy	General	Total
I. Initial assignment					
Cost element					
Indirect labor	$ 3,000	$ 2,500	–0–	$ 5,000	$10,500
Depreciation	2,000	1,000	$ 4,000	500	7,500
Other	10,000	8,500	6,000	9,500	34,000
	$15,000	$12,000	$10,000	$15,000	$52,000
II. Service center costs					
reassigned					
Occupancy	5,000	4,000	(10,000)	1,000	
General	10,000	6,000		(16,000)	
Total overhead costs	$30,000	$22,000	–0–	–0–	$52,000
III. Allocations to products					
Direct labor-hours	7,500	5,000			
Manufacturing overhead					
rate per direct labor-hour	$ 4.00	$ 4.40			

The step method. A special problem was faced in reassigning service center costs in Illustration 21.8, Section II. The two service centers rendered services not only to the production centers but to each other. This implies that some of the costs of each service center should be allocated to the other service center. The question then is: How does one avoid an almost endless process of allocating costs back and forth between the two service centers? One practical solution is to allocate such costs in a prescribed order. Start with one service center, allocate its costs to the production and other service centers; now choose a second service center and allocate its cost. Make no allocation of its costs to the first service center. Proceed in this manner until all service center costs have been allocated. This is known as the **step** *method.* But accountants disagree on how to determine the order in which the service centers' costs are to be allocated. Some argue the most costly service center should be allocated first simply because it provides the most services. Yet others suggest allocating the least significant center first. Significance is judged by the number of cost centers serviced by a given service center. If this test cannot be used, significance can be determined by the dollar amounts of costs incurred. This procedure is used in Illustration 21.8 and results in the occupancy center's costs being allocated first. The allocation was based on relative square feet of floor space occupied: 50 percent to cutting, 40 percent to assembly, and 10 percent to general. The general service center's costs ($16,000) are then allocated on the basis of prime costs (direct materials + direct labor) charged to the two production centers ($50,000 cutting and $30,000 assembly). Thus, the allocations are cutting, ⅝ of $16,000, or $10,000; assembly ⅜ of $16,000, or $6,000.

Task 3.   The total overhead, now accumulated in production centers only, is allocated to the units of product worked on in each center. It is seldom possible to divide the number of units of product into the total overhead costs of a production center to allocate overhead to products for two reasons: (1) different products may be involved—our furniture factory makes benches and tables of different sizes, as well as settees, chairs, chaise lounges, and so forth; and (2) some products may be only partially completed. But all of the products do have things in common. They all have direct materials costs, direct labor costs, have been worked on for a number of direct labor-hours, and may have required a certain amount of machine time. This leads to the computation of an *overhead rate*, wherein the overhead incurred is expressed as an amount per some unit of activity, such as the direct labor-hours used in Section III of Illustration 21.8. In computing overhead rates, the objective is to use a measure of activity that is closely related to the amount of overhead incurred.

After the overhead rates have been computed, overhead cost can readily be allocated to products. For example, if the production of 100 tables required 10 direct labor-hours in the cutting department and 20 hours in the assembly department, the total overhead charged to these tables would be:

$$
\begin{array}{lrl}
\text{Cutting:} & 10 \times \$4.00 = & \$\ \ 40 \\
\text{Assembly:} & 20 \times \$4.40 = & \underline{\ \ \ 88} \\
& \text{Total overhead} & \underline{\underline{\$128}}
\end{array}
$$

Predetermined overhead rates

In the above discussion, overhead rates were determined at the end of a period (say, a month). But, although some companies may follow such a procedure, it is far more common to use a *predetermined* overhead rate to allocate overhead to production. The rate is usually set at the beginning of the year. The reasons for this more common practice include:

1. Overhead costs are seldom incurred uniformly throughout the year as, for example, heating costs will be large in winter. No useful purpose is served in allocating less cost to a unit produced in the summer than one produced in the winter.
2. The volume of goods produced may vary from month to month with accompanying sharp fluctuations in average unit cost if some overhead costs are fixed.
3. Unit costs of production are known sooner. Using a predetermined rate, overhead costs can be assigned to production when direct materials and

direct labor costs are assigned. Without a predetermined rate, unit costs would not be known until the end of the month or even much later if bills for overhead costs are late.

4. Some overhead costs may be better viewed as losses due to inefficiencies rather than costs properly assigned to units of product.

Computing predetermined overhead rates. The mechanics of computing predetermined overhead rates are the same as those used for actual rates except for the use of budgeted rather than actual levels of costs and levels of activity. Budgeted overhead costs are first estimated and charged to the various cost centers. Budgeted service center costs are then reassigned to production centers. Budgeted production center costs are then divided by the estimate of the level of activity to compute the predetermined rates. These budget estimates will normally be available as part of the company's budgeting process, which is discussed in Chapter 25.

Choosing the level of activity to be used in setting predetermined overhead rates is a special problem that will now be discussed.

Levels of activity. Setting overhead rates, especially when large amounts of fixed overhead costs are incurred, involves the problem of choosing the level of activity to be used. As already demonstrated, it would be possible to wait until the end of the period and use actual rates to apply overhead to production. Thus, if $100,000 of fixed overhead costs were incurred and ten units were produced, the overhead cost per unit would be $10,000. If 1,000 units were produced, it would be $100. And the wide fluctuation in unit cost would be due solely to the differing number of units produced.

But suppose the plant was designed to produce 100,000 units per period. Now might it not be logical to argue that the *applied (absorbed) overhead* for each unit should be $1 ($100,000 ÷ 100,000) and that any underapplied overhead from producing less than 100,000 units is a loss from idle capacity? Many accountants would so argue. Thus, the issue is: What level of activity should be used in setting overhead rates?

Among the different levels of activity that might be used, the three most commonly found in practice today are:

1. *Practical capacity*—the maximum attainable output of a plant. It is theoretical capacity less allowance for the fact that individuals can seldom achieve perfection. Its use results in only the costs of the facilities actually used being charged to production. If a plant operated at 60 percent of capacity, 60 percent of its fixed costs would be charged to production, and the remaining 40 percent would be treated as a period cost (loss).
2. *Normal activity*—the level of activity expected to prevail over the long run, say, three to five years. Its use is based on the belief that over the long run all manufacturing costs are to be absorbed in production and recovered through sale of the goods.
3. *Expected activity*—the estimated level of activity for the coming period. This level of activity has the objective of absorbing all fixed overhead for a period in the production of that period.

The level of activity problem illustrated. To illustrate, consider the data in the following schedule. Assume that fixed overhead costs are $480,000 per period and that variable overhead costs amount to $1.50 per direct labor-hour over a range of 40,000 to 100,000 hours.

	Direct labor-hours for the year	Budgeted overhead for the year		
		Variable	Fixed	Total
Practical capacity	100,000	$150,000	$480,000	$630,000
Normal capacity	80,000	120,000	480,000	600,000
Expected activity	60,000	90,000	480,000	570,000

From these data, three predetermined overhead rates could be computed as follows:

1. Practical capacity rate: $630,000 ÷ 100,000 = $6.30 per direct labor-hour.
2. Normal capacity rate: $600,000 ÷ 80,000 = $7.50 per direct labor-hour.
3. Expected activity rate: $570,000 ÷ 60,000 = $9.50 per direct labor-hour.

Note that in each of these rates variable overhead accounts for $1.50 of the total rate. Thus, it is the fixed overhead rate that varies. If the actual overhead costs incurred during the year amounted to $480,000 fixed and $75,000 variable and actual direct labor-hours of services received amounted to 50,000 hours, the actual overhead rate would be $11.10 ($555,000 ÷ 50,000).

Note further the differing amounts of overhead that would be applied to work in process depending upon the level of activity used in setting the rate when 50,000 hours of direct labor services were received:

Practical capacity-based rate: 50,000 × $6.30 = $315,000
Normal capacity-based rate: 50,000 × $7.50 = 375,000
Expected activity-based rate: 50,000 × $9.50 = 475,000

Underapplied or overapplied overhead. When overhead is applied to production using predetermined rates, the manufacturing overhead account is credited with *estimated* amounts applied to work in process inventory. This follows because the rate is based on estimates when it is established. Under these circumstances, it is highly unlikely that the actual costs debited to the account will exactly equal the overhead applied and credited to the account. A *debit balance* will remain if actual overhead exceeds applied overhead and overhead will be *underapplied* or *underabsorbed*. A *credit balance* will remain if applied overhead exceeds actual overhead, and overhead will be *overapplied* or *overabsorbed*.

Refer to Illustration 21.3. If overhead is allocated to production using a predetermined rate of 50 percent of direct labor cost, entry 6 given earlier would read:

Work in Process Inventory 30,000
    Manufacturing Overhead   30,000
  To assign overhead to work in process.

Since $35,000 of actual overhead costs were charged to Manufacturing Overhead, the account would have a $5,000 debit balance representing underapplied overhead for the period.

Reasons for underapplied or overapplied overhead. Underapplied or overapplied overhead may be a result of unexpected events such as price changes, a severe winter, or excessive repairs. Or overhead items may be used inefficiently. But underapplied overhead is more likely to be caused by incurring costs at a higher level than that set in the typical "tight" budget. On the other hand, overapplied overhead is likely to be the result of operating at a higher actual level than that used in setting the overhead rate and to the existence of fixed overhead costs.

Disposition of underapplied or overapplied overhead.   Any under- or overapplied overhead balance can be carried forward in interim statements of financial position if the probability exists that it will be reduced or offset by future operations. At year-end, any remaining balance could be allocated to Work in Process Inventory, Finished Goods Inventory, and Cost of Goods Sold by recomputing the cost of production for the year using actual overhead rates.

As an alternative, charging underapplied overhead off as a loss of the period has particular merit if it results from idle capacity or from unusual circumstances. But, as a practical matter, underapplied or overapplied overhead is frequently transferred to Cost of Goods Sold. Little distortion of net earnings or of assets results from this treatment if the amount transferred is small or if most of the goods produced during the year were sold. Thus, the entry to dispose of the $5,000 of underapplied overhead in the example would read:

Cost of Goods Sold	5,000	
Manufacturing Overhead		5,000
To dispose of underapplied overhead.		

The next two chapters continue with the discussion of accounting for a manufacturing company.

NEW TERMS INTRODUCED IN CHAPTER 21

Administrative or general costs—costs other than manufacturing or selling; includes costs of top administrative functions plus various staff departments.

Applied (absorbed) overhead—indirect factory costs applied to units of product.

Conversion cost—direct labor cost plus manufacturing overhead (indirect factory) cost.

Cost—a money measure of the resources used or the sacrifice made for a stated purpose called the *cost objective.*

Cost center—an accounting unit of activity for accumulating costs having a common cost objective.

Cost of goods manufactured—cost to manufacture plus beginning and less ending work in process inventory.

Cost to manufacture—the cost of all resources put into production during a period; the sum of the costs of direct materials, direct labor, and manufacturing overhead placed in production in a period.

Direct labor—the services of employees actually working on materials to convert them to finished goods.

Direct materials—materials that are clearly traceable to, physically included in, and used as a result of the manufacture of a product.

Expected activity—a level of activity used in setting overhead rates; the estimate of some measure of activity, such as direct labor-hours, that is expected to prevail in the coming period.

Factory cost—*see* Manufacturing cost.

Finished goods (products)—completed manufactured products; also the title of an inventory account maintained for such products.

Fixed cost—a cost that remains constant in total amount despite changes in output or level of activity.

Indirect labor—services of factory employees that cannot or will not, for practical reasons, be traced to the products being manufactured.

Indirect materials—materials used in the manufacture of a product that cannot or will not, for practical reasons, be traced directly to the products being manufactured.

Manufacturing cost—the cost incurred to produce or create a product. It includes direct materials, direct labor, and manufacturing overhead costs.

Manufacturing overhead—all materials and services needed in the manufacture of products, except those accounted for as direct materials and direct labor.

Normal activity—a level of activity used in setting overhead rates, especially the fixed overhead rate, that uses an average of the level of activity that is expected to prevail over a longer period of time such as three to five years.

Overapplied (overabsorbed) overhead—the amount by which the overhead allocated to units of product manufactured in a period exceeds the actual overhead costs incurred in that same period.

Overhead rate—a means of applying overhead to units of product; usually *predetermined* by dividing estimated overhead by some estimate of the number of units in some measure of activity such as direct labor-hours or machine-hours; separate rates may be computed for variable overhead and for fixed overhead.

Practical capacity—a level of activity used in setting overhead rates, especially the fixed overhead rate; equal to the theoretical engineering capacity of a plant less an allowance for the less-than-perfect conduct of the humans involved.

Period cost—a cost usually incurred in the selling or administrative activities of a firm that is treated as an expense of the period in which incurred.

Prime cost—the sum of the direct materials and direct labor costs of a product.

Product cost—(*see also* Manufacturing cost). A cost incurred in the manufacture of a product. It is attached to the product and is treated as an expense when the product is sold.

Production center—a cost center in which work is performed directly on units of product, or a part thereof.

Selling or marketing costs—order getting and order filling costs.

Service center—a cost center in which work indirectly related to the manufacture of a product is performed.

Statement of cost of goods manufactured and sold—a formal accounting report showing (1) the cost to manufacture, (2) the cost of goods manufactured, (3) the cost of goods available for sale, and (4) the cost of goods sold.

Step method—a prescribed order of allocating reciprocal service center costs.

Underapplied (underabsorbed) overhead—the amount by which the actual overhead costs incurred in a period exceed the overhead applied to the units of products manufactured in that period.

Variable cost—a cost that varies in total amount with changes in the level of output or activity.

Work in process—partially completed manufactured products; the title of an inventory account maintained for such products.

DEMONSTRATION PROBLEM

Part 1.   Selected data for the Adams Company for June 1981 are:

Materials inventory, June 1	$ 21,000
Materials purchased	52,000
Materials inventory, June 30	5,000
Direct labor cost	30,000
Work in process inventory, June 1	7,000
Work in process inventory, June 30	51,000
Cost of goods sold	102,000
Finished goods inventory, June 1	41,000
Finished goods inventory, June 30	22,000
Sales	165,000
Selling and administrative expenses	35,000

Required:

a. Give journal entries to record the cost of the materials used and the cost of the goods completed.

b. Compute the amount of manufacturing overhead charged to production in June.

c. Prepare a condensed earnings statement supported by a schedule showing the cost of the goods manufactured and sold.

Part 2.   The following are budget estimates for the Byrnes Company to be used in setting predetermined overhead rates for its two production centers—cutting and assembly. The company operates two service centers—building and personnel—whose costs are to be allocated, building center first, via the step method. Building center fixed costs are to be allocated on the basis of square feet of floor space occupied; personnel center variable costs are to be allocated on the basis of budgeted number of employees; fixed costs on the basis of employees needed at practical capacity.

	Cutting	Assembly	Building	Personnel	Total
Budgeted variable costs	$38,500	$61,500	$ –0–	$10,000	$110,000
Budgeted fixed costs	19,000	32,000	40,000	43,000	134,000
Totals	$57,500	$93,500	$40,000	$53,000	$244,000
Square feet of floor space occupied	8,000	10,000		2,000	20,000
Employees needed at practical capacity ...	110	125	5	5	245
Budgeted number of employees	90	110	4	5	209
Budgeted direct labor-hours	20,000	24,000	—	—	44,000

Required:

a. Allocate the service center costs to the production centers for purposes of setting predetermined overhead rates.(Hint: In computing the number of units in an allocation base, be sure to reduce the total number given by the number in a closed service center and in the center being allocated.)

b. Compute the predetermined overhead rates, based on direct labor-hours, for each production center.

Solution to demonstration problem

Part 1.

a. Work in Process 68,000
       Materials Inventory 68,000
    To record materials used ($21,000 + $52,000 – $5,000).

    Finished Goods 83,000
       Work in Process 83,000
    To record cost of goods completed:

Finished goods, June 30	$ 22,000
Cost of goods sold	102,000
Total	$124,000
Finished goods, June 1	41,000
Cost of goods completed	$ 83,000

b.

Work in process, June 30	$ 51,000
Cost of goods completed	83,000
	$134,000
Less: Work in process, June 1	$ 7,000
Direct materials	68,000
Direct labor	30,000
Total debits to work in process excluding overhead	105,000
Manufacturing overhead applied in June	$ 29,000

c.

```
                    ADAMS COMPANY
                   Earnings Statement
              For the Month Ended June 30, 1981

Sales ..................................................            $165,000
Cost of goods sold ...................................  $102,000
Selling and administrative expenses ..................    35,000    137,000
Net Earnings (before income taxes) ...................            $ 28,000

                    ADAMS COMPANY
        Statement of Cost of Goods Manufactured and Sold
              For the Month Ended June 30, 1981

Direct materials .....................................            $ 68,000
Direct labor .........................................              30,000
Manufacturing overhead ...............................              29,000
Cost to manufacture ..................................            $127,000
Work in process, June 1 ..............................               7,000
                                                                 $134,000
Work in process, June 30 .............................              51,000
Cost of goods manufactured ...........................            $ 83,000
Finished goods, June 1 ...............................              41,000
Cost of goods available for sale .....................            $124,000
Finished goods, June 30 ..............................              22,000
        Cost of goods sold ...........................            $102,000
```

Part 2.
a. and b.

	Cutting	Assembly	Building	Personnel	Total
Budgeted variable costs	$ 38,500	$ 61,500	–0–	$ 10,000	$110,000
Budgeted fixed costs	19,000	32,000	$ 40,000	43,000	134,000
Totals	$ 57,500	$ 93,500	$ 40,000	$ 53,000	$244,000
Allocate building center's fixed costs on basis of square feet of floor space occupied (40:50:10)	16,000	20,000	(40,000)	4,000	
Allocate personnel center variable costs on basis of budgeted number of employees (90:110)......	4,500	5,500		(10,000)	
Allocate personnel center fixed costs on basis of employees needed at practical capacity (110:125)	22,000	25,000		(47,000)	
Totals	$100,000	$144,000	–0–	–0–	$244,000
Budgeted direct labor-hours ...	20,000	24,000			
Predetermined overhead rate per direct labor-hour ...	$5	$6			

QUESTIONS

1. Identify the three broad classifications of costs incurred by manufacturing firms. Indicate why it is important that costs not be incorrectly classified.

2. Identify the three elements of cost incurred in manufacturing a product and indicate the distinguishing characteristics of each.

3. Why might a firm claim that the total cost of employing a person is $10.30 per hour even though the employee's wage rate is $6.50 per hour? How should this difference be classified and why?

4. In general, what is the relationship between cost flows in the accounts and the flow of physical products through a factory?

5. What is meant by the term product cost? State the general principle under which product costs are accumulated.

6. What is the general content of a statement of cost of goods manufactured and sold? What is its relationship to the earnings statement?

7. What is the typical accounting for the overtime wage premium paid a direct laborer? Why? Under what circumstances might an alternative accounting be considered preferable?

8. Why are certain costs referred to as period costs? What are the major types of period costs incurred by a manufacturer?

9. What deficiencies do you see in an accounting system that assigns the actual overhead incurred in a month to the production of that month?

10. Why is the manufacturing overhead rate determined prior to the year in which it is used?

11. What is a manufacturing overhead rate? Why is the application of overhead to production through the use of such a rate almost an absolute necessity?

12. What is the reason, other than errors in estimating costs, for overapplied overhead?

13. When overhead is applied to production via a predetermined overhead rate, is it correct to speak of the per unit product costs computed as actual costs?

14. Indicate the possible dispositions of a balance in the Manufacturing Overhead account and the reasoning or circumstances in which each would seem preferable.

15. What is a service center or department? How does it differ from a production center?

16. Explain the usual accounting for service center costs in setting overhead rates.

17. What levels of capacity or activity could be used in setting overhead rates? What is the main objective sought in the use of each level?

18. What accounting problem is encountered when service centers render services to each other? How can this problem be solved?

EXERCISES

E–1. During a given week $60,000 of direct materials and $5,000 of indirect materials were issued by the storeroom to the production department. Give the required journal entry or entries.

E–2. As prepared by the payroll department, the week's factory labor payroll amounted to $116,000, from which the following were withheld: F.I.C.A. taxes, $5,600; union dues, $2,000; and federal income taxes, $12,000. The payroll is to be paid next Friday. Analysis of the payroll shows that it consists of $98,000 of direct labor and the following wages and salaries: inspectors, $3,800; supervisors, $2,200; electricians, $3,200; timekeepers, $2,400; janitors, $3,600; and warehousemen, $2,800. Give the entry to record the incurrence of the above labor costs and their distribution to proper accounts.

E–3. Given below are some costs incurred by an automobile manufacturer. Classify these costs as direct materials, direct labor, manufacturing overhead, selling, or administrative.

a. Salary of the cost accountant.

b. Cost of automobile radios installed in autos.

c. Cost of stationery used in president's office.

d. Supplies used in cost accountant's office.

e. Wages of a factory inspector.

f. Payroll taxes on assembly-line worker's wages.

g. Repair parts used to repair factory machine.

h. Cost of labor services to install radios in autos.

i. Depreciation on automobiles driven by company's top executives.

j. Cost of magazines purchased for the engineering department.

E–4. Review the list of costs in Exercise E–3 and indicate which of the listed costs is likely to vary directly with the number of autos produced.

E–5. The following data pertain to the Z Company for the year ended June 30, 1981:

Direct materials used	$200,000
Direct labor	400,000
Work in process, 7/1/80	40,000
Work in process, 6/30/81	60,000
Finished goods, 7/1/80	100,000
Finished goods, 6/30/81	140,000
Manufacturing overhead	600,000

Compute the cost of goods manufactured and sold. Also, prepare one entry to summarize the transfer of completed goods for the year.

E–6. Joe Smith was paid for 48 hours of work as a carpenter for Home Constructors, Inc., for last week. His total wages amounted to $312—40 hours at $6 per hour plus 8 hours of Saturday work at $9 per hour (time and a half). He worked 32 hours of regular time on House 124 and 8 hours of regular time and 7 hours of overtime on House 125. He was idle one hour on Saturday waiting for materials to be delivered. Saturday work is common in the construction industry during good weather.

How much of the wages paid Joe Smith should be considered a cost of House 124? Of House 125? As manufacturing overhead? Explain.

E–7. Ace Company sells 25-inch television sets which it assembles from purchased parts. In 1981 it purchased 10,000 picture tubes at $30 each. Of these 10,000 tubes, 25 were used by Ace in testing their product life, 5 were used to replace burned-out tubes in display models, and

9,000 were issued to production. Of the 9,000 placed in production, 7,000 were in units completed, of which 6,000 were sold.

As of December 31, 1981, how much of the $300,000 cost of purchased picture tubes should appear in each of the following accounts?

a. Materials Inventory.

b. Work in Process Inventory.

c. Finished Goods Inventory.

d. Manufacturing Overhead.

e. Selling Expense.

f. Cost of Goods Sold.

E–8. Ames Company applies overhead to production by use of a predetermined overhead rate of $4 per direct labor-hour. During the week ended July 17, Ames received 1,400 hours of direct labor services from its employees that were chargeable to specific units of product. Give the journal entry to record the application of overhead to production.

E–9. Z Company estimated its overhead for 1981 at $400,000 ($100,000 fixed and $300,000 variable) based on a normal activity of 200,000 direct labor-hours. At the end of 1981, manufacturing overhead was overapplied by $3,000 while actual direct labor-hours amounted to 202,000. Analyze the $3,000 as to the reasons for its existence.

E–10. Give the journal entry required in Exercise E–9 to reflect a practical disposition of the overhead balance.

E–11. Assume that at the end of 1981, in Exercise E–9, the costs of the 202,000 actual direct labor-hours were lodged in the following accounts: Work in Process, 20,200 hours; Finished Goods, 50,500 hours; and Cost of Goods Sold, 131,300. Give the journal entry to allocate the overhead balances to these accounts.

E–12. For each of the following cases [*(a)* through *(e)*], fill in the missing data as indicated by the blank spaces. Assume that overhead rates are based on estimated fixed overhead and normalized production.

Case	Fixed overhead rate	Estimated fixed overhead	Normalized production (in units)	Actual production (in units)	Fixed overhead applied
a.	$ 5	$ _____	25,000	_____	$130,000
b.	$ __	90,000	_____	27,000	81,000
c.	__	210,000	30,000	31,000	_____
d.	6		40,000	35,000	_____
e.	8	160,000	_____	_____	144,000

PROBLEMS, SERIES A

P21–1–A. Given below are selected data for the Barnes Company for the month of May:

Direct labor cost incurred	$180,000
Materials issued (including $10,000 of indirect materials).........................	170,000
Work in process inventory, May 1	140,000
Work in process inventory, May 31	200,000
Cost to manufacture in May	770,000
Finished goods inventory, May 1	90,000
Finished goods inventory, May 31	100,000

Required:

a. Compute the amount of manufacturing overhead costs incurred in May.

b. Give journal entries to record the cost of the goods completed in May and the cost of goods sold for May.

P21–2–A. The following data are for the Henson Company for the month of June:

1. Materials purchased on account, $48,000.
2. Direct materials issued, $56,000.
3. Repairs and maintenance on factory buildings, $6,000.
4. Factory depreciation, taxes, and utilities, $41,600.
5. Factory payroll for June, $36,000, including $3,200 of indirect labor.
6. Manufacturing overhead is assigned to production.
7. Cost of goods completed and transferred, $156,000.
8. Cost of goods sold, $160,000.
9. Sales for the month on account, $300,000.

The June 1 inventory account balances were:

Materials	$16,000
Work in process	40,000
Finished goods	12,000

Required:

Prepare a cost and revenue flowchart similar to the one illustrated in the text, incorporating the above data.

P21–3–A. The following data are for the Baker Company for the year ended December 31, 1981:

Sales	$500,000
Direct materials issued	80,000
Factory maintenance	8,000
Depreciation, factory	18,000
Indirect labor	22,000
Work in process, 1/1	30,000
Insurance and taxes, factory	14,000
Utilities, factory	4,000
Other selling expenses	20,000
Other administrative expenses	20,000
Advertising expense........................	30,000

Direct labor cost..........................	100,000
Sales commissions	50,000
Interest expense	10,000
Factory payroll taxes	30,000
Work in process, 12/31	31,000
Finished goods, 1/1	20,000
Finished goods, 12/31	50,000
Administrative salaries	60,000
Indirect materials	5,000

In addition, federal income taxes are estimated at 40 percent of net earnings before income taxes.

Required:

a. Prepare a statement of cost of goods manufactured and sold for 1981.

b. Prepare a condensed earnings statement for the year 1981.

c. Assume Baker Company produced 80,000 units of product in 1981 and that labor wage rates and efficiency remained unchanged from 1980. What was its direct labor cost per unit? If its fixed factory costs consist of factory depreciation and factory insurance and taxes, what was its per unit fixed factory cost?

d. Assume use of the straight-line method of computing depreciation and that tax rates, wages, and prices are expected to remain fairly stable in 1982. If the company expects to produce 100,000 units in 1982, what total direct labor cost should it expect to incur? What per unit direct labor cost? How much total indirect fixed factory cost should it expect to incur? What is its expected per unit fixed indirect factory cost?

e. Explain the differences in total costs and unit costs noted between parts **(c)** and **(d).**

P21–4–A. Klein Company owns a factory building used to house some machines that process a single product. The company has determined from past records and engineering studies that 30 units of product should be processed each machine-hour and that variable overhead costs should amount to $3 per machine-hour. Fixed overhead costs should total $18,000 per month.

Actual production and actual overhead for May and June were:

Month	Units processed	Overhead cost
May	90,000	$27,270
June	100,000	27,800

Required:

a. Compute the amount of overhead cost in total and per unit that should have been incurred in May and in June.

b. Compute the actual total overhead cost, the actual fixed overhead cost, and the actual variable overhead cost per unit for May and for June.

c. Comment on the reasons for the differences in the amounts computed in *(b)*.

P21–5–A. The Marin Company applies overhead to units of product through the use of an overhead rate based on direct labor-hours. Selected budget estimates for 1981 are as follows:

Level of activity	Budgeted direct labor-hours	Budgeted overhead
Practical capacity	75,000	$270,000
Normal activity	60,000	240,000
Expected activity	40,000	200,000

Four direct labor-hours are required to complete one unit of product.

Required:

a. Compute the predetermined overhead rates that Marin might use in applying overhead to production.

b. Compute the fixed and variable portions of each of the rates in *(a)*.

c. Compute the differences in per unit costs that would result from using the different levels of activity in setting overhead rates.

P21–6–A. Gomez Company applies overhead to production using predetermined overhead rates based on direct labor-hours in Production Center A and on machine-hours in Production Center B. A unit of product is worked on in both A and B. Normal activity budget estimates for 1981 are as follows:

	Production Center A	Production Center B
Direct labor cost	$48,000	$56,000
Manufacturing overhead	$72,000	$96,000
Direct labor-hours	12,000	16,000
Machine-hours	8,000	24,000

Cost records for 1981 show the following with respect to one unit of product:

	Production Center A	Production Center B
Actual direct materials cost	$110.00	$34.00
Actual direct labor cost	$ 42.00	$72.00
Direct labor-hours used	5	10
Machine-hours used	3	8

Required:

a. Compute the 1981 overhead rates for each production center.

b. Compute the amount of overhead applied to the unit of product in each production center and compute the unit cost of the product.

c. The actual operating results for 1981 were:

	Production Center A	Production Center B
Manufacturing overhead	$74,000	$98,000
Direct labor-hours	12,000	16,100
Machine-hours	8,200	24,600

Compute the underapplied or overapplied overhead in each production center.

d. Assume that a single plantwide overhead rate based on direct labor-hours is used covering both production centers, rather than separate rates. Compute this single rate, and then compute the cost of the unit referred to above and compare it with the results in *(b)*. Comment on any difference noted in per unit cost.

P21–7–A. The budget prepared for 1981 for the Hamid Company shows the following:

Production centers	Budgeted overhead	Budgeted direct labor-hours
A	$40,000	10,000
B	31,400	4,000
C	50,000	11,000

Service centers	Budgeted total costs	Budgeted hours of service
I	$18,600	
II	14,000	2,000

The above amounts are before any allocations of service center costs. Overhead rates are to be computed for each of the three production centers based on direct labor-hours. Of Service Center II's $14,000 of costs, $10,000 are fixed and are to be allocated 30 percent, 20 percent, 40 percent, and 10 percent to A, B, C, and I, respectively. The $4,000 of variable costs in Service Center II are to be allocated on the basis of hours of service rendered which are budgeted: A—500; B—300; C—1,000; and I—200. The costs charged to Service Center I are then to be allocated to the production centers on the basis of square feet of floor space occupied: A—1,200; B—800; and C—2,000.

Required:

Prepare a schedule showing the allocations of service center costs to the using centers and the computation of predetermined overhead rates for each of the production centers.

P21–8–A. Omata Company intends to start a policy of charging fixed manufacturing overhead to production. Selected actual and budgeted production data and costs for 1981 are:

	Budgeted	Actual
Fixed manufacturing	$600,000	$607,000
Direct labor-hours*	75,000	76,000
Machine-hours*	60,000	59,000
Units of production*	200,000	195,000

* Budgeted amounts are at normal activity level.

Required:

a. Compute three separate, predetermined overhead rates that could be used.

b. Compute, for each of these three rates, the overhead absorbed into production and the underapplied or overapplied fixed overhead for 1981.

c. Theoretically, what disposition should be made for financial reporting of the underapplied or overapplied overhead in part *(b)*?

PROBLEMS, SERIES B

P21–1–B. Selected data for Paper Company for the month of May are as follows:

Materials issued (including $5,000 of indirect materials).........................	$185,000
Factory payrolls (all direct labor except $10,000)	210,000
Finished goods inventory, May 1	70,000
Finished goods inventory, May 31	80,000
Total costs charged to Work in Process in May.............................	580,000
Work in process inventory, May 1	60,000
Work in process inventory, May 31	70,000

Required:

a. Compute the amount of manufacturing overhead costs assigned to production in May.

b. Give journal entries to record the cost of goods completed in May and the cost of the goods sold in May.

P21–2–B. The following data relate to the Ugandi Company for the month of June:

1. Purchased materials on account, $70,000.
2. Materials issued, $80,000, including $2,000 of indirect materials.
3. Factory payroll for the month, $92,000.
4. Payroll costs distributed: direct labor, $80,000; and indirect labor, $12,000.
5. Other overhead costs incurred: factory depreciation, $70,000; property taxes, $16,000; repairs, $10,000; utilities, $8,000; and other, $6,000.
6. Selling expenses incurred, $60,000; and administrative expenses incurred, $55,000.
7. Overhead is assigned to production.
8. Cost of goods completed and transferred, $260,000.

9. Sales on account, $400,000.
10. Cost of goods sold, $250,000.

June 1 inventory balances were:

Materials	$18,000
Work in process	22,000
Finished goods	42,000

Required:

Enter the above data in T-accounts, thus preparing a cost and revenue flowchart similar to the one illustrated in the chapter. You need not prepare or enter closing entries.

P21–3–B. The production and revenue producing activities of the Cabrer Company for the year ended December 31, 1981, are summarized below:

Sales	$800,000
Factory maintenance	14,000
Factory depreciation	32,000
Factory insurance and taxes	16,000
Indirect labor	30,000
Payroll related costs—factory	48,000
Other administrative expenses	24,000
Factory utilities	11,000
Work in process, 12/31	42,000
Finished goods, 12/31	80,000
Sales commissions	70,000
Interest expense	10,000
Direct labor cost............................	180,000
Indirect materials	13,000
Advertising expense........................	50,000
Administrative salaries	96,000
Other selling expenses	30,000
Work in process, 1/1	40,000
Finished goods, 1/1	30,000
Direct materials	128,000

Federal income taxes are estimated at 60 percent of net earnings before such taxes. A total of 40,000 units was manufactured in 1981.

Required:

a. Prepare a statement of cost of goods manufactured and sold for 1981.

b. Prepare a condensed earnings statement for the year 1981.

c. Compute the company's direct labor cost per unit in 1981. Also, assume that fixed overhead consists of factory depreciation, insurance, and taxes; compute the fixed overhead cost per unit for 1981.

d. Assume use of the straight-line method of computing depreciation and that tax rates, wages, and prices are expected to remain fairly stable in 1982. If the company expects to produce 50,000 units in 1982, what is its expected per unit direct labor cost? Its total direct labor cost? How much fixed factory overhead should it expect to incur? What is its expected fixed overhead cost per unit?

e. Give the reasons for the differences and similarities noted in the total and unit costs computed in *(c)* and *(d)*.

P21–4–B. Rossi Company operates a number of machines that process a single product. Study of past records and engineering studies indicates that 15 units of product should be processed per machine-hour at a variable overhead cost of $6 per hour. Fixed overhead costs should amount to $36,000 per month.

Actual production and actual overhead costs for June and July were:

Month	Units processed	Overhead cost
June	50,000	$55,750
July	45,000	54,900

Required:

a. Compute the amount of overhead cost in total and per unit that should have been incurred in June and in July.

b. Compute the per unit actual overhead cost, the per unit actual fixed overhead cost, and the per unit actual variable overhead cost for June and July.

c. Comment on the reasons for the differences noted in the amounts computed in *(b)*.

P21–5–B. Selected budgeted (based on normal activity) and actual data on productive activities and on overhead costs for June Company for 1981 are given below:

	Budgeted	Actual
Total manufacturing overhead	$800,000	$815,000
Direct labor cost	$500,000	$515,000
Direct labor-hours	100,000	101,000
Machine-hours	80,000	81,000

Required:

a. Compute three different overhead rates that might be used to apply overhead to production.

b. For each of the rates computed in *(a)*, compute the amount of overhead applied to production and the amount of underapplied or overapplied overhead for 1981.

c. Assume that one unit of product manufactured in 1981 had an actual materials cost of $40 and an actual direct labor cost of $21. Also assume that the unit required four direct labor-hours and three machine-hours to complete. Compute the unit's total cost under each of the different overhead rates computed in *(a)*.

P21–6–B. Hauer Company applies overhead to production using a predetermined overhead rate based on machine-hours. Budgeted data for 1981 are:

Level of activity	Budgeted machine-hours	Budgeted overhead
Practical capacity	150,000	$780,000
Normal activity	100,000	580,000
Expected activity	120,000	660,000

Two hours of machine time are needed to complete a unit of product.

Required:

a. Without making any calculations, would you expect overhead to be underapplied or overapplied in 1981? Why?

b. Compute the predetermined overhead rates that Hauer might use.

c. Compute the variable and fixed portions of these rates.

d. Assume that the overhead rate used was based on normal activity, that actual overhead amounted to $665,000, and that 122,000 machine-hours were used to process 60,500 units of product in 1981. Compute the underapplied or overapplied overhead for that year.

P21–7–B. Dorf Company's controller, after reviewing the new production processes and recently installed machines, has suggested that the old plantwide, single predetermined overhead rate based on direct labor-hours be replaced by separate rates and that the rate in Production Center A be based on direct labor-hours and in Production Center B on machine-hours. In the company's operations, a unit of product is worked on in both A and B. Budget estimates, based on normal activity, for 1981 are:

	Total	Production Center A	Production Center B
Manufacturing overhead..	$216,000	$96,000	$120,000
Direct labor-hours	72,000	24,000	48,000
Machine-hours	18,000	6,000	12,000

Cost records show the following per unit costs and hours for a unit of product completed in 1981:

	Production Center A	Production Center B
Direct materials used	$50	$28
Direct labor cost	$32	$40
Direct labor-hours used	12	20
Machine-hours used	8	10

Required:

a. Compute the single, plantwide overhead rate that the company would have used prior to the change to separate rates for production centers.

b. Compute the per unit cost of the product using this single rate.

c. Compute the separate production center rates suggested by the controller.

d. Compute the per unit cost of the product using separate production center rates to apply overhead. Compare this per unit cost with the per unit cost computed in **(b)** and comment on any difference.

e. Assume that in 1979 the actual overhead incurred in Center A was $103,000 with 25,020 direct labor-hours received. In Center B, actual overhead was $121,000 with 12,004 machine-hours received. Compute the underapplied or overapplied overhead for each center.

BUSINESS DECISION PROBLEM 21–1

A number of costs that would affect business decisions in the factory operations of different companies are listed below. These costs may be fixed or variable with respect to some measure of volume or output and may be classified as direct materials (DM), direct labor (DL) or manufacturing overhead (MO).

1. Glue used to attach labels to bottles containing a patented medicine.
2. Compressed air used in operating machines turning out products.
3. Insurance on factory building and equipment.
4. A production department supervisor's salary.
5. Rent on factory machinery.
6. Iron ore and coke in a steel mill.
7. Oil, gasoline, and grease for forklift trucks.
8. Services of painters in building construction.
9. Cutting oils used in machining operations.
10. Cost of food in a factory employees' cafeteria.
11. Payroll taxes and fringe benefits related to direct labor.
12. The plant electricians' salaries.
13. Sand in a glass manufacturer.
14. Copy editor's salary in a book publisher.

Required:

a. List the numbers 1 through 14 down the left side of a sheet of paper. After each number write the letters V (for variable) or F (for fixed) and either DM (for direct materials), DL (for direct labor) or MO (for manufacturing overhead) to show how you would classify the similarly numbered cost item given above.

b. With which of your own answers given for part **(a)** could you take issue? Discuss.

BUSINESS DECISION PROBLEM 21–2

The earnings statement for Higgins, Inc., for 1981 was as follows:

HIGGINS, INC.
Earnings Statement
For the Year Ended December 31, 1981

Sales (20,000 units)		$400,000
Cost of goods sold	$360,000	
Other expenses (all fixed)	100,000	460,000
Net Loss		$ (60,000)

The $60,000 loss for 1981 continued a pattern of losses of this size occurring over the past few years. Selling prices and sales volume have remained unchanged over these years. Production volume has amounted to 20,000 units annually at a variable cost of $3 per unit, while fixed manufacturing overhead totals $300,000 annually. There were no inventories at the start or end of 1981.

Despite the fact that costs were incurred in 1982 at the same levels as in 1981, the company's new president proudly presented the following earnings statement to the board of directors:

HIGGINS, INC.
Earnings Statement
For the Year Ended December 31, 1982

Sales (20,000 units)		$400,000
Cost of goods sold	$210,000	
Other expenses (all fixed)	100,000	310,000
Net Earnings		$ 90,000

The board was so delighted with the company's "turnaround" from losses to net earnings that it voted the president a bonus of $20,000. A week later, after collecting the bonus, the president resigned "to pursue other challenges."

Required:

a. Explain carefully, through use of a schedule showing units and dollar amounts, how the president was able to effect the "turnaround" from losses to earnings.

b. How might the above misleading portrayal of $90,000 of net earnings have been prevented, or at least brought to the attention of the board?

BUSINESS DECISION PROBLEM 21–3

Partial earnings statements for the Detroit division of Clair Company for 1979 and 1980 have shown identical results, as follows:

Sales (5,000 units @ $80)		$400,000
Cost of goods sold:		
Variable costs (at $20 per unit)	$100,000	
Fixed costs	240,000	340,000
Gross margin		$ 60,000

Other expenses of the division have amounted to slightly more than $60,000 so that the division has contributed small losses to overall corporate earnings.

A new manager, June O'Donnell, has been placed in charge of the division. She believed it would be possible to reduce the division's inventory from its current level

of 2,000 units (at $68 each) to 1,000 units because of some changes made in production processing. Therefore, she ordered the production of 4,000 units in 1981. Sales volume, selling prices, and fixed overhead are expected to remain unchanged, but variable costs are expected to run $19 per unit because of the changes made. The company sets overhead rates based on expected activity for the coming year, and uses the Fifo inventory method.

Required:

a. Assuming expectations for 1981 are realized exactly, prepare a partial earnings statement for the year.

b. Explain why the actions taken by Ms. O'Donnell did (or did not) lead to increased earnings by the division.

BUSINESS DECISION PROBLEM 21–4

Ed Ralph has taken over a business that had been operated by his father for a number of years. Ed supplies custom-made awnings, boat canvas, convertible tops, interior auto trim, and other canvas and vinyl products. His

business is quite seasonal, picking up quite sharply in the spring and summer from the rather slow winter months. Summarized, the results of operations for the first year that Ed has operated the shop are:

	First quarter	Second quarter	Third quarter	Fourth quarter
Sales	$ 6,100	$31,600	$48,600	$18,800
Cost of goods sold	$ 5,470	$22,900	$35,900	$14,180
Selling and administrative expenses	3,100	2,900	2,850	2,920
Total expenses	$ 8,570	$25,800	$38,750	$17,100
Net Earnings (loss)	$(2,470)	$ 5,800	$ 9,850	$ 1,700

Ed is rather surprised at the sharp fluctuations in quarterly net earnings, especially at the loss in the first quarter. He had followed his father's instructions carefully in bidding on jobs, such bids being basically 200 percent of direct materials costs. He believed the part-time office worker had prepared the above statements following the practices of Ed's father. Digging deeper into the records of the shop, Ed's office worker comes up with the following additional data for the four quarters:

Direct material	$3,020	$15,050	$24,100	$ 9,000
Direct labor	1,040	5,050	7,890	3,080
Variable shop costs	410	1,800	2,910	1,100
Fixed shop costs	1,000	1,000	1,000	1,000
Total production costs	$5,470	$22,900	$35,900	$14,180

The fixed shop costs consist basically of depreciation, insurance, and property taxes. The selling and administrative expenses consist largely of the wages of one office person and utilities expense.

Required:

a. Explain to Ed why his quarterly earnings fluctuate so sharply.

b. Show how, using numbers, a different accounting procedure could be used to reduce these fluctuations.

(Hint: Use a predetermined fixed overhead rate based on an estimated direct labor cost of $17,000.)

c. Ed is thinking about using a different pricing policy in the slow winter months to bring in some business. Expressed as a percentage of direct materials costs, what, approximately, is Ed's lowest possible bid price (assuming such lower prices in the winter do not cause reduced summer business)?

Chapter 22

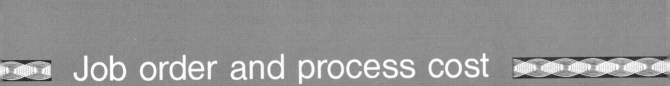

Job order and process cost
systems; variable costing

In previous chapters we have dealt with (1) manufacturing costs and their general flow pattern, (2) the application of overhead to production, and (3) the reporting upon operations of a manufacturing company. Little attention was paid to the procedures and accounting records used in accumulating costs or to the determination of unit costs for units of product.[1] How these costs are determined depends upon the type of cost system employed.

Thus, attention in this chapter is directed to the two major types of cost accumulation systems found in practice—the *job order cost* system and the *process cost* system. In each system the goal is to determine the unit costs of the products manufactured. As already noted, unit costs are needed in determining the cost of the goods sold and the cost of the ending inventories of work in process and finished goods. They may also be used to determine payments to be received under contracts based on "full" cost and in setting selling prices.

JOB ORDER COST SYSTEMS: Timely and useful information

When a *job order cost system* (job costing) is used, costs are accumulated by individual jobs or batches of output. A job may consist of 1,000 chairs, 10 sofas, 5 miles of highway, a single machine, a dam, or a building. A job cost system is generally used when the products being manufactured can be separately identified or when goods are produced to meet a customer's particular needs, such as constructing a house. Job costing is also used in other types of construction, motion pictures, and job printing.

Under job order costing an up-to-date record of the costs incurred on a job is kept in order to provide management with cost data on a timely basis. For example, management may want to know the cost of producing 100 desks when the desks are completed. It can also receive reports as often as desired, even daily, on such matters as materials used, labor costs incurred, goods completed, total and detailed production costs, and whether production costs are in line with expectations.

Basic records in job costing

Illustration 22.1 shows the basic records or source documents used in a job order cost system. These include:

1. The *job order cost sheet* on which is summarized all of the costs—direct materials, direct labor, and applied overhead—of producing a given job or batch of products. It is the key document in the system and is used to control production costs by comparing actual costs with budgeted costs. One sheet is maintained for each job, and the file of job order sheets for unfinished jobs is the subsidiary ledger for the Work in Process Inventory account. When the goods are completed and transferred, the job order sheets are transferred to a completed jobs file and the number of units and their unit costs recorded on inventory cards supporting the Finished Goods Inventory account.

---

[1] It is a mistake to assume that *the* unit cost can be found with any measurement precision. All we have are different techniques for finding *a* cost figure. Assumptions must be made regarding the use of Fifo, Lifo, or weighted-average inventory cost, how much depreciation to charge against a given period and a unit of product, and similar considerations. Reasonable (but arbitrary) allocations must be made. Also, for decision-making purposes future costs rather than past costs often must be used.

Illustration 22.1: Basic records in a job order cost system

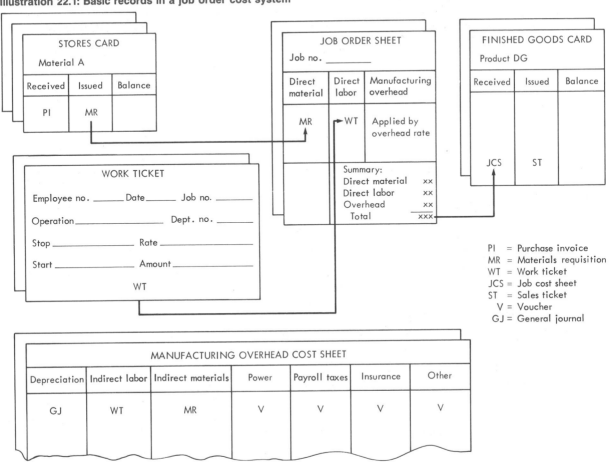

2. The *stores (or materials) card,* one of which is kept for each type of direct and indirect materials maintained in inventory. It shows the quantities (and costs) of each type of materials received, issued, and on hand for which the storekeeper is responsible. When a job is started, direct materials are ordered from the storeroom on a *materials requisition,* which shows the types, cost, and quantities of the materials ordered.

3. The *work (or labor time) ticket* which shows who worked on what job for how many hours and at what wage rate. All of each employee's daily hours must be accounted for on one or more work tickets.

4. The *manufacturing overhead cost sheet* which summarizes the various factory indirect costs incurred. One sheet is maintained for each production center and each service center.

5. The *finished goods card* or *record,* one of which is maintained for each type of product manufactured and sold. Each card contains a running record of units and costs of products completed, sold, and on hand.

Illustration 22.2: Job order system cost flows

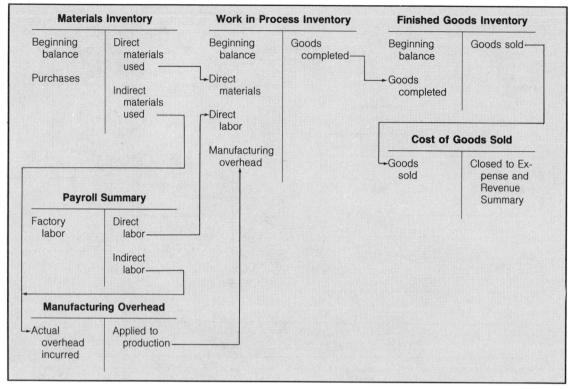

The general flow of costs through the accounting system of a firm using a job order cost system is shown in Illustration 22.2. This illustration should be studied carefully and related to the documents used to record costs that are shown in Illustration 22.1 to gain a full understanding of a job order cost system.

Job order costing—an example

To illustrate a job order cost system, especially the tie-in between the general ledger accounts and the subsidiary records, an example is presented below. The example covers the month of July for which the beginning inventories were:

Materials inventory (Material A, $10,000; Material B, $6,000; various indirect materials, $4,000)	$20,000
Work in process inventory (Job No. 106: direct materials, $4,200; direct labor, $5,000; and overhead, $4,000)	13,200
Finished goods inventory (500 units of Product AB at a cost of $11 per unit)	5,500

The example further assumes that Job No. 106 was completed in July, and that, of the two jobs started in July (Nos. 107 and 108), only Job No. 108 is incomplete at the end of July. The transactions, and the journal entries to record them are given below:

1. Purchased $10,000 of Material A and $15,000 of Material B on account.

```
Materials Inventory ..........................................    25,000
    Accounts Payable .......................................              25,000
    To record purchase of direct materials.
```

2. Issued direct materials: Material A to Job No. 106, $1,000, to Job No. 107, $8,000 to Job No. 108, $2,000; Material B to Job No. 106, $2,000 to Job No. 107, $6,000, to Job No. 108, $4,000. Indirect materials issued to all jobs, $1,000.

```
Work in Process Inventory ....................................    23,000
Manufacturing Overhead .....................................     1,000
    Materials Inventory ....................................              24,000
    To record direct and indirect materials issued.
```

3. Factory payroll for the month, $25,000; social security and income taxes withheld, $4,000.

```
Payroll Summary..........................................    25,000
    Various liability accounts for taxes withheld .................               4,000
    Accrued Wages Payable ..............................              21,000
    To record factory payroll for July.
```

4. Factory payroll paid, $19,000.

```
Accrued Wages Payable ....................................    19,000
    Cash ...............................................              19,000
    To record cash paid to factory employees in July.
```

5. Payroll costs distributed: direct labor, $20,000 (Job No. 106, $5,000; Job No. 107, $12,000; and Job No. 108, $3,000); and indirect labor, $5,000.

```
Work in Process Inventory ....................................    20,000
Manufacturing Overhead ....................................     5,000
    Payroll Summary .......................................              25,000
    To distribute factory labor costs incurred.
```

6. Other manufacturing overhead costs incurred:

```
Payroll taxes accrued ....................................  $ 3,000
Repairs (on account) ....................................     1,000
Property taxes accrued ...................................     4,000
Heat, light, and power (on account) ........................     2,000
Depreciation .............................................     5,000
                                                            $15,000
```

```
Manufacturing Overhead ....................................    15,000
    Accounts Payable .....................................               3,000
    Accrued Payroll Taxes ................................               3,000
    Accrued Property Taxes Payable ........................               4,000
    Accumulated Depreciation .............................               5,000
    To record manufacturing overhead costs incurred.
```

7. Manufacturing overhead applied to production (at rate of 80 percent of direct labor cost):

```
Job No. 106 (0.80 × $5,000)..............................  $ 4,000
Job No. 107 (0.80 × $12,000)..............................     9,600
Job No. 108 (0.80 × $3,000)..............................     2,400
                                                            $16,000
```

```
Work in Process Inventory ..................................    16,000
      Manufacturing Overhead  .............................              16,000
   To record application of overhead to production.
```

8. Jobs completed and transferred to finished goods storeroom (see Illustration 22.3 for details):

```
      Job No. 106 (4,000 units of Product DG @ $6.30) ............   $25,200
      Job No. 107 (10,000 units of Product XY @ $3.56) ............    35,600
                                                                     _____
                                                                     $60,800
                                                                     ========
```

```
Finished Goods Inventory ...................................    60,800
      Work in Process Inventory .............................              60,800
   To record completed production for July.
```

9. Sales on account for the month: 500 units of Product AB for $8,000, cost, $5,500; and 10,000 units of Product XY for $62,000, cost, $35,600 (Job No. 107).

```
Accounts Receivable .......................................    70,000
      Sales .............................................              70,000
   To record sales on account for July.

Cost of Goods Sold ........................................    41,100
      Finished Goods Inventory ..............................              41,100
   To record cost of goods sold in July.
```

After the above entries have been posted to the accounts of the company, the Work in Process Inventory and Finished Goods Inventory accounts would appear (in T-account form) as follows:

Work in Process Inventory

July 1 balance	13,200	Completed	60,800
Direct materials used	23,000		
Direct labor cost incurred	20,000		
Overhead applied	16,000		

Finished Goods Inventory

July 1 balance	5,500	Sold	41,100
Completed	60,800		

The Work in Process Inventory account has a balance at July 31 of $11,400, which agrees with the total costs charged thus far to Job No. 108, as is shown in Illustration 22.3. These costs consist of direct materials, $6,000; direct labor, $3,000; and manufacturing overhead, $2,400. The Finished Goods Inventory account has a balance at July 31 of $25,200. The finished goods inventory card for Product DG supports this amount (see Illustration 22.3) showing that there are indeed units of Product DG on hand having a total cost of $25,200.

Note that the entries in the ledger accounts given above are often made from summaries of costs and thus entered only at the end of the month. On the other hand, in order to keep management informed as to costs incurred, the details of the various costs incurred are recorded more frequently, often daily.

**Illustration 22.3:
Supporting inventory
cards and job
order sheets**

STORES CARD Material A		
Received	Issued	Balance
$10,000		$10,000
		20,000
	$1,000	19,000
	8,000	11,000
	2,000	9,000

STORES CARD Material B		
Received	Issued	Balance
$15,000		$ 6,000
		21,000
	$2,000	19,000
	6,000	13,000
	4,000	9,000

JOB ORDER SHEET (Product DG)   Job No. 106

Date	Direct Materials	Direct Labor	Manufacturing Overhead
July 1	$4,200	$ 5,000	$4,000
July	A: 1,000	5,000	4,000
	B: 2,000	$10,000	$8,000
	$7,200		

Job completed (4,000 units of Product DG @ $6.30). Total cost, $25,200.

JOB ORDER SHEET (Product XY)   Job No. 107

Date	Direct Materials	Direct Labor	Manufacturing Overhead
July	A: $ 8,000	$12,000	$9,600
	B: 6,000		
	$14,000		

Job completed (10,000 units of Product XY @ $3.56). Total cost, $35,600.

JOB ORDER SHEET (Product OR)   Job No. 108

Date	Direct Materials	Direct Labor	Manufacturing Overhead
July	A: $2,000	$3,000	$2,400
	B: 4,000		

Job incomplete (1,000 units of Product OR). Cost to date, $11,400.

FINISHED GOODS CARD Product AB		
Received	Issued	Balance
		$5,500
	$5,500	–0–

FINISHED GOODS CARD Product DG		
Received	Issued	Balance
$25,200		$25,200

FINISHED GOODS CARD Product XY		
Received	Issued	Balance
$35,600		$35,600
	$35,600	–0–

The above example should be studied until the real advantages of using overhead rates (including predetermined rates) are clear. Three jobs were worked on during the month. One (No. 106) was started last month and completed in July. One (No. 107) was started and completed in July. And one (No. 108) was started but not finished in July. Each required different amounts of direct materials and direct labor (and, perhaps, types of direct labor). Under these conditions, there is simply no way to apply overhead to products without the use of a rate based on some level of activity. Note also that the use of a predetermined overhead rate permits the computation of unit costs of Job Nos. 106 and 107 at the time of their completion rather than waiting until the end of the month. But this advantage is secured only at the cost of keeping more detailed records of the costs incurred. As we shall see below, the other major cost system—process costing—requires far less record keeping, but the computation of unit costs is more complex.

PROCESS COST SYSTEMS

Many business firms manufacture huge quantities of a single product or similar products (paint, paper, chemicals, gasoline, rubber, and plastics) on a continuous basis over long periods of time. There is no separate job or specific batch of units; rather production is continuous over the year or several years. Since there is no job, costs cannot be accumulated for the job. Rather, costs must be accumulated for each process which a product undergoes on its way to completion. This calls for another type of cost system, one that yields unit costs by *processes* or by departments for stated periods of *time* rather than by jobs without regard to time periods. Here the processes or departments serve as cost centers for which costs are accumulated for the entire period (month, quarter, or year). These costs are divided by the number of units (tons, pounds, gallons, or feet) produced to get a broad, average unit cost. Such a system is known as a *process cost system (process costing).*

Basic system design

Process cost systems have the same general design as that shown in Illustration 22.2. Costs of the factors of production are first recorded in separate accounts for materials inventory, labor, and overhead. These costs are then transferred to work in process inventory. A process cost system usually has more than one work in process inventory account. Such an account is kept for each processing center in order to determine the unit cost of each process. All products manufactured may be subjected to the same processing in a specified *sequential* order, as depicted in Illustration 22.4. The products are started in Department A, processed, transferred to Department B, processed further, and then transferred to finished goods inventory.

The product manufactured by other firms may require *parallel* processing. Here all products do not undergo the same processing and do not pass through the same departments. For example, a basic material may be entered into Department 1 that yields two products for further processing. One product may be transferred to Department 2 and then to Department 4 for further processing before being transferred to finished goods inventory. The second

Illustration 22.4: Cost flows in a process cost system

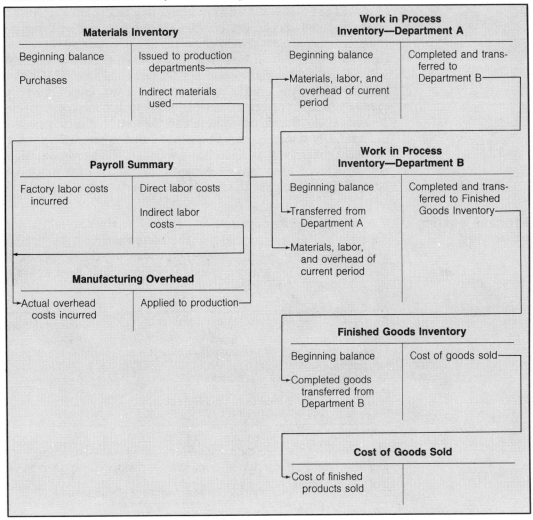

product is processed in Departments 3 and 5 before being transferred to finished goods inventory. Graphically, the processing is:

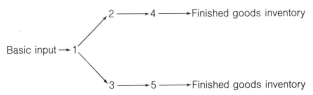

Under the above processing pattern, the accounting system would contain five work in process inventory accounts and unit costs would be determined for the five processes.

Accounting for overhead.   In process costing, manufacturing overhead will be initially recorded in supporting records or accounts for the various producing and service centers. Service center costs will then be allocated to the producing centers. Then, either the actual overhead incurred for the period (usually a month) will be applied to work in process inventory, or overhead will be applied through use of a predetermined rate. If the quantity of units produced and the amounts of overhead costs incurred are roughly equal through time, applying actual overhead to production will yield reasonable product costs. But, if production and the amounts of overhead costs incurred are not fairly stable, the use of a predetermined rate will prevent the reporting of sharp differences in monthly unit costs. For example, if all production employees took their two-week paid vacations in July, unit costs in July may be considerably higher than in June.

Process costing illustrated

Assume that a company sells a chemical product which it processes in two departments. In Department A the basic materials are crushed, powdered, and blended. In Department B the product is tested, packaged and labeled, and transferred to finished goods inventory. The production and cost data for the month of June are:

	Department A	Department B
Units started, completed, and transferred	11,000	9,000
Units on hand at June 30, partially completed	–0–	2,000
Beginning inventory	$ –0–	$ –0–
Direct materials	16,500	1,100
Direct labor	5,500	5,900
Actual manufacturing overhead	4,500	5,600
Applied manufacturing overhead	4,400	5,900

From the above data, the Work in Process Inventory—Department A account can be constructed and, summarized, will appear as follows:

Work in Process Inventory—Department A

Direct materials	16,500	Transferred to Department B—	
Direct labor	5,500	11,000 units @ $2.40	26,400
Overhead (80 percent of direct labor cost)	4,400		

Since all of the units started were completed and transferred, it follows that all of the costs assigned to Department A should be transferred on to Department B. The unit cost in Department A is computed simply by dividing total costs of $26,400 by the 11,000 units completed and transferred to get an average unit cost for the month of $2.40.

But the computations are seldom this simple. One complication is faced whenever partially completed beginning and ending inventories are present. Assume that Department B's Work in Process Inventory account for June, before recording the cost of the units transferred out, is as follows:

Work in Process Inventory—Department B

Transferred from Department A	26,400	
Direct material	1,100	
Direct labor	5,900	
Overhead (100 percent of direct labor)	5,900	

The task now faced is to divide the total costs charged to the department in June, $39,300, between the units transferred out and those remaining on hand in the department. The $39,300 cannot be divided by 11,000 to get an average unit cost because the 11,000 units are not alike; 9,000 are finished, but 2,000 are only partially finished. The problem is solved through use of the concept of equivalent units of production.

Equivalent units.   Essentially, the concept of *equivalent units* involves expressing a given number of partially completed units as a smaller number of fully completed units. For example, it holds that 1,000 units brought to a 50 percent state of completion are the equivalent of 500 units that are 100 percent complete. It is assumed that the same amount of costs must be incurred to bring 1,000 units to a 50 percent level of completion as would be required to complete 500 units.

The first step in computing the equivalent units produced in Department B is to determine the stage of completion of the unfinished units. These units are 100 percent complete as to transferred-in costs or they would not have been transferred out of Department A. But they may have different stages of completion as to the materials, labor, and overhead costs added in Department B. (It is often assumed that the units are at the same stage of completion as to conversion costs—labor and overhead.) All direct materials are added at the start of processing in Department B. Thus, the ending inventory is 100 percent complete as to materials. Since the units transferred out must be complete, equivalent production for materials is 11,000 units—9,000 transferred out and 2,000 on hand, 100 percent complete. Next, assume that the 2,000 units are, on the average, 50 percent complete as to conversion. Equivalent production then for labor and overhead is 10,000 units—9,000 units transferred and 2,000 brought to a 50 percent completion state, which is the equivalent of 1,000 fully complete units.

Let us return to our original example of Department B. With equivalent units of production known, the unit costs of the processing in Department B and the total per unit cost can now be computed:

	Transferred in	Materials	Conversion	Total
Costs to be accounted for:				
Charged to Department B........	$26,400	$ 1,100	$11,800	$39,300
Equivalent units	11,000	11,000	10,000	
Unit costs	$2.40	$0.10	$1.18	$3.68

The conversion cost in the above schedule consists of $5,900 of direct labor and an equal amount of overhead since the latter is applied at a rate of 100 percent of labor cost.

With unit costs computed, the $39,300 of costs charged to Department B in June can now be divided between costs transferred out and costs remaining as the cost of the department's ending inventory:

	Transferred in	Materials	Conversion	Total
Costs accounted for:				
Costs transferred out	$21,600	$ 900	$10,620	$33,120
Cost of inventory	4,800	200	1,180	6,180
Costs accounted for	$26,400	$1,100	$11,800	$39,300

The total costs transferred out of $33,120 consists of $21,600 of Department A's cost (9,000 × $2.40), $900 of materials costs (9,000 × $0.10), and $10,620 of conversion costs (9,000 × $1.18). The cost of the ending inventory in Department B of 2,000 units, complete as to materials and 50 percent complete as to conversion, consists of the following:

Costs from Department A (2,000 × $2.40)		$4,800
Costs added by Department B:		
Materials (2,000 × $0.10)	$ 200	
Conversion (2,000 × 0.5 × $1.18)	1,180	1,380
Total cost of ending inventory		$6,180

The completed units transferred out of Department B will be carried in finished goods inventory at a cost of $3.68 each ($2.40 + $1.28) until sold, at which time they would be charged to the Cost of Goods Sold expense account. The unit costs of production—$2.40 in Department A and $1.28 ($0.10 + $1.18) in Department B—are closely watched by management with explanations sought for unexpected variations.

The journal entries for the above for the month of June are as follows:

1. Work in Process Inventory—Department A 16,500
   Work in Process Inventory—Department B 1,100
       Materials Inventory 17,600
       To record materials placed in production in June.

2. Payroll Summary 11,400
       (Various withholding accounts and accrued
         wages payable) 11,400
       To record factory payroll for June.

3. Work in Process Inventory—Department A 5,500
   Work in Process Inventory—Department B 5,900
       Payroll Summary 11,400
       To distribute factory labor costs (assumed that all such costs are
       chargeable directly to production departments).

4. Manufacturing Overhead 10,100
       (Various accounts—cash, accounts payable, accruals,
         and allowances for depreciation) 10,100
       To record actual overhead costs incurred in June.

5. Work in Process Inventory—Department A 4,400
    Work in Process Inventory—Department B 5,900
        Manufacturing Overhead.................................... 10,300
    To apply overhead to production using predetermined rates based
    on direct labor cost: Department A, 80 percent; and Department B,
    100 percent.

6. Work in Process Inventory—Department B 26,400
        Work in Process Inventory—Department A.................... 26,400
    To record transfer of goods from Department A to Department B.

7. Finished Goods Inventory 33,120
        Work in Process Inventory—Department B.................... 33,120
    To record transfer of completed goods from Department B to finished
    goods.

Assuming that 6,000 units were sold in June at a price of $10 per unit,
the following entries would be required:

8. Accounts Receivable 60,000
        Sales 60,000
    To record sales on account.

9. Cost of Goods Sold 22,080
        Finished Goods Inventory 22,080
    To record cost of goods sold in June, 6,000 units @ $3.68.

The cost of production report

The computation of unit costs is even more complex when there are both beginning and ending inventories in a processing center. This problem, and the key report in process costing, is discussed in this section.

The following data are for Department 3 of the A Company for the month of June 1981:

Units

Units in beginning inventory, complete as to materials, 60% complete as to conversion	6,000
Units transferred in from Department 2	18,000
Units completed and transferred out	16,000
Units in ending inventory, complete as to materials, 50% complete as to conversion	8,000

Costs

Cost of beginning inventory:		
Cost transferred in from preceding department in May	$12,000	
Materials added in May in Department 3	6,000	
Conversion costs (equal amounts of labor and overhead)	3,000	$21,000
Costs transferred in from preceding department in June		37,200
Costs added in Department 3 in June:		
Materials	$18,480	
Conversion (equal amounts of labor and overhead)	18,000	36,480
Total costs in beginning inventory and placed in production in Department 3 in June		$94,680

How the total of $94,680 of costs charged to Department 3 in June is divided between the cost of the units transferred out and the cost of the units remaining on hand in inventory is shown in Illustration 22.5. This report is discussed by explaining the four steps usually undertaken to prepare it.

Illustration 22.5: Cost of
production report

A COMPANY
Cost of Production Report
For the Month of June, 1981

	Actual units	Equivalent units		
		Transferred in	Materials	Conversion
UNITS:				
Units in beginning inventory	6,000			
Units transferred in	18,000			
Units to be accounted for	24,000			
Units completed and transferred	16,000	16,000	16,000	16,000
Units in ending inventory*	8,000	8,000	8,000	4,000
Units accounted for	24,000	24,000	24,000	20,000

* Inventory is complete as to materials added, 50 percent complete as to conversion.

	Transferred in	Materials	Conversion	Total
COSTS:				
Costs to be accounted for:				
Costs in beginning inventory..........	$12,000	$ 6,000	$ 3,000	$21,000
Costs transferred in	37,200			37,200
Costs added in Department 3		18,480	18,000	36,480
Costs to be accounted for	$49,200	$24,480	$21,000	$94,680
Equivalent units (as above)	24,000	24,000	20,000	
Unit costs	$2.05	$1.02	$1.05	$4.12
Costs accounted for:				
Costs in ending inventory	$16,400	$ 8,160	$ 4,200	$28,760
Costs transferred out	32,800	16,320	16,800	65,920
Costs accounted for	$49,200	$24,480	$21,000	$94,680

1. Trace the physical flow of the actual units into and out of the department. The section headed "Units" in Illustration 22.5 shows that 6,000 units were on hand at the beginning of June and that 18,000 units were transferred in, making a total of 24,000 units that must be accounted for. Of these 24,000 units, 16,000 were completed and transferred out, and 8,000 were retained, partially completed, in the department.

2. The actual units are converted to equivalent units. Illustration 22.5 shows the procedures followed to compute *average* unit costs. (Other procedures would be used if unit costs on a Fifo or Lifo basis were desired. Discussion of these methods will be left to a more advanced text.) Equivalent units, under the average method, consist of units completed and transferred plus the equivalent units in the ending inventory, or 24,000 for the costs of units transferred in and for materials, and 20,000 for conversion costs. The observant reader will note that these amounts include units fully or partially completed last month and on hand in Department 3's beginning inventory. The reason for this is explained in Step 3.

3. Compute unit costs for each element of cost, using the equivalent units computed above and the total costs charged to the department. Under the average method, this involves dividing the equivalent units of pro-

duction for the period, *including those in the beginning inventory,* into the costs charged to the department, *including the costs of the beginning inventory. Thus, the costs of the beginning inventory are treated as if incurred in the current period. And the equivalent units of production in the beginning inventory are treated as if produced in the current period.* The unit costs computed are, as a result, averages across the current period and a portion of the prior period, rather than being strictly those of the current period. Despite this lack of exactness, the average method is widely used. It avoids many fine details that emerge under Fifo or Lifo that are of little practical value. As shown in Illustration 22.5, average unit costs for June are costs transferred in, $2.05; materials costs, $1.02; and conversion costs, $1.05. As already noted, management watches these costs closely.

4. The equivalent units transferred out and in inventory can now be multiplied by the unit costs computed to divide the total costs charged to the department into costs to be transferred out and costs that remain in the department's work in process inventory account. Thus, the cost of the ending inventory would be computed as follows:

8,000 equivalent units transferred in @ $2.05	$16,400
8,000 equivalent units of materials costs @ $1.02	8,160
4,000 equivalent units of conversion costs @ $1.05	4,200
Total cost of ending inventory	$28,760

The total cost of the units completed and transferred out can be computed by multiplying 16,000 times the total unit cost ($4.12) and, as shown, amounts to $65,920. The sum of the cost of the ending inventory and the cost of the units transferred out must equal the total of the costs charged to the department, which was used in Step 3 to compute unit costs. Thus, a built-in check upon the accuracy of the procedures followed is provided.

VARIABLE COSTING: Absorption versus variable costing

Currently, the most commonly accepted theory of product costing holds that the cost of producing a product includes direct materials, direct labor, and an apportioned share of the many manufacturing overhead costs. The latter include costs such as factory depreciation and taxes which tend to remain fixed over varying ranges of output. Other costs, such as supplies and power, may vary with production volume. Despite differences in their variability, all of these costs are attached to the units of product manufactured and then traced from work in process inventory to finished goods inventory and finally to cost of goods sold. This method of assigning costs to products is called *absorption or full costing* and is the method generally required for tax purposes.

Because all costs, including fixed overhead costs, are applied to production under full costing, variations in unit product cost may result solely from variations in production volume. If fixed costs are $100,000 and 10,000 units are produced, unit fixed cost is $10; if volume is 20,000, unit fixed cost is $5. Because these variations are not controllable at the production level and may obscure other significant variations in cost, they can be excluded from product cost through use of a costing technique referred to as *variable, direct,* or *marginal costing.*

Illustration 22.6:
Cost flows under
variable costing

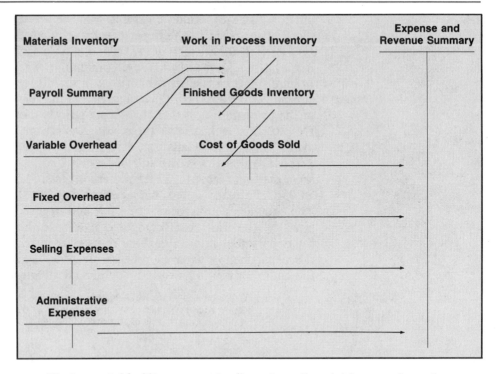

Under *variable (direct, marginal) costing,* all variable manufacturing costs are charged to the product and all fixed costs (including fixed manufacturing costs) are charged to expense. Thus, all manufacturing costs must first be classified as fixed or variable. Direct materials and direct labor costs are usually completely variable. But manufacturing overhead costs must be separated into variable and fixed portions. All variable costs (direct materials, direct labor, and variable overhead) are assigned to production and become part of the unit costs of the products produced. *All fixed costs are assumed to be costs of the period and are charged to expense.* The only difference between full costing and variable costing is in the treatment of fixed manufacturing costs. Under full costing they are treated as product costs and under variable costing they are treated as period costs. The cost flows under variable costing are shown graphically in Illustration 22.6.

Variable and absorption costing compared

The differences between variable and full costing can be seen from an example comparing the earnings statement that would result from applying each technique to the same data. Assume the following data:

Beginning inventory	0	Variable costs (per unit):		
Production (units)	10,000	Direct materials		$2.00
Sales (units)	9,000	Direct labor		1.00
Fixed costs:		Manufacturing overhead		0.30
Manufacturing overhead	$ 6,000	Total		$3.30
Selling expenses	15,000	Variable selling expenses		
Administrative expenses	12,000	(per unit)		$0.20
		Selling price (per unit)		$8.00

Illustration 22.7: Earnings
statement under variable
costing

Sales (9,000 units at $8)		$72,000
Cost of goods sold:		
Variable production costs incurred (10,000 units at $3.30)	$33,000	
Less: Inventory (1,000 units at $3.30)	3,300	29,700
Manufacturing margin		$42,300
Variable selling expenses (9,000 units at $0.20)		1,800
Marginal earnings		$40,500
Period costs:		
Manufacturing overhead	$ 6,000	
Selling expenses	15,000	
Administrative expenses	12,000	33,000
Net Earnings		$ 7,500

Earnings statement under variable costing. Under variable costing the earnings statement for the year would be as is shown in Illustration 22.7. Note that all of the fixed manufacturing costs are considered costs of the period and are not included in inventories.

Earnings statement under conventional costing. Illustration 22.8 contains the earnings statement that would be prepared under full costing. Note that the fixed manufacturing costs are included as part of product cost and some of these costs are included in the ending inventory.

The ending inventory is priced at so-called "full cost." That is, its cost includes fixed manufacturing overhead. Since the total cost of producing 10,000 units is $39,000, then the unit cost is $3.90 and the 1,000 units in inventory are carried at $3,900. Also, under the conventional earnings statement approach, no line of distinction is drawn between fixed and variable selling expenses, and no attempt is made to compute the amount by which sales revenue exceeds the variable costs of the period. Thus, the total selling expenses for the period consisting of $15,000 of fixed expenses, and variable expenses of $1,800 (9,000 units at $0.20) are shown as one lump-sum amount.

Different valuations for inventory. Net earnings under full costing amount to $8,100 and are $600 less, at $7,500, under variable costing. Similarly, the inventory under variable costing is $600 less, at $3,300. In any situation in which the beginning inventories are the same, increasing the value attached

Illustration 22.8: Earnings
statement under
conventional costing

Sales (9,000 units at $8)		$72,000
Cost of goods sold:		
Variable costs of production (10,000 units at $3.30)	$33,000	
Fixed overhead costs	6,000	
Total costs of producing 10,000 units	$39,000	
Less: Inventory (1,000 units at $3.90)	3,900	35,100
Gross margin on sales		$36,900
Operating expenses:		
Selling ($15,000 fixed plus 9,000 at $0.20 each)	$16,800	
Administrative	12,000	28,800
Net Earnings		$ 8,100

to the ending inventory will increase the amount of net earnings reported.

The $600 difference in net earnings can be explained in yet another way. The fixed manufacturing overhead for the period was $6,000. Of the 10,000 units produced, 9,000 were sold and 1,000 are in inventory. Under full costing, 90 percent of the fixed costs is in cost of goods sold and 10 percent is in inventory (0.10 × $6,000 = $600). Under variable costing, none is in inventory, all are in expense.

Analysis is more complicated when both beginning and ending inventories are involved. But the difference in net earnings can be determined by ascertaining whether the amount of fixed overhead in inventory under full costing increased or decreased from the beginning to the end of the year. If it increased, net earnings under variable costing will be less. If it decreased, net earnings under variable costing will be more. As a general guide, the difference in earnings can be related to the *change* in inventories. Assuming a relatively constant level of production, if inventories are increased, production exceeded sales and the net earnings reported under variable costing will be less than under full costing. Conversely, if inventories are decreased, sales exceeded production and net earnings under variable costing will be larger than under full costing.

Variable costing— pro and con

Variable costing is not at present considered an acceptable method of costing for earnings measurement and for inventory valuation, nor is it allowed for tax purposes. It is considered unacceptable because it does not include in inventory all costs of producing the goods and because it misstates the period's charges against revenues. Currently accepted practice requires that all costs of producing a given product be, to the extent possible, attached to that product and treated as expenses only when the product is sold.

Advocates of variable costing prefer to treat the fixed manufacturing costs as part of the costs of being ready to produce. Such costs, they contend, should be charged to the period and not to the production of the period; that is, the relationship between such costs and production is so remote that they should be expensed in the period incurred. In this way, variable costing avoids the reporting of fluctuations in net earnings found under full costing when *production* varies from period to period. Net earnings should be a function of sales, not of production, or so the advocates of variable costing maintain.

The type of information accumulated under variable costing, especially the classification of costs as fixed and variable, is undoubtedly useful to management in gaining a thorough understanding of the relationships between cost, volume, and earnings. And certainly the responsibility for and the control of costs are more readily determined and secured through a proper classification of costs. Variable costing is undoubtedly a useful management tool; and for this reason its usage is likely to increase.

NEW TERMS INTRODUCED IN CHAPTER 22

Absorption or full costing—a concept of costing under which all production costs, including at least some if not all of the fixed factory overhead, are accounted for as product costs and allocated to the units produced during a period.

Equivalent units—a concept or method of measurement of output whereby a larger number of partially completed units of production is expressed in terms of an equivalent number of units of product that could have been brought to the fully completed state with the same productive effort; for example, bringing 1,000 units to a 75 percent level of completion is viewed as the equivalent of bringing 750 units to the 100 percent level of completion.

Finished goods card—contains a running record of units and costs of products completed, sold, and on hand.

Job order cost sheet—a form or record used as a means for accumulating the costs of completing a specific amount of goods called the job; the job order sheets for all of the partially completed jobs form the subsidiary ledger for the Work in Process account.

Job order cost system (job costing)—a cost accounting system in which the costs incurred to produce a product are accumulated by the individual job, such as a building, a dam, 1,000 chairs, or 10 desks.

Manufacturing overhead cost sheet—summarizes the various factory indirect costs incurred.

Materials requisition—a written order directing the stores clerk to issue certain materials to a production center or service center.

Process cost system (process costing)—a cost accounting system in which the costs incurred to produce a product are accumulated by the processes a product undergoes on its way to completion rather than by specific jobs.

Stores (or materials) card—shows the quantities (and costs) of each type of materials received, issued, and on hand.

Variable (direct, marginal) costing—a concept of costing under which costs are classified as fixed and variable with only variable manufacturing costs accounted for as *product costs,* while fixed manufacturing costs are treated as period costs, that is, as expenses incurred.

Work (labor time) ticket—a form or card that shows the amount of time taken by an employee to complete a given assignment; may be prepared for both direct and indirect labor.

DEMONSTRATION PROBLEM

Part 1. Heille Company employs a job order cost system. As of January 1, 1981, its records showed:

Raw materials and supplies .... $ 80,000
Work in process 172,000
Finished goods (50,000 units at $4) 200,000

The work in process inventory consists of two jobs:

No.	Materials	Labor	Manufacturing overhead	Total
212	$30,000	$40,000	$20,000	$ 90,000
213	34,000	32,000	16,000	82,000
	$64,000	$72,000	$36,000	$172,000

Summarized below are manufacturing data for the company for 1979:

1. Raw materials and supplies purchased on account, $330,000.
2. Factory payrolls accrued, $680,000; F.I.C.A. taxes withheld, $34,000; and federal income taxes withheld, $60,000.
3. Manufacturing overhead costs incurred: depreciation, $20,000; heat, light, and power, $8,000; and miscellaneous, $12,000.
4. Direct materials and supplies requisitioned: for Job No. 212, $52,000; Job No. 213, $96,000; Job No. 214, $160,000; and supplies requisitioned, $8,000.
5. Payrolls distributed: direct labor—Job No. 212, $80,000; Job No. 213, $160,000; Job. No. 214, $240,000; factory supervision, $80,000; and indirect labor, $120,000.
6. Overhead is assigned to work in process at the same rate per dollar of direct labor cost as in 1978.
7. Job Nos. 212 and 213 were completed.
8. The cost of goods sold for the year was $688,000.

Required:

Prepare general journal entries to record the above summarized data, as well as all closing entries for which you have sufficient information.

Part 2. AFA, Inc., uses a process cost system to accumulate the costs it incurs to produce aluminum awning stabilizers. The costs incurred in the finishing department are shown for the month of May. The May 1 inventory consisted of 30,000 units, fully complete as to materials, 80 percent complete as to conversion. Its total cost of $240,000 consisted of $180,000 of costs transferred in from the molding department, $25,000 of finishing department material costs, and $35,000 of conversion costs.

Costs from molding department (excluding costs in beginning inventory)		$600,000
Costs added in finishing department in May (excluding costs in beginning inventory):		
Materials	$ 53,000	
Conversion	109,480	162,480
		$762,480

The finishing department received 100,000 units from the molding department; 106,000 units were completed and transferred; 24,000 units, complete as to materials and 60 percent complete as to conversion, were left in the May 31 inventory.

Required:

a. Prepare a cost of production report for the finishing department for the month of May.

b. Compute the average unit cost for conversion for April in the finishing department.

Solution to demonstration problem

Part 1

HEILLE COMPANY General Journal		
a. Raw Materials and Supplies Inventory .... To record raw materials purchased on account.	330,000	
Accounts Payable		330,000

b. Payroll Summary 680,000
        F.I.C.A. Taxes Withheld   34,000
        Federal Income Taxes Withheld   60,000
        Accrued Payroll   586,000
    To record accrued factory payrolls.

c. Manufacturing Overhead 40,000
        Allowance for Depreciation   20,000
        Accounts Payable (Accrued Expenses, Cash, etc.)   20,000
    To record incurrence of various manufacturing overhead costs.

d. Work in Process Inventory 308,000
    Manufacturing Overhead   8,000
        Raw Materials and Supplies Inventory   316,000
    To record requisitions of materials and supplies:

        Job No. 212 .... $ 52,000
            213...   96,000
            214...   160,000
        Supplies .... $ 8,000
                                                              $316,000

e. Work in Process Inventory 480,000
    Manufacturing Overhead 200,000
        Payroll Summary   680,000
    To distribute labor costs:

        Direct labor to Work in Process:
            Job No. 212 .... $ 80,000
                213   160,000
                214 ....   240,000 $480,000

        Manufacturing overhead:
            Factory supervision .... $ 80,000
            Indirect labor   120,000   200,000
                                                              $680,000

f. Work in Process Inventory 240,000
        Manufacturing Overhead   240,000
    Overhead assigned: Job No. 212, $40,000; Job No. 213,
    $80,000; and Job No. 214, $120,000.

g. Finished Goods Inventory 680,000
        Work in Process Inventory   680,000
    Completed jobs transferred:

        No. 212 .... $262,000
        No. 213   418,000
                                                              $680,000

h. Cost of Goods Sold 688,000
        Finished Goods Inventory   688,000
    To record cost of goods sold.

    Cost of Goods Sold   8,000
        Manufacturing Overhead   8,000
    To close underapplied manufacturing overhead.

    Expense and Revenue Summary 696,000
        Cost of Goods Sold   696,000
    To close Cost of Goods Sold expense account.

Part 2
a.

AFA, INC.
Finishing Department
Cost of Production Report
For the Month Ended May 31

| | | Equivalent units | | |
	Actual units	Transferred in	Materials	Conversion
UNITS:				
Units in May 1 inventory	30,000			
Units transferred in	100,000			
Units to be accounted for ...	130,000			
Units completed and transferred ...	106,000	106,000	106,000	106,000
Units in May 31 inventory*	24,000	24,000	24,000	14,400
Units accounted for	130,000	130,000	130,000	120,400

* Inventory is complete as to materials, 60% complete as to conversion.

	Transferred in	Materials	Conversion	Total
COSTS:				
Costs to be accounted for:				
Costs in May 1 inventory	$180,000	$ 25,000	$ 35,000	$ 240,000
Costs transferred in	600,000			600,000
Costs added in department		53,000	109,480	162,480
Costs to be accounted for ..	$780,000	$ 78,000	$144,480	$1,002,480
Equivalent units (as above)	130,000	130,000	120,400	
Unit costs	$6.00	$0.60	$1.20	$7.80
Costs accounted for:				
Costs in May 31 inventory	$144,000	$ 14,400	$ 17,280	$ 175,680
Costs transferred out	636,000	$ 63,600	127,200	826,800
Costs accounted for	$780,000	$ 78,000	$144,480	$1,002,480

b. The unit cost for conversion in the finishing department in April was $1.46 [$35,000 ÷ (0.8 × 30,000)].

QUESTIONS

1. What is the basic purpose of any costing system?

2. In what respects does a process cost system differ from a job order cost system? What factors should be taken into consideration in determining which type of system should be employed?

3. What is a job order sheet? Explain how it is used.

4. What questions might be raised relative to an assertion that a given product has a unit manufacturing cost of $10?

5. What is meant by the term equivalent production? Of what use is the computation of the number of units of equivalent production?

6. Distinguish between the number of units completed and transferred during a period and the equivalent production for the same period.

7. What is the basic information reported in a cost of production report?

8. Under what circumstances would there be a different number of equivalent units of materials than of labor and overhead in the same department in the same period? Under what circumstances would they be the same?

9. Under what circumstances would it be necessary to compute several measures of the equivalent production for a period as regards materials?

10. Should the overtime premium paid on direct labor in a job cost system be charged to the specific jobs worked on? Can you give examples supporting both an affirmative and a negative answer?

11. Under what circumstances in a process cost system is the assignment of overhead to production through

use of a predetermined rate definitely preferable to assigning actual overhead incurred?

12. It requires less effort to operate a job cost system than a process cost system. Agree or disagree? Explain.

13. What essential feature distinguishes variable costing from absorption costing?

14. Under what specific circumstances would you expect the net earnings under variable costing to be larger than under full costing? What is the specific reason for this difference?

EXERCISES

E-1. Job No. 210 has, at the end of the second week in February, an accumulated total cost of $4,200. In the third week, $1,000 of direct materials were used on the job, together with $10 of indirect materials; 200 hours of direct labor were charged to the job at $5 per hour; and manufacturing overhead was applied on the basis of $2.50 per direct labor-hour for fixed overhead and $2 per hour for variable overhead. Job No. 210 was the only job completed in the third week. Compute the cost of Job No. 210 and give the journal entry required to record its completion.

E-2. George Company applies overhead to jobs at a rate of 120 percent of direct labor cost. When completed, Job No. 312 was charged with $1,800 of overhead. Compute the direct labor cost charged to the job.

E-3. Prest Company's Work in Process Inventory account contained the following for June:

a. Units started in production during the month, 30,000; units completed and transferred, 22,000; and units in process at the end of the month (60 percent complete), 8,000.

b. Units in process at beginning of month, 30 percent complete, 5,000; units started during month, 20,000; and units in process at end of month (40 percent complete) 10,000.

E-5. Assume that the data in **(a)** of Exercise E-4 relate to labor for May in Department A. If total labor cost for the department consisted of 2,010 hours at $8 per hour, compute:

a. The labor cost per equivalent unit of production for the month.

b. The labor cost of the ending inventory in the department.

Work in Process Inventory

Direct materials	500,000	Goods completed	700,000
Direct labor	200,000		
Manufacturing overhead	500,000		

Job No. 374 is the only incomplete job at the end of June, and it has been charged with $150,000 of direct materials. Prest applies overhead to its jobs using a rate based on direct labor cost. Compute the direct labor cost and manufacturing overhead charged to Job No. 374.

E-4. Compute the equivalent production in each case given below:

E-6. The Gold Company, which uses a job order cost system, has just completed a job for State Bank—a special order for 200 gold-plated mechanical pencils. Direct material cost was $500; direct labor cost—200 hours at $5 per hour. Budgeted direct labor for this year was $400,000, while overhead was budgeted at $1,000,000. If the overhead rate is expressed as a percentage of direct labor cost, what is the total cost and the unit cost of the bank's order?

E-7. In Department A, materials are added uniformly throughout processing. The beginning inventory was considered 50 percent complete as was the ending inventory. Assume there were 1,000 units in the beginning inventory, 3,000 in the ending inventory, and that 16,000 units were completed and transferred. If average unit costs are to be computed, what is the equivalent production for the period?

E-8. If in Exercise E-7 the total costs charged to the department amounted to $70,000, including the $2,010 cost of the beginning inventory, what is the cost of units completed and transferred?

E-9. Martin Company processes the single product that it manufactures through Process A and Process B sequentially. Records show the following with respect to units processed in May:

	Process A		Process B	
	Units	Percent complete	Units	Percent complete
Inventory May 1	8,000	60	5,000	80
Inventory May 31	4,000	75	6,000	50
Units started in production	20,000		24,000	
Units transferred out	24,000		23,000	

Compute the equivalent production for both processes for May.

E-10. The following data relate to Department A in which all material is added at the start of processing and in which the weight of the finished product is equal to the weight of the direct materials used:

Inventory, June 1:
Materials cost (400 pounds) . . . . $ 780
Conversion cost (20% complete) 110
Direct materials used (2,000
  pounds at $2.01) 4,020
Direct labor (300 hours at $4.40) 1,320
Overhead (at 150% of direct
  labor cost) 1,980

Inventory, June 30:
Materials cost (600 pounds,
  100% complete) . . . . ?
Conversion cost (600 pounds,
  ⅔ complete . . . . ?

Using the above data, compute:

a. The number of pounds transferred out of the department in June.

b. The unit cost per equivalent unit for materials and conversion (use the average method).

c. The cost of the product transferred out.

d. The cost of the ending inventory.

e. The change in the conversion cost per unit from May to June.

E-11. The following data are for a certain company for the year 1981:

Sales (20,000 units) $200,000
Raw materials used (24,000 units at $3) 72,000
Direct labor cost incurred 24,000
Manufacturing overhead incurred:
  Variable 7,200
  Fixed 9,600
Selling and administrative expenses:
  Variable 12,000
  Fixed 40,000

Assume that one unit of raw materials goes into each unit of finished goods, that there is an ending inventory of finished goods of 4,000 units, that there are no other beginning or ending inventories, and that the variable and fixed overhead rates (based on normal activity of 24,000 units) were $0.30 and $0.40, respectively. Compute the earnings before income taxes under **(a)** full costing and **(b)** variable costing.

E-12. Given below are the costs of the finished goods inventories of the M Company:

Cost element	Beginning inventory	Ending inventory
Direct materials	$30,000	$3,000
Direct labor	50,000	5,200
Overhead:		
Variable	20,000	2,000
Fixed	15,000	2,000

Assume that the M Company employs an absorption costing technique in costing its products and that there were no work in process inventories at the beginning or end of the year. State how much its net earnings before income taxes for the year would have differed if it could have used a variable costing technique for tax purposes.

PROBLEMS, SERIES A

P22-1-A. The Ace Company began business on June 1 and engaged in the following activities and incurred the following costs in June:

Raw materials purchased $13,000
Factory payroll costs incurred (all employees are paid
  $5 per hour) 10,500
Factory indirect costs (other than indirect labor) 3,800

The costs charged to the three jobs worked on in June were:

	Job No. 101	Job No. 102	Job No. 103
Direct materials	$2,000	$3,500	$2,500
Direct labor	2,000	4,500	3,500
Overhead applied at $2 per direct labor-hour	?	?	?

Job No. 101 was completed and sold for $8,000; Job No. 102 was completed but not sold; and Job No. 103 is incomplete. No other costs were incurred.

Required:

a. Compute the June 30 balance for each of the three inventory accounts.

b. Prepare an earnings statement for the month of June, assuming selling and administrative expenses were $2,000.

P22-2-A. Hall Company uses a job order cost system, applying overhead through use of a predetermined rate based on direct labor-hours in Department A and machine-hours in Department B. A job may be worked on in either Department A or B. Budget estimates for 1981 are:

	Department A	Department B
Direct labor cost	$60,000	$66,000
Manufacturing overhead	$72,000	$96,000
Direct labor-hours	12,000	16,000
Machine-hours	8,000	24,000

Detailed cost records show the following for Job No. 105 which was completed in 1981:

	Department A	Department B
Materials used	$110	$34
Direct labor cost	$ 42	$72
Direct labor-hours	10	20
Machine-hours	6	16

Required:

a. Compute the overhead rates for 1981 for Departments A and B.

b. Compute the amount of overhead applied to Job No. 105 in each department.

c. Compute the total and unit cost of the 20 units in Job No. 105.

d. Assume the bases upon which the rates were predetermined were switched between the two departments. What would be the difference in the total cost of Job No. 105?

e. The actual operating results for 1981 were:

	Department A	Department B
Actual manufacturing overhead	$74,000	$98,000
Actual direct labor-hours	12,100	16,100
Actual machine-hours	8,200	24,600

Ignore the assumption in part **(d)**. Compute the under- or overapplied overhead for each department for the year.

P22-3-A. Wynn Company employs a job order cost system. As of January 1, 1981, its records showed the following inventory balances:

Raw materials and supplies .... $ 45,000
Work in process 86,000
Finished goods (25,000 units @ $4) 100,000

The work in process inventory consisted of two jobs:

Job No.	Materials	Direct labor	Manufacturing overhead	Total
212	$15,000	$20,000	$10,000	$45,000
213	17,000	16,000	8,000	41,000
	$32,000	$36,000	$18,000	$86,000

Summarized below are production and sales data for the company for 1981.

1. Raw materials and supplies purchased, $160,000.
2. Factory payroll costs incurred, $340,000.
3. Factory indirect costs incurred (other than indirect labor and indirect materials): depreciation, $10,000; heat, light, and power, $4,000; and miscellaneous, $6,000.
4. Raw materials and supplies requisitioned: direct materials for Job No. 212, $26,000, for Job No. 213, $48,000, and for Job No. 214, $80,000; supplies (indirect materials) requisitioned, $4,000.
5. Factory payroll distributed: direct labor to Job No. 212, $40,000, to Job No. 213, $80,000, and to Job No. 214, $120,000; indirect labor, $100,000.
6. Overhead is assigned to work in process at the same rate per dollar of direct labor cost as in 1980.
7. Job Nos. 212 and 213 were completed.

8. Sales for the year amounted to $600,000; cost of goods sold, $344,000.

Required:

a. Prepare journal entires to record the above transactions.

b. Prepare all closing entries for which you have information.

c. Set up T-accounts for Materials Inventory, Payroll Summary, Manufacturing Overhead, Work in Process Inventory, Finished Goods Inventory, and Cost of Goods Sold. Post those parts of the entries made in **(a)** and **(b)** that affect these accounts.

d. Show that the total of the costs charged to incomplete jobs agrees with the balance in fhe Work in Process Inventory account.

P22–4–A. Following are cost and production data of the DBA Company's Department Y, in which all material is added at the beginning of the production process and in which the weight of the finished product is equal to the weight of the raw materials used:

Work in process, June 1, 400 pounds
(¼ complete as to conversion):

Raw materials	$1,600
Direct labor	200
Manufacturing overhead	300
	$2,100

Raw materials placed in production in June, 2,000 pounds	8,000
Direct labor, 600 hours @ $4.80	2,880
Overhead applied, 150% of direct labor cost	4,320
Work in process inventory, June 30, 600 pounds (⅔ complete as to conversion)	?

Required:

Using the above data, compute:

a. The number of pounds of product transferred out of Department Y in June.

b. The unit cost for the month per equivalent unit for materials, labor, and overhead using the average cost method.

c. The cost of the product transferred out of Department Y in June.

d. The cost of the ending work in process inventory in Department Y.

P22–5–A. Strong Company uses a process cost system to account for the costs incurred in making its single product, a health food called Vita-Myte. This product is processed first in Department K and then in Department L, with materials added in both departments. Production for May was as follows:

	Depart-ment K	Depart-ment L
Units started or transferred in	200,000	150,000
Units completed and transferred out	150,000	120,000
Stage of completion of May 31 inventory:		
Materials	100%	80%
Conversion	50%	40%
Direct materials costs	$120,000	$ 21,600
Conversion costs	350,000	237,600

There was no May 1 inventory in either department.

Required:

a. Prepare a cost of production report for Department K for May.

b. Prepare a cost of production report for Department L for May.

P22–6–A. The following data are for the Stein Company for the year 1981:

Sales (10,000 units)	$100,000
Direct materials used (12,000 units at $3)	36,000
Direct labor cost incurred	12,000
Variable manufacturing overhead incurred	3,600
Fixed manufacturing overhead incurred	4,800
Variable selling and administrative expenses	6,000
Fixed selling and administrative expenses	20,000

One unit of direct materials goes into each unit of finished goods. The only beginning or ending inventory is the 2,000 units of finished goods on hand at the end of 1981. Variable and fixed overhead rates (based on 100 percent of capacity of 12,000 units) were $0.30 and $0.40, respectively.

Required:

Prepare an earnings statement under—

a. Variable costing.

b. Full costing.

PROBLEMS, SERIES B

P22-1-B. Blake Corporation employs a job order cost system. Its manufacturing activities in July 1981, its first month of operation, are summarized as follows:

	Job Number			
	201	*202*	*203*	*204*
Direct materials	$8,000	$5,800	$12,600	$6,000
Direct labor cost	$6,600	$6,000	$ 8,400	$2,400
Direct labor-hours . . .	1,100	1,000	1,400	400
Units produced	200	100	1,000	300

Manufacturing overhead is applied at a rate of $2 per direct labor-hour for variable overhead, $3 per hour for fixed overhead.

Job Nos. 201, 202, and 203 were completed in July.

Required:

a. Compute the amount of overhead charged to each job.

b. Compute the total and unit cost of each completed job.

c. Prepare the entry, in general form, to record the transfer of completed jobs to Finished Goods.

d. Compute the balance in the July 31, 1981, Work in Process account and provide a schedule of the costs charged to each incomplete job to support this balance.

P22-2-B. The Littler, Inc., general ledger on June 1, 1981, shows the following balances:

Sales	$4,000,000
Raw materials inventory	200,000
Work in process inventory	90,000
Finished goods inventory	250,000
Manufacturing overhead	1,000 Cr.
Accrued salaries and wages	4,000
Cost of goods sold	3,000,000
Selling expenses	300,000
Administrative expenses	400,000

The work in process inventory consists of the following:

Job No. 1948:		
Material	$66,000
Labor	8,000
Overhead	16,000
	$90,000

Summarized, the transactions occurring in June 1981 were:

1. Raw materials purchased on account, $260,000.
2. Payroll for the month, $44,750; F.I.C.A. taxes withheld, $2,400; and federal income taxes withheld, $4,000.

3. Materials issued during the month: direct, $110,000; and indirect, $16,000. Of the direct materials, $5,000 is assignable to Job No. 1948; the balance to Job No. 1949.
4. Payroll for the month consisted of direct labor $30,000 (Job No. 1948, $6,000; Job No. 1949, $24,000); factory supervision, $800; factory maintenance, $1,200; sales salaries, $4,750; and office and officers' salaries, $8,000.
5. Manufacturing overhead rate is 200 percent of direct labor cost.
6. Other costs incurred in June (on account or accrued except for depreciation and amortization):

Rent (60% factory, 40% administrative)	$20,000
Factory heat, light, and power	11,000
Factory machinery repairs	3,800
Amortization of patents	7,400
Depreciation on factory machinery	9,000
Taxes on factory machinery	1,800
Various selling expenses	20,000

7. Job No. 1948 was completed during the month.
8. Sales for June, $600,000; cost of these sales was $310,000.

Required:

a. Prepare journal entries to record the above summarized data.

b. Prepare any necessary adjusting and closing entries.

c. Prepare a condensed earnings statement for the year ended June 30, 1981.

P22-3-B. The following data are for the initial processing center of the Allan Company for the month of July. All material is added at the beginning of the processing operation.

Work in process inventory, July 1 (10,000 pounds, 40% complete as to conversion):	
Direct materials:	$ 5,000
Direct labor	800
Manufacturing overhead (200% of direct labor cost)	1,600
	$ 7,400
Added in July:	
Direct materials (90,000 pounds)	$45,900
Direct labor (2,000 hours at $8)	16,000
Manufacturing overhead	32,000

The work in process inventory at July 31 consisted of 30,000 units (pounds), one-third complete as to processing.

Required:

Compute the following:

a. Number of pounds completed and transferred out of the processing center.

b. The equivalent units of production for materials, labor, and overhead for July (assuming average unit costs are to be computed).

c. The average unit costs for July for materials, labor, and overhead.

d. The cost of the pounds transferred out in July.

e. The cost of the July 31 work in process inventory.

f. The average unit labor cost last month (June).

P22–4–B. Baker Company manufactures a product called a Savem. It determines product costs using a process cost system. Following are cost and production data for the handle department for the month of June:

	Units	Materials costs	Conversion costs
Inventory, June 1	20,000	$1,790	$2,200
Placed in production			
in June	60,000	5,410	9,560
Inventory, June 30	30,000	?	?

The June 1 inventory was complete as to materials and 50 percent complete as to conversion. The June 30 inventory was complete as to materials and 20 percent complete as to conversion.

Required:

Prepare a cost of production report.

P22–5–B. Castle Drug Company manufactures Sure-Stop, a cold remedy, in a blending department from which the remedy is transferred to the bottling department. Production and cost data for the bottling department for June are as follows:

Work in process, June 1 (40,000 pints):
Transferred-in costs (100% complete) $20,000
Bottling materials (100% complete) 8,000
Conversion costs (50% complete) 4,000

Added in June:
Transferred in (120,000 pints) 61,600
Bottling materials for 120,000 units 25,600
Conversion costs 24,500

All materials in the bottling department are added at the beginning of processing, and their amounts are determined by the number of pints of Sure-Stop transferred in. The ending inventory for June was 20,000 units, 100 percent complete as to materials and 50 percent complete as to conversion.

Required:

a. Prepare a cost of production report for the bottling department for the month of June.

b. Compute the per unit conversion cost in the department for the prior month (May).

c. Give the journal entry needed to record the transfer of the units completed in the bottling department in June.

P22–6–B. Garcia Company employs a full cost system in accounting for the single product it manufactures. Following are selected data for the year 1981:

Sales (10,000 units)	$200,000
Direct materials used (12,000 units at $6)	72,000
Direct labor cost incurred	24,000
Variable manufacturing overhead	7,200
Fixed manufacturing overhead	9,600
Variable selling and administrative expenses	12,000
Fixed selling and administrative expenses	40,000

One unit of direct materials goes into each unit of finished goods. Overhead rates are based on practical capacity of 12,000 units and are $0.60 and $0.80 per unit for variable and fixed overhead. The only beginning or ending inventory is the 2,000 units of finished goods on hand at the end of 1981.

Required:

a. Prepare an earnings statement for 1981 under variable costing.

b. Prepare an earnings statement for 1981 under full costing.

c. Explain the reason for the different net earnings as between *(a)* and *(b)*.

BUSINESS DECISION PROBLEM 22–1

The general manager of the Chicago Division of the Burleson Company submitted its earnings statement for the year ended June 30, 1981 (prepared under full costing), with the comment that the division was at least profitable. The report showed that sales amounted to 80,000 units at $20 per unit and that the following costs had been incurred:

Direct materials	$440,000
Direct labor	190,000
Manufacturing overhead	570,000
Selling and administrative	600,000

A total of 110,000 units was put into process during the year. Of the 30,000 units in the June 30, 1981, inventory, all materials costs have been incurred but the units were only 50 percent complete as to processing. There were no other finished goods or work in process inventories, either beginning or ending.

The Chicago Division's production process is highly automated and its costs are largely fixed—$475,000 of the overhead and $200,000 of the selling and administrative costs are fixed.

Upon receipt of the division's earnings statement, the company's controller made a few quick calculations and commented that the division actually operated at a loss. To this, the general manager of the division took exception, causing a long argument.

Required:

a. Prepare the division's earnings statement under full costing. Include a schedule showing computation of the cost of the ending inventory. Assume fixed overhead is absorbed under expected activity and this equaled actual activity for the year.

b. Repeat part *(a)* under variable costing.

c. State exactly what causes the difference in net earnings between *(a)* and *(b)*.

d. Who is right in this debate? Explain.

BUSINESS DECISION PROBLEM 22–2

The Detroit Division of the Orvis Company produces a single product which it sells for $9 each. Its production costs are $2 per unit variable costs and $480,000 per year of fixed overhead costs. Normal activity for fixed overhead absorption is 160,000 units per year.

On December 31, 1979, the division's finished goods inventory consisted of 20,000 units with a total cost of $100,000 ($40,000, variable; $60,000, fixed). Sales and production data for the years 1980, 1981, and 1982 are:

Year	Sales in units	Dollars of sales	Production in units	Variable production costs
1980	100,000	$900,000	110,000	$220,000
1981	100,000	900,000	80,000	160,000
1982	100,000	900,000	180,000	360,000

Required:

a. Prepare earnings statements for the division for each of the years 1980, 1981, and 1982 under full costing.

b. Repeat part *(a)* under variable costing.

c. Comment briefly on the differences noted and the reasons therefor. Specifically, consider the following questions. Which method shows earnings which vary with sales volume? Which method results in the volume of production affecting earnings? Why might the production for 1982 have been increased to 180,000 units? What are the implications of the above production policy for future earnings in the external financial statements?

Chapter 23

Control through

standard costs

STANDARD COSTS

The job order and process cost systems discussed in Chapter 22 gathered actual historical cost data. But because these data say little about how efficiently operations were conducted, many firms find it helpful to introduce standard costs into their job order or process cost systems. Thus, standard costs can be used in both job order cost and process cost systems. The Appendix at the end of this chapter illustrates how this can be done.

Nature of standard costs

A *standard cost* is a carefully predetermined measure of what a cost *should be* under stated conditions. It is not merely an estimate of what a cost will be; it is more in the nature of a goal to be sought. If properly set, achieving a standard represents a reasonable level of performance.

Standards are set in many ways, but to be of any real value they must be more than mere estimates derived from extending historical trends into the future. Usually engineering and time and motion studies are undertaken to determine the material, labor, and other services required to produce a unit of product. Knowledge of the actual working conditions in a plant is required. Also, general economic conditions must be studied because they will affect the costs of materials and the other services that must be purchased.

The goal is to set a standard cost for each unit of product to be manufactured by determining the standard costs of the direct materials, direct labor, and factory overhead needed to produce it. The standard direct materials cost is made up of a standard number of units of each material required multiplied by a standard price for each. Similarly, the standard direct labor cost consists of the standard number of hours of direct labor needed multiplied by the standard labor or wage rate. The standard overhead cost of a unit is usually based upon a predetermined rate which is computed from standard (budgeted) overhead costs and standard production, although it may be expressed as a rate per unit of some measure of activity such as direct labor-hours. Thus, in both a standard cost system and an actual cost system, overhead is assigned to production through use of a predetermined rate. The two systems differ in that an actual cost system collects actual costs for materials and labor while a standard cost system gathers standard costs and transfers these costs through the system into finished goods.

Advantages of using standard costs

A number of benefits result from the use of a standard cost system. These include (1) cost control, (2) provision of information useful in managerial planning and decision making, (3) more reasonable inventory measurements, (4) cost savings in record keeping, and (5) possibly some reductions in the costs incurred.

Cost control is secured largely by setting standards for each type of cost incurred—materials, labor, and overhead. The amounts by which actual costs differ from standard are recorded in *variance* accounts. These variances provide a starting point in judging the effectiveness of managers in controlling the costs they incur and for which they are held responsible. For example, for such purposes, it is far more useful to know that actual direct materials costs of $52,015 in a certain center exceeded standard by $6,015 than merely to know that actual materials costs amounted to $52,015. Thus, a standard cost system highlights *exceptions;* that is, instances where things are not going as planned. Further investigation will show whether the exception is caused by factors under management's control or not. For example, the exception (the variance) may be caused by inefficient use of materials, or it may be the result of inflation. In either case, the standard cost system has served as an early warning system by highlighting a potential problem for management. On the other hand, little attention is usually paid to actual costs when such costs differ only slightly from standard.

If management develops appropriate standards and succeeds in controlling costs, future actual costs should be fairly close to standard. When this is true, standard costs can be used in preparing budgets and in estimating costs for bidding on jobs.

In a standard cost system, all units of a given product are carried in inventory at the same unit cost. It seems logical that physically identical units should have the same cost. But under an actual cost system, unit costs for batches of identical products may differ because more labor and overhead were assigned to one batch simply because a machine was out of adjustment when the batch was produced. Under a standard cost system, such costs would not be included in inventory. Rather, they would be charged to variance accounts. These accounts are discussed below.

Although standard cost systems may appear to require more detailed record keeping than an actual cost system, actually the reverse is true. For example, in a job order system, detailed accounts or records must be kept of the various types of materials used on each job as well as the various types and quantities of labor services received. In a standard cost system, standard cost sheets may be printed in advance showing quantities, unit costs, and total costs for the materials, labor, and overhead needed to produce a given amount of a certain product. Thus, when a job is started, the job order sheet shows all the various costs that apply to it. There is no need to post individual materials requisitions to individual job order sheets. One entry can be made at the end of the month for the total materials used. Also, since inventories are carried at standard cost, the problems of assumed cost flows—Lifo, Fifo, and so forth—disappear.

The use of standard costs may cause employees to become quite cost conscious and to seek improved methods of completing their tasks. This may result in cost savings.

COMPUTING VARIANCES

As noted above, a variance exists when standard costs differ from actual costs. It is logical to look upon a variance as favorable when actual costs are less than standard costs, and to view the variance as unfavorable when actual costs exceed standard. But it does not follow automatically that these terms should be equated with good and bad as will be explained later. Such an appraisal should be made only after the causes of the variance are known.

Variances cannot serve as essential elements in cost control until they have been isolated. Thus, attention is directed first to the computation of the dollar amount of a variance. The discussion and illustrations that follow are based upon the activities of the Beta Company which manufactures and sells a single product which has the following standard costs:

Materials—5 sheets @ $6	....	$30
Direct labor—2 hours @ $10	....	20
Manufacturing overhead—2 direct labor-hours @ $5	....	10
Total standard cost per unit	....	$60

Additional data regarding the productive activities of the company will be presented as needed.

Materials variances

The standard materials cost of any product is simply the standard *quantity* of materials that should be used multiplied by the *price* that should be paid for those materials. From this it follows that actual costs may differ from standard costs for materials because of the *quantity* of materials used or the *price* paid for the materials. This suggests the need to isolate two variances for materials—a *price variance* and a *usage variance*. But there are other reasons for so doing. First, different individuals may be responsible for each—a purchasing agent for the price variance and a production manager for the usage variance. Second, the materials may not be purchased and used in the same period. The variance associated with the purchase should be isolated in the period of purchase, that associated with usage should be isolated in the period of use. As a general rule, the sooner a variance can be isolated, the greater its value in cost control. And, finally, it is unlikely that a single materials variance—the difference between the standard cost and the actual cost of the materials used—would be of any real value to management.

Materials price variance. The standard price for material meeting certain engineering specifications is usually set by the purchasing and accounting departments. Consideration will, of course, be given to market conditions, vendors' quoted prices, the optimum size of a purchase order, and to other factors. Purchasing materials at a price other than standard gives rise to a *materials price variance*. The materials price variance (MPV) is the difference between actual price (AP) and standard price (SP) multiplied by the actual quantity (AQ) of materials purchased. In equation form, the materials price variance is:

$$MPV = (AP - SP) \times AQ$$

To illustrate, assume that the Beta Company was able, because of the entry into the market of a new foreign supplier, to purchase 60,000 sheets of material at a price of $5.90 each, for a total cost of $354,000. Since the standard price is $6 per sheet, the materials price variance using the above formula is:

$$MPV = (AP - SP) \times AQ$$
$$MPV = (\$5.90 - \$6.00) \times 60,000$$
$$MPV = -\$0.10 \times 60,000$$
$$MPV = -\$6,000$$

The materials price variance of $6,000 is considered favorable since the materials were acquired for a price less than standard. (Why it is expressed as a negative amount will be explained later.) If the actual price had exceeded standard price, the variance would be considered unfavorable because more costs were incurred than allowed by the standard. The entry to record the purchase of the materials is:

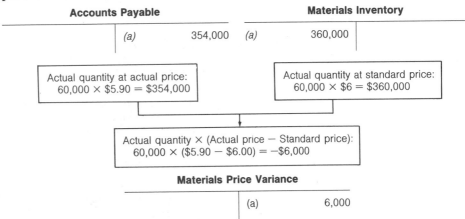

Note that the Accounts Payable account shows the actual debt owed to suppliers, the Materials Inventory account shows the *standard price* of the actual quantity of materials purchased, while the Materials Price Variance account shows the difference between actual price and standard price multiplied by the actual quantity purchased.

Materials usage variance. Since it is largely a matter of physical aspects or product specifications, the standard quantity of materials to be used in making a product is usually set by the engineering department. But if the quality of materials used varies with price, the accounting and purchasing departments may take part in special studies to find the "right" quality.

The *materials usage variance* shows whether the amount of materials used was more or less than the standard amount allowed. It shows only differences from standard caused by the quantity of materials used; it does not include price variances. Thus, the materials usage variance (MUV) is equal to actual quantity used (AQ) minus standard quantity allowed (SQ) multiplied by standard price (SP):

$$MUV = (AQ - SQ) \times SP$$

To illustrate, assume that the Beta Company used 55,500 sheets of materials to produce 11,000 units of a product for which the standard quantity allowed is 55,000 sheets ($5 \times 11,000$). Since the standard price of the material is $6 per sheet, the materials usage variance of $3,000 would be computed as follows:

$$MUV = (AQ - SQ) \times SP$$
$$MUV = (55,500 - 55,000) \times \$6$$
$$MUV = 500 \times \$6$$
$$MUV = \$3,000$$

The variance is unfavorable because more materials were used than the standard amount allowed to complete the job. If the standard quantity allowed had exceeded the quantity actually used, the materials usage variance would have been favorable. The entry to record the use of materials is as follows:

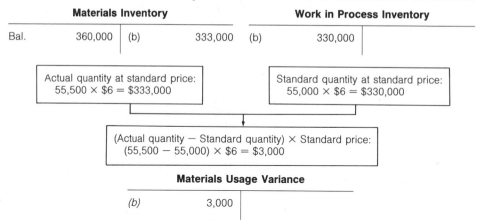

	Materials Inventory				Work in Process Inventory	
Bal.	360,000	(b)	333,000	(b)	330,000	

Actual quantity at standard price:
55,500 × $6 = $333,000

Standard quantity at standard price:
55,000 × $6 = $330,000

(Actual quantity − Standard quantity) × Standard price:
(55,500 − 55,000) × $6 = $3,000

Materials Usage Variance	
(b) 3,000	

The Materials Usage Variance shows the standard cost of the excess materials used. Note, also, that the Work in Process Inventory account contains standard quantities and standard prices.

The equations for both of the above materials variances were expressed in a manner so that positive amounts were unfavorable variances and negative amounts were favorable variances. Unfavorable variances are debits in variance accounts because they add to the costs incurred, which, of course, are recorded as debits. Similarly, favorable variances are shown as negative amounts because they are reductions in costs. It follows that they are recorded in variance accounts as credits. And this format will be used in this text. But a word of caution is in order. Far greater understanding is achieved if a variance is determined to be favorable or unfavorable by reliance upon reason or logic. If more materials were used than standard, or if a price greater than standard was paid, the variance is unfavorable. If the reverse is true, the variance is favorable.

Labor variances

The standard labor cost of any product is equal to the standard quantity of labor time allowed multiplied by the wage rate that should be paid for this time. Here again it follows that the actual labor cost may differ from standard labor cost because of the *quantity* of labor used, the *wages* paid for labor, or both. Both of the labor variances relate to the same period because labor services cannot be purchased in one period, stored, and then used in the next period.

Labor rate variance.   The *labor rate variance* shows how much the actual labor cost of a product differed from its standard cost because actual pay rates differed from standard rates. In this respect, it is similar to the materials price variance. Typically, actual wage rates are set in bargaining between a firm and the employees' union.

The labor rate variance (LRV) is computed by multiplying the difference between the actual rate (AR) paid and the standard rate (SR) allowed by the actual hours (AH) of labor services received:

$$LRV = (AR - SR) \times AH$$

To continue our Beta Company example, assume that the direct labor payroll of the company consisted of 22,200 hours and a total cost of $233,100 (an average actual hourly rate of $10.50). With a standard labor rate of $10 per hour, the labor rate variance is:

$$LRV = (AR - SR) \times AH$$
$$LRV = (\$10.50 - \$10.00) \times 22,200$$
$$LRV = \$0.50 \times 22,200$$
$$LRV = \$11,100$$

The variance is positive and unfavorable since the actual rate paid exceeded the standard rate allowed. If the reverse were true, the variance would be favorable. The recording of the variance will be presented after the labor time variance has been illustrated and discussed.

Labor efficiency variance.   The *labor efficiency variance* is, in effect, a quantity variance. It shows whether the actual labor time required to complete a period's output or a given job was more or less than the standard amount allowed. The standard amount of labor time needed to complete a product is usually set by the firm's engineering department. It may be based on time and motion studies and may be the subject of bargaining with the employees' union.

The labor efficiency variance (LEV) is computed by multiplying the difference between the actual hours (AH) required and the standard hours (SH) allowed by the standard rate (SR) per hour, or

$$LEV = (AH - SH) \times SR$$

To illustrate, assume that the 22,200 hours of labor time received from its employees by the Beta Company resulted in production with a standard labor time of 22,000 hours. Since the standard labor rate is $10 per hour, the labor time variance is $2,000 (unfavorable), computed as follows:

$$LEV = (AH - SH) \times SR$$
$$LEV = (22,200 - 22,000) \times \$10$$
$$LEV = 200 \times \$10$$
$$LEV = \$2,000$$

The variance is unfavorable since more hours than standard were required to complete the period's production. If the reverse had been true, the variance would be favorable.

A graphic illustration may aid in understanding the relationship between standard and actual labor cost and the computation of the labor variances. Illustration 23.1 is deliberately not drawn to scale and is based upon the following data relating to the Beta Company:

Standard labor time per unit	2 hours
Equivalent units produced in period	11,000 units
Standard labor rate per direct labor-hour	$10
Total direct labor wages paid (at average rate of $10.50 per hour)	$233,100
Actual direct labor-hours received	22,200 hours

**Illustration 23.1:
Computation of the
labor variances**

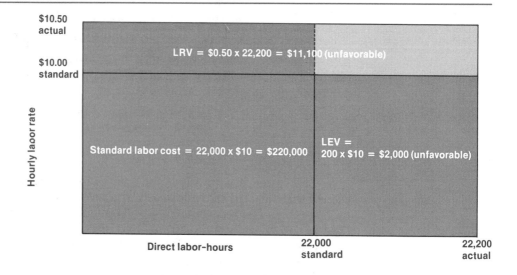

The standard labor time allowed for the period's output was 22,000 hours (11,000 units at 2 hours per unit). The standard labor cost of the output then is $220,000 (22,000 hours at $10 per hour, the standard labor rate). The labor time or efficiency variance is the standard cost of the extra hours of labor required [(22,200 − 22,000) × $10], or $2,000. The actual labor rate is $10.50 per hour. The labor rate variance then is the 50 cents per hour ($10.50 − $10.00) of above-standard wages paid multiplied by the standard hours allowed (22,000) and, by convention. the above-standard wages paid per hour on the extra hours required (200)—the shaded area in the upper right-hand corner of the rectangle. The variation from standard shown by this shaded area is actually caused by both extra hours and above-standard wages per hour. But, as shown, it is included in the labor rate variance as this variance is based on actual hours worked.

The entry to charge Work in Process Inventory with direct labor cost and to set up the two labor variances for the Beta Company would be as follows:

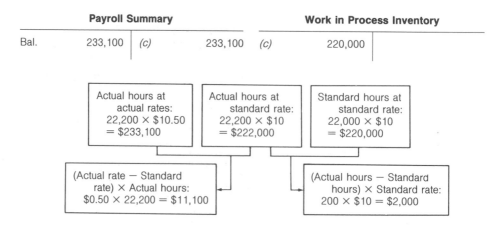

Labor Rate Variance		Labor Efficiency Variance	
(c)	11,100	(c)	2,000

With the above entry, the gross wages earned by direct production employees ($233,100) is distributed as follows: $220,000 (the standard labor cost of the production) to Work in Process Inventory and the balance to the two labor variance accounts. Note that the labor rate variance is not caused by paying employees more wages than they are entitled to receive. The more likely reason is that employees with different pay rates can complete the same task and that too much of the higher hourly rated employee time was used on a given job. Also, if some overtime premium pay is expected in setting standards, then variation from expected amounts can cause a labor rate variance. But, typically, the hours of labor employed are more likely to be under the control of management, and for this reason the labor efficiency variance is watched more closely.

Summary of labor variances. The accuracy of the computation of the two labor variances can be checked readily by comparing their sum with the difference between actual and standard labor cost for a period. In the Beta Company illustration this difference was:

Actual labor cost incurred	$233,100
Standard labor cost allowed	220,000
Total labor variance (unfavorable)	$ 13,100

This $13,100 is made up of two labor variances, both unfavorable:

Labor efficiency variance (200 × $10)	$ 2,000
Labor rate variance (22,200 × $0.50)	11,100
Total labor variance (unfavorable)	$13,100

Overhead variances

In a cost system using standard costs, overhead is applied to the goods produced by means of a standard overhead rate. This rate is set prior to the start of the period through use of a flexible overhead budget. This budget is called a flexible (or variable) budget because it shows the budgeted amount of overhead for various levels of output or volume. Total budgeted overhead will vary as output varies because some overhead costs are variable. But the fixed nature of some overhead costs means that total overhead will not vary in direct proportion with output.

The flexible budget for the Beta Company for the period is shown in Illustration 23.2. Note that it shows the overhead costs expected to be incurred at three levels of activity: 90 percent, 100 percent, and 110 percent of capacity. For product costing purposes, one level of activity must be chosen and a rate set based on that level. *The level chosen is called the standard volume of output.* As stated in Chapter 21, the standard volume may be based on practical capacity, normal activity, or expected activity. This standard volume of output may be expressed in terms of percent of capacity, units of output, and/or direct labor-hours. In our example it is assumed to be at 100 percent of capacity, at which level 10,000 units are expected to be produced and 20,000 direct labor-hours of services are expected to be used. The standard

Illustration 23.2: Flexible overhead budget

BETA COMPANY
Flexible Manufacturing Overhead Budget

	90%	100%	110%
Percent of capacity	90%	100%	110%
Direct labor-hours	18,000	20,000	22,000
Units of output	9,000	10,000	11,000
Variable overhead:			
Indirect materials	$ 7,200	$ 8,000	$ 8,800
Power	9,000	10,000	11,000
Royalties	1,800	2,000	2,200
Other	18,000	20,000	22,000
Total variable overhead	$36,000	$ 40,000	$ 44,000
Fixed overhead:			
Insurance	$ 4,000	$ 4,000	$ 4,000
Property taxes	6,000	6,000	6,000
Depreciation	20,000	20,000	20,000
Other	30,000	30,000	30,000
Total fixed overhead	$60,000	$ 60,000	$ 60,000
Total manufacturing overhead	$96,000	$100,000	$104,000

overhead rate then is $5 per direct labor-hour and consists of $2 per hour of variable and $3 per hour of fixed overhead. Note that the variable rate is $2 per hour at all three levels while the fixed overhead rate decreases from $3.33 ($60,000 divided by 18,000 hours) to $3 to $2.73 ($60,000 divided by 22,000 hours) as volume expands.

Standard overhead rates per direct labor-hour at 100 percent of capacity are:

Variable ($40,000 ÷ 20,000 hours) $2
Fixed ($60,000 ÷ 20,000 hours) 3
Total standard manufacturing overhead rate $5

To continue our illustration, assume that the Beta Company incurred $108,000 of actual manufacturing overhead costs in the period in which 11,000 units of product were produced and for which the standard labor allowed is 22,000 hours. These actual costs would be debited to Manufacturing Overhead and credited to a variety of accounts such as Accounts Payable, Accumulated Depreciation, Unexpired Insurance, Accrued Property Taxes Payable, and so on. The entry to record the application of $110,000 of overhead to production (22,000 hours @ $5 per hour) would be:

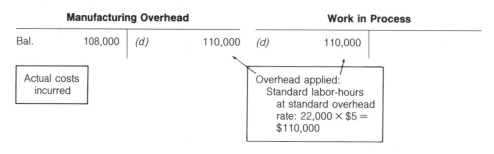

The above accounts show that manufacturing overhead has been overapplied to production by the $2,000 credit balance in the Manufacturing Overhead account. This balance can also be called the *net overhead variance*. It can be divided into a number of variances, of which we will illustrate only two: the overhead volume variance and the overhead budget variance.

The overhead volume variance. The *overhead volume variance* (OVV) results from a combination of two factors: (1) the existence of fixed overhead costs and (2) operating at a level of activity different from that used in setting the standard overhead rate. It shows whether plant assets were used more or less than expected. It is computed as the difference between *(a)* the budgeted fixed overhead (BFO) for the standard direct labor allowed for the actual volume achieved and *(b)* the applied fixed overhead (AFO). Hence,

$$OVV = BFO - AFO$$

In the Beta Company illustration, the 11,000 units produced in the period have a standard labor allowance of 22,000 hours. The flexible budget in Illustration 23.2 shows that the budgeted fixed overhead for 22,000 direct labor-hours is $60,000. The applied fixed overhead is 22,000 hours at $3 per hour, or $66,000. The overhead volume variance then is:

$$OVV = BFO - AFO$$
$$OVV = \$60,000 - \$66,000$$
$$OVV = -\$6,000$$

This variance is considered favorable because applied fixed overhead absorbed in the period's output exceeded the budgeted fixed overhead for the period. That the variance is favorable can also be seen from the fact that the period's output (11,000 units) exceeded the standard volume (10,000) that was used in setting the standard overhead rate.

The overhead budget variance. The *overhead budget variance* (also called the spending or controllable variance) shows in one amount how efficiently operations were conducted in the sense of the prices paid for and the amounts of the overhead services used. It shows for overhead a variance that is similar to a combined price and usage variance for materials or labor. The overhead budget variance (OBV) is equal to the difference between total actual overhead costs (AO) and total budgeted overhead costs (BO) for the *actual* output attained. Since the total actual overhead was $108,000 and the total budgeted overhead was $104,000 (from Illustration 23.2) for 11,000 units (22,000 standard direct labor-hours), the overhead budget variance is computed as follows:

$$OBV = AO - BO$$
$$OBV = \$108,000 - \$104,000$$
$$OBV = \$4,000$$

The variance is unfavorable because actual overhead costs were $108,000 while, according to the flexible budget, they should have amounted to only $104,000.

The relationship between actual, applied, and budgeted overhead and the two overhead variances is presented graphically in Illustration 23.3. It shows that budgeted overhead, y, for any volume level is equal to a fixed amount of overhead, a, plus an amount of variable overhead that is equal to the variable overhead rate, b, times the number of units of volume, x, that is, $y = a + bx$. The line "applied overhead" shows the amount of overhead that would be applied to production at different volumes using the overhead rate. At standard volume (the volume used in setting the standard overhead rate), applied and budgeted overhead are equal (the two lines intersect). With output of less than standard volume, the graph shows that underapplied overhead results, while overapplied overhead results if actual volume exceeds standard volume.

The numerical data in Illustration 23.3 pertain to the Beta Company. They show that at standard volume of 10,000 units (20,000 standard direct labor-hours), budgeted and applied overhead are equal at $100,000. With actual output at 11,000 units, applied overhead is $110,000, while budgeted overhead is $104,000 giving rise to a favorable volume variance of $6,000. Actual overhead amounts to $108,000 while it should have been only $104,000, and this yields an unfavorable budget variance of $4,000. The net overhead variance is $2,000, favorable, and is the sum of the $6,000 favorable volume variance and the $4,000 unfavorable budget variance.

Illustration 23.3: Actual, applied, and budgeted overhead costs

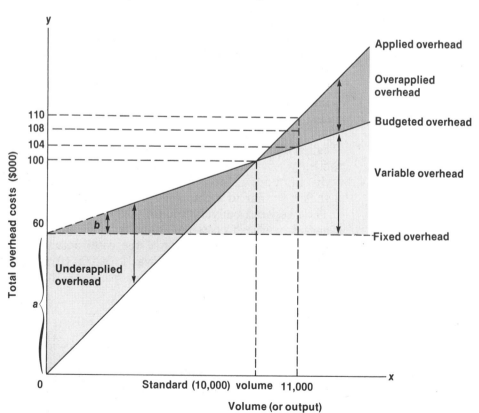

Recording overhead variances. If desired, a formal entry can be made in the accounts showing the two parts of the $2,000 net overhead variance. The entry for the Beta Company would be (the debits and credits keyed with the letter [e]):

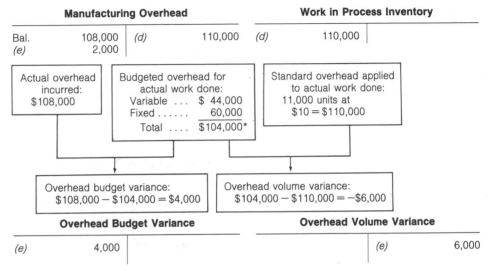

Manufacturing Overhead				Work in Process Inventory	
Bal.	108,000	(d)	110,000	(d)	110,000
(e)	2,000				

Actual overhead incurred: $108,000	Budgeted overhead for actual work done: Variable ... $ 44,000 Fixed ...... 60,000 Total $104,000*	Standard overhead applied to actual work done: 11,000 units at $10 = $110,000

Overhead budget variance: $108,000 − $104,000 = $4,000	Overhead volume variance: $104,000 − $110,000 = −$6,000

Overhead Budget Variance		Overhead Volume Variance	
(e)	4,000	(e)	6,000

* From flexible budget. See Illustration 23.2.

In the entry recorded in the T-accounts, the debit to Manufacturing Overhead of $2,000 reduces that account to a zero balance. The overhead budget variance is recorded as a debit in an account of that title because the $4,000 variance is unfavorable. And the $6,000 favorable overhead volume variance is recorded as a credit in an account of that title. The accounts now contain an analysis of the net overhead variance.

GOODS COMPLETED AND SOLD

To complete our Beta Company example, assume that 11,000 units were completed and transferred to finished goods, that 10,000 units were sold on account at a price equal to 160 percent of standard cost, that there was no beginning or ending work in process inventory, and that there was no finished goods beginning inventory. In the T-accounts below, entry (f) shows the transfer of the standard cost of the units completed, $660,000 (11,000 at $60), from Work in Process Inventory to Finished Goods Inventory. Entry (g) records the sales for the period, while entry (h) records the cost of the goods sold.

Work in Process Inventory				
(b)	Materials	330,000	(f) Completed	660,000
(c)	Labor	220,000		
(d)	Overhead	110,000		

Finished Goods Inventory				
(f)	Completed	660,000	(h) Sold	600,000

Accounts Receivable		Cost of Goods Sold		
(g) 960,000		*(h)* Sold 600,000		

	Sales	
	(g) 960,000	

The work in Process Inventory account has been debited with the standard cost of the materials, labor, and overhead put into production. Therefore, the entry to record the transfer of the standard cost of the completed units, $660,000 (11,000 at $60), reduces the Work in Process Inventory account to a zero balance. Note that the Finished Goods Inventory account is charged with the standard cost of the goods completed and credited with the standard cost of the goods sold. Thus, the ending inventory consists of the units actually on hand (1,000) at their standard cost of $60 each, or $60,000. Sales for the period amount to 10,000 units at $96 each (160 percent of $60). It is fairly common practice to base selling prices (at least partially) on the basis of standard costs.

INVESTIGATING VARIANCES FROM STANDARD

Once variances are isolated, management must decide which ones should be investigated further. Since so many variances occur, they cannot all be investigated. Management needs some selection guides. Possible guides include (1) the absolute size of the variance, (2) the size of the variance relative to the cost incurred, and (3) the type of cost incurred, that is, whether it is considered controllable or noncontrollable. The opinions of knowledgeable operating personnel should be sought.

Statistical analysis may also be used in deciding which variances to investigate. For instance, the mean (average) value of actual costs could be determined for a period of time. It could be agreed that only future variances which deviate from the mean by more than a certain amount or percent would be investigated.

Any analysis of variances is likely to disclose some variances that are controllable within the company and others that are not. Prices paid for materials purchased may be largely beyond the control of the buyer. But amounts used may be controllable internally. Also, although separate variances are isolated, they are not always as independent as they may appear. An unfavorable labor rate variance may result from using higher paid employees in a certain task; but this may result in a favorable labor efficiency variance from greater productivity and possibly a favorable materials usage variance because the more skilled employees caused less spoilage. It follows that variances should be investigated carefully before being used to appraise the performance of a given individual or department.

DISPOSING OF VARIANCES FROM STANDARD

At the end of the year, variances from standard may be (1) viewed as losses due to inefficiency and closed to the Expense and Revenue Summary account; (2) allocated as adjustments of the recorded cost of work in process inventory, finished goods inventory, and cost of goods sold; or (3) closed to Cost of

Goods Sold. Theoretically, the alternative chosen should depend upon whether the standards set were reasonably attainable standards and whether the variance was controllable by company employees. An unfavorable materials price variance caused by an unexpected price change may be considered an added cost since it is likely to be uncontrollable. On the other hand, there is little merit in treating the fixed costs of idle plant capacity as anything but a loss. As a practical matter, and especially if they are small, the variances are usually closed to the Cost of Goods Sold account rather than allocated. They typically are unfavorable (due to the common practice of setting "tight" standards). This tends to reduce reported net earnings below the amounts that would be reported if the variances were treated as cost elements and allocated to the inventory accounts and Cost of Goods Sold.

Entry *i* in the T-accounts below reflects this practical disposition of the variances in our continuing example of the Beta Company:

Materials Price Variance				Materials Usage Variance				Labor Rate Variance		
(i)	6,000	(a)	6,000	(b)	3,000	(i)	3,000	(c)	11,100	(i)	11,100

Labor Efficiency Variance				Overhead Budget Variance				Overhead Volume Variance		
(c)	2,000	(i)	2,000	(e)	4,000	(i)	4,000	(i)	6,000	(e)	6,000

Cost of Goods Sold	
(h)	600,000
(i)	8,100

In journal entry form, entry *i* would read as follows:

Materials Price Variance	6,000	
Overhead Volume Variance	6,000	
Cost of Goods Sold	8,100	
Materials Usage Variance		3,000
Labor Efficiency Variance		2,000
Overhead Budget Variance		4,000
Labor Rate Variance		11,100
To close variance accounts.		

Variances are not reported separately in statements released to the public. They are simply included in the reported cost of goods sold amount. In statements prepared for internal use, the variances may be listed separately after the cost of goods sold at standard cost amount.

APPENDIX: APPLYING STANDARD COSTS IN JOB ORDER AND PROCESS COST SYSTEMS

Standard costs in a job cost system   In a job cost system production quantities are known in advance and this permits a much earlier isolation of some variances than in a process cost system in which equivalent production is known only at the end of a period. This early isolation of variances is illustrated in the following example.

Assume that the A Company accounts for the manufacture of its products in a job cost system in which standard costs are recorded. Its flexible budget monthly amounts (at a standard activity of 8,000 direct labor hours) are variable overhead, $24,000, and fixed overhead, $16,000, yielding a standard variable overhead rate of $3 and a standard fixed overhead rate of $2 per direct labor-hour.

There was no inventory of Work in Process as of June 1. During June two jobs were started for which standard specifications were:

	Job 101	Job 102
Direct materials	$20,000	$50,000
Direct labor:		
2,000 hours at $4	8,000	
5,000 hours at $4		20,000
Overhead:		
2,000 hours at $5	10,000	
5,000 hours at $5		25,000
Total standard cost	$38,000	$95,000

The A Company's activities for June 1981 are summarized as follows:

a. Raw materials with a standard cost of $79,500 were purchased on account at an actual price of $80,150.
b. Standard direct materials were issued for both jobs. In addition, excess materials were requisitioned: Job No. 101, $400; and Job No. 102, $700.
c. Analysis of the factory payrolls debited to Payroll Summary shows they consisted of $10,000 of indirect labor ($4,000 variable and $6,000 fixed) and direct labor of 6,000 hours (Job No. 101, 1,980 hours; and Job No. 102, 4,020 hours) at a total cost of $24,600. Job No. 101 was completed.
d. Various overhead costs incurred: variable, $14,500; and fixed, $10,200.
e. Standard overhead assigned to production: Job No. 101, $10,000; and Job No. 102, 4,020 hours at $5 per hour, $20,100. (Note: standard overhead is assigned to Job No. 101 since it was completed; Job No. 102 is incomplete, but within standard.)
f. Job No. 101 was completed and transferred to finished goods storeroom.
g. Sales for the month—all units in Job No. 101 at a total price of $60,000.

The entries to isolate the variances are as follows:

a. Materials Inventory 79,500
    Materials Price Variance 650
        Accounts Payable 80,150
    To record purchase of materials and to isolate materials
    price variance.

b. Work in Process 70,000
    Materials Usage Variance 1,100
        Materials Inventory 71,100
    To charge standard materials to production and to charge
    excess materials requisitioned to a variance account.

c. Work in Process 24,080
    Manufacturing Overhead 10,000
    Labor Rate Variance 600
        Labor Efficiency Variance 80
        Payroll Summary 34,600

To distribute labor costs and to isolate labor variances:

Job No. 101 (2,000 hours at $4)	$ 8,000
Job No. 102 (4,020 hours at $4)	16,080
Total labor to Work in Process	$24,080

Labor efficiency variance on Job No. 101: (2,000 standard hours − 1,980 actual hours) × $4 = $80 (favorable).
Labor rate variance: ($4.10 actual wage rate − $4.00 standard rate) × 6,000 hours = $600 (unfavorable).

d. Manufacturing Overhead 24,700
   Accounts Payable (and various other accounts) 24,700
   To record incurrence of overhead costs.

e. Work in Process 30,100
   Manufacturing Overhead 30,100
   To apply standard overhead to production: Job No. 101 − $10,000 (standard amount, job completed); Job No. 102 − 4,020 hours at $5 = $20,100 (based on standard labor, job incomplete.

f. Finished Goods 38,000
   Work in Process 38,000
   To record transfer of completed Job No. 101 at standard.

g. Accounts Receivable 60,000
   Sales 60,000
   To record sales for the month.

   Cost of Goods Sold 38,000
   Finished Goods 38,000
   To record cost of goods sold (Job No. 101, $38,000).

Note that in the above entries the materials and labor variances are isolated rather routinely in the recording process. But the overhead variances must be computed separately at the end of the period, unless standard production for the period is known before then. For the A Company, the overhead variances are:

Overhead budget variance:
Actual costs incurred (entries [c] and [d] above)	$34,700	
Standard costs allowed (from flexible budget: $16,000 + 6,020 standard hours at $3)	34,060	
Unfavorable overhead budget variance		$ 640

Overhead volume variance:
Budgeted fixed overhead	$16,000	
Standard fixed overhead applied to production (6,020 hours at $2)	12,040	
Unfavorable overhead volume variance		3,960
Total unfavorable overhead variance		$4,600

If desired, the following entry could be made to isolate the two overhead variances in the accounts:

Overhead Budget Variance	640	
Overhead Volume Variance	3,960	
Manufacturing Overhead		4,600
To set up separate overhead variance amounts.		

Note that the credit to Manufacturing Overhead of $4,600 reduces that account to a zero balance (for previous entries to the account, see entries [c], [d], and [e] above) thus proving the accuracy of the computations.

Typically, the overhead variances and the materials and labor variances will be summarized in a report prepared periodically for internal management. Such a report could be called a "Summary of Variances from Standard."

Standard costs in a process cost system

To provide a brief illustration of how standard costs might be incorporated into a process cost system, the following example is presented.

Assume that the P Company manufactures a product for which the standard specifications are:

Materials—2 pounds at $2 per pound	$4.00
Direct labor—0.5 hours at $4 per hour	2.00
Overhead—0.5 hours at $3 per hour	1.50
Total standard cost	$7.50

The fixed overhead included in the standard cost is based upon a monthly flexible budget which (at standard activity level of 60,000 standard labor-hours) shows budgeted variable overhead of $120,000 and budgeted fixed overhead of $60,000.

P Company charges Work in Process Inventory with actual quantities and actual costs. (An alternative would be to charge Work in Process Inventory with standard quantities at standard costs. This would result in variances being isolated sooner.) Entries made to its Work in Process Inventory account for the month of May 1981 were:

Direct materials (180,500 pounds at $2.02)	$364,610
Direct labor (40,100 hours at $3.95)	158,395
Actual fixed overhead	58,700
Actual variable overhead	80,500
Total cost put into production	$662,205
Standard cost of units completed and transferred (70,000 at $7.50)	525,000
Balance, May 31, 1981	$137,205

Production records show that 70,000 units were completed and transferred and that 20,000 units of product remain in process at the end of the month. These units are complete as regards materials and 50 percent complete as to processing.

From the above information, the equivalent production for the period in terms of standard units of product can be computed as follows:

	Materials	Labor and overhead
Units started and finished	70,000	70,000
Equivalent units in ending inventory	20,000	10,000
Equivalent production	90,000	80,000

Illustration 23.4:
Summary of
variances from
standard

P COMPANY Summary of Variances from Standard Month Ended May 31, 1981		
Materials:		
Price variance (180,500 pounds at $0.02)	$ 3,610	
Usage variance (500 pounds at $2)	1,000	
Total unfavorable materials variance...........................		$ 4,610
Labor:		
Rate variance (40,100 hours at $0.05)	$–2,005	
Efficiency variance (100 hours at $4)	400	
Net favorable labor variance		–1,605
Overhead:		
Budget variance—fixed ($58,700 – $60,000) + variable ($80,500 – $80,000)	$– 800	
Volume variance ($60,000 – $40,000)	20,000	
Net unfavorable overhead variance		19,200
Total variance from standard for the month		$22,205

Now enough information is available to permit the calculation of all of the variances which are summarized in the "Summary of Variances from Standard" shown in Illustration 23.4.

Since the actual price paid for materials was $0.02 per pound above standard, the materials price variance is the actual usage of 180,500 pounds multiplied by $0.02. Since the standard materials allowed for 90,000 equivalent units is 180,000 pounds (90,000 × 2), there is a materials usage variance of 500 pounds times $2. Both variances are unfavorable.

The average wage rate paid employees was $0.05 less than standard; thus a favorable rate variance of this amount multiplied by actual hours of 40,100 emerges. The standard labor allowed for the production of the period (80,000 × 0.5 hours) is 100 hours less than actual. Hence, an unfavorable labor efficiency variance was experienced.

Fixed overhead costs were $1,300 less than budget, while variable overhead costs exceeded their budgeted amount for the actual production in May by $500. Together they yield a net favorable variance of $800. Because the standard fixed overhead applied to production of $40,000 is less than the budgeted fixed overhead for the month of $60,000, there is an unfavorable volume variance of $20,000. These variances amount to $19,200 for overhead and to $22,205 as the total variance (unfavorable) from standard for the month.

The variances shown in Illustration 23.4 can be formally recorded in the accounts and Work in Process Inventory relieved of the month's variances by the following entry:

Materials Price Variance	3,610	
Materials Usage Variance	1,000	
Labor Efficiency Variance	400	
Overhead Volume Variance	20,000	
Labor Rate Variance		2,005
Overhead Budget Variance		800
Work in Process		22,205

To set up variances from standard for the month.

Subtracting the $22,205 from the previously given balance of $137,205 in the Work in Process account leaves a balance of $115,000 which is equal to the standard cost of the ending inventory. The standard cost of the ending inventory can be separately computed as follows:

Direct materials (20,000 units, 2 pounds per unit, 100% complete, unit cost $4)	$ 80,000
Direct labor (20,000 units, 50% complete, unit cost $2)	20,000
Overhead (20,000 units, 50% complete, unit cost $1.50)	15,000
Total standard cost of ending inventory	$115,000

NEW TERMS INTRODUCED IN CHAPTER 23

Labor efficiency variance—a variance from standard caused by using more or less than the standard amount of labor-hours to produce a product or complete a process; computed as (Actual labor-hours − Standard labor-hours) × Standard rate.

Labor rate variance—a variance from standard caused by paying a higher or lower average rate of pay than standard to produce a product or complete a process; computed as (Actual rate − Standard rate) × Actual hours.

Materials price variance—a variance from standard caused by paying a higher or lower price than standard for materials purchased; computed as (Actual price − Standard price) × Actual quantity.

Materials usage variance—a variance from standard caused by using more or less than the standard amount of materials to produce a product or complete a process; computed as (Actual quantity − Standard quantity) × Standard price.

Overhead budget variance—a variance from standard caused by incurring more or less than the standard overhead for the actual production volume experienced as shown by a flexible budget; computed as (Actual variable overhead + Actual fixed overhead) − Budgeted variable and fixed overhead at actual production volume level.

Overhead volume variance—a variance from standard caused by producing at a level other than that used in setting fixed overhead rates; computed as Budgeted fixed overhead − Applied fixed overhead in production of the period.

Standard cost—a carefully refined engineering estimate or projection of the amount of cost that should be incurred to produce a product or complete a process.

Variance—a deviation from standard; may be favorable or unfavorable, that is, actual cost may be less than or more than standard, and may relate to materials, labor, or manufacturing overhead.

DEMONSTRATION PROBLEM

The Baxter Company manufactures children's toys which are all identical. The standard cost of each toy is:

Direct materials:
Three blocks of wood at $0.20 .... $0.60
Direct labor (1 hour at $5) 5.00
Overhead:
    Fixed 0.30
    Variable 0.40
                                    $6.30

In May, 50,000 units were manufactured. Detailed data relative to production are summarized as follows:

Materials purchased:
  160,000 blocks at $0.22
Materials used:
  152,000 blocks of wood
Direct labor: 49,000 hours at $5.10
Fixed overhead: $18,200
Variable overhead: $20,350

The fixed overhead assigned to production is based upon volume of 60,000 units per month.

Required:

From the above data, compute the six variances from standard for the month.

Solution to demonstration problem

Materials price variance:			
160,000 @ $0.02 (unfavorable)		$3,200	
Materials usage variance:			
2,000* @ $0.20 (unfavorable)		400	
Net materials variance (unfavorable)			$3,600
Labor rate variance: (49,000 hours @ $0.10)			
(unfavorable)		$4,900	
Labor efficiency variance: (1,000 hours @ $5)			
(favorable)		5,000	
Total labor variance (favorable)			(100)
Overhead budget variance:			
Actual ($18,200 + $20,350)	$38,550		
Budgeted (18,000 + 50,000 @ $0.40)	38,000		
Overhead budget variance			
(unfavorable)		$ 550	
Overhead volume variance:			
Budgeted—Applied ($18,000 − 50,000 @ $0.30)			
(unfavorable)		3,000	
Total overhead variance (unfavorable)			3,550
Total variance for month (unfavorable)			$7,050

* (50,000 units × 3 blocks) − 152,000.

QUESTIONS

1. Is a standard cost an estimated cost? What is the primary objective of employing standard costs in a cost system? What are some of the other advantages of using standard costs?

2. How can it be maintained that the use of standard costs permits the application of the principle of management by exception?

3. What are some of the problems surrounding the interpretation of variances in a standard cost system?

4. Compute the materials price and usage variances from the following data: .

Standard—1,000 units at $20 per unit.
Purchased—1,200 units at $20.25; used—995 units.

5. What might be a plausible explanation for a given company having a substantial favorable materials price variance and a substantial unfavorable materials usage variance?

6. What is the usual cause of a favorable or unfavorable labor rate variance? What other labor variance is isolated in a standard cost system? Of the two variances, which is more likely to be under the control of management? Explain.

7. Identify the type of variance indicated by each situation below and whether it is a favorable or unfavorable variance.

a. The cutting department of a company during the week ending July 15 cut 12 size S cogged wheels out of three sheets of 12-inch high-tempered steel. Usually three wheels of such size are cut out of each sheet.

b. A company purchased and installed a new expensive cutting machine to handle expanding orders. This purchase and the related depreciation had not been anticipated when the overhead rate was set.

c. Edwards, the band saw operator, was on vacation last week. Lands took his place for the normal 40-hour week. Edwards' wage rate is $5.40 per hour, while Lands' is $5.20 per hour. Production was at capacity last week and the week before.

8. Is the overhead budget variance essentially a "price" or a "usage" variance? Explain.

9. Theoretically, how should variances from standard be disposed of? What is typically their practical disposition?

10. Would you expect the overhead volume variance normally to be favorable or unfavorable? Explain.

11. How do standard costs control?

EXERCISES

E–1. During the month of May a department completed 2,000 units of a product which had a standard material cost of 4,000 square feet at $0.40 per square foot. The actual material used consisted of 4,050 square feet at a cost of $1,660.50. Compute the materials usage and materials price variances and indicate clearly whether each is favorable or unfavorable.

E–2. Compute the labor variances in the following circumstances:

Actual direct labor payroll (19,800 hours)	$81,180
Standard labor allowed per unit, 4 hours at $4	16
Equivalent production for the month (in units)	5,000

E–3. During March, 100 units of a given product were produced. These units have a standard labor cost in Process A of one hour at $4 per hour and two hours in Process B at $3.50 per hour. Assume that Smith worked 95 hours on Process A during the month for which he earned $418 and that Jones worked 205 hours on Process B for which he earned $697. Compute the labor cost variances for each process.

E–4. The following relate to the manufacturing activities of the Glen Company for the month of May 1981:

Standard activity (units)	50,000
Actual production (units)	40,000
Budgeted fixed overhead	$30,000
Variable overhead rate (per unit)	2.00
Actual fixed overhead	30,400
Actual variable overhead	78,300

Compute the overhead budget variance and the overhead volume variance.

E–5. In Exercise E–4, if the actual production had been 65,000 units what would the overhead volume variance have been?

E–6. The standard cost variance accounts of the Martin Company at the end of its fiscal year had the following balances:

Materials usage variance	
(unfavorable)	$ 4,000
Materials price variance	
(unfavorable)	5,000
Labor rate variance (favorable)	3,000
Labor efficiency variance	
(unfavorable)	11,000
Overhead volume variance	
(unfavorable)	6,000
Overhead budget variance	
(favorable)	1,000

Set up T-accounts for the above variances; enter the above balances in these accounts; then prepare one entry to record the closing of these variance accounts in the manner in which they are usually disposed of in practice.

PROBLEMS, SERIES A

P23–1–A. During the month of March a department completed 5,000 units of a product which had a standard material cost of 6,000 square feet at $0.30 per square foot. The actual material used consisted of 6,100 square feet at an actual cost of $1,708. The actual purchase of this material amounted to 9,000 square feet at a total cost of $2,520.

Required:

Using T-accounts, prepare entries **(a)** for the purchase of the materials and **(b)** for the issuance of materials to production.

P23–2–A. The welding department of the Williams Company produced 40,000 units during the month of November. The standard number of direct labor-hours per unit is two hours. The standard rate per hour is $9. During the month, 82,000 direct labor-hours were worked at a cost of $754,400.

Required:

a. Draw a diagram similar to Illustration 23.1 showing the determination of the two labor variances.

b. Record the labor data in a journal entry and post the entry to T-accounts.

P23–3–A. The monthly budgeted fixed overhead of the Buffalo plant of the ABC Company is absorbed into production using a rate based upon a standard volume of output of 100,000 units per month. The flexible budget for the month for overhead allows $75,000 for fixed overhead and $1 per unit of output for variable overhead. Actual overhead for the month consisted of $75,600 of fixed overhead with actual variable overhead given below.

Required:

Compute the overhead budget variance and the overhead volume variance assuming actual production in units and actual variable overhead in dollars were:

a. 75,000 and $76,000.

b. 110,000 and $112,700.

P23–4–A. The Lamp Company manufactures and sells two rather similar table lamps, each of which is assembled and packaged in Department III. The expected volume of activity for this department is 100,000 direct labor-hours, at which level budgeted fixed overhead is $70,000 while variable overhead is budgeted at $1.20 per direct labor-hour.

In May, a total of 81,300 direct labor-hours was worked in the department, 1,300 of which were in excess of the standard labor allowed for the month's production. Actual overhead for the month consisted of $69,700 of fixed overhead and $98,300 of variable overhead.

Required:

Compute the two overhead variances for the month of May showing your computations.

P23–5–A. Based on a standard volume of output of 80,000 units per month, the standard cost of the product manufactured by the Jasper Company is:

Direct materials (0.25 pounds)	$1.00
Direct labor (0.5 hours)	2.00
Variable overhead	1.75
Fixed overhead	0.75
	$5.50

During the month of May, 82,000 units were produced and the following costs incurred:

Direct materials (20,650 pounds at $4.10)	$ 84,665
Direct labor (41,080 hours at $3.90)	160,212
Variable overhead	144,700
Fixed overhead	60,520

Required:

Compute the materials price and usage variances, the labor rate and efficiency variances, and the overhead budget and volume variances.

P23–6–A (based on the Appendix). The Bryant Manufacturing Company employs a job order standard cost accounting system. The standard cost of the material used is $0.80 per square foot, while the standard labor cost is $4 per hour. Overhead is assigned to jobs at the rate of $3 per standard direct labor-hour. Based upon a standard volume of activity of 60,000 direct labor-hours, the flexible budget allows $60,000 of fixed overhead and $2 of variable overhead per direct labor-hour for the month of June 1979.

Work in process is charged with standard quantities

and standard prices. On June 1, 1981, one job (No. 201) was in process, to which the following standard costs have already been assigned:

Material (2,500 square feet)	$2,000
Labor (400 direct labor-hours)	1,600
Manufacturing overhead ($3 per standard direct labor-hour)	1,200
Total	$4,800

When completed, the standard quantities for Job No. 201 are 4,000 square feet of material and 500 hours of direct labor.

During the month of June, 1981, the following transactions and events occurred:

1. Purchased 600,000 square feet of material at $0.78 per square foot.
2. Materials issued:

Job. No.	Actual quantity	Standard quantity
201	1,600 sq. ft.	1,500 sq. ft.
All others	420,000 sq. ft.	421,200 sq. ft.
	421,600 sq. ft.	422,700 sq. ft.

3. The direct labor costs and hours for the month were:

Incurred on—	Actual hours	Standard hours	Actual cost
Job No. 201	104	100	$ 434
All other jobs	51,096	51,000	206,966
	51,200	51,100	$207,400

4. The appropriate amount of overhead was assigned to the jobs.
5. Actual overhead incurred during the month was $155,000.
6. Job. No. 201 was completed during the month. Other production also completed during the month has a standard cost of $520,000.

Required:

a. Prepare general journal entries for each of the numbered transactions given above.

b. Compute and prepare general journal entries to record the overhead budget variance and the overhead volume variance for the month.

P23–7–A (based on the Appendix). The Martinez Company employs a process cost system with standard costs to account for the product it manufacturers in a two-step process through Departments I and II. The standard cost of this product in Department I is:

Direct materials (10 units at $8)	$ 80
Direct labor (5 hours at $6)	30
Variable overhead (5 hours at $4)	20
Fixed overhead (5 hours at $2)	10
	$140

The flexible overhead budget, based on 60,000 direct labor-hours as a standard volume of activity, allows $120,000 of fixed overhead plus $4 per direct labor-hour. Materials price variances are isolated at time of purchase, labor rate variances when payrolls are distributed. Materials usage and labor efficiency variances are isolated at the end of the month when production is known. Standard overhead is assigned to production and overhead variances isolated at the end of the month when production and actual costs are known.

There was no work in process inventory as of July 1, 1981, in Department I. Selected, summarized data for the month are:

1. Purchased 121,000 units of raw material for $963,160.
2. Direct materials requisitioned by Department I, 110,580 units.
3. Of the payroll costs for the month, 49,900 hours with a total cost of $299,760 are chargeable to Department I.
4. Total overhead costs incurred by the department for the month consist of $120,900 of fixed overhead and $201,100 of variable overhead.
5. A total of 9,000 units was completed during the month and 2,000 units remain in process, 100 percent complete as to materials and 50 percent complete as to labor and overhead.
6. Overhead is assigned to production on the basis of standard labor-hours.

Required:

a. Prepare journal entries to record the above summarized data. (In the illustration in the Appendix all variances were isolated at the end of the period. Use logic to isolate them as required in this problem.)

b. Compute the materials usage variance and the labor efficiency variance and prepare journal entries to remove them from work in process.

c. Compute and prepare journal entries to record the overhead budget variance and the overhead volume variance.

d. Assuming the variances isolated are for the year ending July 31, 1981, prepare an entry that represents a practical disposition of these variances.

PROBLEMS, SERIES B

P23–1–B. During the month of June the Zee Company completed 10,000 units of a product which had a standard materials cost of 5,000 pieces at $6 per piece. The actual material used consisted of 5,030 pieces at a cost of $29,677. Actual purchases of the material amounted to 7,000 pieces at a cost of $41,300.

Required:

Using T-accounts, prepare entries **(a)** for the purchase of the materials and **(b)** for the issuance of the materials to production.

P23–2–B. The Handtool Division of the Kelly Company produced 10,000 screwdrivers during the month of August. The standard number of direct labor-hours per screwdriver is 0.5 hours. The standard labor rate is $6 per hour. During the month 5,250 direct labor-hours were worked at a cost of $32,812.50.

Required:

a. Draw a diagram similar to Illustration 23.1 showing the determination of the two labor variances.

b. Record the labor data in a journal entry and post the entry to T-accounts.

P23–3–B. The standard volume of output of the Lansing plant of the Gage Company for the month of April is 100,000 units, while budgeted fixed overhead for the month is $80,000. Actual fixed overhead for the month was $83,500.

Required:

Compute the amount of the overhead volume variance for the month of April under each of the following assumed actual levels of activity in terms of units of output:

a. 60,000.

b. 100,000.

c. 120,000.

P23–4–B. Ludwig Company manufactures a variety of toys, each of which is assembled in the assembly department. The standard production volume for this department is 50,000 direct labor-hours per month for which fixed overhead is budgeted at $250,000 while variable overhead is budgeted at $1.60 per direct labor-hour.

In March, a total of 41,200 direct labor-hours was received in the department, 1,200 of which were in excess of the standard labor-hours allowed for the month's production. The actual overhead for the month consisted of $254,000 of fixed overhead and $67,000 of variable overhead.

Required:

Compute the two overhead variances for the month of March, showing your computations.

P23–5–B. The Ceramic Company manufactures a number of ceramic figurines which, although produced in six colors, are still sufficiently similar to be considered one product for standard costing purposes. The standard cost of each figurine is:

Direct materials:	
2 pounds of clay at $0.80 per pound	$ 1.60
4 ounces of coloring pigment	
at $2.50 per ounce	10.00
Direct labor (0.10 hours at $10)	1.00
Overhead:	
Fixed	0.60
Variable	0.80
	$14.00

In May, 50,000 units were manufactured and 48,000 units were sold. Detailed data relative to production are summarized as follows:

Materials purchased:
  102,000 pounds of clay at $0.76
  210,000 ounces of coloring pigment at $2.52
Materials used:
  101,050 pounds of clay; 200,500 ounces of coloring pigment

Direct labor: 5,030 hours at $10.20
Fixed overhead: $36,400
Variable overhead: $40,700

The fixed overhead assigned to production is based upon a standard volume of output of 60,000 units per month. There were no beginning or ending inventories of work in process.

Required:

From the above data, compute the following:

a. The standard costs for materials, labor, and overhead put into production in May (assuming Work in Process Inventory is charged with standard quantities at standard cost).

b. The standard cost of the goods completed.

c. The standard cost of the goods sold.

d. Six variances from standard for the month.

P23–6–B (based on the Appendix). The Merrill Company maintains a job order standard cost accounting system. The standard cost of the plastic material it uses is $4 per pound, while the standard labor cost is $3 per hour. Overhead is charged to the various jobs at the rate of $4 per direct labor-hour based upon a flexible budget at a standard volume of activity of 200,000 direct labor-hours that shows $400,000 of budgeted fixed overhead and $2 per standard direct labor-hour for variable overhead. Work in process is charged with standard quantities and standard prices. There was no work in process inventory at May 1, 1981.

During May 1981, the following transactions and events occurred:

1. Purchased 200,000 pounds of plastic at $3.92.
2. Started the following jobs during the month:

Job No.	Standard units of material	Standard hours of labor
505	2,500	5,000
506	2,000	4,000
All others	120,500	211,000
	125,000	220,000

3. Materials issued during the month:

Job. No.	Pounds
505	2,550
506	1,975
All others	121,475
	126,000

4. Of the direct labor cost charged to Payroll Summary, the following amounts relate to the various jobs:

Job No.	Actual hours	Standard hours	Actual cost
505	5,100	5,000	$ 15,120
506	4,080	4,000	11,880
All others	184,000	181,000	550,700
	193,180	190,000	$577,700

5. Appropriate overhead was charged to the various jobs.
6. Actual fixed overhead incurred, $408,000; actual variable overhead, $376,000.
7. Job Nos. 505 and 506 were completed along with other production having a standard cost of $1,580,000.

Required:

a. Prepare journal entries to record the above summarized data isolating variances as soon as possible.

b. Compute and prepare journal entries to record the two overhead variances.

c. Assuming that the variances isolated are for the year ending May 31, 1981, prepare an entry that represents a practical disposition of these variances.

P23–7–B (based on the Appendix). The Dent Manufacturing Company manufactures a product by processing it through three successive departments, A, B, and C. A process cost system incorporating standard costs is used. The standard cost of the product in Department A is:

Materials (20 pounds at $1.50)	$30
Labor (3 hours at $6)	18
Fixed overhead	15
Variable overhead	12
	$75

Materials price variances are recorded at the time of purchase with the result that materials are charged to production at actual quantity and standard price. Work in process is charged for actual costs incurred for labor and overhead, and variances are isolated at the end of the period when production is known. Budgeted overhead at the standard volume of output of 25,000 units per month is $375,000 plus $12 per unit completed.

There was no beginning inventory in process on June 1, 1981, in Department A. Following are summarized data for the month of June for Department A:

1. Materials purchased, 450,000 pounds at $1.56.
2. Materials requisitioned, 440,310 pounds.
3. Of the charges to Payroll Summary, $359,940 represents the cost of 59,940 hours of direct labor received in Department A.
4. Actual overhead costs charged to Work in Process: fixed, $378,000; and variable, $242,595.
5. Units completed and transferred to Department B, 18,000; 4,000 units remain on hand in the department, 100 percent complete as to materials (which are added only at the beginning of the processing in the department) and 50 percent complete as to processing.

Required:

a. Prepare journal entries for the above summarized data. (In the illustration in the Appendix all variances were isolated at the end of the period. Use logic to isolate the materials price variances as required in this problem.)

b. Compute the remaining five variances and give one journal entry to remove the variances from the Work in Process Inventory—Department A account.

c. Can the overhead volume variance be logically related to the labor efficiency variance? Explain.

BUSINESS DECISION PROBLEM 23–1

Turn to Exercise E–6 in this chapter. For each of the variances listed give a possible reason for its existence.

BUSINESS DECISION PROBLEM 23–2

Bill Watts, the president of the Able Company, has a problem. It does not involve substantial dollar amounts but does involve the important question of responsibility for variances from standard costs. He has just received the following report:

Total materials costs for the month of May
  (6,900 pounds @ $2.40 per pound) $16,560
Unfavorable materials price variance ($2.40 −
  $2.00) × 6,900 pounds . . . . (2,760)
Unfavorable materials usage variance (6,900
  pounds − 6,000 pounds) × $2 . . . . (1,800)
Standard materials at standard price
  for the actual production in May $12,000

Bill has discussed the unfavorable price variance with Marie Hatter, the purchasing officer. She agrees that under the circumstances she should be held responsible for most of the materials price variance. But she objects to the inclusion of $360 (900 pounds of excess materials used @ $0.40 per pound). This, she argues, is the responsibility of the production department. If it had not been so inefficient in the use of materials, she would not have had to purchase the extra 900 pounds. On the other hand, Ron Sills, the production manager, agrees that he is basically responsible for the excess quantity of materials used. But he does not agree that the above materials usage variance should be revised to include the $360 of unfavorable price variance on the excess materials used. "That's Marie's responsibility," he says.

Bill now turns to you for help. Specifically, he wants you to tell him:

a. Who is responsible for the $360 in dispute?

b. If responsibility cannot be clearly assigned, in which price variance should the accounting department include the variance? Why?

c. Are there likely to be other circumstances where materials variances cannot be considered the responsibility of the person who is most likely to be considered responsible for them. Explain.

Prepare written answers to the three questions asked by Bill.

PART EIGHT

PLANNING, CONTROL,

AND DECISION MAKING

Chapter 24

Responsibility accounting;
segmental analysis

RESPONSIBILITY ACCOUNTING

Responsibility accounting refers to an accounting system that collects, summarizes, and reports accounting data according to the *responsibility* of individual managers. A *responsibility accounting* system seeks to provide information to evaluate each manager on the revenue and expense items over which that manager has primary *control* (the authority to influence). *Each accounting report contains only (or at least clearly segregates) those items which are controllable by the responsible manager.* This is the fundamental principle of responsibility accounting. It should be clear from this description that the business entity must be well organized so that responsibility is assignable to individual managers.

Clear lines of authority and responsibility must exist throughout the organization. The various managers of the company, their responsibility level, and the lines of authority existing within an entity should be as clearly defined as shown in the organization chart in Illustration 24.1. If clear areas of authority cannot be determined, it is very doubtful that responsibility accounting can be implemented. Lines of authority should follow a specified path. For example, a plant supervisor may report to a plant manager, who reports to a vice president of manufacturing, who is responsible to the president. The president is ultimately responsible to the stockholders or their elected representatives, the board of directors. In a sense, the president is responsible for all revenue and expense items of the firms since at the presidential level all items are controllable. But the president will usually delegate authority to various managers since the president cannot keep fully appraised of the day-to-day operating details of each of the segments.

Illustration 24.1: Illustration of a corporate functional organization chart including four levels of management.

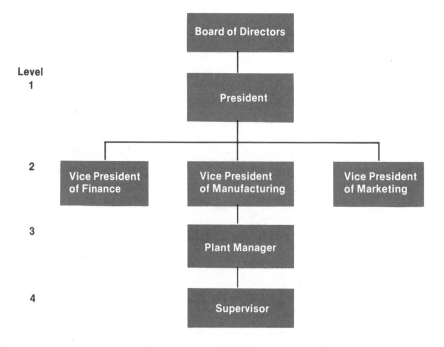

Reference is often made to levels of management. The president is usually considered the first-level manager. All the managers who report directly to the president are second-level managers. Notice on the organization chart in Illustration 24.1 that the individuals within a given level are on a horizontal line across the chart. But it is not to be assumed that all managers within a certain level have equal authority and responsibility. The relative authority of certain types of managers will vary from firm to firm.

While the president may delegate much decision-making power, there are some revenue and expense items that may be exclusively under the president's control. For example, large capital (plant and equipment) expenditures may be approved only by the president. Hence, depreciation, property taxes, and other related expenses should not be designated as the plant manager's responsibility since these costs are not primarily under the plant manager's control. The controllability criterion is crucial to the content of the reports for each manager. For example, at the supervisor level, perhaps only direct materials and direct labor are appropriate for the task of measuring performance. But at the plant manager level many other costs, not controllable at a lower level, are controllable and therefore included in the performance evaluation of the plant manager.

THE CONCEPT OF CONTROL

A manager must be able to exercise primary control over an item before being held responsible for it. Unfortunately, controllability is rarely absolute. Quite frequently, some factors which change the amount of a budgeted item are beyond the control of a manager. For example, the imposition of a 10 percent excise tax by a governmental authority may decrease the sales of certain items in a particular segment. Even though the manager is given authority to control the sales revenue, in this case external factors beyond the manager's control have altered the actual results. Internal factors may also be present. For example, raw material usage may be excessive because, in an effort to save money, the purchasing department bought low-quality materials. Most revenue or expense items have some elements of noncontrollability in them.

The theoretical requirement that a manager has absolute control over items for which that manager is held responsible often must be compromised. The manager is usually responsible for items where *relative* control is present. *Relative control means that the manager has the predominate control over most of the factors which influence a given budget item.* The use of relative control may lead to some motivational problems, since the manager is evaluated on results that may not reflect that manager's efforts. Nevertheless, most budget plans assign control on a relative control basis in order to develop and use segmental budgets.

RESPONSIBILITY REPORTS—HOW THEY RELATE TO EACH OTHER

A unique feature of a responsibility accounting system is the amount of detail in the various reports issued to the different levels of management. For example, a performance report to a particular supervisor would include the dollar amounts, actual and budgeted, of all the revenue and expense items under that supervisor's control. Thus, it shows the *controllable earnings of a segment*. But the report issued to the plant manager would show only the totals from all the supervisors' reports and any additional items subject to the plant manager's control, such as the plant administrative expense. The report to the vice president of manufacturing would contain only the totals of all the plants. Because a responsibility accounting system selectively condenses data, the report to the president does not consist of stapling together all the plant supervisor reports. Only the summary totals of the subordinate levels are reported (see Illustration 24.4). This lack of detail which seems a hindrance to performance analysis actually results in the practice of "management by exception." Since modern business enterprises are becoming increasingly complex, it has become necessary to filter and condense accounting data so that they may be analyzed quickly. Most executives do not have the time to study detailed accounting reports searching for problem areas. Reporting only summary totals highlights those areas that need attention so that the executive can make more efficient use of available time.

The reports issued under the responsibility accounting system are interrelated since the totals from one level are carried forward in the report to the next higher management level. The control reports submitted to the president include all revenue and expense items (in summary form) since the president is responsible for controlling the profitability of the entire firm.

The condensation which occurs at successive levels of management is justified on the basis that the appropriate manager will take the necessary corrective action. Hence, performance details need not be reported except to the particular manager. The manager should be able to describe to the immediate supervisor the action that was taken to correct an undesirable situation. For example, if direct labor cost has been excessively high in a particular department, the supervisor should seek to correct the cause of this variance. The plant manager, upon noticing the unfavorable total budget variance of the department, will investigate. The supervisor should be able to respond that the appropriate corrective action was taken. Hence, it is not necessary to report to the vice president of manufacturing that a particular department within one of the plants is not operating satisfactorily, since the plant manager has already attended to the matter. If the plant as a whole under a plant manager has been performing poorly, then the summary totals which have been reported to the vice president of manufacturing will disclose this situation and an investigation of the plant manager's problems might be indicated.

RESPONSIBILITY REPORTS— NONCONTROL- LABLE ITEMS

In preparing responsibility accounting reports, there are two basic ways of handling revenue or expense items which are noncontrollable at the manager's level. First, they may be omitted entirely from the reports. At the management level at which these items become controllable they are then included in that report. As a result, each level of reports contains only those items which are controllable at that level. But there is some appeal in including all revenue and expense items which can be traced directly or allocated indirectly to a particular manager. This method represents a full-costing approach. Care must be taken to separate controllable from noncontrollable items in such reports.

Timeliness of reports

In order for accounting reports to be of maximum benefit they must be timely. That is, reports should be prepared as soon as possible after the end of the performance measurement period. Timely reports allow prompt corrective action to be taken. Reports that are excessively delayed lose their effectiveness as control devices. For example, a report on the previous month's operations that is not received until the end of the current month is virtually useless for analyzing poor performance areas and taking corrective action. Reports should be issued regularly. Regular reports are desirable since trends can be spotted. The appropriate management action can be initiated before major problems occur. Regularity is also important so that the managers will rely on the reports and become familiar with their contents.

Simplicity of reports

Reports should be relatively simple. Care should be taken to avoid using confusing terminology. Particularly at lower levels of management, aggregate dollar amounts may not be sufficient. Results should also be expressed in physical units when appropriate. It is desirable to report budgeted amounts as well as actual amounts. Often a year-to-date analysis is included in addition to the current period so that the manager can see performance to date. The inclusion of variances from budgeted amounts is desirable so that relative performance can be ascertained. By carefully analyzing budget variances, the significant deviations from the budgeted plan are highlighted. Variance analysis allows management to spot problem areas quickly. The use of variances is helpful in applying the management-by-exception principle.

RESPONSIBILITY REPORTS— ILLUSTRATION

The following illustration is designed to show how responsibility accounting reports in an organization are interrelated.

We will assume an organization with four management levels of which the president, vice president (manufacturing), plant manager, and supervisor are representative (see Illustration 24.2). The fourth level is considered to be the supervisor and so on up to the first level, the president (as shown in Illustration 24.3).

The reports shown in Illustration 24.4 contain only controllable expenses. Notice that only the totals from the supervisor's responsibility report are included in the plant manager's report. In turn, only the totals on the plant manager's report are included on the report for the vice president, and so on. The detailed data from the lower level reports are summarized and carried onto the report for the next higher level. Also, new controllable costs are introduced into the reports for levels 3, 2, and 1 which were not included on a lower level report. For instance, the president's office expense, included as the first item on the president's report, and the vice presidents' salaries were not reported at a lower level (because they were not controllable at a lower level).

The reports also show variation from the budgeted amounts for the month and for the year to date.

On the basis of the reports (see Illustration 24.4), it is probable that the supervisor would take immediate action to see why supplies and overtime

Illustration 24.2:
Organization chart

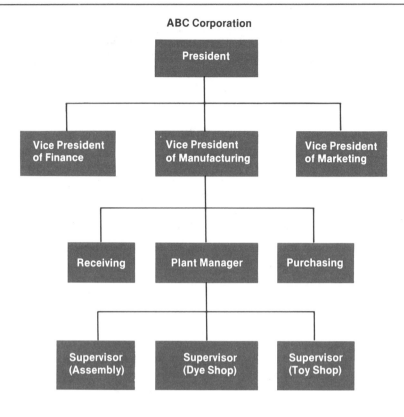

ABC Corporation

Illustration 24.3:
Responsibility reports

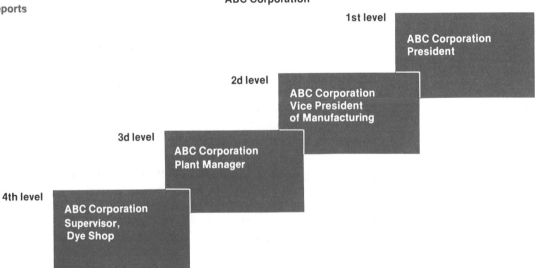

ABC Corporation

Illustration 24.4: Responsibility reports for ABC Corporation

ABC CORPORATION

Fourth level:
  Supervisor, Dye Shop

Controllable expenses	Amount		Over or (under) budget	
	This month	Year to date	This month	Year to date
Repairs and maintenance	$ 200	$ 1,000	$ 10	$ 40
Supplies	180	850	80	95
Tools	100	300	(10)	81
Overtime	200	450	80	14
Total (include in report for next higher level)	$ 680	$ 2,600	$ 160	$ 230

ABC CORPORATION

Third level:
  Plant manager

Controllable expenses	Amount		Over or (under) budget	
	This month	Year to date	This month	Year to date
Plant manager's office expense	$ 800	$ 9,100	$ (50)	$ (100)
Dye shop costs	680	2,600	160	230
Toy shop costs	1,000	5,000	80	130
Assembly	400	1,300	60	240
Salaries of supervisors	5,000	25,000	–0–	–0–
Total (include in report for next higher level)	$ 7,880	$ 43,000	$ 250	$ 500

ABC CORPORATION

Second level:
  Vice president of manufacturing

Controllable expenses	Amount		Over or (under) budget	
	This month	Year to date	This month	Year to date
Vice president's office expense	$ 2,840	$ 9,500	$ (50)	$ (800)
Plant departmental costs	7,880	43,000	250	500
Purchasing	380	2,500	100	200
Receiving	700	3,000	300	900
Salaries of plant manager and heads of purchasing and receiving	7,000	35,000	–0–	–0–
Total (include in report for next higher level)	$18,800	$ 93,000	$ 600	$ 800

ABC CORPORATION

First level:
  President

Controllable expenses	Amount		Over or (under) budget	
	This month	Year to date	This month	Year to date
President's office expense	$ 1,000	$ 5,000	$ 100	$ 200
Vice president, manufacturing	18,800	93,000	600	800
Vice president, sales	8,700	19,000	400	800
Vice president, finance	4,000	15,000	800	900
Vice presidents' salaries	9,000	45,000	–0–	–0–
Total	$41,500	$177,000	$1,900	$2,700

were significantly over the budget this month. The plant manager might ask the supervisor what the problems were and whether they are now under control. The vice president might ask the same question of the plant manager (and of the head of receiving). And the president might ask each of the vice presidents why the budget was exceeded this month.

RESPONSIBILITY CENTERS

Various references have been made to the *segments* of a business enterprise. Examples of segments are divisions, departments, product lines, and service centers. The organization of appropriate business segments is crucial to successful budgeting. The segments of a business enterprise must be defined according to function or product line. For example, companies have traditionally been organized along functional lines. The segments or departments performed a specified function (e.g., marketing, finance, purchasing, production, shipping). Recently, large firms have tended to organize segments according to product line (e.g., the electrical products division, the shoe department, the food division). These segments are to a degree autonomous, self-contained units, each with the various functional units contained within itself. The accounting system must be structured to gather information for each segment. There are three possible types of *responsibility center* for evaluating business segments: the expense (or cost) center, the earnings (or profit) center, and the investment center. The characteristics of a specific segment will limit the selection of an appropriate reporting basis.

Expense or cost centers

Managers of expense centers are held responsible only for specified expense items. The distinguishing feature of expense centers is that they produce no direct revenue from the sale of goods or services. Examples of expense centers are service centers (e.g., the maintenance department, computer section, and the accounting department) or intermediate production facilities which produce parts for assembly into a finished product.

The appropriate goal of an expense center is not necessarily the short-run minimization of expense for any given level of output, but rather the long-run minimization of expense. The time period examined must also be specified. For example, a production supervisor could eliminate maintenance costs during a short period of time. This would cause total short-term costs to be lower. But in the long run, costs might be higher due to more frequent machine breakdowns.

Earnings centers

Because managers are motivated by basing rewards upon earnings, the calculation of segmental earnings has considerable appeal. Accordingly, in an increasing number of firms, the segments are organized as *earnings centers* (having both revenues and expenses). Since segmental earnings are usually defined as segmental revenue minus related expenses, the manager must be able to *control* both of these categories. That is, the manager must have the authority to attempt to control selling price, sales volume, and all of the reported expense items. The manager's authority over all of these measured items is essential to proper performance evaluation.

Transfer prices. When a division or segment does not sell its output to outside parties but only to other segments, it is necessary to establish a *transfer price* which must be "paid" by the other division so that the producing division can have a measured "revenue." This enables the producing unit to become an earnings center rather than an expense center.

In effect, the transfer price is recorded as revenue of one segment and a cost or expense of the other segment. No cash changes hands, and the accounting entry on the corporate books is an internal adjustment. For example, a segment that manufactures a specialized part used in the assembly of a finished product may have no outside market for that part. A transfer price such as $20 per unit must be charged to the assembly segment in order to measure segmental revenue for the segment manufacturing the part. It is essential that the segmental manager have some degree of control over the transfer price. If the manager does not have any control over transfer price and output volume, the use of a profit measure may be undesirable for motivational purposes. Ideally, a transfer price would represent the cost of the part or service if purchased from an outside party. But this market "price" is often not available. In this case, the transfer price sometimes is determined on some cost basis. Examples of cost-based transfer prices are standard full cost or standard marginal cost. These costs may or may not have a predetermined profit margin added to compute the transfer price. In still other cases, transfer prices are negotiated between the two segments.

A method to use in establishing a transfer price in a given situation is given later in the chapter.

Investment centers

Closely related to the earnings center concept is the concept of an investment center. Each segment is considered an *investment center* which is evaluated on the basis of the rate of return that it can earn on a specified investment base. Rate of return is computed by dividing segmental earnings by the appropriate investment base. For example, a segment that earns $100,000 on an investment base of $1,000,000 is said to have a rate of return on investment of 10 percent. Of course, there is a question as to the appropriate investment base that should be utilized in calculating return on investment.

The logic for using investment centers as bases for performance evaluation is that segments with larger resources should produce more earnings than segments with smaller amounts of resources. By calculating rates of return for performance evaluation, the relative effectiveness of a segment is measured. Thus, the segment with the highest percentage return is presumably the most effective in utilizing its resources. When the absolute amount of earnings is used to measure performance, larger segments will have a distinct advantage over smaller segments.

Normally the list of assets available to the division make up the base. But there are differences of opinion among accountants as to whether depreciable assets should be shown at cost less accumulated depreciation, cost, or at current replacement cost. Use of these bases will be discussed later in the chapter.

After the appropriate investment base is selected and valued to the satisfaction of the manager, problems can remain since most segment managers have limited control over certain items. For instance, capital expenditure decisions often are made by the top-level management of the company. Another problem area may exist if the firm has a centralized credit and collection segment. The manager may have little control over the amount of accounts receivable shown as segment assets. It is usually argued that all segments are treated the same and that the inclusion of noncontrollable items in the investment base is therefore appropriate. But it is important that the segment managers agree to this proposition in order to avoid adverse reactions.

SEGMENTAL ANALYSIS

The basic fundamentals of responsibility accounting have been described. Now we will expand the discussion of the investment center concept. Also, some other aspects of segmental analysis will be discussed.

The concept of decentralization is relevant to the discussion. *Decentralization* refers to the extent to which management decision making is dispersed to lower echelons of the organization. In other words, the extent of decentralization refers to the degree of control which segmental managers have over the revenues, expenses, and assets of their segments. When a segment manager has control over all three of these, the investment center concept can be used. Thus, the more decentralized the decision making in an organization, the more applicable is the investment center concept to the segments of the company. The more centralized the decision making, the more likely is one to find responsibility centers established as expense centers.

Typical investment centers are large, autonomous segments of very large companies. They are often separated from one another by location, types of products, functions, and/or necessary management skills. Segments such as these often seem like separate companies to an outside observer. But the investment center concept can be applied wherever the manager has control over revenues, expenses, and assets—even in relatively small companies.

Some of the advantages of decentralization of decision making include the following:

1. Increased control over their segment gives managers experiences which train them for high-level positions in the company. The added responsibility and authority also represent "job enlargement" and often result in increased job satisfaction and motivation.
2. Top management can be more removed from day-to-day decision making at the lower echelons of the company and can manage by the exception principle. By removing top management from everyday problem solving that group can better concentrate on long-range planning and on control of the most significant problem areas.
3. Decisions can be made at the point where problems arise. It is often difficult for members of top management to make appropriate decisions when they are not intimately involved with the problem they are trying to solve.

4. Since decentralization enables the investment center concept to be applied, performance evaluation criteria such as return on investment and residual earnings can be used. These concepts will be explained later in the chapter.

CONCEPTS USED IN SEGMENTAL ANALYSIS

The concepts of variable cost, fixed cost, direct cost, indirect cost, net earnings of a segment, and contribution to indirect expenses need to be understood before the investment center analysis can begin. Variable cost and fixed cost were discussed in Chapter 21. The other terms will now be discussed.

Direct cost and indirect cost

As stated earlier in the chapter, costs may be either directly or indirectly related to a particular *cost objective* (a segment, product, and so on). In other words, a cost is not "direct" or "indirect" in and of itself. It is only "direct" or "indirect" in relation to a given cost objective.

A cost is a *direct cost (expense)* of a cost objective if it is traceable to that cost objective. It is an *indirect cost (expense)* to a cost objective if it is not traceable to that objective but has been allocated to it. A particular cost may be direct to one cost objective and indirect to another cost objective. For instance, the salary of the manager of a segment of a company may be a direct cost of that segment but an indirect cost of one of the products manufactured by that segment.

Since a direct cost is traceable to a cost objective, it is likely that the cost will be eliminated if the cost objective is eliminated. For instance, if the plastics segment of a business is eliminated, it is likely that the salary of the manager of that segment will be eliminated. In any particular case, one may be able to think of a direct cost which would not be eliminated if the cost objective were eliminated, but this is the exception rather than the rule.

An indirect cost is not traceable to a cost objective. Therefore, it only becomes an expense of the cost objective through allocation. An example is where depreciation expense on the company headquarters building is allocated as an expense to each of the segments of the company. If a particular segment is eliminated, it is not likely that the expense will disappear; it will be allocated to the remaining segments. Again, it may be possible in a given situation to identify an indirect cost which would be eliminated if the cost objective were eliminated, but this would be an exception to the general rule.

Since direct costs of a unit are clearly identified with that unit, there is a *tendency* for these items also to be controllable by the manager of that unit. And, since indirect costs become costs of a unit only through allocation, there is a *tendency* for these items to be noncontrollable by the manager of that unit. They are controllable at some higher level, as is true for all costs. But care must be taken not to equate direct and controllable costs. A cost such as the salary of the supervisor of a unit may be direct to that unit and noncontrollable by that supervisor. But many costs are direct to a given unit and controllable by the manager of that unit.

Net earnings of a segment

To measure the contribution which a segment makes to overall company earnings, the earnings statement shown in Illustration 24.5 may be used.

Illustration 24.5:
Segmental net earnings

	Segment		
	A	B	Total
Sales	$1,000,000	$700,000	$1,700,000
Less: Variable expenses (all direct expenses)	500,000	410,000	910,000
Contribution margin	$ 500,000	$290,000	$ 790,000
Less: Direct fixed expenses	120,000	170,000	290,000
Contribution to indirect expenses	$ 380,000	$120,000	$ 500,000
Less: Indirect fixed expenses	90,000	160,000	250,000
Net Earnings	$ 290,000	$ (40,000)	$ 250,000

The *contribution margin* is equal to sales less variable expenses. The same concept can be expressed on a per unit basis, and is used that way in Chapter 26. Notice in the illustration that all variable expenses are direct expenses. Some fixed expenses are direct, while others are indirect.

An alternative format which could be used in reporting for a segment is one which shows gross margin but does not show the contribution margin. It would be as follows:

Sales	$XX
Less: Cost of goods sold	XX
Gross margin	$XX
Less: Other direct expenses	XX
Total*	$XX
Less: Indirect fixed expenses	XX
Net Earnings	$XX

* This total may be labeled "contribution to indirect expenses" only if there are no indirect fixed manufacturing costs included in cost of goods sold.

This format moves the fixed direct manufacturing expenses into the category of cost of goods sold. Since some fixed costs are being deducted from sales immediately, the contribution margin figure cannot be shown. Also some of the variable costs (selling and administrative) move down with the other direct expenses.

To illustrate, assume that detailed data for Segment A of Illustration 24.5 are as shown in the center column in Illustration 24.6. These data can be grouped to show a *Contribution margin format* as shown on the left-hand side of Illustration 24.6 or a *Gross margin format* as shown on the right-hand side. Indirect fixed expenses could be deducted using either format to arrive at net earnings.

In determining the contribution which a segment makes to company earnings, it is tempting to use net earnings of the segment since this figure is used in evaluating the performance of an entire company. But there is a problem with using this means of evaluation for segments within a company. Certain indirect fixed expenses are allocated to the segment, and the bases of allocation are often very arbitrary.

Illustration 24.6: Alternative formats for arriving at contribution to indirect expenses

Contribution margin format		Given:		Gross margin format	
Sales	$1,000,000	Sales	$1,000,000	Sales	$1,000,000
Less: Variable expenses	500,000	Variable manufacturing expenses	450,000	Less: Cost of goods sold	470,000
Contribution margin	500,000	Fixed direct manufacturing expenses ..	20,000	Gross margin	$ 530,000
Less: Direct fixed expenses	120,000	Variable selling and administrative expenses	50,000	Less: Other direct expenses	150,000
Contribution to indirect expenses	$ 380,000	Fixed direct selling and administrative expenses	100,000	Contribution to indirect expenses* ...	$ 380,000

* In situations where indirect fixed manufacturing costs are included in cost of goods sold, this title should not be used. Instead, the title "Total" would be used.

Arbitrary allocations of indirect fixed expenses. As stated above, indirect fixed expenses, such as depreciation on the home office administrative building or on the computer facility maintained at the home office, can only be allocated to segments on some arbitrary basis. An attempt is often made to allocate these expenses on the basis of benefit received, but this is not always possible. For instance, how does one determine the benefit a given segment received by the company making a charitable contribution to a worthy cause? Yet costs such as these must be allocated to the segments on some basis if a net earnings approach is used.

For certain indirect expenses the allocation can be made on the basis of benefit received. For instance, if Segment A of Illustration 24.5 utilized 4,000 hours of the total of 10,000 hours of computer time, it could be charged with 40 percent of the total cost of the computer facility since this is proportional to the benefit received. (Where the benefit received is very clear-cut, one might even argue that the expense should be treated as a direct expense.)

For certain other expenses the allocation is made on the basis of responsibility for incurrence. For instance, assume that Segment A contracts with a magazine to run an advertisement which will benefit it and various other segments of the company. Often the entire cost of the advertisement will be allocated to Segment A since it had the responsibility for incurring that portion of the total advertising expense.

When neither "benefit" nor "responsibility" can be used to allocate indirect fixed expenses, some other basis which seems reasonable in the circumstances must be found. Often they are allocated on the basis of net sales for lack of a better basis for allocation. For instance, if Segment A's net sales are 60 percent of total company sales, then 60 percent of a certain indirect expense would be allocated to Segment A.

Due to the arbitrary nature of allocations of indirect fixed expenses, many companies do not allocate these expenses to their segments. Instead they calculate the contribution to indirect fixed expenses and use this figure to determine the earnings contribution of each segment.

Contribution to indirect expenses

The net earnings figure for a segment does not show the amount by which company earnings would decrease if the segment were discontinued.

If management relied on the net earnings figure for a segment to judge its contribution to earnings, it might conclude that Segment B in Illustration 24.5 should be eliminated. But what would have been the effect on earnings if Segment B had been eliminated? This action would have had the following effect:

Reduction in revenues		$700,000
Reduction in expenses:		
Variable expenses	$410,000	
Direct fixed expenses	170,000	580,000
Reduction in earnings of		
the company		$120,000

Notice that the reduction in earnings of $120,000 which would have resulted from eliminating Segment B is shown by its contribution to indirect expenses in Illustration 24.5.

The *contribution to indirect expenses* is a useful figure for determining whether or not a segment should be retained. For this reason and because the allocations of indirect fixed expenses are so arbitrary, many companies utilize an earnings statement (for internal use) which uses the format shown in Illustration 24.7.

Illustration 24.7: Segmental contribution to indirect expenses

	Segment		
	A	B	Total
Sales	$1,000,000	$700,000	$1,700,000
Less: Variable expenses	500,000	410,000	910,000
Contribution margin	$ 500,000	$290,000	$ 790,000
Less: Direct fixed expenses	120,000	170,000	290,000
Contribution to indirect expenses	$ 380,000	$120,000	$ 500,000
Less: Indirect fixed expenses			250,000
Net Earnings			$ 250,000

The contribution margin format was utilized. The gross margin format could have been used. Notice that no attempt is made to allocate indirect fixed expenses to the segments. This format focuses attention on the amount of dollars which a segment contributes toward covering indirect expenses. If all indirect expenses are covered then, of course, there are net earnings for the period.

Neither the net earnings of a segment nor the contribution to indirect expenses approach has utilized the investment center concept. The "investment base" has not yet been introduced into the analysis.

INVESTMENT CENTER ANALYSIS

Consideration of the investment base transforms the performance criteria into an investment center analysis. You will recall that for a responsibility center to be treated as an investment center, the manager of that center has to have control over revenues, expenses, and assets (investment). The following two criteria include the concept of investment base in the analysis. They are ROI (return on investment) and RE (residual earnings).

Return on investment (ROI)

It seems reasonable that a segment which has a large amount of assets should earn more (in an absolute sense) than a segment that has a small amount of assets. Return on investment gives consideration to this by calculating the return (earnings) as a percentage of the assets employed (investment):

$$ROI = \frac{Earnings}{Investment}$$

To illustrate, assume the facts shown in Illustration 24.8 for a company with three segments.

Illustration 24.8: Computation of return on investment

		Segment			
		(1)	*(2)*	*(3)*	*Total*
a.	Earnings	$ 100,000	$ 250,000	$ 500,000	$ 850,000
b.	Investment	1,000,000	1,250,000	2,000,000	4,250,000
	Return on investment (a) ÷ (b)	10%	20%	25%	20%

Using ROI as a criterion for evaluating the segments, Segment 3 is performing the best (25 percent), Segment 2 is next (20 percent) and Segment 1 is performing the worst (10 percent).

Definitions of earnings and investment. Although this concept appears to be quite simple and forthright, there are several difficulties involved with its use. These difficulties center on what is considered to be "earnings" and what is considered to be "investment." Illustration 24.9 shows the possible combinations of definitions of these terms which may be used and the situations in which they are appropriate.

The first set of definitions could conceivably be used for segmental evaluation, but we do not recommend its use. The indirect fixed expenses which are allocated to a segment prevent its use for evaluating the earnings contribution of the segment. The presence of expenses which are not under the control of the manager prevent its use for evaluating the performance of the manager. Only if an evaluation of the earning power of an entire company is being made should this set of definitions be used. Even then it may be preferable to use an ROI calculation which measures earning power without regard to the sources of assets. This can be done by dividing *net operating earnings* by *operating assets* as was shown in Chapter 20. For definitions of these terms see the bottom of Illustration 24.9.

The second set of definitions is useful in evaluating the *rate* of earnings

Possible definitions of "earnings"	Possible definitions of "investment"	When to use the definitions
1. Net earnings of the segment*	Total assets† directly or indirectly related to the segment (including those related to indirect fixed expenses allocated to the segment)	Not recommended for segmental evaluation, but to evaluate the earning power of an entire company
2. Contribution to indirect expenses	Assets directly used by and identified with the segment	To evaluate the *rate* of earnings contribution of a segment
3. "Controllable" earnings —this would start with contribution to indirect expenses and would eliminate any of the revenues and direct expenses which were not under the "control" of the segment manager. (An example of an item to exclude would be the segment manager's own salary.)	Assets under the "control" of the segment manager	To evaluate the earnings *performance* of the *manager* of the segment

* Often *net operating earnings* are used. This is defined as earnings before interest and taxes (EBIT).
† *Operating assets* are often used in the calculation. Assets not used in normal operations, such as land held for future use, are excluded.

contribution of a segment. Indirect fixed expenses which are allocated to the segment are eliminated from the computation. Also assets which are not directly used by the segment are eliminated from the investment base. This set of definitions is not useful in evaluating the performance of the *manager* since items not under the control of the manager would be included.

The third set of definitions is useful in evaluating the earnings performance of the manager of a segment since all items not under the control of the manager have been eliminated. A fundamental principle of responsibility accounting is to evaluate responsibility center managers only on items under their control.

Valuation base.   Another problem with the denominator is with the *valuation base* to use for plant assets. Some possibilities include original cost less accumulated depreciation, original cost, and current replacement cost. Each of these shall now be considered.

Original cost less accumulated depreciation (or book value) is probably the most widely used valuation base. *Original cost* is the price paid to acquire an asset. One advantage of this method is that the amount can readily be determined. Several disadvantages exist. The first is that many different methods of depreciation exist (straight line, sum-of-the-years' digits, double-declining balance, and so on). This leads to different income amounts and to different asset amounts for two segments which would otherwise be identical. Thus, meaningful interfirm and intrafirm comparisons with other segments are hampered. Also, with this method, the older the plant assets, the higher the ROI tends to be. This results from the fact that the book value of the plant assets decreases as accumulated depreciation increases and earnings remain about the same or increase as a result of inflation. Also when a segment with old plant assets is compared to a segment with new plant assets, the former will have a further advantage in that the original cost of the assets was lower.

The use of *original cost* gets rid of the problem of decreasing book values resulting from the growth in accumulated depreciation. But it does not solve the price-level problem. The ROI may still increase over time because earnings tend to increase due to inflation. Also, the income on old assets needs to be much less than on new assets to achieve the same *rate* of return.

When *current replacement cost* is used, the problem of differing depreciation methods and the price-level problem disappear. Current replacement cost is the cost of replacing the present assets with similar assets which are in the same condition as those now in use. The one disadvantage is that current replacement costs are often difficult to determine. But these data will be more readily available in the future.[1]

Expanded form of ROI computation.   It is useful at times to break the ROI formula into two parts as follows:

$$ROI = \frac{Earnings}{Sales} \times \frac{Sales}{Investment}$$

The first term, $\frac{Earnings}{Sales}$, is called *margin.* It is the percentage relationship of earnings to sales. This percentage also shows the number of cents of earnings that attach to each dollar of sales.

The second term, $\frac{Sales}{Investment}$, is called *turnover.* It is the number of times by which sales per year exceeds the investment in assets.

Breaking the ROI formula into these two components is useful in determining a strategy for increasing the margin or the turnover or the net effect of the two in a particular case. For instance, assume that the manager of a segment is faced with the following return on investment for the past year.

$$ROI = Margin \times Turnover$$

$$ROI = \frac{Earnings}{Sales} \times \frac{Sales}{Investment}$$

$$ROI = \frac{\$100,000}{\$2,000,000} \times \frac{\$2,000,000}{\$1,000,000}$$

$$ROI = 5 \text{ percent} \times 2 \text{ times}$$
$$ROI = 10 \text{ percent}$$

---

[1] The Securities and Exchange Commission requires that large companies report the current replacement cost of plant assets (among other things) in certain reports filed with the SEC. The FASB requires large publicly-held companies to provide both current cost and constant dollar information on a supplemental basis (see Appendix A).

The manager desires to increase ROI for the coming year. The following are illustrative of some of the strategies which might be used (each strategy is independent of all the others):

1. Concentrate on increasing the margin while holding turnover constant. Pursuing this strategy would involve leaving selling prices as they are and making every effort to increase efficiency so as to reduce expenses. By doing so, possibly expenses could be reduced by $40,000 without affecting sales and investment. If so, the new ROI would be:

$$\text{ROI} = \frac{\text{Earnings}}{\text{Sales}} \times \frac{\text{Sales}}{\text{Investment}}$$

$$\text{ROI} = \frac{\$140,000}{\$2,000,000} \times \frac{\$2,000,000}{\$1,000,000}$$

ROI = 7 percent × 2 times
ROI = 14 percent

2. Concentrate on increasing the turnover by reducing the investment in assets while holding income and sales constant. Possibly working capital could be reduced or some land could be sold, reducing investment in assets by $200,000 without affecting sales and earnings. If so, the new ROI would be:

$$\text{ROI} = \frac{\text{Earnings}}{\text{Sales}} \times \frac{\text{Sales}}{\text{Investment}}$$

$$\text{ROI} = \frac{\$100,000}{\$2,000,000} \times \frac{\$2,000,000}{\$800,000}$$

ROI = 5 percent × 2½ times
ROI = 12½ percent

3. Possibly actions could be taken which affect both margin and turnover. An advertising campaign would probably increase sales and earnings. (Getting rid of nonproductive depreciable assets would decrease investment while increasing earnings.) Assume that an advertising campaign increased sales by $500,000 and earnings by $50,000. ROI would then be:

$$\text{ROI} = \frac{\text{Earnings}}{\text{Sales}} \times \frac{\text{Sales}}{\text{Investment}}$$

$$\text{ROI} = \frac{\$150,000}{\$2,500,000} \times \frac{\$2,500,000}{\$1,000,000}$$

ROI = 6 percent × 2.5 times
ROI = 15 percent

In the above example, both margin and turnover were increased as a result of the advertising campaign. But sometimes an increase in one is accompanied by a decrease in the other. For instance, assume that the advertising campaign increased sales by $500,000 but only increased earnings by $12,500. The resulting ROI would be:

$$\text{ROI} = \frac{\text{Earnings}}{\text{Sales}} \times \frac{\text{Sales}}{\text{Investment}}$$

$$\text{ROI} = \frac{\$112,500}{\$2,500,000} \times \frac{\$2,500,000}{\$1,000,000}$$

ROI = 4.5 percent × 2.5 times
ROI = 11.25 percent

In this illustration, the margin decreased from 5 percent to 4.5 percent, but turnover increased from 2 times to 2.5 times. The net result was an increase in ROI from 10 percent to 11.25 percent.

Residual earnings   The use of return on investment (ROI) can result in what is called *suboptimization*. This term is defined as the situation where segment managers take an action which is in their own (their segment's) interest but not in the best interests of the company as a whole.

To illustrate, assume that the manager of Segment 3 in Illustration 24.8 has an opportunity to take on a project involving an investment of $100,000 which will return 22 percent (or $22,000). Since the segment is already realizing a return on investment of 25 percent, the manager may decide to reject the project. But the overall company rate of return is only 20 percent. This would be increased by accepting the project.

To prevent suboptimization, the *residual earnings* concept is sometimes applied. Residual earnings are defined as the amount of earnings of a segment in excess of the desired minimum rate of return. This desired minimum rate is always equal to or greater than the cost of capital (the cost of raising capital—which is explained more fully in Chapter 28). In formula form, residual earnings are:

Residual earnings = Earnings − (Investment × Desired minimun ROI)

When evaluating the earnings contribution of a segment, "earnings" would be "contribution to indirect expenses" and "investment" would be "assets directly used by and identified with the segment." When evaluating the earnings performance of a segment manager, "earnings" would be "controllable earnings" and "investment" would be "assets under the control of the segment manager." The residual earnings concept is generally not used for evaluating an entire company, since the problem of suboptimization does not exist (by definition).

Using the data from Illustration 24.8, residual earnings would be found as shown in Illustration 24.10 (assuming a desired minimum ROI of 10 percent).

If the manager of Segment 3 were to accept the proposal mentioned above (a 22 percent return on an investment of $100,000), the last two columns of Illustration 24.10 would be changed as follows:

		Segment 3	Total
a.	Earnings	$ 522,000	$ 872,000
b.	Investment........................	2,100,000	4,350,000
c.	Desired minimun ROI—		
	(b) × 10%	210,000	435,000
d.	Residual earnings (a) − (c)	312,000	437,000

This example shows that the use of the residual earnings concept will prevent suboptimization in situations such as this. The segment rated as the best is the one with the greatest amount of residual earnings rather than the one with the highest ROI rate. Segment managers will take those actions which will increase their residual earnings.

Illustration 24.10: Computation of residual earnings

		Segment			Total*
		(1)	(2)	(3)	
a.	Earnings	$ 100,000	$ 250,000	$ 500,000	$ 850,000
b.	Investment	1,000,000	1,250,000	2,000,000	4,250,000
c.	Desired minimum ROI—				
	(b) × 10%	100,000	125,000	200,000	425,000
d.	Residual earnings				
	(a) − (c)	–0–	125,000	300,000	425,000

* Depending on the set of definitions used for earnings and investment, the total column may include amounts which do not equal the total when adding across. This is because some expenses will not be allocated and some assets will not be assigned to the segments if definition sets (2) or (3) in Illustration 24.9 are used.

In evaluating the performance of a segment manager, comparisons should be made not only with the current budget and with other segments within the company but also with past performance in that segment and with similar segments in other companies. Consideration must be given to general economic conditions, market conditions for the product being produced, and so on. A superior manager in Company A may be earning a return of 12 percent which is above similar segments in other companies but below other segments in Company A. The other segments in Company A may be more profitable because of market conditions and the nature of the products rather than the performance of the segment manager. Careful judgment must be used whenever evaluating the performance of the manager of a responsibility center.

Transfer prices in segmental reporting

An introductory discussion of transfer prices was presented earlier in the chapter. The topic needs to be covered in greater depth here.

In many companies, segments sell goods or services to other segments within that company. Since the selling segment really has no actual revenues resulting from these transactions, artificial revenues need to be created to use the earnings or investment center concepts. As indicated earlier, there are various means of setting the transfer price. The transfer price will be used as revenue for the selling segment and as expense for the buying segment. Therefore, both segments have a keen interest in what price is set, and conflict may arise.

There does not seem to be consensus in the literature regarding the procedure for establishing a transfer price in a given situation. Some of the possibilities for setting the transfer price include using:

1. Actual variable cost.
2. Actual full cost.
3. Standard variable cost.
4. Standard full cost.
5. Any of the first four above plus a profit margin.
6. Market price.
7. Negotiated price.
8. Arbitrated price.

We would discourage the use of actual cost since this allows the selling segment to pass on its inefficiencies to the buying segment. Thus, standard costs are preferred over actual costs. Also the use of costs (with no profit margin) would severely hamper the use of the earnings center or investment center concepts. (There could be a "return" only in the sense that there might be a positive contribution to indirect expenses if full cost were used as a transfer price.) It seems preferable to include some profit margin in the transfer price.

Ideally, there exists an outside market for the item, and the outside price can be used in setting the transfer price. Where no such price exists, the transfer price may have to be negotiated between the two segments involved. If agreement cannot be reached, an arbitration process may be necessary or the segment may have to be treated as an expense center.

In view of the above discussion, a procedure which seems reasonable in establishing a transfer price in a given situation is as follows:

1. If an outside market for the part exists, the best price of a reputable supplier might be used as the transfer price. Use of this price treats the segments involved as though they actually are separate companies engaging in an "arm's-length" transaction. Occasionally, a price somewhat below the market price can be justified (based on savings in shipping costs, administrative costs, and so on from selling internally). Or, the selling segment may have excess productive capacity which would otherwise lie idle. If it can obtain a transfer price of anything in excess of its variable costs of supplying the good or service, it will increase its earnings. Thus, it may be willing to accept a price below the market price. Use of an impartial arbitration board might be called for in making such adjustments to market price unless they can be negotiated by the two segments involved.

   After the price is established, the two segments must decide whether to "do business" with each other. General rules are as follows:

   a. The buying segment should be required to buy internally as long as the transfer price is not *above* some bona fide available outside price. This assumes that the selling segment can sell its output in the external market. Chapter 27 covers the situation where the decision is to make or buy a part, which is relevant if the selling segment cannot sell its output externally.

b. The selling segment should be required to sell internally as long as the transfer price allows the selling segment to earn as much on internal "sales" as on external sales.

2. If there is no outside market price, have the managers of the two segments involved negotiate a price.

3. Where there is no outside market price and negotiation fails, use arbitration.

a. Each segment could select one member of the arbitration board and then those two could select the third member. The two segments could commit themselves to accepting and using the transfer price for a given period of time.

b. A floor price of standard variable cost of supplying the good or service plus a profit margin, and a ceiling price of full cost of supplying the good or service plus a profit margin, might be used by the board. The case of standard variable cost plus a profit margin could be justified for short-run use, since fixed costs do not change in the short run. Standard full costs plus a profit margin should be used in the long run since all costs must be covered in the long run.

c. If arbitration would create too many hard feelings among representatives of the two segments, the goods should be transferred at standard full cost of supplying the goods or services (or actual full cost if there is no standard cost system in use) and the supplying segment should be treated as an expense center rather than an earnings or investment center.

In every case, top management should determine whether the setting of a transfer price at a particular level will cause segment managers to take actions which result in suboptimization. It must also decide whether to permit some suboptimization in order to promote autonomy of segments or to discourage suboptimization so as to maximize overall company profits.

SEGMENTAL REPORTING IN EXTERNAL FINANCIAL STATEMENTS

Formerly, segmental information was reported only to management for internal decision-making purposes. In December 1976, the Financial Accounting Standards Board issued *Statement of Financial Accounting Standards No. 14* entitled, "Financial Reporting for Segments of a Business Enterprise." This Statement requires publicly held companies to publish certain segmental information in their annual financial statements. Thus, external users of financial statements will also have segmental information to aid them in their decisions regarding these companies.

NEW TERMS INTRODUCED IN CHAPTER 24

Contribution margin—revenues less variable expenses.

Contribution margin format—an earnings statement format for a segment which shows the contribution margin (Sales—Variable expenses).

Contribution to indirect expenses—the earnings of a segment when only direct expenses are deducted from revenues of a segment.

Controllable earnings of a segment—earnings of a segment when expenses under the control of the manager are deducted from the revenues of the segment.

Cost objective—a segment, product, or other item for which costs may be accumulated.

Current replacement cost—the cost of replacing the present assets with similar assets in the same condition as those now in use.

Decentralization—the extent to which management decision making is dispersed to lower levels of the organization.

Direct cost (expense)—a cost which is directly traceable to a given cost objective is said to be a direct cost of that cost objective.

Earnings center—segment of an enterprise having both revenue and expense items.

Expense center—segment of an enterprise having only expense items. (It has no revenue.) Examples include the accounting department and the maintenance department.

Gross margin format—an earnings statement format for a segment which shows the gross margin (Sales—Cost of goods sold).

Indirect cost (expense)—a cost which is not directly traceable to a given cost objective is said to be an indirect cost to that cost objective when it has been allocated to that cost objective.

Investment center—segment of an enterprise having revenues, expenses, and an appropriate investment base.

Margin (as used in ROI)—is equal to $\dfrac{\text{Earnings}}{\text{Sales}}$

Net earnings of a segment—the earnings of a segment when all expenses (direct and indirect) are deducted from revenues of a segment.

Net operating earnings—net earnings adjusted for nonoperating revenues and expenses, such as interest and taxes. Also called earnings before interest and taxes (EBIT).

Operating assets—total assets less nonoperating assets such as land held for future use. They are the assets used to produce the major revenues of the company.

Original cost—the price paid to acquire an asset.

Original cost less accumulated depreciation—is equal to the book value of an asset, the amount paid less total depreciation taken.

Residual earnings—are equal to Earnings—(Investment × Desired minimum ROI).

Responsibility accounting—a system of accounting that seeks to provide information needed to evaluate each manager on the basis of the revenue and expense items over which he (or she) has control.

Responsibility center—a segment of an organization which shows the revenues and expenses charged to a particular executive.

Return on investment (ROI)—is equal to $\dfrac{\text{Earnings}}{\text{Investment}}$ or $\dfrac{\text{Earnings}}{\text{Sales}} \times \dfrac{\text{Sales}}{\text{Investment}}$.

Segments—fairly autonomous units or divisions of a company.

Suboptimization—when an individual within a company takes an action which benefits one segment but is not in the best interest of the company.

Transfer price—an artificial price used when goods or services are transferred from one segment to another segment within the same company.

Turnover—is equal to $\dfrac{\text{Sales}}{\text{Investment}}$.

DEMONSTRATION PROBLEM

The Corey Company has two segments, A and B. Segment A supplies all of its output of a new product to Segment B, which sells it to the general public after altering it slightly at negligible cost. Therefore, the transfer price times the number of units transferred becomes the "sales revenue" of Segment A and the "cost of goods sold" of Segment B. (Inventory amounts in Segment B at the beginning and end of the period are negligible.) Assume there is no outside market price for this new product. The product is protected by a patent so that no other company can produce it or sell it. The question being decided is the amount of the transfer price to use. Following are relevant data:

	Segment A	Segment B
Sales (1,000,000 units)	?	$5,000,000
Cost of goods sold	$2,000,000	?
Other direct costs	1,000,000	900,000

Required:

a. Calculate the contribution to indirect expenses for each segment under each of the following assumed transfer prices:

1. The managers of the two segments negotiate a transfer price of $3.80 per unit.
2. The managers of the two segments are unable to agree on a transfer price. An arbitration board is selected and arrives at a transfer price of $3.70 per unit.
3. The managers are unable to agree on a transfer price, and top management does not believe that an arbitrated price would soothe their ruffled feelings. The transfer price is set at actual full direct cost of supplying the goods. Thus, a transfer price of $3 per unit is set.
4. Assume the same facts as in **(c)** except that the transfer price is set at standard full direct cost of Segment A. Assume this amount to be $2.90 per unit.

b. Comment on the results of the calculations in **(a)**.

Solution to demonstration problem

a.

	Segment A			
	(1)	*(2)*	*(3)*	*(4)*
Sales (1,000,000 units)	$3,800,000	$3,700,000	$3,000,000	$2,900,000
Cost of goods sold	2,000,000	2,000,000	2,000,000	2,000,000
Gross margin	$1,800,000	$1,700,000	$1,000,000	$ 900,000
Less: Other direct costs	1,000,000	1,000,000	1,000,000	1,000,000
Contribution to indirect expenses	$ 800,000	$ 700,000	$ –0–	$ (100,000)

	Segment B			
	(1)	*(2)*	*(3)*	*(4)*
Sales (1,000,000 units)	$5,000,000	$5,000,000	$5,000,000	$5,000,000
Cost of goods sold	3,800,000	3,700,000	3,000,000	2,900,000
Gross margin	$1,200,000	$1,300,000	$2,000,000	$2,100,000
Less: Other direct costs	900,000	900,000	900,000	900,000
Contribution to indirect expenses	$ 300,000	$ 400,000	$1,100,000	$1,200,000

b. Either of the first two transfer prices would work with the investment center concept. Both segments show a positive contribution to indirect expenses.

The third situation does not allow Segment A to show a positive contribution to indirect expenses. It also allows it to pass all of its costs on to Segment B (possibly with some costs of inefficiency). If this transfer price is used, Segment A will have to be treated as an expense center rather than an investment center. But under this method there is little incentive for Segment A to control costs.

The fourth transfer price also dictates that Segment A be treated as an expense center since it allows no profit margin. But there is an incentive to reduce actual costs below standard costs.

QUESTIONS

1. What is the fundamental principle of responsibility accounting?

2. Name three possible reporting bases for evaluating business segments.

3. What is the logic of using an investment center as a basis for performance evaluation?

4. How soon should accounting reports be prepared after the end of the performance measurement period? Explain.

5. Compare and contrast an expense center and an investment center.

6. Which categories of items must a segment manager have control over for the investment center concept to be applicable?

7. What connection is there between the extent of decentralization and the investment center concept?

8. Give some of the advantages of decentralization of decision making.

9. Differentiate between a direct cost and an indirect cost of a segment. What happens to each category if the segment to which they are related is eliminated?

10. Is it possible for a cost to be "direct" to one cost objective and "indirect" to another cost objective? Explain.

11. Indicate how each of the following is calculated for a segment:

a. Gross margin.

b. Contribution margin.

c. Contribution to indirect expenses (under the two different formats).

d. Net earnings.

12. Describe some of the methods by which indirect expenses are usually allocated to a segment.

13. Give the general formula for return on investment (ROI). How may this be split into two components?

14. Give the three sets of definitions for "earnings" and "investment" which may be used in ROI calculations and when each set is applicable.

15. Give the various valuation bases that could be used for plant assets in investment center calculations. Discuss some of the advantages and disadvantages of these methods.

16. In what way is the use of the residual earnings (RE) concept superior to use of return on investment (ROI)?

17. How are residual earnings determined?

18. If the residual earnings for Segment Manager A were $50,000 while the residual earnings for Segment Manager B were $100,000, does this necessarily mean that B is a better manager than A?

19. What purpose is served by setting transfer prices?

20. Assuming that an outside market exists for a part "sold" by Segment 1 to Segment 2, what procedure would you recommend for setting the transfer price? What rules would you have regarding whether the two segments must do business with each other after the transfer price is set?

21. If there is no external market for the part referred to in Question 20, how should the transfer price be set? What if agreement cannot be reached?

EXERCISES

E-1. Describe a segment of a business enterprise that is best treated as an expense center. List four indirect expenses that may be allocated to such an expense center.

E-2. Baxter Company manufactures refrigerators. Below are listed several costs that occur. Indicate whether or not the shop supervisor can control each of the listed items.

a. Depreciation.

b. Repairs.

c. Small tools.

d. Supplies.

e. Bond interest.

E-3. List five important factors that should be considered in designing reports for a responsibility accounting system.

E-4. Given the following data, prepare a schedule which shows contribution margin, contribution to indirect costs, and net earnings of the segment:

Direct fixed expenses	$ 60,000
Indirect fixed expenses	50,000
Sales	500,000
Variable expenses	340,000

What would be the effect on company earnings if the segment were eliminated?

E-5. Three segments (A, B, and C) of the Jacobs Company have net sales of $600,000, $400,000, and $200,000, respectively. A decision is made to allocate the pool of $60,000 of administrative overhead expenses of the home office to the segments based on net sales.

a. How much should be allocated to each of the segments?

b. If Segment C is eliminated, how much would be allocated to A and B?

E-6. Two segments (tires and batteries) showed the following data for the most recent year:

	Tires	Batteries
Contribution to indirect expenses	$ 100,000	$ 288,000
Assets directly used by and identified with the segment	500,000	1,200,000
Sales	2,000,000	3,600,000

a. Calculate return on investment (ROI) for each segment in the most direct manner.

b. Calculate return on investment (ROI) utilizing the margin and turnover components.

E-7. Determine the effect of each of the following on the margin, turnover, and ROI of the tire segment in Exercise E-6. Consider each change independently of the others.

a. Direct variable expenses were reduced by $10,000, and indirect expenses were reduced by $15,000. Sales and assets were unaffected.

b. Assets used by the segment were reduced by $100,000, while earnings and sales were unaffected.

c. An advertising campaign increased sales by $200,000 and earnings by $32,000. Assets directly used by the segment remained unaffected.

E-8. The Trueblood Company has three segments: red, white, and blue. Data concerning "earnings" and "investment" are as follows:

	Red	White	Blue
Contribution to indirect expenses	$ 20,000	$ 45,000	$ 70,000
Assets directly used by and identified with the segment	100,000	300,000	800,000

Assuming that the minimum desired return on investment is 10 percent, calculate the residual earnings of each of the segments. Do the results indicate that any of the segments should be eliminated?

E-9. Assume that for the red segment in Exercise E-8, $5,000 of the direct expenses and $20,000 of the segmental assets are not under the control of the segment manager. Top management wishes to evaluate the segment manager's earnings performance. Calculate the manager's return on investment and residual earnings. (Because certain expenses and assets are not controllable by the segment manager, the minimum desired ROI is 15 percent.)

PROBLEMS, SERIES A

P24–1–A. The Nance Corporation has three product plants (X, Y, and Z). These plants are treated as responsibility centers. The following summarizes the results for the month of March 1981:

Plant	Revenue	Expenses	Investment base (gross assets)
X	$1,000,000	$ 500,000	$10,000,000
Y	2,000,000	800,000	15,000,000
Z	3,000,000	1,100,000	32,000,000

Required:

a. If the plants are treated as earnings centers, which plant manager appears to have done the best job?

b. If the plants are treated as investment centers, which plant manager appears to have done the best job? (Assume that plant managers are evaluated in terms of rate of return on gross assets.)

c. Do the results of earnings center analysis and investment center analysis give different findings? If so, why?

P24–2–A. You are given the following information relevant to the Monroe Company for the year ended December 31, 1981:

Expense and basis of allocation	
Home office building expense (net sales)	$8,000
Buying expenses (net purchases)	7,000
Bad debts (net sales)	1,500
Depreciation of home office equipment (net sales)	2,200
Advertising expense (indirect allocated on basis of relative amounts of direct advertising)	9,000
Insurance expense (relative amounts of equipment plus average inventory in department)	2,400

Additional data:

	Segment A	Segment B	Total
Purchases (net)	$38,000	$12,000	$ 50,000
Sales (net)	80,000	20,000	100,000
Equipment (cost)	15,000	000	25,000
Advertising (direct)	4,000	∠,000	6,000
Average inventory	25,000	10,000	35,000

Required:

a. Prepare a schedule showing the amounts of each type of expense allocable to Segments A and B using the above data and the bases of allocation stated parenthetically above.

P24–2–A. You are given the following information relevant to the Monroe Company for the year ended December 31, 1981:

Controllable expenses	Plant manager		Vice president of manufacturing		President	
	Budget	Actual	Budget	Actual	Budget	Actual
Office expense	$3,000	$4,000	$ 5,000	$ 7,000	$10,000	$ 7,000
Printing shop	2,000	2,000				
Iron shop	1,000	900				
Toaster shop	8,000	7,000				
Purchasing			10,000	11,000		
Receiving			5,000	6,000		
Inspection			8,000	7,000		
Sales manager					80,000	70,000
Controller					60,000	50,000
Treasurer					40,000	30,000
Personnel manager					20,000	30,000

Required:

Prepare the responsibility accounting reports for three levels of management—plant manager, vice president of manufacturing, and president.

P24–3–A. Homewood Company allocates all of its home office expenses to its two segments, A and B. Given below are selected expense account balances and additional data upon which allocations are based:

b. Criticize some of these allocation bases.

P24–4–A. Wilcox, Inc., is a company with two segments, 1 and 2. Its revenues and expenses for 1981 are as follows:

	Segment 1	Segment 2	Total
Sales (net)	$320,000	$480,000	$800,000
Direct expenses:			
Cost of goods sold . . .	150,000	330,000	480,000
Selling	45,600	24,000	69,600
Administrative:			
Bad debts	10,000	6,000	16,000
Insurance	8,000	4,000	12,000
Interest	1,600	800	2,400
Indirect expenses:			
Selling			60,000
Administrative			84,000

Required:

a. Prepare a schedule showing the gross margin and the contribution to indirect expenses of each segment and net earnings for the company as a whole. Do not allocate indirect expenses to the segments.

b. Assume that indirect selling expenses are to be allocated on the basis of net sales and that indirect administrative expenses are to be allocated on the basis of direct administrative expenses. Prepare a statement (starting with the contribution to indirect expenses) which shows the net earnings of each segment.

c. Comment on the meaningfulness of the "earnings" amounts shown in parts *(a)* and *(b)* for determining the earnings contribution of the segments.

P24–5–A. The following data pertain to the operating revenues and expenses for the Keck Company for 1981:

	Segment C	Segment D	Total
Sales	$500,000	$200,000	$700,000
Variable expenses	355,000	112,000	467,000
Direct fixed expenses . . .	40,000	28,000	68,000
Indirect fixed			
expenses			95,000

Of the direct fixed expenses, $8,000 of those shown for Segment C and $6,000 of those shown for Segment D are not under the control of the segment manager.

Of the company's total operating assets of $1,000,000 the following facts exist:

	Segment C	Segment D
Assets directly used by and		
identified with the segment	$400,000	$250,000
Assets under the "control"		
of the segment manager	350,000	200,000

Required:

a. Prepare a statement showing the contribution margin and the contribution to indirect expenses for each segment and the total earnings of the Keck Company.

b. Determine the return on investment for evaluating (1) the earning power of the entire company, (2) the rate of earnings contribution of each segment, and (3) the earnings performance of each segment manager.

c. Comment on the results of part *(b)*.

P24–6–A. The Snyder Company operates with three segments, K, L, and M. Data regarding these segments are as follows:

	Segment K	Segment L	Segment M
Contribution to indirect			
expenses	$ 90,000	$ 50,000	$ 40,000
Earnings controllable by			
the manager	125,000	75,000	64,000
Assets directly used by and			
identified with the segment	500,000	400,000	200,000
Assets under the "control" of			
the segment manager	440,000	355,000	180,000

Required:

a. Calculate the rate of return (ROI) for each segment and each segment manager. Rank them from highest to lowest.

b. Assume the minimum desired rate of return for a segment is 12 percent and for a segment manager is 20 percent. Calculate the residual earnings (RE) for each segment and each manager. Rank them from highest to lowest.

c. Repeat *(b)*, but now assume the desired minimum rate of return for a segment is 17 percent and for a segment manager is 25 percent. Rank them from highest to lowest.

d. Comment of the rankings achieved.

P24–7–A. The manager of the Apex Segment of the Kondrel Corporation was faced with the following data for the year 1981:

Contribution to indirect expenses	$ 500,000
Assets directly used by and identified	
with the segment	6,250,000
Sales	10,000,000

Required:

a. Determine the margin, turnover, and return on investment for the segment in 1981.

b. Determine the effect on margin, turnover, and return on investment of the segment in 1982 if each of the following changes were to occur. Consider each one separately and assume that any items not specifically mentioned remain the same as during 1981.

1. A campaign to control costs results in higher "earnings" of $100,000.

2. Certain nonproductive assets are eliminated. As a result "investment" decreases by $500,000 and expenses decrease by $40,000.

3. An advertising campaign results in increasing sales by $2,000,000, cost of goods sold by $1,500,000, and advertising expense by $300,000.

4. An investment is made in productive assets costing $500,000. As a result sales increase by $200,000 and expenses increase by $30,000.

PROBLEMS, SERIES B

P24–1–B. The Miles Corporation has three product plants (A, B, and C). These plants are treated as responsibility centers. The following summarizes the results for the month of April 1981:

Plant	Revenue	Expenses	Investment base (gross assets)
A......	$ 200,000	$ 100,000	$ 1,000,000
B......	500,000	200,000	1,500,000
C......	2,000,000	1,400,000	10,000,000

Required:

a. If the plants are treated as earnings centers, which plant manager appears to have done the best job?

b. If the plants are treated as investment centers, which plant manager appears to have done the best job? (Assume that plant managers are evaluated in terms of rate of return on gross assets.)

c. Do the results of earnings center analysis and investment center analysis give different findings? If so, why?

P24–2–B. You are given the following information relevant to Mitchell Company for the year ended December 31, 1981. The company is organized according to functions.

Required:

Prepare the responsibility accounting reports for three levels of management—supervisor, plant manager, and vice president of manufacturing.

P24–3–B. Johnson, Inc., allocates expenses and revenues to the two segments that it operates. It extends credit to customers under a revolving charge plan whereby all account balances not paid within 30 days are charged at the rate of 1½ percent per month.

Given below are selected expense and revenue accounts and some additional data needed to complete the allocation of the expenses and the one revenue amount.

Expenses and revenue allocation bases

Revolving charge service revenue (net sales)	$15,000
Home office building occupancy expense (net sales)	12,000
Buying expenses (net purchases)	40,000
General administrative expenses (number of employees in department)	50,000
Insurance expense (relative average inventory plus cost of equipment and fixtures in each department)	4,500
Depreciation of home office equipment (net sales)	7,500

Controllable expenses	Shop "A": supervisor		Plant manager		Vice president of manufacturing	
	Budget	Actual	Budget	Actual	Budget	Actual
Office expense	$2,000	$1,000	$ 4,000	$ 5,000	$10,000	$ 9,000
Supervision	3,000	4,000				
Supplies (manufacturing)	4,000	5,000				
Tools	5,000	6,000				
Shop "B"			9,000	10,000		
Shop "C"			11,000	12,000		
Purchasing					14,000	17,000
Receiving					15,000	15,000
Inspection					16,000	8,000

Additional data:

	Segment R	Segment S	Total
Sales (net)	$100,000	$200,000	$300,000
Purchases (net)	$ 80,000	$120,000	$200,000
Number of employees	3	7	10
Average inventory	$ 20,000	$ 40,000	$ 60,000
Cost of equipment and fixtures	$ 30,000	$ 60,000	$ 90,000

Required:

a. Prepare a schedule showing the allocation of the above items to Segments R and S.

b. Present criticisms of some of these allocation bases.

P24–4–B. Carey, Inc., is a diamond importer which operates two segments, A and B. The revenue and expense data for 1981 are as follows:

	Segment A	Segment B	Total
Net sales	$551,000	$899,000	$1,450,000
Service charges revenue	8,500	24,000	32,500
Direct expenses:			
Cost of goods sold . . .	310,000	470,000	780,000
Selling	53,000	45,000	98,000
Administrative	15,000	10,000	25,000
Bad debts	4,000	11,000	15,000
Indirect expenses:			
Selling			210,000
Administrative			260,000

Required:

a. Prepare a schedule showing the gross margin and the contribution to indirect expenses of each segment and net earnings for the company as a whole. Do not allocate indirect expenses to the segments.

b. Assume that indirect selling expenses are to be allocated to the segments on the basis of net sales and that indirect administrative expenses are to be allocated on the basis of direct administrative expenses. Prepare a statement (starting with the contribution to indirect expenses) which shows the net earnings of each segment.

c. Comment on the meaningfulness of the "earnings" amounts shown in parts *(a)* and *(b)* for determining the earnings contribution of the segments. Should Segment A be eliminated?

P24–5–B. The McKee Corporation operates with three segments. Results of operations for 1981 were the following:

	Segment 1	Segment 2	Segment 3	Total
Sales	$50,000,000	$30,000,000	$20,000,000	$100,000,000
Variable expenses	36,000,000	17,000,000	13,500,000	66,500,000
Fixed expenses:				
Direct	7,000,000	2,500,000	1,000,000	10,500,000
Indirect				5,000,000

The following direct fixed expenses were not under the control of the segment manager: Segment 1, $500,000; Segment 2, $350,000; and Segment 3, $400,000.

For the company's total operating assets of $140,000,000, the following facts exist:

	Segment 1	Segment 2	Segment 3
Assets directly used by and identified with the segment	$70,000,000	$40,000,000	$20,000,000
Assets under the "control" of the segment manager	60,000,000	32,000,000	16,000,000

Required:

a. Prepare a statement showing the contribution margin and the contribution to indirect expenses for each segment and the total earnings of the McKee Corporation.

b. Determine the return on investment for evaluating (1) the earning power of the entire company, (2) the rate of earnings contribution of each segment, and (3) the earnings performance of each segment manager.

c. Comment on the results of part *(b).*

P24–6–B. The Phillips Company has three segments, R, S, and T. Data regarding these segments are as follows:

	Segment R	Segment S	Segment T
Contribution to indirect expenses	$ 600,000	$ 290,000	$100,000
Earnings controllable by the manager	660,000	315,000	120,000
Assets directly used by and identified with the segment.....................	5,000,000	2,000,000	500,000
Assets under the "control" of the segment manager	4,800,000	1,900,000	450,000

Required:

a. Calculate the rate of return (ROI) for each segment and each segment manager. Rank them from highest to lowest.

b. Assume the minimum desired rate of return for a segment is 10 percent and for a segment manager is 12 percent. Calculate the residual earnings (RE) for each segment and for each manager. Rank them from highest to lowest.

c. Repeat **(b)**, but now assume that the desired minimum rate of return for a segment is 14 percent and for a segment manager is 16 percent. Rank them from highest to lowest.

d. Comment on the rankings achieved.

P24–7–B. The Hicks Segment of the Kendrex Corporation reported the following data for 1981:

Contribution to indirect expenses	$ 700,000
Assets directly used by and identified with the segment........................	5,600,000
Sales	11,200,000

Required:

a. Determine the margin, turnover, and return on investment for the segment in 1981.

b. Determine the effect on margin, turnover, and return on investment of the segment in 1982 if each of the following changes were to occur. Consider each one separately, and assume that any items not specifically mentioned remain the same as in 1981.

1. A new labor contract with the union increases expenses by $200,000 for 1982.
2. A strike in early 1982 shuts down operations for two months. Sales decrease by $3,000,000, cost of goods sold by $2,000,000, and other direct expenses by $600,000.
3. Introduction of a new product causes sales to increase by $4,000,000, cost of goods sold by $2,800,000, and other direct expenses by $300,000. Assets increase by $600,000.
4. An advertising campaign is launched. As a result sales increase by $1,000,000, cost of goods sold by $700,000, and other direct expenses by $300,000.

BUSINESS DECISION PROBLEM 24–1

The Alcini Company has two segments, the manufacturing segment and the marketing segment. The manufacturing segment performs all of the activities required to bring the product, electronic air filters, to completion. The marketing segment "purchases" the electronic air filters from the manufacturing segment and markets them to the public for use in home furnaces to electronically clean the air as it recirculates through the furnace. The marketing segment attaches the brand name after it receives the units.

An outside market exists for the units. While the units manufactured by other suppliers have slight variations, they have the same basic features and can be sold at the same price under the marketing segment's brand name. The manufacturing segment can sell its units in the market to other selling organizations.

Required:

Decide whether the two segments should be required to do business with each other in each of the following instances:

a. The outside market price (the best price of a reputable supplier) at which the marketing segment can acquire the units is $300 per unit. This is also the best price at which the manufacturing segment can sell its production. There are no cost savings from selling internally. The transfer price is set at $300 per unit.

b. Assume the same facts as in **(a)** except that there is a $10 per unit cost saving from selling internally. The transfer price is set at $290 per unit.

c. Assume the same facts as in **(a)** except that the manager of the marketing segment insists that the highest acceptable transfer price is $285 per unit.

d. Assume the same facts as in **(a)** except that the manager of the manufacturing segment insists that the lowest acceptable transfer price is $310 per unit.

e. Assume that there is an oversupply in the outside market but that other suppliers of the units refuse to reduce the price. If the manufacturing segment cannot sell its units internally, its facilities will lie idle. To try to undersell its competitors in the external market would only start a price war which could damage the market for years to come. Its variable costs of supplying the goods are $200 per unit. The transfer price is set at $250 per unit.

DECISION PROBLEM 24–2

Respond to each of the following situations.

a. The Dexter Company manufactures swimsuits. The company's business is seasonal so that between August and December usually ten skilled manufacturing employees are "laid off." In order to improve morale the financial vice president suggests that these ten employees not be laid off in the future. Instead it is suggested that they work in general labor from August to December but still be paid their manufacturing wages of $6 per hour. General labor personnel earn $3 per hour. What are the implications of this plan to the assignment of costs to the various segments of the business?

b. The Piper Company builds new homes. Baker is in charge of the construction department. Among other things Baker hires and supervises the carpenters and other workers who build the homes. The Piper Company does not do its own foundation work. The construction of the foundation is done by subcontractors hired by Ruff of the procurement department.

The Piper Company was about to start the development of a 500-home community. Ruff hired the Low Company to build the foundations on the homes. On the day construction was to begin, the Low Company went out of business. Consequently, construction was delayed six weeks while Ruff hired a new subcontractor. Which department should be charged with the cost of the delay in construction? Why?

c. John Calachi is supervisor of Department 39 of the Farrow Company. The annual budget for the department is as follows:

	Annual budget for Department 39
Small tools	$ 9,000
Set up	10,000
Direct labor	11,000
Direct materials	20,000
Supplies	5,000
Supervision	30,000
Property taxes	5,000
Property insurance	1,000
Depreciation, machinery	2,000
Depreciation, building	2,000
Total	$95,000

Identify the budget items that are controllable by Calachi. Calachi's salary of $20,000 is included in supervision. The remaining $10,000 in supervision is the salary of the assistant supervisor who is directly responsible to Calachi.

Chapter 25

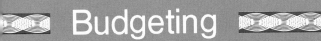

Budgeting

THE BUDGET—FOR PLANNING AND CONTROL

Time and wealth are scarce resources to all individuals and organizations. Effective utilization of either requires planning. But planning alone is insufficient. Control must also be exercised to see that if the plan is feasible, it is actually carried out. A tool widely used in planning and controlling the use of scarce resources is a budget.

There are various types of budgets. *Responsibility budgets* were covered in the preceding chapter. They are designed to judge the performance of an individual manager. *Capital budgets* will be covered in Chapter 28. They are prepared to evaluate particular long term projects such as the addition of equipment or the relocation of a plant. Another type of budget, the *master budget,* is the topic of this chapter. The master budget is made up of two parts, the *operating budget* and the *financial budget.* The operating budget is a projected future earnings statement. The financial budget is a projected future balance sheet.

Before discussing the master budget we will discuss some considerations involved with budgeting in general.

Purposes of budgets

In business, a **budget** is simply a *plan* showing how management intends to acquire and use resources and how it intends to *control* the acquisition and use of resources in a coming time period. The budget often has been referred to as a formal quantitative expression of management plans. Yet it is much more than that. It forces all levels of management to think ahead, anticipate results, and take action to remedy possible poor results.

Budgets may also be used to *motivate* individuals, causing them to strive vigorously to achieve stated goals. They may also be used to *appraise the performance* of individuals. For instance, the standard variable cost of producing a given part in a given cost center is a budget figure against which actual performance can be compared in order to evaluate the performance of that cost center.

Many other benefits result from the preparation and use of budgets. The activities of the business are better *coordinated;* individual members of the management *become aware of the problems of other members* of management; employees may become *cost conscious* and seek to *conserve* resources; the organization plan of the enterprise may be *reviewed* more often and changed where needed; and a breadth of *vision,* which might not otherwise be developed, is fostered. Another important benefit is that a properly prepared budget will allow management to manage by the exception principle. Management by exception means devoting attention to areas where activities are deviating from their planned levels. Thus, expected results must be clearly stated.

Considerations in preparing budget

Uncertainty with regard to future developments is a poor excuse for failure to budget; in fact, the less stable the conditions, the more necessary and desirable is budgeting. Obviously, stable operating conditions permit greater reliance upon past experience as a basis for budgeting. But it must be emphasized that budgets are based on more than past results. Future plans must also be considered.

A budget plan should explicitly spell out management's assumptions relating to such things as (1) the state of the economy over the planning horizon; (2) plans for adding, deleting, or changing product lines; (3) the nature of the industry's competition; and (4) the effect of existing or possible government regulations. If the nature of the assumptions should change during the budget period, an analysis of the effects should be made and reflected upon in the evaluation of the company's performance.

In the preparation of a budget, accounting data play an important part. The details of the budget must be in agreement with the accounts maintained in the company's ledgers. The accounts, in turn, must be designed to facilitate the preparation of the budget and the usual financial statements as well as the numerous reports—cost and financial—that are prepared quarterly, monthly, weekly, or even daily to help exercise operational control.

During the budget period repeated comparisons of accounting data and budgeted projections should be made and the differences investigated. But it should be noted that budgeting is not a substitute for management and that a budget is not self-operating. Instead, the budget is designed as merely a tool—but an important one—of managerial control.

Budget periods vary in length, but usually they coincide with the accounting period. Normally, the budget period is broken into months or quarters, and the greater the uncertainty faced, the more likely is this to be the case.

SOME GENERAL PRINCIPLES OF BUDGETING

Budgeting involves the coordination of financial and nonfinancial planning to satisfy the goals and objectives of the organization. Although there is no foolproof way to prepare an effective budget, the following should be considered carefully when preparing a budget:

A. Top-management support.

All levels of management must be aware of the importance of the budget to the firm. Plans must be stated explicitly, and overemphasis on pure mechanics avoided. Overall broad objectives of the corporation must be decided upon and communicated through the organization.

B. Participation in goal setting.

It is generally believed that an employee is more likely to strive to achieve organization goals if the employee participates in the setting of those goals.

C. Responsibility accounting.

People should know their own performance goals. Only those costs over which an individual has predominant control should be used in the evaluation of the individual's performance.

D. Communication of results.

People should be informed of their own progress in a timely and meaningful manner. Effective communication implies (1) timeliness, (2) reasonable accuracy, and (3) understandability. Results should be communicated in such a manner that adjustments can be made, if needed.

E.   Flexibility.

As basic assumptions underlying the preparation of the budget are altered during the year, the budget should be restated so that the efficiency of the actual level of operations can be analyzed.

BEHAVIORAL IMPLICATIONS

Too often the term budget has very negative connotations to personnel who feel they are *subjected to* a budget. Often in the past, a budget has been imposed by management without giving consideration to the opinions and feelings of the personnel affected. Such imposed budgets may bring on both overt and subtle resistance to the budget. There may be a number of reasons why such resistance is encountered. These might include a lack of understanding about the program, concern about status, expectation of increased pressure, a feeling of unfairness in the method of performance evaluation, a feeling that the goals are unrealistic and unobtainable, lack of confidence in the manner that accounting figures are generated, and a preference for more informal communication and evaluation. Often these fears are completely unfounded, but the important thing is that the employees may not believe they are, and because of their beliefs it will be very difficult to accomplish the objectives of budgeting. The problems encountered by such *imposed* budgets have led the accountant and management to *participatory budgeting.*

Budget participation includes active participation of all levels of management in the setting of operating goals for the forthcoming period. Managers are much more likely to understand, accept, and pursue those goals which they were actively involved in formulating.

Where do the accountants fit into a participatory budget process? Accountants should be the *compiler* or coordinator of the budget, not the *preparer.* They should be on hand during the preparation process to present and explain significant financial data and their relationships. They must identify the relevant cost data that will enable management's objectives to be quantified into dollar terms. Accountants have the responsibility for meaningful budget reports. Everyone must have confidence in the accounting system, and accountants must continually strive to make the accounting system responsive to managerial needs.

The picture of budget participation up to this point has been pretty much one-sided. Studies have shown that budget participation is not effective in some types of organizations. The effectiveness of participation as a tool will vary according to leadership style, organization structure, and organization size. Thus participation is not seen as a panacea for all the problems of budget preparation. Rather, it should be considered as a possible means of achieving better results in most organizations in which the philosophy of participation fits in with the actual managerial philosophy of the organization.

THE MASTER BUDGET

The remainder of this chapter will concentrate on preparing a master budget. The main emphasis will be on the preparation of the operating budget because of its prime importance in the financial planning and control of the business entity. Illustration 25.1 presents in simplified form the major elements in

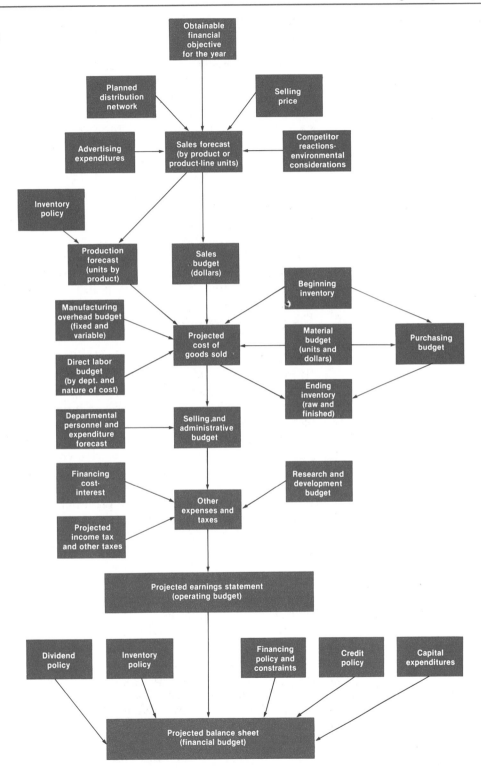

Illustration 25.1: A flowchart of the financial planning process (an overview)

the preparation of the master budget. Some of the more important aspects are seen as follows:

1. The flow (in preparation) proceeds from top to bottom with each lower level derived in part as a function of the previous level.
2. The end result is the preparation of the projected earnings statement and projected balance sheet. The elements making up these statements are contained in the previously prepared budgets.
3. The budgeting process starts with management's plans and objectives for the next period. These plans result in various policy decisions concerning selling price, distribution network, advertising expenditures, and environmental influences from which the sales forecast (by product, or product line) for the period is made.
4. Conversion from units to selling price forms the sales budget in dollars.
5. Projected cost of goods sold is based upon expected volume and inventory policy. Detailed budgets are made for each of the major types of manufacturing expenses on both a cost center (responsibility) basis and in the aggregate. Volume and inventory policy influences the preparation of the purchasing budget.
6. The projected balance sheet is derived from the operating budget, but it is also influenced by policy decisions pertaining to dividends, inventory, and credit, along with capital expenditures and financing plans.

It must be noted that this chapter cannot cover all the areas of budgeting in detail as whole books are devoted to the subject. The presentation that follows, though, does present an overview of a budgeting procedure that has been used successfully by many business enterprises. As you proceed through the chapter, it may be useful to refer back to Illustration 25.1 and examine it in more detail, as it sets a frame of reference for the ensuing discussion.

Since the projected balance sheet in the master budget depends upon many items in the projected earnings statements, the starting place in the preparation of a master budget is the projected earnings statement. The projected earnings statement in budgetary terminology is often referred to as the *operating budget,* while the projected balance sheet is called the *financial budget.* A number of supporting budgets are usually prepared. The sales budget is the key budget supporting the operating budget.

Deriving the operating budget

The sales budget.   Because of its primary importance, careful study and analysis must precede the preparation of the sales budget. The expected general level of economic activity in the budget period must be taken into consideration. The prospects of the industry of which the company is a member must also be considered. These prospects may be influenced in varying degrees by population growth, income per capita, new construction, population migration, and so forth. The relative position of the company in the industry must next be considered and reviewed in the light of any expected or actively sought changes.

Allowances must be made for varying conditions which affect different products or different territories as well as the strength of competitors. Due allowance must also be made for any changes in the expected level of promotional expenditures. Quotas may be developed for salespersons as a result of sales analyses according to territories, customers, products, and so on. The sales budget is usually the responsibility of the sales manager. Based upon expected selling prices, the sales budget may be prepared in units and later converted to dollars. Or a goal in dollars may be set first. Then estimates of selling prices and units of sales must be made and a reasonable combination decided upon based upon management's goal regarding profit maximization, market penetration, or some other objective. In any event, the sales budget should eventually be stated in units to serve as a frame of reference for preparing the rest of the budget.

The production budget. The production budget is geared to the sales budget and the company's inventory policy. It is first developed in terms of units. Unit costs can seldom be developed until production volume is known. The principal objective of the production budget is to achieve agreement in terms of time and quantity between the production of goods and their sale. Careful scheduling must be undertaken to maintain certain minimum quantities of inventory on hand while excessive accumulation is avoided. Also, the cost of carrying inventory on hand must be compared with the higher unit costs frequently encountered in producing relatively small batches of a product.

The production budget is often subdivided into budgets for materials, labor, and overhead. Usually materials and labor will vary directly with production within a given *relevant range* of production. Overhead costs may not vary directly with production, but may be constant in total across the relevant range of production.

Selling, administration, and other expense budgets (schedules). Departmental personnel and expenditure forecasts are used to budget the amounts of selling and administration expenses. Other expenses, such as interest expense, income tax expense, and research and development expenses are also estimated.

Deriving the financial budget

The preparation of a projected balance sheet would ordinarily involve an analysis of each account appearing in that statement. The beginning balance would be taken from the balance sheet at the start of the budget period. The effect of any planned activities upon each account would then be taken into consideration. Many of the accounts will be affected by items appearing in the operating budget and by either cash inflows or outflows.

These cash inflows and outflows are usually shown in a cash budget. The complexities encountered in preparing the financial budget often will require the preparation of work sheets. These analyses include such things as planned accounts receivable collections and balances, planned material purchases, planned inventories, changes in all accounts affected by operating costs, and the amount of federal income taxes payable. Dividend policy, financing policy and constraints, credit policy, and any planned capital expenditures also affect amounts shown in the financial budget.

We will now illustrate the preparation of a master budget for the Leed Company. If you follow the example closely you should be able to prepare a master budget for an actual company.

THE MASTER BUDGET ILLUSTRATED: Preparing the operating budget in units for the Leed Company

The operating budget is first developed in terms of units rather than dollars. Since revenues and the bulk of the costs to be incurred will vary with volume, forecasts of revenues and costs can be derived more easily after quantities are established. After performing the analysis for sales budgets, assume that sales for the year are forecast at 100,000 units. Quarterly sales are expected to be 20,000, 35,000, 20,000, and 25,000 units. In line with company policy of stabilizing production, the 100,000 units will be produced uniformly throughout the year at the rate of 25,000 units per quarter. A simplifying assumption made at this time is to assume away the existence of any beginning or ending work in process inventories. A more realistic assumption would be that work in process inventories remain stable throughout the year.

From the above data, a schedule of budgeted sales and production in terms of units is prepared as shown in Illustration 25.2. Note the fluctuation

Illustration 25.2: Planned sales and production in units

	LEED COMPANY Planned Sales and Production	
	Quarter ending	
	March 31, 1981	*June 30, 1981*
	(in units of product)	
Sales forecast	20,000	35,000
Production planned	25,000	25,000
Increase (decrease) in finished goods inventory................................	5,000	(10,000)
Planned beginning finished goods inventory................................	10,000*	15,000
Planned ending finished goods inventory	15,000	5,000
* Actual on January 1.		

in the ending inventory which must be accepted if sales vary and the management policy of stable production is to be implemented. Thus, the finished goods inventory serves the function of absorbing the difference between production and sales. A management decision has been made that it is less costly to deal with fluctuating inventories than with fluctuating production.

Preparing the operating budget in dollars

The operating budget is now converted from units into dollars. A forecast of expected selling prices must be made. In addition, an analysis of costs must be made along the lines previously outlined. The forecasted selling prices and costs are as shown in Illustration 25.3. Note that the costs are classified according to whether they are variable or fixed in nature and are budgeted accordingly. As described earlier, variable costs are those which vary in total directly with production or sales. Fixed costs are those which are unaffected in total by the relative level of production or sales. Thus, variable costs are budgeted as a constant dollar amount *per unit,* while fixed costs are budgeted

Illustration 25.3: Budget estimate of selling price and costs

```
                        LEED COMPANY
               Budget Estimates of Selling Price and Costs
              For the Quarters Ending March 31, and June 30, 1981

Forecasted selling price ...........................................  $      20

Manufacturing costs:
Variable (per unit manufactured):
  Raw material ................................................         2
  Direct labor ................................................         6
  Overhead ...................................................         1
Fixed overhead (total each quarter) ...........................    75,000

Selling and administrative expenses:
Variable (per unit sold) .......................................         2
Fixed (total each quarter) .....................................   100,000
```

only in total. Individual budgets could be prepared for each of the identifiable units of the entity and accumulated to form the overall budget. This is true for each budget area to be discussed in the remainder of the chapter.

A schedule showing the development of the forecasted cost of goods manufactured and sold is now prepared as shown in Illustration 25.4.

Separate schedules would now be prepared for all of the selling and administrative expenses and their totals entered for each of the first two quarters as is shown in Illustration 25.5.

All of the items appearing in the operating budget (Illustration 25.5) have been explained previously and discussed except the income tax accrual. These taxes are budgeted at an assumed level of 50 percent of net earnings before taxes.

Illustration 25.4: Planned cost of goods manufactured and sold

LEED COMPANY
Planned Cost of Goods Manufactured and Sold

	Quarter ending	
	March 31, 1981	June 30, 1981
Beginning finished goods inventory	$130,000*	$180,000
Cost of goods manufactured:		
Raw materials (25,000 × $2)	$ 50,000	$ 50,000
Direct labor (25,000 × $6)	150,000	150,000
Variable overhead (25,000 × $1)	25,000	25,000
Fixed overhead (per Illustration 25.3)	75,000	75,000
Cost of goods manufactured (25,000 units at $12)	$300,000	$300,000
Goods available for sale	$430,000	$480,000
Ending finished goods inventory:		
(15,000 at $12)†	180,000	
(5,000 at $12)		60,000
Cost of goods sold	$250,000	$420,000

* Actual on January 1.
† First-in, first-out procedure assumed.

LEED COMPANY Projected Earnings Statements For Quarters Ending March 31, and June 30, 1981		
	Quarter ending	
	March 31, 1981	June 30, 1981
Forecasted sales (20,000 and 35,000 at $20) (per Illustration 25.3)	$400,000	$700,000
Cost of goods sold (per Illustration 25.4)	250,000	420,000
Gross margin	$150,000	$280,000
Selling and administrative expenses:		
Variable (20,000 and 35,000 at $2) (per Illustration 25.3)	$ 40,000	$ 70,000
Fixed (per Illustration 25.3)	100,000	100,000
Total expenses	$140,000	$170,000
Net earnings before income taxes	$ 10,000	$110,000
Estimated federal income taxes (assumed to be 50%)	5,000	55,000
Net Earnings	$ 5,000	$ 55,000

The operating budgets illustrated

Illustration 25.5 shows the resulting operating budgets. As noted previously, if the operating budgets do not reveal the desired net earnings, new plans will have to be formulated and new budgets developed. But the purpose of preparing such a plan is to gain some knowledge of what the outcome of a period's activities will be prior to their actual occurrence.

The flexible operating budget

One of the basic principles of budgeting is to adjust the budget for changes in assumptions or changes in the level of operations. To cope with this, a technique known as flexible budgeting has been developed. Preparation of a flexible operating budget will include detailed estimates of expenses at various levels of output. For example, a flexible budget of manufacturing overhead costs at varying levels of output would be as shown in Illustration 25.6.

In the example given in Illustration 25.6, supplies are considered a strictly variable cost, although there are probably few costs that vary in an exact linear relationship with output. Power is a semivariable cost (it varies but not directly with volume) as it is assumed that beyond a minimum level it varies directly with output. Depreciation and supervision are fixed costs, while

Element of overhead	Volume (percent of capacity)			
	70%	80%	90%	100%
Supplies	$ 4,200	$ 4,800	$ 5,400	$ 6,000
Power	11,500	13,000	14,500	16,000
Insurance	4,500	4,500	5,000	5,000
Maintenance	12,000	13,000	14,000	14,800
Depreciation	20,000	20,000	20,000	20,000
Supervision	28,000	28,000	28,000	28,000
	$80,200	$83,300	$86,900	$89,800

insurance and maintenance are semivariable costs. When a flexible budget is prepared, the amount of costs considered to be the budgeted amount in appraising performance is read from the flexible budget for the actual level of output experienced.

Budget variances. A *budget variance* is defined as the difference between an actual cost experienced at a certain level of operations and the budgeted amount for that same level of operations. Budget variances may thus be viewed as indicators or indices of efficiency since they emerge from a comparison of "what was" with "what should have been." To compute a budget variance, a flexible operating budget must be used. As an illustration of a way in which a flexible operating budget may be used, assume that the departmental budget in Illustration 25.6 is prepared based on the expectation of producing 100,000 units of product—the 100 percent of capacity level. Under such expectations, the budgeted amount for supplies would be $6,000, or $0.06 per unit. If at the end of the period, the actual amount of supplies consumed amounted to $5,600, the first impression is that of a favorable variance of $400. But if the production of the period was only 90,000 units, there was actually an unfavorable variance of $200. The flexible operating budget shows that at 90 percent of capacity, the supplies that should have been consumed amount to only $5,400. Consequently, there appears to have been some inefficiency involved in the use of supplies, and an unfavorable budget variance of $200 ($5,600 − $5,400) is said to exist.

In another situation, maintenance may have been budgeted at $13,000 for a given period in the expectation that 80,000 units of product would be produced. This is at the 80 percent of operating capacity level. If actual maintenance costs total $13,900 for the period, this does not mean that an unfavorable variance of $900 has been incurred. Production volume must be known; assume it to be 90,000 units. At this level, maintenance costs are budgeted at $14,000; and, therefore, a favorable variance of $100 was actually experienced.

The main advantage of flexible operating budgets is to allow for appraisal of performance on two levels. First, the deviation from expected output can be analyzed. Then, given the actual level of operations, actual costs can be compared with expected costs for that level of output. The use of flexible or formula operating budgets makes it unnecessary to revise budget estimates when production volume differs from that expected. In the case of directly variable costs, the expected cost at any level can be computed easily. In case of certain semivariable costs which are partially fixed and partially variable, the budget amount for any level of operations other than those presented can be computed from the following formula: Budget amount = Fixed costs + (Variable costs per unit × Units of output). More complicated formulas are needed if the relationship between costs and volume above a minimum level of costs is not linear, that is, if the costs do not vary proportionately with production.

Other semivariable costs may change only when a sufficiently large increase in production occurs as, for example, when one additional inspector must be added for each 20 percent of capacity utilized. Such semivariable costs usually can be read directly from the flexible budget.

The preparation of budgets for selling expenses and for general administrative expenses is similar to the preparation of the manufacturing overhead budget. Several supporting budgets may be involved, such as budgets for advertising, office expenses, and payroll department expenses. In each case the supporting budget may show the fixed expenses and the variable expenses at various levels of sales volume.

The flexible operating budget and budget variances illustrated.   The Leed Company has prepared a detailed flexible operating budget for the quarter ending March 31, 1981. The budget is based on the data in Illustration 25.3. The budgets based on expected sales of 20,000 units and expected production of 25,000 units and actual results for the year are shown in Illustration 25.7.

Assume that (1) actual selling price of all units was $20 per unit, (2) actual production was 25,000 units, and (3) actual sales were 19,000 units.

The comparison of the original budget with actual results yields some useful information. It shows where actual performance deviated from planned performance. Sales were 1,000 units lower than expected; gross margin was $12,500 less than expected; and net earnings were $2,000 more than expected. But the comparison does not show the expected expenditures for the actual level of output attained. This latter comparison is useful for expense control purposes.

Since the company expected to sell 20,000 units but only sold 19,000, a better analysis for expense control purposes can be made by using a flexible

Illustration 25.7:
Comparison of expected
budget and actual results

LEED COMPANY Comparison of Expected Budget and Actual Results	Budget	Actual
Sales	$400,000	$380,000
Cost of goods sold:		
Beginning finished goods inventory	$130,000	$130,000
Cost of goods manufactured:		
Raw materials	$ 50,000	$ 62,500
Direct labor	150,000	143,750
Variable overhead	25,000	31,250
Fixed overhead	75,000	75,000
Cost of goods manufactured	$300,000	$312,500
Goods available for sale	$430,000	$442,500
Ending finished goods inventory	180,000	200,000
Cost of goods sold	$250,000	$242,500
Gross margin	$150,000	$137,500
Selling and administrative expenses:		
Variable	$ 40,000	$ 28,500
Fixed	100,000	95,000
Total expenses	$140,000	$123,500
Net earnings before income taxes	$ 10,000	$ 14,000
Estimated federal income taxes (50%)	5,000	7,000
Net Earnings	$ 5,000	$ 7,000

operating budget for 19,000 units. Such an analysis is presented in Illustration 25.8.

A number of items become readily apparent when a comparison is made between actual expenses incurred and expected expenses for the actual level of output. The flexible operating budget (Illustration 25.8) reveals some inefficiencies. For instance, raw materials cost $2.50 ($62,500/25,000) instead of the $2.00 expected. Direct labor cost was only $5.75 ($143,750/25,000) per unit instead of the $6.00 expected. Variable overhead was $1.25 ($31,250/25,000) per unit instead of the $1.00 expected.

Net earnings were $5,000 more than expected at a sales level of 19,000 units. The main reason for the increase in net earnings was the lower than expected amounts of selling and administrative expenses. Variable selling and administrative expenses were only $1.50 ($28,500/19,000) per unit instead of the $2.00 expected; fixed selling and administrative expenses were only $95,000 instead of the $100,000 expected.

Illustration 25.8: Comparison of flexible operating budget and actual results

LEED COMPANY Comparison of Flexible Operating Budget and Actual Results for Quarter Ended March 31, 1981			
	Budget	Actual	Budget variance (unfavorable)
Sales	$380,000	$380,000	–0–
Cost of goods sold:			
Beginning finished goods inventory	$130,000	$130,000	–0–
Cost of goods manufactured:			
Raw materials	50,000	62,500	$(12,500)
Direct labor	150,000	143,750	6,250
Variable overhead	25,000	31,250	(6,250)
Fixed overhead	75,000	75,000	–0–
Cost of goods manufactured	$300,000	$312,500	$(12,500)
Goods available for sale	$430,000	$442,500	$(12,500)
Ending finished goods inventory	192,000	200,000	8,000
Cost of goods sold	$238,000	$242,500	$ (4,500)
Gross margin	$142,000	$137,500	(4,500)
Selling and administrative expenses:			
Variable	$ 38,000	$ 28,500	$ 9,500
Fixed	100,000	95,000	5,000
Total expenses	$138,000	$123,500	$ 14,500
Net earnings before income taxes	$ 4,000	$ 14,000	$ 10,000
Estimated federal income taxes (50%)	2,000	7,000	(5,000)
Net Earnings	$ 2,000	$ 7,000	$ 5,000

Preparing the financial budget for the Leed Company

The starting point in preparing the financial budget is to examine the balance sheet which existed as of the beginning of the budget period. The balance sheet as of December 31, 1980, is shown in Illustration 25.9.

The operating budget, shown in Illustration 25.5, as well as the other illustrations previously shown will also be helpful in preparing the financial budget. We will identify where the numbers contained in the illustrations

LEED COMPANY
Balance Sheet
December 31, 1980

Assets

Current Assets:		
Cash		$ 130,000
Accounts Receivable		200,000
Inventories:		
Raw materials	$ 40,000	
Finished goods	130,000	170,000
Prepaid expenses		20,000
Total Current Assets		$ 520,000
Plant and Equipment:		
Land		$ 60,000
Buildings	1,000,000	
Less Accumulated Depreciation	400,000	600,000
Equipment	600,000	
Less Accumulated Depreciation	180,000	420,000
Total Plant and Equipment		1,080,000
Total Assets		$1,600,000

Liabilities and Stockholders' Equity

Current Liabilities:		
Accounts payable		$ 80,000
Accrued Liabilities		160,000
Federal income taxes payable		100,000
Total Current Liabilities		$ 340,000
Stockholders' Equity:		
Capital Stock (100,000 shares		
of $10 par value)		$1,000,000
Retained earnings		260,000
Total Stockholder's Equity		1,260,000
Total Liabilities and Stockholders' Equity		$1,600,000

which follow came from so that you will better understand how to prepare the financial budget.

Accounts receivable.   To prepare a financial budget, schedules other than the ones which have already been prepared in connection with the operating budget must be prepared. The first of these is shown in Illustration 25.10. This schedule is prepared under the assumption that 60 percent of the current quarter's sales are collected in that quarter plus all of the uncollected sales of the prior quarter. Thus, collections for the first quarter would be .6($400,000) + $200,000 = $440,000. For the second quarter they would be .6($700,000) + $160,000 = $580,000. These amounts are shown in Illustration 25.10. Several other simplifying assumptions are made, namely, that there are no sales returns or allowances, or discounts, or uncollectible accounts. Obviously, in an actual planning situation, allowance may have to be made for these items. It is also assumed that all sales are made on a credit basis.

Inventories.   A schedule of inventories should be prepared starting with the planned purchases and inventory of raw materials. The planned

LEED COMPANY
Planned Accounts Receivable Collections and Balances

	Quarter ending	
	March 31, 1981	June 30, 1981
Planned balance at beginning of quarter	$200,000*	$160,000
Planned sales for period (per Illustration 25.5)...	400,000	700,000
Total	$600,000	$860,000
Projected collections during quarter (per discussion in text)	440,000	580,000
Planned balance at end of quarter	$160,000	$280,000

* Actual on January 1.

usage and cost per unit are calculated from the production schedules. Assuming no work in process, the ending inventories will consist of raw materials and finished goods.

Illustration 25.11 shows the planned purchases and inventories of raw materials. The raw materials inventory had been built up above the normal level of one half of next quarter's planned usage because of a strike threat in the supplier company. This threat has now passed, and the inventory will be reduced in the first quarter to the normal planned level.

The calculation of planned ending finished goods inventories is included in Illustration 25.4.

LEED COMPANY
Planned Materials Purchases and Inventories

	Quarter ending	
	March 31, 1981	June 30, 1981
Planned usage (25,000 × $2) (per Illustration 25.4)	$50,000	$50,000
Planned ending inventory (½ × 25,000 × $2) (per discussion above)	25,000	25,000
Planned raw materials available for use	$75,000	$75,000
Inventory at beginning of quarter	40,000*	25,000
Planned purchases for the quarter	$35,000	$50,000

* Actual on January 1.

Accounts affected by operating costs.   Although individual schedules could be prepared for each of the accounts affected by operating costs, for illustrative purposes a schedule combining the analyses of all the accounts affected by material purchases or operating costs will be prepared.

The following assumptions are made:

1. All purchases of raw materials are made on account.
2. Direct labor incurred is credited to accrued liabilities.
3. Manufacturing overhead incurred was credited to the following accounts:

	Quarter ending	
	March 31	June 30
Accounts Payable	$ 16,000	$ 13,000
Accrued Liabilities	60,000	64,000
Prepaid Expenses	6,000	5,000
Accumulated Depreciation—Building	5,000	5,000
Accumulated Depreciation—Equipment	13,000	13,000
Total	$100,000	$100,000

4. Selling and administrative expenses incurred were credited to the following accounts:

	Quarter ending	
	March 31	June 30
Accounts Payable	$ 5,000	$ 10,000
Accrued Liabilities	130,000	154,000
Prepaid Expenses	2,000	3,000
Accumulated Depreciation—Building	1,000	1,000
Accumulated Depreciation—Equipment	2,000	2,000
Total	$140,000	$170,000

5. Planned cash payments are as follows:

	Quarter Ending	
	March 31	June 30
Accounts Payable	$ 80,000	$ 56,000
Accrued Liabilities	330,000	354,000
Prepaid Expenses	–0–	10,000
	$410,000	$420,000

Illustration 25.12 shows the analysis of accounts credited as a result of the above data. It provides a considerable amount of information needed in constructing financial budgets for the quarters ended March 31, 1981, and June 30, 1981. The balances for both dates for Accounts Payable, Accrued Liabilities, Prepaid Expenses, Accumulated Depreciation—Building, and Accumulated Depreciation—Equipment are computed in the schedule.

Federal income taxes payable. A separate schedule could be prepared showing the changes in the Federal Income Taxes Payable account. It will be omitted here. The balances reported in the financial budgets are derived under the assumption that one half of the $100,000 liability shown in the December 31, 1980, balance sheet is paid in each of the first two quarters of 1981 (see Illustration 25.12). The accrual for the current quarter is added (see Illustration 25.5). Thus, the balance at March 31, 1981, is $100,000 − $50,000 + $5,000 = $55,000. The balance at June 30, 1981, is $55,000 − $50,000 + $55,000 = $60,000. At June 30, the balance is equal to the accrual for the current year of $5,000 for the first quarter and $55,000 for the second quarter.

Cash budget. After the above analyses have been prepared there should be available information to prepare the cash budget to determine the balance of the cash account at both dates. Since cash flow was dealt with in Chapter 19, only a limited discussion will be undertaken here. Reference is

Illustration 25.12: Analyses of accounts credited for materials purchases and operating costs

LEED COMPANY
Analyses of Accounts Credited for Materials Purchases and Operating Costs

	Total	Accounts payable (Cr.)	Accrued liabilities (Cr.)	Prepaid expenses (Dr.)	Accumulated depreciation Building (Cr.)	Accumulated depreciation Equipment (Cr.)
Purchases or operating costs quarter ending March 31:						
Raw materials (per Illustration 25.11)	$ 35,000	$ 35,000				
Direct labor (per Illustration 25.4)	150,000		$150,000			
Overhead (per Illustration 25.4)	100,000	16,000	60,000	$ 6,000	$ 5,000	$ 13,000
Selling and administrative expense (per Illustration 25.5)	140,000	5,000	130,000	2,000	1,000	2,000
Total	$425,000	$ 56,000	$340,000	$ 8,000	$ 6,000	$ 15,000
Beginning balances (per Illustration 25.9)		80,000	160,000	20,000	400,000	180,000
		$136,000	$500,000	$12,000	$406,000	$195,000
Planned cash payments		80,000	330,000			
Planned balances, March 31		$ 56,000	$170,000	$12,000	$406,000	$195,000
Purchases or operating costs quarter ending June 30:						
Raw materials (per Illustration 25.11)	$ 50,000	$ 50,000				
Direct labor (per Illustration 25.4)	150,000		$150,000			
Overhead (per Illustration 25.4)	100,000	13,000	64,000	$ 5,000	$ 5,000	$ 13,000
Selling and administrative expense (per Illustration 25.5)	170,000	10,000	154,000	3,000	1,000	2,000
Total	$470,000	$ 73,000	$368,000	$ 8,000	$ 6,000	$ 15,000
Total including March 31 balances		$129,000	$538,000	$ 4,000	$412,000	$210,000
Planned cash payments		56,000	354,000	10,000		
Planned balances, June 30		$ 73,000	$184,000	$14,000	$412,000	$210,000

Illustration 25.13: Planned cash flows and cash balances

LEED COMPANY
Planned Cash Flows and Cash Balances

	Quarter ending March 31, 1981	Quarter ending June 30, 1981
Planned balance at beginning of quarter	$130,000*	$ 90,000
Planned cash receipts:		
Collections of accounts receivable (per Illustration 25.10)	440,000	580,000
	$570,000	$670,000
Planned cash disbursements:		
Payment of accounts payable (per Illustration 25.12)	$ 80,000	$ 56,000
Payment of accrued liabilities (per Illustration 25.12)	330,000	354,000
Payment of federal income tax liability	50,000	50,000
Payment of dividends	20,000	40,000
Expenses prepaid (per Illustration 25.12)	–0–	10,000
Total disbursements	$480,000	$510,000
Planned balance at end of quarter	$ 90,000	$160,000

* Actual on January 1.

made in the illustration as to where the information came from with the exception of payment of federal income tax liability and payment of dividends. As stated earlier, it is assumed that the company pays one half of the $100,000 income tax liability shown in the December 31, 1980, balance sheet in each of the first two quarters ($50,000 in each quarter). It is also assumed that $20,000 of dividends will be paid in the first quarter and $40,000 in the second quarter. For the Leed Company the cash budget would be as shown in Illustration 25.13.

The financial budgets illustrated

The financial budgets for the quarters ended March 31, 1981, and June 30, 1981, are now prepared and are as shown in Illustration 25.14.

The completion of the financial budgets for the two quarters completes

Illustration 25.14: Projected balance sheet

LEED COMPANY Projected Balance Sheet	March 31, 1981	June 30, 1981
Assets		
Current Assets:		
Cash (per Illustration 25.13)	$ 90,000	$ 160,000
Accounts receivable (per Illustration 25.10)	160,000	280,000
Inventories:		
Raw materials (per Illustration 25.11)	25,000	25,000
Finished goods (per Illustration 25.4)	180,000	60,000
Prepaid expenses (per Illustration 25.12)	12,000	14,000
Total Current Assets	$ 467,000	$ 539,000
Plant and Equipment:		
Land (per Illustration 25.9)	$ 60,000	$ 60,000
Buildings ($1,000,000 less accumulated depreciation of $406,000 and $412,000) (per Illustrations 25.9 and 25.12)	594,000	588,000
Equipment ($600,000 less accumulated depreciation of $195,000 and $210,000) (per Illustrations 25.9 and 25.12)	405,000	390,000
Total Plant and Equipment	$1,059,000	$1,038,000
Total Assets	$1,526,000	$1,577,000
Liabilities and Stockholders' Equity		
Current Liabilities:		
Accounts payable (per Illustration 25.12)	$ 56,000	$ 73,000
Accrued liabilities (per Illustration 25.12)	170,000	184,000
Federal income taxes payable (per discussion on page 790)	55,000	60,000
Total Current Liabilities	$ 281,000	$ 317,000
Stockholders' Equity:		
Capital stock (100,000 shares of $10 par value) (per Illustration 25.9)	$1,000,000	$1,000,000
Retained earnings (see below)	245,000*	260,000†
Total Stockholders' Equity	$1,245,000	$1,260,000
Total Liabilities and Stockholders' Equity	$1,526,000	$1,577,000

* $260,000 (per Illustration 25.9) + earnings of $5,000 less dividends of $20,000.
† $245,000 + earnings of $55,000 less dividends of $40,000.

the preparation of the master budget. Management now has on hand information which will assist it in appraising the policies it has instituted prior to these policies being actually implemented. If the results of these policies, as shown by the master budget, are unsatisfactory, the policies can be changed before serious difficulty is encountered. For example, the Leed Company management decided to stabilize production. The master budget shows that production can be stabilized even though sales fluctuate widely. The planned ending inventory at June 30 may be considered somewhat low in view of the fluctuations in sales, but management does have advance information of this fact.

NEW TERMS INTRODUCED IN CHAPTER 25

Budget—a plan showing objectives sought and their proposed means of attainment; two major types of budgets are (1) master and (2) control or responsibility budgets.

Budget variance—the difference between an actual amount at an attained level of operations and the budgeted amount for that same level.

Budgeting—the coordination of financial and nonfinancial planning in an attempt to satisfy the goals and objectives of the enterprise.

Control (responsibility) budget—a statement of planned objectives which is used primarily as a means of appraising the performance of an individual unit within an entity.

Financial budget—the projected balance sheet portion of a master budget.

Fixed costs*—those costs which are unaffected by the relative levels of production or sales.

Flexible operating budget*—a budget showing budgeted amounts (of costs usually) for varying levels of output; one that is prepared over a range of outputs.

Master budget—the projected earnings statement and projected balance sheet showing objectives sought and their proposed means of attainment; includes supporting budgets such as for cash, sales, costs, and production; also called master profit plan. It is the overall plan of the enterprise as a whole and ideally consists of all of the various segmental budgets.

Operating budget—the projected earnings statement portion of a master budget.

Participatory budgeting—a method of preparing the budget which includes participation of all levels of management that are responsible for actual performance.

Responsibility budget—see Control budget.

Variable costs*—those costs which vary directly with production and are a constant amount per unit of output over different levels of output or sales.

* These terms were defined and discussed previously but are included again here for your convenience.

DEMONSTRATION PROBLEM

During January 1981, the Phoenix Company plans to sell 20,000 units at a price of $20 per unit. Selling expenses are estimated to be $40,000 plus 2 percent of sales revenue. General and administrative expenses are estimated to be $30,000 plus 1 percent of sales revenue. Income tax expense is estimated to be 40 percent of net operating earnings.

Phoenix plans to produce 25,000 units during January with estimated variable costs per unit as follows: $2 for material, $5 for labor, and $3 for variable overhead. The fixed overhead cost is estimated at $20,000 per month. The finished goods inventory at January 1, 1981, is 4,000 units with a cost per unit of $10. The company uses Fifo inventory procedure.

Required

Prepare a projected earnings statement for January 1981.

Solution to demonstration problem

PHOENIX COMPANY
Projected Earnings Statement
For January 1981

Sales (20,000 × $20)		$400,000
Cost of goods sold (see Schedule 1)		212,800
Gross margin		$187,200
Selling expenses:		
Fixed	$40,000	
Variable (0.02 × $400,000)	8,000	
General and administrative expenses:		
Fixed	30,000	
Variable (0.01 × $400,000)	4,000	82,000
Net earnings before taxes		$105,200
Income taxes (40%)		42,080
Net Earnings		$ 63,120

Schedule 1

PHOENIX COMPANY
Planned Cost of Goods Manufactured and Sold

Beginning finished goods inventory (4,000 × $10)		$ 40,000
Cost of goods manufactured:		
Raw materials (25,000 × $2)	$ 50,000	
Direct labor (25,000 × $5)	125,000	
Variable overhead (25,000 × $3)	75,000	
Fixed overhead	20,000	
Cost of goods manufactured (25,000 × $10.80)		270,000
Cost of goods available for sale		$310,000
Ending finished goods inventory (9,000 × $10.80)		97,200
Cost of goods sold		$212,800

QUESTIONS

1. What are the three main objectives of budgeting?

2. What is meant by the term "management by exception?" How does the concept relate to budgeting?

3. What are five basic principles which, if followed, should improve the possibilities of preparing a meaningful budget? Why is each important?

4. What is the difference between an "imposed" budget and a "participatory" budget?

5. Define and explain a budget variance. A budget variance implies the use of what kind of a budget?

6. What are the two major budgets in the master budget? Which should be prepared first? Why?

7. Distinguish between master and responsibility budgeting.

8. What is a flexible budget? What is meant by the term formula budgeting?

9. The budget established at the beginning of a given period carried an item for supplies in the amount of $40,000. At the end of the period, the supplies used amounted to $44,000. Can it be concluded from these data that either there was inefficient use of supplies or care was not exercised in purchasing the supplies?

10. Management must make certain assumptions about the business environment when preparing a budget. What areas should be considered?

11. Why is budgeted performance better than past performance as a basis for judging actual results?

EXERCISES

E–1. The Lester Shoe Company has decided to produce 60,000 pairs of shoes at a uniform rate throughout 1981. The sales department of Lester Shoe Company has estimated sales for 1981 according to the following schedule:

	Sales in units
First quarter	16,000
Second quarter	13,000
Third quarter	15,000
Fourth quarter	21,000
Total for 1981	65,000

If the December 31, 1980, inventory is estimated to be 8,000 pairs of shoes, prepare a schedule of planned sales and production (in units) for the first two quarters of 1981.

E–2. Labor and materials of Anthony Corporation are considered to be variable costs. Expected production for the year is 100,000 units. At that level of production, labor cost is budgeted at $375,000 and materials cost is expected to be $165,000. Prepare a flexible budget for labor and materials for possible production levels of 70,000, 80,000, and 90,000 units of production.

E–3. Assume that in Exercise E–2, actual production was 80,000 units and material cost was $135,000 while labor cost was $297,000. What is the budget variance?

E–4. The following data apply to the collection of accounts receivable for the Jason Company.

Current balance—February 28—$100,000 (of which $60,000 relates to February sales)
Planned sales for March—$500,000

Assumptions: 70 percent of sales are collected in the month of sale; 20 percent in the following month; and the remaining 10 percent in the second month after the sale. Prepare a schedule of planned collections and ending balance for accounts receivable as of March 31, 1981.

E–5. The Oakes Company expects to sell 30,000 units of Whisbees during the next quarter at a price of $10 per unit. Production costs (all variable) are $3.50 per unit. Selling and administrative expenses are: variable $2.50 per unit, and fixed $80,000 in total. What are the budgeted earnings? (Do not consider taxes.)

E–6. Fixed production costs for the Acorn Company are budgeted at $80,000 assuming 40,000 units of production. Actual sales for the period were 35,000 units while actual production was 40,000 units. Actual fixed costs used in computing cost of goods sold were $70,000. What is the budget variance?

PROBLEMS, SERIES A

P25–1–A. The Kelly Corporation prepares monthly operating and financial budgets. The operating budgets for June and July are based on the following data:

	Units produced	Units sold
June	100,000	90,000
July	90,000	100,000

All sales are at $10 per unit. Raw material, direct labor, and variable overhead are estimated at $1, $2, and $1 per unit, while fixed overhead is budgeted at $180,000 per month. Operating expenses are budgeted at $200,000 plus 10 percent of sales, while federal income taxes are budgeted at 50 percent of net operating earnings. The inventory at June 1 consists of 50,000 units with a cost of $5.70 each.

Required:

a. Prepare monthly budget estimates of cost of goods sold assuming Fifo.

b. Prepare operating budgets for June and July. (Use a single amount for cost of goods sold—as derived above.)

P25–2–A. Net operating earnings for the Bellman Company for 1980 were as follows:

Sales		$2,000,000
Cost of goods sold:		
Raw materials	$400,000	
Direct labor	300,000	
Fixed overhead	200,000	
Variable overhead	120,000	1,020,000
Gross margin		$ 980,000
Selling expenses:		
Variable	$120,000	
Fixed	180,000	300,000
		$ 680,000
General and administrative expenses:		
Variable	$160,000	
Fixed	240,000	400,000
Net Operating Earnings		$ 280,000

An operating budget is prepared for 1981 with sales forecasted at a 20 percent increase solely from volume. Raw materials, direct labor, and all costs labeled variable above are completely variable. Fixed costs are expected to continue as above except for a $20,000 increase in fixed general and administrative costs.

Actual operating data for 1981 are:

Sales	$2,300,000
Raw materials	470,000
Direct labor	350,000
Fixed overhead	205,000
Variable overhead	135,000
Variable selling expense	138,000
Fixed selling expense	182,000
Variable general and administrative expense	190,000
Fixed general and administrative expense	270,000

Required:

a. Prepare a budget report comparing the 1981 operating budget with actual 1981 data.

b. Prepare a budget report which would be useful in appraising the performance of the various persons charged with responsibility to provide satisfactory earnings. (Hint: Prepare budget data on a flexible basis.)

c. Comment on the difference revealed by the two reports.

P25–3–A. The following data are presented for the Jason Oil Company for use in preparing its 1981 operating budget.

Plant capacity	250,000 units
Expected sales volume	225,000 units
Expected production	225,000 units
Actual production	225,000 units
Forecasted sale price	$ 10.00 per unit
Actual selling price	$ 11.25 per unit

Manufacturing costs:	
Variable (per unit of manufacture):	
Raw material	3.00
Direct labor	0.50
Overhead	1.50
Fixed overhead	450,000

Selling and administrative expenses:	
Variable (per unit)	0.75
Fixed	125,000

Assume no beginning inventory. Taxes are 50 percent of pre-tax earnings.

Required:

Part I: Prepare an operating budget for the year ended December 31, 1981.

Part II: The actual results of the Jason Oil Company for the year 1981 were as follows:

Sales		$2,250,000
Cost of goods sold:		
Raw material	$650,000	
Direct labor	100,000	
Variable overhead	300,000	
Fixed overhead	400,000	1,450,000
Gross margin		$ 800,000
Selling and administrative expenses:		
Variable	$200,000	
Fixed	150,000	350,000
Earnings before income tax		$ 450,000
Income taxes—at 50%		225,000
Net Earnings		$ 225,000

Using a flexible operating budget, analyze the efficiency of operations and comment on the company's sales policy.

P25–4–A. The Felkel Company is in the process of preparing its master budget for the year ending December 31, 1981. You are responsible for compiling the detailed budget for selling and administrative expenses. The sales manager and general manager have met with all department heads and have given you the following estimates relating to next year's expectations:

1. Sales for the year are estimated at $7,600,000. About 80 percent of sales are subject to commission. Of the commission sales, approximately 60 percent have a commission of 10 percent going to the salespersons while the remaining 40 percent have a commission rate of 5 percent.
2. In addition to commissions, the company has 30 salespersons with a base salary of $250 per month, plus 10 salespersons with a base salary of $500 per month. Each of the nine regional sales offices has a manager with a base salary of $1,200 per month, who is not entitled to commissions.
3. Administrative salaries were $30,000 per month last year. A 5 percent increase has been granted for next year, beginning on June 1, 1981.
4. Office equipment of $600,000 is depreciated at the rate of 10 percent per year.
5. Building rent is at a rate of $5,000 per month, of which 80 percent is allocable to administrative expenses and 20 percent to sales.
6. Selling supplies are estimated at 2 percent of sales.
7. Office supplies are estimated at 1 percent of sales.
8. Advertising expense is budgeted at a base of $100,000 plus 3 percent of sales.
9. Other expenses include:
   Salesperson's travel—$1,200 per month.
   Other administrative expenses (telephone, etc.)—$600 per month.
   Assume there are no plans to add or terminate any employees.

Required:

Prepare separate sales department budgets and administrative budgets that will be useful in evaluating the two separate functions.

P25–5–A. The Payea Company wants to prepare a schedule of planned cost of goods sold and ending inventory for the quarters ending September 30, 1981, and December 31, 1981. The following data relate to the expected activity for the two quarters:

1. Expected sales for next three quarters are $300,000 (September, 1981), $375,000 (December, 1981), and $204,000 (March, 1982).
2. Selling price is $15 per unit.
3. Due to demand, the company wishes to carry a beginning of the period inventory equal to 25 percent of the following quarter's expected activity.
4. Inventory of finished goods—June 30, 1981, is 5,000 units valued at $12 per unit.
5. Cost of production:

Materials	$2 per unit
Direct labor	4 per unit
Variable overhead	1 per unit
Fixed overhead	100,000 per quarter

6. There is no work in process inventory at the beginning or end of either period.
7. The company computes inventory on a Fifo basis.

Required:

Prepare a schedule of planned cost of goods manufactured and sold for the quarters ending September 30, 1981, and December 31, 1981. (Hint: Prepare production schedules in units first.)

P25–6–A. Samson Corporation prepares annual budgets by quarters for its fiscal year ending June 30. Given below is its post-closing trial balance at December 31, 1980:

	Debits	Credits
Cash	$ 23,000	
Accounts receivable	60,000	
Allowance for doubtful accounts		$ 2,000
Inventories	26,000	
Prepaid expenses	2,000	
Furniture and equipment	30,000	
Allowance for depreciation		2,000
Accounts payable		20,000
Accrued liabilities		6,000
Notes payable, 5% (due 1984)		80,000
Capital stock		50,000
Retained earnings (deficit)	19,000	
	$160,000	$160,000

All of the stock of Samson Corporation was recently acquired by Floyd White after the corporation had suffered losses for a number of years. After the purchase, White loaned substantial sums of money to the corporation, which still owes him $80,000 on a 5 percent note. Because of these past losses there are no accrued federal income taxes payable, but future earnings will be subject to taxation.

White is anxious to withdraw $20,000 from the corpora-
tion (as a payment on the note payable to him) but will
not do so if it reduces the corporation's cash balance
below $20,000. Thus, he is quite interested in the budgets
for the quarter ending March 31, 1981.

Additional data:

1. Sales for the coming quarter are forecasted at
   $200,000; for the following quarter at $250,000. All
   sales are priced to yield a gross margin of 40 percent.
   Inventory is to be maintained on hand at the end of
   any quarter in an amount equal to 20 percent of the
   goods to be sold in the next quarter. All sales are
   on account, and 95 percent of the December 31, 1980,
   receivables plus 70 percent of the current quarter's
   sales will be collected during the quarter ending March
   31, 1981.
2. Selling expenses are budgeted at $8,000 fixed plus
   6 percent of sales; $4,000 will be incurred on account,
   $11,000 accrued, $4,500 from expiration of prepaid
   rent and unexpired insurance, and $500 from allocated
   depreciation.
3. Purchasing expenses are budgeted at $5,800 fixed
   plus 5 percent of purchases for the quarter; $1,500
   will be incurred on account, $8,000 accrued, $2,300
   from expired prepaid expenses, and $200 from allo-
   cated depreciation.
4. Administrative expenses are budgeted at $7,000 plus
   2 percent of sales; $500 will be incurred on account,

$6,000 accrued, $2,200 from expired prepayments,
and $300 from allocated depreciation, while bad debts
are estimated at 1 percent of sales.

5. Interest accrues at 5 percent on the notes payable
   and is credited to Accrued Liabilities.
6. All of the beginning balances in Accounts Payable
   and Accrued Liabilities will be paid during the quarter
   plus 80 percent of the current credits to Accounts Payable and all but $5,000 of the current accrued liabili-
   ties. A $3,000 insurance premium is to be paid prior
   to March 31, and a full year's rent of $24,000 is due
   on January 2.
7. Federal income taxes are budgeted at 50 percent of
   the net earnings before taxes. The taxes should be
   accrued separately, and no payments are due in the
   first quarter.

Required:

   a. Prepare an opening budget for the quarter ending March 31, 1981, including supporting schedules for
planned purchases and operating expenses.

   b. Prepare a financial budget for March 31, 1981. A
supporting schedule analyzing accounts credited for purchases and operating expenses, a schedule showing
planned accounts receivable collections and balances,
and a schedule showing planned cash flows and cash
balances should be included.

   c. Will White be able to collect $20,000 on his note?

PROBLEMS, SERIES B

P25–1–B. The Gleason Company prepares monthly
operating and financial budgets. Estimates of sales (in
units) are made for each month. Production is scheduled
at a level high enough to take care of current needs and
to carry into each month one half of that month's unit sales.
Raw materials, direct labor, and variable overhead are
estimated at $2, $4, and $1 per unit, and fixed overhead
is budgeted at $154,000 per month. Sales for April, May,
June, and July are estimated at 100,000, 120,000,
160,000, and 120,000 units. The inventory at April 1 consists of 50,000 units with a cost of $8.20 per unit.

Required:

   a. Prepare a schedule showing the budgeted production in units for April, May, and June 1981.

   b. Prepare a schedule showing the budgeted cost of
goods sold for the same three months assuming that the
Fifo method is used for inventories.

   P25–2–B. Following is a summary of operating data
of the Grayson Company for the year 1980:

Sales		$10,000,000
Cost of goods manufactured and sold:		
Direct materials	$2,000,000	
Direct labor	1,800,000	
Variable manufacturing overhead	400,000	
Fixed manufacturing overhead	1,200,000	5,400,000
		$ 4,600,000
Selling expenses:		
Variable	$ 500,000	
Fixed	400,000	900,000
		$ 3,700,000
General and administrative expenses:		
Variable	$ 200,000	
Fixed	1,800,000	2,000,000
Net operating earnings		$ 1,700,000

Sales volume for 1981 is budgeted at 90 percent of 1980 volume with no expectation of price change. The 1981 budget amounts for the various other costs and expenses differ from those reported in 1980 only for the expected volume change in the variable items.

The actual operating data for 1981 are:

Sales	$7,800,000
Direct materials	1,820,000
Direct labor	1,650,000
Variable manufacturing overhead	350,000
Fixed manufacturing overhead	1,210,000
Variable selling expenses	660,000
Fixed selling expenses	390,000
Variable general and administrative expenses	184,000
Fixed general and administrative expenses	1,790,000

Required:

a. Prepare a report comparing the operating budget for 1981 with the actual results for that year.

b. Prepare a budget report which would be useful in pinpointing the responsibility for the poor showing in 1981. (Hint: Prepare budget data on a flexible budget basis.)

c. Comment on the differences revealed by the two budget comparisons.

P25–3–B. The following data are presented for the J. W. Porter Company for use in preparing its 1981 operating budget:

Plant capacity	500,000 units
Expected sales	450,000 units
Expected production	450,000 units
Forecasted sales price	$ 5.00 per unit

Manufacturing costs:	
Variable:	
Raw material	2.00
Direct labor	1.00
Overhead	0.50
Fixed	112,500
Selling and administrative expenses:	
Variable	0.25
Fixed	100,000

Assume no beginning inventory. Taxes are 40 percent of pre-tax earnings.

Required:

Part I: Prepare an operating budget for the year ended December 31, 1981.

Part II: The actual results for the J. W. Porter Company for the year ended December 31, 1981, were as follows: (Note: actual sales price was *$4.75 per unit*. Actual production (in units) was equal to actual sales [in units]).

Sales		$2,375,000
Cost of goods sold:		
Materials	$950,000	
Direct labor	525,000	
Variable overhead	300,000	
Fixed overhead	112,500	1,887,500
		$ 487,500
Selling and administrative expense:		
Variable	125,000	
Fixed	100,000	225,000
Earnings before taxes		$ 262,500
Income tax at 40%		105,000
Net Earnings		$ 157,500

Using a flexible operating budget, analyze the efficiency of operations and the company's sales policy. Comment on the results of 1981.

P25–4–B. The Karisma Company is in the process of preparing its master budget for the year ended December 31, 1981. Management is interested in the responsibility budget to be prepared for the sales department. The sales manager and general manager have met with all department heads and have given you the following estimates relating to next year's expectations:

1. The company presently employs 40 full-time salespersons with a base salary of $350 per month. In addition it has eight regional managers with a base salary of $15,000 per year while the one sales manager draws $30,000 per year.
2. Current year sales are estimated at $9,000,000. The 40 full-time salespersons are given commissions on sales of 5 percent on about 70 percent of total sales, 3 percent on 20 percent of sales while the remaining 10 percent of sales are not subject to commission. Approximately one third of the sales are made in the first three months of the year.
3. Advertising commitments have been made with major magazines. These commitments are for $15,000 per month.
4. The company is planning a special in-store promotion during January–February–March. Special incentives are given to the retailers in the form of supplies, aids, and advertising assistance up to 2 percent of total gross sales during the month. Past history has shown the retailers to take advantage of about three fourths of these incentives.
5. A supplementary advertising campaign will also be used during the first quarter of 1981 and will average $30,000 for January and $20,000 during the next two months.
6. Salespersons' travel allowances average $150 per month per salesperson (excluding managers).
7. Selling supplies average 1 percent of gross sales.
8. Sales department clerical salaries are set at $2,500 per month. Rent for sales offices is $6,000 per month.
9. The sales department will conduct a special market test of a new product during the first quarter. Nonrecurring expenses of $45,000 associated with this test are expected to be incurred.

Required:

Prepare a detailed budget for the sales department for the first quarter of 1981.

P25–5–B. The Pasteur Manufacturing Company is in the process of preparing a schedule of planned cost of goods sold and ending inventory for the quarters ended March 31, 1981, and June 30, 1981. The following data relate expected activity for the two quarters:

1. Expected sales:

March quarter	$200,000
June quarter	150,000
September quarter	300,000

2. Selling price per unit is $20.
3. The company policy is to carry a beginning of the period inventory equal to 20 percent of the next period's requirements. Beginning inventory at January 1, 1981, was 2,000 units valued at $12.50 per unit.
4. Cost of production is estimated as follows:

Materials	$3 per unit
Direct labor	7 per unit
Variable overhead	2 per unit
Fixed overhead	19,000 per quarter

5. There is no work in process inventory at the beginning or end of any period.
6. Inventory is computed on a Fifo basis.

Required:

Prepare a schedule of planned cost of goods manufactured and sold for the quarters ended March 31 and June 30, 1981. (Hint: Prepare production schedule in units first.)

P25–6–B.

NELSON CORPORATION
Post-Closing Trial Balance
December 31, 1980

	Debits	Credits
Cash	$ 20,000	
Accounts receivable	40,000	
Allowance for doubtful accounts		$ 3,000
Inventories	50,000	
Prepaid expenses	6,000	
Land	50,000	
Buildings and equipment	150,000	
Accumulated depreciation		20,000
Accounts payable		30,000
Accrued liabilities (including income taxes)		20,000
Capital stock		200,000
Retained earnings		43,000
	$316,000	$316,000

The Nelson Corporation, whose post-closing trial balance at December 31, 1980, appears above, is a rapidly expanding company. Sales in the last quarter of 1980 amounted to $200,000 and are projected at $250,000 and

$400,000 for the first two quarters of 1980. This expansion has created a very tight cash position. Management is especially concerned about the probable cash balance at March 31, 1981, since payment in the amount of $30,000 for some new equipment must be made upon delivery on April 2. The current cash balance of $20,000 is considered to be the minimum workable balance.

Additional data:

1. Purchases, all on account, are to be scheduled so that the inventory at the end of any quarter is equal to one third of the goods expected to be sold in the coming quarter. Cost of goods sold averages 60 percent of sales.
2. Selling expenses are budgeted at $10,000 fixed plus 8 percent of sales; $2,000 is expected to be incurred on account, $24,000 accrued, $2,800 from expired prepayments, and $1,200 from allocated depreciation.
3. Purchasing expenses are budgeted at $7,000 fixed plus 5 percent of purchases; $1,000 will be incurred on account, $13,000 accrued, $1,100 from expired prepayments, and $900 from allocated depreciation.
4. Administrative expenses are budgeted at $12,500 fixed plus 3 percent of sales; $2,000 will be incurred on account, $11,000 accrued, $1,100 from expired prepayments, $900 from allocated depreciation, while bad debts are equal to 2 percent of current sales.
5. Federal income taxes are budgeted at 50 percent of net operating earnings before taxes and are accrued in Accrued Liabilities. Payments on these taxes are included in the payments on Accrued Liabilities discussed below.
6. All December 31, 1980, Accounts Payable will be paid in the current quarter plus 80 percent of current credits to this account. All of the December 31, 1980, accrued liabilities will be paid in the current quarter except for $6,000. Of the current quarter's accrued liabilities, all but $24,000 will be paid during the quarter.
7. Cash outlays for various expenses normally prepaid will amount to $8,000 during the quarter.
8. All sales are made on account, and 80 percent of the sales are collected in the quarter in which made, and all of the remaining sales are collected in the following quarter except for 2 percent which are never collected. The allowance for doubtful accounts shows the estimated amount of accounts receivable at December 31, 1980, arising from 1980 sales which will not be collected.

Required:

a. Prepare an operating budget for the quarter ending March 31, 1981. Supporting schedules for planned purchases and operating expenses should be included.

b. Prepare a financial budget for March 31, 1981. Include supporting schedules analyzing accounts credited for purchases and expenses, showing planned cash flows and cash balance and showing planned collections on and balance of accounts receivable.

c. Will sufficient cash be on hand April 2 to pay for the new equipment?

BUSINESS DECISION PROBLEM

The Scott Company has applied at a local bank for a short-term loan of $25,000 starting on October 1. The loan will be repaid with interest at 10 percent on December 31. The bank's loan officer has requested a cash budget from the company for the quarter ending December 31. The following budget information is needed to prepare the cash budget for the quarter ending December 31:

Sales	$108,000
Purchases	60,000
Salaries and wages to be paid	21,000
Rent payments	1,200
Supplies (payments for)	800
Insurance payments	300
Other cash payments	3,700

A cash balance of $4,000 is planned for October 1. Accounts receivable are expected to be $8,000 on October 1. All of these accounts will be collected in the quarter ending December 31. In general, sales are collected as follows: 90 percent in quarter of sale and 10 percent in quarter after sale. Accounts payable will be $80,000 on October 1 and will be paid during the quarter ending December 31. All purchases are paid for in the quarter after purchase.

Required:

a. Prepare a cash budget for the quarter ending December 31. Assume that the $25,000 loan will be made on October 1 and will be repaid with interest at 10 percent on December 31.

b. Will the company be able to repay the loan on December 31? If the company desires a minimum cash balance of $3,000, will the company be able to repay the loan as planned?

Chapter 26

Cost-volume-earnings analysis for short-term decision making

Cost-volume-earnings analysis is a means of predicting what effect changes in costs and volume will have on a company's net earnings in the *short run.* In the short run plant capacity and certain costs are assumed to be fixed, although all costs are subject to variation in the long run.

Cost-volume-earnings analysis can be used to answer such questions as: At what level of sales will a company break even (i.e., have neither net earnings nor a net loss)? What volume of sales is required to generate a certain level of net earnings? What effect will a change in selling prices, sales volume, or costs have on net earnings?

The relevant earnings statement format for cost-volume-earnings analysis is as follows:

Revenues	$xx
Less: Variable costs	xx
Contribution margin	$xx
Less: Fixed costs	xx
Net Earnings	$xx

Variable costs, fixed costs, and contribution margin all have been discussed previously and will be utilized in this chapter.

THE BEHAVIOR OF COSTS

Knowledge of the behavior and nature of costs is crucial to management for decision-making purposes. Two basic categories of costs are generally used—variable and fixed. As stated previously, *variable costs* (see Illustration 26.1, part [*a*]) are those which vary directly with changes in volume. For example, if volume increases 10 percent, variable costs increase 10 percent. Certain production costs, such as raw materials and the labor used to convert the raw materials into finished products, vary directly with production volume, while other costs, such as sales commissions, vary directly with sales volume.

As stated previously, *fixed costs* (see Illustration 26.1, part [*b*]) are those which remain constant over the entire range of output. They are often described as time-related costs. That is, they will be incurred simply because of the passage of time if the company expects to continue to operate. Depreciation, property insurance, property taxes, and administrative salaries are examples of time-related costs and, therefore, are fixed costs.

Besides these two basic categories of variable and fixed costs, there are two other types of costs which are in part fixed and in part variable. These include mixed (or semivariable) costs (see Illustration 26.1, part [*c*]) and step variable (or step fixed) costs (see Illustration 26.1, part [*d*]).

Illustration 26.1: Four types of cost patterns

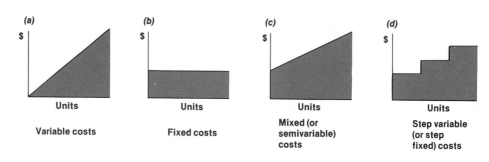

(a)	(b)	(c)	(d)
Units	Units	Units	Units
Variable costs	**Fixed costs**	**Mixed (or semivariable) costs**	**Step variable (or step fixed) costs**

An example of a *mixed cost* occurs when a given amount of maintenance cost has to be incurred while a plant is completely idle. Once production is underway, additional maintenance costs vary with production volume. These costs may be separated into their fixed and variable components as shown:

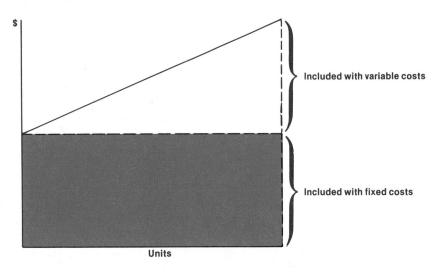

When divided in this way, the top part fits the variable cost pattern as shown in Illustration 26.1, part *(a)*. The bottom part fits the fixed cost pattern as shown in Illustration 26.1, part *(b)*.

The other type, *step variable costs,* is handled in one of two ways. The first is to assume that a straight-line relationship exists as shown below by the slanted dotted line:

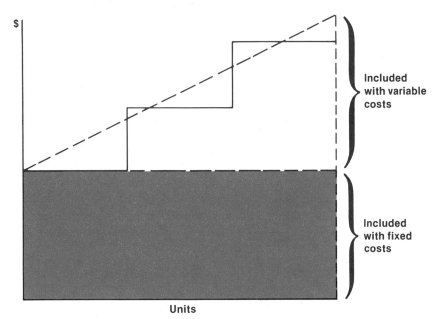

When this method is used, the costs may be separated into their fixed and variable components as was shown for mixed costs.

When step variable costs are present and there are very few steps (one or two usually), it is sometimes useful to treat the costs as "step fixed." To illustrate, assume that between 0–40 percent of capacity a cost is $20,000 and over 40 percent of capacity it becomes $50,000 as shown:

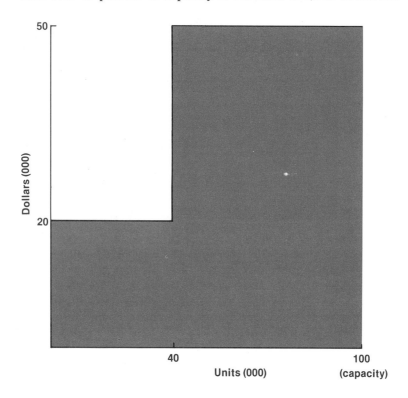

When costs behave in this step fixed manner, the best approach to analyzing operations is to treat the fixed cost as being $20,000 for the 0 to 40 percent level of capacity and as being $50,000 for the 40 to 100 percent level of capacity.

Thus even though there are four different types of cost patterns, it has been shown that two basic categories—variable and fixed—may be used to include all of them. Before proceeding, one other comment is in order. Some variable costs do not vary in a strictly linear relationship with volume. Rather, they vary in a curvilinear pattern—a 10 percent increase in volume may yield an 8 percent change in costs at lower output levels and an 11 percent change in costs at higher output levels. A curvilinear relationship is diagrammed in Illustration 26.2. But in the remainder of this chapter, variable costs are assumed to vary in a linear relationship with volume. The need for this assumption will become more evident as you proceed through this chapter.

Illustration 26.2: Curvilinear cost pattern

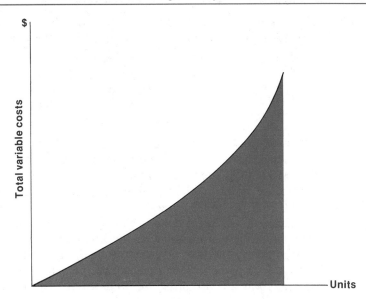

$

Total variable costs

Units

COST-VOLUME-EARNINGS ANALYSIS

In planning future operations, a type of analysis sometimes referred to as *cost-volume-earnings analysis* is undertaken. In such an analysis, the company's break-even point is calculated. A company is said to break even for a given period if the sales revenue and the costs charged to that period are exactly equal. As a result, no element of earnings or loss remains. Thus, *the break-even point is defined as that level of operations at which revenues and costs are equal.*

To undertake a careful and accurate cost-volume-earnings analysis requires knowledge of costs and their behavior as volume changes. Management must be able to distinguish among the different types of costs involved in its operations. Of course, the types and quantities of cost data accumulated will depend on the costs of obtaining the data compared to the benefits resulting from more refined information. Within this constraint, it is desirable to compute break-even points for each area of decision making within the company. Some important classifications of cost data for break-even analysis are by product, territory, salesperson, class of customer, and method of selling.

Several procedures are available for calculating a break-even point. It may be expressed in (1) dollars of sales revenue, (2) number of units produced (sold), or (3) as a percentage of capacity.

Assume that a company manufactures a single product which it sells for $20. Fixed costs per period total $40,000, while variable costs are $12 per unit, or 60 percent of sales price. A linear relationship between variable costs and sales revenue is assumed to exist. Thus, variable costs are, within a given range of sales activity or sales volume, a constant percentage of sales. In this example, variable costs are 60 percent of sales. The sales revenue needed to break even is computed as follows:

$$\text{Sales } (S) = \text{Fixed costs } (FC) + \text{Variable costs } (VC)$$

Fixed costs are known to be $40,000, while variable costs as a percentage of sales are equal to $0.60S$. Substituting, then, the equation becomes:

$$S = \$40,000 + 0.60S$$
$$S - 0.60S = \$40,000$$
$$0.40S = \$40,000$$
$$S = \$40,000 \div 0.40$$
$$S = \$100,000$$

Sales at the break-even point are $100,000, and this can easily be proven. At that level, fixed costs will be $40,000 and variable costs will be $60,000 ($0.60 \times \$100,000$). The break-even point in units can be computed by dividing total sales revenue at the break-even point by the selling price per unit ($\$100,000 \div \$20 = 5,000$ units).

If desired, the break-even point can be expressed in terms of capacity. Newspaper reports often refer to the break-even point of the steel industry, or of a company in that industry, as being a stated percentage of capacity, for example, 65 percent. If in the example presented above the output capacity of the plant was 25,000 units, the break-even point in terms of plant capacity is 20 percent ($5,000 \div 25,000$).

THE BREAK-EVEN CHART

The *break-even chart* in Illustration 26.3 presents graphically the break-even point for the above company. Each *break-even* chart (or analysis) is assumed

Illustration 26.3:
The break-even chart

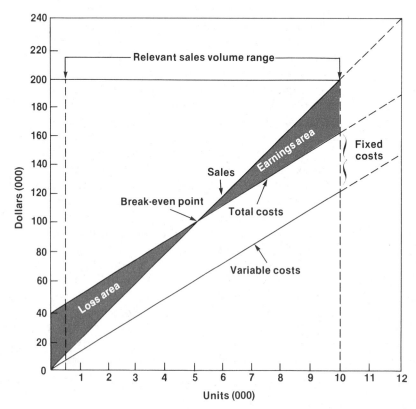

valid only for a specified *relevant range* of volumes. For volumes outside of these ranges, incurrences of different costs will alter the assumed relationship. For example, if only a few units were produced, the variable costs per unit would probably be quite high. Also, to produce more than 10,000 units it may be necessary to add to plant capacity, thus incurring additional fixed costs, or to work extra shifts, thus incurring overtime charges and other inefficiencies. In either case, the cost relationships first assumed are no longer valid. The illustration is based on the data presented previously which are *relevant* for output from 500 to 10,000 units. Different cost and revenue patterns may exist outside these limits.

The chart in Illustration 26.3 shows that the break-even volume of sales is $100,000 (5,000 units at $20). At this level of sales, fixed costs and variable costs are exactly equal to sales revenue as shown:

Revenues	$100,000
Less: Variable costs	60,000
Contribution margin	$ 40,000
Less: Fixed costs	40,000
Net Earnings	$ 0

The break-even (cost-volume-earnings) chart shows that a period of complete idleness would produce a loss of $40,000, the amount of fixed costs, while output of 10,000 units would produce net earnings of $40,000. Other points which can be read show that with sales of 7,500 units total revenue would be $150,000. At that point, total costs would amount to $130,000, leaving net earnings of $20,000.

The break-even point can be lowered by increasing the selling price per unit, decreasing the total fixed costs, or decreasing the variable cost per unit. This can be seen by studying Illustration 26.3 and visually imagining that the slope of the sales line increases, the distance between the variable costs and total costs lines diminishes, or the slope of the variable costs line decreases. The effect of each of these is to lower the break-even point. Taking opposite actions will increase the break-even point.

For example, assume that a company currently has variable costs of $15 per unit, fixed costs of $27,000, and a selling price of $60 per unit. Thus, its break-even point is $36,000 ($27,000/0.75) or 600 ($36,000/$60) units. If the company can increase its selling price by 5 percent while holding variable costs and fixed costs the same, the break-even point will decrease by approximately $562.50 as shown below:

$$S = FC + VC$$

$$S = \$27,000 + \frac{\$15}{\$60 + 0.05(\$60)}\, S$$

$$S = \$27,000 + \frac{15}{63}\, S$$

$$48/63\ S = \$27,000$$
$$S = \$35,437.50 \text{ break-even point if}$$
selling prices increase by 5 percent

Original break-even point	$36,000.00
Break-even point with 5% increase in selling prices	35,437.50
Decrease in break-even volume of sales	$ 562.50

MARGIN OF SAFETY

If a company's current sales are above its break-even point, then the company is said to have a ***margin of safety*** equal to the difference between current sales and sales at the break-even point. The margin of safety is the amount by which sales can decrease before a loss will be incurred. For example, assume current sales are $250,000, and sales at the break-even point are $200,000. The margin of safety is $50,000, or 20 percent of sales, computed as follows:

$$\text{Margin of safety} = \text{Current sales} - \text{Break-even sales}$$
$$= \$250,000 - \$200,000 = \$50,000$$

or

$$\text{Margin of safety} = \frac{\text{Current sales} - \text{Break-even sales}}{\text{Current sales}}$$

$$= \frac{\$250,000 - \$200,000}{\$250,000}$$

$$= 20 \text{ percent}$$

THE CONTRIBUTION MARGIN CONCEPT

As shown at the beginning of this chapter, ***contribution margin*** is defined as the amount by which revenue exceeds the variable costs incurred in securing that revenue. This amount often is referred to as marginal earnings. It may be computed for a given number of units (or dollars of sales) or per unit or per dollar of sales.

Using the preceding data (selling price per unit of $20 and variable costs per unit of $12 with total fixed costs of $40,000), the contribution margin per unit is $8. The sale of one additional unit will add $20 to total revenues, $12 to total costs, and $8 to net earnings (ignoring income taxes). From this information the break-even point in units can be computed. Each unit contributes $8 to the coverage of fixed costs, and fixed costs total $40,000. Thus the sale of 5,000 units will be necessary to cover the fixed costs. The formula is:

$$\text{Break-even point in units} = \text{Fixed costs} \div \text{Contribution margin per unit}$$

At the break-even point, the total contribution margin will equal the total fixed costs as shown in Illustration 26.4.

The break-even point in terms of dollars of sales can also be computed by dividing the fixed costs per period by the ***contribution margin rate.*** This rate is computed by dividing the contribution margin by sales price per unit. In the above data it is 40 percent ($8 ÷ $20), and the break-even point is $100,000 of sales revenue ($40,000 ÷ 0.40).

In addition, the net earnings at any level of output can be computed as the contribution margin per unit multiplied by the number of units sold, less the total fixed costs. Using the above data, the net earnings at the 80

Illustration 26.4:
Break-even chart
showing that
fixed costs equal
contribution margin
at break-even point

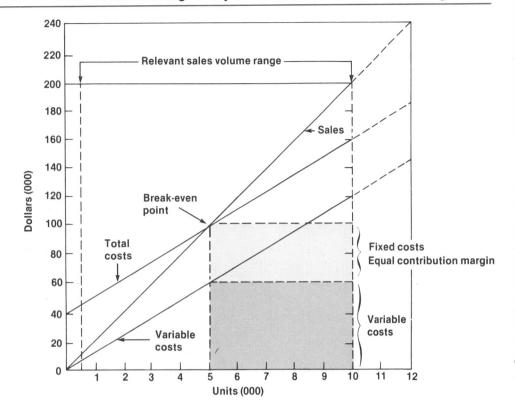

percent level of capacity can be determined. First multiply 8,000 units (0.80 × 10,000) by $8, obtaining $64,000; then subtract the fixed costs of $40,000, leaving net earnings of $24,000. In this case the contribution margin more than covers total fixed costs. The remainder is net earnings (ignoring income taxes) as shown in Illustration 26.5.

A simple example may aid in reinforcing understanding of some of these concepts.

As stated earlier, break-even analysis can be used to analyze the cost-volume-earnings relationships for a venture or project. Suppose that one of the major airlines wanted to know the number of seats that have to be sold on a certain flight for the flight to break even. To solve this problem the costs have to be identified and separated into fixed and variable categories.

The fixed costs are those that do not vary with different levels of seats filled. These include such costs as fuel required to fly the plane with crew (no passengers) to destination; depreciation on the plane and facilities utilized on this flight; salaries of crew members, gate attendants, and maintenance and refueling personnel; and other miscellaneous fixed costs.

The variable costs include those costs which vary directly with the number of passengers. These might include costs such as extra fuel consumed per passenger, food and beverages included in the price of the ticket, baggage handling costs per passenger, and miscellaneous variable costs.

Illustration 26.5:
Break-even chart
showing sales
level for desired
earnings

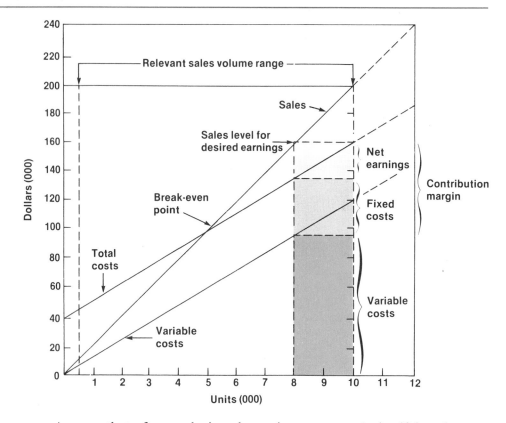

Illustration 26.5:
Break-even chart
showing sales
level for desired
earnings

Assume that after analyzing the various costs and classifying them as fixed or variable, the fixed costs for a given flight are $12,000. The variable costs are $25 per passenger, and tickets are sold at $125. This yields a contribution margin per ticket of $100 ($125 − $25). Assume also that there are 300 seats on the aircraft.

The break-even point can be expressed in dollars, number of passengers, or in percent of capacity.

The sales revenue needed to break even is:

$$\text{Sales } (S) = \text{Fixed costs } (FC) + \text{Variable costs } (VC)$$
$$S = \$12,000 + 0.2\,S$$
$$0.8\,S = \$12,000$$
$$S = \$15,000$$

It also may be found using the contribution margin rate as follows:

$$\text{BEP (dollars)} = \frac{FC}{\text{Contribution margin rate}}$$

$$\text{BEP} = \frac{\$12,000}{80 \text{ percent}}$$

$$\text{BEP} = \$15,000$$

The break even point in terms of number of passengers may be found by dividing the break-even point in dollars ($15,000) by the selling price per unit ($125). Thus, $15,000/$125 = 120 passengers. It also may be found as follows:

$$\text{BEP (units)} = \frac{FC}{\text{Contribution margin}}$$

$$\text{BEP} = \frac{\$12,000}{\$125 - \$25}$$

$$\text{BEP} = 120 \text{ passengers}$$

The break-even point in percent of capacity is:

$$\frac{\text{BEP (units)}}{\text{Total capacity (units)}} = \frac{120 \text{ passengers}}{300 \text{ passengers}} = 40 \text{ percent}$$

Using cost-volume-earnings analysis.   Although cost-volume-earnings analysis alone is insufficient to support managerial decision making, basic cost-volume-earnings relationships should be understood by management. Knowledge of cost-volume-earnings relationships can be used by management to determine the effect on earnings of any change in fixed costs, variable costs, or sales price. For instance, such knowledge may help management to determine (1) whether to increase sales promotion costs in an effort to increase sales volume, (2) whether an order at a lower-than-usual price should be accepted, and (3) whether plant facilities should be expanded. Planning, in general, is facilitated by careful study of break-even charts. Indeed, it has been said that, to be successful, management must become "break-even minded."

This form of analysis may also be useful in determining the level of sales volume that is needed to generate some desired level of net earnings. To illustrate using the preceding data, if management wished to generate $24,000 of net earnings, the chart in Illustration 26.5 shows that sales volume must be 8,000 units, $160,000, or 80 (8,000 ÷ 10,000) percent of capacity.

Now assume that management has the opportunity to operate at 100 percent of capacity if it will increase its fixed costs by investing $10,000 in a sales promotion contract. Will it be profitable for management to make such an investment? The chart in Illustration 26.6 shows that earnings would increase to $30,000, provided the cost and revenue estimates are correct and the objective of management is to maximize net earnings.

To illustrate further, assume that ABC Company's sales are currently $60,000, variable costs are $25,000, and fixed costs are $30,000. Net earnings are $5,000, as computed below:

$$\text{Net earnings } (NE) = \text{Sales } (S) - \text{Variable costs } (VC) - \text{Fixed costs } (FC)$$
$$= \$60,000 - \$25,000 - \$30,000$$
$$= \$5,000$$

Illustration 26.6:
Break-even chart
showing earnings
resulting from
action taken

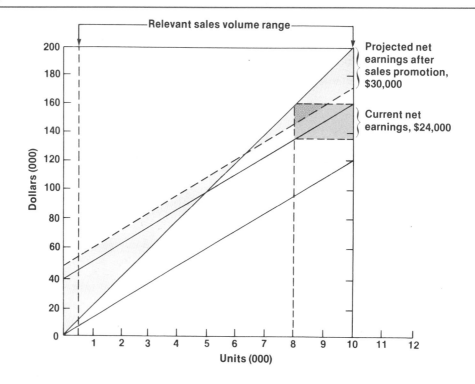

A 5 percent increase in sales price with variable costs and fixed costs remaining the same would have the following effect on the earnings of ABC Company:

$$NE = \$60,000(1.05) - \$25,000 - \$30,000$$
$$= \$63,000 - \$25,000 - \$30,000$$
$$= \$8,000$$

ABC Company's net earnings will increase by \$3,000, or 60 percent (\$3,-000/\$5,000), if sales price increases by 5 percent and variable and fixed costs stay the same.

Now, suppose sales price increases by 5 percent (over \$60,000) and variable costs increase by 10 percent. Net earnings would be \$5,500, as computed below:

$$NE = \$60,000(1.05) - \$25,000(1.10) - \$30,000$$
$$= \$63,000 - \$27,500 - \$30,000$$
$$= \$5,500$$

The result is a \$500, or 10 percent (\$500/\$5,000), increase in net earnings.

Some of the practical aspects of cost-volume-earnings relationships will be discussed in the remainder of the chapter.

SOME PRACTICAL ASPECTS OF COST-VOLUME-EARNINGS ANALYSIS: Cost-volume-earnings analysis for the multiproduct firm

The previous discussion allowed us to talk of the break-even point in terms of either units, sales dollars, or percentage of capacity. When computing the break-even point for a multiproduct firm, we will use sales dollars. Also the assumption must be made that the *product mix*—that is, the number of units of each type of product sold—is known in advance.

To illustrate the situation for a multiproduct firm assume the following historical data:

	Products							
	1		2		3		Total	
	Amt.	%	Amt.	%	Amt.	%	Amt.	%
Sales	$60,000	100	$30,000	100	$10,000	100	$100,000	100
Less: Variable expenses	40,000	67	16,000	53	4,000	40	60,000	60
Contribution margin ..	$20,000	33	$14,000	47	$ 6,000	60	$ 40,000	40

Thus, the sales mix for the products is 60:30:10, respectively. In total, variable costs are 60 percent of total sales. If this sales mix can be expected to hold in the future, the break-even point for a future period can be found as follows (assuming fixed costs are $50,000):

$$S = FC + VC$$
$$S = \$50,000 + 0.6\,S$$
$$0.4\,S = \$50,000$$
$$S = \$125,000$$

The $125,000 can be broken down into products by multiplying the $125,000 by 60 percent, 30 percent and 10 percent respectively.

If historical patterns are not expected to hold in the future, *projected* sales and variable expenses should be used in determining the total expected percentage of variable expenses to total sales.

Methods for estimating mixed costs

Early in the chapter, mixed costs were illustrated (see Illustration 26.1, part [c]). In an actual business situation the accountant might have some difficulty in estimating a particular mixed cost. The fixed portion of a particular mixed cost represents the cost of having a service available for use. The variable portion is the cost associated with various levels of activity (usually defined as production or sales volume).

The scatter diagram. One method for estimating the total amount of a mixed cost at various levels of activity is to prepare a *scatter diagram* in which actual costs incurred are plotted.

Assume that Illustration 26.7 is a scatter diagram representing total actual maintenance costs for a firm's fleet of delivery trucks. The dots on the diagram represent actual costs from the past at various levels of activity. The line is drawn through what appears visually to be the center of the pattern of these dots. In the example above, the fixed element of the mixed

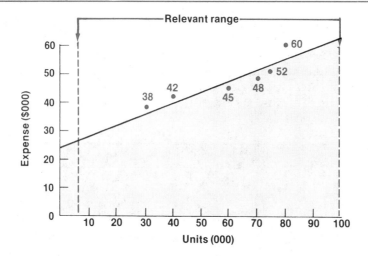

cost is $23,000. Since the line (called a regression line) rises from $23,000 to $63,000 over the range of 100,000 units, the slope of the variable cost portion is

$$\frac{\$63,000 - \$23,000}{100,000 \text{ units}}$$

or $0.40 per unit. Thus, the variable portion of this cost is equal to $0.40 per unit. The data in the chart suggest that the firm's truck maintenance costs can be estimated at $23,000 plus 40 cents for every mile driven.

A more sophisticated method, called the *least squares method*, could be used to draw the regression line. This method is more precise since it involves statistical analysis, but it will not be presented in this text.

The high-low method.   This method is another widely used method for identifying the behavior of mixed costs. The *high-low method* involves the use of only the highest and lowest plots on a scatter diagram to determine the relationship between volume and variable cost.

To illustrate, assume that in Illustration 26.7 the lowest plot is $38,000 of expense at 30,000 units of output and the highest plot is $60,000 at 80,000 units of output. The amount of variable cost per unit is found as follows:

$$\frac{\text{Change in expense}}{\text{Change in output}} = \frac{\$60,000 - \$38,000}{80,000 \text{ units} - 30,000 \text{ units}} = \frac{\$22,000}{50,000} = \$0.44 \text{ per unit}$$

The fixed cost portion is then found as follows:

Total cost at 80,000 units of output	$60,000
Less: Variable cost at that level of output	
(80,000 × $0.44)	35,200
Fixed cost at all levels of output	
within the relevant range	$24,800

The high-low method is less precise than the scatter diagram method since it uses only two data points in the computation. Either or both points may not be representative of the data as a whole.

The meaning of units as a measure of volume

In the various cost-volume-earnings charts included throughout this chapter, the horizontal axis has been labeled "units." A practical question is whether this is units of production or units sold. An implicit assumption in this type of analysis is that production is equal to sales. (In other words, inventories do not vary from the beginning to the end of the period). In the long run we know that production must equal sales. In the short run this might not occur.

Some of the costs which a company will incur vary directly with production (e.g., supplies used in manufacturing) and some vary directly with sales (e.g., sales commissions). One should realize the nature of this problem, but it is best to assume that production is equal to sales for this type of analysis. Therefore, whether "units" is labeled units of output or units of sales is irrelevant.

The nature of fixed costs

Until now in this discussion fixed costs have been treated as if they were all alike. But there are two types of fixed costs which should be identified. They are *committed fixed costs* and *discretionary fixed costs*.

Committed fixed costs.   These costs relate to the basic facilities and organization structure which a company must have to continue operations. They are not changed in the short run without seriously disrupting operations. Examples of committed costs are depreciation on buildings and equipment and salaries of key executives. In the short run costs such as these are viewed as being not subject to the discretion or control of management. They result from past decisions which "committed" the company for a period of several years. For instance, once a company constructs a building to house production operations, it is committed to the use of the building for many years. The depreciation on that building is not as subject to control by management as are some other types of fixed cost.

Discretionary fixed costs.   In contrast to committed fixed costs, discretionary fixed costs are related to fixed cost areas which are subject to management control from year to year. Each year management decides how much to spend on advertising, research and development, and employee training and development programs. Since these decisions are made each year, they are said to be under the "discretion" of management. Management is not locked in or committed to a certain level of expense for any more than one budget period. The next period it may change the level of expense or may eliminate it completely.

The philosophy of management can affect to some extent which fixed costs are committed and which are discretionary. For instance, during the recession of the mid 1970s some companies terminated persons in the upper levels of management while other companies kept their "management team" intact. Thus, in some firms the salaries of top-level managers are discretionary while in others they are committed.

The discussion of committed fixed costs and discretionary fixed costs is relevant to cost-volume-earnings analysis. If a company's fixed costs are almost all committed fixed costs, it is going to have a more difficult time in reducing its break-even point for the next budget period than if most of its fixed costs are discretionary in nature. A company with a large proportion of discretionary fixed costs may be able to reduce fixed costs dramatically in a recessionary period. By doing this it may be able to "run lean" and show some earnings even when economic conditions are difficult. Its chances of long-run survival may be enhanced.

Assumptions made in cost-volume-earnings analysis

The assumptions which must be made in cost-volume-earnings analysis are as follows:

1. Selling price and variable costs per unit remain constant throughout the relevant range. This means that more units can be sold at the same price and there is no change in technical efficiency as volume increases.
2. The number of units produced equals the number of units sold.
3. In multiproduct situations, the product mix is known in advance.
4. Costs can be accurately classified into their fixed and variable portions.

These assumptions have been described as being unrealistic in many situations. But even where there is some truth to this criticism, cost-volume-earnings analysis can serve as a useful planning tool. Although it may lack precision, its use is preferable to pure intuition.

NEW TERMS INTRODUCED IN CHAPTER 26

Break-even chart—a graphic presentation of the relationships between costs, volume, and earnings which also shows the break-even point.

Break-even point—that level of operations at which revenues for a period are equal to the costs assigned to that period so that no element of earnings or loss remains.

Committed fixed costs—those costs relating to the basic facilities and organization structure which a company must have to continue operations. An example is depreciation on the factory building.

Contribution margin*—the amount by which the revenue secured from the sale of products exceeds the variable costs of those products.

Contribution margin rate—contribution margin expressed as a percentage of selling price; sometimes called earnings/volume rate.

Cost-volume-earnings analysis—an analysis of the effects of volume changes upon costs and upon earnings; sometimes referred to as a break-even type of analysis.

Discretionary fixed costs—those fixed costs which are subject to management control from year to year. An example is advertising expense.

Fixed costs*—are those which remain constant (in total) over the entire range of output.

High-low method—a method used in dividing mixed costs into their fixed and variable portions. The high plot and low plot of actual costs are used to draw the line representing a total mixed cost.

Least squares method—a method used for dividing mixed costs into their fixed and variable portions. It utilizes statistical techniques to draw the regression line representing a total mixed cost.

Margin of safety—the difference between current sales and sales at the break-even point.

Mixed cost—a cost which is partly fixed and partly variable such that a minimum cost is often incurred regardless of volume of output but which increases with output.

Product mix—number of units of each type of product sold.

Relevant range—the range of production or sales volume over which the basic assumptions of break-even analysis are valid.

Scatter diagram—a diagram which shows plots of actual costs for various levels of output (sales). It is used in dividing mixed costs into their fixed and variable portions.

Short-run—the period of time over which it is assumed that plant capacity is fixed. Hence it is possible to separate costs into variable and fixed components for analysis.

Step variable costs—are those which remain constant (in total) over a range of output (sales), but then increase in steps at certain points over the entire range of output (sales).

Variable costs*—are those which vary (in total) directly with changes in volume.

> * Although these terms were defined and used in preceding chapters, we include them again here for your convenience.

DEMONSTRATION PROBLEM

The Boston Company has fixed costs of $250,000 per year and variable costs of $6 per unit. Its product sells for $10 per unit. Full capacity is 100,000 units.

Required:

a. Compute the break-even point in terms of (1) sales dollars, (2) units, and (3) percent of capacity.

b. Compute the number of units the company must sell if it wishes to have net earnings of $120,000.

Solution to demonstration problem

a. 1. Sales (S) = Fixed costs (FC) + Variable costs (VC)
$$S = \$250,000 + 0.6S$$
$$0.4S = \$250,000$$
$$S = \$250,000 \div 0.4$$
$$S = \$625,000$$

2. Break-even point in units = $625,000 \div \$10 = \underline{62,500}$

3. Break-even point as percentage of capacity = $62,500 \div 100,000 = \underline{62.5}$ percent

b. Number of units = $\dfrac{\text{Fixed costs} + \text{Desired net earnings}}{\text{Contribution margin}}$

$$= \frac{\$250,000 + \$120,000}{\$4}$$

$$= \frac{\$370,000}{\$4}$$

$$= \underline{92,500}$$

QUESTIONS

1. What format of the earnings statement is used in this chapter?

2. Name and describe the four types of cost patterns.

3. What is meant by the term break-even point? What factors must be taken into consideration in determining it?

4. What are the different ways in which the break-even point may be expressed?

5. How is relevant range related to break-even analysis?

6. Why is break-even analysis considered appropriate only for short-run decisions?

7. What is the formula for calculating the break-even point in sales revenue?

8. What formula is used to solve for the break-even point in units? How can this formula be altered to calculate the number of units which must be sold to achieve a desired level of earnings?

9. Why might a business wish to lower its break-even point? How would it go about lowering the break-even point? What effect would you expect the mechanization and automation of production processes to have upon the break-even point?

10. How is the break-even point calculated for a multi-product firm?

11. What are the various ways in which the cost line for a mixed cost can be determined? Describe each method.

12. What does the label "units" on the horizontal axis of the break-even chart mean?

13. What is a committed fixed cost? Give some examples.

14. What is a discretionary fixed cost? Give some examples.

15. Give an example of a fixed cost which might be considered committed for one firm and discretionary for another.

16. What assumptions are made in cost-volume-earnings analysis?

EXERCISES

E–1. Compute the break-even point for a company in which fixed costs amount to $175,000 and variable costs are 65 percent of sales.

E–2. George Company is currently producing and selling 20,000 units of a given product at $10 per unit. Its average cost of production and sale is $7. It is contemplating attempting to sell 50,000 units at $8. At this level average cost per unit will be $6.50. At which level should it seek to operate?

E–3. If a given company has fixed costs of $50,000 and variable costs of production of $6.75 per unit, how many units will have to be sold at a price of $9.25 each for the company to break even? How many would it have to sell to earn $25,000? If 50,000 units represent 100 percent of capacity, what percentage of capacity does this latter level of operations represent?

E–4. Using the data in Exercise E–3, what would be the effect on the break-even point if (consider each part separately):

a. The price per unit were increased to $9.75?

b. Fixed costs were lowered by $10,000?

c. Variable costs were reduced to $6 per unit?

E–5. Company B sells two products. The sales of Product 1 and Product 2 in the most recent year were $80,000 and $60,000, respectively. The variable costs of the products were $50,000 and $34,000, respectively. The company had fixed costs of $40,000. The sales mix for the next period is estimated to be the same as in the most recent year. What is the break-even point in terms of sales revenue?

E–6. The Walton Company uses the high-low method in determining the cost line for a mixed cost. Assume that the low and high plots are as follows:

Volume	Cost
4,000	$5,000
10,000	8,000

Determine the variable cost per unit and the amount of total fixed costs.

PROBLEMS, SERIES A

P26–1–A.

a. Assume that fixed costs of A Corporation are $400,000 per year, variable costs are $8 per unit, and selling price is $20 per unit. Determine the break-even point.

b. B Company breaks even when sales amount to $4,000,000. In 1981 its sales were $6,000,000 and its variable costs amounted to $1,800,000. Determine the amount of its fixed costs.

c. The sales of C Corporation in 1981 amounted to $80,000,000, its variable costs were $20,000,000, and its fixed costs were $40,000,000. At what level of operations would the C Corporation have exactly broken even?

d. What would have been the net earnings of the C Corporation, part **(c)** above, if sales volume had been 10 percent higher but selling prices had remained unchanged?

e. What would have been the net earnings of the C Corporation, part **(c)** above, if variable costs had been 10 percent lower?

f. What would have been the net earnings of the C Corporation, part **(c)** above, if fixed costs had been 10 percent lower?

g. Determine the break-even point for the C Corporation on the basis of the data given in **(e)** above; in **(f)** above.

P26–2–A. Following are 1981 data for two companies:

	Company Y		Company Z	
Sales		$100,000		$100,000
Costs:				
Fixed	$60,000		$30,000	
Variable	25,000		55,000	
Total ...		85,000		85,000
Net Operating Earnings		$ 15,000		$ 15,000

Required:

a. Prepare a break-even chart for Company Y.

b. Compute the break-even points for both companies.

c. Assume that without changes in selling price, the sales of both companies decreased by 20 percent. Present condensed operating statements, similar to the ones given above, which show the effect of the decrease in sales on the operating earnings of both companies.

P26–3–A.
When the plant of the Wilkerson Company is completely idle, fixed costs amount to $150,000. When the plant operates at levels of 50 percent of capacity and below, its fixed costs are $175,000, and at levels above 50 percent of capacity its fixed costs are $250,000. The company's variable costs at full capacity (100,000 units) amount to $375,000.

Required:

a. Assuming that the company's product sells at $12.50 per unit, what is the company's break-even point?

b. Using only the data given, at what level of operations would it be more economical to close the factory than to operate? In other words, at what level will operating losses approximate the losses if the factory is closed down completely?

c. Assume that when the Wilkerson Company is operating at half its capacity, it decides to reduce the selling price from $12.50 per unit to $7.50 per unit in order to increase its sales. At what percentage of capacity must the company operate in order to break even at the reduced sales price?

P26–4–A.

a. Patrick Corporation is now operating at capacity and reports sales of $300,000, variable costs of $180,000, fixed costs of $50,000, and net earnings of $70,000. If the company invests $200,000 in additional machinery and equipment with a useful life of ten years, it is estimated that sales can be increased by $100,000. Should the company make the additional investment in plant facilities? Show computations to support your answer.

b. Operating data of the Barnes Corporation are as follows: sales, $200,000; fixed costs, $40,000; variable costs, $100,000; and net earnings, $60,000. A proposed addition to the company's plant is estimated by the sales manager to increase sales by a maximum of $150,000. The company's cost accountant states that the proposed addition will increase the company's fixed costs by $80,000 per year. Do you recommend that the proposed expansion be undertaken? Support your answer with computations.

P26–5–A.
The Braxton Company sells three products. It has fixed costs of $100,000. The sales and variable costs of these products for 1981 were as follows:

	Products		
	A	B	C
Sales	$120,000	$80,000	$200,000
Variable costs	80,000	50,000	100,000

Required:

a. Determine the break-even point for 1982 assuming that the sales mix will remain as it was in 1981.

b. Determine the break-even point for 1982 assuming that the sales mix ratio for 1982 is expected to change to 50:30:20.

P26–6–A. The May Company assigns the task of estimating maintenance costs on its productive machinery to you. This cost is a mixed cost. You are supplied with the following data from past years:

Year	Units	Cost
1973	4,000	$5,000
1974	5,000	5,400
1975	4,500	5,500
1976	5,500	5,800
1977	5,000	5,800
1978	6,500	6,200
1979	7,000	6,700
1980	9,000	7,200
1981	10,000	8,000

Required:

a. Using the high-low method, determine the total amount of fixed costs and the amount of variable cost per unit. Draw the cost line.

b. Prepare a scatter diagram, plot the actual costs, and visually fit a linear cost line to the points. Estimate the amount of total fixed costs and the amount of variable costs per unit.

PROBLEMS, SERIES B

P26–1–B. The Wells Corporation has a plant capacity of 100,000 units. Variable costs amount to $400,000 at 100 percent capacity. The fixed costs amount to $300,000, but management thinks this is probably the case only between 20,000 and 80,000 units.

Required:

a. Prepare a break-even chart for the Wells Corporation assuming its product sells for $10 per unit. Be sure to indicate the relevant range, contribution margin, and net earnings on the chart.

b. Compute the break-even point by using the equation to verify your chart.

c. How many units must be sold to have net earnings (ignoring taxes) of $30,000?

P26–2–B. Following is a summary of operations in 1981 for two companies:

	Company C		Company D	
Sales		$500,000		$500,000
Expenses:				
Fixed	$100,000		$350,000	
Variable	300,000		50,000	
Total expenses		400,000		400,000
Net Operating Earnings		$100,000		$100,000

Required:

a. Compute the break-even point for each company.

b. Assume that without changes in selling price the sales of each company decreased by 25 percent. Present condensed operating statements, similar to the ones above, which show the effect of the decrease in sales on the operating earnings of each company.

P26–3–B. The productive capacity of the plant of the Bomare Corporation is 200,000 units, at which level of operations its variable costs amount to $400,000. When the plant is completely idle, fixed costs amount to $100,000. At 60 percent of capacity and below, its fixed costs are $170,000, and at levels above 60 percent of capacity its fixed costs are $250,000.

Required:

a. Determine the company's break-even point assuming that its product sells at $6.25 per unit.

b. Using only the data given, at what level of operations would it be more economical to close the factory than to operate? In other words, at what level will operating losses approximate the losses if the factory is completely closed down?

c. Assume that when the Bomare Corporation is operating at 60 percent of capacity, a decision is made to reduce the selling price from $6.25 per unit to $5 per unit in order to increase its sales. At what percentage of capacity must the company operate in order to be profitable at the reduced sales price?

P26–4–B.

a. The Meyers Company sells its product at $10 per unit; the variable costs of producing and selling it amount to $3 per unit; fixed costs are $210,000 per year. Determine the company's break-even point in dollars of sales revenue.

b. In 1981 the Stokes Company's sales were $750,000 and its variable costs amounted to $187,500. The company's break-even point is at a sales volume of $800,000. Determine the amount of its fixed costs. What were the net earnings for 1981?

c. What would have been the net earnings of the Stokes Company, part **(b)** above, if the 1981 sales volume had been 10 percent higher but selling prices had remained unchanged?

d. What would have been the net earnings of the Stokes Company, part **(b)** above, if 1981 variable costs had been 10 percent lower?

e. What would have been the net earnings of the Stokes Company, part **(b)** above, if fixed costs in 1981 had been 10 percent lower?

f. Determine the break-even point for the Stokes Company on the basis of the data given in **(d)** above; in **(e)** above.

P26–5–B.
The Dawson Company has fixed costs of $80,000. It sells four products. Its sales and variable costs during 1981 were as follows:

	Products			
	W	*X*	*Y*	*Z*
Sales	$60,000	$30,000	$70,000	$40,000
Variable costs ...	40,000	25,000	35,000	15,000

Required:

a. Determine the break-even point for 1982 assuming that the sales mix will remain the same as it was in 1981.

b. Determine the break-even point for 1982 assuming that the sales mix is expected to be in the ratio of 10:30:15:45.

P26–6–B.
The Westly Company has identified various variable and fixed costs in its operations. There is a mixed cost which needs to be divided into its fixed and variable portions. Actual data pertaining to this cost are as follows:

Year	*Units*	*Cost*
1972	5,200	$6,400
1973	5,000	6,000
1974	5,500	6,700
1975	6,400	6,400
1976	7,100	6,500
1977	7,500	6,900
1978	8,200	7,100
1979	8,900	7,600
1980	9,400	8,000
1981	10,000	8,600

Required:

a. Using the high-low method, determine the total amount of fixed costs and the amount of variable cost per unit. Draw the cost line.

b. Prepare a scatter diagram, plot the actual costs, and visually fit a linear cost line to the points. Estimate the amount of total fixed costs and the amount of variable cost per unit.

BUSINESS DECISION PROBLEM 26–1

The Woodson Company is operating at almost 100 percent of capacity. The company expects the demand for its product to increase by 25 percent next year (1982). In order to satisfy the demand for its product, the company is considering two alternatives. The first alternative involves a capital outlay which will increase fixed costs by 15 percent but will have no effect on variable costs. The second alternative will not affect fixed costs but will cause variable costs to increase to 60 percent of the selling price of the company's product.

The Woodson Company's condensed earnings statement for 1981 is shown below:

Sales		$3,000,000
Costs:		
Variable	$1,350,000	
Fixed	550,000	1,900,000
Net earnings before taxes		$1,100,000

Required:

a. Determine the break-even point for 1982 under each of the alternatives.

b. Determine projected net earnings before taxes for 1982 under each of the alternatives.

c. Which alternative would you recommend? Why?

BUSINESS DECISION PROBLEM 26–2

The Easy Listening Company, a leading manufacturer of clock radios, incurred $210,000 of fixed costs while selling 20,000 radios at $50 each. Variable costs amounted to $15 per radio.

A new machine used in the production of clock radios has recently become available and is more efficient than the machine currently being used. The new machine would reduce variable costs by 20 percent but would increase fixed costs by $8,000 because of additional depreciation.

Required:

a. Compute the break-even point *in units* using the old machine.

b. Compute the break-even point *in units* using the new machine.

c. Assuming total sales remain at $1,000,000, compute expected net earnings assuming the new machine is acquired.

d. Should the new machine be acquired? Why?

BUSINESS DECISION PROBLEM 26–3

The Bostwick Company sells a single product at $25 per unit. The company incurs variable costs of $15 per unit and total fixed costs of $100,000 per year. Current year's sales amounted to $750,000.

The company is not satisfied with its current level of net earnings. In order to increase its net earnings, the company is considering the following two alternatives:

1. Spend $30,000 per year on advertising without changing selling prices. Sales volume is expected to increase by 20 percent as a result of this action.
2. Decrease the selling price to $20 per unit. Sales volume is expected to increase by 25 percent as a result of this action.

Required:

a. Compute the company's current break-even point in units.

b. Compute the break-even point in units under each of the two alternatives.

c. Compute expected net earnings under each of the two alternatives. (Ignore income taxes.)

d. Which of the alternatives would you recommend? Why?

Chapter 27

Short-term decision making; taxes

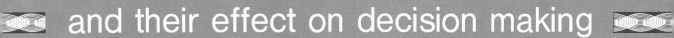

and their effect on decision making

SHORT-TERM DECISION MAKING

Many decisions which managers make can be classified as short-term decisions and are based on incremental or differential analysis. They involve operations and include decisions such as whether to change the price of a product, manufacture rather than buy a part externally, add or drop a product line or department, further process a joint product, and so on. The effects of these decisions are relatively immediate and short run. They can be modified or reversed if things do not proceed as planned. They do not include long-run decisions such as building a new plant or investing in additional machinery. These latter long-run decisions are covered in Chapter 28.

COST AND REVENUE CONCEPTS USED IN DIFFERENTIAL ANALYSIS

Costs which are *relevant costs* in a given situation are *future costs* which *differ* between alternatives. The difference between these costs for two alternatives is called *differential cost* (expense).[1] Past costs are called *sunk costs.* These costs are not relevant in decision making because they have already been incurred, and there is nothing management can do to change history. Also, future costs which do not differ between alternatives may be ignored since they will affect both alternatives similarly.

Assume you had invested $100 in some new clothes thinking you would attend a concert on Saturday afternoon. A friend comes by and invites you to go to an amusement park instead. You believe that you will receive equal enjoyment from either alternative. (In some instances the unquantifiable benefits may differ and they will have to be considered in the final decision.) The cost of admission to attend the concert is $11, while the cost of admission to get into the amusement park is $8. Transportation cost to attend either is $2. In this illustration, the $100 cost of the new clothes is a sunk cost which should be excluded from the decision process. The $2 transportation cost does not differ between the alternatives and may be ignored (although the decision will not be affected if it is left in the analysis). Thus, the relevant costs are the future costs of admission, $11 to attend the concert and $8 to get into the amusement park. The differential cost between the two alternatives is $3 as shown below:

Relevant revenues and expenses (costs) of alternatives

	(1) Concert	(2) Amusement park	Differential
Revenues	$ 0	$0	$0
Costs	11	8	3
Net benefit in favor of choosing amusement park			$3

This framework can be used in many of the decision situations which will be illustrated in this chapter.

---

[1] Some authors equate relevant cost and differential cost. But we use the term "relevant" to identify which costs should be considered in a situation and the term "differential" to identify the amount by which these costs differ.

The example above did not have any relevant revenues. Revenues which are relevant are those future revenues which differ between alternatives. The difference in revenues between two alternatives is called *differential revenue.* For certain decisions the revenues do not differ between alternatives. Then the decision should be to select the alternative with the least cost. In other situations the costs do not differ between alternatives. Then the alternative which results in the greatest revenue should be selected. In many decision situations, both future costs and future revenues differ between alternatives. In these situations, the alternative resulting in the greatest positive difference between future revenues and future expenses (costs) should be selected.

As stated above, differential revenues and costs are the amounts by which future revenues differ and future costs differ between alternative courses of action. In many situations the total variable costs differ between alternatives while the total fixed costs do not. This is true where the alternatives being considered are different levels of output and there are no step variable costs present. If there are step variable costs present, then the differential cost between operating at, say, the 40 percent and at the 60 percent level of capacity might include the increase in total variable costs plus an increment in the "fixed" costs. Thus, differential cost is not synonymous with the difference in variable costs in every instance.

Marginal cost and *marginal revenue* are terms used in economics to describe the increase in total cost and in total revenue resulting from the production and sale of one more unit. But business decisions are more apt to involve choosing between operating levels separated by hundreds or thousands of units, such as seeking to sell 100,000 or 120,000 units in a period. Accountants describe the differences in total revenue and total cost between the two levels as *differential* or *incremental revenue and cost.*

An *opportunity cost* is the potential benefit that is foregone from not following the best alternative course of action. For instance, assume that the two best uses of a plot of land are as a trailer park (annual earnings of $100,000) and as a golf driving range (annual earnings of $60,000). The opportunity cost of utilizing it as a trailer park is $60,000 (the amount which could have been earned in its best alternative use). The opportunity cost of utilizing it as a golf driving range is $100,000, since that is the amount which could have been earned in its best alternative use. These costs are not recorded in the accounting records since they are the costs of *not* doing a certain thing. They come from the discipline of economics.

All of the concepts described so far will be used in this chapter to illustrate the decision process in various types of decisions.

SPECIAL COST STUDIES FOR DECISION MAKING

Accounting records usually are designed to provide full cost and revenue data. Such data are suitable for such general purposes as determination of net earnings, control of costs, and managerial planning in general. There are occasions, however, when management faces problems which require consideration of only selected cost and revenue data. Differential analysis is such an occasion. Several types of short-term decision making involving the use of selected cost and revenue data will now be considered.

Product pricing

Each of the various prices which could be set for a given product represents an alternative course of action. The relevant amounts are the future total sales revenue and the relevant cost (usually only the future variable costs). These are both future amounts which vary between alternatives. Total fixed costs usually remain the same between alternatives and, if so, may therefore be ignored. The goal in selecting a price for a product is to select that price at which total future revenues will exceed total future variable costs by the greatest amount. In other words, select that price which will result in the greatest *total* contribution margin.

A high price is not necessarily the price which will maximize earnings. There may be some good substitutes for the product. If a high price is set, customers may switch to competing products. Thus, the quantity which the company sells would decline substantially. Thus, in the maximization of earnings, the expected volume of sales is as important as the earnings margin per unit of product sold. As stated above, in making any decision regarding the establishment of selling price, management should seek that combination of price and volume which will produce the largest total contribution margin. This is often difficult to do in an actual situation since management may not know how many units can be sold at each price.

Assume that a company has fixed costs of $10,000 and that its variable cost of production per unit is $5. Estimates of the demand for its product are as follows:

20,000 units at $4 per unit
15,000 units at $6 per unit
10,000 units at $8 per unit
5,000 units at $10 per unit

What price should it set for its product? As shown in the calculation below, it should select a price of $8 per unit since this will result in the greatest total contribution margin ($30,000).

Choice	Contribution margin per unit*	×	Number of units	=	Total contribution margin
1	−$1		20,000		−$20,000
2	1		15,000		15,000
3	3		10,000		30,000
4	5		5,000		25,000

* Sales price—variable cost.

Special orders

Not infrequently management is faced with the opportunity to sell its product in two or more different markets at two or more different prices. Price discrimination is unlawful under the **Robinson-Patman Act** unless it is justified by differences in costs of delivery or selling. But since such cost differences often exist, a single product may be marketed at more than one selling price.

The desirability of keeping physical facilities and personnel working at capacity is obvious. Good business management requires keeping the cost of idleness at a minimum. When operations are at a level less than full capacity, additional business should be sought. Such additional business may be accepted at prices lower than average unit costs because only the future additional costs are relevant. They should be matched against the additional future revenue provided. Such costs will be for the most part variable costs such as materials and labor. But the possibility exists that certain fixed costs will also be increased. Regardless of the classification of the costs affected by the increased volume, one point is clear. It is the comparison of differential revenue with differential cost—*not* the average costs—that is the important consideration.

Obviously the effect on regular sales of accepting a special order at a lower-than-usual price must be considered. If regular sales are to be unharmed by the acceptance of such a special order, it is essential that separate markets exist, such as in the case of a foreign and a domestic market.

To illustrate, assume that a given company produces and sells a single product at a variable cost of $8 per unit. Annual capacity is 10,000 units, and annual fixed costs total $48,000. The selling price is $20 per unit, and production and sales are budgeted at 5,000 units. Thus, budgeted net earnings are $12,000, computed as follows:

Sales (5,000 units at $20)		$100,000
Costs:		
Fixed	$48,000	
Variable (5,000 at $8)	40,000	88,000
Net Earnings		$ 12,000

An order for 3,000 units is received from a distributor at a price of $10 per unit. This is only half the regular selling price per unit, and also less than the average cost per unit of $17.60 ($88,000 ÷ 5,000 units). But the $10 price offered exceeds variable cost per unit by $2. If the order is accepted, net earnings will be $18,000, computed as follows:

Sales (5,000 units at $20; 3,000 units at $10)		$130,000
Costs:		
Fixed	$48,000	
Variable (8,000 units at $8)	64,000	112,000
Net Earnings		$ 18,000

To continue to operate at 50 percent of capacity would produce net earnings of only $12,000. Thus, a contribution margin of $2 per unit on the new units will result from acceptance of the order, and net earnings will be increased by $6,000. Because the regular market is unlikely to be affected by the export of the product at a sharply reduced price, the order should be accepted.

Using the decision format illustrated earlier, the analysis would be as follows:

Relevant revenues and expenses (costs) of alternatives

	(1) Accept order	(2) Reject order	Differential
Revenues	$130,000	$100,000	$30,000
Expenses	64,000	40,000	24,000
Net benefit in favor of accepting order			$ 6,000

As a practical matter, *dumping* is the practice of selling excess goods in foreign markets at a price less than full costs. This is usually prohibited by trade agreements. We will assume that no such agreement exists with the foreign country involved in the example.

In summary, variable costs set a floor for selling price in marginal or incremental analyses such as those described above. Even if price exceeds variable costs only slightly, the additional business will make a contribution to earnings. But such "contribution pricing" of marginal business often brings only short-term increases in earnings. Such pricing should be appraised in the light of long-range effects on the entire price structure of the company and the industry. In the long run, full costs must be covered.

Periodically management faces the question of elimination or retention of given products. To assist in the solution of such a problem, a special study of costs and revenues may be called for. Since the earnings statement does not automatically associate costs with given products, costs must be reclassified into those which would be changed by the elimination and those which would remain unaffected. In effect, one must simply assume elimination and compare the reduction in revenues (differential revenue) with the eliminated costs (differential cost). Usually such costs as materials and labor and other variable costs will be eliminated and therefore become part of differential cost. The fixed costs usually will remain unaffected and are therefore not relevant to the decision. But in a given situation, certain fixed costs may be reduced or eliminated if a product is dropped. If revenues resulting from the sale of a product exceed the incremental costs resulting from its sale, a product is making a positive contribution to earnings. It should be retained unless an even more profitable alternative exists.

To illustrate, assume that elimination of Product R is being considered. Product R provides revenue of only $100,000 annually, while the costs with which it is charged by acceptable accounting methods amount to $110,000, producing a loss of $10,000. Assume that a careful analysis of the costs reveals that if Product R were dropped, the reduction in costs would be $80,000, and $30,000 of the costs would continue to be incurred. The latter costs would increase the burden on the remaining products of the company by $30,000 if Product R were dropped. The analysis is as follows:

Relevant revenues and expenses (costs) of alternatives

	(1) Retain Product R	(2) Drop Product R	Differential
Revenues	$100,000	0	$100,000
Expenses	80,000	0	80,000
Net benefit of retaining Product R			$ 20,000

It is easily seen that Product R, even though producing no net earnings, has been contributing $20,000 ($100,000 − $80,000) annually to the net earnings of the business. Its elimination could be a costly mistake unless there were a more profitable use of the resources that would be released from not producing Product R. For instance, possibly the released facilities could be used to produce an alternative product which would make a contribution to earnings of more than $20,000 per year. If so, Product R should be eliminated and production of the alternative product should proceed. The earnings from the alternative product are an opportunity cost of retaining Product R and vice versa.

There may be nonquantifiable reasons for retaining a product even though the quantitative factors indicate that it should be eliminated. Management must consider the effect of elimination or retention on the sales of other products. An unprofitable product may be retained to provide a full line for customers. For example, even if flashbulbs were known to be sold at a loss in a retail drugstore, their sales would probably be continued in order to draw customers into the store and to be able to offer a complete line of photographic products. Likewise, certain services may be retained because of the effect of their elimination on sales of other products. An example is unprofitable warranty work done by a retail automobile dealer. Buyers of new automobiles like to be assured that warranty services are available at their dealer's place of business for the cars they purchase. Even if the service is provided at a loss, it may be wise to retain it.

ELIMINATING A DEPARTMENT

Before a proper decision can be made about the closing of a department, a detailed analysis of all of the operating expenses and other revenues must be made to determine which will be eliminated if the department is eliminated. For example, a statement showing the assumed amounts of expenses and revenues that would be eliminated if the furnishings department of the Moore Company were eliminated is shown in Illustration 27.1. Obviously, if the furnishings department were eliminated, all of its sales revenue would disap-

Illustration 27.1: Effect on revenues and expenses of discontinuing a department

MOORE COMPANY Estimated Effect on Earnings from Discontinuing the Furnishings Department	Current amounts	If department is discontinued	
		Eliminated	Not eliminated
Revenues:			
Net sales	$120,000	$120,000	
Total	$120,000	$120,000	
Expenses:			
Cost of goods sold	$ 74,800	$ 74,800	
Building occupancy	16,000		$16,000
Promotion	6,000	3,000	3,000
Salespeople	11,000	11,000	
Buying	8,600		8,600
Administrative	7,000		7,000
Total	$123,400	$ 88,800	$34,600

pear. Also, it should be quite obvious that the cost of goods sold would be eliminated if the department were closed.

Operating expenses are then analyzed and classified into those which would be eliminated and those which would not be eliminated if the department were closed. If the total expenses which would be eliminated exceed the total revenue which would be eliminated, the department should be eliminated (unless qualitative factors indicate otherwise). If it is the other way around, it should not be eliminated unless a better alternative use of the space and resources is available. Had the furnishings department been eliminated, net earnings would have declined by $31,200 (the difference in the reduction of the incremental revenues and expenses $120,000 − $88,800).

Using the form of analysis used for other decisions, the analysis would appear as follows:

Relevant revenues and expenses (costs) of alternatives

	(1) Keep department	(2) Eliminate department	Differential
Revenue	$120,000	$0	$120,000
Expense	88,800	0	88,800
Net advantage of retaining department			$ 31,200

Possibly the space and facilities now used by the furnishings department could be used to generate future revenues which would exceed future expenses by more than $31,200 per year. If so, the alternative use should be selected.

Expenses which would be eliminated if a department is eliminated normally are the variable expenses and the direct fixed expenses. The allocated fixed expenses normally would continue. But there could be exceptions to these generalizations in any given instance.

DISCONTINUING SALES TO A CERTAIN TYPE OF CUSTOMER

Retention of a given segment of business is usually advisable if its differential revenue exceeds its differential cost (usually variable costs). This form of decision rule has already been illustrated with products and departments. But, as with products or departments, elimination may be in order if there is a more profitable alternative use of resources. This is another way of saying that when the opportunity cost of selling to customers whose purchases are small is considered, an analysis may show that these sales should be discontinued. Assume, for example, that weekly revenues from customers whose orders total less than $20,000 annually exceed weekly incremental costs involved by substantially less than on sales to larger customers. Since the larger customers furnish business which provides a higher contribution margin per week of salesperson effort, it may be advisable to apply greater sales effort to larger customers and to discontinue salespersons' visits to the customers whose purchases are small. Assume there is an adequate supply of new large customers which could be approached for business.

To illustrate, assume the following facts:

	(1) Sell to large customers	(2) Sell to small customers	Differential
Revenue per week	$10,000	$6,000	$4,000
Variable cost per week (including cost of goods sold) ..	4,500	3,750	750
Contribution margin per week	$ 5,500	$2,250	$3,250

* Assume that a salesperson can make one successful call to a large customer per week or three successful calls to small customers per week (average of $2,000 sales revenue per small customer).

Selling to large customers maximizes the contribution margin per unit of time. The company is better off by $3,250 (the difference in the contribution margins) per salesperson per week if sales are to large customers.

FURTHER PROCESSING OF JOINT PRODUCTS

In some manufacturing situations several products result from a common raw material or manufacturing process. These are called *joint products.* An example would be the slaughtering and carving up of any livestock, such as cattle. *Joint product costs* are those costs incurred up to the point where the joint products are split off from each other. These costs are sunk costs in deciding such issues as whether to process a joint product further before selling it or to sell it in its condition at split off.

Assume that Company Y manufactures two products, A and B, from a common manufacturing process. Each of the products could be sold in its present form or could be processed further and sold at a higher price. Assume the following data:

Product	Selling price at split-off point per unit	Cost of further processing per unit	Selling price per unit after further processing
A	$10	$6	$21
B	12	7	18

The differential revenues and costs of further processing of the two products are as follows:

Product	Differential revenue of further processing	Differential cost of further processing	Net advantage (disadvantage) of further processing
A	$11	$6	$5
B	6	7	(1)

Based on this analysis, Product A should be processed further since this will increase earnings by $5 per unit sold. Product B should not be processed further as this will decrease earnings by $1 per unit sold.

This same form of analysis should also be used in deciding whether low value products (often called *by-products*) should be discarded or processed further so that they might be salable. If the differential revenue of further processing exceeds the differential cost, then further processing should be done. If not, the waste products should be discarded.

MAKE-OR-BUY DECISIONS

Another application of differential analysis is in the decision whether to make or buy a part or material used in the manufacture of a product. In such a case a comparison is made between the price which would be paid for the part if it were purchased and the additional costs which would be incurred if the part were to be manufactured. If almost all of the costs of manufacture are fixed and would exist in any case, it is likely that manufacture rather than purchase of the part or material would be more economical.

To illustrate, assume that a company is manufacturing a part used in its final product at a cost of $6. Cost components are materials, $3.00; labor, $1.50; fixed factory costs, $1.05; and other variable factory costs, $0.45. The part could be purchased for $5.25. Since the fixed overhead would presumably continue even if the part were purchased, manufacture of the part should be continued. The added costs of manufacturing amount to only $4.95 ($3.00 + $1.50 + $0.45). This is 30 cents per unit less than the purchase price of the part as shown in the following analysis:

Relevant revenues and expenses (costs) of alternatives

	(1) Make	(2) Buy	Differential
Revenues	$0	$0	$0
Expenses	4.95	5.25	0.30
Net advantage of making			$0.30

In certain situations it may be possible to avoid some of the fixed costs by buying outside. If so, these should be treated the same as the variable costs in the analysis, since they would then be relevant costs.

Also the opportunity cost of not utilizing the space for some other purpose should be considered. If the total opportunity cost of not using the space in its best alternative use is more than 30 cents per unit times the number of units produced, then the part should be purchased from outside.

In some cases the relative cost to manufacture as opposed to purchase may be only a minor consideration. Among the many other factors to be considered are the competency of existing personnel to undertake manufacture of the part or material, the availability of working capital, and the cost of any borrowing that may be necessary.

Maximizing utilization of a scarce resource

Consider the following data for a company which is operating near capacity producing three products:

	Product A	Product B	Product C	Total
Sales (incremental revenue)	$400,000	$300,000	$300,000	$1,000,000
Variable costs (incremental costs)	250,000	200,000	250,000	700,000
Contribution margin..................	$150,000	$100,000	$ 50,000	$ 300,000
Fixed costs (all allocated)	80,000	60,000	60,000	200,000
Earnings	$ 70,000	$ 40,000	$ (10,000)	$ 100,000
Units produced	20,000	20,000	20,000	
Sales price per unit	$20.00	$15.00	$15.00	
Variable cost per unit	12.50	10.00	12.50	
Contribution margin per unit	7.50	5.00	2.50	

In the preceding chapter, computation of the break-even point for a multi-product company was covered. A break-even chart for such a company also can be drawn. The break-even chart for the above firm is shown in Illustration 27.2. Assuming a constant product mix, the computed break-even point is $667,000 (total contribution margin rate, 30 percent, divided into total fixed costs, $200,000).

One might conclude that, to increase earnings, the company should try to expand sales while retaining the same product mix as in the past. But such a strategy is not likely to increase earnings very much. Overlooked is the fact that manufacturing capacity is a *scarce resource* since the company is currently operating near capacity. Thus, a better strategy would be to alter the mix of products within constraints which exist. Suppose that the company has a total annual manufacturing capacity of 6,000 hours. Assume that, after

Illustration 27.2:
Multiproduct break-even
chart

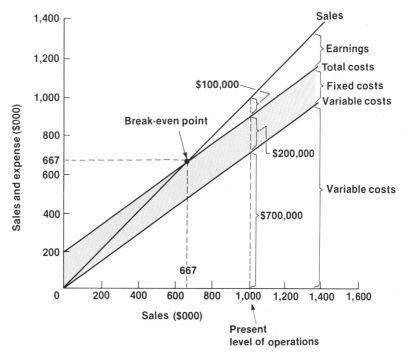

careful analysis, it is found that 8 units of Product A can be produced per hour, 9 units of B per hour, and 20 units of C per hour. These production rates are based on the assumption that the full resources of the factory are devoted to manufacturing *only* that product. Assume further that due to specialized equipment requirements and limited consumer demand the following constraints apply to production and sales:

Product	Maximum production	Maximum demand
A	30,000	24,000
B	40,000	50,000
C	40,000	60,000

If there were no constraints regarding production time, equipment requirements, or consumer demand, one might be tempted to sell only the product with the highest contribution margin per unit. But because production capacity is a scarce resource, the important variable in this situation is maximization of contribution margin per hour of plant capacity. Accordingly, contribution margin per hour of capacity is computed below:

Product	Contribution margin per unit	Units produced per hour	Contribution margin per hour
A	$7.50	8	$60
B	5.00	9	45
C	2.50	20	50

Based upon this analysis Product A still happens to be the most profitable to produce. The maximum production of A, however, is limited by the constraint of estimated consumer demand of 24,000 units. Product C is the next best alternative. Production is limited by equipment constraints to 40,000 units. The balance of plant capacity should be devoted to Product B. The results of this analysis are summarized below:

Product	Contribution margin per hour	Rank	Maximum production	Demand	Units to produce	Time to produce	Contribution margin total
A	$60	1	30,000	24,000	24,000	3,000	$180,000
B	45	3	40,000	50,000	9,000*	1,000	45,000
C	50	2	40,000	60,000	40,000	2,000	100,000
						6,000	$325,000

* After the number of units of A and C have been determined (and the time to produce them), 1,000 hours of productive capacity remains. In that time 9,000 units of B can be produced.

Notice that the full amount of plant capacity is utilized. The new earnings are computed as follows:

Sales:
A (24,000 × $20.00)	$480,000	
B (9,000 × $15.00)	135,000	
C (40,000 × $15.00)	600,000	$1,215,000

Variable costs:
A (24,000 × $12.50)	$300,000	
B (9,000 × $10.00)	90,000	
C (40,000 × $12.50)	500,000	890,000
Contribution margin		$ 325,000
Fixed costs		200,000
Earnings		$ 125,000

It should be noted that switching to other products may result in a temporary increase in fixed costs. These costs may be due to rearranging production lines, retraining workers, and so forth. Also, as pointed out in the previous section there may be other considerations, for example, long-term objectives, that would weigh against dropping a certain product.

The remainder of the chapter is concerned with corporate federal income taxes and their effect on decision making. Certain aspects of income taxes for individuals were presented in Chapter 12.

THE EFFECT OF CORPORATE INCOME TAXATION ON MANAGEMENT DECISION MAKING

Most corporations organized for profit must file a federal income tax return and pay a corporation income tax on their net earnings. Not-for-profit organizations, specifically exempted by law, do not file an income tax return but must file an annual return of information.

NET EARNINGS BEFORE TAXES VERSUS TAXABLE INCOME

Net earnings before taxes (as shown on the earnings statement) and taxable income (as shown in the corporation's tax return) need not necessarily agree. There are various reasons why they might differ. Some of these are:

1. Certain items of revenue and expense included in the computation of business earnings are excluded from the computation of taxable income. For instance, interest earned on state, county, or municipal bonds is not subject to tax. Only "ordinary" and "necessary" business expenses and "reasonable" amounts of salaries can be deducted for tax purposes. Life insurance premiums are not deductible if the corporation is the beneficiary, and proceeds received from life insurance policies are not taxed. Costs of attempting to influence legislation are not deductible. A corporation may deduct from taxable income 85 percent of any dividends received from other domestic corporations. They may deduct charitable contributions only up to 5 percent of taxable income (computed before deducting any contributions). They may deduct capital losses only to the extent of capital gains. In some mining industries depletion deductions (known as percentage depletion) may be deducted in excess of actual cost. Goodwill may not be amortized for tax purposes even though it must be for accounting purposes.

2. The timing of recognition of items of revenue and expense often varies for tax purposes from the timing used in determining business earnings. Interpretations of the tax code generally have held that revenue received in advance is taxable when received and that current expenses based on estimates of future costs (such as costs of performance under service contracts) are not deductible until actually incurred. An exception is bad debts expense. The installment sales method may be used for tax purposes but not for accounting purposes. Under this method, revenue is recognized for tax purposes only when collections are received. Also, elective methods may be used for tax purposes that are different from the ones used for financial statements. For instance, the corporation may be using straight-line depreciation for book purposes and a different method for tax purposes. This is a very common practice.

For a given corporation, the reconciliation between earnings before taxes and taxable income may appear as follows:

Net earnings before taxes per earnings statement		$74,000
Add:		
Life insurance premiums paid	$ 700	
Service revenue received in advance	5,000	
Estimated expenses under service contracts	1,000	6,700
		$80,700
Deduct:		
Interest on New York State Bonds	$3,000	
Difference in depreciation for tax purposes ($8,000) and for book purposes ($6,000)	2,000	5,000
Taxable income		$75,700

The investment credit

The Revenue Act of 1971 included two provisions that are of particular importance to business. The investment credit of the 1960s was reinstated. This permitted taxpayers to deduct 7 percent of the cost of acquisition of machinery and equipment (under certain conditions) from their tax liability in the year of purchase. Also included was a provision allowing a 20 percent speedup in allowable depreciation deductions. These two provisions were included in an attempt to stimulate the economy. For the 1975 tax year the investment credit was increased to 10 percent. The Tax Reform Act of 1976 extended the 10 percent rate through December 31, 1980. The Revenue Act of 1978 made the 10 percent rate permanent. Thus, if a business purchases machinery at a cost of $10,000, it may deduct $1,000 from its tax liability.

Tax rates

In 1974, an ordinary business corporation was subject to two federal income taxes—the normal tax and the surtax. The normal tax (of 22 percent) applied to the first $25,000 of taxable income. Both taxes (the normal tax of 22 percent and a surtax of 26 percent) applied to all taxable income over $25,000. Thus, if a corporation had $40,000 of taxable income, the first $25,000 was taxed at 22 percent and the remaining $15,000 was taxed at 48 percent. A "temporary" reduction in these rates was in effect for the 1975 tax year. For 1975, the first $25,000 of taxable income was taxed at 20 percent, the next $25,000 at 22 percent, and the remainder at 48 percent. The Tax Reform Act of 1976 extended these rates through December 31, 1977.

The Revenue Act of 1978 set corporate income tax rates beginning in 1979 as follows:

Corporate taxable income	Tax rate
$0 to $25,000	17%
$25,000 to $50,000	20
$50,000 to $75,000	30
$75,000 to $100,000	40
Over $100,000	46

The maximum rate of tax on all net long-term capital gains is 28 percent. Capital gains (or losses) result from the sale of capital assets (and certain other assets) which have been held more than one year. Excluded are gains on assets sold in the normal course of business. Thus, a gain on the sale of a building held for more than one year qualifies as a capital gain, while the sale of inventory at a profit does not.

Decisions affected by tax considerations

Management strives to maximize earnings available for common stockholders per share of common stock outstanding. Management can affect the timing of the recognition of revenues and the incurrence of some expenses and thus affect the timing of taxable income. Since money has "time value," there is an incentive for management to defer the incurrence and payment of income taxes.

Form of business organization. The earnings of a proprietorship or partnership are considered income to the individual owners whether they are distributed or not. There is no tax on the business entity itself. Salaries to owners and distributions of earnings are treated the same under the tax law. In fact, salaries are considered merely a means of distributing earnings.

The corporate form of organization creates another taxpayer. The corporation itself is taxed on its earnings. Only when dividends are paid are the stockholders taxed for corporate earnings and then only to the extent of the dividends received. This situation often is described as the double taxation of corporate earnings. Shareholders in high tax brackets often prefer that the corporation retain the earnings rather than paying dividends (although there are limits, and penalties are imposed for unreasonable accumulations of earnings). Then they may later sell their shares with only 40 percent of the gain being taxed (capital gains income) rather than 100 percent of it (ordinary income).

Under the tax law, certain corporations with a limited number of stockholders may elect to be taxed as partnerships. Under this option there is no tax levied on the corporation itself. Instead, all taxable income "flows through" to the individual owners and each pays individual income taxes on his or her share. This tends to negate to some extent the tax implications of the form of organization, although most corporations do not qualify to elect this option.

Size of organization. The owners may also use the corporate form to establish more than one entity, each of which is taxed at 17 percent on the first $25,000, 20 percent of the next $25,000, and 30 percent on the next $25,000, 40 percent on the next $25,000, and 46 percent on earnings of over $100,000 rather than organizing as one entity. For instance, one corporation with $200,000 of taxable earnings could be taxed as follows:

17% on the first $25,000	=	$ 4,250
20% on the next $25,000	=	5,000
30% on the next $25,000	=	7,500
40% on the next $25,000	=	10,000
46% on the remaining $100,000	=	46,000
		$72,750

Organized as eight separate corporations, each with $25,000 of taxable income, the tax may only be 17 percent of $200,000, or $34,000. But unless there are good business reasons for multiple corporations (other than tax reasons), the tax benefit may be reduced or completely disallowed. Certain groups of corporations, controlled by the same five or fewer persons, lost this benefit as of 1975.

Financing arrangements. There are a number of ways of financing business growth. Three external means are by issuing common stock, preferred stock, or bonds. They have been illustrated previously but are included here to emphasize the tax aspects.

Different tax effects result from the use of bonds rather than stock to finance business growth. You should recall that dividends on common and preferred stocks are not deductible in arriving at taxable income. But interest paid on obligations is a deductible business expense in computing taxable income. This tax advantage tends to create a bias toward financing growth through the issuance of bonds rather than by issuing preferred or common stock. Illustration 27.3 supports this contention.

Assume that the Burgess Company is planning to issue $200,000 (at face value) of securities to finance construction of a new building. It is considering issuing either preferred stock with an 8 percent dividend rate on par

Illustration 27.3: Tax effects of comparative forms of financing

	Preferred stock		Bonds	
Earnings before interest and taxes		$140,000		$140,000
Less: Interest at 8% of $200,000		–0–		16,000
Taxable income		$140,000		$124,000
Taxes:				
17% on first $25,000	$ 4,250		$ 4,250	
20% on next $25,000	5,000		5,000	
30% on next $25,000	7,500		7,500	
40% on next $25,000	10,000		10,000	
46% on remainder	18,400	45,150	11,040	37,790
Earnings after taxes		$ 94,850		$ 86,210
Less: Preferred dividends (8% of $200,000)		16,000		–0–
Earnings available for common shareholders		$ 78,850		$ 86,210

value or bonds with an 8 percent interest rate. Assume that either obligation can be issued in the market at its face value.

The higher earnings available for common stockholders if the bonds are issued result from the deductibility of interest which reduces taxes by $7,360 ($16,000 × 46 percent).

Of course there are other considerations in deciding on the method of financing to use. Some of them are the supply and demand conditions in the capital market for bonds and for preferred stock (perhaps one could be issued above its face value and the other below its face value), the amounts of debt already employed, and the stability of earnings. Interest on debt must usually be paid when due if the common stockholders are to retain control of the company, while dividends on preferred stock do not have to be declared and paid. Therefore, the increased risk associated with the issuance of bonds may more than negate the tax advantage.

Tax considerations in mergers.   A provision of the tax law permits corporations to carry losses back three years and forward seven years. This means that if a company has a loss in a given year it can apply it against taxable earnings of other years and recover some or all of the taxes it paid during those years. In doing this, it must apply the loss to the oldest year first, then the next oldest, and so on until the loss has been completely "used up" by offsetting it against ordinary taxable income of these years. The corporation recomputes its taxes for those previous years using the rates then in effect.

An illustration may be helpful. Assume the amounts of taxable income (or loss) shown below (1979 rates are used to compute taxes paid):

Year	Taxable income (or loss)	Taxes paid	Taxes recovered
1979	$ 15,000	$ 2,550	$2,550
1980	20,000	3,400	3,400
1981	5,000	850	850
1982	(100,000)	–0–	–0–
1983	40,000	–0–	–0–
1984	10,000	–0–	–0–
1985	30,000	3,400	–0–
1986	50,000	9,250	–0–
1987	60,000	12,250	–0–

The loss of $100,000 in 1982 would first be offset against the $15,000 of income in 1979, then the $20,000 in 1980, and next the $5,000 in 1981. The company would recover the taxes previously paid of $6,800. At this point it would have a carry-forward of $60,000. It would apply $40,000 of this toward taxable income in 1983 and therefore pay no taxes in that year. This leaves $20,000 of the carry-forward remaining. $10,000 of this would be used to offset income in the next year (1984), and the other $10,000 would be applied against 1985 taxable income.

If the carry-forward had not been used up by the end of the seventh year of carry-forward, the remaining portion would have been lost. The provision has encouraged profitable firms to merge with firms having losses. The acquiring firm could then apply those losses against its *own* profits and thereby have some tax-free earnings. There are certain requirements which must be satisfied which have made this practice applicable in fewer situations in recent years.

Accounting methods used for tax purposes

Cash versus accrual basis. The tax law allows a business to use a modified cash basis of accounting in determining taxable income *unless* inventories are a significant factor in producing earnings. (The basis is described as "modified" because long-term assets cannot be charged to expense when purchased nor can all prepaid expenses (such as a three-year insurance premium) be deducted when paid.) Also revenues must be reported when *constructively received* even though the cash is not yet in the possession of the business. For instance, a check received at the end of the year is considered to be revenue even though it has not been cashed. The accrual basis is mandatory for firms having substantial inventories. Since the timing of revenues and expenses is altered by the use of these two different methods, an executive may determine that either the cash or the accrual basis offers a tax advantage to the company.

Accounting for inventories. There are several different ways of accounting for inventories (see Chapter 9). Each of them assumes a different flow of costs and thus results in different taxable income if used for tax purposes. In recent years many firms have adopted Lifo (last-in, first-out). The last goods purchased are assumed to be the first ones sold. Under this method, during periods of rising prices, the most recent *higher* costs are charged against revenues and the asset, inventory, is shown at lower earlier costs. The result is lower net earnings and lower taxes. The tax law requires that a company may only use the Lifo method for tax purposes if it uses it for financial statement purposes.

Depreciation methods. The tax law permits the use of various methods of depreciation. Two of the best known of these are the sum-of-the-years'-digits method and the uniform-rate-on-declining-balance method. Both of these methods result in depreciation charges higher than those under the straight-line method during the early life of an asset and lower charges during the later years. The use of these methods for tax purposes results initially in lower taxes because taxable income is lower during the early life of the asset. The tax savings in early years can be reinvested and thus increase the earnings per share available for common stockholders for the entire period.

Numerous other examples could be given for showing that business decisions are influenced greatly by their tax effects, but this discussion was intended to be illustrative rather than comprehensive. With the advent of relatively high tax rates, tax planning became an essential function of management.

The tax laws are extremely complicated and are changing constantly. Those who desire to stay current with the status of the law, and with the interpretations of the law made by courts, must specialize in this area.

**INTERPERIOD
INCOME TAX
ALLOCATION**

As already mentioned, taxable income and net earnings before income taxes (for simplicity, pretax earnings) for a corporation may differ sharply for a number of reasons. In fact, the tax return may show a loss, while the earnings statement shows positive net earnings. This raises questions as to what amount of income taxes should be shown in the earnings statement. The answer lies in the nature of the items causing the difference between taxable income and pretax earnings. Some of the differences are *permanent differences*—interest earned on municipal bonds is never taxable, but always is included in net earnings. Such differences cause no problem—the estimated actual amount of income taxes payable for the year is shown on the earnings statement even if this results in reporting only $1,000 of income taxes on $100,000 of pretax earnings.

The reasons for other differences between taxable income and pretax earnings are called *timing differences*—that is, items which will be included in both taxable income and in pretax earnings, but in *different periods*. The items involved thus will have a tax effect. When this is true, generally accepted accounting principles require that *tax allocation* procedures be applied to prevent the presentation of possibly misleading information.

To illustrate, assume (1) that a firm acquires for $200,000 a machine whose estimated life is four years with no salvage value expected; (2) that it uses the straight-line depreciation method for financial reporting purposes and the sum-of-the-years'-digits methods for tax purposes; (3) that net earnings before depreciation and income taxes for each year of the machine's life will be $150,000; (4) that there are no other items which cause differences between pretax earnings and taxable income; and (5) that the tax rate is 40 percent (to simplify the illustration).

Under these circumstances, the actual tax liability for each year will be as shown in Illustration 27.4.

If the amounts of income taxes computed above were shown in the earnings statements for the years 1979–82, net earnings would be as shown in Illustration 27.5. To report net earnings as declining this sharply in the circumstances described would, under generally accepted accounting principles, be considered quite misleading. Especially objectionable is the reporting of sharply increased net earnings for 1979 brought about by deducting only $28,000 of income taxes on $100,000 of pretax earnings when the current tax rate is 40 percent and all of the items making up the $100,000 will appear on the tax return. Under such circumstances, it is contended that the income taxes should be $40,000. This is supported by drawing attention to the fact

**Illustration 27.4:
Calculation of tax liability**

	1979	1980	1981	1982	Total
Earnings before depreciation and income taxes	$150,000	$150,000	$150,000	$150,000	$600,000
Depreciation (sum-of-the years'-digits basis)	80,000	60,000	40,000	20,000	200,000
Taxable income	$ 70,000	$ 90,000	$110,000	$130,000	$400,000
Income taxes	$ 28,000	$ 36,000	$ 44,000	$ 52,000	$160,000

Illustration 27.5:
Net earnings with no tax
allocation

	1979	1980	1981	1982	Total
Earnings before depreciation and income taxes	$150,000	$150,000	$150,000	$150,000	$600,000
Depreciation (straight-line method)	50,000	50,000	50,000	50,000	200,000
Earnings before income taxes	$100,000	$100,000	$100,000	$100,000	$400,000
Income taxes	28,000	36,000	44,000	52,000	160,000
Net Earnings	$ 72,000	$ 64,000	$ 56,000	$ 48,000	$240,000

that there is no actual reduction in taxes. Total income taxes for the four years will be $160,000. Therefore, any taxes not paid in the early years of the machine's life will be paid later—note the $52,000 of taxes in 1982—when, as the accountant puts it, the timing differences reverse. That occurs, in this case, when depreciation is less per tax return than for financial reporting purposes.

Consequently, tax allocation procedures should be applied in the above circumstances. Under such procedures, the earnings statement for each of the four years would be as shown in Illustration 27.6.

Illustration 27.6:
Net earnings with tax
allocation

	Each year	Total for four years
Earnings before depreciation and income taxes..................	$150,000	$600,000
Depreciation	50,000	200,000
Earnings before income taxes	$100,000	$400,000
Income taxes	40,000	160,000
Net Earnings	$ 60,000	$240,000

Under tax allocation, reported net earnings are $60,000 per year. Note especially that reported income taxes are $40,000 in each year which seems logical when pretax earnings are $100,000 and the tax rate is 40 percent.

The entries to record the income tax expense, the income taxes payable, the income taxes paid, and the changes in the deferred income taxes payable are summarized in the T-accounts below. The (1) refers to 1979, the (2) to 1980, and so forth.

Federal Income Tax Expense		Federal Income Taxes Payable				Deferred Federal Income Taxes Payable			
(1)	40,000	(1a)	28,000	(1)	28,000	(3)	4,000	(1)	12,000
(2)	40,000	(2a)	36,000	(2)	36,000	(4)	12,000	(2)	4,000
(3)	40,000	(3a)	44,000	(3)	44,000				
(4)	40,000	(4a)	52,000	(4)	52,000				

The entries keyed with the letter *a* indicate the debits made to record the actual cash paid in settlement of the federal income tax liability. Note that the amount of expense recognized remained constant at $40,000 even though the tax liability increased from $28,000 for 1979 to $52,000 for 1982 by $8,000 increments. The normalizing of the tax expense for each year was accomplished by entries in the Deferred Federal Income Taxes Payable account. As can be seen, the tax expense for the four years is $160,000, and the tax payments for the four years also sum to $160,000. The only difference is that the tax expense is not charged to the year in the same amount as the actual liability for the year. Note, also, that in our simplified example the Deferred Federal Income Taxes Payable account has a zero balance at the end of four years.

Actual business experience has shown that once a Deferred Federal Income Taxes Payable account is established, it is seldom decreased or reduced to zero. The reason is that most businesses acquire new depreciable assets, at perhaps higher prices. The result is that depreciation for tax purposes continues to be greater than depreciation for financial reporting purposes, and the balance in the Deferred Federal Income Taxes Payable account also continues to grow. For this reason, many accountants seriously question the validity of tax allocation in circumstances such as those described above. But discussion of this controversial issue must be left to a more advanced text. In the above example, the Deferred Federal Income Taxes Payable account would be reported as a long-term liability on the balance sheet because the item causing its existence (the machine) is classified as a long-term asset.

In some instances, taxable income will be greater than pretax earnings because of timing differences such as when rent collections received in advance are taxed before they are considered earned revenue for accounting purposes. Application of tax allocation procedures in such circumstances will give rise to a balance in an asset account titled Deferred Federal Income Taxes or possibly Prepaid Federal Income Taxes. This account would be reported as a current asset or a non-current asset depending upon whether the item causing it to exist is classified as a current or long-term liability.

NEW TERMS INTRODUCED IN CHAPTER 27

By-product—the waste material (which sometimes has a small market value compared to the main product) which results from the production of a product or products.

Differential cost (expense)—the difference between the amounts of relevant costs for two alternatives.

Differential revenue—the difference between the amounts of relevant revenues for two alternatives.

Dumping—selling goods in foreign markets at less than full cost; usually prohibited by international trade agreements.

Future costs—costs which would be incurred at some time in the future.

Incremental revenue and cost—see differential revenue and differential expense.

Joint product costs—those costs incurred up to the point where joint products are split off from each other.

Joint products—two or more products resulting from a common raw material or manufacturing process.

Make-or-buy decision—a situation in which management must choose between purchasing or manufacturing a needed part or product.

Marginal cost—the increase in total costs resulting from the production and sale of one more unit.

Opportunity cost—the potential benefit that is foregone from not following the best alternative course of action.

Permanent differences—differences between taxable income and pretax earnings caused by tax provisions which exclude an item of expense or revenue or gain or loss as an element of taxable income.

Relevant costs—future costs which differ between alternatives.

Robinson-Patman Act—makes price discrimination illegal unless it is justified by differences in costs of delivery or selling.

Scarce resource—a factor of production that is absolutely limited in supply.

Sunk costs—past costs about which nothing can be done; they are irrelevant to decisions.

Tax allocation (interperiod)—a procedure whereby the tax effects of an element of expense or revenue, loss or gain, which will affect taxable income are allocated to the period in which the item is recognized for accounting purposes, irrespective of the period in which it is recognized for tax purposes.

Timing differences—items that will affect taxable income and pretax earnings but in different periods.

DEMONSTRATION PROBLEM 27–1

Following are sales and other operating data for the three products made and sold by the Muntz Company:

	Total	Product A	Product B	Product C
Sales	$800,000	$400,000	$250,000	$150,000
Manufacturing costs:				
Fixed	$120,000	$ 50,000	$ 25,000	$ 45,000
Variable	500,000	240,000	200,000	60,000
Total	$620,000	$290,000	$225,000	$105,000
Gross margin	$180,000	$110,000	$ 25,000	$ 45,000
Selling expenses:				
Fixed	$ 15,000	$ 5,000	$ 5,000	$ 5,000
Variable	50,000	15,000	10,000	25,000
Administrative expenses:				
Fixed	20,000	5,000	3,000	12,000
Variable	20,000	10,000	3,000	7,000
Total	$105,000	$ 35,000	$ 21,000	$ 49,000
Operating Earnings	$ 75,000	$ 75,000	$ 4,000	$ (4,000)

In view of the operating loss shown above for Product C, the company's management is considering dropping that product. All variable costs are direct costs and would be eliminated; and all fixed costs are allocated, indirect costs and would not be eliminated. Assume that the space used to produce Product C would be left idle.

Required:

a. Would you recommend elimination of Product C? Give supporting computations.

b. Based upon the information given, determine if it would be profitable to alter the product mix if (assume that total amount of fixed costs and expenses will not change):

1. Dropping Product C allows the company to produce and sell $150,000 more of Product B at the existing selling price and variable cost per unit of Product B.
2. Dropping Product C allows the company to produce and sell $150,000 more of Product A at existing prices and variable cost per unit.
3. What does this tell you about the company's current product mix? Show supporting computations.

Solution to demonstration problem 27-1

a.

Relevant revenues and expenses (costs) of alternatives

	(1) Keep Product C	(2) Eliminate Product C	Differential
Revenues	$150,000	–0–	$150,000
Expenses (all variable)	92,000	–0–	92,000
Net advantage of retaining Product C			$ 58,000

If Product C is dropped, operating earnings will be reduced from $75,000 to $17,000. The difference of $58,000 between sales and variable costs of Product C represents a contribution to the fixed costs of the company which, if Product C is dropped, become chargeable against the remaining products. Product C should not be eliminated.

b.

1. It would not be profitable as Product B has a lower contribution margin than does Product C. Switching to B would decrease profits as follows:

Increase in sales of B	$150,000
Less: Increased variable expenses, 85.2%	127,800
Contribution of B	$ 22,200

This is less than the $58,000 excess of revenue over variable costs furnished by Product C.
   (Note: 85.2 percent computed as $200,000 + $10,000 + $3,000 = $213,000 Variable expenses ÷ $250,000 Sales.)

2. Again, it would not be profitable to switch, as the profit margin is not as great on Product A. Switching to Product A would decrease profits:

Increase in sales of A	$150,000
Less: Variable costs, 66.25%	99,375
Contribution of A	$ 50,625

This is less than the $58,000 contributed by Product C.

3. Product C, which shows a loss on the conventional earnings statement, actually provides the largest percentage contribution margin. Instead of deleting Product C, the company could become more profitable if greater amounts of Product C could be sold and produced at existing prices. Comparison of the three products indicate:

	A	B	C
Sales	$400,000	$250,000	$150,000
Variable costs	265,000	213,000	92,000
Contribution margin	$135,000	$ 37,000	$ 58,000
Percent contribution (contribution margin/sales)	33.75%	14.8%	38.7%

DEMONSTRATION PROBLEM 27–2

The records of the Vista Corporation show the following for the calendar year just ended:

Sales	$375,000
Interest earned on—	
State of New Jersey Bonds	3,000
City of Miami Bonds	1,500
Essex County, Ohio, School District No. 2 Bonds	375
Cost of goods sold and other expenses	315,000
Loss on sale of capital asset	3,000
Gain on sale of capital asset acquired two years ago	7,500
Allowable extra depreciation deduction for tax purposes	4,500
Dividends declared	15,000
Revenue received in advance, considered taxable income of this year	3,000
Contribution made to influence legislation (included in the $315,000 listed above)	300

Required:

a. Present a schedule showing the computation of taxable income.

b. Compute the amount of the corporation's tax that was payable for the current year. (Use the rates mentioned in the text. Also assume the company acquired $100,000 of new equipment during the year and qualified for the full amount of investment credit as a reduction in taxes.)

c. Prepare the adjusting entry necessary to recognize federal income tax expense assuming income tax allocation procedures are followed. (The reduction in taxes caused by the investment credit is to be deducted from federal income tax expense and federal income tax currently payable.) The only permanent differences are the contribution to influence legislation and the non-taxable interest.

Solution to demonstration problem 27–2

a.

VISTA CORPORATION Computation of Taxable Income and Income Taxes Current Year	
Sales	$375,000
Cost of goods sold and other expenses	315,000
Reported earnings from operations	$ 60,000
Add: Revenue received in advance	3,000
Contribution to influence legislation	300
	$ 63,300
Less: Allowable additional depreciation	4,500
Taxable income (exclusive of capital gains)	$ 58,800

b. Computation of tax:

17% of first $25,000	$ 4,250
20% on the next $25,000	5,000
30% on the remaining $8,800	2,640
28% of net capital gain ($7,500 − $3,000 = $4,500); $4,500 × 28%	1,260
Total tax before investment credit	$13,150
Less: Investment credit ($100,000 × 10%)	10,000
Total tax payable	$ 3,150

c.

Federal Income Tax Expense	3,600*	
Federal Income Taxes Payable		3,150
Deferred Federal Income Taxes Payable		450

* Federal income tax expense is computed as follows:

Reported earnings from operations	$60,000
Add permanent difference—contribution to influence legislature.............................	300
Base for computing tax expense	$60,300

Computation of taxes:

$25,000 @ 17%	$ 4,250
$25,000 @ 20%	5,000
$10,300 @ 30%	3,090
Tax on $60,300	$12,340
Add tax on net long-term capital gain	1,260
	$13,600
Deduct reduction in taxes caused by investment credit	10,000
Tax expense	$ 3,600

QUESTIONS

1. Which costs are relevant in deciding between two or more alternative courses of action?

2. What are sunk costs? Why are they not relevant? Give some examples of sunk costs.

3. Define a differential cost and a differential revenue. What other terms are used in place of these terms?

4. How do you calculate the net benefit or advantage of selecting one alternative over another?

5. What is an opportunity cost? How is this cost used in deciding between two or more alternatives?

6. How should management select a selling price for a given product?

7. Why might an American manufacturer sell its product in South America for a price considerably under that which it receives in the United States?

8. What is the decision rule for deciding whether to eliminate a product, a department, or sales to a certain type of customer?

9. In the process of manufacturing gasoline, certain tars are produced which have only a nominal value of $0.01 per gallon. Further processing costs for the tars of $0.03 per gallon are incurred, and then the tars are sold. The average cost per gallon is 6 cents, while sales after processing are made at 5 cents. How would you determine whether this processing of the tars should be discontinued?

10. A company is seeking an additional product to manufacture in presently idle space in a building which it owns. The company currently heats and maintains the entire building. One new product under consideration would require the addition of a number of new employees and some equipment. Indicate how you would proceed to reach a decision with regard to adding the product.

11. You are the president of a small corporation and currently are purchasing a part needed in the product you manufacture and sell. You are considering manufacturing this part yourself. What factors should be taken into consideration in reaching your decision?

12. Suppose that the average fixed cost per unit of a given product is $2 and that the product is being sold at a price which covers only $0.80 of the fixed cost. Should the manufacture and sale of the product be discontinued? Why?

13. You overhear three students arguing. Their discussion proceeds as follows:

Student No. 1: "Management should strive to maximize earnings after taxes."
Student No. 2: "Management should strive to maximize the total dollar amount of earnings available for common stockholders."
Student No. 3: "Management should strive to maximize earnings per share available for common stockholders."

Are they all saying essentially the same thing? If not, which one do you most nearly agree with and why?

14. While the corporate form of organization may have other advantages, it certainly does not offer a tax advantage for the stockholders of a corporation. Comment.

15. A classmate states: "Why all the fuss about deferring revenues and recognizing expenses sooner for tax purposes? All net taxable earnings are taxed eventually anyway. It is only a matter of putting off the payment. I don't think these manipulations are worth the effort." Comment.

16. What factors might cause net earnings on a corporation's earnings statement to differ from its taxable income?

17. Name some specific types of management decisions in which tax considerations play an important part.

18. Classified among the long-term liabilities of the A Corporation is an account entitled, Deferred Federal Income Taxes Payable. Explain the nature of this account.

EXERCISES

E-1. Assume you had invested $240 in a lawn mower to set up a lawn mowing business for the summer. During the first week, you are presented with two opportunities. You can mow the grounds at a housing development (at a fee of $300) or you can help paint a garage (at a fee of $250). The additional costs you will incur are $50 and $20, respectively. These costs include $4 under each alternative for a pair of gloves which will last about one week. Prepare a schedule showing:

a. The relevant revenues and expenses (costs).

b. The differential revenue and expense.

c. The net benefit or advantage of selecting one alternative over the other.

E-2. The Lane Corporation is operating at 80 percent of capacity producing 8,000 units. Variable costs amount to $60 per unit. Wholesaler A offers to buy up to 2,000 units at $70 per unit. Wholesaler B proposes to buy 1,500 units at $75 per unit. Which offer, if any, should the Lane Corporation accept?

E-3. Two companies, Halstead, Inc., and Kelsey and Company, are competitors. Halstead, Inc., has just in-stalled the latest automated equipment so that its fixed costs are $60,000. Kelsey and Company, however, operates in a run-down plant with only $30,000 of fixed costs. Both companies have $100,000 in sales with gross margins of 20 percent. Compute gross margins for the two companies assuming a 10 percent drop in sales volume.

E-4. In the situation described in Exercise E-3 which company can bid lower on a special order to regain lost sales? Why?

E-5. Analysis of Product A reveals that it is losing $5,000 annually. Ten thousand units of Product A are sold at a price of $5 per unit each year. If variable costs are $4 per unit, what would be the increase (decrease) in company earnings if Product A were eliminated?

E-6. Department 1 of the Slate Company has revenues of $100,000, variable expenses of $40,000, direct fixed expenses of $20,000, and allocated, indirect fixed expenses of $50,000. If the department is eliminated what will be the effect on earnings?

E-7. The Lobek Company manufactures two joint products. At the split-off point they have sales values of:

Product 1 . . . . $7/unit
Product 2 . . . . $5/unit

After further processing costing $4 and $3, respectively, they can be sold for $15 and $7, respectively. Should further processing be done on both products? Why?

E–8. The Synder Corporation currently is manufacturing 20,000 units per year of a part used in its final product. The cost of producing this part is $21.50 each. The variable portion of this cost consists of raw materials of $12, direct labor of $6.50, and manufacturing overhead of $1. The company could earn $20,000 per year from the space now used to manufacture this part. Assuming equal quality and availability, what is the maximum price Synder Corporation should pay to buy the part rather than make it?

E–9 a. Wexley Corporation has taxable income of $10,000, $25,000, and $40,000 in its first three years of operations. Determine the amount of federal income taxes it will incur each year.

b. Assume that in the fourth year of operations the Wexley Corporation suffered a loss of $40,000. How much could it recover in back taxes?

E–10. If Ansley Corporation has aftertax earnings of $120,000 what is the amount of reduction in taxes payable (using 1979 rates) produced by its outstanding 6 percent bonds having a face value of $400,000?

E–11. The pretax earnings of the R Corporation for a given year amount to $200,000 while its taxable income is only $160,000. The difference is attributable entirely to additional depreciation taken for tax purposes. If the current income tax rate is assumed to be 40 percent, give the entry to record the income taxes chargeable to the year and the tax liability for the year.

PROBLEMS, SERIES A

P27–1–A. A state government has asked for bids on an order for 200,000 units of Product X. The Rex Company, which has a productive capacity of 1,000,000 units and is currently operating at 80 percent of capacity, is considering making a bid for the government contract. The Rex Company's fixed costs amount to $4,000,000, and its variable costs are $40 per unit.

Required:

a. What is the minimum price to be bid by the company?

b. Present two earnings statements, the first assuming that the bid is unsuccessful and that the price on regular sales is $60 per unit, and the second assuming that the contract is obtained at a bid price of $50 per unit, while regular sales are at $60 per unit.

P27–2–A. The productive capacity of the plant of the Reetz Corporation is 400,000 units, at which level of operations its variable costs amount to $4,800,000. When the plant is completely idle, fixed costs amount to $500,000. At 60 percent of capacity and below, its fixed costs are $720,000, and at levels above 60 percent of capacity its fixed costs are $1,100,000 (this results from the presence of step variable costs). Assume that when the Reetz Corporation is operating at 60 percent of capacity, an order is received from the Foreign Sales Corporation for 160,000 units at $16 each. If its present market for 240,000 units would not be affected, should the order be accepted? Show your computations in support of your answer.

P27–3–A. Bill Grant, the president of Grant's, Inc., is very concerned over the fact that he is unable to generate any net earnings from Department 3. He has devoted considerable time and a disproportionate part of the expenditures of the business to this department and it still shows a loss. He has reached the point where he is considering closing the department and expanding his other two departments equally into the space now occupied by Department 3. He believes, however, that this move will neither increase the sales nor lower the costs of the other two departments but simply will relieve some overcrowding. In condensed form, the earnings statement for the year ended September 30, 1981, is:

	Dept. 1	Dept. 2	Dept. 3	Total
Net sales	$120,000	$80,000	$40,000	$240,000
Cost of goods sold	80,000	$50,000	$25,000	$155,000
Advertising expense	4,000	3,000	4,000	11,000
Sales salaries	10,000	7,000	3,000	20,000
Delivery expense	3,000	2,000	1,000	6,000
Buying expense	6,000	4,000	2,000	12,000
Occupancy expense	5,000	2,500	2,500	10,000
Administrative expense	7,500	5,000	3,500	16,000
Total expenses	$115,500	$73,500	$41,000	$230,000
Net earnings before income taxes	$ 4,500	$ 6,500	$ (1,000)	$ 10,000
Income taxes (credit)	765	1,105	(170)	1,700
Net Earnings (loss)	$ 3,735	$ 5,395	$ (830)	$ 8,300

For all departments, any direct expense would be eliminated if the department were eliminated. Indirect expenses would not be eliminated. Advertising expense is direct to the extent of $3,000 to each of the three departments, while the balance is allocable equally to 1 and 3. All of the sales salaries and related expenses are direct. Delivery expense is all indirect and is allocated on the basis of sales; no reduction is expected if Department 3 is closed. Buying expenses are allocated on the basis of purchases ($90,000, $60,000, and $30,000). If Department 3 is discontinued, these expenses will be reduced by $2,000. Occupancy expenses are all indirect and fixed and are allocated on the basis of square feet of space occupied (10,000, 5,000, and 5,000). Departments 1 and 2 will each take equal amounts of the space formerly occupied by 3 if 3 is closed. Administrative expenses are direct to the extent of $4,000, $1,000, and $2,000 to 1, 2, and 3. The indirect expense is allocated on the basis of estimated direct administrative officer time spent on each department which is in the ratio of $7:8:3$.

Required:

a. Present an earnings statement for the year ended September 30, 1981, showing the departmental earnings that would have resulted if Department 3 had been closed during the year.

b. Should Department 3 be closed? Explain.

P27–4–A. The Arnet Corporation at the present time is purchasing a certain part for assembly into the company's final product. Because the purchase price has been rising steadily during the past several months, the company is considering using its own facilities to manufacture the part. The company's cost accountant has estimated the manufacturing cost per unit to be as follows:

Direct materials	$21.12
Direct labor	28.90
Overhead, fixed	18.48
Overhead, variable	9.62
	$78.12

For the most part, the fixed overhead consists of depreciation on factory buildings and equipment already owned by the company and used in its manufacturing processes. The price being currently paid to the company's supplier of the part is $61.30 per unit.

Required:

a. Assume that the plant of the Arnet company is operating at a level substantially below capacity. Would you recommend that the company undertake to manufacture the part rather than to continue to buy it? Support your answer with computations.

b. Assume that the company's plant is now operating profitably at full capacity. How would you determine whether the company should make or buy the part?

P27–5–A. The Sparks Company is planning to manufacture three products (R, S, and T). Its production capacity is limited to 4,000 hours per year, and it is trying to decide what the proper production-sales mix should be to maximize earnings.

Relevant data are the following:

	Products		
	R	S	T
Contribution margin per unit	$8.00	$5.00	$2.50
No. of units which can be produced per hour	8	10	15
Maximum production if only this product is produced (taking into account specialized equipment requirements) ...	18,000	25,000	35,000
Maximum demand for this product	10,000	35,000	50,000

Required:

Prepare a schedule which includes the—

a. Contribution margin per hour for each product.

b. Ranking of the products in terms of contribution margin per hour.

c. Number of units of each product which should be produced.

d. Time required to produce each product.

e. Total contribution margin (by product and in total).

P27–6–A. The records of the Wilhide Corporation show the following for the calendar year just ended:

Sales	$750,000
Interest earned on—	
State of New York Bonds	6,000
City of Detroit Bonds	3,000
Howard County, Ohio, School District No. 1 Bonds	750
Cost of goods sold and other expenses	630,000
Loss on sale of capital asset	6,000
Gain on sale of capital asset acquired two years ago	15,000
Allowable extra depreciation deduction for tax purposes	9,000
Dividends declared	30,000
Revenue received in advance, considered taxable income	
of this year	6,000
Contribution made to influence legislation (included	
in the $630,000 listed above)	600

Required:

a. Present a schedule showing the computation of taxable income.

b. Compute the corporation's tax for the current year. (Use the tax rates mentioned in this chapter.)

P27–7–A. The Natcher Company had the following amounts of taxable earnings (loss) in the years indicated.

1979	$30,000
1980	20,000
1981	60,000
1982 . . . .[See parts **(a)**, **(b)**, and **(c)** below.]	
1983	40,000
1984	10,000
1985	50,000
1986	70,000
1987	80,000
1988	65,000

Assume that the rates for 1979 are in effect for the entire period.

Required:

a. If the loss in 1982 were $110,000, how much would the company recover in back taxes?

b. If the loss in 1982 were $180,000, how much would the company have to pay in taxes for the period 1983–88?

c. If the loss in 1982 were $400,000, how much would the company have to pay in taxes for the period 1983–88?

d. If there is a remaining unused carry-forward at the end of seven years, what happens to it?

P27–8–A. On January 1 of year 1, Alexander Corporation acquires a machine for $100,000 which is expected to have a four-year life and no salvage value. The company decides to use the sum-of-the-years'-digits method of depreciation for tax purposes and the straight-line method for book purposes. There are no other timing differences. Net earnings before depreciation and income taxes are $100,000 for each of the four years.

Required:

a. Prepare a schedule showing taxable income and income taxes due for each of the four years (assuming a 40 percent tax rate for the sake of simplicity).

b. Prepare a schedule showing net earnings after taxes as it will appear on the earnings statement assuming that income tax allocation procedures are followed.

c. Prepare the year-end adjusting entry required at the end of each of the four years to recognize federal income tax expense.

PROBLEMS, SERIES B

P27–1–B. A company is considering making a bid for a government contract for 100,000 units of its product. The company's productive capacity is 1,000,000 units, and it is currently operating at 80 percent of capacity. Its fixed costs amount to $5,000,000, and its variable expenses are $18 per unit.

Required:

a. Compute the minimum bid to be made by the company.

b. Present two earnings statements, the first assuming that the bid is unsuccessful and that the price on regular sales is $30 per unit, and the second assuming that the contract is obtained at a bid price of $24 per unit and that regular sales continue at $30 per unit.

P27–2–B. When the plant of the Ace Manufacturing Company is completely idle, fixed costs amount to $600,000. When the plant operates at levels of 50 percent of capacity and below, its fixed costs are $700,000, and at levels above 50 percent of capacity its fixed costs are $1,000,000. The company's variable costs at full capacity (100,000 units) amount to $1,500,000.

Assume that when the Ace Manufacturing Company is operating at half its capacity, an order is received from the Overseas Mail Order Company for 50,000 units at $30 each. If its present market for 50,000 units at $50 per unit would not be affected, should the order be accepted? Show computations in support of your answer showing the net earnings from regular sales and the level of earnings which would result if the order is accepted.

P27–3–B. The following data pertain to a given company:

In view of the operating loss shown above for Product 2, the company's management is considering dropping that product. All variable costs are direct costs and would be eliminated and all fixed costs are indirect costs and would not be eliminated. Assuming Product 2's volume would be lost to the company if it were dropped, would you recommend elimination of that product? Give supporting computations.

P27–4–B. Based upon the information given in Problem 27–3–B, assume that the product mix of the firm is technologically interchangeable. The company can delete one product and produce a given amount of the existing other products without changes in unit variable costs, selling price, or total fixed costs.

Assume that dropping Product 2 will allow the company to explore these alternatives:

1. Produce $275,000 more of Product 3 (at selling price).
2. Produce $250,000 more of Product 1.
3. Produce $100,000 more of Product 1 and $200,000 additional of Product 3.
4. Produce $150,000 more of Product 1 and $100,000 additional of Product 3.

Required:

a. What is the best alternative (show computations)?

b. Selecting the best alternative, show what the adjusted sales and net earnings would be.

P27–5–B. The new president, Guy Rex, of Rexford, Inc., is giving serious consideration to discontinuing Department B. He notes that the earnings statements of the

	Total	Product 1	Product 2	Product 3
Sales	$1,000,000	$500,000	$300,000	$200,000
Manufacturing costs:				
Fixed	$ 150,000	$ 75,000	$ 35,000	$ 40,000
Variable	650,000	300,000	250,000	100,000
Total	$ 800,000	$375,000	$285,000	$140,000
Gross margin	$ 200,000	$125,000	$ 15,000	$ 60,000
Selling costs:				
Fixed	$ 25,000	$ 20,000	$ 4,000	$ 1,000
Variable	75,000	20,000	20,000	35,000
Administrative costs:				
Fixed	15,000	10,000	3,000	2,000
Variable	35,000	15,000	5,000	15,000
Total	$ 150,000	$ 65,000	$ 32,000	$ 53,000
Operating Earnings	$ 50,000	$ 60,000	$ (17,000)	$ 7,000

past few years show the department operating at a loss. He also notes that the other two departments seem quite badly crowded and in need of additional space. He doubts, however, that the closing of Department B will increase the sales of these two departments. In condensed form, the earnings statement for the year ending June 30, 1981, is:

Direct materials	$16.86
Direct labor	31.06
Overhead, variable	5.36
Overhead, fixed	15.20
	$68.48

The fixed overhead of $15.20 is composed for the most part of depreciation on factory buildings and equipment

	Dept. A	Dept. B	Dept. C	Total
Net sales	$240,000	$60,000	$100,000	$400,000
Cost of goods sold	$160,000	$37,500	$ 60,000	$257,500
Selling expenses	29,000	15,000	20,000	64,000
Delivery expenses	6,000	1,500	2,500	10,000
Buying expenses	14,500	3,000	5,500	23,000
Occupancy expenses	9,000	3,000	6,000	18,000
Administrative expenses	12,000	3,000	5,000	20,000
Total expenses	$230,500	$63,000	$ 99,000	$392,500
Net earnings from operations	$ 9,500	$ (3,000)	$ 1,000	$ 7,500
Financial charges earned	3,000	750	1,250	5,000
Net earnings before taxes	$ 12,500	$ (2,250)	$ 2,250	$ 12,500
Federal income taxes (credit)	2,125	(382)	382	2,125
Net Earnings (loss)	$ 10,375	$ (1,868)	$ 1,868	$ 10,375

The president of the company has asked you to express your opinion on the desirability of the contemplated closing of Department B. He tells you that he believes that all of the selling expenses and half of the buying, delivery, and administrative expenses charged to Department B will be eliminated upon the closing of the department. Also, all of the financial charges earned and allocated to Department B will be eliminated if the department is closed.

Required:

State your opinion on the desirability of closing Department B. Support your opinion with a schedule showing what the net earnings after taxes for the company as a whole would have been if Department B had been closed at the start of the accounting year ending June 30, 1981.

P27–6–B. In the production of a certain type of machine, the Bilko Products Company uses a part that is made by the company in its own plant at a cost of $68.48, as follows:

which have a variety of uses in the manufacturing process.

The Steven Corporation offers to provide the Bilko Products Company with 100,000 units of the part to meet its total needs at a price of $56.20 per unit.

Required:

a. Bilko Products Company's plant is operating at a level substantially lower than capacity. Should the offer be accepted? Support your answer with computations and explanations.

b. What is the highest acceptable purchase price, assuming that the facilities now used to produce the part could earn $50,000 annually in the best alternative use?

P27–7–B. The Manners Company is currently producing and selling three products (Tic, Tac, Toe). The company has limited production capacity of 5,000 hours per year. Management believes that earnings can be increased by changing the current sales mix.

Relevant data are the following:

	Products		
	Tic	Tac	Toe
Contribution margin per unit	$4	$10	$2
No. of units which can be produced per hour	5	3	12
Maximum production if only this product is produced (taking into account specialized equipment requirements)	15,000	9,000	35,000
Maximum demand for this product	20,000	12,000	18,000

Required:

Prepare a schedule which includes the—

a. Contribution margin per hour for each product.

b. Ranking of the products in terms of contribution margin per hour.

c. Number of units of each product which should be produced.

d. Time required to produce each product.

e. Total contribution margin (by product and in total).

P27–8–B. The Dana Company needed almost $200,-000 in cash to construct a new building. The financial officer for the company discovered that the amount could be raised by issuing $200,000 (face value) of bonds with an interest rate of 9 percent, or preferred stock of the same total par value but with a dividend rate of only 6 percent. The preferred stock is convertible into common stock, but conversion is not expected for a number of years. Which alternative results in greater earnings available for common shareholders in the immediate future under each of the following two different assumptions as to the expected level of earnings:

a. Earnings before interest and taxes (which equal taxable income before interest) of $100,000?

b. Earnings before interest and taxes (all taxable income before interest) of $20,000?

c. How do you explain the difference?

P27–9–B. The Jackson Company expects to have earnings before depreciation and income taxes of $200,000 each year for the period 1981–84. The company acquires a machine for $320,000, which is expected to last four years and have no salvage value at the end of that period. For financial accounting purposes the company uses the straight-line depreciation method, and for tax purposes it uses the sum-of-the-years'-digits method. Assume that the tax rate is 40 percent (for the sake of simplicity) and that there are no other items which cause differences between pretax earnings and taxable income.

Required:

a. Prepare a schedule showing the actual tax liability for each year.

b. Calculate the income tax expense that should be shown each year assuming income tax allocation procedures are to be used.

c. Prepare journal entries to record the tax expense and tax liability for each year.

d. Show how the entries prepared in part *(c)* would be summarized in T-accounts. How would the amounts appearing in these accounts eventually be cleared from the accounts?

BUSINESS DECISION PROBLEM 27–1

Use the data in Problem 27–3–A. The president of Grant's, Inc., has received an offer from the Tie Company, a nationwide retailer of men's ties, to lease the space now occupied by Department 3. The Tie Company offers to sign a long-term lease calling for a flat annual rental of $1,500 plus 5 percent of net sales, with the Grant company to provide the space and to pay all costs of heating, lighting, and air conditioning. The Tie Company states that it normally generates sales of $60,000 annually from a location such as this.

The change in expenses resulting from leasing the space now occupied by Department 3 will be the same as if Department 3 were eliminated except that the advertising in Departments 1 and 2 can be reduced by $500 in each department due to the heavier advertising of the Tie

Company. Deliveries will be made by Grant's for Tie Company without charge, and no change in the level of these expenses is anticipated. The equipment and fixtures now used in Department 3 have only a nominal value and will be sold. The proceeds will be used to redecorate the space for the lessee, so that no change in the level of expenses not already mentioned in Problem 27–3–A is expected from this move.

Required:

a. State your conclusion as to whether the offer to lease should be accepted after preparing schedules comparing the alternatives.

b. What other factors should be taken into consideration before a final decision is reached?

BUSINESS DECISION PROBLEM 27–2

Assume that the earnings statement in Problem 27–5–B is for the Andrews Department Store, Inc., and is representative of the past several years. The manager of the department, Bill Daniels, wishes to go into business for himself and has made an offer to the company to lease the space and the fixtures now being used by Department B. He offers an annual rental of 9 percent of net sales. The company would be expected to provide the heat, light, and air-conditioning services, and to provide the necessary delivery services. The lessee will be responsible for all other services and expenses necessary to operate the department.

You have been asked to review this proposal, to analyze the expenses, and to report on whether it should be accepted. Your analysis of the various expenses incurred reveals the following (all direct expenses of a department would be eliminated if the department were eliminated while the indirect expenses would not):

The direct delivery expenses for Departments A, B, and C are $600, $300, and $350; all of the rest are indirect.

The direct occupancy costs are $1,100, $350, and $500; all of the rest are indirect. The direct selling expenses are $25,000, $13,000, and $17,000, with the balance allocated on the basis of the number of employees (4, 2, and 3) in the three departments.

The buying expenses are direct to the extent of $8,500, $1,500, and $3,000. The balance is allocated in the ratio of 60, 15, and 25 percent, the ratio of gross purchases for the last year. All of the administrative expenses are allocated on the basis of net sales, although bad debts have consistently been 2 percent of net sales of each department.

Required:

a. State your conclusions regarding whether or not the offer to lease should be accepted and support your conclusion with comparative financial data.

b. Cite several other factors that should be considered in reaching a decision.

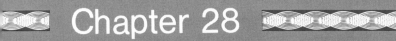

Chapter 28

Capital budgeting:

Long-range planning

INTRODUCTION TO CAPITAL BUDGETING

Business managers always face the problem of planning for the future. This planning includes the acquisition and retirement of buildings, equipment, and other major items of property.

Capital budgeting is the term used to describe the planning and financing for plant assets. Capital expenditures differ from ordinary expenditures in that they—

1. Usually involve very large sums of money;
2. Do not occur as often as expenditures for items such as payroll and inventory; and
3. Commit a firm to a long-term course of action.

The first two characteristics need no further explanation. But let us look at the third characteristic—commitment to a long-term course of action—in more detail. Once a firm builds a plant or undertakes some other capital expenditure, it becomes less flexible. Poor capital budgeting decisions can be very costly. If a poor capital budgeting decision is implemented, the firm can lose all or a part of the funds originally invested. In addition, the capital budgeting decision affects other day-to-day decisions such as the decision to hire and train employees to work with new equipment. If the new equipment is not purchased, the decision to hire and train becomes irrelevant. Other efforts such as marketing and procurement are lost if the capital budgeting decision is revoked. Another price of a poor capital budgeting decision is its harmful effect on the firm's competitive position and image.

Failure to invest enough funds in a good project can also be costly. Ford's Mustang provides an excellent example of such a situation. If Ford had known the reception the Mustang would receive at the time of the original capital budgeting decision, it would have expended more funds earlier. Because of its undercommitment of funds, Ford lost or deferred additional sales. Finally, the amount of funds available for investment is limited. Thus, once a capital investment decision is made, the alternatives to that investment are lost. The benefits or returns lost by rejecting the alternative investments are an opportunity cost.

PROJECT SELECTION: A GENERAL VIEW

The amount of capital available to an enterprise usually is limited. Given this constraint, management must select carefully among capital expenditure proposals. We will discuss the following techniques which are used to evaluate alternative proposals: payback, unadjusted rate of return, net present value, profitability index, and time-adjusted rate of return.

Time value of money

Before describing the various capital budgeting techniques, let us first discuss the important concept of the "time value of money." The meaning of the time value of money concept is that money received today is worth more than the same amount of money received a month or a year from now. This concept, which involves the use of compound interest, is known as the *present value* approach. (This was covered in the Appendix to Chapter 17, but it is briefly reviewed here for your convenience. If you do not need this review go directly to the section, "Net cash benefits.")

Future worth.   The concept of future worth will be explained first. Suppose a student deposits $500 in a savings account at the beginning of the year. Assume that the bank pays interest at a rate of 5 percent each year. At the end of the first year, the original deposit of $500 will have grown to $525 ($500 × 1.05). If the $525 is left in the savings account, then the amount will grow to $551.25 ($525 × 1.05) by the end of the second year. Notice that interest of $26.25 was earned in the second year whereas interest of only $25 was earned in the first year. The reason for the increased amount of interest is that interest in the second year has been earned on the first year's interest in addition to principal. The $25 earned in the first year was left in the account and added to the original deposit. Interest for the second year was computed on the amount of $525 ($500 principal and $25 accumulated interest). When periodic interest is computed on principal and all accumulated interest, interest is said to be compounded. At simple interest, the $500 deposit would have grown to only $550 in two years. At simple interest, the interest for each year would have been $25 ($500 × 0.05).

Note that the $551.25 amount at compound interest was calculated by multiplying $500 × 1.05 × 1.05. Since 1.05 × 1.05 is equal to $(1.05)^2$, a shortcut can be used. The compound amount at the end of two years is simply $500 × $(1.05)^2$, which equals $500 × 1.1025, or $551.25. From this the formula for the compound amount of $1 can be derived as being $(1 + i)^n$, where i is the interest rate per period and n is the number of periods involved.

Interest tables can be used to compute the sum to which any invested amount will grow at a given rate for a stated number of periods. From Table 1, Appendix B, at the end of this text, the amount to which an investment of $1 at 6 percent for five periods will grow can be seen to be $1.338226. The amount to which an investment of $2,000 would grow would be $2,000 times this amount (1.338226), or $2,676.45.

Present value.   While future worth is the value of a specific current investment at some future point in time, present value is the current value of a specified amount to be received at some future date. Present value, then, is the inverse of future worth. It is found by dividing the future sum by $(1 + i)^n$. Thus, the present value of $5,000 to be received one period from now at 6 percent is equal to $5,000 ÷ (1.06). The computation can also be expressed as $5,000 × 1/1.06 which is equal to $5,000 × 0.943396, or $4,716.98. Thus, $4,716.98 invested at 6 percent per period will grow to $5,000 in one period.

The present value of $5,000 due in two periods then is $5,000 ÷ $(1.06)^2$. Here again the computation can be expressed as $5,000 × $1/(1.06)^2$, which simplifies to $5,000 × 0.889996, or $4,449.98. Table 2, Appendix B, at the end of this text, contains the present values of $1 at different interest rates for different periods of time. The use of the table can be illustrated by determining the present value of $20,000 due in 30 periods at 12 percent. The present value of $1 due in 30 periods at 12 percent per period is $0.033. The present value of $20,000 due in 30 periods at 12 percent per period then is $660 ($20,000 × 0.033).

Present value of an annuity.   An *annuity* is defined as a series of equal payments equally spaced in time. The approach to the problem of valuing annuities can be illustrated by finding the present value, at 6 percent per period, of an annuity calling for the payment of $100 at the end of each of the next three periods. Through the use of Table 2, Appendix B, the present value of each of the $100 payments is as follows:

Present value of $100 due in—	
1 period is 0.943396 × $100	$ 94.34
2 periods is 0.889996 × $100	89.00
3 periods is 0.839619 × $100	83.96
Total present value of three $100 payments	$267.30

Such a procedure could become quite tedious if the annuity consisted of 50 or more payments. Fortunately, tables are also available showing the present values of an annuity of $1 per period for varying interest rates and periods. See Table 3, Appendix B. Thus, a single figure can be obtained from the table which represents the present value of an annuity of $1 per period for three periods at an interest rate of 6 percent per period. This figure is 2.673012. Multiplying 2.673012 by $100 (the number of dollars in each payment) yields the present value of the annuity of $267.30.

Net cash benefits   The *net cash benefit* (as used in capital budgeting) is the net cash inflow expected from a project in a period. It is the difference between the periodic cash inflows and the periodic cash outflows for a proposed project.

Asset addition.   Assume, for example, that a firm is considering the purchase of new equipment for $120,000. The equipment is expected to have a useful life of 15 years and no salvage value. It is expected that use of the new equipment will produce cash inflows (revenue) of $75,000 per year and cash outflows (costs) of $50,000 per year. Ignoring depreciation and taxes, the annual net cash inflow is computed as follows:

Cash inflows	$75,000
Cash outflows	50,000
Net cash inflow	$25,000

Depreciation and taxes.   Although depreciation does not involve a cash outflow, it is deductible in arriving at federal taxable income. Thus, depreciation reduces the amount of cash outflow for income taxes. This reduction in cash outflows for income taxes is a tax savings. It is made possible by a depreciation tax shield. A *tax shield* is the total amount of a tax deductible item. Thus, if depreciation is $8,000, the tax shield is $8,000. The tax shield results in a tax saving. The amount of the tax savings can be found by multiplying the tax rate by the amount of the depreciation tax shield. The formula is shown below:

Tax rate × Depreciation tax shield = Tax savings

Using the data in the previous example and assuming straight-line depreciation of $8,000 per year and a 40 percent tax rate, the amount of the tax savings is $3,200 (40 percent × $8,000 depreciation tax shield). Now, considering taxes and depreciation, the annual net cash inflow from the $120,000 of equipment is computed as follows:

	To compute net earnings	To compute cash flow
Cash inflows	$75,000	$75,000
Cash outflows	50,000	50,000
Net cash inflow before taxes	$25,000	$25,000
Depreciation	8,000	
Taxable income	$17,000	
Tax at 40%	6,800	6,800
Net earnings after taxes	$10,200	
Net cash inflow (after taxes)		$18,200

Considering taxes and depreciation, the net cash inflow is $18,200 instead of the $25,000 computed previously.

Asset replacements. Sometimes a firm has to decide whether or not to acquire new plant assets to replace existing plant assets. Such replacement decisions often occur when new and improved—faster and more efficient—machinery and equipment appear on the market.

The computation of the net cash flows is more difficult for a replacement decision than for an addition decision. To illustrate, assume that a company operates two machines that were purchased four years ago at a cost of $18,000 each. The estimated useful life of each machine is 12 years (with no salvage value). Each machine will produce 30,000 units of product each year. The annual cash costs (labor, repairs, etc.) of operating both machines total $14,000.

After the old machines have been used for four years, a new machine becomes available. The new machine can be acquired for $28,000 and has an estimated useful life of eight years (with no salvage value). It will produce 60,000 units annually at a cash cost of $10,000.

There must be a $28,000 cash outflow in the first year to acquire the new machine. The additional annual cash inflow from replacement is computed as follows:

	To compute tax	To compute cash flow
Cash operating costs:		
Old machines	$14,000	
New machines	10,000	
Difference—additional taxable income	$ 4,000	$4,000
Depreciation:		
Old machines ($18,000 ÷ 12) × 2	$ 3,000	
New machine ($28,000 ÷ 8)	3,500	
Difference—additional tax deduction	$ (500)	
Additional taxable income	$ 4,000	
Additional tax deduction	(500)	
Net increase in taxable income	$ 3,500	
Additional tax at 40%	1,400	1,400
Additional cash flow		$2,600

This example used straight-line depreciation. If an accelerated depreciation method is used, the tax shield is larger in the early years and smaller in the later years of the life of the asset.

Out-of-pocket and sunk costs. There is an important distinction between out-of-pocket costs and sunk costs. An *out-of-pocket cost* is one which requires the future use of resources or a future payment. It can be avoided or changed in amount. Future labor and repair costs are examples of out-of-pocket costs.

Sunk costs are costs that have already been incurred. Nothing can be done about sunk costs at the present time. They cannot be avoided or changed in amount. The price paid for a machine the minute it is acquired represents a sunk cost (before that moment it was an out-of-pocket cost). Its amount cannot be changed regardless of whether the machine is scrapped or used. Thus, depreciation is a sunk cost. Depletion and amortization of assets such as ore deposits and patents are also sunk costs. A sunk cost is a *past* cost, while an out-of-pocket cost is a *future* cost. Only the out-of-pocket costs (the future cash outlays) are relevant to capital budgeting decisions, while sunk costs are not.

Initial cost and salvage value. Any cash outflows necessary to acquire an asset and get it ready for use are part of the *initial cost* of the asset. If an investment has a salvage value, that value should be treated as a cash inflow in the year of the asset's disposal.

The cost of capital. The cost of capital is important in project selection. Certainly any acceptable proposal should offer a return that exceeds the cost of the funds used to finance it.

The *cost of capital,* usually expressed as a rate, may be computed on an aftertax basis. It measures the cost of all sources of capital (debt and equity) employed by a firm. For convenience, most current liabilities, such as accounts payable and federal income taxes payable, are treated as being costless. Everything else on the right (equity) side of the balance sheet has a cost.

One approach for determining the cost of capital is the weighted-average method. It considers the cost of funds from all sources.

Assume the following capital structure:

Long-term notes held by an insurance company (8%)	$1,250,000
Long-term notes held by a bank (9%)	625,000
Common stock	1,250,000
Retained earnings	1,875,000
Total	$5,000,000

Let us now compute the weighted-average cost of capital. The philosophy behind this method is that the company will have to maintain (approximately) the present proportions of debt and equity as it expands its capital structure. (We will not evaluate that proposition here.)

If, for the sake of simplicity, we assume a 50 percent income tax rate for corporations, the aftertax costs of the loans are 4 percent and 4.5 percent, respectively (interest expense is tax deductible). Thus, the aftertax cost of

Computation of
weighted-average cost
of capital

	Amount provided	Proportion of total		Aftertax cost	Weighted cost
Insurance company loan	$1,250,000	25.0%	×	4.0%	1.0000%
Bank loan	625,000	12.5	×	4.5	0.5625
Common stock	1,250,000	25.0	×	15.0	3.7500
Retained earnings	1,875,000	37.5	×	9.0	3.3750
	$5,000,000	100.0%			8.6875%

the notes held by the insurance company is found by multiplying the 8 percent interest cost by the 50 percent tax rate. Likewise, aftertax cost of the bank loan is found by multiplying the 9 percent interest cost by the 50 percent tax rate.

In theory, the cost of common stock is the expected earnings per share divided by the market price per share. In our example, we used a 15 percent rate of return under the following assumptions:

1. The market price per share is $100.
2. Expected earnings are $15 per share.

As a result, the cost of common stock is $15 ÷ $100, or 15 percent.

The cost of retained earnings is based on the following factors. The marginal tax bracket of the stockholders must be estimated. If they are all in the 40 percent bracket, they keep only 60 cents of each added dollar of income. If the stockholders keep only 60 cents on the dollar and if the $15 earnings per share were paid out to them, then the stockholders would have only $9 ($15 × 0.60) per share on an aftertax basis. If each stockholder receives $9 on a $100 investment, a 9 percent rate of return is made if all the earnings are paid out in dividends. If the firm can find investments earning more than 9 percent, the earnings should be retained by the firm instead of being distributed to the stockholders.

The 8.6875 percent cost of capital represents the weighted-average cost of all sources of capital currently being used by the firm. The subject of determining the cost of capital is a controversial topic in the literature of accounting and finance. There are various theories for determining it. The above represents only one possible method. We shall assume a cost of capital in the rest of the chapter.

PROJECT SELECTION: PAYBACK PERIOD

The payback period of an outlay is often computed to help in evaluating an investment proposal. The *payback period* is that period of time during which net cash savings from an investment must continue to recover the initial net cash outlay. In effect, it answers the question: How long will it take the new machine to pay for itself? The formula for the payback period is:

$$\text{Payback period} = \frac{\text{Initial cash outlay}}{\text{Annual net cash inflows (or benefits)}}$$

The payback period will be computed for the assets in the addition and replacement examples that begin under the heading "Net cash benefits" earlier in the chapter. The addition example involved equipment costing $120,000 and having a net cash inflow (after taxes) of $18,200 per year. Dividing the initial capital outlay, $120,000, by the annual net cash inflow of $18,200 reveals that 6.6 years would be required for the new equipment to pay for itself.

To compute the payback period for the new machine in the replacement example, the initial cash outlay of $28,000 is divided by the additional annual cash inflow of $2,600. The payback is 10.8 ($28,000 ÷ $2,600) years. But the new machine will last only eight years. Since the payback period is longer than the machine's useful life, the investment will not pay for itself. Therefore, the new machine should not be purchased.

When the payback period is used to evaluate investment proposals, the decision rule may be one of the following:

1. Select the investment with the shortest payback period.
2. Select only those investments that have a payback period of less than a specified number of years.

The payback period type of analysis has several important limitations. First, it ignores the period of time beyond the payback period. For example, consider two alternative investments, each requiring an initial outlay of $30,000. Proposal Y will return $6,000 per year for five years. Thus, it has a five-year payback period. Proposal Z will return $5,000 a year for eight years—a total return of $40,000. Thus, its payback period is six years. If the goal is to maximize earnings, Proposal Y should not be accepted just because it has a shorter payback period. It will take one more year to recover the investment in Proposal Z, but the returns from Proposal Z will continue for two years after the investment has been recovered.

Second, the payback method of analysis also ignores the time value of money. For example, consider the following net cash receipts expected from two capital proposals:

	Proposal A	Proposal B
First year	$15,000	$ 9,000
Second year	12,000	12,000
Third year	9,000	15,000
	$36,000	$36,000

If the cost of each proposal is $36,000, then each has a payback period of three years. But common sense tells us that the two are not equal. Money has a time value; it can be reinvested to increase earnings. Since the larger amounts are received sooner under Proposal A, it is preferable to Proposal B. Despite its faults, the payback method is used extensively in capital budgeting.

When annual cash flows or savings are uniform, the payback period is computed by dividing the initial investment by the annual cash flow (or savings). But, when the annual returns are uneven, a cumulative calculation must be used. For example, assume that a company is considering a proposal which costs $40,000 and is expected to last ten years. The expected annual cash inflows are shown as follows:

Year	Investment	Annual net cash inflows	Cumulative net cash inflows
0	$40,000	—	—
1	—	$8,000	$ 8,000
2	—	6,000	14,000
3	—	7,000	21,000
4	—	5,000	26,000
5	—	8,000	34,000
6	—	6,000	40,000
7	—	3,000	43,000
8	—	2,000	45,000
9	—	3,000	48,000
10	—	1,000	49,000

The payback period in this example is six years—the time it takes to recover the original investment.

PROJECT SELECTION: UNADJUSTED RATE OF RETURN

The *unadjusted rate of return* is computed by dividing the average future annual earnings (after taxes) from the project by the average amount of the investment (original outlay ÷ 2). Notice that annual earnings, and not net cash inflows, are used in the calculation.

To illustrate, assume that a firm is considering two proposals. The firm does not have enough funds to undertake both proposals. Both proposals have a useful life of three years.

Net cash inflow from operations (before taxes)

Proposal	Initial cost	Year 1	Year 2	Year 3	Average depreciation
1	$72,000	$45,000	$45,000	$45,000	$24,000
2	90,000	55,000	55,000	55,000	30,000

Assuming a 40 percent tax rate, the unadjusted rate of return is determined as follows:

	Proposal 1	Proposal 2
1. Average investment:		
Original outlay ÷ 2	$36,000	$45,000
Annual net cash inflow (before taxes)	$45,000	$55,000
Annual depreciation	24,000	30,000
Annual earnings (before taxes)	$21,000	$25,000
Income taxes at 40%	8,400	10,000
2. Average net earnings	$12,600	$15,000
Rate of return (2) ÷ (1)	35%	33⅓%

The unadjusted rate of return can also be computed with the following formula:

$$\text{Rate of return} = \frac{\left(\begin{array}{c}\text{Average annual}\\ \text{net cash inflow}\end{array} - \begin{array}{c}\text{Average annual}\\ \text{depreciation}\end{array}\right)(1 - \text{Tax rate})}{\text{Average investment}}$$

The unadjusted rate of return method does not consider the time value of money or the length of the period over which the return will be earned. It also allows a sunk cost, depreciation, to enter the calculation. In the illustration, Proposal 1 would be selected since it has the higher rate of return. The question of the timing of the cash flows is ignored. There are other variations used in the calculation of the unadjusted rate of return. For example, the rate is sometimes calculated using the gross investment (initial outlay) as the divisor.

PROJECT SELECTION: NET PRESENT VALUE METHOD AND THE PROFITABILITY INDEX

Net present value method.   The *net present value* method uses the concept of the time value of money. Management requires some minimum rate of return on its investments. This required rate of return should be the firm's cost of capital. Since it is difficult to determine the cost of capital, management often selects a target rate of return which it believes to be at or above the cost of capital.

The minimum rate of return is used to discount all expected cash flows (after tax effects) from a proposed investment. The present value of the expected cash flows is then compared with the investment amount. If the present value of the expected cash flows equals or exceeds the investment amount, the investment proposal is acceptable for further consideration. On the other hand, if the present value of the expected cash flows is less than the investment amount, the proposal should be rejected.

To illustrate, assume that a proposed investment will cost $25,000. It is expected that the net cash inflows (after taxes) for the next four years will be $8,000, $7,500, $8,000, and $7,500. Management requires a minimum rate of return of 14 percent. Is the project acceptable? To find out, the following analysis is needed:

	Net cash inflow (after taxes)	Present value of $1 at 14% (from Table II)	Total present value
First year	$8,000	0.877	$ 7,016.00
Second year	7,500	0.769	5,767.50
Third year	8,000	0.675	5,400.00
Fourth Year	7,500	0.592	4,440.00
Total			$22,623.50

Since the present value of the benefits, $22,623.50, is less than the initial outlay of $25,000, the project is not acceptable. Its net present value is equal to the present value of the benefits less the present value of its cost (the investment amount), which in this instance is −$2,376.50 ($22,623.50 − $25,000).

In general, a proposed investment is acceptable if it has a positive net present value. For example, assume the expected benefits from the investment had been $10,000 per year for four years. Then the present value of the benefits would have been (from Table 3, Appendix B):

$$\$10,000 \times 2.914 = \$29,140$$

This yields a net present value of $29,140 − $25,000 = $4,140. Since the net present value is positive, the investment proposal is acceptable. But there may be a competing project that has an even higher net present value. In general, when the net present value method is used to screen projects, those projects that have the highest net present values should be selected.

Profitability index. The *profitability index* is the present value of the expected net cash benefits from an investment divided by the initial cash outlay:

$$PI = \frac{\text{PV of net cash benefits}}{\text{Initial outlay}}$$

Use of the formula allows all possible proposals to be evaluated and ranked according to their desirability. Only those proposals that have a profitability index greater than or equal to 1.00 will be eligible for further consideration. Those with a profitability index of less than 1.00 will not yield the minimum rate of return. The present value of the expected cash benefits of such proposals is less than their required initial cash outlay.

To illustrate, assume that a company is considering two alternative capital outlay proposals which have the following initial costs and expected net cash benefits after taxes:

	Proposal X	Proposal Y
Initial cost	$8,000	$9,500
Expected net cash benefits (after taxes):		
Year 1	$5,000	$9,000
Year 2	4,000	6,000
Year 3	6,000	3,000

Management's minimum desired rate of return is 20 percent. The profitability indices can be computed as follows (using Table 2, Appendix B):

	Present value	
	Proposal X	Proposal Y
Year 1 (cash benefit in Year 1 × 0.833)	$ 4,165	$ 7,497
Year 2 (cash benefit in Year 2 × 0.694)	2,776	4,164
Year 3 (cash benefit in Year 3 × 0.579)	3,474	1,737
Total	$10,415	$13,398
Initial outlay	$ 8,000	$ 9,500

	Proposal X	Proposal Y
Profitability index:	$\dfrac{\$10,415}{\$8,000} = 1.30$	$\dfrac{\$13,398}{\$9,500} = 1.41$

Proposal Y is more desirable than Proposal X since it has a higher profitability index. But the choice of Proposal Y is not automatic. The effect of each proposal on such intangible factors as employee morale and the future flexibility of the firm should also be considered. X may be a more versatile machine than Y for use in manufacturing other products should the demand decline for the present product.

PROJECT SELECTION: THE TIME-ADJUSTED RATE OF RETURN

The *time-adjusted rate of return* is also called the discounted rate of return and internal rate of return. The time-adjusted rate of return is the rate of return which equates the present value of future expected net cash inflows (after tax effects) from an investment with the cost of the investment. It is the rate at which the net present value is zero. If the time-adjusted rate of return equals or exceeds the cost of capital (or target rate of return), then the investment should be considered further. But if the rate of return is less than the minimum rate of return (cost of capital or target rate of return), the proposal should be rejected.

Assume that management is considering several competing proposals and that only one can be accepted. The project with the highest rate of return should be accepted. Of course, the project selected should have a rate of return above that required by management.

Present value tables can be used to approximate the time-adjusted rate of return. To illustrate, assume that a company is considering a $90,000 investment that is expected to last 25 years (with no salvage value). The investment will yield around $15,000 a year (after tax effects) for the next 25 years.

The first step in computing the rate of return involves computing the payback period. In this case, the payback period is six years ($90,000 investment ÷ $15,000 annual cash flow). Next, look at Table 3, Appendix B. It gives the present value of $1 received annually for *n* years. Since the investment is expected to yield returns for 25 years, look at the 25 periods row in the table. In that row, find the factor that is nearest to the payback period of 6. It is 6.097, and the 6.097 present value factor involves an interest rate of 16 percent.

If the annual return of $15,000 is multiplied by the 6.097 factor, the result is $91,455 which is just above the $90,000 cost of the asset. Thus we can say that the actual rate of return is slightly more than 16 percent.

The above example involved level cash flows from year to year. What happens when cash flows are not level? In such instances, a trial and error procedure can be used. For example, assume that a company is considering a $200,000 project that will last four years and yield the following returns (ignoring scrap value):

At the end of—	Net cash inflow (after taxes)
Year 1	$ 20,000
Year 2	40,000
Year 3	80,000
Year 4	150,000
Total	$290,000

The average annual net cash inflow is $72,500 ($290,000 ÷ 4). Based on an average net cash inflow of $72,500, the payback period is 2.76 ($200,000 ÷ $72,500) years. Looking in the four-year row of Table 3, Appendix B, we find that the factor 2.798 is nearest to the payback period of 2.76. But in this case, cash flows are not level. The largest returns occur in the later years of the asset's life. Since the early returns have the largest present value, it is likely that the rate of return will be less than the 16 percent rate that corresponds to the present value factor of 2.798. Thus, we can try various interest rates that are less than 16 percent. Several attempts may be made before we find the discount rate which yields a present value which is the closest to the initial outlay of $200,000. By trial and error we find that the rate of return is slightly higher than 12 percent. The following computation reveals why this is true:

	Return	Present value at 12%	Present value of net cash benefits
Year 1	$ 20,000	0.893	$ 17,860
Year 2	40,000	0.797	31,880
Year 3	80,000	0.712	56,960
Year 4	150,000	0.636	95,400
			$202,100

If the returns had been greater during the earlier years of the asset's life, we would have looked for the correct rate of return among rates that were higher than 16 percent.

The net present value method and the time-adjusted rate of return method theoretically are superior to the payback and unadjusted rate of return methods. But they are also more difficult to apply. If the cost of capital could be calculated precisely, there would be no need to choose between the first two methods.

Since the cost of capital is not a precise percentage, some financial theorists argue that the time-adjusted rate of return method is better than the net present value method. Under the time-adjusted rate of return method, the cost of capital is just used as a *cutoff point* in deciding which projects are acceptable for more consideration. But, under the net present value method, the cost of capital is used in the calculation of the present value of the benefits. Thus, if the cost of capital percentage is wrong, the *ranking* of the projects will be affected. As a result, management may select projects that are really not as profitable as other projects. For our purposes, we will treat both methods as being equally correct.

INVESTMENTS IN WORKING CAPITAL

An investment in plant assets usually must be supported by an investment in working capital such as accounts receivable and inventory. For example, an investment in plant assets often is expected to increase sales. The increase in sales may require an increase in accounts receivable and inventory to support the higher sales level. The increases in the current assets—accounts receivable and inventory—are investments in working capital that usually are recovered in full at the end of a capital project's life. Such investments should be considered in capital budgeting decisions.

To illustrate, assume that a company is considering a capital project that will involve a $50,000 investment in machinery and a $40,000 investment in working capital. The machine, which will be used to produce a new product, has a useful life of eight years. The annual cash inflow (before taxes) is estimated at $25,000 with annual cash outflows (before taxes) of $5,000. The annual net cash flow from the proposal is computed below (assuming straight-line depreciation and a 40 percent tax rate):

	To compute tax	To compute cash flows
Cash inflows	$25,000	$25,000
Cash outflows	5,000	5,000
	$20,000	$20,000
Depreciation ($50,000/8)	6,250	
Taxable income	$13,750	
Tax at 40%	$ 5,500	5,500
Annual net cash inflow, Years 1–8		$14,500

In addition to the $14,500 recovered each year for eight years, the $40,000 investment in working capital will be recovered in Year 8.

The net present value of the proposal is computed as follows (assuming a 14 percent minimum desired rate of return):

Net cash inflow, Years 1–8 ($14,500 × 4.639)	$67,265.50
Recovery of investment in working capital ($40,000 × 0.351)	14,040.00
Present value of net cash inflows	$81,305.50
Initial cash outlay ($50,000 + $40,000)	90,000.00
Net present value	$ (8,694.50)

The investment is not acceptable because it has a negative net present value. If the working capital investment had been ignored, the proposal would have had a rather large positive net present value of $17,265.50 ($67,-265.50 − $50,000.00). Thus, it should be obvious that investments in working capital must be considered if correct capital budgeting decisions are to be made.

THE POSTAUDIT

The last step in the capital budgeting process is the postaudit. Ideally, a disinterested party should perform this review. Management wants to know whether or not the project is living up to its expectations.

The postaudit should be performed early in the life of the project. But enough time should have passed for all of the operational "bugs" to be ironed out. Actual operating costs should be determined. Management would like to know if estimated costs are accurate and if all costs were considered. Also, actual net cash benefits should be compared with the estimated amounts.

Any discrepancies in either costs or revenue estimates should be analyzed. This experience will help in analyzing future capital expenditure proposals.

Annuity—a series of equal cash flows equally spaced in time.

Capital budgeting—the term used to describe the planning, spending, and financing for plant assets.

Cost of capital—the cost of all sources of capital employed by a firm.

Initial cost (of an asset)—any cash outflows necessary to acquire an asset and place it in a position and condition for its intended use.

Net cash benefit—the annual cash inflows from a proposal less the annual cash outflows related to the proposal.

Net present value—a project selection technique that involves discounting all expected cash flows (after taxes) to the present using a minimum rate of return determined by management. If the amount obtained by this process exceeds or equals the investment amount, the proposal is considered acceptable for further consideration.

Out-of-pocket cost—a cost requiring a future outlay of resources, usually cash.

Payback period—that period of time that net cash savings or benefits must continue in order to equal the initial cash outlay required for a capital asset.

Present value—the current value of a specified amount to be received at some future date.

Profitability index—the ratio of the present value of net cash benefits (after taxes) expected from a capital expenditure to the immediate outlay required.

Sunk cost—a past commitment of funds about which nothing can be done at the present time.

Tax shield—the total amount of a tax deductible item, such as depreciation.

Time-adjusted rate of return—a project selection technique that involves finding a rate of return that will equate the present value of future expected cash flows (after taxes) from an investment with the cost of the investment.

Unadjusted rate of return—the rate of return computed by dividing average annual earnings from a project by the average amount of the investment.

DEMONSTRATION PROBLEM

The Logue Company is considering three different investments. Listed below are some data related to these investments:

Investment	Initial outlay	Expected net cash inflow per year	Expected life of proposals
A	$100,000	$20,000	10 years
B	120,000	17,600	15
C	150,000	21,000	20

Management requires a minimum return on investments of 14 percent.

Required:

Rank these proposals using the following selection techniques. (Ignore income taxes and salvage value.)

a. Unadjusted rate of return.

b. Payback period.

c. Time-adjusted rate of return.

d. Profitability index.

Solution to demonstration problem

a. Unadjusted rate of return:

Proposal	(a) Average investment	(b) Average annual net cash inflow	(c) Average depreciation	(b) − (c) = (d) Average annual earnings	(d/a) Rate of return
A	$50,000	$20,000	$10,000	$10,000	20%
B	60,000	17,600	8,000	9,600	16
C	75,000	21,000	7,500	13,500	18

The proposals in order of rank are A, C, and B.

b. Payback period:

Proposal	(a) Investment	(b) Annual cash flow	(a/b) Payback period
A	$100,000	$20,000	5.00 years
B	120,000	17,600	6.82
C	150,000	21,000	7.14

The proposals in order of rank are A, B, and C.

c. Time-adjusted rate of return:

Proposal	Rate
A	16% (slightly below)
B	12 (slightly below)
C	12 (slightly above)

The proposals in order of rank are A, C, and B. (However, neither B nor C earns the minimum rate of return.)

d. Profitability index:

Proposal	(a) Annual net cash inflow	(b) Present value factor at 14%	a × b = (c) Present value of annual net cash inflow	(d) Initial outlay	(c/d) Profitability index
A	$20,000	5.216	$104,320.00	$100,000	1.0432
B	17,600	6.142	108,099.20	120,000	0.9008
C	21,000	6.623	139,083.00	150,000	0.9272

The proposals in order of rank are A, C, and B. (But neither B nor C should be considered acceptable.)

QUESTIONS

1. What is the profitability index and of what value is it?

2. Give an example of an out-of-pocket cost and sunk cost by describing a situation in which both are encountered.

3. A machine currently is being considered for purchase. The salesperson attempting to sell the machine says that it will pay for itself in five years. What is meant by this statement?

4. Why does a capital expenditure commit a firm to a long-term course of action?

5. List three types of external pressures that may affect capital budgeting decisions.

6. Discuss the limitations of the payback method.

7. How do capital expenditures differ from ordinary expenditures?

8. Identify three types of capital investments.

9. What effect does depreciation have on cash flow?

10. What is the time-adjusted rate of return of a capital investment?

11. What role does the cost of capital play in the time-adjusted rate of return method and in the net present value method?

12. What is the purpose of a postaudit? When should a postaudit be performed?

13. What effect would the existence of the investment credit have on the profitability index calculated for capital expenditure projects which qualify for the credit?

EXERCISES

E–1. Given the following annual costs, compute the payback period for the new machine if its net cost is $80,000. (Ignore income taxes.)

	Old machine	New machine
Depreciation	$ 8,000	$16,000
Labor	25,100	22,000
Repairs	6,000	1,500
Other costs	4,000	1,600
	$43,100	$41,100

E–2. The Urono Company is considering investing $75,000 in a new machine. The machine is expected to last five years and to have no salvage value. Yearly net cash inflows from the machine are expected to be $20,000. Calculate the unadjusted rate of return. (Ignore income taxes.)

E–3. Compute the profitability index for each of the following two proposals assuming a desired minimum rate of return of 20 percent. Based upon the profitability indices, which proposal is better?

	Proposal R	Proposal T
Initial outlay	$16,000	$20,600
Cash flow (after taxes):		
First year	10,000	12,000
Second year	9,000	12,000
Third year	6,000	8,000
Fourth year	–0–	5,000

E–4. The Whitehead Company is considering three alternative investment proposals. Using the information presented below, rank the proposals in order of desirability using **(a)** the payback method and **(b)** the unadjusted rate of return method. Assume the net cash inflows occur evenly throughout each year.

	M	O	P
Initial outlay	$ 80,000	$ 80,000	$ 80,000
Net cash inflow (after taxes):			
First year	$ –0–	$ 20,000	$ 20,000
Second year	40,000	60,000	40,000
Third year	40,000	20,000	60,000
Fourth year	20,000	40,000	100,000
	$100,000	$140,000	$220,000

E–5. The Maxey Company is considering the purchase of a new machine. The machine can be bought for $45,000. It is expected to save $9,000 cash per year for ten years. It has an estimated useful life of ten years and an estimated salvage value of zero. Management will not make any investment unless at least an 18 percent rate of return can be earned.

Using the net present value method, determine if the proposal is acceptable.

E–6. Assume the same situation as described in Exercise E–5. Calculate the time-adjusted rate of return. (Ignore income taxes.)

E–7. Rank the following investments in the order of their desirability using **(a)** the payback method, **(b)** the net present value method, and **(c)** the time-adjusted rate of return method. Management requires a minimum rate of return of 14 percent. (Ignore taxes and depreciation.)

Investment	Initial outlay	Expected net cash inflow per year	Expected life of proposal
A	$40,000	$ 6,000	8
B	50,000	8,750	20
C	80,000	16,000	10

PROBLEMS, SERIES A

P28–1–A. The Keep-Pace Manufacturing Company owns five spinning machines which it uses in its manufacturing operations. Each of the machines was purchased four years ago at a cost of $40,000. Each machine has an estimated life of ten years with no expected salvage value. A new machine has become available. One new machine has the same productive capacity as the five old machines combined. The new machine will cost $216,000, is estimated to last six years, and will have a salvage value at the end of that time of $24,000. A trade-in allowance of $8,000 is available for each of the old machines. The new machine can produce 200,000 units each year. Operating costs per unit are compared below:

	Five old machines	New machine
Repairs	$0.453	$0.057
Depreciation	0.100	0.160
Power	0.126	0.069
Other operating costs	0.108	0.033
Operating costs per unit	$0.787	$0.319

Required:

Use the payback method for parts **(a)** and **(b)**.

a. Do you recommend replacement of the old machines? Support your answer with computations. Disregard all factors except those reflected in the data given above.

b. If the old machines were already fully depreciated, would your answer be different? Why?

c. Using the net present value method with a discount rate of 20 percent, present a schedule showing whether or not the new machine should be acquired.

P28–2–A. The Georgia Peach Growers Association has used a particular fruit cooler for several years. The cooler has a zero salvage value. The peach growers are considering buying a technologically improved cooler. The new cooler will cost $58,000. It will save $12,500 per year in cash operating costs. If the peach growers decide not to buy the new cooler, they can use the old cooler for an indefinite period of time by incurring heavy repair costs. The new cooler will have a useful life of eight years.

Required:

a. Compute the time-adjusted rate of return for the new cooler.

b. The peach growers think that the estimated useful life of the new cooler might be more or less than eight years. Compute the time-adjusted rate of return for the new cooler if its useful life is (1) 5 years and (2) 12 years instead of 8 years.

c. Suppose that the new cooler's useful life is eight years but that the annual cost savings are only $10,000. Compute the time-adjusted rate of return.

d. Assume that the annual cost savings will be $11,000 and that the useful life will be ten years. Compute the time-adjusted rate of return.

P28–3–A. The Beechwood Company is considering three different investments. Listed below are some data related to these investments:

Investment	Initial outlay	Expected net cash inflow per year	Expected life of proposal
1	$35,000	$ 7,000	10 years
2	60,000	12,000	20
3	90,000	17,000	10

Management requires a minimum return on investments of 12 percent.

Required:

Rank these proposals using the following selection techniques. (Ignore income taxes and salvage value.)

a. Unadjusted rate of return.

b. Payback period.

c. Time-adjusted rate of return.

d. Profitability index.

P28–4–A. The Brady Company has decided to computerize its accounting system. The company has two alternatives—it can lease a computer under a three-year contract, or it can purchase a computer outright.

If the computer is leased, the lease payment will be $18,000 each year. The first lease payment will be due on the day the lease contract is signed. The other two payments will be due at the end of the first and second years. All repairs and maintenance will be provided by the lessor.

If the computer is purchased outright the following costs will be incurred:

Acquisition cost	$42,000
Repairs and maintenance:	
First year	1,200
Second year	1,000
Third year	1,400

The computer is expected to have only a three-year useful life because of obsolescence and technological advancements. The computer will have no salvage value and will be depreciated on a double-declining-balance basis. The Brady Company's cost of capital is 16 percent.

Required:

Show whether the Brady Company should lease or purchase the computer. (Ignore income taxes.)

P28–5–A. Dixie Athletics, Incorporated, is trying to decide whether or not to add tennis equipment to its existing line of football, baseball, and basketball equipment. Market research studies and cost analyses have provided the following information:

1. Additional machinery and equipment will be needed to manufacture the tennis equipment. The machines and equipment will cost $600,000, have a ten-year useful life, and have a $20,000 salvage value.
2. Sales of tennis equipment for the next ten years have been projected as follows:

Year	Sales in dollars
1	$100,000
2	150,000
3	225,000
4	250,000
5	275,000
6–10 (each year)	300,000

3. Variable costs are equal to 60 percent of selling price, and fixed costs and straight-line depreciation will total $118,000 per year.
4. The company will need to advertise its new product line to gain rapid entry into the market. Its advertising campaign costs will be:

Years	Advertising cost
1–3	$100,000 (each year)
4–10	50,000 (each year)

5. The company requires a 14 percent minimum rate of return on investments.

Required:

Using the net present value method, decide whether or not Dixie Athletics, Incorporated, should add the tennis equipment to its line of products. (Ignore income taxes.)

P28–6–A. The Cardinal Company is considering purchasing new equipment that will cost $600,000. It is estimated that the useful life of the equipment will be five years and that there will be a salvage value of $200,000. The company uses straight-line depreciation. It is estimated that the new equipment will have net cash inflows (before taxes) of $86,000 annually. Assume a tax rate of 40 percent and that management requires a minimum return of 14 percent.

Required:

Using the net present value method determine whether the equipment is an acceptable investment.

P28–7–A. The Large Company has an opportunity to sell some equipment for $10,000. Such a sale will result in a tax-deductible loss of $1,000. If it is not sold, the equipment is expected to produce net cash inflows after taxes of $3,000 for the next ten years. In ten years it is expected that the equipment can be sold for its book value of $1,000. The company's management feels that currently it has other opportunities that will yield 18 percent. Assume a 40 percent tax rate.

Required:

Should the company sell the equipment? Prepare a schedule to support your conclusion.

PROBLEMS, SERIES B

P28–1–B. The Corbett Delivery Company is considering replacement of ten of its delivery vans which originally cost $10,000 each and on each of which $6,250 of depreciation has been taken. They were originally estimated to have useful lives of eight years and no salvage value. Each van travels an average of 75,000 miles per year. The ten new vans, if purchased, will cost $12,000 each. Each van will be driven 75,000 miles per year and will have no salvage value at the end of its three-year estimated useful life. A trade-in allowance of $1,000 is available for each of the old vans.

Following is a comparison of costs of operations:

	Old vans	New vans
Fuel, lubricants, etc.	$0.101	$0.079
Tires	0.045	0.045
Repairs	0.073	0.058
Depreciation	0.017	0.053
Other operating costs (variable)	0.034	0.029
Operating cost per mile	$0.270	$0.264

Required:

Use the payback method for parts (*a*) and (*b*).

a. Do you recommend replacement of the old vans? Support your answer with computations, and disregard all factors not related to the cost data given above.

b. If the old vans were already fully depreciated, would your answer be different? Why?

c. Assume that the tax effects may be ignored (for simplicity), that all cash flows for operating costs fall at the end of each year, and that 18 percent is an appropriate rate for discounting purposes. Using a present value technique, present a schedule showing whether or not the new vans should be acquired.

P28–2–B. The Zebulon Company has been using an old-fashioned forklift for many years. The forklift has a zero salvage value. The company is considering buying a modern forklift. The new forklift will cost $35,000. It will save $7,000 per year in cash operating costs. If the com-

pany decides not to buy the new forklift, it can use the old forklift for an indefinite period of time. The new forklift will have a useful life of ten years.

Required:

a. Compute the time-adjusted rate of return for the new forklift.

b. The company is uncertain about the ten-year useful life. Compute the time-adjusted rate of return for the new forklift if its useful life is (1) 6 years and (2) 15 years instead of 10 years.

c. Suppose that the forklift has a useful life of ten years and that the annual cost savings are only $6,000. Compute the time-adjusted rate of return.

d. Assume that the annual cost savings will be $8,000 and that the useful life will be eight years. Compute the time-adjusted rate of return.

P28–3–B. The Reiner Company is considering three different investments. Listed below are some data related to these investments:

Investment	Initial outlay	Expected net cash inflow per year	Expected life of proposal
1	$15,000	$2,200	20 years
2	40,000	5,000	10
3	55,000	9,200	10

Management requires a minimum return on investments of 12 percent.

Required:

Rank these proposals using the following selection techniques. (Ignore income taxes and salvage value.)

a. Unadjusted rate of return.

b. Payback method.

c. Time-adjusted rate of return.

d. Profitability index.

P28–4–B. Tresp Trucking Company has always purchased its trucks outright and sold them after three years. The company is ready to sell its present fleet of trucks and is trying to decide whether it should continue to purchase trucks or whether it should lease trucks.

If the trucks are purchased, the following costs will be incurred:

	Costs per fleet
Acquisition cost	$52,000
Repairs, first year	600
Repairs, second year	1,100
Repairs, third year	1,500
Other annual costs	1,600

At the end of three years, the trucks could be sold for a total of $16,000. Another fleet of trucks could be purchased then. The costs listed above would be incurred with respect to the second fleet of trucks. The second fleet could also be sold for $16,000 at the end of three years.

If the trucks are leased, the lease contract will run for six years. One fleet of trucks will be provided immediately, and a second fleet of trucks will be provided at the end of three years. The company will pay $21,000 per year under the lease contract.

Required:

Assume the company's cost of capital is 18 percent. Should the company buy or lease the trucks? (Ignore income taxes.)

P28–5–B. Rutledge Manufacturing Company is considering adding a new electronic calculator to its line of products. The following information has been provided by various departments within the company:

1. Additional machinery and equipment will be needed to manufacture the calculator. The machinery and equipment will cost $300,000, have a 15-year useful life, and have a zero salvage value.
2. Sales of Rutledge calculators for the next 15 years have been projected as follows:

Year	Sales in units
1–5	1,500
6–10	1,000
11–15	500

3. Selling price per calculator will be $125.
4. Variable costs will be equal to $50 per calculator. Fixed costs and straight-line depreciation will total $35,000.
5. Advertising campaign costs will be:

Year	Advertising cost
1–5	$25,000
6–10	15,000
11–15	4,000

6. The company requires a 12 percent minimum rate of return on investments.

Required:

Using the net present value method, decide whether or not Rutledge Manufacturing Company should add the calculator to its line of products.

P28–6–B. The Holder Company is considering the purchase of equipment that will cost $300,000. It is estimated that the useful life of the equipment will be ten years and that there will be a salvage value of $75,000 at that time. The company uses straight-line depreciation. It is estimated that the new equipment will have net cash inflows before taxes of $75,000 annually. Assume a tax rate of 35 percent and that management requires a minimum return of 20 percent.

Required:

Using the net present value method determine whether or not the equipment is an acceptable investment.

P28–7–B. The Thin Company has an opportunity to sell a piece of equipment for $30,000. Such a sale will result in a tax-deductible loss of $2,000. If it is not sold, the equipment is expected to produce annual net cash benefits after taxes of $12,000 for the next 20 years. In 20 years it is expected that the equipment will have no salvage value. The company's management feels that currently it has other opportunities that will yield 12 percent. Assume a 30 percent income tax rate.

Required:

Should the company sell the equipment? Prepare a schedule to support your conclusion.

BUSINESS DECISION PROBLEM 28–1

The Biltmore Company has $500,000 which it wishes to invest in capital projects which have a minimum ex-pected rate of return of 14 percent. Five proposals are being evaluated. Acceptance of one proposal does *not* preclude acceptance of any of the other proposals. The company's criteria is to select proposals which have a minimum required rate of return of 14 percent.

The relevant information related to the five proposals is presented below:

Investment	Initial outlay	Expected net cash inflow per year	Expected life of proposal
A	$100,000	$30,000	5 years
B	200,000	40,000	8
C	250,000	55,000	10
D	300,000	52,000	12
E	100,000	21,000	10

Required:

a. Compute the net present value of each of the five proposals.

b. Which projects should be undertaken? Why? In what order should they be undertaken?

BUSINESS DECISION PROBLEM 28–2

The Rockford Company is considering a capital project that will involve a $150,000 investment in machinery and a $30,000 investment in working capital. The machine has a useful life of ten years and no salvage value. The annual cash inflow (before taxes) is estimated at $60,000 with annual cash outflows (before taxes) of $20,000. The company uses straight-line depreciation. The income tax rate is 40 percent.

The company's new bookkeeper computed the net present value of the project using a minimum required rate of return of 16 percent (the company's cost of capital). The bookkeeper's computations are shown below:

Cash inflow	$ 60,000
Cash outflow	−20,000
Net cash inflow	$ 40,000
Present value factor at 16% for 10 years	×4.833
Present value of net cash inflow	$193,320
Initial outlay	150,000
Net present value	$ 43,320

Required:

a. Are the bookkeeper's computations correct? If not, recompute the correct net present value.

b. Is this capital project acceptable to the company? Why or why not?

BUSINESS DECISION PROBLEM 28–3

The Bronson Company is trying to decide whether to purchase or lease a new factory machine. If the machine is purchased, the following costs will be incurred:

Acquisition cost	$200,000
Repairs and maintenance:	
Years 1–5	5,000
Years 6–10	10,000

The machine will be depreciated on a straight-line basis and will have no salvage value.

If the machine is leased, the lease payment will be $30,000 each year for ten years. The first lease payment will be due on the day the lease contract is signed. All repairs and maintenance will be provided by the lessor.

The Bronson Company's cost of capital is 12 percent.

Required:

Do you recommend that the company lease or purchase the machine? Show computations to support your answer. (Ignore income taxes.)

Appendix A

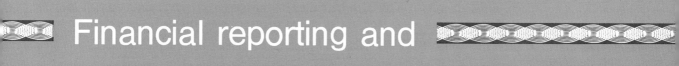

Financial reporting and

changing prices

THE IMPACT OF INFLATION

The impact of inflation upon our economy in most of the years since the early 1940s has become a matter of concern to almost everyone in our society. Many users of financial reports also have begun to question the adequacy of such reports if they do not reveal the impact of inflation upon an entity. In the pages that follow, we deal with what is one of the most serious problems ever faced by accountants—how to account and report in periods of inflation.

The unstable dollar

Most accounting measurements are made using the assumption that the dollar is a stable unit of measure. But we need only to look around us to see that this is not true. The real worth of a dollar is its ability to obtain goods and services, and this has changed significantly in recent years. In periods of inflation (rising prices) these changes represent *purchasing power losses.* In periods of *deflation* (falling prices) they would be *purchasing power gains.*

Changes in the general level of prices are measured by means of a general price index with a base year assigned a value of 100. If prices rise 8 percent in the year following the base year, the index would stand at 108. An index of 200 would mean that prices have doubled. This does not mean that all prices have doubled. A price index is a weighted average of all prices; individual prices may change in a different manner. Available indices include the wholesale price index, the consumer price index, and the most comprehensive index of all, the Gross National Product Implicit Price Deflator. The consumer price index shows that the average price for a "basket" of selected consumer goods and services rose 9 percent in 1978 and that prices have doubled in about 10 years since 1969. Much greater inflation rates have been experienced in some foreign countries.

The current purchasing power of the dollar relative to that of the base year is shown by the reciprocal of the price index. For example, if the index for Year 10 is 200 and for Year 1 (the base year) is 100, the purchasing power of the Year 10 dollar is 50 percent of the base year dollar. Prices have doubled, and the value of the dollar has dropped to one half, or by 50 percent.

The need to adjust historical costs

Accounting measurements consist largely of dollars of historical cost; that is, the unit of measure is the dollar and the attribute measured is historical cost. Such a measurement system has worked very well in periods of stable prices. But it does not work well when the dollar is a sharply changing unit of measure in terms of its purchasing power. To illustrate, assume that you purchased a tract of land for $2,000, held it for several years, and then sold it for $2,500. Under conventional accounting (*historical cost/nominal dollar accounting* as it may also be called), you have recovered your cost of $2,000 and the extra $500 received is called income or earnings. Stated another way, you have recovered the capital invested in the land, and the extra value you now possess can be called income. You are deemed to be better off because you have more dollars now than before. But assume that a general price index rose from 100 to 140 while you held the land. Measured in terms of dollars of constant purchasing power, a far different result is obtained. You have not even recovered your capital, and you certainly have not earned any income. You need $2,800 at current price levels ($2,000 × 140/100) to get back the purchasing power you invested in the land. Since you received only $2,500, you have a loss of $300 in dollars of current purchasing power. To make matters worse, the apparent gain of $500 probably is subject to income taxation. If so, it is a tax on capital, not on income, as measured in terms of purchasing power. And remember, an individual desires money for one reason—its ability to obtain goods and services. From this viewpoint, the $500 of net earnings does not exist.

Time series data may be quite misleading if expressed in unadjusted dollars. For example, a five-year summary of annual sales may show that sales increased 50 percent. But, if sales prices have increased 60 percent in keeping with the rise in the general level of prices, physical sales volume has actually decreased.

Accountants typically take measurements of assets made in dollars of different purchasing power and sum them and report the total as if it had meaning. There is no more validity in this process than adding 100 dollars and 200 French francs and calling the total 300 dollars. Dollars of different purchasing power should be adjusted before being summed.

Other consequences follow from a failure to adjust for the changing value of the dollar. Many are likely to have an effect on net earnings. For instance, understating depreciation by stating it in unadjusted dollars results in overstating net earnings. This may lead to poor allocation of resources and to taxation of capital. This, in turn, may lead to inadequate capital formation and reduced ability to pay debts. The final result may be a lower standard of living and a lesser ability to compete in world markets.

Accounting responses to inflation

There are two basic ways in which accountants might reveal the effects of inflation upon financial data. These are:

1. Change the unit of measure from the nominal dollar to a dollar of constant purchasing power. This is referred to as *general price-level accounting, historical cost/constant dollar accounting,* or *common dollar accounting.*
2. Change the attribute that accountants measure from historical cost to current cost or current value. This approach is sometimes called *current cost/nominal dollar accounting* or *current value accounting.* It often involves reporting of *replacement cost;* if so, it is called *replacement cost accounting.*

The above two changes can be combined and introduced into a single accounting system. This will be discussed briefly in a later section in this Appendix.

Suppose, for example, that you purchased 1,000 units of a product in Year 1 for $3,000 when a general price index was 100 and sold them in Year 2 for $5,000 when the index was 120 and when the replacement cost of the units was $3,900. How much did you earn on the sale? The answer depends upon how cost is measured, and four possible answers are shown below:

	Historical cost/ nominal dollars (HC/N$)	Historical cost/ constant dollars (HC/C$)	Current cost/ nominal dollars (CC/N$)	Current cost/ constant dollars (CC/C$)
Sales revenue	$5,000	$5,000	$5,000	$5,000
Cost of the goods sold	3,000	3,600	3,900	3,900
Earnings (profit)	$2,000	$1,400	$1,100	$1,100

Historical cost/nominal dollar accounting (HC/N$). The $2,000 of earnings shown in this column result from the conventional accounting practice of comparing current sales revenue with the historical cost of the goods sold. The entity is better off because it has not only recovered the original dollar investment, but has $2,000 more than that. No attention is paid to the fact that the dollars recovered do not have the same purchasing power as those originally invested. The fact that the current replacement cost of the goods sold exceeds their historical cost by $900 ($3,900 − $3,000) also is ignored.

Historical cost/constant dollar accounting (HC/C$). In this column, the cost of the goods sold is restated in terms of Year 2 dollars by using a price-level index. The restated amount is then deducted from revenues, which are expressed in Year 2 dollars. The result shows that you increased your purchasing power by $1,400 (Year 2 dollars). You are better off because you have increased your ability to buy goods and services in general. And this is the essence of net earnings—increased ability to buy goods and services. But note, the net earnings are $1,400—not $2,000. The $600 is an adjustment of capital, not an element of income.

Current cost/nominal dollar accounting (CC/N$). In this column, net earnings are computed by deducting the *current cost* of replacing the goods sold from revenues. No adjustments are made for *general* price-level changes (no general price-level index is used), so the measurements are in terms of nominal dollars. Calculating earnings in this manner is supported on the grounds that sale of an inventory item leads directly to a further action—replenishment of the inventory—if the firm is to remain a going concern. A better picture of a firm's ability to compete in its markets may also be provided by comparing current revenues with current costs rather than outdated historical costs. It also is argued that the $1,100 represents "disposable income." Only this amount (or less) can be distributed to owners without reducing the scale of operations.

Some disagreement exists among accountants as to the proper interpretation to be placed on the $900 difference between current cost and historical cost of the goods sold. To many, this increase in the buying prices of goods is a *holding gain* and is to be included in net earnings along with the $1,100 excess of revenues over current cost of the goods sold. Total income is $2,000. To others, the $900 is an adjustment of owners' equity and is not to be reported in the earnings statement. The excess of revenues over all expenses measured in current cost terms is called current operating earnings or profit. Current operating earnings are viewed as resulting from planned management effort and therefore are useful in appraising management's performance. Holding gains are not to be used in this manner.

Current cost/constant dollar accounting (CC/C$). Accounting systems have been advocated that include both current costs and general price-level adjustments. This enables one to distinguish between real and fictional holding gains. A *real holding gain* is the amount by which the current cost of an asset exceeds its historical cost, as adjusted for general price-level change. For example, in the above data, the current cost of the goods sold was $3,900. Their historical cost in constant dollars was $3,600 ($3,000 × 120/100). The $300 difference is a real holding gain. It is the increase in the buying prices of the goods ($900), less the general inflation component of $600. The remaining $600 of holding gains is fictional from a purchasing power point of view. It represents the additional number of current dollars you must have to be as well off as you were when you invested $3,000 in the goods that subsequently were sold. Under this approach, earnings from the sale of goods would equal $1,100 ($5,000 of revenues less $3,900 current cost of goods sold). Income for the period would include the real holding gain of $300.

Choosing the correct method. With four different methods of measuring net earnings available, the question of which is the correct method arises rather automatically. There is no direct answer possible. Each method is correct if one accepts the definitions of cost and earnings implicit in the method. A much more important question is: Which method is the most useful to users of the financial reports? The answer to this question is of considerable concern to many, including the FASB and the SEC. But, as of this writing, the question remains unanswered.

FINANCIAL STATEMENTS UNDER HISTORICAL COST/ CONSTANT DOLLAR ACCOUNTING

As already discussed briefly, the historical dollar amounts in a set of financial statements may be converted or restated into a number of current dollars which have an equivalent amount of purchasing power. Because of inflation it takes a larger number of current dollars to be equivalent to the purchasing power in the historical dollar amount. Conventional financial statements when adjusted are called common dollar statements or *general price-level adjusted financial statements* or are the result of historical cost/constant dollar accounting.

Such statements generally have been recommended, not required, as supplementary information to the conventional financial statements. But recently the FASB issued a new standard that requires certain large publicly held corporations to present certain supplementary information about the effects of inflation.[1] These requirements are discussed further in a later section. Presented below is an example of how financial statements can be adjusted for changes in the general level of prices. Knowing how this is done will lead to a better understanding of the new FASB requirements.

[1] FASB *Statement of Financial Accounting Standards No. 33,* "Financial Reporting and Changing Prices" (Stamford, Conn.: FASB, 1979). Copyright © by Financial Accounting Standards Board, High Ridge Park, Stamford, Connecticut 06905 U.S.A. Portions reprinted with permission. Copies of the complete document are available from the FASB.

Historical cost/constant dollar accounting illustrated

To serve as a basis for illustration, the financial statements of the Carol Company are presented below:

CAROL COMPANY
Comparative Balance Sheets

	December 31	
Assets	1980	1981
Cash	$ 20,000	$ 10,000
Inventory	20,000	40,000
Plant assets, net	64,000	60,000
Land	48,000	48,000
Total Assets	$152,000	$158,000
Liabilities and Owners' Equity		
Accounts payable	$ 8,000	$ 8,000
Bonds payable	40,000	40,000
Capital stock	100,000	100,000
Retained earnings	4,000	10,000
Total Liabilities and Owners' Equity	$152,000	$158,000

CAROL COMPANY
Earnings Statement
For the Year Ended December 31, 1981

Sales		$200,000
Cost of goods sold:		
Inventory, December 31, 1980	$ 20,000	
Purchases	160,000	
Goods available for sale	$180,000	
Inventory, December 31, 1981	40,000	140,000
Gross margin		$ 60,000
Depreciation	$ 4,000	
Other expenses and taxes	46,000	50,000
Net earnings		$ 10,000
Retained earnings December 31, 1980		4,000
Total		$ 14,000
Dividends		4,000
Retained Earnings, December 31, 1981		$ 10,000

Converting the balance sheet. The above comparative balance sheets are presented below with all amounts expressed in terms of the *December 31, 1981, price level*. The adjustments are based upon the assumptions (1) that an index of the general price level stood at 54 when the land and plant assets were acquired and the capital stock was issued; (2) that this same index stood at 100 on December 31, 1980, and at 108 on December 31, 1981; and (3) that the ending Fifo inventories were acquired when the index stood at 98 and 106 for the 1980 and 1981 inventories, respectively.

	Historical dollars	Conversion ratio	Constant dollars
December 31, 1980, balance sheet:			
Cash	$ 20,000	108/100	$ 21,600
Inventory	20,000	108/98	22,040
Plant assets, net	64,000	108/54	128,000
Land	48,000	108/54	96,000
Total	$152,000		$267,640
Accounts payable	$ 8,000	108/100	$ 8,640
Bonds payable	40,000	108/100	43,200
Capital stock	100,000	108/54	200,000
Retained earnings	4,000		15,800
Total	$152,000		$267,640
December 31, 1981, balance sheet:			
Cash	$ 10,000		$ 10,000
Inventory	40,000	108/106	40,755
Plant assets, net	60,000	108/54	120,000
Land	48,000	108/54	96,000
Total	$158,000		$266,755
Accounts payable	$ 8,000		$ 8,000
Bonds payable	40,000		40,000
Capital stock	100,000	108/54	200,000
Retained earnings	10,000		18,755
Total	$158,000		$266,755

In converting the balance sheets, a distinction is drawn between monetary and nonmonetary items. *Monetary items* are cash and fixed claims to cash. They always are automatically expressed in terms of the current price level—a dollar of cash is always worth exactly one dollar of current purchasing power. This explains why no adjustment is needed for cash in the 1981 balance sheet, nor for accounts payable and bonds payable which are also monetary items. But these three items are expressed in 1980 dollars in the 1980 balance sheet. Therefore, to compare with the 1981 amounts, the 1980 amounts must be adjusted to 1981 dollars. Since prices rose 8 percent in 1981, the conversion ratio is 108/100. Thus, the $20,000 of purchasing power held in cash form on December 31, 1980, is equivalent to a purchasing power of $21,600 in December 31, 1981, dollars. The accounts payable and bonds payable are adjusted in the same manner for the same reason. More will be said about monetary items later.

All of the items except the monetary items are called *nonmonetary items.* Their values fluctuate with changing price levels. To adjust their recorded dollar amounts into current price levels, multiply their historical amounts by a ratio whose numerator is the current price index and whose denominator is the index at the acquisition or issuance date. Thus, the ending 1980 inventory is adjusted into December 31, 1981, dollars by the ratio 108/98. Similarly, the ending 1981 inventory is adjusted by the ratio 108/106. The equivalent purchasing power invested in the land in terms of December 31, 1981, dollars is $96,000 ($48,000 × 108/54). This $96,000 *is the cost of the land* in terms of December 31, 1981, purchasing power, *not its current value,* which may be more or less than $96,000. The capital stock is adjusted for both balance sheets in the same manner as land. The retained earnings amount in each converted balance sheet is simply the amount needed to bring the equities side of the balance sheet into balance with the total of the assets. This completes the conversion of the balance sheets from nominal dollars into constant dollars.

The net earnings for the year in constant dollars can now be computed as follows (assuming the dividends were declared and paid on June 30 when the index stood at 104—the average for the year):

Retained earnings, December 31, 1981	$18,755
Dividends ($4,000 × 108/104)	4,154
	$22,909
Retained earnings, December 31, 1980 in December 31, 1981 prices	15,800
Net Earnings for the Year	$ 7,109

The above schedule shows positive net earnings greater than dividends. Thus, it can be argued that capital in a purchasing power sense has been maintained. The converted earnings statement confirms our computation of net earnings.

Converting the earnings statement.   The conversion of the earnings statement into December 31, 1981, dollars is presented below:

	Historical dollars	Conversion ratio	Constant dollars
Sales	$200,000	108/104	$207,692
Cost of goods sold:			
Inventory, December 31, 1980	$ 20,000	108/98	$ 22,040
Purchases	160,000	108/104	166,154
Goods available for sale	$180,000		$188,194
Inventory, December 31, 1981	40,000	108/106	40,755
Cost of goods sold	$140,000		$147,439
Gross margin	$ 60,000		$ 60,253
Depreciation	$ 4,000	108/54	$ 8,000
Other expenses and taxes	46,000	108/104	47,769
Total expenses	$ 50,000		$ 55,769
Net earnings from continuing operations	$ 10,000		$ 4,484
Gain on holding long-term debt			3,200
Loss on holding monetary working capital			(575)
Net Earnings for the Year	$ 10,000		$ 7,109

It is assumed that sales, purchases, and other expenses and taxes were incurred uniformly throughout the year. This means that, on the average, they were incurred when the index stood at 104. To express them in year-end dollars, they are multiplied by the ratio 108/104. The adjustment of the beginning and ending inventories already has been illustrated. The depreciation for the year is converted into 1981 year-end dollars by multiplying its $4,000 historical cost amount by a ratio of 108/54—the current index over the index at time of acquisition of the plant assets.

Gains and losses on monetary items.   The gain or loss that results from holding monetary assets and liabilities through time is easily illustrated. Assume that you hold $1,000 of cash during a year in which the prices in general rose 25 percent. At year-end, you have sustained a loss in purchasing power of 250 year-end dollars. Even though you still have your 1,000 dollars, you have less purchasing power. You need 1,250 year-end dollars to be as well off as you were at the beginning of the year ($1,000 × 125/100). Since you have only $1,000, you have a loss. Conversely, a gain results from being in debt during inflation. Assume that you owe $600 during a period in which prices rise 40 percent. The original debt has a year-end purchasing power equivalent of $840, which is found as follows ($600 × 140/100 = $840). You can satisfy the debt by paying 600 current dollars. Thus, you have experienced a gain of $240.

Carol Company experienced a gain of $3,200 in purchasing power by being in debt $40,000 while prices rose 8 percent ($40,000 × 108/100) − $40,000 = $3,200. It suffered a loss of $575 on monetary working capital (cash minus accounts payable) during the year, as computed in the following schedule:

	Historical dollars	Conversion ratio	Constant dollars
Monetary working capital at beginning of 1981 ($20,000 − $8,000)	$ 12,000	108/100	$ 12,960
Monetary working capital received:			
Sales	200,000	108/104	207,692
	$212,000		$220,652
Monetary working capital paid out:			
Purchases	$160,000	108/104	$166,154
Other expenses and taxes	46,000	108/104	47,769
Dividends	4,000	108/104	4,154
Total monetary working capital paid out	$210,000		$218,077
Monetary working capital at year-end	$ 2,000		
Monetary working capital that should be on hand for no gain or loss			$ 2,575
Actual monetary working capital			2,000
Loss on monetary working capital for the year			$ 575

When we add the purchasing gain on debt of $3,200 and deduct the purchasing power loss on monetary working capital of $575 in the earnings statement, we arrive at net earnings on a constant dollar basis of $7,109, which is nearly 30 percent less than the net earnings under conventional accounting.

In the above illustration, the Carol Company's financial statements were completely adjusted into dollars at the end of the latest fiscal year—December 31, 1981, to make them comparable. Comparability could, of course, be secured by adjusting the measurements into dollars of any given year, such as the base year of the index used, which could be 1960. But because individuals tend to think in terms of the current dollar and often find it difficult in 1981 to conceive of a 1960 dollar or of a price in 1960 dollars, adjustment into current dollars is usually preferred. Some accountants prefer to adjust financial statements into average dollars of the latest year simply because fewer adjustments are required. In the earnings statement, for example, sales, most of the expenses, and taxes are likely to be expressed in average dollars of the year in the conventional (historical cost/nominal dollar) earnings statement without adjustment. Thus, in many cases, only cost of goods sold and depreciation would require restatement or conversion. The conversion of the Carol Company's 1981 earnings statement into average 1981 dollars is shown below:

	Historical dollars	Conversion ratio	Average 1981 dollars
Sales	$200,000		$200,000
Cost of goods sold:			
Inventory, December 31, 1980	$ 20,000	104/98	$ 21,224
Purchases	160,000		160,000
Goods available for sale	$180,000		$181,224
Inventory, December 31, 1981	40,000	104/106	39,245
Cost of goods sold	$140,000		$141,979
Gross margin	$ 60,000		$ 58,021
Depreciation	$ 4,000	104/54	$ 7,704
Other expenses and taxes	46,000		46,000
Total expenses	$ 50,000		$ 53,704
Net earnings from continuing operations	$ 10,000		$ 4,317
Gain on holding long-term debt			3,081
Loss on holding monetary working capital			(554)
Net Earnings for the Year	$ 10,000		$ 6,844

The cost of goods sold of $141,979 could have been computed by multiplying its amount in December 31, 1981, dollars of $147,439 by a conversion factor of 104/108. The gain from holding long-term debt is computed by multiplying its amount in December 31, 1981, dollars ($3,200) by a conversion factor of 104/108 to express it in average 1981 dollars. Since we already have the loss on monetary working capital of $575 expressed in December 31, 1981, dollars, we can convert this loss to average 1981 dollars by use of a conversion factor of 104/108. There is no need to adjust sales or other expenses and taxes. They are already stated in average 1981 dollars.

THE SEC REQUIREMENTS

Just at the time when it appeared that the presentation of supplementary information prepared under a historical cost/constant dollar basis would be required in the U.S. and several foreign countries, the SEC published its *Accounting Series Release No. 190,* "Disclosure of Certain Replacement Cost Data" (March 23, 1976). The release requires, for each year for which a balance sheet is presented, the disclosure in a footnote of:

a)   The current gross replacement cost of year-end inventories, and its excess, if any, over net realizable value.

b)   The estimated current cost of replacing the productive capacity together with the current replacement cost of depreciable, depletable, or amortizable assets net of accumulated depreciation so as to adjust for service potential used up in prior periods.

For each of the two most recent fiscal years it also requires disclosure of:

c) The approximate amount that cost of sales would have been if it had been calculated by estimating the current replacement cost of goods and services sold at the times when the sales were made.

d) The approximate amount of depreciation, depletion, and amortization that would have been recorded if it were estimated on the basis of averge current replacement cost of productive capacity.

Companies are also to include a footnote describing the methods used to approximate replacement cost and the related effects on other costs.[2] The SEC defined *replacement cost* as the lowest amount that would have to be paid in the normal course of business to obtain an asset of equivalent operating or productive capacity. Replacement cost could be determined from *(a)* current quoted market prices, *(b)* historical cost adjusted by a specific price index, *(c)* contract prices in long-term supply contracts, *(d)* current cost of equivalent units, *(e)* estimated cost to replace, or *(f)* currently updated standard costs.

The goal of the SEC in requiring replacement cost disclosures is to help investors gain an understanding of current costs of operations in a business. Subsequent disclosures by companies have revealed that depreciation on a replacement cost basis is often several times that of depreciation on an historical cost basis. Similarly, cost of goods sold is often considerably larger on a replacement cost basis than under conventional accounting. This information does give investors some additional information relating to an entity, but its specific usefulness is yet to be demonstrated. Attempts to measure replacement cost have revealed the rather subjective nature of such estimates, as well as the fact that reasonable estimates are difficult to obtain especially when there have been rather sharp technological advances.

Concern over the relative usefulness of current cost information versus historical cost/constant dollar information is reflected in the new standard by the FASB.

THE FASB REQUIREMENTS

FASB *Statement No. 33* calls for the disclosure by companies in their annual reports of the impact of general inflation and of specific price changes upon earnings and other selected items. The statement does not affect the way in which the basic financial statements are prepared since all required disclosures are to be reported only as supplementary information. The statement applies only to companies with total assets in excess of $1 billion or to those having $125 million (before deducting accumulated depreciation) of property, plant, and equipment and of inventories. Thus, about 1,200 to 1,400 large, publicly-held companies are directly affected. But the long-term implications for financial accounting and reporting are substantial.

The required disclosures

For fiscal years ended on or after December 25, 1979, affected companies are to report:

---

[2] These requirements will be phased out as FASB *Statement No. 33* becomes effective.

a) Earnings (income) from continuing operations adjusted for the effects of general inflation (that is, on a historical cost/constant dollar basis).

b) The purchasing power gain or loss on net monetary items for the current fiscal year (such gain or loss is not to be included in earnings from continuing operations).

c) Earnings (income) from continuing operations for the current fiscal year on a current cost basis.

d) The current cost amounts of inventory and property, plant, and equipment at the end of the current fiscal year.

e) Increases or decreases in current cost amounts for the current fiscal year of inventory and property, plant, and equipment, net of the effects of general inflation (such increases or decreases are not to be included in earnings from continuing operations).

f) A five-year summary of selected financial data including earnings from continuing operations, sales and other revenues, net assets, dividends per common share, and market price per share of common stock at year end.[3]

Current cost is defined as the cost of replacing the service potential of the asset owned. It can be distinguished from current replacement cost which is the amount of cash (or its equivalent) that would have to be paid to acquire currently the best asset available to undertake the function of the asset owned. Thus, current cost relates to the asset owned, while current replacement cost relates to the asset that might be acquired to replace the asset owned. Current cost information can be obtained from *(a)* current invoice prices, *(b)* vendors' price lists or other quotations, *(c)* standard manufacturing costs that reflect current costs, or by *(d)* indexation using either externally or internally generated price indices.

Disclosure formats

The required disclosures in items *(a)* through *(e)* in the previous section can be presented in either statement format (Illustration A.1) or in reconciliation format (Illustration A.2). The statement format provides directly the total amounts for cost of goods sold and for depreciation and amortization expense. Differences in these two expenses are the sole cause of differences in the three earnings (loss) from continuing operations figures provided. The alternative format presented in Illustration A.2 starts with conventional earnings from continuing operations. Adjustments are included for the effects of general inflation upon cost of goods sold and depreciation and amortization expense to arrive at earnings (loss) from continuing operations expressed in historical cost/constant dollars. Further adjustments of the same two expenses are included to reflect the effects of specific price changes. These adjustments yield an earnings or a loss from continuing operations expressed in current cost/constant dollars. Thus, each format provides the required information on earnings from continuing operations under each of three of the four possible bases discussed earlier. The remaining items in each format, including the footnote revealing the fiscal year-end current cost amounts for inventory and property, plant, and equipment, illustrate how other required information may be presented. The item described as "Increase in specific prices (current

---

[3] FASB *Statement No. 33* (para. 29–35).

Illustration A.1

	As reported in the primary statements	Adjusted for general inflation	Adjusted for changes in specific prices (current costs)
	Statement of Income from Continuing Operations Adjusted for Changing Prices For the Year Ended December 31, 1980 ($000)		
Net sales and other operating revenues	$253,000	$253,000	$253,000
Cost of goods sold	$197,000	$204,384	$205,408
Depreciation and amortization expense	10,000	14,130	19,500
Other operating expense	20,835	20,835	20,835
Interest expense	7,165	7,165	7,165
Provision for income taxes	9,000	9,000	9,000
	$244,000	$255,514	$261,908
Income (loss) from continuing operations	$ 9,000	$(2,514)	$(8,908)
Gain from decline in purchasing power of net amounts owed		$ 7,729	$ 7,729
Increase in specific prices (current cost) of inventories and property, plant, and equipment held during the year*			$ 24,608
Effect of increase in general price level			18,959
Excess of increase in specific prices over increase in the general price level			$ 5,649

* At December 31, 1980, current cost of inventory was $65,700, and current cost of property, plant, and equipment, net of accumulated depreciation, was $85,100.

Source: FASB *Statement of Financial Accounting Standards No. 33*, "Financial Reporting and Changing Prices." Appendix A. © 1979 Financial Accounting Standards Board.

cost) . . ." often is referred to as a holding gain in the literature of accounting. Similarly, the "Excess of increase in specific prices over increase in the general price level" is more popularly called a real holding gain.

The new standard also requires footnote disclosure of:

a) The information upon which calculations of current costs are based.
b) The differences, if any, between depreciation methods and estimates used in the primary financial statements and those used for historical cost/constant dollar or current cost calculations.
c) The fact that income tax expense is the same for current cost earnings from continuing operations as it is for conventional earnings from continuing operations; this means that income taxes are not adjusted for or allocated to current cost amounts.

The suggested format in *Statement No. 33* of a five-year summary of required disclosures in a company's 1980 annual report is shown in Illustration A.3. Current cost disclosures for 1979 can be reported for the first time in 1980, if a company has difficulty in obtaining this information in time for the 1979 report. Note that all of the dollar information is expressed in constant average dollars for the latest fiscal year. Alternatively, the data could be expressed in dollars of the base year (1967) of the Consumer Price Index. A company can elect to present comprehensive supplementary financial state-

Illustration A.2

Statement of Income from Continuing Operations Adjusted for Changing Prices For the Year Ended December 31, 1980 (average 1980 $000)		
Income from continuing operations, as reported in the income statement		$ 9,000
Adjustments to restate costs for the effect of general inflation		
Cost of goods sold	(7,384)	
Depreciation and amortization expense	(4,130)	(11,514)
Loss from continuing operations adjusted for general inflation		$(2,514)
Adjustments to reflect the difference between general inflation and changes in specific prices (current costs)		
Cost of goods sold	(1,024)	
Depreciation and amortization expense	(5,370)	(6,394)
Loss from continuing operations adjusted for changes in specific prices		$(8,908)
Gain from decline in purchasing power of net amounts owed		$ 7,729
Increase in specific prices (current cost) of inventories and property, plant, and equipment held during the year*		$ 24,608
Effect of increase in general price level		18,959
Excess of increase in specific prices over increase in the general price level		$ 5,649

* At December 31, 1980, current cost of inventory was $65,700 and current cost of property, plant, and equipment, net of accumulated depreciation, was $85,100.

Source: FASB *Statement of Financial Accounting Standards No. 33,* "Financial Reporting and Changing Prices." Appendix A. © 1979 Financial Accounting Standards Board.

ments on a historical cost/constant dollar basis (as illustrated earlier for the Carol Company) or on a current cost/constant dollar basis. If it does either of these, data for the five-year summary can be expressed in average dollars or end-of-period dollars in accordance with the comprehensive statements, with footnote disclosure.

After a company has provided the above information, together with necessary explanations, and has discussed its significance to the company in its environment, it has met the minimum disclosure requirements of *Statement No. 33*. Note that restatement into constant dollars and in current costs is required only for inventory; property, plant, and equipment; cost of goods sold; and depreciation, depletion, and amortization expense. No other assets need to be restated for disclosure of net assets (assets minus liabilities). No other restatements are required to provide the required disclosures of earnings from continuing operations.

Attention is now directed toward the procedures employed to derive the restated amounts required.

Illustration A.3

Five-Year Comparison of Selected
Supplementary Financial Data Adjusted for Effects of Changing Prices
(average 1980 $000)

	Years ended December 31				
	1976	*1977*	*1978*	*1979*	*1980*
Net sales and other operating revenues	$265,000	$235,000	$240,000	$237,063	$253,000
Historical cost information adjusted for general inflation					
Income (loss) from continuing operations				(2,761)	(2,514)
Income (loss) from continuing operations per comon share				(1.91)	(1.68)
Net assets at year-end				55,518	57,733
Current cost information					
Income (loss) from continuing operations				(4,125)	(8,908)
Income (loss) from continuing operations per common share				(2.75)	(5.94)
Excess of increase in specific prices over increase in the general price level				2,292	5,649
Net assets at year-end				79,996	81,466
Gain from decline in purchasing power of net amounts owed				7,027	7,729
Cash dividends declared per common share	2.59	2.43	2.26	2.16	2.00
Market price per common share at year-end	32	31	43	39	35
Average consumer price index	170.5	181.5	195.4	205.0	220.9

Source: FASB *Statement of Financial Accounting Standards No. 33*, "Financial Reporting and Changing Prices." Appendix A. © 1979 Financial Accounting Standards Board.

Inventory and cost of goods sold computations

For purposes of computing current cost earnings from continuing operations, cost of goods sold is to be measured at current cost or lower recoverable amount at time of sale. Inventories are to be measured at current cost or lower recoverable amount at the measurement date. Recoverable amount for an asset held for sale is its net realizable value, which is equal to cash expected from sale of the asset, less costs incurred to secure the sale.

In the illustrations that follow, the Consumer Price Index (All Urban Consumers) has the following values:

Average for	*Index value*		
1973	133.1		
1974	147.7	Average 4th qtr. 1979	210.0
1975	161.2	Average 4th qtr. 1980	237.8
1976	170.5	December, 1979	212.9
1977	181.5	December, 1980	243.5*
1978	195.4		
1979	205.0		
1980	220.9		

* The above index numbers and the illustrations that follow are adapted from *Statement No. 33*, Appendix E and Appendix F.

The first column in the schedule below contains assumed actual data regarding inventories, production, and cost of goods sold in both units and dollars. The dollar amounts are in nominal dollars as used in the conventional financial statements. Dollars and units are in thousands (000s omitted).

	Nominal dollars	Conversion factor	Average 1980 dollars
Inventory, 1/1/80 (1,000 units)	$ 56,000	220.9/210.0*	$ 58,907
Production (3,036 units)	204,000	†	204,000
Inventory, 12/31/80 (900 units)	(63,000)	220.9/237.8‡	(58,523)
Cost of goods sold (3,136 units)	$197,000		$204,384

* Average index for 1980/index for fourth quarter 1979.
† Assumed to be in average 1980 dollars.
‡ Average index for 1980/index for fourth quarter 1980.

The second two columns show the conversion factors used, and the resulting amounts, to convert the nominal historical amounts to historical cost/ constant dollar amounts expressed in average 1980 dollars. It is assumed that the beginning inventory was acquired during the fourth quarter of 1979 when the index was 210.0—hence the conversion factor of 220.9/210.0 to convert historical costs to average 1980 dollar amounts. It is further assumed that production is in average 1980 dollars so that no adjustment is needed. Finally, it is assumed that the ending inventory was acquired during the fourth quarter of 1980 when the average index was 237.8. The conversion ratio needed to adjust the nominal dollar amount of this inventory to average 1980 dollars then is 220.9/237.8. Note that both cost of goods sold amounts can be traced to Illustration A.1. The difference in the two amounts of $7,384 ($204,384 − $197,000) can be traced to Illustration A.2 as the inflation adjustment to cost of goods sold.

It is assumed that management has determined the current cost of a unit to be $58 at the beginning of the year and $73 per unit at the end of 1980. The average current cost of a unit then is $65.50 [($58 + $73)/2]. Cost of goods sold then at average current cost is:

Average per unit current cost	$ 65.50
Number of units sold (000s)	× 3,136
Average current cost of goods sold (000s)	$205,408

The current cost of the January 1, 1980, inventory and of the December 31, 1980, inventory are computed as follows (amounts in 000):

January 1, 1980 (1,000 units at $58)	$ 58,000
December 31, 1980 (900 units at $73)	65,700

The $65,700 can be traced to the footnote in Illustration A.1 and Illustration A.2.

The above data can now be used to compute the increase in the current cost amount for inventory and the inflation component of this increase (dollar amounts in 000).

	Current cost/ nominal dollars	Conversion factor	Current cost/ average 1980 dollars
Inventory, 1/1/80	$ 58,000	220.9/212.9*	$ 60,179
Production	204,000	†	204,000
Cost of goods sold	(205,408)	†	(205,408)
Inventory, 12/31/80	(65,700)	220.9/243.5‡	(59,602)
Increase in current cost of inventory	$ 9,108		$ 831

* Average index for 1980/index at December 31, 1980.
† Assumed to be in average 1980 dollars.
‡ Average index for 1980/index for December 1980.

The increase in current cost of inventory ($9,108) often is referred to as a holding gain. A simpler example may aid in understanding what the above technique seeks to accomplish. Suppose that one unit of product is purchased for $10 and a debit entered in the inventory account for that amount. After being held for a period of time, the unit is sold and its current cost of $12 is debited to cost of goods sold and credited to inventory. The inventory account now has a credit balance of $2–the difference between the current cost of the unit at time of acquisition and the current cost of the unit at time of sale. This is exactly what a holding gain is, even though the FASB prefers and uses different terminology. The second money column in the above schedule seeks to accomplish exactly the same thing, except that the holding gain is measured in average dollars for 1980.

The data in the above schedule can be used to determine the inflation component (sometimes referred to as a fictional holding gain) of the increase in current cost of the inventory (holding gain):

Increase in current cost (holding gain) in nominal dollars	$9,108
Increase in current cost (holding gain) in constant dollars	831
Inflation component (fictional holding gain)	$8,277

From this brief schedule, we can see that over 90 percent of the increase in the current cost of inventory was caused by general inflation. The dollar amounts immediately above are combined with similar amounts (given below) for property, plant, and equipment and shown in Illustrations A.1 and A.2.

Property, plant, and equipment and depreciation computations

Current cost disclosure requirements call for measuring property, plant, and equipment at current cost or lower recoverable amount of the assets' remaining service potential at the measurement date. Depreciation and amortization expense is to be measured at average current cost or lower recoverable amount of the assets' service potential during the period of use. Recoverable amount for these assets is the net present value of future cash flows expected from the use of the assets. Net present value is to be derived by discounting future cash flows at an appropriate discount rate.

The illustrative computations which follow are based upon these assumed actual data for a company. The details of the property, plant, and equipment (hereafter PPE for the sake of brevity) are (dollar amounts in 000):

Date acquired	Percent depreciated	Historical cost	Accumulated depreciation
1973	80	$ 50,000	$40,000
1974	70	5,000	3,500
1975	60	5,000	3,000
1976	50	5,000	2,500
1977	40	5,000	2,000
1978	30	5,000	1,500
1979	20	10,000	2,000
1980	10	15,000	1,500
		$100,000	$56,000

Depreciation is calculated under the straight-line method at 10 percent per year. A full year's depreciation is charged on acquisitions in the year acquired. There were no disposals.

Assume further that management has determined current costs to be (in nominal dollars):

At December 31, 1979: $170,000 − $95,900 = $74,100 Net current cost.
At December 31, 1980: $220,000 − $134,900 = $85,100 Net current cost.

Now attention is directed toward illustrating how the required disclosures relative to PPE and depreciation expense can be computed. Note that what could be a long and tedious process if applied to individual assets is shortened substantially by dealing with annual totals and assuming that all acquisitions are at the average price level for the year. The Board also suggests that assets acquired many years before a balance sheet date can be summed across a few years, such as for 1945 to 1950, and measured using an average price index for the five years.

The following example shows the type of schedule that would be prepared to convert historical cost/nominal dollar measurements of PPE and of its related accumulated depreciation into historical cost/constant dollar measurements.

Date of acquisition	Historical cost/nominal dollars	Conversion factor	Historical cost/constant dollars	Percent depreciated	Accumulated depreciation
1973	$ 50,000	220.9/133.1	$ 82,983	80	$66,386
1974	5,000	220.9/147.7	7,478	70	5,235
.	.	*	.	.	.
.	.	.	.	.	.
.	.	.	.	.	.
1980	15,000	220.9/220.9	15,000	10	1,500
	$100,000		$141,304		$86,756

* The conversion ratio for 1975 would be 220.9/161.2. For successive years it would be 220.9 (the average index for 1980) divided by the average index for the year of acquisition.

Depreciation expense for 1980 in average 1980 dollars is computed as $141,304 × .10 = $14,130. This amount is reported in Illustration A.1. The difference, $4,130 [.1($141,304 − $100,000)] is reported in Illustration A.2 as an adjustment to restate costs for the effects of general inflation. The $141,304 amount is included in arriving at net assets for purposes of reporting net assets in the section showing historical cost information adjusted for general inflation in Illustration A.3.

In most situations, current cost depreciation expense can be computed by reference to the average current cost of the PPE as determined by averaging the beginning and ending balances. For our illustrative data, current cost depreciation is $19,500, computed as follows:

Current cost, December 31, 1979 (000)	$170,000
Current cost, December 31, 1980 (000)	220,000
	$390,000
Average current cost ($390,000/2)	$195,000
Current cost depreciation expense (.1 × $195,000)	$ 19,500

The $19,500 is reported directly in Illustration A.1. The excess of $19,500 over $14,130 is reported in Illustration A.2. The December 31, 1980, current cost amount for PPE of $85,100 ($220,000 − $134,900) is reported in the footnote in both Illustration A.1 and Illustration A.2. It is also included in determining net assets at current cost for the five-year summary in Illustration A.3.

The increase in current cost (holding gain) of PPE, together with its inflation component, is calculated using the same technique that was used earlier for inventory. Dollar amounts in the following schedule are in thousands.

	Current cost/nominal dollars	Conversion factor	Current cost/average 1980 dollars
Balance, January 1, 1980	$74,100	220.9/212.9*	$76,884
Additions	15,000	†	15,000
Depreciation	(19,500)	†	(19,500)
Balance, December 31, 1980	(85,100)	220.9/243.5‡	(77,202)
Increase in current cost of property, plant, and equipment	$15,500		$ 4,818

* Average index for 1980/index at December 31, 1979.
† Additions and depreciation are expressed in average 1980 dollars.
‡ Average index for 1980/index at December 31, 1980.

The $74,100 shown as the first item in the first column is the net current cost of the PPE and is given in the assumed basic data at the start of this section; it is computed as gross current cost ($170,000) less accumulated depreciation ($95,900). The current cost of the additions is added, while the current cost of the depreciation and the current cost of the ending stock of PPE (net of accumulated depreciation—$220,000 − $134,900) are deducted. The balance ($15,500) is the holding gain, or, in the Board's terminology, the increase in the current cost of the PPE, as measured in nominal dollars.

The second money column shows the calculation of the same increase (or holding gain) in average 1980 (constant) dollars. Beginning net PPE, which is stated at current cost in beginning of the year dollars, is converted to average 1980 dollars by means of the conversion ratio shown. The ending net PPE is restated from December 1980 dollars into average 1980 dollars. The $4,818 often is referred to as a real holding gain. The difference between the $15,500 and the $4,818 is the inflation component of the increase in current cost of the PPE. On occasion, this is referred to as a fictional holding gain.

The following table summarizes the increases in current cost of inventory and of PPE, the inflation component of each, and the increase, net of inflation.

	Increase in current cost	Inflation component	Increase net of inflation
Inventory	$ 9,108	$ 8,277	$ 831
PPE	15,500	10,682	4,818
Totals	$24,608	$18,959	$5,649

The above totals are reported in the schedules of supplementary information, as shown in Illustrations A.1 and A.2.

A concluding note   Uncertainty over whether constant dollar or current cost information was preferable caused the Board to require both types. This uncertainty was shown in responses to the exposure draft of the new standard. Preparers and auditors of financial information preferred historical cost/constant dollar accounting. Users of the information preferred current cost information. The Board foresees a period of experimentation with the new disclosures and has promised to review the new standard in the light of subsequent happenings in five years. Experience in using and in compiling the newly required information is expected to provide badly needed answers to a number of questions.

Usefulness of the newly required disclosures   The exact manner in which readers of financial statements will use the required disclosures of the impact of changing prices upon an entity is not known at the present time. But several possible uses have been mentioned above. For example, the historical cost/constant dollar information may be used in lobbying for changes in our income tax structure by showing that a tax supposedly levied upon income is in fact a tax upon capital. The information will also show whether an entity has increased its purchasing power and whether it was able to pass on to investors an increasing amount of purchasing power. The trend of net assets at year-end will reveal the former. The trend of cash dividends per share in constant dollars will reveal the latter. It also seems obvious that an investor would be quite interested in knowing whether the market price of the common shares owned was steadily increasing through time, as measured in constant dollars. Furthermore, it seems likely that investors will appraise management's performance in terms of its ability to generate purchasing power, rather than cash dividends.

As previously noted, current cost-based information on earnings from continuing operations may provide the best basis for predicting cash flows to investors because it is a measure of disposable income. Because it shows the actual sacrifice made to generate revenues, current cost information may indicate the ability of the firm to survive in the long run. It seems unlikely that a firm can survive in the long run if its revenues are less than the current cost of generating those revenues. Current cost-based information will often reveal the value of an asset to an entity. Its use will lead to a better matching because both revenues and expenses are stated in terms of current market conditions. And by isolating holding gains and losses, it provides information that may be useful in appraising management's performance. Current cost/ constant dollar information will also reveal whether prices in a given industry are rising faster than the general level of prices, which may be significant to investors. Reporting in constant dollar terms will reveal the extent to which an entity was able to pass on to its creditors the impact of inflation on its monetary assets.

NEW TERMS INTRODUCED IN APPENDIX A

Common dollar accounting—a system of accounting that employs a constant unit of measurement based on the purchasing power of the dollar.

Current cost—the outlay avoided by ownership of an asset; the cost of replacing the service potential of an asset owned.

Current cost/constant dollar accounting—a system of accounting in which the unit of measure is a dollar of constant purchasing power and the attribute measured is current cost.

Current cost/nominal dollar accounting—a system of accounting in which current costs are measured in terms of the dollar without adjustment for general price-level change.

Current value accounting—a system of accounting whereby financial statements contain current value information (as opposed to historical cost-based information).

Disposable earnings—a term used at times to describe the excess of revenues over the current cost of the resources consumed in generating those revenues.

Gains and losses on monetary items—the gains or losses from holding monetary assets and liabilities during inflation or deflation.

General price-level accounting—*see* Common dollar accounting.

General price-level adjusted financial statements—historical cost-based financial statements which have been adjusted for changes in the general purchasing power of the dollar through the use of a price index. Also called historical cost/nominal dollar statements.

Historical cost/constant dollar accounting—see general price-level adjusted financial statements.

Historical cost/nominal dollar accounting—the conventional practice of accounting in which historical costs are measured in terms of the dollars expended.

Holding gain (loss)—the increase (decrease) in the value of an asset, usually as measured by current cost, from the date of its acquisition or prior measurement to the date of its sale or current measurement. Fictional holding gain is the inflation component of holding gains. It represents the additional number of current dollars you must have to be as well off as you were when you invested a certain amount in the asset which you subsequently sold or measured. Real holding gain is the amount by which the current cost of an asset exceeds its historical cost, as adjusted for general price-level change. Realized holding gain is a holding gain that has been confirmed by sale of the asset, or in case of a depreciable asset, by recording depreciation on the holding gain.

Monetary items—assets and liabilities whose dollar amounts are fixed by contract and do not vary with changes in the general price level. Examples: cash, accounts receivable, and accounts payable.

Nonmonetary items—items whose values change with changes in the general price level. Examples: inventories, plant assets, capital stock, and retained earnings.

Purchasing power gain—the gain that results from holding monetary liabilities during inflation or monetary assets during deflation.

Purchasing power loss—the loss that results from holding monetary assets during inflation or monetary liabilities during deflation.

Replacement cost—the lowest amount that would have to be paid in the normal course of business to obtain an asset of equivalent operating or productive capacity.

Replacement cost accounting—a system of accounting whereby financial statements contain replacement cost information.

QUESTIONS

1. Distinguish between monetary items and nonmonetary items. Classify the following items as either monetary or nonmonetary:

a. Cash.
b. Retained earnings.
c. Bonds payable.
d. Merchandise inventory.
e. Accounts receivable.
f. Patents.
g. Common stock.
h. Land.
i. Accounts payable.
j. Buildings.

2. What are purchasing power gains and losses? When do purchasing power gains occur? When do purchasing power losses occur?

3. How can replacement costs be estimated?

4. If an index of the general level of prices rose 15 percent in a period, what is the effect upon the value or real worth of the dollar?

5. How might it be argued that a tax supposedly upon earnings or income is in reality a tax upon capital?

6. What are the two basic approaches that might be used to reveal the impact of inflation upon financial statements?

7. Explain what the significance is of the dollar amount attaching to an asset under constant dollar accounting.

8. How is the dollar amount attaching to land adjusted under historical cost/constant dollar accounting?

9. What is the significance of classifying an asset as monetary under constant dollar accounting?

10. Explain the typical adjustment of sales and most expenses under constant dollar accounting.

11. What are the replacement cost disclosures required by the SEC? What is the objective sought in requiring these disclosures?

12. In the supplementary disclosures required by the FASB, what basis of accounting measurement is to be applied?

13. Explain what is meant by "constant dollar income from continuing operations."

14. What is the major deficiency in historical cost/constant dollar accounting?

15. What underlying circumstances must exist to yield an "inflation gain on net monetary items"?

16. How is periodic depreciation calculated under current cost accounting?

17. What does the inclusion of measurement in constant dollars add to the information developed under current cost accounting?

EXERCISES

E–1. R Company was formed in 1980 with a capital investment of $1 million which was invested immediately in land. The index of general prices stood at 100 at this time while an index of land values stood at 150. In 1983 the general price index was 130, while the land index was 450.

a. Compute the holding gain on the land for the three-year period.

b. Compute the inflation component of the holding gain.

c. Compute the purchasing power gain or loss of the R Company for the three years of its existence.

E–2. A general price index stood at 120 on December 31, 1980, and at 132 on December 31, 1981. The accounts payable in the conventional comparative balance sheets for X Company amounted to $20,000 and $25,000, respectively.

a. Compute the dollar amounts to be shown for accounts payable in the comparative constant dollar balance sheets for X Company if such statements are to be prepared in terms of December 31, 1981, dollars.

b. Repeat part **(a)**, expressing the amounts in December 31, 1980, dollars.

the general level of prices rose from 115 to 117.3 during the month. Compute the inflation gain or loss on net monetary items for the month in end-of-month dollars.

E–4. Burns Company purchased a tract of land on 1/2/81 for $200,000 when the general price index stood at 110 and an index of land values stood at 200. Burns still held the land at year-end when the general price index stood at 120 and the land index stood at 230. Compute the holding gain on the land, net of the inflation component.

E–5. The January 1, 1981, inventory of the Ames Company had an historical cost of $4,000 and a current cost of $4,300. Purchases during 1981 amounted to $60,000. The December 31, 1981, inventory had an historical cost of $7,000 and a current cost of $8,100. The current cost of the goods sold was $58,800. Compute the holding gain on the inventory for the year.

E–6. Data needed for the five-year summary of financial data for the Roan Company are:

	1980	1981	1982	1983	1984
Consumer price index (average for year) ..	120	125	135	142	150
Sales (in thousands)	$240	$300	$351	$355	$400
Net assets (in thousands)	48	50	72	71	72
Dividends	$1.20	$1.25	$1.62	$2.13	$2.40

E–3. J Company started a month with $20,000 of cash and $14,000 of accounts payable. No changes occurred in either of these items during the month. An index of

Compute the price-level adjusted sales, net assets, and dividends for the Roan Company with all dollar amounts expressed in terms of average 1984 dollars.

PROBLEMS, SERIES A

PA–1–A. A partial earnings statement for the X Company for the year ended December 31, 1981, in terms of historical dollars is as follows:

X COMPANY
Partial Earnings Statement
For the Year Ended December 31, 1981

Sales		$110,000
Cost of goods sold	$63,000	
Depreciation	6,000	
Other expenses and taxes	12,100	81,100
Earnings from continuing operations		$ 28,900

The sales were made uniformly through the year. The cost of goods sold consisted of goods acquired when the general price index stood at 105. This same index ended the year at 120 and averaged 110 for the year. The current cost of the goods sold was $75,000.

The $6,000 of depreciation reported is on a machine that cost $30,000 when the general price index stood at 90. The machine had a current cost of $50,000 at the beginning of 1981 and a current cost of $60,000 at the end of 1981.

The other expenses and taxes were incurred uniformly through the year, were paid in cash, and are substantially equal to their current cost at time of incurrence.

Required:

a. Prepare a statement showing historical cost/constant dollar earnings from continuing operations in December 31, 1981, dollars for the year ended on that date.

b. Prepare a statement showing historical cost/current cost earnings from continuing operations for the year ended December 31, 1981.

c. Repeat part **(a)** with amounts expressed in average 1981 dollars.

PA–2–A. Barton Company began business on January 2, 1981, when an index of the general level of prices stood at 100. This index rose uniformly through the year, averaging 125 for the year, and ending at 150. Barton's conventional comparative balance sheets for January 2 and December 31, 1981, are as follows:

BARTON COMPANY
Comparative Balance Sheets

Assets	January 2	December 31
Cash	$ 10,000	$ 50,000
Inventory	80,000	30,000
Equipment (net of accumulated depreciation)	60,000	50,000
Total Assets	$150,000	$130,000

Liabilities and Owner's Equity		
Current liabilities	$ 40,000	$ 10,000
Capital stock	110,000	110,000
Retained earnings	–0–	10,000
Total Liabilities and Owners' Equity	$150,000	$130,000

The earnings statement for the year in historical dollars is given below:

BARTON COMPANY
Earnings Statement
For the Year Ended December 31, 1981

Sales		$100,000
Cost of goods sold		50,000
Gross margin		$ 50,000
Depreciation	$10,000	
Other expenses and taxes	20,000	30,000
Net earnings		$ 20,000
Retained earnings, January 2, 1981		–0–
		$ 20,000
Dividends		10,000
Retained Earnings, December 31, 1981		$ 10,000

In 1981, Barton sold goods out of inventory with a cost of $50,000 for cash of $100,000. Expenses and taxes in the amount of $20,000 were incurred uniformly through the year and were paid in cash. A cash dividend of $10,000 was paid on December 31. The useful life of the equipment was estimated at six years.

Required:

a. Prepare a balance sheet for December 31, 1981, with all amounts stated in terms of December 31, 1981, dollars.

b. Prepare an earnings statement for 1981 with all amounts expressed in terms of December 31, 1981, dollars. Include a reconciliation of retained earnings in the statement. Also prepare a schedule showing the computation of the inflation gain or loss on monetary items.

PA–3–A. The following data pertain to the inventory and a machine of the Y Company for the year 1981:

Beginning inventory (historical cost, $5,000)
  at current cost.............................. $ 6,000
Purchases 54,000
Cost of goods sold at current cost 58,000
Ending inventory (historical cost, $7,000)
  at current cost.............................. 10,000
Current cost of machine, beginning of the year 40,000
Current cost of machine, end of the year 60,000
Historical cost of the machine.................... 30,000

Depreciation rate, 10 percent; straight-line method employed.

Machine is 40 percent depreciated at the beginning of 1981.

The Consumer Price Index at 1/1/81 was 100; the average for 1981 was 104.04; at year-end the index stood at 108.24.

Required:

Compute, for both inventory and the machine:

a. The holding gain for the year in average 1981 dollars.

b. The inflation component of the holding gain in average 1981 dollars.

PROBLEMS, SERIES B

PA–1–B. A partial earnings statement for the Reed Company for the year ended December 31, 1981, in terms of historical dollars is given below:

REED COMPANY
Partial Earnings Statement
For the Year Ended December 31, 1981

Sales $210,000
Cost of goods sold................ $135,200
Depreciation 8,000
Other expenses and taxes 42,000   185,200
Earnings from continuing
  operations .... $ 24,800

The sales were made rather uniformly through the year. Other expenses and taxes were also incurred rather uniformly through the year and largely on a cash basis. Thus, their historical cost is substantially equal to their current cost. The depreciation reported relates to a machine acquired at a cost of $80,000 which is being depreciated over a ten-year life on a straight-line basis.

The current cost of the goods sold was $150,000 at the time of their sale. The current cost (gross) of the machine was $130,000 at the beginning of 1981 and $150,000 at the end of the year. An index of the general level of prices stood at 80 when the machine was acquired, at 100 at the beginning of 1981, averaged 105 for 1981 and ended the year at 110. This same index stood at 104 when the goods sold were acquired.

Required:

a. Prepare a statement showing constant dollar earnings from continuing operations in December 31, 1981, dollars for the year ended on that date.

b. Prepare a statement showing current cost earnings

from continuing operations for the year ended December 31, 1981.

c. Repeat part **(a)** with all amounts expressed in average 1981 dollars.

PA–2–B.

MORTON COMPANY
Comparative Balance Sheets

Assets	January 1	December 31
Cash	$ 8,000	$64,000
Supplies	12,000	4,000
Prepaid rent	24,000	–0–
Equipment (net)	40,000	30,000
Total Assets	$84,000	$98,000

Liabilities and Owners' Equity		
Accounts payable and accruals	$ 4,000	$12,000
Capital stock	80,000	80,000
Retained earnings	–0–	6,000
Total Liabilities and Owners' Equity	$84,000	$98,000

Morton Company was organized on December 31, 1980, and received $80,000 for the stock it issued. It immediately paid a year's rent of $24,000 on a building in advance, purchased $12,000 of supplies, and purchased $40,000 of cleaning equipment. It began operations on January 1, 1981, and comparative balance sheets for the year are given above.

During 1981, services were rendered for customers and other expenses and taxes were incurred uniformly through the year. A cash dividend was declared and paid on December 31 in the amount of $12,000. An index of the general level of prices stood at 80 at the beginning of the year, averaged 100 for the year, and ended the year at 120. The earnings statement for the year is as follows:

MORTON COMPANY
Earnings Statement
For the Year Ended December 31, 1981

Service revenue		$100,000
Supplies used	$ 8,000	
Rent expense	24,000	
Depreciation	10,000	
Other expenses and taxes	40,000	82,000
Net earnings		$ 18,000
Retained earnings, January 1, 1981		–0–
		$ 18,000
Dividends		12,000
Retained Earnings, December 31, 1981		$ 6,000

Required:

a. Prepare a schedule showing the conversion of the conventional balance sheet on December 31, 1981, into constant dollars as of that date.

b. Prepare a schedule converting the earnings statement for 1981 into constant December 31, 1981, dollars.

Include the retained earnings data as shown above. Also prepare a schedule showing the computation of the inflation gain or loss on net monetary items.

PA–3–B. The following data are available on the Rollo Company's inventory and machinery for the year 1981:

Inventory at 1/1 (historical cost, $50,000) at current cost	$ 80,000
Inventory at 12/31 (historical cost, $60,000) at current cost	120,000
Purchases	320,000
Cost of goods sold at current cost	360,000
Machinery at current cost on 1/1	700,000
Machinery at current cost on 12/31	900,000
Historical cost of the machinery	500,000

Depreciation rate: 10 percent; straight-line method. The machinery is 45 percent depreciated as of 1/1/81. The appropriate index of the general level of prices stood at 100 on January 1, 1981, averaged 106.1 for the year, and ended the year at 112.5.

Required:

Compute, for both the inventory and the machinery:

a. Holding gain for the year in average 1981 dollars.

b. Inflation components of the holding gain in average 1981 dollars.

BUSINESS DECISION PROBLEM

Kathy Jones had just about decided to invest some of her savings in the common stock of the Arto Company. The conventional financial statements and other data relating to the company show that sales, earnings from continuing operations, earnings per common share and the market price of the company's common stock had increased in a smooth upward trend and had approximately doubled over the past five years. The rate of net earnings to stockholders' equity had increased by nearly 50 percent in this same five years.

Kathy then examined the latest annual report of the company and found the following five-year summary *with all dollar amounts expressed in average 1981 dollars:*

	Years ended December 31				
	1977	*1978*	*1979*	*1980*	*1981*
Net sales	$600,000	$585,000	$560,000	$582,000	$590,000
Historical cost data:					
Income from continuing					
operations	40,000	38,000	37,000	35,000	41,000
Income from continuing					
operations per common share ..	2.00	1.87	1.85	1.80	1.90
Net assets at year-end	310,000	301,000	304,000	305,000	320,000
Current cost data:					
Income from continuing					
operations	36,000	34,000	33,000	32,000	36,000
Income from continuing					
operations per share..........	1.80	1.68	1.65	1.65	1.67
Net assets at year-end	325,000	317,000	319,000	321,000	337,000
Inflation gain (loss) on net					
monetary items	(4,500)	(3,000)	(2,000)	2,000	3,000
Cash dividends declared per					
common share	0.87	0.86	0.84	0.82	0.79
Market price per common share					
at year end	30	28	27	29	32

Required:

Comment on the attractiveness of an investment in Arto common shares, paying specific attention to the differences in the information revealed in the conventional financial statements as compared to the information contained in the above five-year summary.

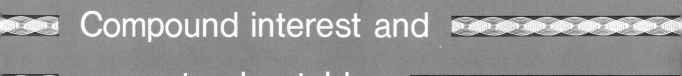
Compound interest and
present value tables

Table 1: Amount of 1 (at compound interest).

$(1 + i)^n$

Periods	2%	2½%	3%	4%	5%	6%
1.....	1.02	1.025	1.03	1.04	1.05	1.06
2.....	1.040 4	1.050 625	1.060 9	1.081 6	1.102 5	1.123 6
3.....	1.061 208	1.076 891	1.092 727	1.124 864	1.157 625	1.191 016
4.....	1.082 432	1.103 813	1.125 509	1.169 859	1.215 506	1.262 477
5.....	1.104 081	1.131 408	1.159 274	1.216 653	1.276 282	1.338 226
6.....	1.126 162	1.159 693	1.194 052	1.265 319	1.340 096	1.418 519
7.....	1.148 686	1.188 686	1.229 874	1.315 932	1.407 100	1.503 630
8.....	1.171 659	1.218 403	1.266 770	1.368 569	1.477 455	1.593 848
9.....	1.195 093	1.248 863	1.304 773	1.423 312	1.551 328	1.689 479
10.....	1.218 994	1.280 085	1.343 916	1.480 244	1.628 895	1 790 848
11.....	1.243 374	1.312 087	1.384 234	1.539 454	1.710 339	1.898 299
12.....	1.268 242	1.344 889	1.425 761	1.601 032	1.795 856	2.012 196
13.....	1.293 607	1.378 511	1.468 534	1.665 074	1.885 649	2.132 928
14.....	1.319 479	1.412 974	1.512 590	1.731 676	1.979 932	2.260 904
15.....	1.345 868	1.448 298	1.557 967	1.800 944	2.078 928	2.396 558
16.....	1.372 786	1.484 506	1.604 706	1.872 981	2.182 875	2.540 352
17.....	1.400 241	1.521 618	1.652 848	1.947 901	2.292 018	2.692 773
18.....	1.428 246	1.559 659	1.702 433	2.025 817	2.406 619	2.854 339
19.....	1.456 811	1.598 650	1.753 506	2.106 849	2.526 950	3.025 600
20.....	1.485 947	1.638 616	1.806 111	2.191 123	2.653 298	3.207 135
21.....	1.515 666	1.679 582	1.860 295	2.278 768	2.785 963	3.399 564
22.....	1.545 980	1.721 571	1.916 103	2.369 919	2.925 261	3.603 537
23.....	1.576 899	1.764 611	1.973 587	2.464 716	3.071 524	3.819 750
24.....	1.608 437	1.808 726	2.032 794	2.563 304	3.225 100	4.048 935
25.....	1.640 606	1.853 944	2.093 778	2.665 836	3.386 355	4.291 871
26.....	1.673 418	1.900 293	2.156 591	2.772 470	3.555 673	4.549 383
27.....	1.706 886	1.947 800	2.221 289	2.883 369	3.733 456	4.822 346
28.....	1.741 024	1.996 495	2.287 928	2.998 703	3.920 129	5.111 687
29.....	1.775 845	2.046 407	2.356 566	3.118 651	4.116 136	5.418 388
30.....	1.811 362	2.097 568	2.427 262	3.243 398	4.321 942	5.743 491
31.....	1.847 589	2.150 007	2.500 080	3.373 133	4.538 039	6.088 101
32.....	1.884 541	2.203 757	2.575 083	3.508 059	4.764 941	6.453 387
33.....	1.922 231	2.258 851	2.652 335	3.648 381	5.003 189	6.840 590
34.....	1.960 676	2.315 322	2.731 905	3.794 316	5.253 348	7.251 025
35.....	1.999 890	2.373 205	2.813 862	3.946 089	5.516 015	7.686 087
36.....	2.039 887	2.432 535	2.898 278	4.103 933	5.791 816	8.147 252
37.....	2.080 685	2.493 349	2.985 227	4.268 090	6.081 407	8.636 087
38.....	2.122 299	2.555 682	3.074 783	4.438 813	6.385 477	9.154 252
39.....	2.164 745	2.619 574	3.167 027	4.616 366	6.704 751	9.703 507
40.....	2.208 040	2.685 064	3.262 038	4.801 021	7.039 989	10.285 718

Table 2: Present value of 1 (at compound interest)

$$\frac{1}{(1+i)^n}$$

Periods	2%	2½%	3%	4%	5%	6%
1.....	0.980 392	0.975 610	0.970 874	0.961 538	0.952 381	0.943 396
2.....	0.961 169	0.951 814	0.942 596	0.924 556	0.907 029	0.889 996
3.....	0.942 322	0.928 599	0.915 142	0.888 996	0.863 838	0.839 619
4.....	0.923 845	0.905 951	0.888 487	0.854 804	0.822 702	0.792 094
5.....	0.905 731	0.883 854	0.862 609	0.821 927	0.783 526	0.747 258
6.....	0.887 971	0.862 297	0.837 484	0.790 315	0.746 215	0.704 961
7.....	0.870 560	0.841 265	0.813 092	0.759 918	0.710 681	0.665 057
8.....	0.853 490	0.820 747	0.789 409	0.730 690	0.676 839	0.627 412
9.....	0.836 755	0.800 728	0.766 417	0.702 587	0.644 609	0.591 898
10.....	0.820 348	0.781 198	0.744 094	0.675 564	0.613 913	0.558 395
11.....	0.804 263	0.762 145	0.722 421	0.649 581	0.584 679	0.526 788
12.....	0.788 493	0.743 556	0.701 380	0.624 597	0.556 837	0.496 969
13.....	0.773 033	0.725 420	0.680 951	0.600 574	0.530 321	0.468 839
14.....	0.757 875	0.707 727	0.661 118	0.577 475	0.505 068	0.442 301
15.....	0.743 015	0.690 466	0.641 862	0.555 265	0.481 017	0.417 265
16.....	0.728 446	0.673 625	0.623 167	0.533 908	0.458 112	0.393 646
17.....	0.714 163	0.657 195	0.605 016	0.513 373	0.436 297	0.371 364
18.....	0.700 159	0.641 166	0.587 395	0.493 628	0.415 521	0.350 344
19.....	0.686 431	0.625 528	0.570 286	0.474 642	0.395 734	0.330 513
20.....	0.672 971	0.610 271	0.553 676	0.456 387	0.376 889	0.311 805
21.....	0.659 776	0.595 386	0.537 549	0.438 834	0.358 942	0.294 155
22.....	0.646 839	0.580 865	0.521 893	0.421 955	0.341 850	0.277 505
23.....	0.634 156	0.566 697	0.506 692	0.405 726	0.325 571	0.261 797
24.....	0.621 721	0.552 875	0.491 934	0.390 121	0.310 068	0.246 979
25.....	0.609 531	0.539 391	0.477 606	0.375 117	0.295 303	0.232 999
26.....	0.597 579	0.526 234	0.463 695	0.360 689	0.281 241	0.219 810
27.....	0.585 862	0.513 400	0.450 189	0.346 817	0.267 848	0.207 368
28.....	0.574 375	0.500 878	0.437 077	0.333 477	0.255 094	0.195 630
29.....	0.563 112	0.488 661	0.424 346	0.320 651	0.242 946	0.184 557
30.....	0.552 071	0.476 743	0.411 987	0.308 319	0.231 377	0.174 110
31.....	0.541 246	0.465 115	0.399 987	0.296 460	0.220 359	0.164 255
32.....	0.530 633	0.453 770	0.388 337	0.285 058	0.209 866	0.154 957
33.....	0.520 229	0.442 703	0.377 026	0.274 094	0.199 873	0.146 186
34.....	0.510 028	0.431 905	0.366 045	0.263 552	0.190 355	0.137 912
35.....	0.500 028	0.421 371	0.355 383	0.253 415	0.181 290	0.130 105
36.....	0.490 223	0.411 094	0.345 032	0.243 669	0.172 657	0.122 741
37.....	0.480 611	0.401 067	0.334 983	0.234 297	0.164 436	0.115 793
38.....	0.471 187	0.391 285	0.325 226	0.225 285	0.156 605	0.109 239
39.....	0.461 948	0.381 741	0.315 754	0.216 621	0.149 148	0.103 056
40.....	0.452 890	0.372 431	0.306 557	0.208 289	0.142 046	0.097 222

Table 2 *(continued)*

8%	10%	12%	14%	16%	18%	20%
0.926	0.909	0.893	0.877	0.862	0.847	0.833
0.857	0.826	0.797	0.769	0.743	0.718	0.694
0.794	0.751	0.712	0.675	0.641	0.609	0.579
0.735	0.683	0.636	0.592	0.552	0.516	0.482
0.681	0.621	0.567	0.519	0.476	0.437	0.402
0.630	0.564	0.507	0.456	0.410	0.370	0.335
0.583	0.513	0.452	0.400	0.354	0.314	0.279
0.540	0.467	0.404	0.351	0.305	0.266	0.233
0.500	0.424	0.361	0.308	0.263	0.225	0.194
0.463	0.386	0.322	0.270	0.227	0.191	0.162
0.429	0.350	0.287	0.237	0.195	0.162	0.135
0.397	0.319	0.257	0.208	0.168	0.137	0.112
0.368	0.290	0.229	0.182	0.145	0.116	0.093
0.340	0.263	0.205	0.160	0.125	0.099	0.078
0.315	0.239	0.183	0.140	0.108	0.084	0.065
0.292	0.218	0.163	0.123	0.093	0.071	0.054
0.270	0.198	0.146	0.108	0.080	0.060	0.045
0.250	0.180	0.130	0.095	0.069	0.051	0.038
0.232	0.164	0.116	0.083	0.060	0.043	0.031
0.215	0.149	0.104	0.073	0.051	0.037	0.026
0.199	0.135	0.093	0.064	0.044	0.031	0.022
0.184	0.123	0.083	0.056	0.038	0.026	0.018
0.170	0.112	0.074	0.049	0.033	0.022	0.015
0.158	0.102	0.066	0.043	0.028	0.019	0.013
0.146	0.092	0.059	0.038	0.024	0.016	0.010
0.135	0.084	0.053	0.033	0.021	0.014	0.009
0.125	0.076	0.047	0.029	0.018	0.011	0.007
0.116	0.069	0.042	0.026	0.016	0.010	0.006
0.107	0.063	0.037	0.022	0.014	0.008	0.005
0.099	0.057	0.033	0.020	0.012	0.007	0.004
0.092	0.052	0.030	0.017	0.010	0.006	0.004
0.085	0.047	0.027	0.015	0.009	0.005	0.003
0.079	0.043	0.024	0.013	0.007	0.004	0.002
0.073	0.039	0.021	0.012	0.006	0.004	0.002
0.068	0.036	0.019	0.010	0.006	0.003	0.002
0.063	0.032	0.017	0.009	0.005	0.003	0.001
0.058	0.029	0.015	0.008	0.004	0.002	0.001
0.054	0.027	0.013	0.007	0.004	0.002	0.001
0.050	0.024	0.012	0.006	0.003	0.002	0.001
0.046	0.022	0.011	0.005	0.003	0.001	0.001

Table 3: Present value of
an annuity of 1

$$\frac{1 - \frac{1}{(1+i)^n}}{i}$$

Periods	2%	2½%	3%	4%	5%	6%
1.....	0.980 392	0.975 610	0.970 874	0.961 539	0.952 381	0.943 396
2.....	1.941 561	1.927 424	1.913 470	1.886 095	1.859 410	1.833 393
3.....	2.883 883	2.856 024	2.828 611	2.775 091	2.723 248	2.673 012
4.....	3.807 729	3.761 974	3.717 098	3.629 895	3.545 951	3.465 106
5.....	4.713 460	4.645 829	4.579 707	4.451 822	4.329 477	4.212 364
6.....	5.601 431	5.508 125	5.417 191	5.242 137	5.075 692	4.917 324
7.....	6.471 991	6.349 391	6.230 283	6.002 055	5.786 373	5.582 381
8.....	7.325 481	7.170 137	7.019 692	6.732 745	6.463 213	6.209 794
9.....	8.162 237	7.970 866	7.786 109	7.435 332	7.107 822	6.801 692
10.....	8.982 585	8.752 064	8.530 203	8.110 896	7.721 735	7.360 087
11.....	9.786 848	9.514 209	9.252 624	8.760 477	8.306 414	7.886 875
12.....	10.575 341	10.257 765	9.954 004	9.385 074	8.863 252	8.383 844
13.....	11.348 374	10.983 185	10.634 955	9.985 648	9.393 573	8.852 683
14.....	12.106 249	11.690 012	11.296 073	10.563 123	9.898 641	9.294 984
15.....	12.849 264	12.381 378	11.937 935	11.118 387	10.379 658	9.712 249
16.....	13.577 709	13.055 003	12.561 102	11.652 296	10.837 770	10.105 895
17.....	14.291 872	13.712 198	13.166 119	12.165 669	11.274 066	10.477 260
18.....	14.992 031	14.353 364	13.753 513	12.659 297	11.689 587	10.827 604
19.....	15.678 462	14.978 891	14.323 799	13.133 939	12.085 321	11.158 117
20.....	16.351 433	15.589 162	14.877 475	13.590 326	12.462 210	11.469 921
21.....	17.011 209	16.184 549	15.415 024	14.029 160	12.821 153	11.764 077
22.....	17.658 048	16.765 413	15.936 917	14.451 115	13.163 003	12.041 582
23.....	18.292 204	17.332 111	16.443 608	14.856 842	13.488 574	12.303 379
24.....	18.913 926	17.884 986	16.935 542	15.246 963	13.798 642	12.550 358
25.....	19.523 457	18.424 376	17.413 148	15.622 080	14.093 945	12.783 356
26.....	20.121 036	18.950 611	17.876 842	15.982 769	14.375 185	13.003 166
27.....	20.706 898	19.464 011	18.327 032	16.329 586	14.643 034	13.210 534
28.....	21.281 272	19.964 889	18.764 108	16.663 063	14.898 127	13.406 164
29.....	21.844 385	20.453 550	19.188 455	16.983 715	15.141 074	13.590 721
30.....	22.396 456	20.930 293	19.600 441	17.292 033	15.372 451	13.764 831
31.....	22.937 702	21.395 407	20.000 429	17.588 494	15.592 811	13.929 086
32.....	23.468 335	21.849 178	20.388 766	17.873 552	15.802 677	14.084 043
33.....	23.988 564	22.291 881	20.765 792	18.147 646	16.002 549	14.230 230
34.....	24.498 592	22.723 786	21.131 837	18.411 198	16.192 904	14.368 141
35.....	24.998 619	23.145 157	21.487 220	18.664 613	16.374 194	14.498 246
36.....	25.488 843	23.556 251	21.832 253	18.908 282	16.546 852	14.620 987
37.....	25.969 453	23.957 318	22.167 235	19.142 579	16.711 287	14.736 780
38.....	26.440 641	24.348 603	22.492 462	19.367 864	16.867 893	14.846 019
39.....	26.902 589	24.730 344	22.808 215	19.584 485	17.017 041	14.949 075
40.....	27.355 479	25.102 775	23.114 772	19.792 774	17.159 086	15.046 297

Table 3 *(continued)*

8%	10%	12%	14%	16%	18%	20%
0.926	0.909	0.893	0.877	0.862	0.847	0.833
1.783	1.736	1.690	1.647	1.605	1.566	1.528
2.577	2.487	2.402	2.322	2.246	2.174	2.106
3.312	3.170	3.037	2.914	2.798	2.690	2.589
3.993	3.791	3.605	3.433	3.274	3.127	2.991
4.623	4.355	4.111	3.889	3.685	3.498	3.326
5.206	4.868	4.564	4.288	4.039	3.812	3.605
5.747	5.335	4.968	4.639	4.344	4.078	3.837
6.247	5.759	5.328	4.946	4.607	4.303	4.031
6.710	6.145	5.650	5.216	4.833	4.494	4.192
7.139	6.495	5.937	5.453	5.029	4.656	4.327
7.536	6.814	6.194	5.660	5.197	4.793	4.439
7.904	7.103	6.424	5.842	5.342	4.910	4.533
8.244	7.367	6.628	6.002	5.468	5.008	4.611
8.559	7.606	6.811	6.142	5.575	5.092	4.675
8.851	7.824	6.974	6.265	5.669	5.162	4.730
9.122	8.022	7.120	6.373	5.749	5.222	4.775
9.372	8.201	7.250	6.467	5.818	5.273	4.812
9.604	8.365	7.366	6.550	5.877	5.316	4.844
9.818	8.514	7.469	6.623	5.929	5.353	4.870
10.017	8.649	7.562	6.687	5.973	5.384	4.891
10.201	8.772	7.645	6.743	6.011	5.410	4.909
10.371	8.883	7.718	6.792	6.044	5.432	4.925
10.529	8.985	7.784	6.835	6.073	5.451	4.937
10.675	9.077	7.843	6.873	6.097	5.467	4.948
10.810	9.161	7.896	6.906	6.118	5.480	4.956
10.935	9.237	7.943	6.935	6.136	5.492	4.964
11.051	9.307	7.984	6.961	6.152	5.502	4.970
11.158	9.370	8.022	6.983	6.166	5.510	4.975
11.258	9.427	8.055	7.003	6.177	5.517	4.979
11.350	9.479	8.085	7.020	6.187	5.523	4.982
11.435	9.526	8.112	7.035	6.196	5.528	4.985
11.514	9.569	8.135	7.048	6.203	5.532	4.988
11.587	9.609	8.157	7.060	6.210	5.536	4.990
11.655	9.644	8.176	7.070	6.215	5.539	4.992
11.717	9.677	8.192	7.079	6.220	5.541	4.993
11.775	9.706	8.208	7.087	6.224	5.543	4.994
11.829	9.733	8.221	7.094	6.228	5.545	4.995
11.879	9.757	8.233	7.100	6.231	5.547	4.996
11.925	9.779	8.244	7.105	6.234	5.548	4.997

Index

This book has been set in 11 and 10 point Times Roman, leaded 1 point. Part numbers and titles are 28 point Spectra (regular) and chapter numbers and titles are 26 point Spectra (regular). The size of the type page is 39 by 49 picas.